LITERATURE
ART AND
ARTIFACT

LITERATURE
ART AND
ARTIFACT

William A. Heffernan
Saddleback College

Mark Johnston
Quinnipiac College

Frank Hodgins
University of Illinois

Harcourt Brace Jovanovich, Publishers

San Diego   New York   Chicago   Austin   Washington, D.C.
London   Sydney   Tokyo   Toronto

Preface

Literature: Art and Artifact is designed for students taking freshman composition and literature courses. As the title indicates, we have made the selections and written the apparatus with a double intention: to present works of literature as works of art worthy of being apprehended and appreciated for their beauty and expressiveness, while at the same time being viewed as objects to be analyzed, evaluated, and written about. The arrangement of the book, along with our consistent emphasis on writing about literature, underscores our belief that the appreciation and analysis of literature should occur simultaneously, that the two intentions should be united.

Literature: Art and Artifact is organized by genre: fiction, poetry, and drama. We have chosen this mode of organization not because it has been perennially popular (which it has), but because it focuses students' attention equally on both the *how* and the *what* of literary art. Moreover, it reminds students that when they write about literature they are writing about techniques and forms as well as ideas.

Each section of *Literature: Art and Artifact* begins with an *exemplary text* or texts, offered without commentary and designed to introduce students to the pleasures of meeting the given genre on its own terms, without mediation from editors or instructors. We believe that this one-on-one encounter between student and text is the most logical place for the study of literature to begin and end. The exemplary texts are followed by apparatus that describes the major elements of the genre in question, and by texts that illustrate that element "in action." Throughout the book we have striven to keep the apparatus as clear as possible for its intended audience; furthermore, we have tried to cover only essential points so that the instructor has full room to supplement or amplify what we have offered. We have attempted to aid the instructor, not to assume his or her proper role.

After each element, we have included a separate section that concerns writing about that element. In these sections we include advice about writing, further general questions concerning analysis, and a sample essay that embodies the key points discussed in the text. Thus the student receives—chapter by chapter—practical suggestions for completing written assignments. These suggestions occur along the way; they are not relegated to an appendix.

After all the elements of a given genre have been described, we have included a section, entitled "Integration and Evaluation," which ties together the concerns of the previous chapters, leaving the student poised to reconsider the *whole* work in light of what he or she has learned and to move more confidently toward answering questions of evaluation. To encourage the student's interest in evaluating literature, we have added to each section a group of "Critical Touchstones," which highlight major critical issues and provide a basis for further discussion and writing.

In the "Further Readings" for each section, as well as in the texts that accompany our description of the elements, we have presented a broad sampling of literature that is varied in its difficulty and in the themes it takes up, but that should inspire students with its consistent high quality.

Predictably, we have incurred many debts in preparing *Literature: Art and Artifact*. At Harcourt Brace Jovanovich, Eleanor Garner provided invaluable assistance with permissions; Melanie Rawn gave us sure and sensitive help in editing the manuscript; and Parma Yarkin, as production editor, steered the book skillfully toward publication. Our principal debt is to Paul H. Nockleby, our acquisitions editor, upon whose patience, intelligence, and care we have always been able to count. To all, our hearty thanks.

WILLIAM A. HEFFERNAN
MARK JOHNSTON
FRANK HODGINS

Contents

PART II   POETRY

Persona, Dramatic Situation, and Tone 639

Meter, Rhythm, and Free Verse   678

Rhyme and Other Sound Devices   710

SECTION **4**   **Poems for Further Reading**   **800**

PART **III**   **DRAMA**

LITERATURE
ART AND ARTIFACT

PART

I

FICTION

1

How to Read Fiction

HOW TO READ FICTION

If a college student has just finished reading a short story she enjoyed and someone asks her how she liked it, she will probably respond—in much the same way she would respond to the question "How are you today?"— by saying "Fine." If asked to elaborate, she will probably recount the plot. In most circumstances, this response is appropriate, even though the student knows that it does not adequately express what she feels about the story. After all, when someone asks "How are you today?" we are not expected to give an exhaustive analysis of our emotional profile or our medical status. So we say "Fine," knowing that that vague, polite, all-purpose word cannot capture all the feelings and thoughts that may be going through our heads at the time.

Unfortunately, the extent to which people think about or respond to what they read rarely goes beyond the level of a passing conversation. Even if they have been affected by a story, been engaged by its characters, or excited by its outcome, they usually do not need to say much more than "It was good." Literature students in college, however, need to respond at uncustomary length to what they have read. To do this well, they must have the ability—the necessary vocabulary and analytical skills—to express complex opinions and ideas about difficult works of literature. In requiring students to read, study, and write about literature more carefully, instructors are merely indicating that in the serious study of literature, such answers as "It was good" will not suffice. But what do we do when we study literature seriously?

Most literature textbooks designed to help students answer these questions begin, as this one does, with the study of short stories. Of all the major **genres** of literature—fiction, poetry, and drama—students usually respond most readily to fiction. Good stories have the power to touch us immediately and deeply. In them, we recognize people like the people we know in conflict with their worlds, with each other, or with themselves. We recognize the places they inhabit—the rooms, houses, communities, regions, countries. We recognize and respond to the situations they are caught up in: a man loses his faith in humanity; a woman tries, with a morbid kind of success, to stop the flow of time; a boy finds his convictions while working in a grocery store. We can imagine ourselves being in these situations. That we respond to them gives us the first indication of why we read fiction—because fiction imitates or reflects the world we all know and deepens our appreciation of that world. Fiction can also introduce us to aspects of the world that we don't know anything about by portraying situations that we have neither encountered nor imagined. Franz Kafka's "A Hunger Artist," for example, gives us insights into the bizarre life of a man who fasts for forty days at a time!

Because we identify with fictional characters, fiction also affects us emotionally. We learn from it and take pleasure in it. We become excited, dismayed, saddened, angered. We learn the effects of a man's excessive pride. We wonder what will happen when a bigoted woman becomes aware of her bigotry. We pity a small child beaten by his angry father. Remember that the Latin word from which *vicarious* is derived means *substituted*. We put ourselves in the places of fictional characters and—by reading about their successes and failures, their thoughts and deeds—we act out, for a time, our own. Fiction confirms what we already know, or contradicts it meaningfully, or calls it into question. Emotion and knowledge begin to merge.

Finally, we read fiction because it represents one of the most ingenious uses of a medium we share with the author and with each other: language. We respond to an author's skillful use of language and to the techniques that authors have developed to render experience in fictional form. The structure of a plot arouses our curiosity; the realism of the dialogue engages us; the way the story is told offers us an unusual perspective on human behavior; or we admire the clarity and the power with which the author has described a place or a character. We respond to the formal means an author has employed. We begin to read more closely to see how one author's technique differs from another's or how a story told in the first person differs from one told in the third person. We begin to make—or to want to make—judgments about the relative quality of different stories. We indeed are far from the answer "It was good."

Or are we? In fact, we are in a better position to say why one story is good, or better than another. We are ready to respond intelligently and thoroughly when we are asked "How did you like it?" We are ready to evaluate a story *critically*.

How we read is nearly as important as why. The first fifteen stories in this book are arranged in three sections—"Exemplary Texts," "The Elements of Fiction," and "Integration and Evaluation"—to suggest three different ways in which we read.

The first three stories in Section 2, "Exemplary Texts," are offered without commentary. They suggest, first of all, that we read for pleasure, for whatever joys the stories may yield if we are attentive on a first, relatively quick, reading. We may think about what we read, talk about it with friends, carry it around with us in our minds—but first we enjoy it.

As pleasant as this kind of reading is, we often feel a need to go beyond it to link enjoyment with knowledge and careful consideration of what we read. We want to know *why* we enjoy what we read and *how* an author produces the effects we find enjoyable. The stories in Section 3, "The Elements of Fiction," suggest ways in which we can begin to answer such questions. For this more thorough kind of reading, we need to equip ourselves with pencil and paper and to allow sufficient time for thought, rereading, and analysis. We might try to summarize the story or ask ourselves questions about it. Here are some of the most common questions, listed with the element that they help us to explore:

1. **Plot:**   What are the main events of the story, and what causes them?
2. **Character:**   Who is the main character of the story? How is this character revealed to us? How does he or she change significantly during the course of the story?
3. **Setting:**   Where is the story set? Is there a significant connection between the setting of the story and its outcome?
4. **Point of View** and **Tone:**   Who tells the story? How does the way the story is told affect our understanding? What is the narrator's attitude toward what he or she is telling?
5. **Symbolism and Allegory:** Do any of the objects, people, or events in the story seem to represent larger concepts?
6. **Theme:**   What is the main idea the author is trying to convey?

To confirm our preliminary answers to these questions, we might want to read the story again to see how these elements work together to make a unified whole or how one element affects others. For example, to what extent do the causes of the events in the story correspond to changes in the characters? Or, how is the main idea of the story supported by the author's description of the setting? We try to see how the story arrives at a coherent effect. Once we have done so, we can begin to ask how powerful or significant that effect is and how it compares with the effects of other stories. Having integrated the elements of the story, we can begin to *evaluate* it critically.

The process described here—one reading for summary, one for analysis, and one for evaluation—may seem excessive. Of course, we don't usually have the need, the desire, or the time to devote this much energy to a single story. There is a time and a proper context for each of three kinds of reading we have described. But careful, thorough reading will not only preserve our enjoyment; it will enhance our enjoyment. We may still say "It was good," but this will be an informed answer, based solidly on the text we've read, that reflects careful reading, precise thought, and considered judgment. It is in such judgment that the richest pleasures of reading lie.

SECTION

2

Exemplary Texts

NATHANIEL HAWTHORNE (1804–1864)

Young Goodman Brown

Nathaniel Hawthorne was born in Salem, Massachusetts, and attended Bowdoin College in Brunswick, Maine. He is best known for his novels, which include *The Scarlet Letter* (1851) and *The House of the Seven Gables* (1852). Along with Edgar Allan Poe, he helped to establish the short story as a major genre in American literature. "Young Goodman Brown" first appeared in 1835.

Young Goodman Brown came forth at sunset into the street at Salem village; but put his head back, after crossing the threshold, to exchange a parting kiss with his young wife. And Faith, as the wife was aptly named, thrust her own pretty head into the street, letting the wind play with the pink ribbons of her cap while she called to Goodman Brown.

"Dearest heart," whispered she, softly and rather sadly, when her lips were close to his ear, "prithee put off your journey until sunrise and sleep in your own bed to-night. A lone woman is troubled with such dreams and such thoughts that she's afeared of herself sometimes. Pray tarry with me this night, dear husband, of all nights in the year."

"My love and my Faith," replied young Goodman Brown, "of all nights in the year, this one night must I tarry away from thee. My journey, as thou callest it, forth and back again, must needs be done 'twixt now and sunrise. What, my sweet, pretty wife, dost thou doubt me already, and we but three months married?"

"Then God bless you!" said Faith, with the pink ribbons; "and may you find all well when you come back."

"Amen!" cried Goodman Brown. "Say thy prayers, dear Faith, and go to bed at dusk, and no harm will come to thee."

So they parted; and the young man pursued his way until, being about to turn the corner by the meeting-house, he looked back and saw the head of Faith still peeping after him with a melancholy air, in spite of her pink ribbons.

"Poor little Faith!" thought he, for his heart smote him. "What a wretch am I to leave her on such an errand! She talks of dreams, too. Methought as she spoke there was trouble in her face, as if a dream had warned her what work is to be done to-night. But no, no; 't would kill her to think it. Well, she's a blessed angel on earth; and after this one night I'll cling to her skirts and follow her to heaven."

With this excellent resolve for the future, Goodman Brown felt himself justified in making more haste on his present evil purpose. He had taken a dreary road, darkened by all the gloomiest trees of the forest, which barely stood aside to let the narrow path creep through, and closed immediately behind. It was all as lonely as could be; and there is this peculiarity in such a solitude, that the traveller knows not who may be concealed by the innumerable trunks and the thick boughs overhead; so that with lonely footsteps he may yet be passing through an unseen multitude.

"There may be a devilish Indian behind every tree," said Goodman Brown to himself; and he glanced fearfully behind him as he added, "What if the devil himself should be at my very elbow!"

His head being turned back, he passed a crook of the road, and, looking forward again, beheld the figure of a man, in grave and decent attire, seated at the foot of an old tree. He arose at Goodman Brown's approach and walked onward side by side with him.

"You are late, Goodman Brown," said he. "The clock of the Old South was striking as I came through Boston, and that is full fifteen minutes agone."

"Faith kept me back a while," replied the young man, with a tremor in his voice, caused by the sudden appearance of his companion, though not wholly unexpected.

It was now deep dusk in the forest, and deepest in that part of it where these two were journeying. As nearly as could be discerned, the second traveller was about fifty years old, apparently in the same rank of life as Goodman Brown, and bearing a considerable resemblance to him, though perhaps more in expression than features. Still they might have been taken for father and son. And yet, though the elder person was as simply clad as the younger, and as simple in manner too, he had an indescribable air of one who knew the world, and who would not have felt abashed at the governor's dinner table or in King William's court, were it possible that his affairs should call him thither. But the only thing about him that could be fixed upon as remarkable was his staff, which bore the likeness of a great black snake, so curiously wrought that it might almost be seen to twist and wriggle itself like a living serpent. This, of course, must have been an ocular deception, assisted by the uncertain light.

"Come, Goodman Brown," cried his fellow-traveller, "this is a dull pace for the beginning of a journey. Take my staff, if you are so soon weary."

"Friend," said the other, exchanging his slow pace for a full stop, "having kept covenant by meeting thee here, it is my purpose now to return whence I came. I have scruples touching the matter thou wot'st of."

"Sayest thou so?" replied he of the serpent, smiling apart. "Let us walk on, nevertheless, reasoning as we go; and if I convince thee not thou shalt turn back. We are but a little way in the forest yet."

"Too far! too far!" exclaimed the goodman, unconsciously resuming his walk. "My father never went into the woods on such an errand, nor his father before him. We have been a race of honest men and good Christians since the days of the martyrs; and shall I be the first of the name of Brown that ever took this path and kept"—

"Such company, thou wouldst say," observed the elder person, interpreting his pause. "Well said, Goodman Brown! I have been as well acquainted with your family as with ever a one among the Puritans; and that's no trifle to say. I helped your grandfather, the constable, when he lashed the Quaker woman so smartly through the streets of Salem; and it was I that brought your father a pitch-pine knot, kindled at my own hearth, to set fire to an Indian village, in King Philip's war. They were my good friends, both; and many a pleasant walk have we had along this path, and returned merrily after midnight. I would fain be friends with you for their sake."

"If it be as thou sayest," replied Goodman Brown, "I marvel they never spoke of these matters; or, verily, I marvel not, seeing that the least rumor of the sort would have driven them from New England. We are a people of prayer, and good works to boot, and abide no such wickedness."

"Wickedness or not," said the traveller with the twisted staff, "I have a very general acquaintance here in New England. The deacons of many a church have drunk the communion wine with me; the selectmen of divers towns make me their chairman; and a majority of the Great and General Court are firm supporters of my interest. The governor and I, too—But these are state secrets."

"Can this be so?" cried Goodman Brown, with a stare of amazement at his undisturbed companion. "Howbeit, I have nothing to do with the governor and council; they have their own ways, and are no rule for a simple husbandman like me. But, were I to go on with thee, how should I meet the eye of that good old man, our minister, at Salem village? Oh, his voice would make me tremble both Sabbath day and lecture day."

Thus far the elder traveller had listened with due gravity; but now burst into a fit of irrepressible mirth, shaking himself so violently that his snake-like staff actually seemed to wriggle in sympathy.

"Ha! ha! ha!" shouted he again and again; then composing himself, "Well, go on, Goodman Brown, go on; but, prithee, don't kill me with laughing."

"Well, then, to end the matter at once," said Goodman Brown, considerably nettled, "there is my wife, Faith. It would break her dear little heart; and I'd rather break my own."

"Nay, if that be the case," answered the other, "e'en go thy ways, Goodman Brown. I would not for twenty old women like the one hobbling before us that Faith should come to any harm."

As he spoke he pointed his staff at a female figure on the path, in whom Goodman Brown recognized a very pious and exemplary dame, who had taught him his catechism in youth, and was still his moral and spiritual adviser, jointly with the minister and Deacon Gookin.

"A marvel, truly that Goody Cloyse should be so far in the wilderness at nightfall," said he. "But with your leave, friend, I shall take a cut through the woods until we have left this Christian woman behind. Being a stranger to you, she might ask whom I was consorting with and whither I was going."

"Be it so," said his fellow-traveller. "Betake you to the woods, and let me keep the path."

Accordingly the young man turned aside, but took care to watch his companion, who advanced softly along the road until he had come within a staff's length of the old dame. She, meanwhile, was making the best of her way, with singular speed for so aged a woman, and mumbling some indistinct words—a prayer, doubtless—as she went. The traveller put forth his staff and touched her withered neck with what seemed the serpent's tail.

"The devil!" screamed the pious old lady.

"Then Goody Cloyse knows her old friend?" observed the traveller, confronting her and leaning on his writhing stick.

"Ah, forsooth, and is it your worship indeed?" cried the good dame. "Yea, truly is it, and in the very image of my old gossip, Goodman Brown, the grandfather of the silly fellow that now is. But—would your worship believe it?—my broomstick hath strangely disappeared, stolen, as I suspect, by that unhanged witch, Goody Cory, and that, too, when I was all anointed with the juice of smallage, and cinquefoil, and wolf's bane"—

"Mingled with fine wheat and the fat of a new-born babe," said the shape of old Goodman Brown.

"Ah, your worship knows the recipe," cried the old lady, cackling aloud. "So, as I was saying, being all ready for the meeting, and no horse to ride on, I made up my mind to foot it; for they tell me there is a nice young man to be taken into communion to-night. But now your good worship will lend me your arm, and we shall be there in a twinkling."

"That can hardly be," answered her friend. "I may not spare you my arm, Goody Cloyse; but here is my staff, if you will."

So saying, he threw it down at her feet, where, perhaps, it assumed life, being one of the rods which its owner had formerly lent to the Egyptian magi. Of this fact, however, Goodman Brown could not take cognizance. He had cast up his eyes in astonishment, and, looking down again, beheld neither Goody Cloyse nor the serpentine staff, but his fellow-traveller alone, who waited for him as calmly as if nothing had happened.

"That old woman taught me my catechism," said the young man; and there was a world of meaning in this simple comment.

They continued to walk onward, while the elder traveller exhorted his companion to make good speed and persevere in the path, discoursing so aptly that his arguments seemed rather to spring up in the bosom of his auditor than to be suggested by himself. As they went, he plucked a branch of maple to serve for a walking stick, and began to strip it of the twigs and little boughs, which were wet with evening dew. The moment his fingers touched them they became strangely withered and dried up as with a week's sunshine. Thus the pair proceeded, at a good free pace, until suddenly, in a gloomy hollow of the road, Goodman Brown sat himself down on the stump of a tree and refused to go any farther.

"Friend," he said, stubbornly, "my mind is made up. Not another step will I budge on this errand. What if a wretched old woman do choose to go to the devil when I thought she was going to heaven: is that any reason why I should quit my dear Faith and go after her?"

"You will think better of this by and by," said his acquaintance, composedly. "Sit here and rest yourself a while; and when you feel like moving again, there is my staff to help you along."

Without more words, he threw his companion the maple stick, and was as speedily out of sight as if he had vanished into the deepening gloom. The young man sat a few moments by the roadside, applauding himself greatly, and thinking with how clear a conscience he should meet the minister in his morning walk, nor shrink from the eye of good old Deacon Gookin. And what calm sleep would be his that very night, which was to have been spent so wickedly, but so purely and sweetly now, in the arms of Faith! Amidst these pleasant and praiseworthy meditations, Goodman Brown heard the tramp of horses along the road, and deemed it advisable to conceal himself within the verge of the forest, conscious of the guilty purpose that had brought him thither, though now so happily turned from it.

On came the hoof tramps and the voices of the riders, two grave old voices, conversing soberly as they drew near. These mingled sounds appeared to pass along the road, within a few yards of the young man's hiding-place; but, owing doubtless to the depth of the gloom at that particular spot, neither the travellers nor their steeds were visible. Though their figures brushed the small boughs by the wayside, it could not be seen that they intercepted, even for a moment, the faint gleam from the strip of bright sky athwart which they must have passed. Goodman Brown alternately crouched and stood on tiptoe, pulling aside the branches and thrusting forth his head as far as he durst without discerning so much as a shadow. It vexed him the more, because he could have sworn, were such a thing possible, that he recognized the voices of the minister and Deacon Gookin, jogging along quietly, as they were wont to do, when bound to some ordination or ecclesiastical council. While yet within hearing, one of the riders stopped to pluck a switch.

"Of the two, reverend sir," said the voice like the deacon's, "I had rather miss an ordination dinner than to-night's meeting. They tell me that some of our community are to be here from Falmouth and beyond, and others from Connecticut and Rhode Island, besides several of the Indian powwows, who, after their fashion, know almost as much deviltry as the best of us. Moreover, there is a goodly young woman to be taken into communion."

"Mighty well, Deacon Gookin!" replied the solemn old tones of the minister. "Spur up, or we shall be late. Nothing can be done, you know, until I get on the ground."

The hoofs clattered again; and the voices, talking so strangely in the empty air, passed on through the forest, where no church had ever been gathered or solitary Christian prayed. Whither, then, could these holy men be journeying so deep into the heathen wilderness? Young Goodman Brown caught hold of a tree for support, being ready to sink down on the ground, faint and overburdened with the heavy sickness of his heart. He looked up to the sky, doubting whether there really was a heaven above him. Yet there was the blue arch, and the stars brightening in it.

"With heaven above and Faith below, I will yet stand firm against the devil!" cried Goodman Brown.

While he still gazed upward into the deep arch of the firmament and had lifted his hands to pray, a cloud, though no wind was stirring, hurried across the zenith and hid the brightening stars. The blue sky was still visible, except directly overhead, where this black mass of cloud was sweeping swiftly northward. Aloft in the air, as if from the depths of the cloud, came a confused and doubtful sound of voices. Once the listener fancied that he could distinguish the accents of towns-people of his own, men and women, both pious and ungodly, many of whom he had met at the communion table, and had seen others rioting at the tavern. The next moment, so indistinct were the sounds, he doubted whether he had heard aught but the murmur of the old forest, whispering without a wind. Then came a stronger swell of those familiar tones, heard daily in the sunshine at Salem village, but never until now from a cloud of night. There was one voice, of a young woman, uttering lamentations, yet with an uncertain sorrow, and entreating for some favor, which, perhaps, it would grieve her to obtain; and all the unseen multitude, both saints and sinners, seemed to encourage her onward.

"Faith!" shouted Goodman Brown, in a voice of agony and desperation; and the echoes of the forest mocked him, crying, "Faith! Faith!" as if bewildered wretches were seeking her all through the wilderness.

The cry of grief, rage, and terror was yet piercing the night, when the unhappy husband held his breath for a response. There was a scream, drowned immediately in a louder murmur of voices, fading into far-off laughter, as the dark cloud swept away, leaving the clear and silent sky above Goodman Brown. But something fluttered lightly down through the air and caught on the branch of a tree. The young man seized it, and beheld a pink ribbon.

"My Faith is gone!" cried he after one stupefied moment. "There is no good on earth; and sin is but a name. Come, devil; for to thee is this world given."

And, maddened with despair, so that he laughed loud and long, did Goodman Brown grasp his staff and set forth again, at such a rate that he seemed to fly along the forest path rather than to walk or run. The road grew wilder and drearier and more faintly traced, and vanished at length, leaving him in the heart of the dark wilderness, still rushing onward with the instinct that guides mortal man to evil. The whole forest was peopled with frightful sounds—the creaking of the trees, the howling of wild beasts, and the yell of Indians; while sometimes the wind tolled like a distant church bell, and sometimes gave a broad roar around the traveller, as if all Nature were laughing him to scorn. But he was himself the chief horror of the scene, and shrank not from its other horrors.

"Ha! ha! ha!" roared Goodman Brown when the wind laughed at him. "Let us hear which will laugh loudest. Think not to frighten me with your deviltry. Come witch, come wizard, come Indian powwow, come devil himself, and here comes Goodman Brown. You may as well fear him as he fear you."

In truth, all through the haunted forest there could be nothing more frightful than the figure of Goodman Brown. On he flew among the black pines, brandishing his staff with frenzied gestures, now giving vent to an inspiration of horrid blasphemy, and now shouting forth such laughter as set all the echoes of the forest laughing like demons around him. The fiend in his own shape is less hideous than when he rages in the breast of man. Thus sped the demoniac on his course, until, quivering among the trees, he saw a red light before him, as when the felled trunks and branches of a clearing have been set on fire, and throw up their lurid blaze against the sky, at the hour of midnight. He paused, in a lull of the tempest that had driven him onward, and heard the swell of what seemed a hymn, rolling solemnly from a distance with the weight of many voices. He knew the tune; it was a familiar one in the choir of the village meeting-house. The verse died heavily away, and was lengthened by a chorus, not of human voices, but of all the sounds of the benighted wilderness pealing in awful harmony together. Goodman Brown cried out, and his cry was lost to his own ear by its unison with the cry of the desert.

In the interval of silence he stole forward until the light glared full upon his eyes. At one extremity of an open space, hemmed in by the dark wall of the forest, arose a rock, bearing some rude, natural resemblance either to an altar or a pulpit, and surrounded by four blazing pines, their tops aflame, their stems untouched, like candles at an evening meeting. The mass of foliage that had overgrown the summit of the rock was all on fire, blazing high into the night and fitfully illuminating the whole field. Each pendent twig and leafy festoon was in a blaze. As the red light arose and fell, a numerous congregation alternately shone forth, then disappeared in shadow, and again grew, as it were, out of the darkness, peopling the heart of the solitary woods at once.

"A grave and dark-clad company," quoth Goodman Brown.

In truth they were such. Among them, quivering to and fro between gloom and splendor, appeared faces that would be seen next day at the council board of the province, and others which, Sabbath after Sabbath, looked devoutly heavenward, and benignantly over the crowded pews, from the holiest pulpits in the land. Some affirm that the lady of the governor was there. At least there were high dames well known to her, and wives of honored husbands, and widows, a great multitude, and ancient maidens, all of excellent repute, and fair young girls, who trembled lest their mothers should espy them. Either the sudden gleams of light flashing over the obscure field bedazzled Goodman Brown, or he recognized a score of the church members of Salem village famous for their especial sanctity. Good old Deacon Gookin had arrived, and waited at the skirts of that venerable saint, his revered pastor. But, irreverently consorting with these grave, reputable, and pious people, these elders of the church, these chaste dames and dewy virgins, there were men of dissolute lives and women of spotted fame, wretches given over to all mean and filthy vice, and suspected even of horrid crimes. It was strange to see that the good shrank not from the wicked, nor were the sinners abashed by the saints. Scattered also among their palefaced enemies were the Indian priests, or powwows, who had often scared their native forest with more hideous incantations than any known to English witchcraft.

"But where is Faith?" thought Goodman Brown; and, as hope came into his heart, he trembled.

Another verse of the hymn arose, a slow and mournful strain, such as the pious love, but joined to words which expressed all that our nature can conceive of sin, and darkly hinted at far more. Unfathomable to mere mortals is the lore of fiends. Verse after verse was sung; and still the chorus of the desert swelled between like the deepest tone of a mighty organ; and with the final peal of that dreadful anthem there came a sound, as if the roaring wind, the rushing streams, the howling beasts, and every other voice of the unconcerted wilderness were mingling and according with the voice of guilty man in homage to the prince of all. The four blazing pines threw up a loftier flame, and obscurely discovered shapes and visages of horror on the smoke wreaths above the impious assembly. At the same moment the fire on the rock shot redly forth and formed a glowing arch above its base, where now appeared a figure. With reverence be it spoken, the figure bore no slight similitude, both in garb and manner, to some grave divine of the New England churches.

"Bring forth the converts!" cried a voice that echoed through the field and rolled into the forest.

At the word, Goodman Brown stepped forth from the shadow of the trees and approached the congregation, with whom he felt a loathful brotherhood by the sympathy of all that was wicked in his heart. He could have well-nigh sworn that the shape of his own dead father beckoned him to advance, looking downward from a smoke wreath, while a woman, with dim features of depair, threw out her hand to warn him back. Was it his mother? But he had no power to retreat one step, nor to resist, even in thought, when the minister and good old Deacon Gookin seized his arms and led him to the blazing rock. Thither came also the slender form of a veiled female, led between Goody Cloyse, that pious teacher of the cate-chism, and Martha Carrier, who had received the devil's promise to be queen of hell. A rampant hag was she. And there stood the proselytes be-neath the canopy of fire.

"Welcome, my children," said the dark figure, "to the communion of your race. Ye have found thus young your nature and your destiny. My children, look behind you!"

They turned; and flashing forth, as it were, in a sheet of flame, the fiend worshippers were seen; the smile of welcome gleamed darkly on every visage.

"There," resumed the sable form, "are all whom ye have reverenced from youth. Ye deemed them holier than yourselves and shrank from your own sin, contrasting it with their lives of righteousness and prayerful aspi-rations heavenward. Yet here are they all in my worshipping assembly. This night it shall be granted you to know their secret deeds: how hoary-bearded elders of the church have whispered wanton words to the young maids of their households; how many a woman, eager for widows' weeds, has given her husband a drink at bedtime and let him sleep his last sleep in her bo-som; how beardless youths have made haste to inherit their fathers' wealth; and how fair damsels—blush not, sweet ones—have dug little graves in the garden, and bidden me, the sole guest, to an infant's funeral. By the sym-pathy of your human hearts for sin ye shall scent out all the places—whether in church, bedchamber, street, field, or forest—where crime has been committed, and shall exult to behold the whole earth one stain of guilt, one mighty blood spot. Far more than this. It shall be yours to pen-etrate, in every bosom, the deep mystery of sin, the fountain of all wicked arts, and which inexhaustibly supplies more evil impulses than human power—than my power at its utmost—can make manifest in deeds. And now, my children, look upon each other."

They did so; and, by the blaze of the hell-kindled torches, the wretched man beheld his Faith, and the wife her husband, trembling before that unhallowed altar.

"Lo, there ye stand, my children," said the figure, in a deep and sol-emn tone, almost sad with its despairing awfulness, as if his once angelic nature could yet mourn for our miserable race. "Depending upon one an-other's hearts, ye had still hoped that virtue were not all a dream. Now are ye undeceived. Evil is the nature of mankind. Evil must be your only hap-piness. Welcome again, my children, to the communion of your race."

"Welcome," repeated the fiend worshippers, in one cry of despair and triumph.

And there they stood, the only pair, as it seemed, who were yet hesitating on the verge of wickedness in this dark world. A basin was hollowed, naturally, in the rock. Did it contain water, reddened by the lurid light? or was it blood? or, perchance, a liquid flame? Herein did the shape of evil dip his hand and prepare to lay the mark of baptism upon their foreheads, that they might be partakers of the mystery of sin, more conscious of the secret guilt of others, both in deed and thought, than they could now be of their own. The husband cast one look at his pale wife, and Faith at him. What polluted wretches would the next glance show them to each other, shuddering alike at what they disclosed and what they saw!

"Faith! Faith!" cried the husband, "look up to heaven, and resist the wicked one."

Whether Faith obeyed he knew not. Hardly had he spoken when he found himself amid calm night and solitude, listening to a roar of the wind which died heavily away through the forest. He staggered against the rock, and felt it chill and damp; while a hanging twig, that had been all on fire, besprinkled his cheek with the coldest dew.

The next morning young Goodman Brown came slowly into the street of Salem village, staring around him like a bewildered man. The good old minister was taking a walk along the graveyard to get an appetite for breakfast and meditate his sermon, and bestowed a blessing, as he passed, on Goodman Brown. He shrank from the venerable saint as if to avoid an anathema. Old Deacon Gookin was at domestic worship, and the holy words of his prayer were heard through the open window. "What God doth the wizard pray to?" quoth Goodman Brown. Goody Cloyse, that excellent old Christian, stood in the early sunshine at her own lattice, catechizing a little girl who had brought her a pint of morning's milk. Goodman Brown snatched away the child as from the grasp of the fiend himself. Turning the corner by the meeting-house, he spied the head of Faith, with the pink ribbons, gazing anxiously forth, and bursting into such joy at sight of him that she skipped along the street and almost kissed her husband before the whole village. But Goodman Brown looked sternly and sadly into her face, and passed on without a greeting.

Had Goodman Brown fallen asleep in the forest and only dreamed a wild dream of a witch-meeting?

Be it so if you will; but, alas! it was a dream of evil omen for young Goodman Brown. A stern, a sad, a darkly meditative, a distrustful, if not a desperate man did he become from the night of that fearful dream. On the Sabbath day, when the congregation were singing a holy psalm, he could not listen because an anthem of sin rushed loudly upon his ear and drowned all the blessed strain. When the minister spoke from the pulpit with power and fervid eloquence, and, with his hand on the open Bible, of the sacred truths of our religion, and of saint-like lives and triumphant deaths, and of future bliss or misery unutterable, then did Goodman Brown turn pale, dreading lest the roof should thunder down upon the gray blasphemer and his hearers. Often, awaking suddenly at midnight, he shrank from the bosom of Faith; and at morning or eventide, when the family knelt down at prayer, he scowled and muttered to himself, and gazed sternly at his wife, and turned away. And when he had lived long, and was borne to his grave a hoary corpse, followed by Faith, an aged woman, and children and grandchildren, a goodly procession, besides neighbors not a few, they carved no hopeful verse upon his tombstone, for his dying hour was gloom.

WILLIAM FAULKNER (1897–1962)

A Rose for Emily

William Faulkner, considered by many to be America's most important twentieth-century novelist, was born in New Albany, Mississippi, and attended the University of Mississippi. Among his major novels, most of which center around a fictional county in Mississippi, are *The Sound and the Fury* (1929), *Light in August* (1932), and *Absalom, Absalom!* (1936). He won the Nobel Prize for Literature in 1950. "A Rose for Emily" first appeared in 1931.

I

When Miss Emily Grierson died, our whole town went to her funeral: the men through a sort of respectful affection for a fallen monument, the women mostly out of curiosity to see the inside of her house, which no one save an old manservant—a combined gardener and cook—had seen in at least ten years.

It was a big, squarish frame house that had once been white, decorated with cupolas and spires and scrolled balconies in the heavily lightsome style of the seventies, set on what had once been our most select street. But garages and cotton gins had encroached and obliterated even the august names of that neighborhood; only Miss Emily's house was left, lifting its stubborn and coquettish decay above the cotton wagons and the gasoline pumps—an eyesore among eyesores. And now Miss Emily had gone to join the representatives of those august names where they lay in the cedar-bemused cemetery among the ranked and anonymous graves of Union and Confederate soldiers who fell at the battle of Jefferson.

Alive, Miss Emily had been a tradition, a duty, and a care; a sort of hereditary obligation upon the town, dating from that day in 1894 when Colonel Sartoris, the mayor—he who fathered the edict that no Negro woman should appear on the streets without an apron—remitted her taxes, the dispensation dating from the death of her father on into perpetuity. Not that Miss Emily would have accepted charity. Colonel Sartoris invented an involved tale to the effect that Miss Emily's father had loaned money to the town, which the town, as a matter of business, preferred this way of repaying. Only a man of Colonel Sartoris' generation and thought could have invented it, and only a woman could have believed it.

When the next generation, with its more modern ideas, became mayors and aldermen, this arrangement created some little dissatisfaction. On the first of the year they mailed her a tax notice. February came, and there was no reply. They wrote her a formal letter, asking her to call at the sheriff's office at her convenience. A week later the mayor wrote her himself, offering to call or to send his car for her, and received in reply a note on paper of an archaic shape, in a thin, flowing calligraphy in faded ink, to the effect that she no longer went out at all. The tax notice was also enclosed, without comment.

They called a special meeting of the Board of Aldermen. A deputation waited upon her, knocked at the door through which no visitor had passed since she ceased giving china-painting lessons eight or ten years earlier. They were admitted by the old Negro into a dim hall from which a stairway mounted into still more shadow. It smelled of dust and disuse—a close, dank smell. The Negro led them into the parlor. It was furnished in heavy, leather-covered furniture. When the Negro opened the blinds of one window, they could see that the leather was cracked; and when they sat down, a faint dust rose sluggishly about their thighs, spinning with slow motions in the single sun-ray. On a tarnished gilt easel before the fireplace stood a crayon portrait of Miss Emily's father.

They rose when she entered—a small, fat woman in black, with a thin gold chain descending to her waist and vanishing into her belt, leaning on an ebony cane with a tarnished gold head. Her skeleton was small and spare; perhaps that was why what would have been merely plumpness in another was obesity in her. She looked bloated, like a body long submerged in motionless water, and of that pallid hue. Her eyes, lost in the fatty ridges of her face, looked like two small pieces of coal pressed into a lump of dough as they moved from one face to another while the visitors stated their errand.

She did not ask them to sit. She just stood in the door and listened quietly until the spokesman came to a stumbling halt. Then they could hear the invisible watch ticking at the end of the gold chain.

Her voice was dry and cold. "I have no taxes in Jefferson. Colonel Sartoris explained it to me. Perhaps one of you can gain access to the city records and satisfy yourselves."

"But we have. We are the city authorities, Miss Emily. Didn't you get a notice from the sheriff, signed by him?"

"I received a paper, yes," Miss Emily said. "Perhaps he considers himself the sheriff . . . I have no taxes in Jefferson."

"But there is nothing on the books to show that, you see. We must go by the—"

"See Colonel Sartoris." (Colonel Sartoris had been dead almost ten years.) "I have no taxes in Jefferson. Tobe!" The Negro appeared. "Show these gentlemen out."

II

So she vanquished them, horse and foot, just as she had vanquished their fathers thirty years before about the smell. That was two years after her father's death and a short time after her sweetheart—the one we believed would marry her—had deserted her. After her father's death she went out very little; after her sweetheart went away, people hardly saw her at all. A few of the ladies had the temerity to call, but were not received, and the only sign of life about the place was the Negro man—a young man then—going in and out with a market basket.

"Just as if a man—any man—could keep a kitchen properly," the ladies said; so they were not surprised when the smell developed. It was another link between the gross, teeming world and the high and mighty Griersons.

A neighbor, a woman, complained to the mayor, Judge Stevens, eighty years old.

"But what will you have me do about it, madam?" he said.

"Why, send her word to stop it," the woman said. "Isn't there a law?"

"I'm sure that won't be necessary," Judge Stevens said. "It's probably just a snake or a rat that nigger of hers killed in the yard. I'll speak to him about it."

The next day he received two more complaints, one from a man who came in diffident deprecation. "We really must do something about it, Judge. I'd be the last one in the world to bother Miss Emily, but we've got to do something." That night the Board of Aldermen met—three graybeards and one younger man, a member of the rising generation.

"It's simple enough," he said. "Send her word to have her place cleaned up. Give her a certain time to do it in, and if she don't . . ."

"Dammit, sir," Judge Stevens said, "will you accuse a lady to her face of smelling bad?"

So the next night, after midnight, four men crossed Miss Emily's lawn and slunk about the house like burglars, sniffing along the base of the brickwork and at the cellar openings while one of them performed a regular sowing motion with his hand out of a sack slung from his shoulder. They broke open the cellar door and sprinkled lime there, and in all the outbuildings. As they recrossed the lawn, a window that had been dark was lighted and Miss Emily sat in it, the light behind her, and her upright torso motionless as that of an idol. They crept quietly across the lawn and into the shadow of the locusts that lined the street. After a week or two the smell went away.

That was when people had begun to feel really sorry for her. People in our town, remembering how old lady Wyatt, her great-aunt, had gone completely crazy at last, believed that the Griersons held themselves a little too high for what they really were. None of the young men were quite good enough for Miss Emily and such. We had long thought of them as a tableau, Miss Emily a slender figure in white in the background, her father a spraddled silhouette in the foreground, his back to her and clutching a horse-whip, the two of them framed by the back-flung front door. So when she got to be thirty and was still single, we were not pleased exactly, but vindicated; even with insanity in the family she wouldn't have turned down all of her chances if they had really materialized.

When her father died, it got about that the house was all that was left to her; and in a way, people were glad. At last they could pity Miss Emily. Being left alone, and a pauper, she had become humanized. Now she too would know the old thrill and the old despair of a penny more or less.

The day after his death all the ladies prepared to call at the house and offer condolence and aid, as is our custom. Miss Emily met them at the door, dressed as usual and with no trace of grief on her face. She told them that her father was not dead. She did that for three days, with the ministers calling on her, and the doctors, trying to persuade her to let them dispose of the body. Just as they were about to resort to law and force, she broke down, and they buried her father quickly.

We did not say she was crazy then. We believed she had to do that. We remembered all the young men her father had driven away, and we knew that with nothing left, she would have to cling to that which had robbed her, as people will.

III

She was sick for a long time. When we saw her again, her hair was cut short, making her look like a girl, with a vague resemblance to those angels in colored church windows—sort of tragic and serene.

The town had just let the contracts for paving the sidewalks, and in the summer after her father's death they began the work. The construction company came with niggers and mules and machinery, and a foreman named Homer Barron, a Yankee—a big, dark, ready man, with a big voice and eyes lighter than his face. The little boys would follow in groups to hear him cuss the niggers, and the niggers singing in time to the rise and fall of picks. Pretty soon he knew everybody in town. Whenever you heard a lot of laughing anywhere about the square, Homer Barron would be in the center of the group. Presently we began to see him and Miss Emily on Sunday afternoons driving in the yellow-wheeled buggy and the matched team of bays from the livery stable.

At first we were glad that Miss Emily would have an interest, because the ladies all said, "Of course a Grierson would not think seriously of a Northerner, a day laborer." But there were still others, older people, who said that even grief could not cause a real lady to forget *noblesse oblige*— without calling it *noblesse oblige*. They just said, "Poor Emily. Her kinsfolk should come to her." She had some kin in Alabama; but years ago her father had fallen out with them over the estate of old lady Wyatt, the crazy woman, and there was no communication between the two families. They had not even been represented at the funeral.

And as soon as the old people said, "Poor Emily," the whispering began. "Do you suppose it's really so?" they said to one another. "Of course it is. What else could . . ." This behind their hands; rustling of craned silk and satin behind jalousies closed upon the sun of Sunday afternoon as the thin, swift clop-clop-clop of the matched team passed: "Poor Emily."

She carried her head high enough—even when we believed that she was fallen. It was as if she demanded more than ever the recognition of her dignity as the last Grierson; as if it had wanted that touch of earthiness to reaffirm her imperviousness. Like when she bought the rat poison, the arsenic. That was over a year after they had begun to say "Poor Emily," and while the two female cousins were visiting her.

"I want some poison," she said to the druggist. She was over thirty then, still a slight woman, though thinner than usual, with cold, haughty black eyes in a face the flesh of which was strained across the temples and about the eye-sockets as you imagine a lighthousekeeper's face ought to look. "I want some poison," she said.

"Yes, Miss Emily. What kind? For rats and such? I'd recom—"

"I want the best you have. I don't care what kind."

The druggist named several. "They'll kill anything up to an elephant. But what you want is—"

"Arsenic," Miss Emily said. "Is that a good one?"

"Is . . . arsenic? Yes, ma'am. But what you want—"

"I want arsenic."

The druggist looked down at her. She looked back at him, erect, her face like a strained flag. "Why, of course," the druggist said. "If that's what you want. But the law requires you to tell what you are going to use it for."

Miss Emily just stared at him, her head tilted back in order to look him eye for eye, until he looked away and went and got the arsenic and wrapped it up. The Negro delivery boy brought her the package; the druggist didn't come back. When she opened the package at home there was written on the box, under the skull and bones: "For rats."

IV

So the next day we all said, "She will kill herself"; and we said it would be the best thing. When she had first begun to be seen with Homer Barron, we had said, "She will marry him." Then we said, "She will persuade him yet," because Homer himself had remarked—he liked men, and it was known that he drank with the younger men in the Elks' Club—that he was not a marrying man. Later we said, "Poor Emily" behind the jalousies as they passed on Sunday afternoon in the glittering buggy, Miss Emily with her head high and Homer Barron with his hat cocked and a cigar in his teeth, reins and whip in a yellow glove.

Then some of the ladies began to say that it was a disgrace to the town and a bad example to the young people. The men did not want to interfere, but at last the ladies forced the Baptist minister—Miss Emily's people were Episcopal—to call upon her. He would never divulge what happened during that interview, but he refused to go back again. The next Sunday they again drove about the streets, and the following day the minister's wife wrote to Miss Emily's relations in Alabama.

So she had blood-kin under her roof again and we sat back to watch developments. At first nothing happened. Then we were sure that they were to be married. We learned that Miss Emily had been to the jeweler's and ordered a man's toilet set in silver, with the letters H.B. on each piece. Two days later we learned that she had bought a complete outfit of men's clothing, including a nightshirt, and we said, "They are married." We were really glad. We were glad because the two female cousins were even more Grierson than Miss Emily had ever been.

So we were not surprised when Homer Barron—the streets had been finished some time since—was gone. We were a little disappointed that there was not a public blowing-off, but we believed that he had gone on to prepare for Miss Emily's coming, or to give her a chance to get rid of the cousins. (By that time it was a cabal, and we were all Miss Emily's allies to help circumvent the cousins.) Sure enough, after another week they departed. And, as we had expected all along, within three days Homer Barron was back in town. A neighbor saw the Negro man admit him at the kitchen door at dusk one evening.

And that was the last we saw of Homer Barron. And of Miss Emily for some time. The Negro man went in and out with the market basket, but the front door remained closed. Now and then we would see her at a window for a moment, as the men did that night when they sprinkled the lime, but for almost six months she did not appear on the streets. Then we knew that this was to be expected too; as if that quality of her father which had thwarted her woman's life so many times had been too virulent and too furious to die.

When we next saw Miss Emily, she had grown fat and her hair was turning gray. During the next few years it grew grayer and grayer until it attained an even pepper-and-salt iron-gray, when it ceased turning. Up to the day of her death at seventy-four it was still that vigorous iron-gray, like the hair of an active man.

From that time on her front door remained closed, save for a period of six or seven years, when she was about forty, during which she gave lessons in china-painting. She fitted up a studio in one of the downstairs rooms, where the daughters and granddaughters of Colonel Sartoris' contemporaries were sent to her with the same regularity and in the same spirit that they were sent to church on Sundays with a twenty-five-cent piece for the collection plate. Meanwhile her taxes had been remitted.

Then the newer generation became the backbone and the spirit of the town, and the painting pupils grew up and fell away and did not send their children to her with boxes of color and tedious brushes and pictures cut from the ladies' magazines. The front door closed upon the last one and remained closed for good. When the town got free postal delivery, Miss Emily alone refused to let them fasten the metal numbers above her door and attach a mailbox to it. She would not listen to them.

Daily, monthly, yearly we watched the Negro grow grayer and more stooped, going in and out with the market basket. Each December we sent her a tax notice, which would be returned by the post office a week later, unclaimed. Now and then we would see her in one of the downstairs windows—she had evidently shut up the top floor of the house—like the carven torso of an idol in a niche, looking or not looking at us, we could never tell which. Thus she passed from generation to generation—dear, inescapable, impervious, tranquil, and perverse.

And so she died. Fell ill in the house filled with dust and shadows, with only a doddering Negro man to wait on her. We did not even know she was sick; we had long since given up trying to get any information from the Negro. He talked to no one, probably not even to her, for his voice had grown harsh and rusty, as if from disuse.

She died in one of the downstairs rooms, in a heavy walnut bed with a curtain, her gray head propped on a pillow yellow and moldy with age and lack of sunlight.

V

The Negro met the first of the ladies at the front door and let them in, with their hushed, sibilant voices and their quick, curious glances, and then he disappeared. He walked right through the house and out the back and was not seen again.

The two female cousins came at once. They held the funeral on the second day, with the town coming to look at Miss Emily beneath a mass of bought flowers, with the crayon face of her father musing profoundly above the bier and the ladies sibilant and macabre; and the very old men—some in their brushed Confederate uniforms—on the porch and the lawn, talking of Miss Emily as if she had been a contemporary of theirs, believing that they had danced with her and courted her perhaps, confusing time with its mathematical progression, as the old do, to whom all the past is not a diminishing road but, instead, a huge meadow which no winter ever quite touches, divided from them now by the narrow bottle-neck of the most recent decade of years.

Already we knew that there was one room in that region above stairs which no one had seen in forty years, and which would have to be forced. They waited until Miss Emily was decently in the ground before they opened it.

The violence of breaking down the door seemed to fill this room with pervading dust. A thin, acrid pall as of the tomb seemed to lie everywhere upon this room decked and furnished as for a bridal: upon the valance curtains of faded rose color, upon the rose-shaded lights, upon the dressing table, upon the delicate array of crystal and the man's toilet things backed with tarnished silver, silver so tarnished that the monogram was obscured. Among them lay a collar and tie, as if they had just been removed, which, lifted, left upon the surface a pale crescent in the dust. Upon a chair hung the suit, carefully folded; beneath it the two mute shoes and the discarded socks.

The man himself lay in the bed.

For a long while we just stood there, looking down at the profound and fleshless grin. The body had apparently once lain in the attitude of an embrace, but now the long sleep that outlasts love, that conquers even the grimace of love, had cuckolded him. What was left of him, rotted beneath what was left of the nightshirt, had become inextricable from the bed in which he lay; and upon him and upon the pillow beside him lay that even coating of the patient and biding dust.

Then we noticed that in the second pillow was the indentation of a head. One of us lifted something from it, and leaning forward, that faint and invisible dust dry and acrid in the nostrils, we saw a long strand of iron-gray hair.

JOHN UPDIKE (b. 1932)

A & P

John Updike, who was born in Shillington, Pennsylvania, has written novels, short stories, poetry, and criticism. He served on the staff of *The New Yorker* and is still a frequent contributor to its pages. Among his most famous works are *Rabbit, Run* (1960), *Couples* (1968), and *Rabbit Redux* (1971). "A & P" was first collected in *Pigeon Feathers* (1962).

In walks these three girls in nothing but bathing suits. I'm in the third checkout slot, with my back to the door, so I don't see them until they're over by the bread. The one that caught my eye first was the one in the plaid green two-piece. She was a chunky kid, with a good tan and a sweet broad soft-looking can with those two crescents of white just under it, where the sun never seems to hit, at the top of the backs of her legs. I stood there with my hand on a box of HiHo crackers trying to remember if I rang it up or not. I ring it up again and the customer starts giving me hell. She's one of these cash-register-watchers, a witch about fifty with rouge on her cheekbones and no eyebrows, and I know it made her day to trip me up. She'd been watching cash registers for fifty years and probably never seen a mistake before.

By the time I got her feathers smoothed and her goodies into a bag— she gives me a little snort in passing, if she'd been born at the right time they would have burned her over in Salem—by the time I get her on her way the girls had circled around the bread and were coming back, without a pushcart, back my way along the counters, in the aisle between the check-outs and the Special bins. They didn't even have shoes on. There was this chunky one, with the two-piece—it was bright green and the seams on the bra were still sharp and her belly was still pretty pale so I guessed she just got it (the suit)—there was this one, with one of those chubby berry-faces, the lips all bunched together under her nose, this one, and a tall one, with black hair that hadn't quite frizzed right, and one of these sunburns right across under the eyes, and a chin that was too long—you know, the kind of girl other girls think is very "striking" and "attractive" but never quite makes it, as they very well know, which is why they like her so much— and then the third one, that wasn't quite so tall. She was the queen. She kind of led them, the other two peeking around and making their shoulders round. She didn't look around, not this queen, she just walked straight on slowly, on these long white prima-donna legs. She came down a little hard on her heels, as if she didn't walk in her bare feet that much, putting down her heels and then letting the weight move along to her toes as if she was testing the floor with every step, putting a little deliberate extra action into it. You never know for sure how girls' minds work (do you really think it's a mind in there or just a little buzz like a bee in a glass jar?) but you got the idea she had talked the other two into coming in here with her, and now she was showing them how to do it, walk slow and hold yourself straight.

She had on a kind of dirty-pink—beige maybe, I don't know—bathing suit with a little nubble all over it and, what got me, the straps were down. They were off her shoulders looped loose around the cool tops of her arms, and I guess as a result the suit had slipped a little on her, so all around the top of the cloth there was this shining rim. If it hadn't been there you wouldn't have known there could have been anything whiter than those shoulders. With the straps pushed off, there was nothing between the top of the suit and the top of her head except just *her*, this clean bare plane of the top of her chest down from the shoulder bones like a dented sheet of metal tilted in the light. I mean, it was more than pretty.

She had sort of oaky hair that the sun and salt had bleached, done up in a bun that was unravelling, and a kind of prim face. Walking into the A & P with your straps down, I suppose it's the only kind of face you *can* have. She held her head so high her neck, coming up out of those white shoulders, looked kind of stretched, but I didn't mind. The longer her neck was, the more of her there was.

She must have felt in the corner of her eye me and over my shoulder Stokesie in the second slot watching, but she didn't tip. Not this queen. She kept her eyes moving across the racks, and stopped, and turned so slow it made my stomach rub the inside of my apron, and buzzed to the other two, who kind of huddled against her for relief, and they all three of them went up the cat-and-dog-food-breakfast-cereal-macaroni-rice-raisins-sea-sonings-spreads-spaghetti-soft-drinks-crackers-and-cookies aisle. From the third slot I look straight up this aisle to the meat counter, and I watched them all the way. The fat one with the tan sort of fumbled with the cookies, but on second thought she put the packages back. The sheep pushing their carts down the aisle—the girls were walking against the usual traffic (not that we have one-way signs or anything)—were pretty hilarious. You could see them, when Queenie's white shoulders dawned on them, kind of jerk, or hop, or hiccup, but their eyes snapped back to their own baskets and on they pushed. I bet you could set off dynamite in an A & P and the people would by and large keep reaching and checking oatmeal off their lists and muttering "Let me see, there was a third thing, began with A, asparagus, no, ah, yes, applesauce!" or whatever it is they do mutter. But there was no doubt, this jiggled them. A few houseslaves in pin curlers even looked around after pushing their carts past to make sure what they had seen was correct.

You know, it's one thing to have a girl in a bathing suit down on the beach, where what with the glare nobody can look at each other much any-way, and another thing in the cool of the A & P, under the fluorescent lights, against all those stacked packages, with her feet paddling along naked over our checkerboard green-and-cream rubber-tile floor.

"Oh Daddy," Stokesie said beside me. "I feel so faint."

"Darling," I said. "Hold me tight." Stokesie's married, with two babies chalked up on his fuselage already, but as far as I can tell that's the only difference. He's twenty-two, and I was nineteen this April.

"Is it done?" he asks, the responsible married man finding his voice. I forgot to say he thinks he's going to be manager some sunny day, maybe in 1990 when it's called the Great Alexandrov and Petrooshki Tea Company or something.

What he meant was, our town is five miles from a beach, with a big summer colony out on the Point, but we're right in the middle of town, and the women generally put on a shirt or shorts or something before they get out of the car into the street. And anyway these are usually women with six children and varicose veins mapping their legs and nobody, including them, could care less. As I say, we're right in the middle of town, and if you stand at our front doors you can see two banks and the Congregational church and the newspaper store and three real-estate offices and about twenty-seven old freeloaders tearing up Central Street because the sewer broke again. It's not as if we're on the Cape; we're north of Boston and there's people in this town haven't seen the ocean for twenty years.

The girls had reached the meat counter and were asking McMahon something. He pointed, they pointed, and they shuffled out of sight behind a pyramid of Diet Delight peaches. All that was left for us to see was old McMahon patting his mouth and looking after them sizing up their joints. Poor kids, I began to feel sorry for them, they couldn't help it.

Now here comes the sad part of the story, at least my family says it's sad but I don't think it's sad myself. The store's pretty empty, it being Thursday afternoon, so there was nothing much to do except lean on the register and wait for the girls to show up again. The whole store was like a pinball machine and I didn't know which tunnel they'd come out of. After a while they come around out of the far aisle, around the light bulbs, re-cords at discount of the Caribbean Six or Tony Martin Sings or some such gunk you wonder they waste the wax on, sixpacks of candy bars, and plastic toys done up in cellophane that fall apart when a kid looks at them anyway. Around they come, Queenie still leading the way, and holding a little gray jar in her hand. Slots Three through Seven are unmanned and I could see her wondering between Stokes and me, but Stokesie with his usual luck draws an old party in baggy gray pants who stumbles up with four giant cans of pineapple juice (what do these bums *do* with all that pineapple juice? I've often asked myself) so the girls come to me. Queenie puts down the jar and I take it into my fingers icy cold. Kingfish Fancy Herring Snacks in Pure Sour Cream: 49¢. Now her hands are empty, not a ring or a bracelet, bare as God made them, and I wonder where the money's coming from. Still with that prim look she lifts a folded dollar bill out of the hollow at the center of her nubbled pink top. The jar went heavy in my hand. Really, I thought that was so cute.

Then every body's luck begins to run out. Lengel comes in from hag-gling with a truck full of cabbages on the lot and is about to scuttle into that door marked MANAGER behind which he hides all day when the girls touch his eye. Lengel's pretty dreary, teaches Sunday school and the rest, but he doesn't miss that much. He comes over and says, "Girls, this isn't the beach."

Queenie blushes, though maybe it's just a brush of sunburn I was no-ticing for the first time, now that she was so close. "My mother asked me to pick up a jar of herring snacks." Her voice kind of startled me, the way voices do when you see the people first, coming out so flat and dumb yet kind of tony, too, the way it ticked over "pick up" and "snacks." All of a sudden I slid right down her voice into her living room. Her father and the other men were standing around in ice-cream coats and bow ties and the women were in sandals picking up herring snacks on toothpicks off a big plate and they were all holding drinks the color of water with olives and sprigs of mint in them. When my parents have somebody over they get lemonade and if it's a real racy affair Schlitz in tall glasses with "They'll Do It Every Time" cartoons stencilled on.

"That's all right," Lengel said. "But this isn't the beach." His repeating this struck me as funny, as if it had just occurred to him, and he had been thinking all these years the A & P was a great big dune and he was the head lifeguard. He didn't like my smiling—as I say he doesn't miss much—but he concentrates on giving the girls that sad Sunday-school-superintendent stare.

Queenie's blush is no sunburn now, and the plump one in plaid, that I liked better from the back—a really sweet can—pipes up, "We weren't doing any shopping. We just came in for the one thing."

"That makes no difference," Lengel tells her, and I could see from the way his eyes went that he hadn't noticed she was wearing a two-piece before. "We want you decently dressed when you come in here."

"We *are* decent," Queenie says suddenly, her lower lip pushing, getting sore now that she remembers her place, a place from which the crowd that runs the A & P must look pretty crummy. Fancy Herring Snacks flashed in her very blue eyes.

"Girls, I don't want to argue with you. After this come in here with your shoulders covered. It's our policy." He turns his back. That's policy for you. Policy is what the kingpins want. What the others want is juvenile delinquency.

All this while, the customers had been showing up with their carts but, you know, sheep, seeing a scene, they had all bunched up on Stokesie, who shook open a paper bag as gently as peeling a peach, not wanting to miss a word. I could feel in the silence everybody getting nervous, most of all Lengel, who asks me, "Sammy, have you rung up this purchase?"

I thought and said "No" but it wasn't about that I was thinking. I go through the punches, 4, 9, GROC, TOT—it's more complicated than you think, and after you do it often enough, it begins to make a little song, that you hear words to, in my case "Hello (*bing*) there, you (*gung*) hap-py *pee-pul* (*splat*)!"—the *splat* being the drawer flying out. I uncrease the bill, tenderly as you may imagine, it just having come from between the two smoothest scoops of vanilla I had ever known were there, and pass a half and a penny into her narrow pink palm, and nestle the herrings in a bag and twist its neck and hand it over, all the time thinking.

The girls, and who'd blame them, are in a hurry to get out, so I say "I quit" to Lengel quick enough for them to hear, hoping they'll stop and watch me, their unsuspected hero. They keep right on going, into the electric eye; the door flies open and they flicker across the lot to their car, Queenie and Plaid and Big Tall Goony-Goony (not that as raw material she was so bad), leaving me with Lengel and a kink in his eyebrow.

"Did you say something, Sammy?"

"I said I quit."

"I thought you did."

"You didn't have to embarrass them."

"It was they who were embarrassing us."

I started to say something that came out "Fiddle-de-doo." It's a saying of my grandmother's, and I know she would have been pleased.

"I don't think you know what you're saying," Lengel said.

"I know you don't," I said. "But I do." I pull the bow at the back of my apron and start shrugging it off my shoulders. A couple customers that had been heading for my slot begin to knock against each other, like scared pigs in a chute.

Lengel sighs and begins to look very patient and old and gray. He's been a friend of my parents for years. "Sammy, you don't want to do this to your Mom and Dad," he tells me. It's true, I don't. But it seems to me that once you begin a gesture it's fatal not to go through with it. I fold the apron, "Sammy" stitched in red on the pocket, and put it on the counter, and drop the bow tie on top of it. The bow tie is theirs, if you've ever wondered. "You'll feel this for the rest of your life," Lengel says, and I know that's true, too, but remembering how he made that pretty girl blush makes me so scrunchy inside I punch the No Sale tab and the machine whirs "pee-pul" and the drawer splats out. One advantage to this scene taking place in summer, I can follow this up with a clean exit, there's no fumbling around getting your coat and galoshes, I just saunter into the electric eye in my white shirt that my mother ironed the night before, and the door heaves itself open, and outside the sunshine is skating around on the asphalt.

I look around for my girls, but they're gone, of course. There wasn't anybody but some young married screaming with her children about some candy they didn't get by the door of a powder-blue Falcon station wagon. Looking back in the big windows, over the bags of peat moss and aluminum lawn furniture stacked on the pavement, I could see Lengel in my place in the slot, checking the sheep through. His face was dark gray and his back stiff, as if he'd just had an injection of iron, and my stomach kind of fell as I felt how hard the world was going to be to me hereafter.

The Elements of Fiction

PLOT

When John Updike begins "A & P" with the words, "In walks these three girls in nothing but bathing suits," he arouses the most basic instinct to which fiction appeals: our curiosity. Above all we want to know what's going to happen. Similarly, when Poe's narrator, Montresor, addresses us in the opening lines of the classic horror story, "The Cask of Amontillado," with "The thousand injuries of Fortunato I had borne as I best could; but when he ventured upon insult, I vowed revenge," the words magically set the story in motion and keep our curiosity alive. The element of fiction that answers our primitive demand to know what happens is called the **narrative**. It consists of the story's sequence of events.

But stories do more than narrate that this happened and that happened. They link incidents of a narrative together with the subtle element of *causation* to form a **plot**. The classic distinction between narrative and plot was made by E. M. Forster, who said that "The king died and the queen died" was simply a narrative. But "The king died, and the queen died of grief" was a plot, because the latter contained the essential element of causation.

Even a relatively simple story like Kate Chopin's "The Storm" uses causation to link the narrative incidents together to form a plot. A sudden summer storm traps Bobinôt and his four-year-old son Bibi at Friedheimer's store, where they wait for the storm to pass. Meanwhile, Bobinôt's wife, Calixta, looks up from her sewing and, seeing the storm gathering, goes out on the front porch to take in Bobinôt's clothes, where she had left them to air. A former admirer, Alcée Laballière, asks for shelter on the porch, but as the porch affords no protection from the driving rain, he enters the house. The door to Calixta's bedroom is open; when a bolt of lightning strikes a nearby tree, Calixta and Alcée find themselves in each other's arms, and they make love in the bedroom. When the storm clears, Alcée rides off. Soon Bobinôt and Bibi are welcomed home by Calixta; the three make a happy family group at the dining-room table. The story concludes with Alcée writing his wife, Clarisse, to tell her she should stay a month longer, if she chooses, in Biloxi; for her part, Clarisse is glad to be temporarily free of the constraints of married life. The final line sums up the results: "The storm passed and everyone was happy." Each of the incidents in Chopin's story forms a link in a chain of cause and effect that inexorably brings the lovers together at the storm's height and then separates them in the ensuing calm.

A story like Chopin's "The Storm" follows a straightforward, chronological order. However, some stories jump back and forth in time, using flashbacks and scrambled chronology. For example, William Faulkner's "A Rose for Emily" begins with the funeral of Miss Emily Grierson, which is actually the next-to-last event in the narrative sequence. Faulkner then flashes back several decades to the remission of Miss Emily's taxes by the town's major in 1894 and then forward to the next generation's attempt to collect those taxes (all in the first several pages of the story). Faulkner continues to move back and forth in time—sometimes telling a portion of the story in chronological sequence, but more often flashing back to events that occurred earlier. Faulkner's purpose is to build *suspense* by momentarily obscuring the cause-and-effect connections between events. The temporary confusion that this causes is compensated for by the surprise ending, which has shock value because we have not anticipated the causal connections. Flashbacks also give a lifelike quality to fiction; in real life, we are rarely presented with information in chronological order and usually find things out in a more haphazard fashion.

In addition to a sequence of events with some causal connection, a plot must have **conflict.** Conflict may be defined as a clash between two opposing forces. The main character, the **protagonist,** is one force; a second force, the **antagonist,** tries to prevent the protagonist from reaching some sort of goal. The antagonist may be a person (or group of people), a physical force (such as a natural barrier), or some quality within the protagonist that must be overcome.

In the case of Goodman Brown, for example, the devil, the forest itself, or the members of the coven may be seen as antagonists preventing Goodman Brown from returning to his innocent wife, Faith. Viewed in this way, the story has an *external conflict,* because all of the opposing forces are outside Goodman Brown. But if Goodman Brown's resemblance to the devil is a clue about the source of evil and if Goodman Brown merely dreamt the "Black Sabbath," then the story's conclusion suggests that Goodman Brown is, himself, both protagonist and antagonist. The story then presents an *internal conflict* in which Goodman Brown's innocence is destroyed by his own cynicism, by his belief in the moral corruption of his wife and neighbors; thus, he becomes "a stern, a sad, a darkly meditative, a distrustful if not desperate man."

At the beginning of a story, we are often given background information to help us understand the nature of the ensuing conflict: Miss Emily's relationship with her father; the purpose of Goodman Brown's midnight errand. This portion of the short story is called the **exposition.** In some twentieth-century fiction (like Faulkner's), the expository information is scattered throughout the story to create a more lifelike impression.

When some event triggers the potential conflict between the opposing forces, the **complications** are underway: Miss Grierson refuses to acknowledge that her father is dead and will not allow him to be buried; Goodman Brown rejects his bride's pleas and enters the dark forest.

Once underway, the clash between the forces reaches a decisive turn at the **climax** or **turning point:** Miss Emily purchases some poison "for rats"; Goodman Brown cries, "My Faith is gone!" The decisive clash does not mean that the story is over; it indicates that one of the forces will soon emerge victorious or assume dominance: Miss Emily will keep her lover from deserting her, one way or another; Goodman Brown will succumb to a diabolical view of life and become a misanthrope.

In the **resolution,** the outcome anticipated in the climax is worked out: Miss Emily grows old and plump, but remains impervious to the forces of change; overnight, Goodman Brown becomes a pessimistic man who shuns his neighbors and turns away from his family.

Sometimes an explanation of the plot is attached as an epilogue. This **denouement** (literally, the "unraveling" or "untying") is an attempt to make the meaning of the conflict explicit to the reader. However, any heavyhanded or preachy prose is a flaw in a short story. Instead, fiction often works through *indirection,* merely hinting at the significance of the action. Faulkner provides the shocking detail of the iron-gray hair lifted from the hollow of the pillow to explain the extent to which Miss Emily refused to acknowledge change. Faulkner's use of the changing color of Miss Emily's hair to a final iron-gray throughout the story is an example of **foreshadowing**—the use of a detail to anticipate something that is about to happen. Hawthorne's denouement consists of his reminder that Goodman Brown's life became so bleak that "they carved no hopeful verse upon his tombstone, for his dying hour was gloom."

Although plot may seem to be one of the most primitive aspects of fiction, because it appeals only to our curiosity, plot is also one of the most subtle elements of fiction. Without an often very complex chain of causation linking together the parts of the plot, there can be no coherent meaning or character development. For example, without the chain of events leading up to the "Black Sabbath" in "Young Goodman Brown," Hawthorne's conclusion that Goodman Brown became a "darkly meditative . . . if not desperate man" would not make any sense; nor in "A & P" would Sammy's statement, "I felt how hard the world was going to be to me hereafter," be a valid summary of his growth without the chain of events that bring Sammy into direct conflict with Lengel. Plot, then, is the scaffolding on which the other elements of fiction depend.

In the two stories that follow, notice that Joyce constructs the plot of "Counterparts" in chronological order; Thurber, however, arouses our curiosity by starting in the middle of things and then flashing back to the initial event in the plot. See if you can locate the different parts of each plot, the ways in which the authors connect events, and whether the endings are foreshadowed by earlier details. You will find other questions about plot at the end of each story.

JAMES JOYCE (1882–1941)

Counterparts

James Joyce, born in Dublin, is Ireland's most famous writer of fiction. His first novel, *A Portrait of the Artist as a Young Man* (1916) depicts his youth in Ireland and suggests his reasons for going into self-exile in Europe from 1904 until his death. His restless experimentation with narrative form and technique culminated in two long novels: *Ulysses* (1922) and *Finnegan's Wake* (1939). "Counterparts" was first collected in *Dubliners* (1914), which includes Joyce's early stories of Irish urban life.

The bell rang furiously and, when Miss Parker went to the tube, a furious voice called out in a piercing North of Ireland accent:

—Send Farrington here!

Miss Parker returned to her machine, saying to a man who was writing at a desk:

—Mr. Alleyne wants you upstairs.

The man muttered *Blast him!* under his breath and pushed back his chair to stand up. When he stood up he was tall and of great bulk. He had a hanging face, dark wine-coloured, with fair eyebrows and moustache: his eyes bulged forward slightly and the whites of them were dirty. He lifted up the counter and, passing by the clients, went out of the office with a heavy step.

He went heavily upstairs until he came to the second landing, where a door bore a brass plate with the inscription *Mr. Alleyne.* Here he halted, puffing with labour and vexation, and knocked. The shrill voice cried:

—Come in!

The man entered Mr. Alleyne's room. Simultaneously Mr. Alleyne, a little man wearing gold-rimmed glasses on a clean-shaven face, shot his head up over a pile of documents. The head itself was so pink and hairless that it seemed like a large egg reposing on the papers. Mr. Alleyne did not lose a moment:

—Farrington? What is the meaning of this? Why have I always to complain of you? May I ask you why you haven't made a copy of that contract between Bodley and Kirwan? I told you it must be ready by four o'clock.

—But Mr. Shelley said, sir—

—*Mr. Shelley said, sir.* . . . Kindly attend to what I say and not to what *Mr. Shelley says, sir.* You have always some excuse or another for shirking work. Let me tell you that if the contract is not copied before this evening I'll lay the matter before Mr. Crosbie. . . . Do you hear me now?

—Yes, sir.

—Do you hear me now? . . . Ay and another little matter! I might as well be talking to the wall as talking to you. Understand once for all that you get a half an hour for your lunch and not an hour and a half. How many courses do you want, I'd like to know. . . . Do you mind me, now?

—Yes, sir.

Mr. Alleyne bent his head again upon his pile of papers. The man stared fixedly at the polished skull which directed the affairs of Crosbie & Alleyne, gauging its fragility. A spasm of rage gripped his throat for a few moments and then passed, leaving after it a sharp sensation of thirst. The man recognized the sensation and felt that he must have a good night's drinking. The middle of the month was passed and, if he could get the copy done in time, Mr. Alleyne might give him an order on the cashier. He stood still, gazing fixedly at the head upon the pile of papers. Suddenly Mr. Alleyne began to upset all the papers, searching for something. Then, as if he had been unaware of the man's presence till that moment, he shot up his head again, saying:

—Eh? Are you going to stand there all day? Upon my word, Farrington, you take things easy!

—I was waiting to see . . .

—Very good, you needn't wait to see. Go downstairs and do your work.

The man walked heavily towards the door and, as he went out of the room, he heard Mr. Alleyne cry after him that if the contract was not copied by evening Mr. Crosbie would hear of the matter.

He returned to his desk in the lower office and counted the sheets which remained to be copied. He took up his pen and dipped it in the ink but he continued to stare stupidly at the last words he had written: *In no case shall the said Bernard Bodley be* . . . The evening was falling and in a few minutes they would be lighting the gas: then he could write. He felt that he must slake the thirst in his throat. He stood up from his desk and, lifting the counter as before, passed out of the office. As he was passing out the chief clerk looked at him inquiringly.

—It's all right, Mr. Shelley, said the man, pointing with his finger to indicate the objective of his journey.

The chief clerk glanced at the hat-rack but, seeing the row complete, offered no remark. As soon as he was on the landing the man pulled a shepherd's plaid cap out of his pocket, put it on his head and ran quickly down the rickety stairs. From the street door he walked on furtively on the inner side of the path towards the corner and all at once dived into a doorway. He was now safe in the dark snug of O'Neill's shop, and, filling up the little window that looked into the bar with his inflamed face, the colour of dark wine or dark meat, he called out:

—Here, Pat, give us a g.p., like a good fellow.

The curate brought him a glass of plain porter. The man drank it at a gulp and asked for a caraway seed. He put his penny on the counter and, leaving the curate to grope for it in the gloom, retreated out of the snug as furtively as he had entered it.

Darkness, accompanied by a thick fog, was gaining upon the dusk of February and the lamps in Eustace Street had been lit. The man went up by the houses until he reached the door of the office, wondering whether he could finish his copy in time. On the stairs a moist pungent odour of perfumes saluted his nose: evidently Miss Delacour had come while he was out in O'Neill's. He crammed his cap back again into his pocket and re-entered the office, assuming an air of absent-mindedness.

—Mr. Alleyne has been calling for you, said the chief clerk severely. Where were you?

The man glanced at the two clients who were standing at the counter as if to intimate that their presence prevented him from answering. As the clients were both male the chief clerk allowed himself a laugh.

—I know that game, he said. Five times in one day is a little bit. . . . Well, you better look sharp and get a copy of our correspondence in the Delacour case for Mr. Alleyne.

This address in the presence of the public, his run upstairs and the porter he had gulped down so hastily confused the man and, as he sat down at his desk to get what was required, he realized how hopeless was the task of finishing his copy of the contract before half past five. The dark damp night was coming and he longed to spend it in the bars, drinking with his friends amid the glare of gas and the clatter of glasses. He got out the Delacour correspondence and passed out of the office. He hoped Mr. Alleyne would not discover that the last two letters were missing.

The moist pungent perfume lay all the way up to Mr. Alleyne's room. Miss Delacour was a middle-aged woman of Jewish appearance. Mr. Alleyne was said to be sweet on her or on her money. She came to the office often and stayed a long time when she came. She was sitting beside his desk now in an aroma of perfumes, smoothing the handle of her umbrella and nodding the great black feather in her hat. Mr. Alleyne had swivelled his chair round to face her and thrown his right foot jauntily upon his left knee. The man put the correspondence on the desk and bowed respectfully but neither Mr. Alleyne nor Miss Delacour took any notice of his bow. Mr. Alleyne tapped a finger on the correspondence and then flicked it towards him as if to say: *That's all right: you can go.*

The man returned to the lower office and sat down again at his desk. He stared intently at the incomplete phrase: *In no case shall the said Bernard Bodley be . . .* and thought how strange it was that the last three words began with the same letter. The chief clerk began to hurry Miss Parker, saying she would never have the letters typed in time for post. The man listened to the clicking of the machine for a few minutes and then set to work to finish his copy. But his head was not clear and his mind wandered away to the glare and rattle of the public-house. It was a night for hot punches. He struggled on with his copy, but when the clock struck five he had still fourteen pages to write. Blast it! He couldn't finish it in time. He longed to execrate aloud, to bring his fist down on something violently. He was so enraged that he wrote *Bernard Bernard* instead of *Bernard Bodley* and had to begin again on a clean sheet.

He felt strong enough to clear out the whole office single-handed. His body ached to do something, to rush out and revel in violence. All the indignities of his life enraged him. . . . Could he ask the cashier privately for an advance? No, the cashier was no good, no damn good: he wouldn't give an advance. . . . He knew where he would meet the boys: Leonard and O'Halloran and Nosey Flynn. The barometer of his emotional nature was set for a spell of riot.

His imagination had so abstracted him that his name was called twice before he answered. Mr. Alleyne and Miss Delacour were standing outside the counter and all the clerks had turned round in anticipation of something. The man got up from his desk. Mr. Alleyne began a tirade of abuse, saying that two letters were missing. The man answered that he knew nothing about them, that he had made a faithful copy. The tirade continued: it was so bitter and violent that the man could hardly restrain his fist from descending upon the head of the manikin before him.

—I know nothing about any other two letters, he said stupidly.

—*You—know—nothing*. Of course you know nothing, said Mr. Alleyne. Tell me, he added, glancing first for approval to the lady beside him, do you take me for a fool? Do you think me an utter fool?

The man glanced from the lady's face to the little egg-shaped head and back again; and, almost before he was aware of it, his tongue had found a felicitous moment:

—I don't think, sir, he said, that that's a fair question to put to me.

There was a pause in the very breathing of the clerks. Everyone was astounded (the author of the witticism no less than his neighbours) and Miss Delacour, who was a stout amiable person, began to smile broadly. Mr. Alleyne flushed to the hue of a wild rose and his mouth twitched with a dwarf's passion. He shook his fist in the man's face till it seemed to vibrate like the knob of some electric machine:

—You impertinent ruffian! You impertinent ruffian! I'll make short work of you! Wait till you see! You'll apologize to me for your impertinence or you'll quit the office instanter! You'll quit this, I'm telling you, or you'll apologize to me!

He stood in a doorway opposite the office watching to see if the cashier would come out alone. All the clerks passed out and finally the cashier came out with the chief clerk. It was no use trying to say a word to him when he was with the chief clerk. The man felt that his position was bad enough. He had been obliged to offer an abject apology to Mr. Alleyne for his impertinence but he knew what a hornet's nest the office would be for him. He could remember the way in which Mr. Alleyne had hounded little Peake out of the office in order to make room for his own nephew. He felt savage and thirsty and revengeful, annoyed with himself and with everyone else. Mr. Alleyne would never give him an hour's rest; his life would be a hell to him. He had made a proper fool of himself this time. Could he not keep his tongue in his cheek? But they had never pulled together from the first, he and Mr. Alleyne, ever since the day Mr. Alleyne had overheard him mimicking his North of Ireland accent to amuse Higgins and Miss Parker: that had been the beginning of it. He might have tried Higgins for the money, but sure Higgins never had anything for himself. A man with two establishments to keep up, of course he couldn't. . . .

He felt his great body again aching for the comfort of the public-house. The fog had begun to chill him and he wondered could he touch Pat in O'Neill's. He could not touch him for more than a bob—and a bob was no use. Yet he must get money somewhere or other: he had spent his last penny for the g.p. and soon it would be too late for getting money anywhere. Suddenly, as he was fingering his watch-chain, he thought of Terry Kelly's pawn-office in Fleet Street. That was the dart! Why didn't he think of it sooner?

He went through the narrow alley of Temple Bar quickly, muttering to himself that they could all go to hell because he was going to have a good night of it. The clerk in Terry Kelly's said *A crown!* but the consignor held out for six shillings; and in the end the six shillings was allowed him literally. He came out of the pawn-office joyfully, making a little cylinder of the coins between his thumb and fingers. In Westmoreland Street the footpaths were crowded with young men and women returning from business and ragged urchins ran here and there yelling out the names of the evening editions. The man passed through the crowd, looking on the spectacle generally with proud satisfaction and staring masterfully at the office-girls. His head was full of the noises of tram-gongs and swishing trolleys and his nose already sniffed the curling fumes of punch. As he walked on he preconsidered the terms in which he would narrate the incident to the boys:

—So, I just looked at him—coolly, you know, and looked at her. Then I looked back at him again—taking my time, you know. *I don't think that that's a fair question to put to me*, says I.

Nosey Flynn was sitting up in his usual corner of Davy Bryne's and, when he heard the story, he stood Farrington a half-one, saying it was as smart a thing as ever he heard. Farrington stood a drink in his turn. After a while O'Halloran and Paddy Leonard came in and the story was repeated to them. O'Halloran stood tailors of malt, hot, all round and told the story of the retort he had made to the chief clerk when he was in Callan's of Fownes's Street; but, as the retort was after the manner of the liberal shepherds in the eclogues, he had to admit that it was not so clever as Farrington's retort. At this Farrington told the boys to polish off that and have another.

Just as they were naming their poisons who should come in but Higgins! Of course he had to join in with the others. The men asked him to give his version of it, and he did so with great vivacity for the sight of five small hot whiskies was very exhilarating. Everyone roared laughing when he showed the way in which Mr. Alleyne shook his fist in Farrington's face. Then he imitated Farrington, saying, *And here was my nabs, as cool as you please*, while Farrington looked at the company out of his heavy dirty eyes, smiling and at times drawing forth stray drops of liquor from his moustache with the aid of his lower lip.

When that round was over there was a pause. O'Halloran had money but neither of the other two seemed to have any; so the whole party left the shop somewhat regretfully. At the corner of Duke Street Higgins and Nosey Flynn bevelled off to the left while the other three turned back towards the city. Rain was drizzling down on the cold streets and, when they reached the Ballast Office, Farrington suggested the Scotch House. The bar was full of men and loud with the noise of tongues and glasses. The three men pushed past the whining match-sellers at the door and formed a little party at the corner of the counter. They began to exchange stories. Leonard introduced them to a young fellow named Weathers who was performing at the Tivoli as an acrobat and knock-about *artiste*. Farrington stood a drink all round. Weathers said he would take a small Irish and Apollinaris. Farrington, who had definite notions of what was what, asked the boys would they have an Apollinaris too; but the boys told Tim to make theirs hot. The talk became theatrical. O'Halloran stood a round and then Farrington stood another round, Weathers protesting that the hospitality was too Irish. He promised to get them in behind the scenes and introduce them to some nice girls. O'Halloran said that he and Leonard would go but that Farrington wouldn't go because he was a married man; and Farrington's heavy dirty eyes leered at the company in token that he understood he was being chaffed. Weathers made them all have just one little tincture at his expense and promised to meet them later on at Mulligan's in Poolbeg Street.

When the Scotch House closed they went round to Mulligan's. They went into the parlour at the back and O'Halloran ordered small hot specials all round. They were all beginning to feel mellow. Farrington was just standing another round when Weathers came back. Much to Farrington's relief he drank a glass of bitter this time. Funds were running low but they had enough to keep them going. Presently two young women with big hats and a young man in a check suit came in and sat at a table close by. Weathers saluted them and told the company that they were out of the Tivoli.

Farrington's eyes wandered at every moment in the direction of one of the young women. There was something striking in her appearance. An immense scarf of peacock-blue muslin was wound round her hat and knotted in a great bow under her chin; and she wore bright yellow gloves, reaching to the elbow. Farrington gazed admiringly at the plump arm which she moved very often and with much grace; and when, after a little time, she answered his gaze he admired still more her large dark brown eyes. The oblique staring expression in them fascinated him. She glanced at him once or twice and, when the party was leaving the room, she brushed against his chair and said *O, pardon!* in a London accent. He watched her leave the room in the hope that she would look back at him, but he was disappointed. He cursed his want of money and cursed all the rounds he had stood, particularly all the whiskies and Apollinaris which he had stood to Weathers. If there was one thing that he hated it was a sponge. He was so angry that he lost count of the conversation of his friends.

When Paddy Leonard called him he found that they were talking about feats of strength. Weathers was showing his biceps muscle to the company and boasting so much that the other two had called on Farrington to uphold the national honour. Farrington pulled up his sleeve accordingly and showed his biceps muscle to the company. The two arms were examined and compared and finally it was agreed to have a trial of strength. The table was cleared and the two men rested their elbows on it, clasping hands. When Paddy Leonard said *Go!* each was to try to bring down the other's hand on to the table. Farrington looked very serious and determined.

The trial began. After about thirty seconds Weathers brought his opponent's hand slowly down on to the table. Farrington's dark wine-coloured face flushed darker still with anger and humiliation at having been defeated by such a stripling.

—You're not to put the weight of your body behind it. Play fair, he said.

—Who's not playing fair? said the other.

—Come on again. The two best out of three.

The trial began again. The veins stood out on Farrington's forehead, and the pallor of Weathers' complexion changed to peony. Their hands and arms trembled under the stress. After a long struggle Weathers again brought his opponent's hand slowly on to the table. There was a murmur of applause from the spectators. The curate, who was standing beside the table, nodded his red head toward the victor and said with loutish familiarity:

—Ah! that's the knack!

—What the hell do you know about it? said Farrington fiercely, turning on the man. What do you put in your gab for?

—Sh, sh! said O'Halloran, observing the violent expression of Farrington's face. Pony up, boys. We'll have just one little smahan more and then we'll be off.

A very sullen-faced man stood at the corner of O'Connell Bridge waiting for the little Sandymount tram to take him home. He was full of
smouldering anger and revengefulness. He felt humiliated and discon-
tented; he did not even feel drunk; and he had only twopence in his pocket.
He cursed everything. He had done for himself in the office, pawned his
watch, spent all his money; and he had not even got drunk. He began to
feel thirsty again and he longed to be back again in the hot reeking public-
house. He had lost his reputation as a strong man, having been defeated
twice by a mere boy. His heart swelled with fury and, when he thought of
the woman in the big hat who had brushed against him and said *Pardon!*
his fury nearly choked him.

His tram let him down at Shelbourne Road and he steered his great
body along in the shadow of the wall of the barracks. He loathed returning
to his home. When he went in by the side-door he found the kitchen empty
and the kitchen fire nearly out. He bawled upstairs:

—Ada! Ada!

His wife was a little sharp-faced woman who bullied her husband when
he was sober and was bullied by him when he was drunk. They had five
children. A little boy came running down the stairs.

—Who is that? said the man, peering through the darkness.

—Me, pa.

—Who are you? Charlie?

—No, pa. Tom.

—Where's your mother?

—She's out at the chapel.

—That's right. . . . Did she think of leaving any dinner for me?

—Yes, pa. I—

—Light the lamp. What do you mean by having the place in darkness?
Are the other children in bed?

The man sat down heavily on one of the chairs while the little boy lit
the lamp. He began to mimic his son's flat accent, saying half to himself:
At the chapel. At the chapel, if you please! When the lamp was lit he banged
his fist on the table and shouted:

—What's for my dinner?

—I'm going . . . to cook it, pa, said the little boy.

The man jumped up furiously and pointed to the fire.

—On that fire! You let the fire out! By God, I'll teach you to do that
again!

He took a step to the door and seized the walking-stick which was
standing behind it.

—I'll teach you to let the fire out! he said, rolling up his sleeve in order
to give his arm free play.

The little boy cried *O, pa!* and ran whimpering round the table, but
the man followed him and caught him by the coat. The little boy looked
about him wildly but, seeing no way of escape, fell upon his knees.

—Now, you'll let the fire out the next time! said the man, striking at him viciously with the stick. Take that, you little whelp!

The boy uttered a squeal of pain as the stick cut his thigh. He clasped his hands together in the air and his voice shook with fright.

—O, pa! he cried. Don't beat me, pa! And I'll . . . I'll say a *Hail Mary* for you. . . . I'll say a *Hail Mary* for you, pa, if you don't beat me. . . . I'll say a *Hail Mary*. . . .

QUESTIONS

1. Joyce entitles his story "Counterparts." Who is the *counterpart* of whom? How does the title anticipate the plot structure?
2. The plot is divided into three episodes, set in three different locales: the office where Farrington works, the pub where he socializes, and his home. How does Joyce link these episodes thematically?
3. Notice that many of the characters (Mr. Alleyne, Farrington, Farrington's son, Tom) repeat their words. For example, Mr. Alleyne says to Farrington, "*You–know–nothing*. Of course you know nothing." In addition, some of the actions are repeated: Farrington loses twice at handwrestling. What is Joyce's reason for including so many examples of repetition? Do they comment on the story's meaning?
4. Why is the physical difference between Farrington and Mr. Alleyne given so much attention in the opening of the story? How are other minor characters (Miss Delacour, Higgins, Weathers) connected to the development of the plot?
5. Where is the climax of the story? Does it occur in the episode at home or in the pub? Why is Farrington's anger connected with Mr. Alleyne's being from Northern Ireland and Weathers being English?

JAMES THURBER (1894–1961)

The Catbird Seat

James Thurber, one of America's most beloved humorists, was born in Columbus, Ohio, and attended Ohio State University there. His cartoons, essays, stories, and humorous sketches appeared frequently in *The New Yorker*. Among his most famous collections are *My Life and Hard Times* (1933) and *The Thurber Carnival* (1945), in which "The Catbird Seat" first appeared.

Mr. Martin bought the pack of Camels on Monday night in the most crowded cigar store on Broadway. It was theater time and seven or eight men were buying cigarettes. The clerk didn't even glance at Mr. Martin, who put the pack in his overcoat pocket and went out. If any of the staff at F & S had seen him buy the cigarettes, they would have been astonished, for it was generally known that Mr. Martin did not smoke, and never had. No one saw him.

It was just a week to the day since Mr. Martin had decided to rub out Mrs. Ulgine Barrows. The term "rub out" pleased him because it suggested nothing more than the correction of an error—in this case an error of Mr. Fitweiler. Mr. Martin had spent each night of the past week working out his plan and examining it. As he walked home now he went over it again. For the hundredth time he resented the element of imprecision, the margin of guesswork that entered into the business. The project as he had worked it out was casual and bold, the risks were considerable. Something might go wrong anywhere along the line. And therein lay the cunning of his scheme. No one would ever see in it the cautious, painstaking hand of Erwin Martin, head of the filing department at F & S, of whom Mr. Fitweiler had once said, "Man is fallible but Martin isn't." No one would see his hand, that is, unless it were caught in the act.

Sitting in his apartment, drinking a glass of milk, Mr. Martin reviewed his case against Mrs. Ulgine Barrows, as he had every night for seven nights. He began at the beginning. Her quacking voice and braying laugh had first profaned the halls of F & S on March 7, 1941 (Mr. Martin had a head for dates). Old Roberts, the personnel chief, had introduced her as the newly appointed special adviser to the president of the firm, Mr. Fitweiler. The woman had appalled Mr. Martin instantly, but he hadn't shown it. He had given her his dry hand, a look of studious concentration, and a faint smile. "Well," she had said, looking at the papers on his desk, "are you lifting the oxcart out of the ditch?" As Mr. Martin recalled that moment, over his milk, he squirmed slightly. He must keep his mind on her crimes as a special adviser, not on her peccadillos as a personality. This he found difficult to do, in spite of entering an objection and sustaining it. The faults of the woman as a woman kept chattering on in his mind like an unruly witness. She had, for almost two years now, baited him. In the halls, in the elevator, even in his own office, into which she romped now and then like a circus horse, she was constantly shouting these silly questions at him. "Are you lifting the oxcart out of the ditch? Are you tearing up the pea patch? Are you hollering down the rain barrel? Are you scraping around the bottom of the pickle barrel? Are you sitting in the catbird seat?"

It was Joey Hart, one of Mr. Martin's two assistants, who had explained what the gibberish meant. "She must be a Dodger fan," he had said. "Red Barber announces the Dodger games over the radio and he uses those expressions—picked 'em up down South." Joey had gone on to explain one or two. "Tearing up the pea patch" meant going on a rampage; "sitting in the catbird seat" meant sitting pretty, like a batter with three balls and no strikes on him. Mr. Martin dismissed all this with an effort. It had been annoying, it had driven him near to distraction, but he was too solid a man to be moved to murder by anything so childish. It was fortunate, he reflected as he passed on to the important charges against Mrs. Barrows, that he had stood up under it so well. He had maintained always an outward appearance of polite tolerance. "Why, I even believe you like the woman," Miss Paird, his other assistant, had once said to him. He had simply smiled.

A gavel rapped in Mr. Martin's mind and the case proper was resumed. Mrs. Ulgine Barrows stood charged with willful, blatant, and persistent attempts to destroy the efficiency and system of F & S. It was competent, material, and relevant to review her advent and rise to power. Mr. Martin had got the story from Miss Paird, who seemed always able to find things out. According to her, Mrs. Barrows had met Mr. Fitweiler at a party, where she had rescued him from the embraces of a powerfully built drunken man who had mistaken the president of F & S for a famous retired Middle Western football coach. She had led him to a sofa and somehow worked upon him a monstrous magic. The aging gentleman had jumped to the conclusion there and then that this was a woman of singular attainments, equipped to bring out the best in him and in the firm. A week later he had introduced her into F & S as his special adviser. On that day confusion got its foot in the door. After Miss Tyson, Mr. Brundage, and Mr. Bartlett had been fired and Mr. Munson had taken his hat and stalked out, mailing in his resignation later, old Roberts had been emboldened to speak to Mr. Fitweiler. He mentioned that Mr. Munson's department had been "a little disrupted" and hadn't they perhaps better resume the old system there? Mr. Fitweiler had said certainly not. He had the greatest faith in Mrs. Barrows' ideas. "They require a little seasoning, a little seasoning, is all," he had added. Mr. Roberts had given it up. Mr. Martin reviewed in detail all the changes wrought by Mrs. Barrows. She had begun chipping at the cornices of the firm's edifice and now she was swinging at the foundation stones with a pickaxe.

Mr. Martin came now, in his summing up, to the afternoon of Monday, November 2, 1942—just one week ago. On that day, at 3 P.M., Mrs. Barrows had bounced into his office. "Boo!" she had yelled. "Are you scraping around the bottom of the pickle barrel?" Mr. Martin had looked at her from under his green eyeshade, saying nothing. She had begun to wander about the office, taking it in with her great, popping eyes. "Do you really need *all* these filing cabinets?" she had demanded suddenly. Mr. Martin's heart had jumped. "Each of these files," he had said, keeping his voice even, "plays an indispensable part in the system of F & S." She had brayed at him, "Well, don't tear up the pea patch!" and gone to the door. From there she had bawled, "But you sure have got a lot of fine scrap in here!" Mr. Martin could no longer doubt that the finger was on his beloved department. Her pickaxe was on the upswing, poised for the first blow. It had not come yet; he had received no blue memo from the enchanted Mr. Fitweiler bearing nonsensical instructions deriving from the obscene woman. But there was no doubt in Mr. Martin's mind that one would be forthcoming. He must act quickly. Already a precious week had gone by. Mr. Martin stood up in his living room, still holding his milk glass. "Gentlemen of the jury," he said to himself, "I demand the death penalty for this horrible person."

The next day Mr. Martin followed his routine, as usual. He polished his glasses more often and once sharpened an already sharp pencil, but not even Miss Paird noticed. Only once did he catch sight of his victim; she swept past him in the hall with a patronizing "Hi!" At five-thirty he walked home, as usual, and had a glass of milk, as usual. He had never drunk anything stronger in his life—unless you could count ginger ale. The late Sam Schlosser, the S of F & S, had praised Mr. Martin at a staff meeting several years before for his temperate habits. "Our most efficient worker neither drinks nor smokes," he had said. "The results speak for themselves." Mr. Fitweiler had sat by, nodding approval.

Mr. Martin was still thinking about that red-letter day as he walked over to the Schrafft's on Fifth Avenue near Forty-sixth Street. He got there, as he always did, at eight o'clock. He finished his dinner and the financial page of the *Sun* at a quarter to nine, as he always did. It was his custom after dinner to take a walk. This time he walked down Fifth Avenue at a casual pace. His gloved hands felt moist and warm, his forehead cold. He transferred the Camels from his overcoat to a jacket pocket. He wondered, as he did so, if they did not represent an unnecessary note of strain. Mrs. Barrows smoked only Luckies. It was his idea to puff a few puffs on a Camel (after the rubbing-out), stub it out in the ashtray holding her lipstick-stained Luckies, and thus drag a small red herring across the trail. Perhaps it was not a good idea. It would take time. He might even choke, too loudly.

Mr. Martin had never seen the house on West Twelfth Street where Mrs. Barrows lived, but he had a clear enough picture of it. Fortunately, she had bragged to everybody about her ducky first-floor apartment in the perfectly darling three-story redbrick. There would be no doorman or other attendants; just the tenants of the second and third floors. As he walked along, Mr. Martin realized that he would get there before nine-thirty. He had considered walking north on Fifth Avenue from Schrafft's to a point from which it would take him until ten o'clock to reach the house. At that hour people were less likely to be coming in or going out. But the procedure would have made an awkward loop in the straight thread of his casualness, and he had abandoned it. It was impossible to figure when people would be entering or leaving the house, anyway. There was a great risk at any hour. If he ran into anybody, he would simply have to place the rubbing-out of Ulgine Barrows in the inactive file forever. The same thing would hold true if there were someone in her apartment. In that case he would just say that he had been passing by, recognized her charming house and thought to drop in.

It was eighteen minutes after nine when Mr. Martin turned into

Twelfth Street. A man passed him, and a man and a woman talking. There was no one within fifty paces when he came to the house, halfway down the block. He was up the steps and in the small vestibule in no time, pressing the bell under the card that said "Mrs. Ulgine Barrows." When the clicking in the lock started, he jumped forward against the door. He got inside fast, closing the door behind him. A bulb in a lantern hung from the hall ceiling on a chain seemed to give a monstrously bright light. There was nobody on the stair, which went up ahead of him along the left wall. A door opened down the hall in the wall on the right. He went toward it swiftly, on tiptoe.

"Well, for God's sake, look who's here!" bawled Mrs. Barrows, and her braying laugh rang out like the report of a shotgun. He rushed past her like a football tackle, bumping her. "Hey, quit shoving!" she said, closing the door behind them. They were in her living room, which seemed to Mr. Martin to be lighted by a hundred lamps. "What's after you?" she said. You're as jumpy as a goat." He found he was unable to speak. His heart was wheezing in his throat. "I—yes," he finally brought out. She was jabbering and laughing as she started to help him off with his coat. "No, no," he said. "I'll put it here." He took it off and put it on a chair near the door. "Your hat and gloves, too," she said. "You're in a lady's house." He put his hat on top of the coat. Mrs. Barrows seemed larger than he had thought. He kept his gloves on. "I was passing by," he said. "I recognized—is there anyone here?" She laughed louder than ever. "No," she said, "we're all alone. You're as white as a sheet, you funny man. Whatever *has* come over you? I'll mix you a toddy." She started toward a door across the room. "Scotch-and-soda be all right? But say, you don't drink, do you?" She turned and gave him her amused look. Mr. Martin pulled himself together. "Scotch-and-soda will be all right," he heard himself say. He could hear her laughing in the kitchen.

Mr. Martin looked quickly around the living room for the weapon. He had counted on finding one there. There were andirons and a poker and something in a corner that looked like an Indian club. None of them would do. It couldn't be that way. He began to pace around. He came to a desk. On it lay a metal paper knife with an ornate handle. Would it be sharp enough? He reached for it and knocked over a small brass jar. Stamps spilled out of it and it fell to the floor with a clatter. "Hey," Mrs. Barrows yelled from the kitchen, "are you tearing up the pea patch?" Mr. Martin gave a strange laugh. Picking up the knife, he tried its point against his left wrist. It was blunt. It wouldn't do.

When Mrs. Barrows reappeared, carrying two highballs, Mr. Martin, standing there with his gloves on, became acutely conscious of the fantasy he had wrought. Cigarettes in his pocket, a drink prepared for him—it was all too grossly improbable. It was more than that; it was impossible. Somewhere in the back of his mind a vague idea stirred, sprouted. "For heaven's sake, take off those gloves," said Mrs. Barrows. "I always wear them in the house," said Mr. Martin. The idea began to bloom, strange and wonderful.

She put the glasses on a coffee table in front of a sofa and sat on the sofa. "Come over here, you odd little man," she said. Mr. Martin went over and sat beside her. It was difficult getting a cigarette out of the pack of Camels, but he managed it. She held a match for him, laughing. "Well," she said, handing him his drink, "this is perfectly marvelous. You with a drink and a cigarette."

Mr. Martin puffed, not too awkwardly, and took a gulp of the highball. "I drink and smoke all the time," he said. He clinked his glass against hers. "Here's nuts to that old windbag, Fitweiler," he said, and gulped again. The stuff tasted awful, but he made no grimace. "Really, Mr. Martin," she said, her voice and posture changing, "you are insulting our employer." Mrs. Barrows was now all special adviser to the president. "I am preparing a bomb," said Mr. Martin, "which will blow the old goat higher than hell." He had only had a little of the drink, which was not strong. It couldn't be that. "Do you take dope or something?" Mrs. Barrows asked coldly. "Heroin," said Mr. Martin. "I'll be coked to the gills when I bump that old buzzard off." "Mr. Martin!" she shouted, getting to her feet. "That will be all of that. You must go at once." Mr. Martin took another swallow of his drink. He tapped his cigarette out in the ashtray and put the pack of Camels on the coffee table. Then he got up. She stood glaring at him. He walked over and put on his hat and coat. "Not a word about this," he said, and laid an index finger against his lips. All Mrs. Barrows could bring out was "Really!" Mr. Martin put his hand on the doorknob. "I'm sitting in the catbird seat," he said. He stuck his tongue out at her and left. Nobody saw him go.

Mr. Martin got to his apartment, walking, well before eleven. No one saw him go in. He had two glasses of milk after brushing his teeth, and he felt elated. It wasn't tipsiness, because he hadn't been tipsy. Anyway, the walk had worn off all effects of the whisky. He got in bed and read a magazine for a while. He was asleep before midnight.

Mr. Martin got to the office at eight-thirty the next morning, as usual. At a quarter to nine, Ulgine Barrows, who had never before arrived at work before ten, swept into his office. "I'm reporting to Mr. Fitweiler now!" she shouted. "If he turns you over to the police, it's no more than you deserve!" Mr. Martin gave her a look of shocked surprise. "I beg your pardon?" he said. Mrs. Barrows snorted and bounced out of the room, leaving Miss Paird and Joey Hart staring after her. "What's the matter with that old devil now?" asked Miss Paird. "I have no idea," said Mr. Martin, resuming his work. The other two looked at him and then at each other. Miss Paird got up and went out. She walked slowly past the closed door of Mr. Fitweiler's office. Mrs. Barrows was yelling inside, but she was not braying. Miss Paird could not hear what the woman was saying. She went back to her desk.

Forty-five minutes later, Mrs. Barrows left the president's office and went into her own, shutting the door. It wasn't until half an hour later that Mr. Fitweiler sent for Mr. Martin. The head of the filing department, neat, quiet, attentive, stood in front of the old man's desk. Mr. Fitweiler was pale and nervous. He took his glasses off and twiddled them. He made a small, bruffing sound in his throat. "Martin," he said, "you have been with us more than twenty years." "Twenty-two, sir," said Mr. Martin. "In that time," pursued the president, "your work and your—uh—manner have been exemplary." "I trust so, sir," said Mr. Martin. "I have understood, Martin," said Mr. Fitweiler, "that you have never taken a drink or smoked." "That is correct, sir," said Mr. Martin. "Ah, yes." Mr. Fitweiler polished his glasses. "You may describe what you did after leaving the office yesterday, Martin," he said. Mr. Martin allowed less than a second for his bewildered pause. "Certainly, sir," he said. "I walked home. Then I went to Schrafft's for dinner. Afterward I walked home again. I went to bed early, sir, and read a magazine for a while. I was asleep before eleven." "Ah, yes," said Mr. Fitweiler again. He was silent for a moment, searching for the proper words to say to the head of the filing department. "Mrs. Barrows," he said finally, "Mrs. Barrows has worked hard, Martin, very hard. It grieves me to report that she has suffered a severe breakdown. It has taken the form of a persecution complex accompanied by distressing hallucinations." "I am very sorry, sir," said Mr. Martin. "Mrs. Barrows is under the delusion," continued Mr. Fitweiler, "that you visited her last evening and behaved yourself in an—uh—unseemly manner." He raised his hand to silence Mr. Martin's little pained outcry. "It is the nature of these psychological diseases," Mr. Fitweiler said, "to fix upon the least likely and most innocent party as the—uh—source of persecution. These matters are not for the lay mind to grasp, Martin. I've just had my psychiatrist, Dr. Fitch, on the phone. He would not, of course, commit himself, but he made enough generalizations to substantiate my suspicions. I suggested to Mrs. Barrows when she had completed her—uh—story to me this morning, that she visit Dr. Fitch, for I suspected a condition at once. She flew, I regret to say, into a rage, and demanded—uh—requested that I call you on the carpet. You may not know, Martin, but Mrs. Barrows had planned a reorganization of your department—subject to my approval, of course, subject to my approval. This brought you, rather than anyone else, to her mind—but again that is a phenomenon for Dr. Fitch and not for us. So, Martin, I am afraid Mrs. Barrows' usefulness here is at an end." "I am dreadfully sorry, sir," said Mr. Martin.

It was at this point that the door to the office blew open with the suddenness of a gas-main explosion and Mrs. Barrows catapulted through it. "Is the little rat denying it?" she screamed. "He can't get away with that!" Mr. Martin got up and moved discreetly to a point beside Mr. Fitweiler's chair. "You drank and smoked at my apartment," she bawled at Mr. Martin, "and you know it! You called Mr. Fitweiler an old windbag and said you were going to blow him up when you got coked to the gills on your heroin!" She stopped yelling to catch her breath and a new glint came into her popping eyes. "If you weren't such a drab, ordinary little man," she said, "I'd think you'd planned it all. Sticking your tongue out, saying you were sitting in the catbird seat, because you thought no one would believe me when I told it! My God, it's really too perfect!" She brayed loudly and hysterically, and the fury was on her again. She glared at Mr. Fitweiler. "Can't you see how he has tricked us, you old fool? Can't you see his little game?" But Mr. Fitweiler had been surreptitiously pressing all the buttons under the top of his desk and employees of F & S began pouring into the room. "Stockton," said Mr. Fitweiler, "you and Fishbein will take Mrs. Barrows to her home. Mrs. Powell, you will go with them." Stockton, who had played a little football in high school, blocked Mrs. Barrows as she made for Mr. Martin. It took him and Fishbein together to force her out of the door into the hall, crowded with stenographers and office boys. She was still screaming imprecations at Mr. Martin, tangled and contradictory imprecations. The hubbub finally died out down the corridor.

"I regret that this has happened," said Mr. Fitweiler. "I shall ask you to dismiss it from your mind, Martin." "Yes, sir," said Mr. Martin, anticipating his chief's "That will be all" by moving to the door. "I will dismiss it." He went out and shut the door, and his step was light and quick in the hall. When he entered his department he had slowed down to his customary gait, and he walked quietly across the room to the W20 file, wearing a look of studious concentration.

QUESTIONS

1. What does Thurber gain by having his story open in the middle of things with Mr. Martin's taking the first step in his plan to "rub out" Mrs. Barrows?
2. At what point in the plot does Mr. Martin change his plans? Why? Does the reader's awareness of his changed plans destroy the suspense or add to the humor? Why?
3. What expository details does Thurber add to the story to make the outcome plausible?
4. In the complications and resolution parts of the plot, how does Mrs. Barrows' character support the inevitability of the outcome?
5. What makes Thurber's title ironical? Why did he choose it rather than another of Mrs. Barrow's expressions?

WRITING ABOUT PLOT

Suppose that you are asked to write about the plot of a story. Your first reaction might be that you have nothing to say beyond retelling the story— and, in one sense, you are probably right. Before you can begin, you need to know the nature of the assignment. If you have been asked to write a "plot summary," then your initial reaction is nearly correct: you are expected to retell the story.

A **plot summary** is a paraphrase of the main events of the story in your own words. It should include an indication of how the most important events in the story are connected and contain passages in which only the author's words or the dialogue give an adequate sense of the events. Normally, a plot summary employs the theme or central idea of the story, without elaborating on it, as a guide for what to include and what to eliminate from the summary.

More often, an instructor will assign a **plot analysis,** which requires you to show how the plot is constructed. Typically, you are asked to do five things in a plot analysis:

1. Explain how this plot fits (or does *not* fit) the classical plot structure (that is, show where the exposition, complications, climax, resolution, and denouement occur in the story).
2. Indicate and explain any use of flashbacks.
3. Call attention to any examples of foreshadowing and their effect on the plot.
4. Discuss the conflict, its connection to the theme, and its development in the plot structure.
5. Point out any patterns in plot development, such as recurring situations, characters, language.

Once you have determined the nature of the assignment, your task is to fulfill its specific requirements. There are many ways in which to write a plot summary or a plot analysis, but they all begin with several common-sense steps preliminary to writing. First, read the story several times. Usually, on the first reading you are paying close attention to the outcome of the story, and you may not notice subtle details. On the second reading, make marginal notations, underlining and circling important elements in the text so that you can locate them more easily when you write your paper. Jot down a "shopping list" of items (not necessarily in sentence form) that will suggest a line of thought later. List the ideas you wish to cover in the order in which they occur to you. Then, regroup these ideas. Decide which elements of the plot you wish to talk about first. If you are writing a plot analysis, will you follow the order of the plot or some other logical order of ideas? For example, will you discuss instances of foreshadowing as they occur in the plot or all together in a single paragraph? If you are writing a plot summary and the story employs flashbacks, will you present the events in chronological order or in the order in which they appear in the story? Additional problems of organization may arise, and you should decide in advance how you will solve them. Once you have grouped your ideas into what appears to be a logical order and established a tentative outline, it's time to begin writing.

What should go into the first paragraph of a paper on "plot"? Whether you are writing a summary or an analysis, you should mention the author and the title of the story by name. Briefly note whether there is a predominant pattern to the way the plot is constructed. Does the plot use some recurring motif, like the doubling motif in Joyce's "Counterparts"? Does the plot fit the pattern of some subgenre of fiction, like the surprise ending of a suspense story, the chase and capture or showdown of a western, the shock of a gothic horror tale? Like any formula, this prescription for an introduction needs to be adapted to the special requirements of the particular story you are writing about.

The rest of your paper should follow your outline and cover those items in the list on page 48 that the reader expects to find in a paper about plot. However, in the process of actually drafting the paper, if you find a better way to arrange the discussion, don't be enslaved by the outline. Follow what seems to be the best arrangement. You're always free to return to your original outline.

In writing the conclusion, restate your key point about the plot but be careful not to introduce any ideas that you have not discussed in the central part of the paper. The key to writing an effective conclusion is to keep it concise; remind the reader of what your essay has covered, but don't expand into any new topics.

Plot summaries and analyses are important exercises in close reading and in determining the patterns of fiction. Practice in this kind of analysis will focus your critical skills, make you aware of what you think, and force you to clarify vague impressions by sending you back again and again to the story for evidence to confirm or alter your critical views. You learn what you think, and you think more clearly because you are required to provide evidence for your written insights. In both ways, closer, more perceptive reading results.

The following plot analysis of Joyce's "Counterparts" explains where each part of the plot is to be found and how the events in the plot are causally connected by a repeated pattern of action. The essay focuses solely on analyzing the plot and does not present a detailed explanation of the characters or the theme. Sample essays analyzing each of these elements will follow in later chapters.

Imitation and Oppression: Plot Structure
in James Joyce's "Counterparts"

The plot of James Joyce's "Counterparts" follows a pattern of resemblances, or counterparts, as the title suggests. Each resemblance brings Farrington, the protagonist, one step closer to the final counterpart of the story: the resemblance between himself and his employer, Mr. Alleyne. Just as Alleyne torments Farrington in the opening of "Counterparts," Farrington himself bullies his son Tom in the story's conclusion.

Joyce plunges us directly into the conflict, bypassing (for the most part) the exposition. He begins with the first of several incidents in the complication that develop Farrington's frustrations and his smoldering anger. Joyce withholds some expository details until the end of the story-- that Farrington is married and the father of five children--and instead dramatizes Farrington's relationship with Mr. Alleyne. The contrasting descriptions of the two characters serve as exposition. Farrington is a tall man of "great bulk," who is slightly seedy and given to drink. In contrast, the diminutive Mr. Alleyne is a bundle of nervous energy and dwarfish passion.

The <u>complications</u> begin when the schoolmasterish Alleyne chastises Farrington for shirking work by mimicking him: "<u>Mr Shelley said, sir.</u> . . . <u>Mr Shelley says, sir.</u>" Alleyne ends his warning with another repetition, "Do you hear me now? . . . Do you mind me now?" A second complicating incident, played out before Miss Delacour, follows the same pattern of mocking mimicry and repeated warning: "<u>You—know—nothing.</u> Of course you know nothing. . . . You'll apologize to me for your impertinence or you'll quit the office instanter! You'll quit this, I'm telling you, or you'll apologize to me!"

A third complicating incident involves a resemblance (a counterpart) between Miss Delacour and an unnamed actress. Miss Delacour, who witnessed Farrington's humiliation, is associated with the erotic ("The moist pungent perfume lay all the way up to Mr. Alleyne's room") and with money ("Mr. Alleyne was said to be sweet on her or on her money"). Later, in Mulligan's pub, Farrington has a mild flirtation, glancing in the direction of a young woman who is in the same acting company as Weathers, the young Englishman who later defeats Farrington at hand wrestling. Like Miss Delacour, she is plump and erotic and wears a hat that attracts attention. As she leaves, she brushes against Farrington's chair saying, "'O, pardon!' in a London accent." Farrington is reminded of his exclusion from the company of such women by his lack of money, and his resentment is touched with Irish anti-British sentiment (Farrington's mimicry of Mr. Alleyne's Northern Irish accent had started Farrington's troubles).

The <u>climax</u> occurs when Farrington loses his reputation as a strong man, and the last vestiges of his male pride are stripped from him as he is defeated twice by a mere boy--a stripling and, what is worse, an Englishman. The counterpart of whom Farrington takes out his anger must therefore be little, like Alleyne, and a boy, like Weathers.

The <u>resolution</u> of the story is enacted when Farrington vents his accumulated rage on his son Tom for letting the fire go out and for not cooking his supper. The scene begins with Farrington interrupting his son's replies to his questions (something Alleyne had done) and mimicking his son's answer as to the whereabouts of the boy's mother: <u>At the chapel. At the chapel, if you please!</u> Suddenly animated by rage, Farrington reaches for a walking stick with which to beat the boy and, like Alleyne, repeats his warning twice: "You let the fire out! By God, I'll teach yo to do that again! . . . I'll teach you to let the fire out!" Like Farrington, who had been forced into an "abject apology," the boy begs to be let off with a repeated litany and the only promise he can think of: "Don't beat me, pa! and I'll . . . I'll say a <u>Hail Mary</u> for you. . . . I'll say a <u>Hail Mary</u> for you, pa, if you don't beat me. . . . I'll say a <u>Hail Mary.</u> . . ." The plot ends without a formal <u>denouement,</u> the final resemblance having made Joyce's point.

Joyce's plot, then, is built around a series of counterparts. Much of the action is repeated. Farrington loses "the two best out of three" in hand wrestling, but he's determined not to lose in the third part of the story. He may lose in the office and in the pub, but he won't lose in his own house-- where he doesn't have to "play fair," where he can "put the weight of [his] body behind it."

SUGGESTIONS FOR WRITING ABOUT PLOT

1. Summarize the plot of Hawthorne's "Young Goodman Brown," focusing on the pattern of encounters in the forest and on the logical connection between the conclusion and the incidents leading up to it.

2. Analyze the plot structure of Faulkner's "A Rose for Emily."
   (a) Give an approximate date for each incident and the textual evidence to support that date.
   (b) Explain the function of each flashback.
3. Write an essay on the plot of Thurber's "The Catbird Seat," showing how flashbacks and foreshadowing account for the effectiveness of the surprise ending.
4. Show how the plot of Updike's "A & P" is built around a series of escalating contrasts.
5. Write an essay on Joyce's "Counterparts," showing how details of the office scene (other than those mentioned in the sample essay) foreshadow subsequent events in the story.

CHARACTER

Plot and *character*, as we have seen, are closely intertwined. We cannot separate the plot of Updike's "A & P" from Sammy's actions and what happens to him. Like plot, the portrayal of character in literature appeals to something elemental. Just as we are curious to know what happens next in a plot, we are interested in how characters act, what they say, and what they learn from their actions. Even when the characters in a story are very much unlike us, we find ourselves intrigued and involved; we wonder what we would do in a similar situation.

In many ways, then, literary characters resemble people we know or could know. They act, they speak, they look a certain way; their acts, speech, and appearance tell us about their interests, their motives, their virtues and vices. As we think about the characters in stories we read, we should take full advantage of our acquired knowledge of human behavior, personality, and motivation. Doing so helps us to enjoy the stories and directs our attention to their significant features.

Although it may seem paradoxical, however, we cannot afford, as careful readers, to be too readily involved in the lives of literary characters. Fictional characters resemble humans, but they are not human. They differ from us in fundamental ways. Being aware of these differences, far from diminishing our enjoyment of literary characters, focuses our attention on the important areas we must think about when we read.

First, literary characters do not exist before or after the works in which they appear. They live only in and through those works. Hence, we know nothing about Young Goodman Brown's youth or the way he would have reacted if Faith's pink ribbon had not floated down out of the sky. We know nothing about Sammy's next job. We are ignorant of these matters because Hawthorne and Updike have chosen not to tell us about them. We can make inferences about Brown's early years, but ultimately we are left with the text and what we find there. Any inferences we make must be solidly based on what we read *in the text*. We must guard against the tendency to treat a literary character as though he or she were our neighbor or our friend.

A second distinction between fictional characters and real people is that the experiences fictional characters undergo are generally *heightened* ones. Authors choose to focus on those moments when their characters gain sudden knowledge, suffer profound misfortune, or encounter unusual dilemmas. To this extent, fiction is unlike the general course of events in our daily lives. We should assume that having chosen their subjects carefully, authors will lavish great care on the creation of their characters. In a good story, nothing should be extraneous or casual. Everything—down to the scar on a character's cheek—should be significant and should contribute to the overall effect of the story. As we read, therefore, we must consider all aspects of character portrayal and development.

A third distinction between literary characters and people is that characters have specific functions in the stories in which they appear and are subject to literary conventions and traditions. For example, in "Young Goodman Brown," Goody Cloyse exists primarily to reveal something to Brown about his fellow townspeople. She is an important character, but we only need to know about her to the extent that she performs this function.

Characters also play a variety of roles. The **protagonist** (Greek for "first actor") is the main character of a story—the one with whose fortunes the story is primarily concerned. This term is in some ways preferable to "hero" or "heroine" because it lacks connotations of goodness or valor, qualities often not found in main characters. The protagonist frequently conflicts with or is opposed by the **antagonist,** who usually provokes some significant change in the main character. In one interpretation, Young Goodman Brown and the "devil figure" he meets in the woods are the protagonist and the antagonist of Hawthorne's story. (Remember that the protagonist and antagonist are not always easy to identify.) Other characters are **confidants** (feminine form, *confidantes*), who exist primarily to receive, for our benefit, information from other, more important characters. Still other characters are **foils** to the main character; they resemble him or her in some ways but differ significantly in others. The writer carefully adjusts and controls all of these roles.

This leads to a final distinction between fictional characters and real people: literary characters are developed to varying degrees. In *Aspects of the Novel* (1927), the British novelist E. M. Forster distinguishes between **flat characters,** two-dimensional figures who reveal only one primary trait, and **round characters,** who are fully developed, viewed from a number of perspectives, and characterized by relatively complex behavior and motivations. When flat characters resemble types found in human society or in other texts, we call them **stereotypes** or **stock characters.** Such figures— the love-sick adolescent, the bragging soldier, the absent-minded professor—afford the author a kind of literary shorthand. When we encounter a stock character, parts of our prior experience vibrate sympathetically.

Regardless of the extent to which they are developed, fictional characters are presented to us through a variety of means. The most common are:

1. By how they are *named*. (Think of the implications of the name "Arnold Friend" in the story by Joyce Carol Oates that follows.)
2. By how they *look*. (When we hear that Emily Grierson "looked bloated, like a body long submerged in motionless water" [page 17], we picture a woman who has become stagnant.)
3. By what they *do, think,* or *say.* These are the most common means of characterization. Pay careful attention to them.
4. By how they *interact* with others. (Think of how Sammy's reactions to the girls in "A & P" help to characterize him.)
5. By what *others,* including the narrator, *say* or *think* about them.

We should pay particular attention to questions of motive, interaction, conflict, development, and outcome. Such questions tie characters to the plot and to the theme their creator is attempting to embody. When we consider that Young Goodman Brown changes from an apparently well-adjusted, married man to a wretched misanthrope, we are ready to ask some telling questions about Hawthorne's story.

As you read the following stories by Isaac Bashevis Singer and Joyce Carol Oates, use your acquired skills as listener, observer, friend, sibling, armchair psychologist, and moralist to come to grips with the characters you meet. But keep your distance. To direct your attention carefully to the text, concentrate on how character is revealed, how each character functions, the extent to which the characters are developed, the changes they undergo, and what these changes reveal about the author's apparent theme. You'll find more specific questions under "Writing about Character."

ISAAC BASHEVIS SINGER (b. 1904)

Gimpel the Fool

Isaac Bashevis Singer was born in Poland and writes in Yiddish. He emigrated to the United States in 1935. His collections of short stories include *Gimpel the Fool and Other Stories* (1957) and *The Spinoza of Market Street and Other Stories* (1961). He has also written novels and children's books. He was awarded the Nobel Prize for Literature in 1978.

I

I am Gimpel the fool. I don't think myself a fool. On the contrary. But that's what folks call me. They gave me the name while I was still in school. I had seven names in all: imbecile, donkey, flax-head, dope, glump, ninny, and fool. The last name stuck. What did my foolishness consist of? I was easy to take in. They said, "Gimpel, you know the rabbi's wife has been brought to childbed?" So I skipped school. Well, it turned out to be a lie. How was I supposed to know? She hadn't had a big belly. But I never looked at her belly. Was that really so foolish? The gang laughed and hee-hawed, stomped and danced and chanted a good-night prayer. And instead of the raisins they give when a woman's lying in, they stuffed my hand full of goat turds. I was no weakling. If I slapped someone he'd see all the way to Cracow. But I'm really not a slugger by nature. I think to myself, Let it pass. So they take advantage of me.

I was coming home from school and heard a dog barking. I'm not afraid of dogs, but of course I never want to start up with them. One of them may be mad, and if he bites there's not a Tartar in the world who can help you. So I made tracks. Then I looked around and saw the whole market place wild with laughter. It was no dog at all but Wolf-Leib the thief. How was I supposed to know it was he? It sounded like a howling bitch.

When the pranksters and leg-pullers found that I was easy to fool, every one of them tried his luck with me. "Gimpel, the Czar is coming to Frampol; Gimpel, the moon fell down in Turbeen; Gimpel, little Hodel Furpiece found a treasure behind the bathhouse." And I like a *golem*[1] believed everyone. In the first place, everything is possible, as it is written in the Wisdom of the Fathers, I've forgotten just how. Second, I had to believe when the whole town came down on me! If I ever dared to say, "Ah, you're kidding!" there was trouble. People got angry. "What do you mean! You want to call everyone a liar?" What was I to do? I believed them, and I hope at least that did them some good.

I was an orphan. My grandfather who brought me up was already bent toward the grave. So they turned me over to a baker, and what a time they gave me there! Every woman or girl who came to bake a pan of cookies or dry a batch of noodles had to fool me at least once. "Gimpel, there's a fair in heaven; Gimpel, the rabbi gave birth to a calf in the seventh month; Gimpel, a cow flew over the roof and laid brass eggs." A student from the *yeshiva*[2] came once to buy a roll, and he said, "You, Gimpel, while you stand here scraping with your baker's shovel the Messiah has come. The dead have arisen." "What do you mean?" I said. "I heard no one blowing the ram's horn!" He said, "Are you deaf?" And all began to cry, "We heard

1. golem: a dolt or simpleton
2. yeshiva: a seminary for the training of orthodox rabbis.

it, we heard!" Then in came Reitze the candle-dipper and called out in her hoarse voice, "Gimpel, your father and mother have stood up from the grave. They're looking for you."

To tell the truth, I knew very well that nothing of the sort had happened, but all the same, as folks were talking, I threw on my wool vest and went out. Maybe something had happened. What did I stand to lose by looking? Well, what a cat music went up! And then I took a vow to believe nothing more. But that was no go either. They confused me so that I didn't know the big end from the small.

I went to the rabbi to get some advice. He said, "It is written, better to be a fool all your days than for one hour to be evil. You are not a fool. They are the fools. For he who causes his neighbor to feel shame loses Paradise himself." Nevertheless the rabbi's daughter took me in. As I left the rabbinical court she said, "Have you kissed the wall yet?" I said, "No; what for?" She answered, "It's a law; you've got to do it after every visit." Well, there didn't seem to be any harm in it. And she burst out laughing. It was a fine trick. She put one over on me, all right.

I wanted to go off to another town, but then everyone got busy matchmaking, and they were after me so they nearly tore my coat tails off. They talked at me and talked until I got water on the ear. She was no chaste maiden, but they told me she was virgin pure. She had a limp, and they said it was deliberate, from coyness. She had a bastard, and they told me the child was her little brother. I cried, "You're wasting your time. I'll never marry that whore." But they said indignantly, "What a way to talk! Aren't you ashamed of yourself? We can take you to the rabbi and have you fined for giving her a bad name." I saw then that I wouldn't escape them so easily and I thought, They're set on making me their butt. But when you're married the husband's the master, and if that's all right with her it's agreeable to me too. Besides, you can't pass through life unscathed, nor expect to.

I went to her clay house, which was built on the sand, and the whole gang, hollering and chorusing, came after me. They acted like bearbaiters. When we came to the well they stopped all the same. They were afraid to start anything with Elka. Her mouth would open as if it were on a hinge, and she had a fierce tongue. I entered the house. Lines were strung from wall to wall and clothes were drying. Barefoot she stood by the tub, doing the wash. She was dressed in a worn hand-me-down gown of plush. She had her hair put up in braids and pinned across her head. It took my breath away, almost, the reek of it all.

Evidently she knew who I was. She took a look at me and said, "Look who's here! He's come, the drip. Grab a seat."

I told her all; I denied nothing. "Tell me the truth," I said, "are you really a virgin, and is that mischievous Yechiel actually your little brother? Don't be deceitful with me, for I'm an orphan."

"I'm an orphan myself," she answered, "and whoever tries to twist you up, may the end of his nose take a twist. But don't let them think they can take advantage of me. I want a dowry of fifty guilders, and let them take up a collection besides. Otherwise they can kiss my you-know-what." She was very plain-spoken. I said, "It's the bride and not the groom who gives a dowry." Then she said, "Don't bargain with me. Either a flat 'yes' or a flat 'no'—go back where you came from."

I thought, No bread will ever be baked from *this* dough. But ours is not a poor town. They consented to everything and proceeded with the wedding. It so happened that there was a dysentery epidemic at the time. The ceremony was held at the cemetery gates, near the little corpse-washing hut. The fellows got drunk. While the marriage contract was being drawn up I heard the most pious high rabbi ask, "Is the bride a widow or a divorced woman?" And the sexton's wife answered for her, "Both a widow and divorced." It was a black moment for me. But what was I to do, run away from under the marriage canopy?

There was singing and dancing. An old granny danced opposite me, hugging a braided white *chalah*.[3] The master of revels made a "God 'a mercy" in memory of the bride's parents. The schoolboys threw burrs, as on *Tishe b' Av* fast day.[4] There were a lot of gifts after the sermon: a noodle board, a kneading trough, a bucket, brooms, ladles, household articles galore. Then I took a look and saw two strapping young men carrying a crib. "What do we need this for?" I asked. So they said, "Don't rack your brains about it. It's all right, it'll come in handy." I realized I was going to be rooked. Take it another way though, what did I stand to lose? I reflected, I'll see what comes of it. A whole town can't go altogether crazy.

II

At night I came where my wife lay, but she wouldn't let me in. "Say, look here, is this what they married us for?" I said. And she said, "My monthly has come." "But yesterday they took you to the ritual bath, and that's afterward, isn't it supposed to be?" "Today isn't yesterday," said she, "and yesterday's not today. You can beat it if you don't like it." In short, I waited.

Not four months later she was in childbed. The townsfolk hid their laughter with their knuckles. But what could I do? She suffered intolerable pains and clawed at the walls. "Gimpel," she cried, "I'm going. Forgive me!" The house filled with women. They were boiling pans of water. The screams rose to the welkin.

The thing to do was to go to the House of Prayer to repeat Psalms, and that was what I did.

The townsfolk liked that, all right. I stood in a corner saying Psalms

---

3.   chalah: a loaf of bread glazed with egg-white
4.   Tishe b' Av: a day of mourning that commemorates disasters

and prayers, and they shook their heads at me. "Pray, pray!" they told me. "Prayer never made any woman pregnant." One of the congregation put a straw to my mouth and said, "Hay for the cows." There was something to that too, by God!

She gave birth to a boy. Friday at the synagogue the sexton stood up before the Ark, pounded on the reading table, and announced, "The wealthy Reb Gimpel invites the congregation to a feast in honor of the birth of a son." The whole House of Prayer rang with laughter. My face was flaming. But there was nothing I could do. After all, I *was* the one responsible for the circumcision honors and rituals.

Half the town came running. You couldn't wedge another soul in. Women brought peppered chick-peas, and there was a keg of beer from the tavern. I ate and drank as much as anyone, and they all congratulated me. Then there was a circumcision, and I named the boy after my father, may he rest in peace. When all were gone and I was left with my wife alone, she thrust her head through the bed-curtain and called me to her.

"Gimpel," said she, "why are you silent? Has your ship gone and sunk?"

"What shall I say?" I answered. "A fine thing you've done to me! If my mother had known of it she'd have died a second time."

She said, "Are you crazy, or what?"

"How can you make such a fool," I said, "of one who should be the lord and master?"

"What's the matter with you?" she said. "What have you taken it into your head to imagine?"

I saw that I must speak bluntly and openly. "Do you think this is the way to use an orphan?" I said. "You have borne a bastard."

She answered, "Drive this foolishness out of your head. The child is yours."

"How can he be mine?" I argued. "He was born seventeen weeks after the wedding."

She told me then that he was premature. I said, "Isn't he a little too premature?" She said she had had a grandmother who carried just as short a time and she resembled this grandmother of hers as one drop of water does another. She swore to it with such oaths that you would have believed a peasant at the fair if he had used them. To tell the plain truth, I didn't believe her; but when I talked it over next day with the schoolmaster he told me that the very same thing had happened to Adam and Eve. Two they went up to bed, and four they descended.

"There isn't a woman in the world who is not the granddaughter of Eve," he said.

That was how it was—they argued me dumb. But then, who really knows how such things are?

I began to forget my sorrow. I loved the child madly, and he loved me too. As soon as he saw me he'd wave his little hands and want me to pick him up, and when he was colicky I was the only one who could pacify him. I bought him a little bone teething ring and a little gilded cap. He was forever catching the evil eye from someone, and then I had to run to get one of those abracadabras for him that would get him out of it. I worked like an ox. You know how expenses go up when there's an infant in the house. I don't want to lie about it; I didn't dislike Elka either, for that matter. She swore at me and cursed, and I couldn't get enough of her. What strength she had! One of her looks could rob you of the power of speech. And her orations! Pitch and sulphur, that's what they were full of, and yet somehow also full of charm. I adored her every word. She gave me bloody wounds though.

In the evening I brought her a white loaf as well as a dark one, and also poppyseed rolls I baked myself. I thieved because of her and swiped everything I could lay hands on, macaroons, raisins, almonds, cakes. I hope I may be forgiven for stealing from the Saturday pots the women left to warm in the baker's oven. I would take out scraps of meat, a chunk of pudding, a chicken leg or head, a piece of tripe, whatever I could nip quickly. She ate and became fat and handsome.

I had to sleep away from home all during the week, at the bakery. On Friday nights when I got home she always made an excuse of some sort. Either she had heartburn, or a stitch in the side, or hiccups, or headaches. You know what women's excuses are. I had a bitter time of it. It was rough. To add to it, this little brother of hers, the bastard, was growing bigger. He'd put lumps on me, and when I wanted to hit back she'd open her mouth and curse so powerfully I saw a green haze floating before my eyes. Ten times a day she threatened to divorce me. Another man in my place would have taken French leave and disappeared. But I'm the type that bears it and says nothing. What's one to do? Shoulders are from God, and burdens too.

One night there was a calamity in the bakery; the oven burst, and we almost had a fire. There was nothing to do but go home, so I went home. Let me, I thought, also taste the joy of sleeping in bed in midweek. I didn't want to wake the sleeping mite and tiptoed into the house. Coming in, it seemed to me that I heard not the snoring of one but, as it were, a double snore, one a thin enough snore and the other like the snoring of a slaughtered ox. Oh, I didn't like that! I didn't like it at all. I went up to the bed, and things suddenly turned black. Next to Elka lay a man's form. Another in my place would have made an uproar, and enough noise to rouse the whole town, but the thought occurred to me that I might wake the child. A little thing like that—why frighten a little swallow like that, I thought. All right then, I went back to the bakery and stretched out on a sack of flour, and till morning I never shut an eye. I shivered as if I had had malaria. "Enough of being a donkey," I said to myself. "Gimpel isn't going to be a sucker all his life. There's a limit even to the foolishness of a fool like Gimpel."

In the morning I went to the rabbi to get advice, and it made a great commotion in the town. They sent the beadle for Elka right away. She came, carrying the child. And what do you think she did? She denied it, denied everything, bone and stone! "He's out of his head," she said. "I know nothing of dreams or divinations." They yelled at her, warned her, hammered on the table, but she stuck to her guns: it was a false accusation, she said.

The butchers and the horse-traders took her part. One of the lads from the slaughterhouse came by and said to me, "We've got our eye on you, you're a marked man." Meanwhile the child started to bear down and soiled itself. In the rabbinical court there was an Ark of the Covenant, and they couldn't allow that, so they sent Elka away.

I said to the rabbi, "What shall I do?"

"You must divorce her at once," said he.

"And what if she refuses?" I asked.

He said, "You must serve the divorce, that's all you'll have to do."

I said, "Well, all right, Rabbi. Let me think about it."

"There's nothing to think about," said he. "You mustn't remain under the same roof with her."

"And if I want to see the child?" I asked.

"Let her go, the harlot," said he, "and her brood of bastards with her."

The verdict he gave was that I mustn't even cross her threshold—never again, as long as I should live.

During the day it didn't bother me so much. I thought, It was bound to happen, the abscess had to burst. But at night when I stretched out upon the sacks I felt it all very bitterly. A longing took me, for her and for the child. I wanted to be angry, but that's my misfortune exactly, I don't have it in me to be really angry. In the first place—this was how my thoughts went—there's bound to be a slip sometimes. You can't live without errors. Probably that lad who was with her led her on and gave her presents and what not, and women are often long on hair and short on sense, and so he got around her. And then since she denies it so, maybe I was only seeing things? Hallucinations do happen. You see a figure or mannikin or something, but when you come up closer it's nothing, there's not a thing there. And if that's so, I'm doing her an injustice. And when I got so far in my thoughts I started to weep. I sobbed so that I wet the flour where I lay. In the morning I went to the rabbi and told him that I had made a mistake. The rabbi wrote on with his quill, and he said that if that were so he would have to reconsider the whole case. Until he had finished I wasn't to go near my wife, but I might send her bread and money by messenger.

III

Nine months passed before all the rabbis could come to an agreement. Letters went back and forth. I hadn't realized that there could be so much erudition about a matter like this.

Meantime Elka gave birth to still another child, a girl this time. On the Sabbath I went to the synagogue and invoked a blessing on her. They called me up to the Torah, and I named the child for my mother-in-law, may she rest in peace. The louts and loudmouths of the town who came into the bakery gave me a going over. All Frampol refreshed its spirits because of my trouble and grief. However, I resolved that I would always believe what I was told. What's the good of not believing? Today it's your wife you don't believe; tomorrow it's God Himself you won't take stock in.

By an apprentice who was her neighbor I sent her daily a corn or a wheat loaf, or a piece of pastry, rolls or bagels, or, when I got the chance, a slab of pudding, a slice of honeycake, or wedding strudel—whatever came my way. The apprentice was a goodhearted lad, and more than once he added something on his own. He had formerly annoyed me a lot, plucking my nose and digging me in the ribs, but when he started to be a visitor to my house he became kind and friendly. "Hey, you, Gimpel," he said to me, "you have a very decent little wife and two fine kids. You don't deserve them."

"But the things people say about her," I said.

"Well, they have long tongues," he said, "and nothing to do with them but babble. Ignore it as you ignore the cold of last winter."

One day the rabbi sent for me and said, "Are you certain, Gimpel, that you were wrong about your wife?"

I said, "I'm certain."

"Why, but look here! You yourself saw it."

"It must have been a shadow," I said.

"The shadow of what?"

"Just of one of the beams, I think."

"You can go home then. You owe thanks to the Yanover rabbi. He found an obscure reference in Maimonides that favored you."

I seized the rabbi's hand and kissed it.

I wanted to run home immediately. It's no small thing to be separated for so long a time from wife and child. Then I reflected, I'd better go back to work now, and go home in the evening. I said nothing to anyone, although as far as my heart was concerned it was like one of the Holy Days. The women teased and twitted me as they did every day, but my thought was, Go on, with your loose talk. The truth is out, like the oil upon the water. Maimonides says it's right, and therefore it is right!

At night, when I had covered the dough to let it rise, I took my share of bread and a little sack of flour and started homeward. The moon was full and the stars were glistening, something to terrify the soul. I hurried onward, and before me darted a long shadow. It was winter, and a fresh snow had fallen. I had a mind to sing, but it was growing late and I didn't want to wake the householders. Then I felt like whistling, but remembered that you don't whistle at night because it brings the demons out. So I was silent and walked as fast as I could.

Dogs in the Christian yards barked at me when I passed, but I thought, Bark your teeth out! What are you but mere dogs? Whereas I am a man, the husband of a fine wife, the father of promising children.

As I approached the house my heart started to pound as though it were the heart of a criminal. I felt no fear, but my heart went thump! thump! Well, no drawing back. I quietly lifted the latch and went in. Elka was asleep. I looked at the infant's cradle. The shutter was closed, but the moon forced its way through the cracks. I saw the newborn child's face and loved it as soon as I saw it—immediately—each tiny bone.

Then I came nearer to the bed. And what did I see but the apprentice lying there beside Elka. The moon went out all at once. It was utterly black, and I trembled. My teeth chattered. The bread fell from my hands and my wife waked and said, "Who is that, ah?"

I muttered, "It's me."

"Gimpel?" she asked. "How come you're here? I thought it was forbidden."

"The rabbi said," I answered and shook as with a fever.

"Listen to me, Gimpel," she said, "go out to the shed and see if the goat's all right. It seems she's been sick." I have forgotten to say that we had a goat. When I heard she was unwell I went into the yard. The nannygoat was a good little creature. I had a nearly human feeling for her.

With hesitant steps I went up to the shed and opened the door. The goat stood there on her four feet. I felt her everywhere, drew her by the horns, examined her udders, and found nothing wrong. She had probably eaten too much bark. "Good night, little goat," I said. "Keep well." And the little beast answered with a "Maa" as though to thank me for the good will.

I went back. The apprentice had vanished.

"Where," I asked, "is the lad?"

"What lad?" my wife answered.

"What do you mean?" I said. "The apprentice. You were sleeping with him."

"The things I have dreamed this night and the night before," she said, "may they come true and lay you low, body and soul! An evil spirit has taken root in you and dazzles your sight." She screamed out, "You hateful creature! You moon calf! You spook! You uncouth man! Get out, or I'll scream all Frampol out of bed!"

Before I could move, her brother sprang out from behind the oven and struck me a blow on the back of the head. I thought he had broken my neck. I felt that something about me was deeply wrong, and I said, "Don't make a scandal. All that's needed now is that people should accuse me of raising spooks and *dybbuks*."[5] For that was what she had meant. "No one will touch bread of my baking."

5. dybbuks: souls of the dead

In short, I somehow calmed her.

"Well," she said, "that's enough. Lie down, and be shattered by wheels."

Next morning I called the apprentice aside. "Listen here, brother!" I said. And so on and so forth. "What do you say?" He stared at me as though I had dropped from the roof or something.

"I swear," he said, "you'd better go to an herb doctor or some healer. I'm afraid you have a screw loose, but I'll hush it up for you." And that's how the thing stood.

To make a long story short, I lived twenty years with my wife. She bore me six children, four daughters and two sons. All kinds of things happened, but I neither saw nor heard. I believed, and that's all. The rabbi recently said to me, "Belief in itself is beneficial. It is written that a good man lives by his faith."

Suddenly my wife took sick. It began with a trifle, a little growth upon the breast. But she evidently was not destined to live long; she had no years. I spent a fortune on her. I have forgotten to say that by this time I had a bakery of my own and in Frampol was considered to be something of a rich man. Daily the healer came, and every witch doctor in the neighborhood was brought. They decided to use leeches, and after that to try cupping. They even called a doctor from Lublin, but it was too late. Before she died she called me to her bed and said, "Forgive me, Gimpel."

I said, "What is there to forgive? You have been a good and faithful wife."

"Woe, Gimpel!" she said. "It was ugly how I deceived you all these years. I want to go clean to my Maker, and so I have to tell you that the children are not yours."

If I had been clouted on the head with a piece of wood it couldn't have bewildered me more.

"Whose are they?" I asked

"I don't know," she said, "there were a lot. . . . But they're not yours." And as she spoke she tossed her head to the side, her eyes turned glassy, and it was all up with Elka. On her whitened lips there remained a smile.

I imagined that, dead as she was, she was saying, "I deceived Gimpel. That was the meaning of my brief life."

IV

One night, when the period of mourning was done, as I lay dreaming on the flour sacks, there came the Spirit of Evil himself and said to me, "Gimpel, why do you sleep?"

I said, "What should I be doing? Eating *kreplach*?"[6]

---

6. kreplach: a filled dumpling

"The whole world deceives you," he said, "and you ought to deceive the world in your turn."

"How can I deceive all the world?" I asked him.

He answered, "You might accumulate a bucket of urine every day and at night pour it into the dough. Let the sages of Frampol eat filth."

"What about judgment in the world to come?" I said.

"There is no world to come," he said. "They've sold you a bill of goods and talked you into believing you carried a cat in your belly. What nonsense!"

"Well then," I said, "and is there a God?"

He answered, "There is no God either."

"What," I said, "*is* there, then?"

"A thick mire."

He stood before my eyes with a goatish beard and horns, longtoothed, and with a tail. Hearing such words, I wanted to snatch him by the tail, but I tumbled from the flour sacks and nearly broke a rib. Then it happened that I had to answer the call of nature, and, passing, I saw the risen dough, which seemed to say to me, "Do it!" In brief, I let myself be persuaded.

At dawn the apprentice came. We kneaded the bread, scattered caraway seeds on it, and set it to bake. Then the apprentice went away, and I was left sitting in the little trench by the oven, on a pile of rags. Well, Gimpel, I thought, you've revenged yourself on them for all the shame they've put on you. Outside the frost glittered, but it was warm beside the oven. The flames heated my face. I bent my head and fell into a doze.

I saw in a dream, at once, Elka in her shroud. She called to me, "What have you done, Gimpel?"

I said to her, "It's all your fault," and started to cry.

"You fool!" she said. "You fool! Because I was false is everything false too? I never deceived anyone but myself. I'm paying for it all, Gimpel. They spare you nothing here."

I looked at her face. It was black. I was startled and waked, and remained sitting dumb. I sensed that everything hung in the balance. A false step now and I'd lose Eternal Life. But God gave me His help. I seized the long shovel and took out the loaves, carried them into the yard, and started to dig a hole in the frozen earth.

My apprentice came back as I was doing it. "What are you doing, boss?" he said, and grew pale as a corpse.

"I know what I'm doing," I said, and I buried it all before his very eyes.

Then I went home, took my hoard from its hiding place, and divided it among the children. "I saw your mother tonight," I said. "She's turning black, poor thing."

They were so astounded they couldn't speak a word.

"Be well," I said, "and forget that such a one as Gimpel ever existed."

I put on my short coat, a pair of boots, took the bag that held my prayer shawl in one hand, my stick in the other, and kissed the *mezzuzah*.[7] When people saw me in the street they were greatly surprised.

"Where are you going?" they said.

I answered, "Into the world." And so I departed from Frampol.

I wandered over the land, and good people did not neglect me. After many years I became old and white; I heard a great deal, many lies and falsehoods, but the longer I lived the more I understood that there were really no lies. Whatever doesn't really happen is dreamed at night. It happens to one if it doesn't happen to another, tomorrow if not today, or a century hence if not next year. What difference can it make? Often I heard tales of which I said, "Now this is a thing that cannot happen." But before a year had elapsed I heard that it actually had come to pass somewhere.

Going from place to place, eating at strange tables, it often happens that I spin yarns—improbable things that could never have happened— about devils, magicians, windmills, and the like. The children run after me, calling, "Grandfather, tell us a story." Sometimes they ask for particular stories, and I try to please them. A fat young boy once said to me, "Grandfather, it's the same story you told us before." The little rogue, he was right.

So it is with dreams too. It is many years since I left Frampol, but as soon as I shut my eyes I am there again. And whom do you think I see? Elka. She is standing by the washtub, as at our first encounter, but her face is shining and her eyes are radiant as the eyes of a saint, and she speaks outlandish words to me, strange things. When I wake I have forgotten it all. But while the dream lasts I am comforted. She answers all my queries, and what comes out is that all is right. I weep and implore, "Let me be with you." And she consoles me and tells me to be patient. The time is nearer then it is far. Sometimes she strokes and kisses me and weeps upon my face. When I awaken I feel her lips and taste the salt of her tears.

No doubt the world is entirely an imaginary world, but it is only once removed from the true world. At the door of the hovel where I lie, there stands the plank on which the dead are taken away. The gravedigger Jew has his spade ready. The grave waits and the worms are hungry; the shrouds are prepared—I carry them in my beggar's sack. Another *shnorrer*[8] is waiting to inherit my bed of straw. When the time comes I will go joyfully. Whatever may be there, it will be real, without complication, without ridicule, without deception. God be praised: there even Gimpel cannot be deceived.

Translated by Saul Bellow

7. mezzuzah: a small parchment inscribed with the shema (from Deuteronomy 6:4–9 and 11:13–21), rolled and put into a case and attached to the doorpost of a home
8. schnorrer: a traveling beggar

QUESTIONS

1. Why does Gimpel choose to believe whatever he is told?
2. How do the citizens of Frampol function in the story?
3. How, if at all, does Elka seem to alter Gimpel's character?
4. Besides gullibility, what are Gimpel's principal traits?
5. Re-read the last paragraph of the story. In what ways has Gimpel's life on earth been a fitting preparation for his life beyond the grave?

JOYCE CAROL OATES (b. 1938)

Where Are You Going, Where Have You Been?

Joyce Carol Oates, born in Lockport, New York, and educated at Syracuse University and the University of Wisconsin, is among the most prolific of contemporary American writers of fiction. Her novels include *Expensive People* (1968). *Them* (1969) and *Bellefleur* (1980). She has also published several volumes of short stories, including *The Wheel of Love* (1970), in which "Where Are Your Going, Where Have You Been?" was first collected.

For Bob Dylan

Her name was Connie. She was fifteen and she had a quick nervous giggling habit of craning her neck to glance into mirrors, or checking other people's faces to make sure her own was all right. Her mother, who noticed everything and knew everything and who hadn't much reason any longer to look at her own face, always scolded Connie about it. "Stop gawking at yourself, who are you? You think you're so pretty?" she would say. Connie would raise her eyebrows at these familiar complaints and look right through her mother, into a shadowy vision of herself as she was right at that moment: she knew she was pretty and that was everything. Her mother had been pretty once too, if you could believe those old snapshots in the album, but now her looks were gone and that was why she was always after Connie.

"Why don't you keep your room clean like your sister? How've you got your hair fixed—what the hell stinks? Hair spray? You don't see your sister using that junk."

Her sister June was twenty-four and still lived at home. She was a secretary in the high school Connie attended, and if that wasn't bad enough—with her in the same building—she was so plain and chunky and steady that Connie had to hear her praised all the time by her mother and her mother's sisters. June did this, June did that, she saved money and helped clean the house and cooked and Connie couldn't do a thing, her mind was all filled with trashy daydreams. Their father was away at work most of the time and when he came home he wanted supper and he read the newspaper at supper and after supper he went to bed. He didn't bother talking much to them, but around his bent head Connie's mother kept picking at her until Connie wished her mother was dead and she herself was dead and it was all over. "She makes me want to throw up sometimes," she complained to her friends. She had a high, breathless, amused voice which made everything she said a little forced, whether it was sincere or not.

There was one good thing: June went places with girl friends of hers, girls who were just as plain and steady as she, and so when Connie wanted to do that her mother had no objections. The father of Connie's best girl friend drove the girls the three miles to town and left them off at a shopping plaza, so that they could walk through the stores or go to a movie, and when he came to pick them up again at eleven he never bothered to ask what they had done.

They must have been familiar sights, walking around that shopping plaza in their shorts and flat ballerina slippers that always scuffed the sidewalk, with charm bracelets jingling on their thin wrists; they would lean together to whisper and laugh secretly if someone passed by who amused or interested them. Connie had long dark blond hair that drew anyone's eye to it, and she wore part of it pulled up on her head and puffed out and the rest of it she let fall down her back. She wore a pullover jersey blouse that looked one way when she was at home and another way when she was away from home. Everything about her had two sides to it, one for home and one for anywhere that was not home: her walk that could be childlike and bobbing, or languid enough to make anyone think she was hearing music in her head, her mouth which was pale and smirking most of the time, but bright and pink on these evenings out, her laugh which was cynical and drawling at home—"Ha, ha, very funny"—but high-pitched and nervous anywhere else, like the jingling of the charms on her bracelet.

Sometimes they did go shopping or to a movie, but sometimes they went across the highway, ducking fast across the busy road, to a drive-in restaurant where older kids hung out. The restaurant was shaped like a big bottle, though squatter than a real bottle, and on its cap was a revolving figure of a grinning boy who held a hamburger aloft. One night in midsummer they ran across, breathless with daring, and right away someone leaned out a car window and invited them over, but it was just a boy from high school they didn't like. It made them feel good to be able to ignore him. They went up through the maze of parked and cruising cars to the bright-lit, fly-infested restaurant, their faces pleased and expectant as if they were entering a sacred building that loomed out of the night to give them what haven and what blessing they yearned for. They sat at the counter and crossed their legs at the ankles, their thin shoulders rigid with excitement and listened to the music that made everything so good: the music was always in the background like music at a church service, it was something to depend upon.

A boy named Eddie came in to talk with them. He sat backwards on his stool, turning himself jerkily around in semi-circles and then stopping and turning again, and after a while he asked Connie if she would like something to eat. She said she did and so she tapped her friend's arm on her way out—her friend pulled her face up into a brave droll look—and Connie said she would meet her at eleven, across the way. "I just hate to leave her like that," Connie said earnestly, but the boy said that she wouldn't be alone for long. So they went out to his car and on the way Connie couldn't help but let her eyes wander over the windshields and faces all around her, her face gleaming with the joy that had nothing to do with Eddie or even this place; it might have been the music. She drew her shoulders up and sucked in her breath with the pure pleasure of being alive, and just at that moment she happened to glance at a face just a few feet from hers. It was a boy with shaggy black hair, in a convertible jalopy painted gold. He stared at her and then his lips widened into a grin. Connie slit her eyes at him and turned away, but she couldn't help glancing back and there he was still watching her. He wagged a finger and laughed and said, "Gonna get you, baby," and Connie turned away again without Eddie noticing anything.

She spent three hours with him, at the restaurant where they ate hamburgers and drank Cokes in wax cups that were always sweating, and then down an alley a mile or so away, and when he left her off at five to eleven only the movie house was still open at the plaza. Her girl friend was there, talking with a boy. When Connie came up the two girls smiled at each other and Connie said, "How was the movie?" and the girl said, "*You* should know." They rode off with the girl's father, sleepy and pleased, and Connie couldn't help but look at the darkened shopping plaza with its big empty parking lot and its signs that were faded and ghostly now, and over at the drive-in restaurant where cars were still circling tirelessly. She couldn't hear the music at this distance.

Next morning June asked her how the movie was and Connie said, "So-so."

She and that girl and occasionally another girl went out several times a week that way, and the rest of the time Connie spent around the house—it was summer vacation—getting in her mother's way and thinking, dreaming, about the boys she met. But all the boys fell back and dissolved into a single face that was not even a face, but an idea, a feeling, mixed up with the urgent insistent pounding of the music and the humid night air of July. Connie's mother kept dragging her back to the daylight by finding things for her to do or saying suddenly, "What's this about the Pettinger girl?"

And Connie would say nervously, "Oh, her. That dope." She always drew thick clear lines between herself and such girls, and her mother was simple and kindly enough to believe her. Her mother was so simple, Connie thought, that it was maybe cruel to fool her so much. Her mother went scuffling around the house in old bedroom slippers and complained over the telephone to one sister about the other, then the other called up and the two of them complained about the third one. If June's name was mentioned her mother's tone was approving, and if Connie's name was mentioned it was disapproving. This did not really mean she disliked Connie and actually Connie thought that her mother preferred her to June because she was prettier, but the two of them kept up a pretense of exasperation, a sense that they were tugging and struggling over something of little value to either of them. Sometimes, over coffee, they were almost friends, but something would come up—some vexation that was like a fly buzzing suddenly around their heads—and their faces went hard with contempt.

One Sunday Connie got up at eleven—none of them bothered with church—and washed her hair so that it could dry all day long, in the sun. Her parents and sister were going to a barbecue at an aunt's house and Connie said no, she wasn't interested, rolling her eyes, to let mother know just what she thought of it. "Stay home alone then," her mother said sharply. Connie sat out back in a lawn chair and watched them drive away, her father quiet and bald, hunched around so that he could back the car out, her mother with a look that was still angry and not at all softened through the windshield, and in the back seat poor old June all dressed up as if she didn't know what a barbecue was, with all the running yelling kids and the flies. Connie sat with her eyes closed in the sun, dreaming and dazed with the warmth about her as if this were a kind of love, the caresses of love, and her mind slipped over onto thoughts of the boy she had been with the night before and how nice he had been, how sweet it always was, not the way someone like June would suppose but sweet, gentle, the way it was in movies and promised in songs; and when she opened her eyes she hardly knew where she was, the back yard ran off into weeds and a fence-line of trees and behind it the sky was perfectly blue and still. The asbestos "ranch house" that was now three years old startled her—it looked small. She shook her head as if to get awake.

It was too hot. She went inside the house and turned on the radio to drown out the quiet. She sat on the edge of her bed, barefoot, and listened for an hour and a half to a program called XYZ Sunday Jamboree, record after record of hard, fast, shrieking songs she sang along with, interspersed by exclamations from "Bobby King": "An' look here you girls at Napoleon's—Son and Charley want you to pay real close attention to this song coming up!"

And Connie paid close attention herself, bathed in a glow of slow-pulsed joy that seemed to rise mysteriously out of the music itself and lay languidly about the airless little room, breathed in and breathed out with each gentle rise and fall of her chest.

After a while she heard a car coming up the drive. She sat up at once, startled, because it couldn't be her father so soon. The gravel kept crunching all the way in from the road—the driveway was long—and Connie ran to the window. It was a car she didn't know. It was an open jalopy, painted a bright gold that caught the sun opaquely. Her heart began to pound and her fingers snatched at her hair, checking it, and she whispered "Christ. Christ," wondering how bad she looked. The car came to a stop at the side door and the horn sounded four short taps as if this were a signal Connie knew.

She went into the kitchen and approached the door slowly, then hung out the screen door, her bare toes curling down off the step. There were two boys in the car and now she recognized the driver: he had shaggy, shabby black hair that looked crazy as a wig and he was grinning at her.

"I ain't late, am I?" he said.

"Who the hell do you think you are?" Connie said.

"Toldja I'd be out, didn't I?"

"I don't even know who you are."

She spoke sullenly, careful to show no interest or pleasure, and he spoke in a fast bright monotone. Connie looked past him to the other boy, taking her time. He had fair brown hair, with a lock that fell onto his forehead. His sideburns gave him a fierce, embarrassed look, but so far he hadn't even bothered to glance at her. Both boys wore sunglasses. The driver's glasses were metallic and mirrored everything in miniature.

"You wanta come for a ride?" he said.

Connie smirked and let her hair fall loose over one shoulder.

"Don'tcha like my car? New paint job," he said. "Hey."

"What?"

"You're cute."

She pretended to fidget, chasing flies away from the door.

"Don'tcha believe me, or what?" he said.

"Look, I don't even know who you are," Connie said in disgust.

"Hey, Ellie's got a radio, see. Mine's broke down." He lifted his friend's arm and showed her the little transistor the boy was holding, and now Connie began to hear the music. It was the same program that was playing inside the house.

"Bobby King?" she said.

"I listen to him all the time. I think he's great."

"He's kind of great," Connie said reluctantly.

"Listen, that guy's *great*. He knows where the action is."

Connie blushed a little, because the glasses made it impossible for her to see just what this boy was looking at. She couldn't decide if she liked him or if he was just a jerk, and so she dawdled in the doorway and wouldn't come down or go back inside. She said, "What's all that stuff painted on your car?"

"Can'tcha read it?" He opened the door very carefully, as if he was afraid it might fall off. He slid out just as carefully, planting his feet firmly on the ground, the tiny metallic world in his glasses slowing down like gelatin hardening and in the midst of it Connie's bright green blouse. "This here is my name, to begin with," he said. ARNOLD FRIEND was written in tar-like black letters on the side, with a drawing of a round grinning face that reminded Connie of a pumpkin, except it wore sunglasses. "I wanta introduce myself, I'm Arnold Friend and that's my real name and I'm gonna be your friend, honey, and inside the car's Ellie Oscar, he's kinda shy." Ellie brought his transistor up to his shoulder and balanced it there. "Now these numbers are a secret code, honey," Arnold Friend explained. He read off the numbers 33, 19, 17 and raised his eyebrows at her to see what she thought of that, but she didn't think much of it. The left rear fender had been smashed and around it was written, on the gleaming gold background: DONE BY CRAZY WOMAN DRIVER. Connie had to laugh at that. Arnold Friend was pleased at her laughter and looked up at her. "Around the other side's a lot more—you wanta come and see them?"

"No."

"Why not?"

"Why should I?"

"Don'tcha wanta see what's on the car? Don'tcha wanta go for a ride?"

"I don't know."

"Why not?"

"I got things to do."

"Like what?"

"Things."

He laughed as if she had said something funny. He slapped his thighs. He was standing in a strange way, leaning back against the car as if he were balancing himself. He wasn't tall, only an inch or so taller than she would be if she came down to him. Connie liked the way he was dressed, which was the way all of them dressed: tight faded jeans stuffed into black, scuffed boots, a belt that pulled his waist in and showed how lean he was, and a white pull-over shirt that was a little soiled and showed the hard small muscles of his arms and shoulders. He looked as if he probably did hard work, lifting and carrying things. Even his neck looked muscular. And his face was a familiar face, somehow: the jaw and chin and cheeks slightly darkened, because he hadn't shaved for a day or two, and the nose long and hawk-like, sniffing as if she were a treat he was going to gobble up and it was all a joke.

"Connie, you ain't telling the truth. This is your day set aside for a ride with me and you know it," he said, still laughing. The way he straightened and recovered from his fit of laughing showed that it had been all fake.

"How do you know what my name is?" she said suspiciously.

"It's Connie."

"Maybe and maybe not."

"I know my Connie," he said, wagging his finger. Now she remembered him even better, back at the restaurant, and her cheeks warmed at the thought of how she sucked in her breath just at the moment she passed him—how she must have looked to him. And he had remembered her. "Ellie and I come out here especially for you," he said. "Ellie can sit in back. How about it?"

"Where?"

"Where what?"

"Where're we going?"

He looked at her. He took off the sunglasses and she saw how pale the skin around his eyes was, like holes that were not in shadow but instead in light. His eyes were like chips of broken glass that catch the light in an amiable way. He smiled. It was as if the idea of going for a ride somewhere, to some place, was a new idea to him.

"Just for a ride, Connie sweetheart."

"I never said my name was Connie," she said.

"But I know what it is. I know your name and all about you, lots of things," Arnold Friend said. He had not moved yet but stood still leaning back against the side of his jalopy. "I took a special interest in you, such a pretty girl, and found out all about you like I know your parents and sister are gone somewheres and I know where and how long they're going to be gone, and I know who you were with last night, and your best friend's name is Betty. Right?"

He spoke in a simple lilting voice, exactly as if he were reciting the words to a song. His smile assured her that everything was fine. In the car Ellie turned up the volume on his radio and did not bother to look around at them.

"Ellie can sit in the back seat," Arnold Friend said. He indicated his friend with a casual jerk of his chin, as if Ellie did not count and she should not bother with him.

"How'd you find out all that stuff?" Connie said.

"Listen: Betty Schultz and Tony Fitch and Jimmy Pettinger and Nancy Pettinger," he said, in a chant. "Raymond Stanley and Bob Hutter—"

"Do you know all those kids?"

"I know everybody."

"Look, you're kidding. You're not from around here."

"Sure."

"But—how come we never saw you before?"

"Sure you saw me before," he said. He looked down at his boots, as if he were a little offended. "You just don't remember."

"I guess I'd remember you," Connie said.

"Yeah?" He looked up at this, beaming. He was pleased. He began to mark time with the music from Ellie's radio, tapping his fists lightly together. Connie looked away from his smile to the car, which was painted so bright it almost hurt her eyes to look at it. She looked at that name, ARNOLD FRIEND. And up at the front fender was an expression that was familiar—MAN THE FLYING SAUCERS. It was an expression kids had used the year before, but didn't use this year. She looked at it for a while as if the words meant something to her that she did not yet know.

"What're you thinking about? Huh?" Arnold Friend demanded. "Not worried about your hair blowing around in the car, are you?"

"No."

"Think I maybe can't drive good?"

"How do I know?"

"You're a hard girl to handle. How come?" he said. "Don't you know I'm your friend? Didn't you see me put my sign in the air when you walked by?"

"What sign?"

"My sign." And he drew an X in the air, leaning out toward her. They were maybe ten feet apart. After his hand fell back to his side the X was still in the air, almost visible. Connie let the screen door close and stood perfectly still inside it, listening to the music from her radio and the boy's blend together. She stared at Arnold Friend. He stood there so stiffly relaxed, pretending to be relaxed, with one hand idly on the door handle as if he were keeping himself up that way and had no intention of ever moving again. She recognized most things about him, the tight jeans that showed his thighs and buttocks and the greasy leather boots and the tight shirt, and even that slippery friendly smile of his, that sleepy dreamy smile that all the boys used to get across ideas they didn't want to put into words. She recognized all this and also the singsong way he talked, slightly mocking, kidding, but serious and a little melancholy, and she recognized the way he tapped one fist against the other in homage to the perpetual music behind him. But all these things did not come together.

She said suddenly, "Hey, how old are you?"

His smile faded. She could see then that he wasn't a kid, he was much older—thirty, maybe more. At this knowledge her heart began to pound faster.

"That's a crazy thing to ask. Can'tcha see I'm your own age?"

"Like hell you are."

"Or maybe a coupla years older, I'm eighteen."

"Eighteen?" she said doubtfully.

He grinned to reassure her and lines appeared at the corners of his mouth. His teeth were big and white. He grinned so broadly his eyes became slits and she saw how thick the lashes were, thick and black as if painted with a black tar-like material. Then he seemed to become embarrassed, abruptly, and looked over his shoulder at Ellie. "*Him*, he's crazy," he said. "Ain't he a riot, he's a nut, a real character." Ellie was still listening to the music. His sunglasses told nothing about what he was thinking. He wore a bright orange shirt unbuttoned halfway to show his chest, which was a pale, bluish chest and not muscular like Arnold Friend's. His shirt collar was turned up all around and the very tips of the collar pointed out past his chin as if they were protecting him. He was pressing the transistor radio up against his ear and sat there in a kind of daze, right in the sun.

"He's kinda strange," Connie said.

"Hey, she says you're kinda strange! Kinda strange!" Arnold Friend cried. He pounded on the car to get Ellie's attention. Ellie turned for the first time and Connie saw with shock that he wasn't a kid either—he had a fair, hairless face, cheeks reddened slightly as if the veins grew too close to the surface of his skin, the face of a forty-year-old baby. Connie felt a wave of dizziness rise in her at this sight and she stared at him as if waiting for something to change the shock of the moment, make it all right again. Ellie's lips kept shaping words, mumbling along with the words blasting his ear.

"Maybe you two better go away," Connie said faintly.

"What? How come?" Arnold Friend cried. "We come out here to take you for a ride. It's Sunday." He had the voice of the man on the radio now. It was the same voice, Connie thought. "Don'tcha know it's Sunday all day and honey, no matter who you were with last night today you're with Arnold Friend and don't you forget it!—Maybe you better step out here," he said, and this last was in a different voice. It was a little flatter, as if the heat was finally getting to him.

"No. I got things to do."

"Hey."

"You two better leave."

"We ain't leaving until you come with us."

"Like hell I am—"

"Connie, don't fool around with me. I mean, I mean, don't *fool around*," he said, shaking his head. He laughed incredulously. He placed his sunglasses on top of his head, carefully, as if he were indeed wearing a wig, and brought the stems down behind his ears. Connie stared at him, another wave of dizziness and fear rising in her so that for a moment he wasn't even in focus but was just a blur, standing there against his gold car and she had the idea that he had driven up the driveway all right but had come from nowhere before that and belonged nowhere and that everything about him and even the music that was so familiar to her was only half real.

"If my father comes and sees you—"

"He ain't coming. He's at a barbecue."

"How do you know that?"

"Aunt Tillie's. Right now they're—uh—they're drinking. Sitting around," he said vaguely, squinting as if he were staring all the way to town and over to Aunt Tillie's back yard. Then the vision seemed to clear and he nodded energetically. "Yeah. Sitting around. There's your sister in a blue dress, huh? And high heels, the poor sad bitch—nothing like you, sweetheart! And your mother's helping some fat woman with the corn, they're cleaning the corn—husking the corn—"

"What fat woman?" Connie cried.

"How do I know what fat woman. I don't know every goddam fat woman in the world!" Arnold Friend laughed.

"Oh, that's Mrs. Hornby. . . . Who invited her?" Connie said. She felt a little light-headed. Her breath was coming quickly.

"She's too fat. I don't like them fat. I like them the way you are, honey," he said, smiling sleepily at her. They stared at each other for a while, through the screen door. He said softly, "Now what you're going to do is this: you're going to come out that door. You're going to sit up front with me and Ellie's going to sit in the back, the hell with Ellie, right? This isn't Ellie's date. You're my date. I'm your lover, honey."

"What? You're crazy—"

"Yes, I'm your lover. You don't know what that is but you will," he said. "I know that too. I know all about you. But look: it's real nice and you couldn't ask for nobody better than me, or more polite. I always keep my word. I'll tell you how it is, I'm always nice at first, the first time. I'll hold you so tight you won't think you have to try to get away or pretend anything because you'll know you can't. And I'll come inside you where it's all secret and you'll give in to me and you'll love me—"

"Shut up! You're crazy!" Connie said. She backed away from the door. She put her hands against her ears as if she'd heard something terrible, something not meant for her. "People don't talk like that, you're crazy," she muttered. Her heart was almost too big now for her chest and its pumping made sweat break out all over her. She looked out to see Arnold Friend pause and then take a step toward the porch lurching. He almost fell. But, like a clever drunken man, he managed to catch his balance. He wobbled in his high boots and grabbed hold of one of the porch posts.

"Honey?" he said. "You still listening?"

"Get the hell out of here!"

"Be nice, honey. Listen."

"I'm going to call the police—"

He wobbled again and out of the side of his mouth came a fast spat curse, an aside not meant for her to hear. But even this "Christ!" sounded forced. Then he began to smile again. She watched this smile come, awkward as if he were smiling from inside a mask. His whole face was a mask, she thought wildly, tanned down onto his throat but then running out as if he had plastered make-up on his face but had forgotten about his throat.

"Honey—? Listen, here's how it is. I always tell the truth and I promise you this: I ain't coming in that house after you."

"You better not! I'm going to call the police if you—if you don't—"

"Honey," he said, talking right through her voice, "honey, I'm not coming in there but you are coming out here. You know why?"

She was panting. The kitchen looked like a place she had never seen before, some room she had run inside but which wasn't good enough, wasn't going to help her. The kitchen window had never had a curtain, after three years, and there were dishes in the sink for her to do—probably—and if you ran your hand across the table you'd probably feel something sticky there.

"You listening, honey? Hey?"

"—going to call the police—"

"Soon as you touch the phone I don't need to keep my promise and can come inside. You won't want that."

She rushed forward and tried to lock the door. Her fingers were shaking. "But why lock it," Arnold Friend said gently, talking right into her face. "It's just a screen door. It's just nothing." One of his boots was at a strange angle, as if his foot wasn't in it. It pointed out to the left, bent at the ankle. "I mean, anybody can break through a screen door and glass and wood and iron or anything else if he needs to, anybody at all and specially Arnold Friend. If the place got lit up with a fire honey you'd come running out into my arms, right into my arms and safe at home—like you knew I was your lover and'd stopped fooling around. I don't mind a nice shy girl but I don't like no fooling around." Part of those words were spoken with a slight rhythmic lilt, and Connie somehow recognized them—the echo of a song from last year, about a girl rushing into her boy friend's arms and coming home again—

Connie stood barefoot on the linoleum floor, staring at him. "What do you want?" she whispered.

"I want you," he said.

"What?"

"Seen you that night and thought, that's the one, yes sir. I never needed to look any more."

"But my father's coming back. He's coming to get me. I had to wash my hair first—" She spoke in a dry, rapid voice, hardly raising it for him to hear.

"No, your daddy is not coming and yes, you had to wash your hair and you washed it for me. It's nice and shining and all for me, I thank you, sweetheart," he said, with a mock bow, but again he almost lost his balance. He had to bend and adjust his boots. Evidently his feet did not go all the way down; the boots must have been stuffed with something so that he would seem taller. Connie stared out at him and behind him Ellie in the car, who seemed to be looking off toward Connie's right, into nothing. This Ellie said, pulling the words out of the air one after another as if he were just discovering them, "You want me to pull out the phone?"

"Shut your mouth and keep it shut," Arnold Friend said, his face red from bending over or maybe from embarrassment because Connie had seen his boots. "This ain't none of your business."

"What—what are you doing? What do you want?" Connie said. "If I call the police they'll get you, they'll arrest you—"

"Promise was not to come in unless you touch that phone, and I'll keep that promise," he said. He resumed his erect position and tried to force his shoulders back. He sounded like a hero in a movie, declaring something important. He spoke too loudly and it was as if he were speaking to someone behind Connie. "I ain't made plans for coming in that house where I don't belong but just for you to come out to me, the way you should. Don't you know who I am?"

"You're crazy," she whispered. She backed away from the door but did not want to go into another part of the house, as if this would give him permission to come through the door. "What do you. . . . You're crazy, you. . . ."

"Huh? What're you saying, honey?"

Her eyes darted everywhere in the kitchen. She could not remember what it was, this room.

"This is how it is, honey: you come out and we'll drive away, have a nice ride. But if you don't come out we're gonna wait till your people come home and then they're all going to get it."

"You want that telephone pulled out?" Ellie said. He held the radio away from his ear and grimaced, as if without the radio the air was too much for him.

"I toldja shut up, Ellie." Arnold Friend said, "you're deaf, get a hearing aid, right? Fix yourself up. This little girl's no trouble and's gonna be nice to me, so Ellie keep to yourself, this ain't your date—right? Don't hem in on me. Don't hog. Don't crush. Don't bird dog. Don't trail me," he said in a rapid meaningless voice, as if he were running through all the expressions he'd learned but was no longer sure which one of them was in style, then rushing on to new ones, making them up with his eyes closed. "Don't crawl under my fence, don't squeeze in my chipmunk hole, don't sniff my glue, suck my popsicle, keep your own greasy fingers on yourself." He shaded his eyes and peered in at Connie, who was backed against the kitchen table. "Don't mind him honey he's just a creep. He's a dope. Right? I'm the boy for you and like I said you come out here nice like a lady and give me your hand, and nobody else gets hurt, I mean, your nice old bald-headed daddy and your mummy and your sister in her high heels. Because listen: why bring them in this?"

"Leave me alone," Connie whispered.

"Hey, you know that old woman down the road, the one with the chickens and stuff—you know her?"

"She's dead!"

"Dead? What? You know her?" Arnold Friend said.

"She's dead—"

"Don't you like her?"

"She's dead—she's—she isn't here any more—"

"But don't you like her, I mean, you got something against her? Some grudge or something?" Then his voice dipped as if he were conscious of rudeness. He touched the sunglasses on top of his head as if to make sure they were still there. "Now you be a good girl."

"What are you going to do?"

"Just two things, or maybe three," Arnold Friend said. "But I promise it won't last long and you'll like me that way you get to like people you're close to. You will. It's all over for you here, so come on out. You don't want your people in any trouble, do you?"

She turned and bumped against a chair or something, hurting her leg, but she ran into the back room and picked up the telephone. Something roared in her ear, a tiny roaring, and she was so sick with fear that she could do nothing but listen to it—the telephone was clammy and very heavy and her fingers groped down to the dial but were too weak to touch it. She began to scream into the phone, into the roaring. She cried out, she cried for her mother, she felt her breath start jerking back and forth in her lungs as if it were something Arnold Friend were stabbing her with again and again with no tenderness. A noisy sorrowful wailing rose all about her and she was locked inside it the way she was locked inside this house.

After a while she could hear again. She was sitting on the floor, with her wet back against the wall.

Arnold Friend was saying from the door, "That's a good girl. Put the phone back."

She kicked the phone away from her.

"No, honey. Pick it up. Put it back right."

She picked it up and put it back. The dial tone stopped.

"That's a good girl. Now you come outside."

She was hollow with what had been fear, but what was now just an emptiness. All that screaming had blasted it out of her. She sat, one leg cramped under her, and deep inside her brain was something like a pinpoint of light that kept going and would not let her relax. She thought, I'm not going to see my mother again. She thought, I'm not going to sleep in my bed again. Her bright green blouse was all wet.

Arnold Friend said, in a gentle-loud voice that was like a stage voice, "The place where you came from ain't there any more, and where you had in mind to go is cancelled out. This place you are now—inside your daddy's house—is nothing but a cardboard box I can knock down any time. You know that and always did know it. You hear me?"

She thought, I have got to think. I have to know what to do.

"We'll go out to a nice field, out in the country here where it smells so nice and it's sunny," Arnold Friend said. "I'll have my arms tight around you so you won't need to try to get away and I'll show you what love is like, what it does. The hell with this house! It looks solid all right," he said. He ran a fingernail down the screen and the noise did not make Connie shiver, as it would have the day before. "Now put your hand on your heart, honey. Feel that? That feels solid too but we know better, be nice to me, be sweet like you can because what else is there for a girl like you but to be sweet and pretty and give in?—and get away before her people come back?"

She felt her pounding heart. Her hands seemed to enclose it. She thought for the first time in her life that it was nothing that was hers, that belonged to her, but just a pounding, living thing inside this body that wasn't hers either.

"You don't want them to get hurt," Arnold Friend went on. "Now get up, honey. Get up all by yourself."

She stood.

"Now turn this way. That's right. Come over here to me—Ellie, put that away, didn't I tell you? You dope. You miserable creepy dope," Arnold Friend said. His words were not angry but only part of an incantation. The incantation was kindly. "Now come out through the kitchen to me honey and let's see a smile, try it, you're a brave sweet little girl and now they're eating corn and hotdogs cooked to bursting over an outdoor fire, and they don't know one thing about you and never did and honey you're better than them because not one of them would have done this for you."

Connie felt the linoleum under her feet; it was cool. She brushed her hair back out of her eyes. Arnold Friend let go of the post tentatively and opened his arms for her, his elbows pointing up toward each other and his wrists limp, to show that this was an embarrassed embrace and a little mocking, he didn't want to make her self-conscious.

She put out her hand against the screen. She watched herself push the door slowly open as if she were safe back somewhere in the other doorway, watching this body and this head of long hair moving out into the sunlight where Arnold Friend waited.

"My sweet little blue-eyed girl," he said, in a half-sung sigh that had nothing to do with her brown eyes but was taken up just the same by the vast sunlit reaches of the land behind him and on all sides of him, so much land that Connie had never seen before and did not recognize except to know that she was going to it.

QUESTIONS

1. How does the description of Connie's household and of her relationship with her parents help prepare us for what happens in the story?
2. How does the description of Arnold Friend's car help to characterize him?
3. What might Arnold Friend symbolize?
4. How is the title of the story significant? Think of the questions as ones Connie's parents might ask her, or as ones we might ask of her.
5. At the end of the story, why does Connie give in to Arnold Friend?

WRITING ABOUT CHARACTER

Writing about character in fiction, while offering great challenges to even the most skillful writers, affords even greater pleasure. Most of us enjoy thinking and learning about human behavior. Because we identify with, or react strongly to, the characters in a story, finding a general subject is usually easy. Two qualities of literary characters, however, may cause difficulty when we try to focus on a suitable subject for a short essay. First, because of our emotional involvement in the characters we read about, we risk selecting a subject that cannot be treated objectively. Second, because of the complexity of carefully developed characters, we may try to say too much and end up with a sprawling, incoherent essay.

Distinguish carefully from the outset between the subject and the thesis of your essay. Young Goodman Brown might be the subject, but you will not get far if you just sit down and start writing about him. To focus and define your essay, consider the following questions.

1. What are the dominant physical traits of the character?
2. What is his or her most distinguishing feature at the beginning of the story? At the end? What other features complement or contradict this dominant feature?
3. What motives (internal) or causes (external) make the character act as he or she does?
4. What, if anything, does the character desire? To what extent is this desire realized or thwarted?
5. What is the turning point in the character's fortune or misfortune?
6. How do other characters perceive the one you are discussing? How accurate are their perceptions?
7. How do the changes the character undergoes affect his or her general world view or relationship with others?
8. How do changes in the character affect or embody what you see as the theme of the story?

After you have selected a fit subject and have jotted down ideas about it, an appropriate strategy may begin to emerge. Most papers analyzing character are developed by example, comparison, definition, causal analysis, or a combination of these. For example, comparison and contrast could be used to delineate the changes Young Goodman Brown undergoes after the meeting in the forest. Or an analysis of cause and effect could reveal the underlying reasons that Sammy leaves his job in "A & P." After you have decided on the approach that works best, you can begin to outline your paper. Write a substantial introductory paragraph that asserts your thesis and suggests the design of your essay. The body of the essay should be organized for maximum persuasiveness. Do not restrict yourself to an organization based on the chronological development of the story. As you revise your first draft, make sure that you support your thesis with accurate, appropriate, and carefully incorporated quotations from the text. Check, too, for logical fallacies—unsupported generalizations, illogical inferences, and faulty analyses of causes. Resist the temptation to oversimplify, and insure that your subject has a significant connection to the main idea of the story. Lastly, do not spend a great deal of time recounting the story's plot. Assume your reader's general familiarity with it, and restrict your remarks about plot to what is essential to your purpose. The concluding paragraph of your essay should show the significance of your thesis and its applicability to the theme of the story.

The following short sample essay (offered as illustration, not as gospel) shows how Hawthorne, in "Young Goodman Brown," uses "minor" characters to reveal the extent of Brown's disillusionment with humankind—how interactions among characters support, and even constitute, the theme of the story.

Isolation and Community:
The Scope of Young Goodman Brown's Disillusionment

Both the structure and the characterization of Hawthorne's "Young Goodman Brown" derive their impulse and meaning from an interplay of the ideas of isolation and community. The relation of individual to group is central to the story. During the first half of the piece, as Brown proceeds to the meeting in the woods, he encounters a series of individuals and groups. First comes his devilish companion with the snake-like staff. Then comes Goody Cloyse. Then come the voices of Deacon Gookin and the minister, who mention how

> some of our community are to be here from Falmouth and beyond, and others from Connecticut and Rhode Island, besides several of the Indian powwows, who, after their fashion, know almost as much deviltry as the best of us. Moreover, there is a goodly young woman to be taken into communion. (page 11)

Finally there is the "unseen multitude" of "saints and sinners" (page 11) who seem to encourage the young woman (very likely Faith) onward toward the meeting.

Thus the narrator implicates Brown's entire milieu in the Satanic doings. The man with the staff is a father-figure ("Still they might have been taken for father and son"). Goody Cloyse, having taught Brown his catechism, stands as a representative of Puritan orthodoxy. The church elders represent local authority. The crowds pouring in from all over New England involve the territory at large. The unseen multitude of saints and sinners suggests the collusion in sin of all those no longer living.

When Brown hears the multitude, he almost turns back. But then Faith's pink ribbons come floating down. Here the procession (at least in Brown's mind), having expanded concentrically to embrace his whole community, suddenly contracts to focus his attention on the person he loves most and whom he has left behind when he goes into the forest to attend the meeting. He suddenly resolves to continue toward the group:

> And maddened with despair, so that he laughed loud and long, did Young Goodman Brown grasp his staff and set forth again, at such a rate that he seemed to fly along the forest path rather than to walk or run.

Ironically, Brown's progress toward the forest gathering both isolates him from and unites him with the "communion of [his] race" (page 14). He is of the company of sinners, having joined the seemingly universal procession of the guilty. He has looked on the possibility that even he and his Faith are tainted, and he is united with the group. But this very union isolates him forever from all that he had formerly loved. After "the dream of evil omen" (page 15), Brown no longer believes that the people he met in the darkness of the forest can lead respectable and righteous lives in the light of everyday. To emphasize this change, Hawthorne brings in, by way of recapitulation, the people Brown had seen in the forest. The minister, Deacon Gookin, Goody Cloyse, Faith--all pass before Brown as he trudges despairingly through the street of his town. Apparently, Brown considers himself wholly cut off from any meaningful human contact. Whether his sense of shared guilt isolates him, or whether, in his pride, he considers himself to be the only righteous person in his community, "his dying hour," as Hawthorne tells us, "was gloom" (page 16).

SUGGESTIONS FOR WRITING ABOUT CHARACTER

1. Show how Faulkner uses the townspeople's changing attitudes toward Emily Grierson to help characterize her.
2. Write an essay detailing how Faulkner uses the description of Emily Grierson's house to help characterize her.
3. Describe and evaluate the behavior of Gimpel's wife Elka in "Gimpel the Fool."
4. Write an essay that shows how Connie's relationship with her parents causes her to gravitate toward Arnold Friend in Oates's "Where Are You Going, Where Have You Been?"
5. Using details of his physique, dress, speech, and actions, "prove" that Arnold Friend is a devil-figure.

SETTING

When we think of a story's setting, we probably think of its historical time and place. This is an accurate but fairly limited view. Leo Tolstoy, for instance, tells us in the opening paragraphs of "The Death of Ivan Ilych" (see page 465) that Ilych died in 1882, and we soon discover that most of the story is set in St. Petersburg, Russia, between 1880 and 1882. Charlie Wales, the main character in F. Scott Fitzgerald's "Babylon Revisited" (see page 310), wanders into the Ritz bar in Paris a few years after the stock market crash of 1929. In each case, the time and place are given, but a more comprehensive view of the setting remains to be developed in subsequent pages in each story.

A more complete definition recognizes that setting includes: (1) the **physical** world within which the action takes place, and (2) **atmosphere** and **mood,** the psychological environment generated by the physical details. Hawthorne's "Young Goodman Brown" contains many passages describing the forest into which Goodman Brown ventures:

> He had taken a dreary road, darkened by all the gloomiest trees of the forest, which barely stood aside to let the narrow path creep through, and closed immediately behind. It was all as lonely as could be; and there is this peculiarity in such a solitude, that the traveler knows not who may be concealed by the innumerable trunks and the thick boughs overhead; so that, with lonely footsteps, he may yet be passing through an unseen multitude.

While this description of the setting contains the physical appearance of the forest path—the darkness and density of the surrounding woods and the narrowness of the way—it also contains atmospheric details that contribute to the mood of the passage: solitude, loneliness, and, paradoxically, Goodman Brown's fear that he is being watched by unseen figures.

In a setting quite different from Hawthorne's wilderness, John Updike sets his action in a modern supermarket in "A & P."

> . . . they all three of them went up the cat-and-dog-food-breakfast-cereal-macaroni-rice-raisins-seasonings-spreads-spaghetti-soft-drinks-crackers-and-cookies aisle . . . The sheep pushing their carts down the aisle—the girls were walking against the usual traffic (not that we have one-way signs or anything)—were pretty hilarious . . . The whole store was like a pinball machine and I didn't know which tunnel they'd come out of. After a while they come around out of the far aisle, around the light bulbs, records at discount of the Caribbean Six or Tony Martin Sings or some such gunk you wonder they waste the wax on, six packs of candy bars, and plastic toys done up in cellophane that fall apart when a kid looks at them anyway.

The description not only gives us a long catalogue of the familiar merchandise sold in the A & P, but also something of the atmosphere: its shoddiness, its anonymity, and the plethora of cheap consumer items that eventually cheapen the quality of life.

The setting of a short story, therefore, includes: (1) the physical environment within which the action takes place; and (2) the atmosphere and mood or psychological effect on the characters created by the accumulation of physical details, especially the dominant ones (darkness and gloom leading to feelings of solitude, loneliness, and fear in Hawthorne; cheapness and shoddiness leading to feelings of boredom and depersonalization in Updike). These two elements of setting work together, and we should view them as integral rather than as separate elements in the setting of a story.

Setting does not stand alone as a passive background in a story. It functions vitally to delineate character or to point to **theme,** or the meaning of the story. Setting can serve either as an influence shaping the personality of a character (as in Goodman Brown's succumbing to the darkness of the forest), or as part of the conflict, an obstacle against which a character will be tested (as in Sammy's rejection of the A & P's values). For some characters the setting may serve both as a shaping influence *and* as an obstacle to overcome. In Joyce Carol Oates' "Where Are you Going, Where Have You Been?", Connie, the fifteen-year-old protagonist, escapes from the harsh criticism of her jealous mother by sneaking across the highway from a suburban mall to a drive-in restaurant where other teenagers hang out. The setting of the restaurant gives us the first clue about the quasi-religious nature of the story, and Connie's ensuing encounter with evil.

> The restaurant was shaped like a big bottle, though squatter than a real bottle, and on its cap was a revolving figure of a grinning boy who held a hamburger aloft. . . . They went up through the maze of parked and cruising cars to the bright-lit, fly-infested restaurant, their faces pleased and expectant as if they were entering a sacred building that loomed out of the night to give them what haven and what blessing they yearned for. They sat at the counter and crossed their legs at the ankles, their thin shoulders rigid with excitement, and listened to the music that made everything so good: the music was always in the background like the music at a church service, it was something to depend upon.

The setting tells us a good deal about Connie: she seeks escape from home by going to the restaurant where, as part of the quasi-congregation, she can lose herself in the group. Her cynicism at home disappears in the restaurant where she is at home with others, and where the atmosphere generated by the music makes everything "nice." Ironically (in view of whom she meets there), the restaurant seems a safe haven for her childlike innocence, a place where she can test out her sexuality without fear of criticism. However, more than the promises of popular songs await her at the story's conclusion when she moves through the screen door of her family's small stucco house "into the vast sunlight reaches of the land . . . that Connie had never seen before and did not recognize except to know that she was going to it."

In addition to delineating character, the setting often contains **symbols** that point directly to the theme. This is especially true of stories with external conflict where the plot may involve the setting as one of the antagonists. For example, one of the most famous passages in American literature opens Stephen Crane's "The Open Boat." The passage describes the setting, a turbulent ocean in which four men try to survive in an open boat after a shipwreck.

> None of them knew the color of the sky. Their eyes glanced level, and were fastened upon the waves that swept toward them. These waves were of the hue of slate, save for the tops, which were of foaming white, and all of the men knew the colors of the sea. The horizon narrowed and widened, and dipped and rose, and at all times its edge was jagged with waves that seemed thrust up in points like rocks.

Crane uses setting here to demonstrate the weakness of men against the forces of nature (hence, the smallness of the boat and the intense concentration of the men upon the waves to maintain their equilibrium), and the indifference of nature to the plight of the men (suggested by the neutral slate-gray color of the waves).

Even when the conflict is internal, we can often discover the theme of the story in some repeated detail of the setting which acts as an **objective correlative,** an external mirror for an internal conflict. The second paragraph of Faulkner's "A Rose for Emily" contains a description of the Grierson house and its surroundings. Not only is the house the setting for most of the story's action, but the contrast between its decay and the commercial encroachments of the twentieth century epitomizes the story's theme.

> It was a big, squarish frame house that had once been white, decorated with cupolas and spires and scrolled balconies in the heavily lightsome style of the seventies, set on what had once been our most select street. But garages and cotton gins had encroached and obliterated even the august names of that neighborhood; only Miss Emily's house was left, lifting its stubborn and coquettish decay above the cotton wagons and the gasoline pumps—an eyesore among eyesores.

The passage contains hints of the plot (Miss Emily Grierson's refusal to acknowledge the passage of time and subsequent decay), and also the theme of the story. Often, these opening passages in short stories not only describe the setting, but also contain valuable clues pointing to the story's meaning. Finally, the **tone** of the story, or the author's attitude toward the characters, is often established in the early paragraphs delineating the setting.

Setting is, therefore, more than just a dramatic backdrop against which a series of actions is played. In short fiction, setting is so often linked with character and theme as to be inseparable from them. You will find that repeated details of the setting accumulate throughout the story to reveal the writer's characters and purpose.

From the first paragraph of "The Open Boat," Crane emphasizes the dangers of the sea to the men in the open boat. Details of the setting, such as the size and color of the waves, herald the story's theme: the indifference of the universe to humanity. A confining setting can be equally destructive, as D. H. Lawrence demonstrates in "An Odor of Chrysanthemums." In this story, the people of a coal-mining town are imprisoned by a claustrophobic setting which chokes off the vital breath of life. The setting of each story plays a central role in revealing the writer's ideas and developing his characters.

STEPHEN CRANE (1871–1900)

The Open Boat

Stephen Crane was born in Newark, New Jersey, and educated at
Lafayette College and Syracuse University. An early exemplar of literary
realism and naturalism in American literature, he is best known for his
novel of the Civil War, *The Red Badge of Courage* (1895). In addition to
his novels, he wrote poems and stories and was a freelance journalist.
"The Open Boat," perhaps his most famous story, was published in 1897.

*A Tale Intended to Be after the Fact,
Being the Experience of Four Men from
the Sunk Steamer* COMMODORE

I

None of them knew the color of the sky. Their eyes glanced level, and
were fastened upon the waves that swept toward them. These waves were
of the hue of slate, save for the tops, which were of foaming white, and all
of the men knew the colors of the sea. The horizon narrowed and widened,
and dipped and rose, and at all times its edge was jagged with waves that
seemed thrust up in points like rocks.

Many a man ought to have a bath-tub larger than the boat which here
rode upon the sea. These waves were most wrongfully and barbarously
abrupt and tall, and each froth-top was a problem in small boat navigation.

The cook squatted in the bottom and looked with both eyes at the six
inches of gunwale which separated him from the ocean. His sleeves were
rolled over his fat forearms, and the two flaps of his unbuttoned vest dangled as he bent to bail out the boat. Often he said: "Gawd! That was a
narrow clip." As he remarked it he invariably gazed eastward over the broken sea.

The oiler, steering with one of the two oars in the boat sometimes
raised himself suddenly to keep clear of water that swirled in over the stern.
It was a thin little oar and it seemed often ready to snap.

The correspondent, pulling at the other oar, watched the waves and
wondered why he was there.

The injured captain, lying in the bow, was at this time buried in that
profound dejection and indifference which comes, temporarily at least, to
even the bravest and most enduring when, willy nilly, the firm fails, the
army loses, the ship goes down. The mind of the master of a vessel is rooted
deep in the timbers of her, though he command for a day or a decade, and
this captain had on him the stern impression of a scene in the grays of dawn

of seven turned faces, and later a stump of a top-mast with a white ball on it that slashed to and fro at the waves, went low and lower, and down. Thereafter there was something strange in his voice. Although steady, it was deep with mourning, and of a quality beyond oration or tears.

"Keep'er a little more south, Billie," said he.

" 'A little more south,' sir," said the oiler in the stern.

A seat in this boat was not unlike a seat upon a bucking broncho, and, by the same token, a broncho is not much smaller. The craft pranced and reared, and plunged like an animal. As each wave came, and she rose for it, she seemed like a horse making at a fence outrageously high. The manner of her scramble over these walls of water is a mystic thing, and, moreover, at the top of them were ordinarily these problems in white water, the foam racing down from the summit of each wave, requiring a new leap, and a leap from the air. Then, after scornfully bumping a crest, she would slide, and race, and splash down a long incline and arrive bobbing and nodding in front of the next menace.

A singular disadvantage of the sea lies in the fact that after successfully surmounting one wave you discover that there is another behind it just as important and just as nervously anxious to do something effective in the way of swamping boats. In a ten-foot dingey one can get an idea of the resources of the sea in the line of waves that is not probable to the average experience, which is never at sea in a dingey. As each slaty wall of water approached, it shut all else from the view of the men in the boat, and it was not difficult to imagine that this particular wave was the final outburst of the ocean, the last effort of the grim water. There was a terrible grace in the move of the waves, and they came in silence, save for the snarling of the crests.

In the wan light, the faces of the men must have been gray. Their eyes must have glinted in strange ways as they gazed steadily astern. Viewed from a balcony, the whole thing would doubtlessly have been weirdly picturesque. But the men in the boat had no time to see it, and if they had had leisure there were other things to occupy their minds. The sun swung steadily up the sky, and they knew it was broad day because the color of the sea changed from slate to emerald-green, streaked with amber lights, and the foam was like tumbling snow. The process of the breaking day was unknown to them. They were aware only of this effect upon the color of the waves that rolled toward them.

In disjointed sentences the cook and the correspondent argued as to the difference between a life-saving station and a house of refuge. The cook had said: "There's a house of refuge just north of the Mosquito Inlet Light, and as soon as they see us, they'll come off in their boat and pick us up."

"As soon as who see us?" said the correspondent.

"The crew," said the cook.

"Houses of refuge don't have crews," said the correspondent. "As I understand them, they are only places where clothes and grub are stored for the benefit of shipwrecked people. They don't carry crews."

"Oh, yes, they do," said the cook.

"No, they don't," said the correspondent.

"Well, we're not there yet, anyhow," said the oiler, in the stern.

"Well," said the cook, "perhaps it's not a house of refuge that I'm thinking of as being near Mosquito Inlet Light. Perhaps it's a life-saving station."

"We're not there yet," said the oiler, in the stern.

II

As the boat bounced from the top of each wave, the wind tore through the hair of the hatless men, and as the craft plopped her stern down again the spray slashed past them. The crest of each of these waves was a hill, from the top of which the men surveyed, for a moment, a broad tumultuous expanse, shining and wind-riven. It was probably splendid. It was probably glorious, this play of the free sea, wild with lights of emerald and white and amber.

"Bully good thing it's an on-shore wind," said the cook. "If not where would we be? Wouldn't have a show."

"That's right," said the correspondent.

The busy oiler nodded his assent.

Then the captain, in the bow, chuckled in a way that expressed humor, contempt, tragedy, all in one. "Do you think we've got a show, now, boys?" said he.

Whereupon the three went silent, save for a trifle of hemming and hawing. To express any particular optimism at this time they felt to be childish and stupid, but they all doubtless possessed this sense of the situation in their mind. A young man thinks doggedly at such times. On the other hand, the ethics of their condition was decidedly against any open suggestion of hopelessness. So they were silent.

"Oh, well," said the captain, soothing his children, "we'll get ashore all right."

But there was that in his tone which made them think, so the oiler quoth: "Yes! If this wind holds!"

The cook was bailing. "Yes! If we don't catch hell in the surf."

Canton flannel gulls flew near and far. Sometimes they sat down on the sea, near patches of brown sea-weed that rolled over the waves with a movement like carpets on a line in a gale. The birds sat comfortably in groups, and they were envied by some in the dingey, for the wrath of the sea was no more to them than it was to a covey of prairie chickens a thousand miles inland. Often they came very close and stared at the men with black bead-like eyes. At these times they were uncanny and sinister in their unblinking scrutiny, and the men hooted angrily at them, telling them to be gone. One came, and evidently decided to alight on the top of the captain's head. The bird flew parallel to the boat and did not circle, but made short sidelong jumps in the air in chicken-fashion. His black eyes were wistfully fixed upon the captain's head. "Ugly brute," said the oiler to the bird. "You look as if you were made with a jack-knife." The cook and the correspondent swore darkly at the creature. The captain naturally wished to knock it away with the end of the heavy painter, but he did not dare do it, because anything resembling an emphatic gesture would have capsized this freighted boat, and so with his open hand, the captain gently and carefully waved the gull away. After it had been discouraged from the pursuit the captain breathed easier on account of his hair, and others breathed easier because the bird struck their minds at this time as being somehow gruesome and ominous.

In the meantime the oiler and the correspondent rowed. And also they rowed.

They sat together in the same seat, and each rowed an oar. Then the oiler took both oars; then the correspondent took both oars; then the oiler; then the correspondent. They rowed and they rowed. The very ticklish part of the business was when the time came for the reclining one in the stern to take his turn at the oars. By the very last star of truth, it is easier to steal eggs from under a hen than it was to change seats in the dingey. First the man in the stern slid his hand along the thwart and moved with care, as if he were of Sèvres. Then the man in the rowing seat slid his hand along the other thwart. It was all done with the most extraordinary care. As the two sidled past each other, the whole party kept watchful eyes on the coming wave, and the captain cried: "Look out now! Steady there!"

The brown mats of sea-weed that appeared from time to time were like islands, bits of earth. They were travelling, apparently, neither one way nor the other. They were, to all intents, stationary. They informed the men in the boat that it was making progress slowly toward the land.

The captain, rearing cautiously in the bow, after the dingey soared on a great swell, said that he had seen the light-house at Mosquito Inlet. Presently the cook remarked that he had seen it. The correspondent was at the oars, then, and for some reason he too wished to look at the light-house, but his back was toward the far shore and the waves were important, and for some time he could not seize an opportunity to turn his head. But at last there came a wave more gentle than the others, and when at the crest of it he swiftly scoured the western horizon.

"See it?" said the captain.

"No," said the correspondent, slowly, "I didn't see anything."

"Look again," said the captain. He pointed. "It's exactly in that direction."

At the top of another wave, the correspondent did as he was bid, and this time his eyes chanced on a small still thing on the edge of the swaying horizon. It was precisely like the point of a pin. It took an anxious eye to find a light-house so tiny.

"Think we'll make it, Captain?"

"If this wind holds and the boat don't swamp, we can't do much else," said the captain.

The little boat, lifted by each towering sea, and splashed viciously by the crests, made progress that in the absence of sea-weed was not apparent to those in her. She seemed just a wee thing wallowing, miraculously, top-up, at the mercy of five oceans. Occasionally, a great spread of water, like white flames, swarmed into her.

"Bail her, cook," said the captian, serenely.

"All right, Captain," said the cheerful cook.

III

It would be difficult to describe the subtle brotherhood of men that was here established on the seas. No one said that it was so. No one mentioned it. But it dwelt in the boat, and each man felt it warm him. They were a captain, an oiler, a cook, and a correspondent, and they were friends, friends in a more curiously iron-bound degree than may be common. The hurt captain, lying against the water-jar in the bow, spoke always in a low voice and calmly, but he could never command a more ready and swiftly obedient crew than the motley three of the dingey. It was more than a mere recognition of what was best for the common safety. There was surely in it a quality that was personal and heartfelt. And after this devotion to the commander of the boat there was this comradeship that the correspondent, for instance, who had been taught to be cynical of men, knew even at the time was the best experience of his life. But no one said that it was so. No one mentioned it.

"I wish we had a sail," remarked the captain. "We might try my over-coat on the end of an oar and give you two boys a chance to rest." So the cook and the correspondent held the mast and spread wide the overcoat. The oiler steered, and the little boat made good way with her new rig. Sometimes the oiler had to scull sharply to keep a sea from breaking into the boat, but otherwise sailing was a success.

Meanwhile the light-house had been growing slowly larger. It had now almost assumed color, and appeared like a little gray shadow on the sky. The man at the oars could not be prevented from turning his head rather often to try for a glimpse of this little gray shadow.

At last, from the top of each wave the men in the tossing boat could see land. Even as the light-house was an upright shadow on the sky, this land seemed but a long black shadow on the sea. It certainly was thinner than paper. "We must be about opposite New Smyrna," said the cook, who had coasted this shore often in schooners. "Captain, by the way, I believe they abandoned that life-saving station there about a year ago."

"Did they?" said the captain.

The wind slowly died away. The cook and the correspondent were not now obliged to slave in order to hold high the oar. But the waves continued their old impetuous swooping at the dingey, and the little craft, no longer under way, struggled woundily over them. The oiler or the corresponhdent took the oars again.

Shipwrecks are *apropos* of nothing. If men could only train for them and have them occur when the men had reached pink condition, there would be less drowning at sea. Of the four in the dingey none had slept any time worth mentioning for two days and two nights previous to embarking in the dingey, and in the excitement of clambering about the deck of a foundering ship they had also forgotten to eat heartily.

For these reasons, and for others, neither the oiler nor the correspondent was fond of rowing at this time. The correspondent wondered ingenuously how in the name of all that was sane could there be people who thought it amusing to row a boat. It was not an amusement; it was a diabolical punishment, and even a genius of mental aberrations could never conclude that it was anything but a horror to the muscles and a crime against the back. He mentioned to the boat in general how the amusement of rowing struck him, and the weary-faced oiler smiled in full sympathy. Previously to the foundering, by the way, the oiler had worked double-watch in the engine-room of the ship.

"Take her easy, now, boys," said the captain. "Don't spend yourselves. If we have to run a surf you'll need all your strength, because we'll sure have to swim for it. Take your time."

Slowly the land arose from the sea. From a black line it became a line of black and a line of white—trees and sand. Finally, the captain said that he could make out a house on the shore. "That's the house of refuge, sure," said the cook. "They'll see us before long, and come out after us."

The distant light-house reared high. "The keeper ought to be able to make us out now, if he's looking through a glass," said the captain. "He'll notify the life-saving people."

"None of those other boats could have got ashore to give word of the wreck," said the oiler, in a low voice. "Else the life-boat would be out hunting us."

Slowly and beautifully the land loomed out of the sea. The wind came again. It had veered from the northeast to the southeast. Finally, a new sound struck the ears of the men in the boat. It was the low thunder of the surf on the shore. "We'll never be able to make the light-house now," said the captain. "Swing her head a little more north, Billie."

" 'A little more north,' sir," said the oiler.

Whereupon the little boat turned her nose once more down the wind, and all but the oarsman watched the shore grow. Under the influence of this expansion doubt and direful apprehension was leaving the minds of the men. The management of the boat was still most absorbing, but it could not prevent a quiet cheerfulness. In an hour, perhaps, they would be ashore.

Their back-bones had become thoroughly used to balancing in the boat and they now rode this wild colt of a dingey like circus men. The correspondent thought that he had been drenched to the skin, but happening to feel in the top pocket of his coat, he found therein eight cigars. Four of them were soaked with seawater; four were perfectly scatheless. After a search, somebody produced three dry matches, and thereupon the four waifs rode impudently in their little boat, and with an assurance of an impending rescue shining in their eyes, puffed at the big cigars and judged well and ill of all men. Everybody took a drink of water.

IV

"Cook," remarked the captain, "there don't seem to be any signs of life about your house of refuge."

"No," replied the cook. "Funny they don't see us!"

A broad stretch of lowly coast lay before the eyes of the men. It was of dunes topped with dark vegetation. The roar of the surf was plain, and sometimes they could see the white lip of a wave as it spun up the beach. A tiny house was blocked out black upon the sky. Southward, the slim light-house lifted its little gray length.

Tide, wind, and waves were swinging the dingey northward. "Funny they don't see us," said the men.

The surf's roar was here dulled, but its tone was, nevertheless, thunderous and mighty. As the boat swam over the great rollers, the men sat listening to this roar. "We'll swamp sure," said everybody.

It is fair to say here that there was not a life-saving station within twenty miles in either direction, but the men did not know this fact and in consequence they made dark and opprobrious remarks concerning the eyesight of the nation's life-savers. Four scowling men sat in the dingey and surpassed records in the invention of epithets.

"Funny they don't see us."

The light-heartedness of a former time had completely faded. To their sharpened minds it was easy to conjure pictures of all kinds of incompetency and blindness and, indeed, cowardice. There was the shore of the populous land, and it was bitter and bitter to them that from it came no sign.

"Well," said the captain, ultimately, "I suppose we'll have to make a try for ourselves. If we stay out here too long, we'll none of us have strength left to swim after the boat swamps."

And so the oiler, who was at the oars, turned the boat straight for the shore. There was a sudden tightening of muscles. There was some thinking.

"If we don't all get ashore—" said the captain. "If we don't all get ashore, I suppose you fellows know where to send news of my finish?"

They then briefly exchanged some addresses and admonitions. As for the reflections of the men, there was a great deal of rage in them. Perchance they might be formulated thus: "If I am going to be drowned—if I am going to be drowned—if I am going to be drowned, why, in the name of the seven mad gods who rule the sea, was I allowed to come thus far and contemplate sand and trees? Was I brought here merely to have my nose dragged away as I was about to nibble the sacred cheese of life? It is preposterous. If this old ninny-woman, Fate, cannot do better than this, she should be deprived of the management of men's fortunes. She is an old hen who knows not her intention. If she has decided to drown me, why did she not do it in the beginning and save me all this trouble. The whole affair is absurd. . . . But, no, she cannot mean to drown me. She dare not drown me. She cannot drown me. Not after all this work." Afterward the man might have had an impulse to shake his fist at the clouds. "Just you drown me, now, and then hear what I call you!"

The billows that came at this time were more formidable. They seemed always just about to break and roll over the little boat in a turmoil of foam. There was a preparatory and long growl in the speech of them. No mind unused to the sea would have concluded that the dingey could ascend these sheer heights in time. The shore was still afar. The oiler was a wily surfman. "Boys," he said, swiftly, "she won't live three minutes more and we're too far out to swim. Shall I take her to sea again, Captain?"

"Yes! Go ahead!" said the captain.

This oiler, by a series of quick miracles, and fast and steady oarsmanship, turned the boat in the middle of the surf and took her safely to sea again.

There was a considerable silence as the boat bumped over the furrowed sea to deeper water. Then somebody in gloom spoke. "Well, anyhow, they must have seen us from the shore by now."

The gulls went in slanting flight up the wind toward the gray desolate east. A squall, marked by dingy clouds, and clouds brick-red, like smoke from a burning building, appeared from the southeast.

"What do you think of those life-saving people? Ain't they peaches?"

"Funny they haven't seen us."

"Maybe they think we're out here for sport! Maybe they think we're fishin'. Maybe they think we're damned fools."

It was a long afternoon. A changed tide tried to force them southward, but wind and wave said northward. Far ahead, where coast-line, sea, and sky formed their mighty angle, there were little dots which seemed to indicate a city on the shore.

"St. Augustine?"

The captain shook his head. "Too near Mosquito Inlet."

And the oiler rowed, and then the correspondent rowed. Then the oiler rowed. It was a weary business. The human back can become the seat of more aches and pains than are registered in books for the composite anatomy of a regiment. It is a limited area, but it can become the theatre of innumerable muscular conflicts, tangles, wrenches, knots, and other comforts.

"Did you ever like to row, Billie?" asked the correspondent.

"No," said the oiler, "Hang it."

When one exchanged the rowing-seat for a place in the bottom of the boat, he suffered a bodily depression that caused him to be careless of everything save an obligation to wiggle one finger. There was cold sea-water swashing to and fro in the boat, and he lay in it. His head, pillowed on a thwart, was within an inch of the swirl of a wave crest, and sometimes a particularly obstreperous sea came in-board and drenched him once more. But these matters did not annoy him. It is almost certain that if the boat had capsized he would have tumbled comfortably out upon the ocean as if he felt sure that it was a great soft mattress.

"Look! There's a man on the shore!"

"Where?"

"There! See 'im? See 'im?"

"Yes, sure! He's walking along."

"Now he's stopped. Look! He's facing us!"

"He's waving at us!"

"So he is! By thunder!"

"Ah, now, we're all right! There'll be a boat out here for us in half an hour."

"He's going on. He's running. He's going up to that house there."

The remote beach seemed lower than the sea, and it required a searching glance to discern the little black figure. The captain saw a floating stick and they rowed to it. A bath-towel was by some weird chance in the boat, and, tying this on the stick, the captain waved it. The oarsman did not dare turn his head, so he was obliged to ask questions.

"What's he doing now?"

"He's standing still again. He's looking, I think. . . . There he goes again. Toward the house. . . . Now he's stopped again."

"Is he waving at us?"

"No, not now! He was, though."

"Look! There comes another man!"

"He's running."

"Look at him go, would you."

"Why, he's on a bicycle. Now he's met the other man. They're both waving at us. Look!"

"There comes something up the beach."

"What the devil is that thing?"

"Why, it looks like a boat."

"Why, certainly it's a boat."

"No, it's on wheels."

"Yes, so it is. Well, that must be the life-boat. They drag them along shore on a wagon."

"That's the life-boat, sure."

"No, by, it's—it's an omnibus."

"I tell you it's a life-boat."

"It is not! It's an omnibus. I can see it plain. See? One of those big hotel omnibuses."

"By thunder, you're right. It's an omnibus, sure as fate. What do you suppose they are doing with an omnibus? Maybe they are going around collecting the life-crew, hey?"

"That's it, likely. Look! There's a fellow waving a little black flag. He's standing on the steps of the omnibus. There come those other two fellows. Now they're all talking together. Look at the fellow with the flag. Maybe he ain't waving it!"

"That ain't a flag, is it? That's his coat. Why, certainly, that's his coat."

"So it is. It's his coat. He's taken it off and is waving it around his head. But would you look at him swing it!"

"Oh, say, there isn't any life-saving station there. That's just a winter resort hotel omnibus that has brought over some of the boarders to see us drown."

"What's that idiot with the coat mean? What's he signaling, anyhow?"

"It looks as if he were trying to tell us to go north. There must be a life-saving station up there."

"No! He thinks we're fishing. Just giving us a merry hand. See? Ah, there, Willie."

"Well, I wish I could make something out of those signals. What do you suppose he means?"

"He don't mean anything. He's just playing."

"Well, if he'd just signal us to try the surf again, or to go to sea and wait, or go north, or go south, or go to hell—there would be some reason in it. But look at him. He just stands there and keeps his coat revolving like a wheel. The ass!"

"There come more people."

"Now there's quite a mob. Look! Isn't that a boat?"

"Where? Oh, I see where you mean. No, that's no boat."

"That fellow is still waving his coat."

"He must think we like to see him do that. Why don't he quit it. It don't mean anything."

"I don't know. I think he is trying to make us go north. It must be that there's a life-saving station there somewhere."

"Say, he ain't tired yet. Look at 'im wave."

"Wonder how long he can keep that up. He's been revolving his coat ever since he caught sight of us. He's an idiot. Why aren't they getting men to bring a boat out. A fishing boat—one of those big yawls—could come out here all right. Why don't he do something?"

"Oh, it's all right, now."

"They'll have a boat out here for us in less than no time, now that they've seen us."

A faint yellow tone came into the sky over the low land. The shadows on the sea slowly deepened. The wind bore coldness with it, and the men began to shiver.

"Holy smoke!" said one, allowing his voice to express his impious mood, "if we keep on monkeying out here! If we've got to flounder out here all night!"

"Oh, we'll never have to stay here all night! Don't you worry. They've seen us now, and it won't be long before they'll come chasing out after us."

The shore grew dusky. The man waving a coat blended gradually into this gloom, and it swallowed in the same manner the omnibus and the group of people. The spray, when it dashed uproariously over the side, made the voyagers shrink and swear like men who were being branded.

"I'd like to catch the chump who waved the coat. I feel like soaking him one, just for luck."

"Why? What did he do?"

"Oh, nothing, but then he seemed so damned cheerful."

In the meantime the oiler rowed, and then the correspondent rowed, and then the oiler rowed. Gray-faced and bowed forward, they mechanically, turn by turn, plied the leaden oars. The form of the light-house had vanished from the southern horizon, but finally a pale star appeared, just lifting from the sea. The streaked saffron in the west passed before the all-merging darkness, and the sea to the east was black. The land had vanished, and was expressed only by the low and drear thunder of the surf.

"If I am going to be drowned—if I am going to be drowned—if I am going to be drowned, why, in the name of the seven mad gods who rule the sea, was I allowed to come thus far and contemplate sand and trees? Was I brought here merely to have my nose dragged away as I was about to nibble the sacred cheese of life?"

The patient captain, drooped over the water-jar, was sometimes obliged to speak to the oarsman.

"Keep her head up! Keep her head up!"

" 'Keep her head up,' sir." The voices were weary and low.

This was surely a quiet evening. All save the oarsman lay heavily and listlessly in the boat's bottom. As for him, his eyes were just capable of noting the tall black waves that swept forward in a most sinister silence, save for an occasional subdued growl of a crest.

The cook's head was on a thwart, and he looked without interest at the water under his nose. He was deep in other scenes. Finally he spoke. "Billie," he murmured, dreamfully, "what kind of pie do you like best?"

V

"Pie," said the oiler and the correspondent, agitatedly. "Don't talk about those things, blast you!"

"Well," said the cook, "I was just thinking about ham sandwiches, and—"

A night on the sea in an open boat is a long night. As darkness settled finally, the shine of the light, lifting from the sea in the south, changed to full gold. On the northern horizon a new light appeared, a small bluish gleam on the edge of the waters. These two lights were the furniture of the world. Otherwise there was nothing but waves.

Two men huddled in the stern, and distances were so magnificent in the dingey that the rower was enabled to keep his feet partly warmed by thrusting them under his companions. Their legs indeed extended far under the rowing-seat until they touched the feet of the captain forward. Sometimes, despite the efforts of the tired oarsman, a wave came piling into the boat, an icy wave of the night, and the chilling water soaked them anew. They would twist their bodies for a moment and groan, and sleep the dead sleep once more, while the water in the boat gurgled about them as the craft rocked.

The plan of the oiler and the correspondent was for one to row until he lost the ability, and then arouse the other from his sea-water couch in the bottom of the boat.

The oiler plied the oars until his head drooped forward, and the over-powering sleep blinded him. And he rowed yet afterward. Then he touched a man in the bottom of the boat, and called his name. "Will you spell me for a little while?" he said, meekly.

"Sure, Billie," said the correspondent, awakening and dragging himself to a sitting position. They exchanged places carefully, and the oiler, cuddling down in the sea-water at the cook's side, seemed to go to sleep instantly.

The particular violence of the sea had ceased. The waves came without snarling. The obligation of the man at the oars was to keep the boat headed so that the tilt of the rollers would not capsize her, and to preserve her from filling when the crests rushed past. The black waves were silent and hard to be seen in the darkness. Often one was almost upon the boat before the oarsman was aware.

In a low voice the correspondent addressed the captain. He was not sure that the captain was awake, although this iron man seemed to be always awake. "Captain, shall I keep her making for that light north, sir?"

The same steady voice answered him. "Yes. Keep it about two points off the port bow."

The cook had tied a life-belt around himself in order to get even the warmth which this clumsy cork contrivance could donate, and he seemed almost stove-like when a rower, whose teeth invariably chattered wildly as soon as he ceased his labor, dropped down to sleep.

The correspondent, as he rowed, looked down at the two men sleeping under foot. The cook's arm was around the oiler's shoulders, and, with their fragmentary clothing and haggard faces, they were the babes of the sea, a grotesque rendering of the old babes in the wood.

Later he must have grown stupid at his work, for suddenly there was a growling of water, and a crest came with a roar and a swash into the boat, and it was a wonder that it did not set the cook afloat in his life-belt. The cook continued to sleep, but the oiler sat up, blinking his eyes and shaking with the new cold.

"Oh, I'm awful sorry, Billie," said the correspondent, contritely.

"That's all right, old boy," said the oiler, and lay down again and was asleep.

Presently it seemed that even the captain dozed, and the correspondent thought that he was the one man afloat on all the oceans. The wind had a voice as it came over the waves, and it was sadder than the end.

There was a long, loud swishing astern of the boat, and a gleaming trail of phosphorescence, like blue flame, was furrowed on the black waters. It might have been made by a monstrous knife.

Then there came a stillness, while the correspondent breathed with the open mouth and looked at the sea.

Suddenly there was another swish and another long flash of bluish light, and this time it was alongside the boat, and might almost have been reached with an oar. The correspondent saw an enormous fin speed like a shadow through the water, hurling the crystalline spray and leaving the long glowing trail.

The correspondent looked over his shoulder at the captain. His face was hidden, and he seemed to be asleep. He looked at the babes of the sea. They certainly were asleep. So, being bereft of sympathy, he leaned a little way to one side and swore softly into the sea.

But the thing did not then leave the vicinity of the boat. Ahead or astern, on one side or the other, at intervals long or short, fled the long sparkling streak, and there was to be heard the whiroo of the dark fin. The speed and power of the thing was greatly to be admired. It cut the water like a gigantic and keen projectile.

The presence of this biding thing did not affect the man with the same horror that it would if he had been a picnicker. He simply looked at the sea dully and swore in an undertone.

Nevertheless, it is true that he did not wish to be alone with the thing. He wished one of his companions to awaken by chance and keep him company with it. But the captain hung motionless over the water-jar and the oiler and the cook in the bottom of the boat were plunged in slumber.

VI

"If I am going to be drowned—if I am going to be drowned—if I am going to be drowned, why, in the name of the seven mad gods who rule the sea, was I allowed to come thus far and contemplate sand and trees?"

During this dismal night, it may be remarked that a man would conclude that it was really the intention of the seven mad gods to drown him, despite the abominable injustice of it. For it was certainly an abominable injustice to drown a man who had worked so hard, so hard. The man felt it would be a crime most unnatural. Other people had drowned at sea since galleys swarmed with painted sails, but still—

When it occurs to a man that nature does not regard him as important, and that she feels she would not maim the universe by disposing of him, he at first wishes to throw bricks at the temple, and he hates deeply the fact that there are no bricks and no temples. Any visible expression of nature would surely be pelleted with his jeers.

Then, if there be no tangible thing to hoot he feels, perhaps, the desire to confront a personification and indulge in pleas, bowed to one knee, and with hands supplicant, saying: "Yes, but I love myself."

A high cold star on a winter's night is the word he feels that she says to him. Thereafter he knows the pathos of his situation.

The men in the dingey had not discussed these matters, but each had, no doubt, reflected upon them in silence and according to his mind. There was seldom any expression upon their faces save the general one of complete weariness. Speech was devoted to the business of the boat.

To chime the notes of his emotion, a verse mysteriously entered the correspondent's head. He had even forgotten that he had forgotten this verse, but it suddenly was in his mind.

In his childhood, the correspondent had been made acquainted with the fact that a soldier of the Legion lay dying in Algiers, but he had never regarded it as important. Myriads of his school-fellows had informed him of the soldier's plight, but the dinning had naturally ended by making him perfectly indifferent. He had never considered it his affair that a soldier of the Legion lay dying in Algiers, nor had it appeared to him as a matter for sorrow. It was less to him than the breaking of a pencil's point.

Now, however, it quaintly came to him as a human, living thing. It was no longer merely a picture of a few throes in the breast of a poet, meanwhile drinking tea and warming his feet at the grate; it was an actuality—stern, mournful, and fine.

The correspondent plainly saw the soldier. He lay on the sand with his feet out straight and still. While his pale left hand was upon his chest in an attempt to thwart the going of his life, the blood came between his fingers. In the far Algerian distance, a city of low square forms was set against a sky that was faint with the last sunset hues. The correspondent, plying the oars and dreaming of the slow and slower movements of the lips of the soldier, was moved by a profound and perfectly impersonal comprehension. He was sorry for the soldier of the Legion who lay dying in Algiers.

The thing which had followed the boat and waited had evidently grown bored at the delay. There was no longer to be heard the slash of the cut-water, and there was no longer the flame of the long trail. The light in the north still glimmered, but it was apparently no nearer to the boat. Sometimes the boom of the surf rang in the correspondent's ears, and he turned the craft seaward then and rowed harder. Southward, some one had evidently built a watch-fire on the beach. It was too low and too far to be seen, but it made a shimmering, roseate reflection upon the bluff back of it, and this could be discerned from the boat. The wind came stronger, and sometimes a wave suddenly raged out like a mountain-cat and there was to be seen the sheen and sparkle of a broken crest.

The captain, in the bow, moved on his water-jar and sat erect. "Pretty long night," he observed to the correspondent. He looked at the shore. "Those life-saving people take their time."

"Did you see that shark playing around?"

"Yes, I saw him. He was a big fellow, all right."

"Wish I had known you were awake."

Later the correspondent spoke into the bottom of the boat.

"Billie!" There was a slow and gradual disentanglement. "Billie, will you spell me?"

"Sure," said the oiler.

As soon as the correspondent touched the cold comfortable sea-water in the bottom of the boat, and had huddled close to the cook's life-belt he was deep in sleep, despite the fact that his teeth played all the popular airs. This sleep was so good to him that it was but a moment before he heard a voice call his name in a tone that demonstrated the last stages of exhaustion. "Will you spell me?"

"Sure, Billie."

The light in the north had mysteriously vanished, but the correspondent took his course from the wide-awake captain.

Later in the night they took the boat farther out to sea, and the captain directed the cook to take one oar at the stern and keep the boat facing the seas. He was to call out if he should hear the thunder of the surf. This plan enabled the oiler and the correspondent to get respite together. "We'll give those boys a chance to get into shape again," said the captain. They curled down and, after a few preliminary chatterings and trembles, slept once more the dead sleep. Neither knew they had bequeathed to the cook the company of another shark, or perhaps the same shark.

As the boat caroused on the waves, spray occasionally bumped over the side and gave them a fresh soaking, but this had no power to break their repose. The ominous slash of the wind and the water affected them as it would have affected mummies.

"Boys," said the cook, with the notes of every reluctance in his voice, "she's drifted in pretty close. I guess one of you had better take her to sea again." The correspondent, aroused, heard the crash of the toppled crests.

As he was rowing, the captain gave him some whiskey and water, and this steadied the chills out of him. "If I ever get ashore and anybody shows me even a photograph of an oar—"

At last there was a short conversation.

"Billie. . . . Billie, will you spell me?"

"Sure," said the oiler.

VII

When the correspondent again opened his eyes, the sea and the sky were each of the gray hue of the dawning. Later, carmine and gold was painted upon the waters. The morning appeared finally, in its splendor, with a sky of pure blue, and the sunlight flamed on the tips of the waves.

On the distant dunes were set many little black cottages, and a tall white wind-mill reared above them. No man, nor dog, nor bicycle appeared on the beach. The cottages might have formed a deserted village.

The voyagers scanned the shore. A conference was held in the boat. "Well," said the captain, "if no help is coming, we might better try a run through the surf right away. If we stay out here much longer we will be too weak to do anything for ourselves at all." The others silently acquiesced in this reasoning. The boat was headed for the beach. The correspondent wondered if none ever ascended the tall wind-tower, and if then they never looked seaward. This tower was a giant, standing with its back to the plight of the ants. It represented in a degree, to the correspondent, the serenity of nature amid the struggles of the individual—nature in the wind, and nature in the vision of men. She did not seem cruel to him then, nor beneficent, nor treacherous, nor wise. But she was indifferent, flatly indifferent. It is, perhaps, plausible that a man in this situation, impressed with the unconcern of the universe, should see the innumerable flaws of his life and have them taste wickedly in his mind and wish for another chance. A distinction between right and wrong seems absurdly clear to him, then, in this new ignorance of the grave-edge, and he understands that if he were given another opportunity he would mend his conduct and his words, and be better and brighter during an introduction, or at a tea.

"Now, boys," said the captain, "she is going to swamp sure. All we can do is to work her in as far as possible, and then when she swamps, pile out and scramble for the beach. Keep cool now, and don't jump until she swamps sure."

The oiler took the oars. Over his shoulders he scanned the surf. "Captain," he said, "I think I'd better bring her about, and keep her head-on to the seas and back her in."

"All right, Billie," said the captain. "Back her in." The oiler swung the boat then and, seated in the stern, the cook and the correspondent were obliged to look over their shoulders to contemplate the lonely and indifferent shore.

The monstrous inshore rollers heaved the boat high until the men were again enabled to see the white sheets of water scudding up the slanted beach. "We won't get in very close," said the captain. Each time a man could wrest his attention from the rollers, he turned his glance toward the shore, and in the expression of the eyes during this contemplation there was a singular quality. The correspondent, observing the others, knew that they were not afraid, but the full meaning of their glances was shrouded.

As for himself, he was too tired to grapple fundamentally with the fact. He tried to coerce his mind into thinking of it, but the mind was dominated at this time by the muscles, and the muscles said they did not care. It merely occurred to him that if he should drown it would be a shame.

There were no hurried words, no pallor, no plain agitation. The men simply looked at the shore. "Now, remember to get well clear of the boat when you jump," said the captain.

Seaward the crest of a roller suddenly fell with a thunderous crash, and the long white comber came roaring down upon the boat.

"Steady now," said the captain. The men were silent. They turned their eyes from the shore to the comber and waited. The boat slid up the incline, leaped at the furious top, bounced over it, and swung down the long back of the wave. Some water had been shipped and the cook bailed it out.

But the next crest crashed also. The tumbling boiling flood of white water caught the boat and whirled it almost perpendicular. Water swarmed in from all sides. The correspondent had his hands on the gunwale at this time, and when the water entered at that place he swiftly withdrew his fingers, as if he objected to wetting them.

The little boat, drunken with this weight of water, reeled and snuggled deeper into the sea.

"Bail her out, cook! Bail her out," said the captain.

"All right, Captain," said the cook.

"Now boys, the next one will do for us, sure," said the oiler. "Mind to jump clear of the boat."

The third wave moved forward, huge, furious, implacable. It fairly swallowed the dingey, and almost simultaneously the men tumbled into the sea. A piece of life-belt had lain in the bottom of the boat, and as the correspondent went overboard he held this to his chest with his left hand.

The January water was icy, and he reflected immediately that it was colder than he had expected to find it off the coast of Florida. This appeared to his dazed mind as a fact important enough to be noted at the time. The coldness of the water was sad; it was tragic. This fact was somehow so mixed and confused with his opinion of his own situation that it seemed almost a proper reason for tears. The water was cold.

When he came to the surface he was conscious of little but the noisy water. Afterward he saw his companions in the sea. The oiler was ahead in the race. He was swimming strongly and rapidly. Off to the correspondent's left, the cook's great white and corked back bulged out of the water, and in the rear the captain was hanging with his one good hand to the keel of the overturned dingey.

There is a certain immovable quality to a shore, and the correspondent wondered at it amid the confusion of the sea.

It seemed also very attractive, but the correspondent knew that it was a long journey, and he paddled leisurely. The piece of life-preserver lay under him, and sometimes he whirled down the incline of a wave as if he were on a hand-sled.

But finally he arrived at a place in the sea where travel was beset with difficulty. He did not pause swimming to inquire what manner of current had caught him, but there his progress ceased. The shore was set before him like a bit of scenery on a stage, and he looked at it and understood with his eyes each detail of it.

As the cook passed, much farther to the left, the captain was calling to him, "Turn over on your back, cook! Turn over on your back and use the oar."

"All right, sir." The cook turned on his back, and, paddling with an oar, went ahead as if he were a canoe.

Presently the boat also passed to the left of the correspondent with the captain clinging with one hand to the keel. He would have appeared like a man raising himself to look over a board fence, if it were not for the extraordinary gymnastics of the boat. The correspondent marvelled that the captain could still hold to it.

They passed on, nearer to shore—the oiler, the cook, the captain—and following them went the water-jar, bouncing gayly over the seas.

The correspondent remained in the grip of this strange new enemy—a current. The shore, with its white slope of sand and its green bluff, topped with little silent cottages, was spread like a picture before him. It was very near to him then, but he was impressed as one who in a gallery looks at a scene from Brittany or Holland.

He thought: "I am going to drown? Can it be possible? Can it be possible? Can it be possible?" Perhaps an individual must consider his own death to be the final phenomenon of nature.

But later a wave perhaps whirled him out of his small deadly current for he found suddenly that he could again make progress toward the shore. Later still, he was aware that the captain, clinging with one hand to the keel of the dingey, had his face turned away from the shore and toward him, and was calling his name. "Come to the boat! Come to the boat!"

In his struggle to reach the captain and the boat, he reflected that when one gets properly wearied, drowning must really be a comfortable arrangement, a cessation of hostilities accompanied by a large degree of relief and he was glad of it, for the main thing in his mind for some moments had been the horror of the temporary agony. He did not wish to be hurt.

Presently he saw a man running along the shore. He was undressing with most remarkable speed. Coat, trousers, shirt, everything flew magically off him.

"Come to the boat," called the captain.

"All right, Captain." As the correspondent paddled, he saw the captain let himself down to bottom and leave the boat. Then the correspondent performed his one little marvel of the voyage. A large wave caught him and flung him with ease and supreme speed completely over the boat and far beyond it. It struck him even then as an event in gymnastics, and a true miracle of the sea. An overturned boat in the surf is not a plaything to a swimming man.

The correspondent arrived in water that reached only to his waist, but his condition did not enable him to stand for more than a moment. Each wave knocked him into a heap, and the under-tow pulled at him.

Then he saw the man who had been running and undressing, and undressing and running, come bounding into the water. He dragged ashore the cook, and then waded toward the captain, but the captain waved him away, and sent him to the correspondent. He was naked, naked as a tree in winter, but a halo was about his head, and he shone like a saint. He gave a strong pull, and a long drag, and a bully heave at the correspondent's hand. The correspondent, schooled in the minor formulae, said: "Thanks, old man." But suddenly the man cried: "What's that?" He pointed a swift finger. The correspondent said: "Go."

In the shallows, face downward, lay the oiler. His forehead touched sand that was periodically, between each wave, clear of the sea.

The correspondent did not know all that transpired afterward. When he achieved safe ground he fell, striking the sand with each particular part of his body. It was as if he had dropped from a roof, but the thud was grateful to him.

It seems that instantly the beach was populated with men with blankets, clothes, and flasks, and women with coffee-pots and all the remedies sacred to their minds. The welcome of the land to the men from the sea was warm and generous, but a still and dripping shape was carried slowly up the beach, and the land's welcome for it could only be the different and sinister hospitality of the grave.

When it came night, the white waves paced to and fro in the moonlight, and the wind brought the sound of the great sea's voice to the men on shore, and they felt that they could then be interpreters.

QUESTIONS

1. Crane's opening description of the setting in section I of "The Open Boat" contains both exposition and symbolism. Cite which portions seem primarily information to further the plot and which details symbolize Crane's idea that "nature is indifferent?"
2. Why does Crane include among the details of the setting the "canton-flannel gulls" and the "dark fin" of the shark?
3. How are the shoreline and the lighthouse described? What details in each of these descriptions further Crane's purpose? Why is it ironical that the life-saving station turns out to be a winter-resort?
4. Among the four characters, only one is given a proper name. Why? What bond develops among the four men?
5. What does the story's last line mean? "The wind brought the sound of the great sea's voice to the men on the shore, and they felt that they could then be interpreters." Interpreters of what? To whom? Does the correspondent's revised attitude toward the soldier who lay dying in Algiers help explain this line?

D. H. LAWRENCE (1885–1930)

Odor of Chrysanthemums

David Herbert Lawrence was born in the mining country of Nottinghamshire, England. His most famous novels, including *Women in Love* (1920) and *Lady Chatterley's Lover* (1928), are renowned for their attacks upon conventional morality and for their effects on the question of literary censorship. A prodigious author, he also wrote poems, stories, criticism, and polemical essays. His short stories, most of which were written between 1914 and 1928, were collected in three volumes in 1961.

I

The small locomotive engine, Number 4, came clanking, stumbling down from Selston with seven full wagons. It appeared round the corner with loud threats of speed, but the colt that it startled from among the gorse, which still flickered indistinctly in the raw afternoon, outdistanced it at a canter. A woman, walking up the railway line to Underwood, drew back into the hedge, held her basket aside, and watched the footplate of the engine advancing. The trucks thumped heavily past, one by one, with slow inevitable movement, as she stood insignificantly trapped between the jolting black wagons and the hedge; then they curved away toward the coppice where the withered oak leaves dropped noiselessly, while the birds, pulling at the scarlet hips beside the track, made off into the dusk that had already crept into the spinney. In the open, the smoke from the engine sank and cleaved to the rough grass. The fields were dreary and forsaken, and in the marshy strip that led to the whimsey, a reedy pit-pond, the fowls had already abandoned their run among the alders, to roost in the tarred fowl-house. The pit-bank loomed up beyond the pond, flames like red sores licking its ashy sides, in the afternoon's stagnant light. Just beyond rose the tapering chimneys and the clumsy black headstocks of Brinsley Colliery. The two wheels were spinning fast up against the sky, and the winding-engine rapped out its little spasms. The miners were being turned up.

The engine whistled as it came into the wide bay of railway lines beside the colliery, where rows of trucks stood in harbor.

Miners, single, trailing and in groups, passed like shadows diverging home. At the edge of the ribbed level of sidings squat a low cottage, three steps down from the cinder track. A large bony vine clutched at the house, as if to claw down the tiled roof. Round the bricked yard grew a few wintry primroses. Beyond, the long garden sloped down to a bush-covered brook course. There were some twiggy apple trees, winter-crack trees, and ragged cabbages. Beside the path hung dishevelled pink chrysanthemums, like pink cloths hung on bushes. A woman came stooping out of the felt-covered fowl-house, halfway down the garden. She closed and padlocked the door, then drew herself erect, having brushed some bits from her white apron.

She was a tall woman of imperious mien, handsome, with definite black eyebrows. Her smooth black hair was parted exactly. For a few moments she stood steadily watching the miners as they passed along the railway: then she turned toward the brook course. Her face was calm and set, her mouth was closed with disillusionment. After a moment she called:

"John!" There was no answer. She waited, and then said distinctly:

"Where are you?"

"Here!" replied a child's sulky voice from among the bushes. The woman looked piercingly through the dusk.

"Are you at that brook?" she asked sternly.

For answer the child showed himself before the raspberry-canes that rose like whips. He was a small, sturdy boy of five. He stood quite still, defiantly.

"Oh!" said the mother, conciliated. "I thought you were down at that wet brook—and you remember what I told you—"

The boy did not move or answer.

"Come, come on in," she said more gently, "it's getting dark. There's your grandfather's engine coming down the line!"

The lad advanced slowly, with resentful, taciturn movement. He was dressed in trousers and waistcoat of cloth that was too thick and hard for the size of the garments. They were evidently cut down from a man's clothes.

As they went slowly toward the house he tore at the ragged wisps of chrysanthemums and dropped the petals in handfuls along the path.

"Don't do that—it does look nasty," said his mother. He refrained, and she, suddenly pitiful, broke off a twig with three or four wan flowers and held them against her face. When mother and son reached the yard her hand hesitated, and instead of laying the flower aside, she pushed it in her apron-band. The mother and son stood at the foot of the three steps looking across the bay of lines at the passing home of the miners. The trundle of the small train was imminent. Suddenly the engine loomed past the house and came to a stop opposite the gate.

The engine-driver, a short man with round gray beard, leaned out of the cab high above the woman.

"Have you got a cup of tea?" he said in a cheery, hearty fashion.

It was her father. She went in, saying she would mash. Directly, she returned.

"I didn't come to see you on Sunday," began the little gray-bearded man.

"I didn't expect you," said his daughter.

The engine-driver winced; then, reassuming his cheery, airy manner, he said:

"Oh, have you heard then? Well, and what do you think—?"

"I think it is soon enough," she replied.

At her brief censure the little man made an impatient gesture, and said coaxingly, yet with dangerous coldness:

"Well, what's a man to do? It's no sort of life for a man of my years, to sit at my hearth like a stranger. And if I'm going to marry again it may as well be soon as late—what does it matter to anybody?"

The woman did not reply, but turned and went into the house. The man in the engine-cab stood assertive, till she returned with a cup of tea and a piece of bread and butter on a plate. She went up the steps and stood near the footplate of the hissing engine.

"You needn't 'a' brought me bread an' butter," said her father. "But a cup of tea"—he sipped appreciatively—"it's very nice." He sipped for a moment or two, then: "I hear as Walter's got another bout on," he said.

"When hasn't he?" said the woman bitterly.

"I heered tell of him in the 'Lord Nelson' braggin' as he was going to spend that b—afore he went: half a sovereign that was."

"When?" asked the woman.

"A' Sat'day night—I know that's true."

"Very likely," she laughed bitterly. "He gives me twenty-three shillings."

"Aye, it's a nice thing, when a man can do nothing with his money but make a beast of himself!" said the gray-whiskered man. The woman turned her head away. Her father swallowed the last of his tea and handed her the cup.

"Aye," he sighed, wiping his mouth. "It's a settler, it is—"

He put his hand on the lever. The little engine strained and groaned, and the train rumbled toward the crossing. The woman again looked across the metals. Darkness was settling over the spaces of the railway and trucks: the miners, in gray somber groups, were still passing home. The winding-engine pulsed hurriedly, with brief pauses. Elizabeth Bates looked at the dreary flow of men, then she went indoors. Her husband did not come.

The kitchen was small and full of firelight; red coals piled glowing up the chimney mouth. All the life of the room seemed in the white, warm hearth and the steel fender reflecting the red fire. The cloth was laid for tea; cups glinted in the shadows. At the back, where the lowest stairs protruded into the room, the boy sat struggling with a knife and a piece of whitewood. He was almost hidden in the shadow. It was half-past four. They had but to await the father's coming to begin tea. As the mother watched her son's sullen little struggle with the wood, she saw herself in his silence and pertinacity; she saw the father in her child's indifference to all but himself. She seemed to be occupied by her husband. He had probably gone past his home, slunk past his own door, to drink before he came in, while his dinner spoiled and wasted in waiting. She glanced at the clock, then took the potatoes to strain them in the yard. The garden and fields beyond the brook were closed in uncertain darkness. When she rose with the saucepan, leaving the drain steaming into the night behind her, she saw the yellow lamps were lit along the high road that went up the hill away beyond the space of the railway lines and the field.

Then again she watched the men trooping home, fewer now and fewer.

Indoors the fire was sinking and the room was dark red. The woman put her saucepan on the hob, and set a batter pudding near the mouth of the oven. Then she stood unmoving. Directly, gratefully, came quick young steps to the door. Someone hung on the latch a moment, then a little girl entered and began pulling off her outdoor things, dragging a mass of curls, just ripening from gold to brown, over her eyes with her hat.

Her mother chid her for coming late from school, and said she would have to keep her at home the dark winter days.

"Why, mother, it's hardly a bit dark yet. The lamp's not lighted, and my father's not home."

"No, he isn't. But it's a quarter to five! Did you see anything of him?"

The child became serious. She looked at her mother with large, wistful blue eyes.

"No, mother, I've never seen him. Why? Has he come up an' gone past, to Old Brinsley? He hasn't, mother, 'cos I never saw him."

"He'd watch that," said the mother bitterly, "he'd take care as you didn't see him. But you may depend upon it, he's seated in the 'Prince o' Wales.' He wouldn't be this late."

The girl looked at her mother piteously.

"Let's have our teas, mother, should we?" said she.

The mother called John to table. She opened the door once more and looked out across the darkness of the lines. All was deserted: she could not hear the winding-engines.

"Perhaps," she said to herself, "he's stopped to get some ripping done."

They sat down to tea. John, at the end of the table near the door, was almost lost in the darkness. Their faces were hidden from each other. The girl crouched against the fender slowly moving a thick piece of bread before the fire. The lad, his face a dusky mark on the shadow, sat watching her who was transfigured in the red glow.

"I do think it's beautiful to look in the fire," said the child.

"Do you?" said her mother. "Why?"

"It's so red, and full of little caves—and it feels so nice, and you can fair smell it."

"It'll want mending directly," replied the mother, "and then if your father comes he'll carry on and say there never is a fire when a man comes home sweating from the pit. A public-house is always warm enough."

There was silence till the boy said complainingly: "Make haste, our Annie."

"Well, I am doing! I can't make the fire do it no faster, can I?"

"She keeps wafflin' it about so's to make 'er slow," grumbled the boy.

"Don't have such an evil imagination, child," replied the mother.

Soon the room was busy in the darkness with the crisp sound of crunching. The mother ate very little. She drank her tea determinedly, and sat thinking. When she rose her anger was evident in the stern unbending of her head. She looked at the pudding in the fender, and broke out:

"It is a scandalous thing as a man can't even come home to his dinner! If it's crozzled up to a cinder I don't see why I should care. Past his very door he goes to get to a public-house, and here I sit with his dinner waiting for him—"

She went out. As she dropped piece after piece of coal on the red fire, the shadows fell on the walls, till the room was almost in total darkness.

"I canna see," grumbled the invisible John. In spite of herself, the mother laughed.

"You know the way to your mouth," she said. She set the dustpan outside the door. When she came again like a shadow on the hearth, the lad repeated, complaining sulkily:

"I canna see."

"Good gracious!" cried the mother irritably, "you're as bad as your father if it's a bit dusk!"

Nevertheless she took a paper spill from a sheaf on the mantelpiece and proceeded to light the lamp that hung from the ceiling in the middle of the room. As she reached up, her figure displayed itself just rounding with maternity.

"Oh, mother—!" exclaimed the girl.

"What?" said the woman, suspended in the act of putting the lamp glass over the flame. The copper reflector shone handsomely on her, as she stood with uplifted arm, turning to face her daughter.

"You've got a flower in your apron!" said the child, in a little rapture at this unusual event.

"Goodness me!" exclaimed the woman, relieved. "One would think the house was afire." She replaced the glass and waited a moment before turning up the wick. A pale shadow was seen floating vaguely on the floor.

"Let me smell!" said the child, still rapturously, coming forward and putting her face to her mother's waist.

"Go along, silly!" said the mother, turning up the lamp. The light revealed their suspense so that the woman felt it almost unbearable. Annie was still bending at her waist. Irritably, the mother took the flowers out from her apron-band.

"Oh, mother—don't take them out!" Annie cried, catching her hand and trying to replace the sprig.

"Such nonsense!" said the mother, turning away. The child put the pale chrysanthemums to her lips, murmuring:

"Don't they smell beautiful!"

Her mother gave a short laugh.

"No," she said, "not to me. It was chrysanthemums when I married him, and chrysanthemums when you were born, and the first time they ever brought him home drunk, he'd got brown chrysanthemums in his button-hole."

She looked at the children. Their eyes and their parted lips were wondering. The mother sat rocking in silence for some time. Then she looked at the clock.

"Twenty minutes to six!" In a tone of fine bitter carelessness she continued: "Eh, he'll not come now till they bring him. There he'll stick! But he needn't come rolling in here in his pit-dirt, for *I* won't wash him. He can lie on the floor—Eh, what a fool I've been, what a fool! And this is what I came here for, to this dirty hole, rats and all, for him to slink past his very door. Twice last week—he's begun now—"

She silenced herself, and rose to clear the table.

While for an hour or more the children played, subduedly intent, fertile of imagination, united in fear of the mother's wrath, and in dread of their father's home-coming, Mrs. Bates sat in her rocking-chair making a "singlet" of thick cream-colored flannel, which gave a dull wounded sound as she tore off the gray edge. She worked at her sewing with energy, listening to the children, and her anger wearied itself, lay down to rest, opening its eyes from time to time and steadily watching, its ears raised to listen. Sometimes even her anger quailed and shrank, and the mother suspended her sewing, tracing the footsteps that thudded along the sleepers outside; she would lift her head sharply to bid the children "hush," but she recovered herself in time, and the footsteps went past the gate, and the children were not flung out of their play-world.

But at last Annie sighed, and gave in. She glanced at her wagon of slippers, and loathed the game. She turned plaintively to her mother.

"Mother!"—but she was inarticulate.

John crept out like a frog from under the sofa. His mother glanced up.

"Yes," she said, "just look at those shirt-sleeves!"

The boy held them out to survey them, saying nothing. Then somebody called in a hoarse voice away down the line, and suspense bristled in the room, till two people had gone by outside, talking.

"It is time for bed," said the mother.

"My father hasn't come," wailed Annie plaintively. But her mother was primed with courage.

"Never mind. They'll bring him when he does come—like a log." She meant there would be no scene. "And he may sleep on the floor till he wakes himself. I know he'll not go to work tomorrow after this!"

The children had their hands and faces wiped with a flannel. They were very quiet. When they had put on their nightdresses, they said their prayers, the boy mumbling. The mother looked down at them, at the brown silken bush of intertwining curls in the nape of the girl's neck, at the little black head of the lad, and her heart burst with anger at their father who caused all three such distress. The children hid their faces in her skirts for comfort.

When Mrs. Bates came down, the room was strangely empty, with a tension of expectancy. She took up her sewing and stitched for some time without raising her head. Meantime her anger was tinged with fear.

II

The clock struck eight and she rose suddenly, dropping her sewing on her chair. She went to the stairfoot door, opened it, listening. Then she went out, locking the door behind her.

Something scuffled in the yard, and she started, though she knew it was only the rats with which the place was overrun. The night was very dark. In the great bay of railway lines, bulked with trucks, there was no trace of light, only away back she could see a few yellow lamps at the pit-top, and the red smear of the burning pit-bank on the night. She hurried along the edge of the track, then, crossing the converging lines, came to the stile by the white gates, whence she emerged on the road. Then the fear which had led her shrank. People were walking up to New Brinsley; she saw the lights in the houses; twenty yards further on were the broad windows of the "Prince of Wales," very warm and bright, and the loud voices of men could be heard distinctly. What a fool she had been to imagine that anything had happened to him! He was merely drinking over there at the "Prince of Wales." She faltered. She had never yet been to fetch him, and she never would go. So she continued her walk toward the long straggling line of houses, standing blank on the highway. She entered a passage between the dwellings.

"Mr. Rigley?—Yes! Did you want him? No, he's not in at this minute."

The raw-boned woman leaned forward from her dark scullery and peered at the other, upon whom fell a dim light through the blind of the kitchen window.

"Is it Mrs. Bates?" she asked in a tone tinged with respect.

"Yes. I wondered if your Master was at home. Mine hasn't come yet."

" 'Asn't 'e! Oh, Jack's been 'ome an' 'ad 'is dinner an' gone out. 'E's just gone for 'alf an hour afore bedtime. Did you call at the 'Prince of Wales'?"

"No—"

"No, you didn't like—! It's not very nice." The other woman was indulgent. There was an awkward pause. "Jack never said nothink about—about your Mester," she said.

"No!—I expect he's stuck in there!"

Elizabeth Bates said this bitterly, and with recklessness. She knew that the woman across the yard was standing at her door listening, but she did not care. As she turned:

"Stop a minute! I'll just go an' ask Jack if 'e knows anythink," said Mrs. Rigley.

"Oh, no—I wouldn't like to put—!"

"Yes, I will, if you'll just step inside an' see as th' childer doesn't come downstairs and set theirselves afire."

Elizabeth Bates, murmuring a remonstrance, stepped inside. The other woman apologized for the state of the room.

The kitchen needed apology. There were little frocks and trousers and childish undergarments on the squab and on the floor, and a litter of playthings everywhere. On the black American cloth of the table were pieces of bread and cake, crusts, slops, and a teapot with cold tea.

"Eh, ours is just as bad," said Elizabeth Bates, looking at the woman, not at the house. Mrs. Rigley put a shawl over her head and hurried out, saying:

"I shanna be a minute."

The other sat, noting with faint disapproval the general untidiness of the room. Then she fell to counting the shoes of various sizes scattered over the floor. There were twelve. She sighed and said to herself, "No wonder!"—glancing at the litter. There came the scratching of two pairs of feet on the yard, and the Rigleys entered. Elizabeth Bates rose. Rigley was a big man, with very large bones. His head looked particularly bony. Across his temple was a blue scar, caused by a wound got in the pit, a wound in which the coal-dust remained blue like tattooing.

" 'Asna 'e come whoam yit?" asked the man, without any form of greeting, but with deference and sympathy. "I couldna say wheer 'e is—'e's non ower theer!"—he jerked his head to signify the "Prince of Wales."

" 'E's 'appen gone up to th' 'Yew,' " said Mrs. Rigley.

There was another pause. Rigley had evidently something to get off his mind:

"Ah left 'im finishin' a stint," he began. "Loose-all 'ad bin gone about ten minutes when we com'n away, an' I shouted, 'Are ter comin', Walt?' an' 'e said, 'Go on, Ah shanna be but a'ef a minnit,' so we com'n ter th' bottom, me an' Bowers, thinkin' as 'e wor just behint, an' 'ud come up i' th' next bantle—"

He stood perplexed, as if answering a charge of deserting his mate. Elizabeth Bates, now again certain of disaster, hastened to reassure him:

"I expect 'e's gone up to th' 'Yew Tree,' as you say. It's not the first time. I've fretted myself into a fever before now. He'll come home when they carry him."

"Ay, isn't it too bad!" deplored the other woman.

"I'll just step up to Dick's an' see if 'e *is* theer," offered the man, afraid of appearing alarmed, afraid of taking liberties.

"Oh, I wouldn't think of bothering you that far," said Elizabeth Bates, with emphasis, but he knew she was glad of his offer.

As they stumbled up the entry, Elizabeth Bates heard Rigley's wife run across the yard and open her neighbor's door. At this, suddenly all the blood in her body seemed to switch away from her heart.

"Mind!" warned Rigley. "Ah've said many a time as Ah'd fill up them ruts in this entry, sumb'dy 'll be breakin' their legs yit."

She recovered herself and walked quickly along with the miner.

"I don't like leaving the children in bed, and nobody in the house," she said.

"No, you dunna!" he replied courteously. They were soon at the gate of the cottage.

"Well, I shanna be many minnits. Dunna you be frettin' now, 'e'll be all right," said the butty.

"Thank you very much, Mr. Rigley," she replied.

"You're welcome!" he stammered, moving away. "I shanna be many minnits."

The house was quiet. Elizabeth Bates took off her hat and shawl, and rolled back the rug. When she had finished, she sat down. It was a few minutes past nine. She was startled by the rapid chuff of the winding-engine at the pit, and the sharp whirr of the brakes on the rope as it descended. Again she felt the painful sweep of her blood, and she put her hand to her side, saying aloud, "Good gracious!—it's only the nine o'clock deputy going down," rebuking herself.

She sat still, listening. Half an hour of this, and she was wearied out.

"What am I working myself up like this for?" she said pitiably to herself, "I s'll only be doing myself some damage."

She took out her sewing again.

At a quarter to ten there were footsteps. One person! She watched for the door to open. It was an elderly woman, in a black bonnet and a black woollen shawl—his mother. She was about sixty years old, pale, with blue eyes, and her face all wrinkled and lamentable. She shut the door and turned to her daughter-in-law peevishly.

"Eh, Lizzie, whatever shall we do, whatever shall we do! she cried.

Elizabeth drew back a little, sharply.

"What is it, mother?" she said.

The elder woman seated herself on the sofa.

"I don't know, child, I can't tell you!"—she shook her head slowly. Elizabeth sat watching her, anxious and vexed.

"I don't know," replied the grandmother, sighing very deeply. "There's no end to my troubles, there isn't. The things I've gone through, I'm sure it's enough—" She wept without wiping her eyes, the tears running.

"But, mother," interrupted Elizabeth, "what do you mean? What is it?"

The grandmother slowly wiped her eyes. The fountains of her tears were stopped by Elizabeth's directness. She wiped her eyes slowly.

"Poor child! Eh, you poor thing!" she moaned. "I don't know what we're going to do, I don't—and you as you are—it's a thing, it is indeed!"

Elizabeth waited.

"Is he dead?" she asked, and at the words her heart swung violently, though she felt a slight flush of shame at the ultimate extravagance of the question. Her words sufficiently frightened the old lady, almost brought her to herself.

"Don't say so, Elizabeth! We'll hope it's not as bad as that; no, may the Lord spare us that, Elizabeth. Jack Rigley came just as I was sittin' down to a glass afore going to bed, an' 'e said, ' 'Appen you'll go down th' line, Mrs. Bates. Walt's had an accident. 'Appen you'll go an' sit wi' 'er till we can get him home.' I hadn't time to ask him a word afore he was gone. An' I put my bonnet on an' come straight down, Lizzie. I thought to myself, 'Eh, that poor blessed child, if anybody should come an' tell her of a sudden, there's no knowin' what'll 'appen to 'er.' You mustn't let it upset you, Lizzie—or you know what to expect. How long is it, six months—or is it five, Lizzie? Ay!"—the old woman shook her head—"time slips on, it slips on! Ay!"

Elizabeth's thoughts were busy elsewhere. If he was killed—would she be able to manage on the little pension and what she could earn?—she counted up rapidly. If he was hurt—they wouldn't take him to the hospital—how tiresome he would be to nurse!—but perhaps she'd be able to get him away from the drink and his hateful ways. She would—while he was ill. The tears offered to come to her eyes at the picture. But what sentimental luxury was this she was beginning? She turned to consider the children. At any rate she was absolutely necessary for them. They were her business.

"Ay!" repeated the old woman, "it seems but a week or two since he brought me his first wages. Ay—he was a good lad, Elizabeth, he was, in his way. I don't know why he got to be such a trouble, I don't. He was a happy lad at home, only full of spirits. But there's no mistake he's been a handful of trouble, he has! I hope the Lord'll spare him to mend his ways. I hope so, I hope so. You've had a sight o'trouble with him, Elizabeth, you have indeed. But he was a jolly enough lad wi' me, he was, I can assure you. I don't know how it is. . . ."

The old woman continued to muse aloud, a monotonous irritating sound, while Elizabeth thought concentratedly, startled once, when she heard the winding-engine chuff quickly, and the brakes skirr with a shriek. Then she heard the engine more slowly, and the brakes made no sound. The old woman did not notice. Elizabeth waited in suspense. The mother-in-law talked, with lapses into silence.

"But he wasn't your son, Lizzie, an' it makes a difference. Whatever he was, I remember him when he was little, an' I learned to understand him and to make allowances. You've got to make allowances for them—"

It was half-past ten, and the old woman was saying: "But it's trouble from beginning to end; you're never too old for trouble, never too old for that—" when the gate banged back, and there were heavy feet on the steps.

"I'll go, Lizzie, let me go," cried the old woman, rising. But Elizabeth was at the door. It was a man in pit-clothes.

"They're bringin' 'im, Missis," he said. Elizabeth's heart halted a moment. Then it surged on again, almost suffocating her.

"Is he—is it bad?" she asked.

The man turned away, looking at the darkness:

"The doctor says 'e'd been dead hours. 'E saw 'im i' th' lamp-cabin."

The old woman, who stood just behind Elizabeth, dropped into a chair, and folded her hands, crying: "Oh, my boy, my boy!"

"Hush!" said Elizabeth, with a sharp twitch of a frown. "Be still, mother, don't waken th' children: I wouldn't have them down for anything!"

The old woman moaned softly, rocking herself. The man was drawing away. Elizabeth took a step forward.

"How was it?" she asked.

"Well, I couldn't say for sure," the man replied, very ill at ease. " 'E wor finishin' a stint an' th' butties 'ad gone, an' a lot o' stuff come down atop 'n 'im."

"And crushed him?" cried the widow, with a shudder.

"No," said the man, "it fell at th' back of 'im. 'E wor under th' face, an' it niver touched 'im. It shut 'im in. It seems 'e wor smothered."

Elizabeth shrank back. She heard the old woman behind her cry:

"What?—what did 'e say it was?"

The man replied, more loudly: " 'E wor smothered!"

Then the old woman wailed aloud, and this relieved Elizabeth.

"Oh, mother," she said, putting her hand on the old woman, "don't waken th' children, don't waken th' children."

She wept a little, unknowing, while the old mother rocked herself and moaned. Elizabeth remembered that they were bringing him home, and she must be ready. "They'll lay him in the parlor," she said to herself, standing a moment pale and perplexed.

Then she lighted a candle and went into the tiny room. The air was cold and damp, but she could not make a fire, there was no fireplace. She set down the candle and looked around. The candlelight glittered on the luster-glasses, on the two vases that held some of the pink chrysanthemums, and on the dark mahogany. There was a cold, deathly smell of chrysanthemums in the room. Elizabeth stood looking at the flowers. She turned away, and calculated whether there would be room to lay him on the floor, between the couch and the chiffonier. She pushed the chairs aside. There would be room to lay him down and to step round him. Then she fetched the old red tablecloth, and another old cloth, spreading them down to save her bit of carpet. She shivered on leaving the parlor; so, from the dresser-drawer she took a clean shirt and put it at the fire to air. All the time her mother-in-law was rocking herself in the chair and moaning.

"You'll have to move from there, mother," said Elizabeth. "They'll be bringing him in. Come in the rocker."

The old mother rose mechanically, and seated herself by the fire, continuing to lament. Elizabeth went into the pantry for another candle, and there, in the little penthouse under the naked tiles, she heard them coming. She stood still in the pantry doorway, listening. She heard them pass the end of the house, and come awkwardly down the three steps, a jumble of shuffling footsteps and muttering voices. The old woman was silent. The men were in the yard.

Then Elizabeth heard Matthews, the manager of the pit, say: "You go in first, Jim. Mind!"

The door came open, and the two women saw a collier backing into the room, holding one end of a stretcher, on which they could see the nailed pit-boots of the dead man. The two carriers halted, the man at the head stooping to the lintel of the door.

"Wheer will you have him?" asked the manager, a short, white-bearded man.

Elizabeth roused herself and came from the pantry carrying the unlighted candle.

"In the parlor," she said.

"In there, Jim!" pointed the manager, and the carriers backed round into the tiny room. The coat with which they had covered the body fell off as they awkwardly turned through the two doorways, and the women saw their man, naked to the waist, lying stripped for work. The old woman began to moan in a low voice of horror.

"Lay th' stretcher at th' side," snapped the manager, "an' put 'im on th' cloths. Mind now, mind! Look you now—!"

One of the men had knocked off a vase of chrysanthemums. He stared awkwardly, then they set down the stretcher. Elizabeth did not look at her husband. As soon as she could get in the room, she went and picked up the broken vase and the flowers.

"Wait a minute!" she said.

The three men waited in silence while she mopped up the water with a duster.

"Eh, what a job, what a job, to be sure!"the manager was saying, rubbing his brow with trouble and perplexity. "Never knew such a thing in my life, never! He'd no business to ha' been left. I never knew such a thing in my life! Fell over him clean as a whistle, an' shut him in. Not four foot of space, there wasn't—yet it scarce bruised him."

He looked down at the dead man, lying prone, half naked, all grimed with coal-dust.

" ' 'Sphyxiated,' the doctor said. It *is* the most terrible job I've ever known. Seems as if it was done o' purpose. Clean over him, an' shut 'im in, like a mouse-trap"—he made a sharp, descending gesture with his hand.

The colliers standing by jerked aside their heads in hopeless comment.

The horror of the thing bristled upon them all.

Then they heard the girl's voice upstairs calling shrilly: "Mother, mother—who is it? Mother, who is it?"

Elizabeth hurried to the foot of the stairs and opened the door:

"Go to sleep!" she commanded sharply. "What are you shouting about? Go to sleep at once—there's nothing—"

Then she began to mount the stairs. They could hear her on the boards, and on the plaster floor of the little bedroom. They could hear her distinctly:

"What's the matter now?—what's the matter with you, silly thing?"— her voice was much agitated, with an unreal gentleness.

"I thought it was some men come," said the plaintive voice of the child. "Has he come?"

"Yes, they've brought him. There's nothing to make a fuss about. Go to sleep now, like a good child."

They could hear her voice in the bedroom, they waited whilst she covered the children under the bedclothes.

"Is he drunk?" asked the girl, timidly, faintly.

"No! No—he's not! He—he's asleep."

"Is he asleep downstairs?"

"Yes—and don't make a noise."

There was silence for a moment, then the men heard the frightened child again:

"What's that noise?"

"It's nothing, I tell you, what are you bothering for?"

The noise was the grandmother moaning. She was oblivious of everything, sitting on her chair rocking and moaning. The manager put his hand on her arm and bade her "Sh—sh!!"

The old woman opened her eyes and looked at him. She was shocked by this interruption, and seemed to wonder.

"What time is it?"—the plaintive thin voice of the child, sinking back unhappily into sleep, asked this last question.

"Ten o'clock," answered the mother more softly. Then she must have bent down and kissed the children.

Matthews beckoned to the men to come away. They put on their caps and took up the stretcher. Stepping over the body, they tiptoed out of the house. None of them spoke till they were far from the wakeful children.

When Elizabeth came down she found his mother alone on the parlor floor, leaning over the dead man, the tears dropping on him.

"We must lay him out," the wife said. She put on the kettle, then returning knelt at the feet, and began to unfasten the knotted leather laces. The room was clammy and dim with only one candle, so that she had to bend her face almost to the floor. At last she got off the heavy boots and put them away.

"You must help me now," she whispered to the old woman. Together they stripped the man.

When they arose, saw him lying in the naïve dignity of death, the women stood arrested in fear and respect. For a few moments they remained still, looking down, the old mother whimpering. Elizabeth felt countermanded. She saw him, how utterly inviolable he lay in himself. She had nothing to do with him. She could not accept it. Stooping, she laid her hand on him, in claim. He was still warm, for the mine was hot where he had died. His mother had his face between her hands, and was murmuring incoherently. The old tears fell in succession as drops from wet leaves; the mother was not weeping, merely her tears flowed. Elizabeth embraced the body of her husband, with cheek and lips. She seemed to be listening, inquiring, trying to get some connection. But she could not. She was driven away. He was impregnable.

She rose, went into the kitchen, where she poured warm water into a bowl, brought soap and flannel and a soft towel.

"I must wash him," she said.

Then the old mother rose stiffly, and watched Elizabeth as she carefully washed his face, carefully brushing the big blond moustache from his mouth with the flannel. She was afraid with a bottomless fear, so she ministered to him. The old woman, jealous, said:

"Let me wipe him!"—and she kneeled on the other side drying slowly as Elizabeth washed, her big black bonnet sometimes brushing the dark head of her daughter-in-law. They worked thus in silence for a long time. They never forgot it was death, and the touch of the man's dead body gave them strange emotions, different in each of the women; a great dread possessed them both, the mother felt the lie was given to her womb, she was denied; the wife felt the utter isolation of the human soul, the child within her was a weight apart from her.

At last it was finished. He was a man of handsome body, and his face showed no traces of drink. He was blond, full-fleshed, with fine limbs. But he was dead.

"Bless him," whispered his mother, looking always at his face, and speaking out of sheer terror. "Dear lad—bless him!" She spoke in a faint, sibilant ecstasy of fear and mother love.

Elizabeth sank down again to the floor, and put her face against his neck, and trembled and shuddered. But she had to draw away again. He was dead, and her living flesh had no place against his. A great dread and weariness held her: he was so unavailing. Her life was gone like his.

"White as milk he is, clear as a twelve-month baby, bless him, the darling!" the old mother murmured to herself. "Not a mark on him, clear and clean and white, beautiful as ever a child was made," she murmured with pride. Elizabeth kept her face hidden.

"He went peaceful, Lizzie—peaceful as sleep. Isn't he beautiful, the lamb? Ay—he must ha' made his peace, Lizzie. 'Appen he made it all right, Lizzie, shut in there. He'd have time. He wouldn't look like this if he hadn't made his peace. The lamb, the dear lamb. Eh, but he had a hearty laugh. I loved to hear it. He had the heartiest laugh, Lizzie, as a lad—"

Elizabeth looked up. The man's mouth was fallen back, slightly open under the cover of the moustache. The eyes, half shut, did not show glazed in the obscurity. Life with its smoky burning gone from him, had left him apart and utterly alien to her. And she knew what a stranger he was to her. In her womb was ice of fear, because of this separate stranger with whom she had been living as one flesh. Was this what it all meant—utter, intact separateness, obscured by heat of living? In dread she turned her face away. The fact was too deadly. There had been nothing between them, and yet they had come together, exchanging their nakedness repeatedly. Each time he had taken her, they had been two isolated beings, far apart as now. He was no more responsible than she. The child was like ice in her womb. For as she looked at the dead man, her mind, cold and detached, said clearly: "Who am I? What have I been doing? I have been fighting a husband who did not exist. *He* existed all the time. What wrong have I done? What was that I have been living with? There lies the reality, this man." And her soul died in her for fear: she knew she had never seen him, he had never seen her, they had met in the dark and had fought in the dark, not knowing whom they met nor whom they fought. And now she saw, and turned silent in seeing. For she had been wrong. She had said he was something he was not; she had felt familiar with him. Whereas he was apart all the while, living as she never lived, feeling as she never felt.

In fear and shame she looked at his naked body, that she had known falsely. And he was the father of her children. Her soul was torn from her body and stood apart. She looked at his naked body and was ashamed, as if she had denied it. After all, it was itself. It seemed awful to her. She looked at his face, and she turned her own face to the wall. For his look was other than hers, his way was not her way. She had denied him what he was—she saw it now. She had refused him as himself. And this had been her life, and his life. She was grateful to death, which restored the truth. And she knew she was not dead.

And all the while her heart was bursting with grief and pity for him. What had he suffered? What stretch of horror for this helpless man! She was rigid with agony. She had not been able to help him. He had been cruelly injured, this naked man, this other being, and she could make no reparation. There were the children—but the children belonged to life. This dead man had nothing to do with them. He and she were only channels through which life had flowed to issue in the children. She was a mother—but how awful she knew it now to have been a wife. And he, dead now, how awful he must have felt it to be a husband. She felt that in the next world he would be a stranger to her. If they met there, in the beyond, they would only be ashamed of what had been before. The children had come, for some mysterious reason, out of both of them. But the children did not unite them. Now he was dead, she knew how eternally he was apart from her, how eternally he had nothing more to do with her. She saw this episode of her life closed. They had denied each other in life. Now he had withdrawn. An anguish came over her. It was finished then: it had become hopeless between them long before he died. Yet he had been her husband. But how little!

"Have you got his shirt, 'Lizabeth?"

Elizabeth turned without answering, though she strove to weep and behave as her mother-in-law expected. But she could not, she was silenced. She went into the kitchen and returned with the garment.

"It is aired," she said, grasping the cotton shirt here and there to try. She was almost ashamed to handle him; what right had she or any one to lay hands on him; but her touch was humble on his body. It was hard work to clothe him. He was so heavy and inert. A terrible dread gripped her all the while: that he could be so heavy and utterly inert, unresponsive, apart. The horror of the distance between them was almost too much for her—it was so infinite a gap she must look across.

At last it was finished. They covered him with a sheet and left him lying, with his face bound. And she fastened the door of the little parlor, lest the children should see what was lying there. Then, with peace sunk heavy on her heart, she went about making tidy the kitchen. She knew she submitted to life, which was her immediate master. But from death, her ultimate master, she winced with fear and shame.

QUESTIONS

1. What contrasting colors are introduced in the first paragraph of Lawrence's story? How do these colors appear later on? What significance does Lawrence attach to them?
2. What impression does the ragged wintry landscape and the glimpse of the Rigley's kitchen have on the reader? Does this impression lend support to Elizabeth Bates' bitterness?
3. How do the different responses of Elizabeth and her son, John, to the "dishevelled pink chrysanthemums" define their characters? Where else are chrysanthemums mentioned?
4. How does Elizabeth's remark to her son, "You're as bad as your father if it's a bit of dusk!" contain more meaning than she realizes? Do any other remarks contain unintentional irony? Is there more than one meaning in the miner's remark, "'E' wor smothered"?
5. In what ways does Bates mother's reaction to her son's death differ from Elizabeth's? Why does his mother call him, "The lamb, the dear lamb"? Why does Elizabeth think, "I have been fighting a husband who did not exist"?

WRITING ABOUT SETTING

In writing about setting you have an opportunity to deal with the element that integrates some of the most important aspects of fiction: character, theme, and symbolism, for setting often has a bearing on each of these elements. As you prepare to write, mark off in the text those passages that describe the setting. There may, of course, be more than one setting in a short story. In Hawthorne's "Young Goodman Brown" there are the dark woods, the forest clearing, and the daytime setting of Salem; in "A Rose for Emily" there are the town, the downstairs of the Grierson house, and the bridal chamber; and in Crane's "The Open Boat" there are the ocean and the distant black-and-white shoreline of sand and trees. Even a story where the action is static, and does not move beyond the original place, may have more than one setting. Updike's "A & P" presents different aspects of the setting as the narrator, Sammy, looks out the store window and describes the street scene in this north-of-Boston town, or up one or another of the aisles, or at another checkstand, or at the manager's office.

As you mark off the passsages describing the setting, look for any repeated patterns: any details repeated, any images (or versions of the same image) that recur, any words that appear more than once in descriptions. For example, Updike's "A & P" is sprinkled with descriptive images of food even when he describes people: "chubby berry-faces," "sweet broad soft-looking can," "sizing up their joints," "two smoothest scoops of vanilla." You need to determine the point behind the repetition; here it is the commercial view of things which the environment of the A & P fosters, and, what is more important in the larger context of the story, which the modern adult world fosters. You therefore need to determine just how this pattern of description relates to the characters and the theme.

Does the environment *determine* the characters' actions, defining or motivating them, or does the setting merely serve as an external reflection of the characters? Is the author using the details of the setting to symbolize human characteristics? In Jean Stafford's "A Country Love Story," the antique sleigh that stands in the yard of the old house Daniel and May buy becomes an external symbol of the decayed marriage (and perhaps even of Daniel). Abandoned in the snow, the sleigh no longer moves, and when May climbs into the sleigh at the end, Stafford shows us May sacrificing her youthful (spring-like) vitality to become "an old man's nurse." Faulkner shows us Miss Emily tenaciously holding on to the things from the past while growing plump and gray amid the dust of her decaying house. Hawthorne gives us a foreshadowed glimpse of Goodman Brown's dark soul through the mirror image of the dark forest. And Sammy rejects the commercial and institutionalized details of life at the A & P.

You also need to ask whether the details of the setting are symbolic pointers to the theme of the short story. For example, what does the harsh fluorescent lighting, the cool temperature, and the "checkerboard green-and-cream rubber-tile floor" of the A & P have to do with the girls' nakedness? Is Updike implying something about what is natural and unnatural, or about youth and age? Answers to these questions about the function of the setting in Updike's story will lead to a discovery of the theme of "A & P." Does the vast landscape at the end of "Where Are You Going, Where Have You Been?" represent the emptiness of the adult world into which Connie moves? Is darkness in "Young Goodman Brown" a sign of misanthropy?

Next you need to determine the tone or the author's attitude toward the characters and toward the reader. The tone may be humorous, ironic, serious, and so on. For example, Sammy's adolescent irony in "A & P" depends on exaggeration to express his attitudes toward the townspeople. He describes the workmen in the street as "twenty-seven old freeloaders tearing up Central Street because the sewer broke again." He describes his boss, Lengel as "haggling with a truck full of cabbages on the lot and . . . about to scuttle into that door marked MANAGER behind which he hides all day." These descriptions establish the tone of "A & P" and tell us about Sammy's and perhaps Updike's attitudes.

After these preliminaries, analyze the assignment. See if it calls for writing about setting and theme, or setting and character, or both. Use only those portions of the setting that have a bearing on the topic assigned. Focus on some specific aspect of the topic assigned, and try to write a sentence summing up your main point. For example, "The dark forest, which Goodman Brown voluntarily enters, is developed by Hawthorne into an external symbol of Goodman Brown's growing misanthropy and loss of faith."

Develop your paper by citing examples to support your subtopics. These subtopics should be suggested by your thesis. They may be arranged according to the different parts of the setting as these are described in the story. For example, the subtopics for a paper on the setting of "A & P" could focus first on the world outside the supermarket, then on different aspects of the setting inside the supermarket. Instead of following the setting in the order in which the author presents it, the subtopics might be logical ideas about the setting arising out of the thesis. Your subtopics should be established in advance of writing so that they provide a framework for your essay.

Your conclusion should be a concise restatement of the thesis and a reminder of the dominant pattern of objects, images, or symbols in the setting. It should include a statement of how the setting affected the characters and/or the thesis. Papers on setting are one very concrete way of learning close reading and of appreciating how writers exercise their craft.

The following essay analyzing the setting of D. H. Lawrence's "An Odor of Chrysanthemums" emphasizes several details prominent in the setting—namely the claustrophobic quality of the mining town and its sombre colors. The essay focuses on how Lawrence contrasts these dark colors with brighter colors to define the relationship between the setting and his characters.

Environment and Character in
Lawrence's "Odor of Chrysanthemums"

D. H. Lawrence's "The Odor of Chrysanthemums" is a poignant story of
a failed relationship in which a wife realizes, only after her husband's death,
that she had never known him, than "she had denied him what he was." As
in many of Lawrence's stories this point can clearly be appreciated only by
understanding the effects of enviornment on his characters' lives, the subtle
interplay between character and setting.

Lawrence sketches the setting, an English coal mining town, in the
early expository paragraphs of the story. He dramatizes the ruthless way in
which a grim setting brutalizes people. The miners, trudging home after a
day's work, are described as a "dreary flow of men . . . in gray somber
groups." They "pass like shadows diverging home." In short, the characters
reflect the paradoxical combination of death and life, somberness and
vitality, which is the atmosphere of the mining town:

The fields were dreary and forsaken, and in the marshy strip that led to
the whimsey, a reedy pit-pond, the fowls had already abandoned their run
among the alders, to roost in the tarred fowl-house. The pit-bank loomed up
beyond the pond, flames like red sores licking its ashy sides, in the
afternoon's stagnant light. Just beyond rose the tapering chimneys and the
clumsy black headstocks of Brinsley Colliery. The two wheels were spinning
fast up against the sky, and the winding engine rapped out its little spasms.
The miners were being turned up.

It is no wonder, then, that in such an enviornment Elizabeth Bates,
wife of a coal miner, and a mother who expects a third child, is disappointed
with her life and resents her plight. Lawrence describes her as a woman
who feels "superior to her circumstances, a woman with an imperious
mien," who "stood defiantly." She resents slaving for her family, her
husband's drinking bouts, and above all, the absence of beauty and love in
her life. At first, Lawrence shows us a sensitive woman who reaches out to
touch the few remnants of beauty in an environment which callously
stamps out beauty. We see her tenderly gaze at a few "ragged whisps of
chrysanthemums" and "suddenly pitifully [break] off a twig with three or
four wan flowers and [hold] them against her face."

Her superiority, however, causes her to remain aloof and unsympathetic
to others. For example, when she seeks a neighbor's aid in locating her
husband, who she believes is carousing in the pub, but who, in reality, lies
dead in the mine, she condescendingly looks down on the disorder of the
neighbor's kitchen. "The kitchen needed apology. There were little frocks
and trousers and childish undergarments on the swab and on the floor, and
a litter of playthings everywhere. . . . Elizabeth sat, noting with faint
disapproval the general untidiness of the room."

Elizabeth Bates, then, is a woman who fails to heed her mother-in-law's
advice, advice which recognizes that circumstances can obscure the
humanity of people. "I learned to understand them and to make allowances.
You've got to make allowances for them. . . ." At this juncture in the story,
the reader is reminded, through a clever metaphor, that a brutalizing
environment can smother the vital flame of life; Lawrence repeats the
metaphor three times when he notes that Bates was literally smothered to
death; "Fell over him clean as a whistle, an' shut him in. . . . 'Sphyxiated,' the
doctor said. It is the most terrible job I've ever known. Seems as if it was on
o' purpose. Clean over him an' shut 'im in, like a mousetrap."

When Bates' corpse lies stripped, and Elizabeth begins to wash away the
coal dust which obscures his features, she comes to recognize that her
husband had remained a stranger to her:

Life with its smoky burning gone from him, had left him apart and utterly alien to her. And she knew what a stranger he was to her. In her womb was ice of fear, because of this separate stranger with whom she had been living as one flesh. Was this what it all meant-- utter, intact separateness, obscured by heat of living? In dread, she turned her face away. The fact was too deadly; there had been nothing between them, and yet they had come together, exchanging their nakedness repeatedly.

The phrase Lawrence employs here, "smoky burning," relates back to the setting. Lawrence has repeatedly referred to burning and fire as signs of life: "All the life of the room seemed in the white, warm hearth and the steel fender reflecting the red fire." On the other hand, coal dust and smokiness (dominant images in the setting) have been referred to as things which obscure life, hiding its essential fires. Again and again, Lawrence reminds us that darkness, dust, and cinders blot out, to those unwilling to look further, the life and humanity of people forced to live in brutalizing circumstances. John Bates, younger son of the miner, is, therefore, like his father associated with the obscuring darkness: "John, at the end of the table near the door, was almost lost in the darkness . . . The lad, his face a dusky mark on the shadow, sat watching her who was transfigured in the red glow."

In the same way, the coal dust has obscured her husband from Elizabeth Bates. Washed clean of the coal dust, the miner becomes to his old mother "clear and clean and white, beautiful as ever a child was made." He is her "dear lamb."

Significantly, Elizabeth thinks not of a white lamb, but of the dark in which she and her husband made love, the dark which hid them from each other. "She knew she had never seen him, he had never seen her, they had met in the dark and had fought in the dark, not knowing whom they met nor whom they fought."

In "An Odor of Chrysanthemums," Lawrence uses setting functionally as an index to his characters' actions. Without the prominence of setting, the characters' conflicts and the thematic direction of the story could not have been so clearly, nor so powerfully, revealed.

SUGGESTIONS FOR WRITING ABOUT SETTING

1. Show how the three settings of "Young Goodman Brown"—the dark forest, the blazing woods, and peaceful Salem—contribute to the character development of Goodman Brown.
2. Analyze the details of the setting in "A Rose for Emily" that directly and indirectly have to do with time.
3. Write an essay showing how details of the setting in the early portions of Joyce Carol Oates' "Where Are You Going, Where Have You Been?" contrast with details of the setting after Arnold Friend drives up to Connie's house.
4. Discuss the unromantic commercial details in the setting of "A & P" and show their relation to Sammy's climactic decision.
5. One of the chief tenets of naturalism, the philosophy which informs Stephen Crane's "The Open Boat," is that nature is "flatly indifferent." Show how the setting and the action reflect this belief.

POINT OF VIEW AND TONE IN FICTION

Actions taken by *people* in particular *places: plot, character,* and *setting* are probably the elements of fiction we think of first when reconsidering stories we've read. But in analyzing fiction, we need to remember more than Sammy's "defense" of the girls in the grocery store, or Young Goodman Brown's vision of Faith's pink ribbon in the forest. We must remember that these events are related to us by someone. That person could be an active participant in the story (or even the main character, as in Sammy's case), a marginal participant who stands on the periphery of the action (as in the case of "A Rose for Emily"), or an apparently disembodied speaker whose voice is so self-assured as to seem the author's own (as in "Young Goodman Brown"). This speaker will be clearly positioned in space and time, will be endowed with knowledge and opinions about the actions he or she is narrating, and will adopt an attitude toward those actions and toward the audience that is hearing about them. When we analyze matters pertaining to the narrator of a story—questions about identity; the use of first person or third person; degree of knowledge, involvement, or objectivity; placement in space and time; attitude—we are concerned with point of view and tone.

Consider one common use of the phrase "point of view." One could say, "From my point of view, I could not see the cello section of the orchestra." This sentence implies four considerations that we must be aware of when we read fiction.

(a) a human agent (the "I" of the sentence)
(b) a position in space (a seat in a concert hall)
(c) a moment in time (the time at which the concert was taking place)
(d) a field of vision (in this case one apparently restricted by the edge of a balcony or a pillar!)

This human agent who tells a story from a particular vantage point of space, time, and vision is called the author's **persona.** This word, taken into English from the Latin word for "mask," implies that the narrator of a story is not the author himself or herself, but a person or voice created by the author to tell one story. He or she can be a first-person narrator, as in "A & P," or a third-person narrator, as in "Young Goodman Brown." Just as we cannot assume that Sammy's opinions about his boss are identical to John Updike's neither can we assume that the narrator's opinions about Young Goodman Brown are identical to Hawthorne's. To do so would be to blur the line between fiction and reality, between story as artistic creation and story as moral, historical, or biographical treatise. Doing so would also cause us to forget that the narrator and his or her point of view are literary devices or conventions which can be exploited, manipulated, misused, or modified like any other element of fiction. The author creates the narrator, who in turn tells the story. That is, the narrator is a medium through whom we learn about the characters and events of the story. How authors employ this medium helps to create some of the distinct challenges, pleasures, and complexities we associate with fiction.

Now consider another common use of the phrase "point of view," as in "My point of view on nuclear weapons is that they should be banned." Here we use the phrase to mean "opinion." We are saying that as we see it— given our limited perspective, our knowledge, judgments, biases, preju- dices, our particular position in space and time—we believe nuclear weap- ons should be banned. Point of view, as used in the analysis of literature, implies a degree of awareness. A fictional narrator can be endowed by its creator, the author, to tell us everything about the story being narrated, or the narrator can be limited in various ways to suit the author's purpose. The narrator of "Young Goodman Brown," for example, can tell us Brown's private, unexpressed thoughts. A narrator with such abilities could, presumably, tell us all about Brown's youth, too. But Brown's youth is not relevant to the story; hence it is left undescribed. We call such nar- rators, who are always third person, **omniscient** (all-knowing) because there is no apparent limit to what they could tell us about the characters in the stories they tell. Conceivably they could tell us about the characters' thoughts, emotions, pasts, and futures, and they could offer judgments based on their encompassing visions.

The use of an omniscient narrator, with its patent lack of realism, re- minds us that the narrator and his or her point of view are conventions adopted for the occasion by an author to tell a story. Most authors limit the point of view in some way to create greater realism, variety, intrigue or immediacy, or to remind us of the tenuousness of subjective responses to human actions and experiences.

Besides the omniscient narrator, five different points of view are used commonly enough in fiction to have been given their own names: **third person limited, first person, dramatic, interior monologue,** and **stream of consciousness.**

When an author uses a third person limited point of view, he or she places us, so to speak, at the side of one of the characters. Our perception of the action is limited to what that character speaks, hears, thinks, feels, or experiences. We cannot gain access to the minds of the other characters or to past and future events except through signals that this "center" (a term first used by the novelist Henry James) can perceive. The "center" can be a main character or a peripheral one. In her short story "A Woman on a Roof" (page 158), Doris Lessing uses a third person limited point of view when she restricts our view of the action to what we can "see" through the eyes and mind of the main character, Tom. James Joyce uses the same point of view in his story "Counterparts" (under "Plot," page 32).

As with any point of view, the use of third person limited has attendant advantages and disadvantages. It creates a greater impression of realism than an omniscient point of view, but it does allow access into at least one character's mind. It balances the detachment of the third person with the sharp focus gained by reporting one character's perceptions and experiences. But as its name implies, it curtails our knowledge of other characters' private thoughts and feelings. Also, it lacks the immediacy possible with a first person point of view.

Third person narrators can be given more or less knowledge about the stories they tell, can mediate between author and reader to varying degrees, and can intrude or not intrude with judgments and summary remarks. Similarly, first person narrators can be central, peripheral, or aloof depending on their connection to the events they narrate (and, of course, on their authors' purposes). To see the effects of this range of possible involvement, consider three stories that use first person narrators: Faulkner's "A Rose for Emily," Herman Melville's "Bartleby, the Scrivener" (page 113), and Updike's "A & P."

In Faulkner's story, we are scarcely aware that the narrator is speaking in the first person. He is, in a sense, a bystander, a representative townsman, someone who knew of Emily, but who had little direct connection with her. He only uses the first person plural, as when he says: "When we saw her again, her hair was cut short, making her look like a girl, with a vague resemblance to those angels in colored church windows—sort of tragic and serene." (page 19) The narrator tends to recede into the background and tell his story without drawing attention to himself. Nevertheless, the quoted sentence—with its use of the corporate "we" and its colloquial style—reminds us that what we are hearing is being filtered through the mind of a character, not a disembodied spokesman. While he may be relatively detached and impartial, his narration has immediacy because he is a fellow townsman of Emily's and, no doubt, because he shares some of her values.

The effect of the first-person narrator in "Bartleby the Scrivener" is markedly different. Here, the narrator is anything but detached. He knows Bartleby well, works with him every day, supports him, and cares for him. He has a distinct emotional involvement in Bartleby's decline and death. He feels guilty, victimized, and indifferent by turns, and his attitudes toward Bartleby cover a range from bewilderment, through impatience and outrage, to an ultimate compassion toward the taciturn scribe. Moreover, the narrator of 'Bartleby" is quick to talk about himself, justify his own actions, and offer judgments about his subordinates. The high profile he keeps reminds us that what we are being told is influenced and colored by the medium through which it passes—so much so that the narrator, though he purports to tell Bartleby's story, becomes, arguably, the main character of the piece. This is in stark contrast to the relatively self-effacing narrator of "A Rose for Emily."

In Updike's "A & P," we hear the main character, Sammy, telling his story in the present tense, almost as it occurs. His tone is informal, and his manner of speaking spontaneous, full of youthful vigor and candor. He seems to be explaining or justifying his actions toward the three girls and toward his boss, but he does so in an apparently more forthright fashion than does the narrator of "Bartleby." "A & P" reminds us that a narrator's temporal placement, spatial location, and attitude have a crucial effect on our understanding.

From these remarks about "A & P," we can see that the tone of a piece of writing is significantly influenced by an author's choice of point of view. As used in literary analysis, *tone* carries a meaning similar to its use in the phrase "tone of voice." When a child speaks angrily to his father, and the father responds "I don't like your tone of voice," he is taking exception to the *way* the child is speaking, not just what he is saying. By adjusting the sounds of our voices, we can, even when using the same words or expressions, convey a wide range of emotions. Think of how we use the word "okay." With it, depending on our tone of voice, we can express glee, anger, boredom, grudging or tentative acceptance, or willing assent.

But we cannot hear narrators, at least not in the same sense we hear the people we talk to. (Again, narrators are fictional creations, not real people.) To create differences in tone in a story, writers make adjustments in the language they use, adjustments that are usually related to the choice of a point of view. Diction can be adjusted to suggest formality or informality. Degree of awareness can be adjusted to suggest naiveté or mature understanding. Modifiers can be used to create sarcasm or bluntness. Sentence structure can be adjusted to create a sense of frenzy or calm. These adjustments are predicated on choices concerning point of view.

To illustrate some of these differences to yourself, do the following. Read Doris Lessing's story "A Woman On A Roof." Lessing uses a third-person limited point of view with the young man Tom as the "center." Now imagine how different the story would be if told from the point of view of Harry, the relatively calm, middle-aged senior workman who accompanies Tom and Stanley. The kinds of things the narrator might notice would be changed because of Harry's age, his status as a family man, and his more mature attitude toward the woman. The tone of his reactions to Tom's fantasized "involvement" with the woman could be sober, or impatient, or sagely tolerant, depending on how Lessing chose to have him view the action. The style and the diction of the piece—and their effect on its tone—would probably be altered by a shift in point of view. The entire story would be changed.

Tone, then, is the attitude an author or narrator adopts toward his or her material or audience. The precise tone of a story may be difficult to pin down or put into words. We may have to settle for such terms as ironic, sarcastic, amused, angry, compassionate, and other such terms that denote feeling.

When we consider the tone of a work of fiction, we must consider possible discrepancies between the attitude of the narrator and the attitude of the author who creates this voice. Such discrepancies, which we can sometimes infer but not necessarily prove, can be crucial to an accurate understanding of any given story. For example, when we read Melville's "Bartleby," we immediately begin to make assumptions about the narrator and his tone. He is by turns garrulous, bewildered, condescending, compassionate, patronizing, and self-justifying. We see the action through his eyes, and, at least provisionally, accept his opinions about these actions and the characters who perform them. However, we must be mindful that, though he tells us the story, he is also part of it. Anything he says, thinks, or does is evidence of *his* character given to us by Melville, who may consider his narrator's actions reprehensible, excusable, understandable, malicious, or benign. Thus a careful analysis of tone involves an ability to "read between the lines"—not to accept as absolute truth all we are told, particularly by a first-person narrator who, like the lawyer in "Bartleby," has a heavy investment in the action he is describing. When we think about tone, we must also think about other elements in the story, particularly point of view.

We have already said that the most common points of view are third person omniscient, third person limited, and first person (participant or non-participant). Other useful terms reveal some of the refined effects that can be obtained within these three basic positions. Many critics use the terms **summary** and **immediate scene.** When a narrator summarizes action he *tells* us that it happened, sometimes giving us opinions and judgments about it, but always mediating between the action and our perception of it.

When, on the other hand, a narrator "stands back" from the story and presents the events as they are happening, focusing our attention on one place and *showing* us the actions and speeches of the characters, he or she is presenting an immediate scene. To get a clearer sense of the difference between summary and immediate scene, compare the beginnings of two stories, Melville's "Bartleby" (summary) and Ernest Hemingway's "Indian Camp" (immediate scene, under "Theme").

When the narrator's presence is suppressed to the extent that he or she merely exhibits the action without any commentary, the point of view is said to be **objective.** Everything is shown, so to speak, from the outside. When the narrator presents only the characters' speeches the point of view is said to be **dramatic.** The point of view of "Indian Camp" is largely objective and dramatic. Taken far enough, the dramatic method changes the short story into something resembling a play, like conversation that is being recorded on tape and transcribed. But we should remember that any seemingly objective or dramatic point of view is, like any other point of view, a convention, a method adopted by the author to enhance (or destroy) the illusion of reality. The author or narrator is still "pulling the strings"—that is, angling the camera and placing the tape recorder. Fiction is not a direct transcription of reality.

Other methods that authors use to create the illusion of reality—this time from the inside rather than the outside—are the **interior monologue** and the **stream of consciousness.** In an interior monologue, we (but no one else in the story) hear the thoughts of a character as though they were being spoken, much as when we hear ourselves talking to ourselves. In stream-of-consciousness narration, we are presented with the apparently unmediated flow of thoughts, impressions, words, and/or reactions experienced by a character. This method of narration, exemplified by parts of James Joyce's famous novel *Ulysses* (1922), usually represents a carefully edited flow of impressions designed, once again, to imitate reality, not transcribe it, and to give us insight into the characters of a story. Writers of fiction have still not found a way to duplicate the richness—or the chaos!—of the human mind at work.

Objective narration, dramatic narration, interior monologue, and stream of consciousness are variations (sometimes brilliant, but just as prone to misuse) on third, or first-person points of view. Resourceful authors can resort to other variations of which, as careful readers of fiction, we should be aware. Some use naive narrators (children, for example) to lend irony to the point of view. Or a narrator can be severely restricted in his or her perceptions—by blindness or deafness, for example. Narrators can also be made unreliable, thus taxing our powers of seeing through what they say to get at the truth. Other authors will use multiple narrators to show us how similar events impinge on different minds.

The above suggests the suppleness and the potential subtlety of point of view as a convention. Point of view is a ubiquitous feature, present in all fiction. One could even make the claim that it is the single most distinguishing feature of fiction, for in no other kind of writing do authors show such an omnipresent, sustained, various, and ingenious use of the device.

As you read the following stories by Melville and Lessing, concentrate on the way each author handles point of view and tone. Consider how each story would be changed if told from a different point of view. Look for consistency or variety within the perspectives the authors adopt. Try to be aware of how point of view affects, or is affected by, other elements of the stories. Above all, be sure to enjoy the stories for what they are: penetrating and amusing observations of human behavior told ingeniously from within a time-honored convention.

HERMAN MELVILLE (1819–1891)

Bartleby, the Scrivener

Herman Melville was born in New York City. After several years as a sailor, he began a series of adventure novels—mostly set at sea or among sailors—that culminated in his masterpiece, *Moby Dick* (1851). During the 1850s and 1860s, Melville's popularity waned, and he spent the last nineteen years of his life as a customs inspector in New York. "Bartleby, the Scrivener," his most haunting tale, first appeared in 1853.

A Story of Wall Street

I am a rather elderly man. The nature of my avocations, for the last thirty years, has brought me into more than ordinary contact with what would seem an interesting and somewhat singular set of men, of whom, as yet, nothing, that I know of, has ever been written—I mean, the law-copyists, or scriveners. I have known very many of them, professionally and privately, and, if I pleased, could relate divers histories, at which goodnatured gentlemen might smile, and sentimental souls might weep. But I waive the biographies of all other scriveners, for a few passages in the life of Bartleby, who was a scrivener, the strangest I ever saw, or heard of. While, of other law-copyists, I might write the complete life, of Bartleby nothing of that sort can be done. I believe that no materials exist for a full and satisfactory biography of this man. It is an irreparable loss to literature. Bartleby was one of those beings of whom nothing is ascertainable, except from the original sources, and, in his case, those are very small. What my own astonished eyes saw of Bartleby, *that* is all I know of him, except, indeed, one vague report, which will appear in the sequel.

Ere introducing the scrivener, as he first appeared to me, it is fit I make some mention of myself, my *employés*, my business, my chambers, and general surroundings, because some such description is indispensable to an adequate understanding of the chief character about to be presented. Imprimis: I am a man who, from his youth upwards, has been filled with a profound conviction that the easiest way of life is the best. Hence, though I belong to a profession proverbially energetic and nervous, even to turbulence, at times, yet nothing of that sort have I ever suffered to invade my peace. I am one of those unambitious lawyers who never address a jury, or in any way draw down public applause; but, in the cool tranquillity of a snug retreat, do a snug business among rich men's bonds, and mortgages, and title-deeds. All who know me, consider me an eminently *safe* man. The late John Jacob Astor, a personage little given to poetic enthusiasm, had no hesitation in pronouncing my first grand point to be prudence; my next, method. I do not speak it in vanity, but simply record the fact, that was not unemployed in my profession by the late John Jacob Astor; a name which, I admit, I love to repeat; for it hath a rounded and orbicular sound to it, and rings like unto bullion. I will freely add, that I was not insensible to the late John Jacob Astor's good opinion.

Some time prior to the period at which this little history begins, my avocations had been largely increased. The good old office, now extinct in the State of New York, of a Master in Chancery, had been conferred upon me. It was not a very arduous office, but very pleasantly remunerative. I seldom lose my temper; much more seldom indulge in dangerous indignation at wrongs and outrages; but I must be permitted to be rash here and declare, that I consider the sudden and violent abrogation of the office of Master in Chancery, by the new Constitution, as a—premature act; inasmuch as I had counted upon a life-lease of the profits, whereas I only received those of a few short years. But this is by the way.

My chambers were up stairs, at No.—Wall Street. At one end, they looked upon the white wall of the interior of a spacious skylight shaft, penetrating the building from top to bottom.

This view might have been considered rather tame than otherwise, deficient in what landscape painters call "life." But, if so, the view from the other end of my chambers offered, at least, a contrast, if nothing more. In that direction, my windows commanded an unobstructed view of a lofty brick wall, black by age and everlasting shade; which wall required no spyglass to bring out its lurking beauties, but, for the benefit of all near-sighted spectators, was pushed up to within ten feet of my window-panes. Owing to the great height of the surrounding buildings, and my chambers being on the second floor, the interval between this wall and mine not a little resembled a huge square cistern.

At the period just preceding the advent of Bartleby, I had two persons as copyists in my employment, and a promising lad as an office-boy. First, Turkey; second, Nippers; third, Ginger Nut. These may seem names, the like of which are not usually found in the Directory. In truth, they were nicknames, mutually conferred upon each other by my three clerks, and were deemed expressive of their respective persons or characters. Turkey was a short, pursy Englishman, of about my own age—that is, somewhere not far from sixty. In the morning, one might say, his face was of a fine florid hue, but after twelve o'clock, meridian—his dinner hour—it blazed like a grate full of Christmas coals; and continued blazing—but, as it were, with a gradual wane—till six o'clock, P.M., or thereabouts; after which, I saw no more of the proprietor of the face, which, gaining its meridian with the sun, seemed to set with it, to rise, culminate, and decline the following day, with the like regularity and undiminished glory. There are many singular coincidences I have known in the course of my life, not the least among which was the fact, that, exactly when Turkey displayed his fullest beams from his red and radiant countenance, just then, too, at that critical moment, began the daily period when I considered his business capacities as seriously disturbed for the remainder of the twenty-four hours. Not that he was absolutely idle, or averse to business then; far from it. The difficulty was, he was apt to be altogether too energetic. There was a strange, inflamed, flurried, flighty recklessness of activity about him. He would be incautious in dipping his pen into his inkstand. All his blots upon my documents were dropped there after twelve o'clock, meridian. Indeed, not only would he be reckless, and sadly given to making blots in the afternoon, but, some days, he went further, and was rather noisy. At such times, too, his face flamed with augmented blazonry, as if cannel coal had been heaped on anthracite. He made an unpleasant racket with his chair; spilled his sand-box; in mending his pens, impatiently split them all to pieces, and threw them on the floor in a sudden passion; stood up, and leaned over his table, boxing his papers about in a most indecorous manner, very sad to behold in an elderly man like him. Nevertheless, as he was in many ways a most valuable person to me, and all the time before twelve o'clock, meridian, was the quickest, steadiest creature, too, accomplishing a great deal of work in a style not easily to be matched—for these reasons, I was willing to overlook his eccentricities, though, indeed, occasionally, I remonstrated with him. I did this very gently, however, because, though the civilest, nay, the blandest and most reverential of men in the morning, yet, in the afternoon, he was disposed, upon provocation, to be slightly rash with his tongue—in fact, insolent. Now, valuing his morning services as I did, and resolved not to lose them—yet, at the same time, made uncomfortable by his inflamed ways after twelve o'clock—and being a man of peace, unwilling by my admonitions to call forth unseemly retorts from him, I took upon me, one Saturday noon (he was always worse on Saturdays) to hint to him, very kindly, that, perhaps, now that he was growing old, it might be well to abridge his labors; in short, he need not come to my chambers after twelve o'clock, but, dinner over, had best go home to his lodgings, and rest himself till tea-time. But no; he insisted upon his afternoon devotions. His countenance became intolerably fervid, as he oratorically assured me—gesticulating with a long ruler at the other end of the room—that if his services in the morning were useful, how indispensable, then, in the afternoon?

"With submission, sir," said Turkey, on this occasion, "I consider myself your right-hand man. In the morning I but marshal and deploy my columns; but in the afternoon I put myself at their head, and gallantly charge the foe, thus"—and he made a violent thrust with the ruler.

"But the blots, Turkey," intimated I.

"True; but, with submission, sir, behold these hairs! I am getting old. Surely, sir, a blot or two of a warm afternoon is not to be severely urged against gray hairs. Old age—even if it blot the page—is honorable. With submission, sir, we *both* are getting old."

This appeal to my fellow-feeling was hardly to be resisted. At all events, I saw that go he would not. So, I made up my mind to let him stay, resolving, nevertheless, to see to it that, during the afternoon, he had to do with my less important papers.

Nippers, the second on my list, was a whiskered, sallow, and, upon the whole, rather piratical-looking young man, of about five-and-twenty. I always deemed him the victim of two evil powers—ambition and indigestion. The ambition was evinced by a certain impatience of the duties of a mere copyist, an unwarrantable usurpation of strictly professional affairs such as the original drawing up of legal documents. The indigestion seemed betokened in an occasional nervous testiness and grinning irritability, causing the teeth to audibly grind together over mistakes committed in copying; unnecessary maledictions, hissed, rather then spoken, in the heat of business; and especially by a continual discontent with the height of the table where he worked. Though of a very ingenious mechanical turn, Nippers could never get this table to suit him. He put chips under it, blocks of various sorts, bits of pasteboard, and at last went so far as to attempt an exquisite adjustment, by final pieces of folded blotting-paper. But no invention would answer. If, for the sake of easing his back, he brought the table-lid at a sharp angle well up towards his chin, and wrote there like a man using the steep roof of a Dutch house for his desk, then he declared that it stopped the circulation in his arms. If now he lowered the table to his waist-bands, and stooped over it in writing, then there was a sore aching in his back. In short, the truth of the matter was, Nippers knew not what he wanted. Or, if he wanted anything, it was to be rid of a scrivener's table altogether. Among the manifestations of his diseased ambition was a fondness he had for receiving visits from certain ambiguous-looking fellows in seedy coats, whom he called his clients. Indeed, I was aware that not only was he, at times, considerable of a ward-politician, but he occasionally did a little business at the justices' courts, and was not unknown on the steps of the Tombs. I have good reason to believe, however, that one individual who called upon him at my chambers, and who, with a grand air, he insisted was his client, was no other than a dun, and the alleged title-deed, a bill. But, with all his failings, and the annoyances he caused me, Nippers, like his compatriot Turkey, was a very useful man to me; wrote a neat, swift hand; and, when he chose, was not deficient in a gentlemanly sort of deportment. Added to this, he always dressed in a gentlemanly sort of way; and so, incidentally, reflected credit upon my chambers. Whereas, with respect to Turkey, I had much ado to keep him from being a reproach to me. His clothes were apt to look oily, and smell of eating-houses. He wore his pantaloons very loose and baggy in summer. His coats were execrable, his hat not to be handled. But while the hat was a thing of indifference to me, inasmuch as his natural civility and deference, as a dependent Englishman, always led him to doff it the moment he entered the room, yet his coat was another matter. Concerning his coats, I reasoned with him; but with no effect. The truth was, I suppose, that a man with so small an income could not afford to sport such a lustrous face and a lustrous coat at one and the same time. As Nippers once observed, Turkey's money went chiefly for red ink. One winter day, I presented Turkey with a highly respectable-looking coat of my own—a padded gray coat, of a most comfortable warmth, and which buttoned straight up from the knee to the neck. I thought Turkey would appreciate the favor, and abate his rashness and obstreperousness of afternoons. But no; I verily believe that buttoning himself up in so downy and blanket-like a coat had a pernicious effect upon him—upon the same principle that too much oats are bad for horses. In fact, precisely as a rash, restive horse is said to feel his oats, so Turkey felt his coat. It made him insolent. He was a man whom prosperity harmed.

Though, concerning the self-indulgent habits of Turkey, I had my own private surmises, yet, touching Nippers, I was well persuaded that, whatever might be his faults in other respects, he was, at least, a temperate young man. But, indeed, nature herself seemed to have been his vintner, and, at his birth, charged him so thoroughly with an irritable, brandy-like disposition, that all subsequent potations were needless. When I consider how, amid the stillness of my chambers, Nippers would sometimes impatiently rise from his seat, and stooping over his table, spread his arms wide apart, seize the whole desk, and move it, and jerk it, with a grim, grinding motion on the floor, as if the table were a perverse voluntary agent, intent on thwarting and vexing him, I plainly perceive that, for Nippers, brandy-and-water were altogether superfluous.

It was fortunate for me that, owing to its peculiar cause—indigestion—the irritability and consequent nervousness of Nippers were mainly observable in the morning, while in the afternoon he was comparatively mild. So that, Turkey's paroxysms only coming on about twelve o'clock, I never had to do with their eccentricities at one time. Their fits relieved each other, like guards. When Nippers' was on, Turkey's was off; and *vice versa*. This was a good natural arrangement, under the circumstances.

Ginger Nut, the third on my list, was a lad, some twelve years old. His father was a carman, ambitious of seeing his son on the bench instead of a cart, before he died. So he sent him to my office, as student at law, errand-boy, cleaner and sweeper, at the rate of one dollar a week. He had a little desk to himself, but he did not use it much. Upon inspection, the drawer exhibited a great array of the shells of various sorts of nuts. Indeed, to this quick-witted youth, the whole noble science of the law was contained in a nutshell. Not the least among the employments of Ginger Nut, as well as one which he discharged with the most alacrity, was his duty as cake and apple purveyor for Turkey and Nippers. Copying lawpapers being proverbially a dry, husky sort of business, my two scriveners were fain to moisten their mouths very often with Spitzenbergs, to be had at the numerous stalls nigh the Custom House and Post Office. Also, they sent Ginger Nut very frequently for that peculiar cake—small, flat, round, and very spicy—after which he had been named by them. Of a cold morning, when business was but dull, Turkey would gobble up scores of these cakes, as if they were mere wafers—indeed, they sell them at the rate of six or eight for a penny—the scrape of his pen blending with the crunching of the crisp particles in his mouth. Of all the fiery afternoon blunders and flurried rashness of Turkey, was his once moistening a ginger-cake between his lips, and clapping it on to a mortgage, for a seal. I came within an ace of dismissing him then. But he mollified me by making an oriental bow, and saying—

"With submission, sir, it was generous of me to find you in stationery on my own account."

Now my original business—that of a conveyancer and title hunter, and drawer-up of recondite documents of all sorts—was considerably increased by receiving the Master's office. There was now great work for scriveners. Not only must I push the clerks already with me, but I must have additional help.

In answer to my advertisement, a motionless young man one morning stood upon my office threshold, the door being open, for it was summer. I can see that figure now—pallidly neat, pitiably respectable, incurably forlorn! It was Bartleby.

After a few words touching his qualifications, I engaged him, glad to have among my corps of copyists a man of so singularly sedate an aspect, which I thought might operate beneficially upon the flighty temper of Turkey, and the fiery one of Nippers.

I should have stated before that ground-glass folding-doors divided my premises into two parts, one of which was occupied by my scriveners, the other by myself. According to my humor, I threw open these doors, or closed them. I resolved to assign Bartleby a corner by the folding-doors, but on my side of them, so as to have this quiet man within easy call, in case any trifling thing was to be done. I placed his desk close up to a small side-window in that part of the room, a window which originally had afforded a lateral view of certain grimy brickyards and bricks, but which, owing to subsequent erections, commanded at present no view at all, though it gave some light. Within three feet of the panes was a wall, and the light came down from far above, between two lofty buildings, as from a very small opening in a dome. Still further to a satisfactory arrangement, I procured a high green folding screen, which might entirely isolate Bartleby from my sight, though not remove him from my voice. And thus, in a manner, privacy and society were conjoined.

At first, Bartleby did an extraordinary quantity of writing. As if long famishing for something to copy, he seemed to gorge himself on my documents. There was no pause for digestion. He ran a day and night line, copying by sunlight and by candle-light. I should have been quite delighted with his application, had he been cheerfully industrious. But he wrote on silently, palely, mechanically.

It is, of course, an indispensable part of a scrivener's business to verify the accuracy of his copy, word by word. Where there are two or more scriveners in an office, they assist each other in this examination, one reading from the copy, the other holding the original. It is a very dull, wearisome, and lethargic affair. I can readily imagine that, to some sanguine temperaments, it would be altogether intolerable. For example, I cannot credit that the mettlesome poet, Byron, would have contentedly sat down with Bartleby to examine a law document of, say five hundred pages, closely written in a crimpy hand.

Now and then, in the haste of business, it had been my habit to assist in comparing some brief document myself, calling Turkey or Nippers for this purpose. One object I had, in placing Bartleby so handy to me behind the screen, was, to avail myself of his services on such trivial occasions. It was on the third day, I think, of his being with me, and before any necessity had arisen for having his own writing examined, that, being much hurried to complete a small affair I had in hand, I abruptly called to Bartleby. In my haste and natural expectancy of instant compliance, I sat with my head bent over the original on my desk, and my right hand sideways, and somewhat nervously extended with the copy, so that, immediately upon emerging from his retreat, Bartleby might snatch it and proceed to business without the least delay.

In this very attitude did I sit when I called to him, rapidly stating what it was I wanted him to do—namely, to examine a small paper with me. Imagine my surprise, nay, my consternation, when, without moving from his privacy, Bartleby, in a singularly mild, firm voice, replied, "I would prefer not to."

I sat awhile in perfect silence, rallying my stunned faculties. Immediately it occured to me that my ears had deceived me, or Bartleby had entirely misunderstood my meaning. I repeated my request in the clearest tone I could assume; but in quite as clear a one came the previous reply, "I would prefer not to."

"Prefer not to," echoed I, rising in high excitement, and crossing the room with a stride. "What do you mean? Are you moonstruck? I want you to help me compare this sheet here—take it," and I thrust it towards him.

"I would prefer not to," said he.

I looked at him steadfastly. His face was leanly composed; his gray eye dimly calm. Not a wrinkle of agitation rippled him. Had there been the least uneasiness, anger, impatience or impertinence in his manner; in other words, had there been anything ordinarily human about him, doubtless I should have violently dismissed him from the premises. But as it was, I should have as soon thought of turning my pale plaster-of-paris bust of Cicero out of doors. I stood gazing at him awhile, as he went on with his own writing, and then reseated myself at my desk. This is very strange, thought I. What had one best do? But my business hurried me. I concluded to forget the matter for the present, reserving it for my future leisure. So, calling Nippers from the other room, the paper was speedily examined.

A few days after this, Bartleby concluded four lengthy documents, being quadruplicates of a week's testimony taken before me in my High Court of Chancery. It became necessary to examine them. It was an important suit, and great accuracy was imperative. Having all things arranged, I called Turkey, Nippers, and Ginger Nut, from the next room, meaning to place the four copies in the hands of my four clerks, while I should read from the original. Accordingly, Turkey, Nippers, and Ginger Nut had taken their seats in a row, each with his document in his hand, when I called to Bartleby to join this interesting group.

"Bartleby! quick, I am waiting."

I heard a slow scrape of his chair legs on the uncarpeted floor, and soon he appeared standing at the entrance of his hermitage.

"What is wanted?" said he, mildly.

"The copies, the copies," said I, hurriedly. "We are going to examine them. There"—and I held towards him the fourth quadruplicate.

"I would prefer not to," he said, and gently disappeared behind the screen.

For a few moments I was turned into a pillar of salt, standing at the head of my seated column of clerks. Recovering myself, I advanced towards the screen, and demanded the reason for such extraordinary conduct.

"*Why* do you refuse?"

"I would prefer not to."

With any other man I should have flown outright into a dreadful passion, scorned all further words, and thrust him ignominiously from my presence. But there was something about Bartleby that not only strangely disarmed me, but, in a wonderful manner, touched and disconcerted me. I began to reason with him.

"These are your own copies we are about to examine. It is labor saving to you, because one examination will answer for your four papers. It is common usage. Every copyist is bound to help examine his copy. Is it not so? Will you not speak? Answer!"

"I prefer not to," he replied in a flute-like tone. It seemed to me that, while I had been addressing him, he carefully revolved every statement that I made; fully comprehended the meaning; I could not gainsay the irresistible conclusion; but, at the same time, some paramount consideration prevailed with him to reply as he did.

"You are decided, then, not to comply with my request—a request made according to common usage and common sense?"

He briefly gave me to understand, that on that point my judgment was sound. Yes: his decision was irreversible.

It is not seldom the case that, when a man is browbeaten in some unprecedented and violently unreasonable way, he begins to stagger in his own plainest faith. He begins, as it were, vaguely to surmise that, wonderful as it may be, all the justice and all the reason is on the other side. Accordingly, if any disinterested persons are present, he turns to them for some reinforcement for his own faltering mind.

"Turkey," said I, "what do you think of this? Am I not right?"

"With submission, sir," said Turkey, in his blandest tone, "I think that you are."

"Nippers," said I, "what do *you* think of it?"

"I think I should kick him out of the office."

(The reader of nice perceptions will have perceived that, it being morning, Turkey's answer is couched in polite and tranquil terms, but Nippers replies in ill-tempered ones. Or, to repeat a previous sentence, Nippers' ugly mood was on duty, and Turkey's off.)

"Ginger Nut," said I, willing to enlist the smallest suffrage in my behalf, "what do *you* think of it?"

"I think, sir, he's a little *luny*," Replied Ginger Nut, with a grin.

"You hear what they say," said I, turning towards the screen, "come forth and do your duty."

But he vouchsafed no reply. I pondered a moment in sore perplexity. But once more business hurried me. I determined again to postpone the consideration of this dilemma to my future leisure. With a little trouble we made out to examine the papers without Bartleby, though at every page or two Turkey deferentially dropped his opinion, that this proceeding was quite out of the common; while Nippers, twitching in his chair with a dyspeptic nervousness, ground out, between his set teeth, occasional hissing maledictions against the stubborn oaf behind the screen. And for his (Nippers') part, this was the first and the last time he would do another man's business without pay.

Meanwhile Bartleby sat in his hermitage, oblivious to everything but his own peculiar business there.

Some days passed, the scrivener being employed upon another lengthy work. His late remarkable conduct led me to regard his ways narrowly. I observed that he never went to dinner; indeed, that he never went anywhere. As yet I had never, of my personal knowledge, known him to be outside of my office. He was a perpetual sentry in the corner. At about eleven o'clock though, in the morning, I noticed that Ginger Nut would advance toward the opening in Bartleby's screen, as if silently beckoned thither by a gesture invisible to me where I sat. The boy would then leave the office, jingling a few pence, and reappear with a handful of ginger-nuts, which he delivered in the hermitage, receiving two of the cakes for his trouble.

He lives, then, on ginger-nuts, thought I; never eats a dinner, properly speaking; he must be a vegetarian, then, but no; he never eats even vegetables, he eats nothing but ginger-nuts. My mind then ran on in reveries concerning the probable effects upon the human constitution of living entirely on ginger-nuts. Ginger-nuts are so called, because they contain ginger as one of their peculiar constituents, and the final flavoring one. Now, what was ginger? A hot, spicy thing. Was Bartleby hot and spicy? Not at all. Ginger, then, had no effect upon Bartleby. Probably he preferred it should have none.

Nothing so aggravates an earnest person as a passive resistance. If the individual so resisted be of a not inhumane temper, and the resisting one perfectly harmless in his passivity, then, in the better moods of the former, he will endeavor charitably to construe to his imagination what proves impossible to be solved by his judgment. Even so, for the most part, I regarded Bartleby and his ways. Poor fellow! thought I, he means no mischief; it is plain he intends no insolence; his aspect sufficiently evinces that his eccentricities are involuntary. He is useful to me. I can get along with him. If I turn him away, the chances are he will fall in with some less indulgent employer, and then he will be rudely treated, and perhaps driven forth miserably to starve. Yes. Here I can cheaply purchase a delicious self-approval. To befriend Bartleby; to humor him in his strange wilfulness, will cost me little or nothing, while I lay up in my soul what will eventually prove a sweet morsel for my conscience. But this mood was not invariable with me. The passiveness of Bartleby sometimes irritated me. I felt strangely goaded on to encounter him in new opposition—to elicit some angry spark from him answerable to my own. But, indeed, I might as well have essayed to strike fire with my knuckles against a bit of Windsor soap. But one afternoon the evil impulse in me mastered me, and the following little scene ensued:

"Bartleby," said I, "when those papers are all copied, I will compare them with you."

"I would prefer not to."

"How? Surely you do not mean to persist in that mulish vagary?"

No answer.

I threw open the folding-doors nearby, and turning upon Turkey and Nippers, exclaimed:

"Bartleby a second time says, he won't examine his papers. What do you think of it, Turkey?"

It was afternoon, be it remembered. Turkey sat glowing like a brass boiler; his bald head steaming; his hands reeling among his blotted papers.

"Think of it?" roared Turkey. "I think I'll just step behind his screen, and black his eyes for him!"

So saying, Turkey rose to his feet and threw his arms into a pugilistic position. He was hurrying away to make good his promise, when I detained him, alarmed at the effect of incautiously rousing Turkey's combativeness after dinner.

"Sit down, Turkey," said I, "and hear what Nippers has to say. What do you think of it, Nippers? Would I not be justified in immediately dismissing Bartleby?"

"Excuse me, that is for you to decide, sir. I think his conduct quite unusual, and, indeed, unjust, as regards Turkey and myself. But it may only be a passing whim."

"Ah," exclaimed I, "you have strangely changed your mind, then—you speak very gently of him now."

"All beer," cried Turkey; "gentleness is effects of beer—Nippers and I dined together today. You see how gentle *I* am, sir. Shall I go and black his eyes?"

"You refer to Bartleby, I suppose. No, not today, Turkey," I replied; "pray, put up your fists."

I closed the doors, and again advanced towards Bartleby. I felt additional incentives tempting me to my fate. I burned to be rebelled against again. I remembered that Bartleby never left the office.

"Bartleby," said I, "Ginger Nut is away; just step around to the Post Office, won't you?" (it was but a three minutes' walk) "and see if there is anything for me."

"I would prefer not to."

"You *will* not?"

"I *prefer* not."

I staggered to my desk, and sat there in a deep study. My blind inveteracy returned. Was there any other thing in which I could procure myself to be ignominiously repulsed by this lean, penniless wight?—my hired clerk? What added thing is there, perfectly reasonable, that he will be sure to refuse to do?

"Bartleby!"

No answer.

"Bartleby," in a louder tone.

No answer.

"Bartleby," I roared.

Like a very ghost, agreeably to the laws of magical invocation, at the third summons, he appeared at the entrance of his hermitage.

"Go to the next room, and tell Nippers to come to me."

"I prefer not to," he respectfully and slowly said, and mildy disappeared.

"Very good, Bartleby," said I, in a quiet sort of serenely-severe self-possessed tone, intimating the unalterable purpose of some terrible retribution very close at hand. At the moment I half intended something of the kind. But upon the whole, as it was drawing towards my dinner-hour, I thought it best to put on my hat and walk home for the day, suffering much from perplexity and distress of mind.

Shall I acknowledge it? The conclusion of this whole business was, that it soon became a fixed fact of my chambers, that a pale young scrivener, by the name of Bartleby, had a desk there; that he copied for me at the usual rate of four cents a folio (one hundred words); but he was permanently exempt from examining the work done by him, that duty being transferred to Turkey and Nippers, out of compliment, doubtless, to their superior acuteness; moreover, said Bartleby was never, on any account, to be dispatched on the most trivial errand of any sort; and that even if entreated to take upon him such a matter, it was if entreated to take upon him such a matter, it was generally understood that he would "prefer not to"—in other words, that he would refuse point-blank.

As days passed on, I became considerably reconciled to Bartleby. His steadiness, his freedom from all dissipation, his incessant industry (except when he chose to throw himself into a standing revery behind his screen), his great stillness, his unalterableness of demeanor under all circumstances, made him a valuable acquisition. One prime thing was this—*he was always there*—first in the morning, continually through the day, and the last at night. I had a singular confidence in his honesty. I felt my most precious papers perfectly safe in his hands. Sometimes, to be sure, I could not, for the very soul of me, avoid falling into sudden spasmodic passions with him. For it was exceeding difficult to bear in mind all the time those strange peculiarities, privileges, and unheard-of exemptions, forming the tacit stipulations on Bartleby's part under which he remained in my office. Now and then, in the eagerness of dispatching pressing business, I would inadvertently summon Bartleby, in a short, rapid tone, to put his finger, say, on the incipient tie of a bit of red tape with which I was about compressing some papers. Of course, from behind the screen the usual answer, "I prefer not to," was sure to come; and then, how could a human creature, with the common infirmities of our nature, refrain from bitterly exclaiming upon such perverseness—such unreasonableness? However, every added repulse of this sort which I received only tended to lessen the probability of my repeating the inadvertence.

Here it must be said, that, according to the custom of most legal gentlemen occupying chambers in densely populated law buildings, there were several keys to my door. One was kept by a woman residing in the attic, which person weekly scrubbed and daily swept and dusted my apartments. Another was kept by Turkey for convenience sake. The third I sometimes carried in my own pocket. The fourth I knew not who had.

Now, one Sunday morning I happened to go to Trinity Church, to hear a celebrated preacher, and finding myself rather early on the ground I thought I would walk round to my chambers for a while. Luckily I had my key with me; but upon applying it to the lock, I found it resisted by something inserted from the inside. Quite surprised, I called out; when to my consternation a key was turned from within; and thrusting his lean visage at me, and holding the door ajar, the apparition of Bartleby appeared, in his shirt-sleeves, and otherwise in a strangely tattered *deshabille*, saying quietly that he was sorry, but he was deeply engaged just then, and—preferred not admitting me at present. In a brief word or two, he moreover added, that perhaps I had better walk round the block two or three times, and by that time he would probably have concluded his affairs.

Now, the utterly unsurmised appearance of Bartleby, tenanting my law-chambers of a Sunday morning, with his cadaverously gentlemanly *nonchalance*, yet withal firm and self-possessed, had such a strange effect upon me, that incontinently I slunk away from my own door, and did as desired. But not without sundry twinges of impotent rebellion against the mild effrontery of this unaccountable scrivener. Indeed, it was his wonderful mild-ness chiefly, which not only disarmed me, but unmanned me, as it were. For I consider that one, for the time, is a sort of unmanned when he tranquilly permits his hired clerk to dictate to him, and order him away from his own premises. Furthermore, I was full of uneasiness as to what Bartleby could possibly be doing in my office in his shirt-sleeves, and in an otherwise dismantled condition of a Sunday morning. Was anything amiss going on? Nay, that was out of the question. It was not to be thought of for a moment that Bartleby was an immoral person. But what could he be doing there?— copying? Nay again, whatever might be his eccentricities, Bartleby was an eminently decorous person. He would be the last man to sit down to his desk in any state approaching to nudity. Besides, it was Sunday; and there was something about Bartleby that forbade the supposition that he would by any secular occupation violate the proprieties of the day.

Nevertheless, my mind was not pacified; and full of a restless curiosity, at last I returned to the door. Without hindrance I inserted my key, opened it, and entered. Bartleby was not to be seen. I looked round anxiously, peeped behind his screen; but it was very plain that he was gone. Upon more closely examining the place, I surmised that for an indefinite period Bartleby must have ate, dressed, and slept in my office, and that too without plate, mirror, or bed. The cushioned seat of a rickety old sofa in one corner bore the faint impress of a lean, reclining form. Rolled away under his desk, I found a blanket; under the empty grate, a blacking box and brush; on a chair, a tin basin, with soap and a ragged towel; in a newspaper a few crumbs of ginger-nuts and a morsel of cheese. Yes, thought I, it is evident enough that Bartleby has been making his home here, keeping bachelor's hall all by himself. Immediately then the thought came sweeping across me, what miserable friendlessness and loneliness are here revealed! His poverty is great; but his solitude, how horrible! Think of it. Of a Sunday, Wall Street is deserted as Petra, and every night of every day it is an emptiness. This building, too, which of week-days hums with industry and life, at nightfall echoes with sheer vacancy, and all through Sunday is forlorn. And here Bartleby makes his home; sole spectator of a solitude which he has seen all populous—a sort of innocent and transformed Marius brooding among the ruins of Carthage!

For the first time in my life a feeling of overpowering stinging melancholy seized me. Before, I had never experienced aught but a not unpleasing sadness. The bond of a common humanity now drew me irresistibly to gloom. A fraternal melancholy! For both I and Bartleby were sons of Adam. I remembered the bright silks and sparkling faces I had seen that day, in gala trim, swan-like sailing down the Mississippi of Broadway; and I contrasted them with the pallid copyist, and thought to myself, Ah, happiness courts the light, so we deem the world is gay; but misery hides aloof, so we deem that misery there is none. These sad fancyings—chimeras, doubtless, of a sick and silly brain—led on to other and more special thoughts, concerning the eccentricities of Bartleby. Presentiments of strange discoveries hovered round me. The scrivener's pale form appeared to me laid out, among uncaring strangers, in its shivering winding-sheet.

Suddenly I was attracted by Bartleby's closed desk, the key in open-sight left in the lock.

I mean no mischief, seek the gratification of no heartless curiosity, thought I; besides, the desk is mine, and its contents, too, so I will make bold to look within. Everything was methodically arranged, the papers smoothly placed. The pigeon-holes were deep, and removing the files of documents, I groped into their recesses. Presently I felt something there, and dragged it out. It was an old bandanna handkerchief, heavy and knotted. I opened it, and saw it was a saving's bank.

I now recalled all the quiet mysteries which I had noted in the man. I remembered that he never spoke but to answer; that, though at intervals he had considerable time to himself, yet I had never seen him reading—no, not even a newspaper; that for long periods he would stand looking out, at his pale window behind the screen, upon the dead brick wall; I was quite sure he never visited any refectory or eating-house; while his pale face clearly indicated that he never drank beer like Turkey; or tea and coffee even, like other men; that he never went anywhere in particular that I could learn; never went out for a walk, unless, indeed, that was the case at present; that he had declined telling who he was, or whence he came, or whether he had any relatives in the world; that though so thin and pale, he never complained of ill-health. And more than all, I remembered a certain unconscious air of pallid—how shall I call it?—of pallid haughtiness, say, or rather an austere reserve about him, which has positively awed me into my tame compliance with his eccentricities, when I had feared to ask him to do the slightest incidental thing for me, even though I might know, from his long-continued motionlessness, that behind his screen he must be standing in one of those dead-wall reveries of his.

Revolving all these things, and coupling them with the recently discovered fact, that he made my office his constant abiding place and home, and not forgetful of his morbid moodiness; revolving all these things, a prudential feeling began to steal over me. My first emotions had been those of pure melancholy and sincerest pity; but just in proportion as the forlornness of Bartleby grew and grew to my imagination, did that same melancholy merge into fear, that pity into repulsion. So true it is, and so terrible, too, that up to a certain point the thought or sight of misery enlists our best affections; but, in certain special cases, beyond that point it does not. They err who would assert that invariably this is owing to the inherent selfishness of the human heart. It rather proceeds from a certain hopelessness of remedying excessive and organic ill. To a sensitive being, pity is not seldom pain. And when at last it is perceived that such pity cannot lead to effectual succor, common sense bids the soul be rid of it. What I saw that morning persuaded me that the scrivener was the victim of innate and incurable disorder. I might give alms to his body; but his body did not pain him; it was his soul that suffered, and his soul I could not reach.

I did not accomplish the purpose of going to Trinity Church that morning. Somehow, the things I had seen disqualified me for the time from church-going. I walked homeward, thinking what I would do with Bartleby. Finally, I resolved upon this—I would put certain calm questions to him the next morning, touching his history, etc., and if he declined to answer them openly and unreservedly (and I supposed he would prefer not), then to give him a twenty dollar bill over and above whatever I might owe him, and tell him his services were no longer required; but that if in any other way I could assist him, I would be happy to do so, especially if he desired to return to his native place, wherever that might be, I would willingly help to defray the expenses. Moreover, if, after reaching home, he found himself at any time in want of aid, a letter from him would be sure of a reply.

The next morning came.

"Bartleby," said I, gently calling to him behind his screen.

No reply.

"Bartleby," said I, in a still gentler tone, "come here; I am not going to ask you to do anything you would prefer not to do—I simply wish to speak to you."

Upon this he noiselessly slid into view.

"Will you tell me, Bartleby, where you were born?"

"I would prefer not to."

"Will you tell me *anything* about yourself?"

"I would prefer not to."

"But what reasonable objection can you have to speak to me? I feel friendly towards you."

He did not look at me while I spoke, but kept his glance fixed upon my bust of Cicero, which, as I then sat, was directly behind me, some six inches above my head.

"What is your answer, Bartleby?" said I, after waiting a considerable time for a reply, during which his countenance remained immovable, only there was the faintest conceivable tremor of the white attenuated mouth.

"At present I prefer to give no answer," he said, and retired into his hermitage.

It was rather weak in me I confess, but his manner, on this occasion, nettled me. Not only did there seem to lurk in it a certain calm disdain, but his perverseness seemed ungrateful, considering the undeniable good usage and indulgence he had received from me.

Again I sat ruminating what I should do. Mortified as I was at his behavior, and resolved as I had been to dismiss him when I entered my office, nevertheless I strangely felt something superstitious knocking at my heart, and forbidding me to carry out my purpose, and denouncing me for a villain if I dared to breathe one bitter word against this forlornest of mankind. At last, familiarly drawing my chair behind his screen, I sat down and said: "Bartleby, never mind, then, about revealing your history; but let me entreat you, as a friend, to comply as far as may be with the usages of this office. Say now, you will help to examine papers tomorrow or next day: in short, say now, that in a day or two you will begin to be a little reasonable:—say so, Bartleby."

"At present I would prefer not to be a little reasonable," was his mildly cadaverous reply.

Just then the folding-doors opened, and Nippers approached. He seemed suffering from an unusually bad night's rest, induced by severer indigestion than common. He overheard those final words of Bartleby.

"*Prefer not*, eh?" gritted Nippers— "I'd *prefer* him, if I were you, sir," addressing me— "I'd *prefer* him; I'd give him preferences, the stubborn mule! What is it, sir, pray, that he *prefers* not to do now?"

Bartleby moved not a limb.

"Mr. Nippers," said I, "I'd prefer that you would withdraw for the present."

Somehow, of late, I had got into the way of involuntarily using this word "prefer" upon all sorts of not exactly suitable occasions. And I trembled to think that my contact with the scrivener had already and seriously affected me in a mental way. And what further and deeper aberration might it not yet produce? This apprehension had not been without efficacy in determining me to summary measures.

As Nippers, looking very sour and sulky, was departing, Turkey blandly and deferentially approached.

"With submission, sir," said he, "yesterday I was thinking about Bartleby here, and I think that if he would but prefer to take a quart of good ale every day, it would do much towards mending him, and enabling him to assist in examining his papers."

"So you have got the word, too," said I, slightly excited.

"With submission, what word, sir?" asked Turkey, respectfully crowding himself into the contracted space behind the screen, and by so doing, making me jostle the scrivener. "What word, sir?"

"I would prefer to be left alone here," said Bartleby, as if offended at being mobbed in his privacy.

"*That's* the word, Turkey,." said I— "*that's* it."

"Oh, *prefer*? oh yes—queer word. I never use it myself. But, sir, as I was saying, if he would but prefer—"

"Turkey," interrupted I, "you will please withdraw."

"Oh certainly, sir, if you prefer that I should."

As he opened the folding-door to retire, Nippers at his desk caught a glimpse of me, and asked whether I would prefer to have a certain paper copied on blue paper or white. He did not in the least roguishly accent the word "prefer." It was plain that it involuntarily rolled from his tongue. I thought to myself, surely I must get rid of a demented man, who already has in some degree turned the tongues, if not the heads of myself and clerks. But I thought it prudent not to break the dismission at once.

The next day I noticed that Bartleby did nothing but stand at his window in his dead-wall revery. Upon asking him why he did not write, he said that he had decided upon doing no more writing.

"Why, how now? what next?" exclaimed I, "do no more writing?"

"No more."

"And what is the reason?"

"Do you not see the reason for yourself?" he indifferently replied.

I looked steadfastly at him, and perceived that his eyes looked dull and glazed. Instantly it occurred to me, that his unexampled diligence in copying by his dim window for the first few weeks of his stay with me might have temporarily impaired his vision.

I was touched. I said something in condolence with him. I hinted that of course he did wisely in abstaining from writing for a while; and urged him to embrace that opportunity of taking wholesome exercise in the open air. This, however, he did not do. A few days after this, my other clerks being absent, and being in a great hurry to dispatch certain letters by the mail, I thought that, having nothing else earthly to do, Bartleby would surely be less inflexible than usual, and carry these letters to the Post Office. But he blankly declined. So, much to my inconvenience, I went myself.

Still added days went by. Whether Bartleby's eyes improved or not, I could not say. To all appearance, I thought they did. But when I asked him if they did, he vouchsafed no answer. At all events, he would do no copying. At last, in replying to my urgings, he informed me that he had permanently given up copying.

"What!" exclaimed I; "suppose your eyes should get entirely well—better than ever before—would you not copy then?"

"I have given up copying," he answered, and slid aside.

He remained as ever, a fixture in my chamber. Nay—if that were possible—he became still more of a fixture than before. What was to be done? He would do nothing in the office; why should he stay there? In plain fact, he had now become a millstone to me, not only useless as a necklace, but afflictive to bear. Yet I was sorry for him. I speak less than truth when I say that, on his own account, he occasioned me uneasiness. If he would but have named a single relative or friend, I would instantly have written, and urged their taking the poor fellow away to some convenient retreat. But he seemed alone, absolutely alone in the universe. A bit of wreck in the mid-Atlantic. At length, necessities connected with my business tyrannized over all other considerations. Decently as I could, I told Bartleby that in six days' time he must unconditionally leave the office. I warned him to take measures, in the interval, for procuring some other abode. I offered to assist him in this endeavor, if he himself would but take the first step towards a removal. "And when you finally quit me, Bartleby," added I, "I shall see that you go not away entirely unprovided. Six days from this hour, remember."

At the expiration of that period, I peeped behind the screen, and lo! Bartleby was there.

I buttoned up my coat, balanced myself; advanced slowly towards him, touched his shoulder, and said, "The time has come; you must quit this place; I am sorry for you; here is money; but you must go."

"I would prefer not," he replied, with his back still towards me.

"You *must*."

He remained silent.

Now I had an unbounded confidence in this man's common honesty. He had frequently restored to me sixpences and shillings carelessly dropped upon the floor, for I am apt to be very reckless in such shirt-button affairs. The proceeding, then, which followed will not be deemed extraordinary.

"Bartleby," said I, "I owe you twelve dollars on account; here are thirty-two; the odd twenty are yours— Will you take it?" and I handed the bills towards him.

But he made no motion.

"I will leave them here, then," putting them under a weight on the table. Then taking my hat and cane and going to the door, I tranquilly turned and added— "After you have removed your things from these offices, Bartleby, you will of course lock the door—since every one is now gone for the day but you—and if you please, slip your key underneath the mat, so that I may have it in the morning. I shall not see you again; so good-bye to you, do not fail to advise me by letter. Good-bye, Bartleby, and fare you well."

But he answered not a word; like the last column of some ruined temple, he remained standing mute and solitary in the middle of the otherwise deserted room.

As I walked home in a pensive mood, my vanity got the better of my pity. I could not but highly plume myself on my masterly management in getting rid of Bartleby. Masterly I call it, and such it must appear to any dispassionate thinker. The beauty of my procedure seemed to consist in its perfect quietness. There was no vulgar bullying, no bravado of any sort, no choleric hectoring, and striding to and fro across the apartment, jerking out vehement commands for Bartleby to bundle himself off with his beggarly traps. Nothing of the kind. Without loudly bidding Bartleby depart—as an inferior genius might have done—I *assumed* the ground that depart he must; and upon that assumption built all I had to say. The more I thought over my procedure, the more I was charmed with it. Nevertheless, next morning, upon awakening, I had my doubts—I had somehow slept off the fumes of vanity. One of the coolest and wisest hours a man has, is just after he awakes in the morning. My procedure seemed as sagacious as ever—but only in theory. How it would prove in practice—there was the rub. It was truly a beautiful thought to have assumed Bartleby's departure; but, after all, that assumption was simply my own, and none of Bartleby's. The great point was, not whether I had assumed that he would quit me, but whether he would prefer to do so. He was more a man of preferences than assumptions.

After breakfast, I walked down town, arguing the probabilities *pro* and *con*. One moment I thought it would prove a miserable failure, and Bartleby would be found all alive at my office as usual; the next moment it seemed certain that I should find his chair empty. And so I kept veering about. At the corner of Broadway and Canal Street, I saw quite an excited group of people standing in earnest conversation.

"I'll take odds he doesn't," said a voice as I passed.

"Doesn't go? —done!" said I, "put up your money."

I was instinctively putting my hand in my pocket to produce my own, when I remembered that this was an election day. The words I had overheard bore no reference to Bartleby, but to the success or non-success of some candidate for the mayoralty. In my intent frame of mind, I had, as it were, imagined that all Broadway shared in my excitement, and were debating the same question with me. I passed on, very thankful that the uproar of the street screened my momentary absent-mindedness.

As I had intended, I was earlier than usual at my office door. I stood listening for a moment. All was still. He must be gone. I tried the knob. The door was locked. Yes, my procedure had worked to a charm; he indeed must be vanished. Yet a certain melancholy mixed with this: I was almost sorry for my brilliant success. I was fumbling under the door mat for the key, which Bartleby was to have left there for me, when accidentally my knee knocked against a panel, producing a summoning sound, and in response a voice came to me from within— "Not yet; I am occupied."

It was Bartleby.

I was thunderstruck. For an instant I stood like the man who, pipe in mouth, was killed one cloudless afternoon long ago in Virginia, by summer lightning; at his own warm open window he was killed, and remained leaning out there upon the dreamy afternoon, till some one touched him, when he fell.

"Not gone!" I murmured at last. But again obeying that wondrous ascendancy which the inscrutable scrivener had over me, and from which ascendancy, for all my chafing, I could not completely escape, I slowly went down stairs and out into the street, and while walking round the block, considered what I should next do in this unheard-of perplexity. Turn the man out by an actual thrusting I could not; to drive him away by calling him hard names would not do; calling in the police was an unpleasant idea; and yet, permit him to enjoy his cadaverous triumph over me—this, too, I could not think of. What was to be done? or, if nothing could be done, was there anything further that I could *assume* in the matter? Yes, as before I had prospectively assumed that Bartleby would depart, so now I might retrospectively assume that departed he was. In the legitimate carrying out of this assumption, I might enter my office in a great hurry, and pretending not to see Bartleby at all, walk straight against him as if he were air. Such a proceeding would in a singular degree have the appearance of a home-thrust. It was hardly possible that Bartleby could withstand such an application of the doctrine of assumption. But upon second thoughts the success of the plan seemed rather dubious. I resolved to argue the matter over with him again.

"Bartleby," said I, entering the office, with a quietly severe expression, "I am seriously displeased. I am pained, Bartleby. I had thought better of you. I had imagined you of such a gentlemanly organization, that in any delicate dilemma a slight hint would suffice—in short, an assumption. But it appears I am deceived. Why," I added, unaffectedly starting, "you have not even touched that money yet," pointing to it, just where I had left it the evening previous.

He answered nothing.

"Will you, or will you not, quit me?" I now demanded in a sudden passion, advancing close to him.

"I would prefer *not* to quit you," he replied, gently emphasizing the *not*.

"What earthly right have you to stay here? Do you pay any rent? Do you pay my taxes? Or is this property yours?"

He answered nothing.

"Are you ready to go on and write now? Are your eyes recovered? Could you copy a small paper for me this morning? or help examine a few lines? or step round to the Post Office? In a word, will you do anything at all, to give a coloring to your refusal to depart the premises?"

He silently retired into his hermitage.

I was now in such a state of nervous resentment that I thought it but prudent to check myself at present from further demonstrations. Bartleby and I were alone. I remembered the tragedy of the unfortunate Adams and the still more unfortunate Colt in the solitary office of the latter; and how poor Colt, being dreadfully incensed by Adams and imprudently permitting himself to get wildly excited, was at unawares hurried into his fatal act—an act which certainly no man could possibly deplore more than the actor himself. Often it had occurred to me in my ponderings upon the subject that had that altercation taken place in the public street, or at a private residence, it would not have terminated as it did. It was the circumstance of being alone in a solitary office, up stairs, of a building entirely unhallowed by humanizing domestic associations—an uncarpeted office, doubtless, of a dusty, haggard sort of appearance—this it must have been, which greatly helped to enhance the irritable desperation of the hapless Colt.

But when this old Adam of resentment rose in me and tempted me concerning Bartleby, I grappled him and threw him. How? Why, simply by recalling the divine injunction: "A new commandment give I unto you, that ye love one another." Yes, this it was that saved me. Aside from higher

considerations, charity often operates as a vastly wise and prudent principle—a great safeguard to its possessor. Men have committed murder for
jealousy's sake, and anger's sake, and hatred's sake, and selfishness' sake,
and spiritual pride's sake; but no man, that ever I heard of, ever committed
a diabolical murder for sweet charity's sake. Mere self-interest, then, if no
better motive can be enlisted, should, especially with high-tempered men,
prompt all beings to charity and philanthropy. At any rate, upon the occasion in question, I strove to drown my exasperated feelings towards the
scrivener by benevolently construing his conduct. Poor fellow, poor fellow!
thought I, he don't mean anything; and besides, he has seen hard times,
and ought to be indulged.

I endeavored, also, immediately to occupy myself, and at the same time
to comfort my despondency. I tried to fancy, that in the course of the morning, at such time as might prove agreeable to him, Bartleby, of his own free
accord, would emerge from his hermitage and take up some decided line of
march in the direction of the door. But no. Half-past twelve o'clock came;
Turkey began to glow in the face, overturn his inkstand, and become generally obstreperous; Nippers abated down into quietude and courtesy; Ginger Nut munched his noon apple; and Bartleby remained standing at his
window in one of his profoundest dead-wall reveries. Will it be credited?
Ought I to acknowledge it? That afternoon I left the office without saying
one further word to him.

Some days now passed, during which, at leisure intervals I looked a
little into "Edwards on the Will," and "Priestley on Necessity." Under the
circumstances, those books induced a salutary feeling. Gradually I slid into
the persuasion that these troubles of mine, touching the scrivener, had been
all predestined from eternity, and Bartleby was billeted upon me for some
mysterious purpose of an all-wise Providence, which it was not for a mere
mortal like me to fathom. Yes, Bartleby, stay there behind your screen,
thought I; I shall persecute you no more; you are harmless and noiseless as
any of these old chairs; in short, I never feel so private as when I know you
are here. At last I see it, I feel it; I penetrate to the predestined purpose of
my life. I am content. Others may have loftier parts to enact; but my mission in this world, Bartleby, is to furnish you with office-room for such
period as you may see fit to remain.

I believe that this wise and blessed frame of mind would have continued with me, had it not been for the unsolicited and uncharitable remarks
obtruded upon me by my professional friends who visited the rooms. But
thus it often is, that the constant friction of illiberal minds wears out at last
the best resolves of the more generous. Though to be sure, when I reflected
upon it, it was not strange that people entering my office should be struck
by the peculiar aspect of the unaccountable Bartleby, and so be tempted to
throw out some sinister observations concerning him. Sometimes an attorney, having business with me, and calling at my office, and finding no one

but the scrivener there, would undertake to obtain some sort of precise information from him touching my whereabouts; but without heeding his idle talk, Bartleby would remain standing immovable in the middle of the room. So after contemplating him in that position for a time, the attorney would depart, no wiser than he came.

Also, when a reference was going on, and the room full of lawyers and witnesses, and business driving fast, some deeply-occupied legal gentleman present, seeing Bartleby wholly unemployed, would request him to run round to his (the legal gentleman's) office and fetch some papers for him. Thereupon, Bartleby would tranquilly decline, and yet remain idle as before. Then the lawyer would give a great stare, and turn to me. And what could I say? At last I was made aware that all through the circle of my professional acquaintance, a whisper of wonder was running round, having reference to the strange creature I kept at my office. This worried me very much. And as the idea came upon me of his possibly turning out a long-lived man, and keeping occupying my chambers, and denying my authority; and perplexing my visitors; and scandalizing my professional reputation; and casting a general gloom over the premises; keeping soul and body together to the last upon his savings (for doubtless he spent but half a dime a day), and in the end perhaps outlive me, and claim possession of my office by right of his perpetual occupancy: as all these dark anticipations crowded upon me more and more, and my friends continually intruded their relentless remarks upon the apparition in my room; a great change was wrought in me. I resolved to gather all my faculties together, and forever rid me of this intolerable incubus.

Ere revolving any complicated project, however, adapted to this end, I first simply suggested to Bartleby the propriety of his permanent departure. In a calm and serious tone, I commended the idea to his careful and mature consideration. But, having taken three days to meditate upon it, he apprised me, that his original determination remained the same; in short, that he still preferred to abide with me.

What shall I do? I now said to myself, buttoning up my coat to the last button. What shall I do? what ought I to do? what does conscience say I *should* do with this man, or, rather, ghost. Rid myself of him, I must; go, he shall. But how? You will not thrust him, the poor, pale, passive mortal—you will not thrust such a helpless creature out of your door? you will not dishonor yourself by such cruelty? No, I will not, I cannot do that. Rather would I let him live and die here, and then mason up his remains in the wall. What, then, will you do? For all your coaxing, he will not budge. Bribes he leaves under your own paper-weight on your table; in short, it is quite plain that he prefers to cling to you.

Then something severe, something unusual must be done. What! Surely you will not have him collared by a constable, and commit his innocent pallor to the common jail? And upon what ground could you procure such a thing to be done? —a vagrant, is he? What! he a vagrant, a wanderer, who refuses to budge? It is because he will *not* be a vagrant, then, that you seek to count him *as* a vagrant. That is too absurd. No visible means of support: there I have him. Wrong again: for indubitably he *does* support himself, and that is the only unanswerable proof that any man can show of his possessing the means so to do. No more, then. Since he will not quit me, I must quit him. I will change my offices; I will move elsewhere, and give him fair notice, that if I find him on my new premises I will then proceed against him as a common trespasser.

Acting accordingly, next day I thus addressed him: "I find these chambers too far from the City Hall; the air is unwholesome. In a word, I propose to remove my offices next week, and shall no longer require your services. I tell you this now, in order that you may seek another place."

He made no reply, and nothing more was said.

On the appointed day I engaged carts and men, proceeded to my chambers, and, having but little furniture, everything was removed in a few hours. Throughout, the scrivener remained standing behind the screen, which I directed to be removed the last thing. It was withdrawn; and, being folded up like a huge folio, left him the motionless occupant of a naked room. I stood in the entry watching him a moment, while something from within me unbraided me.

I re-entered, with my hand in my pocket—and—and my heart in my mouth.

"Good-bye, Bartleby; I am going—good-bye, and God some way bless you; and take that," slipping something in his hand. But it dropped upon the floor, and then—strange to say—I tore myself from him whom I had so longed to be rid of.

Established in my new quarters, for a day or two I kept the door locked, and started at every footfall in the passages. When I returned to my rooms, after any little absence, I would pause at the threshold for an instant, and attentively listen, ere applying my key. But these fears were needless. Bartleby never came nigh me.

I thought all was going well, when a perturbed-looking stranger visited me, inquiring whether I was the person who had recently occupied rooms at No. — Wall Stret.

Full of forebodings, I replied that I was.

"Then, sir," said the stranger who proved a lawyer, "you are responsible for the man you left there. He refuses to do any copying; he refuses to do anything; he says he prefers not to; and he refuses to quit the premises."

"I am very sorry, sir," said I, with assumed tranquillity, but an inward tremor, "but, really, the man you allude to is nothing to me—he is no relation or apprentice of mine, that you should hold me responsible for him."

"In mercy's name, who is he?"

"I certainly cannot inform you. I know nothing about him. Formerly I employed him as a copyist; but he has done nothing for me now for some time past."

"I shall settle him, then—good morning, sir."

Several days passed, and I heard nothing more; and, though I often felt a charitable prompting to call at the place and see poor Bartleby, yet a certain squeamishness, of I know not what, withheld me.

All is over with him, by this time, thought I, at last, when, through another week, no further intelligence reached me. But, coming to my room the day after, I found several persons waiting at my door in a high state of nervous excitement.

"That's the man—here he comes," cried the foremost one, whom I recognized as the lawyer who had previously called upon me alone.

"You must take him away, sir, at once," cried a portly person among them, advancing upon me, and whom I knew to be the landlord of No. — Wall Street. "These gentlemen, my tenants, cannot stand it any longer; Mr. B——," pointing to the lawyer, "has turned him out of his room, and he now persists in haunting the building generally, sitting upon the banisters of the stairs by day, and sleeping in the entry by night. Everybody is concerned; clients are leaving the offices; some fears are entertained of a mob; something you must do, and that without delay."

Aghast at this torrent, I fell back before it, and would fain have locked myself in my new quarters. In vain I persisted that Bartleby was nothing to me—no more than to any one else. In vain—I was the last person known to have anything to do with him, and they held me to the terrible account. Fearful, then of being exposed in the papers (as one person present obscurely threatened), I considered the matter, and, at length, said, that if the lawyer would give me a confidential interview with the scrivener, in his (the lawyer's) own room, I would, that afternoon, strive my best to rid them of the nuisance they complained of.

Going up stairs to my old haunt, there was Bartleby silently sitting upon the banister at the landing.

"What are you doing here, Bartleby?" said I.

"Sitting upon the banister," he mildly replied.

I motioned him into the lawyer's room, who then left us.

"Bartleby," said I, "are you aware that you are the cause of great tribulation to me, by persisting in occupying the entry after being dismissed from the office?"

No answer.

"Now one of two things must take place. Either you must do something, or something must be done to you. Now what sort of business would you like to engage in? Would you like to re-engage in copying for someone?"

"No; I would prefer not to make any change."

"Would you like a clerkship in a dry-goods store?"

"There is too much confinement about that. No, I would not like a clerkship; but I am not particular."

"Too much confinement," I cried, "why, you keep yourself confined all the time!"

"I would prefer not to take a clerkship," he rejoined, as if to settle that little item at once.

"How would a bar-tender's business suit you? There is no trying of the eye-sight in that."

"I would not like it at all; though, as I said before, I am not particular."

His unwonted wordiness inspirited me. I returned to the charge.

"Well, then, would you like to travel through the country collecting bills for the merchants? That would improve your health."

"No, I would prefer to be doing something else."

"How, then, would going as a companion to Europe, to entertain some young gentleman with your conversation—how would that suit you?"

"Not at all. It does not strike me that there is anything definite about that. I like to be stationary. But I am not particular."

"Stationary you shall be, then," I cried, now losing all patience, and, for the first time in all my exasperating connection with him, fairly flying into a passion. "If you do not *go* away from these premises before night, I shall feel bound—indeed, I *am* bound—to—to—to quit the premises myself!" I rather absurdly concluded, knowing not with what possible threat to try to frighten his immobility into compliance. Despairing of all further efforts, I was precipitately leaving him, when a final thought occurred to me—one which had not been wholly unindulged before.

"Bartleby," said I, in the kindest tone I could assume under such exciting circumstances, "will you go home with me now—not to my office, but my dwelling—and remain there till we can conclude upon some convenient arrangement for you at our leisure? Come, let us start now, right away."

"No: at present I would prefer not to make any change at all."

I answered nothing; but, effectually dodging every one by the suddenness and rapidity of my flight, rushed from the building, ran up Wall Street towards Broadway, and, jumping into the first omnibus, was soon removed from pursuit. As soon as tranquility returned, I distinctly perceived that I had now done all that I possibly could, both in respect to the demands of the landlord and his tenants, and with regard to my own desire and sense of duty, to benefit Bartleby, and shield him from rude persecution. I now strove to be entirely care-free and quiescent; and my conscience justified me in the attempt; though, indeed, it was not so successful as I could have wished. So fearful was I of being again hunted out by the incensed landlord and his exasperated tenants, that, surrendering my business to Nippers, for a few days, I drove about the upper part of the town and through the suburbs, in my rockaway; crossed over to Jersey City and Hoboken, and paid fugitive visits to Manhattanville and Astoria. In fact, I almost lived in my rockaway for the time.

When again I entered my office, lo, a note from the landlord lay upon the desk. I opened it with trembling hands. It informed me that the writer had sent to the police, and had Bartleby removed to the Tombs as a vagrant. Moreover, since I knew more about him than any one else, he wished me to appear at that place, and make a suitable statement of the facts. These tidings had a conflicting effect upon me. At first I was indignant; but, at last, almost approved. The landlord's energetic, summary disposition, had led him to adopt a procedure which I do not think I would have decided upon myself; and yet, as a last resort, under such peculiar circumstances, it seemed the only plan.

As I afterwards learned, the poor scrivener, when told that he must be conducted to the Tombs, offered not the slightest obstacle, but, in his pale, unmoving way, silently acquiesced.

Some of the compassionate and curious by-standers joined the party; and headed by one of the constables arm-in-arm with Bartleby, the silent procession filed its way through all the noise, and heat, and joy of the roaring thoroughfares at noon.

The same day I received the note, I went to the Tombs, or, to speak more properly, the Halls of Justice. Seeking the right officer, I stated the purpose of my call, and was informed that the individual I described was, indeed, within. I then assured the functionary that Bartleby was a perfectly honest man, and greatly to be compassionated, however unaccountably eccentric. I narrated all I knew, and closed by suggesting the idea of letting him remain in as indulgent confinement as possible, till something less harsh might be done—though, indeed, I hardly knew what. At all events, if nothing else could be decided upon, the alms-house must receive him. I then begged to have an interview.

Being under no disgraceful charge, and quite serene and harmless in all his ways, they had permitted him freely to wander about the prison, and, especially, in the inclosed grass-platted yards thereof. And so I found him there, standing all alone in the quietest of the yards, his face towards a high wall, while all around, from the narrow slits of the jail windows, I thought I saw peering out upon him the eyes of murderers and thieves.

"Bartleby!"

"I know you," he said, without looking round—"and I want nothing to say to you."

"It was not I that brought you here, Bartleby," said I, keenly pained at him implied suspicion. "And to you, this should not be so vile a place. Nothing reproachful attaches to you by being here. And see, it is not so sad a place as one might think. Look, there is the sky, and here is the grass."

"I know where I am," he replied, but would say nothing more, and so I left him.

As I entered the corridor again, a broad meat-like man, in an apron, accosted me, and, jerking his thumb over his shoulder, said— "Is that your friend?"

"Yes."

"Does he want to starve? If he does, let him live on the prison fare, that's all."

"Who are you?" asked I, not knowing what to make of such an unofficially speaking person in such a place.

"I am the grub-man. Such gentlemen as have friends here, hire me to provide them with something good to eat."

"Is this so?" said I, turning to the turnkey.

He said it was.

"Well, then," said I, slipping some silver into the grub-man's hands (for so they called him), "I want you to give particular attention to my friend there; let him have the best dinner you can get. And you must be as polite to him as possible.'"

"Introduce me, will you?" said the grub-man, looking at me with an expression which seemed to say he was all impatience for an opportunity to give a specimen of his breeding.

Thinking it would prove of benefit to the scrivener, I acquiesced; and, asking the grub-man his name, went up with him to Bartleby.

"Bartleby, this is a friend; you will find him very useful to you."

"Your sarvant, sir, your sarvant," said the grub-man, making a low salutation behind his apron. "Hope you find it pleasant here, sir; nice grounds—cool apartments—hope you'll stay with us some time—try to make it agreeable. What will you have for dinner to-day?"

"I prefer not to dine to-day," said Bartleby, turning away. "It would disagree with me; I am unused to dinners." So saying, he slowly moved to the other side of the inclosure, and took up a position fronting the dead-wall.

"How's this?" said the grub-man, addressing me with a stare of astonishment. "He's odd, ain't he?"

"I think he is a little deranged," said I, sadly.

"Deranged? deranged is it? Well, now, upon my word, I thought that friend of yourn was a gentleman forger; they are always pale and genteel-like, them forgers. I can't help pity 'em—can't help it, sir. Did you know Monroe Edwards?" he added, touchingly, and paused. Then, laying his hand piteously on my shoulder, sighed, "he died of consumption at Sing-Sing. So you weren't acquainted with Monroe?"

"No, I was never socially acquainted with any forgers. But I cannot stop longer. Look to my friend yonder. You will not lose by it. I will see you again."

Some few days after this, I again obtained admission to the Tombs, and went through the corridors in quest of Bartleby; but without finding him.

"I saw him coming from his cell not long ago," said a turnkey, "may be he's gone to loiter in the yards."

So I went in that direction.

"Are you looking for the silent man?" said another turnkey, passing me. "Yonder he lies—sleeping in the yard there. 'Tis not twenty minutes since I saw him lie down."

The yard was entirely quiet. It was not accessible to the common prisoners. The surrounding walls, of amazing thickness, kept off all sounds behind them. The Egyptian character of the masonry weighed upon me with its gloom. But a soft imprisoned turf grew under foot. The heart of the eternal pyramids, it seemed, wherein, by some strange magic, through the clefts, grass-seed, dropped by birds, had sprung.

Strangely huddled at the base of the wall, his knees drawn up, and lying on his side, his head touching the cold stones, I saw the wasted Bartleby. But nothing stirred. I paused; then went close up to him; stooped over, and saw that his dim eyes were open; otherwise he seemed profoundly sleeping. Something prompted me to touch him. I felt his hand, when a tingling shiver ran up my arm and down my spine to my feet.

The round face of the grub-man peered upon me now. "His dinner is ready. Won't he dine to-day, either? Or does he live without dining?"

"Lives without dining," said I, and closed the eyes.

"Eh! — He's asleep, ain't he?"

"With kings and counselors," murmured I.

There would seem little need for proceeding further in this history. Imagination will readily supply the meagre recital of poor Bartleby's interment. But, ere parting with the reader, let me say, that if this little narrative has sufficiently interested him, to awaken curiosity as to who Bartleby was, and what manner of life he led prior to the present narrator's making his acquaintance, I can only reply, that in such curiosity I fully share, but am wholly unable to gratify it. Yet here I hardly know whether I should divulge one little item of rumor, which came to my ear a few months after the scriverer's decease. Upon what basis it rested, I could never ascertain; and hence, how true it is I cannot now tell. But, inasmuch as this vague report has not been without a certain suggestive interest to me, however sad, it may prove the same with some others; and so I will briefly mention it. The report was this: that Bartleby had been a subordinate clerk in the Dead Letter Office at Washington, from which he had been suddenly removed by a change in the administration. When I think over this rumor, hardly can I express the emotions which seize me. Dead letters! does it not sound like dead men? Conceive a man by nature and misfortune prone to a pallid hopelessness, can any business seem more fitted to heighten it than that of continually handling these dead letters, and assorting them for the flames? For by the cart-load they are annually burned. Sometimes from out the folded paper the pale clerk takes a ring—the finger it was meant for, perhaps, moulders in the grave; a bank-note sent in swiftest charity—he whom it would relieve, nor eats nor hungers any more; pardon for those who died despairing; hope for those who died unhoping; good tidings for those who died stifled by unrelieved calamities. On errands of life, these letters speed to death.

Ah, Bartleby! Ah, humanity!

QUESTIONS

1. Locate passages in "Bartleby the Scrivener" where the narrator seems to justify his treatment of Bartleby. How do such passages affect your perception of the story? You may also consider whether the narrator may, at times, be distorting the truth.

2. Wall Street is the setting for "Bartleby." What does this setting at the heart of American commerce, along with Melville's use of interior walls and partitions, imply about the nature of American business or organizational life? In this respect, compare the story to James Joyce's "Counterparts" (page 132).

3. Consider the narrator's treatment of his three other subordinates: Turkey, Nippers, and Ginger Nut. Why is their behavior less objectionable to him than Bartleby's?

4. What is the apparent meaning of the last line of the story?

5. How would "Bartleby" be changed—what effects would be gained or lost—if it were told in the third person by an omniscient narrator?

DORIS LESSING (b. 1919)

A Woman on a Roof

Doris Lessing was born in Persia (Iran), grew up in Rhodesia, and finally settled in London. Like many writers of her generation, she was for a time affiliated with the Communist party, but broke from it in disillusionment. Famous for her studies of the political, social, and sexual complexities of twentieth century life, she is best known for her novels, which include the tetralogy *Children of Violence* (1952–1969) and *The Golden Notebook* (1962). "A Woman on a Roof" first appeared in 1963.

It was during the week of hot sun, that June.

Three men were at work on the roof, where the leads got so hot they had the idea of throwing water on to cool them. But the water steamed, then sizzled; and they made jokes about getting an egg from some woman in the flats under them, to poach it for their dinner. By two it was not possible to touch the guttering they were replacing, and they speculated about what workmen did in regularly hot countries. Perhaps they should borrow kitchen gloves with the egg? They were all a bit dizzy, not used to the heat; and they shed their coats and stood side by side squeezing themselves into a foot-wide patch of shade against a chimney, careful to keep their feet in the thick socks and boots out of the sun. There was a fine view across several acres of roofs. Not far off a man sat in a deck chair reading the newspapers. Then they saw her, between chimneys, about fifty yards away. She lay face down on a brown blanket. They could see the top part of her: black hair, a flushed solid back, arms spread out.

"She's stark naked," said Stanley, sounding annoyed.

Harry, the oldest, a man of about forty-five, said: "Looks like it."

Young Tom, seventeen, said nothing, but he was excited and grinning.

Stanley said: "Someone'll report her if she doesn't watch out."

"She thinks no one can see," said Tom, craning his head all ways to see more.

At this point the woman, still lying prone, brought her two hands up behind her shoulders with the ends of a scarf in them, tied it behind her back, and sat up. She wore a red scarf tied around her breasts and brief red bikini pants. This being the first day of the sun she was white, flushing red. She sat smoking, and did not look up when Stanley let out a wolf whistle. Harry said: "Small things amuse small minds," leading the way back to their part of the roof, but it was scorching. Harry said: "Wait, I'm going to rig up some shade," and disappeared down the skylight into the building. Now that he'd gone, Stanley and Tom went to the farthest point they could to peer at the woman. She had moved, and all they could see were two pink legs stretched on the blanket. They whistled and shouted but the legs did not move. Harry came back with a blanket and shouted: "Come on, then." He sounded irritated with them. They clambered back to him and he said to Stanley: "What about your missus?" Stanley was newly married, about three months. Stanley said, jeering: "What about my missus?" —preserving his independence. Tom said nothing, but his mind was full of the nearly naked woman. Harry slung the blanket, which he had borrowed from a friendly woman downstairs, from the stem of a television aerial to a row of chimney pots. This shade fell across the piece of gutter they had to replace. But the shade kept moving, they had to adjust the blanket, and not much progress was made. At last some of the heat left the roof, and they worked fast, making up for lost time. First Stanley, then Tom, made a trip to the end of the roof to see the woman. "She's on her back," Stanley said, adding a jest which made Tom snicker, and the older man smile tolerantly. Tom's report was that she hadn't moved, but it was a lie. He wanted to keep what he had seen to himself: he had caught her in the act of rolling down the little red pants over her hips, till they were no more than a small triangle. She was on her back, fully visible, glistening with oil.

Next morning, as soon as they came up, they went to look. She was already there, face down, arms spread out, naked except for the little red pants. She had turned brown in the night. Yesterday she was a scarlet and white woman, today she was a brown woman. Stanley let out a whistle. She lifted her head, startled, as if she'd been asleep, and looked straight over at them. The sun was in her eyes, she blinked and stared, then she dropped her head again. At this gesture of indifference, they all three, Stanley, Tom, and old Harry, let out whistles and yells. Harry was doing it in parody of the younger men, making fun of them, but he was also angry. They were all angry because of her utter indifference to the three men watching her.

"Bitch," said Stanley.

"She should ask us over," said Tom, snickering.

Harry recovered himself and reminded Stanley: "If she's married, her old man wouldn't like that."

"Christ," said Stanley virtuously, "if my wife lay about like that, for everyone to see, I'd soon stop her."

Harry said, smiling: "How do you know, perhaps she's sunning herself at this very moment?"

"Not a chance, not on our roof." The safety of his wife put Stanley into a good humour, and they went to work. But today it was hotter than yesterday; and several times one or the other suggested they should tell Matthew, the foreman, and ask to leave the roof until the heat wave was over. But they didn't. There was work to be done in the basement of the big block of flats, but up here they felt free, on a different level from ordinary humanity shut in the streets or the buildings. A lot more people came out onto the roofs that day, for an hour at midday. Some married couples sat side by side in deck chairs, the women's legs stockingless and scarlet, the men in vests with reddening shoulders.

The woman stayed on her blanket, turning herself over and over. She ignored them, no matter what they did, When Harry went off to fetch more screws, Stanley said: "Come on." Her roof belonged to a different system of roofs, separated from theirs at one point by about twenty feet. It meant a scrambling climb from one level to another, edging along parapets, clinging to chimneys, while their big boots slipped and slithered, but at last they stood on a small square projecting roof looking straight down at her, close. She sat smoking, reading a book. Tom thought she looked like a poster, or a magazine cover, with the blue sky behind her and her legs stretched out. Behind her a great crane at work on a new building in Oxford Street swung its black arm across the roofs in a great arc. Tom imagined himself at work on the crane, adjusting the arm to swing over and pick her up and swing her back across the sky to drop her near him.

They whistled. She looked up at them, cool and remote, then went on reading. Again, they were furious. Or rather, Stanley was. His sun-heated face was screwed into rage as he whistled again and again, trying to make her look up. Young Tom stopped whistling. He stood beside Stanley, excited, grinning; but he felt as if he were saying to the woman: "Don't associate me with *him*," for his grin was apologetic. Last night he had thought of the unknown woman before he slept, and she had been tender with him. This tenderness he was remembering as he shifted his feet by the jeering, whistling Stanley, and watched the indifferent, healthy brown woman a few feet off, with the gap that plunged to the street between them. Tom thought it was romantic, it was like being high on two hilltops. But there was a shout from Harry, and they clambered back. Stanley's face was hard, really angry. The boy kept looking at him and wondered why he hated the woman so much, for by now he loved her.

They played their little games with the blanket, trying to trap shade to work under; but again it was not until nearly four that they could work seriously, and they were exhausted, all three of them. They were grumbling about the weather, by now. Stanley was in a thoroughly bad humour. When they made their routine trip to see the woman before they packed up for the day, she was apparently asleep, face down, her back all naked save for the scarlet triangle on her buttocks. "I've got a good mind to report her to the police," said Stanley, and Harry said: "What's eating you? What harm's she doing?"

"I tell you, if she was my wife!"

"But she isn't, is she?" Tom knew that Harry, like himself, was uneasy at Stanley's reaction. He was normally a sharp young man, quick at his work, making a lot of jokes, good company.

"Perhaps it will be cooler tomorrow," said Harry.

But it wasn't, it was hotter, if anything, and the weather forecast said the good weather would last. As soon as they were on the roof, Harry went over to see if the woman were there, and Tom knew it was to prevent Stanley going, to put off his bad humour. Harry had grown-up children, a boy the same age as Tom, and the youth trusted and looked up to him.

Harry came back and said: "She's not there."

"I bet her old man has put his foot down," said Stanley, and Harry and Tom caught each other's eyes and smiled behind the young married man's back.

Harry suggested they should get permission to work in the basement, and they did, that day. But before packing up Stanley said: "Let's have a breath of fresh air." Again Harry and Tom smiled at each other as they followed Stanley up to the roof, Tom in the devout conviction that he was there to protect the woman from Stanley. It was about five-thirty, and a calm, full sunlight lay over the roofs. The great crane still swung its black arm from Oxford Street to above their heads. She was not there. Then there was a flutter of white from behind a parapet, and she stood up, in a belted, white dressing gown. She had been there all day, probably, but on a different patch of roof, to hide from them. Stanley did not whistle, he said nothing, but watched the woman bend to collect papers, books, cigarettes, then fold the blanket over her arm. Tom was thinking: If they weren't here, I'd go over and say . . . what? But he knew from his nightly dreams of her that she was kind and friendly. Perhaps she would ask him down to her flat? Perhaps. . . . He stood watching her disappear down the skylight. As she went, Stanley let out a shrill derisive yell; she started, and it seemed as if she nearly fell. She clutched to save herself, they could hear things falling. She looked straight at them, angry. Harry said, facetiously: "Better be careful on those slippery ladders, love." Tom knew he said it to save her from Stanley, but she could not know it. She vanished, frowning. Tom was full of a secret delight, because he knew her anger was for the others, not for him.

"Roll on some rain," said Stanley, bitter, looking at the blue evening sky.

Next day was cloudless, and they decided to finish the work in the basement. They felt excluded, shut in the grey cement basement fitting pipes, from the holiday atmosphere of London in a heat wave. At lunchtime they came up for some air, but while the married couples, and the men in shirt-sleeves or vests, were there, she was not there, either on her usual patch of roof or where she had been yesterday. They all, even Harry, clambered about, between chimney pots, over parapets, the hot leads stinging their fingers. There was not a sign of her. They took off their shirts and vests and exposed their chests, feeling their feet sweaty and hot. They did not mention the woman. But Tom felt alone again. Last night she had asked him into her flat: it was big and had fitted white carpets and a bed with a padded white leather headtop. She wore a black filmy negligée and her kindness to Tom thickened his throat as he remembered it. He felt she had betrayed him by not being there.

And again after work they climbed up, but still there was nothing to be seen of her. Stanley kept repeating that if it was as hot as this tomorrow he wasn't going to work and that's all there was to it. But they were all there next day. By ten the temperature was in the middle seventies, and it was eighty long before noon. Harry went to the foreman to say it was impossible to work on the leads in that heat; but the foreman said there was nothing else he could put them on, and they'd have to. At midday they stood silent, watching the skylight on her roof open, and then she slowly emerged in her white gown, holding a bundle of blanket. She looked at them, gravely, then went to the part of the roof where she was hidden from them. Tom was pleased. He felt she was more his when the other men couldn't see her. They had taken off their shirts and vests, but now they put them back again, for they felt the sun bruising their flesh. "She must have the hide of a rhino," said Stanley, tugging at guttering and swearing. They stopped work, and sat in the shade, moving around behind chimney stacks. A woman came to water a yellow window box just opposite them. She was middle-aged, wearing a flowered summer dress. Stanley said to her: "We need a drink more than them." She smiled and said: "Better drop down to the pub quick, it'll be closing in a minute." They exchanged pleasantries, and she left them with a smile and a wave.

"Not like Lady Godiva," said Stanley. "She can give us a bit of a chat and a smile."

"You didn't whistle at *her*," said Tom, reproving.

"Listen to him," said Stanley, "you didn't whistle, then?"

But the boy felt as if he hadn't whistled, as if only Harry and Stanley had. He was making plans, when it was time to knock off work, to get left behind and somehow make his way over to the woman. The weather report said the hot spell was due to break, so he had to move quickly. But there was no chance of being left. The other two decided to knock off work at four, because they were exhausted. As they went down, Tom quickly climbed a parapet and hoisted himself higher by pulling his weight up a chimney. He caught a glimpse of her lying on her back, her knees up, eyes closed, a brown woman lolling in the sun. He slipped and clattered down, as Stanley looked for information: "She's gone down," he said. He felt as if he had protected her from Stanley, and that she must be grateful to him. He could feel the bond between the woman and himself.

Next day, they stood around on the landing below the roof, reluctant to climb up into the heat. The woman who had lent Harry the blanket came out and offered them a cup of tea. They accepted gratefully, and sat around Mrs. Pritchett's kitchen an hour or so, chatting. She was married to an airline pilot. A smart blonde, of about thirty, she had an eye for the handsome sharp-faced Stanley; and the two teased each other while Harry sat in a corner, watching, indulgent, though his expression reminded Stanley that he was married. And young Tom felt envious of Stanley's ease in badinage; felt, too, that Stanley's getting off with Mrs. Pritchett left his romance with the woman on the roof safe and intact.

"I thought they said the heat wave'd break," said Stanley, sullen, as the time approached when they really would have to climb up into the sunlight.

"You don't like it, then?" asked Mrs. Pritchett.

"All right for some," said Stanley. "Nothing to do but lie about as if it was a beach up there. Do you ever go up?"

"Went up once," said Mrs. Pritchett, "But it's a dirty place up there, and it's too hot."

"Quite right too," said Stanley.

Then they went up, leaving the cool neat little flat and the friendly Mrs. Pritchett.

As soon as they were up they saw her. The three men looked at her, resentful at her ease in this punishing sun. Then Harry said, because of the expression on Stanley's face: "Come on, we've got to pretend to work, at least."

They had to wrench another length of guttering that ran beside a parapet out of its bed, so that they could replace it. Stanley took it in his two hands, tugged, swore, stood up. "Fuck it," he said, and sat down under a chimney. He lit a cigarette. "Fuck them," he said. "What do they think we are, lizards? I've got blisters all over my hands." Then he jumped up and climbed over the roofs and stood with his back to them. He put his fingers either side of his mouth and let out a shrill whistle. Tom and Harry squatted, not looking at each other, watching him. They could just see the woman's head, the beginnings of her brown shoulders. Stanley whistled again. Then he began stamping with his feet, and whistled and yelled and screamed at the woman, his face getting scarlet. He seemed quite mad, as he stamped and whistled, while the woman did not move, she did not move a muscle.

"Barmy," said Tom.

"Yes," said Harry, disapproving.

Suddenly the older man came to a decision. It was, Tom knew, to save some sort of scandal or real trouble over the woman. Harry stood up and began packing tools into a length of oily cloth. "Stanley," he said, commanding. At first Stanley took no notice, but Harry said: "Stanley, we're packing it in, I'll tell Matthew."

Stanley came back, cheeks mottled, eyes glaring.

"Can't go on like this," said Harry. "It'll break in a day or so. I'm going to tell Matthew we've got sunstroke, and if he doesn't like it, it's too bad." Even Harry sounded aggrieved, Tom noted. The small, competent man, the family man with his grey hair, who was never at a loss, sounded really off balance. "Come on," he said, angry. He fitted himself into the open square in the roof, and went down, watching his feet on the ladder. Then Stanley went, with not a glance at the woman. Then Tom who, his throat beating with excitement, silently promised her in a backward glance: Wait for me, wait, I'm coming.

On the pavement Stanley said: "I'm going home." He looked white now, so perhaps he really did have sunstroke. Harry went off to find the foreman who was at work on the plumbing of some flats down the street. Tom slipped back, not into the building they had been working on, but the building on whose roof the woman lay. He went straight up, no one stopping him. The skylight stood open, with an iron ladder leading up. He emerged onto the roof a couple of yards from her. She sat up, pushing back her black hair with both hands. The scarf across her breasts bound them tight, and brown flesh bulged around it. Her legs were brown and smooth. She stared at him in silence. The boy stood grinning, foolish, claiming the tenderness he expected from her.

"What do you want?" she asked.

"I . . . I came to . . . make your acquaintance," he stammered, grinning, pleading with her.

They looked at each other, the slight, scarlet-faced excited boy, and the serious, nearly naked woman. Then, without a word, she lay down on her brown blanket, ignoring him.

"You like the sun, do you?" he enquired of her glistening back.

Not a word. He felt panic, thinking of how she had held him in her arms, stroked his hair, brought him where he sat, lordly, in her bed, a glass of some exhilarating liquor he had never tasted in life. He felt that if he knelt down, stroked her shoulders, her hair, she would turn and clasp him in her arms.

He said: "The sun's all right for you, isn't it?"

She raised her head, set her chin on two small fists. "Go away," she said. He did not move. "Listen," she said, in a slow reasonable voice, where anger was kept in check, though with difficulty; looking at him, her face weary with anger: "If you get a kick out of seeing women in bikinis, why don't you take a sixpenny bus ride to the Lido? You'd see dozens of them, without all this mountaineering."

She hadn't understood him. He felt her unfairness pale him. He stammered: "But I like you, I've been watching you and . . ."

"Thanks," she said, and dropped her face again, turned away from him.

She lay there. He stood there. She said nothing. She had simply shut him out. He stood, saying nothing at all, for some minutes. He thought: She'll have to say something if I stay. But the minutes went past, with no sign of them in her, except in the tension of her back, her thighs, her arms—the tension of waiting for him to go.

He looked up at the sky, where the sun seemed to spin in heat; and over the roofs where he and his mates had been earlier. He could see the heat quivering where they had worked. "And they expect us to work in these conditions!" he thought, filled with righteous indignation. The woman hadn't moved. A bit of hot wind blew her black hair softly, it shone, and was iridescent. He remembered how he had stroked it last night.

Resentment of her at last moved him off and away down the ladder, through the building, into the street. He got drunk then, in hatred of her.

Next day when he woke the sky was grey. He looked at the wet grey and thought, vicious: "Well, that's fixed you, hasn't it now? That's fixed you good and proper."

The three men were at work early on the cool leads, surrounded by damp drizzling roofs where no one came to sun themselves, black roofs, slimy with rain. Because it was cool now, they would finish the job that day, if they hurried.

QUESTIONS

1. What are the differences among the workers' attitudes toward the woman on the roof?
2. What is the significance of the physical height at which the story takes place? Of the fact that the workers are positioned above the woman?
3. Find evidence of Tom's increasing protectiveness of the sunbather and of his justification of his attitudes toward her. How do you explain his protectiveness and justifications?
4. How do you explain Stanley's extreme anger at the woman as shown in the paragraph beginning "They had to wrench another length of guttering. . . ." (page 163)?
5. Explain the differences which would result in the story if it were told from the woman's point of view, or from Harry's or Stanley's.

WRITING ABOUT POINT OF VIEW AND TONE

When you begin writing about point of view or tone, try starting with six questions reporters often ask when they begin to write an article: who, what, when, where, why, and how? Let's look at each of these questions, for they can be surprisingly complex. Your answers to them will do much to determine the direction your essay takes.

Who? First of all, in which person is the story told? If it is told in the first person, who tells it: the main character? an important character who is not the protagonist? a peripheral figure? an observant outsider? Consider the connections or the relationships between the narrator and the other characters, and between the narrator and the action being described. If the story is narrated in the third person, then how (if at all) are the narrator's perceptions limited? Is the narrator omniscient, seeing at will into the minds of the characters, and into their pasts and futures? Or is he or she limited to what one character could perceive? To what extent, if any, does the narrator intrude upon the action to offer commentary or judgment about it? Try making, particularly if the story is told in the first person, a scratch list of the narrator's principal attributes: age, sex, educational status, profession, mood, and apparent disposition toward the action. Such a list will emphasize aspects of the story that will be helpful whether you are writing about point of view or tone.

What? Obviously, what the narrator tells is important—he or she tells the story! But what sort of story is it? A war story? A love story? A murder mystery? Reconsidering the substance of the story will help keep its details fresh in your mind; will help you see relationships among point of view, tone, and other elements; and will help you to assess the potentially vital relationship between teller and tale. A war story narrated by a battle-scarred sergeant will be substantially different from the same story narrated by a homeless child trapped in the ebb and flow of opposing armies. Remember, if "A Woman on a Roof" were told from Harry's point of view, it would be completely different.

When? At what point in time, relative to the action, is the story told? As it occurs? Just afterward? Long afterward (as a reflection, or a historical account)? Answers to such questions allow you to build up a stock of useful information about the story so that you can appreciate the full complexity and resonance of its point of view or tone. The battle-scarred sergeant's story of the Normandy invasion may change substantially between June 6, 1944, when the sergeant landed on Omaha Beach, and June 6, 1984, when the same sergeant, lying in the sun on Malibu Beach, recounts the story to his friends. Details will be forgotten or added or altered (we all know how memory can embellish even the simplest incidents), or the events can be seen in the broader perspective of historical time rather than on the more crowded canvas of immediate personal perception.

Where? The spatial vantage point from which a story is narrated can be as important as the temporal vantage point. A narrator can see the events of a story from up close, from a distance, or from above. Besides any symbolic significance the use of placement or distance may have in a story, it is another key feature which authors use to "adjust" their narrator's awareness and degree of knowledge, much as a photographer adjusts the placement and focus of a camera. A point of view can be clinical, detached, panoramic, or realistic, depending on the physical placement of the narrator.

How? This question pertains primarily to language and structure—and how they affect point of view and tone. Diction, sentence structure, level of formality: all of these reveal not only a narrator's tone, but also important information about the narrator's personality. And whether an author uses a straight chronological method or shifts in perspective, flashbacks, or alternative points of view—all affect our perception of the story and yield information about the relationship between plot and point of view.

Why? This question applies more to a first-person narrator than to the author or to a third-person narrator. As we have seen with Melville's "Bartleby," the methods of a first person narrator can tell us much about that character's motives and about the tone he or she adopts in telling the story. Narrators, like anyone else, can be motivated by greed, envy, self-interest, pity, or a need to justify their actions. Considering these possible motives will help you appreciate the full resonance of a story told in the first person.

This list of questions may seem long and ponderous, but it should remind you that point of view is a pervasive and often subtle feature of any story. (Remember, too, that the list is meant to "cover all the bases"—all of these questions are not necessarily germane to any given essay assignment.)

Once you have considered these questions, a subject and a thesis statement for your essay may begin to emerge. Critics often address the following topics.

1. The nature of the narrator and the effects of his or her methods upon the story
2. The relationship between point of view and another element in the story (for example, theme, characterization or plot)
3. The consistency or suitability of the point of view
4. Unusual technical elements of the point of view such as multiple narrators, naive narrators, or unusually limited narrators
5. The nature of the tone, how it is revealed, and how it affects our perception of the story

A clearly articulated thesis statement, which will usually concern the importance of point of view or tone to the story, will help keep your essay from sprawling and will help you marshal evidence and cite examples to support what you say. Your essay can usually be developed by exemplification, illustration, or comparison, and organized either chronologically or on the basis of the relative importance of your evidence.

The following essay concerns Doris Lessing's handling of a third person point of view in "A Woman on a Roof." By illustrating Tom's physical and emotional detachment from the woman and from his co-workers, it shows how Lessing uses point of view to reinforce the elements of characterization and theme in her story.

The Detached Point of View of Lessing's "A Woman on a Roof"

In "A Woman on a Roof," Doris Lessing uses a third person point of view. She limits our perception of the action, however, to what could be perceived by Tom, a young roofer who quickly emerges as the protagonist of the story. We see and hear only what Tom can see and hear. We are also privy to his thoughts and fantasies, as we see on page 159 when the narrator says, "Tom said nothing, but his mind was full of the nearly naked woman." But we know nothing about Harry's, Stanley's or the woman's reactions except what Tom could perceive of them from the outside. Lessing's handling of this point of view reinforces Tom's physical and emotional detachment from the other characters and helps to underscore her theme of the dangers inherent in any situation where men treat women as objects.

Lessing's point of view seems almost clinical at times, as, rather like a social scientist, she presents us with the case history of Tom's detachment, which takes three principal forms. First, Tom is physically separated from the woman as she bathes in the sun. She is beneath the men as they work on the roof, "between chimneys, about fifty yards away" (page 159). The woman is, for all practical purposes, unreachable, unattainable for Tom and his co-workers, but their ogling eyes easily bridge the distance between them and the scantily dressed woman. In his infatuation, Tom conjures up romantic images of union with the woman. He imagines them "high on two hilltops" together (page 160). He imagines he is a crane operator who swoops down, picks the woman up, and drops her beside himself. Only in his mind can he overcome his detachment and separation from her.

Tom is also detached from his co-workers. From the first, his fascination with the woman is contrasted with Stanley's angry misogyny, and Harry's sensible, somewhat prudish, indifference. Their three responses to the woman on the second day exemplify their different reactions.

"Bitch," said Stanley.
"She should ask us over," said Tom, snickering.

Harry recovered himself and reminded Stanley:
"If she's married, her old man wouldn't like that." (page 160)

Tom also attempts to disassociate himself from his coworkers (particularly from the "jeering, whistling" Stanley, page 160) so that the woman will recognize the purity of his desire for her. He goes so far that--like any man trying to protect any woman from anyone but himself--he harbors the "devout conviction that he was there to protect the woman from Stanley" (page 161).

Tom's emotional separation from Stanley and Harry occurs simultaneously with (and is in part a product of) a third form of detachment--from reality. As the story progresses, the point of view centers more and more upon Tom's fantasies, and his imaginary encounters with the woman become increasingly elaborate. They are in her bedroom; she's wearing a filmy negligee. Finally, his detachment from reality becomes so extreme--he has no real basis for thinking that she regards him as anything more than an impertinent stranger--that he presents himself to claim "the tenderness he expected from her" (page 164).

Her response to him ("She had simply shut him out", page 165) snaps him back to the reality he had left behind by objectifying her and turning her into a puppet of his fantasy. He becomes resentful, angry, hateful.

Lessing has carefully pre-figured the final gulf which yawns between Tom and the woman by her skillful handling of the point of view. Tom's physical detachment from the woman, his emotional detachment from his co-workers, and his detachment from reality have all been created and emphasized by her use of the selective third person point of view. The perspective that her narrative method affords reinforces her theme: the more men treat women as objects the more likely men are to alienate women and lose any chance of interacting with them as equals.

SUGGESTIONS FOR WRITING ABOUT POINT OF VIEW AND TONE

1. Write an essay that shows the relationship between the first person point of view and the tone of Updike's "A & P."
2. Assess the effects of Faulkner's use of a first person point of view ("we") in "A Rose for Emily."
3. The narrator of "Bartleby the Scrivener" views the action from (at least) three points of view: as Bartleby's employer, as his humanitarian benefactor, and as a confused observer of his behavior. Write an essay that shows how any one of these points of view affects the other two or affects the tone of the story.
4. Write an essay about the tone conveyed by the speeches of three workers in Lessing's "A Woman on a Roof."
5. Show evidence for and describe the effects of the narrator's omniscience, and his ambiguity, in Hawthorne's "Young Goodman Brown."

SYMBOLISM AND ALLEGORY

In one of the best known short stories in American literature, "The Open Boat," Stephen Crane describes the plight of four men tossed about in a small lifeboat after their ship has sunk. Close to the shore but unable to negotiate the heavy surf, one of the men, a newspaper correspondent, gazes wistfully toward the safety of the shore from the precarious boat:

> On the distant dunes were set many little black cottages, and a tall wind-mill reared above them. . . . The correspondent wondered if none ever ascended the tall wind-tower, and if then they never looked seaward. This tower was a giant, standing with its back to the plight of the ants. It represented in a degree to the correspondent, the serenity of nature amid the struggles of the individual—nature in the wind, and nature in the vision of the man. She did not seem cruel to him then, nor beneficent, nor treacherous, nor wise. But she was indifferent, flatly indifferent.

In this passage the wind-tower is explicitly identified as a symbol of the indifference of the universe to mankind's survival. A **symbol** is something which stands for something else: an object (the wind-tower) stands for a concept (Crane's belief that the universe is not concerned with man's fate).

Symbols may be *public* or *private*. We customarily associate a variety of mental concepts with public symbols: a cross or Star of David on a building identifies it as a place of worship; a flag conveys the concept of nation, and by extension, the stars and stripes flying over a building often identifies it as a government building; a red cross identifies a hospital. These rudimentary forms of public symbolism employ the same mechanism used in fiction: information is conveyed indirectly. One thing, usually something tangible— a shape, a flag, a color—embodies a more abstract concept—a religion, a government, medical attention. Fortunately, we share many associations, so the shorthand of symbolism is frequently used in fiction to recall these associations: water is a source of life and frequently suggests rebirth; earth and dust represent death; green often stands for life or hope.

Sometimes, however, we have to rely on the context of the story to clarify a *private symbol,* for without the verbal and physical context of the story, the writer's intentions might either be unclear or misread. For example, in Carson McCullers' "The Sojourner," the protagonist, John Ferris, alludes to the symbolic meaning of an old address book: "There's nothing that makes you so aware of the improvisation of human existence as a song unfinished. Or an old address book." The allusion is confusing even to one of the characters in the story, but not to the perceptive reader since this private symbol is clarified by an earlier passage in the story:

> Ferris pulled out his address book to verify a number. He turned the pages with growing attentiveness. Names and addresses from New York, the capi-

tals of Europe, a few faint ones from his home state in the South. Faded, printed names, sprawled drunken ones. . . . As Ferris closed the address book, he suffered a sense of hazard, transience, almost of fear.

Even without all the other clarifying details, this brief verbal context establishes the address book as a symbol of life's transiency, and thus it becomes the first of a series of symbols indicating Ferris is a sojourner in life.

Closely related to symbolism is **allegory** which is often employed in **parables** and **fables.** In allegory, the main characters are often abstractions in whom we find human equivalents. John Bunyan's *Pilgrim's Progress* tells the story of Christian, who must journey to the Heavenly City but is beset with difficulties and temptations along the way, and at one point falls into the Slough of Despond from which he must be rescued. In the medieval allegorical play *Everyman,* the main character, Everyman, is summoned by Death and seeks to delay his journey; he asks his companions, among whom are Fellowship and Goods, to join him, but at the play's conclusion only Good Deeds can accompany Everyman. Animal fables like Aesop's, or like Orwell's satiric *Animal Farm,* use the standard associations of animals (the cleverness of the fox, the greediness of pigs) to take the place of human abstractions. It is characteristic of allegories to employ a direct and unambiguous system of equivalencies. In *Animal Farm,* Napoleon is a composite portrait of Lenin and Stalin. There is, then, a one-to-one equivalency in the representation of allegories. Parables, a form of allegory, do not employ the usual abstractions of allegory, but they do illustrate the unambiguousness of allegorical constructions. The parable of the mustard seed from the New Testament explains that the mustard seed is "the word of God," and that the seeds which fell on the fertile ground represent those whose "hearts received the word of God." Even a contemporary story like Flannery O'Connor's "Revelation" is based on the biblical parable of the wedding guest, which concludes "the first shall be last, and the last first." The revelation of the title occurs when Mrs. Turpin, the main character, has a vision of the souls of the down-trodden and despised leading the way into heaven, while those who like herself and her husband, Claud, believed themselves among the righteous, are made to bring up the rear.

A visionary light settled in her eyes. She saw the streak as a vast swinging bridge extending upward from the earth through a field of living fire. Upon it a vast horde of souls were rumbling towards heaven. There were whole companies of white trash, clean for the first time in their lives, and bands of black niggers in white robes, and battalions of freaks and lunatics shouting and clapping and leaping like frogs. And bringing up the end of the procession was a tribe of people whom she recognized at once as those who, like herself and Claud, had always had a little of everything and the God-given wit to use it right.

Unlike allegory, symbolism is not limited in its field of reference and is usually much more ambiguous. The allegorical Faith of Hawthorne's "Young Goodman Brown" is more clearly defined than is the symbolic "dust" which appears in several scenes in Faulkner's "A Rose for Emily." The symbol reverberates with potential meaning. At first it stands for the old ways of the Griersons with which the modern South has little patience; later, it suggests the rank common smell which brings the high-and-mighty Griersons down to a more human level. But finally, "the patient and biding dust" symbolizes the ultimate reality, death, that Miss Emily would deny.

One problem we may have is identifying symbols. What kinds of things can be symbols? And how can we tell whether something is symbolic or is merely a literal detail in the story? Anything can be a symbol: a physical object, or a quality of several related objects such as color, texture, or sound. Even a character may be symbolic. In "A Rose for Emily," for example, Emily Grierson herself, is a symbol of the Old South, perverse and utterly mad, denying the passage of time and the reality of death, yet strong-willed, holding out against the encroachments of modernism—symbolized by the eyesores that surround the Grierson house, the taxes that the next modern generation tries to collect, and the street numbers which Miss Emily refuses to allow the town to attach to her house. Sound and color also work symbolically to support the theme of Faulkner's story; the tarnished gold easel and gold-headed cane, her vigorous iron-gray hair, the rose color of the bridal room, and the audible ticking of Miss Emily's invisible watch.

Still, how do we know that these objects, qualities, or characters are symbolic? One useful rule of thumb is to assume that if something is repeated several times in the story it is important, and probably has some symbolic intent. For example, to use Faulkner's story again, the dust that rises when the deputation of aldermen sits down on Miss Emily's furniture ("a faint dust rose sluggishly about their thighs, spinning with slow motes in the single sun ray") is repeated several times in the final scene when another deputation finds Homer Barron: "The violence of breaking down the door seemed to fill the room with pervading dust. . . . and upon him and upon the pillow beside him lay that even coating of the patient and biding dust." This dust is a symbol of the passing of time, transiency, and the irrevocability of death. The same symbolic system is used in many descriptions of Miss Emily's gray hair and in the images of tarnished metal. All three symbols—the dust, the gray hair, the tarnished metal—point to the same thing: death. All three symbols support one another, helping the reader grasp the meaning of Faulkner's story.

Symbols sometimes gain meaning by repetition. By accretion they pick up additional associations in the story, so that what at first appears to be merely a descriptive detail begins to take final shape as a symbol. We may not be aware of this at first reading. That is why many stories need to be reread several times before their meaning becomes clear. Even in a more transparent allegory, like "Young Goodman Brown," Hawthorne feels compelled to remind us several times of the resemblance between Goodman Brown and the stranger he meets in the forest ("they might have been taken for father and son") and of the serpent-like staff the traveller carries. When the stranger touches Goody Cloyse with what appears to be the serpent's tail, she exclaims, "The devil!" and the stranger leans on what appears to be a writhing stick. Repetition establishes the stranger as the Devil, and within the allegory Goodman Brown and his ancestors seem to have some diabolical resemblance.

In addition to looking for repetition, we can sometimes recognize symbols constructed by contrasting one element with another. A detail, innocent of meaning by itself, sometimes gains symbolic import by contrast with a complementary detail. For example, in Jean Stafford's "A Country Love Story," May's imaginary lover, who is youthful and courteous, contrasts with her irritable and aged husband, Daniel; yet the two figures are linked in meaning. If we understand the symbolism of the imaginary lover and, therefore, of May's final dream, we begin to understand Daniel's shortcomings and May's unfulfilled longings.

Since art often works through indirection, you can expect to find both allegory and symbolism in fiction. While it is possible to read stories literally for enjoyment, the richest appreciation of fiction is reserved for those who read patiently, aware of the artistic subtleties of symbolism and allegory.

From the first sentence of Jean Stafford's "A Country Love Story" where the symbol of the sleigh is introduced to the final sentence where May sits passively in the sleigh, Stafford develops the story's major symbol, linking it with a series of other related symbols to reveal her intentions. Franz Kafka's intentions are developed in his allegory "A Hunger Artist," whose protagonist continues to demonstrate his skills even when his talents have gone out of fashion. Despite its surface simplicity, Kafka's allegory has been interpreted in several different ways. For example, sometimes the hunger artist is seen as a kind of Christ figure who continues to fast even after he has been forgotten. Other critics see the story as an allegory of the compulsive artist's life.

FRANZ KAFKA (1883–1924)

A Hunger Artist

Franz Kafka was born in Prague, Czechoslovakia, but wrote in German. He wrote while pursuing a career as a civil servant. Most of his work was published posthumously by his friend and literary executor, Max Brod. Among Kafka's most influential works—whose content is often surrealistic or dream-like—are the novels *The Trial* (1925) and *The Castle* (1926), and his short stories, collected in English translation in 1976. "A Hunger Artist" first appeared in 1922.

During these last decades the interest in professional fasting has markedly diminished. It used to pay very well to stage such great performances under one's own management, but today that is quite impossible. We live in a different world now. At one time the whole town took a lively interest in the hunger artist; from day to day of his fast the excitement mounted; everybody wanted to see him at least once a day; there were people who bought season tickets for the last few days and sat from morning till night in front of his small barred cage; even in the nighttime there were visiting hours, when the whole effect was heightened by torch flares; on fine days the cage was set out in the open air, and then it was the children's special treat to see the hunger artist; for their elders he was often just a joke that happened to be in fashion, but the children stood open-mouthed, holding each other's hands for greater security, marveling at him as he sat there pallid in black tights, with his ribs sticking out so prominently, not even on a seat but down among straw on the ground, sometimes giving a courteous nod, answering questions with a constrained smile, or perhaps stretching an arm through the bars so that one might feel how thin it was, and then again withdrawing deep into himself, paying no attention to anyone or anything, not even to the all-important striking of the clock that was the only piece of furniture in his cage, but merely staring into vacancy with half-shut eyes, now and then taking a sip from a tiny glass of water to moisten his lips.

Besides casual onlookers there were also relays of permanent watchers selected by the public, usually butchers, strangely enough, and it was their task to watch the hunger artist day and night, three of them at a time, in case he should have some secret recourse to nourishment. This was nothing but a formality, instituted to reassure the masses, for the initiates knew well enough that during his fast the artist would never in any circumstances, not even under forcible compulsion, swallow the smallest morsel of food; the honor of his profession forbade it. Not every watcher, of course, was capable of understanding this, there were often groups of night watchers who were very lax in carrying out their duties and deliberately huddled together in a retired corner to play cards with great absorption, obviously intending to give the hunger artist the chance of a little refreshment, which they supposed he could draw from some private hoard. Nothing annoyed the artist more than such watchers; they made him miserable; they made his fast seem unendurable; sometimes he mastered his feebleness sufficiently to sing during their watch for as long as he could keep going, to show them how unjust their suspicions were. But that was of little use; they only wondered at his cleverness in being able to fill his mouth even while singing. Much more to his taste were the watchers who sat close up to the bars, who were not content with the dim night lighting of the hall but focused him in the full glare of the electric pocket torch given them by the impresario. The harsh light did not trouble him at all. In any case he could never sleep properly, and he could always drowse a little, whatever the light, at any hour, even when the hall was thronged with noisy onlookers. He was quite happy at the prospect of spending a sleepless night with such watchers; he was ready to exchange jokes with them, to tell them stories out of his nomadic life, anything at all to keep them awake and demonstrate to them again that he had no eatables in his cage and that he was fasting as not one of them could fast. But his happiest moment was when the morning came and an enormous breakfast was brought them, at his expense, on which they flung themselves with the keen appetite of healthy men after a weary night of wakefulness. Of course there were people who argued that this breakfast was an unfair attempt to bribe the watchers, but that was going rather too far, and when they were invited to take on a night's vigil without a breakfast, merely for the sake of the cause, they made themselves scarce, although they stuck stubbornly to their suspicions.

Such suspicions, anyhow, were a necessary accompaniment to the profession of fasting. No one could possibly watch the hunger artist continuously, day and night, and so no one could produce first-hand evidence that the fast had really been rigorous and continuous; only the artist himself could know that; he was therefore bound to be the sole completely satisfied spectator of his own fast. Yet for other reasons he was never satisfied; it was not perhaps mere fasting that had brought him to such skeleton thinness that many people had regretfully to keep away from his exhibitions, because the sight of him was too much for them, perhaps it was dissatisfaction with himself that had worn him down. For he alone knew, what no other initiate knew, how easy it was to fast. It was the easiest thing in the world. He made no secret of this, yet people did not believe him; at the best they set him down as modest, most of them, however, thought he was out for publicity or else was some kind of cheat who found it easy to fast because he had discovered a way of making it easy, and then had the impudence to admit the fact, more or less. He had to put up with all that, and in the course of time had got used to it, but his inner dissatisfaction always rankled, and never yet, after any term of fasting—this must be granted to his credit—had he left the cage of his own free will. The longest period of fasting was fixed by his impresario at forty days, beyond that term he was not allowed to go, not even in great cities, and there was good reason for it, too. Experience had proved that for about forty days the interest of the public could be stimulated by a steadily increasing pressure of advertisement, but after that the town began to lose interest, sympathetic support began notably to fall off; there were of course local variations as between one town and another or one country and another, but as a general rule forty days marked the limit. So on the fortieth day the flower-bedecked cage was opened, enthusiastic spectators filled the hall, a military band played, two doctors entered the cage to measure the results of the fast, which were announced through a megaphone, and finally two young ladies appeared, blissful at having been selected for the honor, to help the hunger artist down the few steps leading to a small table on which was spread a carefully chosen invalid repast. And at this very moment the artist always turned stubborn. True, he would entrust his bony arms to the outstretched helping hands of the ladies bending over him, but stand up he would not. Why stop fasting at this particular moment, after forty days of it? He had held out for a long time, an illimitably long time; why stop now, when he was in his best fasting form, or rather, not yet quite in his best fasting form? Why should he be cheated of the fame he would get for fasting longer, for being not only the record hunger artist of all time, which presumably he was already, but for beating his own record by a performance beyond human imagination, since he felt that there were no limits to his capacity for fasting? His public pretended to admire him so much, why should it have so little patience with him; if he could endure fasting longer, why shouldn't the public endure it? Besides, he was tired, he was comfortable sitting in the straw, and now he was supposed to lift himself to his full height and go down to a meal the very thought of which gave him a nausea that only the presence of the ladies kept him from betraying, and even that with an effort. And he looked up into the eyes of the ladies who were apparently so friendly and in reality so cruel, and shook his head, which felt too heavy on its strengthless neck. But then there happened yet again what always happened. The impresario came forward, without a word—for the band made speech impossible—lifted his arms in the air above the artist, as if inviting Heaven to look down upon its creature here in the straw, this suffering martyr, which indeed he was, although in quite another sense; grasped him around the emaciated waist, with exaggerated caution, so that the frail condition he was in might be appreciated; and committed him to the care of the blenching ladies, not without secretly giving him a shaking so that his legs and body tottered and swayed. The artist now submitted completely; his head lolled on his breast as if it had landed there by chance; his body was hollowed out; his legs in a spasm of self-preservation clung close to each other at the knees, yet scraped on the ground as if it were not really solid ground, as if they were only trying to find solid ground; and the whole weight of his body, a featherweight after all, relapsed onto one of the ladies, who, looking round for help and panting a little—this post of honor was not at all what she had expected it to be—first stretched her neck as far as she could to keep her face at least free from contact with the artist, then finding this impossible, and her more fortunate companion not coming to her aid but merely holding extended on her own trembling hand the little bunch of knucklebones that was the artist's, to the great delight of the spectators burst into tears and had to be replaced by an attendant who had long been stationed in readiness. Then came the food, a little of which the impresario managed to get between the artist's lips, while he sat in a kind of half-fainting trance, to the accompaniment of cheerful patter designed to distract the public's attention from the artist's condition; after that, a toast was drunk to the public, supposedly prompted by a whisper from the artist in the impresario's ear; the band confirmed it with a mighty flourish, the spectators melted away, and no one had any cause to be dissatisfied with the proceedings, no one except the hunger artist himself, he only, as always.

So he lived for many years, with small regular intervals of recuperation, in visible glory, honored by the world, yet in spite of that troubled in spirit, and all the more troubled because no one would take his trouble seriously. What comfort could he possibly need? What more could he possibly wish for? And if some good-natured person, feeling sorry for him, tried to console him by pointing out that his melancholy was probably caused by fasting, it could happen, especially when he had been fasting for some time, that he reacted with an outburst of fury and to the general alarm began to shake the bars of his cage like a wild animal. Yet the impresario had a way of punishing these outbreaks which he rather enjoyed putting into operation. He would apologize publicly for the artist's behavior, which was only to be excused, he admitted, because of the irritability caused by fasting; a condition hardly to be understood by well-fed people; then by natural transition he went on to mention the artist's equally incomprehensible boast that he could fast for much longer than he was doing; he praised the high ambition, the good will, the great self-denial undoubtedly implicit in such a statement; and then quite simply countered it by bringing out photographs, which were also on sale to the public, showing the artist on the fortieth day of a fast lying in bed almost dead from exhaustion. This perversion of the truth, familiar to the artist though it was, always unnerved him afresh and proved too much for him. What was a consequence of the premature ending of his fast was here presented as the cause of it! To fight against this lack of understanding, against a whole world of non-understanding, was impossible. Time and again in good faith he stood by the bars listening to the impresario, but as soon as the photographs appeared he always let go and sank with a groan back on to his straw, and the reassured public could once more come close and gaze at him.

A few years later when the witnesses of such scenes called them to mind, they often failed to understand themselves at all. For meanwhile the aforementioned change in public interest had set in; it seemed to happen almost overnight; there may have been profound causes for it, but who was going to bother about that; at any rate the pampered hunger artist suddenly found himself deserted one fine day by the amusement seekers, who went streaming past him to other more favored attractions. For the last time the impresario hurried him over half Europe to discover whether the old interest might still survive here and there; all in vain; everywhere, as if by secret agreement, a positive revulsion from professional fasting was in evidence. Of course it could not really have sprung up so suddenly as all that, and many premonitory symptoms which had not been sufficiently remarked or suppressed during the rush and glitter of success now came retrospectively to mind, but it was now too late to take any countermeasures. Fasting would surely come into fashion again at some future date, yet that was no comfort for those living in the present. What, then, was the hunger artist to do? He had been applauded by thousands in his time and could hardly come down to showing himself in a street booth at village fairs, and as for adopting another profession, he was not only too old for that but too fanatically devoted to fasting. So he took leave of the impresario, his partner in an unparalleled career, and hired himself to a large circus; in order to spare his own feelings he avoided reading the conditions of his contract.

A large circus with its enormous traffic in replacing and recruiting men, animals and apparatus can always find a use for people at any time, even for a hunger artist, provided of course that he does not ask too much, and in this particular case anyhow it was not only the artist who was taken on but his famous and long-known name as well; indeed considering the peculiar nature of his performance, which was not impaired by advancing age, it could not be objected that here was an artist past his prime, no longer at the height of his professional skill, seeking a refuge in some quiet corner of a circus; on the contrary, the hunger artist averred that he could fast as well as ever, which was entirely credible; he even alleged that if he were allowed to fast as he liked, and this was at once promised him without more ado, he could astound the world by establishing a record never yet achieved, a statement which certainly provoked a smile among the other professionals, since it left out of account the change in public opinion, which the hunger artist in his zeal conveniently forgot.

He had not, however, actually lost his sense of the real situation and took it as a matter of course that he and his cage should be stationed, not in the middle of the ring as a main attraction, but outside, near the animal cages, on a site that was after all easily accessible. Large and gaily painted placards made a frame for the cage and announced what was to be seen inside it. When the public came thronging out in the intervals to see the animals, they could hardly avoid passing the hunger artist's cage and stopping there for a moment; perhaps they might even have stayed longer had not those pressing behind them in the narrow gangway, who did not understand why they should be held up on their way towards the excitements of the menagerie, made it impossible for anyone to stand gazing quietly for any length of time. And that was the reason why the hunger artist, who had of course been looking forward to these visiting hours as the main achievement of his life, began instead to shrink from them. At first he could hardly wait for the intervals; it was exhilarating to watch the crowds come streaming his way, until only too soon—not even the most obstinate self-deception, clung to almost consciously, could hold out against the fact— the conviction was borne in upon him that these people, most of them, to judge from their actions, again and again, without exception, were all on their way to the menagerie. And the first sight of them from the distance remained the best. For when they reached his cage he was at once deafened by the storm of shouting and abuse that arose from the two contending factions, which renewed themselves continuously, of those who wanted to stop and stare at him—he soon began to dislike them more than the others—not out of real interest but only out of obstinate self-assertiveness, and those who wanted to go straight on to the animals. When the first great rush was past, the stragglers came along, and these, whom nothing could have prevented from stopping to look at him as long as they had breath, raced past with long strides, hardly even glancing at him, in their haste to get to the menagerie in time. And all too rarely did it happen that he had a stroke of luck, when some father of a family fetched up before him with his children, pointed a finger at the hunger artist and explained at length what the phenomenon meant, telling stories of earlier years when he himself had watched similar but much more thrilling performances, and the children, still rather uncomprehending, since neither inside nor outside school had they been sufficiently prepared for this lesson—what did they care about fasting? —yet showed by the brightness of their intent eyes that new and better times might be coming. Perhaps, said the hunger artist to himself many a time, things would be a little better if his cage were set not quite so near the menagerie. That made it too easy for people to make their choice, to say nothing of what he suffered from the stench of the menagerie, the animals' restlessness by night, the carrying past of raw lumps of flesh for the beasts of prey, the roaring at feeding times, which depressed him continually. But he did not dare to lodge a complaint with the management; after all, he had the animals to thank for the troops of people who passed his cage, among whom there might always be one here and there to take an interest in him, and who could tell where they might seclude him if he called attention to his existence and thereby to the fact that, strictly speaking, he was only an impediment on the way to the menagerie.

A small impediment, to be sure, one that grew steadily less. People grew familiar with the strange idea that they could be expected, in times like these, to take an interest in a hunger artist, and with this familiarity the verdict went out against him. He might fast as much as he could, and he did so; but nothing could save him now, people passed him by. Just try to explain to anyone the art of fasting! Anyone who has no feeling for it cannot be made to understand it. The fine placards grew dirty and illegible, they were torn down; the little notice board telling the number of fast days achieved, which at first was changed carefully every day, had long stayed at the same figure, for after the first few weeks even this small task seemed pointless to the staff; and so the artist simply fasted on and on, as he had once dreamed of doing, and it was no trouble to him, just as he had always foretold, but no one counted the days, no one, not even the artist himself, knew what records he was already breaking, and his heart grew heavy. And when once in a time some leisurely passer-by stopped, made merry over the old figure on the board and spoke of swindling, that was in its way the stupidest lie ever invented by indifference and inborn malice, since it was not the hunger artist who was cheating; he was working honestly, but the world was cheating him of his reward.

Many more days went by, however, and that too came to an end. An overseer's eye fell on the cage one day and he asked the attendants why this perfectly good cage should be left standing there unused with dirty straw inside it; nobody knew, until one man, helped out by the notice board, remembered about the hunger artist. They poked into the straw with sticks and found him in it. "Are you still fasting?" asked the overseer. "When on earth do you mean to stop?" "Forgive me, everybody," whispered the hunger artist; only the overseer, who had his ear to the bars, understood him. "Of course," said the overseer, and tapped his forehead with a finger to let the attendants know what state the man was in, "we forgive you." "I always wanted you to admire my fasting," said the hunger artist. "We do admire it," said the overseer, affably. "But you shouldn't admire it," said the hunger artist. "Well, then we don't admire it," said the overseer, "but why shouldn't we admire it?" "Because I have to fast, I can't help it," said the hunger artist. "What a fellow you are," said the overseer; "and why can't you help it?" "Because," said the hunger artist, lifting his head a little and speaking, with his lips pursed, as if for a kiss, right into the overseer's ear, so that no syllable might be lost, "because I couldn't find the food I liked. If I had found it, believe me, I should have made no fuss and stuffed myself like you or anyone else." These were his last words, but in his dimming eyes remained the firm though no longer proud persuasion that he was still continuing to fast.

"Well, clear this out now!" said the overseer, and they buried the hunger artist, straw and all. Into the cage they put a young panther. Even the most insensitive felt it refreshing to see this wild creature leaping around the cage that had so long been dreary. The panther was all right. The food he liked was brought him without hesitation by the attendants; he seemed not even to miss his freedom; his noble body, furnished almost to the bursting point with all that it needed, seemed to carry freedom around with it too; somewhere in his jaws it seemed to lurk; and the joy of life streamed with such ardent passion from his throat that for the onlookers it was not easy to stand the shock of it. But they braced themselves, crowded round the cage, and did not want ever to move away.

Translated by Willa and Edwin Muir

QUESTIONS

1. What details support the interpretation that Kafka's story is an allegory of the artist in society? Are any other interpretations possible? How does the sentence, "He was working honestly, but the world was cheating him of his reward," describe the theme of Kafka's story?

2. Why does Kafka begin the story at the height of the hunger artist's career and trace his descent into obscurity and neglect? What does Kafka mean when he attributes the change in fashion to "amusement seekers" who desert the hunger artist for "more favored attractions"?

3. Explain the function of the conventions of the fast, the impresario, the perma-

nent watchers, the cage, and the circus in the development of the allegory.

4. Why does the hunger artist find it easy to fast? Why does he wish to go beyond the fortieth day? What does Kafka mean when he contends that the hunger artist was a "suffering martyr . . . although in quite another sense"?

5. What does the hunger artist mean by his explanation for his continued fasting: "I couldn't find the food I liked. If I had found it, believe me, I should have made no fuss and stuffed myself like you or anyone else"? Why is it appropriate that he is replaced by a panther which is brought the "food he liked," and which "seemed to carry freedom around with it too"?

JEAN STAFFORD (1915–1979)

A Country Love Story

Jean Stafford was born in California and educated at the University of Colorado and at Heidelberg University. She wrote novels as well as short fiction. *The Collected Stories of Jean Stafford*, from which "A Country Love Story" is taken, appeared in 1969.

An antique sleigh stood in the yard, snow after snow banked up against its eroded runners. Here and there upon the bleached and splintery seat were wisps of horsehair and scraps of the black leather that had once upholstered it. It bore, with all its jovial curves, an air not so much of desuetude as of slowed-down dash, as if weary horses, unable to go another step, had at last stopped here. The sleigh had come with the house. The former owner, a gifted businesswoman from Castine who bought old houses and sold them again with all their pitfalls still intact, had said when she was showing them the place, "A picturesque detail, I think," and, waving it away, had turned to the well, which, with enthusiasm and at considerable length, she said had never gone dry. Actually, May and Daniel had found the detail more distracting than picturesque, so nearly kin was it to outdoor arts and crafts, and when the woman, as they departed in her car, gestured toward it again and said, "Paint that up a bit with something cheery and it will really add no end to your yard," simultaneous shudders coursed them. They had planned to remove the sleigh before they did anything else.

But partly because there were more important things to be done, and partly because they did not know where to put it (a sleigh could not, in the usual sense of the words, be thrown away), and partly because it seemed defiantly a part of the yard, as entitled to be there permanently as the trees, they did nothing about it. Throughout the summer, they saw birds briefly pause on its rakish front and saw the fresh rains wash its runners; in the autumn they watched the golden leaves fill the seat and nestle dryly down; and now, with the snow, they watched this new accumulation.

The sleigh was visible from the windows of the big, bright kitchen where they ate all their meals and, sometimes too bemused with country solitude to talk, they gazed out at it, forgetting their food in speculating on its history. It could have been driven cavalierly by the scion of some sea captain's family, or it could have been used soberly to haul the household's Unitarians to church or to take the womenfolk around the countryside on errands of good will. They did not speak of what its office might have been, and the fact of their silence was often nettlesome to May, for she felt they were silent too much of the time; a little morosely, she thought, If something as absurd and as provocative as this at which we look together—and which is, even though we didn't want it, our own property—cannot bring us to talk, what can? But she did not disturb Daniel in his private musings; she held her tongue, and out of the corner of her eye she watched him watch the winter cloak the sleigh, and, as if she were computing a difficult sum in her head, she tried to puzzle out what it was that had stilled tongues that earlier, before Daniel's illness, had found the days too short to communicate all they were eager to say.

It had been Daniel's doctor's idea, not theirs, that had brought them to the solemn hinterland to stay after all the summer gentry had departed in their beach wagons. The Northern sun, the pristine air, the rural walks and soundless nights, said Dr. Tellenbach, perhaps pining for his native Switzerland, would do more for the "Professor's" convalescent lung than all the doctors and clinics in the world. Privately he had added to May that after so long a season in the sanitarium (Daniel had been there a year), where everything was tuned to a low pitch, it would be difficult and it might be shattering for "the boy" (not now the "Professor," although Daniel, nearly fifty, was his wife's senior by twenty years and Dr. Tellenbach's by ten) to go back at once to the excitements and the intrigues of the university, to what, with finicking humor, the Doctor called "the omnium-gatherum of the schoolmaster's life." The rigors of a country winter would be as nothing, he insisted, when compared to the strain of feuds and cocktail parties. All professors wanted to write books, didn't they? Surely Daniel, a historian with all the material in the world at his fingertips, must have something up his sleeve that could be the *raison d'être* for this year away? May said she supposed he had, she was not sure. She could hear the reluctance in her voice as she escaped the Doctor's eyes and gazed through his windows at the mountains behind the sanitarium. In the dragging months Daniel had been gone, she had taken solace in imagining the time when they *would* return to just that pandemonium the Doctor so deplored, and because it had been pandemonium on the smallest and most discreet scale, she smiled through her disappointment at the little man's Swiss innocence and explained that they had always lived quietly, seldom dining out or entertaining more than twice a week.

"Twice a week!" He was appalled.

"But I'm afraid," she had protested, "that he would find a second year of inactivity intolerable. He does intend to write a book, but he means to write it in England, and we can't go to England now."

"England!" Dr. Tellenbach threw up his hands. "Good *air* is my recommendation for your husband. Good air and little talk."

She said, "It's talk he needs, I should think, after all this time of communing only with himself except when I came to visit."

He had looked at her with exaggerated patience, and then, courtly but authoritative, he said, "I hope you will not think I importune when I tell you that I am very well acquainted with your husband, and, as his physician, I order this retreat. *He* quite agrees."

Stung to see that there was a greater degree of understanding between Daniel and Dr. Tellenbach than between Daniel and herself, May had objected further, citing an occasion when her husband had put his head in his hands and mourned, "I hear talk of nothing but sputum cups and X-rays. Aren't people interested in the state of the world any more?"

But Dr. Tellenbach had been adamant, and at the end, when she had risen to go, he said, "You are bound to find him changed a little. A long illness removes a thoughtful man from his fellow beings. It is like living with an exacting mistress who is not content with half a man's attention but must claim it all." She had thought his figure of speech absurd and disdained to ask him what he meant.

Actually, when the time came for them to move into the new house and she found no alterations in her husband but found, on the other hand, much pleasure in their country life, she began to forgive Dr. Tellenbach. In the beginning, it was like a second honeymoon, for they had moved to a part of the North where they had never been and they explored it together, sharing its charming sights and sounds. Moreover, they had never owned a house before but had always lived in city apartments, and though the house they bought was old and derelict, its lines and doors and window lights were beautiful, and they were possessed by it. All through the summer, they reiterated, "To think that we own all of this! That it actually belongs to us!" And they wandered from room to room marveling at their windows, from none of which was it possible to see an ugly sight. They looked to the south upon a river, to the north upon a lake; to the west of them were pine woods where the wind forever sighed, voicing a vain entreaty; and to the east a rich man's long meadow that ran down a hill to his old, magisterial house. It was true, even in those bewitched days, that there were times on the lake, when May was gathering water lilies as Daniel slowly rowed, that she had seen on his face a look of abstraction and she had known that he was worlds away, in his memories, perhaps, of his illness and the sanitarium (of which he would never speak) or in the thought of the book he was going to write as soon, he said, as the winter set in and there was nothing to do but work. Momentarily the look frightened her and she remembered the Doctor's words, but then, immediately herself again in the security of married love, she caught at another water lily and pulled at its long stem.

Companionably, they gardened, taking special pride in the nicotiana that sent its nighttime fragrance into their bedroom. Together, and with fascination, they consulted carpenters, plasterers, and chimney sweeps. In the blue evenings they read at ease, hearing no sound but that of the night birds—the loons on the lake and the owls in the tops of trees. When the days began to cool and shorten, a cricket came to bless their house, nightly singing behind the kitchen stove. They got two fat and idle tabby cats, who lay insensible beside the fireplace and only stirred themselves to purr perfunctorily.

Because they had not moved in until July and by that time the workmen of the region were already engaged, most of the major repairs of the house were to be postponed until the spring, and in October, when May and Daniel had done all they could by themselves and Daniel had begun his own work, May suddenly found herself without occupation. Whole days might pass when she did nothing more than cook three meals and walk a little in the autumn mist and pet the cats and wait for Daniel to come down from his upstairs study to talk to her. She began to think with longing of the crowded days in Boston before Daniel was sick, and even in the year past, when he had been away and she had gone to concerts and recitals and had done good deeds for crippled children and had endlessly shopped for presents to lighten the tedium of her husband's unwilling exile. And, longing, she was remorseful, as if by desiring another she betrayed this life, and, remorseful, she hid away in sleep. Sometimes she slept for hours in the daytime, imitating the cats, and when at last she got up, she had to push away the dense sleep as if it were a door.

One day at lunch, she asked Daniel to take a long walk with her that afternoon to a farm where the owner smoked his own sausages.

"You never go outdoors," she said, "and Dr. Tellenbach said you must. Besides, it's a lovely day."

"I can't, " he said. "I'd like to, but I can't. I'm busy. You go alone."

Overtaken by a gust of loneliness, she cried, "Oh, Daniel, I have nothing to *do!*"

A moment's silence fell, and then he said, "I'm sorry to put you through this, my dear, but you must surely admit that it's not my fault I got sick."

In her shame, her rapid, overdone apologies, her insistence that nothing mattered in the world except his health and peace of mind, she made everything worse, and at last he said shortly to her, "Stop being a child, May. Let's just leave each other alone."

This outbreak, the very first in their marriage of five years, was the beginning of a series. Hardly a day passed that they did not bicker over something; they might dispute a question of fact, argue a matter of taste, catch each other out in an inaccuracy, and every quarrel ended with Daniel's saying to her, "Why don't you leave me alone?" Once he said, "I've been sick and now I'm busy and I'm no longer young enough to shift the focus of my mind each time it suits your whim." Afterward, there were always apologies, and then Daniel went back to his study and did not open the door of it again until the next meal. Finally, it seemed to her that love, the very center of their being, was choked off, overgrown, invisible. And silent with hostility or voluble with trivial reproach, they tried to dig it out impulsively and could not—could only maul it in its unkempt grave. Daniel, in his withdrawal from her and from the house, was preoccupied with his research, of which he never spoke except to say that it would bore her, and most of the time, so it appeared to May, he did not worry over what was happening to them. She felt the cold old house somehow enveloping her as if it were their common enemy, maliciously bent on bringing them to disaster. Sunken in faithlessness, they stared, at mealtimes, atrophied within the present hour, at the irrelevant and whimsical sleigh that stood abandoned in the mammoth winter.

May found herself thinking, If we redeemed it and painted it, our house would have something in common with Henry Ford's Wayside Inn. And I might make this very observation to him and he might greet it with disdain and we might once again be able to talk to each other. Perhaps we could talk of Williamsburg and how we disapproved of it. Her mind went toiling on. Williamsburg was part of our honeymoon trip; somewhere our feet were entangled in suckers as we stood kissing under a willow tree. Soon she found that she did not care for this line of thought, nor did she care what his response to it might be. In her imagined conversations with Daniel, she never spoke of the sleigh. To the thin, ill scholar whose scholarship and illness had usurped her place, she had gradually taken a weighty but unviolent dislike.

The discovery of this came, not surprising her, on Christmas Day. The knowledge sank like a plummet, and at the same time she was thinking about the sleigh, connecting it with the smell of the barn on damp days, and she thought perhaps it had been drawn by the very animals who had been stabled there and had pervaded the timbers with their odor. There must have been much life within this house once—but long ago. The earth immediately behind the barn was said by everyone to be extremely rich because of the horses, although there had been none there for over fifty years. Thinking of this soil, which earlier she had eagerly sifted through her fingers, May now realized that she had no wish for the spring to come, no wish to plant a garden, and, branching out at random, she found she had no wish to see the sea again, or children, or favorite pictures, or even her own face on a happy day. For a minute or two, she was almost enraptured in this state of no desire, but then, purged swiftly of her cynicism, she knew it to be false, knew that actually she did have a desire—the desire for a desire. And now she felt that she was stationary in a whirlpool, and at the very moment she conceived the notion a bit of wind brought to the seat of the sleigh the final leaf from the elm tree that stood beside it. It crossed her mind that she might consider the wood of the sleigh in its juxtaposition to the living tree and to the horses, who, although they were long since dead, reminded her of their passionate, sweating, running life every time she went to the barn for firewood.

They sat this morning in the kitchen full of sun, and, speaking not to him but to the sleigh, to icicles, to the dark, motionless pine woods, she said, "I wonder if on a day like this they used to take the pastor home after lunch." Daniel gazed abstractedly at the bright-silver drifts beside the well and said nothing. Presently a wagon went past hauled by two oxen with bells on their yoke. This was the hour they always passed, taking to an unknown destination an aged man in a fur hat and an aged woman in a shawl. May and Daniel listened.

Suddenly, with impromptu anger, Daniel said, "What did you just say?"

"Nothing," she said. And then, after a pause, "It would be lovely at Jamaica Pond today."

He wheeled on her and pounded the table with his fist. "I did not ask for this!" The color rose feverishly to his thin cheeks and his breath was agitated. "You are trying to make me sick again. It was wonderful, wasn't it, for you while I was gone?"

"Oh, no, no! Oh, no, Daniel, it was hell!"

"Then, by the same token, this must be heaven." He smiled, the professor catching out a student in a fallacy.

"Heaven." She said the word bitterly.

"Then why do you stay here?" he cried.

It was a cheap impasse, desolate, true, unfair. She did not answer him.

After a while he said, "I almost believe there's something you haven't told me."

She began to cry at once, blubbering across the table at him. "You have said that before. What am I to say? What have I done?"

He looked at her, impervious to her tears, without mercy and yet without contempt. "I don't know. But you've done something."

It was as if she were looking through someone else's scrambled closets and bureau drawers for an object that had not been named to her, but nowhere could she find her gross offense.

Domestically she asked him if he would have more coffee and he peremptorily refused and demanded, "Will you tell me why it is you must badger me? Is it a compulsion? Can't you control it? Are you going mad?"

From that day onward, May felt a certain stirring of life within her solitude, and now and again, looking up from a book to see if the damper on the stove was right, to listen to a rat renovating its house-within-a-house, to watch the belled oxen pass, she nursed her wound, hugged it, repeated his awful words exactly as he had said them, reproduced the way his wasted lips had looked and his bright, farsighted eyes. She could not read for long at any time, nor could she sew. She cared little now for planning changes in her house; she had meant to sand the painted floors to uncover the wood of the wide boards and she had imagined how the long, paneled windows of the drawing room would look when yellow velvet curtains hung there in the spring. Now, schooled by silence and indifference, she was immune to disrepair and to the damage done by the wind and snow, and she looked, as Daniel did, without dislike upon the old and nasty wallpaper and upon the shabby kitchen floor. One day, she knew that the sleigh would stay where it was so long as they stayed there. From every thought, she returned to her deep, bleeding injury. He had asked her if she were going mad.

She repaid him in the dark afternoons while he was closeted away in his study, hardly making a sound save when he added wood to his fire or paced a little, deep in thought. She sat at the kitchen table looking at the sleigh, and she gave Daniel insult for his injury by imagining a lover. She did not imagine his face, but she imagined his clothing, which would be costly and in the best of taste, and his manner, which would be urbane and anticipatory of her least whim, and his clever speech, and his adept court-ship that would begin the moment he looked at the sleigh and said, "I must get rid of that for you at once." She might be a widow, she might be di-vorced, she might be committing adultery. Certainly there was no need to specify in an affair so securely legal. There was no need, that is, up to a point, and then the point came when she took in the fact that she not only believed in this lover but loved him and depended wholly on his compan-ionship. She complained to him of Daniel and he consoled her; she told him stories of her girlhood, when she had gaily gone to parties, squired by boys her own age; she dazzled him sometimes with the wise comments she made on the books she read. It came to be true that if she so much as looked at the sleigh, she was weakened, failing with starvation.

Often, about her daily tasks of cooking food and washing dishes and tending the fires and shopping in the general store of the village, she thought she should watch her step, that it was this sort of thing that *did* make one go mad; for a while, then, she went back to Daniel's question, sharpening its razor edge. But she could not corral her alien thoughts and she trembled as she bought split peas, fearful that the old men loafing by the stove could see the incubus of her sins beside her. She could not avert such thoughts when they rushed upon her sometimes at tea with one of the old religious ladies of the neighborhood, so that, in the middle of a conver-sation about a deaconess in Bath, she retired from them, seeking her lover, who came, faceless, with his arms outstretched, even as she sat up straight in a Boston rocker, even as she accepted another cup of tea. She lingered over the cake plates and the simple talk, postponing her return to her own house and to Daniel, whom she continually betrayed.

It was not long after she recognized her love that she began to wake up even before the dawn and to be all day quick to everything, observant of all the signs of age and eccentricity in her husband, and she compared him in every particular—to his humiliation, in her eyes—with the man whom now it seemed to her she had always loved at fever pitch.

Once when Daniel, in a rare mood, kissed her, she drew back involuntarily and he said gently, "I wish I knew what you had done, poor dear." He looked as if for written words in her face.

"You said you knew," she said, terrified.

"I do."

"Then why do you wish you knew?" Her baffled voice was high and frantic. "You don't talk sense!"

"I do," he said sedately. "I talk sense always. It is you who are oblique." Her eyes stole like a sneak to the sleigh. "But I wish I knew your motive," he said impartially.

For a minute, she felt that they were two maniacs answering each other questions that had not been asked, never touching the matter at hand because they did not know what the matter was. But in the next moment, when he turned back to her spontaneously and clasped her head between his hands and said, like a tolerant father, "I forgive you, darling, because you don't know how you persecute me. No one knows except the sufferer what this sickness is," she knew again, helplessly, that they were not harmonious even in their aberrations.

These days of winter came and went, and on each of them, after breakfast and as the oxen passed, he accused her of her concealed misdeed. She could no longer truthfully deny that she was guilty, for she was in love, and she heard the subterfuge in her own voice and felt the guilty fever in her veins. Daniel knew it, too, and watched her. When she was alone, she felt her lover's presence protecting her—when she walked past the stiff spiraea, with icy cobwebs hung between its twigs, down to the lake, where the black, unmeasured water was hidden beneath a lid of ice; when she walked, instead, to the salt river to see the tar-paper shacks where the men caught smelt through the ice; when she walked in the dead dusk up the hill from the store, catching her breath the moment she saw the sleigh. But sometimes this splendid being mocked her when, freezing with fear of the consequences of her sin, she ran up the stairs to Daniel's room and burrowed her head in his shoulder and cried, "Come downstairs! I'm lonely, please come down!" But he would never come, and at last, bitterly, calmed by his calmly inquisitive regard, she went back alone and stood at the kitchen window, coyly half hidden behind the curtains.

For months she lived with her daily dishonor, rattled, ashamed, stubbornly clinging to her secret. But she grew more and more afraid when, oftener and oftener, Daniel said, "Why do you lie to me? What does this mood of yours mean?" and she could no longer sleep. In the raw nights, she lay straight beside him as he slept, and she stared at the ceiling, as bright as the snow it reflected, and tried not to think of the sleigh out there under the elm tree but could think only of it and of the man, her lover, who was connected with it somehow. She said to herself, as she listened to his breathing, "If I confessed to Daniel, he would understand that I was lonely and he would comfort me, saying, 'I am here, May. I shall never let you be lonely again.' " At these times, she was so separated from the world, so far removed from his touch and his voice, so solitary, that she would have sued a stranger for companionship. Daniel slept deeply, having no guilt to make him toss. He slept, indeed, so well that he never even heard the ditcher on snowy nights rising with a groan over the hill, flinging the snow from the road and warning of its approach by lights that first flashed red, then blue. As it passed their house, the hurled snow swashed like flames. All night she heard the squirrels adding up their nuts in the walls and heard the spirit of the house creaking and softly clicking upon the stairs and in the attics.

In early spring, when the whippoorwills begged in the cattails and the marsh reeds, and the northern lights patinated the lake and the tidal river, and the stars were large, and the huge vine of Dutchman's-pipe had started to leaf out, May went to bed late. Each night she sat on the back steps waiting, hearing the snuffling of a dog as it hightailed it for home, the single cry of a loon. Night after night, she waited for the advent of her rebirth while upstairs Daniel, who had spoken tolerantly of her vigils, slept, keeping his knowledge of her to himself. "A symptom," he had said, scowling in concentration, as he remarked upon her new habit. "Let it run its course. Perhaps when this is over, you will know the reason why you torture me with these obsessions and will stop. You know, you may really have a slight disorder of the mind. It would be nothing to be ashamed of; you could go to a sanitarium."

One night, looking out the window, she clearly saw her lover sitting in the sleigh. His hand was over his eyes and his chin was covered by a red silk scarf. He wore no hat and his hair was fair. He was tall and his long legs stretched indolently along the floorboard. He was younger than she had imagined him to be and he seemed rather frail, for there was a delicate pallor on his high, intelligent forehead and there was an invalid's languor in his whole attitude. He wore a white blazer and gray flannels and there was a yellow rosebud in his lapel. Young as he was, he did not, even so, seem to belong to her generation; rather, he seemed to be the reincarnation of someone's uncle as he had been fifty years before. May did not move until he vanished, and then, even though she knew now that she was truly bedeviled, the only emotion she had was bashfulness, mingled with doubt; she was not sure, that is, that he loved her.

That night, she slept a while. She lay near to Daniel, who was smiling in the moonlight. She could tell that the sleep she would have tonight would be as heavy as a coma, and she was aware of the moment she was overtaken.

She was in a canoe in a meadow of water lilies and her lover was tranquilly taking the shell off a hard-boiled egg. "How intimate," he said, "to eat an egg with you." She was nervous lest the canoe tip over, but at the same time she was charmed by his wit and by the way he lightly touched her shoulder with the varnished paddle.

"May? May? I love you, May."

"Oh!" enchanted, she heard her voice replying. "Oh, I love you, too!"

"The winter is over, May. You must forgive the hallucinations of a sick man."

She woke to see Daniel's fair, pale head bending toward her. "He is old! He is ill!" she thought, but through her tears, to deceive him one last time, she cried, "Oh, thank God, Daniel!"

He was feeling cold and wakeful and he asked her to make him a cup of tea; before she left the room, he kissed her hands and arms and said, "If I am ever sick again, don't leave me, May."

Downstairs, in the kitchen, cold with shadows and with the obtrusion of dawn, she was belabored by a chill. "What time is it?" she said aloud, although she did not care. She remembered, not for any reason, a day when she and Daniel had stood in the yard last October wondering whether they should cover the chimneys that would not be used and he decided that they should not, but he had said, "I hope no birds get trapped." She had replied, "I thought they all left at about this time for the South," and he had answered, with an unintelligible reproach in his voice, "The starlings stay." And she remembered, again for no reason, a day when, in pride and excitement, she had burst into the house crying. "I saw an ermine. It was terribly poised and let me watch it quite a while." He had said categorically, "There are no ermines here."

She had not protested; she had sighed as she sighed now and turned to the window. The sleigh was livid in this light and no one was in it; nor had anyone been in it for many years. But at that moment the blacksmith's cat came guardedly across the dewy field and climbed into it, as if by careful plan, and curled upon the seat. May prodded the clinkers in the stove and started to the barn for kindling. But she thought of the cold and the damp and the smell of the horses, and she did not go but stood there, holding the poker and leaning upon it as if it were an umbrella. There was no place warm to go. "What time is it?" she whimpered, heartbroken, and moved the poker, stroking the lion foot of the fireless stove.

She knew now that no change would come, and that she would never see her lover again. Confounded utterly, like an orphan in solitary confinement, she went outdoors and got into the sleigh. The blacksmith's imperturbable cat stretched and rearranged his position, and May sat beside him with her hands locked tightly in her lap, rapidly wondering over and over again how she would live the rest of her life.

QUESTIONS

1. The antique sleigh, mentioned in the first and third paragraphs, is the major symbol in Stafford's story. What does it symbolize? How do the details of the

description and the action of the story support your interpretation?

2. How does the couple's failure to restore the house contribute to the symbolism of the house itself? Why does Stafford say, "The sleigh had come with the house"?

3. In what way does Daniel's occupation define his character? How does May's name define hers? What do the allusions to Williamsburg, Virginia, and Henry Ford's Wayside Inn contribute to the theme of the story?

4. Why does the imaginary lover seem to be, "the reincarnation of someone's uncle as he had been fifty years ago"? Examine the early scene at the lake in which May gathers water lilies while Daniel rows. How does the later scene in May's dream of the imaginary lover and her in a canoe support the idea that May is sexually repressed?

5. How do the changing seasons act as an ironical counterpart to the progress of Daniel and May's marriage?

WRITING ABOUT SYMBOLISM AND ALLEGORY

Now that you have some grasp of how symbolism and allegory work in fiction, how do you write an essay about a story's symbolism or allegorical content? Before you begin, read the text closely with an eye toward isolating the symbols or the allegorical framework. In simple terms, this means looking for a pattern in the story's structure that lies below the literal plot level.

Symbols are often repeated and develop as a story unfolds; each time a symbol is repeated its meaning is refined or extended. The context of a symbol may remain the same or change, thus clarifying or elaborating more fully a symbol's meaning. For example, if a symbol is associated with a character it may clarify the character's meaning. In Joyce Carol Oates' "Where Are You Going, Where Have You Been?" the boots that Arnold Friend wears do not seem to fit him. Several times Oates mentions that his feet do not seem to go all the way down into the boots, and that the boots may be stuffed with paper. When the reader begins to realize from other details in the story, that Friend's name may be "fiend" (that is, "devil") and that the reason his feet do not fit the boots is because they are actually cloven hooves, the symbolic significance of the character becomes clear.

Before you can fully begin to interpret what the symbolic pattern stands for, you need to determine whether your usual associations of the color, the object, or the character are relevant here, or whether the context of the story has altered them. While you may at first associate an antique sleigh with a Currier and Ives winter scene of nostalgic rural charm, those associations are not entirely relevant for the antique sleigh in Jean Stafford's "A Country Love Story." There the sleigh causes "simultaneous shudders" to course through Daniel and May, and the sleigh eventually becomes a symbol for all that binds and paradoxically separates the couple.

When writing about allegory the case is usually clearer since there is a one-to-one relationship in the allegorical system. Are the names of the characters generalized and do they form some sort of coherent pattern of meaning? Clearly, in the allegorical system of Hawthorne's "Young Goodman Brown," the protagonist's name is meant to represent an "Everyman" from the commonality of his paternal name "Brown" as well as the Puritan title "Goodman," used ironically here. He is also naive and relatively innocent, as the epithet "Young" suggests. The allegorical system is developed further by naming his wife "Faith," and by having his loss of faith represented by Goodman Brown's cry of despair, "My Faith is gone." Similar allegorical names abound in contemporary literature: R. J. Bowman of Eudora Welty's "Death of a Travelling Salesman," who learns to "bow" humbly before backwoods people; Granny Weatherall in Katherine Anne Porter's "The Jilting of Granny Weatherall," a woman who has "weathered" 80 years; and Nick Adams who experiences for the first time the violence of life. Sometimes the names of characters directly reflect their allegorical import—as in Franz Kafka's "A Hunger Artist" in which the characters are simply called "the hunger artist" and "the impresario."

Whether you are writing about symbols or about allegory, ask yourself how the symbols or the generalized names connect to the main purpose of the story. Sometimes the title of the story helps. For example, Oates' "Where Are you Going, Where Have You Been?" is not only a question that Connie's parents fail to ask her, but as the dedication to Bob Dylan suggests, the title is an allusion to a line in one of his songs ("Oh where have you been, my darling young one?" from "A Hard Rain's A-gonna Fall"), the complete lyrics of which describe the innocent's encounter with evil in the world.

A paper about symbols or allegory should begin by noting any pattern of symbols or allegorical framework that supports the story's meaning. Symbols may fall into several interrelated patterns. Arnold Friend's cloven hooves, his putting his sign on Connie, the quasi-religious nature of the drive-in restaurant, Friend's clairvoyance, and the diminishing size and substance of the family home combine to form a pattern of symbols that turns a contemporary tale of teenage rebellion into a classic encounter of innocence and evil, much like "Young Goodman Brown." The body of your paper should develop the allegorical framework: who represents what, how the theme is related to the allegorical actions and characters. Or, it should show how the clusters of symbols—the interrelated network of symbols—connect to form the meaning lying below the surface plot.

This last step is complicated by two common pitfalls: 1) seeing everything in literal terms, or 2) "reading into" the story meanings not intended by the writer. While it may be an intentional fallacy to limit the meaning of a work only to what the author has explicitly said it meant, nevertheless symbols are neither Rorschach inkblots, neutral shapes to which the viewer attributes meaning, nor thematic apperception tests intended to reveal through associations an individual's personality. Instead symbols are fraught with meanings that reveal the writer's purpose. It *is* true that art expresses itself through ambiguity, and that the symbolic or allegorical framework is flexible enough to accommodate a variety of interpretations, but the author has established defined areas of meaning, and part of the task of reading and writing about the symbolic or allegorical content of a work is to discover and document what those defined areas are. Much of the task of writing about symbols or allegory lies in the demonstration of how the cross-referencing of symbols and allegorical allusions is sufficient to block off any unintended meanings. It is therefore a good idea to outline the references so they can be discussed logically and coherently. A topical discussion of the symbols is preferable to following the plot and discussing them in the order in which they occur. The following discussion of the symbols in Jean Stafford's "A Country Love Story" arranges the three clusters of symbols in their order of importance to the theme.

Finally, there is a feeling of logical satisfaction when the pattern of a story is revealed and you are able to articulate it clearly and coherently. The satisfaction stems not just from the pleasure you get by solving a complicated puzzle. Understanding a piece of fiction and being able to communicate completely with the mind of the writer and to participate in some way in the aesthetic pleasure which the writer enjoyed in creating the story in the first place.

The following essay about the major symbols in Jean Stafford's "A Country Love Story" demonstrates how symbolism unifies all the elements of a short story. The marital conflict is embodied in the old sleigh, and the couple's age difference (the heart of the conflict) is revealed by their association with winter or spring; the characters of Daniel and May are defined by their connection to the sleigh, the old house, and by other details of the setting. Finally, the choice of a limited omniscient point of view, anchored in May's consciousness, is dictated by Stafford's decision to include the imaginary lover among the story's symbols.

Symbols of Change in Jean Stafford's
"A Country Love Story"

Jean Stafford's "A Country Love Story" uses three types of symbols: seasonal symbols, animal symbols, and most importantly, symbols of decay to explore the implications of the story's theme. By juxtaposing these symbols with the characters' conflict, Stafford creates dramatic tension in her story ultimately leading her main characters, Daniel and May, to an impasse in their marriage at the story's conclusion.

When Stafford introduces Daniel and May, the season is summer, and together the couple garden "companionably." They look forward to restoring the old house which they have purchased, as well as to mending their marriage, which has suffered a breach during the year Daniel has spent in a tuberculosis sanitarium. However, with the coming of fall, repairs on the house must be postponed until spring since no handyman is available. As winter sets in, the couple begin to quarrel. Daniel, who has changed psychologically during his stay in the sanitarium, shuts himself off in his study to write the book Dr. Tellenbach assumed "the professor" had "up his sleeve"; May, twenty years Daniel's junior, becomes lethargic, but when she mentions her boredom to Daniel, she touches off their first argument. "I'm no longer young enough to shift the focus of my mind to suit your whim," Daniel angrily replies to May's complaints. As the antique sleigh, which had come with the house, continues to sit in the yard, "snow after snow banked up against its eroded runners," it begins to grow into an unspoken accusation between the couple, reminding them that they have nothing to say to each other, and that their marriage, like the antique sleigh, is not some thing that can easily be "thrown away." Instead of the rebirth May had hoped for, the return of spring brings the chilling cold of Daniel's "winter," his old age. Despite Daniel's assertion that "the winter is over," May feels there is no place warm to go, and can only ask over and over, "What time is it?" Clearly, the seasonal symbolism dramatizes the outcome of this December-May relationship.

Animal symbols are introduced with each new season. Prominent among them are the horses which had once pulled the old sleigh. At first May wonders about the horses which took the family on outings; they come to stand for "passionate, sweating, running life," the past life of the old house, and everything opposite of her and Daniel's life of "desuetude [and] slowed down dash." Later, May comes to fear the horses, for they remind her of all that's missing in her life. At the story's conclusion, May wishes to avoid going into the barn where the soil is rich from all the years the horses were kept there. The reader is reminded of May's youthful fecundity, and of an earlier scene on a lake when May, happy in "the security of a married love," pulled at the "long stem" of a water lily. By the story's conclusion, the horses are merely a memory, and the sleigh sits immobile with its dry and splintering seat.

When winter first sets in, May and Daniel acquire two fat idle tabby cats. Since Daniel is preoccupied with writing his book, May imitates the cats, losing herself in sleep: "Sometimes she slept for hours in the daytime imitating the cats, and when at last she got up, she had to push away the dense sleep as if it were a door." When she climbs into the sleigh at the story's conclusion, May sits next to the blacksmith's cat, combining two motifs in the story: May's lethargy and boredom (represented by the two tabby cats), and her relinquishment of the warm life of passion. At this juncture in the story, Stafford links together the symbols of the sleigh, the blacksmith's cat, and the horses to dramatically emphasize the significance of May's choice in joining the blacksmith's cat in the sleigh:

> The sleigh was livid in this light and no one was in it; nor had anyone been in it for many years. But at that moment the blacksmith's cat came guardedly across the dewy field and climbed into it, as if by careful plan, and curled up on the seat. May prodded the clinkers in the stove and started to the barn for kindling. But she thought of the cold and the damp and the smell of the horses, and she did not go but stood there. . . There was no warm place to go.

Climbing into the sleigh next to the cat, May accepts a passionless life, one reduced to the sole problem of how to get through the years with Daniel: "The blacksmith's imperturbable cat stretched and rearranged his position, and May sat beside him with her hands locked tightly in her lap, rapidly wondering over and over again how she would live the rest of her life."

Several other references to animals underscore the growing antagonism between Daniel and May. While Daniel closes up the chimneys for winter so that no birds will get trapped, May comments that she thought Daniel had said all the birds left; unaccountably, Daniel caustically replies, "The starlings stay." On another occasion, the professor reproves May's youthful enthusiasm when he deflates her excited discovery of an ermine with the categorical denial, "There are no ermines here." Finally, Stafford employs the oxen, traditionally associated with patience and stolidity, as a reminder of the uneventful life of routine which awaits May in taking care of an invalid, "an ill scholar." Each day Daniel and May, without comment, watch an old couple in a sleigh drawn by oxen, routinely going on an inexplicable journey (the journey, itself, a symbol of May's pointless life). Clearly, the old couple represents what Daniel and May are in the process of becoming: a patiently stolid routinized couple on a journey to nowhere.

Most important of all the symbols in Stafford's story are the symbols of decay: the house and the sleigh. May's early meditation juxtaposes the splintery wood of the sleigh with the living tree which it stands next to. "The sleigh," writes Stafford, "bore not so much an air of desuetude as of slowed-down dash." She also tells us that the sleigh "came with the house." Like the house, it belongs to another era. They never get rid of the sleigh, just as they never restore the house. It is May's imaginary lover who says, "I must get rid of that for you." At first the couple are full of plans for the house, and consider themselves lucky, but summer gives way to fall, and since no workman can be found, the house remains unrestored. There is, throughout the story, a hint of futility about the possibility of recapturing the past through restoration, as if once something has decayed, it is too late to repair it. Both Daniel and May despised Henry Ford's restoration of the famous Wayside Inn, and, ironically, they both disapproved of the restored colonial Williamsburg, even though they had honeymooned there. Clearly, the one restored figure in the story, the imaginary lover who looked like someone's uncle fifty years ago (Daniel is fifty), is a surrogate for Daniel. But his restored figure is imaginary, and disappears when May is awakened from her dream by Daniel, who is now clearly old and ill. A shadow of his former self, Daniel has been transformed by a year in the sanitorium into an old man, an old historian who lives in the past; his marriage to May cannot be restored, and like the antique sleigh which neither can speak about, the marriage has reached its final resting place. In climbing into the decayed sleigh, May has resigned herself to a life without change.

Jean Stafford's "A Country Love Story" is a symbolic evocation of a failed relationship. The story derives its power and its concentrated energy from the three main clusters of symbols: seasonal symbols, animal symbols, and symbols of decay. Through these symbols, Stafford evokes Francis Bacon's cynical definition of a wife in his essay "Of Marriage and Single Life": "Wives are young men's mistresses, companions for middle age, and old men's nurses."

SUGGESTIONS FOR WRITING ABOUT SYMBOLISM AND ALLEGORY

1. Trace how the symbols in Hawthorne's "Young Goodman Brown" form an allegorical pattern.
2. Write an essay on Faulkner's "A Rose for Emily" showing how Miss Emily Grierson is a symbol of timelessness for the town. Focus especially on the narrator's conception of her as an idol and a monument.
3. Develop the idea that Kafka's "The Hunger Artist" is an allegory of the misunderstood and maligned artist. In your essay cite details from the allegorical framework such as the different attitudes of the watchers

toward the hunger artist, the response of children, his relationship with the impresario, and his life in the circus—to demonstrate that Kafka's allegory describes the plight of the artist in society.

4. Select details from "A & P" which cumulatively develop the conflict in the story between youth, nonconformity and idealism on the one hand and age, conformity, and cynicism on the other. What details combine to form symbols? Which symbols work by contrast?

THEME IN FICTION

A musician, a businesswoman, and a college student might all use the word "theme" in ways that elucidate the literary use of the term. The musician might speak of a theme as the principal melodic subject in a composition, such as the four-note theme at the beginning of Beethoven's Fifth Symphony. This theme could be announced, varied, or repeated, but it would dominate the composition and give it a unique character. The businesswoman might say that the theme of a conference she is organizing is the improvement of employee morale in a large firm. This use of the word "theme" implies a controlling idea or purpose, one to which all other conference proceedings are subordinate.

For a college student, the word "theme" could have quite different connotations: hours of hard work and hair-pulling, the struggle to discover what to say, the effort of putting complex words in a graceful order, the care needed for revision, the satisfaction of reading a polished essay.

In talking about **theme** in works of fiction (or in literary works generally), we could offer suggestions for a definition that could include such phrases as "the main idea" or "the author's message," or "the 'point' he or she is trying to make in the story." Though each of these definitions contains some truth, we might be better off remembering our three uses of the word "theme" and put aside any attempt at an absolute definition that might limit our appreciation of the word's full resonance. Rather, let us examine Hawthorne's "Young Goodman Brown" for recurrent ideas, for the dominant idea emerging from its combined elements, and for a unity of effect to which all of these elements contribute. This search may uncover some valid ideas about Hawthorne's story; it may also reveal the slippery nature of theme in fiction.

Among the ideas Hawthorne returns to again and again in the story are mystery, revelry in sin, human wickedness, and disillusionment. These recurrent "themes," made up largely of clusters of recurrent images or ideas called *motifs* (also a musical term), have the value of sharpening our focus upon the story. They are unarguably present in the piece, but by themselves they fall short of encapsulating the shattering effect of Brown's experiences.

Suppose we think that disillusionment and gloom are the main ideas of the story. What then? Does that mean the theme is Brown's disillusionment at discovering that all the apparently virtuous people in his community are gleeful sinners, or that the theme is his awareness that the world is a gloomy place where he alone does not worship the devil?

Each of these ideas contains some truth, but each seems inadequate to explain the total impact of Hawthorne's story. Our sense of their inadequacy reminds us of two important ideas about theme in fiction: (1) a story may have multiple themes, and (2) most attempts to expound *the* theme of a story will leave us with a sense of dissatisfaction and incompleteness. Themes do not "solve" stories as clues solve mysteries. A good story resists a convenient summation that proclaims its moral or lesson. Some stories, in fact, seem to have no recognizable theme at all.

Various "themes" recur in "Young Goodman Brown." What if we select one of these—the theme of disillusionment—and examine it further? We may recall and list exemplars of Brown's disillusionment. His catechism teacher, the church elders, the local citizenry, his wife Faith—one after the other Brown sees the people he admires or loves march through the story on their way to meet the devil. He is shocked by what he sees. Surely, we say to ourselves, the theme of the story must be the damaging effects of realizing that people whom we thought to be virtuous are instead tainted with sin.

To cite Brown's disillusionment and the gloomy, misanthropic outlook it causes as the theme of the story, however, may be to see it too much from his point of view. Having noted the recurrent ideas of the story, and having analyzed them thoroughly, we may still find ourselves searching for the one main idea that everything else supports or leads up to. We may suspect that the theme of the story is larger than Brown's perception of his situation. If we continue to think about Brown's reactions to the sinners, we may discern that his gloom is really, unbeknownst to him, the result of his spiritual pride in thinking that only he has been left untainted by sin. Perhaps, without realizing it, he goes to the woods so that his suspicions about the sinfulness of humankind can be confirmed. All the evidence of the story suggests that humankind generally is in league with the devil. Yet Brown, at the end of the story, sees himself set apart from this rout of sinners, a virtuous but disillusioned man who believes that only he has resisted the devil's temptations. The entire story, seen from this perspective, seems to support the idea that spiritual pride is the most damaging quality humans can possess.

If it proves little else, this analysis of the theme of "Young Goodman Brown" proves that we can make true statements about the theme of a story without exhausting the truth the story contains. If it is a good one, the story will transcend our attempts to sum it up with a clever formulation. In the face of the best fiction, we find ourselves in the position of the reader who, in attempting to underline passages important to the theme of the story, underlines everything. The truth of the fiction lies in our perception of its unity.

As you think about the themes of the two stories that follow (Thomas Mann's "Little Herr Friedemann" and Ernest Hemingway's "Indian Camp") look for recurrent ideas, dominant ideas, and for the unity of each story that all of its details seem to create and support. Also consider the following points:

1. The theme of a story will usually concern the main character and the changes undergone as a result of interactions with others. Pay attention to the main character and to what is learned, suffered, or experienced.
2. The theme will usually be anticipated before the end of the story. Note the "progress" of the main character as the story unfolds. Consider the story in retrospect to see how its development leads to its conclusion.
3. The theme of a story will usually be supported by other elements. Analyzing a story for its theme will help produce an integrated, balanced reading. Make note of how plot, character, setting, point of view, and symbolism support and create theme.
4. The theme of a story will usually be complex, not a moral as in a fable from Aesop, but a dramatized event or series of events that engages our emotions as well as our thoughts. When "boiled down" to simple statements, the themes of most stories will not seem profound. But remember that we should be less concerned with this relatively simple statement than with the emotional and intellectual appeals the story offers.
5. The theme of a story may go unperceived by any of the characters. Give thought not only to what the characters perceive about their actions and situations, but also to what these actions and situations imply about human behavior and the human condition. Sometimes the theme of a story can lie in the discrepancy between the characters' perceptions and the implications of what they do.

THOMAS MANN (1875–1955)

Little Herr Friedemann

Thomas Mann, born in Lubeck, Germany, achieved instant
recognition with his novel *Buddenbrooks* (1900). His most famous novel,
The Magic Mountain, was published in 1924. In 1929, he was awarded the
Nobel Prize for Literature. From 1933 to 1945, he lived and taught in the
United States and became an American citizen in 1944. "Little Herr
Friedemann," one of his earliest stories, first appeared in 1897.

It was the nurse's fault. When they first suspected, Frau Consul Friedemann had spoken to her very gravely about the need of controlling her
weakness. But what good did that do? Or the glass of red wine which she
got daily besides the beer which was needed for the milk? For they suddenly discovered that she even sank so low as to drink the methylated spirit
which was kept for the spirit lamp. Before they could send her away and
get someone to take her place, the mischief was done. One day the mother
and sisters came home to find that little Johannes, then about a month old,
had fallen from the couch and lay on the floor, uttering an appallingly faint
little cry, while the nurse stood beside him quite stupefied.

The doctor came and with firm, gentle hands tested the little creature's
contracted and twitching limbs. He made a very serious face. The three
girls stood sobbing in a corner and the Frau Consul in the anguish of her
heart prayed aloud.

The poor mother, just before the child's birth, had already suffered a
crushing blow: her husband, the Dutch Consul, had been snatched away
from her by sudden and violent illness, and now she was too broken to
cherish any hope that little Johannes would be spared to her. But by the
second day the doctor had given her hand an encouraging squeeze and told
her that all immediate danger was over. There was no longer any sign that
the brain was affected. The facial expression was altered, it had lost the
fixed and staring look. . . . Of course, they must see how things went on—
and hope for the best, hope for the best.

The grey gabled house in which Johannes Friedemann grew up stood
by the north gate of the little old commercial city. The front door led into
a large flag-paved entry, out of which a stair with a white wooden balustrade
led up into the second storey. The faded wall-paper in the living-room had
a landscape pattern, and straight-backed chairs and sofas in dark-red plush
stood round the heavy mahogany table.

Often in his childhood Johannes sat here at the window, which always
had a fine showing of flowers, on a small footstool at his mother's feet,
listening to some fairy-tale she told him, gazing at her smooth grey head,
her mild and gentle face, and breathing in the faint scent she exhaled. She

showed him the picture of his father, a kindly man with grey side-whiskers—he was now in heaven, she said, and awaiting them there.

Behind the house was a small garden where in summer they spent much of their time, despite the smell of burnt sugar which came over from the refinery close by. There was a gnarled old walnut tree in whose shade little Johannes would sit, on a low wooden stool, cracking walnuts, while Frau Friedemann and her three daughters, now grown women, took refuge from the sun under a grey canvas tent. The mother's gaze often strayed from her embroidery to look with sad and loving eyes at her child.

He was not beautiful, little Johannes, as he crouched on his stool industriously cracking his nuts. In fact, he was a strange sight, with his pigeon breast, humped back, and disproportionately long arms. But his hands and feet were delicately formed, he had soft red-brown eyes like a doe's, a sensitive mouth, and fine, light-brown hair. His head, had it not sat so deep between his shoulders, might almost have been called pretty.

When he was seven he went to school, where time passed swiftly and uniformly. He walked every day, with the strut deformed people often have, past the quaint gabled houses and shops to the old schoolhouse with the vaulted arcades. When he had done his preparation he would read in his books with the lovely title-page illustrations in colour, or else work in the garden, while his sisters kept house for their invalid mother. They went out too, for they belonged to the best society of the town; but unfortunately they had not married, for they had not much money nor any looks to recommend them.

Johannes too was now and then invited out by his schoolmates, but it is not likely that he enjoyed it. He could not take part in their games, and they were always embarrassed in his company, so there was no feeling of good fellowship.

There came a time when he began to hear certain matters talked about, in the courtyard at school. He listened wide-eyed and large-eared, quite silent, to his companions' raving over this or that little girl. Such things, though they entirely engrossed the attention of these others, were not, he felt, for him; they belonged in the same category as the ball games and gymnastics. At times he felt a little sad. But at length he had become quite used to standing on one side and not taking part.

But after all it came about—when he was sixteen—that he felt suddenly drawn to a girl of his own age. She was the sister of a classmate of his, a blonde, hilarious hoyden, and he met her when calling at her brother's house. He felt strangely embarrassed in her neighbourhood; she too was embarrassed and treated him with such artificial cordiality that it made him sad.

One summer afternoon as he was walking by himself on the wall outside the town, he heard a whispering behind a jasmine bush and peeped cautiously through the branches. There she sat on a bench beside a long-legged, red-haired youth of his acquaintance. They had their arms about each other and he was imprinting on her lips a kiss, which she returned amid giggles. Johannes looked, turned round, and went softly away.

His head was sunk deeper than ever between his shoulders, his hands trembled, and a sharp pain shot upwards from his chest to his throat. But he choked it down, straightening himself as well as he could. "Good," said he to himself. "That is over. Never again will I let myself in for any of it. To the others it brings joy and happiness, for me it can only mean sadness and pain. I am done with it. For me that is all over. Never again."

The resolution did him good. He had renounced, renounced forever. He went home, took up a book, or else played on his violin, which despite his deformed chest he had learned to do.

At seventeen Johannes left school to go into business, like everybody else he knew. He was apprenticed to the big lumber firm of Herr Schlievogt down on the river-bank. They were kind and considerate, he on his side was responsive and friendly, time passed with peaceful regularity. But in his twenty-first year his mother died, after a lingering illness.

This was a sore blow for Johannes Friedemann, and the pain of it endured. He cherished this grief, he gave himself up to it as one gives oneself to a great joy, he fed it with a thousand childhood memories; it was the first important event in his life and he made the most of it.

Is not life in and for itself a good, regardless of whether we may call its content "happiness"? Johannes Friedemann felt that it was so, and he loved life. He, who had renounced the greatest joy it can bring us, taught himself with infinite, incredible care to take pleasure in what it had still to offer. A walk in the springtime in the parks surrounding the town; the fragrance of a flower; the song of a bird—might not one feel grateful for such things as these?

And that we need to be taught how to enjoy, yes, that our education is always and only equal to our capacity for enjoyment—he knew that too, and he trained himself. Music he loved, and attended all the concerts that were given in the town. He came to play the violin not so badly himself, no matter what a figure of fun he made when he did it; and took delight in every beautiful soft tone he succeeded in producing. Also, by much reading he came in time to possess a literary taste the like of which did not exist in the place. He kept up with the new books, even the foreign ones; he knew how to savour the seductive rhythm of a lyric or the ultimate flavour of a subtly told tale—yes, one might almost call him a connoisseur.

He learned to understand that to everything belongs its own enjoyment and that it is absurd to distinguish between an experience which is "happy" and one which is not. With a right good will he accepted each emotion as it came, each mood, whether sad or gay. Even he cherished the unfulfilled desires, the longings. He loved them for their own sakes and told himself that with fulfilment the best of them would be past. The vague, sweet, painful yearning and hope of quiet spring evenings—are they not richer in joy than all the fruition the summer can bring? Yes, he was a connoisseur, our little Herr Friedemann.

But of course they did not know that, the people whom he met on the street, who bowed to him with the kindly, compassionate air he knew so well. They could not know that this unhappy cripple, strutting comically along in his light overcoat and shiny top hat—strange to say, he was a little vain—they could not know how tenderly he loved the mild flow of his life, charged with no great emotions, it is true, but full of a quiet and tranquil happiness which was his own creation.

But Herr Friedemann's great preference, his real passion, was for the theatre. He possessed a dramatic sense which was unusually strong; at a telling theatrical effect or the catastrophe of a tragedy his whole small frame would shake with emotion. He had his regular seat in the first row of boxes at the opera-house; was an assiduous frequenter and often took his sisters with him. Since their mother's death they kept house for their brother in the old home which they all owned together.

It was a pity they were unmarried still; but with the decline of hope had come resignation—Friederike, the eldest, was seventeen years further on than Herr Friedemann. She and her sister Henriette were over-tall and thin, whereas Pfiffi, the youngest, was too short and stout. She had a funny way, too, of shaking herself as she talked, and water came in the corners of her mouth.

Little Herr Friedemann did not trouble himself overmuch about his three sisters. But they stuck together loyally and were always of one mind. Whenever an engagement was announced in their circle they with one voice said how very gratifying that was.

Their brother continued to live with them even after he became independent, as he did by leaving Herr Schlievogt's firm and going into business for himself, in an agency of sorts, which was no great tax on his time. His offices were in a couple of rooms on the ground floor of the house so that at mealtimes he had but the pair of stairs to mount—for he suffered now and then from asthma.

His thirtieth birthday fell on a fine warm June day, and after dinner he sat out in the grey canvas tent, with a new head-rest embroidered by Henriette. He had a good cigar in his mouth and a good book in his hand. But sometimes he would put the latter down to listen to the sparrows chirping blithely in the old nut tree and look at the clean gravel path leading up to the house between lawns bright with summer flowers.

Little Herr Friedemann wore no beard, and his face had scarcely changed at all, save that the features were slightly sharper. He wore his fine light-brown hair parted on one side.

Once, as he let the book fall on his knee and looked up into the sunny blue sky, he said to himself: "Well, so that is thirty years. Perhaps there may be ten or even twenty more, God knows. They will mount up without a sound or a stir and pass by like those that are gone; and I look forward to them with peace in my heart."

Now, it happened in July of the same year that a new appointment to the office of District Commandant had set the whole town talking. The stout and jolly gentleman who had for many years occupied the post had been very popular in social circles and they saw him go with great regret. It was in compliance with goodness knows what regulations that Herr von Rinnlingen and no other was sent hither from the capital.

In any case the exchange was not such a bad one. The new Commandant was married but childless. He rented a spacious villa in the southern suburbs of the city and seemed to intend to set up an establishment. There was a report that he was very rich—which received confirmation in the fact that he brought with him four servants, five riding and carriage horses, a landau and a light hunting-cart.

Soon after their arrival the husband and wife left cards on all the best society, and their names were on every tongue. But it was not Herr von Rinnlingen, it was his wife who was the centre of interest. All the men were dazed, for the moment too dazed to pass judgment; but their wives were quite prompt and definite in the view that Gerda von Rinnlingen was not their sort.

"Of course, she comes from the metropolis, her ways would naturally be different," Frau Hagenström, the lawyer's wife, said, in conversation with Henriette Friedemann. "She smokes, and she rides. That is of course. But it is her manners—they are not only free, they are positively brusque, or even worse. You see, no one could call her ugly, one might even say she is pretty; but she has not a trace of feminine charm in her looks or gestures or her laugh—they completely lack everything that makes a man fall in love with a woman. She is not a flirt—and goodness knows I would be the last to disparage her for that. But it is strange to see so young a woman—she is only twenty-four—so entirely wanting in natural charm. I am not expressing myself very well, my dear, but I know what I mean. All the men are simply bewildered. In a few weeks, you will see, they will be disgusted."

"Well," Fräulein Friedemann said, "she certainly has everything she wants."

"Yes," cried Frau Hagenström, "look at her husband! And how does she treat him? You ought to see it—you will see it! I would be the first to approve of a married woman behaving with a certain reserve towards the other sex. But how does she behave to her own husband? She has a way of fixing him with an ice-cold stare and saying 'My dear friend!' with a pitying expression that drives me mad. For when you look at him—upright, correct, gallant, a brilliant officer and a splendidly preserved man of forty! They have been married four years, my dear."

Herr Friedemann was first vouchsafed a glimpse of Frau von Rinnlingen in the main street of the town, among all the rows of shops, at midday, when he was coming from the Bourse, where he had done a little bidding.

He was strolling along beside Herr Stephens, looking tiny and important, as usual. Herr Stephens was in the wholesale trade, a huge stocky man with round side-whiskers and bushy eyebrows. Both of them wore top hats; their overcoats were unbuttoned on account of the heat. They tapped their canes along the pavement and talked of the political situation; but half-way down the street Stephens suddenly said:

"Deuce take it if there isn't the Rinnlingen driving along."

"Good," answered Herr Friedemann in his high, rather sharp voice, looking expectantly ahead. "Because I have never yet set eyes on her. And here we have the yellow cart we hear so much about."

It was in fact the hunting-cart which Frau von Rinnlingen was herself driving today with a pair of thoroughbreds; a groom sat behind her, with folded arms. She wore a loose beige coat and skirt and a small round straw hat with a brown leather band, beneath which her well-waved red-blond hair, a good, thick crop, was drawn into a knot at the nape of her neck. Her face was oval, with a dead-white skin and faint bluish shadows lurking under the close-set eyes. Her nose was short but well-shaped, with a becoming little saddle of freckles; whether her mouth was as good or no could not be told, for she kept it in continual motion, sucking the lower and biting the upper lip.

Herr Stephens, as the cart came abreast of them, greeted her with a great show of deference; little Herr Friedemann lifted his hat too and looked at her with wide-eyed attention. She lowered her whip, nodded slightly, and drove slowly past, looking at the houses and shop-windows.

After a few paces Herr Stephens said:

"She has been taking a drive and was on her way home."

Little Herr Friedemann made no answer, but stared before him at the pavement. Presently he started, looked at his companion, and asked: "What did you say?"

And Herr Stephens repeated his acute remark.

Three days after that Johannes Friedemann came home at midday from his usual walk. Dinner was at half past twelve, and he would spend the interval in his office at the right of the entrance door. But the maid came across the entry and told him that there were visitors.

"In my office?" he said

"No, upstairs with the mistresses."

"Who are they?"

"Herr and Frau Colonel von Rinnlingen."

"Ah," said Johannes Friedemann. "Then I will—"

And he mounted the stairs. He crossed the lobby and laid his hand on the knob of the high white door leading into the "landscape room." And then he drew back, turned round, and slowly returned as he had come. And spoke to himself, for there was no one else there, and said: "No, better not."

He went into his office, sat down at his desk, and took up the paper. But after a little he dropped it again and sat looking to one side out of the window. Thus he sat until the maid came to say that luncheon was ready; then he went up into the dining-room where his sisters were already waiting, and sat down in his chair, in which there were three music-books.

As she ladled the soup Henriette said:

"Johannes, do you know who were here?"

"Well?" he asked.

"The new Commandant and his wife."

"Indeed? That was friendly of them."

"Yes," said Pfiffi, a little water coming in the corners of her mouth. "I found them both very agreeable."

"And we must lose no time in returning the call," said Friederike. "I suggest that we go next Sunday, the day after tomorrow."

"Sunday," Henriette and Pfiffi said.

"You will go with us, Johannes?" asked Friederike.

"Of course he will," said Pfiffi, and gave herself a little shake. Herr Friedemann had not heard her at all; he was eating his soup, with a hushed and troubled air. It was as though he were listening to some strange noise he heard.

Next evening *Lohengrin* was being given at the opera, and everybody in society was present. The small auditorium was crowded, humming with voices and smelling of gas and perfumery. And every eye-glass in the stalls was directed towards box thirteen, next to the stage; for this was the first appearance of Herr and Frau von Rinnlingen and one could give them a good looking-over.

When little Herr Friedemann, in flawless dress clothes and glistening white pigeon-breasted shirt-front, entered his box, which was number thirteen, he started back at the door, making a gesture with his hand towards his brow. His nostrils dilated feverishly. Then he took his seat, which was next to Frau von Rinnlingen's.

She contemplated him for a little while, with her under lip stuck out; then she turned to exchange a few words with her husband, a tall, broad-shouldered gentleman with a brown, good-natured face and turned-up moustaches.

When the overture began and Frau von Rinnlingen leaned over the balustrade Herr Friedemann gave her a quick, searching side glance. She wore a light-coloured evening frock, the only one in the theatre which was slightly low in the neck. Her sleeves were full and her white gloves came up to her elbows. Her figure was statelier then it had looked under the loose coat; her full bosom slowly rose and fell and the knot of red-blond hair hung low and heavy at the nape of her neck.

Herr Friedemann was pale, much paler than usual, and little beads of perspiration stood on his brow beneath the smoothly parted brown hair. He could see Frau von Rinnlingen's left arm, which lay upon the balustrade. She had taken off her glove and the rounded, dead-white arm and ringless hand, both of them shot with pale blue veins, were directly under his eye— he could not help seeing them.

The fiddles sang, the trombones crashed, Telramund was slain, general jubilation reigned in the orchestra, and little Herr Friedemann sat there motionless and pallid, his head drawn in between his shoulders, his forefinger to his lips and one hand thrust into the opening of his waistcoat.

As the curtain fell, Frau von Rinnlingen got up to leave the box with her husband. Johannes Friedemann saw her without looking, wiped his handkerchief across his brow, then rose suddenly and went as far as the door into the foyer, where he turned, came back to his chair, and sat down in the same posture as before.

When the bell rang and his neighbours re-entered the box he felt Frau von Rinnlingen's eyes upon him, so that finally against his will he raised his head. As their eyes met, hers did not swerve aside; she continued to gaze without embarrassment until he himself, deeply humiliated, was forced to look away. He turned a shade paler and felt a strange, sweet pang of anger and scorn. The music began again.

Towards the end of the act Frau von Rinnlingen chanced to drop her fan; it fell at Herr Friedemann's feet. They both stooped at the same time, but she reached it first and gave a little mocking smile as she said: "Thank you."

Their heads were quite close together and just for a second he got the warm scent of her breast. His face was drawn, his whole body twitched, and his heart thumped so horribly that he lost his breath. He sat without moving for half a minute, then he pushed back his chair, got up quietly, and went out.

He crossed the lobby, pursued by the music; got his top hat from the cloak-room, his light overcoat and his stick, went down the stairs and out of doors.

It was a warm, still evening. In the gas-lit street the gabled houses towered towards a sky where stars were softly beaming. The pavement echoed the steps of a few passers-by. Someone spoke to him, but he heard and saw nothing; his head was bowed and his deformed chest shook with the violence of his breathing. Now and then he murmured to himself:

"My God, my God!"

He was gazing horror-struck within himself, beholding the havoc which had been wrought with his tenderly cherished, scrupulously managed feelings. Suddenly he was quite overpowered by the strength of his tortured longing. Giddy and drunken he leaned against a lamp-post and his quivering lips uttered the one word: "Gerda!"

The stillness was complete. Far and wide not a soul was to be seen. Little Herr Friedemann pulled himself together and went on, up the street in which the opera-house stood and which ran steeply down to the river, then along the main street northwards to his home.

How she had looked at him! She had forced him, actually, to cast down his eyes! She had humiliated him with her glance. But was she not a woman and he a man? And those strange brown eyes of hers—had they not positively glittered with unholy joy?

Again he felt the same surge of sensual, impotent hatred mount up in him; then he relived the moment when her head had touched his, when he had breathed in the fragrance of her body—and for the second time he halted, bent his deformed torso backwards, drew in the air through clenched teeth, and murmured helplessly, desperately, uncontrollably: "My God, my God!"

Then went on again, slowly, mechanically, through the heavy evening air, through the empty echoing streets until he stood before his own house. He paused a minute in the entry, breathing the cool, dank inside air; then he went into his office.

He sat down at his desk by the open window and stared straight ahead of him at a large yellow rose which somebody had set there in a glass of water. He took it up and smelt it with his eyes closed, then put it down with a gesture of weary sadness. No, no. That was all over. What was even that fragrance to him now? What any of all those things that up to now had been the well-springs of his joy?

He turned away and gazed into the quiet street. At intervals steps passed and the sound died away. The stars stood still and glittered. He felt so weak, so utterly tired to death. His head was quite vacant, and suddenly his despair began to melt into a gentle, pervading melancholy. A few lines of a poem flickered through his head, he heard the *Lohengrin* music in his ears, he saw Frau von Rinnlingen's face and her round white arm on the red velvet—then he fell into a heavy fever-burdened sleep.

Often he was near waking, but feared to do so and managed to sink back into forgetfulness again. But when it had grown quite light, he opened his eyes and looked round him with a wide and painful gaze. He remembered everything, it was as though the anguish had never been intermitted by sleep.

His head was heavy and his eyes burned. But when he had washed up and bathed his head with cologne he felt better and sat down in his place by the still openwindow. It was early, perhaps only five o'clock. Now and then a baker's boy passed; otherwise there was no one to be seen. In the opposite house the blinds were down. But birds were twittering and the sky was luminously blue. A wonderfully beautiful Sunday morning.

A feeling of comfort and confidence came over little Herr Friedemann. Why had he been distressing himself? Was not everything just as it had been? The attack of yesterday had been a bad one. Granted. But it should be the last. It was not too late, he could still escape destruction. He must avoid every occasion of a fresh seizure; he felt sure he could do this. He felt the strength to conquer and suppress his weakness.

It struck half past seven and Friederike came in with the coffee, setting it on the round table in front of the leather sofa against the the rear wall.

"Good morning, Johannes," said she; "here is your breakfast."

"Thanks," said little Herr Friedemann. And then: "Dear Friederike, I am sorry, but you will have to pay your call without me, I do not feel well enough to go. I have slept badly and have a headache—in short, I must ask you—"

"What a pity!" answered Friederike. "You must go another time. But you do look ill. Shall I lend you my menthol pencil?"

"Thanks," said Herr Friedemann. "It will pass." And Friederike went out.

Standing at the table he slowly drank his coffee and ate a croissant. He felt satisfied with himself and proud of his firmness. When he had finished he sat down again by the open window, with a cigar. The food had done him good and he felt happy and hopeful. He took a book and sat reading and smoking and blinking into the sunlight.

Morning had fully come, wagons rattled past, there were many voices and the sound of the bells on passing trams. With and among it all was woven the twittering and chirping; there was a radiant blue sky, a soft mild air.

At ten o'clock he heard his sisters cross the entry; the front door creaked, and he idly noticed that they passed his window. An hour went by. He felt more and more happy.

A sort of hubris mounted in him. What a heavenly air—and how the birds were singing! He felt like taking a little walk. Then suddenly, without any transition, yet accompanied by a terror namelessly sweet came the thought: "Suppose I were to go to her!" And suppressing, as though by actual muscular effort, every warning voice within him, he added with blissful resolution: "I will go to her!"

He changed into his Sunday clothes, took his top hat and his stick, and hurried with quickened breath through the town and into the southern suburbs. Without looking at a soul he kept raising and dropping his head with each eager step, completely rapt in his exalted state until he arrived at the avenue of chestnut trees and the red brick villa with the name of Commandant von Rinnlingen on the gate-post.

But here he was seized by a tremor, his heart throbbed and pounded in his breast. He went across the vestibule and rang at the inside door. The die was cast, there was no retreating now. "Come what come may," thought he, and felt the stillness of death within him.

The door suddenly opened and the maid came towards him across the vestibule; she took his card and hurried away up the red-carpeted stair. Herr Friedemann gazed fixedly at the bright colour until she came back and said that her mistress would like him to come up.

He put down his stick beside the door leading into the salon and stole a look at himself in the glass. His face was pale, the eyes red, his hair was sticking to his brow, the hand that held his top hat kept on shaking.

The maid opened the door and he went in. He found himself in a rather large, half-darkened room, with drawn curtains. At his right was a piano, and about the round table in the centre stood several arm-chairs covered in brown silk. The sofa stood along the left-hand wall, with a landscape painting in a heavy gilt frame hanging above it. The wall-paper too was dark in tone. There was an alcove filled with potted palms.

A minute passed, then Frau von Rinnlingen opened the portières on the right and approached him noiselessly over the thick brown carpet. She wore a simply cut frock of red and black plaid. A ray of light, with motes dancing in it, streamed from the alcove and fell upon her heavy red hair so that it shone like gold. She kept her strange eyes fixed upon him with a searching gaze and as usual stuck out her under lip.

"Good morning, Frau Commandant," began little Herr Friedemann, and looked up at her, for he came only as high as her chest. "I wished to pay you my respects too. When my sisters did so I was unfortunately out . . . I regretted sincerely . . ."

He had no idea at all what else he should say; and there she stood and gazed ruthlessly at him as though she would force him to go on. The blood rushed to his head. "She sees through me," he thought, "she will torture and despise me. Her eyes keep flickering. . . ."

But at last she said, in a very high, clear voice:

"It is kind of you to have come. I have also been sorry not to see you before. Will you please sit down?"

She took her seat close beside him, leaned back, and put her arm along the arm of the chair. He sat bent over, holding his hat between his knees. She went on:

"Did you know that your sisters were here a quarter of an hour ago? They told me you were ill."

"Yes," he answered, "I did not feel well enough to go out, I thought I should not be able to. That is why I am late."

"You do not look very well even now," said she tranquilly, not shifting her gaze. "You are pale and your eyes are inflamed. You are not very strong, perhaps?"

"Oh," said Herr Friedemann, stammering, "I've not much to complain of, as a rule."

"I am ailing a good deal too," she went on, still not turning her eyes from him, "but nobody notices it. I am nervous, and sometimes I have the strangest feelings."

She paused, lowered her chin to her breast, and looked up expectantly at him. He made no reply, simply sat with his dreamy gaze directed upon her. How strangely she spoke, and how her clear and thrilling voice affected him! His heart beat more quietly and he felt as though he were in a dream. She began again:

"I am not wrong in thinking that you left the opera last night before it was over?"

"Yes, madam."

"I was sorry to see that. You listened like a music-lover—though the performance was only tolerable. You are fond of music, I am sure. Do you play the piano?"

"I play the violin, a little," said Herr Friedemann. "That is, really not very much—"

"You play the violin?" she asked, and looked past him consideringly. "But we might play together," she suddenly said. "I can accompany a little. It would be a pleasure to find somebody here—would you come?"

"I am quite at your service—with pleasure," said he, stiffly. He was still as though in a dream. A pause ensued. Then suddenly her expression changed. He saw it alter for one of cruel, though hardly perceptible mockery, and again she fixed him with that same searching, uncannily flickering gaze. His face burned, he knew not where to turn; drawing his head down between his shoulders he stared confusedly at the carpet, while there shot through him once more that strangely sweet and torturing sense of impotent rage.

He made a desperate effort and raised his eyes. She was looking over his head at the door. With the utmost difficulty he fetched out a few words:

"And you are so far not too dissatisfied with your stay in our city?"

"Oh, no," said Frau Rinnlingen indifferently. "No, certainly not; why should I not be satisfied? To be sure, I feel a little hampered, as though everybody's eyes were upon me, but—oh, before I forget it," she went on quickly, "we are entertaining a few people next week, a small, informal company. A little music, perhaps, and conversation. . . . There is a charming garden at the back, it runs down to the river. You and your sisters will be receiving an invitation in due course, but perhaps I may ask you now to give us the pleasure of your company?"

Herr Friedemann was just expressing his gratitude for the invitation when the door-knob was seized energetically from without and the Commandant entered. They both rose and Frau von Rinnlingen introduced the two men to each other. Her husband bowed to them both with equal courtesy. His bronze face glistened with the heat.

He drew off his gloves, addressing Herr Friedemann in a powerful, rather sharp-edged voice. The latter looked up at him with large vacant eyes and had the feeling that he would presently be clapped benevolently on the shoulder. Heels together, inclining from the waist, the Commandant turned to his wife and asked, in a much gentler tone:

"Have you asked Herr Friedemann if he will give us the pleasure of his company at our little party, my love? If you are willing I should like to fix the date for next week and I hope that the weather will remain fine so that we can enjoy ourselves in the garden."

"Just as you say," answered Frau von Rinnlingen, and gazed past him.

Two minutes later Herr Friedemann got up to go. At the door he turned and bowed to her once more, meeting her expressionless gaze still fixed upon him.

He went away, but he did not go back to the town; unconsciously he struck into a path that led away from the avenue towards the old ruined fort by the river, among well-kept lawns and shady avenues with benches.

He walked quickly and absently, with bent head. He felt intolerably hot, as though aware of flames leaping and sinking within him, and his head throbbed with fatigue.

It was as though her gaze still rested on him—not vacantly as it had at the end, but with that flickering cruelty which went with the strange still way she spoke. Did it give her pleasure to put him beside himself, to see him helpless? Looking through and through him like that, could she not feel a little pity?

He had gone along the river-bank under the moss-grown wall; he sat down on a bench within a half-circle of blossoming jasmine. The sweet, heavy scent was all about him, the sun brooded upon the dimpling water.

He was weary, he was worn out; and yet within him all was tumult and anguish. Were it not better to take one last look and then to go down into that quiet water; after a brief struggle to be free and safe and at peace? Ah, peace, peace—that was what he wanted! Not peace in an empty and sound-less void, but a gentle, sunlit peace, full of good, of tranquil thoughts.

All his tender love of life thrilled through him in that moment, all his profound yearning for his vanished "happiness." But then he looked about him into the silent, endlessly indifferent peace of nature, saw how the river went its own way in the sun, how the grasses quivered and the flowers stood up where they blossomed, only to fade and be blown away; saw how all that was bent submissively to the will of life; and there came over him all at once that sense of acquaintance and understanding with the inevitable which can make those who know it superior to the blows of fate.

He remembered the afternoon of his thirtieth birthday and the peaceful happiness with which he, untroubled by fears or hopes, had looked forward to what was left of his life. He had seen no light and no shadow there, only a mild twilight radiance gently declining into the dark. With what a calm and superior smile had he contemplated the years still to come—how long ago was that?

Then this woman had come, she had to come, it was his fate that she should, for she herself was his fate and she alone. He had known it from the first moment. She had come—and though he had tried his best to de-fend his peace, her coming had roused in him all those forces which from his youth up he had sought to suppress, feeling, as he did, that they spelled torture and destruction. They had seized upon him with frightful, irresistible power and flung him to the earth.

They were his destruction, well he knew it. But why struggle, then, and why torture himself? Let everything take its course. He would go his appointed way, closing his eyes before the yawning void, bowing to his fate, bowing to the overwhelming, anguishingly sweet, irresistible power.

The water glittered, the jasmine gave out its strong, pungent scent, the birds chattered in the tree-tops that gave glimpses among them of a heavy, velvety-blue sky. Little hump-backed Herr Friedemann sat long upon his bench; he sat bent over, holding his head in his hands.

Everybody agreed that the Rinnlingens entertained very well. Some thirty guests sat in the spacious dining-room, at the long, prettily decorated table, and the butler and two hired waiters were already handing round the ices. Dishes clattered, glasses rang, there was a warm aroma of food and perfumes. Here were comfortable merchants with their wives and daughters; most of the officers of the garrison; a few professional men, lawyers and the popular old family doctor—in short, all the best society.

A nephew of the Commandant, on a visit, a student of mathematics, sat deep in conversation with Fräulein Hagenström, whose place was directly opposite Herr Friedemann's, at the lower end of the table. Johannes Friedemann sat there on a rich velvet cushion, beside the unbeautiful wife of the Colonial Director and not far off Frau von Rinnlingen, who had been escorted to table by Consul Stephens. It was astonishing, the change which had taken place in little Herr Friedemann in these few days. Perhaps the incandescent lighting in the room was partly to blame; but his cheeks looked sunken, he made a more crippled impression even than usual, and his inflamed eyes, with their dark rings, glowed with an inexpressibly tragic light. He drank a great deal of wine and now and then addressed a remark to his neighbour.

Frau von Rinnlingen had not so far spoken to him at all; but now she leaned over and called out:

"I have been expecting you in vain these days, you and your fiddle."

He looked vacantly at her for a while before he replied. She wore a light-coloured frock with a low neck that left the white throat bare; a Maréchal Niel rose in full bloom was fastened in her shining hair. Her cheeks were a little flushed, but the same bluish shadows lurked in the corners of her eyes.

Herr Friedemann looked at his plate and forced himself to make some sort of reply; after which the school superintendent's wife asked him if he did not love Beethoven and he had to answer that too. But at this point the Commandant, sitting at the head of the table, caught his wife's eye, tapped on his glass and said:

"Ladies and gentlemen, I suggest that we drink our coffee in the next room. It must be fairly decent out in the garden too, and whoever wants a little fresh air, I am for him."

Lieutenant von Deidesheim made a tactful little joke to cover the ensuing pause, and the table rose in the midst of laughter. Herr Friedemann and his partner were among the last to quit the room; he escorted her through the "old German" smoking-room to the dim and pleasant living-room, where he took his leave.

He was dressed with great care: his evening clothes were irreproachable, his shirt was dazzlingly white, his slender, well-shaped feet were encased in patent-leather pumps, which now and then betrayed the fact that he wore red silk stockings.

He looked out into the corridor and saw a good many people descending the steps into the garden. But he took up a position at the door of the smoking-room, with his cigar and coffee, where he could see into the living-room.

Some of the men stood talking in this room, and at the right of the door a little knot had formed round a small table, the centre of which was the mathematics student, who was eagerly talking. He had made the assertion that one could draw through a given point more than one parallel to a straight line; Frau Hagenström had cried that this was impossible, and he had gone on to prove it so conclusively that his hearers were constrained to behave as though they understood.

At the rear of the room, on the sofa beside the red-shaded lamp, Gerda von Rinnlingen sat in conversation with young Fräulein Stephens. She leaned back among the yellow silk cushions with one knee slung over the other, slowly smoking a cigarette, breathing out the smoke through her nose and sticking out her lower lip. Fräulein Stephens sat stiff as a graven image beside her, answering her questions with an assiduous smile.

Nobody was looking at little Herr Friedemann, so nobody saw that his large eyes were constantly directed upon Frau von Rinnlingen. He sat rather droopingly and looked at her. There was no passion in his gaze nor scarcely any pain. But there was something dull and heavy there, a dead weight of impotent, involuntary adoration.

Some ten minutes went by. Then as though she had been secretly watching him the whole time, Frau von Rinnlingen approached and paused in front of him. He got up as he heard her say:

"Would you care to go into the garden with me, Herr Friedemann?"

He answered:

"With pleasure, madam."

"You have never seen our garden?" she asked him as they went down the steps. "It is fairly large. I hope that there are not too many people in it; I should like to get a breath of fresh air. I got a headache during supper;

perhaps the red wine was too strong for me. Let us go this way." They passed through a glass door, the vestibule, and a cool little courtyard, whence they gained the open air by descending a couple more steps.

The scent of all the flower-beds rose into the wonderful, warm, starry night. The garden lay in full moonlight and the guests were strolling up and down the white gravel paths, smoking and talking as they went. A group had gathered round the old fountain, where the much-loved old doctor was making them laugh by sailing paper boats.

With a little nod Frau von Rinnlingen passed them by, and pointed ahead of her, where the fragrant and well-cared-for garden blended into the darker park.

"Shall we go down this middle path?" asked she. At the beginning of it stood two low, squat obelisks.

In the vista at the end of the chestnut alley they could see the river shining green and bright in the moonlight. All about them was darkness and coolness. Here and there side paths branched off, all of them probably curving down to the river. For a long time there was not a sound.

"Down by the water," she said, "there is a pretty spot where I often sit. We could stop and talk a little. See the stars glittering here and there through the trees."

He did not answer, gazing, as they approached it, at the river's shimmering green surface. You could see the other bank and the park along the city wall. They left the alley and came out on the grassy slope down to the river, and she said:

"Here is our place, a little to the right, and there is no one there."

The bench stood facing the water, some six paces away, with its back to the trees. It was warmer here in the open. Crickets chirped among the grass, which at the river's edge gave way to sparse reeds. The moonlit water gave off a soft light.

For a while they both looked in silence. Then he heard her voice; it thrilled him to recognize the same low, gentle, pensive tone of a week ago, which now as then moved him so strangely:

"How long have you had your infirmity, Herr Friedemann? Were you born so?"

He swallowed before he replied, for his throat felt as though he were choking. Then he said, politely and gently:

"No, *gnädige Frau*. It comes from their having let me fall, when I was an infant."

"And how old are you now?" she asked again.

"Thirty years old."

"Thirty years old," she repeated. "And these thirty years were not happy ones?"

Little Herr Friedemann shook his head, his lips quivered.

"No," he said, "that was all lies and my imagination."

"Then you have thought that you were happy?" she asked.

"I have tried to be," he replied, and she responded:

"That was brave of you."

A minute passed. The crickets chirped and behind them the boughs rustled lightly.

"I understand a good deal about unhappiness," she told him. "These summer nights by the water are the best thing for it."

He made no direct answer, but gestured feebly across the water, at the opposite bank, lying peaceful in the darkness.

"I was sitting over there not long ago," he said.

"When you came from me?" she asked. He only nodded.

Then suddenly he started up from his seat, trembling all over; he sobbed and gave vent to a sound, a wail which yet seemed like a release from strain, and sank slowly to the ground before her. He had touched her hand with his as it lay beside him on the bench, and clung to it now, seizing the other as he knelt before her, this little cripple, trembling and shuddering; he buried his face in her lap and stammered between his gasps in a voice which was scarcely human:

"You know, you understand . . . . let me . . . . I can no longer . . . . my God, oh, my God!"

She did not repulse him, neither did she bend her face towards him. She sat erect, leaning a little away, and her close-set eyes, wherein the liquid shimmer of the water seemed to be mirrored, stared beyond him into space.

Then she gave him an abrupt push and uttered a short, scornful laugh. She tore her hands from his burning fingers, clutched his arm, and flung him sidewise upon the ground. Then she sprang up and vanished down the wooded avenue.

He lay there with his face in the grass, stunned, unmanned, shudders coursing swiftly through his frame. He pulled himself together, got up somehow, took two steps, and fell again, close to the water. What were his sensations at this moment? Perhaps he was feeling that same luxury of hate which he had felt before when she had humiliated him with her glance, degenerated now, when he lay before her on the ground and she had treated him like a dog, into an insane rage which must at all costs find expression even against himself—a disgust, perhaps of himself, which filled him with a thirst to destroy himself, to tear himself to pieces, to blot himself utterly out.

On his belly he dragged his body a little further, lifted its upper part, and let it fall into the water. He did not raise his head nor move his legs, which still lay on the bank.

The crickets stopped chirping a moment at the noise of the little splash. Then they went on as before, the boughs lightly rustled, and down the long alley came the faint sound of laughter.

QUESTIONS

1. What is the function of the short introductory section of the story? What is the symbolic significance of the fall that Little Herr Friedemann suffers?
2. What is the impact of Little Herr Friedemann's deformed physique on the other characters of the story?
3. Toward the end of the story (page 213) Mann uses the phrase "a dead weight of impotent, involuntary adoration" to describe Little Herr Friedemann's feelings toward Gerda von Rinnlingen. What is the significance of this phrase?
4. Why does Gerda reject Little Herr Friedemann?
5. Gerda's rejection of him may be the immediate cause of Little Herr Friedemann's suicide. What are other, more general, causes?

ERNEST HEMINGWAY (1899–1961)

Indian Camp

Ernest Hemingway was born in Oak Park, Illinois. After serving as an ambulance driver in World War I, he settled in Paris and worked as a correspondent. His novels, which include *The Sun Also Rises* (1926), *A Farewell to Arms* (1929), and *The Old Man and the Sea* (1952), are among the most popular of major twentieth century American novels. He won the Nobel Prize for Literature in 1954. "Indian Camp," one of many stories that concern Hemingway's fictional hero Nick Adams, was collected in *In Our Time* (1925).

At the lake shore there was another rowboat drawn up. The two Indians stood waiting.

Nick and his father got in the stern of the boat and the Indians shoved it off and one of them got in to row. Uncle George sat in the stern of the camp rowboat. The young Indian shoved the camp boat off and got in to row Uncle George.

The two boats started off in the dark. Nick heard the oarlocks of the other boat quite a way ahead of them in the mist. The Indians rowed with quick choppy strokes. Nick lay back with his father's arm around him. It was cold on the water. The Indian who was rowing them was working very hard, but the other boat moved further ahead in the mist all the time.

"Where are we going, Dad?" Nick asked.

"Over to the Indian camp. There is an Indian lady very sick."

"Oh," said Nick.

Across the bay they found the other boat beached. Uncle George was smoking a cigar in the dark. The young Indian pulled the boat way up on the beach. Uncle George gave both the Indians cigars.

They walked up from the beach through a meadow that was soaking wet with dew, following the young Indian who carried a lantern. Then they went into the woods and followed a trail that led to the logging road that ran back into the hills. It was much lighter on the logging road as the timber was cut away on both sides. The young Indian stopped and blew out his lantern and they all walked on along the road.

They came around a bend and a dog came out barking. Ahead were the lights of the shanties where the Indian bark-peelers lived. More dogs rushed out at them. The two Indians sent them back to the shanties. In the shanty nearest the road there was a light in the window. An old woman stood in the doorway holding a lamp.

Inside on a wooden bunk lay a young Indian woman. She had been trying to have her baby for two days. All the old women in the camp had been helping her. The men had moved off up the road to sit in the dark and smoke out of range of the noise she made. She screamed just as Nick and the two Indians followed his father and Uncle George into the shanty. She lay in the lower bunk, very big under a quilt. Her head was turned to one side. In the upper bunk was her husband. He had cut his foot very badly with an ax three days before. He was smoking a pipe. The room smelled very bad.

Nick's father ordered some water to be put on the stove, and while it was heating he spoke to Nick.

"This lady is going to have a baby, Nick," he said.

"I know," said Nick.

"You don't know," said his father. "Listen to me. What she is going through is called being in labor. The baby wants to be born and she wants it to be born. All her muscles are trying to get the baby born. That is what is happening when she screams."

"I see," Nick said.

Just then the woman cried out.

"Oh, Daddy, can't you give her something to make her stop screaming?" asked Nick.

"No. I haven't any anesthetic," his father said. "But her screams are not important. I don't hear them because they are not important."

The husband in the upper bunk rolled over against the wall.

The woman in the kitchen motioned to the doctor that the water was hot. Nick's father went into the kitchen and poured about half of the water out of the big kettle into a basin. Into the water left in the kettle he put several things he unwrapped from a handkerchief.

"Those must boil," he said, and began to scrub his hands in the basin of hot water with a cake of soap he had brought from the camp. Nick watched his father's hands scrubbing each other with the soap. While his father washed his hands very carefully and thoroughly, he talked.

"You see, Nick, babies are supposed to be born head first but sometimes they're not. When they're not they make a lot of trouble for everybody. Maybe I'll have to operate on this lady. We'll know in a little while."

When he was satisfied with his hands he went in and went to work.

"Pull back that quilt, will you, George?" he said. "I'd rather not touch it."

Later when he started to operate Uncle George and three Indian men held the woman still. She bit Uncle George on the arm and Uncle George said, "Damn squaw bitch!" and the young Indian who had rowed Uncle George over laughed at him. Nick held the basin for his father. It all took a long time.

His father picked the baby up and slapped it to make it breathe and handed it to the old woman.

"See, it's a boy, Nick," he said. "How do you like being an interne?"

Nick said, "All right." He was looking away so as not to see what his father was doing.

"There. That gets it," said his father and put something into the basin.

Nick didn't look at it.

"Now," his father said, "there's some stitches to put in. You can watch this or not, Nick, just as you like. I'm going to sew up the incision I made."

Nick did not watch. His curiosity had been gone for a long time.

His father finished and stood up. Uncle George and the three Indian men stood up. Nick put the basin out in the kitchen.

Uncle George looked at his arm. The young Indian smiled reminiscently.

"I'll put some peroxide on that, George," the doctor said.

He bent over the Indian woman. She was quiet now and her eyes were closed. She looked very pale. She did not know what had become of the baby or anything.

"I'll be back in the morning," the doctor said, standing up. "The nurse should be here from St. Ignace by noon and she'll bring everything we need."

He was feeling exalted and talkative as football players are in the dressing room after a game.

"That's one for the medical journal, George," he said. "Doing a Cæsarian with a jack-knife and sewing it up with nine-foot, tapered gut leaders."

Uncle George was standing against the wall, looking at his arm.

"Oh, you're a great man, all right," he said.

"Ought to have a look at the proud father. They're usually the worst sufferers in these little affairs," the doctor said. "I must say he took it all pretty quietly."

He pulled back the blanket from the Indian's head. His hand came away wet. He mounted on the edge of the lower bunk with the lamp in one hand and looked in. The Indian lay with his face toward the wall. His throat had been cut from ear to ear. The blood had flowed down into a pool where his body sagged the bunk. His head rested on his left arm. The open razor lay, edge up, in the blankets.

"Take Nick out of the shanty, George," the doctor said.

There was no need of that. Nick, standing in the door of the kitchen, had a good view of the upper bunk when his father, the lamp in one hand, tipped the Indian's head back.

It was just beginning to be daylight when they walked along the logging road back toward the lake.

"I'm terribly sorry I brought you along, Nickie," said his father, all his post-operative exhilaration gone. "It was an awful mess to put you through."

"Do ladies always have such a hard time having babies?" Nick asked.

"No, that was very, very exceptional."

"Why did he kill himself, Daddy?"

"I don't know, Nick. He couldn't stand things, I guess."

"Do many men kill themselves, Daddy?"

"Not very many, Nick."

"Do many women?"

"Hardly ever."

"Don't they ever?"

"Oh, yes. They do sometimes."

"Daddy?"

"Yes."

"Where did Uncle George go?"

"He'll turn up all right."

"Is dying hard, Daddy?"

"No, I think it's pretty easy, Nick. It all depends."

They were seated in the boat, Nick in the stern, his father rowing. The sun was coming up over the hills. A bass jumped, making a circle in the water. Nick trailed his hand in the water. It felt warm in the sharp chill of the morning.

In the early morning on the lake sitting in the stern of the boat with his father rowing, he felt quite sure that he would never die.

QUESTIONS

1. What are Uncle George's attitudes toward Nick's father (the doctor) and toward the events of the story? How do these attitudes affect our perception of Nick's father?
2. Hemingway's point of view in this story is generally objective or dramatic. This causes us to make inferences about the responses of the characters. Cite all the evidence you can to show that Nick is repelled by the woman's labor and the delivery of the baby and frightened by the death of her husband.
3. How do the father's responses to Nick differ in the death scene from what they were in the birth scene? What causes these differences?
4. How does the last sentence of the story support your conception of its theme?
5. Some critics have viewed "Indian Camp" as essentially a story of initiation. Into what is Nick being initiated? By whom—or by what?

WRITING ABOUT THEME

Writing an essay about the theme of a short story is a complex task that can be fraught with frustration, bewilderment, false confidence and over-generalization. It is tempting to oversimplify a story (which makes it easier to understand, of course), to settle for the obvious while ignoring the accurate, and to reduce the story to a clear-cut "moral" which makes it tidy and manageable.

To combat these temptations you should, after reading the story quickly to find out what happens in it, read it again carefully for evidence about the theme. Also, allow sufficient time for the intellectual and emotional impact of the story to sink in. Only by doing so can you obtain the principal benefit of grappling with the theme of a story: the opportunity to see the story as an integrated, unified whole wherein all details work together to support one another, like the various instruments in a symphony orchestra. Writing about a story's theme enables a reader to view its essential harmony, its coherence, and the way *all* of its voices or elements (plot, character, setting, point of view, tone) make *one* voice.

Finding a suitable topic for the paper can be a difficult task, for you are being asked to write about nothing less than the essential idea of the story. This difficulty can be helpful, however, for it will force you to look carefully at the entire story. As you think about your paper, consider the following five questions; each of which will help you think about theme.

1. What was your *original* notion of the main idea of the story? This may not be your final notion, but it may at least give you something to disprove. Be flexible.
2. Are there repeated or varied patterns of language, sensory detail, or situation in the story? Such patterns often reveal what authors consider important. They also can signal changes that help reveal the theme of the story.
3. How do the elements of the story affect each other? For example, does point of view help to reveal character? Is the plot of the story linked to changes in the setting? Are the characters of the story linked significantly to the settings they occupy? Answers to such questions will help reveal the unity of the story and will perhaps clarify its dominant idea.
4. Do any of the characters change significantly during the story? Do they differ at the end of the story from what they were at the beginning? If you think of Brown in "Young Goodman Brown," Emily in "A Rose for Emily," or Sammy in "A & P," you will see that the theme of a story usually concerns a significant change in the main character.
5. What is the tone of the story? Does it seem that the author is being ironic or satirical—that things aren't exactly as they seem? Consider point of view, and be wary of surprises.

The thesis statement of an essay about theme will concern the "thesis" or main idea of the story. Make the thesis statement broad enough to cover the principal theme or themes of the story, but narrow enough to be manageable in a short composition. Try to make the thesis a wholly predicated statement, not just a simple equation using "is." For example, instead of saying "the theme of 'Young Goodman Brown' is pride," try something like " 'Young Goodman Brown' shows the destructive, embittering effects of the pride that causes one man to consider himself the only human untainted by sin." This statement provides key words or phrases—"embittering," "destructive," "pride," "tainted by sin"—which should promote unity and may suggest an organizational pattern for your essay. In the case of "Young Goodman Brown," a cause-and-effect pattern suggested by the terms of the thesis statement might be workable. As you think about ways of organizing your essay, and as you look for details to support your thesis, take full advantage of the modes of expository writing you have used before. For example, use a comparison of Sammy's reactions to the girls and his boss's reactions to them to write about the theme of Updike's "A & P." Or use an analysis of cause and effect to get at the theme of Faulkner's "A Rose for Emily," or an extended definition of spiritual pride to analyze "Young Goodman Brown."

Another expository mode, the use of examples, could help you avoid the most common pitfall in writing about theme: the lack of concrete detail or "evidence" to support the thesis. Overgeneralization and a refusal to see the theme of the story in all its complexity are particular perils in writing about theme. Try to extract evidence from the whole story to show the reader that you have considered all of its elements. Also avoid reductiveness and excessive didacticism. The writer of the story did not preach to you, so don't preach to your reader. And remember—stick to what the text says.

The following sample essay uses the principle of contrast to comment on the theme of initiation in Ernest Hemingway's "Indian Camp." Note its thesis statement (at the end of the first paragraph), the way it uses a series of contrasts as its organizational pattern, and the way it draws evidence from the entire story, not just the conclusion.

Nick's Double Confrontation:
Initiation and Denial in Hemingway's "Indian Camp"

In Ernest Hemingway's "Indian Camp," the main character, Nick, is initiated into the mysteries of birth and death. This double confrontation draws him out momentarily from his secure naïveté, but he quickly retreats to security. The themes of initiation and retreat are signalled by three sets of contrasts.

The first contrast is between the way Nick is repelled by the childbirth he witnesses, but fascinated by the suicide that the childbirth causes. He crosses the lake to the Indian camp secure in his father's arms, but his security soon turns to fear and repulsion when he sees and hears the woman in labor. He says, "Oh, Daddy, can't you give her something to make her stop screaming?" Nick's father tries to teach him about labor and delivery. But Nick's "curiosity had been gone a long time." (page 218)

Contrasting with this fear of birth is the obvious fascination with which Nick considers the suicide of the Indian father. He stares at the corpse while his father examines it, and, as he and his father leave the camp, he questions his father about suicide and death.

The second contrast that bears on Nick's initiation is that between his father's reaction to the birth and his reaction to the subsequent suicide. As the birth occurs, Nick's father is in complete control of the situation. He tries to teach and show Nick about childbirth. Furthermore, in spite of the crude instruments and unpleasant conditions, he manages to deliver the child successfully. Afterwards he feels "exalted and talkative as football players are in the dressing room after a game." (page 218)

When he discovers that the Indian has committed suicide, however, Nick's father tries to shelter Nick from the grisly scene. He tells Uncle George to take Nick out of the shanty, and says "I'm terribly sorry I brought you along, Nickie." (page 219) In the concluding dialogue, Nick's father does not emphasize the Indian's death, but insists, when questioned, that dying is "pretty easy." (page 219)

The third contrast is between the events of birth and death themselves, as Nick sees them. Birth is difficult, loud, and painful; death is relatively easy, quiet, and sudden. Children may watch birth, but must be sheltered from death. A delivering woman causes a man to kill himself. Birth causes death: herein lies the key to Nick's final reaction.

In experiencing his double confrontation, Nick has not only been initiated into the mysteries of birth and death; he has also been initiated into his father's adult reactions to them. Moreover, because of the proximity in time of birth and death, Nick has naively drawn a causal connection between them. The difficult, agonizing labor of the Indian woman has apparently made him resolve never to subject himself to such a scene again. Since birth "causes" death, and since his father is a source of protection from both, Nick, at the end of the story, returns to his state of security in the boat with his father. He "felt sure that he would never die." (page 219) Experience has tested his character, and, with his father's help, he has become stronger as a result of what he has seen.

SUGGESTIONS FOR WRITING ABOUT THEME

1. Write an essay on "the danger of suppressed emotion" as the theme of Mann's "Little Herr Friedemann."
2. Explain the connection between the gruesome attic scene at the end of "A Rose for Emily" and what you consider to be the theme of the story.
3. Compare "A & P" and "Little Herr Friedemann" as stories of youthful and adult infatuation.
4. Write an essay comparing "Young Goodman Brown" and "Indian Camp" as stories of initiation.

5. Show how Faulkner uses images of time and resistance to change to support the theme of "A Rose for Emily."
6. Demonstrate how the different settings (town, then forest, then town again) support the theme of "Young Goodman Brown."
7. Write an essay that shows how the theme of Updike's "A & P" centers around Sammy's youthful defiance of his boss.

INTEGRATION AND EVALUATION

Classes in literature are sometimes criticized for being like classes in anatomy: after you have dissected the specimen, it's no longer recognizable. John Steinbeck once justified a trip to gather marine specimens in the Gulf of California by saying that only by feeling the tug of the fish on the line could he claim to have experienced the whole phenomenon; taking a grey object out of a jar of formaldehyde to count the number of spines on its dorsal fin was not experiencing the reality of "fish." So it is with literature. As the poet William Wordsworth wrote, "We murder to dissect." If the story remains in pieces as a result of analysis, and the whole is not reassembled for full enjoyment of the living thing, then you have not learned to appreciate the whole experience of literature. It should come to more than an intellectual pursuit—or counting spines on dorsal fins.

To fully appreciate William Faulkner's "A Rose for Emily," you need to see the interplay among the elements that comprise the short story; to see, for example, that Faulkner's use of flashbacks in the construction of the plot affects not only his choice of point of view, but also how the main character is conceived and the theme presented. Faulkner begins the story with the penultimate event, the funeral of Miss Emily Grierson, an old maid who had become a hereditary care for the town. The shocking ending, presented last in the sequence of events, has its desired effect on the reader because Faulkner has interrupted the normal sequence of events, creating suspense and involving the reader in the recreation of the events as they might actually have happened. Faulkner deliberately presents the incident of the smell coming from Miss Emily's house in part II, but doesn't introduce Homer Barron, the Yankee road construction foreman, until part III. He further confuses the true sequence of events by introducing the smell within the context of the generational differences between the new aldermen of the emerging South and the older, more genteel generation. At the same time he includes examples of foreshadowing in part II; for instance, when Miss Emily denies her father's death, Faulkner introduces a hint of congenital insanity. Like the townsman-narrator, the reader is drawn into discovering the truth about Miss Emily in stages. Faulkner uses the first-person-observer point of view to suggest that there is some responsibility on the town's part for the discovered "skeleton in the closet." What is unexpected is the discovery of necrophilia, the final macabre revelation coming when "the long strand of iron-grey hair" is lifted from the pillow. This strand of grey hair is one of the time markers Faulkner places in the story, giving his otherwise scrambled narrative coherence. We can place events on a chronological time line through the changing colors of Miss Emily's hair, the growing infirmity of her Negro servant, her increasing plumpness, and the changes in the generations of town leaders.

Like the blending of point of view and plot, character and theme are linked together and mingled with other elements in Faulkner's story. For all her uniqueness, Miss Emily remains a flat character, a symbol, in the way she is presented by the spokesman for the town. She is called at various times in the story "an idol in a niche," "a hereditary obligation," "a fallen monument." At the beginning of the story in the "cedar-bemused cemetery," she officially enters the town's legends, and the old Confederate veterans further confuse time at her funeral by misremembering, believing that they had danced with her. The passing of Miss Emily is the passing of an era, the passing of the Old South, "dear, inescapable, impervious, tranquil, and perverse." The ambivalence about Miss Emily is precisely the ambivalence of the townspeople toward the past: she sleeps with the corpse of Homer Barron, a Yankee who flouted Southern customs; yet she is admired for preserving her position as the last of the Griersons against the ravages of time. Throughout the story, the setting supports this ambivalence. In the second paragraph, Faulkner emphasizes the contrast between the formerly elegant but now decayed Grierson mansion and its surrounding industrial wasteland. Later, he refers to signs of progress and improvement (postal service and roads) and he regrets the loss of gentility and its replacement by the harsher efficiency of the "rising generation." Like much of Faulkner's fiction, this story laments the changes that have brought to the South some of the worst aspects of an over-efficiency that has dehumanized people.

The dominant symbol in Faulkner's tale is, of course, the rose of the title, which appears only in the final scene of the story when the bridal chamber is broken into and a rosy hue seems to suffuse the entire tomb-like room: "A thin, acrid pall as of the tomb seemed to lie everywhere upon this room decked and furnished as for a bridal: upon the valance curtains of faded rose color, upon the rose-shaded lights. . . " A rose is a flower given in love, but this rose is given partly as a funereal offering, and partly to make amends for what the town had done to Miss Emily. The townspeople had frozen her in time, prevented her from growing and changing, and from having a full life. Through the townsman-spokesman's eyes, we see her unchanged, "bloated, like a body long submerged in motionless water."

Earlier, as young a woman, while all about her was changing, her image in the town's eyes remained static: "We had long thought of them as a tableau, Miss Emily a slender figure in white in the background, her father a spraddled silhouette in the foreground, his back to her and clutching a horsewhip, the two of them framed by the back-flung front door." Social customs had kept her from participating in life, and the town thought of her always in public, yet static terms: "angels in colored church windows," "a strained flag," "motionless as that of an idol," "the carven torso of an idol in a niche." Twice in her life Miss Emily had clung to the only life (and love) she had known: she held fast to the bodies of Homer and her father. So, at the story's conclusion, we are shocked by the necrophilia, yet we feel pity for Miss Emily.

How are we to evaluate a story which produces such an ambiguous reaction? Is a story good because it is ambiguous? What are the responsibilities of the author to help clarify his purpose, and at least partly resolve his intentions? Evaluating a short story calls for: 1) apprehending the author's purpose, intention, or theme; 2) objectively determining (without limiting the author to our own theological, philosophical, or social beliefs) whether such a theme has "high seriousness"; that is, whether its significance is proportionate to the aims of literature; and 3) deciding whether the means by which the story is told are appropriate to the theme the author has incorporated. Apply these three tests to Faulkner's story to see whether it passes or fails. If it passes, does it deserve to be called a "classic"—a story that not only fulfills the criteria, but fulfills them so well that it becomes an example of its kind, perhaps attracting other imitators?

By using the first-person-observer point of view, Faulkner creates the public voice of the town itself, making us as dependent as the town for our information and our view of Miss Emily. Part of the ambiguity of "A Rose for Emily" comes from this method of narration; yet Faulkner clarifies the ambiguity of action and narrative perspective with unambiguous language. The language of the descriptions—that of the Grierson house, for example, "lifting its stubborn and coquetish decay above the cotton wagons and the gasoline pumps"—reveals a nostalgia for the old ways. Similarly, the town's evolving emotions run the gamut from resentment toward "the high and mighty Griersons," to pity ("they could at last pity Miss Emily"), to sympathy ("we were all Miss Emily's allies"), to finally seeing her as "a tradition, a duty, and a care; a sort of hereditary obligation on the town." But the town fails to understand its collective responsibility for Miss Emily's withdrawal from life. Faulkner's ambiguity is within his purpose: to show the seductive charm of the Old South in the Grierson house with its charming "cupolas and spires and scrolled balconies," and in Miss Emily's haughty disregard for conventions. But his purpose is also to reveal through the gothic horror of the ending the unnaturalness and madness resulting from denying history's lesson: time cannot be resisted and the past must be relinquished.

Faulkner's story passes tests one and two—it has a clear theme, which is significant in terms of Southern history and in psychological terms. But does his story pass test three? Does the gothic horror story mix well with the historical theme of Faulkner's fiction? Here the case is less clear. While the allegory is unmistakable in "A Rose for Emily," the horror elements may seem to be a distraction from the *real* point Faulkner is making. Only by introducing what Harry Levin has called in another Southern writer, Edgar Allan Poe, "the power of blackness," can Faulkner find an antidote of sufficient strength to counter the danger of his story's slipping into the mawkish sentimentality of a romantic Southern local color story that celebrates the values of a South which no longer exists. The success of Faulkner's antidote—gothic horror; black humor; grotesque, flat characters—can be seen in the many imitators spawned by this type of fiction. Southern writers like Carson McCullers, Flannery O'Connor, Eudora Welty, and Walker Percy have borrowed, each in his or her own unique way, one or more of Faulkner's antidotes. Judged on the basis of appropriateness of means to an end, Faulkner's story once more passes our test. "A Rose for Emily" is, therefore, a "classic" Southern gothic horror story, one that goes beyond the merely entertaining aspects of most gothic horror fiction to capture a Southern and even a social dilemma about the present's relationship to the past. The horror is functional, and the resulting integration of the parts to the artistic whole makes "A Rose for Emily" a timeless example of the modern short story.

As you discover the "Stories for Further Reading" that follow, see if you can find classics—or potential classics—among them. Note how they go beyond mere entertainment, and, by matching means and ends successfully, tell us something important about the human condition.

SECTION
4

Stories for Further Reading

TONI CADE BAMBARA (b. 1939)
The Lesson

Toni Cade Bambara was born in New York City and educated at Queens College and the City College of New York. She has written essays as well as fiction. "The Lesson" first appeared in *Gorilla, My Love* (1972), a collection of her short stories. Her most recent novel is *The Salt Eaters* (1980).

Back in the days when everyone was old and stupid or young and foolish and me and Sugar were the only ones just right, this lady moved on our block with nappy hair and proper speech and no makeup. And quite naturally we laughed at her, laughed the way we did at the junk man who went about his business like he was some big-time president and his sorry-ass horse his secretary. And we kinda hated her too, hated the way we did the winos who cluttered up our parks and pissed on our handball walls and stank up our hallways and stairs so you couldn't halfway play hide-and-seek without a goddamn gas mask. Miss Moore was her name. The only woman on the block with no first name. And she was black as hell, cept for her feet, which were fish-white and spooky. And she was always planning these boring-ass things for us to do, us being my cousin, mostly, who lived on the block cause we all moved North the same time and to the same apartment then spread out gradual to breathe. And our parents would yank our heads into some kinda shape and crisp up our clothes so we'd be presentable for travel with Miss Moore, who always looked like she was going to church, though she never did. Which is just one of things the grownups talked about when they talked behind her back like a dog. But when she came calling with some sachet she'd sewed up or some gingerbread she'd made or some book, why then they'd all be too embarrassed to turn her down and we'd get handed out all spruced up. She'd been to college and said it only right that she should take responsibility for the young ones' education, and she not even related by marriage or blood. So they'd go for it. Specially Aunt Gretchen. She was the main gofer in the family. You got some ole dumb shit foolishness you want somebody to go for, you send for Aunt Gretchen. She been screwed into the go-along for so long, it's a blood-deep natural thing with her. Which is how she got saddled with me and Sugar and Junior in the first place while our mothers were in a la-de-da apartment up the block having a good ole time.

So this one day Miss Moore rounds us all up at the mailbox and it's puredee hot and she's knockin herself out about arithmetic. And school suppose to let up in summer I heard, but she don't never let up. And the starch in my pinafore scratching the shit outta me and I'm really hating this nappy-head bitch and her goddamn college degree. I'd much rather go to the pool or to the show where it's cool. So me and Sugar leaning on the mailbox being surly, which is a Miss Moore word. And Flyboy checking out what everybody brought for lunch. And Fat Butt already wasting his peanut-butter-and-jelly sandwich like the pig he is. And Junebug punchin on Q.T.'s arm for potato chips. And Rose Giraffe shifting from one hip to the other waiting for somebody to step on her foot or ask her if she from Georgia so she can kick ass, preferably Mercedes'. And Miss Moore asking us do we know what money is, like we a bunch of retards. I mean real money, she say, like it's only poker chips or monopoly papers we lay on the grocer. So right away I'm tired of this and say so. And would much rather snatch Sugar and go to the Sunset and terrorize the West Indian kids and take their hair ribbons and their money too. And Miss Moore files that remark away for next week's lesson on brotherhood, I can tell. And finally I say we oughta get to the subway cause it's cooler and besides we might meet some cute boys. Sugar done swiped her mama's lipstick, so we ready.

So we heading down the street and she's boring us silly about what things cost and what our parents make and how much goes for rent and how money ain't divided up right in this country. And then she gets to the part about we all poor and live in the slums, which I don't feature. And I'm ready to speak on that, but she steps out in the street and hails two cabs just like that. Then she hustles half the crew in with her and hands me a five-dollar bill and tells me to calculate 10 percent tip for the driver. And we're off. Me and Sugar and Junebug and Flyboy hangin out the window and hollering to everybody, putting lipstick on each other cause Flyboy a faggot anyway, and making farts with our sweaty armpits. But I'm mostly trying to figure how to spend this money. But they all fascinated with the meter ticking and Junebug starts laying bets as to how much it'll read when Flyboy can't hold his breath no more. Then Sugar lays bets as to how much it'll be when we get there. So I'm stuck. Don't nobody want to go for my plan, which is to jump out at the next light and run off to the first bar-b-que we can find. Then the driver tells us to get the hell out cause we are there already. And the meter reads eighty-five cents. And I'm stalling to figure out the tip and Sugar say give him a dime. And I decide he don't need it bad as I do, so later for him. But then he tries to take off with Junebug foot still in the door so we talk about his mama something ferocious. Then we check out that we on Fifth Avenue and everybody dressed up in stockings. One lady in a fur coat, hot as it is. White folks crazy.

"This is the place," Miss Moore say, presenting it to us in the voice she uses at the museum. "Let's look in the windows before we go in."

"Can we steal?" Sugar asks very serious like she's getting the ground rules squared away before she plays. "I beg your pardon," say Miss Moore, and we fall out. So she leads us around the windows of the toy store and me and Sugar screamin, "This is mine, that's mine, I gotta have that, that was made for me, I was born for that," till Big Butt drowns us out.

"Hey, I'm goin to buy that there."

"That there? You don't even know what it is, stupid."

"I do so," he say punchin on Rosie Giraffe. "It's a microscope."

"Whatcha gonna do with a microscope, fool?"

"Look at things."

"Like what, Ronald?" ask Miss Moore. And Big Butt ain't got the first notion. So here go Miss Moore gabbing about the thousands of bacteria in a drop of water and the somethinorother in a speck of blood and the million and one living things in the air around us is invisible to the naked eye. And what she say that for? Junebug go to town on that "naked" and we rolling. Then Miss Moore ask what it cost. So we all jam into the window smudgin it up and the price tag say $300. So then she ask how long'd take for Big Butt and Junebug to save up their allowances. "Too long," I say. "Yeh," adds Sugar, "outgrown it by that time." And Miss Moore say no, you never outgrow learning instruments. "Why, even medical students and interns and," blah, blah, blah. And we ready to choke Big Butt for bringing it up in the first damn place.

"This here costs four hundred eighty dollars," say Rosie Giraffe. So we pile up all over her to see what she pointin out. My eyes tell me it's a chunk of glass cracked with something heavy, and different-color inks dripped into the splits, then the whole thing put into a oven or something. But for $480 it don't make sense.

"That's a paperweight made of semi-precious stones fused together under tremendous pressure," she explains slowly, with her hands doing the mining and all the factory work.

"So what's paperweight?" asks Rosie Giraffe.

"To weight paper with, dumbbell," say Flyboy, the wise man from the East.

"Not exactly," say Miss Moore, which is what she say when you warm or way off too. "It's to weigh paper down so it won't scatter and make your desk untidy." So right away me and Sugar curtsy to each other and then to Mercedes who is more the tidy type.

"We don't keep paper on top of the desk in my class," say Junebug, figuring Miss Moore crazy or lyin one.

"At home, then," she say. "Don't you have a calendar and a pencil case and a blotter and a letter-opener on your desk at home where you do your homework?" And she know damn well what our homes look like cause she nosys around in them every chance she gets.

"I don't even have a desk," say Junebug. "Do we?"

"No. And I don't get no homework neither," say Big Butt.

"And I don't even have a home," say Flyboy like he do at school to keep the white folks off his back and sorry for him. Send this poor kid to camp posters, is his speciality.

"I do," say Mercedes. "I have a box of stationery on my desk and a picture of my cat. My godmother bought the stationery and the desk. There's a big rose on each sheet and the envelopes smell like roses."

"Who wants to know about your smelly-ass stationery," say Rosie Giraffe fore I can get my two cents in.

"It's important to have a work area all your own so that . . ."

"Will you look at this sailboat, please," say Flyboy, cuttin her off and pointin to the thing like it was his. So once again we tumble all over each other to gaze at this magnificent thing in the toy store which is just big enough to maybe sail two kittens across the pond if you strap them to the posts tight. We all start reciting the price tag like we in assembly. "Handcrafted sailboat of fiberglass at one thousand one hundred ninety-five dollars."

"Unbelievable," I hear myself say and am really stunned. I read it again for myself just in case the group recitation put me in a trance. Same thing. For some reason this pisses me off. We look at Miss Moore and she lookin at us, waiting for I dunno what.

"Who'd pay all that when you can buy a sailboat set for a quarter at Pop's, a tube of glue for a dime, and a ball of string for eight cents? It must have a motor and a whole lot else besides," I say. "My sailboat cost me about fifty cents."

"But will it take water?" say Mercedes with her smart ass.

"Took mine to Alley Pond Park once," say Flyboy. "String broke. Lost it. Pity."

"Sailed mine in Central Park and it keeled over and sank. Had to ask my father for another dollar."

"And you got the strap," laugh Big Butt. "The jerk didn't even have a string on it. My old man wailed on his behind."

Little Q.T. was staring hard at the sailboat and you could see he wanted it bad. But he too little and somebody'd just take it from him. So what the hell. "This boat for kids, Miss Moore?"

"Parents silly to buy something like that just to get all broke up," say Rosie Giraffe.

"That much money it should last forever," I figure.

"My father'd buy it for me if I wanted it."

"Your father, my ass," say Rosie Giraffe getting a chance to finally push Mercedes.

"Must be rich people shop here," say Q.T.

"You are a very bright boy," say Flyboy. "What was your first clue?" And he rap him on the head with the back of his knuckles, since Q.T. the only one he could get away with. Though Q.T. liable to come up behind you years later and get his licks in when you half expect it.

"What I want to know is," I says to Miss Moore though I never talk to her, I wouldn't give the bitch that satisfaction, "is how much a real boat costs? I figure a thousand'd get you a yacht any day."

"Why don't you check that out," she says, "and report back to the group?" Which really pains my ass. If you gonna mess up a perfectly good swim day least you could do is have some answers. "Let's go in," she say like she got something up her sleeve. Only she don't lead the way. So me and Sugar turn the corner to where the entrance is, but when we get there I kinda hang back. Not that I'm scared, what's there to be afraid of, just a toy store. But I feel funny, shame. But what I got to be shamed about? Got as much right to go in as anybody. But somehow I can't seem to get hold on the door, so I step away for Sugar to lead. But she hangs back too. And I look at her and she looks at me and this is ridiculous. I mean, damn, I have never ever been shy about doing nothing or going nowhere. But then Mercedes steps up and then Rosie Giraffe and Big Butt crowd in behind and shove, and next thing we all stuffed into the doorway with only Mercedes squeezing past us, smoothing out her jumper and walking right down the aisle. Then the rest of us tumble in like a glued-together jigsaw done all wrong. And people lookin at us. And it's like the time me and Sugar crashed into the Catholic church on a dare. But once we got in there and everything so hushed and holy and the candles and the bowin and the handkerchiefs on all the drooping heads, I just couldn't go through with the plan. Which was for me to run up to the altar and do a tap dance while Sugar played the nose flute and messed around in the holy water. And Sugar kept givin me the elbow. Then later teased me so bad I tied her up in the shower and turned it on and locked her in. And she'd be there till this day if Aunt Gretchen hadn't finally figured I was lying about the boarder takin a shower.

Same thing in the store. We all walkin on tiptoe and hardly touchin the games and puzzles and things. And I watched Miss Moore who is steady watchin us like she waitin for a sign. Like Mama Drewery watches the sky and sniffs the air and takes note of just how much slant is in the bird formation. Then me and Sugar bump smack into each other, so busy gazing at the toys, 'specially the sailboat. But we don't laugh and go into our fat-lady bump-stomach routine. We just stare at that price tag. Then Sugar run a finger over the whole boat. And I'm jealous and want to hit her. Maybe not her, but I sure want to punch somebody in the mouth.

"Watcha bring us here for, Miss Moore?"

"You sound angry, Sylvia. Are you mad about something?" Give me one of them grins like she tellin a grown-up joke that never turns out to be funny. And she's lookin very closely at me like maybe she plannin to do my portrait from memory. I'm mad, but I won't give her that satisfaction. So I slouch around the store bein very bored and say, "Let's go."

Me and Sugar at the back of the train watchin' the tracks whizzin by large then small then gettin gobbled up in the dark. I'm thinkin about this tricky toy I saw in the store. A clown that somersaults on a bar then does chin-ups just cause you yank lightly at his leg. Cost $35. I could see me askin my mother for a $35 birthday clown. "You wanna who that costs what?' she'd say, cocking her head to the side to get a better view of the hole in my head. Thirty-five dollars, could buy new bunk beds for Junior and Gretchen's boy. Thirty-five dollars and the whole household could go visit Granddaddy Nelson in the country. Thirty-five dollars would pay for the rent and the piano bill too. Who are these people that spend that much for performing clowns and $1,000 for toy sailboats? What kinda work they do and how they live and how come we ain't in on it? Where we are is who we are, Miss Moore always pointin out. But it don't necessarily have to be that way, she always adds then waits for somebody to say that poor people have to wake up and demand their share of the pie and don't none of us know what kind of pie she talkin about in the first damn place. But she ain't so smart cause I still got her four dollars from the taxi and she sure ain't getting it. Messin up my day with this shit. Sugar nudges me in my pocket and winks.

Miss Moore lines us up in front of the mailbox where we started from, seem like years ago, and I got a headache for thinkin so hard. And we lean all over each other so we can hold up under the draggy-ass lecture she always finishes us off with at the end before we thank her for borin us to tears. But she just looks at us like she readin tea leaves. Finally she say, "Well, what did you think of F.A.O. Schwartz?"

Rosie Giraffe mumbles, "White folks crazy."

"I'd like to go in there again when I get my birthday money," says Mercedes, and we shove her out the pack so has to lean on the mailbox by herself.

"I'd like a shower. Tiring day," say Flyboy.

Then Sugar surprises me by sayin, "You know, Miss Moore, I don't think all of us here put together eat in a year what that sailboat costs." And Miss Moore lights up like somebody goosed her. "And?" she say, urging Sugar on. Only I'm standin on her foot so she don't continue.

"Imagine for a minute what kind of society it is in which some people can spend on a toy what it would cost to feed a family of six or seven. What do you think?"

"I think," say Sugar pushing me off her feet like she never done before, cause I whip her ass in a minute, "that this is not much of a democracy if you ask me. Equal chance to pursue happiness means an equal crack at the dough, don't it?" Miss Moore is besides herself and I am disgusted with Sugar's treachery. So I stand on her foot one more time to see if she'll shove me. She shuts up, and Miss Moore looks at me, sorrowfully I'm thinkin. And somethin weird is goin on, I can feel it in my chest.

"Anybody else learn anything today?" lookin dead at me. I walk away and Sugar has to run to catch up and don't even seem to notice when I shrug her arm off my shoulder.

"Well, we got four dollars anyway," she says.

"Uh hunh."

"We could go to Hascombs and get half a chocolate layer and then go to the Sunset and still have plenty money for potato chips and ice-cream sodas."

"Uh hunh."

"Race you to Hascombs," she say.

We start down the block and she gets ahead which is O.K. by me cause I'm goin to the West End and then over to the Drive to think this day through. She can run if she want to and even run faster. But ain't nobody gonna beat me at nuthin.

JOHN BARTH (b. 1930)

Night-Sea Journey

John Barth was born in Cambridge, Maryland, and educated at Johns Hopkins University. His novels, renowned for their experimentation with narrative technique, include *The Sot-Weed Factor* (1960), *Giles Goat-Boy* (1966), *Letters* (1979), and *Sabbatical: A Romance* (1982). "Night-Sea Journey" appeared in *Lost in the Funhouse* (1968), a collection of Barth's short fiction.

"One way or another, no matter which theory of our journey is correct, it's myself I address; to whom I rehearse as to a stranger our history and condition, and will disclose my secret hope though I sink for it.

"Is the journey my invention? Do the night, the sea, exist at all, I ask myself, apart from my experience of them? Do I myself exist, or is this a dream? Sometimes I wonder. And if I am, who am I? The Heritage I supposedly transport? But how can I be both vessel and contents? Such are the questions that beset my intervals of rest.

"My trouble is, I lack conviction. Many accounts of our situation seem plausible to me—where and what we are, why we swim and whither. But implausible ones as well, perhaps especially those, I must admit as possibly correct. Even likely. If at times, in certain humors—stroking in unison, say, with my neighbors and chanting with them 'Onward! Upward!'—I have supposed that we have after all a common Maker, Whose nature and motives we may not know, but Who engendered us in some mysterious wise and launched us forth toward some end known but to Him—if (for a moodslength only) I have been able to entertain such notions, very popular in certain quarters, it is because our night-sea journey partakes of their absurdity. One might even say: I can believe them *because* they are absurd.

"Has that been said before?

"Another paradox: it appears to be these recesses from swimming that sustain me in the swim. Two measures onward and upward, flailing with the rest, then I float exhausted and dispirited, brood upon the night, the sea, the journey, while the flood bears me a measure back and down: slow progress, but I live, I live, and make my way, aye, past many a drowned comrade in the end, stronger, worthier than I, victims of their unremitting *joie de nager*. I have seen the best swimmers of my generation go under. Numberless the number of the dead! Thousands drown as I think this thought, millions as I rest before returning to the swim. And scores, hundreds of millions have expired since we surged forth, brave in our innocence, upon our dreadful way. 'Love! Love!' we sang then, a quarter-billion strong, and churned the warm sea white with joy of swimming! Now all are gone down—the buoyant, the sodden, leaders and followers, all gone under, while wretched I swim on. Yet these same reflective intervals that keep me afloat have led me into wonder, doubt, despair—strange emotions for a swimmer!—have led me, even, to suspect . . . that our night-sea journey is without meaning.

"Indeed, if I have yet to join the hosts of the suicides, it is because (fatigue apart) I find it no meaningfuller to drown myself then to go on swimming.

"I know that there are those who seem actually to enjoy the night-sea; who claim to love swimming for its own sake, or sincerely believe that 'reaching the Shore,' 'transmitting the Heritage' (*Whose* Heritage, I'd like to know? And to whom?) is worth the staggering cost. I do not. Swimming itself I find at best not actively unpleasant, more often tiresome, not infrequently a torment. Arguments from function and design don't impress me: granted that we can and do swim, that in a manner of speaking our long tails and streamlined heads are 'meant for' swimming; it by no means follows—for me, at least—that we *should* swim, or otherwise endeavor to 'fulfill our destiny.' Which is to say, Someone Else's destiny, since ours, so far as I can see, is merely to perish, one way or another, soon or late. The heartless zeal of our (departed) leaders, like the blind ambition and good cheer of my own youth, appalls me now; for the death of my comrades I am inconsolable. If the night-sea journey has justification, it is not for us swimmers ever to discover it.

"Oh, to be sure, 'Love!' one heard on every side: 'Love it is that drives and sustains us!' I translate: we don't know *what* drives and sustains us, only that we are most miserably driven and, imperfectly, sustained. *Love* is how we call our ignorance of what whips us. 'To reach the Shore,' then: but what if the Shore exists in the fancies of us swimmers merely, who dream it to account for the dreadful fact that we swim, have always and only swum, and continue swimming without respite (myself excepted) until we die? Supposing even that there *were* a Shore—that, as a cynical companion of mine once imagined, we rise from the drowned to discover all those vulgar superstitions and exalted metaphors to be literal truth: the giant Maker of us all, the Shores of Light beyond our night-sea journey!—whatever would a swimmer do there? The fact is, when we imagine the Shore, what comes to mind is just the opposite of our condition: no more night, no more sea, no more journeying. In short, the blissful estate of the drowned.

" 'Ours not to stop and think; ours but to swim and sink. . . .' Because a moment's thought reveals the pointlessness of swimming. 'No matter,' I've heard some say, even as they gulped their last: 'The night-sea journey may be absurd, but here we swim, will-we nill-we, against the flood, onward and upward, toward a Shore that may not exist and couldn't be reached if it did.' The thoughtful swimmer's choices, then, they say, are two: give over thrashing and go under for good, or embrace the absurdity; affirm in and for itself the night-sea journey; swim on with neither motive nor destination, for the sake of swimming, and compassionate moreover with your fellow swimmer, we being all at sea and equally in the dark. I find neither course acceptable. If not even the hypothetical Shore can justify a sea-full of drowned comrades, to speak of the swim-in-itself as somehow doing so strikes me as obscene. I continue to swim—but only because blind habit, blind instinct, blind fear of drowning are still more strong than the horror of our journey. And if on occasion I have assisted a fellow-thrasher, joined in the cheers and songs, even passed along to others strokes of genius from the drowned great, it's that I shrink by temperament from making myself conspicuous. To paddle off in one's own direction, assert one's independent right-of-way, overrun one's fellows without compunction, or dedicate oneself entirely to pleasures and diversions without regard for conscience—I can't finally condemn those who journey in this wise; in half my moods I envy them and despise the weak vitality that keeps me from following their example. But in reasonabler moments I remind myself that it's their very freedom and self-responsibility I reject, as more dramatically absurd, in our senseless circumstances, than tailing along in conventional fashion. Suicides, rebels, affirmers of the paradox—nay-sayers and yea-sayers alike to our fatal journey—I finally shake my head at them. And splash sighing past their corpses, one by one, as past a hundred sorts of others: friends, enemies, brothers, fools, sages, brutes—and nobodies, million upon million. I envy them all.

"A poor irony: that I, who find abhorrent and tautological the doctrine of survival of the fittest (*fitness* meaning, in my experience, nothing more than survivalability, a talent whose only demonstration is the fact of survival, but whose chief ingredients seem to be strength, guile, callousness), may be the sole remaining swimmer! But the doctrine is false as well as repellent: Chance drowns the worthy with the unworthy, bears up the unfit with the fit by whatever definition, and makes the night-sea journey essentially *haphazard* as well as murderous and unjustified.

" 'You only swim once.' Why bother, then?

" 'Except ye drown, ye shall not reach the Shore of Life.' Poppycock.

"One of my late companions—that same cynic with the curious fancy, among the first to drown—entertained us with odd conjectures while we waited to begin our journey. A favorite theory of his was that the Father does exist, and did indeed make us and the sea we swim—but not a-purpose or even consciously; He made us, as it were, despite Himself, as we make waves with every tail-thrash, and may be unaware of our existence. Another was that He knows we're here but doesn't care what happens to us, inasmuch as He created (voluntarily or not) other seas and swimmers at more or less regular intervals. In bitterer moments, such as just before he drowned, my friend even supposed that our Maker wished us unmade; there was indeed a Shore, he'd argue, which could save at least some of us from drowning and toward which it was our function to struggle—but for reasons unknowable to us He wanted desperately to prevent our reaching that happy place and fulfilling our destiny. Our 'Father,' in short, was our adversary and would-be killer! No less outrageous, and offensive to traditional opinion, were the fellow's speculations on the nature of our Maker: that He might well be no swimmer Himself at all, but some sort of monstrosity, perhaps even tailless; that He might be stupid, malicious, insensible, perverse, or asleep and dreaming; that the end for which He created and launched us forth, and which we flagellate ourselves to fathom, was perhaps immoral, even obscene. Et cetera, et cetera: there was no end to the chap's conjectures, or the impoliteness of his fancy; I have reason to suspect that his early demise, whether planned by 'our Maker' or not, was expedited by certain fellow-swimmers indignant at his blasphemies.

"In other moods, however (he was given to moods as I), his theorizing would become half-serious, so it seemed to me, especially upon the subjects of Fate and Immortality, to which our youthful conversations often turned. Then his harangues, if no less fantastical, grew solemn and obscure, and if he was still baiting us, his passion undid the joke. His objection to popular opinions of the hereafter, he would declare, was their claim to general validity. Why need believers hold that *all* the drowned rise to be judged at journey's end, and non-believers that drowning is final without exception? In *his* opinion (so he'd vow at least), nearly everyone's fate was permanent death; indeed he took a sour pleasure in supposing that every 'Maker' made thousands of separate seas in His creative life-time, each populated like ours with millions of swimmers, and that in almost every instance both sea and swimmers were utterly annihilated, whether accidentally or by malevolent design. (Nothing if not pluralistical, he imagined there might be millions and billions of 'Fathers,' perhaps in some 'night-sea' of their own!) However—and here he turned infidels against him with the faithful—he professed to believe that in possibly a single night-sea per thousand, say, one of its quarter-billion swimmers (that is, one swimmer in two hundred fifty billions) achieved a qualified immortality. In some cases the rate might be slightly higher; in others it was vastly lower, for just as there are swimmers of every degree of proficiency, including some who drown before the journey starts, unable to swim at all, and others created drowned, as it were, so he imagined what can only be termed impotent Creators, Makers unable to Make, as well as uncommonly fertile ones and all grades between. And it pleased him to deny any necessary relation between a Maker's productivity and His other virtues—including, even, the quality of His creatures.

"I could go on (*he* surely did) with his elaboration of these mad notions—such as that swimmers in other night-seas needn't be of our kind; that Makers themselves might belong to different species, so to speak; that our particular Maker mightn't Himself be immortal, or that we might be not only His emissaries but His 'immortality,' continuing His life and our own, transmogrified, beyond our individual deaths. Even this modified immortality (meaningless to me) he conceived as relative and contingent, subject to accidental or deliberate termination: his pet hypothesis was that Makers and swimmers *each generate the other*—against all odds, their number being so great—and that any given 'immortal' (still speaking relatively) was only the cyclic process of incarnation, which itself might have a beginning and an end. Alternatively he liked to imagine cycles within cycles, either finite or infinite: for example, the 'night-sea,' as it were, in which Makers 'swam' and created night-seas and swimmers like ourselves, might be the creation of a larger Maker, Himself one of many, Who in turn et cetera. Time itself he regarded as relative to our experience, like magnitude: who knew but what, with each thrash of our tails, minuscule seas and swimmers, whole eternities, came to pass—as ours, perhaps, and our Maker's Maker's, was elapsing between the strokes of some supertail, in a slower order of time?

"Naturally I hooted with the others at this nonsense. We were young then, and had only the dimmest notion of what lay ahead; in our ignorance we imagined night-sea journeying to be a positively heroic enterprise. Its meaning and value we never questioned; to be sure, some must go down by the way, a pity no doubt, but to win a race requires that others lose, and like all my fellows I took for granted that I would be the winner. We milled and swarmed, impatient to be off, never mind where or why, only to try our youth against the realities of night and sea; if we indulged the skeptic at all, it was as a droll, half-contemptible mascot. When he died in the initial slaughter, no one cared.

"And even now I don't subscribe to all his views—but I no longer scoff. The horror of our history has purged me of opinions, as of vanity, confidence, spirit, charity, hope, vitality, everything—except dull dread and a kind of melancholy, stunned persistence. What leads me to recall his fancies is my growing suspicion that I, of all swimmers, may be the sole survivor of this fell journey, tale-bearer of a generation. This suspicion, together with the recent sea-change, suggests to me now that nothing is impossible, not even my late companion's wildest visions, and brings me to a certain desperate resolve, the point of my chronicling.

"Very likely I have lost my senses. The carnage at our setting out; our decimation by whirlpool, poisoned cataract, sea-convulsion; the panic stampedes, mutinies, slaughters, mass suicides; the mounting evidence that none will survive the journey—add to these anguish and fatigue; it were a miracle if sanity stayed afloat. Thus I admit, with the other possibilities, that the present sweetening and calming of the sea, and what seems to be a kind of vasty presence, song, or summons from the near upstream, may be hallucinations of disordered sensibility . . . .

"Perhaps, even, I am drowned already. Surely I was never meant for the rough-and-tumble of the swim; not impossibly I perished at the outset and have only imagined the night-sea journey from some final deep. In any case, I'm no longer young, and it is we spent old swimmers, disabused of every illusion, who are most vulnerable to dreams.

"Sometimes I think I am my drowned friend.

"Out with it: I've begun to believe, not only that *She* exists, but that She lies not far ahead, and stills the sea, and draws me Herward! Aghast, I recollect his maddest notion: that our destination (which existed, mind, in but one night-sea out of hundreds and thousands) was no Shore, as commonly conceived, but a mysterious being, indescribable except by paradox and vaguest figure: wholly different from us swimmers, yet our complement; the death of us, yet our salvation and resurrection; simultaneously our journey's end, mid-point, and commencement; not membered and thrashing like us, but a motionless or hugely gliding sphere of unimaginable dimension; self-contained, yet dependent absolutely, in some wise, upon the chance (always monstrously improbable) that one of us will survive the night-sea journey and reach . . . Her! *Her,* he called it, or *She,* which is to say, Other-than-a-he. I shake my head; the thing is too preposterous; it is myself I talk to, to keep my reason in this awful darkness. There is no She! There is no You! I rave to myself; it's Death alone that hears and summons. To the drowned, all seas are calm . . . .

"Listen: my friend maintained that in every order of creation there are two sorts of creators, contrary yet complementary, one of which gives rise to seas and swimmers, the other to the Night-which-contains-the-sea and to What-waits-at-the-journey's-end: the former, is short, to destiny, the latter to destination (and both profligately, involuntarily, perhaps indifferently or unwittingly). The 'purpose' of the night-sea journey—but not necssarily of the journeyer or of either Maker!—my friend could describe only in abstractions: *consummation, transfiguration, union of contraries, transcension of categories.* When we laughed, he would shrug and admit that he understood the business no better than we, and thought it ridiculous, dreary, possibly obscene. 'But one of you,' he'd add with his wry smile, 'may be the Hero destined to complete the night-sea journey and be one with Her. Chances are, of course, you won't make it.' He himself, he declared, was not even going to try; the whole idea repelled him; if we chose to dismiss it as an ugly fiction, so much the better for us; thrash, splash, and be merry, we were soon enough drowned. But there it was, he could not say how he knew or why he bothered to tell us, any more than he could say what would happen after She and Hero, Shore and Swimmer, 'merged identities' to become something both and neither. He quite agreed with me that if the issue of that magical union had no memory of the night-sea journey, for example, it enjoyed a poor sort of immortality; even poorer if, as he rather imagined, a swimmer-hero plus a She equalled or became merely another Maker of future night-seas and the rest, at such incredible expense of life. This being the case—he was persuaded it was—the merciful thing to do was refuse to participate; the genuine heroes, in his opinion, were the suicides, and the hero of heroes would be the swimmer who, in the very presence of the Other, refused Her proffered 'immortality' and thus put an end to at least one cycle of catastrophes.

"How we mocked him! Our moment came, we hurtled forth, pretending to glory in the adventure, thrashing, singing, cursing, strangling, rationalizing, rescuing, killing, inventing rules and stories and relationships, giving up, struggling on, but dying all, and still in darkness, until only a battered remnant was left to croak 'Onward, upward,' like a bitter echo. Then they too fell silent—victims, I can only presume, of the last frightful wave—and the moment came when I also, utterly desolate and spent, thrashed my last and gave myself over to the current, to sink or float as might be, but swim no more. Whereupon, marvelous to tell, in an instant the sea grew still! Then warmly, gently, the great tide turned, began to bear me, as it does now, onward and upward will-I nill-I, like a flood of joy—and I recalled with dismay my dead friend's teaching.

"I am not deceived. This new emotion is Her doing; the desire that possesses me is Her bewitchment. Lucidity passes from me; in a moment I'll cry 'Love!' bury myself in Her side, and be 'transfigured.' Which is to say, I die already; this fellow transported by passion is not I; *I am he who abjures and rejects the night-sea journey!* I. . . .

"I am all love. 'Come!' She whispers, and I have no will.

"You who I may be about to become, whatever You are: with the last twitch of my real self I beg You to listen. It is *not* love that sustains me! No; though Her magic makes me burn to sing the contrary, and though I drown even now for the blasphemy, I will say truth. What has fetched me across this dreadful sea is a single hope, gift of my poor dead comrade: that You may be stronger-willed than I, and that by sheer force of concentration

I may transmit to You, along with Your official Heritage, a private legacy of awful recollection and negative resolve. Mad as it may be, my dream is that some unimaginable embodiment of myself (or myself plus Her if that's how it must be) will come to find itself expressing, in however garbled or radical a translation, some reflection of these reflections. If against all odds this comes to pass, may You to whom, through whom I speak, do what I cannot: terminate this aimless, brutal business! Stop Your hearing against Her song! Hate Love!

"Still alive, afloat, afire. Farewell then my penultimate hope: that one may be sunk for direst blasphemy on the very shore of the Shore. Can it be (my old friend would smile) that only utterest nay-sayers survive the night? But even that were Sense, and there is no sense, only senseless love, senseless death. Whoever echoes these reflections: be more courageous than their author! An end to night-sea journeys! Make no more! And forswear me when I shall forswear myself, deny myself, plunge into her who summons, singing . . .

" 'Love! Love! Love!' "

DONALD BARTHELME (b. 1931)

Bishop

Donald Barthelme was born in Philadelphia and raised in Texas. He now lives in New York City. His novels include *Snow White* (1967) and *The Dead Father* (1975). His unconventional and humorous stories have been collected in several books, including *Come Back, Dr. Caligari* (1964), *Amateurs* (1976), and *Overnight to Many Distant Cities* (1983).

Bishop's standing outside his apartment building.

An oil truck double-parked, its hose coupled with the sidewalk, the green-uniformed driver reading a paperback called *Name Your Baby*.

Bishop's waiting for Cara.

The martini rule is not before quarter to twelve.

Eyes go out of focus. He blinks them back again.

He had a beer for breakfast, as usual, a Pilsner Urquell. Imported beer is now ninety-nine cents a bottle at his market.

The oil truck's pump shuts off with a click. The driver tosses his book into the cab and begins uncoupling.

Cara's not coming.

The painter John Frederick Peto made a living playing cornet in a camp meeting for the last twenty years of his life, according to Alfred Frankenstein.

Bishop goes back inside the building and climbs one flight of stairs to his apartment.

His bank has lost the alimony payment he cables twice a month to his second wife, in London. He switches on the FM, dialing past two classical stations to reach Fleetwood Mac.

Bishop's writing a biography of the nineteenth-century American painter William Michael Harnett. But today he can't make himself work.

Cara's been divorced, once.

At twenty minutes to twelve he makes himself a martini.

Hideous bouts of black anger in the evening. Then a word or a sentence in the tone she can't bear. The next morning he remembers nothing about it.

The artist Peto was discovered when, after his death, his pictures were exhibited with the faked signatures of William Michael Harnett, according to Alfred Frankenstein.

His second wife, working in London, recently fainted at her desk. The company doctor sent her home with something written on a slip of paper— a diagnosis. For two days she stared at the piece of paper, then called Bishop and read him the word: *lipothymia*. Bishop checked with the public library, called her again in London. "It means fainting," he said.

On the FM, a program called *How to Protect Against Radiation Through Good Nutrition*. He switches it off.

In the morning he remembers nothing of what had been said the previous night. But, coming into the kitchen and seeing her harsh, set face, he knows there's been a quarrel.

His eyes ache.

He's not fat.

She calls.

"I can't make it."

"I noticed."

"I'm sorry."

"How about tonight?"

"I'll have to see. I'll let you know."

"When?"

"As soon as I can."

"Can you give me a rough idea?"

"Before six."

Bishop types a letter to a university declining a speaking engagement.

He's been in the apartment for seventeen years.

His rent has just been raised forty-nine dollars a month.

Bishop is not in love with Cara, and she is certainly not in love with him. Still, they see each other rather often, sleep together rather often.

When he's given up on Cara, on a particular evening, he'll make a Scotch to take to bed with him. He lies on one elbow in the dark, smoking and sipping the Scotch.

He has a birthday in July, he'll be forty-nine.

Waking in the middle of the night he notices, again and again and again, that he sleeps with one fist jammed against his jaw—forearm, upper arm, and jaw making a rigid defensive triangle.

Cara says: "Everyone's got good taste, it just doesn't mean that much."

She's in textiles, a designer.

He rarely goes to lunch with anyone now.

On the street, he greets a neighbor he's never even nodded to before, a young man who is, he's heard, a lawyer. Bishop remembers the young man as a tall thin child with evasive eyes.

He buys flowers, daffodils.

In front of his liquor store there are six midday drunks in a bunch, youngish men, perhaps late thirties. They're lurching about and harassing passersby, a couple of open half pints visible (but this liquor store, Bishop knows, doesn't sell half pints). One of them, a particularly clumsy man with a red face under red stubble, makes a grab for his paper-wrapped flowers, Bishop sidesteps him easily, so early in the day, where do they get the money?

He thinks of correspondences between himself and the drunks.

He's not in love with Cara but he admires her, especially her ability to survive the various men she takes up with from time to time, all of whom (he does not include himself) seem intent on tearing her down (she confides to him), on tearing her to pieces. . . .

When Bishop puts out a grease fire in the oven by slapping at it with a dish towel she criticizes his performance, even though he's burned his arm.

"You let too much oxygen in."

He's convinced that his grandfather and grandmother, who are dead, will come back to life one day.

Bishop's telephone bill is a nightmare of long-distance charges: Charleston, Beverly Hills, New Orleans, Charleston, Charleston, London, Norfolk, Boston, Beverly Hills, London—

When they make love in the darkness of his very small bedroom, with a bottle of indifferent California wine on the night table, she locks her hands in the small of his back, exerting astonishing pressure.

Gray in beard, three wavy lines across his forehead.

"He would frequently paint one picture over another and occasionally a third picture over the second." Frankenstein, on Peto.

The flowers remain in their paper wrapping in the kitchen, on the butcher-block bar.

He watches the four o'clock movie, a film he's seen possibly forty times, Henry Fonda as Colonel Thursday dancing with Sergeant Major Ward Bond's wife at the Fort Apache noncommissioned officers' ball. . . .

Cara calls. Something's come up.

"Have a good evening."

"You too."

Bishop makes himself a Scotch, although it's only four-thirty and the rule about Scotch is not before five.

Robert Young says: "Sanka brand coffee *is* real coffee."

He remembers driving to his grandparents' ranch, the stack of saddles in a corner of the ranch house's big inner room, the rifles on pegs over the doors, sitting on the veranda at night and watching the headlights of cars coming down the steep hill across the river.

During a commercial he gets out the television schedule to see what he can expect of the evening.

6:00 (2, 4, 7, 31) News
      (5) I Love Lucy
      (9) Joker's Wild
    (11) Sanford and Son
    (13) As We See It
    (21) Once Upon a Classic
    (25) Mister Rogers

A good movie, *Edison*, with Spencer Tracy, at eight.

He could call his brother in Charleston.

He could call a friend in Beverly Hills.

He could make a couple of quarts of chili, freeze some of it.

Bishop stands in front of a mirror, wondering why his eyes hurt.

He could read some proofs that have been sitting on his desk for two weeks.

Another Scotch. *Fort Apache* is over.

He walks from the front of the apartment to the back, approving of the furniture, the rugs, the peeling paint.

Bishop puts on his down jacket and goes out to the market. At the meat counter a child in a stroller points at him and screams: *"Old man!"*

The child's mother giggles and says: "Don't take it personally, it's the beard."

What's easiest? Steak, outrageously priced, what he doesn't eat will be there for breakfast.

He picks out two bunches of scallions to chop up for his baked potato.

He looks around for something foolish to buy, to persuade himself he's on top of things.

His right arm still has three ugly red blotches from the episode of the grease fire.

Caviar is sixty-seven dollars for four ounces. But he doesn't like caviar.

Bishop once bought records, Poulenc to Bob Wills, but now does not.

Also, he formerly bought prints. He has a Jim Dine and a de Chirico and a Bellmer and a Richard Hamilton. It's been years since he's bought a print.

(Although he reads the art magazines religiously.)

A shrink once said to him: "Big Daddy, is that it?"

He's had wives, thick in emotional texture, with many lovely problems, his advice is generally good.

Diluted by caution perhaps.

When his grandfather and grandmother come back to life, Bishop sits with them on the veranda of the ranch house looking down to the river, they seem just the same and talk about the things they've always talked about. He walks with his grandfather over the terrain studded with caliche like half-buried skulls, a dirty white, past a salt lick and the windmill and then another salt lick, and his grandfather points out the place where his aunt had been knocked off her horse by a low-lying tree branch. His grandmother is busy burning toast and then scraping it (the way they like it), and is at the same time reading the newspaper, crying aloud "Ben!" and then reading him something about the Stewart girl, you remember who she is, getting married to that fellow who, you remember, got in all the trouble. . . .

With his Scotch in bed, Bishop summons up an image of felicity: walking in the water, the shallow river, at the edge of the ranch, looking for minnows in the water under the overhanging trees, skipping rocks across the river, intent . . .

JORGE LUIS BORGES (1899–1986)

The Garden of Forking Paths

Jorge Luis Borges, Argentina's most famous writer, was born in Buenos Aires and educated in Switzerland. His mysterious and allusive stories appeared in several collections, including *Ficciones* (1945), *The Aleph* (1949), and *Labyrinths* (1964). He also published poetry and essays. "The Garden of Forking Paths" first appeared in 1941.

To Victoria Ocampo

In his *A History of the World War* (page 212), Captain Liddell Hart reports that a planned offensive by thirteen British divisions, supported by fourteen hundred artillery pieces, against the German line at Serre-Montauban, scheduled for July 24, 1916, had to be postponed until the morning of the 29th. He comments that torrential rain caused this delay—which lacked any special significance. The following deposition, dictated by, read over, and then signed by Dr. Yu Tsun, former teacher of English at the Tsingtao *Hochschule*, casts unsuspected light upon this event. The first two pages are missing.

★ ★ ★ ★ ★ ★ ★ ★ ★ ★

. . . and I hung up the phone. Immediately I recollected the voice that had spoken in German. It was that of Captain Richard Madden. Madden, in Viktor Runeberg's office, meant the end of all our work and—though this seemed a secondary matter, *or should have seemed so to me*—of our lives also. His being there meant that Runeberg had been arrested or murdered.* Before the sun set on this same day, I ran the same risk. Madden was implacable. Rather, to be more accurate, he was obliged to be implacable. An Irishman in the service of England, a man suspected of equivocal feelings if not of actual treachery, how could he fail to welcome and seize upon this extraordinary piece of luck: the discovery, capture and perhaps the deaths of two agents of Imperial Germany?

I went up to my bedroom. Absurd though the gesture was, I closed and locked the door. I threw myself down on my narrow iron bed, and waited on my back. The never changing rooftops filled the window, and the hazy six o'clock sun hung in the sky. It seemed incredible that this day, a day without warnings or omens, might be that of my implacable death. In despite of my dead father, in despite of having been a child in one of the symmetrical gardens of Hai Feng, was I to die now?

Then I reflected that all things happen, happen to one, precisely *now*. Century follows century, and things happen only in the present. There are countless men in the air, on land and at sea, and all that really happens happens to me. . . . The almost unbearable memory of Madden's long horseface put an end to these wandering thoughts.

In the midst of my hatred and terror (now that it no longer matters to me to speak of terror, now that I have outwitted Richard Madden, not that my neck hankers for the hangman's noose), I knew that the fast-moving and doubtless happy soldier did not suspect that I possessed the Secret— the name of the exact site of the new British artillery park on the Ancre. A bird streaked across the misty sky and, absently, I turned it into an airplane and then that airplane into many in the skies of France, shattering the artillery park under a rain of bombs. If only my mouth, before it should be silenced by a bullet, could shout this name in such a way that it could be heard in Germany. . . . My voice, my human voice, was weak. How could it reach the ear of the Chief? The ear of that sick and hateful man who knew nothing of Runeberg or of me except that we were in Staffordshire. A man who, sitting in his arid Berlin office, leafed infinitely through newspapers, looking in vain for news from us. I said aloud, "I must flee."

---

*A malicious and outlandish statement. In point of fact, Captain Richard Madden had been attacked by the Prussian spy Hans Rabener, alias Viktor Runeberg, who drew an automatic pistol when Madden appeared with orders for the spy's arrest. Madden, in self defense, had inflicted wounds of which the spy later died.—*Note by the manuscript editor.*

I sat up on the bed, in senseless and perfect silence, as if Madden was already peering at me. Somthing—perhaps merely a desire to prove my total penury to myself—made me empty out my pockets. I found just what I knew I was going to find. The American watch, the nickel-plated chain and the square coin, the key ring with the useless but compromising keys to Runeberg's office, the notebook, a letter which I decided to destroy at once (and which I did not destroy), a five shilling piece, two single shillings and some pennies, a red and blue pencil, a handkerchief—and a revolver with a single bullet. Absurdly I held it and weighed it in my hand, to give myself courage. Vaguely I thought that a pistol shot can be heard for a great distance.

In ten minutes I had developed my plan. The telephone directory gave me the name of the one person capable of passing on the information. He lived in a suburb of Fenton, less than half an hour away by train.

I am a timorous man. I can say it now, now that I have brought my incredibly risky plan to an end. It was not easy to bring about, and I know that its execution was terrible. I did not do it for Germany—no! Such a barbarous country is of no importance to me, particularly since it had degraded me by making me become a spy. Furthermore, I knew an Englishman—a modest man—who, for me, is as great as Goethe. I did not speak with him for more than an hour, but during that time, he *was* Goethe.

I carried out my plan because I felt the Chief had some fear of those of my race, of those uncountable forebears whose culmination lies in me. I wished to prove to him that a yellow man could save his armies. Besides, I had to escape the Captain. His hands and voice could, at any moment, knock and beckon at my door.

Silently, I dressed, took leave of myself in the mirror, went down the stairs, sneaked a look at the quiet street, and went out. The station was not far from my house, but I thought it more prudent to take a cab. I told myself that I thus ran less chance of being recognized. The truth is that, in the deserted street, I felt infinitely visible and vulnerable. I recall that I told the driver to stop short of the main entrance. I got out with a painful and deliberate slowness.

I was going to the village of Ashgrove, but took a ticket for a station further on. The train would leave in a few minutes, at eight-fifty. I hurried, for the next would not go until half past nine. There was almost no one on the platform. I walked through the carriages. I remember some farmers, a woman dressed in mourning, a youth deep in Tacitus' *Annals* and a wounded, happy soldier.

At last the train pulled out. A man I recognized ran furiously, but vainly, the length of the platform. It was Captain Richard Madden. Shattered, trembling, I huddled in the distant corner of the seat, as far as possible from the fearful window.

From utter terror I passed into a state of almost abject happiness. I told myself that the duel had already started and that I had won the first encounter by besting my adversary in his first attack—even if it was only for forty minutes—by an accident of fate. I argued that so small a victory prefigured a total victory. I argued that it was not so trivial, that were it not for the precious accident of the train schedule, I would be in prison or dead. I argued, with no less sophism, that my timorous happiness was proof that I was man enough to bring this adventure to a successful conclusion. From my weakness I drew strength that never left me.

I foresee that man will resign himself each day to new abominations, that soon only soldiers and bandits will be left. To them I offer this advice: *Whosoever would undertake some atrocious enterprise should act as if it were already accomplished, should impose upon himself a future as irrevocable as the past.*

Thus I proceeded, while with the eyes of a man already dead, I contemplated the fluctuations of the day which would probably be my last, and watched the diffuse coming of night.

The train crept along gently, amid ash trees. It slowed down and stopped, almost in the middle of a field. No one called the name of a station. "Ashgrove?" I asked some children on the platform. "Ashgrove," they replied. I got out.

A lamp lit the platform, but the children's faces remained in a shadow. One of them asked me: "Are you going to Dr. Stephen Albert's house?" Without waiting for my answer, another said: "The house is a good distance away but you won't get lost if you take the road to the left and bear to the left at every crossroad." I threw them a coin (my last), went down some stone steps and started along a deserted road. At a slight incline, the road ran downhill. It was a plain dirt way, and overhead the branches of trees intermingled, while a round moon hung low in the sky as if to keep me company.

For a moment I thought that Richard Madden might in some way have divined my desperate intent. At once I realized that this would be impossible. The advice about turning always to the left reminded me that such was the common formula for finding the central courtyard of certain labyrinths. I know something about labyrinths. Not for nothing am I the great-grandson of Ts'ui Pên. He was Governor of Yunnan and gave up temporal power to write a novel with more characters than there are in the *Hung Lou Mêng*, and to create a maze in which all men would lose themselves. He spent thirteen years on these oddly assorted tasks before he was assassinated by a stranger. His novel had no sense to it and nobody ever found his labyrinth.

Under the trees of England I meditated on this lost and perhaps mythical labyrinth. I imagined it untouched and perfect on the secret summit of some mountain; I imagined it drowned under rice paddies or beneath the sea; I imagined it infinite, made not only of eight-sided pavilions and of twisting paths but also of rivers, provinces and kingdoms. . . . I thought of a maze of mazes, of a sinuous, ever growing maze which would take in both past and future and would somehow involve the stars.

Lost in these imaginary illusions I forgot my destiny—that of the hunted. For an undetermined period of time I felt myself cut off from the world, an abstract spectator. The hazy and murmuring countryside, the moon, the decline of the evening, stirred within me. Going down the gently sloping road I could not feel fatigue. The evening was at once intimate and infinite.

The road kept descending and branching off, through meadows misty in the twilight. A high-pitched and almost syllabic music kept coming and going, moving with the breeze, blurred by the leaves and by distance.

I thought that a man might be an enemy of other men, of the differing moments of other men, but never an enemy of a country: not of fireflies, words, gardens, streams, or the West wind.

Meditating thus I arrived at a high, rusty iron gate. Through the railings I could see an avenue bordered with poplar trees and also a kind of summer house or pavilion. Two things dawned on me at once, the first trivial and the second almost incredible: the music came from the pavilion and that music was Chinese. That was why I had accepted it fully, without paying it any attention. I do not remember whether there was a bell, a push-button, or whether I attracted attention by clapping my hands. The stuttering sparks of the music kept on.

But from the end of the avenue, from the main house, a lantern approached; a lantern which alternately, from moment to moment, was crisscrossed or put out by the trunks of the trees; a paper lantern shaped like a drum and colored like the moon. A tall man carried it. I could not see his face for the light blinded me.

He opened the gate and spoke slowly in my language.

"I see that the worthy Hsi P'eng has troubled himself to see to relieving my solitude. No doubt you want to see the garden?"

Recognizing the name of one of our consuls, I replied, somewhat taken aback.

"The garden?"

"The garden of forking paths."

Something stirred in my memory and I said, with incomprehensible assurance:

"The garden of my ancestor, Ts'ui Pên."

"Your ancestor? Your illustrious ancestor? Come in."

The damp path zigzagged like those of my childhood. When we reached the house, we went into a library filled with books from both East and West. I recognized some large volumes bound in yellow silk—manuscripts of the Lost Encyclopedia which was edited by the Third Emperor of the Luminous Dynasty. They had never been printed. A phonograph record was spinning near a bronze phoenix. I remember also a rose-glazed jar and yet another, older by many centuries, of that blue color which our potters copied from the Persians. . . .

Stephen Albert was watching me with a smile on his face. He was, as I have said, remarkably tall. His face was deeply lined and he had gray eyes and a gray beard. There was about him something of the priest, and something of the sailor. Later, he told me he had been a missionary in Tientsin before he "had aspired to become a Sinologist."

We sat down, I upon a large, low divan, he with his back to the window and to a large circular clock. I calculated that my pursuer, Richard Madden, could not arrive in less than an hour. My irrevocable decision could wait.

"A strange destiny," said Stephen Albert, "that of Ts'ui Pên—Governor of his native province, learned in astronomy, in astrology and tireless in the interpretation of the canonical books, a chess player, a famous poet and a calligrapher. Yet he abandoned all to make a book and a labyrinth. He gave up all the pleasures of oppression, justice, of a well-stocked bed, of banquets, and even of erudition, and shut himself up in the Pavilion of the Limpid Sun for thirteen years. At his death, his heirs found only a mess of manuscripts. The family, as you doubtless know, wished to consign them to the fire, but the executor of the estate—a Taoist or a Buddhist monk—insisted on their publication."

"Those of the blood of Ts'ui Pên," I replied, "still curse the memory of that monk. Such a publication was madness. The book is a shapeless mass of contradictory rough drafts. I examined it once upon a time: the hero dies in the third chapter, while in the fourth he is alive. As for the other enterprise of Ts'ui Pên . . . his Labyrinth. . . ."

"Here is the Labyrinth," Albert said, pointing to a tall, laquered writing cabinet.

"An ivory labyrinth?" I exclaimed. "A tiny labyrinth indeed . . . . !"

"A symbolic labyrinth," he corrected me. "An invisible labyrinth of time. I, a barbarous Englishman, have been given the key to this transparent mystery. After more than a hundred years most of the details are irrecoverable, lost beyond all recall, but it isn't hard to image what must have happened. At one time, Ts'ui Pên must have said; 'I am going into seclusion to write a book,' and at another, 'I am retiring to construct a maze.' Everyone assumed these were separate activities. No one realized that the book and the labyrinth were one and the same. The Pavilion of the Limpid Sun was set in the middle of an intricate garden. This may have suggested the idea of a physical maze.

"Ts'ui Pên died. In all the vast lands which once belonged to your family, no one could find the labyrinth. The novel's confusion suggested that *it* was the labyrinth. Two circumstances showed me the direct solution to the problem. First, the curious legend that Ts'ui Pên had proposed to create an infinite maze, second, a fragment of a letter which I discovered."

Albert rose. For a few moments he turned his back to me. He opened the top drawer in the high black and gilded writing cabinet. He returned holding in his hand a piece of paper which had once been crimson but which had faded with the passage of time: it was rose colored, tenuous, quadrangular. Ts'ui Pên's calligraphy was justly famous. Eagerly, but without understanding, I read the words which a man of my own blood had written with a small brush: "I leave to various future times, but not to all, my garden of forking paths."

I handed back the sheet of paper in silence. Albert went on:

"Before I discovered this letter, I kept asking myself how a book could be infinite. I could not imagine any other than a cyclic volume, circular. A volume whose last page would be the same as the first and so have the possibility of continuing indefinitely. I recalled, too, the night in the middle of *The Thousand and One Nights* when Queen Scheherezade, through a magical mistake on the part of her copyist, started to tell the story of *The Thousand and One Nights*, with the risk of again arriving at the night upon which she will relate it, and thus on to infinity. I also imagined a Platonic hereditary work, passed on from father to son, to which each individual would add a new chapter or correct, with pious care, the work of his elders.

"These conjectures gave me amusement, but none seemed to have the remotest application to the contradictory chapters of Ts'ui Pên. At this point, I was sent from Oxford the manuscript you have just seen.

"Naturally, my attention was caught by the sentence, 'I leave to various future times, but not to all, my garden of forking paths.' I had no sooner read this, than I understood. *The Garden of Forking Paths* was the chaotic novel itself. The phrase 'to various future times, but not to all' suggested the image of bifurcating in time, not in space. Rereading the whole work confirmed this theory. In all fiction, when a man is faced with alternatives he chooses one at the expense of the others. In the almost unfathomable Ts'ui Pên, he chooses—simultaneously—all of them. He thus *creates* various futures, various times which start others that will in their turn branch out and bifurcate in other times. This is the cause of the contradictions in the novel.

"Fang, let us say, has a secret. A stranger knocks at his door. Fang makes up his mind to kill him. Naturally there are various possible outcomes. Fang can kill the intruder, the intruder can kill Fang, both can be saved, both can die and so on and so on. In Ts'ui Pên's work, all the possible solutions occur, each one being the point of departure for other bifurcations. Sometimes the pathways of this labyrinth converge. For example, you come to this house; but in other possible pasts you are my enemy; in others my friend.

"If you will put up with my atrocious pronunciation, I would like to read you a few pages of your ancestor's work."

His countenance, in the bright circle of lamplight, was certainly that of an ancient, but it shone with something unyielding, even immortal.

With slow precision, he read two versions of the same epic chapter. In the first, an army marches into battle over a desolate mountain pass. The bleak and somber aspect of the rocky landscape made the soldiers feel that life itself was of little value, and so they won the battle easily. In the second, the same army passes through a palace where a banquet is in progress. The splendor of the feast remained a memory throughout the glorious battle, and so victory followed.

With proper veneration I listened to these old tales, although perhaps with less admiration for them in themselves than for the fact that they had been thought out by one of my own blood, and that a man of a distant empire had given them back to me, in the last stage of a desperate adventure, on a Western island. I remember the final words, repeated at the end of each version like a secret command: "Thus the heroes fought, with tranquil heart and bloody sword. They were resigned to killing and to dying."

At that moment I felt within me and around me something invisible and intangible pullulating. It was not the pullulation of two divergent, parallel, and finally converging armies, but an agitation more inaccessible, more intimate, prefigured by them in some way. Stephen Albert continued:

"I do not think that your illustrious ancestor toyed idly with variations. I do not find it believable that he would waste thirteen years laboring over a never ending experiment in rhetoric. In your country the novel is an inferior genre; in Ts'ui Pên's period, it was a despised one. Ts'ui Pên was a fine novelist but he was also a man of letters who, doubtless, considered himself more than a mere novelist. The testimony of his contemporaries attests to this, and certainly the known facts of his life confirm his leanings toward the metaphysical and the mystical. Philosophical conjectures take up the greater part of his novel. I know that of all problems, none disquieted him more, and none concerned him more than the profound one of time. Now then, this is the *only* problem that does not figure in the pages of *The Garden*. He does not even use the word which means *time*. How can these voluntary omissions be explained?"

I proposed various solutions, all of them inadequate. We discussed them. Finally Stephen Albert said: "In a guessing game to which the answer is chess, which word is the only one prohibited?" I thought for a moment and then replied:

"The word is *chess*."

"Precisely," said Albert. "*The Garden of Forking Paths* is an enormous guessing game, or parable, in which the subject is time. The rules of the game forbid the use of the word itself. To eliminate a word completely, to refer to it by means of inept phrases and obvious paraphrases, is perhaps the best way of drawing attention to it. This, then, is the tortuous method of approach preferred by the oblique Ts'ui Pên in every meandering of his interminable novel. I have gone over hundreds of manuscripts, I have corrected errors introduced by careless copyists, I have worked out the plan from this chaos, I have restored, or believe I have restored, the original. I have translated the whole work. I can state categorically that not once has the word *time* been used in the whole book.

"The explanation is obvious. *The Garden of Forking Paths* is a picture, incomplete yet not false, of the universe such as Ts'ui Pên conceived it to be. Differing from Newton and Schopenhauer, your ancestor did not think of time as absolute and uniform. He believed in an infinite series of times, in a dizzily growing, ever spreading network of diverging, converging and parallel times. This web of time—the strands of which approach one another, bifurcate, intersect or ignore each other through the centuries—embraces *every* possibility. We do not exist in most of them. In some you exist and not I, while in others I do, and you do not, and in yet others both of us exist. In this one, in which chance has favored me, you have come to my gate. In another, you, crossing the garden, have found me dead. In yet another, I say these very same words, but am an error, a phantom."

"In all of them," I enunciated, with a tremor in my voice. "I deeply appreciate and am grateful to you for the restoration of Ts'ui Pên's garden."

"Not in *all*," he murmured with a smile. "Time is forever dividing itself toward innumerable futures and in one of them I am your enemy."

Once again I sensed the pullulation of which I have already spoken. It seemed to me that the dew-damp garden surrounding the house was infinitely saturated with invisible people. All were Albert and myself, secretive, busy and multiform in other dimensions of time. I lifted my eyes and the short nightmare disappeared. In the black and yellow garden there was only a single man, but this man was as strong as a statue and this man was walking up the path and he was Captain Richard Madden.

"The future exists now," I replied. "But I am your friend. Can I take another look at the letter?"

Albert rose from his seat. He stood up tall as he opened the top drawer of the high writing cabinet. For a moment his back was again turned to me. I had the revolver ready. I fired with the utmost care: Albert fell without a murmur, at once. I swear that his death was instantaneous, as if he had been struck by lightning.

What remains is unreal and unimportant. Madden broke in and arrested me. I have been condemned to hang. Abominably, I have yet triumphed! The secret name of the city to be attacked got through to Berlin. Yesterday it was bombed. I read the news in the same English newspapers which were trying to solve the riddle of the murder of the learned Sinologist Stephen Albert by the unknown Yu Tsun. The Chief, however, had already solved this mystery. He knew that my problem was to shout, with my feeble voice, above the tumult of war, the name of the city called Albert, and that I had no other course open to me than to kill someone of that name. He does not know, for no one can, of my infinite penitence and sickness of the heart.

Translated by Helen Temple and Ruthven Todd

RAYMOND CARVER (b. 1939)

So Much Water So Close to Home

Raymond Carver was born in Oregon. He has published poetry, essays, and fiction. His most recent collections of stories are *What We Talk About When We Talk About Love* (1981) and *The Cathedral* (1983). *Fires* (1983), from which this version of "So Much Water So Close to Home" is taken, is a collection of his poetry and prose.

My husband eats with good appetite but he seems tired, edgy. He chews slowly, arms on the table, and stares at something across the room. He looks at me and looks away again. He wipes his mouth on the napkin. He shrugs and goes on eating. Something has come between us though he would like me to believe otherwise.

"What are you staring at me for?" he asks. "What is it?" he says and puts his fork down.

"Was I staring?" I say and shake my head stupidly, stupidly.

The telephone rings. "Don't answer it," he says.

"I might be your mother," I say. "Dean—it might be something about Dean."

"Watch and see," he says.

I pick up the receiver and listen for a minute. He stops eating. I bite my lip and hang up.

"What did I tell you?" he says. He starts to eat again, then throws the napkin onto his plate. "Goddamn it, why can't people mind their own business? Tell me what I did wrong and I'll listen! It's not fair. She was dead, wasn't she? There were other men there besides me. We talked it over and we all decided. We'd only just got there. We'd walked for hours. We couldn't just turn around, we were five miles from the car. It was opening day. What the hell, I don't see anything wrong. No, I don't. And don't look at me that way, do you hear? I won't have you passing judgment on me. Not you."

"You know," I say and shake my head.

"What do I know, Claire? Tell me. Tell me what I know. I don't know anything except one thing: you hadn't better get worked up over this." He gives me what he thinks is a *meaningful* look. "She was dead, dead, dead, do you hear?" he says after a minute. "It's a damn shame, I agree. She was a young girl and it's a shame, and I'm sorry, as sorry as anyone else, but she was dead, Claire, dead. Now let's leave it alone. Please, Claire. Let's leave it alone now."

"That's the point," I say. "She was dead. But don't you see? She needed help."

"I give up," he says and raises his hands. He pushes his chair away from the table, takes his cigarettes and goes out to the patio with a can of beer. He walks back and forth for a minute and then sits in a lawn chair and picks up the paper once more. His name is there on the first page along with the names of his friends, the other men who made the "grisly find."

I close my eyes for a minute and hold onto the drainboard. I must not dwell on this any longer. I must get over it, put it out of sight, out of mind, etc., and "go on." I open my eyes. Despite everything, knowing all that may be in store, I rake my arm across the drainboard and send the dishes and glasses smashing and scattering across the floor.

He doesn't move. I know he has heard, he raises his head as if listening, but he doesn't move otherwise, doesn't turn around to look. I hate him for that, for not moving. He waits a minute, then draws on his cigarette and leans back in the chair. I pity him for listening, detached, and then settling back and drawing on his cigarette. The wind takes the smoke out of his mouth in a thin stream. Why do I notice that? He can never know how much I pity him for that, for sitting still and listening, and letting the smoke stream out of his mouth. . . .

He planned his fishing trip into the mountains last Sunday, a week before the Memorial Day weekend. He and Gordon Johnson, Mel Dorn, Vern Williams. They play poker, bowl, and fish together. They fish together every spring and early summer, the first two or three months of the season, before family vacations, little league baseball, and visiting relatives can intrude. They are decent men, family men, responsible at their jobs. They have sons and daughters who go to school with our son, Dean. On Friday afternoon these four men left for a three day fishing trip to the Naches River. They parked the car in the mountains and hiked several miles to where they wanted to fish. They carried their bedrolls, food and cooking utensils, their playing cards, their whisky. The first evening at the river, even before they could set up camp, Mel Dorn found the girl floating face down in the river, nude, lodged near the shore in some branches. He called the other men and they all came to look at her. They talked about what to do. One of the men—Stuart didn't say which—perhaps it was Vern Williams, he is a heavy-set, easy man who laughs often—one of them thought they should start back to the car at once. The others stirred the sand with their shoes and said they felt inclined to stay. They pleaded fatigue, the late hour, the fact the the girl "wasn't going anywhere." In the end they all decided to stay. They went ahead and set up the camp and built a fire and drank their whisky. They drank a lot of whisky and when the moon came up they talked about the girl. Someone thought they should do something to prevent the body from floating away. Somehow they thought that this might create a problem for them if it floated away during the night. They took flashlights and stumbled down to the river. The wind was up, a cold wind, and waves from the river lapped the sandy bank. One of the men, I don't know who, it might have been Stuart, he could have done it, waded into the water and took the girl by the fingers and pulled her, still face down, closer to shore, into shallow water, and then took a piece of nylon cord and tied it around her wrist and then secured the cord to tree roots, all the while the flashlights of the other men played over the girl's body. Afterwards, they went back to camp and drank more whisky. Then they went to sleep. The next morning, Saturday, they cooked breakfast, drank lots of coffee, more whisky, and then split up to fish, two men upriver, two men down.

That night, after they had cooked their fish and potatoes and had more coffee and whisky, they took their dishes down to the river and rinsed them off a few yards from where the body lay in the water. They drank again and then they took out their cards and played and drank until they couldn't see the cards any longer. Vern Williams went to sleep, but the others told coarse stories and spoke of vulgar or dishonest escapades out of their past, and no one mentioned the girl until Gordon Johnson, who'd forgotten for a minute, commented on the firmness of the trout they'd caught, and the terrible coldness of the river water. They stopped talking then but continued to drink until one of them tripped and fell cursing against the lantern, and then they climbed into their sleeping bags.

The next morning they got up late, drank more whisky, fished a little as they kept drinking whisky. Then, at one o'clock in the afternoon, Sunday, a day earlier then they'd planned, they decided to leave. They took down their tents, rolled their sleeping bags, gathered their pans, pots, fish and fishing gear, and hiked out. They didn't look at the girl again before they left. When they reached the car they drove the highway in silence until they came to a telephone. Stuart made the call to the sheriff's office while the others stood around in the hot sun and listened. He gave the man on the other end of the line all of their names—they had nothing to hide, they weren't ashamed of anything—and agreed to wait at the service station until someone could come for more detailed directions and individual statements.

He came home at eleven o'clock that night. I was asleep but woke when I heard him in the kitchen. I found him leaning against the refrigerator drinking a can of beer. He put his heavy arms around me and rubbed his hands up and down my back, the same hands he'd left with two days before, I thought.

In bed he put his hands on me again and then waited, as if thinking of something else. I turned slightly and then moved my legs. Afterwards, I know he stayed awake for a long time, for he was awake when I fell asleep; and later, when I stirred for a minute, opening my eyes at a slight noise, a rustle of sheets, it was almost daylight outside, birds were singing, and he was on his back smoking and looking at the curtained window. Half-asleep I said his name, but he didn't answer. I fell asleep again.

He was up this morning before I could get out of bed—to see if there was anything about it in the paper, I suppose. The telephone began to ring shortly after eight o'clock.

"Go to hell," I heard him shout into the receiver. The telephone rang again a minute later, and I hurried into the kitchen. "I have nothing else to add to what I've already said to the sheriff. That's right!" He slammed down the receiver.

"What is going on?" I said, alarmed.

"Sit down," he said slowly. His fingers scraped, scraped against his stubble of whiskers. "I have to tell you something. Something happened while we were fishing." We sat across from each other at the table, and then he told me.

I drank coffee and stared at him as he spoke. Then I read the account in the newspaper that he shoved across the table: ". . . unidentified girl eighteen to twenty-four years of age . . . body three to five days in the water . . . rape a possible motive . . . preliminary results show death by strangulation . . . cuts and bruises on her breasts and pelvic area . . . autopsy . . . rape, pending further investigation."

"You've got to understand," he said. "Don't look at me like that. Be careful now, I mean it. Take it easy, Claire."

"Why didn't you tell me last night?" I asked.

"I just . . . didn't. What do you mean?" he said.

"You know what I mean," I said. I looked at his hands, the broad fingers, knuckles covered with hair, moving, lighting a cigarette now, fingers that had moved over me, into me last night.

He shrugged. "What difference does it make, last night, this morning? It was late. You were sleepy, I thought I'd wait until this morning to tell you." He looked out to the patio: a robin flew from the lawn to the picnic table and preened its feathers.

"It isn't true," I said. "You didn't leave her there like that?"

He turned quickly and said, "What'd I do? Listen to me carefully now, once and for all. Nothing happened. I have nothing to be sorry for or feel guilty about. Do you hear me?"

I got up from the table and went to Dean's room. He was awake and in his pajamas, putting together a puzzle. I helped him find his clothes and then went back to the kitchen and put his breakfast on the table. The telephone rang two or three more times and each time Stuart was abrupt while he talked and angry when he hung up. He called Mel Dorn and Gordon Johnson and spoke with them, slowly, seriously, and then he opened a beer and smoked a cigarette while Dean ate, asked him about school, his friends, etc., exactly as if nothing had happened.

Dean wanted to know what he'd done while he was gone, and Stuart took some fish out of the freezer to show him.

"I'm taking him to your mother's for the day," I said.

"Sure," Stuart said and looked at Dean who was holding one of the frozen trout. "If you want to and he wants to, that is. You don't have to, you know. There's nothing wrong."

"I'd like to anyway," I said.

"Can I go swimming there?" Dean asked and wiped his fingers on his pants.

"I believe so," I said. "It's a warm day so take your suit, and I'm sure your grandmother will say it's okay."

Stuart lighted a cigarette and looked at us.

Dean and I drove across town to Stuart's mother's. She lives in an apartment building with a pool and a sauna bath. Her name is Catherine Kane. Her name, Kane, is the same as mine, which seems impossible. Years ago, Stuart has told me, she used to be called Candy by her friends. She is a tall, cold woman with white-blonde hair. She gives me the feeling that she is always judging, judging. I explain briefly in a low voice what has happened (she hasn't yet read the newspaper) and promise to pick Dean up that evening. "He brought his swimming suit," I say. "Stuart and I have to talk about some things," I add vaguely. She looks at me steadily from over her glasses. Then she nods and turns to Dean, saying "How are you, my little man?" She stoops and puts her arms around him. She looks at me again as I open the door to leave. She has a way of looking at me without saying anything.

When I return home Stuart is eating something at the table and drinking beer. . . .

After a time I sweep up the broken dishes and glassware and go outside. Stuart is lying on his back on the grass now, the newspaper and can of beer within reach, staring at the sky. It's breezy but warm out and birds call.

"Stuart, could we go for a drive?" I say. "Anywhere."

He rolls over and looks at me and nods. "We'll pick up some beer," he says. "I hope you're feeling better about this. Try to understand, that's all I ask." He gets to his feet and touches me on the hip as he goes past. "Give me a minute and I'll be ready."

We drive through town without speaking. Before we reach the country he stops at a roadside market for beer. I notice a great stack of papers just inside the door. On the top step a fat woman in a print dress holds out a licorice stick to a little girl. In a few minutes we cross Everson Creek and turn into a picnic area a few feet from the water. The creek flows under the bridge and into a large pond a few hundred yards away. There are a dozen or so men and boys scattered around the banks of the pond under the willows, fishing.

So much water so close to home, why did he have to go miles away to fish?

"Why did you have to go there of all places?" I say.

"The Naches? We always go there. Every year, at least once." We sit on a bench in the sun and he opens two cans of beer and gives one to me. "How the hell was I to know anything like that would happen?" He shakes his head and shrugs, as if it had all happened years ago, or to someone else. "Enjoy the afternoon, Claire. Look at this weather."

"They said they were innocent."

"Who? What are you talking about?"

"The Maddox brothers. They killed a girl named Arlene Hubly near the town where I grew up, and then cut off her head and threw her into the Cle Elum River. She and I went to the same high school. It happened when I was a girl."

"What a hell of a thing to be thinking about," he says. "Come on, get off it. You're going to get me riled in a minute. How about it now? Claire?"

I look at the creek. I float toward the pond, eyes open, face down, staring at the rocks and moss on the creek bottom until I am carried into the lake where I am pushed by the breeze. Nothing will be any different. We will go on and on and on and on. We will go on even now, as if nothing had happened. I look at him across the picnic table with such intensity that his face drains.

"I don't know what's wrong with you," he says. "I don't—"

I slap him before I realize. I raise my hand, wait a fraction of a second, and then slap his cheek hard. This is crazy, I think as I slap him. We need to lock our fingers together. We need to help one another. This is crazy.

He catches my wrist before I can strike again and raises his own hand. I crouch, waiting, and see something come into his eyes and then dart away. He drops his hand. I drift even faster around and around in the pond.

"Come on, get in the car," he says. "I'm taking you home."

"No, no," I say, pulling back from him.

"Come on," he says. "Goddamn it."

"You're not being fair to me," he says later in the car. Fields and trees and farmhouses fly by outside the window. "You're not being fair. To either one of us. Or to Dean, I might add. Think about Dean for a minute. Think about me. Think about someone else besides your goddamn self for a change."

There is nothing I can say to him now. He tries to concentrate on the road, but he keeps looking into the rearview mirror. Out of the corner of his eye, he looks across the seat to where I sit with my knees drawn up under my chin. The sun blazes against my arm and the side of my face. He opens another beer while he drives, drinks from it, then shoves the can between his legs and lets out breath. He knows. I could laugh in his face. I could weep.

II

Stuart believes he is letting me sleep this morning. But I was awake long before the alarm sounded, thinking, lying on the far side of the bed, away from his hairy legs and his thick, sleeping fingers. He gets Dean off for school, and then he shaves, dresses, and leaves for work. Twice he looks into the bedroom and clears his throat, but I keep my eyes closed.

In the kitchen I find a note from him signed "Love." I sit in the breakfast nook in the sunlight and drink coffee and make a coffee ring on the note. The telephone has stopped ringing, that's something. No more calls since last night. I look at the paper and turn it this way and that on the table. Then I pull it close and read what it says. The body is still unidentified, unclaimed, apparently unmissed. But for the last twenty-four hours men have been examining it, putting things into it, cutting, weighing, measuring, putting back again, sewing up, looking for the exact cause and moment of death. Looking for evidence of rape. I'm sure they hope for rape. Rape would make it easier to understand. The paper says the body will be taken to Keith & Keith Funeral Home pending arrangements. People are asked to come forward with information, etc.

Two things are certain: 1) people no longer care what happens to other people; and 2) nothing makes any real difference any longer. Look at what has happened. Yet nothing will change for Stuart and me. Really change, I mean. We will grow older, both of us, you can see it in our faces already, in the bathroom mirror, for instance, mornings when we use the bathroom at the same time. And certain things around us will change, become easier or harder, one thing or the other, but nothing will ever really be any different. I believe that. We have made our decisions, our lives have been set in motion, and they will go on and on until they stop. But if that is true, then what? I mean, what if you believe that, but you keep it covered up, until one day something happens that should change something, but then you see nothing is going to change after all. What then? Meanwhile, the people around you continue to talk and act as if you were the same person as yesterday, or last night, or five minutes before, but you are really undergoing a crisis, your heart feels damaged. . . .

The past is unclear. It's as if there is a film over those early years. I can't even be sure that the things I remember happening really happened to me. There was a girl who had a mother and father—the father ran a small cafe where the mother acted as waitress and cashier—who moved as if in a dream through grade school and high school and then, in a year or two, into secretarial school. Later, much later—what happened to the time in between?—she is in another town working as a receptionist for an electronics parts firm and becomes acquainted with one of the engineers who asks her for a date. Eventually, seeing that's his aim, she lets him seduce her. She had an intuition at the time, an insight about the seduction that later, try as she might, she couldn't recall. After a short while they decide to get married, but already the past, her past, is slipping away. The future is something she can't imagine. She smiles, as if she has a secret, when she thinks about the future. Once, during a particularly bad argument, over what she can't now remember, five years or so after they were married, he tells her that someday this affair (his words: "this affair") will end in violence. She remembers this. She files this away somewhere and begins repeating it aloud from time to time. Sometimes she spends the whole morning on her knees in the sandbox behind the garage playing with Dean and one or two of his friends. But every afternoon at four o'clock her head begins to hurt. She holds her forehead and feels dizzy with the pain. Stuart asks her to see a doctor and she does, secretly pleased at the doctor's solicitous attention. She goes away for a while to a place the doctor recommends. Stuart's mother comes out from Ohio in a hurry to care for the child. But she, Claire, spoils everything and returns home in a few weeks. His mother moves out of the house and takes an apartment across town and perches there, as if waiting. One night in bed when they are both near sleep, Claire tells him that she heard some women patients at the clinic discussing fellatio. She thinks this is something he might like to hear. Stuart is pleased at hearing this. He strokes her arm. Things are going to be okay, he says. From now on everything is going to be different and better for them. He has received a promotion and a substantial raise. They've even bought another car, a station wagon, her car. They're going to live in the here and now. He says he feels able to relax for the first time in years. In the dark, he goes on stroking her arm. . . . He continues to bowl and play cards regularly. He goes fishing with three friends of his.

That evening three things happen: Dean says that the children at school told him that his father found a dead body in the river. He wants to know about it.

Stuart explains quickly, leaving out most of the story, saying only that, yes, he and three other men did find a body while they were fishing.

"What kind of body?" Dean asks. "Was it a girl?"

"Yes, it was a girl. A woman. Then we called the sheriff." Stuart looks at me.

"What'd he say?" Dean asks.

"He said he'd take care of it."

"What did it look like? Was it scary?"

"That's enough talk," I say. "Rinse your plate, Dean, and then you're excused."

"But what'd it look like?" he persists. "I want to know."

"You heard me," I say. "Did you hear me, Dean? Dean!" I want to shake him. I want to shake him until he cries.

"Do what your mother says," Stuart tells him quietly. "It was just a body, and that's all there is to it."

I am clearing the table when Stuart comes up behind and touches my arm. His fingers burn. I start, almost losing a plate.

"What's the matter with you?" he says, dropping his hand. "Claire, what is it?"

"You scared me," I say.

"That's what I mean. I should be able to touch you without you jumping out of your skin." He stands in front of me with a little grin, trying to catch my eyes, and then he puts his arm around my waist. With his other hand he takes my free hand and puts it on the front of his pants.

"Please, Stuart." I pull away and he steps back and snaps his fingers.

"Hell with it then," he says. "Be that way if you want. But just remember."

"Remember what?" I say quickly. I look at him and hold my breath.

He shrugs. "Nothing, nothing," he says.

The second thing that happens is that while we are watching television that evening, he in his leather recliner chair, I on the sofa with a blanket and magazine, the house quiet except for the television, a voice cuts into the program to say that the murdered girl has been identified. Full details will follow on the eleven o'clock news.

We look at each other. In a few minutes he gets up and says he is going to fix a nightcap. Do I want one?

"No," I say.

"I don't mind drinking alone," he says. "I thought I'd ask."

I can see he is obscurely hurt, and I look away, ashamed and yet angry at the same time.

He stays in the kitchen a long while, but comes back with his drink just when the news begins.

First the announcer repeats the story of the four local fishermen finding the body. Then the station shows a high school graduation photograph of the girl, a dark-haired girl with a round face and full, smiling lips. There's a film of the girl's parents entering the funeral home to make the identification. Bewildered, sad, they shuffle slowly up the sidewalk to the front steps to where a man in a dark suit stands waiting, holding the door. Then, it seems as if only seconds have passed, as if they have merely gone inside the door and turned around and come out again, the same couple is shown leaving the building, the woman in tears, covering her face with a handkerchief, the man stopping long enough to say to a reporter, "It's her, it's Susan. I can't say anything right now. I hope they get the person or persons who did it before it happens again. This violence. . . ." He motions feebly at the television camera. Then the man and woman get into an old car and drive away into the late afternoon traffic.

The announcer goes on to say that the girl, Susan Miller, had gotten off work as a cashier in a movie theater in Summit, a town 120 miles north of our town. A green, late model car pulled up in front of the theater and the girl, who according to witnesses looked as if she'd been waiting, went over to the car and got in, leading the authorities to suspect that the driver of the car was a friend, or at least an acquaintance. The authorities would like to talk to the driver of the green car.

Stuart clears his throat then leans back in the chair and sips his drink.

The third thing that happens is that after the news Stuart stretches, yawns, and looks at me. I get up and begin making a bed for myself on the sofa.

"What are you doing?" he says, puzzled.

"I'm not sleepy," I say, avoiding his eyes. "I think I'll stay up a while longer and then read something until I fall asleep."

He stares as I spread a sheet over the sofa. When I start to go for a pillow, he stands at the bedroom door, blocking the way.

"I'm going to ask you once more," he says. "What the hell do you think you're going to accomplish by this?"

"I need to be by myself tonight," I say. "I need to have time to think."

He lets out breath. "I'm thinking you're making a big mistake by doing this. I'm thinking you'd better think again about what you're doing. Claire?"

I can't answer. I don't know what I want to say. I turn and begin to tuck in the edges of the blanket. He stares at me a minute longer and then I see him raise his shoulders. "Suit yourself then. I could give a fuck less what you do," he says. He turns and walks down the hall scratching his neck.

This morning I read in the paper that services for Susan Miller are to be held in Chapel of the Pines, Summit, at two o'clock the next afternoon. Also, that police have taken statements from three people who saw her get into the green Chevrolet. But they still have no license number for the car. They are getting warmer, though, and the investigation is continuing. I sit for a long while holding the paper, thinking, then I call to make an appointment at the hairdresser's.

I sit under the dryer with a magazine on my lap and let Millie do my nails.

"I'm going to a funeral tomorrow," I say after we have talked a bit about a girl who no longer works there.

Millie looks up at me and then back at my fingers. "I'm sorry to hear that, Mrs. Kane. I'm real sorry."

"It's a young girl's funeral," I say.

"That's the worst kind. My sister died when I was a girl, and I'm still not over it to this day. Who died?" she says after a minute.

"A girl. We weren't all that close, you know, but still."

"Too bad. I'm real sorry. But we"ll get you fixed up for it, don't worry. How's that look?"

"That looks . . . fine. Millie, did you ever wish you were somebody else, or else just nobody, nothing, nothing at all?"

She looks at me. "I can't say I ever felt that, no. No, if I was somebody else I'd be afraid I might not like who I was." She holds my fingers and seems to think about something for a minute. "I don't know, I just don't know. . . . Let me have your other hand now, Mrs. Kane."

At eleven o'clock that night I make another bed on the sofa and this time Stuart only looks at me, rolls his tongue behind his lips, and goes down the hall to the bedroom. In the night I wake and listen to the wind slamming the gate against the fence. I don't want to be awake, and I lie for a long while with my eyes closed. Finally I get up and go down the hall with my pillow. The light is burning in our bedroom and Stuart is on his back with his mouth open, breathing heavily. I go into Dean's room and get into bed with him. In his sleep he moves over to give me space. I lie there for a minute and then hold him, my face against his hair.

"What is it, mama?" he says.

"Nothing, honey. Go back to sleep. It's nothing, it's all right."

I get up when I hear Stuart's alarm, put on coffee and prepare breakfast while he shaves.

He appears in the kitchen doorway, towel over his bare shoulder, appraising.

"Here's coffee," I say. "Eggs will be ready in a minute."

He nods.

I wake Dean and the three of us have breakfast. Once or twice Stuart looks at me as if he wants to say something, but each time I ask Dean if he wants more milk, more toast, etc.

"I'll call you today," Stuart says as he opens the door.

"I don't think I'll be home today," I say quickly. "I have a lot of things to do today. In fact, I may be late for dinner."

"All right. Sure." He moves his briefcase from one hand to the other. "Maybe we'll go out for dinner tonight? How would you like that?" He keeps looking at me. He's forgotten about the girl already. "Are you all right?"

I move to straighten his tie, then drop my hand. He wants to kiss me goodbye. I move back a step. "Have a nice day then," he says finally. He turns and goes down the walk to his car.

I dress carefully. I try on a hat that I haven't worn in several years and look at myself in the mirror. Then I remove the hat, apply a light makeup, and write a note for Dean.

Honey, Mommy has things to do this afternoon, but will be home later. You are to stay in the house or in the back/yard until one of us comes home.

Love

I look at the word "Love" and then I underline it. As I am writing the note I realize I don't know whether *back yard* is one word or two. I have never considered it before. I think about it and then I draw a line and make two words of it.

I stop for gas and ask directions to Summit. Barry, a forty-year-old mechanic with a moustache, comes out from the restroom and leans against the front fender while the other man, Lewis, puts the hose into the tank and begins to slowly wash the windshield.

"Summit," Barry says, looking at me and smoothing a finger down each side of his moustache. "There's no best way to get to Summit, Mrs. Kane. It's about a two, two-and-a-half-hour drive each way. Across the mountains. It's quite a drive for a woman. Summit? What's in Summit, Mrs. Kane?"

"I have business," I say, vaguely uneasy. Lewis has gone to wait on another customer.

"Ah. Well, if I wasn't tied up there"—he gestures with his thumb toward the bay—"I'd offer to drive you to Summit and back again. Road's not all that good. I mean it's good enough, there's just a lot of curves and so on."

"I'll be all right. But thank you." He leans against the fender. I can feel his eyes as I open my purse.

Barry takes the credit card. "Don't drive it at night," he says. "It's not all that good a road, like I said. And while I'd be willing to bet you wouldn't have car trouble with this, I know this car, you can never be sure about blowouts and things like that. Just to be on the safe side I'd better check these tires." He taps one of the front tires with his shoe. "We'll run it onto the hoist. Won't take long."

"No, no, it's all right. Really, I can't take any more time. The tires look fine to me."

"Only takes a minute," he says. "Be on the safe side."

"I said no. No! They look fine to me. I have to go now. Barry. . . ."

"Mrs. Kane?"

"I have to go now."

I sign something. He gives me the receipt, the card, some stamps. I put everything into my purse. "You take it easy," he says. "Be seeing you."

As I wait to pull into the traffic, I look back and see him watching. I close my eyes, then open them. He waves.

I turn at the first light, then turn again and drive until I come to the highway and read the sign: SUMMIT 117 Miles. It is ten-thirty and warm.

The highway skirts the edge of town, then passes through farm country, through fields of oats and sugar beets and apple orchards, with here and there a small herd of cattle grazing in open pastures. Then everything changes, the farms become fewer and fewer, more like shacks now than houses, and stands of timber replace the orchards. All at once I'm in the mountains and on the right, far below, I catch glimpses of the Naches River.

In a little while I see a green pickup truck behind me, and it stays behind me for miles. I keep slowing at the wrong times, hoping it will pass, and then increasing my speed, again at the wrong times. I grip the wheel until my fingers hurt. Then on a clear stretch he does pass, but he drives along beside for a minute, a crew-cut man in a blue workshirt in his early thirties, and we look at each other. Then he waves, toots the horn twice, and pulls ahead of me.

I slow down and find a place, a dirt road off of the shoulder. I pull over and turn off the ignition. I can hear the river somewhere down below the trees. Ahead of me the dirt road goes into the trees. Then I hear the pickup returning.

I start the engine just as the truck pulls up behind me. I lock the doors and roll up the windows. Perspiration breaks on my face and arms as I put the car in gear, but there is no place to drive.

"You all right?" the man says as he comes up to the car. "Hello. Hello in there." He raps the glass. "You okay?" He leans his arms on the door and brings his face close to the window.

I stare at him and can't find any words.

"After I passed I slowed up some," he says. "But when I didn't see you in the mirror I pulled off and waited a couple of minutes. When you still didn't show I thought I'd better drive back and check. Is everything all right? How come you're locked up in there?"

I shake my head.

"Come on, roll down your window. Hey, are you sure you're okay? You know it's not good for a woman to be batting around the country by herself." He shakes his head and looks at the highway, then back at me. "Now come on, roll down the window, how about it? We can't talk this way."

"Please, I have to go."

"Open the door, all right?" he says, as if he isn't listening. "At least roll the window down. You're going to smother in there." He looks at my breasts and legs. The skirt has pulled up over my knees. His eyes linger on my legs, but I sit still, afraid to move.

"I want to smother," I say. "I am smothering, can't you see?"

"What in the hell?" he says and moves back from the door. He turns and walks back to his truck. Then, in the side mirror, I watch him returning, and I close my eyes.

"You don't want me to follow you toward Summit or anything? I don't mind. I got some extra time this morning," he says.

I shake my head.

He hesitates and then shrugs. "Okay, lady, have it your way then," he says. "Okay."

I wait until he has reached the highway, and then I back out. He shifts gears and pulls away slowly, looking back at me in his rearview mirror. I stop the car on the shoulder and put my head on the wheel.

The casket is closed and covered with floral sprays. The organ begins soon after I take a seat near the back of the chapel. People begin to file in and find chairs, some middle-aged and older people, but most of them in their twenties or even younger. They are people who look uncomfortable in their suits and ties, sport coats and slacks, their dark dresses and leather gloves. One boy in flared pants and a yellow short-sleeved shirt takes the chair next to mine and begins to bite his lips. A door opens at one side of the chapel and I look up and for a minute the parking lot reminds me of a meadow. But then the sun flashes on car windows. The family enters in a group and moves into a curtained area off to the side. Chairs creak as they settle themselves. In a few minutes a slim, blond man in a dark suit stands and asks us to bow our heads. He speaks a brief prayer for us, the living, and when he finishes he asks us to pray in silence for the soul of Susan Miller, departed. I close my eyes and remember her picture in the newspaper and on television. I see her leaving the theater and getting into the green Chevrolet. Then I imagine her journey down the river, the nude body hitting rocks, caught at by branches, the body floating and turning, her hair streaming in the water. Then the hands and hair catching in the overhanging branches, holding, until four men come along to stare at her. I can see a man who is drunk (Stuart?) take her by the wrist. Does anyone here know about that? What if these people knew that? I look around at the other faces. There is a connection to be made of these things, these events, these faces, if I can find it. My head aches with the effort to find it.

He talks about Susan Miller's gifts: cheerfulness and beauty, grace and enthusiasm. From behind the closed curtain someone clears his throat, someone else sobs. The organ music begins. The service is over.

Along with the others I file slowly past the casket. Then I move out onto the front steps and into the bright, hot afternoon light. A middle-aged woman who limps as she goes down the stairs ahead of me reaches the sidewalk and looks around, her eyes falling on me. "Well, they got him," she says. "If that's any consolation. They arrested him this morning. I heard it on the radio before I came. A guy right here in town. A longhair, you might have guessed." We move a few steps down the hot sidewalk. People are starting cars. I put out my hand and hold on to a parking meter. Sunlight glances off polished hoods and fenders. My head swims. "He's admitted having relations with her that night, but he says he didn't kill her." She snorts. "They'll put him on probation and then turn him loose."

"He might not have acted alone," I say. "They'll have to be sure. He might be covering up for someone, a brother, or some friends."

"I have known that child since she was a little girl," the woman goes on, and her lips tremble. "She used to come over and I'd bake cookies for her and let her eat them in front of the TV." She looks off and begins shaking her head as the tears roll down her cheeks.

III

Stuart sits at the table with a drink in front of him. His eyes are red and for a minute I think he has been crying. He looks at me and doesn't say anything. For a wild instant I feel something has happened to Dean, and my heart turns.

"Where is he?" I say. "Where is Dean?"

"Outside," he says.

"Stuart, I'm so afraid, so afraid," I say, leaning against the door.

"What are you afraid of, Claire? Tell me, honey, and maybe I can help. I'd like to help, just try me. That's what husbands are for."

"I can't explain," I say. "I'm just afraid. I feel like, I feel like, I feel like. . . ."

He drains his glass and stands up, not taking his eyes from me. "I think I know what you need, honey. Let me play doctor, okay? Just take it easy now." He reaches an arm around my waist and with his other hand begins to unbutton my jacket, then my blouse. "First things first," he says, trying to joke.

"Not now, please," I say.

"Not now, please," he says, teasing. "Please nothing." Then he steps behind me and locks an arm around my waist. One of his hands slips under my brassiere.

"Stop, stop, stop," I say. I stamp on his toes.

And then I am lifted up and then falling. I sit on the floor looking up at him and my neck hurts and my skirt is over my knees. He leans down and says, "You go to hell then, do you hear, bitch? I hope your cunt drops off before I touch it again." He sobs once and I realize he can't help it, he can't help himself either. I feel a rush of pity for him as he heads for the living room.

He didn't sleep at home last night.

This morning, flowers, red and yellow chrysanthemums. I am drinking coffee when the doorbell rings.

"Mrs. Kane?" the young man says, holding his box of flowers.

I nod and pull the robe tighter at my throat.

"The man who called, he said you'd know." The boy looks at my robe, open at the throat, and touches his cap. He stands with his legs apart, feet firmly planted on the top step. "Have a nice day," he says.

A little later the telephone rings and Stuart says, "Honey, how are you? I'll be home early, I love you. Did you hear me? I love you, I'm sorry, I'll make it up to you. Goodbye, I have to run now."

I put the flowers into a vase in the center of the dining room table and then I move my things into the extra bedroom.

Last night, around midnight, Stuart breaks the lock on my door. He does it just to show me that he can, I suppose, for he doesn't do anything when the door springs open except stand there in his underwear looking surprised and foolish while the anger slips from his face. He shuts the door slowly, and a few minutes later I hear him in the kitchen prying open a tray of ice cubes.

I'm in bed when he calls today to tell me that he's asked his mother to come stay with us for a few days. I wait a minute, thinking about this, and then hang up while he is still talking. But in a little while I dial his number at work. When he finally comes on the line I say, "It doesn't matter, Stuart. Really, I tell you it doesn't matter one way or the other."

"I love you," he says.

He says something else and I listen and nod slowly. I feel sleepy. Then I wake up and say, "For God's sake, Stuart, she was only a child."

ANTON CHEKHOV (1860–1904)

In Exile

Anton Chekhov, Russia's most famous story writer and dramatist, was born in Taganrog, Russia. Though he was trained as a physician at Moscow University, Checkhov's true vocation was literature. His major plays include *The Three Sisters* (1901) and *The Cherry Orchard* (1904). His short stories and novellas have exerted a profound influence on the international development of the short story. "In Exile" first appeared in 1892.

Old Semyon, nicknamed Preacher, and a young Tatar, whom no one knew by name, were sitting on the riverbank by the campfire; the other three ferry-men were in the hut. Semyon, an old man of sixty, lean and toothless, but broad-shouldered and still healthy-looking, was drunk; he would have gone in to sleep long before, but he had a bottle in his pocket and he was afraid that the fellows in the hut would ask him for vodka. The Tatar was ill and weary, and wrapping himself up in his rags was describing how nice it was in the Simbirsk province, and what a beautiful and clever wife he had left behind at home. He was not more than twenty-five, and now, by the light of the campfire, with his pale and sick, mournful face, he looked like a boy.

"To be sure, it is not paradise here," said Preacher. "You can see for yourself, the water, the bare banks, clay, and nothing else. . . . Easter has long passed and yet there is ice on the river, and this morning there was snow. . . ."

"It's bad! it's bad!" said the Tatar, and looked round him in terror.

The dark, cold river was flowing ten paces away; it grumbled, lapped against the hollow clay banks and raced on swiftly towards the faraway sea. Close to the bank there was the dark blur of a big barge, which the ferry-men called a "karbas." Far away on the further bank, lights, dying down and flickering up again, zigzagged like little snakes; they were burning last year's grass. And beyond the little snakes there was darkness again. There little icicles could be heard knocking against the barge. It was damp and cold. . . .

The Tatar glanced at the sky. There were as many stars as at home, and the same blackness all round, but something was lacking. At home in Simbirsk province the stars were quite different, and so was the sky.

"It's bad! it's bad!" he repeated.

"You will get used to it," said Semyon, and he laughed. "Now you are young and foolish, the milk is hardly dry on your lips, and it seems to you in your foolishness that you are more wretched than anyone; but the time will come when you will say to yourself: 'I wish no one a better life than mine.' You look at me. Within a week the floods will be over and we shall set up the ferry; you will all go wandering off about Siberia while I shall stay and shall begin going from bank to bank. I've been going like that for twenty-two years, day and night. The pike and the salmon are under the water while I am on the water. And thank God for it, I want nothing; God give everyone such a life."

The Tatar threw some dry twigs on the campfire, lay down closer to the blaze, and said:

"My father is a sick man. When he dies my mother and wife will come here. They have promised."

"And what do you want your wife and mother for?" asked Preacher. "That's mere foolishness, my lad. It's the Devil confounding you, damn his soul! Don't you listen to him, the cursed one. Don't let him have his way. He is at you about the women, but you spite him; say, 'I don't want them!' He is on at you about freedom, but you stand up to him and say: 'I don't want it!' I want nothing, neither father nor mother, nor wife, nor freedom, nor post, nor paddock; I want nothing, damn their souls!"

Semyon took a pull at the bottle and went on:

"I am not a simple peasant, not of the working class, but the son of a deacon, and when I was free I lived at Kursk; I used to wear a frock-coat, and now I have brought myself to such a pass that I can sleep naked on the ground and eat grass. And I wish no one a better life. I want nothing and I am afraid of nobody, and the way I look at it is that there is nobody richer and freer than I am. When they sent me here from Russia from the first day I stuck it out; I want nothing! The Devil was at me about my wife and about my home and about freedom, but I told him: 'I want nothing.' I stuck to it, and here you see I live well, and I don't complain, and if anyone gives way to the Devil and listens to him, if but once, he is lost, there is no salvation for him: he is sunk in the bog to the crown of his head and will never get out.

"It is not only a foolish peasant like you, but even gentlemen, well-educated people, are lost. Fifteen years ago they sent a gentleman here from Russia. He hadn't shared something with his brothers and had forged something in a will. They did say he was a prince or a baron, but maybe he was simply an official—who knows? Well, the gentleman arrived here, and first thing he bought himself a house and land in Mukhortinskoe. 'I want to live by my own work,' says he, 'in the sweat of my brow, for I am not a gentleman now,' says he, 'but a settler.' 'Well,' says I, 'God help you, that's the right thing.' He was a young man then, busy and careful; he used to mow himself and catch fish and ride sixty miles on horseback. Only this is what happened: from the very first year he took to riding to Gyrino for the post; he used to stand on my ferry and sigh: 'Ech, Semyon, how long it is since they sent me any money from home!' 'You don't want money, Vassily Sergeyich,' says I. 'What use is it to you? You cast away the past, and forget it as though it had never been at all, as though it had been a dream, and begin to live anew. Don't listen to the Devil,' says I; 'he will bring you to no good, he'll draw you into a snare. Now you want money,' says I, 'but in a very little while you'll be wanting something else, and then more and more. If you want to be happy,' says I, 'the chief thing is not to want anything. Yes. . . . If,' says I, 'if Fate has wronged you and me cruelly, it's no good asking for her favor and bowing down to her, but you despise her and laugh at her, or else she will laugh at you.' That's what I said to him. . . .

"Two years later I ferried him across to this side, and he was rubbing his hands and laughing. 'I am going to Gyrino to meet my wife,' says he. 'She was sorry for me,' says he; 'she has come. She is good and kind.' And he was breathless with joy. So a day later he came with his wife. A beautiful young lady in a hat; in her arms was a baby girl. And lots of luggage of all sorts. And my Vassily Sergeyich was fussing round her; he couldn't take his eyes off her and couldn't say enough in praise of her. 'Yes, brother Semyon, even in Siberia people can live!' 'Oh, all right,' thinks I, 'it will be a different tale presently.' And from that time forward he went almost every week to inquire whether money had not come from Russia. He wanted a lot of money. 'She is losing her youth and beauty here in Siberia for my sake,' says he, 'and sharing my bitter lot with me, and so I ought,' says he, 'to provide her with every comfort. . . .'

"To make it livelier for the lady he made acquaintance with the officials and all sorts of riffraff. And of course he had to give food and drink to all that crew, and there had to be a piano and a shaggy lapdog on the sofa— plague take it! . . . Luxury, in fact, self-indulgence. The lady did not stay with him long. How could she? The clay, the water, the cold, no vegetables for you, no fruit. All around you ignorant and drunken people and no sort of manners, and she was a spoiled lady from Petersburg or Moscow. . . . To be sure she moped. Besides, her husband, say what you like, was not a gentleman now, but a settler—not the same rank.

"Three years later, I remember, on the eve of the Assumption, there was shouting from the further bank. I went over with the ferry, and what do I see but the lady, all wrapped up, and with her a young gentleman, an official. A sleigh with three horses. . . . I ferried them across here, they got in and away like the wind. They were soon lost to sight. And towards morning Vassily Sergeyich galloped down to the ferry. 'Didn't my wife come this way with a gentleman in spectacles, Semyon?' 'She did,' said I; 'you may look for the wind in the fields!' He galloped in pursuit of them. For five days and nights he was riding after them. When I ferried him over to the other side afterwards, he flung himself on the ferry and beat his head on the boards of the ferry and howled. 'So that's how it is,' says I. I laughed, and reminded him 'people can live even in Siberia!' And he beat his head harder than ever. . . .

"Then he began longing for freedom. His wife had slipped off to Russia, and of course he was drawn there to see her and to get her away from her lover. And he took, my lad, to galloping almost every day, either to the post or the town to see the commanding officer; he kept sending in petitions for them to have mercy on him and let him go back home; and he used to say that he had spent some two hundred rubles on telegrams alone. He sold his land and mortgaged his house to the Jews. He grew gray and bent, and yellow in the face, as though he was in consumption. If he talked to you he would go, khee—khee—khee, . . . and there were tears in his eyes. He kept rushing about like this with petitions for eight years, but now he has grown brighter and more cheerful again: he has found another whim to give way to. You see, his daughter has grown up. He looks at her, and she is the apple of his eye. And to tell the truth she is all right, good-looking, with black eyebrows and a lively disposition. Every Sunday he used to ride with her to church in Gyrino. They used to stand on the ferry, side by side, she would laugh and he could not take his eyes off her. 'Yes, Semyon,' says he, 'people can live even in Siberia. Even in Siberia there is happiness. Look,' says he, 'what a daughter I have got! I warrant you wouldn't find another like her for a thousand versts round.' 'Your daughter is all right,' says I, 'that's true, certainly.' But to myself I thought: 'Wait a bit, the wench is young, her blood is dancing, she wants to live, and there is no life here.' And she did begin to pine, my lad. . . . She faded and faded, and now she can hardly crawl about. Consumption.

"So you see what Siberian happiness is, damn its soul! You see how people can live in Siberia. . . . He has taken to going from one doctor to another and taking them home with him. As soon as he hears that two or three hundred miles away there is a doctor or a sorcerer, he will drive to fetch him. A terrible lot of money he spent on doctors, and to my thinking he had better have spent the money on drink. . . . She'll die just the same. She is certain to die, and then it will be all over with him. He'll hang himself from grief or run away to Russia—that's a sure thing. He'll run away and they'll catch him, then he will be tried, sent to prison, he will have a taste of the lash. . . ."

"Good! Good!" said the Tatar, shivering with cold.

"What is good?" asked Preacher.

"His wife, his daughter. . . . What of prison and what of sorrow!—anyway, he did see his wife and his daughter. . . . You say, want nothing. But 'nothing' is bad! His wife lived with him three years—that was a gift from God. 'Nothing' is bad, but three years is good. 'How not understand?'"

Shivering and hesitating, with effort picking out the Russian words of which he knew but few, the Tatar said that God forbid one should fall sick and die in a strange land, and be buried in the cold and dark earth; that if his wife came to him for one day, even for one hour, that for such happiness he would be ready to bear any suffering and to thank God. Better one day of happiness than nothing.

Then he described again what a beautiful and clever wife he had left at home. Then, clutching his head in both hands, he began crying and assuring Semyon that he was not guilty, and was suffering for nothing. His two brothers and an uncle had carried off a peasant's horses, and had beaten the old man till he was half dead, and the peasant commune had not judged fairly, but had contrived a sentence by which all the three brothers were sent to Siberia, while the uncle, a rich man, was left at home.

"You will get used to it!" said Semyon.

The Tatar was silent, and stared with tear-stained eyes at the fire; his face expressed bewilderment and fear, as though he still did not understand why he was here in the darkness and the wet, beside strangers, and not in the Simbirsk province.

Preacher lay near the fire, chuckled at something, and began humming a song in an undertone.

"What joy has she with her father?" he said a little later. "He loves her and he rejoices in her, that's true; but, mate, you must mind your p's and q's with him, he is a strict old man, a harsh old man. And young wenches don't want strictness. They want petting and ha-ha-ha! and ho-ho-ho! and scent and pomade. Yes. . . . Ech! life, life," sighed Semyon, and he got up heavily. "The vodka is all gone, so it is time to sleep. Eh? I am going, my lad. . . ."

Left alone, the Tatar put on more twigs, lay down and stared at the fire; he began thinking of his own village and of his wife. If his wife could only come for a month, for a day; and then if she liked she might go back again. Better a month or even a day than nothing. But if his wife kept her promise and came, what would he have to feed her on? Where could she live here?

"If there were not something to eat, how could she live?" the Tatar asked aloud.

He was paid only ten kopeks for working all day and all night at the oar; it is true that travelers gave him tips for tea and for vodka, but the men shared all they received among themselves, and gave nothing to the Tatar, but only laughed at him. And from poverty he was hungry, cold, and frightened. . . . Now, when his whole body was aching and shivering, he ought to go into the hut and lie down to sleep; but he had nothing to cover him there, and it was colder than on the riverbank; here he had nothing to cover him either, but at least he could make up the fire. . . .

In another week, when the floods were quite over and they set the ferry going, none of the ferrymen but Semyon would be wanted, and the Tatar would begin going from village to village begging for alms and for work. His wife was only seventeen; she was beautiful, spoiled, and shy; could she possibly go from village to village begging alms with her face unveiled? No, it was terrible even to think of that. . . .

It was already getting light; the barge, the bushes of willow on the water, and the waves could be clearly discerned, and if one looked round there was the steep clay slope; at the bottom of it the hut thatched with dingy brown straw, and the huts of the village lay clustered higher up. The cocks were already crowing in the village.

The rusty red clay slope, the barge, the river, the strange, unkind people, hunger, cold, illness, perhaps all that was not real. Most likely it was all a dream, thought the Tatar. He felt that he was asleep and heard his own snoring. . . . Of course he was at home in Simbirsk province, and he had only to call his wife by name for her to answer; and in the next room was his mother. . . . What terrible dreams there are, though! What are they for? The Tatar smiled and opened his eyes. What river was this, the Volga?

Snow was falling.

"Boat!" was shouted on the further side. "Boat!"

The Tatar woke up, and went to wake his mates and row over to the other side. The ferrymen came on to the riverbank, putting on their torn sheepskins as they walked, swearing with voices husky from sleepiness and shivering from the cold. On waking from their sleep, the river, from which came a breath of piercing cold, seemed to strike them as revolting and horrible. They jumped into the barge without hurrying themselves. . . . The Tatar and the three ferrymen took the long, broad-bladed oars, which in the darkness looked like the claws of crabs; Semyon leaned his stomach against the tiller. The shout on the other side still continued, and the two shots were fired from a revolver, probably with the idea that the ferrymen were asleep or had gone to the tavern in the village.

"All right, you have plenty of time," said Semyon in the tone of a man convinced that there was no necessity in this world to hurry—that it would lead to nothing, anyway.

The heavy, clumsy barge moved away from the bank and floated between the willow-bushes, and only the willows slowly moving back showed that the barge was not standing still but moving. The ferrymen swung the oars evenly in time; Semyon lay with his stomach on the tiller and, describing a semicircle in the air, flew from one side to the other. In the darkness it looked as though the men were sitting on some antediluvian animal with long paws, and were moving on it through a cold, desolate land, the land of which one sometimes dreams in nightmares.

They passed beyond the willows and floated out into the open. The creak and regular splash of the oars was heard on the further shore, and a shout came: "Make haste; make haste!"

Another ten minutes passed, and the barge banged heavily against the landing-stage.

"And it keeps sprinkling and sprinkling," muttered Semyon, wiping the snow from his face; "and where it all comes from God only knows."

On the bank stood a thin man of medium height, in a jacket lined with fox-fur and in a white lambskin cap. He was standing at a little distance from his horses and not moving; he had a gloomy, concentrated expression, as though he were trying to remember something and was angry with his untrustworthy memory. When Semyon went up to him and took off his cap, smiling, he said:

"I am hastening to Anastasyevka. My daughter's worse again, and they say that there is a new doctor at Anastasyevka."

They dragged the carriage on to the barge and floated back. The man whom Semyon addressed as Vassily Sergeyich stood all the time motionless, tightly compressing his thick lips and staring off into space; when his coachman asked permission to smoke in his presence he made no answer, as though he had not heard. Semyon, lying with his stomach on the tiller, looked mockingly at him and said:

"Even in Siberia people can live—can li-ive!"

There was a triumphant expression on Preacher's face, as though he had proved something and was delighted that things had happened as he had foretold. The unhappy helplessness of the man in the foxskin coat evidently afforded him great pleasure.

"It's muddy driving now, Vassily Sergeyich," he said when the horses were harnessed again on the bank. "You should have put off going for another fortnight, when it will be drier. Or else not have gone at all. . . . If any good would come of your going—but as you know yourself, people have been driving about for years and years, day and night, and it's always been no use. That's the truth."

Vassily Sergeyich tipped him without a word, got into his carriage and drove off.

"There, he has galloped off for a doctor!" said Semyon, shrinking from the cold. "But looking for a good doctor is like chasing the wind in the fields or catching the Devil by the tail, plague take your soul! What a queer chap, Lord forgive me a sinner!"

The Tatar went up to Preacher, and, looking at him with hatred and repulsion, shivering, and mixing Tatar words with his broken Russian, said: "He is good . . . good; but you are bad! You are bad! The gentleman is a good soul, excellent, and you are a beast, bad! The gentleman is alive, but you are a dead carcass. . . . God created man to be alive, and to have joy and grief and sorrow; but you want nothing, so you are not alive, you are stone, clay! A stone wants nothing and you want nothing. You are a stone, and God does not love you, but He loves the gentleman!"

Everyone laughed; the Tatar frowned contemptuously, and with a wave of his hand wrapped himself in his rags and went to the campfire. The ferrymen and Semyon sauntered to the hut.

"It's cold," said one ferryman huskily as he stretched himself on the straw with which the damp clay floor was covered.

"Yes, it's not warm," another assented. "It's a dog's life. . . ."

They all lay down. The door was thrown open by the wind and the snow drifted into the hut; nobody felt inclined to get up and shut the door: they were cold, and it was too much trouble.

"I am all right," said Semyon as he began to doze. "I wouldn't wish anyone a better life."

"You are a tough one, we all know. Even the devils won't take you!"

Sounds like a dog's howling came from outside.

"What's that? Who's there?"

"It's the Tatar crying."

"I say. . . . He's a queer one!"

"He'll get u-used to it!" said Semyon, and at once fell asleep.

The others were soon asleep too. The door remained unclosed.

KATE CHOPIN (1851–1904)

The Storm

Kate Chopin was born in St. Louis and spent her married life in Louisiana, where most of her stories are set. Her stories were collected in *Bayou Folk* (1894) and *A Night in Acadia* (1897), from which "The Storm" is taken. Her one novel, *The Awakening* (1899) was condemned for its frank sensuality and its treatment of marital infidelity.

I

The leaves were so still that even Bibi thought it was going to rain. Bobinôt, who was accustomed to converse on terms of perfect equality with his little son, called the child's attention to certain sombre clouds that were rolling with sinister intention from the west, accompanied by a sullen, threatening roar. They were at Friedheimer's store and decided to remain there till the storm had passed. They sat within the door on two empty kegs. Bibi was four years old and looked very wise.

"Mama'll be 'fraid, yes," he suggested with blinking eyes.

"She'll shut the house. Maybe she got Sylvie helpin' her this evenin'," Bobinôt responded reassuringly.

"No; she ent got Sylvie. Sylvie was helpin' her yistiday," piped Bibi.

Bobinôt arose and going across to the counter purchased a can of shrimps, of which Calixta was very fond. Then he returned to his perch on the keg and sat stolidly holding the can of shrimps while the storm burst. It shook the wooden store and seemed to be ripping great furrows in the distant field. Bibi laid his little hand on his father's knee and was not afraid.

II

Calixta, at home, felt no uneasiness for their safety. She sat at a side window sewing furiously on a sewing machine. She was greatly occupied and did not notice the approaching storm. But she felt very warm and often stopped to mop her face on which the persipiration gathered in beads. She unfastened her white sacque at the throat. It began to grow dark, and suddenly realizing the situation she got up hurriedly and went about closing windows and doors.

Out on the small front gallery she had hung Bobinôt's Sunday clothes to air and she hastened out to gather them before the rain fell. As she stepped outside, Alcée Laballière rode in at the gate. She had not seen him very often since her marriage, and never alone. She stood there with Bobinôt's coat in her hands, and the big rain drops began to fall. Alcée rode his horse under the shelter of a side projection where the chickens had huddled and there were plows and a harrow piled up in the corner.

"May I come and wait on your gallery till the storm is over, Calixta?" he asked.

"Come 'long in, M'sieur Alcée."

His voice and her own startled her as if from a trance, and she seized Bobinôt's vest. Alcée, mounting to the porch, grabbed the trousers and snatched Bibi's braided jacket that was about to be carried away by a sudden gust of wind. He expressed an intention to remain outside, but it was soon apparent that he might as well have been out in the open: the water beat in upon the boards in driving sheets, and he went inside, closing the door after him. It was even necessary to put something beneath the door to keep the water out.

"My! what a rain! It's good two years sence it rain' like that," exclaimed Calixta as she rolled up a piece of bagging and Alcée helped her to thrust it beneath the crack.

She was a little fuller of figure than five years before when she married; but she had lost nothing of her vivacity. Her blue eyes still retained their melting quality; and her yellow hair, dishevelled by the wind and rain, kinked more stubbornly than ever about her ears and temples.

The rain beat upon the low, shingled roof with a force and clatter that threatened to break an entrance and deluge them there. They were in the dining room—the sitting room—the general utility room. Adjoining was her bed room, with Bibi's couch along side her own. The door stood open, and the room with its white, monumental bed, its closed shutters, looked dim and mysterious.

Alcée flung himself into a rocker and Calixta nervously began to gather up from the floor the lengths of a cotton sheet which she had been sewing.

"If this keeps up, *Dieu sait* if the levees goin' to stan' it!" she exclaimed.

"What have you got to do with the levees?"

"I got enough to do! An' there's Bobinôt with Bibi out in that storm— if he only didn' left Friedheimer's!"

"Let us hope, Calixta, that Bobinôt's got sense enough to come in out of a cyclone."

She went and stood at the window with a greatly disturbed look on her face. She wiped the frame that was clouded with moisture. It was stiflingly hot. Alcée got up and joined her at the window, looking over her shoulder. The rain was coming down in sheets obscuring the view of far-off cabins and enveloping the distant wood in a gray mist. The playing of the lightning was incessant. A bolt struck a tall chinaberry tree at the edge of the field. It filled all visible space with a blinding glare and the crash seemed to invade the very boards they stood upon.

Calixta put her hands to her eyes, and with a cry, staggered backward. Alcée's arm encircled her, and for an instant he drew her close and spasmodically to him.

"*Bonte!*" she cried, releasing herself from his encircling arm and retreating from the window, "the house'll go next! If I only knew w'ere Bibi was!" She would not compose herself; she would not be seated. Alcée clasped her shoulders and looked into her face. The contact of her warm, palpitating body when he had unthinkingly drawn her into his arms, had aroused all the old-time infatuation and desire for her flesh.

"Calixta," he said, "don't be frightened. Nothing can happen. The house is to low too be struck, with so many tall trees standing about. There! aren't you going to be quiet? say, aren't you?" He pushed her hair back from her face that was warm and steaming. Her lips were as red and moist as pomegranate seed. Her white neck and a glimpse of her full, firm bosom disturbed him powerfully. As she glanced up at him the fear in her liquid blue eyes had given place to a drowsy gleam that unconsciously betrayed a sensuous desire. He looked down into her eyes and there was nothing for him to do but to gather her lips in a kiss. It reminded him of Assumption.

"Do you remember—in Assumption, Calixta?" he asked in a low voice broken by passion. Oh! she remembered; for in Assumption he had kissed her and kissed and kissed her; until his senses would well nigh fail, and to save her he would resort to a desperate flight. If she was not an immaculate dove in those days, she was still inviolate; a passionate creature whose very defenselessness had made her defense, against which his honor forbade him to prevail. Now—well, now—her lips seemed in a manner free to be tasted, as well as her round, white throat and her whiter breasts.

They did not heed the crashing torrents, and the roar of the elements made her laugh as she lay in his arms. She was a revelation in that dim, mysterious chamber; as white as the couch she lay upon. Her firm, elastic flesh that was knowing for the first time its birthright, was like a creamy lily that the sun invites to contribute its breath and perfume to the undying life of the world.

The generous abundance of her passion, without guile or trickery, was like a white flame which penetrated and found response in depths of his own sensuous nature that had never yet been reached.

When he touched her breasts they gave themselves up in quivering ecstasy, inviting his lips. Her mouth was a fountain of delight. And when he possessed her, they seemed to swoon together at the very borderland of life's mystery.

He stayed cushioned upon her, breathless, dazed, enervated, with his heart beating like a hammer upon her. With one hand she clasped his head, her lips lightly touching his forehead. The other hand stroked with a soothing rhythm his muscular shoulders.

The growl of the thunder was distant and passing away. The rain beat softly upon the shingles, inviting them to drowsiness and sleep. But they dared not yield.

The rain was over; and the sun was turning the glistening green world into a palace of gems. Calixta, on the gallery, watched Alcée ride away. He turned and smiled at her with a beaming face; and she lifted her pretty chin in the air and laughed aloud.

III

Bobinôt and Bibi, trudging home, stopped without at the cistern to make themselves presentable.

"My! Bibi, w'at will yo' mama say! You ought to be ashame'. You oughtn' put on those good pants. Look at 'em! An' that mud on yo' collar! How you got that mud on yo' collar, Bibi? I never saw such a boy!" Bibi was the picture of pathetic resignation. Bobinôt was the embodiment of serious solicitude as he strove to remove from his own person and his son's the signs of their tramp over heavy roads and through wet fields. He scraped the mud off Bibi's bare legs and feet with a stick and carefully removed all traces from his heavy brogans. Then, prepared for the worst— the meeting with an over-scrupulous housewife, they entered cautiously at the back door.

Calixta was preparing supper. She had set the table and was dripping coffee at the hearth. She sprang up as they came in.

"Oh, Bobinôt! You back! My! but I was uneasy. W'ere you been during the rain? An' Bibi? he ain't wet? he ain't hurt?" She had clasped Bibi and was kissing him effusively. Bobinôt's explanations and apologies which he had been composing all along the way, died on his lips as Calixta felt him to see if he were dry, and seemed to express nothing but satisfaction at their safe return.

"I brought you some shrimps, Calixta," offered Bobinôt, hauling the can from his ample side pocket and laying it on the table.

"Shrimps! Oh, Bobinôt! you too good fo' anything!" and she gave him a smacking kiss on the cheek that resounded. "*J'vous reponds*, we'll have a feas' to night! umph-umph!"

Bobinôt and Bibi began to relax and enjoy themselves, and when the three seated themselves at table they laughed much and so loud that anyone might have heard them as far away as Laballière's.

IV

Alcée Laballière wrote to his wife, Clarisse, that night. It was a loving letter, full of tender solicitude. He told her not to hurry back, but if she and the babies liked it at Biloxi, to stay a month longer. He was getting on nicely; and though he missed them, he was willing to bear the separation a while longer—realizing that their health and pleasure were the first things to be considered.

V

As for Clarisse, she was charmed upon receiving her husband's letter. She and the babies were doing well. The society was agreeable; many of her old friends and acquaintances were at the bay. And the first free breath since her marriage seemed to restore the pleasant liberty of her maiden days. Devoted as she was to her husband, their intimate conjugal life was something which she was more than willing to forego for a while.

So the storm passed and everyone was happy.

JOSEPH CONRAD (1857–1924)
The Secret Sharer

Joseph Conrad is perhaps the world's most famous example of a writer who achieved fame writing in an adopted language. Born in Poland as Josef Korzeniowksi, he spent twenty years as a sailor and attained the rank of captain in the British merchant fleet. His novels and stories, which often reflect his adventurous years as a sailor, include *Lord Jim* (1900), *Nostromo* (1904), and *Victory* (1915). "The Secret Sharer" first appeared in 1913.

I

On my right hand there were lines of fishing stakes resembling a mysterious system of half-submerged bamboo fences, incomprehensible in its division of the domain of tropical fishes, and crazy of aspect as if abandoned forever by some nomad tribe of fishermen now gone to the other end of the ocean; for there was no sign of human habitation as far as the eye could reach. To the left a group of barren islets, suggesting ruins of stone walls, towers, and blockhouses, had its foundations set in a blue sea that itself looked solid, so still and stable did it lie below my feet; even the track of light from the westering sun shone smoothly, without that animated glitter which tells of an imperceptible ripple. And when I turned my head to take a parting glance at the tug which had just left us anchored outside the bar, I saw the straight line of the flat shore joined to the stable sea, edge to edge, with a perfect and unmarked closeness, in one leveled floor half brown, half blue under the enormous dome of the sky. Corresponding in their insignificance to the islets of the sea, two small clumps of trees, one on each side of the only fault in the impeccable joint, marked the mouth of the river Meinam we had just left on the first preparatory stage of our homeward journey; and, far back on the inland level, a larger and loftier mass, the grove surrounding the great Paknam pagoda, was the only thing on which the eye could rest from the vain task of exploring the monotonous sweep of the horizon. Here and there gleams as of a few scattered pieces of silver marked the windings of the great river; and on the nearest of them, just within the bar, the tug steaming right into the land become lost to my sight, hull and funnel and masts, as though the impassive earth had swallowed her up without an effort, without a tremor. My eye followed the light cloud of her smoke, now here, now there, above the plain, according to the devious curves of the stream, but always fainter and farther away, till I lost it at last behind the miter-shaped hill of the great pagoda. And then I was left alone with my ship, anchored at the head of the Gulf of Siam.

She floated at the starting point of a long journey, very still in an immense stillness, the shadows of her spars flung far to the eastward by the setting sun. At that moment I was alone on her decks. There was not a sound in her—and around us nothing moved, nothing lived, not a canoe on the water, not a bird in the air, not a cloud in the sky. In this breathless pause at the threshold of a long passage we seemed to be measuring our fitness for a long and arduous enterprise, the appointed task of both our existences to be carried out, far from all human eyes, with only sky and sea for spectators and for judges.

There must have been some glare in the air to interfere with one's sight, because it was only just before the sun left us that my roaming eyes made out beyond the highest ridge of the principal islet of the group something which did away with the solemnity of perfect solitude. The tide of darkness flowed on swiftly; and with tropical suddenness a swarm of stars came out above the shadowy earth, while I lingered yet, my hand resting lightly on my ship's rail as if on the shoulder of a trusted friend. But, with all that multitude of celestial bodies staring down at one, the comfort of quiet communion with her was gone for good. And there were also disturbing sounds by this time—voices, footsteps forward; the steward flitted along the main deck, a busily ministering spirit; a hand bell tinkled urgently under the poop deck. . . .

I found my two officers waiting for me near the supper table, in the lighted cuddy. We sat down at once, and as I helped the chief mate, I said:

"Are you aware that there is a ship anchored inside the islands? I saw her mastheads above the ridge as the sun went down."

He raised sharply his simple face, overcharged by a terrible growth of whisker, and emitted his usual ejaculations: "Bless my soul, sir! You don't say so!"

My second mate was a sound-cheeked, silent young man, grave beyond his years, I thought; but as our eyes happened to meet I detected a slight quiver on his lips. I looked down at once. It was not my part to encourage sneering on board my ship. It must be said, too, that I knew very little of my officers. In consequence of certain events of no particular significance, except to myself, I had been appointed to the command only a fortnight before. Neither did I know much of the hands forward. All these people had been together for eighteen months or so, and my position was that of the only stranger on board. I mention this because it has some bearing on what is to follow. But what I felt most was my being a stranger to the ship; and if truth must be told, I was somewhat of a stranger to myself. The youngest man on board (barring the second mate), and untried as yet by a position of the fullest responsibility, I was willing to take the adequacy of the others for granted. They had simply to be equal to their tasks: but I wondered how far I should turn out faithful to that ideal conception of one's own personality every man sets up for himself secretly.

Meantime the chief mate, with an almost visible effect of collaboration on the part of his round eyes and frightful whiskers, was trying to evolve a theory of the anchored ship. His dominant trait was to take all things into earnest consideration. He was of a painstaking turn of mind. As he used to say, he "liked to account to himself" for practically everything that came in his way, down to a miserable scorpion he had found in his cabin a week before. The why and the wherefore of that scorpion—how it got on board and came to select his room rather than the pantry (which was a dark place and more what a scorpion would be partial to), and how on earth it managed to drown itself in the inkwell of his writing desk—had exercised him infinitely. The ship within the islands was much more easily accounted for; and just as we were about to rise from the table he made his pronouncement. She was, he doubted not, a ship from home lately arrived. Probably she drew too much water to cross the bar except at the top of spring tides. Therefore she went into that natural harbor to wait for a few days in preference to remaining in an open roadstead.

"That's so," confirmed the second mate, suddenly, in his slightly hoarse voice. "She draws over twenty feet. She's the Liverpool ship *Sephora* with a cargo of coal. Hundred and twenty-three days from Cardiff."

We looked at him in surprise.

"The tugboat skipper told me when he came on board for your letters, sir," explained the young man. "He expects to take her up the river the day after tomorrow."

After thus overwhelming us with the extent of his information he slipped out of the cabin. The mate observed regretfully that he "could not account for that young fellow's whims." What prevented him telling us all about it at once, he wanted to know.

I detained him as he was making a move. For the last two days the crew had had plenty of hard work, and the night before they had very little sleep. I felt painfully that I—a stranger—was doing something unusual when I directed him to let all hands turn in without setting an anchor watch. I proposed to keep on deck myself till one o'clock or thereabouts. I would get the second mate to relieve me at that hour.

"He will turn out the cook and the steward at four," I concluded, "and then give you a call. Of course at the slightest sign of any sort of wind we'll have the hands up and make a start at once."

He concealed his astonishment. "Very well, sir." Outside the cuddy he put his head in the second mate's door to inform him of my unheard-of caprice to take a five hours' anchor watch on myself. I heard the other raise his voice incredulously: "What? The captain himself?" Then a few more murmurs, a door closed, then another. A few moments later I went on deck.

My strangeness, which had made me sleepless, had prompted that unconventional arrangement, as if I had expected in those solitary hours of the night to get on terms with the ship of which I knew nothing, manned by men of whom I knew very little more. Fast alongside a wharf, littered like any ship in port with a tangle of unrelated things, invaded by unrelated shore people, I had hardly seen her yet properly. Now, as she lay cleared for sea, the stretch of her main deck seemed to me very fine under the stars. Very fine, very roomy for her size, and very inviting. I descended the poop and paced the waist, my mind picturing to myself the coming passage through the Malay Archipelago, down the Indian Ocean, and up the Atlantic. All its phases were familiar enough to me, every characteristic, all the alternatives which were likely to face me on the high seas—everything! . . . except the novel responsibility of command. But I took heart from the reasonable thought that the ship was like other ships, the men like other men, and that the sea was not likely to keep any special surprises expressly for my discomfiture.

Arrived at that comforting conclusion, I bethought myself of a cigar and went below to get it. All was still down there. Everybody at the after end of the ship was sleeping profoundly. I came out again on the quarterdeck, agreeably at ease in my sleeping suit on that warm breathless night, barefooted, a glowing cigar in my teeth, and, going forward, I was met by the profound silence of the fore end of the ship. Only as I passed the door of the forecastle I heard a deep, quiet, trustful sigh of some sleeper inside. And suddenly I rejoiced in the great security of the sea as compared with the unrest of the land, in my choice of that untempted life presenting no disquieting problems, invested with an elementary moral beauty by the absolute straightforwardness of its appeal and by the singleness of its purpose.

The riding light in the fore-rigging burned with a clear, untroubled, as if symbolic, flame, confident and bright in the mysterious shades of the night. Passing on my way aft along the other side of the ship, I observed that the rope side ladder, put over, no doubt, for the master of the tug when he came to fetch away our letters, had not been hauled in as it should have been. I became annoyed at this, for exactitude in small matters is the very soul of discipline. Then I reflected that I had myself peremptorily dismissed my officers from duty, and by my own act had prevented the anchor watch being formally set and things properly attended to. I asked myself whether it was wise ever to interfere with the established routine of duties even from the kindest of motives. My action might have made me appear eccentric. Goodness only knew how that absurdly whiskered mate would "account" for my conduct, and what the whole ship thought of that informality of their new captain. I was vexed with myself.

Not from compunction certainly, but, as it were mechanically, I proceeded to get the ladder in myself. Now a side ladder of that sort is a light affair and comes in easily, yet my vigorous tug, which should have brought it flying on board, merely recoiled upon my body in a totally unexpected jerk. What the devil! . . . I was so astounded by the immovableness of that ladder that I remained stock-still, trying to account for it to myself like that imbecile mate of mine. In the end, of course, I put my head over the rail.

The side of the ship made an opaque belt of shadow on the darkling glassy shimmer of the sea. But I saw at once something elongated and pale floating very close to the ladder. Before I could form a guess a faint flash of phosphorescent light, which seemed to issue suddenly from the naked body of a man, flickered in the sleeping water with the elusive, silent play of summer lightning in a night sky. With a gasp I saw revealed to my stare a pair of feet, the long legs, a broad livid back immersed right up to the neck in a greenish cadaverous glow. One hand, awash, clutched the bottom rung of the ladder. He was complete but for the head. A headless corpse! The cigar dropped out of my gaping mouth with a tiny plop and a short hiss quite audible in the absolute stillness of all things under heaven. At that I suppose he raised up his face, a dimly pale oval in the shadow of the ship's side. But even then I could only barely make out down there the shape of his black-haired head. However, it was enough for the horrid, frost-bound sensation which had gripped me about the chest to pass off. The moment of vain exclamations was past, too. I only climbed on the spare spar and leaned over the rail as far as I could, to bring my eyes nearer to that mystery floating alongside.

As he hung by the ladder, like a resting swimmer, the sea lightning played about his limbs at every stir; and he appeared in it ghastly, silvery, fishlike. He remained as mute as a fish, too. He made no motion to get out of the water, either. It was inconceivable that he should not attempt to come on board, and strangely troubling to suspect that perhaps he did not want to. And my first words were prompted by just that troubled incertitude.

"What's the matter?" I asked in my ordinary tone, speaking down to the face upturned exactly under mine.

"Cramp," is answered, no louder. Then slightly anxious, "I say, no need to call anyone."

"I was not going to," I said.

"Are you alone on deck?"

"Yes."

I had somehow the impression that he was on the point of letting go the ladder to swim away beyond my ken—mysterious as he came. But, for the moment, this being appearing as if he had risen from the bottom of the sea (it was certainly the nearest land to the ship) wanted only to know the time. I told him. And he, down there, tentatively:

"I suppose your captain's turned in?"

"I am sure he isn't," I said.

He seemed to struggle with himself, for I heard something like the low, bitter murmur of doubt. "What's the good?" His next words came out with a hesitating effort.

"Look here, my man. Could you call him out quietly?"

I thought the time had come to declare myself.

"I am the captain."

I heard a "By Jove!" whispered at the level of the water. The phosphorescence flashed in the swirl of the water all about his limbs, his other hand seized the ladder.

"My name's Leggatt."

The voice was calm and resolute. A good voice. The self-possession of that man had somehow induced a corresponding state in myself. It was very quietly that I remarked:

"You must be a good swimmer."

"Yes. I've been in the water practically since nine o'clock. The question for me now is whether I am to let go this ladder and go on swimming till I sink from exhaustion, or—to come on board here.

I felt this was no mere formula of desperate speech, but a real alternative in the view of a strong soul. I should have gathered from this that he was young; indeed, it is only the young who are ever confronted by such clear issues. But at this time it was pure intuition on my part. A mysterious communication was established already between us two—in the face of that silent darkened tropical sea. I was young, too; young enough to make no comment. The man in the water began suddenly to climb up the ladder, and I hastened away from the rail to fetch some clothes.

Before entering the cabin I stood still, listening in the lobby at the foot of the stairs. A faint snore came through the closed door of the chief mate's room. The second mate's door was on the hook, but the darkness in there was absolutely soundless. He, too, was young and could sleep like a stone. Remained the steward, but he was not likely to wake up before he was called. I got a sleeping suit out of my room and, coming back on deck, saw the naked man from the sea sitting on the main hatch, glimmering white in the darkness, his elbows on his knees and his head in his hands. In a moment he had concealed his damp body in a sleeping suit of the same gray-stripe pattern as the one I was wearing and followed me like my double on the poop. Together we moved right aft, barefooted, silent.

"What is it?" I asked in a deadened voice, taking the lighted lamp out of the binnacle, and raising it to his face.

"An ugly business."

He had rather regular features; a good mouth; light eyes under some-what heavy, dark eyebrows; a smooth, square forehead; no growth on his cheeks; a small, brown mustache, and a well-shaped, round chin. His expression was concentrated, meditative, under the inspecting light of the lamp I held up to his face; such as a man thinking hard in solitude might wear. My sleeping suit was just right for his size. A well-knit young fellow of twenty-five at most. He caught his lower lip with the edge of white, even teeth.

"Yes," I said, replacing the lamp in the binnacle. The warm, heavy tropical night closed upon his head again.

"There's a ship over there," he murmured.

"Yes, I know. The *Sephora*. Did you know of us?"

"Hadn't the slightest idea. I am the mate of her—" He paused and corrected himself. "I should say I *was*."

"Aha! Something wrong?"

"Yes. Very wrong indeed. I've killed a man."

"What do you mean? Just now?"

"No, on the passage. Weeks ago. Thirty-nine south. When I say a man—"

"Fit of temper," I suggested, confidently.

The shadowy, dark head, like mine, seemed to nod imperceptibly above the ghostly gray of my sleeping suit. It was, in the night, as though I had been faced by my own reflection in the depths of a somber and im-mense mirror.

"A pretty thing to have to own up to for a Conway boy," murmured my double, distinctly.

"You're a Conway boy?"

"I am," he said, as if startled. Then slowly . . . "Perhaps you too—"

It was so; but being a couple of years older I had left before he joined. After a quick interchange of dates a silence fell; and I thought suddenly of my absurd mate with his terrific whiskers and the "Bless my soul—you don't say so" type of intellect. My double gave me an inkling of his thoughts by saying:

"Mr father's a parson in Norfolk. Do you see me before a judge and jury on that charge? For myself I can't see the necessity. There are fellows that an angel from heaven—And I am not that. He was one of those crea-tures that are just simmering all the time with a silly sort of wickedness. Miserable devils that have no business to live at all. He wouldn't do his duty and wouldn't let anybody else do theirs. But what's the good of talk-ing! You know well enough the sort of ill-conditioned snarling cur—"

He appealed to me as if our experiences had been as identical as our clothes. And I knew well enough the pestiferous danger of such a character where there are no means of legal repression. And I knew well enough also that my double there was no homicidal ruffian. I did not think of asking him for details, and he told me the story roughly in brusque, disconnected sentences. I needed no more. I saw it all going on as though I were myself inside that other sleeping suit.

"It happened while we were setting a reefed foresail, at dusk. Reefed foresail! You understand the sort of weather. The only sail we had left to keep the ship running; so you may guess what it had been like for days. Anxious sort of job, that. He gave me some of his cursed insolence at the sheet. I tell you I was overdone with this terrific weather that seemed to have no end to it. Terrific, I tell you—and a deep ship. I believe the fellow himself was half crazed with funk. It was no time for gentlemanly reproof, so I turned round and felled him like an ox. He up and at me. We closed just as an awful sea made for the ship. All hands saw it coming and took to the rigging, but I had him by the throat, and went on shaking him like a rat, the men above us yelling, 'Look out! look out!' Then a crash as if the sky had fallen on my head. They say that for over ten minutes hardly anything was to be seen of the ship—just the three masts and a bit of the forecastle head and of the poop all awash driving along in a smother of foam. It was a miracle that they found us, jammed together behind the forebits. It's clear that I meant business, because I was holding him by the throat still when they picked us up. He was black in the face. It was too much for them. It seems they rushed us aft together, gripped as we were, screaming 'Murder!' like a lot of lunatics, and broke into the cuddy. And the ship running for her life, touch and go all the time, any minute her last in a sea fit to turn your hair gray only a-looking at it. I understand that the skipper, too, started raving like the rest of them. The man had been deprived of sleep for more than a week, and to have this sprung on him at the height of a furious gale nearly drove him out of his mind. I wonder they didn't fling me overboard after getting the carcass of their precious shipmate out of my fingers. They had rather a job to separate us, I've been told. A sufficiently fierce story to make an old judge and a respectable jury sit up a bit. The first thing I heard when I came to myself was the maddening howling of that endless gale, and on that the voice of the old man. He was hanging on to my bunk, staring into my face out of his sou'wester.

" 'Mr. Leggatt, you have killed a man. You can act no longer as chief mate of this ship.' "

His care to subdue his voice made it sound monotonous. He rested a hand on the end of the skylight to steady himself with, and all that time did not stir a limb, so far as I could see. "Nice little tale for a quiet tea party," he concluded in the same tone.

One of my hands, too, rested on the end of the skylight; neither did I stir a limb, so far as I knew. We stood less than a foot from each other. It occurred to me that if old "Bless my soul—you don't say so" were to put his head up the companion and catch sight of us, he would think he was seeing double, or imagine himself come upon a scene of weird witchcraft; the strange captain having a quiet confabulation by the wheel with his own gray ghost. I became very much concerned to prevent anything of the sort. I heard the other's soothing undertone.

"My father's a parson in Norfolk," it said. Evidently he had forgotten he had told me this important fact before. Truly a nice little tale.

"You had better slip down into my stateroom now," I said, moving off stealthily. My double followed my movements; our bare feet made no sound; I let him in, closed the door with care, and, after giving a call to the second mate, returned on deck for my relief.

"Not much sign of any wind yet," I remarked when he approached.

"No, sir. Not much," he assented, sleepily, in his hoarse voice, with just enough deference, no more, and barely suppressing a yawn.

"Well, that's all you have to look out for. You have got your orders."

"Yes, sir."

I paced a turn or two on the poop and saw him take up his position face forward with his elbow in the rat-lines of the mizzen-rigging before I went below. The mate's faint snoring was still going on peacefully. The cuddy lamp was burning over the table on which stood a vase with flowers, a polite attention from the ships' provision merchant—the last flowers we should see for the next three months at the very least. Two bunches of bananas hung from the beam symmetrically, one on each side of the rudder casing. Everything was as before in the ship—except that two of her captain's sleeping suits were simultaneously in use, one motionless in the cuddy, the other keeping very still in the captain's stateroom.

It must be explained here that my cabin had the form of the capital letter L, the door being within the angle and opening into the short part of the letter. A couch was to the left, the bed-place to the right; my writing desk and the chronometers' table faced the door. But anyone opening it, unless he stepped right inside, had no view of what I call the long (or vertical) part of the letter. It contained some lockers surmounted by a bookcase; and a few clothes, a thick jacket or two, caps, oilskin coat, and such like, hung on the hooks. There was at the bottom of that part a door opening into my bathroom, which could be entered also directly from the saloon. But that way was never used.

The mysterious arrival had discovered the advantage of this particular shape. Entering my room, lighted strongly by a big bulkhead lamp swung on gimbals above my writing desk, I did not see him anywhere till he stepped out quietly from behind the coats hung in the recessed part.

"I heard somebody moving about, and went in there at once," he whispered.

I, too, spoke under my breath.

"Nobody is likely to come in here without knocking and getting permission."

He nodded. His face was thin and the sunburn faded, as though he had been ill. And no wonder. He had been, I heard presently, kept under arrest in his cabin for nearly seven weeks. But there was nothing sickly in his eyes or in his expression. He was not a bit like me, really; yet, as we stood leaning over my bed-place, whispering side by side, with our dark heads together and our backs to the door, anybody bold enough to open it stealthily would have been treated to the uncanny sight of a double captain busy talking in whispers with his other self.

"But all this doesn't tell me how you came to hang on to our side ladder," I inquired, in the hardly audible murmurs we used, after he had told me something more of the proceedings on board the *Sephora* once the bad weather was over.

"When we sighted Java Head I had had time to think all those matters out several times over. I had six weeks of doing nothing else, and with only an hour or so every evening for a tramp on the quarter-deck."

He whispered, his arms folded on the side of my bed-place, staring through the open port. And I could imagine perfectly the manner of this thinking out—a stubborn if not a steadfast operation; something of which I should have been perfectly incapable.

"I reckoned it would be dark before we closed with the land," he continued, so low that I had to strain my hearing, near as we were to each other, shoulder touching shoulder almost. "So I asked to speak to the old man. He always seemed very sick when he came to see me—as if he could not look me in the face. You know, that foresail saved the ship. She was too deep to have run long under bare poles. And it was I that managed to set it for him. Anyway, he came. When I had him in my cabin—he stood by the door looking at me as if I had the halter around my neck already—I asked him right away to leave my cabin door unlocked at night while the ship was going through Sunda Straits. There would be the Java coast within two or three miles, off Angier Point. I wanted nothing more. I've had a prize for swimming my second year in the Conway."

"I can believe it," I breathed out.

"God only knows why they locked me in every night. To see some of their faces you'd have thought they were afraid I'd go about at night strangling people. Am I a murdering brute? Do I look it? By Jove! if I had been he wouldn't have trusted himself like that into my room. You'll say I might have chucked him aside and bolted out, there and then—it was dark already. Well, no. And for the same reason I wouldn't think of trying to smash the door. There would have been a rush to stop me at the noise, and I did not mean to get into a confounded scrimmage. Somebody else might have got killed—for I would not have broken out only to get chucked back, and I did not want any more of that work. He refused, looking more sick than ever. He was afraid of the men, and also of that old second mate of his who had been sailing with him for years—a gray-headed old humbug; and his steward, too, had been with him devil knows how long—seventeen years or more—a dogmatic sort of loafer who hated me like poison, just because I was the chief mate. No chief mate ever made more than one voyage in the *Sephora*, you know. Those two old chaps ran the ship. Devil only knows what the skipper wasn't afraid of (all his nerve went to pieces altogether in that hellish spell of bad weather we had)—of what the law would do to him—of his wife, perhaps. Oh, yes! she's on board. Though I don't think she would have meddled. She would have been only too glad to have me out of the ship in any way. The 'brand of Cain' business, don't you see. That's all right. I was ready enough to go off wandering on the face of the earth—and that was price enough to pay for an Abel of that sort. Anyhow, he wouldn't listen to me. 'This thing must take its course. I represent the law here.' He was shaking like a leaf. 'So you won't?' 'No!' 'Then I hope you will be able to sleep on that,' I said, and turned my back on him. 'I wonder that *you* can,' cries he, and locks the door.

"Well, after that, I couldn't. Not very well. That was three weeks ago. We have had a slow passage through the Java Sea; drifted about Carimata for ten days. When we anchored here they thought, I suppose, it was all right. The nearest land (and that's five miles) is the ship's destination; the consul would soon set about catching me; and there would have been no object in bolting to these islets there. I don't suppose there's a drop of water on them. I don't know how it was, but tonight that steward, after bringing me my supper, went out to let me eat it, and left the door unlocked. And I ate it—all there was, too. After I had finished I strolled out on the quarter-deck. I don't know that I meant to do anything. A breath of fresh air was all I wanted, I believe. Then a sudden temptation came over me. I kicked off my slippers and was in the water before I had made up my mind fairly. Somebody heard the splash and they raised an awful hullabaloo. 'He's gone! Lower the boats! He's committed suicide! No, he's swimming.' Certainly I was swimming. It's not so easy for a swimmer like me to commit suicide by drowning. I landed on the nearest islet before the boat left the ship's side. I heard them pulling about in the dark, hailing, and so on, but after a bit they gave up. Everything quieted down and the anchorage became as still as death. I sat down on a stone and began to think. I felt certain they would start searching for me at daylight. There was no place to hide on those stony things—and if there had been, what would have been the good? But now I was clear of that ship, I was not going back. So after a while I took off all my clothes, tied them up in a bundle with a stone inside, and dropped them in the deep water on the outer side of the islet. That was suicide enough for me. Let them think what they liked, but I didn't mean to drown myself. I meant to swim till I sank—but that's not the same thing. I struck out for another of these little islands, and it was from that one that I first saw your riding light. Something to swim for. I went on easily, and on the way I came upon a flat rock a foot or two above water. In the daytime, I dare say, you might make it out with a glass from your poop. I scrambled up on it and rested myself for a bit. Then I made another start. That last spell must have been over a mile."

His whisper was getting fainter and fainter, and all the time he stared straight out through the porthole, in which there was not even a star to be seen. I had not interrupted him. There was something that made comment impossible in his narrative, or perhaps in himself; a sort of feeling, a quality, which I can't find a name for. And when he ceased, all I found was a futile whisper: "So you swam for our light?"

"Yes—straight for it. It was something to swim for. I couldn't see any stars low down because the coast was in the way, and I couldn't see the land, either. The water was like glass. One might have been swimming in a confounded thousand-feet deep cistern with no place for scrambling out anywhere; but what I didn't like was the notion of swimming round and round like a crazed bullock before I gave out; and as I didn't mean to go back . . . No. Do you see me being hauled back, stark naked, off one of these little islands by the scruff of the neck and fighting like a wild beast? Somebody would have got killed for certain, and I did not want any of that. So I went on. Then your ladder—"

"Why didn't you hail the ship?" I asked, a little louder.

He touched my shoulder lightly. Lazy footsteps came right over our heads and stopped. The second mate had crossed from the other side of the poop and might have been hanging over the rail, for all we knew.

"He couldn't hear us talking—could he?" My double breathed into my very ear, anxiously.

His anxiety was an answer, a sufficient answer, to the question I had put to him. An answer containing all the difficulty of that situation. I closed the porthole quietly, to make sure. A louder word might have been overheard.

"Who's that?" he whispered then.

"My second mate. But I don't know much more of the fellow than you do."

And I told him a little about myself. I had been appointed to take charge while I least expected anything of the sort, not quite a fortnight ago. I didn't know either the ship or the people. Hadn't had the time in port to look about me or size anybody up. And as to the crew, all they knew was that I was appointed to take the ship home. For the rest, I was almost as much of a stranger on board as himself, I said. And at the moment I felt it most acutely. I felt that it would take very little to make me a suspect person in the eyes of the ship's company.

He had turned about meantime; and we, the two strangers in the ship, faced each other in identical attitudes.

"Your ladder—" he murmured, after a silence. "Who'd have thought of finding a ladder hanging over at night in a ship anchored out here! I felt just then a very unpleasant faintness. After the life I've been leading for nine weeks, anybody would have got out of condition. I wasn't capable of swimming round as far as your rudder chains. And, lo and behold! there was a ladder to get hold of. After I gripped it I said to myself, 'What's the good?" When I saw a man's head looking over I thought I could swim away presently and leave him shouting—in whatever language it was. I didn't mind being looked at. I—I liked it. And then you speaking to me so quietly—as if you had expected me—made me hold on a little longer. It had been a confounded lonely time—I don't mean while swimming. I was glad to talk a little to somebody that didn't belong to the *Sephora*. As to asking for the captain, that was a mere impulse. It could have been no use, with all the ship knowing about me and the other people pretty certain to be round here in the morning. I don't know—I wanted to be seen, to talk with somebody, before I went on. I don't know what I would have said. . . . 'Fine night, isn't it?' or something of the sort."

"Do you think they will be round here presently?" I asked with some incredulity.

"Quite likely," he said, faintly.

He looked extremely haggard all of a sudden. His head rolled on his shoulders.

"H'm. We shall see then. Meantime get into that bed," I whispered. "Want help? There."

It was a rather high bed-place with a set of drawers underneath. This amazing swimmer really needed the lift I gave him by seizing his leg. He tumbled in rolled over on his back, and flung one arm across his eyes. And then, with his face nearly hidden, he must have looked exactly as I used to look in that bed. I gazed upon my other self for a while before drawing across carefully the two green serge curtains which ran on a brass rod. I thought for a moment of pinning them together for greater safety, but I sat down on the couch, and once there I felt unwilling to rise and hunt for a pin. I would do it in a moment. I was extremely tired, in a peculiarly intimate way, by the strain of stealthiness, by the effort of whispering and the general secrecy of this excitement. It was three o'clock by now and I had been on my feet since nine, but I was not sleepy; I could not have gone to sleep. I sat there, fagged out, looking at the curtains, trying to clear my mind of the confused sensation of being in two places at once, and greatly bothered by an exasperating knocking in my head. It was a relief to discover suddenly that it was not in my head at all, but on the outside of the door. Before I could collect myself the words "Come in" were out of my mouth, and the steward entered with a tray, bringing in my morning coffee. I had slept, after all, and I was so frightened that I shouted, "This way! I am here, steward," as though he had been miles away. He put down the tray on the table next the couch and only then said, very quietly, "I can see you are here, sir." I felt him give me a keen look, but I dared not meet his eyes just then. He must have wondered why I had drawn the curtains of my bed before going to sleep on the couch. He went out, hooking the door open as usual.

I heard the crew washing decks above me. I knew I would have been told at once if there had been any wind. Calm, I thought, and I was doubly vexed. Indeed, I felt dual more than ever. The steward reappeared suddenly in the doorway. I jumped up from the couch so quickly that he gave a start.

"What do you want here?"

"Close your port, sir—they are washing decks."

"It is closed," I said, reddening.

"Very well, sir." But he did not move from the doorway and returned my stare in an extraordinary, equivocal manner for a time. Then his eyes wavered, all his expressions changed, and in a voice unusually gentle, almost coaxingly:

"May I come in to take the empty cup away, sir?"

"Of course!" I turned my back on him while he popped in and out. Then I unhooked and closed the door and even pushed the bolt. This sort of thing could not go on very long. The cabin was as hot as an oven, too. I took a peep at my double, and discovered that he had not moved, his arm was still over his eyes; but his chest heaved; his hair was wet; his chin glistened with perspiration. I reached over him and opened the port.

"I must show myself on deck," I reflected.

Of course, theoretically, I could do what I liked, with no one to say nay to me within the whole circle of the horizon; but to lock my cabin door and take the key away I did not dare. Directly I put my head out of the companion I saw the group of my two officers, the second mate barefooted, the chief mate in long india-rubber boots, near the break of the poop, and the stewart halfway down the poop ladder talking to them eagerly. He happened to catch sight of me and dived, the second ran down on the main deck shouting some order or other, and the chief mate came to meet me, touching his cap.

There was a sort of curiosity in his eye that I did not like. I don't know whether the steward had told them that I was "queer" only, or downright drunk, but I know the man meant to have a good look at me. I watched him coming with a smile which, as he got into point-blank range, took effect and froze his very whiskers. I did not give him time to open his lips.

"Square the yards by lifts and braces before the hands go to breakfast."

It was the first particular order I had given on board that ship; and I stayed on deck to see it executed, too. I had felt the need of asserting myself without loss of time. That sneering young cub got taken down a peg or two on that occasion, and I also seized the opportunity of having a good look at the face of every foremast man as they filed past me to go to the after braces. At breakfast time, eating nothing myself, I presided with such frigid dignity that the two mates were only too glad to escape from the cabin as soon as decency permitted; and all the time the dual working of my mind distracted me almost to the point of insanity. I was constantly watching myself, my secret self, as dependent on my actions as my own personality, sleeping in that bed, behind that door which faced me as I sat at the head of the table. It was very much like being mad, only it was worse because one was aware of it.

I had to shake him for a solid minute, but when at last he opened his eyes it was in the full possession of his senses, with an inquiring look.

"All's well so far," I whispered. "Now you must vanish into the bath-room."

He did so, as noiseless as a ghost, and I then rang for the steward, and facing him boldly, directed him to tidy up my stateroom while I was having my bath—"and be quick about it." As my tone admitted of no excuses, he said, "Yes, sir," and ran off to fetch his dustpan and brushes. I took a bath and did most of my dressing, splashing, and whistling softly for the steward's edification, while the secret sharer of my life stood drawn up bolt upright in that little space, his face looking very sunken in daylight, his eyelids lowered under the stern, dark line of his eyebrows drawn together by a slight frown.

When I left him there to go back to my room the steward was finished dusting. I sent for the mate and engaged him in some insignificant conversation. It was, as it were, trifling with the terrific character of whiskers; but my object was to give him an opportunity for a good look at my cabin. And then I could at last shut, with a clear conscience, the door of my stateroom and get my double back into the recessed part. There was nothing else for it. He had to sit still on a small folding stool, half smothered by the heavy coats hanging there. We listened to the steward going into the bathroom out of the saloon, filling the water bottles there, scrubbing the bath, setting things to rights, whisk, bang, clatter—out again into the saloon—turn the key—click. Such was my scheme for keeping my second self invisible. Nothing better could be contrived under the circumstances. And there we sat; I at my writing desk ready to appear busy with some papers, he behind me, out of sight of the door. It would not have been prudent to talk in daytime; and I could not have stood the excitement of that queer sense of whispering to myself. Now and then, glancing over my shoulder, I saw him far back there, sitting rigidly on the low stool, his bare feet close together, his arms folded, his head hanging on his breast—and perfectly still. Anybody would have taken him for me.

I was fascinated by it myself. Every moment I had to glance over my shoulder. I was looking at him when a voice outside the door said:

"Beg pardon, sir."

"Well!" . . . I kept my eyes on him, and so, when the voice outside the door announced, "There's a ship's boat coming our way, sir," I saw him give a start—the first movement he had made for hours. But he did not raise his bowed head.

"All right. Get the ladder over."

I hesitated. Should I whisper something to him? But what? His immobility seemed to have been never disturbed. What could I tell him he did not know already? . . . Finally I went on deck.

II

The skipper of the *Sephora* had a thin red whisker all round his face, and the sort of complexion that goes with hair of that color; also the particular, rather smeary shade of blue in the eyes. He was not exactly a showy figure; his shoulders were high, his stature but middling—one leg slightly more bandy than the other. He shook hands, looking vaguely around. A spiritless tenacity was his main characteristic, I judged. I behaved with a politeness which seemed to disconcert him. Perhaps he was shy. He mumbled to me as if he were ashamed of what he was saying; gave his name (it was something like Archbold—but at this distance of years I hardly am sure), his ship's name, and a few other particulars of that sort, in the manner of a criminal making a reluctant and doleful confession. He had had terrible weather on the passage out—terrible—terrible—wife aboard, too.

By this time we were seated in the cabin and the steward brought in a tray with a bottle and glasses. "Thanks! No." Never took liquor. Would have some water, though. He drank two tumblerfuls. Terrible thirsty work. Ever since daylight had been exploring the islands round his ship.

"What was that for—fun?" I asked, with an appearance of polite interest.

"No!" He sighed. "Painful duty."

As he persisted in his mumbling and I wanted my double to hear every word, I hit upon the notion of informing him that I regretted to say I was hard of hearing.

"Such a young man, too!" he nodded, keeping his smeary blue, unintelligent eyes fastened upon me. What was the cause of it—some disease? he inquired, without the least sympathy and as if he thought that, if so, I'd got no more than I deserved.

"Yes; disease," I admitted in a cheerful tone which seemed to shock him. But my point was gained, because he had to raise his voice to give me his tale. It is not worth while to record that version. It was just over two months since all this had happened, and he had thought so much about it that he seemed completely muddled as to its bearings, but still immensely impressed.

"What would you think of such a thing happening on board your own ship? I've had the *Sephora* for these fifteen years. I am a well-known shipmaster."

He was densely distressed—and perhaps I should have sympathized with him if I had been able to detach my mental vision from the unsuspected sharer of my cabin as though he were my second self. There he was on the other side of the bulkhead, four or five feet from us, no more, as we sat in the saloon. I looked politely at Captain Archbold (if that was his name), but it was the other I saw, in a gray sleeping suit, seated on a low stool, his bare feet close together, his arms folded, and every word said between us falling into the ears of his dark head bowed on his chest.

"I have been at sea now, man and boy, for seven-and-thirty years, and I've never heard of such a thing happening in an English ship. And that it should be my ship. Wife on board, too."

I was hardly listening to him.

"Don't you think," I said, "that the heavy sea which, you told me, came aboard just then might have killed the man? I have seen the sheer weight of a sea kill a man very neatly, by simply breaking his neck."

"Good God!" he uttered, impressively, fixing his smeary blue eyes on me. "The sea! No man killed by the sea ever looked like that." He seemed positively scandalized at my suggestion. And as I gazed at him, certainly not prepared for anything original on his part, he advanced his head close to mine and thrust his tongue out at me so suddenly that I couldn't help starting back.

After scoring over my calmness in this graphic way he nodded wisely. If I had seen the sight, he assured me, I would never forget it as long as I lived. The weather was too bad to give the corpse a proper sea burial. So next day at dawn they took it up on the poop, covering its face with a bit of bunting; he read a short prayer, and then, just as it was, in its oilskins and long boots, they launched it amongst those mountainous seas that seemed ready every moment to swallow up the ship herself and the terrified lives on board of her.

"That reefed foresail saved you," I threw in.

"Under God—it did." he exclaimed fervently. "It was by a special mercy, I firmly believe, that it stood some of those hurricane squalls."

"It was the setting of that sail which—" I began.

"God's own hand in it," he interrupted me. "Nothing less could have done it. I don't mind telling you that I hardly dared give the order. It seemed impossible that we could touch anything without losing it, and then our last hope would have been gone."

The terror of that gale was on him yet. I let him go on for a bit, then said, casually—as if returning to a minor subject:

"You were very anxious to give up your mate to the shore people, I believe?"

He was. To the law. His obscure tenacity on that point had in it something incomprehensible and a little awful; something, as it were, mystical, quite apart from his anxiety that he should not be suspected of "countenancing any doings of that sort." Seven-and-thirty virtuous years at sea, of which over twenty of immaculate command, and the last fifteen in the *Sephora*, seemed to have laid him under some pitiless obligation.

"And you know," he went on, groping shamefacedly amongst his feelings, "I did not engage that young fellow. His people had some interest with my owners. I was in a way forced to take him on. He looked very smart, very gentlemanly, and all that. But do you know—I never liked him, somehow. I am a plain man. You see, he wasn't exactly the sort for the chief mate of a ship like the *Sephora*."

I had become so connected in thoughts and impressions with the secret sharer of my cabin that I felt as if I, personally, were being given to understand that I, too, was not the sort that would have done for the chief mate of a ship like the *Sephora*. I had no doubt of it in my mind.

"Not at all the style of man. You understand," he insisted, superfluously, looking hard at me.

I smiled urbanely. He seemed at a loss for a while.

"I suppose I must report a suicide."

"Beg pardon?"

"Sui-cide! That's what I'll have to write to my owners directly I get in."

"Unless you manage to recover him before tomorrow," I assented, dispassionately. . . . "I mean, alive."

He mumbled something which I really did not catch, and I turned my ear to him in a puzzled manner. He fairly bawled:

"The land—I say, the mainland is at least seven miles off my anchorage."

"About that."

My lack of excitement, of curiosity, of surprise, of any sort of pronounced interest, began to arouse his distrust. But except for the felicitous pretense of deafness I had not tried to pretend anything. I had felt utterly incapable of playing the part of ignorance properly, and therefore was afraid to try. It is also certain that he had brought some ready-made suspicions with him, and that he viewed my politeness as a strange and unnatural phenomenon. And yet how else could I have received him? Not heartily! That was impossible for psychological reasons, which I need not state here. My only object was to keep off his inquiries. Surlily? Yes, but surliness might have provoked a point-blank question. From its novelty to him and from its nature, punctilious courtesy was the manner best calculated to restrain the man. But there was the danger of his breaking through my defense bluntly. I could not, I think, have met him by a direct lie, also for psychological (not moral) reasons. If he had only known how afraid I was of his putting my feeling of identity with the other to the test! But, strangely enough—(I thought of it only afterward)—I believe that he was not a little disconcerted by the reverse side of that weird situation, by something in me that reminded him of the man he was seeking—suggested a mysterious similitude to the young fellow he had distrusted and disliked from the first.

However that might have been, the silence was not very prolonged. He took another oblique step.

"I reckon I had no more than a two-mile pull to your ship. Not a bit more."

"And quite enough, too, in this awful heat," I said.

Another pause full of mistrust followed. Necessity, they say, is mother of invention, but fear, too, is not barren of ingenious suggestions. And I was afraid he would ask me point-blank for news of my other self.

"Nice little saloon, isn't it?" I remarked, as if noticing for the first time the way his eyes roamed from one closed door to the other. "And very well fitted out, too. Here, for instance," I continued reaching over the back of my seat negligently and flinging the door open, "is my bathroom."

He made an eager movement, but hardly gave it a glance. I got up, shut the door of the bathroom, and invited him to have a look round, as if

I were very proud of my accommodation. He had to rise and be shown round, but he went through the business without any raptures whatever.

"And now we'll have a look at my stateroom," I declared, in a voice as loud as I dared to make it, crossing the cabin to the starboard side with purposely heavy steps.

He followed me in and gazed around. My intelligent double had vanished. I played my part.

"Very convenient—isn't it?"

"Very nice. Very comf . . ." He didn't finish, and went out brusquely as if to escape from some unrighteous wiles of mine. But it was not to be. I had been too frightened not to feel vengeful; I felt I had him on the run, and I meant to keep him on the run. My polite insistence must have had something menacing in it, because he gave in suddenly. And I did not let him off a single item; mate's room, pantry, storerooms, the very sail locker which was also under the poop—he had to look into them all. When at last I showed him out on the quarter-deck he drew a long, spiritless sigh, and mumbled dismally that he must really be going back to his ship now. I desired my mate, who had joined us, to see to the captain's boat.

The man of whiskers gave a blast on the whistle which he used to wear hanging round his neck, and yelled, "*Sephora* away!" My double down there in my cabin must have heard, and certainly could not feel more relieved than I. Four fellows came running out from somewhere forward and went over the side, while my own men, appearing on deck too, lined the rail. I escorted my visitor to the gangway ceremoniously, and nearly overdid it. He was a tenacious beast. On the very ladder he lingered, and in that unique, guiltily conscientious manner of sticking to the point:

"I say . . . you . . . you don't think that—"

I covered his voice loudly:

"Certainly not. . . . I am delighted. Good-by."

I had an idea of what he meant to say, and just saved myself by the privilege of defective hearing. He was too shaken generally to insist, but my mate, close witness of that parting, looked mystified and his face took on a thoughtful cast. As I did not want to appear as if I wished to avoid all communication with my officers, he had the opportunity to address me.

"Seems a very nice man. His boat's crew told our chaps a very extraordinary story, if what I am told by the steward is true. I suppose you had it from the captain, sir?"

"Yes. I had a story from the captain."

"A very horrible affair—isn't it, sir?"

"It is."

"Beats all these tales we hear about murders in Yankee ships."

"I don't think it beats them. I don't think it resembles them in the least."

"Bless my soul—you don't say so! But of course I've no acquaintance whatever with American ships, not I, so I couldn't go against your knowledge.

It's horrible enough for me. . . . But the queerest part is that these fellows seemed to have some idea the man was hidden aboard here. They had really. Did you ever hear of such a thing?"

"Preposterous—isn't it?"

We were walking to and fro athwart the quarter-deck. No one of the crew forward could be seen (the day was Sunday), and the mate pursued:

"There was some little dispute about it. Our chaps took offense. 'As if we would harbor a thing like that,' they said. 'Wouldn't you like to look for him in our coal hole?' Quite a tiff. But they made it up in the end. I suppose he did drown himself. Don't you, sir?"

"I don't suppose anything."

"You have no doubt in the matter, sir?"

"None whatever."

I left him suddenly. I felt I was producing a bad impression, but with my double down there it was most trying to be on deck. And it was almost as trying to be below. Altogether a nerve-trying situation. But on the whole I felt less torn in two when I was with him. There was no one in the whole ship whom I dared take into my confidence. Since the hands had got to know his story, it would have been impossible to pass him off for anyone else, and an accidental discovery was to be dreaded now more than ever. . . .

The steward being engaged in laying the table for dinner, we could talk only with our eyes when I first went down. Later in the afternoon we had a cautious try at whispering. The Sunday quietness of the ship was against us; the stillness of air and water around her was against us; the elements, the men were against us—everything was against us in our secret partnership; time itself—for this could not go on forever. The very trust in Providence was, I suppose, denied to his guilt. Shall I confess that this thought cast me down very much? And as to the chapter of accidents which counts for so much in the book of success, I could only hope that it was closed. For what favorable accident could be expected?

"Did you hear everything?" were my first words as soon as we took up our position side by side, leaning over my bed-place.

He had. And the proof of it was his earnest whisper, "The man told you he hardly dared to give the order."

I understood the reference to be to that saving foresail.

"Yes. He was afraid of it being lost in the setting."

"I assure you he never gave the order. He may think he did, but he never gave it. He stood there with me on the break of the poop after the maintopsail blew away, and whimpered about our last hope—positively whimpered about it and nothing else—and the night coming on! To hear one's skipper go on like that in such weather was enough to drive any fellow out of his mind. It worked me up into a sort of desperation. I just took it into my hands and went away from him, boiling, and—But what's the use telling you? *You* know! . . . Do you think that if I had not been pretty fierce with them I should have got the men to do anything? Not it! The bosun perhaps? Perhaps! It wasn't a heavy sea—it was a sea gone mad! I suppose the end of the world will be something like that; and a man may have the heart to see it coming once and be done with it—but to have to face it day after day—I don't blame anybody. I was precious little better than the rest. Only—I was an officer of that old coal-wagon, anyhow—"

"I quite understand," I conveyed that sincere assurance into his ear. He was out of breath with whispering; I could hear him pant slightly. It was all very simple. The same strung-up force which had given twenty-four men a chance, at least, for their lives, had, in a sort of recoil, crushed an unworthy mutinous existence.

But I had no leisure to weigh the merits of the matter—footsteps in the saloon, a heavy knock. "There's enough wind to get under way with, sir." Here was the call of a new claim upon my thoughts and even upon my feelings.

"Turn the hands up," I cried through the door. "I'll be on deck directly."

I was going out to make the acquaintance of my ship. Before I left the cabin our eyes met—the eyes of the only two strangers on board. I pointed to the recessed part where the little campstool awaited him and laid my finger on my lips. He made a gesture—somewhat vague—a little mysterious, accompanied by a faint smile, as if of regret.

This is not the place to enlarge upon the sensations of a man who feels for the first time a ship move under his feet to his own independent word. In my case they were not unalloyed. I was not wholly alone with my command; for there was that stranger in my cabin. Or rather, I was not completely and wholly with her. Part of me was absent. That mental feeling of being in two places at once affected me physically as if the mood of secrecy had penetrated my very soul. Before an hour had elapsed since the ship had begun to move, having occasion to ask the mate (he stood by my side) to take a compass bearing of the Pagoda, I caught myself reaching up to his ear in whispers. I say I caught myself, but enough had escaped to startle the man. I can't describe it otherwise than by saying that he shied. A grave, preoccupied manner, as though he were in possession of some perplexing intelligence, did not leave him henceforth. A little later I moved away from the rail to look at the compass with such a stealthy gait that the helmsman noticed it—and I could not help noticing the unusual roundness of his eyes. These are trifling instances, though it's to no commander's advantage to be suspected of ludicrous eccentricities. But I was also more seriously affected. There are to a seaman certain words, gestures, that should in given conditions come as naturally, as instinctively as the winking of a menaced eye. A certain order should spring on to his lips without thinking; a certain sign should get itself made, so to speak, without reflection. But all unconscious alertness had abandoned me. I had to make an effort of will to recall myself back (from the cabin) to the conditions of the moment. I felt that I was appearing an irresolute commander to those people who were watching me more or less critically.

And, besides, there were the scares. On the second day out, for instance, coming off the deck in the afternoon (I had straw slippers on my bare feet) I stopped at the open pantry door and spoke to the steward. He was doing something there with his back to me. At the sound of my voice he nearly jumped out of his skin, as the saying is, and incidentally broke a cup.

"What on earth's the matter with you?" I asked, astonished.

He was extremely confused. "Beg your pardon, sir. I made sure you were in your cabin."

"You see I wasn't."

"No, sir. I could have sworn I had heard you moving in there not a moment ago. It's most extraordinary . . . very sorry, sir."

I passed on with an inward shudder. I was so identified with my secret double that I did not even mention the fact in those scanty, fearful whispers we exchanged. I suppose he had made some slight noise of some kind or other. It would have been miraculous if he hadn't at one time or another. And yet, haggard as he appeared, he looked always perfectly self-controlled, more than calm—almost invulnerable. On my suggestion he remained almost entirely in the bathroom, which, upon the whole, was the safest place. There could be really no shadow of an excuse for anyone ever wanting to go in there, once the steward had done with it. It was a very tiny place. Sometimes he reclined on the floor, his legs bent, his head sustained on one elbow. At others I would find him on the campstool, sitting in his gray sleeping suit and with his cropped dark hair like a patient, unmoved convict. At night I would smuggle him into my bed-place, and we would whisper together, with the regular footfalls of the officer of the watch passing and repassing over our heads. It was an infinitely miserable time. It was lucky that some tins of fine preserves were stowed in a locker in my stateroom; hard bread I could always get hold of; and so he lived on stewed chicken, paté de foie gras, asparagus, cooked oysters, sardines—on all sorts of abominable sham delicacies out of tins. My early morning coffee he always drank; and it was all I dared do for him in that respect.

Every day there was the horrible maneuvering to go through so that my room and then the bathroom should be done in the usual way. I came to hate the sight of the steward, to abhor the voice of that harmless man. I felt that it was he who would bring on the disaster of discovery. It hung like a sword over our heads.

The fourth day out, I think (we were working down the east side of the Gulf of Siam, tack for tack, in light winds and smooth water)—the fourth day, I say, of this miserable juggling with the unavoidable, as we sat at our evening meal, that man, whose slightest movement I dreaded, after putting down the dishes ran up on deck busily. This could not be dangerous. Presently he came down again; and then it appeared that he had remembered a coat of mine which I had thrown over a rail to dry after having been wetted in a shower which had passed over the ship in the afternoon. Sitting stolidly at the head of the table I became terrified at the sight of the garment on his arm. Of course he made for my door. There was no time to lose.

"Steward," I thundered. My nerves were so shaken that I could not govern my voice and conceal my agitation. This was the sort of thing that made my terrifically whiskered mate tap his forehead with his forefinger. I had detected him using that gesture while talking on deck with a confidential air to the carpenter. It was too far to hear a word, but I had no doubt that his pantomime could only refer to the strange new captain.

"Yes, sir," the pale-faced steward turned resignedly to me. It was this maddening course of being shouted at, checked without rhyme or reason, arbitrarily chased out of my cabin, suddenly called into it, sent flying out of his pantry on incomprehensible errands, that accounted for the growing wretchedness of his expression.

"Where are you going with that coat?"

"To your room, sir."

"Is there another shower coming?"

"I'm sure I don't know, sir. Shall I go up again and see, sir?"

"No! never mind."

My object was attained, as of course my other self in there would have heard everything that passed. During this interlude my two officers never raised their eyes off their respective plates; but the lip of that confounded cub, the second mate, quivered visibly.

I expected the steward to hook my coat on and come out at once. He was very slow about it; but I dominated my nervousness sufficiently not to shout after him. Suddenly I became aware (it could be heard plainly enough) that the fellow for some reason or other was opening the door of the bathroom. It was the end. The place was literally not big enough to swing a cat in. My voice died in my throat and I went stony all over. I expected to hear a yell of surprise and terror, and made a movement, but had not the strength to get on my legs. Everything remained still. Had my second self taken the poor wretch by the throat? I don't know what I would have done next moment if I had not seen the steward come out of my room, close the door, and then stand quietly by the sideboard.

Saved, I thought. But, no! Lost! Gone! He was gone!

I laid my knife and fork down and leaned back in my chair. My head swam. After a while, when sufficiently recovered to speak in a steady voice, I instructed my mate to put the ship round at eight o'clock himself.

"I won't come on deck," I went on. "I think I'll turn in, and unless the wind shifts I don't want to be disturbed before midnight. I feel a bit seedy."

"You did look middling bad a little while ago," the chief mate remarked without showing any great concern.

They both went out, and I stared at the steward clearing the table. There was nothing to be read on the wretched man's face. But why did he avoid my eyes I asked myself. Then I thought I should like to hear the sound of his voice.

"Steward!"

"Sir!" Startled as usual.

"Where did you hang up that coat?"

"In the bathroom, sir." The usual anxious tone. "It's not quite dry yet, sir."

For some time longer I sat in the cuddy. Had my double vanished as he had come? But of his coming there was an explanation, whereas his disappearance would be inexplicable. . . . I went slowly into my dark room, shut the door, lighted the lamp, and for a time dared not turn round. When at last I did I saw him standing bolt upright in the narrow recessed part. It would not be true to say I had a shock, but an irresistible doubt of his bodily existence flitted through my mind. Can it be, I asked myself, that he is not visible to other eyes than mine? It was like being haunted. Motionless, with a grave face, he raised his hands slightly at me in a gesture which meant clearly, "Heavens! what a narrow escape!" Narrow indeed. I think I had come creeping quietly as near insanity as any man who has not actually gone over the border. That gesture restrained me, so to speak.

The mate with the terrific whiskers was now putting the ship on the other tack. In the moment of profound silence which follows upon the hands going to their stations I heard on the poop his raised voice: "Hard alee!" and the distant shout of the order repeated on the maindeck. The sails, in that light breeze, made but a faint fluttering noise. It ceased. The ship was coming round slowly; I held my breath in the renewed stillness of expectation; one wouldn't have thought that there was a single living soul on her decks. A sudden brisk shout, "Mainsail haul!" broke the spell, and in the noisy cries and rush overhead of the men running away with the main brace we two, down in my cabin, came together in our usual position by the bed-place.

He did not wait for my question. "I heard him fumbling here and just managed to squat myself down in the bath," he whispered to me. "The fellow only opened the door and put his arm in to hang the coat up. All the same—"

"I never thought of that," I whispered back, even more appalled than before at the closeness of the shave, and marveling at that something un-yielding in his character which was carrying him through so finely. There was no agitation in his whisper. Whoever was being driven distracted, it was not he. He was sane. And the proof of his sanity was continued when he took up the whispering again.

"It would never do for me to come to life again."

It was something that a ghost might have said. But what he was allud-ing to was his old captain's reluctant admission of the theory of suicide. It would obviously serve his turn—if I had understood at all the view which seemed to govern the unalterable purpose of his action.

"You must maroon me as soon as ever you can get amongst these islands off the Cambodje shore," he went on.

"Maroon you! We are not living in a boy's adventure tale," I protested. His scornful whispering took me up.

"We aren't indeed! There's nothing of a boy's tale in this. But there's nothing else for it. I want no more. You don't suppose I am afraid of what can be done to me? Prison or gallows or whatever they may please. But you don't see me coming back to explain such things to an old fellow in a wig and twelve respectable tradesmen, do you? What can they know whether I am guilty or not—or of *what* I am guilty, either? That's my affair. What does the Bible say? 'Driven off the face of the earth.' Very well. I am off the face of the earth now. As I came at night so I shall go."

"Impossible!" I murmured. "You can't."

"Can't? . . . Not naked like a soul on the Day of Judgment. I shall freeze on to this sleeping suit. The Last Day is not yet—and . . . you have understood thoroughly. Didn't you?"

I felt suddenly ashamed of myself. I may say truly that I understood—and my hesitation in letting that man swim away from my ship's side had been mere sham sentiment, a sort of cowardice.

"It can't be done now till next night," I breathed out. "The ship is on the offshore tack and the wind may fail us."

"As long as I know that you understand," he whispered. "But of course you do. It's a great satisfaction to have got somebody to understand. You seem to have been there on purpose." And in the same whisper, as if we two whenever we talked had to say things to each other which were not fit for the world to hear, he added, "It's very wonderful."

We remained side by side talking in our secret way—but sometimes silent or just exchanging a whispered word or two at long intervals. And as usual he stared through the port. A breath of wind came now and again into our faces. The ship might have been moored in dock, so gently and on an even keel she slipped through the water, that did not murmur even at our passage, shadowy and silent like a phantom sea.

At midnight I went on deck, and to my mate's great surprise put the ship round on the other tack. His terrible whiskers flitted round me in silent criticism. I certainly should not have done it if it had been only a question of getting out of that sleepy gulf as quickly as possible. I believe he told the second mate, who relieved him, that it was a great want of judgment. The other only yawned. That intolerable cub shuffled about so sleepily and lolled against the rails in such a slack, improper fashion that I came down on him sharply.

"Aren't you properly awake yet?"

"Yes, sir! I am awake."

"Well, then, be good enough to hold yourself as if you were. And keep a lookout. If there's any current we'll be closing with some islands before daylight.

The east side of the gulf is fringed with islands, some solitary, others in groups. On the blue background of the high coast they seem to float on silvery patches of calm water, arid and gray, or dark green and rounded like clumps of evergreen bushes, with the larger ones, a mile or two long, showing the outlines of ridges, ribs of gray rock under the dark mantle of matted leafage. Unknown to trade, to travel, almost to geography, the manner of life they harbor is an unsolved secret. There must be villages—settlements of fishermen at least—on the largest of them, and some communication with the world is probably kept up by native craft. But all forenoon, as we headed for them, fanned along by the faintest of breezes, I saw no sign of man or canoe in the field of the telescope I kept on pointing at the scattered group.

At noon I gave no orders for a change of course, and the mate's whiskers became much concerned and seemed to be offering themselves unduly to my notice. At last I said:

"I am going to stand right in. Quite in—as far as I can take her."

The stare of extreme surprise imparted an air of ferocity also to his eyes, and he looked truly terrific for a moment.

"We're not doing well in the middle of the gulf," I continued, casually. "I am going to look for the land breezes tonight."

"Bless my soul! Do you mean, sir, in the dark amongst the lot of all them islands and reefs and shoals?"

"Well—if there are any regular land breezes at all on this coast one must get close inshore to find them, mustn't one?"

"Bless my soul!" he exclaimed again under his breath. All that afternoon he wore a dreamy, contemplative appearance which in him was a mark of perplexity. After dinner I went into my stateroom as if I meant to take some rest. There we two bent our dark heads over a half-unrolled chart lying on my bed.

"There," I said. "It's got to be Koh-ring. I've been looking at it ever since sunrise. It has got two hills and a low point. It must be inhabited. And on the coast opposite there is what looks like the mouth of a biggish river—with some town, no doubt, not far up. It's the best chance for you that I can see."

"Anything. Koh-ring let it be."

He looked thoughtfully at the chart as if surveying chances and distances from a lofty height—and following with his eyes his own figure wandering on the blank land of Cochin China, and then passing off that piece of paper clean out of sight into uncharted regions. And it was as if the ship had two captains to plan her course for her. I had been so worried and restless running up and down that I had not had the patience to dress that day. I had remained in my sleeping suit, with straw slippers and a soft floppy hat. The closeness of the heat in the gulf had been most oppressive, and the crew were used to see me wandering in that airy attire.

"She will clear the south point as she heads now," I whispered into his ear. "Goodness only knows when, though, but certainly after dark. I'll edge her in to half a mile, as far as I may be able to judge in the dark—"

"Be careful," he murmured, warningly—and I realized suddenly that all my future, the only future for which I was fit, would perhaps go irretrievably to pieces in any mishap to my first command.

I could not stop a moment longer in the room. I motioned him to get out of sight and made my way on the poop. That unplayful cub had the watch. I walked up and down for a while thinking things out, then beckoned him over.

"Send a couple of hands to open the two quarter-deck ports," I said, mildly.

He actually had the impudence, or else so forgot himself in his wonder at such an incomprehensible order, as to repeat:

"Open the quarter-deck ports! What for, sir?"

"The only reason you need concern yourself about is because I tell you to do so. Have them open wide and fastened properly."

He reddened and went off, but I believe made some jeering remark to the carpenter as to the sensible practice of ventilating a ship's quarter-deck. I know he popped into the mate's cabin to impart the fact to him because the whiskers came on deck, as it were by chance, and stole glances at me from below—for signs of lunacy or drunkenness, I suppose.

A little before supper, feeling more restless than ever, I rejoined, for a moment, my second self. And to find him sitting so quietly was surprising, like something against nature, inhuman.

I developed my plan in a hurried whisper.

"I shall stand in as close as I dare and then put her round. I shall presently find means to smuggle you out of here into the sail locker, which communicates with the lobby. But there is an opening, a sort of square for hauling the sails out, which gives straight on the quarter-deck and which is never closed in fine weather, so as to give air to the sails. When the ship's way is deadened in stays and all the hands are aft at the main braces you shall have a clear road to slip out and get overboard through the open quarter-deck port. I've had them both fastened up. Use a rope's end to lower yourself into the water so as to avoid a splash—you know. It could be heard and cause some beastly complication."

He kept silent for a while, then whispered, "I understand."

"I won't be there to see you go," I began with an effort. "The rest . . . I only hope I have understood, too."

"You have. From first to last," and for the first time there seemed to be a faltering, something strained in his whisper. He caught hold of my arm, but the ringing of the supper bell made me start. He didn't, though; he only released his grip.

After supper I didn't come below again till well past eight o'clock. The faint, steady breeze was loaded with dew; and the wet, darkened sails held all there was of propelling power in it. The night, clear and starry, sparkled darkly, and the opaque, lightless patches shifting slowly against the low stars were the drifting islets. On the port bow there was a big one more distant and shadowily imposing by the great space of sky it eclipsed.

On opening the door I had a back view of my very own self looking at a chart. He had come out of the recess and was standing near the table.

"Quite dark enough," I whispered.

He stepped back and leaned against my bed with a level, quiet glance. I sat on the couch. We had nothing to say to each other. Over our heads the officer of the watch moved here and there. Then I heard him move quickly. I knew what that meant. He was making for the companion; and presently his voice was outside my door.

"We are drawing in pretty fast, sir. Land looks rather close."

"Very well," I answered. "I am coming on deck directly."

I waited till he was gone out of the cuddy, then rose. My double moved too. The time had come to exchange our last whispers, for neither of us was ever to hear each other's natural voice.

"Look here!" I opened a drawer and took out three sovereigns. "Take this, anyhow. I've got six and I'd give you the lot, only I must keep a little money to buy some fruit and vegetables for the crew from native boats as we go through Sunda Straits."

He shook his head.

"Take it," I urged him, whispering desperately. "No one can tell what—"

He smiled and slapped meaningly the only pocket of the sleeping jacket. It was not safe, certainly. But I produced a large old silk handkerchief of mine, and tying the three pieces of gold in a corner, pressed it on him. He was touched, I suppose, because he took it at last and tied it quickly round his waist under the jacket, on his bare skin.

Our eyes met; several seconds elapsed, till, our glances still mingled, I extended my hand and turned the lamp out. Then I passed through the cuddy, leaving the door of my room wide open. . . . "Steward!"

He was still lingering in the pantry in the greatness of his zeal, giving a rub up to a plated cruet stand the last thing before going to bed. Being careful not to wake up the mate, whose room was opposite, I spoke in an undertone.

He looked round anxiously. "Sir!"

"Can you get me a little hot water from the galley?"

"I am afraid, sir, the galley fire's been out for some time now."

"Go and see."

He fled up the stairs.

"Now," I whispered, loudly, into the saloon—too loudly, perhaps, but I was afraid I couldn't make a sound. He was by my side in an instant—the double captain slipped past the stairs—through the tiny dark passage . . . a sliding door. We were in the sail locker, scrambling on our knees over the sails. A sudden thought struck me. I saw myself wandering barefooted, bareheaded, the sun beating on my dark poll. I snatched off my floppy hat and tried hurriedly in the dark to ram it on my other self. He dodged and fended off silently. I wonder what he thought had come to me before he understood and suddenly desisted. Our hands met gropingly, lingered united in a steady, motionless clasp for a second. . . . No word was breathed by either of us when they separated.

I was standing quietly by the pantry door when the steward returned.

"Sorry, sir. Kettle barely warm. Shall I light the spirit lamp?"

"Never mind."

I came out on deck slowly. It was now a matter of conscience to shave the land as close as possible—for now he must go overboard whenever the ship was put in stays. Must! There could be no going back for him. After a moment I walked over to leeward and my heart flew into my mouth at the nearness of the land on the bow. Under any other circumstances I would not have held on a minute longer. The second mate had followed me anxiously.

I looked on till I felt I could command my voice.

"She will weather," I said then in a quiet tone.

"Are you going to try that, sir?" he stammered out incredulously.

I took no notice of him and raised my tone just enough to be heard by the helmsman.

"Keep her good full."

"Good full, sir."

The wind fanned my cheek, the sails slept, the world was silent. The strain of watching the dark loom of the land grow bigger and denser was too much for me. I had shut my eyes—because the ship must go closer. She must! The stillness was intolerable. Were we standing still?

When I opened my eyes the second view started my heart with a thump. The black southern hill of Koh-ring seemed to hang right over the ship like a towering fragment of the everlasting night. On that enormous mass of blackness there was not a gleam to be seen, not a sound to be heard. It was gliding irresistibly toward us and yet seemed already within reach of the hand. I saw the vague figures of the watch grouped in the waist, gazing in awed silence.

"Are you going on, sir?" inquired an unsteady voice at my elbow.

I ignored it. I had to go on.

"Keep her full. Don't check her way. That won't do now," I said warningly.

"I can't see the sails very well," the helmsman answered me, in strange, quavering tones.

Was she close enough? Already she was, I won't say in the shadow of the land, but in the very blackness of it, already swallowed up as it were, gone too close to be recalled, gone from me altogether.

"Give the mate a call," I said to the young man who stood at my elbow still as death. "And turn all hands up."

My tone had a borrowed loudness reverberated from the height of the land. Several voices cried out together: "We are all on deck, sir."

Then stillness again, with the great shadow gliding closer, towering higher, without a light, without a sound. Such a hush had fallen on the ship that she might have been a bark of the dead floating in slowly under the very gate of Erebus.

"My God! Where are we?"

It was the mate moaning at my elbow. He was thunderstruck, and as it were deprived of the moral support of his whiskers. He clapped his hands and absolutely cried out, "Lost!"

"Be quiet," I said sternly.

He lowered his tone, but I saw the shadowy gesture of his despair. "What are we doing here?"

"Looking for the land wind."

He made as if to tear his hair, and addressed me recklessly.

"She will never get out. You have done it, sir. I knew it'd end in something like this. She will never weather, and you are too close now to stay. She'll drift ashore before she's round. O my God!"

I caught his arm as he was raising it to batter his poor devoted head, and shook it violently.

"She's ashore already," he wailed, trying to tear himself away.

"Is she? . . . Keep good full there!"

"Good full, sir," cried the helmsman in a frightened, thin, childlike voice.

I hadn't let go the mate's arm and went on shaking it. "Ready about, do you hear? You go forward"—shake—"and stop there"—shake—"and hold your noise"—shake—"and see these head sheets properly over-hauled"—shake, shake—shake.

And all the time I dared not look toward the land lest my heart should fail me. I released my grip at last and he ran forward as if fleeing for dear life.

I wondered what my double there in the sail locker thought of this commotion. He was able to hear everything—and perhaps he was able to understand why, on my conscience, it had to be thus close—no less. My first order "Hard alee!" re-echoed ominously under the towering shadow of Koh-ring as if I had shouted in a mountain gorge. And then I watched the land intently. In that smooth water and light wind it was impossible to feel the ship coming-to. No! I could not feel her. And my second self was making now ready to slip out and lower himself overboard. Perhaps he was gone already . . . ?

The great black mass brooding over our very mastheads began to pivot away from the ship's side silently. And now I forgot the secret stranger ready to depart, and remembered only that I was a total stranger to the ship. I did not know her. Would she do it? How was she to be handled?

I swung the mainyard and waited helplessly. She was perhaps stopped, and her very fate hung in the balance, with the black mass of Koh-ring like the gate of the everlasting night towering over her taffrail. What would she do now? Had she way on her yet? I stepped to the side swiftly, and on the shadowy water I could see nothing except a faint phosphorescent flash revealing the glassy smoothness of the sleeping surface. It was impossible to tell—and I had not learned yet the feel of my ship. Was she moving? What I needed was something easily seen, a piece of paper, which I could throw overboard and watch. I had nothing on me. To run down for it I didn't dare. There was no time. All at once my strained, yearning stare distinguished a white object floating within a yard of the ship's side. White on the blackwater. A phosphorescent flash passed under it. What was that thing? . . . I recognized my own floppy hat. It must have fallen off his head . . . and he didn't bother. Now I had what I wanted—the saving mark for my eyes. But I hardly thought of my other self, now gone from the ship, to be hidden forever from all friendly faces, to be a fugitive and a vagabond on the earth, with no brand of the curse on his sane forehead to stay a slaying hand . . . too proud to explain.

And I watched the hat—the expression of my sudden pity for his mere flesh. It had been meant to save his homeless head from the dangers of the sun. And now—behold—it was saving the ship, by serving me for a mark to help out the ignorance of my strangeness. Ha! It was drifting forward, warning me just in time that the ship had gathered sternway.

"Shift the helm," I said in a low voice to the seaman standing still like a statue.

The man's eyes glistened wildly in the binnacle light as he jumped round to the other side and spun round the wheel.

I walked to the break of the poop. On the overshadowed deck all hands stood by the forebraces waiting for my order. The stars ahead seemed to be gliding from right to left. And all was so still in the world that I heard the quiet remark "She's round," passed in a tone of intense relief between two seaman.

"Let go and haul."

The foreyards ran round with a great noise, amidst cheery cries. And now the frightful whiskers made themselves heard giving various orders. Already the ship was drawing ahead. And I was alone with her. Nothing! no one in the world should stand now between us, throwing a shadow on the way of silent knowledge and mute affection, the perfect communion of a seaman with his first command.

Walking to the taffrail, I was in time to make out, on the very edge of a darkness thrown by a towering black mass like the very gateway of Erebus—yes, I was in time to catch an evanescent glimpse of my white hat left behind to mark the spot where the secret sharer of my cabin and of my thoughts, as though he were my second self, had lowered himself into the water to take his punishment: a free man, a proud swimmer striking out for a new destiny.

F. SCOTT FITZGERALD (1896–1940)

Babylon Revisited

F. Scott Fitzgerald was born in St. Paul, Minnesota, and attended Princeton University. Along with Ernest Hemingway and William Faulkner, he is one of America's three most famous novelists of the first half of the twentieth century and is particularly renowned as a spokesman for the "Jazz Age" of the 1920s. Among his most famous novels are *The Great Gatsby* (1925) and *Tender is the Night* (1934). "Babylon Revisited" appeared in *Taps at Reveille* (1935).

"And where's Mr. Campbell?" Charlie asked.

"Gone to Switzerland. Mr. Campbell's a pretty sick man, Mr. Wales."

"I'm sorry to hear that. And George Hardt?" Charlie inquired.

"Back in America, gone to work."

"And where is the Snow Bird?"

"He was in here last week. Anyway, his friend, Mr. Schaeffer, is in Paris."

Two familiar names from the long list of a year and a half ago. Charlie scribbled an address in his notebook and tore out the page.

"If you see Mr. Schaeffer, give him this," he said. "It's my brother-in-law's address. I haven't settled on a hotel yet."

He was not really disappointed to find Paris was so empty. But the stillness in the Ritz bar was strange and portentous. It was not an American bar any more—he felt polite in it, and not as if he owned it. It had gone back into France. He felt the stillness from the moment he got out of the taxi and saw the doorman, usually in a frenzy of activity at this hour, gossiping with a *chasseur* by the servants' entrance.

Passing through the corridor, he heard only a single, bored voice in the once-clamorous women's room. When he turned into the bar he traveled the twenty feet of green carpet with his eyes fixed straight ahead by old habit; and then, with his foot firmly on the rail, he turned and surveyed the room, encountering only a single pair of eyes that fluttered up from a newspaper in the corner. Charlie asked for the head barman, Paul, who in the latter days of the bull market had come to work in his own custom-built car—disembarking, however, with due nicety at the nearest corner. But Paul was at his country house today and Alix giving him information.

"No, no more," Charlie said, "I'm going slow these days."

Alix congratulated him: "You were going pretty strong a couple of years ago."

"I'll stick to it all right," Charlie assured him. "I've stuck to it for over a year and a half now."

"How do you find conditions in America?"

"I haven't been to America for months. I'm in business in Prague, representing a couple of concerns there. They don't know about me down there."

Alix smiled.

"Remember the night of George Hardt's bachelor dinner here?" said Charlie. "By the way, what's become of Claude Fessenden?"

Alix lowered his voice confidentially: "He's in Paris, but he doesn't come here any more. Paul doesn't allow it. He ran up a bill of thirty thousand francs, charging all his drinks and his lunches, and usually his dinner, for more than a year. And when Paul finally told him he had to pay, he gave him a bad check."

Alix shook his head sadly.

"I don't understand it, such a dandy fellow. Now he's all bloated up—" He made a plump apple of his hands.

Charlie watched a group of strident queens installing themselves in a corner.

"Nothing affects them," he thought. "Stocks rise and fall, people loaf or work, but they go on forever." The place oppressed him. He called for the dice and shook with Alix for the drink.

"Here for long, Mr. Wales?"

"I'm here for four or five days to see my little girl."

"Oh-h! You have a little girl?"

Outside, the fire-red, gas-blue, ghost-green signs shone smokily through the tranquil rain. It was late afternoon and the streets were in movement; the *bistros* gleamed. At the corner of the Boulevard des Capucines he took a taxi. The Place de la Concorde moved by in pink majesty; they crossed the logical Seine, and Charlie felt the sudden provincial quality of the Left Bank.

Charlie directed his taxi to the Avenue de l'Opéra, which was out of his way. But he wanted to see the blue hour spread over the magnificent façade, and imagine that the cab horns, playing endlessly the first few bars of *Le Plus que Lent*, were the trumpets of the Second Empire. They were closing the iron grill in front of Brentano's Bookstore, and people were already at dinner behind the trim little bourgeois hedge of Duval's. He had never eaten at a really cheap restaurant in Paris. Five-course dinner, four francs fifty, eighteen cents, wine included. For some odd reason he wished that he had.

As they rolled on to the Left Bank and he felt its sudden provincialism, he thought, "I spoiled this city for myself. I didn't realize it, but the days came along one after another, and then two years were gone, and everything was gone, and I was gone."

He was thirty-five, and good to look at. The Irish mobility of his face was sobered by a deep wrinkle between his eyes. As he rang his brother-in-law's bell in the Rue Palatine, the wrinkle deepened till it pulled down his brows; he felt a cramping sensation in his belly. From behind the maid who opened the door darted a lovely little girl of nine who shrieked "Daddy!" and flew up, struggling like a fish, into his arms. She pulled his head around by one ear and set her cheek against his.

"My old pie," he said.

"Oh, daddy, daddy, daddy, daddy, dads, dads, dads!"

She drew him into the salon, where the family waited, a boy and a girl his daughter's age, his sister-in-law and her husband. He greeted Marion with his voice pitched carefully to avoid either feigned enthusiasm or dislike, but her response was more frankly tepid, though she minimized her expression of unalterable distrust by directing her regard toward his child. The two men clasped hands in a friendly way and Lincoln Peters rested his for a moment on Charlie's shoulder.

The room was warm and comfortably American. The three children moved intimately about, playing through the yellow oblongs that led to other rooms; the cheer of six o'clock spoke in the eager smacks of the fire and the sounds of French activity in the kitchen. But Charlie did not relax; his heart sat up rigidly in his body and he drew confidence from his daughter, who from time to time came close to him, holding in her arms the doll he had brought.

"Really extremely well," he declared in answer to Lincoln's question. "There's a lot of business there that isn't moving at all, but we're doing even better than ever. In fact, damn well. I'm bringing my sister over from America next month to keep house for me. My income last year was bigger than it was when I had money. You see, the Czechs—"

His boasting was for a specific purpose; but after a moment, seeing a faint restiveness in Lincoln's eye, he changed the subject:

"Those are fine children of yours, well brought up, good manners."

"We think Honoria's a great little girl too."

Marion Peters came back from the kitchen. She was a tall woman with worried eyes, who had once possessed a fresh American loveliness. Charlie had never been sensitive to it and was always surprised when people spoke of how pretty she had been. From the first there had been an instinctive antipathy between them.

"Well, how do you find Honoria?" she asked.

"Wonderful. I was astonished how much she's grown in ten months. All the children are looking well."

"We haven't had a doctor for a year. How do you like being back in Paris?"

"It seems very funny to see so few Americans around."

"I'm delighted," Marion said vehemently. "Now at least you can go into a store without their assuming you're a millionaire. We've suffered like everybody, but on the whole it's a good deal pleasanter."

"But it was nice while it lasted," Charlie said. "We were a sort of royalty, almost infallible, with a sort of magic around us. In the bar this afternoon" —he stumbled, seeing his mistake— "there wasn't a man I knew."

She looked at him keenly. "I should think you'd have had enough of bars."

"I only stayed a minute. I take one drink every afternoon, and no more."

"Don't you want a cocktail before dinner?" Lincoln asked.

"I take only one drink every afternoon, and I've had that."

"I hope you keep to it," said Marion.

Her dislike was evident in the coldness with which she spoke, but Charlie only smiled; he had larger plans. Her very aggressiveness gave him an advantage, and he knew enough to wait. He wanted them to initiate the discussion of what they knew had brought him to Paris.

At dinner he couldn't decide whether Honoria was most like him or her mother. Fortunate if she didn't combine the traits of both that had brought them to disaster. A great wave of protectiveness went over him. He thought he knew what to do for her. He believed in character; he wanted to jump back a whole generation and trust in character again as the eternally valuable element. Everything else wore out.

He left soon after dinner, but not to go home. He was curious to see Paris by night with clearer and more judicious eyes than those of other days. He bought a *strapontin* for the Casino and watched Josephine Baker go through her chocolate arabesques.

After an hour he left and strolled toward Montmartre, up the Rue Pigalle into the Place Blanche. The rain had stopped and there were a few people in evening clothes disembarking from taxis in front of cabarets, and *cocottes* prowling singly or in pairs, and many Negroes. He passed a lighted door from which issued music, and stopped with the sense of familiarity; it was Bricktop's, where he had parted with so many hours and so much money. A few doors farther on he found another ancient rendezvous and incautiously put his head inside. Immediately an eager orchestra burst into sound, a pair of professional dancers leaped to their feet and a maître d'hôtel swooped toward him, crying, "Crowd just arriving, sir!" But he withdrew quickly.

"You have to be damn drunk," he thought.

Zelli's was closed, the bleak and sinister cheap hotels surrounding it were dark; up in the Rue Blanche there was more light and a local, colloquial French crowd. The Poet's Cave had disappeared, but the two great mouths of the Café of Heaven and the Café of Hell still yawned—even devoured, as he watched, the meager contents of a tourist bus—a German, a Japanese, and an American couple who glanced at him with frightened eyes.

So much for the effort and ingenuity of Montmartre. All the catering to vice and waste was on an utterly childish scale, and he suddenly realized the meaning of the word "dissipate"—to dissipate into thin air; to make nothing out of something. In the little hours of the night every move from place to place was an enormous human jump, an increase of paying for the privilege of slower and slower motion.

He remembered thousand-franc notes given to an orchestra for playing a single number, hundred-franc notes tossed to a doorman for calling a cab.

But it hadn't been given for nothing.

It had been given, even the most wildly squandered sum, as an offering to destiny that he might not remember the things most worth remembering, the things that now he would always remember—his child taken from his control, his wife escaped to a grave in Vermont.

In the glare of a *brasserie* a woman spoke to him. He bought her some eggs and coffee, and then, eluding her encouraging stare, gave her a twenty-franc note and took a taxi to his hotel.

II

He woke upon a fine fall day—football weather. The depression of yesterday was gone and he liked the people on the streets. At noon he sat opposite Honoria at Le Grand Vatel, the only restaurant he could think of not reminiscent of champagne dinners and long luncheons that began at two and ended in a blurred and vague twilight.

"Now, how about vegetables? Oughtn't you to have some vegetables?"

"Well, yes."

"Here's *épinards* and *chou-fleur* and carrots and *haricots*."

"I'd like *chou-fleur*."

"Wouldn't you like to have two vegetables?"

"I usually only have one at lunch."

The waiter was pretending to be inordinately fond of children. "*Qu'elle est mignonne la petite! Elle parle exactement comme une Française.*"

"How about dessert? Shall we wait and see?"

The waiter disappeared. Honoria looked at her father expectantly.

"What are we going to do?"

"First, we're going to that toy store in the Rue Saint-Honoré and buy you anything you like. And then we're going to the vaudeville at the Empire."

She hesitated. "I like it about the vaudeville, but not the toy store."

"Why not?"

"Well, you brought me this doll." She had it with her. "And I've got lots of things. And we're not rich any more, are we?"

"We never were. But today you are to have anything you want."

"All right," she agreed resignedly.

When there had been her mother and a French nurse he had been inclined to be strict; now he extended himself, reached out for a new tolerance; he must be both parents to her and not shut any of her out of communication.

"I want to get to know you," he said gravely. "First let me introduce myself. My name is Charles J. Wales, of Prague."

"Oh, daddy!" her voice cracked with laughter.

"And who are you, please?" he persisted, and she accepted a rôle immediately: "Honoria Wales, Rue Palatine, Paris."

"Married or single?"

"No, not married. Single."

He indicated the doll. "But I see you have a child, madame."

Unwilling to disinherit it, she took it to her heart and thought quickly: "Yes, I've been married, but I'm not married now. My husband is dead."

He went on quickly, "And the child's name?"

"Simone. That's after my best friend at school."

"I'm very pleased that you're doing so well at school.

"I'm third this month," she boasted. "Elsie"—that was her cousin—"is only about eighteenth, and Richard is about at the bottom."

"You like Richard and Elsie, don't you?"

"Oh, yes. I like Richard quite well and I like her all right."

Cautiously and casually he asked: "And Aunt Marion and Uncle Lincoln—which do you like best?"

"Oh, Uncle Lincoln, I guess."

He was increasingly aware of her presence. As they came in, a murmur of ". . . adorable" followed them, and now the people at the next table bent all their silences upon her, staring as if she were something no more conscious than a flower.

"Why don't I live with you?" she asked suddenly. "Because mamma's dead?"

"You must stay here and learn more French. It would have been hard for daddy to take care of you so well."

"I don't really need much taking care of any more. I do everything for myself."

Going out of the restaurant, a man and a woman unexpectedly hailed him.

"Well, the old Wales!"

"Hello there, Lorraine. . . . Dunc."

Sudden ghosts out of the past: Duncan Schaeffer, a friend from college. Lorraine Quarrles, a lovely, pale blonde of thirty; one of a crowd who had helped them make months into days in the lavish times of three years ago.

"My husband couldn't come this year," she said, in answer to his question. "We're poor as hell. So he gave me two hundred a month and told me I could do my worst on that. . . . This your little girl?"

"What about coming back and sitting down?" Duncan asked.

"Can't do it." He was glad for an excuse. As always, he felt Lorraine's passionate, provocative attraction, but his own rhythm was different now.

"Well, how about dinner?" she asked.

"I'm not free. Give me your address and let me call you."

"Charlie, I believe you're sober," she said judicially. "I honestly believe he's sober, Dunc. Pinch him and see if he's sober."

Charlie indicated Honoria with his head. They both laughed.

"What's your address?" said Duncan skeptically.

He hesitated, unwilling to give the name of his hotel.

"I'm not settled yet. I'd better call you. we're going to see the vaude-ville at the Empire."

"There! That's what I want to do," Lorraine said. "I want to see some clowns and acrobats and jugglers. That's just what we'll do, Dunc."

"We've got to do an errand first," said Charlie. "Perhaps we'll see you there."

"All right, you snob. . . . Good-by, beautiful little girl."

"Good-by."

Honoria bobbed politely.

Somehow, an unwelcome encounter. They liked him because he was functioning, because he was serious; they wanted to see him, because he was stronger than they were now, because they wanted to draw a certain sustenance from his strength.

At the Empire, Honoria proudly refused to sit upon her father's folded coat. She was already an individual with a code of her own, and Charlie was more and more absorbed by the desire of putting a little of himself into her before she crystallized utterly. It was hopeless to try to know her in so short a time.

Between the acts they came upon Duncan and Lorraine in the lobby where the band was playing.

"Have a drink?"

"All right, but not up at the bar. We'll take a table."

"The perfect father."

Listening abstractedly to Lorraine, Charlie watched Honoria's eyes leave their table, and he followed them wistfully about the room, wondering what they saw. He met her glance and she smiled.

"I liked that lemonade," she said.

What had she said? What had he expected? Going home in a taxi after-ward, he pulled her over until her head rested against his chest.

"Darling, do you ever think about your mother?"

"Yes, sometimes," she answered vaguely.

"I don't want you to forget her. Have you got a picture of her?"

"Yes, I think so. Anyhow, Aunt Marion has. Why don't you want me to forget her?"

"She loved you very much."

"I loved her too."

They were silent for a moment.

"Daddy, I want to come and live with you," she said suddenly.

His heart leaped; he had wanted it to come like this.

"Aren't you perfectly happy?"

"Yes, but I love you better than anybody. And you love me better than anybody, don't you, now that mummy's dead?"

"Of course I do. But you won't always like me best, honey. You'll grow up and meet somebody your own age and go marry him and forget you ever had a daddy."

"Yes, that's true," she agreed tranquilly.

He didn't go in. He was coming back at nine o'clock and he wanted to keep himself fresh and new for the thing he must say then.

"When you're safe inside, just show yourself in that window."

"All right. Good-by, dads, dads, dads, dads."

He waited in the dark street until she appeared, all warm and glowing, in the window above and kissed her fingers out into the night.

III

They were waiting. Marion sat behind the coffee service in a dignified black dinner dress that just faintly suggested mourning. Lincoln was walking up and down with the animation of one who had already been talking. They were as anxious as he was to get into the question. He opened it almost immediately:

"I suppose you know what I want to see you about—why I really came to Paris."

Marion played with the black stars on her necklace and frowned.

"I'm awfully anxious to have a home," he continued. "And I'm awfully anxious to have Honoria in it. I appreciate your taking in Honoria for her mother's sake, but things have changed now" —he hesitated and then continued more forcibly— "changed radically with me, and I want to ask you to reconsider the matter. It would be silly for me to deny that about three years ago I was acting badly—"

Marion looked up at him with hard eyes.

"—but all that's over. As I told you, I haven't had more than a drink a day for over a year, and I take that drink deliberately, so that the idea of alcohol won't get too big in my imagination. You see the idea?"

"No," said Marion succinctly.

"It's a sort of stunt I set myself. It keeps the matter in proportion."

"I get you," said Lincoln. "You don't want to admit it's got any attraction for you."

"Something like that. Sometimes I forget and don't take it. But I try to take it. Anyway, I couldn't afford to drink in my position. The people I represent are more than satisfied with what I've done, and I'm bringing my sister over from Burlington to keep house for me, and I want awfully to have Honoria too. You know that even when her mother and I weren't getting along well we never let anything that happened touch Honoria. I know she's fond of me and I know I'm able to take care of her and—well, there you are. How do you feel about it?"

He knew that now he would have to take a beating. It would last an hour or two hours, and it would be difficult, but if he modulated his inevitable resentment to the chastened attitude of the reformed sinner, he might win his point in the end.

Keep your temper, he told himself. You don't want to be justified. You want Honoria.

Lincoln spoke first: "We've been talking it over ever since we got your letter last month. We're happy to have Honoria here. She's a dear little thing, and we're glad to be able to help her, but of course that isn't the question—"

Marion interrupted suddenly. "How long are you going to stay sober, Charlie?" she asked.

"Permanently, I hope."

"How can anybody count on that?"

"You know I never did drink heavily until I gave up business and came over here with nothing to do. Then Helen and I began to run around with—"

"Please leave Helen out of it. I can't bear to hear you talk about her like that."

He stared at her grimly; he had never been certain how fond of each other the sisters were in life.

"My drinking only lasted about a year and a half—from the time we came over until I—collapsed."

"It was time enough."

"It was time enough," he agreed.

"My duty is entirely to Helen," she said. "I try to think what she would have wanted me to do. Frankly, from the night you did that terrible thing you haven't really existed for me. I can't help that. She was my sister."

"Yes."

"When she was dying she asked me to look out for Honoria. If you hadn't been in a sanitarium then, it might have helped matters."

He had no answer.

"I'll never in my life be able to forget that morning when Helen knocked at my door, soaked to the skin and shivering and said you'd locked her out."

Charlie gripped the sides of the chair. This was more difficult than he expected; he wanted to launch out into a long expostulation and explanation, but he only said: "The night I locked her out—" and she interrupted, "I don't feel up to going over that again."

After a moment's silence Lincoln said: "We're getting off the subject. You want Marion to set aside her legal guardianship and give you Honoria. I think the main point for her is whether she has confidence in you or not."

"I don't blame Marion," Charlie said slowly, "but I think she can have entire confidence in me. I had a good record up to three years ago. Of course, it's within human possibilities I might go wrong any time. But if we wait much longer I'll lose Honoria's childhood and my chance for a home." He shook his head, "I'll simply lose her, don't you see?"

"Yes, I see," said Lincoln.

"Why didn't you think of all this before?" Marion asked.

"I suppose I did, from time to time, but Helen and I were getting along badly. When I consented to the guardianship, I was flat on my back in a sanitarium and the market had cleaned me out. I knew I'd acted badly, and I thought if it would bring any peace to Helen, I'd agree to anything. But now it's different. I'm functioning, I'm behaving damn well, so far as—"

"Please don't swear at me," Marion said.

He looked at her, startled. With each remark the force of her dislike became more and more apparent. She had built up all her fear of life into one wall and faced it toward him. This trivial reproof was possibly the result of some trouble with the cook several hours before. Charlie became increasingly alarmed at leaving Honoria in this atmosphere of hostility against himself; sooner or later it would come out, in a word here, a shake of the head there, and some of that distrust would be irrevocably implanted in Honoria. But he pulled his temper down out of his face and shut it up inside him; he had won a point, for Lincoln realized the absurdity of Marion's remark and asked her lightly since when she had objected to the word "damn."

"Another thing," Charlie said: "I'm able to give her certain advantages now. I'm going to take a French governess to Prague with me. I've got a lease on a new apartment—"

He stopped, realizing that he was blundering. They couldn't be expected to accept with equanimity the fact that his income was again twice as large as their own.

"I suppose you can give her more luxuries than we can," said Marion. "When you were throwing away money we were living along watching every ten francs. . . . I suppose you'll start doing it again."

"Oh, no," he said. "I've learned. I worked hard for ten years, you know—until I got lucky in the market, like so many people. Terribly lucky. It won't happen again."

There was a long silence. All of them felt their nerves straining, and for the first time in a year Charlie wanted a drink. He was sure now that Lincoln Peters wanted him to have his child.

Marion shuddered suddenly; part of her saw that Charlie's feet were planted on the earth now, and her own maternal feeling recognized the naturalness of his desire; but she had lived for a long time with a prejudice—a prejudice founded on a curious disbelief in her sister's happiness, and which, in the shock of one terrible night, had turned to hatred for him. It had all happened at a point in her life where the discouragement of ill health and adverse circumstances made it necessary for her to believe in tangible villainy and a tangible villain.

"I can't help what I think!" she cried out suddenly. "How much you were responsible for Helen's death, I don't know. It's something you'll have to square with your own conscience."

An electric current of agony surged through him; for a moment he was almost on his feet, an unuttered sound echoing in his throat. He hung on to himself for a moment, another moment.

"Hold on there," said Lincoln uncomfortably. "I never thought you were responsible for that."

"Helen died of heart trouble," Charlie said dully.

"Yes, heart trouble." Marion spoke as if the phrase had another meaning for her.

Then, in the flatness that followed her outburst, she saw him plainly and she knew he had somehow arrived at control over the situation. Glancing at her husband, she found no help from him, and as abruptly as if it were a matter of no importance, she threw up the sponge.

"Do what you like!" she cried, springing up from her chair. "She's your child. I'm not the person to stand in your way. I think if it were my child I'd rather see her—" She managed to check herself. "You two decide it. I can't stand this. I'm sick. I'm going to bed."

She hurried from the room; after a moment Lincoln said:

"This has been a hard day for her. You know how strongly she feels—" His voice was almost apologetic: "When a woman gets an idea in her head."

"Of course."

"It's going to be all right. I think she sees now that you—can provide for the child, and so we can't very well stand in your way or Honoria's way."

"Thank you, Lincoln."

"I'd better go along and see how she is."

"I'm going."

He was still trembling when he reached the street, but a walk down the Rue Bonaparte to the *quais* set him up, and as he crossed the Seine, fresh and new by the *quai* lamps, he felt exultant. But back in his room he couldn't sleep. The image of Helen haunted him. Helen whom he had loved so until they had senselessly begun to abuse each other's love, tear it into shreds. On that terrible February night that Marion remembered so vividly, a slow quarrel had gone on for hours. There was a scene at the Florida, and then he attempted to take her home, and then she kissed young Webb at a table; after that there was what she had hysterically said. When he arrived home alone he turned the key in the lock in wild anger. How could he know she would arrive an hour later alone, that there would be a snowstorm in which she wandered about in slippers, too confused to find a taxi? Then the aftermath, her escaping pneumonia by a miracle, and all the attendant horror. They were "reconciled," but that was the beginning of the end, and Marion, who had seen with her own eyes and who imagined it to be one of many scenes from her sister's martyrdom, never forgot.

Going over it again brought Helen nearer, and in the white, soft light that steals upon half sleep near morning he found himself talking to her again. She said that he was perfectly right about Honoria and that she wanted Honoria to be with him. She said she was glad he was being good and doing better. She said a lot of other things—very friendly things—but she was in a swing in a white dress, and swinging faster and faster all the time, so that at the end he could not hear clearly all that she said.

IV

He woke up feeling happy. The door of the world was open again. He made plans, vistas, futures for Honoria and himself, but suddenly he grew sad, remembering all the plans he and Helen had made. She had not planned to die. The present was the thing—work to do and someone to love. But not to love too much, for he knew the injury that a father can do to a daughter or a mother to a son by attaching them too closely: afterward, out in the world, the child would seek in the marriage partner the same blind tenderness and, failing probably to find it, turn against love and life.

It was another bright, crisp day. He called Lincoln Peters at the bank where he worked and asked if he could count on taking Honoria when he left for Prague. Lincoln agreed that there was no reason for delay. One thing—the legal guardianship. Marion wanted to retain that a while longer. She was upset by the whole matter, and it would oil things if she felt that the situation was still in her control for another year. Charlie agreed, wanting only the tangible, visible child.

Then the question of a governess. Charles sat in a gloomy agency and talked to a cross Béarnaise and to a buxom Breton peasant, neither of whom he could have endured. There were others whom he would see tomorrow.

He lunched with Lincoln Peters at Griffons, trying to keep down his exultation.

"There's nothing quite like your own child," Lincoln said. "But you understand how Marion feels too."

"She's forgotten how hard I worked for seven years there," Charlie said. "She just remembers one night."

"There's another thing." Lincoln hesitated. "While you and Helen were tearing around Europe throwing money away, we were just getting along. I didn't touch any of the prosperity because I never got ahead enough to carry anything but my insurance. I think Marion felt there was some kind of injustice in it—you not even working toward the end, and getting richer and richer."

"It went just as quick as it came," said Charlie.

"Yes, a lot of it stayed in the hands of *chasseurs* and saxophone players and maîtres d'hôtel—well, the big party's over now. I just said that to explain Marion's feeling about those crazy years. If you drop in about six o'clock tonight before Marion's too tired, we'll settle the details on the spot."

Back at his hotel, Charlie found a *pneumatique* that had been redirected from the Ritz bar where Charlie had left his address for the purpose of finding a certain man.

DEAR CHARLIE: You were so strange when we saw you the other day that I wondered if I did something to offend you. If so, I'm not conscious of it. In fact, I have thought about you too much for the last year, and it's always been in the back of my mind that I might see you if I came over here. We *did* have such good times that crazy spring, like the night you and I stole the butcher's tricycle, and the time we tried to call on the president and you had the old derby rim and the wire cane. Everybody seems so old lately, but I don't feel old a bit. Couldn't we get together some time today for old time's sake? I've got a vile hang-over for the moment, but will be feeling better this afternoon and will look for you about five in the sweatshop at the Ritz.

Always devotedly,

LORRAINE.

His first feeling was one of awe that he had actually, in his mature years, stolen a tricycle and pedaled Lorraine all over the Étoile between the small hours and dawn. In retrospect it was a nightmare. Locking out Helen didn't fit in with any other act of his life, but the tricycle incident did—it was one of many. How many weeks or months of dissipation to arrive at the condition of utter irresponsibility?

He tried to picture how Lorraine had appeared to him then—very attractive; Helen was unhappy about it, though she said nothing. Yesterday, in the restaurant, Lorraine had seemed trite, blurred, worn away. He emphatically did not want to see her, and he was glad Alix had not given away his hotel address. It was a relief to think, instead, of Honoria, to think of Sundays spent with her and of saying good morning to her and of knowing she was there in his house at night, drawing her breath in the darkness.

At five he took a taxi and bought presents for all the Peters—a piquant cloth doll, a box of Roman soldiers, flowers for Marion, big linen handkerchiefs for Lincoln.

He saw, when he arrived in the apartment, that Marion had accepted the inevitable. She greeted him now as though he were a recalcitrant member of the family, rather than a menacing outsider. Honoria had been told she was going; Charlie was glad to see that her tact made her conceal her excessive happiness. Only on his lap did she whisper her delight and the question "When?" before she slipped away with the other children.

He and Marion were alone for a minute in the room, and on an impulse he spoke out boldly:

"Family quarrels are bitter things. They don't go according to any rules. They're not aches or wounds; they're more like splits in the skin that won't heal because there's not enough material. I wish you and I could be on better terms."

"Some things are hard to forget," she answered. "It's a question of confidence." There was no answer to this and presently she asked, "When do you propose to take her?"

"As soon as I can get a governess. I hoped the day after tomorrow."

"That's impossible. I've got to get her things in shape. Not before Saturday."

He yielded. Coming back into the room, Lincoln offered him a drink. "I'll take my daily whisky," he said.

It was warm here, it was a home, people together by a fire. The children felt very safe and important; the mother and father were serious, watchful. They had things to do for the children more important than his visit here. A spoonful of medicine was, after all, more important than the strained relations between Marion and himself. They were not dull people, but they were very much in the grip of life and circumstances. He wondered if he couldn't do something to get Lincoln out of his rut at the bank.

A long peal at the door-bell; the *bonne à tout faire* passed through and went down the corridor. The door opened upon another long ring, and then voices, and the three in the salon looked up expectantly; Richard moved to bring the corridor within his range of vision, and Marion rose. Then the maid came back along the corridor, closely followed by the voices, which developed under the light into Duncan Schaeffer and Lorraine Quarrles.

They were gay, they were hilarious, they were roaring with laughter. For a moment Charlie was astounded; unable to understand how they ferreted out the Peters' address.

"Ah-h-h-!" Duncan wagged his finger roguishly at Charlie. "Ah-h-h!"

They both slid down another cascade of laughter. Anxious and at a loss, Charlie shook hands with them quickly and presented them to Lincoln and Marion. Marion nodded, scarcely speaking. She had drawn back a step toward the fire; her little girl stood beside her, and Marion put an arm about her shoulder.

With growing annoyance at the intrusion, Charlie waited for them to explain themselves. After some concentration Duncan said:

"We came to invite you out to dinner. Lorraine and I insist that all this shishi, cagy business 'bout your address got to stop."

Charlie came closer to them, as if to force them backward down the corridor.

"Sorry, but I can't. Tell me where you'll be and I'll phone you in half an hour."

This made no impression. Lorraine sat down suddenly on the side of a chair, and focusing her eyes on Richard, cried, "Oh, what a nice little boy! Come here, little boy." Richard glanced at his mother, but did not move. With a perceptible shrug of her shoulders, Lorraine turned back to Charlie:

"Come and dine. Sure your cousins won' mine. See you so sel'om. Or solemn."

"I can't," said Charlie sharply. "You two have dinner and I'll phone you."

Her voice became suddenly unpleasant. "All right, we'll go. But I remember once when you hammered on my door at four A.M. I was enough of a good sport to give you a drink. Come on, Dunc."

Still in slow motion, with blurred, angry faces, with uncertain feet, they retired along the corridor.

"Good night," Charlie said.

"Good night!" responded Lorraine emphatically.

When he went back into the salon Marion had not moved, only now her son was standing in the circle of her other arm. Lincoln was still swinging Honoria back and forth like a pendulum from side to side.

"What an outrage!" Charlie broke out. "What an absolute outrage!"

Neither of them answered. Charlie dropped into an armchair, picked up his drink, set it down again and said:

"People I haven't seen for two years having the colossal nerve—"

He broke off. Marion had made the sound "Oh!" in one swift, furious breath, turned her body from him with a jerk and left the room.

Lincoln set down Honoria carefully.

"You children go in and start your soup," he said, and when they obeyed, he said to Charlie:

Marion's not well and she can't stand shocks. That kind of people make her really physically sick."

"I didn't tell them to come here. They wormed your name out of somebody. They deliberately—"

"Well, it's too bad. It doesn't help matters. Excuse me a minute."

Left alone, Charlie sat tense in his chair. In the next room he could hear the children eating, talking in monosyllables, already oblivious to the scene between their elders. He heard a murmur of conversation from a farther room and then the ticking bell of a telephone receiver picked up, and in a panic he moved to the other side of the room and out of earshot.

In a minute Lincoln came back. "Look here, Charlie. I think we'd better call off dinner for tonight. Marion's in bad shape."

"Is she angry with me?"

"Sort of," he said, almost roughly. "She's not strong and—"

"You mean she's changed her mind about Honoria?"

"She's pretty bitter right now. I don't know. You phone me at the bank tomorrow."

"I wish you'd explain to her I never dreamed these people would come here. I'm just as sore as you are."

"I couldn't explain anything to her now."

Charlie got up. He took his coat and hat and started down the corridor. Then he opened the door of the dining room and said in a strange voice, "Good night, children."

Honoria rose and ran around the table to hug him.

"Good night, sweetheart," he said vaguely, and then trying to make his voice more tender, trying to conciliate something, "Good night, dear children."

V

Charlie went directly to the Ritz bar with the furious idea of finding Lorraine and Duncan, but they were not there, and he realized that in any case there was nothing he could do. He had not touched his drink at the Peters, and now he ordered a whisky-and-soda. Paul came over to say hello.

"It's a great change," he said sadly. "We do about half the business we did. So many fellows I hear about back in the States lost everything, maybe not in the first crash, but then in the second. Your friend George Hardt lost every cent, I hear. Are you back in the States?"

"No, I'm in business in Prague."

"I heard that you lost a lot in the crash."

"I did," and he added grimly, "but I lost everything I wanted in the boom."

"Selling short."

"Something like that."

Again the memory of those days swept over him like a nightmare—the people they had met travelling; then people who couldn't add a row of figures or speak a coherent sentence. The little man Helen had consented to dance with at the ship's party, who had insulted her ten feet from the table; the women and girls carried screaming with drink or drugs out of public places—

—The men who locked their wives out in the snow, because the snow of twenty-nine wasn't real snow. If you didn't want it to be snow, you just paid some money.

He went to the phone and called the Peters' apartment; Lincoln answered.

"I called up because this thing is on my mind. Has Marion said anything definite?"

"Marion's sick," Lincoln answered shortly. "I know this thing isn't altogether your fault, but I can't have her go to pieces about it. I'm afraid we'll have to let it slide for six months; I can't take the chance of working her up to this state again."

"I see."

"I'm sorry, Charlie."

He went back to his table. His whisky glass was empty, but he shook his head when Alix looked at it questioningly. There wasn't much he could do now except send Honoria some things; he would send her a lot of things tomorrow. He thought rather angrily that this was just money—he had given so many people money. . . .

"No, no more," he said to another waiter. "What do I owe you?"

He would come back some day; they couldn't make him pay forever. But he wanted his child, and nothing was much good now, beside that fact. He wasn't young any more, with a lot of nice thoughts and dreams to have by himself. He was absolutely sure Helen wouldn't have wanted him to be so alone.

CHARLOTTE PERKINS GILMAN (1860–1935)

The Yellow Wallpaper

Charlotte Perkins Gilman was born in Hartford, Connecticut. She worked in both the labor and women's rights movements, and advocated economic independence for women in her book *Women and Economics* (1898). "The Yellow Wallpaper," her most famous work of fiction, appeared in 1899.

It is very seldom that mere ordinary people like John and myself secure ancestral halls for the summer.

A colonial mansion, a hereditary estate, I would say a haunted house, and reach the height of romantic felicity—but that would be asking too much of fate!

Still I will proudly declare that there is something queer about it.

Else, why should it be let so cheaply? And why have stood so long untenanted?

John laughs at me, of course, but one expects that in marriage.

John is practical in the extreme. He has no patience with faith, an intense horror of superstition, and he scoffs openly at any talk of things not to be felt and seen and put down in figures.

John is a physician, and *perhaps*— (I would not say it to a living soul, of course, but this is dead paper and a great relief to my mind)— *perhaps* that is one reason I do not get well faster.

You see he does not believe I am sick!

And what can one do?

If a physician of high standing, and one's own husband, assures friends and relatives that there is really nothing the matter with one but temporary nervous depression—a slight hysterical tendency—what is one to do?

My brother is also a physician, and also of high standing, and he says the same thing.

So I take phosphates or phosphites—whichever it is, and tonics, and journeys, and air, and exercise, and am absolutely forbidden to "work" until I am well again.

Personally, I disagree with their ideas.

Personally, I believe that congenial work, with excitement and change, would do me good.

But what is one to do?

I did write for a while in spite of them; but it *does* exhaust me a good deal—having to be so sly about it, or else meet with heavy opposition.

I sometimes fancy that in my condition if I had less opposition and more society and stimulus—but John says the very worst thing I can do is to think about my condition, and I confess it always makes me feel bad.

So I will let it alone and talk about the house.

The most beautiful place! It is quite alone, standing well back from the road, quite three miles from the village. It makes me think of English places that you read about, for there are hedges and walls and gates that lock, and lots of separate little houses for the gardeners and people.

There is a *delicious* garden! I never saw such a garden—large and shady, full of box-bordered paths, and lined with long grape-covered arbors with seats under them.

There were greenhouses, too, but they are all broken now.

There was some legal trouble, I believe, something about the heirs and coheirs; anyhow, the place has been empty for years.

That spoils my ghostliness, I am afraid, but I don't care—there is something strange about the house—I can feel it.

I even said so to John one moonlight evening, but he said what I felt was a *draught*, and shut the window.

I get unreasonably angry with John sometimes. I'm sure I never used to be so sensitive. I think it is due to this nervous condition.

But John says if I feel so, I shall neglect proper self-control; so I take pains to control myself—before him, at least, and that makes me very tired.

I don't like our room a bit. I wanted one downstairs that opened on the piazza and had roses all over the window, and such pretty old-fashioned chintz hanging! but John would not hear of it.

He said there was only one window and not room for two beds, and no near room for him if he took another.

He is very careful and loving, and hardly lets me stir without special direction.

I have a schedule prescription for each hour in the day; he takes all care from me, and so I feel basely ungrateful not to value it more.

He said we came here solely on my account, that I was to have perfect rest and all the air I could get. "Your exercise depends on your strength, my dear," said he, "and your food somewhat on your appetite; but air you can absorb all the time." So we took the nursery at the top of the house.

It is a big, airy room, the whole floor nearly, with windows that look all ways, and air and sunshine galore. It was nursery first and then playroom and gymnasium, I should judge; for the windows are barred for little children, and there are rings and things in the walls.

The paint and paper look as if a boys' school had used it. It is stripped off—the paper—in great patches all around the head of my bed, about as far as I can reach, and in a great place on the other side of the room low down. I never saw a worse paper in my life.

One of those sprawling flamboyant patterns committing every artistic sin.

It is dull enough to confuse the eye in following, pronounced enough to constantly irritate and provoke study, and when you follow the lame uncertain curves for a little distance they suddenly commit suicide—plunge off at outrageous angles, destroy themselves in unheard of contradictions.

The color is repellent, almost revolting; a smouldering unclean yellow, strangely faded by the slow-turning sunlight.

It is a dull yet lurid orange in some places, a sickly sulphur tint in others.

No wonder the children hated it! I should hate it myself if I had to live in this room long.

There comes John, and I must put this away, —he hates to have me write a word.

We have been here two weeks, and I haven't felt like writing before, since that first day.

I am sitting by the window now, up in this atrocious nursery, and there is nothing to hinder my writing as much as I please, save lack of strength.

John is away all day, and even some nights when his cases are serious.

I am glad my case is not serious!

But these nervous troubles are dreadfully depressing.

John does not know how much I really suffer. He knows there is no *reason* to suffer, and that satisfies him.

Of course it is only nervousness. It does weigh on me so not to do my duty in any way!

I meant to be such a help to John, such a real rest and comfort, and here I am a comparative burden already!

Nobody would believe what an effort it is to do what little I am able, —to dress and entertain, and order things.

It is fortunate Mary is so good with the baby. Such a dear baby!

And yet I *cannot* be with him, it makes me so nervous.

I suppose John never was nervous in his life. He laughs at me so about this wallpaper!

At first he meant to repaper the room, but afterwards he said that I was letting it get the better of me, and that nothing was worse for a nervous patient than to give way to such fancies.

He said that after the wallpaper was changed it would be the heavy bedstead, and then the barred windows, and then that gate at the head of the stairs, and so on.

"You know the place is doing you good," he said, "and really, dear, I don't care to renovate the house just for a three months' rental."

"Then do let us go downstairs," I said, "there are such pretty rooms there."

Then he took me in his arms and called me a blessed little goose, and said he would go down to the cellar, if I wished, and have it whitewashed into the bargain.

But he is right enough about the beds and windows and things.

It is an airy and comfortable room as any one need wish, and, of course, I would not be so silly as to make him uncomfortable just for a whim.

I'm really getting quite fond of the big room, all but that horrid paper.

Out of one window I can see the garden, those mysterious deepshaded arbors, the riotous old-fashioned flowers, and bushed and gnarly trees.

Out of another I get a lovely view of the bay and a little private wharf belonging to the estate. There is a beautiful shaded lane that runs down there from the house. I always fancy I see people walking in these numerous paths and arbors, but John has cautioned me not to give way to fancy in the least. He says that with my imaginative power and habit of story-making, a nervous weakness like mine is sure to lead to all manner of excited fancies, and that I ought to use my will and good sense to check the tendency. So I try.

I think sometimes that if I were only well enough to write a little it would relieve the press of ideas and rest me.

But I find I get pretty tired when I try.

It is so discouraging not to have any advice and companionship about my work. When I get really well, John says we will ask Cousin Henry and Julia down for a long visit; but he says he would as soon put fireworks in my pillow-case as to let me have those stimulating people about now.

I wish I could get well faster.

But I must not think about that. This paper looks to me as if it *knew* what a vicious influence it had!

There is a recurrent spot where the pattern lolls like a broken neck and two bulbous eyes stare at you upside down.

I get positively angry with the impertinence of it and the everlastingness. Up and down and sideways they crawl, and those absurd, unblinking eyes are everywhere. There is one place where two breadths didn't match, and the eyes go all up and down the line, one a little higher than the other.

I never saw so much expression in an inanimate thing before, and we all know how much expression they have! I used to lie awake as a child and get more entertainment and terror out of blank walls and plain furniture than most children could find in a toystore.

I remember what a kindly wink the knobs of our big, old bureau used to have, and there was one chair that always seemed like a strong friend.

I used to feel that if any of the other things looked too fierce I could always hop into that chair and be safe.

The furniture in this room is no worse than inharmonious, however, for we had to bring it all from downstairs. I suppose when this was used as a playroom they had to take the nursery things out, and no wonder! I never saw such ravages as the children have made here.

The wallpaper, as I said before, is torn off in spots, and it sticketh closer than a brother—they must have had perseverance as well as hatred.

Then the floor is scratched and gouged and splintered, the plaster itself is dug out here and there, and this great heavy bed which is all we found in the room, looks as if it had been through the wars.

But I don't mind it a bit—only the paper.

There comes John's sister. Such a dear girl as she is, and so careful of me! I must not let her find me writing.

She is a perfect and enthusiastic housekeeper, and hopes for no better profession. I verily believe she thinks it is the writing which made me sick!

But I can write when she is out, and see her a long way off from these windows.

There is one that commands the road, a lovely shaded winding road, and one that just looks off over the country. A lovely country, too, full of great elms and velvet meadows.

This wallpaper has a kind of sub-pattern in a different shade, a particularly irritating one, for you can only see it in certain lights, and not clearly then.

But in the places where it isn't faded and where the sun is just so—I can see a strange, provoking, formless sort of figure, that seems to skulk about behind that silly and conspicuous front design.

There's sister on the stairs!

Well, the Fourth of July is over! The people are all gone and I am tired out. John thought it might do me good to see a little company, so we just had mother and Nellie and the children down for a week.

Of course I didn't do a thing. Jennie sees to everything now.

But it tired me all the same.

John says if I don't pick up faster he shall send me to Weir Mitchell in the fall.

But I don't want to go there at all. I had a friend who was in his hands once, and she says he is just like John and my brother, only more so!

Besides, it is such an undertaking to go so far.

I don't feel as if it was worth while to turn my hand over for anything, and I'm getting dreadfully fretful and querulous.

I cry at nothing, and cry most of the time.

Of course I don't when John is here, or anybody else, but when I am alone.

And I am alone a good deal just now. John is kept in town very often by serious cases, and Jennie is good and lets me alone when I want her to.

So I walk a little in the garden or down that lovely lane, sit on the porch under the roses, and lie down up here a good deal.

I'm getting really fond of the room in spite of the wallpaper. Perhaps *because* of the wallpaper.

It dwells in my mind so!

I lie here on this great immovable bed—it is nailed down, I believe—and follow that pattern about by the hour. It is as good as gymnastics, I assure you. I start, we'll say, at the bottom, down in the corner over there where it has not been touched, and I determine for the thousandth time that I *will* follow that pointless pattern to some sort of a conclusion.

I know a little of the principle of design, and I know this thing was not arranged on any laws of radiation, or alternation, or repetition, or symmetry, or anything else that I ever heard of.

It is repeated, of course, by the breadths, but not otherwise.

Looked at in one way each breadth stands alone, the bloated curves and flourishes—a kind of "debased Romanesque" with *delirium tremens*—go waddling up and down in isolated columns of fatuity.

But, on the other hand, they connect diagonally, and the sprawling outlines run off in great slanting waves of optic horror, like a lot of wallowing seaweeds in full chase.

The whole thing goes horizontally, too, at least it seems so, and I exhaust myself in trying to distinguish the order of its going in that direction.

They have used a horizontal breadth for a frieze, and that adds wonderfully to the confusion.

There is one end of the room where it is almost intact, and there, when the crosslights fade and the low sun shines directly upon it, I can almost fancy radiation after all, —the interminable grotesques seem to form around a common center and rush off in headlong plunges of equal distraction.

It makes me tired to follow it. I will take a nap I guess.

I don't know why I should write this.

I don't want to.

I don't feel able.

And I know John would think it absurd. But I *must* say what I feel and think in some way—it is such a relief!

Half the time now I am awfully lazy, and lie down ever so much.

John says I mustn't lose my strength, and has me take cod liver oil and lots of tonics and things, to say nothing of ale and wine and rare meat.

Dear John! He loves me very dearly, and hates to have me sick. I tried to have a real earnest reasonable talk with him the other day, and tell him how I wish he would let me go and make a visit to Cousin Henry and Julia.

But he said I wasn't able to go, nor able to stand it after I got there; and I did not make out a very good case for myself, for I was crying before I had finished.

It is getting to be a great effort for me to think straight. Just this nervous weakness I suppose.

And dear John gathered me up in his arms, and just carried me upstairs and laid me on the bed, and sat by me and read to me till it tired my head.

He said I was his darling and his comfort and all he had, and that I must take care of myself for his sake, and keep well.

He says no one but myself can help me out of it, that I must use my will and self-control and not let any silly fancies run away with me.

There's one comfort, the baby is well and happy, and does not have to occupy this nursery with the horrid wallpaper.

If we had not used it, that blessed child would have! What a fortunate escape! Why, I wouldn't have a child of mine, an impressionable little thing, live in such a room for worlds.

I never thought of it before, but it is lucky that John kept me here after all, I can stand it so much easier than a baby, you see.

Of course I never mention it to them any more—I am too wise, —but I keep watch of it all the same.

There are things in that paper that nobody knows but me, or ever will.

Behind that outside pattern the dim shapes get clearer every day.

It is always the same shape, only very numerous.

And it is like a woman stooping down and creeping about behind that pattern. I don't like it a bit. I wonder—I begin to think—I wish John would take me away from here!

It is so hard to talk with John about my case, because he is so wise, and because he loves me so.

But I tried it last night.

It was moonlight. The moon shines in all around just as the sun does.

I hate to see it sometimes, it creeps so slowly, and always comes in by one window or another.

John was asleep and I hated to waken him, so I kept still and watched the moonlight on that undulating wallpaper till I felt creepy.

The faint figure behind seemed to shake the pattern, just as if she wanted to get out.

I got up softly and went to feel and see if the paper *did* move, and when I came back John was awake.

"What is it, little girl?" he said. "Don't go walking about like that— you'll get cold."

I thought it was a good time to talk, so I told him that I really was not gaining here, and that I wished he would take me away.

"Why darling!" said he, "our lease will be up in three weeks, and I can't see how to leave before.

"The repairs are not done at home, and I cannot possibly leave town just now. Of course if you were in any danger, I could and would, but you really are better, dear, whether you can see it or not. I am a doctor, dear, and I know. You are gaining flesh and color, your appetite is better, I feel really much easier about you."

"I don't weigh a bit more," said I, "nor as much; and my appetite may be better in the evening when you are here, but it is worse in the morning when you are away!"

"Bless her little heart!" said he with a big hug, "she shall be as sick as she pleases! But now let's improve the shining hours by going to sleep, and talk about it in the morning!"

"And you won't go away?" I asked gloomily.

"Why, how can I, dear? It is only three weeks more and then we will take a nice little trip of a few days while Jennie is getting the house ready. Really dear you are better!"

"Better in body perhaps—" I began, and stopped short, for he sat up straight and looked at me with such a stern, reproachful look that I could not say another word.

"My darling," said he, "I beg of you, for my sake and for our child's sake, as well as for your own, that you will never for one instant let that idea enter your mind! There is nothing so dangerous, so fascinating, to a temperament like yours. It is a false and foolish fancy. Can you not trust me as a physician when I tell you so?"

So of course I said no more on that score, and we went to sleep before long. He thought I was asleep first, but I wasn't, and lay there for hours trying to decide whether that front pattern and the back pattern really did move together or separately.

On a pattern like this, by daylight, there is a lack of sequence, a defiance of law, that is a constant irritant to a normal mind.

The color is hideous enough, and unreliable enough, and infuriating enough, but the pattern is torturing.

You think you have mastered it, but just as you get well underway in following, it turns a back-somersault and there you are. It slaps you in the face, knocks you down, and tramples upon you. It is like a bad dream.

The outside pattern is a florid arabesque, reminding one of a fungus. If you can imagine a toadstool in joints, an interminable string of toadstools, budding and sprouting in endless convolutions—why, that is something like it.

That is, sometimes!

There is one marked peculiarity about this paper, a thing nobody seems to notice but myself, and that is that it changes as the light changes.

When the sun shoots in through the east window—I always watch for that first long, straight ray—it changes so quickly that I never can quite believe it.

That is why I watch it always.

By moonlight—the moon shines in all night when there is a moon—I wouldn't know it was the same paper.

At night in any kind of light, in twilight, candle light, lamp-light, and worst of all by moonlight, it becomes bars! The outside pattern I mean, and the woman behind it is as plain as can be.

I didn't realize for a long time what the thing was that showed behind, that dim sub-pattern, but now I am quite sure it is a woman.

By daylight she is subdued, quiet. I fancy it is the pattern that keeps her so still. It is so puzzling. It keeps me quiet by the hour.

I lie down ever so much now. John says it is good for me, and to sleep all I can.

Indeed he started the habit by making me lie down for an hour after each meal.

It is a very bad habit I am convinced, for you see I don't sleep.

And that cultivates deceit, for I don't tell them I'm awake—O no!

The fact is I am getting a little afraid of John.

He seems very queer sometimes, and even Jennie has an inexplicable look.

It strikes me occasionally, just as a scientific hypothesis,—that perhaps it is the paper!

I have watched John when he did not know I was looking, and come into the room suddenly on the most innocent excuses, and I've caught him several times *looking at the paper!* And Jennie too. I caught Jennie with her hand on it once.

She didn't know I was in the room, and when I asked her in a quiet, a very quiet voice, with the most restrained manner possible, what she was doing with the paper—she turned around as if she had been caught stealing, and looked quite angry—asked me why I should frighten her so!

Then she said that the paper stained everything it touched, that she had found yellow smooches on all my clothes and John's, and she wished we would be more careful!

Did not that sound innocent? But I know she was studying that pattern, and I am determined that nobody shall find it out but myself!

Life is very much more exciting now than it used to be. You see I have something more to expect, to look forward to, to watch. I really do eat better, and am more quiet than I was.

John is so pleased to see me improve! He laughed a little the other day, and said I seemed to be flourishing in spite of my wallpaper.

I turned it off with a laugh. I had no intention of telling him it was *because* of the wallpaper—he would make fun of me. He might even want to take me away.

I don't want to leave now until I have found it out. There is a week more, and I think that will be enough.

I'm feeling ever so much better! I don't sleep much at night, for it is so interesting to watch developments; but I sleep a good deal in the day-time.

In the daytime it is tiresome and perplexing.

There are always new shoots on the fungus, and new shades of yellow all over it. I cannot keep count of them, though I have tried conscientiously.

It is the strangest yellow, that wallpaper! It makes me think of all the yellow things I ever saw—not beautiful ones like butter-cups, but old foul, bad yellow things.

But there is something else about that paper—the smell! I noticed it the moment we came into the room, but with so much air and sun it was not bad. Now we have had a week of fog and rain, and whether the windows are open or not, the smell is here.

It creeps all over the house.

I find it hovering in the dining-room, skulking in the parlor, hiding in the hall, lying in wait for me on the stairs.

It gets into my hair.

Even when I go to ride, if I turn my head suddenly and surprise it—there is that smell!

Such a peculiar odor, too! I have spent hours in trying to analyze it, to find what it smelled like.

It is not bad—at first, and very gentle, but quite the subtlest, most enduring odor I ever met.

In this damp weather it is awful, I wake up in the night and find it hanging over me.

It used to disturb me at first. I thought seriously of burning the house—to reach the smell.

But now I am used to it. The only thing I can think of that it is like is the *color* of the paper! A yellow smell.

There is a very funny mark on this wall, low down, near the mop-board. A streak that runs round the room. It goes behind every piece of furniture, except the bed, a long, straight, even *smooch*, as if it had been rubbed over and over.

I wonder how it was done and who did it, and what they did it for. Round and round and round—round and round and round—it makes me dizzy!

I really have discovered something at last.

Through watching so much at night, when it changes so, I have finally found out.

The front pattern *does* move—and no wonder! The woman behind shakes it!

Sometimes I think there are a great many women behind, and sometimes only one, and she crawls around fast, and her crawling shakes it all over.

Then in the very bright spots she keeps still, and in the very shady spots she just takes hold of the bars and shakes them hard.

And she is all the time trying to climb through. But nobody could climb through that pattern—it strangles so; I think that is why it has so many heads.

They get through, and then the pattern strangles them off and turns them upside down, and makes their eyes white!

If those heads were covered or taken off it would not be half so bad.

I think that woman gets out in the daytime!

And I'll tell you why—privately—I've seen her!

I can see her out of every one of my windows!

It is the same woman, I know, for she is always creeping, and most women do not creep by daylight.

I see her on that long road under the trees, creeping along, and when a carriage comes she hides under the blackberry vines.

I don't blame her a bit. It must be very humiliating to be caught creeping by daylight!

I always lock the door when I creep by daylight. I can't do it at night, for I know John would suspect something at once.

And John is so queer now, that I don't want to irritate him. I wish he would take another room! Besides, I don't want anybody to get that woman out at night but myself.

I often wonder if I could see her out of all the windows at once.

But, turn as fast as I can, I can only see out of one at one time.

And though I always see her, she *may* be able to creep faster than I can turn!

I have watched her sometimes away off in the open country, creeping as fast as a cloud shadow in a high wind.

If only that top pattern could be gotten off from the under one! I mean to try it, little by little.

I have found out another funny thing, but I shan't tell it this time! It does not do to trust people too much.

There are only two more days to get this paper off, and I believe John is beginning to notice. I don't like the look in his eyes.

And I heard him ask Jennie a lot of professional questions about me. She had a very good report to give.

She said I slept a good deal in the daytime.

John knows I don't sleep very well at night, for all I'm so quiet!

He asked me all sorts of questions, too, and pretended to be very loving and kind.

As if I couldn't see through him!

Still, I don't wonder he acts so, sleeping under this paper for three months.

It only interests me, but I feel sure John and Jennie are secretly affected by it.

Hurrah! This is the last day, but it is enough. John to stay in town over night, and won't be out until this evening.

Jennie wanted to sleep with me—the sly thing! But I told her I should undoubtedly rest better for a night all alone.

That was clever, for really I wasn't alone a bit! As soon as it was moonlight and that poor thing began to crawl and shake the pattern, I got up and ran to help her.

I pulled and she shook, I shook and she pulled, and before morning we had peeled off yards of that paper.

A strip about as high as my head and half around the room.

And then when the sun came and that awful pattern began to laugh at me, I declared I would finish it to-day!

We go away to-morrow, and they are moving all my furniture down again to leave things as they were before.

Jennie looked at the wall in amazement, but I told her merrily that I did it out of pure spite at the vicious thing.

She laughed and said she wouldn't mind doing it herself, but I must not get tired.

How she betrayed herself that time!

But I am here, and no person touches this paper but me—not *alive!*

She tried to get me out of the room—it was too patent! But I said it was so quiet and empty and clean now that I believed I would lie down again and sleep all I could; and not to wake me even for dinner—I would call when I woke.

So now she is gone, and the servants are gone, and the things are gone, and there is nothing left but that great bedstead nailed down, with the canvas mattress we found on it.

We shall sleep downstairs to-night, and take the boat home to-morrow.

I quite enjoy the room, now it is bare again.

How those children did tear about here!

This bedstead is fairly gnawed!

But I must get to work.

I have locked the door and thrown the key down into the front path.

I don't want to go out, and I don't want to have anybody come in, till John comes.

I want to astonish him.

I've got a rope up here that even Jennie did not find. If that woman does get out, and tries to get away, I can tie her!

But I forgot I could not reach far without anything to stand on!

This bed will *not* move!

I tried to lift and push it until I was lame, and then I got so angry I bit off a little piece at one corner—but it hurt my teeth.

Then I peeled off all the paper I could reach standing on the floor. It sticks horribly and the pattern just enjoys it! All those strangled heads and bulbous eyes and waddling fungus growths just shriek with derision!

I am getting angry enough to do something desperate. To jump out of the window would be admirable exercise, but the bars are too strong even to try.

Besides I wouldn't do it. Of course not. I know well enough that a step like that is improper and might be misconstrued.

I don't like to *look* out of the windows even—there are so many of those creeping women, and they creep so fast.

I wonder if they all come out of that wallpaper as I did?

But I am securely fastened now by my well-hidden rope—you don't get *me* out in the road there!

I suppose I shall have to get back behind the pattern when it comes night, and that is hard!

It is so pleasant to be out in this great room and creep around as I please!

I don't want to go outside. I won't, even if Jennie asks me to.

For outside you have to creep on the ground, and everything is green instead of yellow.

But here I can creep smoothly on the floor, and my shoulder just fits in that long smooch around the wall, so I cannot lose my way.

Why there's John at the door!

It is no use, young man, you can't open it!

How he does call and pound!

Now he's crying for an axe.

It would be a shame to break down that beautiful door!

"John dear!" said I in the gentlest voice, "the key is down by the front steps, under a plantain leaf!"

That silenced him for a few moments.

Then he said—very quietly indeed, "Open the door, my darling!"

"I can't," said I. "The key is down by the front door under a plantain leaf!"

And then I said it again, several times, very gently and slowly, and said it so often that he had to go and see, and he got it of course, and came in. He stopped short by the door.

"What is the matter?" he cried. "For God's sake, what are you doing!"

I kept on creeping just the same, but I looked at him over my shoulder.

"I've got out at last," said I, "in spite of you and Jane. And I've pulled off most of the paper, so you can't put me back!"

Now why should that man have fainted? But he did, and right across my path by the wall, so that I had to creep over him every time!

STANISLAW LEM (b. 1921)

How the World Was Saved

Stanislaw Lem, Polish critic, novelist, and futurologist, was born in Lvov (now part of the Soviet Union). He is co-founder of the Polish Astronautical Society and is a member of the Polish Cybernetics Association. His novels include *Solaris* (1961) and *The Invincible* (1967). "How the World Was Saved" originally appeared in *The Cyberiad: Fables for the Cybernetic Age* (1967).

One day Trurl the constructor put together a machine that could create anything starting with *n*. When it was ready, he tried it out, ordering it to make needles, then nankeens and negligees, which it did, then nail the lot to narghiles filled with nepenthe and numerous other narcotics. The machine carried out his instructions to the letter. Still not completely sure of its ability, he had it produce, one after the other, nimbuses, noodles, nuclei, neutrons, naphtha, noses, nymphs, naiads, and *natrium*. This last it could not do, and Trurl, considerably irritated, demanded an explanation.

"Never heard of it," said the machine.

"What? But it's only sodium. You know, the metal, the element . . ."

"Sodium starts with an *s*, and I work only in *n*."

"But in Latin it's *natrium*."

"Look, old boy," said the machine, "if I could do everything starting with *n* in every possible language, I'd be a Machine That Could Do Everything in the Whole Alphabet, since any item you care to mention undoubtedly starts with *n* in one foreign language or another. It's not that easy. I can't go beyond what you programmed. So no sodium."

"Very well," said Trurl and ordered it to make Night, which it made at once—small perhaps, but perfectly nocturnal. Only then did Trurl invite over his friend Klapaucius the constructor, and introduced him to the machine, praising its extraordinary skill at such length, that Klapaucius grew annoyed and inquired whether he too might not test the machine.

"Be my guest," said Trurl. "But it has to start with *n*."

"*N?*" said Klapaucius. "All right, let it make Nature."

The machine whined, and in a trice Trurl's front yard was packed with naturalists. They argued, each publishing heavy volumes, which the others tore to pieces; in the distance one could see flaming pyres, on which martyrs to Nature were sizzling; there was thunder, and strange mushroom-shaped columns of smoke rose up; everyone talked at once, no one listened, and there were all sorts of memoranda, appeals, subpoenas and other documents, while off to the side sat a few old men, feverishly scribbling on scraps of paper.

"Not bad, eh?" said Trurl with pride. "Nature to a T, admit it!"

But Klapaucius wasn't satisfied.

"What, that mob? Surely you're not going to tell me that's Nature?"

"Then give the machine something else," snapped Trurl. "Whatever you like." For a moment Klapaucius was at a loss for what to ask. But after a little thought he declared that he would put two more tasks to the machine; if it could fulfill them, he would admit that it was all Trurl said it was. Trurl agreed to this, whereupon Klapaucius requested Negative.

"Negative?!" cried Trurl. "What on earth is Negative?"

"The opposite of positive, of course," Klapaucius coolly replied. "Negative attitudes, the negative of a picture, for example. Now don't try to pretend you never heard of Negative. All right, machine, get to work!"

The machine, however, had already begun. First it manufactured antiprotons, then antielectrons, antineutrons, antineutrinos, and labored on, until from out of all this antimatter an antiworld took shape, glowing like a ghostly cloud above their heads.

"H'm," muttered Klapaucius, displeased. "That's supposed to be Negative? Well . . . let's say it is, for the sake of peace. . . . But now here's the third command: Machine, do Nothing!"

The machine sat still. Klapaucius rubbed his hands in triumph, but Trurl said:

"Well, what did you expect? You asked it to do nothing, and it's doing nothing."

"Correction: I asked it to do Nothing, but it's doing nothing."

"Nothing is nothing!"

"Come, come. It was supposed to do Nothing, but it hasn't done anything, and therefore I've won. For Nothing, my dear and clever colleague, is not your run-of-the-mill nothing, the result of idleness and inactivity, but dynamic, aggressive Nothingness, that is to say, perfect, unique, ubiquitous, in other words Nonexistence, ultimate and supreme, in its very own nonperson!"

"You're confusing the machine!" cried Trurl. But suddenly its metallic voice rang out:

"Really, how can you two bicker at a time like this? Oh yes, I know what Nothing is, and Nothingness, Nonexistence, Nonentity, Negation, Nullity and Nihility, since all these come under the heading of n, n as in Nil. Look then upon your world for the last time, gentlemen! Soon it shall no longer be . . ."

The constructors froze, forgetting their quarrel, for the machine was in actual fact doing Nothing, and it did it in this fashion: one by one, various things were removed from the world, and the things, thus removed, ceased to exist, as if they had never been. The machine had already disposed of nolars, nightzebs, nocs, necs, nallyrakers, neotremes and nonmalrigers. At moments, though, it seemed that instead of reducing, diminishing and subtracting, the machine was increasing, enhancing and adding, since it liquidated, in turn: nonconformists, nonentities, nonsense, nonsupport, nearsightedness, narrowmindedness, naughtiness, neglect, nausea, necrophilia and nepotism. But after a while the world very definitely began to thin out around Trurl and Klapaucius.

"Omigosh!" said Trurl. "If only nothing bad comes out of all this . . ."

"Don't worry," said Klapaucius. "You can see it's not producing Universal Nothingness, but only causing the absence of whatever starts with n. Which is really nothing in the way of nothing, and nothing is what your machine, dear Trurl, is worth!"

"Do not be deceived," replied the machine. "I've begun, it's true, with everything in n, but only out of familiarity. To create however is one thing, to destroy, another thing entirely. I can blot out the world for the simple reason that I'm able to do anything and everything—and everything means everything—in *n*, and consequently Nothingness is child's play for me. In less than a minute now you will cease to have existence, along with everything else, so tell me now, Klapaucius, and quickly, that I am really and truly everything I was programmed to be, before it is too late."

"But—" Klapaucius was about to protest, but noticed, just then, that a number of things were indeed disappearing, and not merely those that started with *n*. The constructors were no longer surrounded by the gruncheons, the targalisks, the shupops, the calinatifacts, the thists, worches and pritons.

"Stop! I take it all back! Desist! Whoa! Don't do Nothing!!" screamed Klapaucius. But before the machine could come to a full stop, all the brashations, plusters, laries and zits had vanished away. Now the machine stood motionless. The world was a dreadful sight. The sky had particularly suffered: there were only a few, isolated points of light in the heavens—no trace of the glorious worches and zits that had, till now, graced the horizon!

"Great Gauss!" cried Kalpaucius. "And where are the gruncheons? Where my dear, favorite pritons? Where now the gentle zits?!"

"They no longer are, nor ever will exist again," the machine said calmly. "I executed, or rather only began to execute, your order . . ."

"I tell you to do Nothing, and you . . . you . . ."

"Klapaucius, don't pretend to be a greater idiot than you are," said the machine. "Had I made Nothing outright, in one fell swoop, everything would have ceased to exist, and that includes Trurl, the sky, the Universe, and you—and even myself. In which case who could say and to whom could it be said that the order was carried out and I am an efficient and capable machine? And if no one could say it to no one, in what way then could I, who also would not be, be vindicated?"

"Yes, fine, let's drop the subject," said Klapaucius. "I have nothing more to ask of you, only please, dear machine, please return the zits, for without them life loses all its charm . . ."

"But I can't, they're in z," said the machine. "Of course, I can restore nonsense, narrowmindedness, nausea, necrophilia, neuralgia, nefariousness and noxiousness. As for the other letters, however, I can't help you."

"I want my zits!" bellowed Klapaucius.

"Sorry, no zits," said the machine. "Take a good look at this world, how riddled it is with huge, gaping holes, how full of Nothingness, the Nothingness that fills the bottomless void between the stars, how everything about us has become lined with it, how it darkly lurks behind each shred of matter. This is your work, envious one! And I hardly think the future generations will bless you for it . . ."

"Perhaps . . . they won't find out, perhaps they won't notice," groaned the pale Klapaucius, gazing up incredulously at the black emptiness of space and not daring to look his colleague, Trurl, in the eye. Leaving him beside the machine that could do everything in *n*, Klapaucius skulked home—and to this day the world has remained honeycombed with nothingness, exactly as it was when halted in the course of its liquidation. And as all subsequent attempts to build a machine on any other letter met with failure, it is to be feared that never again will we have such marvelous phenomena as the worches and the zits—no, never again.

BERNARD MALAMUD (1914–1986)

The Magic Barrel

Bernard Malamud was born in Brooklyn and educated in the City College of New York and at Columbia University. *The Magic Barrel,* in which the following story first appeared, won the National Book Award in 1958. Malamud's novels include *The Natural* (1952) and *The Fixer (1966). His Collected Stories* appeared in 1983.

Not long ago there lived in uptown New York, in a small, almost meager room, though crowded with books, Leo Finkle, a rabbinical student in the Yeshivah University. Finkle, after six years of study, was to be ordained in June and had been advised by an acquaintance that he might find it easier to win himself a congregation if he were married. Since he had no present prospects of marriage, after two tormented days of turning it over in his mind, he called in Pinye Salzman, a marriage broker whose two-line advertisement he had read in the *Forward*.

The matchmaker appeared one night out of the dark fourth-floor hallway of the graystone rooming house where Finkle lived, grasping a black, strapped portfolio that had been worn thin with use. Salzman, who had been long in the business, was of slight but dignified build, wearing an old hat, and an overcoat too short and tight for him. He smelled frankly of fish, which he loved to eat, and although he was missing a few teeth, his presence was not displeasing, because of an amiable manner curiously contrasted with mournful eyes. His voice, his lips, his wisp of beard, his bony fingers were animated, but give him a moment of repose and his mild blue eyes revealed a depth of sadness, a characteristic that put Leo a little at ease although the situation, for him, was inherently tense.

He at once informed Salzman why he had asked him to come, explaining that his home was in Cleveland, and that but for his parents, who had married comparatively late in life, he was alone in the world. He had for six years devoted himself almost entirely to his studies, as a result of which, understandably, he had found himself without time for a social life and the company of young women. Therefore he thought it the better part of trial and error—of embarrassing fumbling—to call in an experienced person to advise him on these matters. He remarked in passing that the function of the marriage broker was ancient and honorable, highly approved in the Jewish community, because it made practical the necessary without hindering joy. Moreover, his own parents had been brought together by a match-maker. They had made, if not a financially profitable marriage—since nei-ther had possessed any worldly goods to speak of—at least a successful one in the sense of their everlasting devotion to each other. Salzman listened in embarrassed surprise, sensing a sort of apology. Later, however, he expe-rienced a glow of pride in his work, an emotion that had left him years ago, and he heartily approved of Finkle.

The two went to their business. Leo had led Salzman to the only clear place in the room, a table near a window that overlooked the lamp-lit city. He seated himself at the matchmaker's side but facing him, attempting by an act of will to suppress the unpleasant tickle in his throat. Salzman ea-gerly unstrapped his portfolio and removed a loose rubber band from a thin packet of much-handled cards. As he flipped through them, a gesture and sound that physically hurt Leo, the student pretended not to see and gazed steadfastly out the window. Although it was still February, winter was on its last legs, signs of which he had for the first time in years begun to notice. He now observed the round white moon, moving high in the sky through a cloud menagerie, and watched with half-open mouth as it penetrated a huge hen, and dropped out of her like an egg laying itself. Salzman, though pretending through eyeglasses he had just slipped on, to be engaged in scan-ning the writing on the cards, stole occasional glances at the young man's distinguished face, noting with pleasure the long, severe scholar's nose, brown eyes heavy with learning, sensitive yet ascetic lips, and a certain, almost hollow quality of the dark cheeks. He gazed around at shelves upon shelves of books and let out a soft, contented sigh.

When Leo's eyes fell upon the cards, he counted six spread out in Salzman's hand.

"So few?" he asked in disappointment.

"You wouldn't believe me how much cards I got in my office," Salz-man replied. "The drawers are already filled to the top, so I keep them now in a barrel, but is every girl good for a new rabbi?"

Leo blushed at this, regretting all he had revealed of himself in a cur-riculum vitae he had sent to Salzman. He had thought it best to acquaint him with his strict standards and specifications, but in having done so, felt he had told the marriage broker more than was absolutely necessary.

He hesitantly inquired, "Do you keep photographs of your clients on file?"

"First comes family, amount of dowry, also what kind promises," Salz-man replied, unbuttoning his tight coat and settling himself in the chair. "After comes pictures, rabbi."

"Call me Mr. Finkle. I'm not yet a rabbi."

Salzman said he would, but instead called him doctor, which he changed to rabbi when Leo was not listening too attentively.

Salzman adjusted his horn-rimmed spectacles, gently cleared his throat and read in an eager voice the contents of the top card:

"Sophie P. Twenty-four years. Widow one year. No children.

Educated high school and two years college. Father promises eight thousand dollars. Has wonderful wholesale business. Also real estate. On the mother's side comes teachers, also one actor. Well known on Second Avenue."

Leo gazed up in surprise. "Did you say a widow?"

"A widow don't mean spoiled, rabbi. She lived with her husband maybe four months. He was a sick boy she made a mistake to marry him."

"Marrying a widow has never entered my mind."

"This is because you have no experience. A widow, especially if she is young and healthy like this girl, is a wonderful person to marry. She will be thankful to you the rest of her life. Believe me, if I was looking now for a bride, I would marry a widow."

Leo reflected, then shook his head.

Salzman hunched his shoulders in an almost imperceptible gesture of disappointment. He placed the card down on the wooden table and began to read another:

"Lily H. High school teacher. Regular. Not a substitute. Has savings and new Dodge car. Lived in Paris one year. Father is successful dentist thirty-five years. Interested in professional man. Well Americanized family. Wonderful opportunity."

"I knew her personally," said Salzman. "I wish you could see this girl. She is a doll. Also very intelligent. All day you could talk to her about books and theyater and what not. She also knows current events."

"I don't believe you mentioned her age?"

"Her age?" Salzman said, raising his brows. "Her age is thirty-two years."

Leo said after a while, "I'm afraid that seems a little too old."

Salzman let out a laugh. "So how old are you, rabbi?"

"Twenty-seven."

"So what is the difference, tell me, between twenty-seven and thirty-two? My own wife is seven years older than me. So what did I suffer?— Nothing. If Rothschild's daughter wants to marry you, would you say on account her age, no?"

"Yes," Leo said dryly.

Salzman shook off the no in the yes. "Five years don't mean a thing. I give you my word that when you will live with her for one week you will forget her age. What does it mean five years—that she lived more and knows more than somebody who is younger? On this girl, God bless her, years are not wasted. Each one that it comes makes better the bargain."

"What subject does she teach in high school?"

"Languages. If you heard the way she speaks French, you will think it is music. I am in the business twenty-five years, and I recommend her with my whole heart. Believe me, I know what I'm talking, rabbi."

"What's on the next card?" Leo said abruptly.

Salzman reluctantly turned up the third card:

"Ruth K. Nineteen years. Honor student. Father offers thirteen thousand cash to the right bridegroom. He is a medical doctor. Stomach specialist with marvelous practice. Brother–in–law owns own garment business. Particular people."

Salzman looked as if he had read his trump card.

"Did you say nineteen?" Leo asked with interest.

"On the dot."

"Is she attractive?" He blushed. "Pretty?"

Salzman kissed his finger tips. "A little doll. On this I give you my word. Let me call the father tonight and you will see what means pretty."

But Leo was troubled. "You're sure she's that young?"

"This I am positive. The father will show you the birth certificate."

"Are you positive there isn't something wrong with her?" Leo insisted.

"Who says there is anything wrong?"

"I don't understand why an American girl her age should go to a marriage broker."

A smile spread over Salzman's face.

"So for the same reason you went, she comes."

Leo flushed. "I am pressed for time."

Salzman, realizing he had been tactless, quickly explained. "The father came, not her. He wants she should have the best, so he looks around himself. When we will locate the right boy he will introduce him and encourage. This makes a better marriage than if a young girl without experience takes for herself. I don't have to tell you this."

"But don't you think this young girl believes in love?" Leo spoke uneasily.

Salzman was about to guffaw but caught himself and said soberly, "Love comes with the right person, not before."

Leo parted dry lips but did not speak. Noticing that Salzman had snatched a glance at the next card, he cleverly asked, "How is her health?"

"Perfect," Salzman said, breathing with difficulty. "Of course, she is a little lame on her right foot from an auto accident that it happened to her when she was twelve years, but nobody notices on account she is so brilliant and also beautiful."

Leo got up heavily and went to the window. He felt curiously bitter and upbraided himself for having called in the marriage broker. Finally, he shook his head.

"Why not?" Salzman persited, the pitch of his voice rising.

"Because I detest stomach specialists."

"So what do you care what is his business? After you marry her do you need him? Who says he must come every Friday night in your house?"

Ashamed of the way the talk was going, Leo dismissed Salzman, who went home with heavy, melancholy eyes.

Though he had felt only relief at the marriage broker's departure, Leo was in low spirits the next day. He explained it as arising from Salzman's failure to produce a suitable bride for him. He did not care for his type of clientele. But when Leo found himself hesitating whether to seek out another matchmaker, one more polished than Pinye, he wondered if it could be—his protestations to the contrary, and although he honored his father and mother—that he did not, in essence, care for the matchmaking institution? This thought he quickly put out of mind yet found himself still upset. All day he ran around in the woods—missed an important appointment, forgot to give out his laundry, walked out of a Broadway cafeteria without paying and had to run back with the ticket in his hand; had even not recognized his landlady in the street when she passed with a friend and courteously called out, "A good evening to you, Doctor Finkle." By nightfall, however, he had regained sufficient calm to sink his nose into a book and there found peace from his thoughts.

Almost at once there came a knock on the door. Before Leo could say enter, Salzman, commercial cupid, was standing in the room. His face was gray and meager, his expression hungry, and he looked as if he would expire on his feet. Yet the marriage broker managed, by some trick of the muscles, to display a broad smile.

"So good evening. I am invited?"

Leo nodded, disturbed to see him again, yet unwilling to ask the man to leave.

Beaming still, Salzman laid his portfolio on the table. "Rabbi, I got for you tonight good news."

"I've asked you not to call me rabbi. I'm still a student."

"Your worries are finished. I have for you a first-class bride."

"Leave me in peace concerning this subject." Leo pretended lack of interest.

"The world will dance at your wedding."

"Please, Mr. Salzman, no more."

"But first must come back my strength," Salzman said weakly. He fumbled with the portfolio straps and took out of the leather case an oily paper bag, from which he extracted a hard, seeded roll and a small, smoked white fish. With a quick motion of his hand he stripped the fish out of its skin and began ravenously to chew. "All day in a rush," he muttered.

Leo watched him eat.

"A sliced tomato you have maybe?" Salzman hesitantly inquired.

"No."

The marriage broker shut his eyes and ate. When he had finished he carefully cleaned up the crumbs and rolled up the remains of the fish, in the paper bag. His spectacled eyes roamed the room until he discovered, amid some piles of books, a one-burner gas stove. Lifting his hat he humbly asked, "A glass tea you got, rabbi?"

Conscience-stricken, Leo rose and brewed the tea. He served it with a chunk of lemon and two cubes of lump sugar, delighting Salzman.

After he had drunk his tea, Salzman's strength and good spirits were restored.

"So tell me, rabbi," he said amiably, "you considered some more the three clients I mentioned yesterday?"

"There was no need to consider."

"Why not?"

"None of them suits me."

"What then suits you?"

Leo let it pass because he could give only a confused answer.

Without waiting for a reply, Salzman asked, "You remember this girl I talked to you—the high school teacher?"

"Age thirty-two?"

But, surprisingly, Salzman's face lit in a smile. "Age twenty-nine."

Leo shot him a look. "Reduced from thirty-two?"

"A mistake," Salzman avowed. "I talked today with the dentist. He took me to his safety deposit box and showed me the birth certificate. She was twenty-nine years last August. They made her a party in the mountains where she went for her vacation. When her father spoke to me the first time I forgot to write the age and I told you thirty-two, but now I remember this was a different client, a widow."

"The same one you told me about? I thought she was twenty-four?"

"A different. Am I responsible that the world is filled with widows?"

"No, but I'm not interested in them, nor for that matter, in school teachers."

Salzman pulled his clasped hands to his breast. Looking at the ceiling he devoutly exclaimed, "Yiddishe kinder, what can I say to somebody that he is not interested in high school teachers? So what then you are interested?"

Leo flushed but controlled himself.

"In what else will you be interested," Salzman went on, "if you not interested in this fine girl that she speaks four languages and has personally in the bank ten thousand dollars? Also her father guarantees further twelve thousand. Also she has a new car, wonderful clothes, talks on all subjects, and she will give you a first-class home and children. How near do we come in our life to paradise?"

"If she's so wonderful, why wasn't she married ten years ago?"

"Why?" said Salzman with a heavy laugh. "—Why? Because she is *partikiler*. This is why. She wants the *best*."

Leo was silent, amused at how he had entangled himself. But Salzman had aroused his interest in Lily H., and he began seriously to consider calling on her. When the marriage broker observed how intently Leo's mind was at work on the facts he had supplied, he felt certain they would soon come to an agreement.

Late Saturday afternoon, conscious of Salzman, Leo Finkle walked with Lily Hirschorn along Riverside Drive. He walked briskly and erectly, wearing with distinction the black fedora he had that morning taken with trepidation out of the dusty hat box on his closet shelf, and the heavy black Saturday coat he had thoroughly whisked clean. Leo also owned a walking stick, a present from a distant relative, but quickly put temptation aside and did not use it. Lily, petite and not unpretty, had on something signifying the approach of spring. She was au courant, animatedly, with all sorts of subjects, and he weighed her words and found her surprisingly sound— score another for Salzman, whom he uneasily sensed to be somewhere around, hiding perhaps high in a tree along the street, flashing the lady signals with a pocket mirror; or perhaps a cloven-hoofed Pan, piping nuptial ditties as he danced his invisible way before them, strewing wild buds on the walk and purple grapes in their path, symbolizing fruit of a union, though there was of course still none.

Lily startled Leo by remarking, "I was thinking of Mr. Salzman, a curious figure, wouldn't you say?"

Not certain what to answer, he nodded.

She bravely went on, blushing, "I for one am grateful for his introducing us. Aren't you?"

He courteously replied, "I am."

"I mean," she said with a little laugh—and it was all in good taste, or at least gave the effect of being not in bad— "do you mind that we came together so?"

He was not displeased with her honesty, recognizing that she meant to set the relationship aright, and understanding that it took a certain amount of experience in life, and courage, to want to do it quite that way. One had to have some sort of past to make that kind of beginning.

He said that he did not mind. Salzman's function was traditional and honorable—valuable for what it might achieve, which, he pointed out, was frequently nothing.

Lily agreed with a sigh. They walked on for a while and she said after a long silence, again with a nervous laugh, "Would you mind if I asked you something a little bit personal? Frankly, I find the subject fascinating." Although Leo shrugged, she went on half embarrassedly, "How was it that you came to your calling? I mean was it a sudden passionate inspiration?"

Leo after a time, slowly replied, "I was always interested in the Law."

"You saw revealed in it the presence of the Highest?"

He nodded and changed the subject. "I understand that you spent a little time in Paris, Miss Hirschorn?"

"Oh, did Mr. Salzman tell you, Rabbi Finkle?" Leo winced but she went on, "It was ages ago and almost forgotten. I remember I had to return for my sister's wedding."

And Lily would not be put off. "When," she asked in a trembly voice, "did you become enamored of God?"

He stared at her. Then it came to him that she was talking not about Leo Finkle, but of a total stranger, some mystical figure, perhaps even passionate prophet that Salzman had dreamed up for her—no relation to the living or dead. Leo trembled with rage and weakness. The trickster had obviously sold her a bill of goods, just as he had him, who'd expected to become acquainted with a young lady of twenty-nine, only to behold, the moment he laid eyes upon her strained and anxious face, a woman past thirty-five and aging rapidly. Only his self-control had kept him this long in her presence.

"I am not," he said gravely, "a talented religious person," and in seeking words to go on, found himself possessed by shame and fear. "I think," he said in a strained manner, "that I came to God not because I loved Him, but because I did not."

This confession he spoke harshly because its unexpectedness shook him.

Lily wilted. Leo saw a profusion of loaves of bread go flying like ducks high over his head, not unlike the winged loaves by which he had counted himself to sleep last night. Mercifully, then, it snowed, which he would not put past Salzman's machinations.

He was infuriated with the marriage broker and swore he would throw him out of the room the minute he reappeared. But Salzman did not come that night, and when Leo's anger had subsided, an unaccountable despair grew in its place. At first he thought this was caused by his disappointment in Lily, but before long it became evident that he had involved himself with Salzman without a true knowledge of his own intent. He gradually realized—with an emptiness that seized him with six hands—that he had called in the broker to find him a bride because he was incapable of doing it himself. This terrifying insight he had derived as a result of his meeting and conversation with Lily Hirschorn. Her probing questions had somehow irritated him into revealing—to himself more than her—the true nature of his relationship to God, and from that it had come upon him, with shocking force, that apart from his parents, he had never loved anyone. Or perhaps it went the other way, that he did not love God so well as he might, because he had not loved man. It seemed to Leo that his whole life stood starkly revealed and he saw himself for the first time as he truly was—unloved and loveless. This bitter but somehow not fully unexpected revelation brought him to a point of panic, controlled only by extraordinary effort. He covered his face with his hands and cried.

The week that followed was the worst of his life. He did not eat and lost weight. His beard darkened and grew ragged. He stopped attending seminars and almost never opened a book. He seriously considered leaving the Yeshivah, although he was deeply troubled at the thought of the loss of all his years of study—saw them like pages torn from a book, strewn over the city—and at the devastating effect of this decision upon his parents. But he had lived without knowledge of himself, and never in the Five Books and all the Commentaries—mea culpa—had the truth been revealed to him. He did not know where to turn, and in all this desolating loneliness there was no *to whom*, although he often thought of Lily but not once could bring himself to go downstairs and make the call. He became touchy and irritable, especially with his landlady, who asked him all manner of personal questions; on the other hand, sensing his own disagreeableness, he waylaid her on the stairs and apologized abjectly, until mortified, she ran from him. Out of this, however, he drew the consolation that he was a Jew and that a Jew suffered. But gradually, as the long and terrible week drew to a close, he regained his composure and some idea of purpose in life: to go on as planned. Although he was imperfect, the ideal was not. As for his quest of a bride, the thought of continuing afflicted him with anxiety and heartburn, yet perhaps with this new knowledge of himself he would be more successful than in the past. Perhaps love would now come to him and a bride to that love. And for this sanctified seeking who needed a Salzman?

The marriage broker, a skeleton with haunted eyes, returned that very night. He looked, withal, the picture of frustrated expectancy—as if he had steadfastly waited the week at Miss Lily Hirschorn's side for a telephone call that never came.

Casually coughing, Salzman came immediately to the point: "So how did you like her?"

Leo's anger rose and he could not refrain from chiding the matchmaker: "Why did you lie to me, Salzman?"

Salzman's pale face went dead white, the world had snowed on him.

"Did you not state that she was twenty-nine?" Leo insisted.

"I give you my word—"

"She was thirty-five, if a day. *At least* thirty-five."

"Of this don't be too sure. Her father told me—"

"Never mind. The worst of it was that you lied to her."

"How did I lie to her, tell me?"

"You told her things about me that weren't true. You made me out to be more, consequently less than I am. She had in mind a totally different person, a sort of semi-mystical Wonder Rabbi."

"All I said, you was a religious man."

"I can imagine."

Salzman sighed. "This is my weakness that I have," he confessed. "My wife says to me I shouldn't be a salesman, but when I have two fine people that they would be wonderful to be married, I am so happy that I talk too much." He smiled wanly. "This is why Salzman is a poor man."

Leo's anger left him. "Well, Salzman, I'm afraid that's all."

The marriage broker fastened hungry eyes on him.

"You don't want any more a bride?"

"I do," said Leo, "but I have decided to seek her in a different way. I am no longer interested in an arranged marriage. To be frank, I now admit the necessity of premarital love. That is, I want to be in love with the one I marry."

"Love?" said Salzman, astounded. After a moment he remarked, "For us, our love is our life, not for the ladies. In the ghetto they—"

"I know, I know," said Leo. "I've thought of it often. Love, I have said to myself, should be a by-product of living and worship rather than its own end. Yet for myself I find it necessary to establish the level of my need and fulfill it."

Salzman shrugged but answered, "Listen, rabbi, if you want love, this I can find for you also. I have such beautiful clients that you will love them the minute your eyes will see them."

Leo smiled unhappily. "I'm afraid you don't understand."

But Salzman hastily unstrapped his portfolio and withdrew a manila packet from it.

"Pictures," he said, quickly laying the envelope on the table.

Leo called after him to take the pictures away, but as if on the wings of the wind, Salzman had disappeared.

March came. Leo had returned to his regular routine. Although he felt not quite himself yet—lacked energy—he was making plans for a more active social life. Of course it would cost something, but he was an expert in cutting corners; and when there was no corners left he would make circles rounder. All the while Salzman's pictures had lain on the table, gathering dust. Occasionally as Leo sat studying, or enjoying a cup of tea, his eyes fell on the manila envelope, but he never opened it.

The days went by and no social life to speak of developed with a member of the opposite sex—it was difficult, given the circumstances of his situation. One morning Leo toiled up the stairs to his room and stared out the window at the city. Although the day was bright his view of it was dark. For some time he watched the people in the street below hurrying along and then turned with a heavy heart to his little room. On the table was the packet. With a sudden relentless gesture he tore it open. For a half-hour he stood by the table in a state of excitement, examining the photographs of the ladies Salzman had included. Finally, with a deep sigh he put them down. There were six, of varying degrees of attractiveness, but look at them long enough and they all became Lily Hirschorn: all past their prime, all starved behind bright smiles, not a true personality in the lot. Life, despite their frantic yoohooings, had passed them by; they were pictures in a brief case that stank of fish. After a while, however, as Leo attempted to return the photographs into the envelope, he found in it another, a snapshot of the type taken by a machine for a quarter. He gazed at it a moment and let out a cry.

Her face deeply moved him. Why, he could at first not say. It gave him the impression of youth—spring flowers, yet age—a sense of having been used to the bone, wasted; this came from the eyes, which were hauntingly familiar, yet absolutely strange. He had a vivid impression that he had met her before, but try as he might he could not place her although he could almost recall her name, as if he had read it in her own handwriting. No, this couldn't be; he would have remembered her. It was not, he affirmed, that she had an extraordinary beauty—no, though her face was attractive enough; it was that *something* about her moved him. Feature for feature, even some of the ladies of the photographs could do better; but she leaped forth to his heart—had *lived*, or wanted to—more than just wanted, perhaps regretted how she had lived—had somehow deeply suffered: it could be seen in the depths of those reluctant eyes, and from the way the light enclosed and shone from her, and within her, opening realms of possibility: this was her own. Her he desired. His head ached and eyes narrowed with the intensity of his gazing, then as if an obscure fog had blown up in the mind, he experienced fear of her and was aware that he had received an impression, somehow, of evil. He shuddered, saying softly, it is thus with us all. Leo brewed some tea in a small pot and sat sipping it without sugar, to calm himself. But before he had finished drinking, again with excitement he examined the face and found it good: good for Leo Finkle. Only such a one could understand him and help him seek whatever he was seeking. She might, perhaps, love him. How she had happened to be among the discards in Salzman's barrel he could never guess, but he knew he must urgently go find her.

Leo rushed downstairs, grabbed up the Bronx telephone book, and searched for Salzman's home address. He was not listed, nor was his office. Neither was he in the Manhattan book. But Leo remembered having written down the address on a slip of paper after he had read Salzman's advertisement in the "personals" column of the *Forward*. He ran up to his room and tore through his papers, without luck. It was exasperating. Just when he needed the matchmaker he was nowhere to be found. Fortunately Leo remembered to look in his wallet. There on a card he found his name written and a Bronx address. No phone number was listed, the reason—Leo now recalled—he had originally communicated with Salzman by letter. He got on his coat, put a hat on over his skull cap and hurried to the subway station. All the way to the far end of the Bronx he sat on the edge of his seat. He was more than once tempted to take out the picture and see if the girl's face was as he remembered it, but he refrained, allowing the snapshot to remain in his inside coat pocket, content to have her so close. When the train pulled into the station he was waiting at the door and bolted out. He quickly located the street Salzman had advertised.

The building he sought was less than a block from the subway, but it was not an office building, nor even a loft, nor a store in which one could rent office space. It was a very old tenement house. Leo found Salzman's name in pencil on a soiled tag under the bell and climbed three dark flights to his apartment. When he knocked, the door was opened by a thin, asthmatic, gray-haired woman, in felt slippers.

"Yes?" she said, expecting nothing. She listened without listening. He could have sworn he had seen her, too, before but knew it was an illusion.

"Salzman—does he live here? Pinye Salzman," he said, "the matchmaker?"

She stared at him a long minute. "Of course."

He felt embarrassed. "Is he in?"

"No." Her mouth, though left open, offered nothing more.

"The matter is urgent. Can you tell me where his office is?"

"In the air." She pointed upward.

"You mean he has no office?" Leo asked.

"In his socks."

He peered into the apartment. It was sunless and dingy, one large room divided by a half-open curtain, beyond which he could see a sagging metal bed. The near side of a room was crowded with rickety chairs, old bureaus, a three-legged table, racks of cooking utensils, and all the apparatus of a kitchen. But there was no sign of Salzman or his magic barrel, probably also a figment of the imagination. An odor of frying fish made Leo weak to the knees.

"Where is he?" he insisted. "I've got to see your husband."

At length she answered, "So who knows where he is? Every time he thinks a new thought he runs to a different place. Go home, he will find you."

"Tell him Leo Finkle."

She gave no sign she had heard.

He walked downstairs, depressed.

But Salzman, breathless, stood waiting at his door.

Leo was astounded and overjoyed. "How did you get here before me?"

"I rushed."

"Come inside."

They entered. Leo fixed tea, and a sardine sandwich for Salzman. As they were drinking he reached behind him for the packet of pictures and handed them to the marriage broker.

Salzman put down his glass and said expectantly, "You found somebody you like?"

"Not among these."

The marriage broker turned away.

"Here is the one I want." Leo held forth the snapshot.

Salzman slipped on his glasses and took the picture into his trembling hand. He turned ghastly and let out a groan.

"What's the matter?" cried Leo.

"Excuse me. Was an accident this picture. She isn't for you."

Salzman frantically shoved the manila packet into his portfolio. He thrust the snapshot into his pocket and fled down the stairs.

Leo, after momentary paralysis, gave chase and cornered the marriage broker in the vestibule. The landlady made hysterical outcries but neither of them listened.

"Give me back the picture, Salzman."

"No." The pain in his eyes was terrible.

"Tell me who she is then."

"This I can't tell you. Excuse me."

He made to depart, but Leo, forgetting himself, seized the matchmaker by his tight coat and shook him frenziedly.

"Please," sighed Salzman. *"Please."*

Leo ashamedly let him go. "Tell me who she is," he begged. "It's very important for me to know."

"She is not for you. She is a wild one—wild, without shame. This is not a bride for a rabbi."

"What do you mean wild?"

"Like an animal. Like a dog. For her to be poor was a sin. This is why to me she is dead now."

"In God's name, what do you mean?"

"Her I can't introduce to you," Salzman cried.

"Why are you so excited?"

"Why, he asks," Salzman said, bursting into tears. "This is my baby, my Stella, she should burn in hell."

Leo hurried up to bed and hid under the covers. Under the covers he thought his life through. Although he soon fell asleep he could not sleep her out of his mind. He woke, beating his breast. Though he prayed to be rid of her, his prayers went unanswered. Through days of torment he endlessly struggled not to love her; fearing success, he escaped it. He then concluded to convert her to goodness, himself to God. The idea alternately nauseated and exalted him.

He perhaps did not know that he had come to a final decision until he encountered Salzman in a Broadway cafeteria. He was sitting alone at a rear table, sucking the bony remains of a fish. The marriage broker appeared haggard, and transparent to the point of vanishing.

Salzman looked up at first without recognizing him. Leo had grown a pointed beard and his eyes were weighted with wisdom.

"Salzman," he said, "love has at last come to my heart."

"Who can love from a picture?" mocked the marriage broker.

"It is not impossible."

"If you can love her, then you can love anybody. Let me show you some new clients that they just sent me their photographs. One is a little doll."

"Just her I want," Leo murmured.

"Don't be a fool, doctor. Don't bother with her."

"Put me in touch with her, Salzman," Leo said humbly. "Perhaps I can be of service."

Salzman had stopped eating and Leo understood with emotion that it was now arranged.

Leaving the cafeteria, he was, however, afflicted by a tormenting suspicion that Salzman had planned it all to happen this way.

Leo was informed by letter that she would meet him on a certain corner, and she was there one spring night, waiting under a street lamp. He appeared, carrying a small bouquet of violets and rosebuds. Stella stood by the lamp post, smoking. She wore white with red shoes, which fitted his expectations, although in a troubled moment he had imagined the dress red, and only the shoes white. She waited uneasily and shyly. From afar he saw that her eyes—clearly her father's—were filled with desperate innocence. He pictured, in her, his own redemption. Violins and lit candles revolved in the sky. Leo ran forward with flowers outthrust.

Around the corner, Salzman, leaning against a wall, chanted prayers for the dead.

GABRIEL GARCIA MARQUEZ (b. 1928)

The Woman Who Came at Six O'Clock

Gabriel Garcia Marquez, one of the Latin America's most renowned and influential writiers, was born in Colombia and educated at the University of Bogota. His novels include *One Hundred Years of Solitude* (translated in 1970) and *Chronicle of a Death Foretold* (1981). His stories have been collected in several volumes, including *No One Writes to the Colonel and Other Stories* (1968) and *Innocent Erendira and Other Stories* (1978), in which "The Woman Who Came at Six O'Clock" appeared. Garcia Marquez was awarded the Nobel Prize for Literature in 1982.

The swinging door opened. At that hour there was nobody in José's restaurant. It had just struck six and the man knew that the regular customers wouldn't begin to arrive until six-thirty. His clientele was so conservative and regular that the clock hadn't finished striking six when a woman entered, as on every day at that hour, and sat down on the stool without saying anything. She had an unlighted cigarette tight between her lips.

"Hello, queen," José said when he saw her sit down. Then he went to the other end of the counter, wiping the streaked surface with a dry rag. Whenever anyone came into the restaurant José did the same thing. Even with the woman, with whom he'd almost come to acquire a degree of intimacy, the fat and ruddy restaurant owner put on his daily comedy of a hard-working man. He spoke from the other end of the counter.

"What do you want today?" he said.

"First of all I want to teach you how to be a gentleman," the woman said. She was sitting at the end of the stools, her elbows on the counter, the extinguished cigarette between her lips. When she spoke, she tightened her mouth so that José would notice the unlighted cigarette.

"I didn't notice," José said.

"You still haven't learned to notice anything," said the woman.

The man left the cloth on the counter, walked to the dark cupboards which smelled of tar and dusty wood, and came back immediately with the matches. The woman leaned over to get the light that was burning in the man's rustic, hairy hands. José saw the woman's lush hair, all greased with cheap, thick Vaseline. He saw her uncovered shoulder above the flowered brassiere. He saw the beginning of her twilight breast when the woman raised her head, the lighted butt between her lips now.

"You're beautiful tonight, queen," José said.

"Stop your nonsense," the woman said. "Don't think that's going to help me pay you."

"That's not what I meant, queen," José said. "I'll bet your lunch didn't agree with you today."

The woman sucked in the first drag of thick smoke, crossed her arms, her elbows still on the counter, and remained looking at the street through the wide restaurant window. She had a melancholy expression. A bored and vulgar melancholy.

"I'll fix you a good steak," José said.

"I still haven't got any money," the woman said.

"You haven't had any money for three months and I always fix you something good," José said.

"Today's different," said the woman somberly, still looking out at the street.

"Every day's the same," José said. "Every day the clock says six, then you come in and say you're hungry as a dog and then I fix you something good. The only difference is this: today you didn't say you were as hungry as a dog but that today is different."

"And it's true," the woman said. She turned to look at the man, who was at the other end of the counter checking the refrigerator. She examined him for two or three seconds. Then she looked at the clock over the cupboard. It was three minutes after six. "It's true, José. Today is different," she said. She let the smoke out and kept on talking with crisp, impassioned words. "I didn't come at six today, that's why it's different, José."

The man looked at the clock.

"I'll cut off my arm if that clock is one minute slow," he said.

"That's not it, José. I didn't come at six o'clock today," the woman said.

"It just struck six, queen," José said. "When you came in it was just finishing."

"I've got a quarter of an hour that says I've been here," the woman said.

José went over to where she was. He put his great puffy face up to the woman while he tugged on one of his eyelids with his index finger.

"Blow on me here," he said.

The woman threw her head back. She was serious, annoyed, softened, beautified by a cloud of sadness and fatigue.

"Stop your foolishness, José. You know I haven't had a drink for six months."

"Tell it to somebody else," he said, "not to me. I'll bet you've had a pint or two at least."

"I had a couple of drinks with a friend," she said.

"Oh, now I understand," José said.

"There's nothing to understand," the woman said. "I've been here for a quarter of an hour."

The man shrugged his shoulders.

"Well, if that's the way you want it, you've got a quarter of an hour that says you've been here," he said. "After all, what difference does it make, ten minutes this way, ten minutes that way?"

"It makes a difference, José," the woman said. And she stretched her arms over the glass counter with an air of careless abandon. She said: "And it isn't that I wanted it that way; it's just that I've been here for a quarter of an hour." She looked at the clock again and corrected herself: "What am I saying—it's been twenty minutes."

"O.K., queen," the man said. "I'd give you a whole day and the night that goes with it just to see you happy."

During all this time José had been moving about behind the counter, changing things, taking something from one place and putting it in another. He was playing his role.

"I want to see you happy," he repeated. He stopped suddenly, turning to where the woman was. "Do you know that I love you very much?"

The woman looked at him coldly.

"Ye-e-es . . .? What a discovery, José. Do you think I'd go with you even for a million pesos?"

"I didn't mean that, queen," José said. "I repeat, I bet your lunch didn't agree with you."

"That's not why I said it," the woman said. And her voice became less indolent. "No woman could stand a weight like yours, even for a million pesos."

José blushed. He turned his back to the woman and began to dust the bottles on the shelves. He spoke without turning his head.

"You're unbearable today, queen. I think the best thing is for you to eat your steak and go home to bed."

"I'm not hungry," the woman said. She stayed looking out at the street again, watching the passers-by of the dusking city. For an instant there was a murky silence in the restaurant. A peacefulness broken only by José's fiddling about in the cupboard. Suddenly the woman stopped looking out into the street and spoke with a tender, soft, different voice.

"Do you really love me, Pepillo?"

"I do," José said dryly, not looking at her.

"In spite of what I've said to you?" the woman asked.

"What did you say to me?" José asked, still without any inflection in his voice, still without looking at her.

"That business about a million pesos," the woman said.

"I'd already forgotten," José said.

"So do you love me?" the woman asked.

"Yes," said José.

There was a pause. José kept moving about, his face turned toward the cabinets, still not looking at the woman. She blew out another mouthful of smoke, rested her bust on the counter, and then, cautiously and roguishly, biting her tongue before saying it, as if speaking on tiptoe:

"Even if you didn't go to bed with me?" she asked.

And only then did José turn to look at her.

"I love you so much that I wouldn't go to bed with you," he said. Then he walked over to where she was. He stood looking into her face, his powerful arms leaning on the counter in front of her, looking into her eyes. He said: "I love you so much that every night I'd kill the man who goes with you."

At the first instant the woman seemed perplexed. Then she looked at the man attentively, with a wavering expression of compassion and mockery. Then she had a moment of brief disconcerted silence. And then she laughed noisily.

"You're jealous, José. That's wild, you're jealous!"

José blushed again with frank, almost shameful timidity, as might have happened to a child who'd revealed all his secrets all of a sudden. He said:

"This afternoon you don't seem to understand anything, queen." And he wiped himself with the rag. He said:

"This bad life is brutalizing you."

But now the woman had changed her expression.

"So, then," she said. And she looked into his eyes again, with a strange glow in her look, confused and challenging at the same time.

"So you're not jealous."

"In a way I am," José said. "But it's not the way you think."

He loosened his collar and continued wiping himself, drying his throat with the cloth.

"So?" the woman asked.

"The fact is I love you so much that I don't like your doing it," José said.

"What?" the woman asked.

"This business of going with a different man every day," José said.

"Would you really kill him to stop him from going with me?" the woman asked.

"Not to stop him from going with you, no," José said. "I'd kill him because he *went* with you."

"It's the same thing," the woman said.

The conversation had reached an exciting density. The woman was speaking in a soft, low, fascinated voice. Her face was almost stuck up against the man's healthy, peaceful face, as he stood motionless, as if bewitched by the vapor of the words.

"That's true," José said.

"So," the woman said, and reached out her hand to stroke the man's rough arm. With the other she tossed away her butt. "So you're capable of killing a man?"

"For what I told you, yes," José said. And his voice took on an almost dramatic stress.

The woman broke into convulsive laughter, with an obvious mocking intent.

"How awful, José. How awful," she said, still laughing. "José killing a man. Who would have known that behind the fat and sanctimonious man who never makes me pay, who cooks me a steak every day and has fun talking to me until I find a man, there lurks a murderer. How awful, José! You scare me!"

José was confused. Maybe he felt a little indignation. Maybe, when the woman started laughing, he felt defrauded.

"You're drunk, silly," he said. "Go get some sleep. You don't even feel like eating anything."

But the woman had stopped laughing now and was serious again, pensive, leaning on the counter. She watched the man go away. She saw him open the refrigerator and close it again without taking anything out. Then she saw him move to the other end of the counter. She watched him polish the shining glass, the same as in the beginning. Then the woman spoke again with the tender and soft tone of when she said: "Do you really love me, Pepillo?"

"José," she said.

The man didn't look at her.

"José!"

"Go home and sleep," José said. "And take a bath before you go to bed so you can sleep it off."

"Seriously, José," the woman said. "I'm not drunk."

"Then you've turned stupid," José said.

"Come here, I've got to talk to you," the woman said.

The man came over stumbling, halfway between pleasure and mistrust.

"Come closer!"

He stood in front of the woman again. She leaned forward, grabbed him by the hair, but with a gesture of obvious tenderness.

"Tell me again what you said at the start," she said.

"What do you mean?" José asked. He was trying to look at her with his head turned away, held by the hair.

"That you'd kill a man who went to bed with me," the woman said.

"I'd kill a man who went to bed with you, queen. That's right," José said.

The woman let him go.

"In that case you'd defend me if I killed him, right?" she asked affirmatively, pushing José's enormous pig head with a movement of brutal coquettishness. The man didn't answer anything. He smiled.

"Answer me, José," the woman said. "Would you defend me if I killed him?"

"That depends," José said. "You know it's not as easy as you say."

"The police wouldn't believe anyone more than you," the woman said.

José smiled, honored, satisfied. The woman leaned over toward him again, over the counter.

"It's true, José. I'm willing to bet that you've never told a lie in your life," she said.

"You won't get anywhere this way," José said.

"Just the same," the woman said. "The police know you and they'll believe anything without asking you twice."

José began pounding on the counter opposite her, not knowing what to say. The woman looked out at the street again. Then she looked at the clock and modified the tone of her voice, as if she were interested in finishing the conversation before the first customers arrived.

"Would you tell a lie for me, José?" she asked. "Seriously."

And then José looked at her again, sharply, deeply, as if a tremendous idea had come pounding up in his head. An idea that had entered through one ear, spun about for a moment, vague, confused, and gone out through the other, leaving behind only a warm vestige of terror.

"What have you got yourself into, queen?" José asked. He leaned forward, his arms folded over the counter again. The woman caught the strong and ammonia-smelling vapor of his breathing, which had become difficult because of the pressure that the counter was exercising on the man's stomach.

"This is really serious, queen. What have you got yourself into?" he asked.

The woman made her head spin in the opposite direction.

"Nothing," she said. "I was just talking to amuse myself."

Then she looked at him again.

"Do you know you may not have to kill anybody?"

"I never thought about killing anybody," José said, distressed.

"No, man," the woman said. "I mean nobody goes to bed with me."

"Oh!" José said. "Now you're talking straight out. I always thought you had no need to prowl around. I'll make a bet that if you drop all this I'll give you the biggest steak I've got every day, free."

"Thank you, José," the woman said. "But that's not why. It's because I *can't* go to bed with anyone any more."

"You're getting things all confused again," José said. He was becoming impatient.

"I'm not getting anything confused," the woman said. She stretched out on the seat and José saw her flat, sad breasts underneath her brassiere.

"Tomorrow I'm going away and I promise you I won't come back and bother you ever again. I promise you I'll never go to bed with anyone."

"Where'd you pick up that fever?" José asked.

"I decided just a minute ago," the woman said. "Just a minute ago I realized it's a dirty business."

José grabbed the cloth again and started to clean the glass in front of her. He spoke without looking at her.

He said:

"Of course, the way you do it it's a dirty business. You should have known that a long time ago."

"I was getting to know it a long time ago," the woman said, "but I was only convinced of it just a little while ago. Men disgust me."

José smiled. He raised his head to look at her, still smiling, but he saw her concentrated, perplexed, talking with her shoulders raised, twirling on the stool with a taciturn expression, her face gilded by premature autumnal grain.

"Don't you think they ought to lay off a woman who kills a man because after she's been with him she feels disgust with him and everyone who's been with her?"

"There's no reason to go that far," José said, moved, a thread of pity in his voice.

"What if the woman tells the man he disgusts her while she watches him get dressed because she remembers that she's been rolling around with him all afternoon and feels that neither soap nor sponge can get his smell off her?"

"That all goes away, queen," José said, a little indifferent now, polishing the counter. "There's no reason to kill him. Just let him go."

But the woman kept on talking, and her voice was a uniform, flowing, passionate current.

"But what if the woman tells him he disgusts her and the man stops getting dressed and runs over to her again, kisses her again, does . . .?"

"No decent man would ever do that," José says.

"What if he does?" the woman asks, with exasperating anxiety. "What if the man isn't decent and does it and then the woman feels that he disgusts her so much that she could die, and she knows that the only way to end it all is to stick a knife in under him?"

"That's terrible," José said. "Luckily there's no man who would do what you say."

"Well," the woman said, completely exasperated now. "What if he did? Suppose he did."

"In any case it's not that bad," José said. He kept on cleaning the counter without changing position, less intent on the conversation now.

The woman pounded the counter with her knuckles. She became affirmative, emphatic.

"You're a savage, José," she said. "You don't understand anything." She grabbed him firmly by the sleeve. "Come on, tell me that the woman should kill him."

"O.K.," José said with a conciliatory bias. "It's all probably just the way you say it is."

"Isn't that self-defense?" the woman asked, grabbing him by the sleeve.

Then José gave her a lukewarm and pleasant look.

"Almost, almost," he said. And he winked at her, with an expression that was at the same time a cordial comprehension and a fearful compromise of complicity. But the woman was serious. She let go of him.

"Would you tell a lie to defend a woman who does that?" she asked.

"That depends," said José.

"Depends on what?" the woman asked.

"Depends on the woman," said José.

"Suppose it's a woman you love a lot," the woman said. "Not to be with her, but like you say, you love her a lot."

"O.K., anything you say, queen," José said, relaxed, bored.

He'd gone off again. He'd looked at the clock. He'd seen that it was going on half-past six. He'd thought that in a few minutes the restaurant would be filling up with people and maybe that was why he began to polish the glass with greater effort, looking at the street through the window. The woman stayed on her stool, silent, concentrating, watching the man's movements with an air of declining sadness. Watching him as a lamp about to go out might have looked at a man. Suddenly, without reacting, she spoke again with the unctuous voice of servitude.

"José!"

The man looked at her with a thick, sad tenderness, like a maternal ox. He didn't look at her to hear her, just to look at her, to know that she was there, waiting for a look that had no reason to be one of protection or solidarity. Just the look of a plaything.

"I told you I was leaving tomorrow and you didn't say anything," the woman said.

"Yes," José said. "You didn't tell me where."

"Out there," the woman said. "Where there aren't any men who want to sleep with somebody."

José smiled again.

"Are you really going away?" he asked, as if becoming aware of life, quickly changing the expression on his face.

"That depends on you," the woman said. "If you know enough to say what time I got here, I'll go away tomorrow and I'll never get mixed up in this again. Would you like that?"

José gave an affirmative nod, smiling and concrete. The woman leaned over to where he was.

"If I come back here someday I'll get jealous when I find another woman talking to you, at this time and on this same stool."

"If you come back here you'll have to bring me something," José said.

"I promise you that I'll look everywhere for the tame bear, bring him to you," the woman said.

José smiled and waved the cloth through the air that separated him from the woman, as if he were cleaning an invisible pane of glass. The woman smiled too, with an expression of cordiality and coquetry now. Then the man went away, polishing the glass to the other end of the counter.

"What, then?" José said without looking at her.

"Will you really tell anyone who asks you that I got here at a quarter to six?" the woman said.

"What for?" José said, still without looking at her now, as if he had barely heard her.

"That doesn't matter," the woman said. "The thing is that you do it."

José then saw the first customer come in through the swinging door and walk over to a corner table. He looked at the clock. It was six-thirty on the dot.

"O.K., queen," he said distractedly. "Anything you say. I always do whatever you want."

"Well," the woman said. "Start cooking my steak, then."

The man went to the refrigerator, took out a plate with a piece of meat on it, and left it on the table. Then he lighted the stove.

"I'm going to cook you a good farewell steak, queen," he said.

"Thank you, Pepillo," the woman said.

She remained thoughtful as if suddenly she had become sunken in a strange subworld peopled with muddy, unknown forms. Across the counter she couldn't hear the noise that the raw meat made when it fell into the burning grease. Afterward she didn't hear the dry and bubbling crackle as José turned the flank over in the frying pan and the succulent smell of the marinated meat by measured moments saturated the air of the restaurant. She remained like that, concentrated, reconcentrated, until she raised her head again, blinking as if she were coming back out of a momentary death. Then she saw the man beside the stove, lighted up by the happy, rising fire.

"Pepillo."

"What!"

"What are you thinking about?" the woman asked.

"I was wondering whether you could find the little windup bear some-place," José said.

"Of course I can," the woman said. "But what I want is for you to give me everything I asked for as a going-away present."

José looked at her from the stove.

"How often have I got to tell you?" he said. "Do you want something besides the best steak I've got?"

"Yes," the woman said.

"What is it?" José asked.

"I want another quarter of an hour."

José drew back and looked at the clock. Then he looked at the customer, who was still silent, waiting in the corner, and finally at the meat roasting in the pan. Only then did he speak.

"I really don't understand, queen," he said.

"Don't be foolish, José," the woman said. "Just remember that I've been here since five-thirty."

CARSON MCCULLERS (1917–1967)

The Sojourner

Carson McCullers was born in Georgia and studied writing at Columbia University. She achieved fame at the age of twenty-three with her novel *The Heart is a Lonely Hunter* (1940). *The Member of the Wedding* (1946) was successful both as a novel and as a play (adapted for the theater by McCullers herself). "The Sojourner" appeared in *The Ballad of the Sad Cafe and Other Stories* (1951).

The twilight border between sleep and waking was a Roman one this morning; splashing fountains and arched, narrow streets, the golden lavish city of blossoms and age-soft stone. Sometimes in this semi-consciousness he sojourned again in Paris, or war German rubble, or Swiss skiing and a snow hotel. Sometimes, also, in a fallow Georgia field at hunting dawn. Rome it was this morning in the yearless region of dreams.

John Ferris awoke in a room in a New York hotel. He had the feeling that something unpleasant was awaiting him—what it was, he did not know. The feeling, submerged by matinal necessities, lingered even after he had dressed and gone downstairs. It was a cloudless autumn day and the pale sunlight sliced between the pastel skyscrapers. Ferris went into the next-door drugstore and sat at the end booth next to the window glass that overlooked the sidewalk. He ordered an American breakfast with scrambled eggs and sausage.

Ferris had come from Paris to his father's funeral which had taken place the week before in his home town in Georgia. The shock of death had made him aware of youth already passed. His hair was receding and the veins in his now naked temples were pulsing and prominent and his body was spare except for an incipient belly bulge. Ferris had loved his father and the bond between them had once been extraordinarily close—but the years had somehow unraveled this filial devotion; the death, expected for a long time, had left him with an unforeseen dismay. He had stayed as long as possible to be near his mother and brothers at home. His plane for Paris was to leave the next morning.

Ferris pulled out his address book to verify a number. He turned the pages with growing attentiveness. Names and addresses from New York, the capitals of Europe, a few faint ones from his home state in the South. Faded, printed names, sprawled drunken ones. Betty Wills: a random love, married now. Charlie Williams: wounded in the Hürtgen Forest, unheard of since. Grand old Williams—did he live or die? Don Walker: a B.T.O. in television, getting rich. Henry Green: hit the skids after the war, in a sanitarium now, they say. Cozie Hall: he had heard that she was dead. Heedless, laughing Cozie—it was strange to think that she too, silly girl, could die. As Ferris closed the address book, he suffered a sense of hazard, transience, almost of fear.

It was then that his body jerked suddenly. He was staring out of the window when there, on the sidewalk, passing by, was his ex-wife. Elizabeth passed quite close to him, walking slowly. He could not understand the wild quiver of his heart, nor the following sense of recklessness and grace that lingered after she was gone.

Quickly Ferris paid his check and rushed out to the sidewalk. Elizabeth stood on the corner waiting to cross Fifth Avenue. He hurried toward her meaning to speak, but the lights changed and she crossed the street before he reached her. Ferris followed. On the other side he could easily have overtaken her, but he found himself lagging unaccountably. Her fair brown hair was plainly rolled, and as he watched her Ferris recalled that once his father had remarked that Elizabeth had a 'beautiful carriage.' She turned at the next corner and Ferris followed, although by now his intention to overtake her had disappeared. Ferris questioned the bodily disturbance that the sight of Elizabeth aroused in him, the dampness of his hands, the hard heart-strokes.

It was eight years since Ferris had last seen his ex-wife. He knew that long ago she had married again. And there were children. During recent years he had seldom thought of her. But at first, after the divorce, the loss had almost destroyed him. Then after the anodyne of time, he had loved again, and then again, Jeannine, she was now. Certainly his love for his ex-wife was long since past. So why the unhinged body, the shaken mind? He knew only that his clouded heart was oddly dissonant with the sunny, candid autumn day. Ferris wheeled suddenly and, walking with long strides, almost running, hurried back to the hotel.

Ferris poured himself a drink, although it was not yet eleven o'clock. He sprawled out in an armchair like a man exhausted, nursing his glass of bourbon and water. He had a full day ahead of him as he was leaving by plane the next morning for Paris. He checked over his obligations: take luggage to Air France, lunch with his boss, buy shoes and an overcoat. And something—wasn't there something else? Ferris finished his drink and opened the telephone directory.

His decision to call his ex-wife was impulsive. The number was under Bailey, the husband's name, and he called before he had much time for self-debate. He and Elizabeth had exchanged cards at Christmastime, and Ferris had sent a carving set when he received the announcement of her wedding. There was no reason *not* to call. But as he waited, listening to the ring at the other end, misgiving fretted him.

Elizabeth answered; her familiar voice was a fresh shock to him. Twice he had to repeat his name, but when he was identified, she sounded glad. He explained he was only in town for that day. They had a theater engagement, she said—but she wondered if he would come by for an early dinner. Ferris said he would be delighted.

As he went from one engagement to another, he was still bothered at odd moments by the feeling that something necessary was forgotten. Ferris bathed and changed in the late afternoon, often thinking about Jeannine:

he would be with her the following night. 'Jeannine,' he would say, 'I happened to run into my ex-wife when I was in New York. Had dinner with her. And her husband, of course. It was strange seeing her after all these years.'

Elizabeth lived in the East Fifties, and as Ferris taxied uptown he glimpsed at intersections the lingering sunset, but by the time he reached his destination it was already autumn dark. The place was a building with a marquee and a doorman, and the apartment was on the seventh floor.

'Come in, Mr. Ferris.'

Braced for Elizabeth or even the unimagined husband, Ferris was astonished by the freckled red-haired child; he had known of the children, but his mind had failed somehow to acknowledge them. Surprise made him step back awkwardly.

'This is our apartment,' the child said politely. 'Aren't you Mr. Ferris? I'm Billy. Come in.'

In the living room beyond the hall, the husband provided another surprise; he too had not been acknowledged emotionally. Bailey was a lumbering red-haired man with a deliberate manner. He rose and extended a welcoming hand.

'I'm Bill Bailey. Glad to see you. Elizabeth will be in, in a minute. She's finishing dressing.'

The last words struck a gliding series of vibrations, memories of the other years. Fair Elizabeth, rosy and naked before her bath. Half-dressed before the mirror of her dressing table, brushing her fine, chestnut hair. Sweet, casual intimacy, the soft-fleshed loveliness indisputably possessed. Ferris shrank from the unbidden memories and compelled himself to meet Bill Bailey's gaze.

'Billy, will you please bring that tray of drinks from the kitchen table?'

The child obeyed promptly, and when he was gone Ferris remarked conversationally, 'Fine boy you have there.'

'We think so.'

Flat silence until the child returned with a tray of glasses and a cocktail shaker of Martinis. With the priming drinks they pumped up conversation: Russia, they spoke of, and the New York rain-making, and the apartment situation in Manhattan and Paris.

'Mr. Ferris is flying all the way across the ocean tomorrow,' Bailey said to the little boy who was perched on the arm of his chair, quiet and well behaved. 'I bet you would like to be a stowaway in his suitcase.'

Billy pushed back his limp bangs. 'I want to fly in an airplane and be a newspaperman like Mr. Ferris.' He added with sudden assurance, 'That's what I would like to do when I am big.'

Bailey said, 'I thought you wanted to be a doctor.'

'I do!' said Billy. 'I would like to be both. I want to be a atom-bomb scientist too.'

Elizabeth came in carrying in her arms a baby girl.

'Oh, John!' she said. She settled the baby in the father's lap. 'It's grand to see you. I'm awfully glad you could come.'

The little girl sat demurely on Bailey's knees. She wore a pale pink crêpe de Chine frock, smocked around the yoke with rose, and a matching silk hair ribbon tying back her pale soft curls. Her skin was summer tanned and her brown eyes flecked with gold and laughing. When she reached up and fingered her father's horn-rimmed glasses, he took them off and let her look through them a moment. 'How's my old Candy?'

Elizabeth was very beautiful, more beautiful perhaps than he had ever realized. Her straight clean hair was shining. Her face was softer, glowing and serene. It was a madonna loveliness, dependent on the family ambiance.

'You've hardly changed at all,' Elizabeth said, 'but it has been a long time.'

'Eight years.' His hand touched his thinning hair self-consciously while further amenities were exchanged.

Ferris felt himself suddenly a spectator—an interloper among these Baileys. Why had he come? He suffered. His own life seemed so solitary, a fragile column supporting nothing amidst the wreckage of the years. He felt he could not bear much longer to stay in the family room.

He glanced at his watch. 'You're going to the theater?'

'It's a shame,' Elizabeth said, 'but we've had this engagement for more than a month. But surely, John, you'll be staying home one of these days before long. You're not going to be an expatriate, are you?'

'Expatriate,' Ferris repeated. 'I don't much like the word.'

'What's a better word?' she asked.

He thought for a moment. 'Sojourner might do.'

Ferris glanced again at his watch, and again Elizabeth apologized. 'If only we had known ahead of time—'

'I just had this day in town. I came home unexpectedly. You see, Papa died last week.'

'Papa Ferris is dead?'

'Yes, at Johns Hopkins. He had been sick there nearly a year. The funeral was down home in Georgia.'

'Oh, I'm so sorry, John. Papa Ferris was always one of my favorite people.'

The little boy moved from behind the chair so that he could look into his mother's face. He asked, 'Who is dead?'

Ferris was oblivious to apprehension; he was thinking of his father's death. He saw again the outstretched body on the quilted silk within the coffin. The corpse flesh was bizarrely rouged and the familiar hands lay massive and joined above a spread of funeral roses. The memory closed and Ferris awakened to Elizabeth's calm voice.

'Mr. Ferris' father, Billy. A really grand person. Somebody you didn't know.'

'But why did you call him *Papa* Ferris?'

Bailey and Elizabeth exchanged a trapped look. It was Bailey who answered the questioning child. 'A long time ago,' he said, 'your mother and Mr. Ferris were once married. Before you were born—a long time ago.'

'Mr. Ferris?'

The little boy stared at Ferris, amazed and unbelieving. And Ferris' eyes, as he returned the gaze, were somehow unbelieving too. Was it indeed true that at one time he had called this stranger, Elizabeth, Little Butterduck during nights of love, that they had lived together, shared perhaps a thousand days and nights and—finally—endured in the misery of sudden solitude the fiber by fiber (jealousy, alcohol and money quarrels) destruction of the fabric of married love.

Bailey said to the children, 'It's somebody's suppertime. Come on now.'

'But Daddy! Mama and Mr. Ferris—I—'

Billy's everlasting eyes—perplexed and with a glimmer of hostility—reminded Ferris of the gaze of another child. It was the young son of Jeannine—a boy of seven with a shadowed little face and knobby knees whom Ferris avoided and usually forgot.

'Quick march!' Bailey gently turned Billy toward the door. 'Say good night now, son.'

'Good night, Mr. Ferris.' He added resentfully, 'I thought I was staying up for the cake.'

'You can come in afterward for the cake,' Elizabeth said. 'Run along now with Daddy for your supper.'

Ferris and Elizabeth were alone. The weight of the situation descended on those first moments of silence. Ferris asked permission to pour himself another drink and Elizabeth set the cocktail shaker on the table at his side. He looked at the grand piano and noticed the music on the rack.

'Do you still play as beautifully as you used to?'

'I still enjoy it.'

'Please play, Elizabeth.'

Elizabeth arose immediately. Her readiness to perform when asked had always been one of her amiabilities; she never hung back, apologized. Now as she approached the piano there was the added readiness of relief.

She began with a Bach prelude and fugue. The prelude was as gaily iridescent as a prism in a morning room. The first voice of the fugue, an announcement pure and solitary, was repeated intermingling with a second voice, and again repeated within an elaborated frame, the multiple music, horizontal and serene, flowed with unhurried majesty. The principal melody was woven with two other voices, embellished with countless ingenuities—now dominant, again submerged, it had the sublimity of a single thing that does not fear surrender to the whole. Toward the end, the density of the material gathered for the last enriched insistence on the dominant first motif and with a chorded final statement the fugue ended. Ferris rested his head on the chair back and closed his eyes. In the following silence a clear, high voice came from the room down the hall.

'Daddy, how *could* Mama and Mr. Ferris—' A door was closed.

The piano began again—what was this music? Unplaced, familiar, the limpid melody had lain a long while dormant in his heart. Now it spoke to him of another time, another place—it was the music Elizabeth used to play. The delicate air summoned a wilderness of memory. Ferris was lost in the riot of past longings, conflicts, ambivalent desires. Strange that the music, catalyst for this tumultuous anarchy, was so serene and clear. The singing melody was broken off by the appearance of the maid.

'Miz Bailey, dinner is out on the table now.'

Even after Ferris was seated at the table between his host and hostess, the unfinished music still overcast his mood. He was a little drunk.

'*L'improvisation de la vie humaine*,' he said. 'There's nothing that makes you so aware of the improvisation of human existence as a song unfinished. Or an old address book.'

'Address book?' repeated Bailey. Then he stopped, noncommittal and polite.

'You're still the same old boy, Johnny,' Elizabeth said with a trace of the old tenderness.

It was a Southern dinner that evening, and the dishes were his old favorites. They had fried chicken and corn pudding and rich, glazed candied sweet potatoes. During the meal Elizabeth kept alive a conversation when the silences were overlong. And it came about that Ferris was led to speak of Jeannine.

'I first knew Jeannine last autumn—about this time of the year—in Italy. She's a singer and she had an engagement in Rome. I expect we will be married soon.'

The words seemed so true, inevitable, that Ferris did not at first acknowledge to himself the lie. He and Jeannine had never in that year spoken of marriage. And indeed, she was still married—to a White Russian money-changer in Paris from whom she had been separated for five years. But it was too late to correct the lie. Already Elizabeth was saying: 'This really makes me glad to know. Congratulations, Johnny.'

He tried to make amends with truth. 'The Roman autumn is so beautiful. Balmy and blossoming.' He added, 'Jeannine has a little boy of six. A curious trilingual little fellow. We go to the Tuileries sometimes.'

A lie again. He had taken the boy once to the gardens. The sallow foreign child in shorts that bared his spindly legs had sailed his boat in the concrete pond and ridden the pony. The child had wanted to go in to the puppet show. But there was not time, for Ferris had an engagement at the Scribe Hotel. He had promised they would go to the guignol another afternoon. Only once had he taken Valentin to the Tuileries.

There was a stir. The maid brought in a white-frosted cake with pink candles. The children entered in their night clothes. Ferris still did not understand.

'Happy birthday, John,' Elizabeth said. 'Blow out the candles.'

Ferris recognized his birthday date. The candles blew out lingeringly and there was the smell of burning wax. Ferris was thirty-eight years old. The veins in his temples darkened and pulsed visibly.

'It's time you started for the theater.'

Ferris thanked Elizabeth for the birthday dinner and said the appropriate good-byes. The whole family saw him to the door.

A high, thin moon shone above the jagged, dark skyscrapers. The streets were windy, cold. Ferris hurried to Third Avenue and hailed a cab. He gazed at the nocturnal city with the deliberate attentiveness of departure and perhaps farewell. He was alone. He longed for flighttime and the coming journey.

The next day he looked down on the city from the air, burnished in sunlight, toylike, precise. Then America was left behind and there was only the Atlantic and the distant European shore. The ocean was milky pale and placid beneath the clouds. Ferris dozed most of the day. Toward dark he was thinking of Elizabeth and the visit of the previous evening. He thought of Elizabeth among her family with longing, gentle envy and inexplicable regret. He sought the melody, the unfinished air, that had so moved him. The cadence, some unrelated tones, were all that remained; the melody itself evaded him. He had found instead the first voice of the fugue that Elizabeth had played—it came to him, inverted mockingly and in a minor key. Suspended above the ocean the anxieties of transience and solitude no longer troubled him and he thought of his father's death with equanimity. During the dinner hour the plane reached the shore of France.

At midnight Ferris was in a taxi crossing Paris. It was a clouded night and mist wreathed the lights of the Place de la Concorde. The midnight bistros gleamed on the wet pavements. As always after a transocean flight the change of continents was too sudden. New York at morning, this midnight Paris. Ferris glimpsed the disorder of his life: the succession of cities, of transitory loves; and time, the sinister glissando of the years, time always.

'Vite! Vite!' he called in terror. 'Dépêchez-vous.'

Valentin opened the door to him. The little boy wore pajamas and an outgrown red robe. His grey eyes were shadowed and, as Ferris passed into the flat, they flickered momentarily.

'J'attends Maman.'

Jeannine was singing in a night club. She would not be home before another hour. Valentin returned to a drawing, squatting with his crayons over the paper on the floor. Ferris looked down at the drawing—it was a banjo player with notes and wavy lines inside a comic-strip balloon.

'We will go again to the Tuileries.'

The child looked up and Ferris drew him closer to his knees. The melody, the unfinished music that Elizabeth had played, came to him suddenly. Unsought, the load of memory jettisoned—this time bringing only recognition and sudden joy.

'Monsieur Jean,' the child said, 'did you see him?'

Confused, Ferris thought only of another child—the freckled, family-loved boy. 'See who, Valentin?'

'Your dead papa in Georgia.' The child added, 'Was he okay?'

Ferris spoke with rapid urgency: 'We will go often to the Tuileries. Ride the pony and we will go into the guignol. We will see the puppet show and never be in a hurry any more.'

'Monsieur Jean,' Valentin said. 'The guignol is now closed.'

Again, the terror the acknowledgment of wasted years and death. Valentin, responsive and confident, still nestled in his arms. His cheek touched the soft cheek and felt the brush of the delicate eyelashes. With inner desperation he pressed the child close—as though an emotion as protean as his love could dominate the pulse of time.

JAMES ALAN MCPHERSON (b. 1943)

Elbow Room

James Alan McPherson was born in Savannah, Georgia, and received a law degree from Harvard University. His first collection of stories, *Hue and Cry,* appeared in 1969. "Elbow Room" is the title story from a collection which was awarded the Pulitzer Prize in 1977.

> "Boone's genius was to recognize the difficulty as neither material nor political but one purely moral and aesthetic."
> —*"The Discovery of Kentucky"*
> WILLIAM CARLOS WILLIAMS

Narrator is unmanageable. Demonstrates a disregard for form bordering on the paranoid. Questioned closely, he declares himself the open enemy of conventional narrative categories. When pressed for reasons, narrator became shrill in insistence that "borders," "structures," "frames," "order," and even "form" itself, are regarded by him with the highest suspicion. Insists on unevenness as a virtue. Flaunts an almost barbaric disregard for the moral mysteries, or integrities, of traditional narrative modes. This flaw in his discipline is well demonstrated here. In order to save this narration, editor feels compelled to clarify slightly, not to censor but to impose at least the illusion of order. This was an effort toward preserving a certain morality of technique. Editor speaks here of a morality of morality, of that necessary corroboration between unyielding material and the discerning eye of absolute importance in the making of a final draft.

This is the essence of what he said:

I

Paul Frost was one of thousands of boys who came out of those little Kansas towns back during that time. He was one of the few who did not go back. When he came out it was easy moving forward by not going to the war. But after a while it got harder. Paul was in school up in Chicago when he determined to stand pat and take his blows. He returned home briefly and confronted his family and the members of a selective service committee. These were people who had watched his growing up. They were outraged at his refusal. Watching their outrage and remaining silent made Paul cry inside himself. He went back up to Chicago and did alternate service in a hospital for the insane. He began attending a Quaker meeting. Nights in the hospital, he read heavily in history, literature, and moral philosophy. Soon he began to see that many of the inmates were not insane. This frightened him enough to make him stop talking and begin watching things very closely. He was living, during this time, in a rented room out near Garfield Park. He went out only for work, meals, and to the library for more books. He knew no women and wanted none. Because he lived inside himself, he was soon taken by other people for an idiot. Their assumptions enabled Paul to maintain and nourish a secret self. He held conversations with it nights in his room. His first public speech, after many months of silence, was to a mental defective one evening at the hospital over a checkerboard down in the recreation room. "I don't think you're crazy," he whispered to the man. "So what are you *doing* here?" This patient looked warily at Paul and then smiled. He had that wistful, wide-eyed smile of the uncaring doomed. He leaned across the board and looked directly into Paul Frost's bright brown eyes. "What are *you* doing here?" he said. This question unsettled Paul. The more he thought about it the more nervous he became. He began walking LaSalle Street during his free time, picking conversations with total strangers. But everyone seemed to be in a great hurry. In the second year of his alternative service, he secured a transfer to another hospital out on the Coast. There, in Oakland, he did a number of wild things. Activity kept him from thinking about being crazy and going back to Kansas. His last act as a madman was to marry, in San Francisco, a black girl named Virginia Valentine, from a little town called Warren outside Knoxville, Tennessee.

II

Virginia Valentine had come out of Warren some ten years before, on the crest of that great wave of jailbreaking peasants. To people like her, imprisoned for generations, the outside world seemed absolutely clear in outline and full of sweet choices. Many could not cope with freedom and moved about crazily, much like long-chained pets anticipating the jerks of their leashes. Some committed suicide. Others, seeking safety, rushed into other prisons. But a few, like Virginia, rose and ranged far and wide in flight, like aristocratic eagles seeking high, free peaks on which to build their nests.

Virginia's quest was an epic of idealism. At nineteen she joined the Peace Corps and took the poor man's grand tour of the world. She was gregarious in a rough and country way. She had a talent for locating quickly the human core in people. And she had great humor. At twenty she was nursing babies in Ceylon. At twenty-one she stood watching people in a market in Jamshedpur, India, learning how to count the castes. Deciding then that Hindus were more "black" than anyone she had ever seen at home, she began calling herself "nigger" in an affirmative and ironic way. She developed a most subtle and delicious sense of humor. In Senegal, among the fishermen, she acquired the habit of eating with her hands. On holiday, in Kenya, she climbed up Kilimanjaro and stood on its summit, her hands on her hips in the country manner, her eyes looking up for more footholds. In the sweaty, spice-smelling markets of Cairo, Port Said, and Damascus she learned to outhaggle conniving traders. Seeing slaves and women still being sold, she developed the healthy habit of browbeating Arabs. There are stories she tells about old man Leakey, about squatting beside him in a Masai compound in north Tanzania, about helping herself to a drink of milk and cow's blood. The old man, she says, was curt, but eager to show his bones. The drink, she says, was not bad. The Masai did not dance. She entered the areas behind the smiles of Arabs, Asians, Africans, Israelis, Indians. In the stories they told she found implanted different ways of looking at the world.

When she returned home, at twenty-two, she was bursting with stories to tell. There were many like her. In Boston, New York, Philadelphia, Chicago, and all parts of California, people gathered in groups and told similar stories. They thought in terms new to them. In conversation they remarked on common points of reference in the four quarters of the world. The peasants among them had become aristocratic without any of the telling affectations. The aristocrats by birth had developed an easy, common touch. They considered themselves a new tribe.

But then their minds began to shift. In the beginning it was a subtle process. During conversation someone might say a casual "You know?" and there would be a hesitation, slight at first, denying affirmation. Virginia had painful stories to tell about increases in the periods of silence during the reacculturation. People began to feel self-conscious and guilty. If pushed, she will tell about the suicide in her group. People saw less and less of each other. Soon they were nodding on the street. Inevitably, many people in conversation began saying, "I don't understand!" At first this was tentative, then it became a defensive assertion. It took several months before they became black and white. Those who tried to fight grew confused and bitter. This was why Virginia, like many of the more stubborn, abandoned the East and ran off to California. Like a wounded bird fearful of landing with its wings still spread, she went out to the territory in search of some soft, personal space to cushion the impact of her grounding.

III

I went to the territory to renew my supply of stories. There were no new ones in the East at the time I left. Ideas and manners had coalesced into old and cobwebbed conventions. The old stories wre still being told, but their tellers seemed to lack confidence in them. Words seemed to have become detached from emotion and no longer flowed on the rhythm of passion. Even the great myths floated apart from their rituals. Cynical salesmen hawked them as folklore. There was no more bite in humor. And language, mother language, was being whored by her best sons to suit the appetites of wealthy patrons. There were no new stories. Great energy was spent describing the technology of fucking. Black folk were back into entertaining with time-tested acts. Maupassant's whores bristled with the muscle of union organizers. The life-affirming peasants of Chekhov and Babel sat wasted and listless on their porches, oblivious to the beats in their own blood. Even Pushkin's firebrands and noble brigands seemed content with the lackluster: mugging old ladies, killing themselves, snatching small change from dollar-and-dime grocers. During this time little men became afflicted with spells of swaggering. Men with greatness in them spoke on the telephone, and in private, as if bouncing safe clichés off the ear of a listener into an expectant and proprietary tape recorder. Everywhere there was this feeling of grotesque sadness, far, far past honest tears.

And the caste curtains were drawn, resegregating all imaginations. In restaurants, on airplanes, even in the homes of usually decent people, there was retrenchment, indifference, and fear. More than a million stories died in the East back during that time: confessions of fear, screams of hatred orchestrated into prayers, love and trust and need evolving, murders, retribution, redemption, honestly expressed rage. If I had approached a stranger and said, "Friend, I need your part of the story in order to complete my sense of self," I would have caused him to shudder, tremble, perhaps denounce me as an assailant. Yet to not do this was to default on my responsibility to narrate fully. There are stories that *must* be told, if only to be around when fresh dimensions are needed. But in the East, during that time, there was no thought of this. A narrator cannot function without new angles of vision. I needed new eyes, regeneration, fresh forms, and went hunting for them out in the territory.

A point of information. What has form to do with caste restrictions?
Everything.
You are saying you want to be white?

A narrator needs as much access to the world as the advocates of that mythology.

You are ashamed then of being black?

Only of not being nimble enough to dodge other people's straitjackets.

Are you not too much obsessed here with integration?

I was cursed with a healthy imagination.

What have caste restrictions to do with imagination?

Everything.

A point of information. What is your idea of personal freedom?

Unrestricted access to new stories forming.

Have you paid strict attention to the forming of this present one?

Once upon a time there was a wedding in San Francisco.

Virginia I valued for her stock of stories. I was suspicious of Paul Frost for claiming first right to these. They were a treasure I felt sure he would exploit. The girl was not at all pretty, and at first I could not see how he could love her. She was a little plump, had small breasts, and habitually wore Levi's and that flat, broad-brimmed type of cap popularized by movie gangsters in the forties. But the more I looked into her costume, the more I recognized it as the disguise of a person trying to deflect attention away from a secret self. When she laughed, it was loudly, and behind the laugh I heard a hand reaching out secretly to tug down loose corners of the costume. Even her affection of a swagger seemed contrived to conceal a softness of heart. Listening to the rough muscles of her voice, when she laughed, I sensed they were being flexed to keep obscure a sensitivity too finely tuned to risk exposure to the world. She employed a complicated kind of defensive irony. When her voice boomed, "Don't play with me now, nigger!" it said on the underside of the very same rhythm, *Don't come too close, I hurt easily.* Or when the voice said, "Come on in here and meet my fiancé, and if you don't like it you can go to hell!", the quick, dark eyes, watching closely for reactions, said in their silent language, *Don't hurt my baby! Don't hurt my baby!* She spiced her stories with this same delicious irony. Virginia Valentine was a country raconteur with a stock of stories flavored by international experience. Telling them, she spoke with her whole presence in very complicated ways. She was unique. She was a classic kind of narrator. Virginia Valentine was a magic woman.

Paul Frost seemed attracted to her by this outward display of strength. I am convinced he was by this time too mature to view her as just exotic. He was the second generation of a Kansas family successful in business matters, and he must have had keen eyes for value. But because of this, and perhaps for reasons still unclear to him, his family and the prairies were now in his past. I think he felt the need to redeem the family through works of great art, to release it from the hauntings of those lonely prairie towns. I know that when I looked I saw dead Indians living in his eyes. But I also saw a wholesome glow in their directness. They seemed in earnest need of answers to honest questions always on the verge of being asked. This aura of intense interest hung close to his face, like a bright cloud, or like a glistening second coat of skin not yet thick enough to be attached to him. It seemed to inquire of whomever his eyes addressed, "Who am I?" But this was only an outward essence. Whatever else he was eluded my inspection of his face. And as I grew aware of myself in pursuit of its definition, I began to feel embarrassed, and a little perverse. Because the thing that illuminated him, that provided the core of his mystery, might have been simple guilt, or outright lust, or a passion to dominate, or a need to submit to a fearful-seeming object. All such motives enter into the convention of love.

And yet at times, watching Virginia's eyes soften as they moved over his face, I could read in them the recognition of extraordinary spiritual forces, quietly commanded, but so self-assured as to be unafraid of advertising themselves. I am sure he was unaware of his innocence. And perhaps this is why Virginia's eyes pleaded, when he openly approached a soul-crushed stranger, *Don't hurt my baby! Don't hurt my baby!*, even while her voice laughed, teased, or growled. She employed her country wits with the finesse and style of a magic woman. And after I had come to understand them better, I began to see deeper into their bond. She was an eagle with broken wings spread, somewhat awkwardly, over the aristocratic soul of a simple farm boy. Having his soul intact made him a vulnerable human being. But having flown so high herself, and having been severely damaged, she still maintained too much grace, and too complete a sense of the treachery in the world, to allow any roughnesses to touch the naked thing. Paul Frost was a very lucky innocent. Virginia Valentine was protecting him to heal herself.

This wedding was a quiet affair in a judge's chambers. Paul's brother was best man. A tall, strapping fellow, he had flown out from Kansas to stand beside his brother. He held the ring with a gentle dignity. Paul's parents did not attend. They had called many times making the usual pleas. When these failed they sent a telegram saying BEST. But Virginia's parents were there from Tennessee. They were pleasant, country folk who had long begged her to come home. But when they saw they could not change her mind, they flew out with country-cured hams, a homemade cake, and a wedding quilt sewn by Virginia's grandmother, who was a full-blooded Cherokee living far back in the Tennessee woods. They also brought a handful of recipes from well-wishing neighbors. The mother wore a light blue dress and a white hat. A very dark-skinned little woman, she sat on the judge's leather chair looking as solemn as an usher at Sunday church service. Mr. Daniel Valentine, the father, a large-framed, handsome, brown man, smiled nervously when the judge had finished, and shook hands all around. He had the delicate facial features of an Indian, with curly black hair and high cheekbones. Virginia's color was deep reddish brown. She wore a simple white dress with a red sash. She smiled often and reassuringly at her brooding mother, as if to say, "It's all right. I told you so." Paul, in a black suit and black bow tie, looked as responsible and as sober as a banquet steward in a plush private club.

At the reception, in a sunny corner of the Golden Gate Park, Mr. Daniel Valentine offered around cigars. Then he strolled slowly about the grounds, his hands in his pockets. It was a warm November afternoon, much warmer than his body said it had a right to be. He was out of his proper environment and was obviously ill at ease. I walked along with him, smoking my cigar. In his brown face I saw fear and pride and puzzlement. He felt obliged to explain to himself how one of the most certain things in the world had miscarried. He had assumed that color was the highest bond, and I think he must have felt ashamed for someone. "We told her many the time to come home," he said while we walked. He stared at the late-blooming flowers, the green trees just starting to brown, the shirtless young men throwing Frisbees. He said, "I don't pretend to know the world no more, but I know enough about the lay of the land to have me a good, long talk with him. I laid it *right on the line*, too. My baby come from a long line of family, and her mama and me's proud of that. Right there in the South, there's plenty white women that have chase me, so I know a little something about how the world go round. But I ain't nobody's pretty plaything, and my baby ain't neither." He swelled out his chest and breathed deeply, inspecting closely the greenness of the grass, the spread of the trees. I sensed that his body was trying desperately to remember the coolness of the Tennessee autumn. He was sweating a little. He said, "Now, I don't give a *damn* about *his* family. They can go to hell for all of me. But I care a lot about *mine*! And last night I told him, 'If you *ever* hurt my baby, if you *ever* make her cry about something that ain't the fault of her womanly ways, I'm gonna come *looking* for you.' I told him I'd wear out a stick on him." He said this to me as one black man to another, as if he owed me reassurance. And I had no way of telling him that his daughter, in her private mind and treasured, secret self, had long ago moved a world away from that small living room in which conventional opinion mattered. "That's just what I told him, too," Mr. Daniel Valentine said. Then he averted his eyes, puffed his cigar, and nodded toward where the others stood crowded around a eucalyptus tree. Mrs. Valentine was unpacking the lunch. Paul was laughing like a little boy and swinging Virginia's hand. "But they do make a fine couple, don't they now?" he asked me.

They made a very fine couple. Paul rented an apartment in the Mission district and brought all their possessions under one roof. Virginia's posters, paintings, and sculpture acquired while traveling were unpacked from their boxes and used to decorate the walls and end tables. Paul's many books were stacked neatly in high brown bookcases in the small living room. The few times I saw them after the wedding they seemed very happy. They seemed eager to pick up and mend the broken pieces of fragmented lives.

Virginia worked as a clerk for a state agency. Paul worked for a construction company during the day and studied for his degree nights in a community college. Paul worked very hard, with the regularity and order of a determined man. I think the steady rhythms of the prairie were still in him, and he planned ahead with the memory of winter still in mind. But they made special efforts to live in cosmopolitan style. Both of them were learning Spanish from their Chicano neighbors. They chose their friends carefully with an eye on uniqueness and character. They were the most democratic people I have ever seen. They simply allowed people to present themselves, and they had relationships with Chicanos, Asians, French, Brazilians, black and white Americans. But they lived in a place where people were constantly coming and going. And they lived there at a time when a certain structure was settling in. It was not as brutal as it was in the East, but it was calculated to ensure the same results.

During this time Paul's father, back in Kansas, was putting on the pressure. I think the idea of Virginia had finally entered his imagination and he was frightened for the future of his name. He called long-distance periodically, vowing full support for Paul when he finally reconsidered. He seemed to have no doubt this would occur. They argued back and forth by telephone. The father accused the son of beginning to think like a Negro. The father accused the son of being deluded. The son accused the father of being narrow-minded. The son accused the father of being obtuse. Nothing was ever resolved, but the discussions were most rational. The father was simply a good businessman. In his mind he had a sharp impression of the market. I am sure he thought his son had made a bad investment that was bound to be corrected as soon as Virginia's stock declined. There was, after all, no permanent reification of color. From his point of view it was this simple. But from Paul's point of view it was not.

When they invited me to dinner in early December, Virginia said, "This old rascal thinks that one day he'll have to kiss a pickaninny. If I had a cold heart I'd send him one of them minstrel pictures." She laughed when she said this, but there was not the usual irony in her voice. She pushed her hands into the back pockets of her Levi's and leaned her butt against the kitchen stove.

Paul was at the kitchen table drinking wine. He seemed upset and determined. He said, "My father is a very decent man in his own way. He just knows a little part of the world. He's never talked seriously with anybody that's not like him. He doesn't understand black people, and he would have a hard time understanding Ginny." He laughed, his clear eyes flashing. "She's a bundle of contradictions. She breaks all the rules. All of you do."

I sat down at the table and poured myself a glass of the red wine. Virginia was baking a spicy Spanish dish, and the smell of it made me more relaxed than I should have been. After draining the glass I said, "I can understand your father's worry. According to convention, one of you is supposed to die, get crippled for life, or get struck down by a freak flash of lightning while making love on a sunny day."

Paul laughed. He sipped from his glass of wine. "This is real life," he said, "not the movies. And in any case, *I* don't have to worry."

Virginia was stirring a dish of red sauce on the stove. The air was heavy with the smell of pungent spices.

I said to Paul, "The producers in Hollywood are recycling."

Paul laughed again. "This is *real* life," he told me. But he was getting a little drunk. He sipped his wine and said, "In this house we pay close attention to reality. By public definition Ginny is black, but in fact she's a hybrid of African, European, and Indian bloodlines. Out in the world she roughhouses, but here at home she's gentle and sweet. Before anybody else she pretends to be tough, but with me she's a *softy*. It took me a long time to understand these contradictions, and it'll take my family longer. My father has a very unsubtle, orderly mind. I'm willing to wait. I see my marriage as an investment in the future. When my father has mellowed some, I'll take my wife home. As I said, *I* don't have to worry."

Virginia called from the stove, "That old rascal might at least *speak* to me when he calls."

Paul fingered his wineglass, looking guilty and cornered.

It was not my story, but I could not help intruding upon its materials. It seemed to me to lack perspective. I poured myself another glass of wine and looked across the table at Paul. Above us the naked light bulb reflected eerily in my glass of red wine. I said, "Time out here is different from time in the East. When we say 'Good afternoon' here, in the East people are saying 'Good night.' It's a matter of distance, not of values. Ideas that start in the East move very fast in media, but here the diversity tends to slow them down. Still, a mind needs media to reinforce a sense of self. There are no imaginations pure enough to be self-sustaining."

Paul looked hard at me. He looked irritated. He said, "I don't understand what you're talking about."

I said, "Someone is coming here to claim you. Soon you may surprise even yourself. While there is still time, you must force the reality of your wife into your father's mind and run toward whatever cover it provides."

He really did not understand. I think he still believed he was a free agent. He sat erect at the kitchen table, sipping from his glass of wine. He looked confused, hurt, almost on the edge of anger. I felt bad for having intruded into his story, but there was a point I wanted very much for him to see. I pointed toward a Nigerian ceremonial mask nailed to the wall just over the kitchen door. The white light from the bulb above us glowed on the brown, polished wood of the mask. "Do you think it's beautiful?" I asked.

Paul looked up and inspected the mask. It was an exaggeration of the human face, a celebration in carved wood of the mobile human personality. The eyes were mere slits. Teeth protruded from a broad mouth at unexpected angles. From the forehead of the face, curving upward, were appendages resembling a mountain goat's horns. Paul sipped his wine. He said, "It's very nice. Ginny bought it from a trader in Ibadan. There's a good story behind it."

I said, "But do you think it's beautiful?"

"The story or the mask?" Virginia called from the stove. She laughed with just a hint of self-derision, but the sound contained the image of a curtain being pulled across a private self.

"The mask, of course!" Paul called to her coolly. Then he looked at me with great emotion in his eyes. "It's nice," he said.

I said, "You are a dealer in art. You have extraordinary taste. But your shop is in a small town. You want to sell this mask by convincing your best customer it is beautiful and of interest to the eye. Every other dealer in town says it is ugly. How do you convince the customer and make a sale?"

Paul's eyes widened and flashed. He started to get up, then sat back down. "I don't like *condescension*," he said. "I don't much like being talked down to!" He was angry, but in a controlled way. He started to get up again.

Virginia shouted, "*Dinner!*"

I said to Paul, "You have enlisted in a psychological war."

He looked trapped. He turned to face his wife. But she had her back to him, making great noises while opening the stove. I think she was singing an old Negro hymn. He turned toward me again, a great fear claiming control of his entire face. "Why don't you just *leave!*" he shouted. "Why don't you just *get out!*"

I looked past him and saw Virginia standing by the stove. She was holding a hot red dish with her bare hands. She was trembling like a bird. In her face was the recognition of a profound defeat. She cried, "Go away! Please, go *away!* No matter what you think, this is my husband!"

I left them alone with their dinner. It was not my story. It was not ripe for telling until they had got it under better control.

Analysis of this section is needed. It is too subtle and needs to be more clearly explained.

I tried to enter his mind and failed.

Explain.

I had confronted him with color and he became white.

Unclear. Explain.

There was a public area of personality in which his "I" existed. The nervous nature of this is the basis of what is miscalled arrogance. In reality it was the way his relationship with the world was structured. I attempted to challenge this structure by attacking its assumptions too directly and abruptly. He sensed the intrusion and reacted emotionally to protect his sense of form. He simply shut me out of his world.

Unclear. Explain:

I am I. I am we. You are.

Clarity is essential on this point. Explain.

More than a million small assumptions, reaffirmed year after year, had become as routine as brushing teeth. The totality guarded for him an area of personality he was under no obligation to develop. All necessary development preexisted for him, long before his birth, out there in the world, in the images, actions, power, and status of others. In that undefined "I" existed an ego that embraced the outlines, but only the outlines, of the entire world. This was an unconscious process over which he had little control. It defined his self for him. It was a formal structure that defined his sense of order. It was one geared unconsciously to the avoidance of personal experience challenging that order. I tried to enter this area uninvited and was pushed back. This was his right. A guest does not enter a very private room without knocking carefully. Nor does a blind man continue moving when he hears an unfamiliar sound.

Clarity is essential on this point. Please explain.

I think he understood enough to know that he was on a moral mission.

After Christmas, Virginia contacted me by telephone and said, "No matter what you think, he has a good heart and he's sorry. But you *did* provoke him. One thing I learned from traveling is you accept people the way they are and try to work from there. Africans can be a cruel people. Arabs I never *did* learn to trust. And there's a lot of us *niggers* that ain't so hot. But them raggedy-ass Indians taught me something about patience and faith. They ain't never had nothing, but they *still* going strong. In Calcutta you see crippled beggars out in the street, and people just walk on around them. Now a Westerner would say that's cruel, but them fucking Indians so damn complicated they probably look at that same beggar and see a reincarnated raja that lived in us a thousand years ago, ate too much of them hot spices, and died of gout. *Shit!* He don't *need* nothing else! So they don't worry about how he looks now. But patience is a Christmas-morning thing. You have to accept what's under the tree and keep on believing there's a Santa Claus. Both you *and* that nigger of mine have to learn that. I ain't giving up on *nothing!* I ain't giving up on *shit!* So why don't you heist up your raggedy ass and come with us to Mass on New Year's Eve?"

I have said Virginia Frost was a magic woman.

The cathedral was massive, chilly and dark. Huge arched stained-glass windows reflected the outlines of sacred images in the flickering lights of red and yellow candle flames. Two Episcopal priests, in flowing white albs, stood in the chancel and read invocations from their missals. Little boys in black cassocks paced reverently up and down the aisles, censing from gray-smoking thuribles. Seated on the benches around us were people—young and old and middle-aged, the well dressed and the shabby, the hopeful and the forlorn. Young men with great scraggly beards sat silently with lowered heads. Beside them were young women, pale and hard-faced, looking as beaten and worn as pioneer women after too many years of frontier life. Single girls wore sequined denim jackets over long frocks with ruffled bottoms. Many wore leather boots. Here and there, almost invisible in the crowd, men and men and women and women, segregated by sex, sat holding hands with heads bowed. Virginia was wearing her mug's cap, and it sat rakishly on her strong curly hair. I sat on her right, Paul on her left. We sat close together. The place projected the mood of a sanctuary.

Above us, in the balconies, two choirs in black and white robes sang a mass. Their voices cried like wounded angels bent on calling back to earth a delinquent God. The effort was magnificent. But all around us, people looked abstracted, beaten, drained of feeling. There was a desperate concentration on the choir, an effort of such intensity it almost made its own sound. It seemed to be asking questions of the songs floating down from the choir. We closed our eyes and said private prayers. It was nearing midnight, and we heard the faith of Bach insisted on in the collective voices of the choir. And in response, breathing in the stillness of the people, one sensed a profound imploring. But then a voice behind us imposed itself on the silence. "Young man," it rasped, "if you're too *dumb* to take your hat off in church, get out!" From all along the two rows came the sounds of stiff necks creaking. "Young man," the voice demanded of Virginia, "did you hear me? Or are you too *dumb* to know the English language?" I opened my eyes and turned. Beside me, Virginia was closing her eyes tighter. Beside her, I saw Paul lift his own head and turn fierce eyes on the old gentleman's face. In his voice was a familiar arrogance from a source he had just begun to consciously tap. "You old *fart!*" he said, his tone disrupting the harmony floating down from above us. "You old fart!" he said. "This is *my wife*. If you don't like what she's wearing, *that's tough!*"

The choir lifted their voices, as if bent on erasing the incident with the strength of their sound. Around us people coughed softly. Paul put his arm around Virginia's shoulder. He closed his eyes and whispered in her ear. I closed my own eyes and tried to lose myself in the music. But I was made humble and hopeful by that other thing, and I thought to myself, *This one's a man*.

From January on, Paul began confronting the hidden dimensions of his history. Something in his mind seemed to have opened, and he was hungry for information. He read books hungrily for other points of view, sifting through propaganda for facts. He underlined a great deal, scribbled questions in the margins, asked questions openly. He discarded much of what he read, but what stuck in that private place in his mind made him pensive, and silent, and a little sad. I watched him closely, though I kept my distance. I admired him for his heroic attempt to look back.

But in early February, while he was with Virginia in the parking lot of a supermarket, a carful of children called him nigger. Their dog barked along with the sing-song rhythm. "I just laughed at the little crumbsnatchers," Virginia said.

She said she could not understand why Paul became so upset.

In late February, when he was walking with Virginia in the rain through the Sunset district, two younger children called him nigger.

"What's a nigger?" he asked me on the telephone. "I mean, what does it *really* mean to you?"

I said, "A descendant of Proteus, an expression of the highest form of freedom."

He hung up on me.

I did not call him back. I was convinced he had to earn his own definitions.

In early March Virginia found out she was pregnant.

That same month Paul disclosed that his father, during one of their arguments, had mentioned to him the full name of the black janitor who swept out his office. But the old man was most upset about the baby.

During the months after Christmas I saw very little of them. I had become interested in a man recently paroled after more than fifty years in prison. He had many rich stories to tell. I visited him often in his room at a half-way-house, playing chess and listening while he talked. He sang eloquent praises to the luxuries of freedom. He detailed for me the epic nature of the effort that had got him sprung. He was alive with ambition, lust, large appetites. And yet, in his room, he seemed to regulate his movements by the beat of an invisible clock. He would begin walking toward the door, then stop and look puzzled, then return to his chair beside the bed. His window faced the evening sun just where it sank into the ocean, but the window shade was never lifted. He invited me once to have lunch with him, then opened a can of peaches and insisted that we share a single spoon. He invited me to attend a party with him, given in his honor by one of his benefactors. There, he sat on a chair in the corner of the room and smiled broadly only when a curious stranger expressed interest in his recollections. He told the same stories line for line. Late in the evening, I spoke briefly with the hostess. This woman looked me straight in the eye while denouncing prisons with a passionate indignation. Periodically, she swung her empty martini glass in a confident arc to the right of her body. There, as always, stood a servant holding a tray at just the point where, without ever having to look, my hostess knew a perfect arc and a flat surface were supposed to intersect. I saw my own face reflected roundly in the hostess's blue-tinted spectator's sunglasses, and I began to laugh.

The above section is totally unclear. It should be cut.

I would leave it in. It was attempting to suggest the nature of the times.

But here the narrative begins to drift. There is a shift in subject, mood, and focus of narration. Cutting is advised.

Back during that time there was little feeling and no focus.

Narrator has a responsibility to make things clear.

Narrator fails in this respect. There was no clarity. There was no focus. There was no control. The hands of a great clock seemed to be spinning wildly, and there was no longer any great difference between East and West.

This thing affected everyone. There was a feeling of a great giving up. I sensed a bombed-out place inside me. I watched people clutch at bottles, pills, the robes of Jesus, and I began to feel cynical and beaten. Inside myself, and out there in the world, I heard only sobs; and sighs and moans. There was during this time a great nakedness, exposed everywhere, and people dared you to look. I looked. I saw. I saw Virginia Frost losing control of her stories. As her belly grew, her recollections began to lose their structure. The richness was still there, but her accounts became more anecdotal than like stories. They lacked clarity and order. She still knew the names, the accents, the personal quirks of individual Indians, Asians, Israelis, but more and more they fragmented into pieces of memory. There was no longer the sense of a personal epic. She no longer existed inside her own stories. They began bordering dangerously on the exotic and nostalgic. At times, telling them, she almost became a performer—one capable of brilliant flashes of recollection that stunned briefly, lived, and then were gone. She had inside her an epic adventure, multinational in scope, but the passion needed to give it permanent shape was obviously fading. One part of her was a resigned mother-to-be, but the other part was becoming a country teller of tall stories with an international cast.

I have said it was the nature of the times.

Something was also happening to Paul. In his mind, I think, he was trying desperately to unstructure and flesh out his undefined "I." But he seemed unable to locate the enemy and, a novice in thinking from the defensive point of view, had not yet learned the necessary tactics. Still, he seemed to sense there were some secrets to survival that could be learned from books, conversations, experiences with people who lived very close to the realities of life. He cut himself off from the company of most white males. He got a job with a landscaping crew and spent most of his days outdoors. His muscles hardened and his face grew brown. He grew a long black beard. He read the Bible, Sören Kierkegaard, abstract treatises on ethics. He underlined heavily. The beard merged with his intense, unblinking eyes to give him the appearance of a suffering, pain-accepting Christ. During this time he flirted with the clothing styles of the street-corner dandy. Often in conversation he spoke bitterly about the neglect of the poor. He quoted from memory long passages from Isaiah, Jeremiah, the book of Lamentations. He denounced his father as a moral coward. He was self-righteous, struggling, and abysmally alone. But his face still maintained its aura. His large brown eyes still put the same question, though now desperately asked, "Who am I?"

And many times, watching him conceal his aloneness, I wanted to answer, "The abstract white man of mythic dimensions, if being that will make you whole again." But the story was still unfinished, and I did not want to intrude on its structure again. The chaos was his alone, as were the contents he was trying desperately to reclaim from an entrenched and determined form. But to his credit it must be said that, all during this time, I never once heard him say to Virginia, "I don't understand." For the stoic nature of this silence, considering the easy world waiting behind those words, one could not help but love him.

Then, in early June, both sets of parents began making gestures. Virginia's people called up often, proposing treasured family names for the baby. Paul's mother sent money for a bassinet. She hinted, in strictest confidence to Paul, that more than European bloodlines ran in her veins. But the father was still unyielding. His arguments had grown more complex: If he recognized the baby he would have to recognize Virginia's family, and if he ever visited the family they would have to visit him. From this new perspective the objection was grounded in a simple matter of class distinction. His mind lacked subtlety, but one had to admire its sense of order. On his personal initiative, he told his son, he had engineered the hiring of a black employee by his company. Paul told his father this would not do. The mother told Paul the father would think it over, and after he had thought it over Virginia and the baby would be welcome in their home. But Virginia told Paul this would not do either.

They had never seen the problem from her point of view.

Virginia said, "I don't want my baby to be an honorary white."

She said this to me toward midsummer, in the park, during a conversation at the Japanese Tea Garden. Around us under the pavilion sat tourists munching cookies, sipping warm tea, huddled against the coolness of the morning mist. Virginia now wore a maternity smock over her pants, but her mug's cap still rode defiantly atop her curly hair. Her belly protruded with the expanding child. Her brown cheeks were fleshy and her eyes looked very tired. She said, "I'm black. I've accepted myself as that. But didn't I make some elbow room, though?" She tapped her temple with her forefinger. "I mean up *here!*" Then she laughed bitterly and sipped her tea. "When times get tough, *anybody* can pass for white. Niggers been doing *that* for *centuries*, so it ain't nothing new. But shit, wouldn't it of been something to be a nigger that could relate to white and black and everything else in the world out of a self as big as the world is?" She laughed. Then she said, "That would have been *some* nigger!"

We sipped our tea and watched the mist lifting from the flowers. On the walkways below us the tourists kept taking pictures.

I said, "You were game. You were bold all right. *You* were some nigger."

She said, "I was *whiter* than white and *blacker* than black. Hell, at least I got to *see* through the fog."

I said, "You were game all right."

A tourist paused, smiled nervously, and snapped our picture.

Virginia said, "It's so *fucked up!* You get just two choices, and either one leaves you blind as a bat at noon. You want both, just for starters, and then you want everything else in the world. But what you wind up with is one eye and a bunch of memories. But I don't want my baby to be one-eyed and honorary white. At least the black eye can peep round corners."

Inside myself I suddenly felt a coolness as light as the morning mist against my skin. Then I realized that I was acting. I did not care about them and their problems any more. I did not think they had a story worth telling. I looked away from her and said, "Life is tough, all right."

Virginia was turning her teacup. She turned it around and around on the hand-painted tray. She looked out over the garden and said, "But I'm worried about that nigger of mine. I told you he had heart. In his mind he's still working through all that shit. Underneath that soft front he's strong as a mule, and he's stubborn. Right now both his eyes are a little open, but if he ever got his jaws tight he might close one eye and become blacker than I ever thought about being. That's the way it's rigged."

I did not feel I owed them anything more. But because she had once shared with me the richness of her stories, I felt obliged. I looked at the tourists moving clumsily between the hanging red and purple fuchsia. They knocked many of the delicate petals to the ground. The pavilion was completely surrounded by tramping tourists. I looked down at Virginia's belly and said, "Then for the sake of your child don't be black. Be more of a classic kind of nigger."

She laughed then and slapped my back.

I walked with Paul around the city before I returned East. This was in the late summer, several months before the baby was due, and I felt I owed him something. It was on a Sunday. Paul had attended a Quaker meeting that morning and seemed at peace with himself. We walked all afternoon. Along the avenues, on the sidewalk, paralleling the beach, down the broad roads through the park, we strolled aimlessly and in silence. The people we saw seemed resigned, anomic, vaguely haunted by lackluster ghosts. My own eyes seemed drawn to black people. In Golden Gate Park I watched a black man, drunk or high on dope, making ridiculous gestures at a mother wheeling a baby in its carriage. The man seemed intent on parodying a thought already in the young mother's mind. I stopped and pointed and said to Paul, "That's a nigger." On the Panhandle we paused to study an overdressed black man, standing in a group of casually dressed whites, who smiled with all his teeth exposed. His smile seemed to be saying, even to strangers, "You know everything about me. I know you know I know I have nothing to hide." I nodded toward him and said to Paul, "That's a nigger." Paul looked about more freely. On Lincoln Way, walking back toward the bus stop, he directed my eyes to a passing car with stickers plastered on its bumpers. They boosted various mundane causes, motor lubricants, and the Second Coming of Jesus. In the middle of the back bumper there was a white sticker with great black letters reading, BE PROUD TO BE A NIGGER.

Paul laughed. I think he must have thought it a subtle joke.

But a few blocks from the park I nodded toward a heavily bearded young white man on a sparkling, red ten-speed bike. He was red-faced and unwashed. His black pants and black sweatshirt seemed, even from a distance, infested with dirt and sweat and crawling things. As he pedaled, crusty, dirt-covered toes protruded from sandals made from the rubber casings of tires. He seemed conscious of himself as the survivor of something. He maneuvered through the afternoon traffic, against all lights, with a bemused arrogance etched into the creases of his red face. When he was far down the block, I said to Paul, "That one is only passing. He is a bad parody of a part-time nigger."

He did not laugh. He did not understand.

I said, "Imagine two men on this street. One is white and dressed like that. The other is black and seems to be a parading model for a gentleman's tailor. In your mind, or in your father's mind, which of them would seem unnatural?"

Paul stopped walking. He looked very hurt. He said, "Now it's finally out in the open. You think I'm a racist."

I felt very cool and spacious inside myself. I felt free of any obligation to find a new story. I felt free enough to say to Paul, "I think you were born in a lonely place where people value a certain order. I saw a picture on a calendar once of a man posed between the prairie and the sky. He seemed pressured by all that space, as if he were in a crucible. He seemed humbled by the simplistic rhythm of the place. I think that in his mind he must have to be methodical, to think in very simple terms, in order to abide with those rhythms."

But he still thought I was accusing him, or calling him to account. He said, "People *do* grow. You may not think much of *me*, but my children will be great!"

I said, "They will be black and blind or passing for white and self-blinded. Those are the only choices."

Paul walked on ahead of me, very fast.

On Nineteenth Avenue, at the bus stop, he turned to me and said, "Don't bother to come all the way back. Ginny's probably taking a nap." He looked away up the street to where several buses were waiting for the light to change. The fog had come in, it was getting darker, and in the light of the traffic his eyes looked red and tired. I was not standing close enough to him to see his face, but I am sure that by this time his aura had completely disappeared. He looked beaten and drained, like everything else in sight.

We shook hands and I began to walk away, convinced there were no new stories in the world.

Both buses passed me on their ways to the corner. But above the squeaks and hissing of their brakes I heard Paul's voice calling, "At *least* I tried! At *least* I'm *fighting!* And I know what a *nigger* is, too. It's what you are when you begin thinking of yourself as a work of art!"

I did not turn to answer, although I heard him clearly. I am certain there was no arrogance at all left in his voice.

Almost two months later, when I called their apartment before leaving for the East, the telephone was disconnected. When I went there to say goodbye they were gone. A Chicano couple, just up from LA, was moving in. They spoke very poor English. When I described the couple I was looking for they shook their heads slowly. Then the husband, a big-bellied man with a handlebar mustache, rummaged in a pile of trash in the hall and pulled out a sign painted on a piece of cardboard. He held it up across his chest. The sign said, WE ARE PARENTS. GO AWAY.

I went back to the East resigned to telling the old stories.

But six months later, while I was trying to wrestle my imagination into the cold heart of a recalcitrant folktale, a letter from a small town in Kansas was forwarded to me by way of San Francisco. It was the announcement of a baby's birth, seven or eight months old. Also enclosed were three color pictures. The first, dated in October, was a mass of pink skin and curly black hair. The second, a more recent snapshot, was of a chubby brown boy, naked on his back, his dark brown eyes staring out at the world. On the back of this picture was printed: "Daniel P. Frost, four months, eight days." The third picture was of Virginia and Paul standing on either side of an elderly couple. Virginia was smiling triumphantly, wearing her mug's cap. The old man looked solemn. The woman, with purple-white hair, was holding the baby. Paul stood a little apart from the others, his arms crossed. His beard was gone and he looked defiant. There was a familiar intensity about his face. On the back of this picture someone had written: "He will be a *classic* kind of nigger."

Clarify the meaning of this comment.

I would find that difficult to do. It was from the beginning not my story. I lack the insight to narrate its complexities. But it may still be told. The mother is, after all, a country raconteur with cosmopolitan experience. The father sees clearly with both eyes. And when I called Kansas they had already left for the backwoods of Tennessee, where the baby has an odd assortment of relatives. I will wait. The mother is a bold woman. The father has a sense of how things should be. But while waiting, I will wager my reputation on the ambition, if not the strength, of the boy's story.

Comment is unclear. Explain. Explain.

FLANNERY O'CONNOR (1925–1964)

Revelation

Flannery O'Connor was born in Georgia and educated at the Georgia State College for Women and at the University of Iowa. Her novels were *Wise Blood* (1952) and *The Violent Bear It Away* (1960). She is, however, most renowned as a writer of short fiction. "Revelation" appeared in *Everything That Rises Must Converge* (1965).

The doctor's waiting room, which was very small, was almost full when the Turpins entered and Mrs. Turpin, who was very large, made it look even smaller by her presence. She stood looming at the head of the magazine table set in the center of it, a living demonstration that the room was inadequate and ridiculous. Her little bright black eyes took in all the patients as she sized up the seating situation. There was one vacant chair and a place on the sofa occupied by a blond child in a dirty blue romper who should have been told to move over and make room for the lady. He was five or six, but Mrs. Turpin saw at once that no one was going to tell him to move over. He was slumped down in the seat, his arms idle at his sides and his eyes idle in his head; his nose ran unchecked.

Mrs. Turpin put a firm hand on Claud's shoulder and said in a voice that included anyone who wanted to listen, "Claud, you sit in that chair there," and gave him a push down into the vacant one. Claud was florid and bald and sturdy, somewhat shorter than Mrs. Turpin, but he sat down as if he were accustomed to doing what she told him to.

Mrs. Turpin remained standing. The only man in the room besides Claud was a lean stringy old fellow with a rusty hand spread out on each knee, whose eyes were closed as if he were asleep or dead or pretending to be so as not to get up and offer her his seat. Her gaze settled agreeably on a well-dressed grey-haired lady whose eyes met hers and whose expression said: if that child belonged to me, he would have some manners and move over—there's plenty of room there for you and him too.

Claud looked up with a sigh and made as if to rise.

"Sit down," Mrs. Turpin said. "You know you're not supposed to stand on that leg. He has an ulcer on his leg," she explained.

Claud lifted his foot onto the magazine table and rolled his trouser leg up to reveal a purple swelling on a plump marble-white calf.

"My!" the pleasant lady said. "How did you do that?"

"A cow kicked him," Mrs. Turpin said.

"Goodness!" said the lady.

Claud rolled his trouser leg down.

"Maybe the little boy would move over," the lady suggested, but the child did not stir.

"Somebody will be leaving in a minute," Mrs. Turpin said. She could not understand why a doctor—with as much money as they made charging five dollars a day to just stick their head in the hospital door and look at you—couldn't afford a decent-sized waiting room. This one was hardly bigger than a garage. The table was cluttered with limp-looking magazines and at one end of it there was a big green glass ash tray full of cigaret butts and cotton wads with little blood spots on them. If she had had anything to do with the running of the place, that would have been emptied every so often. There were no chairs against the wall at the head of the room. It had a rectangular-shaped panel in it that permitted a view of the office where the nurse came and went and the secretary listened to the radio. A plastic fern in a gold pot sat in the opening and trailed its fronds down almost to the floor. The radio was softly playing gospel music.

Just then the inner door opened and a nurse with the highest stack of yellow hair Mrs. Turpin had ever seen put her face in the crack and called for the next patient. The woman sitting beside Claud grasped the two arms of her chair and hoisted herself up; she pulled her dress free from her legs and lumbered through the door where the nurse had disappeared.

Mrs. Turpin eased into the vacant chair, which held her tight as a corset. "I wish I could reduce," she said, and rolled her eyes and gave a comic sigh.

"Oh, *you* aren't fat," the stylish lady said.

"Ooooo I am too," Mrs. Turpin said. "Claud he eats all he wants to and never weighs over one hundred and seventy-five pounds, but me I just look at something good to eat and I gain some weight," and her stomach and shoulders shook with laughter. "You can eat all you want to, can't you, Claud?" she asked, turning to him.

Claud only grinned.

"Well, as long as you have such a good disposition," the stylish lady said, "I don't think it makes a bit of difference what size you are. You just can't beat a good disposition."

Next to her was a fat girl of eighteen or nineteen, scowling into a thick blue book which Mrs. Turpin saw was entitled *Human Development*. The girl raised her head and directed her scowl at Mrs. Turpin as if she did not like her looks. She appeared annoyed that anyone should speak while she tried to read. The poor girl's face was blue with acne and Mrs. Turpin thought how pitiful it was to have a face like that at that age. She gave the girl a friendly smile but the girl only scowled the harder. Mrs. Turpin herself was fat but she had always had good skin, and, though she was forty-seven years old, there was not a wrinkle in her face except around her eyes from laughing too much.

Next to the ugly girl was the child, still in exactly the same position, and next to him was a thin leathery old woman in a cotton print dress. She and Claud had three sacks of chicken feed in their pump house that was in the same print. She had seen from the first that the child belonged with the old woman. She could tell by the way they sat—kind of vacant and white-trashy, as if they would sit there until Doomsday if nobody called and told them to get up. And at right angles but next to the well-dressed pleasant lady was a lank-faced woman who was certainly the child's mother. She had on a yellow sweat shirt and wine-colored slacks, both gritty-looking, and the rims of her lips were stained with snuff. Her dirty yellow hair was tied behind with a little piece of red paper ribbon. Worse than niggers any day, Mrs. Turpin thought.

The gospel hymn playing was, "When I looked up and He looked down," and Mrs. Turpin, who knew it, supplied the last line mentally, "And wona these days I know I'll we-eara crown."

Without appearing to, Mrs. Turpin always noticed people's feet. The well-dressed lady had on red and grey suede shoes to match her dress. Mrs. Turpin had on her good black patent leather pumps. The ugly girl had on Girl Scout shoes and heavy socks. The old woman had on tennis shoes and the white-trashy mother had on what appeared to be bedroom slippers, black straw with gold braid threaded through them—exactly what you would have expected her to have on.

Sometimes at night when she couldn't go to sleep, Mrs. Turpin would occupy herself with the question of who she would have chosen to be if she couldn't have been herself. If Jesus had said to her before he made her, "There's only two places available for you. You can either be a nigger or white-trash," what would she have said? "Please, Jesus, please," she would have said, "just let me wait until there's another place available," and he would have said, "No, you have to go right now and I have only those two places so make up your mind." She would have wiggled and squirmed and begged and pleaded but it would have been no use and finally she would have said, "All right, make me a nigger then—but that don't mean a trashy one." And he would have made her a neat clean respectable Negro-woman, herself but black.

Next to the child's mother was a red-headed youngish woman, reading one of the magazines and working a piece of chewing gum, hell for leather, as Claud would say. Mrs. Turpin could not see the woman's feet. She was not white-trash, just common. Sometimes Mrs. Turpin occupied herself at night naming the classes of people. On the bottom of the heap were most colored people, not the kind she would have been if she had been one, but most of them; then next to them—not above, just away from—were the white-trash; then above them were the home-owners, and above them the home-and-land owners, to which she and Claud belonged. Above she and Claud were people with a lot of money and much bigger houses and much more land. But here the complexity of it would begin to bear in on her, for some of the people with a lot of money were common and ought to be below she and Claud and some of the people who had good blood had lost their money and had to rent and then there were colored people who owned their homes and land as well. There was a colored dentist in town who had two red Lincolns and a swimming pool and a farm with registered white-face cattle on it. Usually by the time she had fallen asleep all the classes of people were moiling and roiling around in her head, and she would dream they were all crammed in together in a box car, being ridden off to be put in a gas oven.

"That's a beautiful clock," she said and nodded to her right. It was a big wall clock, the face encased in a brass sunburst.

"Yes, it's very pretty," the stylish lady said agreeably. "And right on the dot too," she added, glancing at her watch.

The ugly girl beside her cast an eye upward at the clock, smirked, then looked directly at Mrs. Turpin and smirked again. Then she returned her eyes to her book. She was obviously the lady's daughter because, although they didn't look anything alike as to disposition, they both had the same shape of face and the same blue eyes. On the lady they sparkled pleasantly but in the girl's seared face they appeared alternately to smolder and to blaze.

What if Jesus had said, "All right, you can be white-trash or a nigger or ugly"!

Mrs. Turpin felt an awful pity for the girl, though she thought it was one thing to be ugly and another to act ugly.

The woman with the snuff-stained lips turned around in her chair and looked up at the clock. Then she turned back and appeared to look a little to the side of Mrs. Turpin. There was a cast in one of her eyes. "You want to know wher you can get you one of themther clocks?" she asked in a loud voice.

"No, I already have a nice clock," Mrs. Turpin said. Once somebody like her got a leg in the conversation, she would be all over it.

"You can get you one with green stamps," the woman said. "That's most likely wher he got hisn. Save you up enough, you can get you most anythang. I got me some joo'ry."

Ought to have got you a wash rag and some soap, Mrs. Turpin thought.

"I get contour sheets with mine," the pleasant lady said.

The daughter slammed her book shut. She looked straight in front of her, directly through Mrs. Turpin and on through the yellow curtain and the plate glass window which made the wall behind her. The girl's eyes seemed lit all of a sudden with a peculiar light, an unnatural light like night road signs give. Mrs. Turpin turned her head to see if there was anything going on outside that she should see, but she could not see anything. Figures passing cast only a pale shadow through the curtain. There was no reason the girl should single her out for her ugly looks.

"Miss Finley," the nurse said, cracking the door. The gum-chewing woman got up and passed in front of her and Claud and went into the office. She had on red high-heeled shoes.

Directly across the table, the ugly girl's eyes were fixed on Mrs. Turpin as if she had some very special reason for disliking her.

"This is wonderful weather, isn't it?" the girl's mother said.

"It's good weather for cotton if you can get the niggers to pick it," Mrs. Turpin said, "but niggers don't want to pick cotton any more. You can't get the white folks to pick it and now you can't get the niggers— because they got to be right up there with the white folks."

"They gonna *try* anyways," the white-trash woman said, leaning forward.

"Do you have one of those cotton-picking machines?" the pleasant lady asked.

"No," Mrs. Turpin said, "they leave half the cotton in the field. We don't have much cotton anyway. If you want to make it farming now, you have to have a little of everything. We got a couple of acres of cotton and a few hogs and chickens and just enough white-face that Claud can look after them himself."

"One thang I don't want," the white-trash woman said, wiping her mouth with the back of her hands. "Hogs. Nasty stinking things, a-gruntin and a-rootin all over the place."

Mrs. Turpin gave her the merest edge of her attention. "Our hogs are not dirty and they don't stink," she said. "They're cleaner than some children I've seen. Their feet never touch the ground. We have a pig-parlor— that's where you raise them on concrete," she explained to the pleasant lady, "and Claud scoots them down with the hose every afternoon and washes off the floor." Cleaner by far than that child right there, she thought. Poor nasty little thing. He had not moved except to put the thumb of his dirty hand into his mouth.

The woman turned her face away from Mrs. Turpin. "I know I wouldn't scoot down no hog with no hose," she said to the wall.

You wouldn't have no hog to scoot down, Mrs. Turpin said to herself.

"A-gruntin and a-rootin and a-groanin," the woman muttered.

"We got a little of everything," Mrs. Turpin said to the pleasant lady. "It's no use in having more than you can handle yourself with help like it is. We found enough niggers to pick our cotton this year but Claud he has to go after them and take them home again in the evening. They can't walk that half a mile. No they can't. I tell you," she said and laughed merrily, "I sure am tired of buttering up niggers, but you got to love em if you want em to work for you. When they come in the morning, I run out and I say, 'Hi yawl this morning?' and when Claud drives them off to the field I just wave to beat the band and they just wave back." And she waved her hand rapidly to illustrate.

"Like you read out of the same book," the lady said, showing she understood perfectly.

"Child, yes," Mrs. Turpin said. "And when they come in from the field, I run out with a bucket of icewater. That's the way it's going to be from now on," she said. "You may as well face it."

"One thang I know," the white-trash woman said. "Two thangs I ain't going to do: love no niggers or scoot down no hog with no hose." And she let out a bark of contempt.

The look that Mrs. Turpin and the pleasant lady exchanged indicated they both understood that you had to *have* certain things before you could *know* certain things. But every time Mrs. Turpin exchanged a look with the lady, she was aware that the ugly girl's peculiar eyes were still on her, and she had trouble bringing her attention back to the conversation.

"When you got something," she said, "you got to look after it." And when you ain't got a thing but breath and britches, she added to herself, you can afford to come to town every morning and just sit on the Court House coping and spit.

A grotesque revolving shadow passed across the curtain behind her and was thrown palely on the opposite wall. Then a bicycle clattered down against the outside of the building. The door opened and a colored boy glided in with a tray from the drug store. It had two large red and white paper cups on it with tops on them. He was a tall, very black boy in discolored white pants and a green nylon shirt. He was chewing gum slowly, as if to music. He set the tray down in the office opening next to the fern and stuck his head through to look for the secretary. She was not in there. He rested his arms on the ledge and waited, his narrow bottom stuck out, swaying slowly to the left and right. He raised a hand over his head and scratched the base of his skull.

"You see that button there, boy?" Mrs. Turpin said. "You can punch that and she'll come. She's probably in the back somewhere."

"Is thas right?" the boy said agreeably, as if he had never seen the button before. He leaned to the right and put his finger on it. "She sometime out," he said and twisted around to face his audience, his elbows behind him on the counter. The nurse appeared and he twisted back again. She handed him a dollar and he rooted in his pocket and made the change and counted it out to her. She gave him fifteen cents for a tip and he went out with the empty tray. The heavy door swung to slowly and closed at length with the sound of suction. For a moment no one spoke.

"They ought to send all them niggers back to Africa," the white-trash woman said. "That's wher they come from in the first place."

"Oh, I couldn't do without my good colored friends," the pleasant lady said.

"There's a heap of things worse than a nigger," Mrs. Turpin agreed. "It's all kinds of them just like it's all kinds of us."

"Yes, and it takes all kinds to make the world go round," the lady said in her musical voice.

As she said it, the raw-complexioned girl snapped her teeth together. Her lower lip turned downwards and inside out, revealing the pale pink inside of her mouth. After a second it rolled back up. It was the ugliest face Mrs. Turpin had ever seen anyone make and for a moment she was certain that the girl had made it at her. She was looking at her as if she had known and disliked her all her life—all of Mrs. Turpin's life, it seemed too, not just all the girl's life. Why, girl, I don't even know you, Mrs. Turpin said silently.

She forced her attention back to the discussion. "It wouldn't be practical to send them back to Africa," she said. "They wouldn't want to go. They got it too good here."

"Wouldn't be what they wanted—if I had anythang to do with it," the woman said.

"It wouldn't be a way in the world you could get all the niggers back over there," Mrs. Turpin said. "They'd be hiding out and lying down and turning sick on you and wailing and hollering and raring and pitching. It wouldn't be a way in the world to get them over there."

"They got over here," the trashy woman said. "Get back like they got over."

"It wasn't so many of them then," Mrs. Turpin explained.

The woman looked at Mrs. Turpin as if here was an idiot indeed but Mrs. Turpin was not bothered by the look, considering where it came from.

"Nooo," she said, "they're going to stay here where they can go to New York and marry white folks and improve their color. That 's what they all want to do, every one of them, improve their color."

"You know what comes of that, don't you?" Claud asked.

"No, Claud, what?" Mrs. Turpin said.

Claud's eyes twinkled. "White-faced niggers," he said with never a smile.

Everybody in the office laughed except the white-trash and the ugly girl. The girl gripped the book in her lap with white fingers. The trashy woman looked around her from face to face as if she thought they were all idiots. The old woman in the feed sack dress continued to gaze expressionless across the floor at the high-top shoes of the man opposite her, the one who had been pretending to be asleep when the Turpins came in. He was laughing heartily, his hands still spread out on his knees. The child had fallen to the side and was lying now almost face down in the old woman's lap.

While they recovered from their laughter, the nasal chorus on the radio kept the room from silence.

"You go to blank blank
And I'll go to mine
But we'll all blank along
To-geth-ther,
And all along the blank
We'll hep each other out
Smile-ling in any kind of
Weath-ther!"

Mrs. Turpin didn't catch every word but she caught enough to agree with the spirit of the song and it turned her thoughts sober. To help anybody out that needed it was her philosophy of life. She never spared herself when she found somebody in need, whether they were white or black, trash or decent. And of all she had to be thankful for, she was most thankful that this was so. If Jesus had said, "You can be high society and have all the money you want and be thin and svelte-like, but you can't be a good woman with it," she would have had to say, "Well don't make me that then. Make me a good woman and it don't matter what else, how fat or how ugly or how poor!" Her heart rose. He had not made her a nigger or white-trash or ugly! He had made her herself and given her a little of everything. Jesus, thank you! she said. Thank you thank you thank you! Whenever she counted her blessings she felt as buoyant as if she weighed one hundred and twenty-five pounds instead of one hundred and eighty.

"What's wrong with your little boy?" the pleasant lady asked the white-trashy woman.

"He has a ulcer," the woman said proudly. "He ain't give me a minute's peace since he was born. Him and her are just alike," she said, nodding at the old woman, who was running her leathery fingers through the child's pale hair. "Look like I can't get nothing down them two but Co' Cola and candy."

That's all you try to get down em, Mrs. Turpin said to herself. Too lazy to light the fire. There was nothing you could tell her about people like them that she didn't know already. And it was not just that they didn't have anything. Because if you gave them everything, in two weeks it would all be broken or filthy or they would have chopped it up for lightwood. She knew all this from her own experience. Help them you must, but help them you couldn't.

All at once the ugly girl turned her lips inside out again. Her eyes were fixed like two drills on Mrs. Turpin. This time there was no mistaking that there was something urgent behind them.

Girl, Mrs. Turpin exclaimed silently, I haven't done a thing to you! The girl might be confusing her with somebody else. There was no need to sit by and let herself be intimidated. "You must be in college," she said boldly, looking directly at the girl. "I see you reading a book there."

The girl continued to stare and pointedly did not answer.

Her mother blushed at this rudeness. "The lady asked you a question, Mary Grace," she said under her breath.

"I have ears," Mary Grace said.

The poor mother blushed again. "Mary Grace goes to Wellesley College," she explained. She twisted one of the buttons on her dress. "In Massachusetts," she added with a grimace. "And in the summer she just keeps right on studying. Just reads all the time, a real book worm. She's done real well at Wellesley; she's taking English and Math and History and Psychology and Social Studies," she rattled on, "and I think it's too much. I think she ought to get out and have fun."

The girl looked as if she would like to hurl them all through the plate glass window.

"Way up north," Mrs. Turpin murmured and thought, well, it hasn't done much for her manners.

"I'd almost rather to have him sick," the white-trash woman said, wrenching the attention back to herself. "He's so mean when he ain't. Look like some children just take natural to meanness. It's some gets bad when they get sick but he was the opposite. Took sick and turned good. He don't give me no trouble now. It's me waitin to see the doctor," she said.

If I was going to send anybody back to Africa, Mrs. Turpin thought, it would be your kind, woman. "Yes, indeed," she said aloud, but looking up at the ceiling, "it's a heap of things worse than a nigger." And dirtier than a hog, she added to herself.

"I think people with bad dispositions are more to be pitied than anyone on earth," the pleasant lady said in a voice that was decidedly thin.

"I thank the Lord he has blessed me with a good one," Mrs. Turpin said. "The day has never dawned that I couldn't find something to laugh at."

"Not since she married me anyways," Claud said with a comical straight face.

Everybody laughed except the girl and the white-trash.

Mrs. Turpin's stomach shook. "He's such a caution," she said, "that I can't help but laugh at him."

The girl made a loud ugly noise through her teeth.

Her mother's mouth grew thin and tight. "I think the worst thing in the world," she said, "is an ungrateful person. To have everything and not appreciate it. I know a girl," she said, "who has parents who would give her anything, a little brother who loves her dearly, who is getting a good education, who wears the best clothes, but who can never say a kind word to anyone, who never smiles, who just criticizes and complains all day long."

"Is she too old to paddle?" Claud asked.

The girl's face was almost purple.

"Yes," the lady said, "I'm afraid there's nothing to do but leave her to her folly. Some day she'll wake up and it'll be too late."

"It never hurt anyone to smile," Mrs. Turpin said. "It just makes you feel better all over."

"Of course," the lady said sadly, "but there are just some people you can't tell anything to. They can't take criticism."

"If it's one thing I am," Mrs. Turpin said with feeling, "it's grateful. When I think who all I could have been besides myself and what all I got, a little of everything, and a good disposition besides, I just feel like shouting, 'Thank you, Jesus, for making everything the way it is!' It could have been different!" For one thing, somebody else could have got Claud. At the thought of this, she was flooded with gratitude and a terrible pang of joy ran through her. "Oh thank you, Jesus, Jesus, thank you!" she cried aloud.

The book struck her directly over her left eye. It struck almost at the same instant that she realized the girl was about to hurl it. Before she could utter a sound, the raw face came crashing across the table toward her, howling. The girl's fingers sank like clamps into the soft flesh of her neck. She heard the mother cry out and Claud shout, "Whoa!" There was an instant when she was certain that she was about to be in an earthquake.

All at once her vision narrowed and she saw everything as if it were happening in a small room far away, or as if she were looking at it through the wrong end of a telescope. Claud's face crumpled and fell out of sight. The nurse ran in, then out, then in again. Then the gangling figure of the doctor rushed out of the inner door. Magazines flew this way and that as the table turned over. The girl fell with a thud and Mrs. Turpin's vision suddenly reversed itself and she saw everything large instead of small. The eyes of the white-trashy woman were staring hugely at the floor. There the girl, held down on one side by the nurse and on the other by her mother, was wrenching and turning in their grasp. The doctor was kneeling astride her, trying to hold her arm down. He managed after a second to sink a long needle into it.

Mrs. Turpin felt entirely hollow except for her heart which swung from side to side as if it were agitated in a great empty drum of flesh.

"Somebody that's not busy call for the ambulance," the doctor said in the off-hand voice young doctors adopt for terrible occasions.

Mrs. Turpin could not have moved a finger. The old man who had been sitting next to her skipped numbly into the office and made the call, for the secretary still seemed to be gone.

"Claud!" Mrs. Turpin called.

He was not in his chair. She knew she must jump up and find him but she felt like some one trying to catch a train in a dream, when everything moves in slow motion and the faster you try to run the slower you go.

"Here I am," a suffocated voice, very unlike Claud's, said.

He was doubled up in the corner on the floor, pale as paper, holding his leg. She wanted to get up and go to him but she could not move. Instead, her gaze was drawn slowly downward to the churning face on the floor, which she could see over the doctor's shoulder.

The girl's eyes stopped rolling and focused on her. They seemed a much lighter blue than before, as if a door that had been tightly closed behind them was now open to admit light and air.

Mrs. Turpin's head cleared and her power of motion returned. She leaned forward until she was looking directly into the fierce brilliant eyes. There was no doubt in her mind that the girl did know her, knew her in some intense and personal way, beyond time and place and condition. "What you got to say to me?" she asked hoarsely and held her breath, waiting, as for a revelation.

The girl raised her head. Her gaze locked with Mrs. Turpin's. "Go back to hell where you came from, you old wart hog," she whispered. Her voice was low but clear. Her eyes burned for a moment as if she saw with pleasure that her message had struck its target.

Mrs. Turpin sank back in her chair.

After a moment the girl's eyes closed and she turned her head wearily to the side.

The doctor rose and handed the nurse the empty syringe. He leaned over and put both hands for a moment on the mother's shoulders, which were shaking. She was sitting on the floor, her lips pressed together, holding Mary Grace's hand in her lap. The girl's fingers were gripped like a baby's around her thumb. "Go on to the hospital," he said. "I'll call and make the arrangements."

"Now let's see that neck," he said in a jovial voice to Mrs. Turpin. He began to inspect her neck with his first two fingers. Two little moon-shaped lines like pink fish bones were indented over her windpipe. There was the beginning of an angry red swelling above her eye. His fingers passed over this also.

"Lea' me be," she said thickly and shook him off. "See about Claud. She kicked him."

"I'll see about him in a minute," he said and felt her pulse. He was a thin grey-haired man, given to pleasantries. "Go home and have yourself a vacation the rest of the day," he said and patted her on the shoulder.

Quit your pattin me, Mrs. Turpin growled to herself.

"And put an ice pack over that eye," he said. Then he went and squatted down beside Claud and looked at his leg. After a moment he pulled him up and Claud limped after him into the office.

Until the ambulance came, the only sounds in the room were the tremulous moans of the girl's mother, who continued to sit on the floor. The white-trash woman did not take her eyes off the girl. Mrs. Turpin looked straight ahead at nothing. Presently the ambulance drew up, a long dark shadow, behind the curtain. The attendants came in and set the stretcher down beside the girl and lifted her expertly onto it and carried her out. The nurse helped the mother gather up her things. The shadow of the ambulance moved silently away and the nurse came back in the office.

"That ther girl is going to be a lunatic, ain't she?" the white-trash woman asked the nurse, but the nurse kept on to the back and never answered her.

"Yes, she's going to be a lunatic," the white-trash woman said to the rest of them.

"Po' critter," the old woman murmured. The child's face was still in her lap. His eyes looked idly out over her knees. He had not moved during the disturbance except to draw one leg up under him.

"I thank Gawd," the white-trash woman said fervently, "I ain't a lunatic."

Claud came limping out and the Turpins went home.

As their pick-up truck turned into their own dirt road and made the crest of the hill, Mrs. Turpin gripped the window ledge and looked out suspiciously. The land sloped gracefully down through a field dotted with lavender weeds and at the start of the rise their small yellow frame house, with its little flower beds spread out around it like a fancy apron, sat primly in its accustomed place between two giant hickory trees. She would not have been startled to see a burnt wound between two blackened chimneys.

Neither of them felt like eating so they put on their house clothes and lowered the shade in the bedroom and lay down, Claud with his leg on a pillow and herself with a damp washcloth over her eye. The instant she was flat on her back, the image of a razor-backed hog with warts on its face and horns coming out behind its ears snorted into her head. She moaned, a low quiet moan.

"I am not," she said tearfully, "a wart hog. From hell." But the denial had no force. The girl's eyes and her words, even the tone of her voice, low but clear, directed only to her, brooked no repudiation. She had been singled out for the message, though there was trash in the room to whom it might justly have been applied. The full force of this fact struck her only now. There was a woman there who was neglecting her own child but she had been overlooked. The message had been given to Ruby Turpin, a respectable, hard-working, church-going woman. The tears dried. Her eyes began to burn instead with wrath.

She rose on her elbow and the washcloth fell into her hand. Claud was lying on his back, snoring. She wanted to tell him what the girl had said. At the same time, she did not wish to put the image of herself as a wart hog from hell into his mind.

"Hey, Claud," she muttered and pushed his shoulder.

Claud opened one pale baby blue eye.

She looked into it warily. He did not think about anything. He just went his way.

"Wha, whasit?" he said and closed the eye again.

"Nothing," she said. "Does your leg pain you?"

"Hurts like hell," Claud said.

"It'll quit terreckly," she said and lay back down. In a moment Claud was snoring again. For the rest of the afternoon they lay there. Claud slept. She scowled at the ceiling. Occasionally she raised her fist and made a small stabbing motion over her chest as if she was defending her innocence to invisible guests who were like the comforters of Job, reasonable-seeming but wrong.

About five-thirty Claud stirred. "Got to go after those niggers," he sighed, not moving.

She was looking straight up as if there were unintelligible handwriting on the ceiling. The protuberance over her eye had turned a greenish-blue. "Listen here," she said.

"What?"

"Kiss me."

Claud leaned over and kissed her loudly on the mouth. He pinched her side and their hands interlocked. Her expression of ferocious concentration did not change. Claud got up, groaning and growling, and limped off. She continued to study the ceiling.

She did not get up until she heard the pick-up truck coming back with the Negroes. Then she rose and thrust her feet in her brown oxfords, which she did not bother to lace, and stumped out onto the back porch and got her red plastic bucket. She emptied a tray of ice cubes into it and filled it half full of water and went out into the back yard. Every afternoon after Claud brought the hands in, one of the boys helped him put out hay and the rest waited in the back of the truck until he was ready to take them home. The truck was parked in the shade under one of the hickory trees.

"Hi yawl this evening?" Mrs. Turpin asked grimly, appearing with the bucket and the dipper. There were three women and a boy in the truck.

"Us doin nicely," the oldest woman said. "Hi you doin?" and her gaze stuck immediately on the dark lump on Mrs. Turpin's forehead. "You done fell down, ain't you?" she asked in a solicitous voice. The old woman was dark and almost toothless. She had on an old felt hat of Claud's set back on her head. The other two women were younger and lighter and they both had new bright green sun hats. One of them had hers on her head; the other had taken hers off and the boy was grinning beneath it.

Mrs. Turpin set the bucket down on the floor of the truck. "Yawl hep yourselves," she said. She looked around to make sure Claud had gone. "No. I didn't fall down," she said, folding her arms. "It was something worse than that."

"Ain't nothing bad happen to you!" the old woman said. She said it as if they all knew that Mrs. Turpin was protected in some special way by Divine Providence. "You just had you a little fall."

"We were in town at the doctor's office for where the cow kicked Mr. Turpin," Mrs. Turpin said in a flat tone that indicated they could leave off their foolishness. "And there was this girl there. A big fat girl with her face all broke out. I could look at that girl and tell she was peculiar but I couldn't tell how. And me and her mama were just talking and going along and all of a sudden WHAM! She throws this big book she was reading at me and . . ."

"Naw!" the old woman cried out.

"And then she jumps over the table and commences to choke me."

"Naw!" they all exclaimed, "naw!"

"Hi come she do that?" the old woman asked. "What ail her?"

Mrs. Turpin only glared in front of her.

"Somethin ail her," the old woman said.

"They carried her off in an ambulance," Mrs. Turpin continued, "but before she went she was rolling on the floor and they were trying to hold her down to give her a shot and she said something to me." She paused. "You know what she said to me?"

"What she say?" they asked.

"She said," Mrs. Turpin began, and stopped, her face very dark and heavy. The sun was getting whiter and whiter, blanching the sky overhead so that the leaves of the hickory tree were black in the face of it. She could not bring forth the words. "Something real ugly," she muttered.

"She sho shouldn't said nothin ugly to you," the old woman said. "You so sweet. You the sweetest lady I know."

"She pretty too," the one with the hat on said.

"And stout, the other one said. "I never knowed no sweeter white lady."

"That's the truth befo' Jesus," the old woman said. "Amen! You des as sweet and pretty as you can be."

Mrs. Turpin knew just exactly how much Negro flattery was worth and it added to her rage. "She said," she began again and finished this time with a fierce rush of breath, "that I was an old wart hog from hell."

There was an astounded silence.

"Where she at?" the youngest woman cried in a piercing voice. "Lemme see her. I'll kill her!"

"I'll kill her with you!" the other one cried.

"She b'long in the sylum," the old woman said emphatically. "You the sweetest white lady I know.

"She pretty too," the other two said. "Stout as she can be and sweet. Jesus satisfied with her!"

"Deed he is," the old woman declared.

Idiots! Mrs. Turpin growled to herself. You could never say anything intelligent to a nigger. You could talk at them but not with them. "Yawl ain't drunk your water," she said shortly. "Leave the bucket in the truck when you're finished with it. I got more to do than just stand around and pass the time of day," and she moved off and into the house.

She stood for a moment in the middle of the kitchen. The dark protuberance over her eye looked like a miniature tornado cloud which might any moment sweep across the horizon of her brow. Her lower lip protruded dangerously. She squared her massive shoulders. Then she marched into the front of the house and out the side door and started down the road to the pig parlor. She had the look of a woman going single-handed, weaponless, into battle.

The sun was a deep yellow now like a harvest moon and was riding westward very fast over the far tree line as if it meant to reach the hogs before she did. The road was rutted and she kicked several good-sized stones out of her path as she strode along. The pig parlor was on a little knoll at the end of a lane that ran off from the side of the barn. It was a square of concrete as large as a small room, with a board fence about four feet high around it. The concrete floor sloped slightly so that the hog wash could drain off into a trench where it was carried to the field for fertilizer. Claud was standing on the outside, on the edge of the concrete, hanging onto the top board, hosing down the floor inside. The hose was connected to the faucet of a water trough nearby.

Mrs. Turpin climbed up beside him and glowered down at the hogs inside. There were seven long-snouted bristly shoats in it—tan with liver-colored spots—and an old sow a few weeks off from farrowing. She was lying on her side grunting. The shoats were running about shaking themselves like idiot children, their little slit pig eyes searching the floor for anything left. She had read that pigs were the most intelligent animal. She doubted it. They were supposed to be smarter than dogs. There had even been a pig astronaut. He had performed his assignment perfectly but died of a heart attack afterwards because they left him in his electric suit, sitting upright throughout his examination when naturally a hog should be on all fours.

A-gruntin and a-rootin and a-groanin.

"Gimme that hose," she said, yanking it away from Claud. "Go on and carry them niggers home and then get off that leg."

"You look like you might have swallowed a mad dog," Claud observed, but he got down and limped off. He paid no attention to her humors.

Until he was out of earshot, Mrs. Turpin stood on the side of the pen, holding the hose and pointing the stream of water at the hind quarters of any shoat that looked as if it might try to lie down. When he had had time to get over the hill, she turned her head slightly and her wrathful eyes scanned the path. He was nowhere insight. She turned back again and seemed to gather herself up. Her shoulders rose and she drew in her breath.

"What do you send me a message like that for?" she said in a low fierce voice, barely above a whisper but with the force of a shout in its concentrated fury. "How am I a hog and me both? How am I saved and from hell too?" Her free fist was knotted and with the other she gripped the hose, blindly pointing the stream of water in and out of the eye of the old sow whose outraged squeal she did not hear.

The pig parlor commanded a view of the back pasture where their twenty beef cows were gathered around the hay-bales Claud and the boy had put out. The freshly cut pasture sloped down to the highway. Across it was their cotton field and beyond that a dark green dusty wood which they owned as well. The sun was behind the wood, very red, looking over the paling of trees like a farmer inspecting his own hogs.

"Why me?" she rumbled. "It's no trash around here, black or white, that I haven't given to. And break my back to the bone every day working. And do for the church."

She appeared to be the right size woman to command the arena before her. "How am I a hog?" she demanded. "Exactly how am I like them?" and she jabbed the stream of water at the shoats. "There was plenty of trash there. It didn't have to be me.

"If you like trash better, go get yourself some trash then." she railed. "You could have made me trash. Or a nigger. If trash is what you wanted why didn't you make me trash?" She shook her fist with the hose in it and a watery snake appeared momentarily in the air. "I could quit working and take it easy and be filthy," she growled. "Lounge about the sidewalks all day drinking root beer. Dip snuff and spit in every puddle and have it all over my face. I could be nasty.

"Or you could have made me a nigger. It's too late for me to be a nigger," she said with deep sarcasm, "but I could act like one. Lay down in the middle of the road and stop traffic. Roll on the ground."

In the deepening light everything was taking on a mysterious hue. The pasture was growing a peculiar glassy green and the streak of highway had turned lavender. She braced herself for a final assault and this time her voice rolled out over the pasture. "Go on," she yelled, "call me a hog! Call me a hog again. From hell. Call me a wart hog from hell. Put that bottom rail on top. There'll still be a top and bottom!"

A garbled echo returned to her.

A final surge of fury shook her and she roared, "Who do you think you are?"

The color of everything, field and crimson sky, burned for a moment with a transparent intensity. The question carried over the pasture and across the highway and the cotton field and returned to her clearly like an answer from beyond the wood.

She opened her mouth but no sound came out of it.

A tiny truck, Claud's, appeared on the highway, heading rapidly out of sight. Its gears scraped thinly. It looked like a child's toy. At any moment a bigger truck might smash into it and scatter Claud's and the niggers' brains all over the road.

Mrs. Turpin stood there, her gaze fixed on the highway, all her muscles rigid, until in five or six minutes the truck reappeared, returning. She waited until it had had time to turn into their own road. Then like a monumental statue coming to life, she bent her head slowly and gazed, as if through the very heart of mystery, down into the pig parlor at the hogs. They had settled all in one corner around the old sow who was grunting softly. A red glow suffused them. They appeared to pant with a secret life.

Until the sun slipped finally behind the tree line, Mrs. Turpin remained there with her gaze bent to them as if she were absorbing some abysmal life-giving knowledge. At last she lifted her head. There was only a purple streak in the sky, cutting through a field of crimson and leading, like an extension of the highway, into the descending dusk. She raised her hands from the side of the pen in a gesture hieratic and profound. A visionary light settled in her eyes. She saw the streak as a vast swinging bridge extending upward from the earth through a field of living fire. Upon it a vast horde of souls were rumbling toward heaven. There were whole companies of white-trash, clean for the first time in their lives, and bands of black niggers in white robes, and battalions of freaks and lunatics shouting and clapping and leaping like frogs. And bringing up the end of the procession was a tribe of people whom she recognized at once as those who, like herself and Claud, had always had a little of everything and the God-given wit to use it right. She leaned forward to observe them closer. They were marching behind the others with great dignity, accountable as they had always been for good order and common sense and respectable behavior.

They alone were on key. Yet she could see by their shocked and altered faces that even their virtues were being burned away. She lowered her hands and gripped the rail of the hog pen, her eyes small but fixed unblinkingly on what lay ahead. In a moment the vision faded but she remained where she was, immobile.

At length she got down and turned off the faucet and made her slow way on the darkening path to the house. In the woods around her the invisible cricket choruses had struck up, but what she heard were the voices of the souls climbing upward into the starry field and shouting hallelujah.

EDGAR ALLAN POE (1809–1849)
The Cask of Amontillado

The name of Edgar Allan Poe has become almost synonymous with the short story. He is the father of the detective story and, along with Nathaniel Hawthorne, Poe, a Virginia native, stands at the beginning of a long line of great American short story writers. In addition to writing poetry and criticism, he wrote such famous tales as "The Tell-Tale Heart," "The Pit and the Pendulum," and "The Fall of the House of Usher." "The Cask of Amontillado" first appeared in 1846.

The thousand injuries of Fortunato I had borne as I best could; but when he ventured upon insult, I vowed revenge. You, who so well know the nature of my soul, will not suppose, however, that I gave utterance to a threat. *At length* I would be avenged; this was a point definitely settled—but the very definitiveness with which it was resolved precluded the idea of risk. I must not only punish, but punish with impunity. A wrong is unredressed when retribution overtakes its redresser. It is equally unredressed when the avenger fails to make himself felt as such to him who has done the wrong.

It must be understood, that neither by word nor deed had I given Fortunato cause to doubt my good-will. I continued, as was my wont, to smile in his face, and he did not perceive that my smile *now* was at the thought of his immolation.

He had a weak point—this Fortunato—although in other regards he was a man to be respected and even feared. He prided himself on his connoisseurship in wine. Few Italians have the true virtuoso spirit. For the most part their enthusiasm is adopted to suit the time and opportunity—to practise imposture upon the British and Austrian *millionnaires*. In painting and gemmary Fortunato, like his countrymen, was a quack—but in the matter of old wines he was sincere. In this respect I did not differ from him materially: I was skilful in the Italian vintages myself, and bought largely whenever I could.

It was about dusk, one evening during the supreme madness of the carnival season, that I encountered my friend. He accosted me with excessive warmth, for he had been drinking much. The man wore motley. He had on a tight-fitting parti-striped dress, and his head was surmounted by the conical cap and bells. I was so pleased to see him, that I thought I should never have done wringing his hand.

I said to him: "My dear Fortunato, you are luckily met. How remarkably well you are looking to-day! But I have received a pipe of what passes for Amontillado, and I have my doubts."

"How?" said he. "Amontillado? A pipe? Impossible! And in the middle of the carnival!"

"I have my doubts," I replied; "and I was silly enough to pay the full Amontillado price without consulting you in the matter. You were not to be found, and I was fearful of losing a bargain."

"Amontillado!"

"I have my doubts."

"Amontillado!"

"And I must satisfy them."

"Amontillado!"

"As you are engaged, I am on my way to Luchesi. If any one has a critical turn, it is he. He will tell me—"

"Luchesi cannot tell Amontillado from Sherry."

"And yet some fools will have it that his taste is a match for your own."

"Come, let us go."

"Whither?"

"To your vaults."

"My friend, no; I will not impose upon your good nature. I perceive you have an engagement. Luchesi—"

"I have no engagement;—come."

"My friend, no. It is not the engagement, but the severe cold with which I perceive you are afflicted. The vaults are insufferably damp. They are encrusted with nitre."

"Let us go, nevertheless. The cold is merely nothing. Amontillado. You have been imposed upon. And as for Luchesi, he cannot distinguish Sherry from Amontillado."

Thus speaking, Fortunato possessed himself of my arm. Putting on mask of black silk, and drawing a *roquelaire* closely about my person, suffered him to hurry me to my palazzo.

There were no attendants at home; they had absconded to make merry in honor of the time. I had told them that I should not return until the morning, and had given them explicit orders not to stir from the house. These orders were sufficient, I well knew, to insure their immediate disappearance, one and all, as soon as my back was turned.

I took from their sconces two flambeaux, and giving one to Fortunato bowed him through several suites of rooms to the archway that led into the vaults. I passed down a long and winding staircase, requesting him to be cautious as he followed. We came at length to the foot of the descent, and stood together on the damp ground of the catacombs of the Montresors.

The gait of my friend was unsteady, and the bells upon his cap jingled as he strode.

"The pipe?" said he.

"It is farther on," said I; "but observe the white web-work which gleams from these cavern walls."

He turned toward me, and looked into my eyes with two filmy orbs that distilled the rheum of intoxication.

"Nitre?" he asked, at length.

"Nitre," I replied. "How long have you had that cough?"

"Ugh! ugh! ugh!—ugh! ugh! ugh!—ugh! ugh! ugh!—ugh! ugh! ugh!—ugh! ugh! ugh!"

My poor friend found it impossible to reply for many minutes.

"It is nothing," he said, at last.

"Come," I said, with decision, "we will go back; your health is precious. You are rich, respected, admired, beloved; you are happy, as once I was. You are a man to be missed. For me it is no matter. We will go back; you will be ill, and I cannot be responsible. Besides, there is Luchesi—"

"Enough," he said; "the cough is a mere nothing; it will not kill me. I shall not die of a cough."

"True—true," I replied; "and, indeed, I had no intention of alarming you unnecessarily; but you should use all proper caution. A draught of this Medoc will defend us from the damps."

Here I knocked off the neck of a bottle which I drew from a long row of its fellows that lay upon the mould.

"Drink," I said, presenting him the wine.

He raised it to his lips with a leer. He paused and nodded to me familiarly, while his bells jingled.

"I drink," he said, "to the buried that repose around us."

"And I to your long life."

He again took my arm, and we proceeded.

"These vaults," he said, "are extensive."

"The Montresors," I replied. "were a great and numerous family."

"I forget your arms."

"A huge human foot d'or, in a field azure; the foot crushes a serpent rampant whose fangs are imbedded in the heel."

"And the motto?"

"*Nemo me impune lacessit.*"[1]

"Good!" he said.

---

1. Latin: "No one attacks me with impunity."

The wine sparkled in his eyes and the bells jingled. My own fancy grew warm with the Medoc. We had passed through walls of piled bones, with casks and puncheons intermingling, into the inmost recesses of the catacombs. I paused again, and this time I made bold to seize Fortunato by an arm above the elbow.

"The nitre!" I said; "see, it increases. It hangs like moss upon the vaults. We are below the river's bed. The drops of moisture trickle among the bones. Come, we will go back ere it is too late. Your cough—"

"It is nothing," he said; "let us go on. But first, another draught of the Medoc."

I broke and reached him a flagon of De Grâve. He emptied it at a breath. His eyes flashed with a fierce light. He laughed and threw the bottle upward with a gesticulation I did not understand.

I looked at him in surprise. He repeated the movement—a grotesque one.

"You do not comprehend?" he said.

"Not I," I replied.

"Then you are not of the brotherhood."

"How?"

"You are not of the masons."

"Yes, yes," I said; "yes, yes."

"You? Impossible! A mason?"

"A mason," I replied.

"A sign," he said.

"It is this," I answered, producing a trowel from beneath the folds of my *roquelaire*.

"You jest," he exclaimed, recoiling a few paces. "But let us proceed to the Amontillado."

"Be it so," I said, replacing the tool beneath the cloak, and again offering him my arm. He leaned upon it heavily. We continued our route in search of the Amontillado. We padded through a range of low arches, descended, passed on, and descending again, arrived at a deep crypt, in which the foulness of the air caused our flambeaux rather to glow than flame.

At the most remote end of the crypt there appeared another less spacious. Its walls had been lined with human remains, piled to the vault overhead, in the fashion of the great catacombs of Paris. Three side of this interior crypt were still ornamented in this manner. From the fourth the bones had been thrown down, and lay promiscuously upon the earth, forming at one point a mound of some size. Within the wall thus exposed by the displacing of the bones, we perceived a still interior recess, in depth about four feet, in width three, in height six or seven. It seemed to have been constructed for no especial use within itself, but formed merely the interval between two of the colossal supports of the roof of the catacombs, and was backed by one of their circumscribing walls of solid granite.

It was in vain that Fortunato, uplifting his dull torch, endeavored to pry into the depth of the recess. Its termination the feeble light did not enable us to see.

"Proceed," I said; "herein is the Amontillado. As for Luchesi—"

"He is an ignoramus," interrupted my friend, as he stepped unsteadily forward, while I followed immediately at his heels. In an instant he had reached the extremity of the niche, and finding his progress arrested by the rock, stood stupidly bewildered. A moment more and I had fettered him to the granite. In its surface were two iron staples, distant from each other about two feet, horizontally. From one of these depended a short chain, from the other a padlock. Throwing the links about his waist, it was but the work of a few seconds to secure it. He was too much astounded to resist. Withdrawing the key I stepped back from the recess.

"Pass your hand," I said, "over the wall; you cannot help feeling the nitre. Indeed it is *very* damp. Once more let me *implore* you to return. No? Then I must positively leave you. But I must first render you all the little attentions in my power."

"The Amontillado!" ejaculated my friend, not yet recovered from his astonishment.

"True," I replied; "the Amontillado."

As I said these words I busied myself among the pile of bones of which I have before spoken. Throwing them aside, I soon uncovered a quantity of building stone and mortar. With these materials and with the aid of my trowel, I began vigorously to wall up the entrance of the niche.

I had scarcely laid the first tier of the masonry when I discovered that the intoxication of Fortunato had in a great measure worn off. The earliest indication I had of this was a low moaning cry from the depth of the recess. It was *not* the cry of a drunken man. There was then a long and obstinate silence. I laid the second tier, and the third, and the fourth; and then I heard the furious vibrations of the chain. The noise lasted for several minutes, during which, that I might hearken to it with the more satisfaction, I ceased my labors and sat down upon the bones. When at last the clanking subsided, I resumed the trowel, and finished without interruption the fifth, the sixth, and the seventh tier. The wall was now nearly upon a level with my breast. I again paused, and holding the flambeaux over the masonwork, threw a few feeble rays upon the figure within.

A succession of loud and shrill screams, bursting suddenly from the throat of the chained form, seemed to thrust me violently back. For a brief moment I hesitated—I trembled. Unsheathing my rapier, I began to grope with it about the recess; but the thought of an instant reassured me. I placed my hand upon the solid fabric of the catacombs, and felt satisfied. I reapproached the wall. I replied to the yells of him who clamored. I re-echoed—I aided—I surpassed them in volume and in strength. I did this, and the clamorer grew still.

It was now midnight, and my task was drawing to a close. I had completed the eighth, the ninth, and the tenth tier. I had finished a portion of the last and the eleventh; there remained but a single stone to be fitted and plastered in. I struggled with its weight; I placed it partially in its destined position. But now there came from out the niche a low laugh that erected the hairs upon my head. It was succeeded by a sad voice, which I had difficulty in recognizing as that of the noble Fortunato. The voice said—

"Ha! ha! ha!—he! he!—a very good joke indeed—an excellent jest. We will have many a rich laugh about it at the palazzo—he! he! he!—over our wine—he! he! he!"

"The Amontillado!" I said.

"He! he! he!—he! he! he!—yes, the Amontillado. But is it not getting late? Will not they be awaiting us at the palazzo, the Lady Fortunato and the rest? Let us be gone."

"Yes," I said, "let us be gone."

For *the love of God, Montresor!*"

"Yes," I said, "for the love of God!"

But to these words I hearkened in vain for a reply. I grew impatient. I called aloud:

"Fortunato!"

No answer. I called again:

"Fortunato!"

No answer still. I thrust a torch through the remaining aperture and let it fall within. There came forth in return only a jingling of the bells. My heart grew sick—on account of the dampness of the catacombs. I hastened to make an end of my labor. I forced the last stone into its position; I plastered it up. Against the new masonry I re-erected the old rampart of bones. For the half of a century no mortal has disturbed them. *In pace requiescat!*

KATHERINE ANNE PORTER (1890–1980)

The Jilting of Granny Weatherall

Katherine Anne Porter (1890–1980) was born in Indian Creek, Texas. As a young woman she worked as a journalist. "The Jilting of Granny Weatherall" appeared in her first collection of stories, *Flowering Judas and Other Stories* (1930). Her one novel, *Ship of Fools*, was begun in the 1930s but not published until 1962. In 1965, her *Collected Stories* won both the Pulitzer Prize and the National Book Award.

She flicked her wrist neatly out of Doctor Harry's pudgy careful fingers and pulled the sheet up to her chin. The brat ought to be in knee breeches. Doctoring around the country with spectacles on his nose! "Get along now, take your schoolbooks and go. There's nothing wrong with me."

Doctor Harry spread a warm paw like a cushion on her forehead where the forked green vein danced and made her eyelids twitch. "Now, now, be a good girl, and we'll have you up in no time."

"That's no way to speak to a woman nearly eighty years old just because she's down. I'd have you respect your elders, young man."

"Well, Missy, excuse me." Doctor Harry patted her cheek. "But I've got to warn you, haven't I? You're a marvel, but you must be careful or you're going to be good and sorry."

"Don't tell me what I'm going to be. I'm on my feet now, morally speaking. It's Cornelia. I had to go to bed to get rid of her."

Her bones felt loose, and floated around in her skin, and Doctor Harry floated like a balloon around the foot of the bed. He floated and pulled down his waistcoat and swung his glasses on a cord. "Well, stay where you are, it certainly can't hurt you."

"Get along and doctor your sick," said Granny Weatherall. "Leave a well woman alone. I'll call for you when I want you. . . . Where were you forty years ago when I pulled through milk-leg and double pneumonia? You weren't even born. Don't let Cornelia lead you on," she shouted, because Doctor Harry appeared to float up to the ceiling and out. "I pay my own bills, and I don't throw my money away on nonsense!"

She meant to wave good-by, but it was too much trouble. Her eyes closed of themselves, it was like a dark curtain drawn around the bed. The pillow rose and floated under her, pleasant as a hammock in a light wind. She listened to the leaves rustling outside the window. No, somebody was swishing newspapers: no, Cornelia and Doctor Harry were whispering together. She leaped broad awake, thinking they whispered in her ear.

"She was never like this, *never* like this!" "Well, what can we expect?" "Yes, eighty years old. . . ."

Well, and what if she was? She still had ears. It was like Cornelia to whisper around doors. She always kept things secret in such a public way. She was always being tactful and kind. Cornelia was dutiful; that was the trouble with her. Dutiful and good: "So good and dutiful," said Granny, "that I'd like to spank her." She saw herself spanking Cornelia and making a fine job of it.

"What'd you say, Mother?"

Granny felt her face tying up in hard knots.

"Can't a body think, I'd like to know?"

"I thought you might want something."

"I do. I want a lot of things. First off, go away and don't whisper."

She lay and drowsed, hoping in her sleep that the children would keep out and let her rest a minute. It had been a long day. Not that she was tired. It was always pleasant to snatch a minute now and then. There was always so much to be done, let me see: tomorrow.

Tomorrow was far away and there was nothing to trouble about. Things were finished somehow when the time came; thank God there was always a little margin over for peace: then a person could spread out the plan of life and tuck in the edges orderly. It was good to have everything clean and folded away, with the hair brushes and tonic bottles sitting straight on the white embroidered linen: the day started without fuss and the pantry shelves laid out with rows of jelly glasses and brown jugs and white stone-china jars with blue whirligigs and words painted on them: coffee, tea, sugar, ginger, cinnamon, allspice: and the bronze clock with the lion on top nicely dusted off. The dust that lion could collect in twenty-four hours! The box in the attic with all those letters tied up, well, she'd have to go through that tomorrow. All those letters—George's letters and John's letters and her letters to them both—lying around for the children to find afterwards made her uneasy. Yes, that would be tomorrow's business. No use to let them know how silly she had been once.

While she was rummaging around she found death in her mind and it felt clammy and unfamiliar. She had spent so much time preparing for death there was no need for bringing it up again. Let it take care of itself now. When she was sixty she had felt very old, finished, and went around making farewell trips to see her children and grandchildren, with a secret in her mind: This is the very last of your mother, children! Then she made her will and came down with a long fever. That was all just a notion like a lot of other things, but it was lucky too, for she had once for all got over the idea of dying for a long time. Now she couldn't be worried. She hoped she had better sense now. Her father had lived to be one hundred and two years old and had drunk a noggin of stong hot toddy on his last birthday. He told the reporters it was his daily habit, and he owed his long life to that. He had made quite a scandal and was very pleased about it. She believed she'd just plague Cornelia a little.

"Cornelia! Cornelia!" No footsteps, but a sudden hand on her cheek. "Bless you, where have you been?"

"Here, Mother."

"Well, Cornelia, I want a noggin of hot toddy."

"Are you cold, darling?"

"I'm chilly, Cornelia. Lying in bed stops the circulation. I must have told you that a thousand times."

Well, she could just hear Cornelia telling her husband that Mother was getting a little childish and they'd have to humor her. The thing that most annoyed her was that Cornelia thought she was deaf, dumb, and blind. Little hasty glances and tiny gestures tossed around her and over her head saying, "Don't cross her, let her have her way, she's eighty years old," and she sitting there as if she lived in a thin glass cage. Sometimes Granny almost made up her mind to pack up and move back to her own house where nobody could remind her every minute that she was old. Wait, wait, Cornelia, till your own children whisper behind your back!

In her day she had kept a better house and had got more work done. She wasn't too old yet for Lydia to be driving eighty miles for advice when one of the children jumped the track, and Jimmy still dropped in and talked things over: "Now, Mammy, you've a good business head, I want to know what you think of this? . . ." Old. Cornelia couldn't change the furniture around without asking. Little things, little things! They had been so sweet when they were little. Granny wished the old days were back again with the children young and everything to be done over. It had been a hard pull, but not too much for her. When she thought of all the food she had cooked, and all the clothes she had cut and sewed, and all the gardens she had made—well, the children showed it. There they were, made out of her, and they couldn't get away from that. Sometimes she wanted to see John again and point to them and say, Well, I didn't do so badly, did I? But that would have to wait. That was for tomorrow. She used to think of him as a man, but now all the children were older than their father, and he would be a child beside her if she saw him now. It seemed strange and there was something wrong in the idea. Why, he couldn't possibly recognize her. She had fenced in a hundred acres once, digging the post holes herself and clamping the wires with just a negro boy to help. That changed a woman. John would be looking for a young woman with the peaked Spanish comb in her hair and the painted fan. Digging post holes changed a woman. Riding country roads in the winter when women had their babies was another thing: sitting up nights with sick horses and sick negroes and sick children and hardly ever losing one. John, I hardly ever lost one of them! John would see that in a minute, that would be something he could understand, she wouldn't have to explain anything!

It made her feel like rolling up her sleeves and putting the whole place to rights again. No matter if Cornelia was determined to be everywhere at once, there were a great many things left undone on this place. She would start tomorrow and do them. It was good to be strong enough for everything, even if all you made melted and changed and slipped under your hands, so that by the time you finished you almost forgot what you were working for. What was it I set out to do? she asked herself intently, but she could not remember. A fog rose over the valley, she saw it marching across the creek swallowing the trees and moving up the hill like an army of ghosts. Soon it would be at the near edge of the orchard, and then it was time to go in and light the lamps. Come in, children, don't stay out in the night air.

Lighting the lamps had been beautiful. The children huddled up to her and breathed like little calves waiting at the bars in the twilight. Their eyes followed the match and watched the flame rise and settle in a blue curve, then they moved away from her. The lamp was lit, they didn't have to be scared and hang on to mother any more. Never, never, never more. God, for all my life I thank Thee. Without thee, my God, I could never have done it. Hail, Mary, full of grace.

I want you to pick all the fruit this year and see that nothing is wasted. There's always someone who can use it. Don't let good things rot for want of using. You waste life when you waste good food. Don't let things get lost. It's bitter to lose things. Now, don't let me get to thinking, not when I am tired and taking a little nap before supper. . . .

The pillow rose about her shoulders and pressed against her heart and the memory was being squeezed out of it: oh, push down the pillow, somebody: it would smother her if she tried to hold it. Such a fresh breeze blowing and such a green day with no threats in it. But he had not come, just the same. What does a woman do when she has put on the white veil and set out the white cake for a man and he doesn't come? She tried to remember. No, I swear he never harmed me but in that. He never harmed me but in that . . . and what if he did? There was the day, the day, but a whirl of dark smoke rose and covered it, crept up and over into the bright field where everything was planted so carefully in orderly rows. That was hell, she knew hell when she saw it. For sixty years she had prayed against remembering him and against losing her soul in the deep pit of hell, and now the two things were mingled in one and the thought of him was a smoky cloud from hell that moved and crept in her head when she had just got rid of Doctor Harry and was trying to rest a minute. Wounded vanity, Ellen, said a sharp voice in the top of her mind. Don't let your wounded vanity get the upper hand of you. Plenty of girls get jilted. You were jilted, weren't you? Then stand up to it. Her eyelids wavered and let in streamers of blue-gray light like tissue paper over her eyes. She must get up and pull the shades down or she'd never sleep. She was in bed again and the shades were not down. How could that happen? Better turn over, hide from the light, sleeping in the light gave you nightmares. "Mother, how do you feel now?" and a stinging wetness on her forehead. But I don't like having my face washed in cold water!

Hapsy? George? Lydia? Jimmy? No, Cornelia, and her features were swollen and full of little puddles. "They're coming, darling, they'll all be here soon." Go wash your face, child, you look funny.

Instead of obeying, Cornelia knelt down and put her head on the pillow. She seemed to be talking but there was no sound. "Well, are you tongue-tied? Whose birthday is it? Are you going to give a party?"

Cornelia's mouth moved urgently in strange shapes. "Don't do that, you bother me, daughter."

"O, no, Mother. Oh, no. . . ."

Nonsense. It was strange about children. They disputed your every word. "No what, Cornelia?"

"Here's Doctor Harry."

"I won't see that boy again. He just left five minutes ago."

"That was this morning, Mother. It's night now. Here's the nurse."

"This is Doctor Harry, Mrs. Weatherall. I never saw you look so young and happy!"

"Ah, I'll never be young again—but I'd be happy if they'd let me lie in peace and get rested."

She thought she spoke up loudly, but no one answered. A warm weight on her forehead, a warm bracelet on her wrist, and a breeze went on whispering, trying to tell her something. A shuffle of leaves in the everlasting hand of God. He blew on them and they danced and rattled. "Mother, don't mind, we're going to give you a little hypodermic." "Look here, daughter, how do ants get in this bed? I saw sugar ants yesterday." Did you send for Hapsy too?

It was Hapsy she really wanted. She had to go a long way back through a great many rooms to find Hapsy standing with a baby on her arm. She seemed to herself to be Hapsy also, and the baby on Hapsy's arm was Hapsy and himself and herself, all at once, and there was no surprise in the meeting. Then Hapsy melted from within and turned flimsy as gray gauze and the baby was a gauzy shadow, and Hapsy came up close and said, "I thought you'd never come," and looked at her very searchingly and said, "You haven't changed a bit!" They leaned forward to kiss, when Cornelia began whispering from a long way off, "Oh, is there anything you want to tell me? Is there anything I can do for you?"

Yes, she had changed her mind after sixty years and she would like to see George. I want you to find George. Find him and be sure to tell him I forgot him. I want him to know I had my husband just the same and my children and my house like any other woman. A good house too and a good husband that I loved and fine children out of him. Better than I hoped for even. Tell him I was given back everything he took away and more. Oh, no, oh, God, no, there was something else besides the house and the man and the children. Oh, surely they were not all? What was it? Something not given back. . . . Her breath crowded down under her ribs and grew into a monstrous frightening shape with cutting edges; it bored up into her head, and the agony was unbelievable: Yes, John, get the Doctor now, no more talk, my time has come.

When this one was born it should be the last. The last. It should have been born first, for it was the one she had truly wanted. Everything came in good time. Nothing left out, left over. She was strong, in three days she would be as well as ever. Better. A woman needed milk in her to have her full health.

"Mother, do you hear me?"

"I've been telling you—"

"Mother, Father Connolly's here."

"I went to Holy Communion only last week. Tell him I'm not so sinful as all that."

"Father just wants to speak to you."

He could speak as much as he pleased. It was like him to drop in and inquire about her soul as if it were a teething baby, and then stay on for a cup of tea and a round of cards and gossip. He always had a funny story of some sort, usually about an Irishman who made his little mistakes and confessed them, and the point lay in some absurd thing he would blurt out in the confessional showing his struggles between native piety and original sin. Granny felt easy about her soul. Cornelia, where are your manners? Give Father Connolly a chair. She had her secret comfortable understanding with a few favorite saints who cleared a straight road to God for her. All as surely signed and sealed as the papers for the new Forty Acres. Forever . . . heirs and assigns forever. Since the day the wedding cake was not cut, but thrown out and wasted. The whole bottom dropped out of the world, and there she was blind and sweating with nothing under her feet and the walls falling away. His hand had caught her under the breast, she had not fallen, there was the freshly polished floor with the green rug on it, just as before. He had cursed like a sailor's parrot and said, "I'll kill him for you." Don't lay a hand on him, for my sake leave something to God. "Now, Ellen, you must believe what I tell you. . . ."

So there was nothing, nothing to worry about any more, except sometimes in the night one of the children screamed in a nightmare, and they both hustled out shaking and hunting for the matches and calling, "There, wait a minute, here we are!" John, get the doctor now, Hapsy's time has come. But there was Hapsy standing by the bed in a white cap. "Cornelia, tell Hapsy to take off her cap. I can't see her plain."

Her eyes opened very wide and the room stood out like a picture she had seen somewhere. Dark colors with the shadows rising towards the ceiling in long angles. The tall black dresser gleamed with nothing on it but John's picture, enlarged from a little one, with John's eyes very black when they should have been blue. You never saw him, so how do you know how he looked? But the man insisted the copy was perfect, it was very rich and handsome. For a picture, yes, but it's not my husband. The table by the bed had a linen cover and a candle and a crucifix. The light was blue from Cornelia's silk lampshades. No sort of light at all, just frippery. You had to live forty years with kerosene lamps to appreciate honest electricity. She felt very strong and she saw Doctor Harry with a rosy nimbus around him.

"You look like a saint, Doctor Harry, and I vow that's as near as you'll ever come to it."

"She's saying something."

"I heard you, Cornelia. What's all this carrying-on?"

"Father Connolly's saying—"

Cornelia's voice staggered and bumped like a cart in a bad road. It rounded corners and turned back again and arrived nowhere. Granny stepped up in the cart very lightly and reached for the reins, but a man sat beside her and she knew him by his hands, driving the cart. She did not look in his face, for she knew without seeing, but looked instead down the road where the trees leaned over and bowed to each other and a thousand birds were singing a Mass. She felt like singing too, but she put her hand in the bosom of her dress and pulled out a rosary, and Father Connolly murmured Latin in a very solemn voice and tickled her feet. My God, will you stop that nonsense? I'm a married woman. What if he did run away and leave me to face the priest by myself? I found another a whole world better. I wouldn't have exchanged my husband for anybody except St. Michael himself, and you may tell him that for me with a thank you in the bargain.

Light flashed on her closed eyelids, and a deep roaring shook her. Cornelia, is that lightning? I hear thunder. There's going to be a storm. Close all the windows. Call the children in. . . . "Mother, here we are, all of us." "Is that you, Hapsy?" "Oh, no, I'm Lydia. We drove as fast as we could." Their faces drifted above her, drifted away. The rosary fell out of her hands and Lydia put it back. Jimmy tried to help, their hands fumbled together, and Granny closed two fingers around Jimmy's thumb. Beads wouldn't do, it must be something alive. She was so amazed her thoughts ran round and round. So, my dear Lord, this is my death and I wasn't even thinking about it. My children have come to see me die. But I can't, it's not time. Oh, I always hated surprises. I wanted to give Cornelia the amethyst set—Cornelia, you're to have the amethyst set, but Hapsy's to wear it when she wants, and, Doctor Harry, do shut up. Nobody sent for you. Oh, my dear Lord, do wait a minute. I meant to do something about the Forty Acres, Jimmy doesn't need it and Lydia will later on, with that worthless husband of hers. I meant to finish the altar cloth and send six bottles of wine to Sister Borgia for her dyspepsia. I want to send six bottles of wine to Sister Borgia, Father Connolly, now don't let me forget.

Cornelia's voice made short turns and tilted over and crashed. "Oh, Mother, oh, Mother, oh, Mother. . . ."

"I'm not going, Cornelia. I'm taken by surprise. I can't go."

You'll see Hapsy again. What about her? "I thought you'd never come." Granny made a long journey outward, looking for Hapsy. What if I don't find her? What then? Her heart sank down and down, there was no bottom to death, she couldn't come to the end of it. The blue light from Cornelia's lampshade drew into a tiny point in the center of her brain, it flickered and winked like an eye, quietly it fluttered and dwindled. Granny lay curled down within herself, amazed and watchful, staring at the point of light that was herself; her body was now only a deeper mass of shadow in an endless darkness and this darkness would curl around the light and swallow it up. God, give a sign!

For the second time there was no sign. Again no bridegroom and the priest in the house. She could not remember any other sorrow because this grief wiped them all away. Oh, no, there's nothing more cruel than this— I'll never forgive it. She stretched herself with a deep breath and blew out the light.

J. F. POWERS (b. 1917)

The Forks

J. F. Powers was born in Jacksonville, Illinois, and attended
Northwestern University. His stories, which often concern the Catholic
priesthood, have appeared in several collections, including *Prince of
Darkness and Other Stories* (1947), from which "The Forks" is taken. His
one novel, *Morte D'Urban*, appeared in 1962.

That summer when Father Eudex got back from saying Mass at the or-
phanage in the morning, he would park Monsignor's car, which was long
and black and new like a politician's, and sit down in the cool of the porch
to read his office. If Monsignor was not already standing in the door, he
would immediately appear there, seeing that his car had safely returned,
and inquire:

"Did you have any trouble with her?"

Father Eudex knew too well the question meant, Did you mistreat my
car?

"No trouble, Monsignor."

"Good," Monsignor said, with imperfect faith in his curate, who was
not a car owner. For a moment Monsignor stood framed in the screen door,
fumbling his watch fob as for a full-length portrait, and then he was suddenly not there.

"Monsignor," Father Eudex said, rising nervously, "I've got a chance
to pick up a car."

At the door Monsignor slid into his frame again. His face expressed
what was for him intense interest.

"Yes? Go on."

"I don't want to have to use yours every morning."

"It's all right."

"And there are other times." Father Eudex decided not to be maudlin
and mention sick calls, nor be entirely honest and admit he was tired of
busses and bumming rides from parishioners. "And now I've got a chance
to get one—cheap."

Monsignor, smiling, came alert at *cheap*.

"New?"

"No, I wouldn't say it's new."

Monsignor was openly suspicious now. "What kind?"

"It's a Ford."

"And not new?"

"Not new, Monsignor—but in good condition. It was owned by a retired farmer and had good care."

Monsignor sniffed. He *knew* cars. "V-Eight, Father?"

"No," Father Eudex confessed. "It's a Model A."

Monsignor chuckled as though this were indeed the damnedest thing he had ever heard.

"But in very good condition, Monsignor."

"You said that."

"Yes. And I could take it apart if anything went wrong. My uncle had one."

"No doubt." Monsignor uttered a laugh at Father Eudex's rural origins. Then he delivered the final word, long delayed out of amusement. "It wouldn't be prudent, Father. After all, this isn't a country parish. You know the class of people we get here."

Monsignor put on his Panama hat. Then, apparently mistaking the obstinacy in his curate's face for plain ignorance, he shed a little more light. "People watch a priest, Father. *Damnant quod non intelligunt.*[1] It would never do. You'll have to watch your tendencies."

Monsignor's eyes tripped and fell hard on the morning paper lying on the swing where he had finished it.

"Another flattering piece about that crazy fellow. . . . There's a man who might have gone places if it weren't for his mouth! A bishop doesn't have to get mixed up in all that stuff!"

Monsignor, as Father Eudex knew, meant unions, strikes, race riots—all that stuff.

"A parishioner was saying to me only yesterday it's getting so you can't tell the Catholics from the Communists, with the priests as bad as any. Yes, and this fellow is the worst. He reminds me of that bishop a few years back—at least he called himself a bishop, a Protestant—that was advocating companionate marriages. It's not that bad, maybe, but if you listened to some of them you'd think that Catholicity and capitalism were incompatible!"

"The Holy Father—"

"The Holy Father's in Europe, Father. Mr. Memmers lives in this parish. I'm his priest. What can I tell him?"

"Is it Mr. Memmers of the First National, Monsignor?"

"It is, Father. And there's damned little cheer I can give a man like Memmers. Catholics, priests, and laity alike—yes, and princes of the Church, all talking atheistic communism!"

This was the substance of their conversation, always, the deadly routine in which Father Eudex played straight man. Each time it happened he seemed to participate, and though he should have known better he justified his participation by hoping that it would not happen again, or in quite the same way. But it did, it always did, the same way, and Monsignor, for all his alarms, had nothing to say really and meant one thing only, the thing he never said—that he dearly wanted to be, and was not, a bishop.

Father Eudex could imagine just what kind of bishop Monsignor

1. Latin: "They damn what they do not understand."

would be. His reign would be a wise one, excessively so. His mind was made up on everything, excessively so. He would know how to avoid the snares set in the path of the just man, avoid them, too, in good taste and good conscience. He would not be trapped as so many good shepherds before him had been trapped, poor souls—caught in fair-seeming dilemmas of justice that were best left alone, like the first apple. It grieved him, he said, to think of those great hearts broken in silence and solitude. It was the worst kind of exile, alas! But just give him the chance and he would know what to do, what to say, and, more important, what not to do, not to say—neither yea nor nay for him. He had not gone to Rome for nothing. For him the dark forest of decisions would not exist; for him, thanks to hours spent in prayer and meditation, the forest would vanish as dry grass before fire, his fire. He knew the mask of evil already—birth control, indecent movies, salacious books—and would call these things by their right names and dare to deal with them for what they were, these new occasions for the old sins of the cities of the plains.

But in the meantime—oh, to have a particle of the faith that God had in humanity! Dear, trusting God forever trying them beyond their feeble powers, ordering terrible tests, fatal trials by nonsense (the crazy bishop). And keeping Monsignor steadily warming up on the side lines, ready to rush in, primed for the day that would perhaps never dawn.

At one time, so the talk went, there had been reason to think that Monsignor was headed for a bishopric. Now it was too late; Monsignor's intercessors were all dead; the cupboard was bare; he knew it at heart, and it galled him to see another man, this *crazy* man, given the opportunity, and making such a mess of it.

Father Eudex searched for and found a little salt for Monsignor's wound. "The word's going around he'll be the next archbishop," he said.

"I won't believe it," Monsignor countered hoarsely. He glanced at the newspaper on the swing and renewed his horror. "If that fellow's right, Father, I'm"—his voice cracked at the idea—"*wrong!*"

Father Eudex waited until Monsignor had started down the steps to the car before he said, "It could be."

"I'll be back for lunch, Father. I'm taking her for a little spin."

Monsignor stopped in admiration a few feet from the car—her. He was as helpless before her beauty as a boy with a birthday bicycle. He could not leave her alone. He had her out every morning and afternoon and evening. He was indiscriminate about picking people up for a ride in her. He kept her on a special diet—only the best of gas and oil and grease, with daily rubdowns. He would run her only on the smoothest roads and at so many miles an hour. That was to have stopped at the first five hundred, but only now, nearing the thousand mark, was he able to bring himself to increase her speed, and it seemed to hurt him more than it did her.

Now he was walking around behind her to inspect the tires. Apparently O.K. He gave the left rear fender an amorous chuck and eased into the front seat. Then they drove off, the car and he, to see the world, to explore each other further on the honeymoon.

Father Eudex watched the car slide into the traffic, and waited, on edge. The corner cop, fulfilling Father Eudex's fears, blew his whistle and waved his arms up in all four directions, bringing traffic to a standstill. Monsignor pulled expertly out of line and drove down Clover Boulevard in a one-car parade; all others stalled respectfully. The cop, as Monsignor passed, tipped his cap, showing a bald head. Monsignor, in the circumstances, could not acknowledge him, though he knew the man well—a parishioner. He was occupied with keeping his countenance kindly, grim, and exalted, that the cop's faith remain whole, for it was evidently inconceivable to him that Monsignor should ever venture abroad unless to bear the Holy Viaticum, always racing with death.

Father Eudex, eyes baleful but following the progress of the big black car, saw a hand dart out of the driver's window in a wave. Monsignor would combine a lot of business with pleasure that morning, creating what he called "good will for the Church"—all morning in the driver's seat toasting passers-by with a wave that was better than a blessing. How he loved waving to people!

Father Eudex overcame his inclination to sit and stew about things by going down the steps to meet the mailman. He got the usual handful for the Monsignor—advertisements and amazing offers, the unfailing crop of chaff from dealers in church goods, organs, collection schemes, insurance, and sacramental wines. There were two envelopes addressed to Father Eudex, one a mimeographed plea from a missionary society which he might or might not acknowledge with a contribution, depending upon what he thought of the cause—if it was really lost enough to justify a levy on his poverty—and the other a check for a hundred dollars.

The check came in an eggshell envelope with no explanation except a tiny card, "Compliments of the Rival Tractor Company," but even that was needless. All over town clergymen had known for days that the checks were on the way again. Some, rejoicing, could hardly wait. Father Eudex, however, was one of those who could.

With the passing of hard times and the coming of the fruitful war years, the Rival Company, which was a great one for public relations, had found the best solution to the excess-profits problem to be giving. Ministers and even rabbis shared in the annual jack pot, but Rival employees were largely Catholic and it was the checks to the priests that paid off. Again, some thought it was a wonderful idea, and others thought that Rival, plagued by strikes and justly so, had put their alms to work.

There was another eggshell envelope, Father Eudex saw, among the letters for Monsignor, and knew his check would be for two hundred, the premium for pastors.

Father Eudex left Monsignor's mail on the porch table by his cigars. His own he stuck in his back pocket, wanting to forget it, and went down the steps into the yard. Walking back and forth on the shady side of the rectory where the lilies of the valley grew and reading his office, he gradually drifted into the back yard, lured by a noise. He came upon Whalen, the janitor, pounding pegs into the ground.

Father Eudex closed the breviary on a finger. "What's it all about, Joe?"

Joe Whalen snatched a piece of paper from his shirt and handed it to Father Eudex. "He gave it to me this morning."

He—it was the word for Monsignor among them. A docile pronoun only, and yet when it meant the Monsignor it said, and concealed, nameless things.

The paper was a plan for a garden drawn up by the Monsignor in his fine hand. It called for a huge fleur-de-lis bounded by smaller crosses—and these Maltese—a fountain, a sundial, and a cloister walk running from the rectory to the garage. Later there would be birdhouses and a ten-foot wall of thick gray stones, acting as a moat against the eyes of the world. The whole scheme struck Father Eudex as expensive and, in this country, Presbyterian.

When Monsignor drew the plan, however, he must have been in his medieval mood. A spouting whale jostled with Neptune in the choppy waters of the fountain. North was indicated in the legend by a winged cherub huffing and puffing.

Father Eudex held the plan up against the sun to see the watermark. The stationery was new to him, heavy, simulated parchment, with the Church of the Holy Redeemer and Monsignor's name embossed, three initials, W. F. X., William Francis Xavier. With all those initials the man could pass for a radio station, a chancery wit had observed, or if his last name had not been Sweeney, Father Eudex added now, for high Anglican.

Father Eudex returned the plan to Whalen, feeling sorry for him and to an extent guilty before him—if only because he was a priest like Monsignor (now turned architect) whose dream of a monastery garden included the overworked janitor under the head of "labor."

Father Eudex asked Whalen to bring another shovel. Together, almost without words, they worked all morning spading up crosses, leaving the big fleur-de-lis to the last. Father Eudex removed his coat first, then his collar, and finally was down to his undershirt.

Toward noon Monsignor rolled into the driveway.

He stayed in the car, getting red in the face, recovering from the pleasure of seeing so much accomplished as he slowly recognized his curate in Whalen's helper. In a still, appalled voice he called across the lawn, "Father," and waited as for a beast that might or might not have sense enough to come.

Father Eudex dropped his shovel and went over to the car, shirtless.

Monsignor waited a moment before he spoke, as though annoyed by the everlasting necessity, where this person was concerned, to explain. "Father," he said quietly at last, "I wouldn't do any more of that—if I were you. Rather, in any event, I wouldn't."

"All right, Monsignor."

"To say the least, it's not prudent. If necessary"—he paused as Whalen came over to dig a cross within earshot—"I'll explain later. It's time for lunch now."

The car, black, beautiful, fierce with chromium, was quiet as Monsignor dismounted, knowing her master. Monsignor went around to the rear, felt a tire, and probed a nasty cinder in the tread.

"Look at that," he said, removing the cinder.

Father Eudex thought he saw the car lift a hoof, gaze around, and thank Monsignor with her headlights.

Monsignor proceeded at a precise pace to the back door of the rectory. There he held the screen open momentarily, as if remembering something or reluctant to enter before himself—such was his humility—but then called to Whalen with an intimacy that could never exist between them.

"Better knock off now, Joe."

Whalen turned in on himself. "*Joe*—is it!"

Father Eudex removed his clothes from the grass. His hands were all blisters, but in them he found a little absolution. He apologized to Joe for having to take the afternoon off. "I can't make it, Joe. Something turned up."

"Sure, Father."

Father Eudex could hear Joe telling his wife about it that night—yeah, the young one got in wrong with the old one again. Yeah, the old one, he don't believe in it, work, for them.

Father Eudex paused in the kitchen to remember he knew not what. It was in his head, asking to be let in, but he did not place it until he heard Monsignor in the next room complaining about the salad to the housekeeper. It was the voice of dear, dead Aunt Hazel, coming from the summer he was ten. He translated the past into the present: I can't come out and play this afternoon, Joe, on account of my monsignor won't let me.

In the dining room Father Eudex sat down at the table and said grace. He helped himself to a chop, creamed new potatoes, pickled beets, jelly, and bread. He liked jelly. Monsignor passed the butter.

"That's supposed to be a tutti-frutti salad," Monsignor said, grimacing at his. "But she used green olives."

Father Eudex said nothing.

"I said she used green olives."

"I like green olives all right."

"I like green olives, but *not* in tutti-frutti salad."

Father Eudex replied by eating a green olive, but he knew it could not end there.

"Father," Monsignor said in a new tone. "How would you like to go away and study for a year?"

"Don't think I'd care for it, Monsignor. I'm not the type."

"You're no canonist, you mean?"

"That's one thing."

"Yes. Well, there are other things it might not hurt you to know. To be quite frank with you, Father, I think you need broadening."

"I guess so," Father Eudex said thickly.

"And still, with your tendencies . . . and with the universities honeycombed with Communists. No, that would never do. I think I meant seasoning, not broadening."

"Oh."

"No offense?"

"No offense."

Who would have thought a little thing like an olive could lead to all this, Father Eudex mused—who but himself, that is, for his association with Monsignor had shown him that anything could lead to everything. Monsignor was a master at making points. Nothing had changed since the day Father Eudex walked into the rectory saying he was the new assistant. Monsignor had evaded Father Eudex's hand in greeting, and a few days later, after he began to get the range, he delivered a lecture on the whole subject of handshaking. It was Middle West to shake hands, or South West, or West in any case, and it was not done where he came from, and—why had he ever come from where he came from? Not to be reduced to shaking hands, you could bet! Handshaking was worse than foot washing and unlike that pious practice there was nothing to support it. And from handshaking Monsignor might go into a general discussion of Father Eudex's failings. He used the open forum method, but he was the only speaker and there was never time enough for questions from the audience. Monsignor seized his examples at random from life. He saw Father Eudex coming out of his bedroom in pajama bottoms only and so told him about the dressing gown, its purpose, something of its history. He advised Father Eudex to barber his armpits, for it was being done all over now. He let Father Eudex see his bottle of cologne, "Steeple," special for clergymen, and said he should not be afraid of it. He suggested that Father Eudex shave his face oftener, too. He loaned him his Rogers Peet catalogue, which had sketches of clerical blades togged out in the latest, and prayed that he would stop going around looking like a rabbinical student.

He found Father Eudex reading *The Catholic Worker* one day and had not trusted him since. Father Eudex's conception of the priesthood was evangelical in the worst sense, barbaric, gross, foreign to the mind of the Church, which was one of two terms he used as sticks to beat him with. The other was taste. The air of the rectory was often heavy with The Mind of the Church and Taste.

Another thing. Father Eudex could not conduct a civil conversation. Monsignor doubted that Father Eudex could even think to himself with anything like agreement. Certainly any discussion with Father Eudex ended inevitably in argument or sighing. Sighing! Why didn't people talk up if they had anything to say? No, they'd rather sigh! Father, don't ever, ever sigh at me again!

Finally, Monsignor did not like Father Eudex's table manners. This came to a head one night when Monsignor, seeing his curate's plate empty and all the silverware at his place unused except for a single knife, fork, and spoon, exploded altogether, saying it had been on his mind for weeks, and then descending into the vernacular he declared that Father Eudex did not know the forks—now perhaps he could understand that! Meals, unless Monsignor had guests or other things to struggle with, were always occasions of instruction for Father Eudex, and sometimes of chastisement.

And now he knew the worst—if Monsignor was thinking of recommending him for a year of study, in a Sulpician seminary probably, to learn the forks. So this was what it meant to be a priest. *Come, follow me. Going forth, teach ye all nations. Heal the sick, raise the dead, cleanse the lepers, cast out devils.* Teach the class of people we get here? Teach Mr. Memmers? Teach Communists? Teach Monsignors? And where were the poor? The lepers of old? The lepers were in their colonies with nuns to nurse them. The poor were in their holes and would not come out. Mr. Memmers was in his bank, without cheer. The Communists were in their universities, awaiting a sign. And he was at table with Monsignor, and it was enough for the disciple to be as his master, but the housekeeper had used green olives.

Monsignor inquired, "Did you get your check today?"

Father Eudex, looking up, considered. "I got *a* check," he said.

"From the Rival people, I mean?"

"Yes."

"Good. Well, I think you might apply it on the car you're wanting. A decent car. That's a worthy cause." Monsignor noticed that he was not taking it well. "Not that I mean to dictate what you shall do with your little windfall, Father. It's just that I don't like to see you mortifying yourself with a Model A—and disgracing the Church."

"Yes," Father Eudex said, suffering.

"Yes. I dare say you don't see the danger, just as you didn't a while ago when I found you making a spectacle of yourself with Whalen. You just don't see the danger because you just don't think. Not to dwell on it, but I seem to remember some overshoes."

The overshoes! Monsignor referred to them as to the Fall. Last winter Father Eudex had given his overshoes to a freezing picket. It had got back to Monsignor and—good Lord, a man could have his sympathies, but he had no right clad in the cloth to endanger the prestige of the Church by siding in these wretched squabbles. Monsignor said he hated to think of all the evil done by people doing good! Had Father Eudex ever heard of the Albigensian heresy, or didn't the seminary teach that any more?

Father Eudex declined dessert. It was strawberry mousse.

"Delicious," Monsignor said. "I think I'll let her stay."

At that moment Father Eudex decided that he had nothing to lose. He placed his knife next to his fork on the plate, adjusted them this way and that until they seemed to work a combination in his mind, to spring a lock which in turn enabled him to speak out.

"Monsignor," he said. "I think I ought to tell you I don't intend to make use of that money. In fact—to show you how my mind works—I have even considered endorsing the check to the strikers' relief fund."

"So," Monsignor said calmly—years in the confessional had prepared him for anything.

"I'll admit I don't know whether I can in justice. And even if I could I don't know that I would. I don't know why . . . I guess hush money, no matter what you do with it, is lousy."

Monsignor regarded him with piercing baby blue eyes. "You'd find it pretty hard to prove, Father, that *any* money *in se* is . . . what you say it is. I would quarrel further with the definition 'hush money.' It seems to me nothing if not rash that you would presume to impugn the motive of the Rival Company in sending out these checks. You would seem to challenge the whole concept of good works—not that I am ignorant of the misuses to which money can be put." Monsignor, changing tack, tucked it all into a sigh. "Perhaps I'm just a simple soul, and it's enough for me to know personally some of the people in the Rival Company and to know them good people. Many of them Catholic . . ." A throb had crept into Monsignor's voice. He shut it off.

"I don't mean anything that subtle, Monsignor," Father Eudex said. "I'm just telling you, as my pastor, what I'm going to do with the check. Or what I'm not going to do with it. I don't know what I'm going to do with it. Maybe send it back."

Monsignor rose from the table, slightly smiling. "Very well, Father. But there's always the poor."

Monsignor took leave of Father Eudex with a laugh. Father Eudex felt it was supposed to fool him into thinking that nothing he had said would be used against him. It showed, rather, that Monsignor was not winded, that he had broken wild curates before, plenty of them, and that he would ride again.

Father Eudex sought the shade of the porch. He tried to read his office, but was drowsy. He got up for a glass of water. The saints in Ireland used to stand up to their necks in cold water, but not for drowsiness. When he came back to the porch a woman was ringing the doorbell. She looked like a customer for rosary beads.

"Hello," he said.

"I'm Mrs. Klein, Father, and I was wondering if you could help me out."

Father Eudex straightened a porch chair for her. "Please sit down."

"It's a German name, Father. Klein was German descent," she said, and added with a silly grin, "It ain't what you think, Father."

"I beg your pardon."

"Klein. Some think it's a Jew name. But they stole it from Klein."

Father Eudex decided to come back to that later. "You were wondering if I could help you?"

"Yes, Father. It's personal."

"Is it a matter for confession?"

"Oh no, Father." He had made her blush.

"Then go ahead."

Mrs. Klein peered into the honeysuckle vines on either side of the porch for alien ears.

"No one can hear you, Mrs. Klein."

"Father—I'm just a poor widow," she said, and continued as though Father Eudex had just slandered the man. "Klein was awful good to me, Father."

"I'm sure he was."

"So good . . . and he went and left me all he had." She had begun to cry a little.

Father Eudex nodded gently. She was after something, probably not money, always the best bet—either that or a drunk in the family—but this one was not Irish. Perhaps just sympathy.

"I come to get your advice, Father. Klein always said, 'If you got a problem, Freda, see the priest.' "

"Do you need money?"

"I got more than I can use from the bakery."

"You have a bakery?"

Mrs. Klein nodded down the street. "That's my bakery. It was Klein's. The Purity."

"I go by there all the time," Father Eudex said, abandoning himself to her. He must stop trying to shape the conversation and let her work it out.

"Will you give me your advice, Father?" He felt that she sensed his indifference and interpreted it as his way of rejecting her. She either had no idea how little sense she made or else supreme faith in him, as a priest, to see into her heart.

"Just what is it you're after, Mrs. Klein?"

"He left me all he had, Father, but it's just laying in the bank."

"And you want me to tell you what to do with it?"

"Yes, Father."

Father Eudex thought this might be interesting, certainly a change. He went back in his mind to the seminary and the class in which they had considered the problem of inheritances. Do we have any unfulfilled obligations? Are we sure? . . . Are there any impedimenta? . . .

"Do you have any dependents, Mrs. Klein—any children?"

"One boy, Father. I got him running the bakery. I pay him good—too much, Father."

"Is 'too much' a living wage?"

"Yes, Father. He ain't got a family."

"A living wage is not too much," Father Eudex handed down, sailing into the encyclical style without knowing it.

Mrs. Klein was smiling over having done something good without knowing precisely what it was.

"How old is your son?"

"He's thirty-six, Father."

"Not married?"

"No, Father, but he's got him a girl." She giggled, and Father Eudex, embarrassed, retied his shoe.

"But you don't care to make a will and leave this money to your son in the usual way?"

"I guess I'll have to . . . if I die," Mrs. Klein was suddenly crushed and haunted, but whether by death or charity, Father Eudex did not know.

"You don't have to, Mrs. Klein. There are many worthy causes. And the worthiest is the cause of the poor. My advice to you, if I understand your problem, is to give what you have to someone who needs it."

Mrs. Klein just stared at him.

"You could even leave it to the archdiocese," he said, completing the sentence to himself: but I don't recommend it in your case . . . with your tendencies. You look like an Indian giver to me.

But Mrs. Klein had got enough. "Huh!" she said, rising. "Well! You *are* a funny one!"

And then Father Eudex realized that she had come to him for a broker's tip. It was in the eyes. The hat. The dress. The shoes. "If you'd like to speak to the pastor," he said, "come back in the evening."

"You're a nice young man," Mrs. Klein said, rather bitter now and bent on getting away from him. "But I got to say this—you ain't much of a priest. And Klein said if I got a problem, see the priest—huh! You ain't much of a priest! What time's your boss come in?"

"In the evening," Father Eudex said. "Come any time in the evening."

Mrs. Klein was already down the steps and making for the street.

"You might try Mr. Memmers at the First National," Father Eudex called, actually trying to help her, but she must have thought it was just some more of his nonsense and did not reply.

After Mrs. Klein had disappeared Father Eudex went to his room. In the hallway upstairs Monsignor's voice, coming from the depths of the clerical nap, halted him.

"Who was it?"

"A woman," Father Eudex said. "A woman seeking good counsel."

He waited a moment to be questioned, but Monsignor was not awake enough to see anything wrong with that, and there came only a sigh and a shifting of weight that told Father Eudex he was simply turning over in bed.

Father Eudex walked into the bathroom. He took the Rival check from his pocket. He tore it into little squares. He let them flutter into the toilet. He pulled the chain—hard.

He went to his room and stood looking out the window at nothing. He could hear the others already giving an account of their stewardship, but could not judge them. I bought baseball uniforms for the school. I bought the nuns a new washing machine. I purchased a Mass kit for a Chinese missionary. I bought a set of matched irons. Mine helped pay for keeping my mother in a rest home upstate. I gave mine to the poor.

And you, Father?

PHILIP ROTH (b. 1933)
Eli, The Fanatic

Philip Roth was born in Newark and educated at Bucknell University and at the University of Chicago. "Eli, the Fanatic" appeared in *Goodbye, Columbus* (1959), which established Roth's reputation and won the National Book Award. Roth's novels include *When She Was Good* (1967), *Portnoy's Complaint* (1969), and *The Ghost Writer* (1979).

Leo Tzuref stepped out from back of a white column to welcome Eli Peck, Eli jumped back, surprised; then they shook hands and Tzuref gestured him into the sagging old mansion. At the door Eli turned, and down the slope of lawn, past the jungle of hedges, beyond the dark, untrampled horse path, he saw the street lights blink on in Woodenton. The stores along Coach House Road tossed up a burst of yellow—it came to Eli as a secret signal from his townsmen: "Tell this Tzuref where we stand, Eli. This is a modern community, Eli, we have our families, we pay taxes . . ." Eli, burdened by the message, gave Tzuref a dumb, weary stare.

"You must work a full day," Tzuref said, steering the attorney and his briefcase into the chilly hall.

Eli's heels made a racket on the cracked marble floor, and he spoke above it. "It's the commuting that's killing," he said, and entered the dim room Tzuref waved open for him. "Three hours a day . . . I came right from the train." He dwindled down into a harp-backed chair. He expected it would be deeper than it was and consequently jarred himself on the sharp bones of his seat. It woke him, this shiver of the behind, to his business. Tzuref, a bald shaggy-browed man who looked as if he'd once been very fat, sat back of an empty desk, halfway hidden, as though he were settled on the floor. Everything around him was empty. There were no books in the bookshelves, no rugs on the floor, no draperies on the big casement windows. As Eli began to speak Tzuref got up and swung a window back on one noisy hinge. "May and it's like August," he said, and with his back to Eli, he revealed the black circle on the back of his head. The crown of his head was missing! He returned through the dimness—the lamps had no bulbs—and Eli realized all he'd seen was a skullcap. Tzuref struck a match and lit a candle, just as the half-dying shouts of children at play rolled in through the open window. It was as though Tzuref had opened it so Eli could hear them.

"Aah, now," he said. "I received your letter."

Eli poised, waiting for Tzuref to swish open a drawer and remove the letter from his file. Instead the old man leaned forward onto his stomach, worked his hand into his pants pocket, and withdrew what appeared to be a week-old handkerchief. He uncrumpled it; he unfolded it; he ironed it on the desk with the side of his hand. "So," he said.

Eli pointed to the grimy sheet which he'd gone over word-by-word with his partners, Lewis and McDonnell. "I expected an answer," Eli said. "It's a week."

"It was so important, Mr. Peck, I knew you would come."

Some children ran under the open window and their mysterious babble—not mysterious to Tzuref, who smiled—entered the room like a third person. Their noise caught up against Eli's flesh and he was unable to restrain a shudder. He wished he had gone home, showered and eaten dinner, before calling on Tzuref. He was not feeling as professional as usual—the place was too dim, it was too late. But down in Woodenton they would be waiting, his clients and neighbors. He spoke for the Jews of Woodenton, not just himself and his wife.

"You understood?" Eli said.

"It's not hard."

"It's a matter of zoning . . ." and when Tzuref did not answer, but only drummed his fingers on his lips, Eli said, "We didn't make the laws . . ."

"You respect them."

"They protect us . . . the community."

"The law is the law," Tzuref said.

"Exactly!" Eli had the urge to rise and walk about the room.

"And then of course"—Tzuref made a pair of scales in the air with his hands—"the law is not the law. When is the law that is the law not the law?" He jiggled the scales. "And vice versa."

"Simply," Eli said sharply. "You can't have a boarding school in a residential area." He would not allow Tzuref to cloud the issue with issues. "We thought it better to tell you before any action is undertaken."

"But a house in a residential area?"

"Yes. That's what residential means." The DP's English was perhaps not as good as it seemed at first. Tzuref spoke slowly, but till then Eli had mistaken it for craft—or even wisdom. "Residence means home," he added.

"So this is my residence."

"But the children?"

"It is their residence."

"*Seventeen* children?"

"Eighteen," Tzuref said.

"But you *teach* them here."

"The Talmud. That's illegal?"

"That makes it school."

Tzuref hung the scales again, tipping slowly the balance.

"Look, Mr. Tzuref, in America we call such a place a boarding school."

"Where they teach the Talmud?"

"Where they teach period. You are the headmaster, they are the students."

Tzuref placed his scales on the desk. "Mr. Peck," he said, "I don't believe it . . ." but he did not seem to be referring to anything Eli had said.

"Mr. Tzuref, that is the law. I came to ask what you intend to do."

"What I *must* do?"

"I hope they are the same."

"They are." Tzuref brought his stomach into the desk. "We stay." He smiled. "We are tired. The headmaster is tired. The students are tired."

Eli rose and lifted his briefcase. It felt so heavy packed with the grievances, vengeances, and schemes of his clients. There were days when he carried it like a feather—in Tzuref's office it weighed a ton.

"Goodbye, Mr. Tzuref."

"Sholom," Tzuref said.

Eli opened the door to the office and walked carefully down the dark tomb of a corridor to the door. He stepped out on the porch and, leaning against a pillar, looked down across the lawn to the children at play. Their voices whooped and rose and dropped as they chased each other round the old house. The dusk made the children's game look like a tribal dance. Eli straightened up, started off the porch, and suddenly the dance was ended. A long piercing scream trailed after. It was the first time in his life anyone had run at the sight of him. Keeping his eyes on the lights of Woodenton, he headed down the path.

And then, seated on a bench beneath a tree, Eli saw him. At first it seemed only a deep hollow of blackness—then the figure emerged. Eli recognized him from the description. There he was, wearing the hat, that hat which was the very cause of Eli's mission, the source of Woodenton's upset. The town's lights flashed their message once again: "Get the one with the hat. What a nerve, what a nerve . . ."

Eli started towards the man. Perhaps he was less stubborn than Tzuref, more reasonable. After all, it was the law. But when he was close enough to call out, he didn't. He was stopped by the sight of the black coat that fell down below the man's knees, and the hands which held each other in his lap. By the round-topped, wide-brimmed Talmudic hat, pushed onto the back of his head. And by the beard, which hid his neck and was so soft and thin it fluttered away and back again with each heavy breath he took. He was asleep, his sidelocks curled loose on his cheeks. His face was no older than Eli's.

Eli hurried towards the lights.

The note on the kitchen table unsettled him. Scribblings on bits of paper had made history this past week. This one, however, was unsigned. "Sweetie," it said, "I went to sleep. I had a sort of Oedipal experience with the baby today. Call Ted Heller."

She had left him a cold soggy dinner in the refrigerator. He hated cold soggy dinners, but would take one gladly in place of Miriam's presence. He was ruffled, and she never helped that, not with her infernal analytic powers. He loved her when life was proceeding smoothly—and that was when she loved him. But sometimes Eli found being a lawyer surrounded him like quicksand—he couldn't get his breath. Too often he wished he were pleading for the other side; though if he were on the other side, then he'd wish he were on the side he was. The trouble was that sometimes the law didn't seem to be the answer, *law* didn't seem to have anything to do with what was aggravating everybody. And that, of course, made him feel foolish and unnecessary . . . Though that was not the situation here—the townsmen had a case. But not *exactly,* and if Miriam were awake to see Eli's upset, she would set about explaining his distress to him, understanding him, forgiving him, so as to get things back to Normal, for Normal was where they loved one another. The difficulty with Miriam's efforts was they only upset him more; not only did they explain little to him about himself or his predicament, but they convinced him of *her* weakness. Neither Eli nor Miriam, it turned out, was terribly strong. Twice before he'd faced this fact, and on both occasions had found solace in what his neighbors forgivingly referred to as "a nervous breakdown."

Eli ate his dinner with his briefcase beside him. Halfway through, he gave in to himself, removed Tzuref's notes, and put them on the table, beside Miriam's. From time to time he flipped through the notes, which had been carried into town by the one in the black hat. The first note, the incendiary:

To whom it may concern:

Please give this gentleman the following: Boys shoes with rubber heels and soles.

> 5 prs size 6c
> 3 prs size 5c
> 3 prs size 5b
> 2 prs size 4a
> 3 prs size 4c
> 1 pr size 7b
> 1 pr size 7c

Total 18 prs. boys shoes. This gentleman has a check already signed. Please fill in correct amount.

L. Tzuref
Director, Yeshivah of
Woodenton, N.Y.
(5/8/48)

"Eli, a regular greenhorn," Ted Heller had said. "He didn't say a word. Just handed me the note and stood there, like in the Bronx the old guys who used to come around selling Hebrew trinkets."

"A Yeshivah!" Artie Berg had said. "Eli, in Woodenton, a Yeshivah! If I want to live in Brownsville, Eli, I'll live in Brownsville."

"Eli," Harry Shaw speaking now, "the old Puddington place. Old man Puddington'll roll over in his grave. Eli, when I left the city, Eli, I didn't plan the city should come to me."

Note number two:

Dear Grocer:
    Please give this gentleman ten pounds of sugar. Charge it to our account, Yeshivah of Woodenton, NY—which we will now open with you and expect a bill each month. The gentleman will be in to see you once or twice a week.
L. Tzuref, Director
(5/10/48)

P.S. Do you carry kosher meat?

"He walked right by my window, the greenie," Ted had said, "and he nodded, Eli. He's my *friend* now."

"Eli," Artie Berg had said, "he handed the damn thing to a *clerk* at Stop N' Shop—and in that hat yet!"

"Eli," Harry Shaw again, "it's not funny. Someday, Eli, it's going to be a hundred little kids with little *yamalkahs* chanting their Hebrew lessons on Coach House Road, and then it's not going to strike you funny."

"Eli, what goes on up there—my kids hear strange sounds."

"Eli, this is a modern community."

"Eli, we pay taxes."

"Eli."

"Eli!"

"*Eli!*"

At first it was only another townsman crying in his ear; but when he turned he saw Miriam, standing in the doorway, behind her belly.

"Eli, sweetheart, how was it?"

"He said no."

"Did you see the other one?" she asked.

"Sleeping, under a tree."

"Did you let him know how people feel?"

"He was sleeping."

"Why didn't you wake him up? Eli, this isn't an everyday thing."

"He was tired!"

"Don't shout, please," Miriam said.

" ' Don't shout. I'm pregnant. The baby is heavy.' " Eli found he was getting angry at nothing she'd said yet; it was what she was going to say.

"He's a very heavy baby the doctor says," Miriam told him.

"Then sit *down* and make my dinner."

Now he found himself angry about her not being present at the dinner which he'd just been relieved that she wasn't present at. It was as though he had a raw nerve for a tail, that he kept stepping on. At last Miriam herself stepped on it.

"Eli, you're upset. I understand."

"You *don't* understand."

She left the room. From the stairs she called, "I do, sweetheart."

It was a trap! He would grow angry knowing she would be "understanding." She would in turn grow more understanding seeing his anger. He would in turn grow angrier . . . The phone rang.

"Hello," Eli said.

"Eli, Ted. So?"

"So nothing."

"Who is Tzuref? He's an American guy?"

"No. A DP. German."

"And the kids?"

"DP's too. He teaches them."

"What? What subjects?" Ted asked.

"I don't know."

"And the guy with the hat, you saw the guy with the hat?"

"Yes. He was sleeping."

"Eli, he sleeps with the *hat?*"

"He sleeps with the hat."

"Goddam fanatics," Ted said. "This is the twentieth century, Eli. Now it's the guy with the hat. Pretty soon all the little Yeshivah boys'll be spilling down into town."

"Next thing they'll be after our daughters."

"Michele and Debbie wouldn't look at them."

"Then," Eli mumbled, "You've got nothing to worry about, Teddie," and he hung up.

In a moment the phone rang. "Eli? We got cut off. We've got nothing to worry about? You worked it out?"

"I have to see him again tomorrow. We can work something out."

"That's fine, Eli. I'll call Artie and Harry."

Eli hung up.

"I thought you said *nothing* worked out." It was Miriam.

"I did."

"Then why did you tell Ted *something* worked out?"

"It did."

"Eli, maybe you should get a little more therapy."

"That's enough of that, Miriam."

"You can't function as a lawyer by being neurotic. That's no answer."

"You're ingenious, Miriam."

She turned, frowning, and took her heavy baby to bed. The phone rang.

"Eli, Artie. Ted called. You worked it out? No trouble?"

"Yes."

"When are they going?"

"Leave it to me, will you, Artie? I'm tired. I'm going to sleep."

In bed Eli kissed his wife's belly and laid his head upon it to think. He laid it lightly, for she was that day entering the second week of her ninth month. Still, when she slept, it was a good place to rest, to rise and fall with her breathing and figure things out. "If that guy would take off that crazy hat. I know it, what eats them. If he'd take off that crazy hat everything would be all right."

"What?" Miriam said.

"I'm talking to the baby."

Miriam pushed herself up in bed. "Eli, please, baby, shouldn't you maybe stop in to see Dr. Eckman, just for a little conversation?"

"I'm fine."

"Oh, sweetie!" she said, and put her head back on the pillow.

"You know what your mother brought to this marriage—a sling chair and a goddam New School enthusiasm for Sigmund Freud."

Miriam feigned sleep, he could tell by the breathing.

"I'm telling the kid the truth, aren't I, Miriam? A sling chair, three months to go on a *New Yorker* subscription, and *An Introduction to Psychoanalysis*. Isn't that right?"

"Eli, must you be aggressive?"

"That's all you worry about, is your insides. You stand in front of the mirror all day and look at yourself being pregnant."

"Pregnant mothers have a relationship with the fetus that fathers can't understand."

"Relationship my ass. What is my liver doing now? What is my small intestine doing now? Is my island of Langerhans on the blink?"

"Don't be jealous of a little fetus, Eli."

"I'm jealous of your island of Langerhans!"

"Eli, I can't argue with you when I know it's not me you're really angry with. Don't you see, sweetie, you're angry with yourself."

"You and Eckman."

"Maybe he could help, Eli."

"Maybe he could help you. You're practically lovers as it is."

"You're being hostile again," Miriam said.

"What do you care—it's only *me* I'm being hostile towards."

"Eli, we're going to have a beautiful baby, and I'm going to have a perfectly simple delivery, and you're going to make a fine father, and there's absolutely no reason to be obsessed with whatever is on your mind. All we have to worry about—" she smiled at him "—is a name."

Eli got out of bed and slid into his slippers. "We'll name the kid Eckman if it's a boy and Eckman if it's a girl."

"Eckman Peck sounds terrible."

"He'll have to live with it," Eli said, and he went down to his study where the latch on his briefcase glinted in the moonlight that came through the window.

He removed the Tzuref notes and read through them all again. It unnerved him to think of all the flashy reasons his wife could come up with for his reading and rereading the notes. "Eli, why are you so *preoccupied* with Tzuref?" "Eli, stop getting *involved*. Why do you think you're getting *involved*, Eli?" Sooner or later, everybody's wife finds their weak spot. His goddam luck he had to be neurotic! Why couldn't he have been born with a short leg.

He removed the cover from his typewriter, hating Miriam for the edge she had. All the time he wrote the letter, he could hear what she would be saying about his not being *able* to let the matter drop. Well, her trouble was that she wasn't *able* to face the matter. But he could hear her answer already: clearly, he was guilty of "a reaction formation." Still, all the fancy phrases didn't fool Eli: all she wanted really was for Eli to send Tzuref and family on their way, so that the community's temper would quiet, and the calm circumstances of their domestic happiness return. All she wanted were order and love in her private world. Was she so wrong? Let the world bat its brains out—in Woodenton there should be peace. He wrote the letter anyway:

Dear Mr. Tzuref:

Our meeting this evening seems to me inconclusive. I don't think there's any reason for us not to be able to come up with some sort of compromise that will satisfy the Jewish community of Woodenton and the Yeshivah and yourself. It seems to me that what most disturbs my neighbors are the visits to town by the gentleman in the black hat, suit, etc. Woodenton is a progressive suburban community whose members, both Jewish and Gentile, are anxious that their families live in comfort and beauty and serenity. This is, after all, the twentieth century, and we do not think it too much to ask that the members of our community dress in a manner appropriate to the time and place.

Woodenton, as you may not know, has long been the home of well-to-do Protestants. It is only since the war that Jews have been able to buy property here, and for Jews and Gentiles to live beside each other in amity. For this adjustment to be made, both Jews and Gentiles alike have had to give up some of their more extreme practices in order not to threaten or offend the other. Certainly such amity is to be desired. Perhaps if such conditions had existed in prewar Europe, the persecution of the Jewish people, of which you and those 18 children have been victims, could not have been carried out with such success—in fact, might not have been carried out at all.

Therefore, Mr. Tzuref, will you accept the following conditions? If you can, we will see fit not to carry out legal action against the Yeshivah for failure to comply with township Zoning ordinances No. 18 and No. 23. The conditions are simply:

1. The religious, educational, and social activities of the Yeshivah of Woodenton will be confined to the Yeshivah grounds.

2. Yeshivah personnel are welcomed in the streets and stores of Woodenton provided they are attired in clothing usually associated with American life in the 20th century.

If these conditions are met, we see no reason why the Yeshivah of Woodenton cannot live peacefully and satisfactorily with the Jews of Woodenton—as Jews of Woodenton have come to live with the Gentiles of Woodenton. I would appreciate an immediate reply.

> Sincerely,
> ELI PECK, Attorney

Two days later Eli received his immediate reply:

> Mr. Peck:
> The suit the gentleman wears is all he's got.
> Sincerely,
> LEO TZUREF, Headmaster

Once again, as Eli swung around the dark trees and onto the lawn, the children fled. He reached out with his briefcase as if to stop them, but they were gone so fast all he saw moving was a flock of skullcaps.

"Come, come . . ." a voice called from the porch. Tzuref appeared from behind a pillar. Did he *live* behind those pillars? Was he just watching the children at play? Either way, when Eli appeared, Tzuref was ready, with no forewarning.

"Hello," Eli said.

"Sholom."

"I didn't mean to frighten them."

"They're scared, so they run."

"I didn't do anything."

Tzuref shrugged. The little movement seemed to Eli strong as an accusation. What he didn't get at home, he got here.

Inside the house they took their seats. Though it was lighter than a few evenings before, a bulb or two would have helped. Eli had to hold his briefcase towards the window for the last gleamings. He removed Tzuref's letter from a manila folder. Tzuref removed Eli's letter from his pants pocket. Eli removed the carbon of his own letter from another manila folder. Tzuref removed Eli's first letter from his back pocket. Eli removed the carbon from his briefcase. Tzuref raised his palms. ". . . It's all I've got . . . It's all I've got . . ."

Those upraised palms, the mocking tone—another accusation. It was a crime to keep carbons! Everybody had an edge on him—Eli could do no right.

"I offered a compromise, Mr. Tzuref. You refused."

"Refused, Mr. Peck? What is, is."

"The man could get a new suit."

"That's all he's got."

"So you told me," Eli said.

"So I told you, so you know."

"It's not an insurmountable obstacle, Mr. Tzuref. We have stores."

"For that too?"

"On Route 12, a Robert Hall—"

"To take away the one thing a man's got?"

"Not take away, *replace*."

"But I tell you he has nothing. *Nothing*. You have that word in English? Nicht? Gornisht?"

"Yes, Mr. Tzuref, we have the word."

"A mother and a father?" Tzuref said. "No. A wife? No. A baby? A little ten-month-old baby? No! A village full of friends? A synagogue where you knew the feel of every seat under your pants? Where with your eyes closed you could smell the cloth of the Torah?" Tzuref pushed out of his chair, stirring a breeze that swept Eli's letter to the floor. At the window he leaned out, and looked, beyond Woodenton. When he turned he was shaking a finger at Eli. "And a medical experiment they performed on him yet! That leaves nothing, Mr. Peck. Absolutely nothing!"

"I misunderstood."

"No news reached Woodenton?"

"About the suit, Mr. Tzuref. I thought he couldn't afford another."

"He can't."

They were right where they'd begun. "Mr. Tzuref!" Eli demanded. *"Here?"* He smacked his hand to his billfold.

"Exactly!" Tzuref said, smacking his own breast.

"Then we'll buy him one!" Eli crossed to the window and taking Tzuref by the shoulders, pronounced each word slowly. "We-will-pay-for-it. All right?"

"Pay? What, diamonds!"

Eli raised a hand to his inside pocket, then let it drop. Oh stupid! Tzuref, father to eighteen, had smacked not what lay under his coat, but deeper, under the ribs.

"Oh . . ." Eli said. He moved away along the wall. "The suit is all he's got then."

"You got my letter," Tzuref said.

Eli stayed back in the shadow, and Tzuref turned to his chair. He swished Eli's letter from the floor, and held it up. "You say too much . . . all this reasoning . . . all these conditions . . ."

"What can I do?"

"You have the word 'suffer' in English?"

"We have the word suffer. We have the word law too."

"Stop with the law! You have the word suffer. Then try it. It's a little thing."

"They won't," Eli said.

"But you, Mr. Peck, how about you?"

"I am them, they are me, Mr. Tzuref."

"Aach! You are us, we are you!"

Eli shook and shook his head. In the dark he suddenly felt that Tzuref might put him under a spell. "Mr. Tzuref, a little light?"

Tzuref lit what tallow was left in the holders. Eli was afraid to ask if they couldn't afford electricity. Maybe candles were all they had left.

"Mr. Peck, who made the law, may I ask you that?"

"The people."

"No."

"Yes."

"Before the people."

"No one. Before the people there was no law." Eli didn't care for the conversation, but with only candlelight, he was being lulled into it.

"Wrong," Tzuref said.

"We make the law, Mr. Tzuref. It is our community. These are my neighbors. I am their attorney. They pay me. Without law there is chaos."

"What you call law, I call shame. The heart, Mr. Peck, the heart is law! God!" he announced.

"Look, Mr. Tzuref, I didn't come here to talk metaphysics. People use the law, it's a flexible thing. They protect what they value, their property, their well-being, their happiness—"

"Happiness? They hide their shame. And you, Mr. Peck, you are shameless?"

"We do it," Eli said, wearily, "for our children. This is the twentieth century . . ."

"For the goyim maybe. For me the Fifty-eighth." He pointed at Eli. "That is too old for shame."

Eli felt squashed. Everybody in the world had evil reasons for his actions. Everybody! With reasons so cheap, who buys bulbs. "Enough wisdom, Mr. Tzuref. Please. I'm exhausted."

"Who isn't?" Tzuref said.

He picked Eli's papers from his desk and reached up with them. "What do you intend for us to do?"

"What you must," Eli said. "I made the offer."

"So he must give up his suit?"

"Tzuref, Tzuref, leave me be with that suit! I'm not the only lawyer in the world. I'll drop the case, and you'll get somebody who won't talk compromise. Then you'll have no home, no children, nothing. Only a lousy black suit! Sacrifice what you want. I know what I would do."

To that Tzuref made no answer, but only handed Eli his letters.

"It's not me, Mr. Tzuref, it's them."

"They are you."

"No," Eli intoned, "I am me. They are them. You are you."

"You talk about leaves and branches. I'm dealing with under the dirt."

"Mr. Tzuref, you're driving me crazy with Talmudic wisdom. This is that, that is the other thing. Give me a straight answer."

"Only for straight questions."

"Oh, God!"

Eli returned to his chair and plunged his belongings into his case. "Then, that's all," he said angrily.

Tzuref gave him the shrug.

"Remember, Tzuref, you called this down on yourself."

"*I* did?"

Eli refused to be his victim again. Double-talk proved nothing.

"Goodbye," he said.

But as he opened the door leading to the hall, he heard Tzuref.

"And your wife, how is she?"

"Fine, just fine." Eli kept going.

"And the baby is due when, any day?"

Eli turned. "That's right."

"Well," Tzuref said, rising. "Good luck."

"You know?"

Tzuref pointed out the window—then, with his hands, he drew upon himself a beard, a hat, a long, long coat. When his fingers formed the hem they touched the floor. "He shops two, three times a week, he gets to know them."

"He *talks* to them?"

"He sees them."

"And he can tell which is my wife?"

"They shop at the same stores. He says she is beautiful. She has a kind face. A woman capable of love . . . though who can be sure."

"*He* talks about *us*, to *you?*" demanded Eli.

"You talk about us, to her?"

"Goodbye, Mr. Tzuref."

Tzuref said, "Sholom. And good luck—I know what it is to have children. Sholom," Tzuref whispered, and with the whisper the candles went out. But the instant before, the flames leaped into Tzuref's eyes, and Eli saw it was not luck Tzuref wished him at all.

Outside the door, Eli waited. Down the lawn the children were holding hands and whirling around in a circle. At first he did not move. But he could not hide in the shadows all night. Slowly he began to slip along the front of the house. Under his hands he felt where bricks were out. He moved in the shadows until he reached the side. And then, clutching his briefcase to his chest, he broke across the darkest spots of the lawn. He aimed for a distant glade of woods, and when he reached it he did not stop, but ran through until he was so dizzied that the trees seemed to be running beside him, fleeing not towards Woodenton but away. His lungs were nearly ripping their seams as he burst into the yellow glow of the Gulf station at the edge of town.

"Eli, I had pains today. Where were you?"

"I went to Tzuref."

"Why didn't you call? I was worried."

He tossed his hat past the sofa and onto the floor. "Where are my winter suits?"

"In the hall closet. Eli, it's May."

"I need a strong suit." He left the room, Miriam behind him.

"Eli, talk to me. Sit down. Have dinner. Eli, what are you doing? You're going to get moth balls all over the carpet."

He peered out from the hall closet. Then he peered in again—there was a zipping noise, and suddenly he swept a greenish tweed suit before his wife's eyes.

"Eli, I love you in that suit. But not now. Have something to eat. I made dinner tonight—I'll warm it."

"You've got a box big enough for this suit?"

"I got a Bonwit's box, the other day. Eli, *why?*"

"Miriam, you see me doing something, let me do it."

"You haven't eaten."

"I'm *doing* something." He started up the stairs to the bedroom.

"Eli, would you please tell me what it is you want, and why?"

He turned and looked down at her. "Suppose this time you give me the reasons *before* I tell you what I'm doing. It'll probably work out the same anyway."

"Eli, I want to help."

"It doesn't concern you."

"But I want to help *you*," Miriam said.

"Just be quiet, then."

"But you're upset," she said, and she followed him up the stairs, heavily, breathing for two.

"Eli, what now?"

"A shirt." He yanked open all the drawers of their new teak dresser. He extracted a shirt.

"Eli, batiste? With a tweed suit?" she inquired.

He was at the closet now, on his knees. "Where are my cordovans?"

"Eli, why are you doing this so compulsively? You look like you *have* to do something."

"Oh, Miriam, you're supersubtle."

"Eli, stop this and talk to me. Stop it or I'll call Dr. Eckman."

Eli was kicking off the shoes he was wearing. "Where's the Bonwit box?"

"Eli, do you want me to have the baby right *here!*"

Eli walked over and sat down on the bed. He was draped not only with his own clothing, but also with the greenish tweed suit, the batiste shirt, and under each arm a shoe. He raised his arms and let the shoes drop onto the bed. Then he undid his necktie with one hand and his teeth and added that to the booty.

"Underwear," he said. "He'll need underwear."

"Who!"

He was slipping out of his socks.

Miriam kneeled down and helped him ease his left foot out of the sock. She sat with it on the floor. "Eli, just lie back. Please."

"Plaza 9-3103."

"What?"

"Eckman's number," he said, "It'll save you the trouble."

"Eli—"

"You've got the goddam tender 'You need help' look in your eyes, Miriam, don't tell me you don't."

"I don't."

"I'm not flipping," Eli said.

"I know, Eli."

"Last time I sat in the bottom of the closet and chewed on my bedroom slippers. That's what I did."

"I know."

"And I'm not doing that. This is not a nervous breakdown, Miriam, let's get that straight."

"Okay," Miriam said. She kissed the foot she held. Then, softly, she asked, "What *are* you doing?"

"Getting clothes for the guy in the hat. Don't tell me why, Miriam. Just let me do it."

"That's all?" she asked.

"That's all."

"You're not leaving?"

"No."

"Sometimes I think it gets too much for you, and you'll just leave."

"What gets too much?"

"I don't *know*, Eli. Something gets too much. Whenever everything's peaceful for a long time, and things are nice and pleasant, and we're expecting to be even happier. Like now. It's as if you don't think we *deserve* to be happy."

"Damn it, Miriam! I'm giving this guy a new suit, is that all right? From now on he comes into Woodenton like everybody else, is that all right with you?"

"And Tzuref moves?"

"I don't even know if he'll take the suit, Miriam! What do you have to bring up moving!"

"Eli, I didn't bring up moving. Everybody did. That's what everybody wants. Why make everybody un*happy*. It's even a law, Eli."

"Don't tell me what's the law."

"All right, sweetie. I'll get the box."

"*I'll* get the box. Where is it?"

"In the basement."

When he came up from the basement, he found all the clothes neatly folded and squared away on the sofa: shirt, tie, shoes, socks, underwear, belt, and an old gray flannel suit. His wife sat on the end of the sofa, looking like an anchored balloon.

"Where's the green suit?" he said.

"Eli, it's your loveliest suit. It's my favorite suit. Whenever I think of you, Eli, it's in that suit."

"Get it out."

"Eli, it's a Brooks Brothers suit. You say yourself how much you love it."

"Get it out."

"But the gray flannel's more practical. For shopping."

"Get it out."

"You go overboard, Eli. That's your trouble. You won't do anything in moderation. That's how people destroy themselves."

"I do *everything* in moderation. That's my trouble. The suit's in the closet again?"

She nodded, and began to fill up with tears. "Why does it have to be *your* suit? Who are you even to decide to give a suit? What about the others?" She was crying openly, and holding her belly. "Eli, I'm going to have a baby. Do we need all *this?* and she swept the clothes off the sofa to the floor.

At the closet Eli removed the green suit. "It's a J. Press," he said, looking at the lining.

"I hope to hell he's happy with it!" Miriam said, sobbing.

A half hour later the box was packed. The cord he'd found in the kitchen cabinet couldn't keep the outfit from popping through. The trouble was there was too much: the gray suit *and* the green suit, an oxford shirt as well as the batiste. But let him have two suits! Let him have three, four, if only this damn silliness would stop! And a hat—of course! God, he'd almost forgotten the hat. He took the stairs two at a time and in Miriam's closet yanked a hatbox from the top shelf. Scattering hat and tissue paper to the floor, he returned downstairs, where he packed away the hat he'd worn that day. Then he looked at his wife, who lay outstretched on the floor before the fireplace. For the third time in as many minutes she was saying, "Eli, this is the real thing."

"Where?"

"Right under the baby's head, like somebody's squeezing oranges."

Now that he'd stopped to listen he was stupefied. He said, "But you have two more weeks . . ." Somehow he'd really been expecting it was to go on not just another two weeks, but another nine months. This led him to suspect, suddenly, that his wife was feigning pain so as to get his mind off delivering the suit. And just as suddenly he resented himself for having such a thought. God, what had he become! He'd been an unending bastard towards her since this Tzuref business had come up—just when her pregnancy must have been most burdensome. He'd allowed her no access to him but still, he was sure, for good reasons: she might tempt him out of his confusion with her easy answers. He could be tempted all right, it was why he fought so hard. But now a sweep of love came over him at the thought of her contracting womb, and his child. And yet he would not indicate it to her. Under such splendid marital conditions, who knows but she might extract some promise from him about his concern with the school on the hill.

Having packed his second bag of the evening, Eli sped his wife to Woodenton Memorial. There she proceeded not to have her baby, but to lie hour after hour through the night having at first oranges, then bowling balls, then basketballs, squeezed back of her pelvis. Eli sat in the waiting room, under the shattering African glare of a dozen rows of fluorescent bulbs, composing a letter to Tzuref.

> Dear Mr. Tzuref:
>   The clothes in this box are for the gentleman in the hat. In a life of sacrifice what is one more? But in a life of no sacrifices even one is impossible. Do you see what I'm saying, Mr. Tzuref? I am not a Nazi who would drive eighteen children, who are probably frightened at the sight of a firefly, into homelessness. But if you want a home here, you must accept what we have to offer. The world is the world, Mr. Tzuref. As you would say, what is, is. All we say to this man is change your clothes. Enclosed are two suits and two shirts, and everything else he'll need, including a new hat. When he needs new clothes let me know.
>   We await his appearance in Woodenton, as we await friendly relations with the Yeshivah of Woodenton.

He signed his name and slid the note under a bursting flap and into the box. Then he went to the phone at the end of the room and dialed Ted Heller's number.

"Hello."

"Shirley, it's Eli."

"Eli, we've been calling all night. The lights are on in your place, but nobody answers. We thought it was burglars."

"Miriam's having the baby."

"At home?" Shirley said. "Oh, Eli, what a fun-idea!"

"Shirley, let me speak to Ted."

After the ear-shaking clatter of the phone whacking the floor, Eli heard footsteps, breathing, throat-clearing, then Ted. "A boy or a girl?"

"Nothing yet."

"You've given Shirley the bug, Eli. Now she's going to have *our* next one at home."

"Good."

"That's a terrific way to bring the family together, Eli."

"Look, Ted, I've settled with Tzuref."

"When are they going?"

"They're not exactly going, Teddie. I settled it—you won't even know they're there."

"A guy dressed like 1000 B.C. and I won't know it? What are you thinking about, pal?"

"He's changing his clothes."

"Yeah, to what? Another funeral suit?"

"Tzuref promised me, Ted. Next time he comes to town, he comes dressed like you and me."

"What! Somebody's kidding somebody, Eli."

Eli's voice shot up. "If he says he'll do it, he'll do it!"

"And, Eli," Ted asked, "he said it?"

"He said it." It cost him a sudden headache, this invention.

"And suppose he doesn't change, Eli. Just suppose. I mean that *might* happen, Eli. This might just be some kind of stall or something."

"No," Eli assured him.

The other end was quiet a moment. "Look, Eli," Ted said, finally, "he changes. Okay? All right? But they're still up there, aren't they? *That* doesn't change."

"The point is you won't know it."

Patiently Ted said, "Is this what we asked of you, Eli? When we put our faith and trust in you, is that what we were asking? We weren't concerned that this guy should become a Beau Brummell, Eli, believe me. We just don't think this is the community for them. And, Eli, we isn't me. The Jewish members of the community appointed me, Artie, and Harry to see what could be done. And we appointed you. And what's happened?"

Eli heard himself say, "What happened, happened."

"Eli, you're talking in crossword puzzles."

"My wife's having a baby," Eli explained, defensively.

"I realize that, Eli. But this is a matter of zoning, isn't it? Isn't that what we discovered? You don't abide by the ordinance, you go. I mean I can't raise mountain goats, say, in my backyard—"

"This isn't so simple, Ted. People are involved—"

"People? Eli, we've been through this and through this. We're not just dealing with people—these are religious fanatics is what they are. Dressing like that. What I'd really like to find out is what goes on up there. I'm getting more and more skeptical, Eli, and I'm not afraid to admit it. It smells like a lot of hocus-pocus abracadabra stuff to me. Guys like Harry, you know, they think and they think and they're afraid to admit what they're thinking. I'll tell you. Look, I don't even know about this Sunday school business. Sundays I drive my oldest kid all the way to Scarsdale to learn Bible stories . . . and you know what she comes up with? This Abraham in the Bible was going to kill his own *kid* for a sacrifice. She gets nightmares from it, for God's sake! You call that religion? Today a guy like that they'd lock him up. This is an age of science, Eli. I size people's feet with an X-ray machine, for God's sake. They've disproved all that stuff, Eli, and I refuse to sit by and watch it happening on my own front lawn.

"Nothing's happening on your front lawn, Teddie. You're exaggerating, nobody's sacrificing their kid."

"You're damn right, Eli—I'm not sacrificing mine. You'll see when you have your own what it's like. All the place is, is a hideaway for people who can't face life. It's a matter of *needs*. They have all these superstitions, and why do you think? Because they can't face the world, because they can't take their place in society. That's no environment to bring kids up in, Eli."

"Look, Ted, see it from another angle. We can convert them," Eli said, with half a heart.

"What, make a bunch of Catholics out of them? Look, Eli—pal, there's a good healthy relationship in this town because it's modern Jews and Protestants. That's the point, isn't it, Eli? Let's not kid each other, I'm not Harry. The way things are now are fine—like human beings. There's going to be no pogroms in Woodenton. Right? 'Cause there's no fanatics, no crazy people—" Eli winced, and closed his eyes a second—"just people who respect each other, and leave each other be. Common sense is the ruling thing, Eli. I'm for common sense. Moderation."

"Exactly, exactly, Ted. I agree, but common sense, maybe, says make this guy change his clothes. Then maybe—"

"Common sense says that? Common sense says to me they go and find a nice place somewhere else, Eli. New York is the biggest city in the world, it's only 30 miles away—why don't they go there?"

"Ted, give them a chance. Introduce them to common sense."

"Eli, You're dealing with *fanatics*. Do they display common sense? Talking a dead language, that makes sense? Making a big thing out of suffering, so you're going oy-oy-oy all your life, that's common sense? Look, Eli, we've been through all this. I don't know if you know—but there's talk that *Life* magazine is sending a guy out to the Yeshivah for a story. With pictures."

"Look, Teddie, you're letting your imagination get inflamed. I don't think *Life's* interested."

"But I'm interested, Eli. And we thought you were supposed to be."

"I am," Eli said, "I am. Let him just change the clothes, Ted. Let's see what happens."

"They live in the medieval ages, Eli—it's some superstition, some *rule*."

"Let's just *see*," Eli pleaded.

"Eli, every day—"

"One more day," Eli said. "If he doesn't change in one more day . . . ."

"What?"

"Then I get an injunction first thing Monday. That's that."

"Look, Eli—it's not up to me. Let me call Harry—"

"You're the spokesman, Teddie. I'm all wrapped up here with Miriam having a baby. Just give me the day—them the day."

"All right, Eli. I want to be fair. But tomorrow, that's all. Tomorrow's the judgment day, Eli, I'm telling you."

"I hear trumpets," Eli said, and hung up. He was shaking inside—Teddie's voice seemed to have separated his bones at the joints. He was still in the phone booth when the nurse came to tell him that Mrs. Peck would positively not be delivered of a child until the morning. He was to go home and get some rest, he looked like *he* was having the baby. The nurse winked and left.

But Eli did not go home. He carried the Bonwit box out into the street with him and put it in the car. The night was soft and starry, and he began to drive the streets of Woodenton. Square cool windows, apricot-colored, were all one could see beyond the long lawns that fronted the homes of the townsmen. The stars polished the permanent baggage carriers atop the station wagons in the driveways. He drove slowly, up, down, around. Only his tires could be heard taking the gentle curves in the road.

What peace. What incredible peace. Have children ever been so safe in their beds? Parents—Eli wondered—so full in their stomachs? Water so warm in its boilers? Never. Never in Rome, never in Greece. Never even did walled cities have it so good! No wonder then they would keep things just as they were. Here, after all, were peace and safety—what civilization had been working toward for centuries. For all his jerkiness, that was all Ted Heller was asking for, peace and safety. It was what his parents had asked for in the Bronx, and his grandparents in Poland, and theirs in Russia or Austria, or wherever else they'd fled to or from. It was what Miriam was asking for. And now they had it—the world was at last a place for families, even Jewish families. After all these centuries, maybe there just had to be this communal toughness—or numbness—to protect such a blessing. Maybe that was the trouble with the Jews all along—too soft. Sure, to live takes guts . . . Eli was thinking as he drove on beyond the train station, and parked his car at the darkened Gulf station. He stepped out, carrying the box.

At the top of the hill one window trembled with light. What *was* Tzuref doing up there in that office? Killing babies—probably not. But studying a language no one understood? Practicing customs with origins long forgotten? Suffering sufferings already suffered once too often? Teddie was right—why keep it up! However, if a man chose to be stubborn, then he couldn't expect to survive. The world is give-and-take. What sense to sit and brood over a suit. Eli would give him one last chance.

He stopped at the top. No one was around. He walked slowly up the lawn, setting each foot into the grass, listening to the shh shhh shhhh his shoes made as they bent the wetness into the sod. He looked around. Here there was nothing. Nothing! An old decaying house—and a suit.

On the porch he slid behind a pillar. He felt someone was watching him. But only the stars gleamed down. And at his feet, off and away, Woodenton glowed up. He set his package on the step of the great front door. Inside the cover of the box he felt to see if his letter was still there. When he touched it, he pushed it deeper into the green suit, which his fingers still remembered from winter. He should have included some light bulbs. Then he slid back by the pillar again, and this time there was something on the lawn. It was the second sight he had of him. He was facing Woodenton and barely moving across the open space towards the trees. His right fist was beating his chest. And then Eli heard a sound rising with each knock on the chest. What a moan! It could raise hair, stop hearts, water eyes. And it did all three to Eli, plus more. Some feeling crept into him for whose deepness he could find no word. It was strange. He listened—it did not hurt to hear this moan. But he wondered if it hurt to make it. And so, with only stars to hear, he tried. And it did hurt. Not the bumble-bee of noise that turned at the back of his throat and winged out his nostrils. What hurt buzzed down. It stung and stung inside him, and in turn the moan sharpened. It became a scream, louder, a song, a crazy song that whined through the pillars and blew out the grass, until the strange hatted creature on the lawn turned and threw his arms wide, and looked in the night like a scarecrow.

Eli, ran, and when he reached the car the pain was only a bloody scratch across his neck where a branch had whipped back as he fled the greenie's arms.

The following day his son was born. But not till one in the afternoon, and by then a great deal had happened.

First, at nine-thirty the phone rang. Eli leaped from the sofa—where he'd dropped the night before—and picked it screaming from the cradle. He could practically smell the hospital as he shouted into the phone, "Hello, yes!"

"Eli, it's Ted. Eli, he *did* it. He just walked by the store. I was opening the door, Eli, and I turned around and I swear I thought it was you. But it was him. He still walks like he did, but the clothes, Eli, the clothes."

"Who?"

"The greenie. He has on man's regular clothes. And the suit, it's a beauty."

The suit barreled back into Eli's consciousness, pushing all else aside. "What color suit?"

"Green. He's just strolling in the green suit like it's a holiday. Eli . . . is it a Jewish holiday?"

"Where is he now?"

"He's walking straight up Coach House Road, in this damn tweed job. Eli, it worked. You were right."

"We'll see."

"What next?"

"We'll see."

He took off the underwear in which he'd slept and went into the kitchen where he turned the light under the coffee. When it began to perk he held his head over the pot so it would steam loose the knot back of his eyes. It still hadn't when the phone rang.

"Eli, Ted again. Eli, the guy's walking up and down every street in town. Really, he's on a tour or something. Artie called me, Herb called me. Now Shirley calls that he just walked by our house. Eli, go out on the porch you'll see."

Eli went to the window and peered out. He couldn't see past the bend in the road, and there was no one in sight.

"Eli?" He heard Ted from where he dangled over the telephone table. He dropped the phone into the hook, as a few last words floated up to him—"Eliyousawhim . . . ?" He threw on the pants and shirt he'd worn the night before and walked barefoot onto his front lawn. And sure enough, his apparition appeared around the bend: in a brown hat a little too far down on his head, a green suit too far back on the shoulders, an unbuttoned-down button-down shirt, a tie knotted so as to leave a two-inch tail, trousers that cascaded onto his shoes—he was shorter than that black hat had made him seem. And moving the clothes was that walk that was not a walk, the tiny-stepped shlumpy gait. He came round the bend, and for all his strangeness—it clung to his whiskers, signaled itself in his locomotion—he looked as if he belonged. Eccentric, maybe, but he belonged. He made no moan, nor did he invite Eli with wide-flung arms. But he did stop when he saw him. He stopped and put a hand to his hat. When he felt for its top, his hand went up too high. Then it found the level and fiddled with the brim. The fingers fiddled, fumbled, and when they'd finally made their greeting, they traveled down the fellow's face and in an instant seemed to have touched each one of his features. They dabbed the eyes, ran the length of the nose, swept over the hairy lip, until they found their home in the hair that hid a little of his collar. To Eli the fingers said, *I have a face, I have a face at least*. Then his hand came through the beard and when it stopped at his chest it was like a pointer—and the eyes asked a question as tides of water shifted over them. *The face is all right, I can keep it?* Such a look was in those eyes that Eli was still seeing them when he turned his head away. They were the hearts of his jonquils, that only last week had appeared—they were the leaves on his birch, the bulbs in his coach lamp, the droppings on his lawn: those eyes were the eyes in his head. They were his, he had made them. He turned and went into his house and when he peeked out the side of the window, between shade and molding, the green suit was gone.

The phone.

"Eli, Shirley."

"I saw him, Shirley," and he hung up.

He sat frozen for a long time. The sun moved around the windows. The coffee steam smelled up the house. The phone began to ring, stopped, began again. The mailman came, the cleaner, the bakery man, the gardener, the ice cream man, the League of Women Voters lady. A Negro woman spreading some strange gospel calling for the revision of the Food and Drug Act knocked at the front, rapped the windows, and finally scraped a half-dozen pamphlets under the back door. But Eli only sat, without underwear, in last night's suit. He answered no one.

Given his condition, it was strange that the trip and crash at the back door reached his inner ear. But in an instant he seemed to melt down into the crevices of the chair, then to splash up and out to where the clatter had been. At the door he waited. It was silent, but for a fluttering of damp little leaves on the trees. When he finally opened the door, there was no one there. He'd expected to see green, green green, big as the doorway, topped by his hat, waiting for him with those eyes. But there was no one out there, except for the Bonwit's box which lay bulging at his feet. No string tied it and the top rode high on the bottom.

The coward! He couldn't do it! He couldn't!

The very glee of that idea pumped fuel to his legs. He tore out across his back lawn, past his new spray of forsythia, to catch a glimpse of the bearded one fleeing naked through yards, over hedges and fences, to the safety of his hermitage. In the distance a pile of pink and white stones— which Harriet Knudson had painted the previous day—tricked him. "Run," he shouted to the rocks, "run, you . . ." but he caught his error before anyone else did, and though he peered and craned there was no hint anywhere of a man about his own size, with white, white, terribly white skin (how white must be the skin of his body!) in cowardly retreat. He came slowly, curiously, back to the door. And while the trees shimmered in the light wind, he removed the top from the box. The shock at first was the shock of having daylight turned off all at once. Inside the box was an eclipse. But black soon sorted from black, and shortly there was the glassy black of lining, the coarse black of trousers, the dead black of fraying threads, and in the center the mountain of black: the hat. He picked the box from the doorstep and carried it inside. For the first time in his life he *smelled* the color of blackness: a little stale, a little sour, a little old, but nothing that could overwhelm you. Still, he held the package at arm's length and deposited it on the dining room table.

Twenty rooms on a hill and they store their old clothes with me! What am I supposed to do with them? Give them to charity? That's where they came from. He picked up the hat by the edges and looked inside. The crown was smooth as an egg, the brim practically threadbare. There is nothing else to do with a hat in one's hands but put it on, so Eli dropped the thing on his head. He opened the door to the hall closet and looked at himself in the full-length mirror. The hat gave him bags under the eyes. Or perhaps he had not slept well. He pushed the brim lower till a shadow touched his lips. Now the bags under his eyes had inflated to become his face. Before the mirror he unbuttoned his shirt, unzipped his trousers, and then, shedding his clothes, he studied what he was. What a silly disappointment to see yourself naked in a hat. Especially in that hat. He sighed, but could not rid himself of the great weakness that suddenly set on his muscles and joints, beneath the terrible weight of the stranger's strange hat.

He returned to the dining room table and emptied the box of its contents: jacket, trousers, and vest (*it* smelled deeper than blackness). And under it all, sticking between the shoes that looked chopped and bitten, came the first gleam of white. A little fringed serape, a gray piece of semi-underwear, was crumpled at the bottom, its thready border twisted into itself. Eli removed it and let it hang free. What is it? For warmth? To wear beneath underwear in the event of a chest cold? He held it to his nose but it did not smell from Vick's or mustard plaster. It was something special, some Jewish thing. Special food, special language, special prayers, why not special BVD's? So fearful was he that he would be tempted back into wearing his traditional clothes—reasoned Eli—that he had carried and buried in Woodenton everything, including the special underwear. For that was how Eli now understood the box of clothes. The greenie was saying, Here, I give up. I refuse even to be tempted. We surrender. And that was how Eli continued to understand it until he found he'd slipped the white fringy surrender flag over his hat and felt it clinging to his chest. And now, looking at himself in the mirror, he was momentarily uncertain as to who was tempting who into what. Why *did* the greenie leave his clothes? Was it even the greenie? Then who was it? And why? But, Eli, for Christ's sake, in an age of science things don't happen like that. Even the goddam pigs take drugs . . .

Regardless of who was the source of the temptation, what was its end, not to mention its beginning, Eli, some moments later, stood draped in black, with a little white underneath, before the full-length mirror. He had to pull down on the trousers so they would not show the hollow of his ankle. The greenie, didn't he wear socks? Or had he forgotten them? The mystery was solved when Eli mustered enough courage to investigate the trouser pockets. He had expected some damp awful thing to happen to his fingers should he slip them down and out of sight—but when at last he jammed bravely down he came up with a khaki army sock in each hand. As he slipped them over his toes, he invented a genesis: a G.I.'s present in 1945. Plus everything else lost between 1938 and 1945, he had also lost his socks. Not that he had lost the socks, but that he'd had to stoop to accepting these, made Eli almost cry. To calm himself he walked out the back door and stood looking at his lawn.

On the Knudson back lawn, Harriet Knudson was giving her stones a second coat of pink. She looked up just as Eli stepped out. Eli shot back in again and pressed himself against the back door. When he peeked between the curtain all he saw were paint bucket, brush, and rocks scattered on the Knudson's pink-spattered grass. The phone rang. Who was it—Harriet Knudson? Eli, there's a Jew at your door. *That's me.* Nonsense, Eli, I saw him with my own eyes. *That's me, I saw you too, painting your rocks pink.* Eli, You're having a nervous breakdown again. Jimmy, Eli's having a nervous breakdown again. Eli, this is Jimmy, hear you're having a little breakdown, anything I can do, boy? Eli, this is Ted, Shirley says you need help. Eli, this is Artie, you need help. Eli, Harry, you need help you need help . . . The phone rattled its last and died.

"God helps them who help themselves," intoned Eli, and once again he stepped out the door. This time he walked to the center of his lawn and in full sight of the trees, the grass, the birds, and the sun, revealed that it was he, Eli, in the costume. But nature had nothing to say to him, and so stealthily he made his way to the hedge separating his property from the field beyond and he cut his way through, losing his hat twice in the underbrush. Then, clamping the hat to his head, he began to run, the threaded tassels jumping across his heart. He ran through the weeds and wild flowers, until on the old road that skirted the town he slowed up. He was walking when he approached the Gulf station from the back. He supported himself on a huge tireless truck rim, and among tubes, rusted engines, dozens of topless oil cans, he rested. With a kind of brainless cunning, he readied himself for the last mile of his journey.

"How are you, Pop?" It was the garage attendant, rubbing his greasy hands on his overalls, and hunting among the cans.

Eli's stomach lurched and he pulled the big black coat round his neck.

"Nice day," the attendant said and started around to the front.

"Sholom," Eli whispered and zoomed off towards the hill.

The sun was directly overhead when Eli reached the top. He had come by way of the woods, where it was cooler, but still he was perspiring beneath his new suit. The hat had no sweatband and the cloth clutched his head. The children were playing. The children were always playing, as if it was that alone that Tzuref had to teach them. In their shorts, they revealed such thin legs that beneath one could see the joints swiveling as they ran. Eli waited for them to disappear around a corner before he came into the open. But something would not let him wait—his green suit. It was on the porch, wrapped around the bearded fellow, who was painting the base of a pillar. His arm went up and down, up and down, and the pillar glowed like white fire. The very sight of him popped Eli out of the woods onto the lawn. He did not turn back, though his insides did. He walked up the lawn, but the children played on; tipping the black hat, he mumbled, "Shhh . . . shhhh," and they hardly seemed to notice.

At last he smelled paint.

He waited for the man to turn to him. He only painted. Eli felt suddenly that if he could pull the black hat down over his eyes, over his chest and belly and legs, if he could shut out all light, then a moment later he would be home in bed. But the hat wouldn't go past his forehead. He couldn't kid himself—he was there. No one he could think of had forced him to do this.

The greenie's arm flailed up and down on the pillar. Eli breathed loudly, cleared his throat, but the greenie wouldn't make life easier for him. At last, Eli had to say "Hello."

The arm swished up and down; it stopped—two fingers went out after a brush hair stuck to the pillar.

"Good day," Eli said.

The hair came away; the swishing resumed.

"Sholom," Eli whispered and the fellow turned.

The recognition took some time. He looked at what Eli wore. Up close, Eli looked at what he wore. And then Eli had the strange notion that he was two people. Or that he was one person wearing two suits. The greenie looked to be suffering from a similar confusion. They stared long at one another. Eli's heart shivered, and his brain was momentarily in such a mixed-up condition that his hands went out to button down the collar of his shirt that somebody else was wearing. What a mess! The greenie flung his arms over his face.

"What's the matter . . ." Eli said. The fellow had picked up his bucket and brush and was running away. Eli ran after him.

"I wasn't going to hit . . ." Eli called. "Stop . . ." Eli caught up and grabbed his sleeve. Once again, the greenie's hands flew up to his face. This time, in the violence, white paint spattered both of them.

"I only want to . . ." But in that outfit Eli didn't really know what he wanted. "To talk . . ." he said finally. "For you to look at me. Please just *look* at me . . ."

The hands stayed put, as paint rolled off the brush onto the cuff of Eli's green suit.

"Please . . . please," Eli said, but he did not know what to do. "Say something, speak *English*," he pleaded.

The fellow pulled back against the wall, back, back, as though some arm would finally reach out and yank him to safety. He refused to uncover his face.

"Look," Eli said, pointing to himself. "It's your suit. I'll take care of it."

No answer—only a little shaking under the hands, which led Eli to speak as gently as he knew how.

"We'll . . . we'll moth-proof it. There's a button missing" —Eli pointed— I'll have it fixed. I'll have a zipper put in . . . Please, please— just look at me . . ." He was talking to himself, and yet how could he stop? Nothing he said made any sense—that alone made his heart swell. Yet somehow babbling on, he might babble something that would make things easier between them. "Look . . ." He reached inside his shirt to pull the frills of underwear into the light. "I'm wearing the special underwear, even . . . Please," he said, "*please, please, please*" he sang, as if it were some sacred word. "Oh, *please* . . ."

Nothing twitched under the tweed suit—and if the eyes watered, or twinkled, or hated, he couldn't tell. It was driving him crazy. He had dressed like a fool, and for what? For this? He reached up and yanked the hands away.

"There!" he said—and in that first instant all he saw of the greenie's face were two white droplets stuck to each cheek.

"Tell me—" Eli clutched his hands down to his sides— "Tell me, what can I do for you, I'll do it . . ."

Stiffly, the greenie stood there, sporting his two white tears.

"Whatever I can do . . . Look, look, what I've done *already*." He grabbed his black hat and shook it in the man's face.

And in exchange, the greenie gave him an answer. He raised one hand to his chest, and then jammed it, finger first, towards the horizon. And with what a pained look! As though the air were full of razors! Eli followed the finger and saw beyond the knuckle, out past the nail, Woodenton.

"What do you want?" Eli said. "I'll bring it!"

Suddenly the greenie made a run for it. But then he stopped, wheeled, and jabbed that finger at the air again. It pointed the same way. Then he was gone.

And then, all alone, Eli had the revelation. He did not question his understanding, the substance or the source. But with a strange, dreamy elation, he started away.

On Coach House Road, they were double-parked. The Mayor's wife pushed a grocery cart full of dog food from Stop N' Shop to her station wagon. The President of the Lions Club, a napkin around his neck, was jamming pennies into the meter in front of the Bit-in-Teeth Restaurant. Ted Heller caught the sun as it glazed off the new Byzantine mosaic entrance to his shoe shop. In pinkened jeans, Mrs. Jimmy Knudson was leaving Halloway's Hardware, a paint bucket in each hand. Roger's Beauty Shoppe had its doors open—women's heads in silver bullets far as the eye could see. Over by the barbershop the pole spun, and Artie Berg's youngest sat on a red horse, having his hair cut; his mother flipped through *Look*, smiling: the greenie had changed his clothes.

And into this street, which seemed paved with chromium, came Eli Peck. It was not enough, he knew, to walk up one side of the street. That was not enough. Instead he walked ten paces up one side, then on an angle, crossed to the other side, where he walked ten more paces, and crossed back. Horns blew, traffic jerked, as Eli made his way up Coach House

Road. He spun a moan high up in his nose as he walked. Outside no one could hear him, but he felt it vibrate the cartilage at the bridge of his nose.

Things slowed around him. The sun stopped rippling on spokes and hubcaps. It glowed steadily as everyone put on brakes to look at the man in black. They always paused and gaped, whenever he entered the town. Then in a minute, or two, or three, a light would change, a baby squawk, and the flow continue. Now, though lights changed, no one moved.

"He shaved his beard," Eric the barber said.

"Who?" asked Linda Berg.

"The . . . the guy in the suit. From the place there."

Linda looked out the window.

"It's Uncle Eli," little Kevin Berg said, spitting hair.

"Oh, God," Linda said, "Eli's having a nervous breakdown."

"A nervous breakdown!" Ted Heller said, but not immediately. Immediately he had said "Hoooly . . ."

Shortly, everybody in Coach House Road was aware that Eli Peck, the nervous young attorney with the pretty wife, was having a breakdown. Everybody except Eli Peck. He knew what he did was not insane, though he felt every inch of its strangeness. He felt those black clothes as if they were the skin of his skin—the give and pull as they got used to where he bulged and buckled. And he felt eyes, every eye on Coach House Road. He saw headlights screech to within an inch of him, and stop. He saw mouths: first the bottom jaw slides forward, then the tongue hits the teeth, the lips explode, a little thunder in the throat, and they've said it: Eli Peck Eli Peck Eli Peck Eli Peck. He began to walk slowly, shifting his weight down and forward with each syllable: E–li–Peck–E–li–Peck–E–li–Peck. Heavily he trod, and as his neighbors uttered each syllable of his name, he felt each syllable shaking all his bones. He knew who he was down to his marrow— they were telling him. Eli Peck. He wanted them to say it a thousand times, a million times, he would walk forever in that black suit, as adults whispered of his strangeness and children made "Shame . . . shame" with their fingers.

"It's going to be all right, pal . . ." Ted Heller was motioning to Eli from his doorway. "C'mon, pal, it's going to be all right . . ."

Eli saw him, past the brim of his hat. Ted did not move from his doorway, but leaned forward and spoke with his hand over his mouth. Behind him, three customers peered through the doorway. "Eli, it's Ted, remember Ted . . ."

Eli crossed the street and found he was heading directly towards Harriet Knudson. He lifted his neck so she could see his whole face.

He saw her forehead melt down to her lashes. "Good morning, Mr. Peck."

"Sholom," Eli said, and crossed the street where he saw the President of the Lions.

"Twice before . . ." he heard someone say, and then he crossed again, mounted the curb, and was before the bakery, where a delivery man charged past with a tray of powdered cakes twirling above him. "Pardon me, Father," he said, and scooted into his truck. But he could not move it. Eli Peck had stopped traffic.

He passed the Rivoli Theater, Beekman Cleaners, Harris' Westinghouse, the Unitarian Church, and soon he was passing only trees. At Ireland Road he turned right and started through Woodenton's winding streets. Baby carriages stopped whizzing and creaked—"Isn't that . . ." Gardeners held their clipping. Children stepped from the sidewalk and tried the curb. And Eli greeted no one, but raised his face to all. He wished passionately that he had white tears to show them . . . And not till he reached his own front lawn, saw his house, his shutters, his new jonquils, did he remember his wife. And the child that must have been born to him. And it was then and there he had the awful moment. He could go inside and put on his clothes and go to his wife in the hospital. It was not irrevocable, even the walk wasn't. In Woodenton memories are long but fury short. Apathy works like forgiveness. Besides, when you've flipped, you've flipped—it's Mother Nature.

What gave Eli the awful moment was that he turned away. He knew exactly what he could do but he chose not to. To go inside would be to go halfway. There was more . . . So he turned and walked towards the hospital and all the time he quaked an eighth of an inch beneath his skin, that he'd *chosen* to be crazy! But if you chose to be crazy, then you weren't crazy. It's when you didn't choose. No, he wasn't flipping. He had a child to see.

"Name?"

"Peck."

"Fourth floor." He was given a little blue card.

In the elevator everybody stared. Eli watched his black shoes rise four floors.

"Four."

He tipped his hat, but knew he couldn't take it off.

"Peck," he said. He showed the card.

"Congratulations." the nurse said, ". . . the grandfather?"

"The father. Which room?"

She led him to 412. "A joke on the Mrs.?" she said, but he slipped in the door without her.

"Miriam?"

"Yes?"

"Eli."

She rolled her white face towards her husband. "Oh, Eli . . . Oh, Eli."

He raised his arms. "What could I do?"

"You have a son. They called all morning."

"I came to see him."

"Like *that!*" she whispered harshly. "Eli, you can't go around like that."

"I have a son. I want to see him."

"Eli, why are you doing this to me!" Red seeped back into her lips. "*He's* not your fault," she explained. "Oh, Eli, sweetheart, why do you feel guilty about everything? Eli, change your clothes. I forgive you."

"Stop forgiving me. Stop understanding me."

"But I love you."

"That's something else."

"But, sweetie, you *don't* have to dress like that. You didn't do anything. You don't have to feel guilty because . . . because everything's all right. Eli, can't you see that?"

"Miriam, enough reasons. Where's my son?"

"Oh, please, Eli, don't flip now. I need you now. Is that why you're flipping—because I need you?"

"In your selfish way, Miriam, you're very generous. I want my son."

"Don't flip now. I'm afraid, now that he's out." She was beginning to whimper. "I don't know if I love him, now that he's out. When I look in the mirror, Eli, he won't be there . . . Eli, Eli, you look like you're going to your own funeral. Please, can't you leave well enough *alone?* Can't we just have a family?"

"No."

In the corridor he asked the nurse to lead him to his son. The nurse walked on one side of him, Ted Heller on the other.

"Eli, do you want some help? I thought you might want some help."

"No."

Ted whispered something to the nurse; then to Eli he whispered, "Should you be walking around like this?"

"Yes."

In his ear Ted said, "You'll . . . frighten the kid . . ."

"There," the nurse said. She pointed to a bassinet in the second row and looked, puzzled, to Ted. "Do I go in?" Eli said.

"No," the nurse said. "She'll roll him over." She rapped on the enclosure full of babies. "Peck," she mouthed to the nurse on the inside.

Ted tapped Eli's arm. "You're not thinking of doing something you'll be sorry for . . . are you, Eli? Eli—I mean you know you're still Eli, don't you?"

In the enclosure, Eli saw a bassinet had been wheeled before the square window.

"Oh, Christ . . ." Ted said. "You don't have this Bible stuff on the brain—" And suddenly he said, "You wait, pal." He started down the corridor, his heels tapping rapidly.

Eli felt relieved—he leaned forward. In the basket was what he'd come to see. Well, now that he was here, what did he think he was going to say to it? I'm your father, Eli, the Flipper? I am wearing a black hat, suit, and fancy underwear, all borrowed from a friend? How could he admit to this reddened ball—*his* reddened ball—the worst of all: that Eckman would shortly convince him he wanted to take off the whole business. He couldn't admit it! He wouldn't do it!

Past his hat brim, from the corner of his eye, he saw Ted had stopped in a doorway at the end of the corridor. Two interns stood there smoking, listening to Ted. Eli ignored it.

No, even Eckman wouldn't make him take it off! No! He'd wear it, if he chose to. He'd make the kid wear it! Sure! Cut it down when the time came. A smelly hand-me-down, whether the kid liked it or not!

Only Teddie's heels clacked; the interns wore rubber soles—for they were there, beside him, unexpectedly. Their white suits smelled, but not like Eli's.

"Eli," Ted said, softly, "visiting time's up, pal."

"How are you feeling, Mr. Peck? First child upsets everyone . . ."

He'd just pay no attention; nevertheless, he began to perspire, thickly, and his hat crown clutched his hair.

"Excuse me—Mr. Peck . . ." It was a new rich bass voice. "Excuse me, rabbi, but you're wanted . . . in the temple." A hand took his elbow, firmly; then another hand the other elbow. Where they grabbed, his tendons went taut.

"Okay, rabbi. Okay okay okay okay okay okay . . ." He listened; it was a very soothing word, that okay. "Okay okay everything's going to be okay." His feet seemed to have left the ground some, as he glided away from the window, the bassinet, the babies. "Okay easy does it everything's all right all right—"

But he rose, suddenly, as though up out of a dream, and flailing his arms, screamed: *"I'm the father!"*

But the window disappeared. In a moment they tore off his jacket—it gave so easily, in one yank. Then a needle slid under his skin. The drug calmed his soul, but did not touch it down where the blackness had reached.

PETER TAYLOR (b. 1917)

First Heat

Peter Taylor was born in Tennessee and educated at Vanderbilt University and at Kenyon College. He has written a novel, *A Woman of Means* (1950) as well as numerous collections of short stories. "First Heat" appeared in his *Collected Stories* (1969).

He turned up the air conditioning and lay across the bed, wearing only his jockey shorts. But it didn't stop. Two showers already since he came in from the afternoon session! Showers had done no good. Still, he might take another presently if it continued. The flow of perspiration was quite extraordinary. Perhaps it was the extra sleeping pill he took last night. He had never been one to sweat so. It was rather alarming. It really was. And with the air conditioner going full blast he was apt to give himself pneumonia.

What he needed of course was a drink, and that was impossible. He was not going to have a single drink before she arrived. He was determined to be cold sober. She would telephone up from the desk—or from one of the house phones nearby. He always thought of her as telephoning directly from the desk. Somehow that made the warning more official. But she did always telephone, did so out of fear he might not have his regular room. So she said. He knew better, of course. Married for nearly fifteen years, and at home she still knocked on doors—on the door to his study, on the door to the bathroom, even on the door to their bedroom. She even had the children trained to knock on doors, even each other's doors. Couldn't she assume that since he knew she was on the way, knew she was by now wheeling along the Interstate—doing seventy-five and more in her old station wagon—couldn't she assume that whatever kind of fool, whatever kind of philanderer she might suspect him of being, he would have the sense to have set matters right by the time she got there? But what rot! As if he didn't *have* a problem, as if he needed to make one up!

He could hear his own voice in the Senate Chamber that afternoon. Not his words, just his guilty voice. Suddenly he got up off the bed, pulled back the spread, the blanket, the top sheet. He threw himself down on his back, stuck his legs in the air, and pulled off his shorts. They were wringing wet with his damnable perspiration! He wadded them into a ball and, still lying on his back, still holding his legs in the air, he hurled the underwear at the ceiling, where it made a faintly damp spot before falling to the carpeted floor. And she—she would already know what his voice in the Senate Chamber had said. (His legs still in the air.) And knowing how the voting went, know who betrayed whom, who let whom down, who let what bill that was supposed to go through intact be amended. It would all have been reported on the local six o'clock state news, perhaps even with his taped voice uttering the words of betrayal. She would have picked it up on the radio in the station wagon just after she set out, with her evening dress in a suitbox beside her. Maybe she would even have turned back, feeling she just couldn't face certain people at the mansion reception tonight . . . or couldn't face him.

Now—only now—he let his legs drop to the bed, his feet coming down wide apart on the firm, first-rate-hotel mattress. And he threw out his arms, one hand palm upward landing on each pillow of the double bed. He *would* relax, *would* catch a quick nap. But a new charge of sweat pressed out through every pore of his skin, on his forehead, on his neck, in the soft area just above his collarbone, from the exposed inner sides of his thighs and his ankles, from the exposed armpits and upper arms and forearms, from the palms of his hands and the soles of his feet. He felt he was aware of every infinitesimal modicum of sweat that was passing through every pore of every area of his body. Somehow it made him feel more utterly, thoroughly naked than he had ever before felt in his entire life. Yes, and this time the sweat came before the thought—just a little before the thought this time. The thought of what he had done and left undone concerning the amendment, said and left unsaid concerning the amendment, the thought of the discrepancy between his previously announced position and the position he finally took on the floor, all thought of *that* seemed something secondary and consequential to the sweat. Perhaps he was ill, really ill! Perhaps it was only a coincidence that this sickening sweat had come over his body. But no, he was not that sort—to claim illness. One thing for certain, though, the sweat was already like ice water on his skin.

Now he would have to get up and dry himself off again. There was a scratching sensation in his throat. He even coughed once. He would have to turn *down* the air conditioner. And he would have to find something else to focus his mind on. After all, he had not betrayed his country or his family. And not, God knew, his constituents. Was it only old man Nat Haley he was worrying about? He had agreed to support Nat Haley's waterways bill, had been quite outspoken in favor of it. The newspapers all over the state had quoted him. And then, yesterday, he had received promises from other sources, promises so much to the interest of his constituents that he could not resist. By God, it was the sort of thing he—*and* she—had known he would have to do if he stood for the legislature and got elected, the sort of thing he would have to face up to if he went into politics, where everybody had said *he* ought not to go. He and she had looked each other in the eye one day—before he ever announced—and said as much . . . Well, at the last minute he had agreed to support the very amendment which Nat Haley had said would be ruinous, would take all the bite out of his bill. But Nat Haley was, himself, the damnedest kind of double-dealer. Even *he* had observed that. Ah, he was beginning to know politics. And he was beginning to understand what "everybody" had meant. Old Nat Haley was well known for the deals he arranged and didn't live up to. Everyone knew about Nat Haley. Nat Haley wouldn't have hesitated to fight this bill itself if he had discovered, even at the last minute, that that was to his advantage.

Who then, was he betraying? And it wasn't a bill of any great import, either.

He sat up and swung his feet over the side of the bed. His hand came down briefly on the moisture his body had left on the otherwise starchy hotel sheet. He glanced backward and saw the wet shadow of himself that his perspiration had left there, and he turned away from it. But as he turned away from his silhouette on the sheet, there he was, in all his nakedness, in the large rectangular mirror above the dresser. And there he was in the mirror on the open bathroom door. He reached to the floor and took up a bath towel he had dropped there earlier and began drying himself—and hiding himself. He stood up and went over his body roughly with the towel; then, his eyes lighting on the mirror on the bathroom door, he wadded up the towel, just as he had the jockey shorts, and hurled it at the door. It came right up against his face there! And when it had fallen, he realized that this time it wasn't—as so often—his face in the mirror that offended him. He didn't care about the face. He knew it too well and what its every line and look meant. The body interested him as never before, or as it had not in years. For a moment, it was like meeting someone from the past, someone he had almost forgotten—an old friend, and old enemy. It was— almost—a young man's body still; he was not forty yet and he exercised as much as he ever had and ate and drank with moderation. The body in the door mirror and in the large mirror over the dresser had good tone, was only a little heavier about the hips than it had once been, and the arm muscles were really better developed than when he was twenty. Taking in the different views he had of the body in the two mirrors he recalled that as late as his college days he had sometimes shadow-boxed before mirrors, usually wearing his ordinary boxer shorts and imagining they were made of silk, with his name, or some title, like *The Killer*, embroidered on them in purple or orange letters. He didn't smile over the recollection. But neither did he take any such stance before the mirrors now. The body in the mirrors was tense, as if prepared to receive a blow; and he looked at it objectively as a painter or a sculptor might, as a physician might. He observed features that particularized it: the modest island of dark hair on the chest, which narrowed into a peninsula pointing down below the navel and over the slightly rounded belly, almost joining the pubic hair above the too-innocent-looking penis; the elongated thighs; the muscular calves; the almost hairless arms; the shoulders, heavy and slightly stooped. Presently, his interest in himself seemed entirely anatomical. And all at once it was as though his eyes were equipped with x-rays. He could see beneath the skin and under the flesh to the veins and tendons and the ropelike muscles, the heart and lungs, the liver, the intestines, the testicles, as well as every bone and joint of the skeleton. And now it was as though a klieg light—no, a supernatural light—shone from behind him and through him. Only when at last he moved one foot, shifting his weight from one leg to the other, did the flesh and the covering skin return. Had it been a dream? A vision? It seemed to him now that he was not naked at all, or that this was not the nakedness he had sought when he removed his clothes. At any rate, his body had ceased to sweat.

He stepped back to the bed and lay down on his side, his back to the mirrors. He experienced momentary relief. It was as though he had seen beyond mere nakedness of body and spirit, had looked beyond all that which particularized him and made his body and his life meaningful, human. Was that the ultimate nakedness? Why, it could just as well have been old Nat Haley's insides he had seen. And he did relax now. He closed his eyes . . . But then it came on again. Only this time there was no sweat. There was just the explicit dread of that moment—soon now, soon—when he would open the door to her. And he thought of how other, older politicians would laugh at his agonizing over so small a matter. *They* would know what a mistake politics was for him. Or perhaps they would know that, like them, he was *made* for politics. Wasn't this merely his baptism—in betrayal? In politics the ends were what mattered, had to matter. In politics that was the only absolute. If you were loyal to other men, you were apt to betray your constituency. Or did he have it all backward? No, he had it right, he was quite sure. And for that very reason, wasn't the state Senate as far as he would go and farther than he should have gone? Friends had warned him against state politics especially. His father had said to him: "You are the unlikeliest-looking political candidate I have ever seen." But it was a decision she and he had made together, and together they had agreed that one's political morality could not always coincide with one's private morality. They had read that somewhere, hadn't they? At any rate, one had to be prepared to face up to that morality . . . And now, though he felt chilled to the bone, the sweat came on again. He rolled over and reached for the towel on the floor, forgettting he had thrown it at the mirror. As he got off the bed, the same hand that had reached for the towel reached out to the wall and turned down the air conditioner. He went into the bathroom and got a dry towel and came back drying himself—or those two hands were drying him. He stopped before the long mirror on the bathroom door, the hands still drying him. He remembered something else his father had said to him once when they were on a fishing trip at Tellico Plains. He had gone for a swim in the river and stood on a rocky slab beside the water afterward, first rubbing his chest and his head with a towel and then fanning his body with it before and aft. His father, watching the way he was fanning himself with the towel, said, "You do cherish that body of yours, don't y'?" But what mistaken notions his father had always had about him. Or perhaps it was only wishful thinking on his father's part. Perhaps he had only *wished* that kind of concern for him. Ah, if only his body *had* been his great care and concern in life—his problem! And no doubt that's what his sweating meant! He *wished* it were only a bodily ill!

He wasn't, as a matter of fact, a man who was given to lolling about this way with no clothes on—either at home or in a hotel room. And it occurred to him now that it wasn't the sweat alone that had made him do so today. As soon as he had walked into the room and closed the door after him he had begun pulling off his clothes. It seemed to him almost that the sweat began *after* he had stripped off his clothes. But he couldn't definitely recall now whether it had begun before or after he got to the room. At any rate, he wasn't *sure* it had begun before. Had it? Else, why had he undressed at once? . . . He lay down on the bed again and his eye lit on the black telephone beside the bed. The first thing some men did when alone in a hotel room, he knew, was to take up the telephone and try to arrange for a woman to come up. Or that was what he always understood they did. The point was, he should have *known*. But he—he would hardly know nowadays how to behave with such a woman. He would hardly know what to say or do if one of those hotel creatures came into the room. Or would he know very well, indeed! Yes, how simple it all would be. What a great satisfaction, and how shameful it would seem afterward. How sinful—how clearly sinful—he would know himself to be. There the two of them are, in bed. But suddenly there comes a knock on the door! He will have to hide her. His wife is out there in the passage. The baby-sitter came a little early. And the traffic was not as bad as she had anticipated. With the new Interstate, a forty-mile drive is nothing. He has no choice. There isn't anything else he can do: he will have to hide the creature. She will have to stand naked, her clothes clutched in her arms, behind the drapery or in the closet, while he and his wife dress for the reception at the governor's mansion. If only—But the telephone, the real, black telephone was ringing now, there on the real bedside table.

He let it ring for thirty seconds or so. Finally, he took up the instrument. He said nothing, only lay on his side breathing into the mouthpiece.

"Hello," she said on the house phone. He could hear other voices laughing and talking in the lobby.

"Hello," he managed.

"I'm downstairs," she said, as she always said, waiting for him to invite her to come up. He invited her now, and she replied, "Is everything all right? You sound funny."

"Everything's fine. Come on up," he said. "You've heard the news?"

"I listened in the car, on the way over."

"I changed my mind about the bill," he said.

"Is Mr. Haley pretty angry?"

"He cut me cold on the Capitol steps afterward."

"I thought so," she said. "He was icy to me when I passed him in the lobby just now. Or I imagined he was."

"Do you still want to go to the reception?"

She laughed. "Of course I do. I'm sure you had good reasons."

"Oh, yes, I had good reasons."

"Then, shall I come on up?"

"Do," he said. But then he caught her before she hung up. "Wait," he said. He sat on the bed, pulling the sheet up about his hips. "Why don't you wait down there? Why don't we go somewhere and have a drink and something to eat before we dress for the reception? I'm starved."

"I'm starved, too," she said. "I had only a very small snack with the children at four-thirty."

"I'll be right down," he said.

"Well—" She hesitated and then said, "No, I have my dress with me in a box—my dress for tonight. I want to put it on a hanger. I'll be right up—that is, if you don't mind."

"Good," he said.

"And why don't we have our drink up there? It might be easier."

"Good," he said.

As soon as he had put down the telephone, he sprang from the bed, ran to pick up his sweaty shorts and the sweaty hotel towels. He began straightening the room and pulling on his clothes at the same time, with desperate speed. She must not find him undressed, this way. It would seem too odd. And if he should begin the sweating again, he was lost, he told himself. He would have to try to ignore it, but she would notice, and she would know . . . She would be on the elevator now, riding up with other members of the legislature and their wives, wives who had also come to town for the reception at the mansion. He felt utterly empty, as though not even those veins and tendons and bones and organs were inside him. Wearing only his shirt and fresh shorts and his black socks and supporters, he stopped dressing long enough to give the bed a haphazard making up. He yanked the sheet and blanket and spread about. Fluffed the pillows. But if only there were something besides his body, something else tangible to hide. Catching a glimpse of himself in the mirror, he blushed bashfully and began pulling on his trousers to cover his naked legs. While slipping his tie under his collar, he was also pushing his feet into his shoes. As he tied the necktie and then tied the shoe strings, he was listening for her footsteps in the passage. Oh, if only, if only—if only there were a woman, herself covered with sweat, and still—still panting, for him to hide. What an innocent, simple thing it would be. But there was only himself . . . When the knock came at the door, he was pulling on his jacket. "Just a second," he called. And for no reason at all, before opening the door he went to the glass-topped desk on which lay his open briefcase and closed the lid to the case, giving a quick snap to the lock. Then he threw open the door.

It was as though only a pair of blue eyes—bodiless, even lidless—hung there in the open doorway, suspended by invisible wires from the lintel. He read the eyes as he had not been able to read the voice on the telephone. They were not accusing. They had done their accusing in the car, no doubt, while listening to the radio. Now they were understanding and forgiving . . . He bent forward and kissed the inevitable mouth beneath the eyes. It too was understanding and forgiving. But if only the mouth and eyes would not forgive, not yet. He wanted their censure, first. She entered the room, with the suitbox under her arm, and went straight over to the closet. He held his breath, his eyes fixed on the closet door. She paused with her hand on the doorknob and looked back at him. Suddenly he understood the kind of sympathy she felt for him. Is it the lady or the tiger? her hesitation seemed to say. If only, she seemed to say with him, if only it *were* the lady, naked and clutching her bundle of clothing to her bosom. But he knew of course, as did she, it would be the tiger, the tiger whose teeth they had drawn beforehand, whose claws they had filed with their talk about the difference between things private and things political. The tiger was that very difference, that very discrepancy, and the worst of it was that they could never admit to each other again that the discrepancy existed. They stood facing each other well and fully clothed. When, finally, she would open the closet door, they would see only his formal evening clothes hanging there, waiting to be worn to the governor's mansion tonight. And while he looked over her shoulder, she would open the cardboard box and hang her full-length white evening gown beside his tuxedo. And after a while the tuxedo and the evening gown would leave the hotel room together and go down the elevator to the lobby and ride in a cab across town to the governor's mansion. And there was no denying that when the tuxedo and the evening gown got out of the taxi and went up the steps to the mansion and then moved slowly along in the receiving line, he and she, for better or for worse, would be inside them. But when the reception was over and the gown and the tuxedo came down the steps from the mansion, got into another taxi, and rode back across town to their empty hotel room, who was it that would be in them then? Who?

LEO TOLSTOY (1828–1910)

The Death of Ivan Ilych

Leo Tolstoy, generally considered to be Russia's most important novelist, was born at Yasnaya Polyana, Russia. He served in the Russian army and fought in the Crimean War. His major novels are *War and Peace* (1869), which chronicles Napoleon's attempted conquest of Russia in 1812, and *Anna Karenina* (1877). One of the most famous novellas of world literature, "The Death of Ivan Ilych" appeared in 1886.

I

During an interval in the Melvinski trial in the large building of the Law Courts, the members and public prosecutor met in Ivan Egorovich Shebek's private room, where the conversation turned on the celebrated Krasovski case. Fëdor Vasilievich warmly maintained that it was not subject to their jurisdiction, Ivan Egorovich maintained the contrary, while Peter Ivanovich, not having entered into the discussion at the start, took no part in it but looked through the *Gazette* which had just been handed in.

"Gentlemen," he said, "Ivan Ilych has died!"

"You don't say so!"

"Here, read it yourself," replied Peter Ivanovich, handing Fëdor Vasilievich the paper still damp from the press. Surrounded by a black border were the words: "Praskovya Fëdorovna Golovina, with profound sorrow, informs relatives and friends of the demise of her beloved husband Ivan

Ilych Golovin, Member of the Court of Justice, which occurred on February the 4th of this year 1882. The funeral will take place on Friday at one o'clock in the afternoon."

Ivan Ilych had been a colleague of the gentlemen present and was liked by them all. He had been ill for some weeks with an illness said to be incurable. His post had been kept open for him, but there had been conjectures that in case of his death Alexeev might receive his appointment, and that either Vinnikov or Shtabel would succeed Alexeev. So on receiving the news of Ivan Ilych's death the first thought of each of the gentlemen in that private room was of the changes and promotions it might occasion among themselves or their acquaintances.

"I shall be sure to get Shtabel's place or Vinnikov's," thought Fëdor Vasilievich. "I was promised that long ago, and the promotion means an extra eight hundred rubles a year for me besides the allowance."

"Now I must apply for my brother-in-law's transfer from Kaluga," thought Peter Ivanovich. "My wife will be very glad, and then she won't be able to say that I never do anything for her relations."

"I thought he would never leave his bed again," said Peter Ivanovich aloud. "It's very sad."

"But what really was the matter with him?"

"The doctors couldn't say—at least they could, but each of them said something different. When last I saw him I thought he was getting better."

"And I haven't been to see him since the holidays. I always meant to go."

"Had he any property?"

"I think his wife had a little—but something quite trifling."

"We shall have to go to see her, but they live so terribly far away."

"Far away from you, you mean. Everything's far away from your place."

"You see, he never can forgive my living on the other side of the river," said Peter Ivanovich, smiling at Shebek. Then, still talking of the distances between different parts of the city, they returned to the Court.

Besides considerations as to the possible transfers and promotions likely to result from Ivan Ilych's death, the mere fact of the death of a near acquaintance aroused, as usual, in all who heard of it the complacent feeling that, "it is he who is dead and not I."

Each one thought or felt, "Well, he's dead but I'm alive!" But the more intimate of Ivan Ilych's acquaintances, his so-called friends, could not help thinking also that they would now have to fulfill the very tiresome demands of propriety by attending the funeral service and paying a visit of condolence to the widow.

Fëdor Vasilievich and Peter Ivanovich had been his nearest acquaintances. Peter Ivanovich had studied law with Ivan Ilych and had considered himself to be under obligations to him.

Having told his wife at dinner-time of Ivan Ilych's death and of his conjecture that it might be possible to get her brother transferred to their circuit, Peter Ivanovich sacrificed his usual nap, put on his evening clothes, and drove to Ivan Ilych's house.

At the entrance stood a carriage and two cabs. Leaning against the wall in the hall downstairs near the cloak-stand was a coffin-lid covered with cloth of gold, ornamented with gold cord and tassels, that had been polished up with metal powder. Two ladies in black were taking off their fur cloaks. Peter Ivanovich recognized one of them as Ivan Ilych's sister, but the other was a stranger to him. His colleague Schwartz was just coming downstairs. but on seeing Peter Ivanovich enter he stopped and winked at him, as if to say: "Ivan Ilych has made a mess of things—not like you and me."

Schwartz's face, with his Piccadilly whiskers and his slim figure in evening dress, had as usual an air of elegant solemnity which contrasted with the playfulness of his character and had a special piquance here, or so it seemed to Peter Ivanovich.

Peter Ivanovich allowed the ladies to precede him and slowly followed them upstairs. Schwartz did not come down but remained where he was, and Peter Ivanovich understood that he wanted to arrange where they should play bridge that evening. The ladies went upstairs to the widow's room, and Schwartz, with seriously compressed lips but a playful look in his eyes, indicated by a twist of his eyebrows the room to the right where the body lay.

Peter Ivanovich, like everyone else on such occasions, entered feeling uncertain what he would have to do. All he knew was that at such times it is always safe to cross oneself. But he was not quite sure whether one should make obeisances while doing so. He therefore adopted a middle course. On entering the room he began crossing himself and made a slight movement resembling a bow. At the same time, as far as the motion of his head and arm allowed, he surveyed the room. Two young men—apparently nephews, one of whom was a high-school pupil—were leaving the room, crossing themselves as they did so. An old woman was standing motionless, and a lady with strangely arched eyebrows was saying something to her in a whisper. A vigorous, resolute Church Reader, in a frock-coat, was reading something in a loud voice with an expression that precluded any contradiction. The butler's assistant, Gerasim, stepping lightly in front of Peter Ivanovich, was strewing something on the floor. Noticing this, Peter Ivanovich was immediately aware of a faint odor of a decomposing body.

The last time he had called on Ivan Ilych, Peter Ivanovich had seen Gerasim in the study. Ivan Ilych had been particularly fond of him and he was performing the duty of a sick nurse.

Peter Ivanovich continued to make the sign of the cross slightly inclining his head in an intermediate direction between the coffin, the Reader, and the icons on the table in a corner of the room. Afterwards, when it seemed to him that this movement of his arm in crossing himself had gone on too long, he stopped and began to look at the corpse. The dead man lay, as dead men always lie, in a specially heavy way, his rigid limbs sunk in the soft cushions of the coffin, with the head forever bowed on the pillow. His yellow waxen brow with bald patches over his sunken temples was thrust up in the way peculiar to the dead, the protruding nose seeming to press on the upper lip. He was much changed and had grown even thinner since Peter Ivanovich had last seen him, but, as is always the case with the dead, his face was handsomer and above all more dignified than when he was alive. The expression on the face said that what was necessary had been accomplished, and accomplished rightly. Besides this there was in that expression a reproach and a warning to the living. This warning seemed to Peter Ivanovich out of place, or at least not applicable to him. He felt a certain discomfort and so he hurriedly crossed himself once more and turned and went out the door—too hurriedly and too regardless of propriety, as he himself was aware.

Schwartz was waiting for him in the adjoining room with legs spread wide apart and both hands toying with his top-hat behind his back. The mere sight of that playful, well-groomed, and elegant figure refreshed Peter Ivanovich. He felt that Schwartz was above all these happenings and would not surrender to any depressing influences. His very look said that this incident of a church service for Ivan Ilych could not be a sufficient reason for infringing the order of the session—in other words, that it would certainly not prevent his unwrapping a new pack of cards and shuffling them that evening while a footman placed four fresh candles on the table: in fact, that there was no reason for supposing that this incident would hinder their spending the evening agreeably. Indeed he said this in a whisper as Peter Ivanovich passed him, proposing that they should meet for a game at Fëdor Vasilievich's. But apparently Peter Ivanovich was not destined to play bridge that evening. Praskovya Fëdorovna (a short, fat woman who despite all efforts to the contrary had continued to broaden steadily from her shoulders downwards and who had the same extraordinarily arched eyebrows as the lady who had been standing by the coffin), dressed all in black, her head covered with lace, came out of her own room with some other ladies, conducted them to the room where the dead body lay, and said: "The service will begin immediately. Please go in."

Schwartz, making an indefinite bow, stood still, evidently neither accepting nor declining this invitation. Praskovya Fëdorovna, recognizing Peter Ivanovich, sighed, went close up to him, took his hand, and said: "I know you are a true friend to Ivan Ilych . . ." and looked at him awaiting some suitable response. And Peter Ivanovich knew that, just as it had been the right thing to cross himself in that room, so what he had to do here was to press her hand, sigh, and say, "Believe me . . ." So he did all this and as he did it felt that the desired result had been achieved: that both he and she were touched.

"Come with me. I want to speak to you before it begins." said the widow. "Give me your arm."

Peter Ivanovich gave her his arm and they went to the inner rooms, passing Schwartz, who winked at Peter Ivanovich compassionately.

"That does for our bridge! Don't object if we find another player. Perhaps you can cut in when you do escape," said his playful look.

Peter Ivanovich sighed still more deeply and despondently, and Praskovya Fëdorovna pressed his arm gratefully. When they reached the drawing-room, upholstered in pink cretonne and lighted by a dim lamp, they sat down at the table—she on a sofa and Peter Ivanovich on a low pouffe, the springs of which yielded spasmodically under his weight. Praskovya Fëdorovna had been on the point of warning him to take another seat, but felt that such a warning was out of keeping with her present condition and so changed her mind. As he sat down on the pouffe Peter Ivanovich recalled how Ivan Ilych had arranged this room and had consulted him regarding this pink cretonne with green leaves. The whole room was full of furniture and knick-knacks, and on her way to the sofa the lace of the widow's black shawl caught on the carved edge of the table. Peter Ivanovich rose to detach it, and the springs of the pouffe, relieved of his weight, rose also and gave him a push. The widow began detaching her shawl herself, and Peter Ivanovich again sat down, suppressing the rebellious springs of the pouffe under him. But the widow had not quite freed herself and Peter Ivanovich got up again, and again the pouffe rebelled and even creaked. When this was all over she took out a clean cambric handkerchief and began to weep. The episode with the shawl and the struggle with the pouffe had cooled Peter Ivanovich's emotions and he sat there with a sullen look on his face. This awkward situation was interrupted by Sokolov, Ivan Ilych's butler, who came to report that the plot in the cemetery that Praskovya Fëdorovna had chosen would cost two hundred rubles. She stopped weeping and, looking at Peter Ivanovich with the air of a victim, remarked in French that it was very hard for her. Peter Ivanovich made a silent gesture signifying his full conviction that it must indeed be so.

"Please smoke," she said in a magnanimous yet crushed voice, and turned to discuss with Sokolov the price of the plot for the grave.

Peter Ivanovich while lighting his cigarette heard her inquiring very circumstantially into the price of different plots in the cemetery and finally decided which she would take. When that was done she gave instructions about engaging the choir. Sokolov then left the room.

"I look after everything myself," she told Peter Ivanovich, shifting the albums that lay on the table; and noticing that the table was endangered by his cigarette-ash, she immediately passed him an ashtray, saying as she did so: "I consider it an affectation to say that my grief prevents my attending to practical affairs. On the contrary, if anything can—I won't say console me, but—distract me, it is seeing to everything concerning him." She again took out her handkerchief as if preparing to cry, but suddenly, as if mastering her feeling, she shook herself and began to speak calmly. "But there is something I want to talk to you about."

Peter Ivanovich bowed, keeping control of the springs of the pouffe, which immediately began quivering under him.

"He suffered terribly the last few days."

"Did he?" said Peter Ivanovich.

"Oh, terribly! He screamed unceasingly, not for minutes but for hours. For the last three days he screamed incessantly. It was unendurable. I cannot understand how I bore it; you could hear him three rooms off. Oh, what I have suffered!"

"Is it possible that he was conscious all that time?" asked Peter Ivanovich.

"Yes," she whispered. "To the last moment. He took leave of us a quarter of an hour before he died, and asked us to take Vasya away."

The thought of the sufferings of this man he had known so intimately, first as a merry little boy, then as a school-mate, and later as a grown-up colleague, suddenly struck Peter Ivanovich with horror, despite an unpleasant consciousness of his own and this woman's dissimulation. He again saw that brow, and that nose pressing down on the lip, and felt afraid for himself.

"Three days of frightful suffering and then death! Why, that might suddenly, at any time, happen to me," he thought, and for a moment felt terrified. But—he did not himself know how—the customary reflection at once occurred to him that this had happened to Ivan Ilych and not to him, and that it should not and could not happen to him, and that to think that it could would be yielding to depression which he ought not to do, as Schwartz's expression plainly showed. After which reflection Peter Ivanovich felt reassured, and began to ask with interest about the details of Ivan Ilych's death, as though death was an accident natural to Ivan Ilych but certainly not to himself.

After many details of the really dreadful physical sufferings Ivan Ilych had endured (which details he learnt only from the effect those sufferings had produced on Praskovya Fëdorovna' nerves) the widow apparently found it necessary to get to business.

"Oh, Peter Ivanovich, how hard is it! How terribly, terribly hard!" and she again began to weep.

Peter Ivanovich sighed and waited for her to finish blowing her nose. When she had done so he said, "Believe me . . ." and she again began talking and brought out what was evidently her chief concern with him—namely, to question him as to how she could obtain a grant of money from the government on the occasion of her husband's death. She made it appear that she was asking Peter Ivanovich's advice about her pension, but he soon saw that she already knew about that to the minutest detail, more even than he did himself. She knew how much could be got out of the government in consequence of her husband's death, but wanted to find out whether she could not possibly extract something more. Peter Ivanovich tried to think of some means of doing so, but after reflecting for a while and, out of propriety, condemning the government for its niggardliness, he said he thought that nothing more could be got. Then she sighed and evidently began to devise means of getting rid of her visitor. Noticing this, he put out his cigarette, rose, pressed her hand, and went out into the ante-room.

In the dining-room where the clock stood that Ivan Ilych had liked so much and had bought at an antique shop, Peter Ivanovich met a priest and a few acquaintances who had come to attend the service, and he recognized Ivan Ilych's daughter, a handsome young woman. She was in black and her slim figure appeared slimmer than ever. She had a gloomy, determined, almost angry expression, and bowed to Peter Ivanovich as though he were in some way to blame. Behind her, with the same offended look, stood a wealthy young man, an examining magistrate, whom Peter Ivanovich also knew and who was her fiancé, as he had heard. He bowed mournfully to them and was about to pass into the death-chamber, when from under the stairs appeared the figure of Ivan Ilych's schoolboy son, who was extremely like his father. He seemed a little Ivan Ilych, such as Peter Ivanovich remembered when they studied law together. His tear-stained eyes had in them the look that is seen in the eyes of boys of thirteen or fourteen who are not pure-minded. When he saw Peter Ivanovich he scowled morosely and shamefacedly. Peter Ivanovich nodded to him and entered the death-chamber. The service began: candles, groans, incense, tears, and sobs. Peter Ivanovich stood looking gloomily down at his feet. He did not look once at the dead man, did not yield to any depressing influence, and was one of the first to leave the room. There was no one in the anteroom, but Gerasim darted out of the dead man's room, rummaged with his strong hands among the fur coats to find Peter Ivanovich's and helped him on with it.

"Well, friend Gerasim," said Peter Ivanovich, so as to say something. "It's a sad affair, isn't it?"

"It's God's will. We shall all come to it some day." said Gerasim, displaying his teeth—the even, white teeth of a healthy peasant—and, like a man in the thick of urgent work, he briskly opened the front door, called the coachman, helped Peter Ivanovich into the sledge, and sprang back to the porch as if in readiness for what he had to do next.

Peter Ivanovich found the fresh air particularly pleasant after the smell of incense, the dead body, and carbolic acid.

"Where to, sir?" asked the coachman.

"It's not too late even now . . . I'll call round on Fëdor Vasilievich."

He accordingly drove there and found them just finishing the first rubber, so that it was quite convenient for him to cut in.

II

Ivan Ilych's life had been most simple and most ordinary and therefore most terrible.

He had been a member of the Court of Justice, and died at the age of forty-five. His father had been an official who after serving in various ministries and departments in Petersburg had made the sort of career which brings men to positions from which by reason of their long service they cannot be dismissed, though they were obviously unfit to hold any responsible position, and for whom therefore posts are specially created, which though fictitious carry salaries of from six to ten thousand rubles that are not fictitious, and in receipt of which they live on to a great age.

Such was the Privy Councillor and superfluous member of various superfluous institutions, Ilya Epimovich Golovin.

He had three sons, of whom Ivan Ilych was the second. The eldest son was following in his father's footsteps only in another department, and was already approaching that stage in the service at which a similar sinecure would be reached. The third son was a failure. He had ruined his prospects in a number of positions and was now serving in the railway department. His father and brothers, and still more their wives, not merely disliked meeting him, but avoided remembering his existence unless compelled to do so. His sister had married Baron Greff, a Petersburg official of her father's type. Ivan Ilych was *le phénix de la famille*[1] as people said. He was neither as cold and formal as his elder brother nor as wild as the younger, but was a happy mean between them—an intelligent, polished, lively and agreeable man. He had studied with his younger brother at the School of Law, but the latter had failed to complete the course and was expelled when he was in the fifth class. Ivan Ilych finished the course well. Even when he was at the School of Law he was just what he remained for the rest of his life: a capable, cheerful, good-natured, and sociable man, though strict in the fulfillment of what he considered to be his duty: and he considered his duty to be what was so considered by those in authority. Neither as a boy nor as a man was he a toady, but from early youth was by nature attracted to people of high station as a fly is drawn to the light, assimilating their ways and views of life and establishing friendly relations with them. All the enthusiasms of childhood and youth passed without leaving much trace on him; he succumbed to sensuality, to vanity, and latterly among the highest classes to liberalism, but always within limits which his instinct unfailingly indicated to him as correct.

At school he had done things which had formerly seemed to him very horrid and made him feel disgusted with himself when he did them; but when later on he saw that such actions were done by people of good position

1. The pride of the family. (Unless otherwise indicated, all foreign phrases are in French—often the everyday language of middle-class and upper-class Russians of Tolstoy's time.)

and that they did not regard them as wrong, he was able not exactly to regard them as right, but to forget about them entirely or not be at all troubled at remembering them.

Having graduated from the School of Law and qualified for the tenth rank of the civil service, and having received money from his father for his equipment, Ivan Ilych ordered himself clothes at Scharmer's, the fashionable tailor, hung a medallion inscribed *respice finem*[2] on his watch-chain, took leave of his professor and the prince who was patron of the school, had a farewell dinner with his comrades at Donon's first-class restaurant, and with his new and fashionable portmanteau, linen, clothes, shaving and other toilet appliances, and a traveling rug, all purchased at the best shops, he set off for one of the provinces where, through his father's influence he had been attached to the Governor as an official for special service.

In the province Ivan Ilych soon arranged as easy and agreeable a position for himself as he had had at the School of Law. He performed his official tasks, made his career, and at the same time amused himself pleasantly and decorously. Occasionally he paid official visits to country districts, where he behaved with dignity both to his superiors and inferiors, and performed the duties entrusted to him, which related chiefly to the sectarians, with an exactness and incorruptible honesty of which he could not but feel proud.

In official matters, despite his youth and taste for frivolous gaiety, he was exceedingly reserved, punctilious, and even severe; but in society he was often amusing and witty, and always good-natured, correct in his manner, and *bon enfant*,[3] as the governor and his wife—with whom he was like one of the family—used to say of him.

In the province he had an affair with a lady who made advances to the elegant young lawyer, and there was also a milliner; and there were carousals with aides-de-camp who visited the district, and after-supper visits to a certain outlying street of doubtful reputation; and there was too some obsequiousness to his chief and even to his chief's wife, but all this was done with such a tone of good breeding that no hard names could be applied to it. It all came under the heading of the French saying: *"Il faut que jeunesse se passe."*[4] It was all done with clean hands, in clean linen, with French phrases, and above all among people of the best society and consequently with the approval of people of rank.

So Ivan Ilych served for five years and then came a change in his official life. The new and reformed judicial institutions were introduced, and new men were needed. Ivan Ilych became such a new man. He was offered the post of examining magistrate, and he accepted it though the post was in another province and obliged him to give up the connections he had formed

2. "Consider your end," that is, your death (Latin).
3. One of the boys (literally, "a good child").
4. "Youth will have its day."

and to make new ones. His friends met to give him a send-off; they had a group-photograph taken and presented him with a silver cigarette case, and he set off to his new post.

As examining magistrate Ivan Ilych was just as *comme il faut*[5] and decorous a man, inspiring general respect and capable of separating his official duties from his private life, as he had been when acting as an official on special service. His duties now as examining magistrate were far more interesting and attractive than before. In his former position it had been pleasant to wear an undress uniform made by Scharmer, and to pass through the crowd of petitioners and officials who were timorously awaiting an audience with the governor, and who envied him as with free and easy gait he went straight into his chief's private room to have a cup of tea and a cigarette with him. But not many people had then been directly dependent on him—only police officials and the sectarians when he went to special missions—and he liked to treat them politely, almost as comrades, as if he were letting them feel that he who had the power to crush them was treating them in this simple, friendly way. There were then but few such people. But now, as an examining magistrate, Ivan Ilych felt that everyone without exception, even the most important and self-satisfied, was in his power, and that he need only write a few words on a sheet of paper with a certain heading, and this or that important, self-satisfied person would be brought before him in the role of an accused person or a witness, and if he did not choose to allow him to sit down, would have to stand before him and answer his questions. Ivan Ilych never abused his power; he tried on the contrary to soften its expression, but the consciousness of it and of the possibility of softening its effect, supplied the chief interest and attraction of his office. In his work itself, especially in his examinations, he very soon acquired a method of eliminating all considerations irrelevant to the legal aspect of the case, and reducing even the most complicated case to a form in which it would be presented on paper only in its externals, completely excluding his personal opinion of the matter, while above all observing every prescribed formality. The work was new and Ivan Ilych was one of the first men to apply the new Code of 1864.[6]

On taking up the post of examining magistrate in a new town, he made new acquaintances and connections, placed himself on a new footing, and assumed a somewhat different tone. He took up an attitude of rather dignified aloofness towards the provincial authorities, but picked out the best circle of legal gentlemen and wealthy gentry living in the town and assumed a tone of slight dissatisfaction with the government, of moderate liberalism, and of enlightened citizenship. At the same time, without at all altering the elegance of his toilet, he ceased shaving his chin and allowed his beard to grow as it pleased.

5. Proper (literally, "as it should be").
6. The emancipation of the serfs in 1861 was followed by a thorough all-round reform of judicial proceedings. [Translator's note]

Ivan Ilych settled down very pleasantly in this new town. The society there, which inclined towards opposition to the Governor, was friendly, his salary was larger, and he began to play *vint*,[7] which he found added not a little to the pleasure of life, for he had a capacity for cards, played good-humoredly, and calculated rapidly and astutely, so that he usually won.

After living there for two years he met his future wife, Praskofvya Fëdorovna Mikhel, who was the most attractive, clever, and brilliant girl of the set in which he moved, and among other amusements and relaxations from his labors as examining magistrate, Ivan Ilych established light and playful relations with her.

While he had been an official on special service he had been accustomed to dance, but now as an examining magistrate it was exceptional for him to do so. If he danced now, he did it as if to show that though he served under the reformed order of things, and had reached the fifth official rank, yet when it came to dancing he could do it better than most people. So at the end of an evening he sometimes danced with Praskovya Fëdorovna, and it was chiefly during these dances that he captivated her. She fell in love with him. Ivan Ilych had at first no definite intention of marrying, but when the girl fell in love with him he said to himself: "Really, why shouldn't I marry?"

Praskovya Fëdorovna came of a good family, was not bad looking, and had some little property. Ivan Ilych might have aspired to a more brilliant match, but even this was good. He had his salary, and she, he hoped, would have an equal income. She was well connected, and was a sweet, pretty, and thoroughly correct young woman. To say that Ivan Ilych married because he fell in love with Praskovya Fëdorovna and found that she sympathized with his views of life would be as incorrect as to say that he married because his social circle approved of the match. He was swayed by both these considerations: the marriage gave him personal satisfaction, and at the same time it was considered the right thing by the most highly placed of his associates.

So Ivan Ilych got married.

The preparations for marriage and the beginning of married life, with its conjugal caresses, the new furniture, new crockery, and new linen, were very pleasant until his wife became pregnant—so that Ivan Ilych had begun to think that marriage would not impair the easy, agreeable, gay and always decorous character of his life, approved of by society and regarded by himself as natural, but would even improve it. But from the first months of his wife's pregnancy, something new, unpleasant, depressing, and unseemly, and from which there was no way of escape, unexpectedly showed itself.

His wife, without any reason—*de gaieté de coeur*[8] as Ivan Ilych expressed it to himself—began to disturb the pleasure and propriety of their

---

7. A form of bridge. [Translator's note]
8. From sheer exuberance.

life. She began to be jealous without any cause, expected him to devote his whole attention to her, found fault with everything, and made coarse and ill-mannered scenes.

At first Ivan Ilych hoped to escape from the unpleasantness of this state of affairs by the same easy and decorous relation to life that had served him heretofore: he tried to ignore his wife's disagreeable moods, continued to live in his usual easy and pleasant way, invited friends to his house for a game of cards, and also tried going out to his club or spending his evenings with friends. But one day his wife began upbraiding him so vigorously, using such coarse words, and continued to abuse him every time he did not fulfil her demands, so resolutely and with such evident determination not to give way till he submitted—that is, till he stayed at home and was bored just as she was—that he became alarmed. He now realized that matrimony—at any rate with Praskovya Fëdorovna—was not always conducive to the pleasures and amenities of life, but on the contrary often infringed both comfort and propriety, and that he must therefore entrench himself against such infringement. And Ivan Ilych began to seek for means of doing so. His official duties were the one thing that imposed upon Praskovya Fëdorovna, and by means of his official work and the duties attached to it he began struggling with his wife to secure his own independence.

With the birth of their child, the attempts to feed it and the various failures in doing so, and with the real and imaginary illnesses of mother and child, in which Ivan Ilych's sympathy was demanded but about which he understood nothing, the need of securing for himself an existence outside his family life became still more imperative.

As his wife grew more irritable and exacting and Ivan Ilych transferred the center of gravity of his life more and more to his official work so did he grow to like his work better and became more ambitious than before.

Very soon, within a year of his wedding, Ivan Ilych had realized that marriage, though it may add some comforts to life, is in fact a very intricate and difficult affair towards which in order to perform one's duty, that is, to lead a decorous life approved of by society, one must adopt a definite attitude just as towards one's official duties.

And Ivan Ilych evolved such an attitude towards married life. He only required of it those conveniences—dinner at home, housewife, and bed—which it could give him, and above all that propriety of external forms required by public opinion. For the rest he looked for light-hearted pleasure and propriety, and was very thankful when he found them, but if he met with antagonism and querulousness he at once retired into his separate fenced-off world of official duties, where he found satisfaction.

Ivan Ilych was esteemed a good official, and after three years was made Assistant Public Prosecutor. His new duties, their importance, the possibility of indicting and imprisoning anyone he chose, the publicity his speeches received, and the success he had in all these things made his work still more attractive.

More children came. His wife became more and more querulous and ill-tempered, but the attitude Ivan Ilych had adopted towards his home life rendered him almost impervious to her grumbling.

After seven years' service in that town he was transferred to another province as Public Prosecutor. They moved, but were short of money and his wife did not like the place they moved to. Though the salary was higher the cost of living was greater, besides which two of their children died and family life became still more unpleasant for him.

Praskovya Fëdorovna blamed her husband for every inconvenience they encountered in their new home. Most of the conversations between husband and wife, especially as to the children's education, led to topics which recalled former disputes, and those disputes were apt to flare up again at any moment. There remained only those rare periods of amorousness which still came to them at times but did not last long. These were islets at which they anchored for a while and then again set out upon that ocean of veiled hostility which showed itself in their aloofness from one another. This aloofness might have grieved Ivan Ilych had he considered that it ought not to exist, but he now regarded the position as normal, and even made it the goal at which he aimed in family life. His aim was to free himself more and more from those unpleasantnesses and to give them a semblance of harmlessness and propriety. He attained this by spending less and less time with his family, and when obliged to be at home he tried to safeguard his position by the presence of outsiders. The chief thing however was that he had his official duties. The whole interest of his life now centered in the official world and that interest absorbed him. The consciousness of his power, being able to ruin anybody he wished to ruin, the importance, even the external dignity of his entry into court, or meetings with his subordinates, his success with superiors and inferiors, and above all his masterly handling of cases, of which he was conscious—all this gave him pleasure and filled his life, together with chats with his colleagues, dinners, and bridge. So that on the whole Ivan Ilych's life continued to flow as he considered it should do—pleasantly and properly.

So things continued for another seven years. His eldest daughter was already sixteen, another child had died, and only one son was left, a schoolboy and a subject of dissension. Ivan Ilych wanted to put him in the School of Law, but to spite him Praskovya Fëdorovna entered him at the High School. The daughter had been educated at home and had turned out well: the boy did not learn badly either.

III

So Ivan Ilych lived for seventeen years after his marriage. He was already a Public Prosecutor of long standing, and had declined several proposed transfers while awaiting a more desirable post, when an unanticipated and unpleasant occurrence quite upset the peaceful course of his life. He was expecting to be offered the post of presiding judge in a University town, but Happe somehow came to the front and obtained the appointment instead. Ivan Ilych became irritable, reproached Happe, and quarreled both with him and with his immediate superiors—who became colder to him and again passed him over when other appointments were made.

This was in 1880, the hardest year of Ivan Ilych's life. It was then that it became evident on the one hand that his salary was insufficient for them to live on, and on the other that he had been forgotten, and not only this, but that what was for him the greatest and most cruel injustice appeared to others a quite ordinary occurrence. Even his father did not consider it his duty to help him. Ivan Ilych felt himself abandoned by everyone, and that they regarded his position with a salary of 3,500 rubles as quite normal and even fortunate. He alone knew that with the consciousness of the injustices done him, with his wife's incessant nagging, and with the debts he had contracted by living beyond his means, his position was far from normal.

In order to save money that summer he obtained leave of absence and went with his wife to live in the country at her brother's place.

In the country, without his work, he experienced *ennui* for the first time in his life, and not only *ennui* but intolerable depression, and he decided that it was impossible to go on living like that, and that it was necessary to take energetic measures.

Having passed a sleepless night pacing up and down the veranda, he decided to go to Petersburg and bestir himself, in order to punish those who had failed to appreciate him and to get transferred to another ministry.

Next day, despite many protests from his wife and her brother, he started for Petersburg with the sole object of obtaining a post with a salary of five thousand rubles a year. He was no longer bent on any particular department, or tendency, or kind of activity. All he now wanted was an appointment to another post with a salary of five thousand rubles, either in the administration, in the banks, with the railways, in one of the Empress Marya's Institutions, or even in the customs—but it had to carry with it a salary of five thousand rubles and be in a ministry other than that in which they had failed to appreciate him.

And this quest of Ivan Ilych's was crowned with remarkable and unexpected success. At Kursk an acquaintance of his, F. I. Ilyin, got into the first-class carriage, sat down beside Ivan Ilych, and told him of a telegram just received by the Governor of Kursk announcing that a change was about to take place in the ministry: Peter Ivanovich was to be superseded by Ivan Semënovich.

The proposed change, apart from its significance for Russia, had a special significance for Ivan Ilych, because by bringing forward a new man, Peter Petrovich, and consequently his friend Zachar Ivanovich, it was highly favorable for Ivan Ilych, since Zachar Ivanovich was a friend and colleague of his.

In Moscow this news was confirmed, and on reaching Petersburg Ivan

Ilych found Zachar Ivanovich and received a definite promise of an appointment in his former department of Justice.

A week later he telegraphed to his wife: "Zachar in Miller's place. I shall receive appointment on presentation of report."

Thanks to this change of personnel, Ivan Ilych had unexpectedly obtained an appointment in his former ministry which placed him two stages above his former colleagues besides giving him five thousand rubles salary and three thousand five hundred rubles for expenses connected with his removal. All his ill humor towards his former enemies and the whole department vanished, and Ivan Ilych was completely happy.

He returned to the country more cheerful and contented than he had been for a long time. Praskovya Fëdorovna also cheered up and a truce was arranged between them. Ivan Ilych told of how he had been fêted by everybody in Petersburg, how all those who had been his enemies were put to shame and now fawned on him, how envious they were of his appointment, and how much everybody in Petersburg had liked him.

Praskovya Fëdorovna listened to all this and appeared to believe it. She did not contradict anything, but only made plans for their life in the town to which they were going. Ivan Ilych saw with delight that these plans were his plans, that he and his wife agreed, and that, after a stumble, his life was regaining its due and natural character of pleasant lightheartedness and decorum.

Ivan Ilych had come back for a short time only, for he had to take up his new duties on the 10th of September. Moreover, he needed time to settle into the new place, to move all his belongings from the province, and to buy and order many additional things: in a word, to make such arrangements as he had resolved on, which were almost exactly what Praskovya Fëdorovna too had decided on.

Now that everything had happened so fortunately, and that he and his wife were at one in their aims and moreover saw so little of one another, they got on together better than they had done since the first years of marriage. Ivan Ilych had thought of taking his family away with him at once, but the insistence of his wife's brother and her sister-in-law, who had suddenly become particularly amiable and friendly to him and his family, induced him to depart alone.

So he departed, and the cheerful state of mind induced by his success and by the harmony between his wife and himself, the one intensifying the other, did not leave him. He found a delightful house, just the thing both he and his wife had dreamt of. Spacious, lofty reception rooms in the old style, a convenient and dignified study, rooms for his wife and daughter, a study for his son—it might have been specially built for them. Ivan Ilych himself superintended the arrangements, chose the wallpapers, supplemented the furniture (preferably with antiques which he considered particularly *comme il faut*), and supervised the upholstering. Everything progressed and approached the ideal he had set himself: even when things were only half completed they exceeded his expectations. He saw what a refined and elegant character, free from vulgarity, it would all have when it was ready. On falling asleep he pictured to himself how the reception-room would look. Looking at the yet unfinished drawing-room he could see the fireplace, the screen, the what-not, the little chairs dotted here and there, the dishes and plates on the walls, and the bronzes, as they would be when everything was in place. He was pleased by the thought of how his wife and daughter, who shared his taste in this matter, would be impressed by it. They were certainly not expecting as much. He had been particularly successful in finding, and buying cheaply, antiques which gave a particularly aristocratic character to the whole place. But in his letters he intentionally understated everything in order to be able to surprise them. All this so absorbed him that his new duties—though he liked his official work—interested him less than he had expected. Sometimes he even had moments of absent-mindedness during the Court Sessions, and would consider whether he should have straight or curved cornices for his curtains. He was so interested in it all that he often did things himself, rearranging the furniture, or rehanging the curtains. Once when mounting a step-ladder to show the upholsterer, who did not understand, how he wanted the hangings draped, he made a false step and slipped, but being a strong and agile man he clung on and only knocked his side against the knob of the window frame. The bruised place was painful but the pain soon passed, and he felt particularly bright and well just then. He wrote: "I feel fifteen years younger." He thought he would have everything ready by September, but it dragged on till mid-October. But the result was charming not only in his eyes but to everyone who saw it.

In reality it was just what is usually seen in the houses of people of moderate means who want to appear rich, and therefore succeed only in resembling others like themselves: there were damasks, dark wood, plants, rugs, and dull and polished bronzes—all the things people of a certain class have in order to resemble other people of that class. His house was so like the others that it would never have been noticed, but to him it all seemed to be quite exceptional. He was very happy when he met his family at the station and brought them to the newly furnished house all lit up, where a footman in a white tie opened the door into the hall decorated with plants, and when they went on into the drawing-room, and the study uttering exclamations of delight. He conducted them everywhere, drank in their praises eagerly, and beamed with pleasure. At tea that evening, when Praskovya Fëdorovna among other things asked him about his fall, he laughed and showed them how he had gone flying and had frightened the upholsterer.

"It's a good thing I'm a bit of an athlete. Another man might have been killed, but I merely knocked myself, just here; it hurts when it's touched, but it's passing off already—it's only a bruise."

So they began living in their new home—in which, as always happens, when they got thoroughly settled in they found they were just one room short—and with the increased income, which as always was just a little (some five hundred rubles) too little, but it was all very nice.

Things went particularly well at first, before everything was finally arranged and while something had still to be done: this thing bought, that thing ordered, another thing moved, and something else adjusted. Though there were some disputes between husband and wife, they were both so well satisfied and had so much to do that it all passed off without any serious quarrels. When nothing was left to arrange it became rather dull and something seemed to be lacking, but they were then making acquaintances, forming habits, and life was growing fuller.

Ivan Ilych spent his mornings at the law court and came home to dinner, and at first he was generally in a good humor, though he occasionally became irritable just on account of his house. (Every spot on the tablecloth or the upholstery, and every broken windowblind string, irritated him. He had devoted so much trouble to arranging it all that every disturbance of it distressed him.) But on the whole his life ran its course as he believed life should do: easily, pleasantly, and decorously.

He got up at nine, drank his coffee, read the paper, and then put on his undress uniform and went to the law courts. There the harness in which he worked had already been stretched to fit him and he donned it without a hitch: petitioners, inquiries at the chancery, the chancery itself, and the sittings public and administrative. In all this the thing was to exclude everything fresh and vital, which always disturbs the regular course of official business, and to admit only official relations with people, and then only on official grounds. A man would come, for instance, wanting some information. Ivan Ilych, as one in whose sphere the matter did not lie, would have nothing to do with him: but if the man had some business with him in his official capacity, something that could be expressed on officially stamped paper, he would do everything, positively everything he could within the limits of such relations, and in doing so would maintain the semblance of friendly human relations, that is, would observe the courtesies of life. As soon as the official relations ended, so did everything else. Ivan Ilych possessed this capacity to separate his real life from the official side of affairs and not mix the two, in the highest degree, and by long practice and natural aptitude had brought it to such a pitch that sometimes, in the manner of a virtuoso, he would even allow himself to let the human and official relations mingle. He let himself do this just because he felt that he could at any time he chose resume the strictly official attitude again and drop the human relation. And he did it all easily, pleasantly, correctly, and even artistically. In the intervals between the sessions he smoked, drank tea, chatted a little about politics, a little about general topics, a little about cards, but most of all about official appointments. Tired, but with the feelings of a virtuoso—one of the first violins who has played his part in an orchestra with precision—he would return home to find that his wife and daughter had been out paying calls, or had a visitor, and that his son had been to school, had done his homework with his tutor, and was duly learning what is taught at High Schools. Everything was as it should be. After dinner, if they had no visitors, Ivan Ilych sometimes read a book that was being much discussed at the time, and in the evening settled down to work, that is, read official papers, compared the depositions of witnesses, and noted paragraphs of the Code applying to them. This was neither dull nor amusing. It was dull when he might have been playing bridge, but if no bridge was available it was at any rate better than doing nothing or sitting with his wife. Ivan Ilych's chief pleasure was giving little dinners to which he invited men and women of good social position, and just as his drawing-room resembled all other drawing-rooms so did his enjoyable little parties resemble all other such parties.

Once they even gave a dance. Ivan Ilych enjoyed it and everything went off well, except that it led to a violent quarrel with his wife about the cakes and sweets. Praskovya Fëdorovna had made her own plans, but Ivan Ilych insisted on getting everything from an expensive confectioner and ordered too many cakes, and the quarrel occurred because some of those cakes were left over and the confectioner's bill came to forty-five rubles. It was a great and disagreeable quarrel. Praskovya Fëdorovna called him "a fool and an imbecile," and he clutched at his head and made angry allusions to divorce.

But the dance itself had been enjoyable. The best people were there and Ivan Ilych had danced with Princess Trufonova, a sister of the distinguished founder of the Society "Bear My Burden."

The pleasures connected with his work were pleasures of ambition; his social pleasures were those of vanity; but Ivan Ilych's greatest pleasure was playing bridge. He acknowledged that whatever disagreeable incident happened in his life, the pleasure that beamed like a ray of light above everything else was to sit down to bridge with good players, not noisy partners and of course to four-handed bridge (with five players it was annoying to have to stand out, though one pretended not to mind), to play a clever and serious game (when the cards allowed it) and then to have supper and drink a glass of wine. After a game of bridge, especially if he had won a little (to win a large sum was unpleasant), Ivan Ilych went to bed in specially good humor.

So they lived. They formed a circle of acquaintances among the best people and were visited by people of importance and by young folk. In their views as to their acquaintances, husband, wife, and daughter were entirely agreed, and tacitly and unanimously kept at arm's length and shook off the various shabby friends and relations who, with much show of affection, gushed into the drawing-room with its Japanese plates on the walls. Soon these shabby friends ceased to obtrude themselves and only the best people remained in the Golovins' set.

Young men made up to Lisa, and Petrishchev, an examining magistrate and Dmitri Ivanovich Petrishchev's son and sole heir, began to be so attentive to her that Ivan Ilych had already spoken to Praskovya Fëdorovna about it, and considered whether they should not arrange a party for them, or get up some private theatricals.

So they lived, and all went well, without change, and life flowed pleasantly.

IV

They were all in good health. It could not be called ill health if Ivan Ilych sometimes said that he had a queer taste in his mouth and felt some discomfort in his left side.

But this discomfort increased and, though not exactly painful, grew into a sense of pressure in his side accompanied by ill humor. And his irritability became worse and worse and began to mar the agreeable, easy, and correct life that had established itself in the Golovin family. Quarrels between husband and wife became more and more frequent, and soon the ease and amenity disappeared and even the decorum was barely maintained. Scenes again became frequent, and very few of those islets remained on which husband and wife could meet without an explosion. Praskovya Fëdorovna now had good reason to say that her husband's temper was trying. With characteristic exaggeration she said he had always had a dreadful temper, and that it had needed all her good nature to put up with it for twenty years. It was true that now the quarrels were started by him. His bursts of temper always came just before dinner, often just as he began to eat his soup. Sometimes he noticed that a plate or dish was chipped, or the food was not right, or his son put his elbow on the table, or his daughter's hair was not done as he liked it, and for all this he blamed Praskovya Fëdorovna. At first she retorted and said disagreeable things to him, but once or twice he fell into such a rage at the beginning of dinner that she realized it was due to some physical derangement brought on by taking food, and so she restrained herself and did not answer, but only hurried to get the dinner over. She regarded this self-restraint as highly praiseworthy. Having come to the conclusion that her husband had a dreadful temper and made her life miserable, she began to feel sorry for herself, and the more she pitied herself the more she hated her husband. She began to wish he would die; yet she did not want him to die because then his salary would cease. And this irritated her against him still more. She considered herself dreadfully unhappy just because not even his death could save her, and though she concealed her exasperation, that hidden exasperation of hers increased his irritation also.

After one scene in which Ivan Ilych had been particularly unfair and after which he had said in explanation that he certainly was irritable but that it was due to his not being well, she said that if he was ill it should be attended to, and insisted on his going to see a celebrated doctor.

He went. Everything took place as he had expected and as it always does. There was the usual waiting and the important air assumed by the doctor, with which he was so familiar (resembling that which he himself assumed in court), and the sounding and listening, and the questions which called for answers that were foregone conclusions and were evidently unnecessary, and the look of importance which implied that "if only you put yourself in our hands we will arrange everything—we know indubitably how it has to be done, always in the same way for everybody alike." It was all just as it was in the law courts. The doctor put on just the same air towards him as he himself put on towards an accused person.

The doctor said that so-and-so indicated that there was so-and-so-inside the patient, but if the investigation of so-and-so did not confirm this, then he must assume that and that. If he assumed that and that, then . . . and so on. To Ivan Ilych only one question was important: was his case serious or not? But the doctor ignored that inappropriate question. From his point of view it was not the one under consideration, the real question was to decide between a floating kidney, chronic catarrh, or appendicitis. It was not a question of Ivan Ilych's life or death, but one between a floating kidney and appendicitis. And that question the doctor solved brilliantly, as it seemed to Ivan Ilych, in favor of the appendix, with the reservation that should an examination of the urine give fresh indications the matter would be reconsidered. All this was just what Ivan Ilych had himself brilliantly accomplished a thousand times in dealing with men on trial. The doctor summed up just as brilliantly, looking over his spectacles triumphantly and even gaily at the accused. From the doctor's summing up Ivan Ilych concluded that things were bad, but that for the doctor, and perhaps for everybody else, it was a matter of indifference, though for him it was bad. And this conclusion struck him painfully, arousing in him a great feeling of pity for himself and of bitterness towards the doctor's indifference to a matter of such importance.

He said nothing of this, but rose, placed the doctor's fee on the table, and remarked with a sigh: "We sick people probably often put inappropriate questions. But tell me, in general, is this complaint dangerous, or not? . . ."

The doctor looked at him sternly over his spectacles with one eye, as if to say: "Prisoner, if you will not keep the questions put to you, I shall be obliged to have you removed from the court."

"I have already told you what I consider necessary and proper. The analysis may show something more." And the doctor bowed.

Ivan Ilych went out slowly, seated himself disconsolately in his sledge, and drove home. All the way home he was going over what the doctor had said, trying to translate those complicated, obscure, scientific phrases into plain language and find in them an answer to the question: "Is my condition bad? Is it very bad? Or is there as yet nothing much wrong?" And it seemed to him that the meaning of what the doctor had said was that it was very bad. Everything in the streets seemed depressing. The cabmen, the houses, the passers-by, and the shops, were dismal. His ache, this dull gnawing ache that never ceased for a moment, seemed to have acquired a new and more serious significance from the doctor's dubious remarks. Ivan Ilych now watched it with a new and oppressive feeling.

He reached home and began to tell his wife about it. She listened, but in the middle of his account his daughter came in with her hat on, ready to go out with her mother. She sat down reluctantly to listen to this tedious story, but could not stand it long, and her mother too did not hear him to the end.

"Well, I am very glad," she said. "Mind now to take your medicine regularly. Give me the prescription and I'll send Gerasim to the chemist's." And she went to get ready to go out.

While she was in the room Ivan Ilych had hardly taken time to breathe, but he sighed deeply when she left it.

"Well," he though, "perhaps it isn't so bad after all."

He began taking his medicine and following the doctor's directions, which had been altered after the examination of the urine. But then it happened that there was a contradiction between the indications drawn from the examination of the urine and the symptoms that showed themselves. It turned out that what was happening differed from what the doctor had told him, and that he had either forgotten, or blundered, or hidden something from him. He could not, however, be blamed for that, and Ivan Ilych still obeyed his orders implicitly and at first derived some comfort from doing so.

From the time of his visit to the doctor, Ivan Ilych's chief occupation was the exact fulfilment of the doctor's instructions regarding hygiene and the taking of medicine, and the observation of his pain and his excretions. His chief interests came to be people's ailments and people's health. When sickness, deaths, or recoveries were mentioned in his presence, expecially when the illness resembled his own, he listened with agitation which he tried to hide, asked questions, and applied what he heard to his own case.

The pain did not grow less, but Ivan Ilych made efforts to force himself to think that he was better. And he could do this so long as nothing agitated him. But as soon as he had any unpleasantness with his wife, any lack of success in his official work, or held bad cards at bridge, he was at once acutely sensible of his disease. He had formerly borne such mischances, hoping soon to adjust what was wrong, to master it and attain success, or make a grand slam. But now every mischance upset him and plunged him into despair. He would say to himself: "There now, just as I was beginning to get better and the medicine had begun to take effect, comes this accursed misfortune, or unpleasantness . . ." And he was furious with the mishap, or with the people who were causing the unpleasantness and killing him, for he felt that this fury was killing him but could not restrain it. One would have thought that it should have been clear to him that this exasperation with circumstances and people aggravated his illness, and that he ought therefore to ignore unpleasant occurrences. But he drew the very opposite conclusion: he said that he needed peace, and he watched for everything that might disturb it and became irritable at the slightest infringement of it. His condition was rendered worse by the fact that he read medical books and consulted doctors. The progress of his disease was so gradual that he could deceive himself when comparing one day with another—the difference was so slight. But when he consulted the doctors it seemed to him that he was getting worse, and even very rapidly. Yet despite this he was continually consulting them.

That month he went to see another celebrity, who told him almost the same as the first had done but put his questions rather differently, and the interview with this celebrity only increased Ivan Ilych's doubts and fears. A friend of a friend of his, a very good doctor, diagnosed his illness again quite differently from the others, and though he predicted recovery, his questions and suppositions bewildered Ivan Ilych still more and increased his doubts. A homoeopathist diagnosed the disease in yet another way, and prescribed medicine which Ivan Ilych took secretly for a week. But after a week, not feeling any improvement and having lost confidence both in the former doctor's treatment and in this one's, he became still more despondent. One day a lady acquaintance mentioned a cure effected by a wonder-working icon. Ivan Ilych caught himself listening attentively and beginning to believe that it had occurred. This incident alarmed him. "Has my mind really weakened to such an extent?" he asked himself. "Nonsense! It's all rubbish. I mustn't give way to nervous fears but having chosen a doctor must keep strictly to his treatment. That is what I will do. Now it's all settled. I won't think about it, but will follow the treatment seriously till summer, and then we shall see. From now there must be no more of this wavering!" This was easy to say but impossible to carry out. The pain in this side oppressed him and seemed to grow worse and more incessant, while the taste in his mouth grew stranger and stranger. It seemed to him that his breath had a disgusting smell, and he was conscious of a loss of appetite and strength. There was no deceiving himself: something terrible, new, and more important than anything before in his life, was taking place within him of which he alone was aware. Those about him did not understand or would not understand it, but thought everything in the world was going on as usual. That tormented Ivan Ilych more than anything. He saw that his household, especially his wife and daughter who were in a perfect whirl of visiting, did not understand anything of it and were annoyed that he was so depressed and so exacting, as if he were to blame for it. Though they tried to disguise it he saw that he was an obstacle in their path, and that his wife had adopted a definite line in regard to his illness and kept to it regardless of anything he said or did. Her attitude was this. "You know," she would say to her friends, "Ivan Ilych can't do as other people do, and keep to the treatment prescribed for him. One day he'll take his drops and keep strictly to his diet and go to bed in good time, but the next day unless I watch him he'll suddenly forget his medicine, eat sturgeon—which is forbidden—and sit up playing cards till one o'clock in the morning."

"Oh come, when was that?" Ivan Ilych would ask in vexation. "Only once at Peter Ivanovich's."

"And yesterday with Shebek."

"Well, even if I hadn't stayed up, this pain would have kept me awake."

"Be that as it may you'll never get well like that, but will always make us wretched."

Praskovya Fëdorovna's attitude to Ivan Ilych's illness, as she expressed it both to others and to him, was that it was his own fault and was another of the annoyances he caused her. Ivan Ilych felt that this opinion escaped her involuntarily—but that did not make it easier for him.

At the law courts too, Ivan Ilych noticed, or thought he noticed, a strange attitude towards himself. It sometimes seemed to him that people were watching him inquisitively as a man whose place might soon be vacant. Then again, his friends would suddenly begin to chaff him in a friendly way about his low spirits, as if the awful, horrible, and unheard-of thing that was going on within him, incessantly gnawing at him and irresistibly drawing him away, was a very agreeable subject for jests. Schwartz in particular irritated him by his jocularity, vivacity, and *savior-faire*, which reminded him of what he himself had been ten years ago.

Friends came to make up a set and they sat down to cards. They dealt, bending the new cards to soften them, and he sorted the diamonds in his hand and found he had seven. His partner said "No trumps" and supported him with two diamonds. What more could be wished for? It ought to be jolly and lively. They would make a grand slam. But suddenly Ivan Ilych was conscious of that gnawing pain, that taste in his mouth, and it seemed ridiculous that in such circumstances he should be pleased to make a grand slam.

He looked at his partner Mikhail Mikhaylovich, who rapped the table with his strong hand and instead of snatching up the tricks pushed the cards courteously and indulgently towards Ivan Ilych that he might have the pleasure of gathering them up without the trouble of stretching out his hand for them. "Does he think I am too weak to stretch out my arm?" thought Ivan Ilych, and forgetting what he was doing he over-trumped his partner, missing the grand slam by three tricks. And what was most awful of all was that he saw how upset Mikhail Mikhaylovich was about it but did not himself care. And it was dreadful to realize why he did not care.

They all saw that he was suffering, and said: "We can stop if you are tired. Take a rest." Lie down? No, he was not at all tired, and he finished the rubber. All were gloomy and silent, Ivan Ilych felt that he had diffused this gloom over them and could not dispel it. They had supper and went away, and Ivan Ilych was left alone with the consciousness that his life was poisoned and was poisoning the lives of others, and that this poison did not weaken but penetrated more and more deeply into his whole being.

With this consciousness, and with physical pain besides the terror, he must go to bed, often to lie awake the greater part of the night. Next morn-

ing he had to get up again, dress, go to the law courts, speak, and write; or
if he did not go out, spend at home those twenty-four hours a day each of
which was a torture. And he had to live thus all alone on the brink of an
abyss, with no one who understood or pitied him.

V

So one month passed and then another. Just before the New Year his
brother-in-law came to town and stayed at their house. Ivan Ilych was at
the law courts and Praskovya Fëdorovna had gone shopping. When Ivan
Ilych came home and entered his study he found his brother-in-law there—
a healthy, florid man—unpacking his portmanteau himself. He raised his
head on hearing Ivan Ilych's footsteps and looked up at him for a moment
without a word. That stare told Ivan Ilych everything. His brother-in-law
opened his mouth to utter an exclamation of surprise but checked himself,
and that action confirmed it all.

"I have changed, eh?"

"Yes, there is a change."

And after that, try as he would to get his brother-in-law to return to
the subject of his looks, the latter would say nothing about it. Praskovya
Fëdorovna came home and her brother went out to her. Ivan Ilych locked
the door and began to examine himself in the glass, first full face, then in
profile. He took up a portrait of himself taken with his wife, and compared
it with what he saw in the glass. The change in him was immense. Then he
bared his arms to the elbow, looked at them, drew the sleeves down again,
sat down on an ottoman, and grew blacker than night.

"No, no, this won't do!" he said to himself, and jumped up, went to
the table, took up some law papers and began to read them, but could not
continue. He unlocked the door and went into the reception-room. The
door leading to the drawing-room was shut. He approached it on tiptoe and
listened.

"No, you are exaggerating!" Praskovya Fëdorovna was saying.

"Exaggerating! Don't you see it? Why, he's a dead man! Look at his
eyes—there's no light in them. But what is it that is wrong with him?"

"No one knows. Nikolaevich said something, but I don't know what.
And Leshchetitsky[9] said quite the contrary . . ."

Ivan Ilych walked away, went to his own room, lay down, and began
musing: "The kidney, a floating kidney." He recalled all the doctors had
told him of how it detached itself and swayed about. And by an effort of
imagination he tried to catch that kidney and arrest it and support it. So
little was needed for this, it seemed to him. "No, I'll go to see Peter
Ivanovich again." He rang, ordered the carriage, and got ready to go.

"Where are you going, Jean?" asked his wife, with a specially sad and
exceptionally kind look.

9. Two doctors, the latter a celebrated specialist. [Translator's note]

This exceptionally kind look irritated him. He looked morosely at her. "I must go to see Peter Ivanovich."[10]

He went to see Peter Ivanovich, and together they went to see his friend, the doctor. He was in, and Ivan Ilych had a long talk with him.

Reviewing the anatomical and physiological details of what in the doctor's opinion was going on inside him, he understood it all.

There was something, a small thing, in the vermiform appendix. It might all come right. Only stimulate the energy of one organ and check the activity of another, then absorption would take place and everything would come right. He got home rather late for dinner, ate his dinner, and conversed cheerfully, but could not for a long time bring himself to go back to work in his room. At last, however, he went to his study and did what was necessary, but the consciousness that he had put something aside—an important, intimate matter which he would revert to when his work was done—never left him. When he had finished his work he remembered that this intimate matter was the thought of his vermiform appendix. But he did not give himself up to it, and went to the drawing-room for tea. There were callers there, including the examining magistrate who was a desirable match for his daughter, and they were conversing, playing the piano, and singing. Ivan Ilych, as Praskovya Fëdorovna remarked, spent that evening more cheerfully than usual, but he never for a moment forgot that he had postponed the important matter of the appendix. At eleven o'clock he said good-night and went to his bedroom. Since his illness he had slept alone in a small room next to his study. He undressed and took up a novel by Zola,[11] but instead of reading it he fell into thought, and in his imagination that desired improvement in the vermiform appendix occurred. There were the absorption and evacuation and the re-establishment of normal activity. "Yes, that's it!" he said to himself. "One need only assist nature, that's all." He remembered his medicine, rose, took it, and lay down on his back watching for the beneficent action of the medicine and for it to lessen the pain. "I need only take it regularly and avoid all injurious influences. I am already feeling better, much better." He began touching his side: it was not painful to the touch. "There, I really don't feel it. It's much better already." He put out the light and turned on his side . . . "The appendix is getting better, absorption is occurring." Suddenly he felt the old, familiar dull, gnawing pain, stubborn and serious. There was the same familiar loathsome taste in his mouth. His heart sank and he felt dazed. "My God! My God!" he muttered. "Again, again! and it will never cease." And suddenly the matter presented itself in a quite different aspect. "Vermiform appendix! Kidney!" he said to himself. "It's not a question of appendix or kidney, but of life and . . . death. Yes, life was there and now it is going, going and I cannot stop it. Yes. Why deceive myself? Isn't it obvious to

10. That was the friend whose friend was a doctor. [Translator's note]
11. Émile Zola (1840–1902), French novelist.

everyone but me that I'm dying, and that it's only a question of weeks, days . . . it may happen this moment. There was light and now there is darkness. I was here and now I'm going there! Where?" A chill came over him, his breathing ceased, and he felt only the throbbing of his heart.

"When I am not, what will there be? There will be nothing. Then where shall I be when I am no more? Can this be dying? No, I don't want to!" He jumped up and tried to light the candle, felt for it with trembling hands, dropped candle and candlestick on the floor, and fell back on his pillow.

"What's the use? It makes no difference," he said to himself, staring with wide-open eyes into the darkness. "Death. Yes, Death. And none of them know or wish to know it, and they have no pity for me. Now they are playing." (He heard through the door the distant sound of a song and its accompaniment.) "It's all the same to them, but they will die too! Fools! I first, and they later, but it will be the same for them. And now they are merry . . . the beasts!"

Anger choked him and he was agonizingly, unbearably miserable. "It is impossible that all men have been doomed to suffer this awful horror!" He raised himself.

"Something must be wrong. I must calm myself—must think it all over from the beginning." And he again began thinking. "Yes, the beginning of my illness: I knocked my side, but I was still quite well that day and the next. It hurt a little, then rather more. I saw the doctors, then followed despondency and anguish, more doctors, and I drew nearer to the abyss. My strength grew less and I kept coming nearer and nearer, and now I have wasted away and there is no light in my eyes. I think of the appendix—but this is death! I think of mending the appendix, and all the while here is death! Can it really be death?" Again terror seized him and he gasped for breath. He leant down and began feeling for the matches, pressing with his elbow on the stand beside the bed. It was in his way and hurt him, he grew furious with it, pressed on it still harder, and upset it. Breathless and in despair he fell on his back, expecting death to come immediately.

Meanwhile the visitors were leaving. Praskovya Fëdorovna was seeing them off. She heard something fall and came in.

"What has happened?"

"Nothing. I knocked it over accidentally."

She went out and returned with a candle. He lay there panting heavily, like a man who has run a thousand yards, and stared upwards at her with a fixed look.

"What is it, Jean?"

"No . . . no . . . thing. I upset it." ("Why speak of it? She won't understand," he thought.)

And in truth she did not understand. She picked up the stand, lit his candle, and hurried away to see another visitor off. When she came back he still lay on his back, looking upwards.

"What is it? Do you feel worse?"

"Yes."

She shook her head and sat down.

"Do you know, Jean, I think we must ask Leshchetitsky to come and see you here."

This meant calling in the famous specialist, regardless of expense. He smiled malignantly and said "No." She remained a little longer and then went up to him and kissed his forehead.

While she was kissing him he hated her from the bottom of his soul and with difficulty refrained from pushing her away.

"Good-night. Please God you'll sleep."

"Yes."

VI

Ivan Ilych saw that he was dying, and he was in continual despair.

In the depth of his heart he knew he was dying, but not only was he not accustomed to the thought, he simply did not and could not grasp it.

The syllogism he had learnt from Kiezewetter's Logic: "Caius is a man, men are mortal, therefore Caius is mortal," had always seemed to him correct as applied to Caius, but certainly not as applied to himself. That Caius—man in the abstract—was mortal, was perfectly correct, but he was not Caius, not an abstract man, but a creature quite, quite separate from all others. He had been little Vanya, with a mama and a papa, with Mitya and Volodya, with the toys, a coachman and a nurse, afterwards with Katenka and with all the joys, griefs, and delights of childhood, boyhood, and youth. What did Caius know of the smell of that striped leather ball Vanya had been so fond of? Had Caius kissed his mother's hand like that, and did the silk of her dress rustle so for Caius? Had he rioted like that at school when the pastry was bad? Had Caius been in love like that? Could Caius preside at a session as he did? "Caius really was mortal, and it was right for him to die; but for me, little Vanya, Ivan Ilych, with all my thoughts and emotions, it's altogether a different matter. It cannot be that I ought to die. That would be too terrible."

Such was his feeling.

"If I had to die like Caius I should have known it was so. An inner voice would have told me so, but there was nothing of the sort in me and I and all my friends felt that our case was quite different from that of Caius. And now here it is!" he said to himself. "It can't be. It's impossible! But here it is. How is this? How is one to understand it?"

He could not understand it, and tried to drive this false, incorrect, morbid thought away and to replace it by other proper and healthy thoughts. But that thought, and not the thought only but the reality itself, seemed to come and confront him.

And to replace that thought he called up a succession of others, hoping to find in them some support. He tried to get back into the former current of thoughts that had once screened the thought of death from him, But strange to say, all that formerly shut off, hidden, and destroyed, his consciousness of death, no longer had that effect. Ivan Ilych now spent most of his time in attempting to re-establish that old current. He would say to himself: "I will take up my duties again—after all I used to live by them." And banishing all doubts he would go to the law courts, enter into conversation with his colleagues, and sit carelessly as was his wont, scanning the crowd with a thoughtful look and leaning both his emaciated arms on the arms of his oak chair; bending over as usual to a colleague and drawing his papers nearer he would interchange whispers with him, and then suddenly raising his eyes and sitting erect would pronounce certain words and open the proceedings. But suddenly in the midst of those proceedings the pain in his side, regardless of the stage the proceedings had reached, would begin its own gnawing work. Ivan Ilych would turn his attention to it and try to drive the thought of it away, but without success. *It* would come and stand before him and look at him, and he would be petrified and the light would die out of his eyes, and he would again begin asking himself whether *It* alone was true. And his colleagues and subordinates would see with surprise and distress that he, the brilliant and subtle judge, was becoming confused and making mistakes. He would shake himself, try to pull himself together, manage somehow to bring the sitting to a close, and return home with the sorrowful consciousness that his judicial labors could not as formerly hide from him what he wanted them to hide, and could not deliver him from *It*. And what was worst of all was that *It* drew his attention to itself not in order to make him take some action but only that he should look at *It*, look it straight in the face: look at it and without doing anything, suffer inexpressibly.

And to save himself from this condition Ivan Ilych looked for consolations—new screens—and new screens were found and for a while seemed to save him, but then they immediately fell to pieces or rather became transparent, as if *It* penetrated them and nothing could veil *It*.

In these latter days he would go into the drawing-room he had arranged—that drawing-room where he had fallen and for the sake of which (how bitterly ridiculous it seemed) he had sacrificed his life—for he knew that his illness originated with that knock. He would enter and see that something had scratched the polished table. He would look for the cause of this and find that it was the bronze ornamentation of an album, that had got bent. He would take up the expensive album which he had lovingly arranged, and feel vexed with his daughter and her friends for their untidiness—for the album was torn here and there and some of the photographs turned upside down. He would put it carefully in order and bend the ornamentation back into position. Then it would occur to him to place all those things in another corner of the room, near the plants. He could call the footman, but his daughter or wife would come to help him. They would not agree, and his wife would contradict him, and he would dispute and grow angry. But that was all right, for then he did not think about *It*. *It* was invisible.

But then, when he was moving something himself, his wife would say: "Let the servants do it. You will hurt yourself again." And suddenly *It* would flash through the screen and he would see it. It was just a flash, and he hoped it would disappear, but he would involuntarily pay attention to his side. "It sits there as before, gnawing just the same!" And he could no longer forget *It*, but could distinctly see it looking at him from behind the flowers. "What is it all for?"

"It really is so! I lost my life over that curtain as I might have done when storming a fort. Is that possible? How terrible and how stupid. It can't be true! It can't, but it is."

He would go to his study, lie down, and again be alone with *It:* face to face with *It*. And nothing could be done with *It* except to look at it and shudder.

VII

How it happened it is impossible to say because it came about step by step, unnoticed, but in the third month of Ivan Ilych's illness, his wife, his daughter, his son, his acquaintances, the doctors, the servants, and above all he himself, were aware that the whole interest he had for other people was whether he would soon vacate his place, and at last release the living from the discomfort caused by his presence and be himself released from his sufferings.

He slept less and less. He was given opium and hypodermic injections of morphine, but this did not relieve him. The dull depression he experienced in a somnolent condition at first gave him a little relief, but only as something new, afterwards it became as distressing as the pain itself or even more so.

Special foods were prepared for him by the doctors' orders, but all those foods became increasingly distasteful and disgusting to him.

For his excretions also special arrangements had to be made, and this was a torment to him every time—a torment from the uncleanliness, the unseemliness, and the smell, and from knowing that another person had to take part in it.

But just through this most unpleasant matter, Ivan Ilych obtained comfort. Gerasim, the butler's young assistant, always came in to carry the things out. Gerasim was a clean, fresh peasant lad, grown stout on town food and always cheerful and bright. At first the sight of him, in his clean Russian peasant costume, engaged on that disgusting task embarrassed Ivan Ilych.

Once when he got up from the commode too weak to draw up his trousers, he dropped into a soft armchair and looked with horror at his bare, enfeebled thighs with the muscles so sharply marked on them.

Gerasim with a firm light tread, his heavy boots emitting a pleasant smell of tar and fresh winter air, came in wearing a clean Hessian apron, the sleeves of his print shirt tucked up over his strong bare young arms; and refraining from looking at his sick master out of consideration for his feelings, and restraining the joy of life that beamed from his face, he went up to the commode.

"Gerasim!" said Ivan Ilych in a weak voice.

Gerasim started, evidently afraid he might have committed some blunder, and with a rapid movement turned his fresh, kind, simple young face which just showed the first downy signs of a beard.

"Yes, sir?"

"That must be very unpleasant for you. You must forgive me. I am helpless."

"Oh, why, sir," and Gerasim's eyes beamed and he showed his glistening white teeth, "what's a little trouble? It's a case of illness with you, sir."

And his deft strong hands did their accustomed task, and he went out of the room stepping lightly. Five minutes later he as lightly returned.

Ivan Ilych was still sitting in the same position in the armchair.

"Gerasim," he said when the latter had replaced the freshly-washed utensil. "Please come here and help me." Gerasim went up to him. "Lift me up. It is hard for me to get up, and I have sent Dmitri away."

Gerasim went up to him, grasped his master with his strong arms deftly but gently, in the same way that he stepped—lifted him, supported him with one hand, and with the other drew up his trousers and would have set him down again, but Ivan Ilych asked to be led to the sofa. Gerasim, without an effort and without apparent pressure, led him, almost lifting him, to the sofa and placed him on it.

"Thank you. How easily and well you do it all!"

Gerasim smiled again and turned to leave the room. But Ivan Ilych felt his presence such a comfort that he did not want to let him go.

"One thing more, please move up that chair. No, the other one—under my feet. It is easier for me when my feet are raised."

Gerasim brought the chair, set it down gently in place, and raised Ivan Ilych's legs on to it. It seemed to Ivan Ilych that he felt better while Gerasim was holding up his legs.

"It's better when my legs are higher," he said. "Place that cushion under them."

Gerasim did so. He again lifted the legs and placed them, and again Ivan Ilych felt better while Gerasim held his legs. When he set them down Ivan Ilych fancied he felt worse.

"Gerasim," he said. "Are you busy now?"

"Not at all, sir," said Gerasim, who had learnt from the townsfolk how to speak to gentlefolk.

"What have you still to do?"

"What have I to do? I've done everything except chopping the logs for tomorrow."

"Then hold my legs up a bit higher, can you?"

"Of course I can. Why not?" And Gerasim raised his master's legs higher and Ivan Ilych thought that in that position he did not feel any pain at all.

"And how about the logs?"

"Don't trouble about that, sir. There's plenty of time."

Ivan Ilych told Gerasim to sit down and hold his legs, and began to talk to him. And strange to say it seemed to him that he felt better while Gerasim held his legs up.

After that Ivan Ilych would sometimes call Gerasim and get him to hold his legs on his shoulders, and he liked talking to him. Gerasim did it all easily, willingly, simply, and with a good nature that touched Ivan Ilych. Health, strength, and vitality in other people were offensive to him, but Gerasim's strength and vitality did not mortify but soothed him.

What tormented Ivan Ilych most was the deception, the lie, which for some reason they all accepted, that he was not dying but was simply ill, and that he only need keep quiet and undergo a treatment and then something very good would result. He however knew that do what they would nothing would come of it, only still more agonizing suffering and death. This deception tortured him—their not wishing to admit what they all knew and what he knew, but wanting to lie to him concerning his terrible condition, and wishing and forcing him to participate in that lie. Those lies—lies enacted over him on the eve of his death and destined to degrade this awful, solemn act to the level of their visitings, their curtains, their sturgeon for dinner—were a terrible agony for Ivan Ilych. And strangely enough, many times when they were going through their antics over him he had been within a hairbreadth of calling out to them: "Stop lying! You know and I know that I am dying. Then at least stop lying about it!" But he had never had the spirit to do it. The awful, terrible act of his dying was, he could see, reduced by those about him to the level of a casual, unpleasant, and almost indecorous incident (as if someone entered a drawing-room diffusing an unpleasant odor) and this was done by that very decorum which he had served all his life long. He saw that no one felt for him, because no one even wished to grasp his position. Only Gerasim recognized it and pitied him. And so Ivan Ilych felt at ease only with him. He felt comforted when Gerasim supported his legs (sometimes all night long) and refused to go to bed, saying: "Don't you worry, Ivan Ilych. I'll get sleep enough later on," or when he suddenly became familiar and exclaimed: "If you weren't sick it would be another matter, but as it is, why should I grudge a little trouble?" Gerasim alone did not lie; everything showed that he alone understood the facts of the case and did not consider it necessary to disguise them, but simply felt sorry for his emaciated and enfeebled master. Once when Ivan Ilych was sending him away he even said straight out: "We shall all of us die, so why should I grudge a little trouble?"—expressing the fact that he did not think his work burdensome, because he was doing it for a dying man and hoped someone would do the same for him when his time came.

Apart from this lying, or because of it, what most tormented Ivan Ilych was that no one pitied him as he wished to be pitied. At certain moments after prolonged suffering he wished most of all (though he would have been ashamed to confess it) for someone to pity him as a sick child is pitied. He longed to be petted and comforted. He knew he was an important functionary, that he had a beard turning grey, and that therefore what he longed for was impossible, but still he longed for it. And in Gerasim's attitude towards him there was something akin to what he wished for, and so that attitude comforted him. Ivan Ilych wanted to weep, wanted to be petted and cried over, and then his colleague Shebek would come, and instead of weeping and being petted, Ivan Ilych would assume a serious, severe, and profound air, and by force of habit would express his opinion on a decision of the Court of Cassation and would stubbornly insist on that view. This falsity around him and within him did more than anything else to poison his last days.

VIII

It was morning. He knew it was morning because Gerasim had gone, and Peter the footman had come and put out the candles, drawn back one of the curtains, and begun quietly to tidy up. Whether it was morning or evening, Friday or Sunday, made no difference, it was all just the same: the gnawing, unmitigated, agonizing pain, never ceasing for an instant the consciousness of life inexorably waning but not yet extinguished, the approach of that ever dreaded and hateful Death which was the only reality, and always the same falsity. What were days, weeks, hours, in such a case?

"Will you have some tea, sir?"

"He wants things to be regular, and wishes the gentlefolk to drink tea in the morning," thought Ivan Ilych, and only said "No."

"Wouldn't you like to move onto the sofa, sir?"

"He wants to tidy up the room, and I'm in the way. I am uncleanliness and disorder," he thought, and said only:

"No, leave me alone."

The man went on bustling about. Ivan Ilych stretched out his hand. Peter came up, ready to help.

"What is it, sir?"

"My watch."

Peter took the watch which was close at hand and gave it to his master.

"Half-past eight. Are they up?"

"No, sir, except Vasily Ivanich" (the son) "who has gone to school.

Praskovya Fëdorovna ordered me to wake her if you asked for her. Shall I do so?"

"No, there's no need to." "Perhaps I'd better have some tea," he thought, and added aloud: "Yes, bring me some tea."

Peter went to the door, but Ivan Ilych dreaded being left alone. "How can I keep him here? Oh yes, my medicine." "Peter, give me my medicine." "Why not? Perhaps it may still do me some good." He took a spoonful and swallowed it. "No, it won't help. It's all tomfoolery, all deception," he decided as soon as he became aware of the familiar, sickly, hopeless taste. "No, I can't believe in it any longer. But the pain, why this pain? If it would only cease just for a moment!" and he moaned. Peter turned towards him. "It's all right. Go and fetch me some tea."

Peter went out. Left alone Ivan Ilych groaned not so much with pain, terrible though that was, as from mental anguish. Always and for ever the same, always these endless days and nights. If only it would come quicker! If only *what* would come quicker? Death, darkness? . . . No, no! Anything rather than death!

When Peter returned with the tea on a tray, Ivan Ilych stared at him for a time in perplexity, not realizing who and what he was. Peter was disconcerted by that look and his embarrassment brought Ivan Ilych to himself.

"Oh, tea! All right, put it down. Only help me to wash and put on a clean shirt."

And Ivan Ilych began to wash. With pauses for rest, he washed his hands and then his face, cleaned his teeth, brushed his hair, and looked in the glass. He was terrified by what he saw, expecially by the limp way in which his hair clung to his pallid forehead.

While his shirt was being changed he knew that he would be still more frightened at the sight of his body, so he avoided looking at it. Finally he was ready. He drew on a dressing-gown, wrapped himself in a plaid, and sat down in the armchair to take his tea. For a moment he felt refreshed, but as soon as he began to drink the tea he was again aware of the same taste, and the pain also returned. He finished it with an effort, and then lay down stretching out his legs, and dismissed Peter.

Always the same. Now a spark of hope flashes up, then a sea of despair rages, and always pain; always pain, always despair, and always the same. When alone he had a dreadful and distressing desire to call someone, but he knew beforehand that with others present it would be still worse. "Another dose of morphine—to lose consciousness. I will tell him, the doctor, that he must think of something else. It's impossible, impossible, to go on like this."

An hour and another pass like that. But now there is a ring at the door bell. Perhaps it's the doctor? It is. He comes in fresh, hearty, plump, and cheerful, with that look on his face that seems to say: "There now, you're in a panic about something, but we'll arrange it all for you directly!" The doctor knows this expression is out of place here, but he has put it on once for all and can't take it off—like a man who has put on a frock-coat in the morning to pay a round of calls.

The doctor rubs his hands vigorously and reassuringly.

"Brr! How cold it is! There's such a sharp frost; just let me warm myself!" he says, as if it were only a matter of waiting till he was warm, and then he would put everything right.

"Well now, how are you?"

Ivan Ilych feels that the doctor would like to say: "Well, how are our affairs?" but that even he feels that this would not do, and says instead: "What sort of a night have you had?"

Ivan Ilych looks at him as much as to say: "Are you really never ashamed of lying?" But the doctor does not wish to understand this question, and Ivan Ilych says: "Just as terrible as ever. The pain never leaves me and never subsides. If only something . . ."

"Yes, you sick people are always like that . . . There, now I think I am warm enough. Even Praskovya Fëdorovna, who is so particular, could find no fault with my temperature. Well, now I can say good-morning," and the doctor presses his patient's hand.

Then, dropping his former playfulness, he begins with a most serious face to examine the patient, feeling his pulse and taking his temperature, and then begins the sounding and auscultation.

Ivan Ilych knows quite well and definitely that all this is nonsense and pure deception, but when the doctor, getting down on his knee, leans over him, putting his ear first higher then lower, and performs various gymnastic movements over him with a significant expression on his face. Ivan Ilych submits to it all as he used to submit to the speeches of the lawyers, though he knew very well that they were all lying and why they were lying.

The doctor, kneeling on the sofa, is still sounding him when Praskovya Fëdorovna's silk dress rustles at the door and she is heard scolding Peter for not having let her know of the doctor's arrival.

She comes in, kisses her husband, and at once proceeds to prove that she has been up a long time already, and only owing to a misunderstanding failed to be there when the doctor arrived.

Ivan Ilych looks at her, scans her all over, sets against her the whiteness and plumpness and cleanness of her hands and neck, the gloss of her hair, and the sparkle of her vivacious eyes. He hates her with his whole soul. And the thrill of hatred he feels for her makes him suffer from her touch.

Her attitude towards him and his disease is still the same. Just as the doctor had adopted a certain relation to his patient which he could not abandon, so had she formed one towards him—that he was not doing something he ought to do and was himself to blame, and that she reproached him lovingly for this—and she could not now change that attitude.

"You see he doesn't listen to me and doesn't take his medicine at the proper time. And above all he lies in a position that is no doubt bad for him—with his legs up."

She described how he made Gerasim hold his legs up.

The doctor smiled with a contemptuous affability that said: "What's to be done? These sick people do have foolish fancies of that kind, but we must forgive them."

When the examination was over the doctor looked at his watch, and then Praskovya Fëdorovna announced to Ivan Ilych that it was of course as he pleased, but she had sent today for a celebrated specialist who would examine him and have a consultation with Michael Danilovich (their regular doctor).

"Please don't raise any objections. I am doing this for my own sake," she said ironically, letting it be felt that she was doing it all for his sake and only said this to leave him no right to refuse. He remained silent, knitting his brows. He felt that he was so surrounded and involved in a mesh of falsity that it was hard to unravel anything.

Everything she did for him was entirely for her own sake, and she told him she was doing for herself what she actually was doing for herself, as if that was so incredible that he must understand the opposite.

At half-past eleven the celebrated specialist arrived. Again the sounding began and the significant conversations in his presence and in another room, about the kidneys and the appendix, and the questions and answers, with such an air of importance that again, instead of the real question of life and death which now alone confronted him, the question arose of the kidney and appendix which were not behaving as they ought to and would now be attacked by Michael Danilovich and the specialist and forced to amend their ways.

The celebrated specialist took leave of him with a serious though not hopeless look, and in reply to the timid question Ivan Ilych, with eyes glistening with fear and hope, put to him as to whether there was a chance of recovery, said that he could not vouch for it but there was a possibility. The look of hope with which Ivan Ilych watched the doctor out was so pathetic that Praskovya Fëdorovna, seeing it, even wept as she left the room to hand the doctor his fee.

The gleam of hope kindled by the doctor's encouragement did not last long. The same room, the same pictures, curtains, wallpaper, medicine bottles, were all there, and the same aching suffering body, and Ivan Ilych began to moan. They gave him a subcutaneous injection and he sank into oblivion.

It was twilight when he came to. They brought him his dinner and he swallowed some beef tea with difficulty, and then everything was the same again and night was coming on.

After dinner, at seven o'clock, Praskovya Fëdorovna came into the room in evening dress, her full bosom pushed up by her corset, and with traces of powder on her face. She had reminded him in the morning that they were going to the theater. Sarah Bernhardt was visiting the town and they had a box, which he had insisted on their taking. Now he had forgotten about it and her toilet offended him, but he concealed his vexation when he remembered that he had himself insisted on their securing a box and going because it would be an instructive and aesthetic pleasure for the children.

Praskovya Fëdorovna came in, self-satisfied but yet with a rather guilty air. She sat down and asked how he was, but as he saw, only for the sake of asking and not in order to learn about it, knowing that there was nothing to learn—and then went on to what she really wanted to say: that she would not on any account have gone but that the box had been taken and Helen and their daughter were going, as well as Petrishchev (the examining magistrate, their daughter's fiancé) and that it was out of the question to let them go alone; but that she would have much preferred to sit with him for a while; and he must be sure to follow the doctor's orders while she was away.

"Oh, and Fëdor Petrovich" (the fiancé) "would like to come in. May he? And Lisa?"

"All right."

Their daughter came in in full evening dress, her fresh young flesh exposed (making a show of that very flesh which in his own case caused so much suffering), strong, healthy, evidently in love, and impatient with illness, suffering, and death, because they interfered with her happiness.

Fëdor Petrovich came in too, in evening dress, his hair curled *á la Capoul*,[12] a tight stiff collar round his long sinewy neck, an enormous white shirt-front and narrow black trousers tightly stretched over his strong thighs. He had one white glove tightly drawn on, and was holding his opera hat in his hand.

Following him the schoolboy crept in unnoticed, in a new uniform, poor little fellow, and wearing gloves. Terribly dark shadows showed under his eyes, the meaning of which Ivan Ilych knew well.

His son had always seemed pathetic to him, and now it was dreadful to see the boy's frightened look of pity. It seemed to Ivan Ilych that Vasya was the only one besides Gerasim who understood and pitied him.

They all sat down and again asked how he was. A silence followed. Lisa asked her mother about the opera-glasses, and there was an altercation between mother and daughter as to who had taken them and where they had been put. This occasioned some unpleasantness.

Fëdor Petrovich inquired of Ivan Ilych whether he had ever seen Sarah Bernhardt. Ivan Ilych did not at first catch the question, but then replied: "No, have you seen her before?"

"Yes, in *Adrienne Lecouvreur*.[13]

Praskovya Fëdorovna mentioned some rôles in which Sarah Bernhardt was particularly good. Her daughter disagreed. Conversation sprang up as to the elegance and realism of her acting—the sort of conversation that is always repeated and is always the same.

12. An elaborate hair styling for men. Capoul was a famous French singer.
13. Comedy by French playwrights Eugène Scribe and Ernest Legouvé.

In the midst of the conversation Fёdor Petrovich glanced at Ivan Ilych and became silent. The others also looked at him and grew silent. Ivan Ilych was staring with glittering eyes straight before him, evidently indignant with them. This had to be rectified, but it was impossible to do so. The silence had to be broken, but for a time no one dared to break it and they all became afraid that the conventional deception would suddenly become obvious and the truth become plain to all. Lisa was the first to pluck up courage and break that silence, but by trying to hide what everybody was feeling, she betrayed it.

"Well, if we are going it's time to start," she said, looking at her watch, a present from her father, and with a faint and significant smile at Fёdor Petrovich relating to something known only to them. She got up with a rustle of her dress.

They all rose, said good-night, and went away.

When they had gone it seemed to Ivan Ilych that he felt better; the falsity had gone with them. But the pain remained—that same pain and that same fear that made everything monotonously alike, nothing harder and nothing easier. Everything was worse.

Again minute followed minute and hour followed hour. Everything remained the same and there was no cessation. And the inevitable end of it all became more and more terrible.

"Yes, send Gerasim here," he replied to a question Peter asked.

IX

His wife returned late at night. She came in on tiptoe, but he heard her, opened his eyes, and made haste to close them again. She wished to send Gerasim away and to sit with him herself, but he opened his eyes and said: "No, go away."

"Are you in great pain?"

"Always the same."

"Take some opium."

He agreed and took some. She went away.

Till about three in the morning he was in a state of stupefied misery. It seemed to him that he and his pain were being thrust into a narrow, deep black sack, but though they were pushed further and further in they could not be pushed to the bottom. And this, terrible enough in itself, was accompanied by suffering. He was frightened yet wanted to fall through the sack, he struggled but yet co-operated. And suddenly he broke through, fell, and regained consciousness. Gerasim was sitting at the foot of the bed dozing quietly and patiently, while he himself lay with his emaciated stockinged legs resting on Gerasim's shoulders; the same shaded candle was there and the same unceasing pain.

"Go away, Gerasim," he whispered.

"It's all right, sir. I'll stay a while."

"No. Go away."

He removed his legs from Gerasim's shoulders, turned sideways onto his arm, and felt sorry for himself. He only waited till Gerasim had gone into the next room and then restrained himself no longer but wept like a child. He wept on account of his helplessness, his terrible loneliness, the cruelty of man, the cruelty of God, and the absence of God.

"Why hast Thou done all this? Why hast Thou brought me here? Why, why dost Thou torment me so terribly?"

He did not expect an answer and yet wept because there was no answer and could be none. The pain again grew more acute, but he did not stir and did not call. He said to himself: "Go on! Strike me! But what is it for? What have I done to Thee? What is it for?"

Then he grew quiet and not only ceased weeping but even held his breath and became all attention. It was as though he were listening not to an audible voice but to the voice of his soul, to the current of thoughts arising within him.

"What is it you want?" was the first clear conception capable of expression in words, that he heard.

"What do you want? What do you want?" he repeated to himself.

"What do I want? To live and not to suffer," he answered.

And again he listened with such concentrated attention that even his pain did not distract him.

"To live? How?" asked his inner voice.

"Why, to live as I used to—well and pleasantly."

"As you lived before, well and pleasantly?" the voice repeated.

And in imagination he began to recall the best moments of his pleasant life. But strange to say none of those best moments of his pleasant life now seemed at all what they had then seemed—none of them except the first recollections of childhood. There, in childhood, there had been something really pleasant with which it would be possible to live if it could return. But the child who had experienced that happiness existed no longer, it was like a reminiscence of somebody else.

As soon as the period began which had produced the present Ivan Ilych, all that had then seemed joys now melted before his sight and turned into something trivial and often nasty.

And the further he departed from childhood and the nearer he came to the present the more worthless and doubtful were the joys. This began with the School of Law. A little that was really good was still found there—there was light-heartedness, friendship, and hope. But in the upper classes there had already been fewer of such good moments. Then during the first years of his official career, when he was in the service of the Governor, some pleasant moments again occurred: they were the memories of love for a woman. Then all became confused and there was still less of what was good; later on again there was still less that was good, and the further he went the less there was. His marriage, a mere accident, then the disenchantment that followed it, his wife's bad breath and the sensuality and hypocrisy: then the deadly official life and those preoccupations about money, a year of it, and two, and ten, and twenty, and always the same thing. And the longer it lasted the more deadly it became. "It is as if I had been going downhill while I imagined I was going up. And that is really what it was. I was going up in public opinion, but to the same extent life was ebbing away from me. And now it is all done and there is only death."

"Then what does it mean? Why? It can't be that life is so senseless and horrible. But if it really has been so horrible and senseless, why must I die and die in agony? There is something wrong!"

"Maybe I did not live as I ought to have done," it suddenly occurred to him."But how could that be, when I did everything properly?" he replied, and immediately dismissed from his mind this, the sole solution of all the riddles of life and death, as something quite impossible.

"Then what do you want now? To live? Live how? Live as you lived in the law courts when the usher proclaimed 'The judge is coming!' The judge is coming, the judge!" he repeated to himself. "Here he is, the judge. But I am not guilty!" he exclaimed angrily. "What is it for?" And he ceased crying, but turning his face to the wall continued to ponder on the same question: Why, and for what purpose, is there all this horror? But however much he pondered he found no answer. And whenever the thought occurred to him, as it often did, that it all resulted from his not having lived as he ought to have done, he at once recalled the correctness of his whole life and dismissed so strange an idea.

X

Another fortnight passed. Ivan Ilych now no longer left his sofa. He would not lie in bed but lay on the sofa, facing the wall nearly all the time. He suffered ever the same unceasing agonies and in his loneliness pondered always on the same insoluble question: "What is this? Can it be that it is Death?" And the inner voice answered: "Yes, it is Death."

"Why these sufferings? And the voice answered, "For no reason—they just are so." Beyond and besides this there was nothing.

From the very beginning of his illness, ever since he had first been to see the doctor, Ivan Ilych's life had been divided between two contrary and alternating moods: now it was despair and the expectation of this uncomprehended and terrible death, and now hope and an intently interested observation of the functioning of his organs. Now before his eyes there was only a kidney or an intestine that temporarily evaded its duty, and now only that incomprehensible and dreadful death from which it was impossible to escape.

These two states of mind had alternated from the very beginning of his illness, but the further it progressed the more doubtful and fantastic became the conception of the kidney, and the more real the sense of impending death.

He had but to call to mind what he had been three months before and what he was now, to call to mind with what regularity he had been going downhill, for every possibility of hope to be shattered.

Latterly during that loneliness in which he found himself as he lay facing the back of the sofa, a loneliness in the midst of a populous town and surrounded by numerous acquaintances and relations but that yet could not have been more complete anywhere—either at the bottom of the sea or under the earth—during that terrible loneliness Ivan Ilych had lived only in memories of the past. Pictures of his past rose before him one after another. They always began with what was nearest in time and then went back to what was most remote—to his childhood—and rested there. If he thought of the stewed prunes that had been offered him that day, his mind went back to the raw shrivelled French plums of his childhood, their peculiar flavor and the flow of saliva when he sucked their stones, and along with the memory of that taste came a whole series of memories of those days: his nurse, his brother, and their toys. "No, I mustn't think of that . . . It is too painful," Ivan Ilych said to himself, and brought himself back to the present—to the button on the back of the sofa and the creases in its morocco. "Morocco is expensive, but it does not wear well: there had been a quarrel about it. It was a different kind of quarrel and a different kind of morocco that time when we tore father's portfolio and were punished, and mama brought us some tarts . . ." And again his thoughts dwelt on his childhood, and again it was painful and he tried to banish them and fix his mind on something else.

Then again together with that chain of memories another series passed through his mind—of how his illness had progressed and grown worse. There also the further back he looked the more life there had been. There had been more of what was good in life and more of life itself. The two merged together. "Just as the pain went on getting worse and worse, so my life grew worse and worse," he thought. "There is one bright spot there at the back, at the beginning of life, and afterwards all becomes blacker and blacker and proceeds more and more rapidly—in inverse ratio to the square of the distance from death," thought Ivan Ilych. And the example of a stone falling downwards with increasing velocity entered his mind. Life, a series of increasing sufferings, flies further and further towards its end—the most terrible suffering. "I am flying . . ." He shuddered, shifted himself, and tried to resist, but was already aware that resistance was impossible, and again with eyes weary of gazing but unable to cease seeing what was before them, he stared at the back of sofa and waited—awaiting that dreadful fall and shock and destruction.

"Resistance is impossible!" he said to himself. "If I could only understand what it is all for! But that too is impossible. An explanation would be possible if it could be said that I have not lived as I ought to. But it is impossible to say that," and he remembered all the legality, correctitude, and propriety of his life. "That at any rate can certainly not be admitted," he thought, and his lips smiled ironically as if someone could see that smile and be taken in by it. "There is no explanation! Agony, death . . . What for?"

XI

Another two weeks went by in this way and during that fortnight an event occurred that Ivan Ilych and his wife had desired. Petrishchev formally proposed. It happened in the evening. The next day Praskovya Fëdorovna came into her husband's room considering how best to inform him of it, but that very night there had been a fresh change for the worse in his condition. She found him still lying on the sofa but in a different position. He lay on his back, groaning and staring fixedly straight in front of him.

She began to remind him of his medicines, but he turned his eyes towards her with such a look that she did not finish what she was saying; so great an animosity, to her in particular, did that look express.

"For Christ's sake let me die in peace!" he said.

She would have gone away, but just then their daughter came in and went up to say good morning. He looked at her as he had done at his wife, and in reply to her inquiry about his health said dryly that he would soon free them all of himself. They were both silent and after sitting with him for a while went away.

"Is it our fault?" Lisa said to her mother. "It's as if we were to blame! I am sorry for Papa, but why should we be tortured?"

The doctor came at his usual time. Ivan Ilych answered "Yes" and "No," never taking his angry eyes from him, and at last said: "You know you can do nothing for me, so leave me alone."

"We can ease your sufferings."

"You can't even do that. Let me be."

The doctor went into the drawing-room and told Praskovya Fëdorovna that the case was very serious and that the only resource left was opium to allay her husband's sufferings, which must be terrible.

It was true, as the doctor said, that Ivan Ilych's physical sufferings were terrible, but worse that the physical sufferings were his mental sufferings, which were his chief torture.

His mental sufferings were due to the fact that that night, as he looked at Gerasim's sleepy, good-natured face with its prominent cheek-bones, the question suddenly occurred to him: "What if my whole life has really been wrong?"

It occurred to him that what had appeared perfectly impossible before, namely that he had not spent his life as he should have done, might after all be true. It occurred to him that his scarcely perceptible attempts to struggle against what was considered good by the most highly placed people, those scarcely noticeable impulses which he had immediately suppressed, might have been the real thing, and all the rest false. And his professional duties and the whole arrangement of his life and of his family, and all his social and official interest, might all have been false. He tried to defend all those things to himself and suddenly felt the weakness of what he was defending. There was nothing to defend.

"But if that is so," he said to himself, "and I am leaving this life with the consciousness that I have lost all that was given me and it is impossible to rectify it—what then?"

He lay on his back and began to pass his life in review in quite a new way. In the morning when he saw first his footman, then his wife, then his daughter, and then the doctor, their every word and movement confirmed to him the awful truth that had been revealed to him during the night. In them he saw himself—all that for which he had lived—and saw clearly that it was not real at all, but a terrible and huge deception which had hidden both life and death. This consciousness intensified his physical suffering tenfold. He groaned and tossed about, and pulled at his clothing which choked and stifled him. And he hated them on that account.

He was given a large dose of opium and became unconscious, but at noon his sufferings began again. He drove everybody away and tossed from side to side.

His wife came to him and said:

"Jean, my dear, do this for me. It can't do any harm and often helps. Healthy people often do it."

He opened his eyes wide.

"What? Take communion? Why? It's unnecessary! However. . . ."

She began to cry.

"Yes, do, my dear. I'll send for our priest. He is such a nice man."

"All right. Very well," he muttered.

When the priest came and heard his confession, Ivan Ilych was softened and seemed to feel a relief from his doubts and consequently from his sufferings, and for a moment there came a ray of hope. He again began to think of the vermiform appendix and the possibility of correcting it. He received the sacrament with tears in his eyes.

When they laid him down again afterwards he felt a moment's ease, and the hope that he might live awoke in him again. He began to think of the operation that had been suggested to him. "To live! I want to live!" he said to himself.

His wife came in to congratulate him after his communion, and when uttering the usual conventional words she added:

"You feel better, don't you?"

Without looking at her he said "Yes."

Her dress, her figure, the expression of her face, the tone of her voice, all revealed the same thing. "This is wrong, it is not as it should be. All you have lived for and still live for is falsehood and deception, hiding life and death from you." And as soon as he admitted that thought, his hatred and his agonizing physical suffering again sprang up, and with that suffering a consciousness of the unavoidable, approaching end. And to this was added a new sensation of grinding shooting pain and a feeling of suffocation.

The expression of his face when he uttered that "yes" was dreadful. Having uttered it, he looked her straight in the eyes, turned on his face with a rapidity extraordinary in his weak state and shouted:

"Go away! Go away and leave me alone!"

XII

From that moment the screaming began that continued for three days, and was so terrible that one could not hear it through two closed doors without horror. At the moment he answered his wife he realized that he was lost, that there was no return, that the end had come, the very end, and his doubts were still unsolved and remained doubts.

"Oh! Oh! Oh!" he cried in various intonations. He had begun by screaming "I won't!" and continued screaming on the letter *O*.

For three whole days, during which time did not exist for him, he struggled in that black sack into which he was being thrust by an invisible, resistless force. He struggled as a man condemned to death struggles in the hands of the executioner, knowing that he cannot save himself. And every moment he felt that despite all his efforts he was drawing nearer and nearer to what terrified him. He felt that his agony was due to his being thrust into that black hole and still more to his not being able to get right into it. He was hindered from getting into it by his conviction that his life had been a good one. That very justification of his life held him fast and prevented his moving forward, and it caused him most torment of all.

Suddenly some force struck him in the chest and side, making it still harder to breathe, and he fell through the hole and there at the bottom was a light. What had happened to him was like the sensation one sometimes experiences in a railway carriage when one thinks one is going backwards while one is really going forwards and suddenly becomes aware of the real direction.

"Yes, it was all not the right thing," he said to himself, "but that's no matter. It can be done. But what *is* the right thing?" he asked himself, and suddenly grew quiet.

This occurred at the end of the third day, two hours before his death. Just then his schoolboy son had crept softly in and gone up to the bedside. The dying man was still screaming desperately and waving his arms. His hand fell on the boy's head, and the boy caught it, pressed it to his lips, and began to cry.

At that very moment Ivan Ilych fell through and caught sight of the light, and it was revealed to him that though his life had not been what it should have been, this could still be rectified. He asked himself, "What *is* the right thing?" and grew still, listening. Then he felt that someone was kissing his hand. He opened his eyes, looked at his son, and felt sorry for him. His wife came up to him and he glanced at her. She was gazing at him open-mouthed, with undried tears on her nose and cheek and a despairing look on her face. He felt sorry for her too.

"Yes, I am making them wretched," he thought. "They are sorry, but it will be better for them when I die." He wished to say this but had not the strength to utter it. "Besides, why speak? I must act," he thought. With a look at his wife he indicated his son and said: "Take him away . . . sorry for him . . . sorry for you too. . . ." He tried to add, "forgive me," but said "forgo" and waved his hand, knowing that He whose understanding mattered would understand.

And suddenly it grew clear to him that what had been oppressing him and would not leave him was all dropping away at once from two sides, from ten sides, and from all sides. He was sorry for them, he must act so as not to hurt them: release them and free himself from these sufferings. "How good and how simple!" he thought. "And the pain?" he asked himself. "What has become of it? Where are you, pain?"

He turned his attention to it.

"Yes, here it is. Well, what of it? Let the pain be."

"And death . . . where is it?"

He sought his former accustomed fear of death and did not find it. "Where is it? What death?" There was no fear because there was no death.

In place of death there was light.

"So that's what it is!" he suddenly exclaimed aloud. "What joy!"

To him all this happened in a single instant, and the meaning of that instant did not change. For those present his agony continued for another two hours. Something rattled in his throat, his emaciated body twitched, then the gasping and rattle became less and less frequent.

"It is finished!" said someone near him.

He heard these words and repeated them in his soul.

"Death is finished," he said to himself. "It is no more!"

He drew in a breath, stopped in the midst of a sigh, stretched out, and died.

Translated by Louise and Aylmer Maude

ALICE WALKER (b. 1944)

Everyday Use

Alice Walker, born in Georgia, has written novels, short stories, and poetry. Her novels include *The Third Life of Grange Copeland* (1970) and *The Color Purple* (1982), which was awarded the Pulitzer Prize for Fiction. "Everyday Use" is taken from *In Love and Trouble: Stories of Black Women* (1973).

for your grandmama

I will wait for her in the yard that Maggie and I made so clean and wavy yesterday afternoon. A yard like this is more comfortable than most people know. It is not just a yard. It is like an extended living room. When the hard clay is swept clean as a floor and the fine sand around the edges lined with tiny, irregular grooves, anyone can come and sit and look up into the elm tree and wait for the breezes that never come inside the house.

Maggie will be nervous until after her sister goes: she will stand hopelessly in corners, homely and ashamed of the burn scars down her arms and legs, eying her sister with a mixture of envy and awe. She thinks her sister has held life always in the palm of one hand, that "no" is a word the world never learned to say to her.

You've no doubt seen those TV shows where the child who has "made it" is confronted, as a surprise, by her own mother and father, tottering in weakly from backstage. (A pleasant surprise, of course: What would they do if parent and child came on the show only to curse out and insult each other?) On TV mother and child embrace and smile into each other's faces. Sometimes the mother and father weep, the child wraps them in her arms and leans across the table to tell how she would not have made it without their help. I have seen these programs.

Sometimes I dream a dream in which Dee and I are suddenly brought together on a TV program of this sort. Out of a dark and soft-seated limousine I am ushered into a bright room filled with many people. There I meet a smiling, gray, sporty man like Johnny Carson who shakes my hand and tells me what a fine girl I have. Then we are on the stage and Dee is embracing me with tears in her eyes. She pins on my dress a large orchid, even though she has told me once that she thinks orchids are tacky flowers.

In real life I am a large, big-boned woman with rough, man-working hands. In the winter I wear flannel nightgowns to bed and overalls during the day. I can kill and clean a hog as mercilessly as a man. My fat keeps me hot in zero weather. I can work outside all day, breaking ice to get water for washing; I can eat pork liver cooked over the open fire minutes after it comes steaming from the hog. One winter I knocked a bull calf straight in the brain between the eyes with a sledge hammer and had the meat hung up to chill before nightfall. But of course all this does not show on television. I am the way my daughter would want me to be: a hundred pounds lighter, my skin like an uncooked barley pancake. My hair glistens in the hot bright lights. Johnny Carson has much to do to keep up with my quick and witty tongue.

But that is a mistake. I know even before I wake up. Who ever knew a Johnson with a quick tongue? Who can even imagine me looking a strange white man in the eye? It seems to me I have talked to them always with one foot raised in flight, with my head turned in whichever way is farthest from them. Dee, though. She would always look anyone in the eye. Hesitation was no part of her nature.

"How do I look, Mama?" Maggie says, showing just enough of her thin body enveloped in pink skirt and red blouse for me to know she's there, almost hidden by the door.

"Come out into the yard," I say.

Have you ever seen a lame animal, perhaps a dog run over by some careless person rich enough to own a car, sidle up to someone who is ignorant enough to be kind to him? That is the way my Maggie walks. She has been like this, chin on chest, eyes on ground, feet in shuffle, ever since the fire that burned the other house to the ground.

Dee is lighter than Maggie, with nicer hair and a fuller figure. She's a woman now, though sometimes I forget. How long ago was it that the other house burned? ten, twelve years? Sometimes I can still hear the flames and feel Maggie's arms sticking to me, her hair smoking and her dress falling off her in little black papery flakes. Her eyes seemed stretched open, blazed open by the flames reflected in them. And Dee. I see her standing off under the sweet gum tree she used to dig gum out of; a look of concentration on her face as she watched the last dingy gray board of the house fall in toward the red-hot brick chimney. Why don't you do a dance around the ashes? I'd wanted to ask her. She had hated the house that much.

I used to think she hated Maggie, too. But that was before we raised the money, the church and me, to send her to Augusta to school. She used to read to us without pity; forcing words, lies, other folks' habits, whole lives upon us two, sitting trapped and ignorant underneath her voice. She washed us in a river of make-believe, burned us with a lot of knowledge we didn't necessarily need to know. Pressed us to her with the serious way she read, to shove us away at just the moment, like dimwits, we seemed about to understand.

Dee wanted nice things. A yellow organdy dress to wear to her graduation from high school; black pumps to match a green suit she'd made from an old suit somebody gave me. She was determined to stare down any disaster in her efforts. Her eyelids would not flicker for minutes at a time. Often I fought off the temptation to shake her. At sixteen she had a style of her own: and knew what style was.

I never had an education myself. After second grade the school was closed down. Don't ask my why: in 1927 colored asked fewer questions than they do now. Sometimes Maggie reads to me. She stumbles along good-naturedly but can't see well. She knows she is not bright. Like good looks and money, quickness passed her by. She will marry John Thomas (who has mossy teeth in an earnest face) and then I'll be free to sit here and I guess just sing church songs to myself. Although I never was a good singer. Never could carry a tune. I was always better at a man's job. I used to love to milk till I was hooked in the side in '49. Cows are soothing and slow and don't bother you, unless you try to milk them the wrong way.

I have deliberately turned my back on the house. It is three rooms, just like the one that burned, except the roof is tin; they don't make shingle roofs any more. There are no real windows, just some holes cut in the sides, like the portholes in a ship, but not round and not square, with rawhide holding the shutters up on the outside. This house is in a pasture, too, like the other one. No doubt when Dee sees it she will want to tear it down. She wrote me once that no matter where we "choose" to live, she will manage to come see us. But she will never bring her friends. Maggie and I thought about this and Maggie asked me, "Mama, when did Dee ever *have* any friends?"

She had a few. Furtive boys in pink shirts hanging about on washday after school. Nervous girls who never laughed. Impressed with her they worshiped the well-turned phrase, the cute shape, the scalding humor that erupted like bubbles in lye. She read to them.

When she was courting Jimmy T she didn't have much time to pay to us, but turned all her faultfinding power on him. He *flew* to marry a cheap city girl from a family of ignorant flashy people. She hardly had time to recompose herself.

When she comes I will meet—but there they are!

Maggie attempts to make a dash for the house, in her shuffling way, but I stay her with my hand. "Come back here," I say. And she stops and tries to dig a well in the sand with her toe.

It is hard to see them clearly through the strong sun. But even the first glimpse of leg out of the car tells me it is Dee. Her feet were always neat-looking, as if God himself had shaped them with a certain style. From the other side of the car comes a short, stocky man. Hair is all over his head a foot long and hanging from his chin like a kinky mule tail. I hear Maggie suck in her breath. "Uhnnnh," is what it sounds like. Like when you see the wriggling end of a snake just in front of your foot on the road. "Uhnnnh."

Dee next. A dress down to the ground, in this hot weather. A dress so loud it hurts my eyes. There are yellows and oranges enough to throw back the light of the sun. I feel my whole face warming from the heat waves it throws out. Earrings gold, too, and hanging down to her shoulders. Bracelets dangling and making noises when she moves her arm up to shake the folds of the dress out of her armpits. The dress is loose and flows, and as she walks closer, I like it. I hear Maggie go "Uhnnnh" again. It is her sister's hair. It stands straight up like the wool on a sheep. It is black as night and around the edges are two long pigtails that rope about like small lizards disappearing behind her ears.

"Wa-su-zo-Tean-o!" she says, coming on in that gliding way the dress makes her move. The short stocky fellow with the hair to his navel is all grinning and he follows up with "Asalamalakim, my mother and sister!" He moves to hug Maggie but she falls back, right up against the back of my chair. I feel her trembling there and when I look up I see the perspiration falling off her chin.

"Don't get up," says Dee. Since I am stout it takes something of a push. You can see me trying to move a second or two before I make it. She turns, showing white heels through her sandals, and goes back to the car. Out she peeks next with a Polaroid. She stoops down quickly and lines up picture after picture of me sitting there in front of the house with Maggie cowering behind me. She never takes a shot without making sure the house is included. When a cow comes nibbling around the edge of the yard she snaps it and me and Maggie *and* the house. Then she puts the Polaroid in the back seat of the car, and comes up and kisses me on the forehead.

Meanwhile Asalamalakim is going through motions with Maggie's hand. Maggie's hand is as limp as a fish, and probably as cold, despite the sweat, and she keeps trying to pull it back. It looks like Asalamalakim wants to shake hands but wants to do it fancy. Or maybe he don't know how people shake hands. Anyhow, he soon gives up on Maggie.

"Well," I say. "Dee."

"No, Mama," she says. "Not 'Dee,' Wangero Leewanika Kemanjo!"

"What happened to 'Dee'?" I wanted to know.

"She's dead," Wangero said. "I couldn't bear it any longer being named after the people who oppress me."

"You know as well as me you was named after your aunt Dicie," I said. Dicie is my sister. She named Dee. We called her "Big Dee" after Dee was born.

"But who was *she* named after?" asked Wangero.

"I guess after Grandma Dee," I said.

"And who was she named after?" asked Wangero.

"Her mother," I said, and saw Wangero was getting tired. "That's about as far back as I can trace it," I said.

Though, in fact, I probably could have carried it back beyond the Civil War through the branches.

"Well," said Asalamalakim, "there you are."

"Uhnnnh," I heard Maggie say.

"There I was not," I said, "before 'Dicie' cropped up in our family, so why should I try to trace it that far back?"

He just stood there grinning, looking down on me like somebody inspecting a Model A car. Every once in a while he and Wangero sent eye signals over my head.

"How do you pronounce this name?" I asked.

"You don't have to call me by it if you don't want to," said Wangero.

"Why shouldn't I?" I asked. "If that's what you want us to call you, we'll call you."

"I know it might sound awkward at first," said Wangero.

"I'll get used to it," I said. "Ream it out again."

Well, soon we got the name out of the way. Asalamalakim had a name twice as long and three times as hard. After I tripped over it two or three times he told me to just call him Hakim-a-barber. I wanted to ask him was he a barber, but I didn't really think he was, so I didn't ask.

"You must belong to those beef-cattle peoples down the road," I said. They said "Asalamalakim" when they met you, too, but they didn't shake hands. Always too busy: feeding the cattle, fixing the fences, putting up salt-lick shelters, throwing down hay. When the white folks poisoned some of the herd the men stayed up all night with rifles in their hands. I walked a mile and a half just to see the sight.

Hakim-a-barber said, "I accept some of their doctrines, but farming and raising cattle is not my style." (They didn't tell me, and I didn't ask, whether Wangero (Dee) had really gone and married him.)

We sat down to eat and right away he said he didn't eat collards and pork was unclean. Wangero, though, went on through the chitlins and corn bread, the greens and everything else. She talked a blue streak over the sweet potatoes. Everything delighted her. Even the fact that we still used the benches her daddy made for the table when we couldn't afford to buy chairs.

"Oh, Mama!" she cried. Then turned to Hakim-a-barber. "I never knew how lovely these benches are. You can feel the rump prints," she said, running her hands underneath her and along the bench. Then she gave a sigh and her hand closed over Grandma Dee's butter dish. "That's it!" she said. "I knew there was something I wanted to ask you if I could have." She jumped up from the table and went over in the corner where the churn stood, the milk in it clabber by now. She looked at the churn and looked at it.

"This churn top is what I need," she said. "Didn't Uncle Buddy whittle it out of a tree you all used to have?"

"Yes," I said.

"Uh huh," she said happily. "And I want the dasher, too."

"Uncle Buddy whittle that, too?" asked the barber.

Dee (Wangero) looked up at me.

"Aunt Dee's first husband whittled the dash," said Maggie so low you almost couldn't hear her. "His name was Henry, but they called him Stash."

"Maggie's brain is like an elephant's," Wangero said, laughing. "I can use the churn top as a centerpiece for the alcove table," she said, sliding a plate over the churn, "and I'll think of something artistic to do with the dasher."

When she finished wrapping the dasher the handle stuck out. I took it for a moment in my hands. You didn't even have to look close to see where hands pushing the dasher up and down to make butter had left a kind of sink in the wood. In fact, there were a lot of small sinks; you could see where thumbs and fingers had sunk into the wood. It was beautiful light yellow wood, from a tree that grew in the yard where Big Dee and Stash had lived.

After dinner Dee (Wangero) went to the trunk at the foot of my bed and started rifling through it. Maggie hung back in the kitchen over the dishpan. Out came Wangero with two quilts. They had been pieced by Grandma Dee and then Big Dee and me had hung them on the quilt frames on the front porch and quilted them. One was in the Lone Star pattern. The other was Walk Around the Mountain. In both of them were scraps of dresses Grandma Dee had worn fifty and more years ago. Bits and pieces of Grandpa Jarrell's Paisley shirts. And one teeny faded blue piece, about the size of a penny matchbox, that was from Great Grandpa Ezra's uniform that he wore in the Civil War.

"Mama," Wangero said sweet as a bird. "Can I have these old quilts?"

I heard something fall in the kitchen, and a minute later the kitchen door slammed.

"Why don't you take one or two of the others?" I asked. "These old things was just done by me and Big Dee from some tops your grandma pieced before she died."

"No," said Wangero. "I don't want those. They are stitched around the borders by machine."

"That'll make them last better," I said.

"That's not the point," said Wangero. "These are all pieces of dresses Grandma used to wear. She did all this stitching by hand. Imagine!" She held the quilts securely in her arms, stroking them.

"Some of the pieces, like those lavender ones, come from old clothes her mother handed down to her," I said, moving up to touch the quilts. Dee (Wangero) moved back just enough so that I couldn't reach the quilts. They already belonged to her.

"Imagine!" she breathed again, clutching them closely to her bosom.

"The truth is," I said, "I promised to give them quilts to Maggie, for when she marries John Thomas."

She gasped like a bee had stung her.

"Maggie can't appreciate these quilts! she said. "She'd probably be backward enough to put them to everyday use."

"I reckon she would," I said. "God knows I been saving 'em for long enough with nobody using 'em. I hope she will!" I didn't want to bring up how I had offered Dee (Wangero) a quilt when she went away to college. Then she had told me they were old-fashioned, out of style.

"But they're *priceless!*" she was saying now, furiously; for she has a temper. "Maggie would put them on the bed and in five years they'd be in rags. Less than that!"

"She can always make some more," I said. "Maggie knows how to quilt."

Dee (Wangero) looked at me with hatred. "You just will not understand. The point is these quilts, *these* quilts!"

"Well," I said, stumped. "What would *you* do with them?"

"Hang them," she said. As if that was the only thing you *could* do with quilts.

Maggie by now was standing in the door. I could almost hear the sound her feet made as they scraped over each other.

"She can have them, Mama," she said, like somebody used to never winning anything, or having anything reserved for her. "I can 'member Grandma Dee without the quilts."

I looked at her hard. She had filled her bottom lip with checkerberry snuff and it gave her face a kind of dopey, hangdog look. It was Grandma Dee and Big Dee who taught her how to quilt herself. She stood there with her scarred hands hidden in the folds of her skirt. She looked at her sister with something like fear but she wasn't mad at her. This was Maggie's portion. This was the way she knew God to work.

When I looked at her like that something hit me in the top of my head and ran down to the soles of my feet. Just like when I'm in church and the spirit of God touches me and I get happy and shout. I did something I never had done before: hugged Maggie to me, then dragged her on into the room, snatched the quilts out of Miss Wangero's hands and dumped them into Maggie's lap. Maggie just sat there on my bed with her mouth open.

"Take one or two of the others," I said to Dee.

But she turned without a word and went out to Hakim-a-barber.

"You just don't understand," she said, as Maggie and I came out to the car.

"What don't I understand?" I wanted to know.

"Your heritage," she said. And then she turned to Maggie, kissed her, and said, "You ought to try to make something of yourself, too, Maggie. It's really a new day for us. But from the way you and Mama still live you'd never know it."

She put on some sunglasses that hid everything above the tip of her nose and her chin.

Maggie smiled; maybe at the sunglasses. But a real smile, not scared. After we watched the car dust settle I asked Maggie to bring me a dip of snuff. And then the two of us sat there just enjoying, until it was time to go in the house and go to bed.

EUDORA WELTY (b. 1909)

The Death of a Travelling Salesman

Eudora Welty, another of America's great southern writers of short fiction, was born in Jackson, Mississippi. Her first book of stories, *A Curtain of Green and Other Stories* appeared in 1941. She has also written novels, the most famous of which is *Delta Wedding* (1946). Her *Collected Stories*—which includes "The Death of a Travelling Salesman"—was published in 1980.

R. J. Bowman, who for fourteen years had traveled for a shoe company through Mississippi, drove his Ford along a rutted dirt path. It was a long day! The time did not seem to clear the noon hurdle and settle into soft afternoon. The sun, keeping its strength here even in winter, stayed at the top of the sky, and every time Bowman stuck his head out of the dusty car to stare up the road, it seemed to reach a long arm down and push against the top of his head, right through his hat—like the practical joke of an old drummer, long on the road. It made him feel all the more angry and helpless. He was feverish, and he was not quite sure of the way.

This was his first day back on the road after a long siege of influenza. He had had a very high fever, and dreams, and had become weakened and pale, enough to tell the difference in the mirror, and he could not think clearly . . . All afternoon, in the midst of his anger, and for no reason, he had thought of his dead grandmother. She had been a comfortable soul. Once more Bowman wished he could fall into the big feather bed that had been in her room . . . Then he forgot her again.

This desolate hill country! And he seemed to be going the wrong way— it was as if he were going back, far back. There was not a house in sight . . . There was no use wishing he were back in bed, though. By paying the hotel doctor his bill he had proved his recovery. He had not even been sorry when the pretty trained nurse said good-bye. He did not like illness, he distrusted it, as he distrusted the road without signposts. It angered him. He had given the nurse a really expensive bracelet, just because she was packing up her bag and leaving.

But now—what if in fourteen years on the road he had never been ill before and never had an accident? His record was broken, and he had even begun almost to question it . . . He had gradually put up at better hotels, in the bigger towns, but weren't they all, eternally, stuffy in summer and drafty in winter? Women? He could only remember little rooms within little rooms, like a nest of Chinese paper boxes, and if he thought of one woman he saw the worn loneliness that the furniture of that room seemed built of. And he himself—he was a man who always wore rather wide-brimmed black hats, and in the wavy hotel mirrors had looked something like a bull-fighter, as he paused for that inevitable instant on the landing, walking downstairs to supper . . . He leaned out of the car again, and once more the sun pushed at his head.

Bowman had wanted to reach Beulah by dark, to go to bed and sleep off his fatigue. As he remembered, Beulah was fifty miles away from the last town, on a graveled road. This was only a cow trail. How had he ever come to such a place? One hand wiped the sweat from his face, and he drove on.

He had made the Beulah trip before. But he had never seen this hill or this petering-out path before—or that cloud, he thought shyly, looking up and then down quickly—any more than he had seen this day before. Why did he not admit he was simply lost and had been for miles? . . . He was not in the habit of asking the way of strangers, and these people never knew where the very roads they lived on went to; but then he had not even been close enough to anyone to call out. People standing in the fields now and then, or on top of the haystacks, had been too far away, looking like leaning sticks or weeds, turning a little at the solitary rattle of his car across their countryside, watching the pale sobered winter dust where it chunked out behind like big squashes down the road. The stares of thse distant people had followed him solidly like a wall, impenetrable, behind which they turned back after he had passed.

The cloud floated there to one side like the bolster on his grandmother's bed. It went over a cabin on the edge of a hill, where two bare chinaberry trees clutched at the sky. He drove through a heap of dead oak leaves, his wheels stirring their weightless sides to make a silvery melancholy whistle as the car passed through their bed. No car had been along this way ahead of him. Then he saw that he was on the edge of a ravine that fell away, a red erosion, and that this was indeed the road's end.

He pulled the brake. But it did not hold, though he put all his strength into it. The car, tipped toward the edge, rolled a little. Without doubt, it was going over the bank.

He got out quietly, as though some mischief had been done him and he had his dignity to remember. He lifted his bag and sample case out, set them down, and stood back and watched the car roll over the edge. He heard something—not the crash he was listening for, but a slow, unuproarious crackle. Rather distastefully he went to look over, and he saw that his car had fallen into a tangle of immense grapevines as thick as his arm, which caught it and held it, rocked it like a grotesque child in a dark cradle, and then, as he watched, concerned somehow that he was not still inside it, released it gently to the ground.

He sighed.

Where am I? he wondered with a shock. Why didn't I do something? All his anger seemed to have drifted away from him. There was the house, back on the hill. He took a bag in each hand and with almost childlike willingness went toward it. But his breathing came with difficulty, and he had to stop to rest.

It was a shotgun house, two rooms and an open passage between, perched on the hill. The whole cabin slanted a little under the heavy heaped-up vine that covered the roof, light and green, as though forgotten from summer. A woman stood in the passage.

He stopped still. Then all of a sudden his heart began to behave strangely. Like a rocket set off, it began to leap and expand into uneven patterns of beats which showered into his brain, and he could not think. But in scattering and falling it made no noise. It shot up with great power, almost elation, and fell gently, like acrobats into nets. It began to pound profoundly, then waited irresponsibly, hitting in some sort of inward mockery first at his ribs, then against his eyes, then under his shoulder blades, and against the roof of his mouth when he tried to say, "Good afternoon, madam." But he could not hear his heart—it was as quiet as ashes falling. This was rather comforting; still, it was shocking to Bowman to feel his heart beating at all.

Stock-still in his confusion, he dropped his bags, which seemed to drift in slow bulks gracefully through the air and to cushion themselves on the gray prostrate grass near the doorstep.

As for the woman standing there, he saw at once that she was old. Since she could not possibly hear his heart, he ignored the pounding and now looked at her carefully, and yet in his distraction dreamily, with his mouth open.

She had been cleaning the lamp, and held it, half blackened, half clear, in front of her. He saw her with the dark passage behind her. She was a big woman with a weather-beaten but unwrinkled face; her lips were held tightly together, and her eyes looked with a curious dulled brightness into his. He looked at her shoes, which were like bundles. If it were summer she would be barefoot . . . Bowman, who automatically judged a woman's age on sight, set her age at fifty. She wore a formless garment of some gray coarse material rough-dried from a washing, from which her arms appeared pink and unexpectedly round. When she never said a word, and sustained her quiet pose of holding the lamp, he was convinced of the strength in her body.

"Good afternoon, madam," he said.

She stared on, whether at him or at the air around him he could not tell, but after a moment she lowered her eyes to show that she would listen to whatever he had to say.

"I wonder if you would be interested—" He tried once more. "An accident—my car . . ."

Her voice emerged low and remote, like a sound across a lake. "Sonny he ain't here."

"Sonny?"

"Sonny ain't here now."

Her son—a fellow able to bring my car up, he decided in blurred relief.

He pointed down the hill. "My car's in the bottom of the ditch. I'll need help."

"Sonny ain't here, but he'll be here."

She was becoming clearer to him and her voice stronger, and Bowman saw that she was stupid.

He was hardly surprised at the deepening postponement and tedium of his journey. He took a breath, and heard his voice speaking over the silent blows of his heart. "I was sick. I am not strong yet . . . May I come in?"

He stooped and laid his big black hat over the handle on his bag. It was a humble motion, almost a bow, that instantly struck him as absurd and betraying of all his weakness. He looked up at the woman, the wind blowing his hair. He might have continued for a long time in this unfamiliar attitude; he had never been a patient man, but when he was sick he had learned to sink submissively into the pillows, to wait for his medicine. He waited on the woman.

Then she, looking at him with blue eyes, turned and held open the door, and after a moment Bowman, as if convinced in his action, stood erect and followed her in.

Inside, the darkness of the house touched him like a professional hand, the doctor's. The woman set the half-cleaned lamp on a table in the center of the room and pointed, also like a professional person, a guide, to a chair with a yellow cowhide seat. She herself crouched on the hearth, drawing her knees up under the shapeless dress.

At first he felt hopefully secure. His heart was quieter. The room was enclosed in the gloom of yellow pine boards. He could see the other room, with the foot of an iron bed showing, across the passage. The bed had been made up with a red-and-yellow pieced quilt that looked like a map or a picture, a little like his grandmother's girlhood painting of Rome burning.

He had ached for coolness, but in this room it was cold. He stared at the hearth with dead coals lying on it and iron pots in the corners. The hearth and smoked chimney were of the stone he had seen ribbing the hills, mostly slate. Why is there no fire? he wondered.

And it was so still. The silence of the fields seemed to enter and move familiarly through the house. The wind used the open hall. He felt that he was in a mysterious, quiet, cool danger. It was necessary to do what? . . . To talk.

"I have a nice line of women's low-priced shoes . . ." he said.

But the woman answered, "Sonny'll be here. He's strong. Sonny'll move your car."

"Where is he now?"

"Farms for Mr. Redmond."

Mr. Redmond. Mr. Redmond. That was someone he would never have to encounter, and he was glad. Somehow the name did not appeal to him . . . In a flare of touchiness and anxiety, Bowman wished to avoid even mention of unknown men and their unknown farms.

"Do you two live here alone?" He was surprised to hear his old voice, chatty, confidential, inflected for selling shoes, asking a question like that— a thing he did not even want to know.

"Yes. We are alone."

He was surprised at the way she answered. She had taken a long time to say that. She had nodded her head in a deep way too. Had she wished to affect him with some sort of premonition? he wondered unhappily. Or was it only that she would not help him, after all, by talking with him? For he was not strong enough to receive the impact of unfamiliar things without a little talk to break their fall. He lived a month in which nothing had happened except in his head and his body—an almost inaudible life of heartbeats and dreams that came back, a life of fever and privacy, a delicate life which had left him weak to the point of—what? Of begging. The pulse in his palm leapt like a trout in a brook.

He wondered over and over why the woman did not go ahead with cleaning the lamp. What prompted her to stay there across the room, silently bestowing her presence upon him? He saw that with her it was not a time for doing little tasks. Her face was grave; she was feeling how right she was. Perhaps it was only politeness. In docility he held his eyes stiffly wide; they fixed themselves on the woman's clasped hands as though she held the cord they were strung on.

Then, "Sonny's coming," she said.

He himself had not heard anything, but there came a man passing the window and then plunging in at the door, with two hounds beside him, Sonny was a big enough man, with his belt slung low about his hips. He looked at least thirty. He had a hot, red face that was yet full of silence. He wore muddy blue pants and an old military coat stained and patched. World War? Bowman wondered. Great God, it was a Confederate coat. On the back of his light hair he had a wide filthy black hat which seemed to insult Bowman's own. He pushed down the dogs from his chest. He was strong, with dignity and heaviness in his way of moving. . . . There was the resemblance to his mother.

They stood side by side . . . He must account again for his presence here.

"Sonny, this man, he had his car to run off over the prec'pice an' wants to know if you will git it out for him," the woman said after a few minutes.

Bowman could not even state his case.

Sonny's eyes lay upon him.

He knew he should offer explanations and show money—at least appear either penitent or authoritative. But all he could do was to shrug slightly.

Sonny brushed by him going to the window, followed by the eager dogs, and looked out. There was effort even in the way he was looking, as if he could throw his sight out like a rope. Without turning Bowman felt that his own eyes could have seen nothing: it was too far.

"Got me a mule out there an' got me a block an' tackle," said Sonny meaningfully. "I *could* catch me my mule an' git me my ropes, an' before long I'd git your car out the ravine."

He looked completely around the room, as if in meditation, his eyes roving in their own distance. Then he pressed his lips firmly and yet shyly together, and with the dogs ahead of him this time, he lowered his head and strode out. The hard earth sounded, cupping to his powerful way of walking—almost a stagger.

Mischievously, at the suggestion of those sounds, Bowman's heart leapt again. It seemed to walk about inside him.

"Sonny's goin' to do it." the woman said. She said it again, singing it almost, like a song. She was sitting in her place by the hearth.

Without looking out, he heard some shouts and the dogs barking and the pounding of hoofs in short runs on the hill. In a few minutes Sonny passed under the window with a rope, and there was a brown mule with quivering, shining, purple-looking ears. The mule actually looked in the window. Under its eyelashes it turned target-like eyes into his. Bowman averted his head and saw the woman looking serenely back at the mule, with only satisfaction in her face.

She sang a little more, under her breath. It occurred to him, and it seemed quite marvelous, that she was not really talking to him, but rather following the thing that came about with words that were unconscious and part of her looking.

So he said nothing, and this time when he did not reply he felt a curious and strong emotion, not fear, rise up in him.

This time, when his heart leapt, something—his soul—seemed to leap too, like a little colt invited out of a pen. He stared at the woman while the frantic nimbleness of his feeling made his head sway. He could not move; there was nothing he could do, unless perhaps he might embrace this woman who sat there growing old and shapeless before him.

But he wanted to leap up, to say to her, I have been sick and I found out then, only then, how lonely I am. Is it too late? My heart puts up a struggle inside me, and you may have heard it, protesting against emptiness . . . It should be full, he would rush on to tell her, thinking of his heart now as a deep lake, it should be holding love like other hearts. It should be flooded with love. There would be a warm spring day . . . Come and stand in my heart, whoever you are, and a whole river would cover your feet and rise higher and take your knees in whirlpools, and draw you down to itself, your whole body, your heart too.

But he moved a trembling hand across his eyes, and looked at the placid crouching woman across the room. She was still as a statue. He felt ashamed and exhausted by the thought that he might, in one more moment, have tried by simple words and embraces to communicate some strange thing—something which seemed always to have just escaped him. . . .

Sunlight touched the furthest pot on the hearth. It was late afternoon. This time tomorrow he would be somewhere on a good graveled road, driving his car past things that happened to people, quicker than their happening. Seeing ahead to the next day, he was glad, and knew that this was no time to embrace an old woman. He could feel in his pounding temples the readying of his blood for motion and for hurrying away.

"Sonny's hitched up your car by now," said the woman. "He'll git it out the ravine right shortly."

"Fine!" he cried with his customary enthusiasm.

Yet it seemed a long time that they waited. It began to get dark. Bowman was cramped in his chair. Any man should know enough to get up and walk around while he waited. There was something like guilt in such stillness and silence.

But instead of getting up, he listened . . . His breathing restrained, his eyes powerless in the growing dark, he listened uneasily for a warning sound, forgetting in wariness what it would be. Before long he heard something—soft, continuous, insinuating.

"What's that noise?" he asked, his voice jumping into the dark. Then wildly he was afraid it would be his heart beating so plainly in the quiet room, and she would tell him so.

"You might hear the stream," she said grudgingly.

Her voice was closer. She was standing by the table. He wondered why she did not light the lamp. She stood there in the dark and did not light it.

Bowman would never speak to her now, for the time was past. I'll sleep in the dark, he thought, in his bewilderment pitying himself.

Heavily she moved on to the window. Her arm, vaguely white, rose straight from her full side and she pointed out into the darkness.

"That white speck's Sonny," she said, talking to herself.

He turned unwillingly and peered over her shoulder; he hesitated to rise and stand beside her. His eyes searched the dusky air. The white speck floated smoothly toward her finger, like a leaf on a river, growing whiter in the dark. It was as if she had shown him something secret, part of her life, but had offered no explanation. He looked away. He was moved almost to tears, feeling for no reason that she had made a silent declaration equivalent to his own. His hand waited upon his chest.

Then a step shook the house, and Sonny was in the room. Bowman felt how the woman left him there and went to the other man's side.

"I done got your car out, mister," said Sonny's voice in the dark. "She's settin' awaitin' in the road, turned to go back where she come from."

"Fine!" said Bowman, projecting his own voice to loudness. "I'm surely much obliged—I could never have done it myself—I was sick . . ."

"I could do it easy," said Sonny.

Bowman could feel them both waiting in the dark, and he could hear the dogs panting out in the yard, waiting to bark when he should go. He felt strangely helpless and resentful. Now that he could go, he longed to stay. Of what was he being deprived? His chest was rudely shaken by the violence of his heart. These people cherished something here that he could not see, they withheld some ancient promise of food and warmth and light. Between them they had a conspiracy. He thought of the way she had moved away from him and gone to Sonny, she had flowed toward him. He was shaking with cold, he was tired, and it was not fair. Humbly and yet angrily he stuck his hand into his pocket.

"Of course I'm going to pay you for everything—"

"We don't take money for such," said Sonny's voice belligerently.

"I want to pay. But do something more . . . Let me stay— tonight. . . ." He took another step toward them. If only they could see him, they would know his sincerity, his real need! His voice went on, "I'm not very strong yet, I'm not able to walk far, even back to my car, maybe, I don't know—I don't know exactly where I am—"

He stopped. He felt as if he might burst into tears. What would they think of him!

Sonny came over and put his hands on him. Bowman felt them pass (they were professional too) across his chest, over his hips. He could feel Sonny's eyes upon him in the dark.

"You ain't no revenuer come sneakin' here, mister, ain't got no gun?"

To this end of nowhere! And yet *he* had come. He made a grave answer. "No."

"You can stay."

"Sonny," said the woman, "You'll have to borry some fire."

"I'll go git it from Redmond's," said Sonny.

"What?" Bowman strained to hear their words to each other.

"Our fire, it's out, and Sonny's got to borry some, because its dark an' cold," she said.

"But matches—I have matches—"

"We don't have no need for 'em," she said proudly. "Sonny's goin' after his own fire."

"I'm goin' to Redmond's," said Sonny with an air of importance, and he went out.

After they had waited a while, Bowman looked out the window and saw a light moving over the hill. It spread itself out like a little fan. It zigzagged along the field, darting and swift, not like Sonny at all . . . Soon enough, Sonny staggered in, holding a burning stick behind him in tongs, fire flowing in his wake, blazing light into the corners of the room.

"We'll make a fire now," the woman said, taking the brand.

When that was done she lit the lamp. It showed its dark and light. The whole room turned golden-yellow like some sort of flower, and the walls smelled of it and seemed to tremble with the quiet rushing of the fire and the waving of the burning lampwick in its funnel of light.

The woman moved among the iron pots. With the tongs she dropped hot coals on top of the iron lids. They made a set of soft vibrations, like the sound of a bell far away.

She looked up and over at Bowman, but he could not answer. He was trembling . . .

"Have a drink, mister?" Sonny asked. He had brought in a chair from the other room and sat astride it with his folded arms across the back. Now we are all visible to one another, Bowman thought, and cried, "Yes sir, you bet, thanks!"

"Come after me and do just what I do," said Sonny.

It was another excursion into the dark. They went through the hall, out to the back of the house, past a shed and a hooded well. They came to a wilderness of thicket.

"Down on your knees," said Sonny.

"What?" Sweat broke out on his forehead.

He understood when Sonny began to crawl through a sort of tunnel that the bushes made over the ground. He followed, started in spite of himself when a twig or a thorn touched him gently without making a sound, clinging to him and finally letting him go.

Sonny stopped crawling and, crouched on his knees, began to dig with both his hands into the dirt. Bowman shyly struck matches and made a light. In a few minutes Sonny pulled up a jug. He poured out some of the whisky into a bottle from his coat pocket, and buried the jug again. "You never know who's liable to knock at your door," he said, and laughed. "Start back," he said, almost formally. "Ain't no need for us to drink outdoors, like hogs.

At the table by the fire, sitting opposite each other in their chairs, Sonny and Bowman took drinks out of the bottle, passing it across. The dogs slept; one of them was having a dream.

"This is good," said Bowman. "This is what I needed." It was just as though he were drinking the fire off the hearth.

"He makes it," said the woman with quiet pride.

She was pushing the coals off the pots, and the smells of corn bread and coffee circled the room. She set everything on the table before the men, with a bone-handled knife stuck into one of the potatoes, splitting out its golden fiber. Then she stood for a minute looking at them, tall and full above them where they sat. She leaned a little toward them.

"You all can eat now," she said, and suddenly smiled.

Bowman had just happened to be looking at her. He set his cup back on the table in unbelieving protest. A pain pressed at his eyes. He saw that she was not an old woman. She was young, still young. He could think of no number of years for her. She was the same age as Sonny, and she belonged to him. She stood with the deep dark corner of the room behind her, the shifting yellow light scattering over her head and her gray formless dress, trembling over her tall body when it bent over them in its sudden communication. She was young. Her teeth were shining and her eyes glowed. She turned and walked slowly and heavily out of the room, and he heard her sit down on the cot and then lie down. The pattern on the quilt moved.

"She's goin' to have a baby," said Sonny, popping a bite into his mouth.

Bowman could not speak. He was shocked with knowing what was really in this house. A marriage, a fruitful marriage. That simple thing. Anyone could have had that.

Somehow he felt unable to be indignant or protest, although some sort of joke had certainly been played upon him. There was nothing remote or mysterious here—only something private. The only secret was the ancient communication between two people. But the memory of the woman's waiting silently by the cold hearth, of the man's stubborn journey a mile away to get fire, and how they finally brought out their food and drink and filled the room proudly with all they had to show, was suddenly too clear and too enormous within him for response. . . .

"You ain't as hungry as you look," said Sonny.

The woman came out of the bedroom as soon as the men had finished, and ate her supper while her husband stared peacefully into the fire.

Then they put the dogs out, with the food that was left.

"I think I'd better sleep here by the fire, on the floor," said Bowman.

He felt that he had been cheated, and that he could afford now to be generous. Ill though he was, he was not going to ask them for their bed. He was through with asking favors in this house, now that he understood what was there.

"Sure, mister."

But he had not known yet how slowly he understood. They had not meant to give him their bed. After a little interval they both rose and looking at him gravely went into the other room.

He lay stretched by the fire until it grew low and dying. He watched every tongue of blaze lick out and vanish. "There will be special reduced prices on all footwear during the month of January," he found himself repeating quietly, and then he lay with his lips tight shut.

How many noises the night had! He heard the stream running, the fire dying, and he was sure now that he heard his heart beating, too, the sound it made under his ribs. He heard breathing, round and deep, of the man and his wife in the room across the passage. And that was all. But emotion swelled patiently within him, and he wished that the child were his.

He must get back to where he had been before. He stood weakly before the red coals and put on his overcoat. It felt too heavy on his shoulders. As he started out he looked and saw that the woman had never got through with cleaning the lamp. On some impulse he put all the money from his billfold under its fluted glass base, almost ostentatiously.

Ashamed, shrugging a little, and then shivering, he took his bags and went out. The cold of the air seemed to lift him bodily. The moon was in the sky.

On the slope he began to run, he could not help it. Just as he reached the road, where his car seemed to sit in the moonlight like a boat, his heart began to give off tremendous explosions like a rifle, bang bang bang.

He sank in fright onto the road, his bags falling about him. He felt as if all this had happened before. He covered his heart with both hands to keep anyone from hearing the noise it made.

But nobody heard it.

5

Critical Touchstones

EDGAR ALLAN POE (1809–1849)

[*The Single Effect of the Tale*]

In 1847, Edgar Allan Poe reviewed Nathaniel Hawthorne's *Twice-Told Tales* for *Godey's Lady's Book,* a popular magazine of the day. In this review Poe argues for the importance of brevity in both the poem and the story. He also contends that a good short story must have a "unique or single effect" to be successful, and that all the details of the story should support or help to create this one effect. According to Poe the story cannot achieve the heights of beauty attainable by the poem; however, the story offers a broader terrain, capable of many different kinds of effects and suitable for a wider variety of subjects. See the headnote for Poe on page 405.

The tale proper, in my opinion, affords unquestionably the fairest field for the exercise of the loftiest talent, which can be afforded by the wide domains of mere prose. Were I bidden to say how the highest genius could be most advantageously employed for the best display of its own powers, I should answer, without hesitation—in the composition of a rhymed poem, not to exceed in length what might be perused in an hour. Within this limit alone can the highest order of true poetry exist. I need only here say, upon this topic, that, in almost all classes of compositon, the unity of effect or impression is a point of the greatest importance. It is clear, moreover, that this unity cannot be thoroughly preserved in productions whose perusal cannot be completed at one sitting. We may continue the reading of a prose composition, from the very nature of prose itself, much longer than we can persevere, to any good purpose, in the perusal of a poem. This latter, if truly fulfilling the demands of the poetic sentiment, induces an exaltation of the soul which cannot be long sustained. All high excitements are necessarily transient. Thus a long poem is a paradox. And, without unity of impression, the deepest effects cannot be brought about. Epics were the off-spring of an imperfect sense of Art, and their reign is no more. A poem *too* brief may produce a vivid, but never an intense or enduring impression. Without a certain continuity of effort—without a certain duration of repetition or purpose—the soul is never deeply moved. There must be the dropping of the water upon the rock. De Béranger has wrought brilliant things—pungent and spirit-stirring—but, like all immassive bodies, they lack *momentum,* and thus fail to satisfy the poetic Sentiment. They sparkle and excite, but, from want of continuity, fail deeply to impress. Extreme brevity will degenerate into epigrammatism; but the sin of extreme length is more unpardonable. *In medio tutissimus ibis.*[1]

Were I called upon, however, to designate that class of composition which, next to such a poem as I have suggested, should best fulfil the demands of high genius—should offer it the most advantageous field of exertion—I should unhesitatingly speak of the prose tale as Mr. Hawthorne has here exemplified it. I allude to the short prose narrative, requiring from a half-hour to one or two hours in its perusal. The ordinary novel is objectionable, from its length, for reasons already stated in substance. As it cannot be read at one sitting, it deprives itself, of course, of the immense force derivable from *totality*. Worldly interests intervening during the pauses of perusal, modify, annul, or counteract, in a greater or less degree, the impressions of the book. But simple cessation in reading would, of itself, be sufficient to destroy the true unity. In the brief tale, however, the author is enabled to carry out the fulness of his intention, be it what it may. During the hour of perusal the soul of the reader is at the writer's control. There are no external or extrinsic influences—resulting from weariness or interruption.

A skillfull literary artist has constructed a tale. If wise, he has not fashioned his thoughts to accommodate his incidents; but having conceived, with deliberate care, a certain unique or single *effect* to be wrought out, he then invents such incidents—he then combines such events as may best aid him in establishing this preconceived effect. If his very initial sentence tend not to the outbringing of this effect, then he has failed in his first step. In the whole composition there should be no word written, of which the tendency, direct or indirect, is not to the one preestablished design. And by such means, with such care and skill, a picture is at length painted which leaves in the mind of him who contemplates it with a kindred art, a sense of the fullest satisfaction. The idea of the tale has been presented unblemished, because undisturbed; and this is an end unattainable by the novel. Undue brevity is just as exceptionable here as in the poem; but undue length is yet more to be avoided.

We have said that the tale has a point of superiority even over the

1. "You will travel with greatest safety in the middle."

poem. In fact, while the *rhythm* of this latter is an essential aid in the development of the poem's highest idea—the idea of the Beautiful—the artificialities of this rhythm are an inseparable bar to the development of all points of thought or expression which have their basis in *Truth*. But Truth is often, and in very great degree, the aim of the tale. Some of the finest tales are tales of ratiocination. Thus the field of this species of composition, if not in so elevated a region on the mountain of Mind, is a table-land of far vaster extent than the domain of the mere poem. Its products are never so rich, but infinitely more numerous, and more appreciable by the mass of mankind. The writer of the prose tale, in short, may bring to his theme a vast variety of modes or inflections of thought and expression—(the ratiocinative, for example, the sarcastic or the humorous) which are not only antagonistical to the nature of the poem, but absolutely forbidden by one of its most peculiar and indispensable adjuncts; we allude, of course, to rhythm. It may be added, here, *par parenthèse*, that the author who aims at the purely beautiful in a prose tale is laboring at a great disadvantage. For Beauty can be better treated in the poem. Not so with terror, or passion, or horror, or a multitude of such other points. And here it will be seen how full of prejudice are the usual animadversions against those *tales of effect*, many fine examples of which were found in the earlier numbers of Blackwood. The impressions produced were wrought in a legitimate sphere of action, and constituted a legitimate although sometimes an exaggerated interest. They were relished by every man of genius: although there were found many men of genius who condemned them without just ground. The true critic will but demand that the design intended be accomplished, to the fullest extent, by means most advantageously applicable.

HENRY JAMES (1843–1916)
[The House of Fiction]

Henry James was born in New York, travelled widely in Europe, and, in 1915, became a British citizen. He and Mark Twain are commonly considered America's two greatest novelists of the period between 1880 and 1910. Among James's most famous novels are *The Portrait of a Lady* (1881), *The Ambassadors* (1903), and *The Golden Bowl* (1904). He was a painstaking craftsman and also a penetrating analyst of the craft of fiction. In the early twentieth century, he wrote a series of prefaces for the New York edition of his work. In the following selection from the Preface to *The Portrait of a Lady*, James quotes a passage from the Russian novelist and short story writer Ivan Turgenev (1818–1883) and comments about the origin of fiction in the availability or disposability (*disponibilité*) of imagined characters. He ends the selection with his famous image of the "house of fiction," a comparison suggesting the remarkable variety of fiction and the importance of the individual artist's moral vision.

I have always fondly remembered a remark that I heard fall years ago from the lips of Ivan Turgenieff in regard to his own experience of the usual origin of the fictive picture. It began for him almost always with the vision of some person or persons, who hovered before him, soliciting him, as the active or passive figure, interesting him and appealing to him just as they were and by what they were. He saw them in that fashion, as *disponibles*, saw them subject to the chances, the complications of existence, and saw them vividly, but then had to find for them the right relations, those that would most bring them out; to imagine, to invent and select and piece together the situations most useful and favourable to the sense of the creatures themselves, the complications they would be most likely to produce and to feel.

"To arrive at these things is to arrive at my 'story'," he said, "and that's the way I look for it. The result is that I'm often accused of not having 'story' enough. I seem to myself to have as much as I need—to show my people, to exhibit their relations with each other; for that is all my measure. If I watch them long enough I see them come together, I see them *placed*, I see them engaged in this or that act and in this or that difficulty. How they look and move and speak and behave, always in the setting I have found for them is my account of them—of which I dare say, alas, *que cela manque souvent d'architecture*.[1] But I would rather, I think, have too little architecture than too much—when there's danger of its interfering with my measure of the truth. The French of course like more of it than I give—having by their own genius such a hand for it; and indeed one must give all one can. As for the origin of one's wind-blown germs themselves, who shall say, as you ask, where *they* come from? We have to go too far back, too far behind, to say. Isn't it all we can say that they come from every quarter of heaven, that they are *there* at almost any turn of the road? They accumulate, and we are always picking them over, selecting among them. They are the breath of life—by which I mean that life, in its own way, breathes them upon us. They are so, in a manner prescribed and imposed—floated into our minds by the current of life. That reduces to imbecility the vain critic's quarrel, so often, with one's subject, when he hasn't the wit to accept it. Will he point out then which other it should properly have been?—his office being, essentially *to* point out. *Il en serait bien embarrassé.*[2] Ah, when he points out what I've done or failed to do with it, that's another matter: there he's on his ground. I give him up my 'architecture,'" my distinguished friend concluded, "as much as he will."

So this beautiful genius, and I recall with comfort the gratitude I drew from his reference to the intensity of suggestion that may reside in the stray figure, the unattached character, the image *en disponibilité*.[3] It gave me higher warrant than I seemed then to have met for just that blest habit of

1. French: "that it often fails in its architecture."
2. French: "He would be quite embarrassed."
3. French: "unattached."

one's own imagination, the trick of investing some conceived or encountered individual, some brace or group of individuals, with the germinal property and authority. I was myself so much more antecedently conscious of my figures than of their setting—a too preliminary, a preferential interest in which struck me as in general such a putting of the cart before the horse. I might envy, though I couldn't emulate, the imaginative writer so constituted as to see his fable first and to make out its agents afterwards: I could think so little of any fable that it didn't need its agents positively to launch it; I could think so little of any situation that didn't depend for its interest on the nature of the persons situated, and thereby on their way of taking it. There are methods of so-called presentation, I believe—among novelists who have appeared to flourish—that offer the situation as indifferent to that support; but I have not lost the sense of the value for me, at the time, of the admirable Russian's testimony to my not needing, all superstitiously, to try and perform any such gymnastic. Other echoes from the same source linger with me, I confess, as unfadingly—if it be not all indeed one much-embracing echo. It was impossible after that not to read, for one's uses, high lucidity into the tormented and disfigured and bemuddled question of the objective value, and even quite into that of the critical appreciation of "subject" in the novel.

One had had from an early time, for that matter, the instinct of the right estimate of such values and of its reducing to the inane the dull dispute over the "immoral" subject and the moral. Recognising so promptly the one measure of the worth of a given subject, the question about it that, rightly answered, disposes of all others—is it valid, in a word, is it genuine, is it sincere, the result of some direct impression or perception of life? —I had found small edification, mostly, in a critical pretension that had neglected from the first all delimitation of ground and all definition of terms. The air of my earlier time shows, to memory, as darkened, all round, with that vanity—unless the difference to-day be just in one's own final impatience, the lapse of one's attention. There is, I think, no more nutritive or suggestive truth in this connexion than that of the perfect dependence of the "moral" sense of a work of art on the amount of felt life concerned in producing it. The question comes back thus, obviously, to the kind and the degree of the artist's prime sensibility, which is the soil out of which his subject springs. The quality and capacity of that soil, its ability to "grow" with due freshness and straightness any vision of life, represents, strongly or weakly, the projected morality. That element is but another name for the more or less close connexion of the subject with some mark made on the intelligence, with some sincere experience. By which, at the same time, of course, one is far from contending that this enveloping air of the artist's humanity—which gives the last touch to the worth of the work—is not a widely and wondrously varying element; being on one occasion a rich and magnificent medium and on another a comparatively poor and ungenerous one. Here we get exactly the high price of the novel as a literary form—its power not only, while preserving that form with closeness, to range through all the differences of the individual relation to its general subject-matter, all the varieties of outlook on life, of disposition to reflect and project, created by conditions that are never the same from man to man (or, so far as that goes, from man to woman), but positively to appear more true to its character in proportion as it strains, or tends to burst, with a latent extravagance, its mould.

The house of fiction has in short not one window, but a million—a number of possible windows not to be reckoned; rather, every one of which has been pierced, or is still pierceable, in its vast front, by the need of the individual vision and by the pressure of the individual will. These apertures, of dissimilar shape and size, hang so, all together, over the human scene that we might have expected of them a greater sameness of report than we find. They are but windows at the best, mere holes in a dead wall, disconnected, perched aloft; they are not hinged doors opening straight upon life. But they have this mark of their own that at each of them stands a figure with a pair of eyes, or at least with a fieldglass, which forms, again and again, for observation, a unique instrument, insuring to the person making use of it an impression distinct from every other. He and his neighbors are watching the same show, but one seeing more where the other sees less, one seeing black where the other sees white, one seeing big where the other sees small, one seeing coarse where the other sees fine. And so on, and so on; there is fortunately no saying on what, for the particular pair of eyes, the window may *not* open; "fortunately" by reason, precisely, of this incalculability of range. The spreading field, the human scene, is the "choice of subject"; the pierced aperture, either broad or balconied or slit-like and low-browed, is the "literary form"; but they are, singly or together, as nothing without the posted presence of the watcher—without, in other words, the consciousness of the artist. Tell me what the artist is, and I will tell you of what he has *been* conscious. Thereby I shall express to you at once his boundless freedom and his "moral" reference.

JOSEPH CONRAD (1857–1924)

[Realism and Romanticism]

In the following excerpt from the Preface to *Within the Tides* (1915), Joseph Conrad comments on the relationship between realistic and romantic elements in works of fiction. His own life as a sailor had put him in touch with some of the more unusual, even exotic, aspects of life. His problem as a writer of fiction was to imbue these romantic elements with "their proper atmosphere of actuality." If he moved too far in either direction, he would risk being faithless to his own experience or to the familiar experiences of his readers. See the headnote for Conrad on page 279.

I have not sought for special imaginative freedom or a larger play of fancy in my choice of characters and subjects. The nature of the knowledge, suggestions or hints used in my imaginative work has depended directly on the conditions of my active life. It depended more on contacts, and very slight contacts at that, than on actual experience; because my life as a matter of fact was far from being adventurous in itself. Even now when I look back on it with a certain regret (who would not regret his youth?) and positive affection, its colouring wears the sober hue of hard work and exacting calls of duty, things which in themselves are not much charged with a feeling of romance. If these things appeal strongly to me even in retrospect it is, I suppose, because the romantic feeling of reality was in me an inborn faculty. This in itself may be a curse but when disciplined by a sense of personal responsibility and a recognition of the hard facts of existence shared with the rest of mankind becomes but a point of view from which the very shadows of life appear endowed with an internal glow. And such romanticism is not a sin. It is none the worse for the knowledge of truth. It only tries to make the best of it, hard as it may be; and in this hardness discovers a certain aspect of beauty.

I am speaking here of romanticism in relation to life, not of romanticism in relation to imaginative literature, which, in its early days, was associated simply with medieval subjects sought for in a remote past. My subjects are not medieval and I have a natural right to them because my past is very much on my own. If their course lie out of the beaten path of organized social life, it is, perhaps, because I myself did in a short break away from it early in obedience to an impulse which must have been very genuine since it has sustained me through all the dangers of disillusion. But that origin of my literary work was very far from giving a larger scope to my imagination. On the contrary, the mere fact of dealing with matters outside the general run of everyday experience laid me under the obligation of a more scrupulous fidelity to the truth of my own sensations. The problem was to make unfamiliar things credible. To do that I had to create for them, to reproduce for them, to envelop them in their proper atmosphere of actuality. This was the hardest task of all and the most important, in view of that conscientious rendering of truth in thought and fact which has always been my aim.

E. M. FORSTER (1879–1970)

Flat and Round Characters

E. M. Forster was born in London and educated at King's College, Cambridge. His most important novels are *Howard's End* (1910) and *A Passage to India* (1924). He also wrote stories, essays, and literary criticism. In the following excerpt from *Aspects of the Novel* (1927), Forster contrasts what he was the first to call "flat" and "round" characters in fiction, that is, those who are one-dimensional and static and those who are multi-dimensional and dynamic. Using examples drawn primarily from works of British fiction, he reveals the virtues of using flat characters, but concludes that only round characters are "fit to perform tragically."

We may divide characters into flat and round.

Flat characters were called "humorous" in the seventeenth century, and are sometimes called types, and sometimes caricatures. In their purest form, they are constructed round a single idea or quality: when there is more than one factor in them, we get the beginning of the curve towards the round. The really flat character can be expressed in one sentence such as "I never will desert Mr. Micawber." There is Mrs. Micawber—she says she won't desert Mr. Micawber, she doesn't, and there she is. Or: "I must conceal, even by subterfuges, the poverty of my master's house." There is Caleb Balderstone in *The Bride of Lammermoor*. He does not use the actual phrase, but it completely describes him; he has no existence outside it, no pleasures, none of the private lusts and aches that must complicate the most consistent of servitors. Whatever he does, wherever he goes, whatever lies he tells or plates he breaks, it is to conceal the poverty of his master's house. It is not his *idée fixe*, because there is nothing in him into which the idea can be fixed. He is the idea, and such life as he possesses radiates from its edges and from the scintillations it strikes when other elements in the novel impinge. Or take Proust. There are numerous flat characters in Proust, such as the Princess of Parma, or Legrandin. Each can be expressed in a single sentence, the Princess's sentence being, "I must be particularly careful to be kind." She does nothing except to be particularly careful, and those of the other characters who are more complex than herself easily see through the kindness, since it is only a by-product of the carefulness.

One great advantage of flat characters is that they are easily recognized whenever they come in—recognized by the reader's emotional eye, not by the visual eye, which merely notes the recurrence of a proper name. In Russian novels, where they so seldom occur, they would be a decided help. It is a convenience for an author when he can strike with his full force at once, and flat characters are very useful to him, since they never need reintroducing, never run away, have not to be watched for development, and provide their own atmosphere—little luminous disks of a pre-arranged size, pushed hither and thither like counters across the void or between the stars; most satisfactory.

A second advantage is that they are easily remembered by the reader afterwards. They remain in his mind as unalterable for the reason that they were not changed by circumstances; they moved through circumstances, which gives them in retrospect a comforting quality, and preserves them when the book that produced them may decay. The Countess in *Evan Harrington* furnishes a good little example here. Let us compare our memories of her with our memories of Becky Sharp. We do not remember what the Countess did or what she passed through. What is clear is her figure and the formula that surrounds it, namely, "Proud as we are of dear papa, we must conceal his memory." All her rich humour proceeds from this. She is a flat character. Becky is round. She, too, is on the make, but she cannot be summed up in a single phrase, and we remember her in connection with the great scenes through which she passed and as modified by those scenes—that is to say, we do not remember her so easily because she waxes and wanes and has facets like a human being. All of us, even the sophisticated, yearn for permanence, and to the unsophisticated permanence is the chief excuse for a work of art. We all want books to endure, to be refuges, and their inhabitants to be always the same, and flat characters tend to justify themselves on this account.

All the same, critics who have their eyes fixed severely upon daily life—as were our eyes last week—have very little patience with such renderings of human nature. Queen Victoria, they argue, cannot be summed up in a single sentence, so what excuse remains for Mrs. Micawber? One of our foremost writers, Mr. Norman Douglas, is a critic of this type, and the passage from him which I will quote puts the case against flat characters in a forcible fashion. The passage occurs in an open letter to D. H. Lawrence, with whom he is quarrelling: a doughty pair of combatants, the hardness of whose hitting makes the rest of us feel like a lot of ladies up in a pavilion. He complains that Lawrence, in a biography, has falsified the picture by employing "the novelist's touch," and he goes on to define what this is:

> It consists, I should say, in a failure to realize the complexities of the ordinary human mind; it selects for literary purposes two or three facets of a man or woman, generally the most spectacular, and therefore useful ingredients of their character and disregards all the others. Whatever fails to fit in with these specially chosen traits is eliminated—must be eliminated, for otherwise the description would not hold water. Such and such are the data: everything incompatible with those data has to go by the board. It follows that the novelist's touch argues, often logically, from a wrong premise: it takes what it likes and leaves the rest. The facets may be correct as far as they go but there are too few of them: what the author says may be true and yet by no means the truth. That is the novelist's touch. It falsifies life.

Well, the novelist's touch as thus defined is, of course, bad in biography, for no human being is simple. But in a novel it has its place: a novel that is at all complex often requires flat people as well as round, and the outcome of their collisions parallels life more accurately than Mr. Douglas implies. The case of Dickens is significant. Dickens' people are nearly all flat (Pip and David Copperfield attempt roundness, but so diffidently that they seem more like bubbles than solids). Nearly every one can be summed up in a sentence, and yet there is this wonderful feeling of human depth. Probably the immense vitality of Dickens causes his characters to vibrate a little, so that they borrow his life and appear to lead one of their own. It is a conjuring trick; at any moment we may look at Mr. Pickwick edgeways and find him no thicker than a gramophone record. But we never get the sideway view. Mr. Pickwick is far too adroit and well-trained. He always has the air of weighing something, and when he is put into the cupboard of the young ladies' school he seems as heavy as Falstaff in the buck-basket at Windsor. Part of the genius of Dickens is that he does use types and caricatures, people whom we recognize the instant they re-enter, and yet achieves effects that are not mechanical and a vision of humanity that is not shallow. Those who dislike Dickens have an excellent case. He ought to be bad. He is actually one of our big writers, and his immense success with types suggests that there may be more in flatness than the severer critics admit.

Or take H. G. Wells. With the possible exceptions of Kipps and the aunt in *Tono Bungay*, all Wells' characters are as flat as a photograph. But the photographs are agitated with such vigour that we forget their complexities lie on the surface and would disappear if it were scratched or curled up. A Wells character cannot indeed be summed up in a single phrase; he is tethered much more to observation, he does not create types. Nevertheless his people seldom pulsate by their own strength. It is the deft and powerful hands of their maker that shake them and trick the reader into a sense of depth. Good but imperfect novelists, like Wells and Dickens, are very clever at transmitting force. The part of their novel that is alive galvanizes the part that is not, and causes the characters to jump about and speak in a convincing way. They are quite different from the perfect novelist who touches all his material directly, who seems to pass the creative finger down every sentence and into every word. Richardson, Defoe, Jane Austen, are perfect in this particular way; their work may not be great but their hands are always upon it; there is not the tiny interval between the touching of the button and the sound of the bell which occurs in novels where the characters are not under direct control.

For we must admit that flat people are not in themselves as big achievements as round ones, and also that they are best when they are comic. A serious or tragic flat character is apt to be a bore. Each time he enters crying "Revenge!" or "My heart bleeds for humanity!" or whatever his formula is, our hearts sink. One of the romances of a popular contemporary writer is constructed round a Sussex farmer who says, "I'll plough up that bit of gorse." There is the farmer, there is the gorse; he says he'll plough it up, he does plough it up, but it is not like saying "I'll never desert Mr. Micawber," because we are so bored by his consistency that we do not care whether he succeeds with the gorse or fails. If his formula were analysed and connected up with the rest of the human outfit, we should not be bored any longer, the formula would cease to be the man and become an obsession in the man; that is to say he would have turned from a flat farmer into a round one. It is only round people who are fit to perform tragically for any length of time and can move us to any feelings except humour and appropriateness. . . .

. . . The test of a round character is whether it is capable of surprising in a convincing way. If it never surprises, it is flat. If it does not convince, it is a flat pretending to be round. It has the incalculability of life about it—life within the pages of a book. And by using it sometimes alone, more often in combination with the other kind, the novelist achieves his task of acclimatization and harmonizes the human race with the other aspects of his work.

WILLIAM FAULKNER (1897–1962)

[*The Writer's Sources*]

In the academic year 1957–58, William Faulkner was invited to be writer-in-residence at the University of Virginia in Charlottesville. *Faulkner in the University* (1959), from which the following selection is taken, is a collection of interviews and public remarks he made about his writing or about writing in general. In the following excerpt he speaks of the writer's three sources—"imagination, observation, and experience"— and of the relationship between fiction and autobiography. See the headnote for Faulkner on page 16.

Q. Sir, a few minutes ago you mentioned that people in your home town were looking into your books for familiar characters. Realizing that you've got a rich legacy in your experiences, but it seems to me that nowadays the modern novelist is writing merely thinly disguised autobiography. Which do you think is really more valuable from the sense of the artist, the disguised autobiography, or making it up from whole cloth, as it were?

A. I would say that the writer has three sources, imagination, observation, and experience. He himself doesn't know how much of which he uses at any given moment because each of the sources themselves are not too important to him. That he is writing about people, and he uses his material from the three sources as the carpenter reaches into his lumber room and finds a board that fits the particular corner he's building. Of course, any writer, to begin with, is writing his own biography because he has discovered the world and then suddenly discovered that the world is important enough or moving enough or tragic enough to put down on paper or in music or on canvas, and at that time all he knows is what has happened to him because he has not developed his capacity to perceive, to draw conclusions, to have an insight into people. His only insight in it is into himself, and it's a biography because that's the only gauge he has to measure—is what he has experienced himself. As he gets older and works more, imagination is like any muscle, it improves with use. Imagination develops, his observation gets shrewder as he gets older, as he writes, so that when he reaches his peak, his best years, when his work is best, he himself doesn't know and doesn't have time to bother and doesn't really care how much of what comes from each of these sources, that then he is writing about people, writing about the aspirations, the troubles, the anguishes, the courage, and the cowardice, the baseness and the splendor of man, of the human heart.

EUDORA WELTY (b. 1909)

[Some Notes on Time in Fiction]

In addition to her stories and novels, Eudora Welty has also written two books abut the craft of fiction: *The Eye of the Story: Selected Essays and Reviews* (1978) and *One Writer's Beginnings* (1984). In the following excerpt from the first of these, Welty compares the importance of place and time to the fiction writer and comments on the relationship of time to the element of plot. She sees change, causality, and suspense as being central to the writer's concerns. See the headnote for Welty on page 516.

Time and place, the two bases of reference upon which the novel, in seeking to come to grips with human experience, must depend for its validity, operate together, of course. They might be taken for granted as ordinary factors, until the novelist at his work comes to scrutinize them apart.

Place, the accessible one, the inhabited one, has blessed identity—a proper name, a human history, a visible character. Time is anonymous; when we give it a face, it's the same face the world over. While place is in itself as informing as an old gossip, time tells us nothing about itself except by the signals that it is passing. It has never given anything away.

Unlike time, place has surface, which will take the imprint of man—his hand, his foot, his mind; it can be tamed, domesticized. It has shape, size, boundaries; man can measure himself against them. It has atmosphere and temperature, change of light and show of season, qualities to which man spontaneously responds. Place has always nursed, nourished and instructed man; he in turn can rule it and ruin it, take it and lose it, suffer if he is exiled from it, and after living on it he goes to it in his grave. It is the stuff of fiction, as close to our living lives as the earth we can pick up and rub between our fingers, something we can feel and smell. But time is like the wind of the abstract. Beyond its all-pervasiveness, it has no quality that we apprehend but rate of speed, and our own acts and thoughts are said to give it that. Man can feel love for place; he is prone to regard time as something of an enemy.

Yet the novelist lives on closer terms with time than he does with place. The reasons for this are much older than any novel; they reach back into our oldest lore. How many of our proverbs are little nutshells to pack the meat of time in! ("He that diggeth a pit shall fall into it." "Pride goeth before destruction, and a haughty spirit before a fall.") The all-withstanding devices of myth and legend (the riddle of the Sphinx, Penelope's web, the Thousand and One Nights) are constructed of time. And time goes to make that most central device of all, the plot itself—as Scheherazade showed us in her own telling.

Indeed, these little ingots of time are ingots of plot too. Not only do they contain stories, they convey the stories—they speak of life-in-the-movement, with a beginning and an end. All that needed to be added was the middle; then the novel came along and saw to that.

Only the nursery fairy tale is not answerable to time, and time has no effect upon it; time winds up like a toy, and toy it is: when set to "Once upon a time" it spins till it runs down at "Happy ever after." Fairy tales don't come from old wisdom, they come from old foolishness—just as potent. They follow rules of their own that are quite as strict as time's (the magic of number and repetition, the governing of the spell); their fairy perfection forbids the existence of choices, and the telling always has to be the same. Their listener is the child, whose gratification comes of the fairy tale's having no suspense. The tale is about wishes, and thus grants a wish itself.

Real life is not wished, it is lived; stories and novels, whose subject is human beings in relationship with experience to undergo, make their own difficult way, struggle toward their own resolutions. Instead of fairy immunity to change, there is the vulnerability of human imperfection caught up in human emotion, and so there is growth, there is crisis, there is fulfillment, there is decay. Life moves toward death. The novel's progress is one of causality, and with that comes suspense. Suspense is a necessity in a novel because it is a main condition of our existence. Suspense is known only to mortals, and its agent and messenger is time.

The novel is time's child— "I could a talk *unfold*" —and bears all the earmarks, and all the consequences.

WAYNE C. BOOTH (b. 1921)

Narrators and Their Qualities

Wayne C. Booth is an American literary critic and educator (at the University of Chicago). His best known work is *The Rhetoric of Fiction* (1961), from which the following excerpt is taken. Booth argues that the conventional distinction between first and third person narrators is too reductive and simplistic, and that it fails to take into account many "variables" concerning point of view that writers of fiction can adjust to create special effects. His remarks remind us that skillful readers must pay careful attention to *how* stories are told and that rhetoric, the art of persuasion, is just as important in narrative writing as it is in exposition.

PERSON

Perhaps the most overworked distinction is that of person. To say that a story is told in the first or the third person will tell us nothing of importance unless we become more precise and describe how the particular qualities of the narrators relate to specific effects. It is true that choice of the first person is sometimes unduly limiting; if the "I" has inadequate access to necessary information, the author may be led into improbabilities. And there are other effects that may dictate a choice in some cases. But we can hardly expect to find useful criteria in a distinction that throws all fiction into two, or at most three, heaps.

Further evidence that this distinction is less important than has often been claimed is seen in the fact that all of the following functional distinctions apply to both first- and third-person narration alike.

DRAMATIZED AND UNDRAMATIZED NARRATORS

Perhaps the most important differences in narrative effect depend on whether the narrator is dramatized in his own right and on whether his beliefs and characteristics are shared by the author.

The implied author (the author's "second self").—Even the novel in which no narrator is dramatized creates an implicit picture of an author who stands behind the scenes, whether as stage manager, as puppeteer, or as an indifferent God, silently paring his fingernails. This implied author is always distinct from the "real man" —whatever we may take him to be— who creates a superior version of himself, a "second self," as he creates his work.

In so far as a novel does not refer directly to this author, there will be no distinction between him and the implied, undramatized narrator; in Hemingway's "The Killers," for example, there is no narrator other than the implicit second self that Hemingway creates as he writes.

Undramatized narrators.—Stories are usually not so rigorously impersonal as "The Killers"; most tales are presented as passing through the consciousness of a teller, whether an "I" or a "he. . . ." As soon as we encounter an "I," we are conscious of an experiencing mind whose views of the experience will come between us and the event. When there is no such "I," as in "The Killers," the inexperienced reader may make the mistake of thinking that the story comes to him unmediated. But no such mistake can be made from the moment that the author explicitly places a narrator into the tale, even if he is given no personal characteristics whatever.

Dramatized narrators.—In a sense even the most reticent narrator has been dramatized as soon as he refers to himself as "I," or, like Flaubert, tells us that "we" were in the classroom when Charles Bovary entered. . . . The range of human types that have been dramatized as narrators is almost as great as the range of other fictional characters—one must say "almost" because there are some characters who are not fully qualified to narrate or "reflect" a story (Faulkner can use the idiot for *part* of his novel only because the other three parts exist to set off and clarify the idiot's jumble).

We should remind ourselves that many dramatized narrators are never explicitly labeled as narrators at all. In a sense, every speech, every gesture, narrates; most works contain disguised narrators who are used to tell the audience what it needs to know, while seeming merely to act out their roles.

Though disguised narrators of this kind are seldom labeled so explicitly as God in Job, they often speak with an authority as sure as God's.

The most important unacknowledged narrators in modern fiction are the third-person "centers of consciousness" through whom authors have filtered their narratives. Whether such "reflectors," as James sometimes called them, are highly polished mirrors reflecting complex mental experience, or the rather turbid, sense-bound "camera eyes" of much fiction since James, they fill precisely the function of avowed narrators—though they can add intensities of their own.

The very real advantages of this method, for some purposes, have provided a dominant theme in modern criticism. Indeed, so long as our attention is on such qualities as naturalness and vividness, the advantages seem overwhelming. Only as we break out of the fashionable assumption that all good fiction tries for the same kind of vivid illusion in the same way are we forced to recognize disadvantages. The third-person reflector is only one mode among many, suitable for some effects but cumbersome and even harmful when other effects are desired.

Observers and Narrator-Agents

Among dramatized narrators there are mere observers, and there are narrator-agents, who produce some measurable effect on the course of events. Clearly, any rules we might discover about observers may not apply to narrator-agents, yet the distinction is seldom made in talk about point of view.

SCENE AND SUMMARY

All narrators and observers, whether first or third person, can relay their tales to us primarily as scene, primarily as summary or what Lubbock called "picture," or, most commonly, as a combination of the two.

Like Aristotle's distinction between dramatic and narrative manners, the somewhat different modern distinction between showing and telling does cover the ground. But the trouble is that it pays for broad coverage with gross imprecision. Narrators of all shapes and shades must either report dialogue alone or support it with "stage directions" and description of setting. But when we think of the radically different effect of a scene reported by Huck Finn and a scene reported by Poe's Montresor, we see that the quality of being "scenic" suggests very little about literary effect. The contrast between scene and summary, between showing and telling, is likely to be of little use until we specify the kind of narrator who is providing the scene or the summary.

COMMENTARY

Narrators who allow themselves to tell as well as show vary greatly depending on the amount and kind of commentary allowed in addition to a direct relating of events in scene and summary. Such commentary can, of course, range over any aspect of human experience, and it can be related to the main business in innumerable ways and degrees. To treat it as a single device is to ignore important differences between commentary that is merely ornamental, commentary that serves a rhetorical purpose but is not part of the dramatic structure, and commentary that is integral to the dramatic structure.

SELF-CONSCIOUS NARRATORS

Cutting across the distinction between observers and narrator-agents of all these kinds is the distinction between *self-conscious narrators,* aware of themselves as writers, and narrators or observers who rarely if ever discuss their writing chores (*Huckleberry Finn*) or who seem unaware that they are writing, thinking, speaking, or "reflecting" a literary work.

VARIATIONS OF DISTANCE

Whether or not they are involved in the action as agents or as sufferers, narrators and third-person reflectors differ markedly according to the degree and kind of distance that separates them from the author, the reader, and the other characters of the story. In any reading experience there is an implied dialogue among author, narrator, the other characters, and the reader. Each of the four can range, in relation to each of the others, from identification to complete opposition, on any axis of value, moral, intellectual, aesthetic, and even physical. The elements usually discussed under "aesthetic distance" enter in of course; distance in time and space, differences of social class or conventions of speech or dress—these and many others serve to control our sense that we are dealing with an aesthetic object, just as the paper moons and other unrealistic stage effects of some modern drama have had an "alienation" effect. But we must not confuse these with the equally important effects of personal beliefs and qualities, in author, reader, narrator, and all others in the cast of characters.

1. The *narrator* may be more or less distant from the *implied author*. The distance may be moral. . . . It may be intellectual. . . . It may be physical or temporal: most authors are distant from even the most knowing narrator in that they presumably know how "everything turns out in the end."

2. The *narrator* also may be more or less distant from the characters in the story he tells. He may differ morally, intellectually, and temporally; morally and intellectually . . . ; morally and emotionally . . . ; and thus on through every possible trait.

3. The *narrator* may be more or less distant from the reader's own norms. With the repudiation of omniscient narration, and in the face of inherent limitations in dramatized reliable narrators, it is hardly surprising that modern authors have experimented with unreliable narrators whose characteristics change in the course of the works they narrate. Ever since Shakespeare taught the modern world what the Greeks had overlooked in neglecting character change (compare Macbeth and Lear with Oedipus), stories of character development or degeneration have become more and more popular. But it was not until authors had discovered the full uses of the third-person reflector that they could effectively show a narrator changing *as he narrates*. . . . But the third-person reflector can be shown, technically in the past tense but in effect present before our eyes, moving toward or away from values that the reader holds dear. Authors in the twentieth century have proceeded almost as if determined to work out all of the possible plot forms based on such shifts: start far and end near; start near, move far, and end near; start far and move farther; and so on. Perhaps the most characteristic, however, have been the astonishing achievements in the first of these, taking extremely unsympathetic characters like Faulkner's Mink Snopes and transforming them, both through character change and technical manipulation, into characters of dignity and power.

4. The *implied author* may be more or less distant from the *reader*. The distance may be intellectual . . . moral . . . , or aesthetic. From the author's viewpoint, a successful reading of his book must eliminate all distance between the essential norms of his implied author and the norms of the postulated reader. Often enough, there is very little fundamental distance to begin with. . . . A bad book . . . is often most clearly recognizable because the implied author asks that we judge according to norms that we cannot accept.

5. The *implied author* (carrying the reader with him) may be more or less distant from *other characters*. Again, the distance can be on any axis of value. Some successful authors keep most of their characters very far "away" in every respect. . . . Others present a wider range from far to near, on a variety of axes.

For practical criticism probably the most important of these kinds of distance is that between the fallible or unreliable narrator and the implied author who carries the reader with him in judging the narrator. If the reason for discussing point of view is to find how it relates to literary effects, then surely the moral and intellectual qualities of the narrator are more important to our judgment than whether he is referred to as "I" or "he," or whether he is privileged or limited. If he is discovered to be untrustworthy, then the total effect of the work he relays to us is transformed.

Our terminology for this kind of distance in narrators is almost hopelessly inadequate. For lack of better terms, I have called a narrator *reliable* when he speaks for or acts in accordance with the norms of the work (which is to say, the implied author's norms), *unreliable* when he does not. It is true that most of the great reliable narrators indulge in large amounts of incidental irony, and they are thus "unreliable" in the sense of being potentially deceptive. But difficult irony is not sufficient to make a narrator unreliable. Nor is unreliability ordinarily a matter of lying, although deliberately deceptive narrators have been a major resource of some modern novelists. It is most often a matter of what James calls *inconscience;* the narrator is mistaken, or he believes himself to have qualities which the author denies him. Or, as in *Huckleberry Finn*, the narrator claims to be naturally wicked while the author silently praises his virtues behind his back.

Unreliable narrators thus differ markedly depending on how far and in what direction they depart from their author's norms; the older term "tone," like the currently fashionable terms "irony" and "distance" covers many effects that we should distinguish. Some narrators are placed as far "away" from author and reader as possible, in respect to every virtue except a kind of interesting vitality. Some, like Fleda Vetch, the reflector in James's *The Spoils of Poynton*, some close to representing the author's ideal of taste, judgment, and moral sense. All of them make stronger demands on the reader's powers of inference than do reliable narrators.

VARIATIONS IN SUPPORT OR CORRECTION

Both reliable and unreliable narrators can be unsupported or uncorrected by other narrators or supported or corrected. Sometimes it is almost impossible to infer whether or to what degree a narrator is fallible; sometimes explicit corroborating or conflicting testimony makes the inference easy. Support or correction differs radically, it should be noted, depending on whether it is provided from within the action, so that the narrator-agent might benefit from it in sticking to the right line or in changing his own views, or is simply provided externally, to help the reader correct or reinforce his own views as against the narrator's. Obviously, the effects of isolation will be extremely different in the two cases.

PRIVILEGE

Observers and narrator-agents, whether self-conscious or not, reliable or not, commenting or silent, isolated or supported, can be either privileged to know what could not be learned by strictly natural means or limited to realistic vision and inference. Complete privilege is what we usually call omniscience. But there are many kinds of privilege, and very few "omniscient" narrators are allowed to know or show as much as their authors know.

The most important single privilege is that of obtaining an inside view of another character, because of the rhetorical power that such a privilege conveys upon a narrator. There is a curious ambiguity in the term "omniscience." Many modern works that we usually classify as narrated dramatically, with everything relayed to us through the limited views of the characters, postulate fully as much omniscience in the silent author as Fielding claims for himself. . . . In short, impersonal narration is really no escape from omniscience—the true author is as "unnaturally" all-knowing as he ever was. If evident artificiality were a fault—which it is not—modern narration would be as faulty as Trollope's.

INSIDE VIEWS

Finally, narrators who provide inside views differ in the depth and the axis of their plunge. Boccaccio can give inside views, but they are extremely shallow. Jane Austen goes relatively deep morally, but scarcely skims the surface psychologically. All authors of stream-of-consciousness narration presumably attempt to go deep psychologically, but some of them deliberately remain shallow in the moral dimension. We should remind ourselves that any sustained inside view, of whatever depth, temporarily turns the character whose mind is shown into a narrator; inside views are thus subject to variations in all of the qualities we have described above, and most importantly in the degree of unreliability. Generally speaking, the deeper our plunge, the more unreliability we will accept without loss of sympathy.

Narration is an art, not a science, but this does not mean that we are necessarily doomed to fail when we attempt to formulate principles about it. There are systematic elements in every art, and criticism of fiction can never avoid the responsibility of trying to explain technical successes and failures by reference to general principles. But we must always ask where the general principles are to be found.

It is not surprising to hear practicing novelists report that they have never had any help from critics about point of view. In dealing with point of view the novelist must always deal with the individual work: which particular character shall tell this particular story, or part of a story, with what precise degree of reliability, privilege, freedom to comment, and so on. Shall he be given dramatic vividness? Even if the novelist has decided on a narrator who will fit one of the critic's classifications— "omniscient," "first person," "limited omniscient," "objective," "roving," "effaced," or whatever—his troubles have just begun. He simply cannot find answers to his immediate, precise, practical problems by referring to statements such as that the "omniscient is the most flexible method," or that "the objective is the most rapid or vivid." Even the soundest of generalizations at this level will be of little use to him in his page-by-page progress through his novel.

As Henry James's detailed records show, the novelist discovers his narrative technique as he tries to achieve for his readers the potentialities of his developing idea. The majority of his choices are consequently choices of degree, not kind. To decide that your narrator shall not be omniscient decides practically nothing. The hard question is: Just how *inconscient* shall he be? Again, to decide on first-person narration settles only a part of one's problem, perhaps the easiest part. What kind of first person? How fully characterized? How much aware of himself as narrator? How reliable? How much confined to realistic inference; how far privileged to go beyond realism? At what points shall he speak truth and at what points utter no judgment or even utter falsehood? These questions can be answered only by reference to the potentialities and necessities of particular works, not by reference to fiction in general, or the novel, or rules about point of view.

There are no doubt *kinds* of effect to which the author can refer; for example, if he wants to make a scene more amusing, poignant, vivid, or ambiguous, or if he wants to make a character more sympathetic or more convincing, such-and-such practices may be indicated. But we can understand why in his search for help in his decisions, the novelist should find the practice of his peers more helpful than the abstract rules of the textbooks: the sensitive author who reads the great novels finds in them a storehouse of precise examples, of how *this* effect, as distinct from all other possible effects, was heightened by the proper narrative choice. In dealing with the types of narration, the critic must always limp behind, referring constantly to the varied practice which alone can correct his temptations to overgeneralize. In place of our modern "fourth unity," in place of abstract rules about consistency and objectivity in the use of point of view, we need more painstaking, specific accounts of how great tales are told.

JOHN UPDIKE (b. 1932)

[The Virtues of Sloppy Writing]

In this selection from *The Paris Review Interviews* (fourth series, edited by George Plimpton, 1976), John Updike speaks of the dangers of writing too carefully. A glance back at his story "A & P" (page 23) will show that he has not lost the power to record experience spontaneously, with "the rhythm of utterance, the happiness." He also says that although psychological insights are important in fiction, readers are ultimately won over by the author's "instinct for action and pattern, and a perhaps savage wish to hold, through [his or her] voice, another soul in thrall." See the headnote for Updike on page 23.

INTERVIEWER: You mentioned Kerouac a moment ago. How do you feel about his work?

UPDIKE: Somebody like Kerouac who writes on teletype paper as rapidly as he can once slightly alarmed me. Now I can look upon this more kindly. There may be some reason to question the whole idea of fineness and care in writing. Maybe something can get into sloppy writing that would elude careful writing. I'm not terribly careful myself, actually. I write fairly rapidly if I get going, and don't change much, and have never been one for making outlines or taking out whole paragraphs or agonizing much. If a thing goes, it goes for me, and if it doesn't go, I eventually stop and get off.

INTERVIEWER: What is it that you think gets into sloppy writing that eludes more careful prose?

UPDIKE: It comes down to what is language. Up to now, until this age of mass literacy, language has been something spoken. In utterance there's a minimum of slowness. In trying to treat words as chisel strokes, you run the risk of losing the quality of utterance, the rhythm of utterance, the happiness. A phrase out of Mark Twain—he describes a raft hitting a bridge and says that it "went all to smash and scatteration like a box of matches struck by lightning." The beauty of "scatteration" could only have occurred to a talkative man, a man who had been brought up among people who were talking and who loved to talk himself. I'm aware myself of a certain dryness of this reservoir, this backlog of spoken talk. A Rumanian once said to me that Americans are always telling stories. I'm not sure this is as true as it once was. Where we once used to spin yarns, now we sit in front of the TV and receive pictures. I'm not sure the younger generation even knows how to gossip. But, as for a writer, if he has something to tell, he should perhaps type it almost as fast as he could talk it. We must look to the organic world, not the inorganic world, for metaphors; and just as the organic world has periods of repose and periods of great speed and exercise, so I think the writer's process should be organically varied. But there's a kind of tautness that you should feel within yourself no matter how slow or fast you're spinning out the reel.

INTERVIEWER: In "The Sea's Green Sameness" you deny that characterization and psychology are primary goals of fiction. What do you think is more important?

UPDIKE: I wrote "The Sea's Green Sameness" years ago and meant, I believe, that narratives should not be *primarily* packages for psychological insights, though they can contain them, like raisins in buns. But the substance is the dough, which feeds the storytelling appetite, the appetite for motion, for suspense, for resolution. The author's deepest pride, as I have experienced it, is not in his incidental wisdom but in his ability to keep an organized mass of images moving forward, to feel life engendering itself under his hands. But no doubt, fiction is also a mode of spying; we read it as we look in windows or listen to gossip, to learn what other people *do*. Insights of all kinds are welcome; but no wisdom will substitute for an instinct for action and pattern, and a perhaps savage wish to hold, through your voice, another soul in thrall.

INTERVIEWER: In view of this and your delight in the "noncommittal luminosity of fact," do you think you're much like the "nouvelle vague" novelists?

UPDIKE: I used to. I wrote *The Poorhouse Fair* as an anti-novel, and have found Nathalie Sarraute's description of the modern novelistic predicament a helpful guide. I am attracted to the cool surface of some contemporary French novels, and like them, do want to give inanimate or vegetable presences some kind of vote in the democracy of narrative. Basically, though, I describe things not because their muteness mocks our subjectivity but because they seem to be masks for God. And I should add that there is, in fiction, an image-making function, above image-retailing. To create a coarse universal figure like Tarzan is in some ways more of an accomplishment than the novels of Henry James.

INTERVIEWER: As a technician, how unconventional would you say you were?

UPDIKE: As unconventional as I need to be. An absolute freedom exists on the blank page, so let's use it. I have from the start been wary of the fake, the automatic. I tried not to force my sense of life as many-layered and ambiguous, while keeping in mind some sense of transaction, of a bargain struck, between me and the ideal reader. Domestic fierceness within the middle class, sex and death as riddles for the thinking animal, social existence as sacrifice, unexpected pleasures and rewards, corruption as a kind of evolution—these are some of the themes. I have tried to achieve objectivity in the form of narrative. My work is meditation, not pontification, so that interviews like this one feel like a forcing of the growth, a posing. I think of my books not as sermons or directives in a war of ideas but as objects, with different shapes and textures and the mysteriousness of anything that exists. My first thought about art, as a child, was that the artist brings something into the world that didn't exist before, and that he does it without destroying something else. A kind of refutation of the conservation of matter. That still seems to me its central magic, its core of joy.

ALICE WALKER (b. 1944)

From *The Black Writer and the Southern Experience*

In the following passage from an essay in *In Search of Our Mother's Gardens* (1983), Alice Walker explains the importance of the American South as a distinct region to black writers such as herself. Tragic as its history might at times have been, Walker sees the social milieu of the South as part of a fertile and "advantageous" heritage. See the headnote for Walker on page 509.

In large measure, black Southern writers owe their clarity of vision to parents who refused to diminish themselves as human beings by succumbing to racism. Our parents seemed to know that an extreme negative emotion held against other human beings for reasons they do not control can be blinding. Blindness about other human beings, especially for a writer, is equivalent to death. Because of this blindness, which is, above all, racial, the works of many Southern writers have died. Much that we read today is fast expiring.

My own slight attachment to William Faulkner was rudely broken by realizing, after reading statements he made in *Faulkner in the University*, that he believed whites superior morally to blacks; that whites had a duty (which at their convenience they would assume) to "bring blacks along" politically, since blacks, in Faulkner's opinion, were "not ready" yet to function properly in a democratic society. He also thought that a black man's intelligence is directly related to the amount of white blood he had.

For the black person coming of age in the sixties, where Martin Luther King stands against the murderers of Goodman, Chaney, and Schwerner, there appears no basis for such assumptions. Nor was there any in Garvey's day, or in Du Bois's or in Douglass's or in Nat Turner's. Nor at any other period in our history, from the very founding of the country; for it was hardly incumbent upon slaves to be slaves and saints too. Unlike Tolstoy, Faulkner was not prepared to struggle to change the structure of the society he was born in. One might concede that in his fiction he did seek to examine the reasons for its decay, but unfortunately, as I have learned while trying to teach Faulkner to black students, it is not possible, from so short a range, to separate the man from his works.

One reads Faulkner knowing that his "colored" people had to come through "Mr. William's" back door, and one feels uneasy, and finally enraged that Faulkner did not burn the whole house down. When the provincial mind starts out *and continues* on a narrow and unprotesting course, "genius" itself must run on a track.

Flannery O'Connor at least had the conviction that "reality" is at best superficial and that the puzzle of humanity is less easy to solve than that of race. But Miss O'Connor was not so much of Georgia, as in it. The majority of southern writers have been too confined by prevailing social customs to probe deeply into mysteries that the Citizens Councils insist must never be revealed.

Perhaps my Northern brothers will not believe me when I say there is a great deal of positive material I can draw from my "underprivileged" background. But they have never lived, as I have, at the end of a long road in a house that was faced by the edge of the world on one side and nobody for miles on the other. They have never experienced the magnificent quiet of a summer day when the heat is intense and one is so very thirsty, as one moves across the dusty cotton fields, that one learns forever that water is the essence of all life. In the cities it cannot be so clear to one that he is a creature of the earth, feeling the soil between the toes, smelling the dust thrown up by the rain, loving the earth so much that one longs to taste it and sometimes does.

Nor do I intend to romanticize the Southern black country life. I can recall that I hated it, generally. The hard work in the fields, the shabby houses, the evil greedy men who worked my father to death and almost broke the courage of that strong woman, my mother. No, I am simply saying that Southern black writers, like most writers, have a heritage of love and hate, but that they also have enormous richness and beauty to draw from. And, having been placed, as Camus says, "halfway between misery and the sun," they, too, know that "though all is not well under the sun, history is not everything."

No one could wish for a more advantageous heritage than that bequeathed to the black writer in the South: a compassion for the earth, a trust in humanity beyond our knowledge of evil, and an abiding love of justice. We inherit a great responsibility as well, for we must give voice to centuries not only of silent bitterness and hate but also of neighborly kindness and sustaining love.

II

POETRY

SECTION
1

How To Read
Poetry

HOW TO READ POETRY

Many college readers approach poetry with preconceptions that are also misconceptions—the products of hearsay, early reading experiences, or even prior classroom instruction. Like many preconceptions, they contain some truth. Perhaps by addressing them at the outset, we can help sift truth from half-truth and thus facilitate our understanding of a difficult type of literature. Here are some common preconceptions.

1. That poems mean anything the reader wants them to. This idea is similar to the notion that "beauty is in the eye of the beholder." Tastes about poetry can and do differ. What one reader likes, another dislikes. What a world it would be without such disagreement! But poems say what *they* say and mean what *they* mean—not what *we* want them to say or mean. They can be ambiguous or have many levels of meaning; these are possibilities that we appreciate and look for. But the words of poetry are generally the words we all use, and they have the meanings we customarily attach to them. When Matthew Arnold says in "Dover Beach" that "the sea is calm tonight," he may be making the sea stand for something beyond itself, its calmness reflecting the mood of the speaker. But, on one level at least, the statement means exactly what it says: the sea is calm tonight. When you read a poem, then, read it first for what it says. Be aware that there may be diverse intepretations and disagreement about the meaning of the poem and the importance of that meaning. But take heart; you have the basic tool required to read it effectively and enjoyably. You understand the language.
2. That poems are unnecessarily difficult. This second idea is related to the

first. When something is difficult, we often do not make the effort required to understand it. In our desire to convince ourselves (or others) that we do understand it, however, we may search for meanings that are not there. We confuse the meaning of a part with the meaning of the whole, arriving at interpretations that are inconsistent, narrow, or even nonsensical. Poems *are* difficult. They are carefully made, and they draw upon many of the resources of the language—including meaning, sound, word order, rhetorical devices, and typography. To understand them, we must spend proportionately more time with them than we would with a story or a novel.

3. That poems record the nebulous or imprecise thoughts of "dreamy" people. Because poems are difficult, and because their meaning is sometimes difficult to pin down, we often think they are vague expressions of ideas that could be stated more clearly. Bad poems sometimes display this fault. In good poetry, however, we encounter precise language that records highly intense and complex emotional and mental states. We must study this language with care and attentiveness.

Though poets use language familiar to all, they use it with special precision, subtlety, and skill. Attentive readers of poetry should pay special attention to those features of language that poets use for special effects. Among the more conventionally familiar of these are **rhyme** and other properties of sound in language, **rhythm** and **meter** (the way a poem "moves" or has a beat), and **lines.** These are the elements that most people would mention first if asked to define poetry, and there is good reason to do so. The line is a vital element of poetic form; in fact, the line as a structural unit distinguishes poetry from all other kinds of writing. Furthermore, poets use meter, rhythm, and rhyme to give lines their special character. Poets adjust these elements to give force to their meaning and to give their work a characteristic "voice." The universality of lines and rhythm in poetry, therefore, should serve to remind us of their significance.

Poetry employs other devices besides those commonly associated with it, however. Your study of fiction, in fact, should be of some help as you approach the poems that follow. Poems have speakers (called, as in fiction, **personae**), and they often have recognizable dramatic situations, plots, and characters whose actions we are asked to consider. These "fictional" elements may make poetry seem less foreign.

Above all, we must pay attention to the language of poetry, for it is used with great care and subtlety. This language is, first of all, often highly condensed. Every word in a good poem counts, and poets take great pains to make their use of language as efficient as possible. They may use unusual words, or familiar ones invested with significant connotations that affect the tone of their work. They usually employ more sensory imagery than prose writers, and they are adept at using complex and often ingenious figures of speech that clarify meaning and convey striking pictures to us with great economy. We must be sensitive to all of these. In the chapters that follow, the language of poetry will be one of our most important concerns.

Reading and understanding poetry are difficult tasks, but they yield great pleasures and benefits. To read poetry effectively, we must struggle to come to grips with language at a fundamental level and learn to appreciate the myriad effects writers can achieve by handing words carefully. Even if we don't always win this struggle, it helps us to read any text with greater care and sensitivity. Here are some tips that may help you as you read the poems that follow.

Read each poem several times, and at least once out loud. This will help acclimate you to the work at hand, and will help you appreciate the sound of the poem, its sentence structure, and its overall organization. If you can read a poem correctly, you are well on your way to understanding what it emphasizes.

Know the words. Clearly, since the language of a poem is usually condensed and charged with meaning, we should scrutinize the individual words that poets use. Pay heed to the contexts of the words you read. A good dictionary, a desk encyclopedia, and even a dictionary of classical mythology can all help you make greater sense of a poem. And of course do not be afraid to mark in your book; careful annotation can be of great help.

Pay attention to the line breaks. Lines are one of the most distinctive features of poetry. A poem on a ticker tape would lose one of its essential elements. Try to determine why poets choose to break lines where they do. But be cautious, when you are reading, that you do not stop at the ends of lines where you are not supposed to. The sense of an important line may "curl" around to the next line along with the words. Watch punctuation.

Be mindful of the sentence structure used in the poem. Most poems employ phrases, clauses, and sentences just as other kinds of writing do. An awareness of grammatical patterns will help you understand the rhetorical practices of the writer and will help make any poem more comprehensible and readable.

Visualize what you read. As with drama, poems are made more vivid if we attempt to *see* what the author is telling us. Using your imagination can help you come to terms with the situation the poem describes, and may even help you appreciate its tone.

Enter the poem where you can. When you read a poem, you may understand the final stanzas before you understand the middle ones, or the whole poem may not fall into place until you reread the beginning in light of the end. Be flexible in your approach. Use one part of the poem to help you understand another. There will be plenty of time to integrate all your isolated insights.

Try to achieve some sense of the overall organization of the poem. Does it have structural parts that may convey meaning in segments? Are there significant repetitions? Are there changes of setting or time? Are there stages in an argument or statement the poem is making? Being aware of how poems are organized will help you to understand and to write about them more effectively.

Try to determine the speaker, the occasion, and the dramatic situation of the poem. This will usually not be easy, and sometimes won't even be possible, but making the attempt will help you visualize the poem and enhance your interest in it.

Perhaps more than any other kind of writing, poetry reminds us of the axiom that you only get out of something what you put into it. Poems demand a significant expenditure of time and energy to become familiar and clear to us. But reading poetry with understanding is one of the great rewards of literature.

SECTION

2

Exemplary Texts

JOHN KEATS (1795–1821)

Born in London, Keats studied medicine but abandoned it in 1816 to devote his time to writing poetry. A small volume, *Poems,* appeared in 1817, and its modest success encouraged Keats to continue with a long mythological poem entitled *Endymion* (1818). Keats's reputation as one of England's greatest lyric poets rests largely on his famous odes and upon the other poems published in *Lamia, Isabella, The Eve of St. Agnes and Other Poems* (1820). He died in Rome of tuberculosis.

On First Looking into Chapman's Homer

Much have I traveled in the realms of gold,
  And many goodly states and kingdoms seen;
  Round many western islands have I been
Which bards in fealty to Apollo hold.
Oft of one wide expanse had I been told   5
  That deep-browed Homer ruled as his demesne;
  Yet did I never breathe its pure serene
Till I heard Chapman speak out loud and bold:
Then felt I like some watcher of the skies
  When a new planet swims into his ken;   10
Or like stout Cortez when with eagle eyes
  He stared at the Pacific—and all his men
Looked at each other with a wild surmise—
  Silent, upon a peak in Darien.

Ode On a Grecian Urn

I

Thou still unravished bride of quietness,
    Thou foster-child of silence and slow time,
Sylvan historian, who canst thus express
    A flowery tale more sweetly than our rhyme:
What leaf-fringed legend haunts about thy shape   5
    Of deities or mortals, or of both,
        In Tempe or the dales of Arcady?
What men or gods are these? What maidens loath?
    What mad pursuit? What struggle to escape?
        What pipes and timbrels? What wild ecstasy?   10

II

Heard melodies are sweet, but those unheard
    Are sweeter; therefore, ye soft pipes, play on;
Not to the sensual ear, but, more endeared,
    Pipe to the spirit ditties of no tone:
Fair youth, beneath the trees, thou canst not leave   15
    Thy song, nor ever can those trees be bare;
        Bold Lover, never, never canst thou kiss,
Though winning near the goal—yet, do not grieve;
She cannot fade, though thou hast not thy bliss,
    For ever wilt thou love, and she be fair!   20

III

Ah, happy, happy boughs! that cannot shed
    Your leaves, nor ever bid the Spring adieu;
And, happy melodist, unweariéd,
    For ever piping songs for ever new;
More happy love! more happy, happy love!   25
    For ever warm and still to be enjoyed,
        For ever panting, and for ever young;
All breathing human passion far above,
    That leaves a heart high-sorrowful and cloyed,
        A burning forehead, and a parching tongue.   30

IV

Who are these coming to the sacrifice?
  To what green altar, O mysterious priest,
Lead'st thou that heifer lowing at the skies,
  And all her silken flanks with garlands dressed?
What little town by river or sea shore, 35
  Or mountain-built with peaceful citadel,
    Is emptied of this folk, this pious morn?
And, little town, thy streets for evermore
  Will silent be; and not a soul to tell
    Why thou art desolate, can e'er return. 40

V

O Attic shape! Fair attitude! with brede
  Of marble men and maidens overwrought,
With forest branches and the trodden weed;
  Thou, silent form, dost tease us out of thought
As doth eternity: Cold Pastoral! 45
  When old age shall this generation waste,
    Thou shalt remain, in midst of other woe
Than ours, a friend to man, to whom thou say'st,
  Beauty is truth, truth beauty—that is all
    Ye know on earth, and all ye need to know. 50

La Belle Dame Sans Merci

O what can ail thee, Knight at arms,
  Alone and palely loitering?
The sedge has withered from the Lake
  And no birds sing!

O what can ail thee, Knight at arms, 5
  So haggard, and so woebegone?
The squirrel's granary is full,
  And the harvest's done.

I see a lily on thy brow
  With anguish moist and fever dew, 10
And on thy cheeks a fading rose
  Fast withereth too.

"I met a Lady in the Meads,
    Full beautiful, a faery's child,
Her hair was long, her foot was light   15
    And her eyes were wild.

"I made a Garland for her head,
    And bracelets too, and fragrant Zone;
She looked at me as she did love
    And made sweet moan.   20

"I set her on my pacing steed
    And nothing else saw all day long,
For sidelong would she bend and sing
    A faery's song.

"She found me roots of relish sweet,   25
    And honey wild, and manna dew,
And sure in language strange she said
    'I love thee true.'

"She took me to her elfin grot
    And there she wept and sighed full sore,   30
And there I shut her wild wild eyes
    With kisses four.

"And there she lulléd me asleep,
    And there I dreamed, Ah Woe betide!
The latest dream I ever dreamt   35
    On the cold hill side.

"I saw pale Kings, and Princes too,
    Pale warriors, death-pale were they all;
They cried, 'La belle dame sans merci
    Hath thee in thrall!'   40

"I saw their starved lips in the gloam
    With horrid warning gapéd wide,
And I awoke, and found me here
    On the cold hill's side.

"And this is why I sojourn here,   45
    Alone and palely loitering;
Though the sedge is withered from the Lake
    And no birds sing."

EMILY DICKINSON (1830–1886)

Along with Walt Whitman, Emily Dickinson is generally considered America's greatest nineteenth century poet. Her short and carefully-structured lyric poems, drawn from her contemplative and often reclusive life in Amherst, Massachusetts, contrast starkly with Whitman's sprawling and raucous free verse hymns to American democracy (see pp. 691, 905). Dickinson attended Amherst Academy and Mt. Holyoke Female Seminary. Only seven of her more than 1800 poems were published during her lifetime, and her complete poems were not published until 1955. Her influence on her contemporaries was thus nil—but a century later the beauty and insights of her best poems continue to delight and surprise every reader of her work.

There's a certain Slant of light

There's a certain Slant of light,
Winter Afternoons—
That oppresses, like the Heft
Of Cathedral Tunes—

Heavenly Hurt, it gives us—   5
We can find no scar,
But internal difference,
Where the Meanings, are—

None may teach it—Any—
'Tis the Seal Despair—   10
An imperial affliction
Sent us of the Air—

When it comes, the Landscape listens—
Shadows—hold their breath—
When it goes, 'tis like the Distance   15
On the look of Death—

A narrow Fellow in the Grass

A narrow Fellow in the Grass
Occasionally rides—
You may have met Him—did you not
His notice sudden is—

The Grass divides as with a Comb— 5
A spotted shaft is seen—
And then it closes at your feet
And opens further on—

He likes a Boggy Acre
A Floor too cool for Corn— 10
Yet when a Boy, and Barefoot—
I more than once at Noon
Have passed, I thought, a Whip lash
Unbraiding in the Sun
When stooping to secure it 15
It wrinkled, and was gone—

Several of Nature's People
I know, and they know me—
I feel for them a transport
Of cordiality— 20

But never met this Fellow
Attended, or alone
Without a tighter breathing
And Zero at the Bone—

Much Madness is divinest Sense

Much Madness is divinest Sense—
To a discerning Eye—
Much Sense—the starkest Madness—
'Tis the Majority
In this, as All, prevail— 5
Assent—and you are sane—
Demur—you're straightway dangerous—
And handled with a Chain—

WILLIAM BUTLER YEATS (1865–1939)

Born and educated in Dublin, Ireland, Yeats had become an
important contributor to the Irish literary revival by the 1890s. His studies
of Irish folklore and legends influenced his first book, *The Wanderings of
Oisin and Other Poems* (1889). After 1900 his poetry, always highly lyrical,
become increasingly symbolic and political in its orientation. Yeats in fact
served as a senator in the newly-formed Irish Free State from 1923 to
1928. He was awarded the Nobel Prize in 1923. Among his most famous
books are *The Tower* (1928) and *The Winding Stair* (1933).

Leda and the Swan

A sudden blow: the great wings beating still
Above the staggering girl, her thighs caressed
By the dark webs, her nape caught in his bill,
He holds her helpless breast upon his breast.

How can those terrified vague fingers push   5
The feathered glory from her loosening thighs?
And how can body, laid in that white rush,
But feel the strange heart beating where it lies?

A shudder in the loins engenders there
The broken wall, the burning roof and tower   10
And Agamemnon dead.
                    Being so caught up,
So mastered by the brute blood of the air,
Did she put on his knowledge with his power
Before the indifferent beak could let her drop?

Sailing to Byzantium

I

That is no country for old men. The young
in one another's arms, birds in the trees
—Those dying generations—at their song,
The salmon-falls, the mackerel-crowded seas,
Fish, flesh, or fowl, commend all summer long   5
Whatever is begotten, born, and dies.
Caught in that sensual music all neglect
Monuments of unaging intellect.

II

An aged man is but a paltry thing,
A tattered coat upon a stick, unless   10
Soul clap its hands and sing, and louder sing
For every tatter in its mortal dress,
Nor is there singing school but studying
Monuments of its own magnificence;
And therefore I have sailed the seas and come   15
To the holy city of Byzantium.

III

O sages standing in God's holy fire
As in the gold mosaic of a wall,
Come from the holy fire, perne in a gyre,
And be the singing-masters of my soul.   20
Consume my heart away; sick with desire
And fastened to a dying animal
It knows not what it is; and gather me
Into the artifice of eternity.

IV

Once out of nature I shall never take   25
My bodily form from any natural thing,
But such a form as Grecian goldsmiths make
Of hammered gold and gold enameling
To keep a drowsy Emperor awake;
Or set upon a golden bough to sing   30
To lords and ladies of Byzantium
Of what is past, or passing, or to come.

Lapis Lazuli

For Harry Clifton

I have heard that hysterical women say
They are sick of the palette and fiddle-bow,
Of poets that are always gay,
For everybody knows or else should know
That if nothing drastic is done   5
Aeroplane and Zeppelin will come out,
Pitch like King Billy bomb-balls in
Until the town lie beaten flat.

All perform their tragic play,
There struts Hamlet, there is Lear,   10
That's Ophelia, that Cordelia;
Yet they, should the last scene be there,
The great stage curtain about to drop,
If worthy their prominent part in the play,
Do not break up their lines to weep.   15

They know that Hamlet and Lear are gay;
Gaiety transfiguring all that dread.
All men have aimed at, found and lost,
Black out; Heaven blazing into the head:
Tragedy wrought to its uttermost.   20
Though Hamlet rambles and Lear rages,
And all the drop-scenes drop at once
Upon a hundred thousand stages,
It cannot grow by an inch or an ounce.

On their own feet they came, or on shipboard,   25
Camelback, horseback, ass-back, mule-back,
Old civilizations put to the sword.
Then they and their wisdom went to rack:
No handiwork of Callimachus,
Who handled marble as if it were bronze,   30
Made draperies that seemed to rise
When sea-wind swept the corner, stands;
His long lamp-chimney shaped like the stem
Of a slender palm, stood but a day;
All things fall and are built again,   35
And those that build them again are gay.

Two Chinamen, behind them a third,
Are carved in lapis lazuli,
Over them flies a long-legged bird,
A symbol of longevity;   40
The third, doubtless a serving-man,
Carries a musical instrument.

Every discoloration of the stone,
Every accidental crack or dent,
Seems a water-course or an avalanche,   45
Or lofty slope where it still snows
Though doubtless plum or cherry-branch
Sweetens the little half-way house
Those Chinamen climb towards, and I
Delight to imagine them seated there;   50
There, on the mountain and the sky,
On all the tragic scene they stare.
One asks for mournful melodies;
Accomplished fingers begin to play.
Their eyes mid many wrinkles, their eyes,   55
Their ancient, glittering eyes, are gay.

ROBERT LOWELL (1917–1977)

Born in Boston, among Lowell's famous literary ancestors were James Russell Lowell, the nineteenth century poet, and Amy Lowell, the twentieth century imagist poet. Lowell entered Harvard, but after two years there he transferred to Kenyon College in Ohio, from which he graduated in 1940. His first book, *Land of Unlikeness*, appeared in 1944. Lowell was a master of many poetic styles, from his formal, carefully-ordered early verse to the looser, personally revealing, "confessional" poems of *Life Studies* (1959). He was perhaps the greatest poet of his generation in America, and his influence on later work has been pervasive.

For the Union Dead

"Relinquunt Omnia Servare Rem Publicam"[1]

The old South Boston Aquarium stands
in a Sahara of snow now. Its broken windows are boarded.
The bronze weathervane cod has lost half its scales.
The airy tanks are dry.

Once my nose crawled like a snail on the glass;   5
my hand tingled
to burst the bubbles
drifting from the noses of the cowed, compliant fish.

My hand draws back. I often sigh still
for the dark downward and vegetating kingdom   10
of the fish and reptile. One morning last March,
I pressed against the new barbed and galvanized

fence on the Boston Common. Behind their cage,
yellow dinosaur steam shovels were grunting
as they cropped up tons of mush and grass   15
to gouge their underworld garage.

Parking spaces luxuriate like civic
sandpiles in the heart of Boston.
A girdle of orange, Puritan-pumpkin colored girders
braces the tingling Statehouse,   20

1. "They give up everything to serve the Republic"

shaking over the excavations, as it faces Colonel Shaw
and his bell-cheeked Negro infantry
on St. Gaudens' shaking Civil War relief,
propped by a plank splint against the garage's earthquake.

Two months after marching through Boston,   25
half the regiment was dead;
at the dedication,
William James could almost hear the bronze Negroes breathe.

Their monument sticks like a fishbone
in the city's throat.   30
Its Colonel is as lean
as a compass-needle.

He has an angry wrenlike vigilance,
a greyhound's gentle tautness;
he seems to wince at pleasure,   35
and suffocate for privacy.

He is out of bounds now. He rejoices in man's lovely,
peculiar power to choose life and die—
when he leads his black soldiers to death,
he cannot bend his back.   40

On a thousand small town New England greens,
the old white church holds their air
of sparse, sincere rebellion; frayed flags
quilt the graveyards of the Grand Army of the Republic.

The stone statues of the abstract Union Soldier   45
grow slimmer and younger each year—
wasp-waisted, they doze over muskets
and muse through their sideburns . . .

Shaw's father wanted no monument
except the ditch,   50
where his son's body was thrown
and lost with his "niggers."

The ditch is nearer.
There are no statues for the last war here;
on Boylston Street, a commercial photograph   55
shows Hiroshima boiling

over a Mosler Safe, the "Rock of Ages"
that survived the blast. Space is nearer.
When I crouch to my television set,
the drained faces of Negro school-children rise like balloons.   60

Colonel Shaw
is riding on his bubble,
he waits
for the blesséd break.

The Aquarium is gone. Everywhere,   65
giant finned cars nose forward like fish;
a savage servility
slides by on grease.

Memories of West Street and Lepke

Only teaching on Tuesdays, book-worming
in pajamas fresh from the washer each morning,
I hog a whole house on Boston's
"hardly passionate Marlborough Street,"
where even the man   5
scavenging filth in the back alley trash cans,
has two children, a beach wagon, a helpmate,
and is a "young Republican."
I have a nine months' daughter,
young enough to be my grandaughter.   10
Like the sun she rises in her flame-flamingo infants' wear.

These are the tranquillized *Fifties*,
and I am forty. Ought I to regret my seedtime?
I was a fire-breathing Catholic C.O.,
and made my manic statement,   15
telling off the state and president, and then
sat waiting sentence in the bull pen
beside a Negro boy with curlicues
of marijuana in his hair.

Given a year,   20
I walked on the roof of the West Street Jail, a short
enclosure like my school soccer court,
and saw the Hudson River once a day
through sooty clothesline entanglements
and bleaching khaki tenements.   25

Strolling, I yammered metaphysics with Abramowitz,
a jaundice-yellow ("it's really tan")
and fly-weight pacifist,
so vegetarian,
he wore rope shoes and preferred fallen fruit.   30
He tried to convert Bioff and Brown,
the Hollywood pimps, to his diet.
Hairy, muscular, suburban,
wearing chocolate double-breasted suits,
they blew their tops and beat him black and blue.   35

I was so out of things, I'd never heard
of the Jehovah's Witnesses.
"Are you a C.O.?" I asked a fellow jailbird.
"No," he answered, "I'm a J.W."
He taught me the "hospital tuck,"   40
and pointed out the T-shirted back
of *Murder Incorporated's* Czar Lepke,
there piling towels on a rack,
or dawdling off to his little segregated cell full
of things forbidden the common man: 45
a portable radio, a dresser, two toy American
flags tied together with a ribbon of Easter palm.
Flabby, bald, lobotomized,
he drifted in a sheepish calm,
where no agonizing reappraisal   50
jarred his concentration on the electric chair—
hanging like an oasis in his air
of lost connections. . . .

Children of Light

Our fathers wrung their bread from stocks and stones
And fenced their gardens with the Redman's bones;
Embarking from the Nether Land of Holland,
Pilgrims unhouseled by Geneva's night,
They planted here the Serpent's seeds of light;   5
And here the pivoting searchlights probe to shock
The riotous glass houses built on rock,
And candles gutter by an empty altar,
And light is where the landless blood of Cain
Is burning, burning the unburied grain.   10

DENISE LEVERTOV (b. 1923)

Denise Levertov was born in London of a Welsh mother and an
Anglican clergyman father who was a Russian Jew by birth. She was
educated entirely at home, attending neither school nor college. She came
to the United States in 1948. Although some of her most famous poems
are political, she defies inclusion in any "school" or group of poets such as
the Beat Poets of the 1950s or the Confessional Poets of the 1960s and
1970s. Among her many volumes of poems are *The Jacob's Ladder* (1961),
The Sorrow Dance (1967), *Life in the Forest* (1978), *and Candles in Babylon*
(1982).

Merrit Parkway

As if it were
forever that they move, that we
    keep moving—

    Under a wan sky where
    as the lights went on a star   5
        pierced the haze and now
    follows steadily
               a constant
    above our six lanes
    the dreamlike continuum . . .   10

And the people—ourselves!
    the humans from inside the
    cars, apparent
    only at gasoline stops
               unsure,   15
        eyeing each other
        drink coffee hastily at the
        slot machines and hurry
    back to the cars
    vanish   20
    into them forever, to
    keep moving—

Houses now and then beyond the
sealed road, the trees / trees, bushes
passing by, passing   25
    the cars that
        keep moving ahead of

us, past us, pressing behind us
and
over left, those that come   30
toward us shining too brightly
moving relentlessly

in six lanes, gliding
north and south, speeding with
a slurred sound—   35

The Ache of Marriage

The ache of marriage:

thigh and tongue, beloved,
are heavy with it,
it throbs in the teeth

We look for communion   5
and are turned away, beloved,
each and each

It is leviathan and we
in its belly
looking for joy, some joy   10
not to be known outside it

two by two in the ark of
the ache of it.

An English Field in the Nuclear Age

To render it!—*this* moment,
haze and halos of
sunbless'd particulars, knowing
no one,
not lost and dearest nor   5
the unfound,
could,
though summoned,
though present,
partake nor proffer vision unless   10
(named, spun, tempered, stain of it

sunk into steel of utterance) it
be wrought:
(centuries furrowed in oakbole, *this* oak,
these dogrose pallors, that very company   15
of rooks plodding
from stile to stile of the sky):
to render that isolate knowledge, certain
(shadow of oakleaves, larks
urging the green wheat into spires)   20
there is no sharing save in the furnace,
the transubstantiate, acts
of passion:
(the way

air, *this* minute, searches   25
warm bare shoulders, blind, a lover,

and how among
thistles, nettles, subtle silver
of long-dried cowpads,

gold mirrors of buttercup satin   30
assert eternity as they reflect
nothing, everything, absolute instant,
and dread

holds its breath, for
this minute at least was   35
not the last).

SEAMUS HEANEY (b. 1939)

Born in County Derry, Ireland, Heaney has taught at the University
of Belfast in Northern Ireland and has held several visiting professorships
in the United States, including one at Harvard. His work has been
collected in *Poems 1965–1975*, which contains his first four books of
poems and *Preoccupations: Selected Prose 1968–1978*, a collection of critical
essays and reviews.

Digging

Between my finger and my thumb
The squat pen rests; snug as a gun.
Under my window, a clean rasping sound
When the spade sinks into gravelly ground:
My father, digging. I look down   5

Till his straining rump among the flowerbeds
Bends low, comes up twenty years away
Stooping in rhythm through potato drills
Where he was digging.

The coarse boot nestled on the lug, the shaft   10
Against the inside knee was levered firmly.
He rooted out tall tops, buried the bright edge deep
To scatter new potatoes that we picked
Loving their cool hardness in our hands.

By God, the old man could handle a spade.   15
Just like his old man.

My grandfather cut more turf in a day
Than any other man on Toner's bog.
Once I carried him milk in a bottle
Corked sloppily with paper. He straightened up   20
To drink it, then fell to right away

Nicking and slicing neatly, heaving sods
Over his shoulder, going down and down
For the good turf. Digging.

The cold smell of potato mould, the squelch and slap   25
Of soggy peat, the curt cuts of an edge
Through living roots awaken in my head.
But I've no spade to follow men like them.

Between my finger and my thumb
The squat pen rests.   30
I'll dig with it.

Mid-Term Break

I sat all morning in the college sick bay
Counting bells knelling classes to a close.
At two o'clock our neighbors drove me home.

In the porch I met my father crying—
He had always taken funerals in his stride—   5
And Big Jim Evans saying it was a hard blow.

The baby cooed and laughed and rocked the pram
When I came in, and I was embarrassed
By old men standing up to shake my hand

And tell me they were "sorry for my trouble," 10
Whispers informed strangers I was the eldest,
Away at school, as my mother held my hand

In hers and coughed out angry tearless sighs.
At ten o'clock the ambulance arrived
With the corpse, stanched and bandaged by the nurses. 15

Next morning I went up into the room. Snowdrops
And candles soothed the bedside; I saw him
For the first time in six weeks. Paler now,

Wearing a poppy bruise on his left temple,
He lay in the four foot box as in his cot. 20
No gaudy scars, the bumper knocked him clear.

A four foot box, a foot for every year.

Punishment

I can feel the tug
of the halter at the nape
of her neck, the wind
on her naked front.

It blows her nipples
to amber beads, 5
it shakes the frail rigging
of her ribs.

I can see her drowned
body in the bog, 10
the weighing stone,
the floating rods and boughs.

Under which at first
she was a barked sapling
that is dug up 15
oak-bone, brain-firkin:

her shaved head
like a stubble of black corn,
her blindfold a soiled bandage,
her noose a ring 20

to store
the memories of love.
Little adulteress,
before they punished you

you were flaxen-haired,   25
undernourished, and your
tar-black face was beautiful.
My poor scapegoat,

I almost love you
but would have cast, I know,   30
the stones of silence.
I am the artful voyeur

of your brain's exposed
and darkened combs,
your muscles' webbing   35
and all your numbered bones:

I who have stood dumb
when your betraying sisters,
cauled in tar,
wept by the railings,   40

who would connive
in civilized outrage
yet understand the exact
and tribal, intimate revenge.

SECTION

3

The Elements of Poetry

WORDS

To love poetry, or even to appreciate it, is to love words: their sounds, their meanings, even the way they feel in our mouths when we say them. Say "sprawl" over and over again, slowly, and the word spreads out like its meaning. Say "cease" and notice how your tongue helps make the hissing sound, how the word itself ceases when you withdraw your tongue. Hear the hopping of the syllables in "incredible"; the clipped, curt end of "cook." Words, even before we know what they mean, appeal to us on a fundamental physiological level. We not only take pleasure from hearing them, but also from saying them. Reading poetry aloud more than repays us for the time it takes. The following poem by D. H. Lawrence resounds, quite literally, when read aloud.

D. H. LAWRENCE (1885–1930)

Piano

Softly, in the dusk, a woman is singing to me;
Taking me back down the vista of years, till I see
A child sitting under the piano, in the boom of the tingling strings
And pressing the small, poised feet of a mother who smiles as she sings.

In spite of myself, the insidious master of song
Betrays me back, till the heart of me weeps to belong
To the old Sunday evenings at home, with winter outside
And hymns in the cozy parlor, the tinkling piano our guide.

5

So now it is vain for the singer to burst into clamor
With the great black piano appassionato. The glamour   10
Of childish days is upon me, my manhood is cast
Down in the flood of remembrance, I weep like a child for the past.

This poem reverberates, and its subject is reverberation. In Lawrence's words we hear the piano, and in the piano we hear his nostalgic emotions. The words he uses, words we share with him as common property, have expressed his thoughts and affected ours. We are drawn into the poem by our kinship with the English language.

Notice that not one of the words Lawrence uses is in any way foreign to the vocabulary of the average adult. Perhaps "insidious" and "appassionato" are the only ones we would have to look up in a dictionary if asked to define them. Lawrence's words reach out to us across almost seventy years. His language is distinctive, and no doubt chosen with great care, but it is free of the archaisms, clipped contractions, and flowery diction that are often associated with poetry. The language of the poem is familiar, but made fresh by the way it is arranged. As students of poetry we must pay attention not only to words themselves, but also to their contexts.

English offers a living testimony to the vitality of language, and it is not surprising that some of the world's best poetry, by common acknowledgement, is written in English. The plays of Shakespeare, the poetry of Milton, Keats, Tennyson, T. S. Eliot, and Wallace Stevens—because we share the language in which they are written, these rich creations link us with an important literary and linguistic tradition reflecting the more than 1500 years of history that are preserved in modern English.

English is commonly divided into three broad historical periods, as follows:

440–1066   Old English
1066–1500   Middle English
1500–present   Modern English

Old English, also called Anglo-Saxon, was a Germanic language only slightly influenced by Latin. Most monosyllabic words in modern English (including common words like prepositions, pronouns, and conjunctions) remain from Anglo-Saxon. *Leg, book, earth, man, ice,* and *sea* are typical English words derived from this Germanic ancestor.

Old English produced an important body of literary prose and poetry, but ceased to be written after about 1100 because of the Norman conquest of England in 1066. The language of the conquering Normans—French—was superimposed upon Anglo-Saxon, and the resulting fusion gives modern English its special character, including its flexible and varied vocabulary. French is a derivative of Latin; hence **Middle English,** the language of Chaucer's *Canterbury Tales,* represents an amalgamation of a Germanic language with a Latin-based language. No other modern language exhibits such a fusion. Most polysyallabic words in modern English—the hard or "learned" words—are derived from French or Latin. *Celebration, dominant, engendered, bellicose,* and *rudimentary* are typical examples.

By 1500 the use of the printing press had solidified the spelling of the language. Almost anything written before this date in English has to be read with the help of a glossary or a dictionary, but after this period **Modern English** assumed its character. English thus preserves the grammars and the vocabularies of two major language systems. This distinction between Anglo-Saxon and French/Latin borrowings is one of the properties that we must be aware of when considering the diction and the style of modern English poetry.

Besides their origins, their number of syllables (and of course their definitions!) all words have qualities we must be sensitive to in order to appreciate the effects poets are able to create through word choice. Like other users of the language, poets choose their words with several considerations in mind.

1. Level of formality. Although words cannot be placed into social classes, the fact remains that some words are "proper" in some contexts and others not; some are "fancy" and difficult, some are plain and easy to understand. *Evening repast* is a formal term for the meal we have at 6:00 P.M.; *supper* is the middle range term we might normally use in everyday speech; *grub* is decidedly less formal than either. Depending upon their perceived audience, their aims, and their backgrounds, poets will use terms that lie somewhere along this spectrum of formality.

2. Level of concreteness or abstractness. For practical purposes, words are concrete or abstract depending upon whether or not they conjure up some kind of sensory image in our minds. *Smoke,* for example, causes images of sight, smell, or even taste to enter our minds. *Smoke* is concrete. *Hope* or *liberty,* conversely, create no particular sensory images. We cannot imagine touching or tasting them. They are abstract. Although abstract words of course have their place in poetry, poets usually prefer concrete words because they have the ability to affect the reader's imagination.

3. Level of specificity or generality. Think of the words *vehicle, automobile, Chevrolet,* and *Corvette.* As we move from the first to the last, the words become more specific, take on narrower and narrower definitions. There can be more kinds of vehicles, but few kinds of Corvettes. Specificity will tend to coincide with concreteness but the two are not the same. *Fruit* is a concrete term, but *plum* is a specific one. Again, poets will usually prefer specific words to general words because they are more likely to affect the reader's imagination.

Examine the following two poems by William Blake and see how Blake handles the three levels mentioned above. To get a sense of how these levels are significant, try changing the diction of one of the poems to make it general rather than specific (for example, change *tyger* to *animal*).

WILLIAM BLAKE (1757–1827)

The Lamb

Little Lamb, who made thee?
  Dost thou know who made thee?
Gave thee life & bid thee feed,
By the stream & o'er the mead;
Gave thee clothing of delight,   5
Softest clothing wooly bright;
Gave thee such a tender voice,
Making all the vales rejoice!
  Little Lamb who made thee?
  Dost thou know who made thee?   10

  Little Lamb I'll tell thee,
  Little Lamb I'll tell thee!
He is callèd by thy name,
For he calls himself a Lamb:
He is meek & he is mild,   15
He became a little child:
I a child & thou a lamb,
We are callèd by his name.
  Little Lamb God bless thee.
  Little Lamb God bless thee.   20

The Tyger

Tyger! Tyger! burning bright
In the forests of the night,
What immortal hand or eye
Could frame thy fearful symmetry?

In what distant deeps or skies   5
Burnt the fire of thine eyes?
On what wings dare he aspire?
What the hand, dare seize the fire?

And what shoulder, & what art,
Could twist the sinews of thy heart? 10
And when thy heart began to beat,
What dread hand? & what dread feet?

What the hammer? what the chain?
In what furnace was thy brain?
What the anvil? what dread grasp 15
Dare its deadly terrors clasp?

When the stars threw down their spears,
And water'd heaven with their tears,
Did he smile his work to see?
Did he who made the Lamb make thee? 20

Tyger! Tyger! burning bright
In the forests of the night,
What immortal hand or eye
Dare frame thy fearful symmetry?

To begin to understand Blake's poems, we must understand the meanings of his words. That much is clear enough. But we must also pay attention to how these words are used in context. We all know what *burning* means in "The Tyger," but the word takes on a different cast when we perceive that the burning takes place in the eyes of the ferocious, threatening tiger at night. Awareness of the context sharpens and deepens our sense of the meaning of the word and of its significance in the whole poem. Awareness of context, as well as other properties such as sound and grammatical function, is crucial to an understanding of the following "nonsense" poem by Lewis Carroll. See if you can "define" some of the unusual words he uses.

LEWIS CARROLL (1832–1898)

Jabberwocky

'Twas brillig, and the slithy toves
  Did gyre and gimble in the wabe;
All mimsy were the borogoves,
  And the mome raths outgrabe.

"Beware the Jabberwock, my son!   5
   The jaws that bite, the claws that catch!
Beware the Jubjub bird and shun
   The frumious Bandersnatch!"

He took his vorpal sword in hand
   Long time the manxome foe he sought—   10
So rested he by the Tumtum tree,
   And stood awhile in thought.

And, as in uffish thought he stood,
   The Jabberwock, with eyes of flame,
Came whiffling through the tulgey wood,   15
   And burbled as it came!

One, two! One, two! And through and through
   The vorpal blade went snicker-snack!
He left it dead, and with its head
   He went galumphing back.   20

"And hast thou slain the Jabberwock?
   Come to my arms, my beamish boy!
O frabjous day! Callooh! Callay!"
   He chortled in his joy.

'Twas brillig, and the slithy toves   25
   Did gyre and gimble in the wabe;
All mimsy were the borogoves,
   And the mome raths outgrabe.

Even though we cannot define *frabjous* (line 23), we can, because of its
context, make reasonable inferences about it. We know it is an adjective
because of its placement before the noun *day*. We could assume it has a
positive happy meaning because it is chortled in joy. The assumption might
be supported by the resemblance the word bears to "happy" words like
fabulous and *joyous*. These assumptions lead us to the conclusion that, no
matter what the *denotation* or dictionary definition of *frabjous* might be, it
has a decidedly positive connotation.

The **connotation** of a word refers to the range of associations the word
calls into our minds. These associations may be private or nearly universal.
The denotation of *dust*, for instance, might be "powdery earth capable of
being suspended in air." For one person, this word may also call up the
picture of a friend's name written in dust on a table top. To many Christians it might, by suggesting "earth to earth, ashes to ashes, dust to dust,"
call up a picture of a funeral, or even the general idea of mortality. Good

poets are usually adept at choosing words charged with significant connotations. These connotations create density, promote economy of utterance, and serve to support or create the ideas and themes the poet is trying to convey.

Read the following poems by Wilfred Owen, and Ted Hughes, then go back over each one to see how the poets have used connotation to affect our responses to the situations depicted. Try changing some particularly charged words in a way that destroys the connotation or that contradicts the impression the poet is trying to create.

WILFRED OWEN (1893–1918)

Dulce et Decorum Est

Bent double, like old beggars under sacks,
Knock-kneed, coughing like hags, we cursed through sludge,
Till on the haunting flares we turned our backs
And towards our distant rest began to trudge.
Men marched asleep. Many had lost their boots   5
But limped on, blood-shod. All went lame; all blind;
Drunk with fatigue, deaf even to the hoots
Of tired, outstripped Five-Nines that dropped behind.

GAS! GAS! Quick, boys!—An ecstasy of fumbling,
Fitting the clumsy helmets just in time;   10
But someone still was yelling out and stumbling
And flound'ring like a man in fire or lime . . .
Dim, through the misty panes and thick green light,
As under a green sea, I saw him drowning.

In all my dreams, before my helpless sight,   15
He plunges at me, guttering, choking, drowning.

If in some smothering dreams you too could pace
Behind the wagon that we flung him in,
And watch the white eyes writhing in his face,
His hanging face, like a devil's sick of sin;   20
If you could hear, at every jolt, the blood
Come gargling from the froth-corrupted lungs,
Obscene as cancer, bitter as the cud
Of vile, incurable sores on innocent tongues,—
My friend, you would not tell with such high zest   25
To children ardent for some desperate glory,
The old Lie: Dulce et decorum est
Pro patria mori.

TED HUGHES (b. 1930)

Secretary

If I should touch her she would shriek and weeping
Crawl off to nurse the terrible wound: all
Day like a starling under the bellies of bulls
She hurries among men, ducking, peeping.

Off in a whirl at the first move of a horn.   5
At dusk she scuttles down the gauntlet of lust
Like a clockwork mouse. Safe home at last
She mends socks with holes, shirts that are torn,

For father and brother, and a delicate supper cooks:
Goes to bed early, shuts out with the light   10
Her thirty years, and lies with buttocks tight,
Hiding her lovely eyes until day break.

Notice how, in Owen's "Dulce et Decorum Est," the tone of the poem is affected by such words as *lame, hag, haunting, trudge,* and *limp.* The picture of forlornness these words create helps to reflect the bitterness Owen feels toward war and its ravages. This, he is saying, is a condition to which young men should not be encouraged to subject themselves.

The way word choice affects tone in Owen's poem reminds us that all the elements of a poem are affected, indeed created, by the poet's use of words. Students of poetry must consider word choice with particular care when discussing elements such as sound, imagery, figurative language, tone, meter, rhythm, and theme. Although we can isolate words as a subject for study in poetry, we must also learn to see them as means to other ends. As you read the five poems that follow, note the individual choices of words that the authors make, but also try to see how these choices affect (a) the sound of the poems, (b) the sensory vividness of the poems, and (c) the tone or attitude that the author or speaker adopts toward his subject.

WILLIAM BLAKE (1757–1827)

London

I wander thro' each charter'd street,
Near where the charter'd Thames does flow,
And mark in every face I meet
Marks of weakness, marks of woe.

In every cry of every man,   5
In every Infant's cry of fear,
In every voice, in every ban,
The mind-forg'd manacles I hear.

How the Chimney-sweeper's cry
Every blackning Church appalls;   10
And the hapless Soldier's sigh
Runs in blood down Palace walls.

But most thro' midnight streets I hear
How the youthful Harlot's curse
Blasts the new-born Infant's tear,   15
And blights with plagues the Marriage hearse.

RALPH WALDO EMERSON (1803–1882)

The Snow-Storm

ANNOUNCED by all the trumpets of the sky,
Arrives the snow, and, driving o'er the fields,
Seems nowhere to alight: the whited air
Hides hills and woods, the river, and the heaven,
And veils the farm-house at the garden's end.   5
The sled and traveller stopped, the courier's feet
Delayed, all friends shut out, the housemates sit
Around the radiant fireplace, enclosed
In a tumultuous privacy of storm.

 Come see the north wind's masonry.   10
Out of an unseen quarry evermore
Furnished with tile, the fierce artificer
Curves his white bastions with projected roof
Round every windward stake or tree, or door.
Speeding, the myriad-handed, his wild work   15
So fanciful, so savage, nought cares he
For number or proportion. Mockingly,
On coop or kennel he hangs Parian wreaths;
A swan-like form invests the hidden thorn;
Fills up the farmer's lane from wall to wall,   20
Maugre the farmer's sighs; and at the gate
A tapering turret overtops the work.
And when his hours are numbered, and the world
Is all his own, retiring, as he were not,

Leaves, when the sun appears, astonished Art   25
To mimic in slow structures, stone by stone,
Built in an age, the mad wind's night-work,
The frolic architecture of the snow.

1. Circle the words in the poem that concern building or architecture.
   What do their meanings contribute to the overall effect of the poem?
2. What words in the poem are used to compare the snow-storm to a person—specifically, an artist?

ROBERT HERRICK (1591–1674)

Delight in Disorder

A sweet disorder in the dress
Kindles in clothes a wantonness.
A lawn about the shoulders thrown
Into a fine distractiön;
An erring lace, which here and there   5
Enthralls the crimson stomacher;
A cuff neglectful, and thereby
Ribbons to flow confusedly;
A winning wave, deserving note,
In the tempestuous petticoat;   10
A careless shoestring, in whose tie
I see a wild civility;
Do more bewitch me than when art
Is too precise in every part.

1. Look up the etymology (or derivation) of *distraction, enthrall, tempestuous,* and *civility.* How are the original meanings of these words appropriate in the context of the poem?
2. Circle the words that record the *disorder* of the title.

JOHN CROWE RANSOM (1888–1974)

Bells for John Whiteside's Daughter

There was such speed in her little body,
And such lightness in her footfall,
It is no wonder her brown study
Astonishes us all.

Her wars were bruited in our high window. 5
We looked among orchard trees and beyond
Where she took arms against her shadow,
Or harried unto the pond

The lazy geese, like a snow cloud
Dripping their snow on the green grass, 10
Tricking and stopping, sleepy and proud,
Who cried in goose, Alas,

For the tireless heart within the little
Lady with rod that made them rise
From their noon apple-dreams and scuttle 15
Goose-fashion under the skies!

But now go the bells, and we are ready,
In one house we are sternly stopped
To say we are vexed at her brown study,
Lying so primly propped. 20

1. What is a *brown study*? How is this phrase significant in the poem?
2. What words of the poem make its occasion clear?
3. What words in the three middle stanzas are used to suggest the girl's former liveliness?

THEODORE ROETHKE (1908–1963)

Elegy for Jane

My Student, Thrown by a Horse

I remember the neckcurls, limp and damp as tendrils;
And her quick look, a sidelong pickerel smile;
And how, once startled into talk, the light syllables leaped for her,
And she balanced in the delight of her thought,
A wren, happy, tail into the wind, 5
Her song trembling the twigs and small branches.
The shade sang with her;
The leaves, their whispers turned to kissing;
And the mold sang in the bleached valleys under the rose.
Oh, when she was sad, she cast herself down into such a pure depth, 10
Even a father could not find her:
Scraping her cheek against straw;
Stirring the clearest water.

My sparrow, you are not here,
Waiting like a fern, making a spiny shadow.   15
The sides of wet stones cannot console me,
Nor the moss, wound with the last light.

If only I could nudge you from this sleep,
My maimed darling, my skittery pigeon.
Over this damp grave I speak the words of my love: 20
I, with no rights in this matter,
Neither father nor lover.

1. What words of the poem link Jane to the world of plants and animals
   that she apparently loved?
2. List the words whose denotation or connotation impart Roethke's feeling
   for Jane.

WRITING ABOUT WORDS IN POETRY

If we study painting we learn about color and line. If we study architecture we learn about building materials and geometric design. But we do
not grow up using colors, lines, building materials, and geometrical designs
in our everyday lives. To study poetry, we must study words. But we have
been using words since infancy; this familiarity, while it may give us an
advantage in talking about poetry, may also create difficulties. Most of us
are not linguists, and we have not taken up the study of language for professional purposes. Still, we think we know about language because we use it
all the time. Why, we might ask, would we want to devote time to the study
of words in a poem, and where would we begin?

A poet's words are like fingerprints: each poet's words look the same
to the unpracticed eye, but are in fact unique and characteristic. Words
represent choices at the most fundamental level, and to get at a poet's real
character we must spend time considering his or her words. Word choice
leads to, and is affected by, other kinds of choices that must be considered
when we begin to analyze a poem in all its complexity. But as students of
poetry, we must first begin with words because they afford a microscopic
view of a text. Writing about them forces us to think carefully about the
poem and to get into the habit of looking at the specific details of poems
when making general statements about them. We learn, by studying the
words of a poem, how to use inductive reasoning in literary analysis, how
to move from the specific to the general, without relying on pre-conceived
or predetermined notions. We learn, in short, to think for ourselves.

The assignments described here presume no special knowledge about
language on your part. Rather, they are designed to help you take advantage

of what you already know and to use that knowledge with some objectivity and with a growing sensitivity to the details of the poems you read. They are meant to pique your interest in the "nuts and bolts" of poems. As you continue to study poetry, other and perhaps more sophisticated reasons for paying attention to diction when writing about poetry will emerge. For now, we suggest three kinds of assignments that center around the analysis of the language of poetry.

Essays on the formality, concreteness, specificity, or derivation of the words poets use. For example, picking apart a poem to see whether its author generally employs simple monosyllabic words derived from Anglo-Saxon or more ornate and complex words derived from Latin may tell us something about that writer's directness, range, formality, poetic style, and sense of the language proper to poetry, or at least to *this* poetry. We begin to understand what makes one writer differ from another and to appreciate these differences. We can use this information for its own sake, or as an aid in analyzing other features of a poet's work such as sensory language or tone. The essay at the end of this chapter, on Seamus Heaney's "Digging," is not primarily concerned with interpreting the meaning of the poem, but rather with describing the kinds of words Heaney uses. This kind of paper directs our attention to the details of the text and helps bring Heaney into focus as a craftsman. The modest aims of such essays are worthy, and fulfilling them can yield useful information that can help us when we analyze a poem to consider its imagery and theme. They thus become preliminary steps toward interpretation.

Essays about connotation. This kind of essay is slightly more complex because we must pay attention to something other than superficial properties of words, and because we must look out for the ways in which the language of poems reverberates, extends beyond itself, and works subtly on our emotions. Paying attention to connotation reveals how words can help us see two things at once—how an attitude affects a perception. Essays of this kind also allow us to make our first attempts at judging a poet's skill in choosing words with connotations consistent with and appropriate to the context and meaning of the whole poem.

Essays about the effects of word choice on other elements. Attention should be paid to language when assessing any aspect of a poem: sensory detail, tone or attitude, figurative comparisons, rhythm, and theme. This kind of essay affords us the opportunity to investigate how the elements of a poem work together to make a single coherent effect. This in turn forces us to synthesize our impressions and takes us still nearer to the heart of the poem.

These three kinds of essays are increasingly complex and make increasingly strict demands on our abilities to consider the entire poem. As exercises, they keep our attention carefully focussed on the text, not the author or the period when the poem was written. Moreover, they remind us that a poem is more than its reducible meaning; it is also a technical performance, a product of craftsmanship and art. We begin to see that *what* the poem says and *how* it is written cannot really be distinguished.

Potential difficulties in writing about words lie in the areas of evidence, organization, and logic. Be sure that you quote freely from the text to support what you say, and use your dictionary as needed to insure that your statements about the language of the poem are accurate. The *Oxford English Dictionary* can be of invaluable help in this regard. Be sure that any count you make of words or syllables is done carefully.

Essays about words are commonly developed by using examples of the qualities being discussed. A line-by-line organization does not usually work well; rather, try using an arrangement that moves from the least to the most important or striking feature. Also, avoid the logical fallacies that arise when conclusions are based on meager evidence. It is difficult to generalize from one or two examples. The text, again, is your principal source of evidence. Do not approach it with preconceived notions of what you will find; let it assert its own arguments.

Using quantitative means and some etymological information readily available in any dictionary, the following essay attempts to describe the language of Seamus Heaney's poem "Digging" (page 572). The "terrain" of the essay is small, but it yields useful information that could spur a reader's interest in Heaney's poetic style and methods or aid in a full interpretation of the poem.

Simple Tools: The Language of Seamus Heaney's "Digging"

Seamus Heaney's poem "Digging" is about tools—the spade of the gardener or turf-cutter and the pen of the writer. The poem implies a transmission of skill and values through the generations from grandfather to father to son. Heaney's tool—his pen and the language flowing from it—is seen as a kind of descendant of the spades used by his forebears. Using blunt, direct, and simple words, Heaney fondly remembers the physical prowess and skill of these forebears, but admits he will never to able to dig as they did ("I've no spade to follow men like them"). He is, however, able to dig up the past; to do so, he uses diction that is appropriate to the youth he recollects and to the strong men he memorializes.

The first two lines of the poem typify its diction: "Between my finger and my thumb/ The squat pen rests; snug as a gun." The words of the poem are simple, everyday words used as comfortably and efficiently as Heaney's father wielded a spade. The sounds of snug and gun suggest this comfort, and the image of the pen as gun reminds us, perhaps, of the power and efficiency Heaney feels when he wields the pen. Spurning "hard" words of foreign derivation, Heaney relies heavily on Anglo-Saxon diction. The poem is 218 words long (excluding "Toner's") and uses 142 different words. Of these, 118 are of Germanic origin, and the vast majority drawn from Old English. Most of the remaining 24 words (such as bottle, slice, squat, and firm) are derived from Old French and have been in the language for centuries. Only two words, themselves simple (curt and peat), come directly from Latin. Heaney's diction underscores the simple, enduring virtues he praises: hard work, and a son's reverence for his father and grandfather. Language is part of the tradition they share.

As we might expect, given Heaney's reliance on Old English diction, most of the words in the poem are monosyllabic (164 out of 218). Of the 54 polysyllabic words, only eight have more than two syllables (potato is used three times), and seventeen are polysyllabic only because inflections such as -ing have been added to monosyllabic words. Most of these monosyllabic words are vigorous and abrupt, words like squat, snug, rump, lug, cut, turf, slap, and curt. These words suggest a simple, earth-bound environment and direct communication between men at work. Heaney uses the end position of many lines (24 out of 31) to heighten this emphasis on short and powerful words.

In "Digging," Heaney is recalling days when men worked hard using tools they knew well and could handle with great skill. His own tools, drawn as they are from a simple lexicon, place him firmly in the tradition of his ancestors, who would no doubt have been proud of the deft and seemingly effortless simplicity with which he has composed this poem in praise of them. Heaney joins himself with his hard-working ancestors: he shares their work ethic, their language, and their directness.

SUGGESTIONS FOR WRITING ABOUT WORDS

1. Write an essay that proposes and justifies "real" meanings for the nonsense words in Carroll's "Jabberwocky."
2. Compare the diction of Blake's "The Lamb" and "The Tyger." Show how the denotations and connotations of the words support the contrasting themes of the two poems.
3. Write an informal etymological analysis of the words in Seamus Heaney's "Punishment" (page 574). Describe the stylistic tendencies your study reveals.
4. Show how connotation is used to support theme in either Roethke's "Elegy for Jane" or Owen's "Dulce et Decorum Est."

IMAGERY AND FIGURATIVE LANGUAGE

Imagine that you are walking across a field with a friend, who says, "A big ox is following us." Before you turn, the image of an ox enters your mind: four legs, a swishing tail, a wide head, short ears. These are literal images your mind produces when you confront the word *ox*. When you turn to look, however, you see not an ox but a man: two legs, no tail, human head and ears. You realize that your friend was employing a **figure of speech**—language used in something other than the customary way.

As soon as you realize that your friend's usage is figurative, your mind begins to operate in curious ways. To the "ox-man" following you, you may ascribe one or more of these qualities: dullness, stupidity, slowness, clumsiness, diligence, strength, and so forth. If your friend's figurative description of the man proves accurate, you may begin to appreciate the economy, color, and clarity that figurative language affords.

Imagery of all kinds—literal or figurative, and pertaining to any sense—is central to poetry. It lends familiarity, interest, and vividness to what we read, engages our emotions, promotes economy and even organization, and implies judgments about experience. Poets employ imagery and figurative language for all of these purposes. In "The Fish," Elizabeth Bishop uses both literal and figurative images to convey her impressions of her subject.

ELIZABETH BISHOP (1911–1979)

The Fish

I caught a tremendous fish
and held him beside the boat
half out of water, with my hook
fast in a corner of his mouth.
He didn't fight.   5
He hadn't fought at all.
He hung a grunting weight,
battered and venerable
and homely. Here and there
his brown skin hung in strips   10
like ancient wallpaper,
and its pattern of darker brown
was like wallpaper: shapes like full-blown roses
stained and lost through age.
He was speckled with barnacles,   15
fine rosettes of lime,
and infested with tiny white sea-lice,
and underneath two or three
rags of green weed hung down.   20
While his gills were breathing in
the terrible oxygen—the frightening gills,
fresh and crisp with blood,
that can cut so badly—   25
I thought of the coarse white flesh
packed in like feathers,
the big bones and the little bones,
the dramatic reds and blacks   30
of his shiny entrails,
and the pink swim-bladder
like a big peony.

I looked into his eyes
which were far larger than mine   35
but shallower, and yellowed,
the irises backed and packed
with tarnished tinfoil
seen through the lenses
of old scratched isinglass.   40
They shifted a little, but not
to return my stare.
—It was more like the tipping
of an object toward the light.
I admired his sullen face,   45
the mechanism of his jaw,
and then I saw
that from his lower lip
—if you could call it a lip—
grim, wet, and weaponlike,   50
hung five old pieces of fish-line,
or four and a wire leader
with the swivel still attached,
with all their five big hooks
grown firmly in his mouth.   55
A green line, frayed at the end
where he broke it, two heavier lines,
and a fine black thread
still crimped from the strain and snap
when it broke and he got away.   60
Like medals with their ribbons
frayed and wavering,
a five-haired beard of wisdom
trailing from his aching jaw.
I stared and stared   65
and victory filled up
the little rented boat,
from the pool of bilge
where oil had spread a rainbow
around the rusted engine   70
to the bailer rusted orange,
the sun-cracked thwarts,
the oarlocks on their strings,
the gunnels—until everything
was rainbow, rainbow, rainbow!   75
And I let the fish go.

Note that when Bishop refers to the "green line" (line 56) hanging from the fish's mouth, she is using a literal image. But when she compares the

lines to "medals with their ribbons" (line 61) or a "five-haired beard of
wisdom" (line 63), she is employing figurative images, comparisons which
serve to clarify her meaning. Can you find other examples of literal and
figurative images in the poem?

Considered in the simplest way, **imagery** means any language which
appeals or refers to any of our senses. The following terms are sometimes
used to label the senses: *visual* (sight), *auditory* (hearing), *gustatory* (taste),
olfactory (smell), *tactile* (touch, including kinetic imagery for motion and
thermal imagery for heat). As you read the following poem by T. S. Eliot,
note the individual senses to which his words refer.

T. S. ELIOT (1888–1965)

Preludes

I

The winter evening settles down
With smell of steaks in passageways.
Six o'clock.
The burnt-out ends of smoky days.
And now a gusty shower wraps   5
The grimy scraps
Of withered leaves about your feet
And newspapers from vacant lots;
The showers beat
On broken blinds and chimney-pots,   10
And at the corner of the street
A lonely cab-horse steams and stamps.
And then the lighting of the lamps.

II

The morning comes to consciousness
Of faint stale smells of beer   15
From the sawdust-trampled street
With all its muddy feet that press
To early coffee-stands.
With the other masquerades
That time resumes,   20
One thinks of all the hands
That are raising dingy shades
In a thousand furnished rooms.

III

You tossed a blanket from the bed,
You lay upon your back, and waited;   25
You dozed, and watched the night revealing
The thousand sordid images
Of which your soul was constituted;
They flickered against the ceiling.
And when all the world came back   30
And the night crept up between the shutters
And you heard the sparrows in the gutters,
You had such a vision of the street
As the street hardly understands;
Sitting along the bed's edge, where   35
You curled the papers from your hair,
Or clasped the yellow soles of feet
In the palms of both soiled hands.

IV

His soul stretched tight across the skies
That fade behind a city block,   40
Or trampled by insistent feet
At four and five and six o'clock;
And short square fingers stuffing pipes,
And evening newspapers, and eyes
Assured of certain certainties,   45
The conscience of a blackened street
Impatient to assume the world.

I am moved by fancies that are curled
Around these images, and cling:
The notion of some infinitely gentle   50
Infinitely suffering thing.

Wipe your hand across your mouth, and laugh;
The worlds revolve like ancient-women
Gathering fuel in vacant lots.

Figurative language almost always involves some sort of sensory imagery, but it goes beyond literal imagery to draw comparisons or connections between things, and to augment, extend, or contradict customary usage so that the unfamiliar is made more familiar. Figures of speech are sometimes called *tropes* (from Greek "turns") to show how they turn or transfer meaning from one object to another.

Where is the trope, or transfer of meaning, in our ox-man example? And how are our minds affected by our friend's figurative usage? When we turn and see the man, and realize our friend has spoken figuratively in referring to him as an ox, our minds set up a kind of screen or filter that admits and applies certain features about oxen (dullness, clumsiness) but prohibits certain other features (four legs, tail) from being applied. The figure of speech is thus both restrictive and extensive at the same time. It restricts the meanings or associations we transfer to the man, but it extends our ideas about the man far beyond the mere word *man*. In the following poem, Sylvia Plath uses a series of metaphors to describe her pregnancy. Note that when she calls herself a "melon strolling on two tendrils," that is, a woman with a large stomach walking on two thin legs, we do not think of her as being green, but as being full and round. The comparison also suggests a connection with the "ripening" aspect of the natural life cycle. Plath's metaphor thus blocks out some meanings and admits others.

SYLVIA PLATH (1932–1963)

Metaphors

I'm a riddle in nine syllables,
An elephant, a ponderous house,
A melon strolling on two tendrils.
O red fruit, ivory, fine timbers!
This loaf's big with its yeasty rising.   5
Money's new-minted in this fat purse.
I'm a means, a stage, a cow in calf.
I've eaten a bag of green apples,
Boarded the train there's no getting off.

Many different kinds of figures of speech have been identified and named by readers and literary scholars. Among the simplest is the **simile**, a direct comparison using "like" or "as" to connect two different objects of ideas. The following stanza by Robert Burns contains two famous similes.

O my Luve's like a red, red rose,
   That's newly sprung in June
O my Luve's like the melodie
   That's sweetly play'd in tune.

What qualities do roses have that loved ones might too?
   The following poem by Langston Hughes relies almost entirely on a series of similes which suggest what happens to "A Dream Deferred."

LANGSTON HUGHES (1902–1967)

A Dream Deferred

What happens to a dream deferred?
   Does it dry up
   like a raisin in the sun?
   Or fester like a sore—
   And then run?   5
   Does it stink like rotten meat?
   Or crust and sugar over—
   like a syrupy sweet?

   Maybe it just sags
   like a heavy load.   10

   Or does it explode?

When you encounter similes or other figures of speech in the poems you read, try to visualize or sense them along with the poem. Doing so should greatly enhance your enjoyment and understanding of poetry. You could also, as at least a first step, assess the originality and appropriateness of the figures of speech you encounter. If Hughes had said that a dream deferred is like a luscious bunch of grapes rather than like a raisin drying in the sun, you would have every reason to question the applicability of the comparison in the context of the poem. Notice that in the last line of the poem, Hughes uses a comparison without "like" or "as" to imply that a dream deferred may resemble a bomb about to explode.

Instead of using "like" or "as" to show comparison, the **metaphor** uses an explicit or implicit comparison of two things, one of which clarifies the other. Consider these statements:

Simile: He is like a bull.
Explicit Metaphor: He is a bull.
Implicit Metaphor: I wouldn't want him in my China closet.

As we move down the list, we have to work harder, so to speak, to see how the term being clarified, called the **tenor** ("he" in this case) is in fact clarified by the term to which it is compared, the **vehicle** (the bull). The **grounds** of the comparison (clumsiness) is the point where tenor and vehicle coincide. Here is a famous short poem by Ezra Pound.

EZRA POUND (1885–1972)

In a Station of the Metro

The apparition of these faces in the crowd;
Petals on a wet, black bough.

The *tenor* of Pound's metaphor is the faces in the crowd at a subway station. The *vehicle* (that to which the tenor is compared) is the petals on the bough. The *grounds* could be the indistinctness, or the radiant beauty, of the faces against the dark background.

Three important sub-classes of metaphor are used with sufficient frequency that they have been given individual names. In **personification** human characteristics are attributed to nonhuman or inanimate things. William Wordsworth's "I Wandered Lonely as a Cloud" exemplifies the kind of vividness or sympathy that can result from such a comparison.

WILLIAM WORDSWORTH (1770–1850)

I Wandered Lonely as a Cloud

I wandered lonely as a cloud
That floats on high o'er vales and hills,
When all at once I saw a crowd,
A host, of golden daffodils;
Beside the lake, beneath the trees,   5
Fluttering and dancing in the breeze.

Continuous as the stars that shine
And twinkle on the milky way,
They stretched in never-ending line
Along the margin of a bay: 10
Ten thousand saw I at a glance,
Tossing their heads in sprightly dance.

The waves beside them danced; but they
Outdid the sparkling waves in glee;
A poet could not but be gay,   15
In such a jocund company;
I gazed—and gazed—but little thought
What wealth the show to me had brought:

For oft, when on my couch I lie
In vacant or in pensive mood,   20
They flash upon that inward eye
Which is the bliss of solitude;
And then my heart with pleasure fills,
And dances with the daffodils.

Wordsworth makes the daffodils seem human by comparing them to a *crowd* or a *host* and by showing them "Tossing their heads in sprightly dance." It is no wonder that thinking of the daffodils fills the speaker of the poem with happiness.

Metonymy and **synecdoche**, though similar in meaning, can be distinguished in the following way. In *metonymy*, a quality or attribute or object usually associated with something is used to stand for that thing, as the "Oval Office" stands for the President of the United States. In "Aunt Jennifer's Tigers" (page 624), Adrienne Rich uses the aunt's wedding band to represent the weight of an apparently restrictive marriage. In *synecdoche*, a part of something is used to stand for the whole, as when we use "farm hands" to mean the people who help with farm work. Notice how Theodore Roethke uses the word *bones* in the last stanza of "I Knew a Woman."

THEODORE ROETHKE (1908–1963)

I Knew a Woman

I knew a woman, lovely in her bones,
When small birds sighed, she would sigh back at them;
Ah, when she moved, she moved more ways than one:
The shapes a bright container can contain!
Of her choice virtues only gods should speak,   5
Or English poets who grew up on Greek
(I'd have them sing in chorus, cheek to cheek).

How well her wishes went! She stroked my chin,
She taught me Turn, and Counter-turn, and Stand;
She taught me Touch, that undulant white skin;   10
I nibbled meekly from her proffered hand;
She was the sickle; I, poor I, the rake,
Coming behind her for her pretty sake
(But what prodigious mowing we did make).

Love likes a gander, and adores a goose: 15
Her full lips pursed, the errant note to seize;
She played it quick, she played it light and loose;
My eyes, they dazzled at her flowing knees;
Her several parts could keep a pure repose,
Or one hip quiver with a mobile nose 20
(She moved in circles, and those circles moved).

Let seed be grass, and grass turn into hay:
I'm martyr to a motion not my own;
What's freedom for? To know eternity.
I swear she cast a shadow white as stone. 25
But who would count eternity in days?
These old bones live to learn her wanton ways:
(I measure time by how a body sways).

Theorists of poetry and language (not to mention poets themselves) do not agree on what metaphors actually do to us or exactly how they work. Common to all metaphor is a kind of confrontation or double vision of two words (or groups of words) and the objects or ideas they refer to. Additionally, there is the filtering process referred to above, a process in part controlled by the context of the metaphor. We might also speak of the way a metaphor extends, or projects, or energizes our consciousness of language and reality. Whichever of these effects—confrontation, filtering, or extension—one chooses to emphasize, the fact remains that metaphors and figures of speech in general provide much of the precision, economy, and intense emotion we associate with poetry.

Three other familiar figures of speech are exemplified in the following poem by John Donne.

JOHN DONNE (1572–1631)

Elegy #19: To His Mistress, Going to Bed

Come, madam, come, all rest my powers defy,
Until I labor, I in labor lie.
The foe oft-times having the foe in sight,
Is tired with standing though he never fight.
Off with that girdle, like heaven's zone glistering,
But a far fairer world encompassing.
Unpin that spangled breastplate which you wear,
That th' eyes of busy fools may be stopped there.
Unlace yourself, for that harmonious chime
Tells me from you that now it is bed time.

Off with that happy busk, which I envy,
That still can be, and still can stand so nigh.
Your gown, going off, such beauteous state reveals,
As when from flowry meads th' hill's shadow steals.
Off with that wiry coronet and show   15
The hairy diadem which on you doth grow:
Now off with those shoes, and then safely tread
In this love's hallowed temple, this soft bed.
In such white robes, heaven's angels used to be
Received by men; thou, Angel, bring'st with thee   20
A heaven like Mahomet's paradise; and though
Ill spirits walk in white, we easily know
By this these angels from an evil sprite:
Those set our hairs, but these our flesh upright.
   License my roving hands, and let them go   25
Before, behind, between, above, below.
O my America! my new-found-land,
My kingdom, safeliest when with one man manned,
My mine of precious stones, my empery,
How blest am I in this discovering thee!   30
To enter in these bonds is to be free;
Then where my hand is set, my seal shall be.
   Full Nakedness! All joys are due to thee,
As souls unbodied, bodies unclothed must be
To taste whole joys.
   Gems which you women use   35
Are like Atalanta's balls, cast in men's views,
That when a fool's eye lighteth on a gem,
His earthly soul may covet theirs, not them.
Like pictures, or like book's gay coverings made
For lay-men, are all women thus arrayed;   40
Themselves are mystic books, which only we
(Whom their imputed grace will dignify)
Must see revealed.
   Then, since that I may know,
As liberally as to a midwife, show
Thyself: cast all, yea, this white linen hence,   45
There is no penance due to innocence.
   To teach thee, I am naked first; why then,
What needst thou have more covering than a man?

    In line 33 Donne says, "Full nakedness, all joys are due to thee." This figure of speech, **apostrophe,** involves addressing an abstraction or object as though it were a person, or an absent or dead person as though he or she were living or present. A **paradox** (line 31) is a statement that contradicts itself, but which is still in some sense true, as when Donne says, "To enter in these bonds is to be free." Only by entering into the bonds of love can he attain the freedom of affection and sexuality that he obviously desires. Donne uses **hyperbole** when he calls his mistress his *America* (line 27), his *empery* (or *empire*, line 29), or when he says she brings him "a heaven like Mahomet's Paradise" (line 21). These statements are exaggerations that go beyond what is literally accurate, but that contain figurative truth. We use overstatement freely in everyday conversation as when we say, "I almost died" or "You could have knocked me over with a feather" to convey extreme surprise.

In **understatement,** the counterpart of overstatement, the writer says *less* that what he or she intends. If an instructor says, "These aren't bad papers," he or she really means that they are good ones. Robert Frost employs a significant understatement in his poem "Birches." When at the end of this poem he says "One could do worse than be a swinger of birches," he means that one could hardly do better.

Two somewhat more specialized figures of speech remain to be mentioned. The **conceit** is a metaphor which brings together two radically dissimilar things, for which no ground of comparison is obvious or even apparently possible. When T. S. Eliot, in his poem "The Love-Song of J. Alfred Prufrock" (page 663) says, ". . . the evening is spread out against the sky/ Like a patient etherized upon a table," he is using a conceit. The figure of speech implies a deadened atmosphere, with perhaps a ridge of clouds in the skies. Some elaborate conceits, like the one which concludes the following poem by John Donne, resemble ingenious analogies in which two objects or ideas are compared on a number of points. Before you read Donne's poem, try to think of ways in which two lovers resemble the legs of a geometrician's compass.

JOHN DONNE (1572–1631)

A Valediction: Forbidding Mourning

As virtuous men pass mildly away,
And whisper to their souls to go,
Whilst some of their sad friends do say,
"The breath goes now," and some say,"No,"

So let us melt and make no noise,   5
No tear-floods, nor sigh-tempests move;
'Twere profanation of our joys
To tell the laity our love.

Moving of th' earth brings harm and fears;
Men reckon what it did and meant.   10
But trepidation of the spheres,
Though greater far, is innocent.

Dull sublunary lovers' love
(Whose soul is sense) cannot admit
Absence, because it doth remove   15
Those things which elemented it.

But we by a love so much refined
That ourselves know not what it is,
Inter-assurèd of the mind,
Care less eyes, lips, and hands to miss.   20

Our two souls, therefore, which are one,
Though I must go, endure not yet
A breach, but an expansion,
Like gold to airy thinness beat.

If they be two, they are two so   25
As stiff twin compasses are two;
Thy soul, the fixed foot, makes no show
To move, but doth if th' other do.

And though it in the center sit,
Yet when the other far doth roam,   30
It leans and hearkens after it,
And grows erect as that comes home.

Such wilt thou be to me, who must,
Like th' other foot, obliquely run;
Thy firmness makes my circle just,   35
And makes me end where I begun.

If, now that you have read the poem, you get a compass and actually work out Donne's comparison, you will see that it is strikingly accurate and appropriate for its context.

    Symbols present more difficulties for most readers. They are easy to miss, and, if found, difficult to pin down. Since they are one of the most prevalent and dynamic figures of speech in contemporary poetry, however, they warrant our special attention. Like symbols in fiction, poetic symbols can be objects, people, or events that stand for something else—some larger idea that the poet is trying to convey to us. Symbols differ from simple metaphor in that they are actually present in the works that contain them; that is, they are not merely referred to for purposes of comparison. Donne simply refers to the compass to clarify the relationship between the lovers. The compass is not actually present at the scene of the lovers' parting from one another. Notice, on the other hand, how the ship *Titanic*, in the following poem by Thomas Hardy, is not only invested with significance by the poet, but also stands in its own right as an object in the poem.

THOMAS HARDY (1840–1928)

The Convergence of the Twain

Lines on the Loss of the Titanic

1

In a solitude of the sea
Deep from human vanity,
And the Pride of Life that planned her, stilly couches her.

2

Steel chambers, late the pyres
Of her salamandrine fires,   5
Cold currents thrid, and turn to rhythmic tidal lyres.

3

Over the mirrors meant
To glass the opulent
The sea-worm crawls—grotesque, slimed, dumb, indifferent.

4

Jewels in joy designed   10
To ravish the sensuous mind
Lie lightless, all their sparkles bleared and black and blind.

5

Dim moon-eyed fishes near
Gaze at the gilded gear
And query: "What does this vaingloriousness down here?"   15

6

Well: while was fashioning
This creature of cleaving wing,
The Immanent Will that stirs and urges everything

7

Prepared a sinister mate
For her—so gaily great—   20
A Shape of Ice, for the time far and dissociate.

8

And as the smart ship grew
In stature, grace, and hue,
In shadowy silent distance grew the Iceberg too.

9

Alien they seemed to be: 25
No mortal eye could see
The intimate welding of their later history,

10

Or sign that they were bent
By paths coincident
One being anon twin halves of one august event,   30

11

Till the Spinner of the Years
Said "Now!" And each one hears,
And consummation comes, and jars two hemispheres.

If we speculate about what the *Titanic* symbolizes in the poem, and about how the symbolism works, we begin to understand why symbols are such a rich and popular vehicle for literary expression. For example, does the ship symbolize human pride, human vanity, the unforeseeable nature of events, the necessary working out of fate? It could mean all of these things. That each of these ideas could serve as a possible meaning proves that the symbol is dynamic: it is *in* the poem, and can therefore be acted upon, changed, or augmented by other objects in the poem. The symbol is also persistent; even, in some longer works, recurrent. Its meanings can shift; it can gather other ideas to itself. Notice the effect that Hardy creates by having the worm crawl across the mirror in "The Convergence of the Twain." Most symbols, then, are durable, persistent, variable, and extensible. Try rereading the first poem in this chapter, Elizabeth Bishop's "The Fish," to see how the symbol of the fish possesses these qualities.

Critics customarily distinguish among four kinds of symbols. *Natural symbols* comprise those objects occurring in nature that are invested with the same meaning by virtually all cultures worldwide. The sun is commonly a symbol of light, vitality, knowledge, and power. Roses are symbols of beauty.

In *conventional symbols*, an object made by humans is invested with a significance agreed upon by all members of a cultural group. The cross, the lamb, the Star of David, and national flags of all kinds are appropriate examples. Dylan Thomas's "Fern Hill" (page 632) abounds with natural and conventional symbols of various kinds.

Nonce symbols are those used "for the nonce," or for the time being, by a given poet. They are the most common kind of symbol. Like the *Titanic* or the fish, they can mean different things at different times—to the same poet or to different poets. *Private symbols* are those used recurrently by a poet with consistent significance in a variety of works. The gyre, or cone-shaped spiral, is a private symbol used by the Irish poet William Butler Yeats to suggest the cyclical patterns of history. (See "Sailing to Byzantium," page 563 and "The Second Coming," page 789.)

The ability to identify or label figures of speech is important when writing about a poem. The names are a kind of shorthand. More important for readers is the ability to respond intellectually and emotionally to the figures of speech encountered and to see how they function, how they contribute to the overall sense a poem makes. Figures of speech have a wide variety of potential functions: by making abstract ideas relatively concrete, they increase our knowledge of what the poet is talking about while lending vividness or animation to the poem's statements. They help provide shape or structure to individual lines or even to whole poems. They convey judgments and emotions, and help set the tone and atmosphere of the poem. They create economy by allowing poets to telescope many meanings and suggestions into one carefully chosen comparison. And, by providing ornamentation to the language of poetry, they help distinguish that language from ordinary discourse.

As you read the following poems, try to see how their figures of speech accomplish these functions. You might also want to make some tentative judgments about the effectiveness of the figurative language by asking yourself the following questions: Are the figures of speech appropriate to their context? Do they work well with the other elements to help advance the poem's apparent meaning or effect? Are they consistent, not only within themselves, but also in light of other figures of speech in the poem? Are they reasonably original, fresh, and vivid?

ROBERT BURNS (1759–1796)

A Red, Red Rose

O my luve's like a red, red rose,
   That's newly sprung in June;
O my luve's like the melodie
   That's sweetly played in tune.

As fair art thou, my bonnie lass,   5
   So deep in luve am I;
And I will luve thee still, my dear,
   Till a' the seas gang dry.

Till a' the seas gang dry, my dear,
   And the rocks melt wi' the sun: 10
O I will love thee still, my dear,
   While the sands o' life shall run.

And fare thee weel, my only luve,
   And fare thee weel awhile!
And I will come again, my luve,   15
   Though it were ten thousand mile.

HART CRANE (1899–1932)

Proem: To Brooklyn Bridge

How many dawns, chill from his rippling rest
The seagull's wings shall dip and pivot him,
Shedding white rings of tumult, building high
Over the chained bay waters Liberty—

Then, with inviolate curve, forsake our eyes   5
As apparitional as sails that cross
Some page of figures to be filed away;
—Till elevators drop us from our day . . .

I think of cinemas, panoramic sleights
With multitudes bent toward some flashing scene   10
Never disclosed, but hastened to again,
Foretold to other eyes on the same screen;

And Thee, across the harbor, silver-paced
As though the sun took step of thee, yet left
Some motion ever unspent in thy stride,—   15
Implicitly thy freedom staying thee!

Out of some subway scuttle, cell or loft
A bedlamite speeds to thy parapets,
Tilting there momently, shrill shirt ballooning,
A jest falls from the speechless caravan.   20

Down Wall, from girder into street noon leaks,
A rip-tooth of the sky's acetylene;
All afternoon the cloud-flown derricks turn . . .
Thy cables breath the North Atlantic still.

And obscure as that heaven of the Jews,   25
Thy guerdon . . . Accolade thou dost bestow
Of anonymity time cannot raise:
Vibrant reprieve and pardon thou dost show.

O harp and altar, of the fury fused,
(How could mere toil align thy choiring strings!)   30
Terrific threshold of the prophet's pledge,
Prayer of pariah, and the lover's cry,—

Again the traffic lights that skim thy swift
Unfractioned idiom, immaculate sigh of stars,
Beading thy path—condense eternity: 35
And we have seen night lifted in thine arms.

Under thy shadow by the piers I waited;
Only in darkness is thy shadow clear.
The City's fiery parcels all undone,
Already snow submerges an iron year . . .   40

O Sleepless as the river under thee,
Vaulting the sea, the prairies' dreaming sod,
Unto us lowliest sometime sweep, descend
And of the curveship lend a myth to God.

1. How do Crane's images of daily life in New York City contribute, by
   contrast or otherwise, to his description of the bridge?
2. Which of the images of the poem give the bridge the mythic dimensions
   implied in the last line?

JAMES DICKEY (b. 1923)

Falling

> *A 29-year old stewardess fell . . . to her death
> tonight when she was swept through an emer-
> gency door that suddenly sprang open . . .
> The body . . . was found . . . three hours
> after the accident.*
> —*New York Times*

The states when they black out and lie there rolling   when they
    turn

To something transcontinental   move by   drawing moonlight
      out of the great
One-sided stone hung off the starboard wingtip   some sleeper
      next to
An engine is groaning for coffee   and there is faintly coming in
Somewhere the vast beast-whistle of space. In the galley with its
      racks   5
Of trays   she rummages for a blanket   and moves in her slim
      tailored
Uniform to pin it over the cry at the top of the door. As though
      she blew

The door down with a silent blast from her lungs   frozen   she
      is black
Out finding herself   with the plane nowhere and her body
      taking by the throat
The undying cry of the void   falling   living   beginning to be
      something   10
That no one has ever been and lived through   screaming
without enough air
Still neat   lipsticked   stockinged   girdled by regulation
her hat
Still on   her arms and legs in no world   and yet spaced also
      strangely
With utter placid rightness on thin air   taking her time
      she holds it
In many places   and now, still thousands of feet from her death
      she seems   15
To slow   she develops interest   she turns in her maneuverable
      body

To watch it. She is hung high up in the overwhelming middle of
      things in her
Self   in low body-whistling wrapped intensely   in all her dark
      dance-weight
Coming down from a marvellous leap   with the delaying,
      dumbfounding ease
Of a dream of being drawn   like endless moonlight to the
      harvest soil   20
Of a central state of one's country   with a great gradual warmth
      coming
Over her floating   finding more and more breath in what she has
      been using
For breath   as the levels become more human   seeing clouds
      placed honestly

Below her left and right   riding slowly toward them   she
    clasps it all
To her and can hang her hands and feet in it in peculiar ways
    and   25
Her eyes opened wide by wind, can open her mouth as wide
    wider and suck
All the heat from the cornfields   can go down on her back with
    a feeling
Of stupendous pillows stacked under her   and can turn   turn
    as to someone
In bed   smile, understood in darkness   can go away   slant
    slide
Off tumbling   into the emblem of a bird with its wings half-
    spread   30
Or whirl madly on herself   in endless gymnastics in the growing
    warmth
Of wheatfields rising toward the harvest moon.   There is time to
    live
In superhuman health   seeing mortal unreachable lights far
    down seeing
An ultimate highway with one late priceless car probing it
    arriving
In a square town   and off her starboard arm the glitter of water
    catches   35

The moon by its one shaken side   scaled, roaming silver   My
    God it is good
And evil   lying in one after another of all the positions for love
Making   dancing   sleeping   and now cloud wisps at her no
Raincoat   no matter   all small towns brokenly brighter from
    inside
Cloud   she walks over them like rain   bursts out to behold a
    Greyhound   40
Bus shooting light through its sides   it is the signal to go
    straight
Down like a glorious diver   then feet first   her skirt stripped
    beautifully
Up   her face in fear-scented cloths   her legs deliriously bare
    then
Arms out   she slow-rolls over   steadies out   waits for
    something great
To take control of her   trembles near feathers   planes head-
    down   45
The quick movements of bird-necks turning her head   gold eyes
    the insight-

eyesight of owls blazing into the hencoops   a taste for chicken
    overwhelming
Her   the long-range vision of hawks enlarging all human lights
    of cars
Freight trains   looped bridges   enlarging the moon racing
    slowly
Through all the curves of a river   all the darks of the midwest
    blazing   50
From above. A rabbit in a bush turns white   the smothering
    chickens
Huddle   for over them there is still time for something to live
With the streaming half-idea of a long stoop   a hurtling   a fall
That is controlled   that plummets as it wills   turns gravity
Into a new condition, showing its other side like a moon
    shining   55
New Powers   there is still time to live on a breath made of
    nothing
But the whole night   time for her to remember to arrange her
    skirt
Like a diagram of a bat   tightly it guides her   she has this
    flying-skin
Made of garments   and there are also those sky-divers on
    TV   sailing
In sunlight   smiling under their goggles   swapping batons
    back and forth   60
And He who jumped without a chute and was handed one by a
    diving
Buddy. She looks for her grinning companion   white teeth
    nowhere
She is screaming   singing hymns   her thin human wings
    spread out
From her neat shoulders   the air beast-crooning to her
    warbling
And she can no longer behold the huge partial form of the
    world   now   65
She is watching her country lose its evoked master shape
    watching it lose
And gain   get back its houses and peoples   watching it bring up
Its local lights   single homes   lamps on barn roofs   if she fell
Into water she might live   like a diver   cleaving   perfect
    plunge

Into another   heavy silver   unbreathable   slowing   saving   70
Element: there is water   there is time to perfect all the fine

Points of diving   feet together   toes pointed   hands shaped
 right
To insert her into water like a needle   to come out healthily
 dripping
And be handed a Coca-Cola   there they are   there are the
 waters
Of life   the moon packed and coiled in a reservoir   so let me
 begin   75
To plane across the night air of Kansas   opening my eyes
 superhumanly
Bright   to the dammed moon   opening the natural wings of my
 jacket
By Don Loper   moving like a hunting owl toward the glitter of
 water
One cannot just fall   just tumble screaming all that time   one must
 use
It   she is now through with all   through all   clouds
 damp   hair   80
Straightened   the last wisp of fog pulled apart on her face like
 wool revealing
New darks   new progressions of headlights along dirt roads
 from chaos.
And night   a gradual warming   a new-made, inevitable world
 of one's own
Country   a great stone of light in its waiting waters   hold
 hold out
For water: who knows when what correct young woman must
 take up her body   85
And fly   and head for the moon-crazed inner eye of midwest
 imprisoned
Water   stored up for her for years   the arms of her jacket
 slipping
Air up her sleeves to go   all over her? What final things can be
 said
Of one who starts out sheerly in her body in the high middle of
 night
Air   to track down water like a rabbit where it lies like life
 itself   90
Off to the right in Kansas? She goes toward   the blazing-bare
 lake
Her skirts neat   her hands and face warmed more and more by
 the air
Rising from pastures of beans   and under her   under chenille
 bedspreads

The farm girls are feeling the goddess in them struggle and rise
    brooding
On the scratch-shining posts of the bed   dreaming of female
    signs   95
Of the moon   male blood like iron   of what is really said by
    the moan
Of airliners passing over them at dead of midwest midnight
    passing
Over brush fires   burning out in silence on little hills   and will
    wake
To see the woman they should be   struggling on the roof tree to
    become
Stars: for her the ground is closer   water is nearer   she
    passes   100
It   then banks   turns   her sleeves fluttering differently as she
    rolls
Out to face the east, where the sun shall come up from wheat
    fields she must
Do something with water   fly to it   fall in it   drink it   rise
From it   but there is none left upon earth   the clouds have
    drunk it back
The plants have sucked it down   there are standing toward her only 105
The common fields of death   she comes back from flying to
    falling
Returns to a powerful cry   the silent scream with which she
    blew down
The coupled door of the airliner   nearly   nearly losing hold
Of what she has done   remembers   remembers the shape at
    the heart
Of cloud   fashionably swirling   remembers she still has time
    to die   110
Beyond explanation. Let her now take off her hat in summer air
    the contour
Of cornfields   and have enough time to kick off her one
    remaining
Shoe with the toes   of the other foot   to unhook her stockings
With calm fingers, noting how fatally easy it is to undress in
    midair
Near death   when the body will assume without effort any
    position   115
Except the one that will sustain it   enable it to rise   live
Not die   nine farms hover close   widen   eight of them
    separate, leaving
One in the middle   then the fields of that farm do the same
    there is no

Way to back off   from her chosen ground   but she sheds the
    jacket
With its silver sad impotent wings   sheds the bat's guiding
    tailpiece   120
Of her skirt   the lightning-charged clinging of her blouse   the
    intimate
Inner flying-garment of her slip in which she rides like the holy
    ghost
Of a virgin   sheds the long windsocks of her stockings   absurd
Brassiere   then feels the girdle required by regulations
    squirming
Off her: no longer monobuttocked   she feels the girdle flutter
    shake   125
In her hand   and float   upward   her clothes rising off
    her ascending
Into cloud   and fights away from her head the last sharp
    dangerous shoe
Like a dumb bird   and now will drop in   SOON   now will
    drop

In like this   the greatest thing that ever came to Kansas   down
    from all
Heights   all levels of American breath   layered in the lungs
    from the frail   130
Chill of space to the loam where extinction slumbers in corn
    tassels thickly
And breathes like rich farmers counting: will come among them
    after
Her last superhuman act   the last slow careful passing of her
    hands
All over her unharmed body   desired by every sleeper in his
    dream:
Boys finding for the first time their loins filled with heart's blood   135
Widowed farmers whose hands float under light covers to
    find themselves
Arisen as sunrise   the splendid position of blood unearthly
    drawn
Toward clouds   all feel something   pass over them as she
    passes
Her palms over *her* long legs   *her* small breasts   and deeply
    between
Her thighs   her hair shot loose from all pins   streaming in the
    wind   140
Of her body   let her come openly   trying at the last second to
    land

On her back   That is it   THIS
                             All those who find her impressed
In the soft loam   gone down   driven well into the image of her
    body
The furrows for miles flowing in upon her where she lies very
    deep   145
In   her mortal outline   in the earth as it is in cloud   can tell
    nothing
But that she is there   inexplicable   unquestionable   and
    remember
That something broke in them as well   and began to live and
    die more
When they walked for no reason into their fields to where the
    whole earth
Caught her   interrupted her maiden flight   told her how to lie
    she cannot   150
Turn   go away   cannot move   cannot slide off it and assume
    another
Position   no sky-diver with any grin could save her   hold her
    in his arms
Plummet with her   unfold above her his wedding silks   she
    can no longer
Mark the rain with whirling women that take the place of a dead
    wife
Or the goddess in Norwegian farm girls   or all the back-
    breaking whores   155
Of Wichita. All the known air above her is not giving up quite
    one
Breath   it is all gone   and yet not dead   not anywhere else
Quite   lying still in the field on her back   sensing the smells
Of incessant growth try to lift her   a little sight left in the
    corner
Of one eye   fading   seeing something wave   lies believing   160
That she could have made it   at the best part of her brief
    goddess
State   to water   gone in headfirst   come out smiling
    invulnerable
Girl in a bathing-suit ad   but she is lying like a sunbather at
    the last
Of moonlight   half-buried in her impact on the earth   not far
From a railroad trestle   a water tank   she could see if she
    could   165
Raise her head from her modest hole   with her clothes
    beginning

To come down all over Kansas   into bushes   on the dewy
    sixth green
Of a golf course   one shoe   her girdle coming down
    fantastically
On a clothesline, where it belongs   her blouse on a lightning
    rod:

Lies in the fields   in *this* field   on her broken back as though
    on   170
A cloud she cannot drop through   while farmers sleepwalk
    without
Their women from houses   a walk like falling toward the far
    waters
Of life   in moonlight   toward the dreamed eternal meaning of
    their farms
Toward the flowering of the harvest in their hands   that tragic
    cost
Feels herself go   go toward   go outward   breathes at last
    fully   175
Not   and tries   less   once   tries   tries   AH, GOD—

ROBERT FROST (1874–1963)

Birches

When I see birches bend to left and right
Across the lines off straighter darker trees,
I like to think some boy's been swinging them.
But swinging doesn't bend them down to stay
As ice-storms do. Often you must have seen them   5
Loaded with ice a sunny winter morning
After a rain. They click upon themselves
As the breeze rises, and turn many-colored
As the stir cracks and crazes their enamel.
Soon the sun's warmth makes them shed crystal shells   10
Shattering and avalanching on the snowcrust—
Such heaps of broken glass to sweep away
You'd think the inner dome of heaven had fallen.
They are dragged to the withered bracken by the load,
And they seem not to break; though once they are bowed   15
So low for long, they never right themselves:
You may see their trunks arching in the woods
Years afterwards, trailing their leaves on the ground

Like girls on hands and knees that throw their hair
Before them over their heads to dry in the sun.   20
But I was going to say when Truth broke in
With all her matter-of-fact about the ice-storm,
I should prefer to have some boy bend them
As he went out and in to fetch the cows—
Some boy too far from town to learn baseball,   25
Whose only play was what he found himself,
Summer or winter, and could play alone.
One by one he subdued his father's trees
By riding them down over and over again
Until he took the stiffness out of them   30
And not one but hung limp, not one was left
For him to conquer. He learned all there was
To learn about not launching out too soon
And so not carrying the tree away
Clear to the ground. He always kept his poise.   35
To the top branches, climbing carefully
With the same pains you use to fill a cup
Up to the brim, and even above the brim.
Then he flung outward, feet first, with a swish,
Kicking his way down through the air to the ground.   40
So was I once myself a swinger of birches.
And so I dream of going back to be.
It's when I'm weary of considerations,
And life is too much like a pathless wood
Where your face burns and tickles with the cobwebs   45
Broken across it, and one eye is weeping
From a twig's having lashed across it open.
I'd like to get away from earth awhile
And then come back to it and begin over.
May no fate willfully misunderstand me   50
And half grant what I wish and snatch me away
Not to return. Earth's the right place for love:
I don't know where it's likely to go better.
I'd like to go by climbing a birch tree,
And climb black branches up a snow-white trunk,   55
Toward heaven, till the tree could bear no more,
But dipped its top and set me down again.
That would be good both going and coming back.
One could do worse than be a swinger of birches.

1. What does swinging on birch trees symbolize for the speaker?
2. How does the descriptive imagery of lines 1–20 prepare us for the conclusion of the poem?

S. S. GARDONS
[W. D. SNODGRASS] (b. 1926)

To A Child

We've taken the dog for his walk
To the practice football field;
We sit on a dead branch, concealed
  In the tall grass and the trees
Near the old spring; we talk the usual talk   5
  About the birds and the bees.

How strange we should come here.
In the thick, matted grass, ten feet away
Some twenty years ago I lay
  With my first girl; half-dead   10
Or half-demented by my fear,
  I left her there and fled.

I always seem to choose
Odd spots; we used to go stone dapping
On the riverbanks where lovers lay   15
Abandoned in each other's arms all day
  By their beached green canoes;
  You asked why were they napping.

We've sat on cemetery
Stones to sing; found a toad   20
  Flat on the graveyard road
That no one had seen fit to bury;
  There we deciphered dark
Names carved in stone, names carved in white birch bark.

We've waded up the creek   25
Over sharp stones, and through deep
Slime, to its source; caught a turtle
  And carried him home to keep.
  At best, he lived a week;
We said *that* ought to make the garden fertile.   30

We've named the animals in the park;
  Watched a caged squirrel caper,
  Patted the baby tapir,

Fed milk to the llamas, fawns and goats that roam
Loose, in a sort of Noah's Ark   35
  Or home away from home.

We heard a bantie chick there that had wandered
  Into the wrong pen;
  It kept on peeping, scurrying
  To a huge indignant hen   40
  That fled. You said we'd bring
Our feather duster for it to crawl under.

  And I mailed you long letters
Though you were still too young to read;
Sent you the maple wings that fly,   45
Linden gliders and torqued ailanthus seeds,
  The crisp pine flyers that flutter
  Like soft moths down the sky;

  Told you how Fall winds bear
The tree seeds out, like airmailed letters,   50
To distant ground so, when they come up later,
  They may find, possibly,
The rain they need, some sun and air,
  Far from the parent tree.

  They threw my letters out.   55
They said I had probably forgotten.
We have seen the sheen and glow of rotten
Wood, the glimmering being that consumes
  The flesh of a dead trout.
  We've been in livingrooms;   60

  We have seen the dodder,
That parasitic pale love-vine that thrives
Coiling the zinnias in the ardor
  Of its close embrace.
  We have seen men abase   65
Themselves to their embittered wives;

And I have let you see my mother,
  That old sow in her stye
  Who would devour her farrow;
We have seen my sister in her narrow   70
Grave. Without love we die;
  With love we kill each other.

You are afraid, now, of dying;
  Sick of change and loss;
You think of your own self lying   75
Still in the ground while someone takes your room.
Today, you felt the small life toss
  In your step-mother's womb.

I sit here with you in the summer's lull
By the lost handkerchiefs of lovers   80
  To tell you when your brother
  Will be born; how, and why.
I tell you love is possible.
  We have to try.

PHILIP BOOTH (b. 1925)

After the Rebuilding

After the rebuilding was done, and
the wood stove finally installed, after
the ripping out of walls, tearing back to
its beams the house he'd lived in, frozen, for over
fifty years, he started mornings up with the world's   5
most expensive kindling. Not just scraps of red oak from
new flooring, ends of clear birch from kitchen trim, and
knots from #2 pine, but odd-lot pieces of his old life:
window frames clawed from his daughter's lost room,
his grandfather's coat peg, shelving his mother   10
had rolled her crust on, and lathing first plastered
the year Thoreau moved to Walden. The wood stove itself
was new: the prime heat for four new rooms descended
from seven, the central logic for all the opening up,
for revisions hammered out daily, weeks of roughing-in,   15
and after months of unfigured costs, the final bevels
and the long returning. Oh, when he first got up to
rekindle the fire of November mornings, he found
that everything held heat: he sweat as he tossed
the chunks in; he found himself burning, burning.   20

RANDALL JARRELL (1914–1965)

The Death of the Ball Turret Gunner

From my mother's sleep I fell into the State,
And I hunched in its belly till my wet fur froze.
Six miles from earth, loosed from its dream of life,
I woke to black flak and the nightmare fighters.
When I died they washed me out of the turret with a hose.   5

1. Which of the poem's images are designed to suggest that the ball turret
   is like a womb?
2. What does Jarrell mean by "I fell into the State" (line 1)?

ARCHIBALD MACLEISH (1892–1982)

Ars Poetica

A poem should be palable and mute
as a globed fruit,

Dumb
As old medallions to the thumb,

Silent as the sleeve-worn stone   5
Of casement ledges where the moss has grown—

A poem should be wordless
As the flight of birds.

A poem should be motionless in time
As the moon climbs,   10

Leaving, as the moon releases
Twig by twig the night-entangled trees,

Leaving, as the moon behind the winter leaves,
Memory by memory the mind—

A poem should be motionless in time   15
As the moon climbs.

A poem should be equal to:
Not true.

For all the history of grief
An empty doorway and a maple leaf.   20

For love
The leaning grasses and two lights above the sea—

A poem should not mean
But be.

1. What are the tenor, vehicle, and grounds for the metaphors in lines 19–
   20 and 21–22?
2. How can the assertion of the last couplet be applied to other arts besides
   poetry?

ANDREW MARVELL (1621–1678)

The Definition of Love

My Love is of a birth as rare
As 'tis, for object, strange and high;
It was begotten by Despair
Upon Impossibility.

Magnanimous Despair alone   5
Could show me so divine a thing,
Where feeble Hope could ne'er have flown
But vainly flapped its tinsel wing.

And yet I quickly might arrive
Where my extended soul is fixed;   10
But Fate does iron wedges drive,
And always crowds itself betwixt.

For Fate with jealous eye does see
Two perfect loves, nor lets them close;
Their union would her ruin be,   15
And her tyrannic power depose.

And therefore her decrees of steel
Us as the distant poles have placed
(Though Love's whole world on us doth wheel),
Not by themselves to be embraced.   20

Unless the giddy heaven fall,
And earth some new convulsion tear,
And, us to join, the world should all
Be cramped into a planisphere.

As lines, so loves oblique may well   25
Themselves in every angle greet;
But ours, so truly parallel,
Though infinite, can never meet.

Therefore the love which us doth bind,
But Fate so enviously debars,   30
Is the conjuction of the mind,
And opposition of the stars.

1. Explain the significance of geometrical images in this poem.
2. How does Marvell use personification to give life and clarity to such abstractions as "Despair," "Hope," and "Fate"?

GEORGE OPPEN (1908–1984)

Image of the Engine

I

Likely as not a ruined head gasket
Spitting at every power stroke, if not a crank shaft
Bearing knocking at the roots of the thing like a pile-driver:
A machine involved with itself, a concentrated
Hot lump of a machine   5
Geared in the loose mechanics of the world with the valves jumping
And the heavy frenzy of the pistons. When the thing stops,
Is stopped, with the last slow cough
In the manifold, the flywheel blundering
Against compression, stopping, finally   10
Stopped, compression leaking
From the idle cylinders will one imagine
Then because he can imagine
That squeezed from the cooling steel
There hovers in that moment, wraith-like and like a plume   15
    of steam, an aftermath,
A still and quiet angel of knowledge and of comprehension.

II

Endlessly, endlessly,
The definition of mortality

The image of the engine

That stops.   20
We cannot live on that.
I know that no one would live out
Thirty years, fifty years if the world were ending
With his life.
The machine stares out,   25
Stares out
With all its eyes

Thru the glass
With the ripple in it, past the sill
Which is dusty—If there is someone   30
In the garden!
Outside, and so beautiful.

III

What ends
is that.
          Even companionship   35
Ending.

'I want to ask if you remember
When we were happy! As tho all travels

Ended untold, all embarkations
Foundered   40

IV

On that water
Grey with morning
The gull will fold its wings
And sit. And with its two eyes
There as much as anything   45
Can watch a ship and all its hallways
And all companions sink.

V

Also he has set the world
In their hearts. From lumps, chunks,

We are locked out: like children, seeking love   50
At last among each other. With their first full strength
The young go search for it,

Native in the native air.
But even in the beautiful bony children
Who arise in the morning have left behind   55
Them worn and squalid toys in the trash

Which is a grimy death of love. The lost
Glitter of the stores!
The streets of stores!
Crossed by the streets of stores   60
And every crevice of the city leaking
Rubble: concrete, conduit, pipe, a crumbling
Rubble of our roots

                But they will find
In flood, storm, ultimate mishap: 65
Earth, water, the tremendous
Surface, the heart thundering
Absolute desire.

ADRIENNE RICH (b. 1929)

Aunt Jennifer's Tigers

Aunt Jennifer's tigers prance across a screen,
Bright topaz denizens of a world of green.
They do not fear the men beneath the tree;
They pace in sleek chivalric certainty.

Aunt Jennifer's fingers fluttering through her wool   5
Find even the ivory needle hard to pull.
The massive weight of Uncle's wedding band
Sits heavily upon Aunt Jennifer's hand.

When Aunt is dead, her terrified hands will lie
Still ringed with ordeals she was mastered by.   10
The tigers in the panel that she made
Will go on prancing, proud and unafraid.

DELMORE SCHWARTZ (1913–1966)
The Heavy Bear Who Goes With Me

'the withness of the body'

The heavy bear who goes with me,
A manifold honey to smear his face,
Clumsy and lumbering here and there,
The central ton of every place,
The hungry beating brutish one   5
In love with candy, anger, and sleep,
Crazy factotum, disheveling all,
Climbs the building, kicks the football,
Boxes his brother in the hate-ridden city.

Breathing at my side, that heavy animal,   10
That heavy bear who sleeps with me,
Howls in his sleep for a world of sugar,
A sweetness intimate as the water's clasp,
Howls in his sleep because the tight-rope
Trembles and shows the darkness beneath.   15
–The strutting show-off is terrified,
Dressed in his dress-suit, bulging his pants,
Trembles to think that his quivering meat
Must finally wince to nothing at all.

That inescapable animal walks with me,   20
Has followed me since the black womb held,
Moves where I move, distorting my gesture,
A caricature, a swollen shadow,
A stupid clown of the spirit's motive,
Perplexes and affronts with his own darkness,   25
The secret life of belly and bone,
Opaque, too near, my private, yet unknown,
Stretches to embrace the very dear
With whom I would walk without him near,
Touches her grossly, although a word   30
Would bare my heart and make me clear,
Stumbles, flounders, and strives to be fed
Dragging me with him in his mouthing care,
Amid the hundred million of his kind,
The scrimmage of appetite everywhere.   35

1. Which images of the poem suggest that the bear represents an uncontrollable force in the speaker's life?
2. What kinds of impulses might the bear represent?
3. What is "the scrimmage of appetite everywhere"?

CHARLES SIMIC (b. 1938)

Breasts

I love breasts, hard
Full brests, guarded
By a button.

They come in the night.
The bestiaries of the ancients   5
Which include the unicorn
Have kept them out.

Pearly, like the east
An hour before sunrise,
Two ovens of the only   10
Philosopher's stone
Worth bothering about.

They bring on their nipples
Beads of inaudible sighs,
Vowels of delicious clarity   15
For the little red schoolhouse of our mouths.

Elsewhere, solitude
Makes another gloomy entry
In its ledger, misery
Borrows another cup of rice.   20

They draw nearer: Animal
Presence. In the barn
The milk shivers in the pail.

I like to come up to them
From underneath, like a kid   25
Who climbs on a chair
To reach a jar of forbidden jam.

Gently, with my lips,
Loosen the button.
Have them slip into my hands   30
Like two freshly poured beer-mugs.

I spit on fools who fail to include
Breasts in their metaphysics,
Star-gazers who have not enumerated them
Among the moons of the earth . . .   35

They give each finger
Its true shape, its joy:
Virgin soap, foam
On which our hands are cleansed.

And how the tongue honors   40
These two sour buns,
For the tongue is a feather
Dipped in a egg-yolk.

I insist that a girl
Stripped to the waist   45
Is the first and last miracle,

That the old janitor on his deathbed
Who demands to see the breasts of his wife
For one last time
Is the greatest poet who ever lived.   50

O my sweet, my wistful bagpipes.
Look, everyone is asleep on the earth.
Now, in the absolute immobility
Of time, drawing the waist
Of the one I love to mine,   55

I will tip each breast
Like a dark heavy grape
Into the hive
Of my drowsy mouth.

WALLACE STEVENS (1879–1955)

Thirteen Ways of Looking at a Blackbird

I

Among twenty snowy mountains,
The only moving thing
Was the eye of the blackbird.

II

I was of three minds,
Like a tree   5
In which there are three blackbirds.

III

The blackbird whirled in the autumn winds.
It was a small part of the pantomime.

IV

A man and a woman
Are one.   10
A man and a woman and a blackbird
Are one.

V

I do not know which to prefer,
The beauty of inflections
Or the beauty of innuendoes,   15
The blackbird whistling
Or just after.

VI

Icicles filled the long window
With barbaric glass.
The shadow of the blackbird   20
Crossed it to and fro.
The mood
Traced in the shadow
An indecipherable cause.

VII

O thin men of Haddam,   25
Why do you imagine golden birds?
Do you not see how the blackbird
Walks around the feet
Of the women about you?

VIII

I know noble accents   30
And lucid, inescapable rhythms:
But I know, too,
That the blackbird is involved
In what I know.

IX

When the blackbird flew out of sight,   35
It marked the edge
Of one of many circles.

X

At the sight of blackbirds
Flying in a green light,
Even the bawds of euphony   40
Would cry out sharply.

XI

He rode over Connecticut
In a glass coach.
Once, a fear pierced him,
In that he mistook   45
The shadow of his equipage
For blackbirds.

XII

The river is moving.
The blackbird must be flying.

XIII

It was evening all afternoon.   50
It was snowing
And it was going to snow.
The blackbird sat
In the cedar-limbs.

1. Do you sense any progression in the image of the blackbird as you move
   through the poem's thirteen parts?
2. Isolate the images of motion in the poem.
3. What seems to be their significance?

WALLACE STEVENS (1879–1955)

The World as Meditation

> *J'ai passé trop de temps à travailler mon vio-*
> *lon, à voyager. Mais l'exercise essentiel du*
> *compositeur—la méditation—rien ne l'a ja-*
> *mais suspendu en moi . . . Je vis un rêve per-*
> *manent, qui ne s'arrête ni nuit ni jour.*
> GEORGES ENESCO

Is it Ulysses that approaches from the east,
The interminable adventurer? The trees are mended.
That winter is washed away. Someone is moving

On the horizon and lifting himself up above it.
A form of fire approaches the cretonnes of Penelope,   5
Whose mere savage presence awakens the world in which she dwells.

She has composed, so long, a self with which to welcome him,
Companion to his self for her, which she imagined,
Two in a deep-founded sheltering, friend and dear friend.

The trees had been mended, as an essential exercise   10
In an inhuman meditation, larger than her own.
No winds like dogs watched over her at night.

She wanted nothing he could not bring her by coming alone.
She wanted no fetchings. His arms would be her necklace
And her belt, the final fortune of their desire.   15

But was it Ulysses? Or was it only the warmth of the sun
On her pillow? The thought kept beating in her like her heart.
The two kept beating together. It was only day.

It was Ulysses and it was not. Yet they had met,
Friend and dear friend and a planet's encouragement.   20
The barbarous strength within her would never fail.

She would talk a little to herself as she combed her hair,
Repeating his name with its patient syllables,
Never forgetting him that kept coming constantly so near.

JONATHAN SWIFT (1667–1745)

A Description of the Morning

Now hardly here and there a hackney-coach
Appearing, showed the ruddy morn's approach.
Now Betty from her master's bed had flown,
And softly stole to discompose her own;
The slip-shod 'prentice from his master's door   5
Had pared the dirt and sprinkled round the floor.
Now Moll had whirled her mop with dext'rous airs,
Prepared to scrub the entry and the stairs.
The youth with broomy stumps began to trace
The kennel-edge, where wheels had worn the place.   10
The small-coal man was heard with cadence deep,
Till drowned in shriller notes of chimney-sweep:
Duns at his lordship's gate began to meet;
And brickdust Moll had screamed through half the street.
The turnkey now his flock returning sees,   15
Duly let out a-nights to steal for fees:
The watchful bailiffs take their silent stands,
And schoolboys lag with satchels in their hands.

1. Which images of the poem imply its tone?
2. What is that tone? Upon what principles does the imagery of the poem
   seem to be organized?
3. Isolate the different senses to which Swift's description appeals.

DYLAN THOMAS (1914–1953)

Fern Hill

Now as I was young and easy under the apple boughs
About the lilting house and happy as the grass was green,
    The night above the dingle starry,
        Time let me hail and climb
    Golden in the heydays of his eyes,   5
And honored among wagons I was prince of the apple towns
And once below a time I lordly had the trees and leaves
    Trail with daisies and barley
    Down the rivers of the windfall light.

And as I was green and carefree, famous among the barns   10
About the happy yard and singing as the farm was home,
    In the sun that is young once only,
        Time let me play and be
    Golden in the mercy of his means,
And green and golden I was huntsman and herdsman, the calves   15
Sang to my horn, the foxes on the hills barked clear and cold,
    And the sabbath rang slowly
    In the pebbles of the holy streams.

All the sun long it was running, it was lovely, the hay
Fields high as the house, the tunes from the chimneys, it was air   20
    And playing, lovely and watery
        And fire green as grass.
    And nightly under the simple stars
As I rode to sleep the owls were bearing the farm away,
All the moon long I heard, blessed among stables, the night-jars   25
    Flying with the ricks, and the horses
    Flashing into the dark.

And then to awake, and the farm, like a wanderer white
With the dew, come back, the cock on his shoulder: it was all
    Shining, it was Adam and maiden,   30
        The sky gathered again
    And the sun grew round that very day.
So it must have been after the birth of the simple light
In the first spinning place, the spellbound horses walking warm
    Out of the whinnying green stable   35
    On to the fields of praise.

And honored among foxes and pheasants by the gay house
Under the new made clouds and happy as the heart was long,
    In the sun born over and over,
        I ran my heedless ways,   40
    My wishes raced through the house high hay
And nothing I cared, at my sky blue trades, that time allows
In all his tuneful turning so few and such morning songs
    Before the children green and golden
        Follow him out of grace,   45

Nothing I cared, in the lamb white days, that time would take me
Up to the swallow thronged loft by the shadow of my hand,
    In the moon that is always rising,
        Nor that riding to sleep
I should hear him fly with the high fields   50
And wake to the farm forever fled from the childless land.
Oh as I was young and easy in the mercy of his means,
        Time held me green and dying
    Though I sang in my chains like the sea.

1. How does Thomas use color imagery to reinforce the ideas of youth and innocence in the poem?
2. How does religious imagery function in the poem?

JEAN TOOMER (1894–1967)

Reapers

Black reapers with the sound of steel on stones
Are sharpening scythes. I see them place the hones
In their hip-pockets as a thing that's done,
And start their silent swinging, one by one.
Black horses drive a mower through the weeds,   5
And there, a field rat, startled, squealing bleeds,
His belly close to ground. I see the blade,
Blood-stained, continue cutting weeds and shade.

JAMES WRIGHT (1923–1980)
Three Sentences for a Dead Swan

I

There they are now,
The wings,
And I heard them beginning to starve
Between two cold white shadows,
But I dreamed they would rise   5
Together,
My black Ohioan swan.

II

Now one after another I let the black scales fall
From the beautiful black spine
Of this lonesome dragon that is born on the earth at last,   10
My black fire,
Ovoid of my darkness,
Machine-gunned and shattered hillsides of yellow trees
In the autumn of my blood where the apples
Purse their wild lips and smirk knowingly   15
That my love is dead.

III

Here, carry his splintered bones
Slowly, slowly
Back into the
Tar and chemical strangled tomb,   20
The strange water,
the Ohio river, that is not tomb to
Rise from the dead
From.

1. Where do you find images of destruction or damage in the poem?
2. What is the significance of calling the swan a "lonesome dragon"?

WRITING ABOUT FIGURATIVE LANGUAGE

Although it is often difficult, writing about figurative language in a poem offers an excellent opportunity to move toward an analysis of the whole poem. Unlike rhyme and diction, which are often tangential to the essential effect of the poem, figurative language is usually prevalent, noticeable, and characteristic of the way a poet sees a subject. As such, it gives something to "get our teeth into," something particularly challenging and important. Moreover, writing about figurative language taxes our skills of locating figures of speech, identifying them, "unravelling" them, correlating them, drawing inferences from them, and presenting our ideas about them in a unified and coherent way.

Coherence—an organizational pattern that makes sense and has significance—is especially important in this kind of paper. There are a variety of fruitful ways to approach the imagery and figurative language of poems, but not all approaches will work with all poems. The sample essay at the end of this chapter, for instance, analyzes Wiliam Butler Yeats's poem "Leda and the Swan" to discover how Yeats uses bodily imagery to imply answers to the questions the poem poses. The essay would have less merit had it approached the poem from the point of view of Yeats's use of simile or color images. If you quickly reread Yeats's poem (page 563), you will see that imagery pertaining to the body abounds in it, but that there are no similes and no references to color beyond the use of *dark* in line three and the whiteness of the swan.

The lesson here, though it may seem obvious, is subtle and worth emphasizing: do not force a particular kind of analysis upon an intractable poem. Take what the poem gives you. Unless your instructor makes a very specific assignment—for example, "Write about personification in Wordsworth's 'I Wandered Lonely as a Cloud'"—base your analysis on a principle revealed by a close reading. Then use that principle to discover as much significance as possible in the poem.

There are several principles that can be used to focus your attention on a poem and to organize your thinking about it. Three have to do with types of images, three with more complex concerns. We offer them here not as the only means of approaching imagery and figurative language, but as consistently productive "avenues of attack." Feel free to combine them or to restrict them further.

Images and figures of speech can be classified in any of three ways: by the *sense* to which they appeal, by the *kind of figure* employed, or by the *sphere* from which they are drawn. Any astute reader should have a general sense of a poem's imagery from these points of view. Writers in search of a meaningful approach to a paper topic should be particularly aware of them.

One effective type of essay about imagery and figurative language uses as its organizational basis the senses to which a poet appeals. You could, for example, analyze how a poet uses images of smell in a poem about memory, or images of sight in a poem about the kinship between poetry and painting. Once you select a poem to write about, examine it carefully from the perspective of the senses the poet appeals to. Which one predominates? Are a variety of senses appealed to, or does the poet seem to prefer one or two at the expense of others? Is there a shift in the range of appeal as the poem proceeds? Is there a connection between the senses engaged and the theme or organization of the poem?

Viewing the poem in terms of the figures of speech it employs can also yield appropriate subject matter for an analytical paper. Does a poet rely on similes or standard metaphors, or lean more toward the use of personification? Are conceits or symbols employed? Try to get a sense of the figure of speech that seems characteristic of the poem. Note the range of figures employed or any shifts in their use as the poem develops. Or write a paper that extensively evaluates one key figure of speech, like the elaborate conceit in Donne's "A Valediction: Forbidding Mourning" (page 601) or the symbol of the urn in John Keats's "Ode on a Grecian Urn" (page 558).

The spheres from which poets draw their imagery constitute a particularly rich and challenging vein that writers can explore. In "Fern Hill" (page 632), for example, Dylan Thomas draws most of his imagery from the spheres of religion and nature. In "Death of the Ball Turret Gunner" (page 620) Randall Jarrell uses imagery of gestation and childbirth (or abortion, depending on the interpretation). Other poems might employ flower imagery, legal imagery, military imagery, hunting imagery, and so forth. Looking at a poem from the point of view of the kind of imagery it employs can give insight into what a poet considers significant and can help us appreciate the unity and consistency of the poem.

There are other ways to analyze a poem's imagery and figurative language. Attend to the patterns, repetitions, or connections among the kinds of images employed. Does the imagery develop, recur, change, or become elaborated as we read? Does the poet use contrasts among the images to advance the poem? Does one kind of imagery (for example, color in "Fern Hill") augment the significance of another (the religious symbolism)? One may also examine the relationship between imagery and figurataive language and some other element in the poem with the intent of expressing the range of purposes the imagery serves. Does the imagery help to support the theme of the poem? Create its tone? Characterize the speaker of the poem? Give insight into the dramatic situation it records? How, for example, is the character or the situation of the aunt in Adrienne Rich's "Aunt Jennifer's Tigers" (page 624) made clearer to us by the figures of speech Rich uses?

A final way to approach the analysis of imagery and figurative language in a poem is to assess their quality. Judgments of this kind can be difficult because we tend to consider ineffective those images or figures of speech we cannot understand. The obvious way to avoid this fault, of course, is to know as much as possible about all aspects of the poem we are analyzing. This knowledge requires an integrated "vivisection" of the whole poem as well as an isolation of the element of imagery and figurative language that we are examining. Needless to say, seeing a whole simultaneously with a part is no easy task. Below are some questions about the quality of imagery in a poem that lead in both directions: toward part and whole.

First, is the imagery fresh and original, or is it trite and shopworn? In most imagery, there is scant virtue in familiarity, unless a customary image or comparison has been given a fresh twist. Are the figures of speech mixed ("iron out the bottlenecks" is a good example of a mixed metaphpor), or are the analogies used by the poet incomplete or inconsistent? Having a clear sense of the general meaning, theme, or direction the poem takes is important. Only in this way can you determine whether a particular image or figure of speech advances the tone and theme of the poem or contradicts them. Bear in mind that some images can be intentionally discordant.

Reread Sylvia Plath's poem "Metaphors" (page 595). Are the figures of speech used to describe pregnancy consistent with each other, or do they pull awkwardly in different directions? Do they all serve to clarify Plath's pregnant state? Do they accumulate in any way or help to augment each other? What do the comparisons say about her attitude? These kinds of questions can help you understand the imagery of most poems you read.

There are several common pitfalls in analyzing imagery or figurative language. Be sure that you locate and use all important examples that will help to advance your thesis statement, but be cautious not to "over-read" and thus make false evidence out of something incidental or irrelevant to the points you are trying to make. Try not to oversimplify the poem by failing to appreciate the full range of functions the imagery serves, and pay careful attention to how imagery and figurative language affect other elements such as tone, organization, and theme.

The following sample essay attempts to show the significance of bodily imagery in William Butler Yeats's "Leda and the Swan" (page 563). Whatever historical or mythological significance this poem may have is grounded in particulars about the bodies of Leda and Zeus—who assumed the form of a swan and made love to her. This bodily imagery tells us much about their struggle and its consequences.

Images of the Body in "Leda and the Swan"

An analysis of William Butler Yeats's "Leda and the Swan" might reasonably focus on the poem's concluding question. The whole poem seems to lead to it; it is isolated in the final three-and-one-half lines (and the final sentence); and its key terms knowledge and power appropriately combine the violent and the noble connotations of Zeus's act. If the question is meant rhetorically, it would seem to be the kind of rhetorical question that has no answer—not the kind that presumes a definite one. However, Yeats's careful use of images pertaining to the bodies of the lovers provides the reader with at least suggestions for an answer.

The first four lines of the poem describe how Zeus, king of the gods in the Greek pantheon, assumed the form of a swan and assaulted the mortal Leda. The lines emphasize Zeus's superhuman power and Leda's helplessness: his wings beat above her, her whole body staggers. Caressed and caught show his activity and her passivity. Her human body (thighs and nape) are enthralled by his animal body (webs and bill). Significantly,

Yeats uses the word <u>breast</u> twice to suggest their union and to prepare us for one of the key questions of the second stanza.

Lines five and six extend the image of violent rape. With her "terrified vague fingers," Leda attempts to repel the swan, but he is too strong. Her thighs begin to loosen. The answer to the rhetorical question posed in these two lines (can Leda's fingers push Zeus away?) is obviously, "They can't."

Lines seven and eight remind us of the last line of the first stanza by focusing our attention upon the beating of Zeus's heart as he lies against Leda. The answer to this question (can Leda's body feel Zeus's heart beating?) would have to be "It can't." However, this negative answer leads in a decidedly different direction from the first. Leda cannot repel Zeus, but she can feel his godly swan's heart beating against her human one. The union of their hearts as well as their loins prepares us for the poem's conclusion.

The first two-and-one-half lines of the last stanza refer to Helen, the beautiful queen of Menelaus abducted to Troy, and Clytemnestra, the treacherous wife of the Greek warrior Agamemnon. They were the issue (along with Castor and Pollux) of the union of Zeus and Leda. The "shudder" in Leda's loins prefigures the rape of Helen by Paris, the siege of Troy, and the murder of Agamemnon by Clytemnestra upon his return from the Trojan war. We do not need Homer to tell us that both the immortal swan and the mortal woman play important roles in the destiny of the Greeks. The imagery of the poem has always demonstrated that the mortal's body can be the instrument of the divine agency.

The question posed in the last sentence of the poem (concerning whether Leda put on Zeus's knowledge with his power) may be rhetorical, but the bodily imagery Yeats has used in his description certainly leads us to something more provocative than a mere shrug of the shoulders. Leda is still "mastered by the brute blood" and dropped by the "indifferent" beak, but her life, as well as her body, has become charged with a portentous power. She is the weaker, but her children will change history. She is not as knowledgeable as Zeus, but she has wrestled with the king of Olympus. She has felt the heartbeat of their compatibility and sympathy.

SUGGESTIONS FOR WRITING ABOUT IMAGERY AND FIGURATIVE LANGUAGE

1. Compare the symbolism of the art objects described in Keats's "Ode on a Grecian Urn" (page 558) with those in Yeats's "Sailing to Byzantium" (page 563).
2. Write an essay about the accumulation of symbolic meaning in Dickey's "Falling" (page 607).
3. Analyze the images of clothing and nakedness in Donne's "To His Mistress, Going to Bed" (page 599).
4. Describe the relationship between imagery and tone in Eliot's "Preludes" (page 593).
5. Show how the theme of Thomas's "Fern Hill" (page 632) arises from the interplay of images of freedom and entrapment in the poem.

PERSONA, DRAMATIC SITUATION, AND TONE

Imagine having had several telephone conversations with someone you have never actually met. When you finally meet, he or she appears quite different from the way you had imagined. What made you picture the person differently? Was it what was said? The tone of voice, or the pauses and emphases in the conversation? Maybe it was the choice of words or attitude. Perhaps it was all of these things.

In a way, reading a poem is like listening to a voice and making conjectures about the person behind that voice. Basically, we use the same clues as when we picture the telephone caller; the difference is that poems are written with greater care so that the voice is more accurately presented. Poets represent the *voice* of the poem through the details selected, the words chosen, the arrangement of those words and details, the tone of voice or attitude of that voice, and the context of what is said. Consider the voice in the following poem. What can we tell about the speaker from his voice?

CHARLES BUKOWSKI (b. 1920)

Yellow

Seivers was one of the hardest running backs since
Jimmy Brown, and lateral motion too,
like a chorus girl, really, until one day he got hit on
the blind side by Basil Skronski; we carried Seivers off the field
but Skronski had gotten one rib and cracked another.   5

the next year Seivers wasn't even good in practice, gun shy as a
squirrel in deer season; he stopped contact, fumbled, couldn't even
hold a look-in pass or a handoff—all that wasted and he could go
    the 100 in 9.7

I'm 45 years old, out of shape, too much beer, but one of the best
assistant coaches in the pro game, and I can't stand to see a man   10
jaking it. I got him in the locker room the other day when the whole
squad was in there. I told him, "Seivers, you used to be a player
but now you're chickenshit!"

"you can't talk that way to me, Manny!" he said, and I turned him
around, he was lacing on a shoe, and I right-cracked him   15
right on the chin. he fell against a locker
and then he began to cry—the greatest since Brown,
crying there against the locker, one shoe off, one on.

"come on, men, let's get outa here!" I told the gang, and we ran
on out, and when we got back he had cleared out, he was gone, his   20
gear was gone. we got some kid from Illinois running his spot now,
head down, knees high, he don't care where he's going.

guys like Seivers end up washing dishes for a buck an hour
and that's just what they deserve.

From the details of the poem, we know that the speaker is named
"Manny," he is a 45 year-old assistant football coach, and he hates players
who have become "yellow." But these biographical details do not tell us
much about what the coach is like. He reveals himself in his account of his
actions—criticizing Seivers before the entire team and "right-cracking him/
right on the chin"—and in what he says: "You used to be a player/but now
you're a chickenshit." Over-the-hill himself, Manny approves of younger
foolish players who take risks. Injuries and a devil-may-care recklessness
are signs that a player is not "jaking it." Manny's use of slang, his calling
the rest of the team "men," and his concluding that "guys like Seivers (get)
just what they deserve" characterize Manny as someone whose ideals are
those of an older macho man who is perhaps unsure of his own virility.
Bukowski has created a stereotypic character, the virile coach (ironically
named "Manny"), who is clearly different from his creator. Manny's voice
is certainly not Bukowski's. We know this not from Manny's own self-
characterization, which even while admitting to being out of shape still
rings with a certain macho pride ("too much beer"), but from the inadver-
tent revelations with which the poet deftly fills in the outlines even of so
stereotypic a character. Manny's choice of similes ("like a chorus girl," "gun
shy as a squirrel in deer season"), the dramatic juxtaposition of Seivers'
crying and Manny's disgust—it comes after the second reference to the
great running back Jimmy Brown—show us that Bukowski and not Manny
is controlling how certain details and their strategic location will reveal
Manny's persona.

We call the voice of the poem the **persona** from the Latin, meaning
mask. Just as actors wore masks in Greek tragedies to represent the characters they were playing, the poet wears a mask or assumes a role like an
actor when writing a poem. Sometimes the poet will assume a completely
fictitious role, as Bukowski does in "Yellow." At other times, the poet will
present some aspect of himself, even in what seems to be an undisguised
autobiographical utterance. Even when the details of the poem seem to
match autobiographical details of the poet's own life and the utterance
seems a "confessional" poem, it is usually best to assume that the mask is
donned for the moment, that the poet is objectifying the situation by isolating one aspect of his or her personality. Think how often we do this when
we speak to friends. We choose a separate persona, a separate stance, when

we are with certain friends. Our interests are different, our attitudes may change, and even our vocabulary shifts with circumstances. Transplanted Easterners adopt the appropriate accent and stance when reaching the West Coast. But place them in a setting with other transplanted Easterners, and they soon revert to their native dialect. None of these aspects is the complete person. They are all personae. In the following poem, notice that John Berryman has given the name "Henry" to an aspect of himself, an alter ego; yet also notice that another voice competes for our attention, someone called Sir Bones, or Mr. Bones, who comments on Henry's thoughts. Henry seems a libidinous person, someone who chooses impossible situations and is basically lonely. Mr. Bones, on the other hand, handles the self-pitying Henry roughly, having little sympathy with this side of Henry's character.

JOHN BERRYMAN (1914–1972)

Dream Song #4

Filling her compact & delicious body
with chicken páprika, she glanced at me
twice.
Fainting with interest, I hungered back
and only the fact of her husband & four other people   5
kept me from springing on her

or falling at her little feet and crying
'You are the hottest one for years of night
Henry's dazed eyes
have enjoyed, Brilliance,' I advanced upon   10
(despairing) my spumoni. —Sir Bones: is stuffed,
de world, wif feeding girls.

—Black hair, complexion Latin, jewelled eyes
downcast . . . the slob beside her   feasts . . . What wonders is
she sitting on, over there?   15
The restaurant buzzes. She might as well be on Mars.
Where did it all go wrong? There ought to be a law against Henry.
—Mr. Bones: there is.

Berryman protested that Henry is "not the poet, not me," yet there are aspects of the character that resemble Berryman: his alienation and feeling of rejection (like his father, Berryman committed suicide). But the narrow approach of searching for autobiographical parallels misses the essential voice and experience of the poem, and even some of its humor. We all carry on a silent mental dialogue with ourselves, or with aspects of ourselves. Henry refers to himself in the third person, and even sees himself in a comic vaudeville routine in blackface playing straightman to Mr. Bones' ironic comments on his own foolishness. The situation—a visual flirtation between a woman and Henry across a crowded restaurant—is simultaneously funny, tantalizing and frustrating. The words Henry chooses show him to be an incorrigible flirt who admires at a distance. He's aware of the obvious parallels between food and sex and shows some wit when he describes the woman as simultaneously a diner and a dinner: "Filling her compact & delicious body/with chicken páprika." But all Henry can make advances on is his spumoni. Listening to Henry we soon understand, even from this brief fragment of his interior monologue, that he is self-mocking; he yearns to get closer to the beauty that he admires, but is afraid and deliberately chooses situations that will end in frustration and defeat.

If poems have speakers, it follows that they also have listeners, **auditors** to whom the words are spoken. Sometimes the auditor may be simply the reader who, if not addressed directly, eavesdrops on the utterance of the persona. Compare the two following love poems, each addressed to the speaker's lover. In the first, the voice is that of a young wife (she is 16 years of age) addressing her absent husband in a letter. The occasion for the letter is his anticipated return. In the letter she traces the course of their relationship from when they were children, to their arranged marriage, to the stages of the growth of her love for her husband.

EZRA POUND (1885–1972)

The River Merchant's Wife: A Letter

While my hair was still cut straight across my forehead
I played about the front gate, pulling flowers.
You came by on bamboo stilts, playing horse,
You walked about my seat, playing with blue plums.
And we went on living in the village of Chokan:⁣   5
Two small people, without dislike or suspicion.

At fourteen I married My Lord you.
I never laughed, being bashful.
Lowering my head, I looked at the wall.
Called to, a thousand times, I never looked back.   10

At fifteen I stopped scowling,
I desired my dust to be mingled with yours
Forever and forever and forever.
Why should I climb the look out?

At sixteen you departed,   15
You went into far Ku-to-yen, by the river of swirling eddies,
And you have been gone five months.
The monkeys make sorrowful noise overhead.

You dragged your feet when you went out.
By the gate now, the moss is grown, the different mosses,   20
Too deep to clear them away!
The leaves fall early this autumn, in wind.
The paired butterflies are already yellow with August
Over the grass in the West garden;
They hurt me. I grow older.   25
If you are coming down through the narrows of the river Kiang,
Please let me know beforehand,
And I will come out to meet you
    As far as Cho-fu-Sa.

           By *Rihaku*

  We learn from the speaker that she and her husband played innocently together as children, that she remained faithful to him even though others flirted with her, and that she fell in love with her husband after the first year of their marriage. We also learn that both husband and wife are suffering through this enforced separation of five months. She tells her husband that when he left, "You dragged your feet when you went out." Like the changing nature imagery of the poem, small details contribute to the characterization of the speaker and the auditor.

  Like Ezra Pound's translation of Li Po's poem, Matthew Arnold's poem depends for its characterizations on the details of the speaker's observations. The speaker does not tell us much about the auditor except that he shares with her his innermost thoughts about the state of the world without the comforts of religious faith. Her love seems to be a bulwark against the harsh realities of an anarchic world. Her asked-for faithfulness seems the only antidote to the pageant of human misery. Written in the mid-nineteenth century when discoveries in biology and geology were threatening to the old world view of the earth's age, the poem describes the world without the comforts of religious faith which was "like the folds of a bright girdle furled," covering the unpleasant aspects of life, "the vast edges drear/And naked shingles of the world." The Greek dramatist Sophocles had perceived even twenty-four centuries before the essential sadness of life that was compensated for by the comforts of faith.

MATTHEW ARNOLD (1822–1888)

Dover Beach

The sea is calm tonight.
The tide is full, the moon lies fair
Upon the straits; on the French coast the light
Gleams and is gone; the cliffs of England stand,
Glimmering and vast, out in the tranquil bay.　　　　　5
Come to the window, sweet is the night-air!
Only, from the long line of spray
Where the sea meets the moon-blanched land,
Listen! you hear the grating roar
Of pebbles which the waves draw back, and fling,　　　10
At their return, up the high strand,
Begin, and cease, and then again begin,
With tremulous cadence slow, and bring
The eternal note of sadness in.

Sophocles long ago　　　　　　　　　　　　　　　15
Heard it on the Aegean, and it brought
Into his mind the turbid ebb and flow
Of human misery; we
Find also in the sound a thought,
Hearing it by this distant northern sea.　　　　　20

The Sea of Faith
Was once, too, at the full, and round earth's shore
Lay like the folds of a bright girdle furled.
But now I only hear
Its melancholy, long, withdrawing roar,　　　　　　25
Retreating, to the breath
Of the night-wind, down the vast edges drear
And naked shingles of the world.
Ah, love, let us be true
To one another! for the world, which seems　　　　30
To lie before us like a land of dreams,
So various, so beautiful, so new,
Hath really neither joy, nor love, nor light,
Nor certitude, nor peace, nor help for pain;
And we are here as on a darkling plain　　　　　　35
Swept with confused alarms of struggle and flight,
Where ignorant armies clash by night.

The real dramatic situation of the poem begins in the fourth and final stanza when the speaker addresses the woman beside him; turning to her for some compensatory stability which faith had formerly provided, his "Ah, love, let us be true to one another!" seems a desperate utterance. The speaker is looking for some light in the dark place of strife which the world has become. He may not have been honest enough to accept a world without illusion and needs some kind of stability to counteract the disillusionment of modern life without faith. Arnold's "Dover Beach" raises some complicated questions about the complex interrelationship among the elements of dramatic situation, persona, auditor and tone.

A poem like Arnold's, since it presents the voice of one speaker who addresses a silent listener, is a soliloquy or monologue. But a special sort of monologue, the **dramatic monologue,** presents the voice of a speaker who unintentionally and often ironically reveals himself or herself to the silent auditor. When the auditor is an imaginary or absent person, or the person is treated as if he were absent, the poet is using a form of *apostrophe* (see page 600). In the following poem, an unwed mother silently addresses her infant child. She refuses to speak aloud until line 43. Why? Does the title help explain why? How does the last line of the first stanza foreshadow the eventual outcome of the dramatic scene presented in the monologue?

ANNE SEXTON (1928–1974)

Unknown Girl in the Maternity Ward

Child, the current of your breath is six days long.
You lie, a small knuckle on my white bed;
lie, fisted like a snail, so small and strong
at my breast. Your lips are animals; you are fed
with love. At first hunger is not wrong.   5
The nurses nod their caps; you are shepherded
down starch halls with the other unnested throng
in wheeling baskets. You tip like a cup; your head
moving to my touch. You sense the way we belong.
But this is an institution bed.   10
You will not know me very long.

The doctors are enamel. They want to know
the facts. They guess about the man who left me,
some pendulum soul, going the way men go
and leave you full of child. But our case history   15
stays blank. All I did was let you grow.
Now we are here for all the ward to see.

They thought I was strange, although
I never spoke a word. I burst empty
of you, letting you learn how the air is so.   20
The doctors chart the riddle they ask of me
and I turn my head away. I do not know.

Yours is the only face I recognize.
Bone at my bone, you drink my answers in.
Six times a day I prize   25
your need, the animals of your lips, your skin
growing warm and plump. I see your eyes
lifting their tents. They are blue stones, they begin
to outgrow their moss. You blink in surprise
and I wonder what you can see, my funny kin,   30
as you trouble my silence. I am a shelter of lies.
Should I learn to speak again, or hopeless in
such sanity will I touch some face I recognize?

Down the hall the baskets start back. My arms
fit you like a sleeve, they hold   35
catkins of your willows, the wild bee farms
of your nerves, each muscle and fold
of your first days. Your old man's face disarms
the nurses. But the doctors return to scold
me. I speak. It is you my silence harms.   40
I should have known; I should have told
them something to write down. My voice alarms
my throat. 'Name of father—none.' I hold
you and name you bastard in my arms.

And now that's that. There is nothing more   45
that I can say or lose.
Others have traded life before
and could not speak. I tighten to refuse
your owling eyes, my fragile visitor.
I touch your cheeks, like flowers. You bruise   50
against me. We unlearn. I am a shore
rocking you off. You break from me. I choose
your only way, my small inheritor
and hand you off, trembling the selves we lose.
Go child, who is my sin and nothing more.   55

Notice that we learn a good deal about the mother from the language
she uses to refer to her child. She uses natural things to compare with the

child ("fisted like a snail" line 3, "Your lips are animals" line 4, "catkins of your willows" line 36, "The wild bee farms of your nerves" lines 36–37, "your owling eyes" line 44, "your cheeks, like flowers" line 50) revealing her true feelings for her natural but "illegitimate" child. Notice how the tone shifts in lines 44 ("name you bastard in my arms") and 55 ("Go child, who is my sin and nothing more.") Are the final words sincerely spoken?

Sexton's poem illustrates another important step in reading a poem literally: it is not only necessary to identify the persona, and the listener, but it is equally important to identify the dramatic situation. Like stage plays, many poems present dramatic situations and have some of the elements of a play: characters, setting, and conflict. Many times poems will present us with more than one voice. If different speakers are not named or otherwise identified, we need to be able to hear the different voices of the speakers. As in monologue, this is done by attending to the choice of words, the attitude, the tone, and the details mentioned. Consider, for instance, the following poem by Josephine Miles. There are four speakers presented in the dramatic situation of the poem: the driver who has stopped in the loading zone in front of a movie theater, the driver of the car behind who wants him to move up, the bystander who sides with the driver of the second car, and the usher who tries to arbitrate.

JOSEPHINE MILES (1911–1985)

Reason

Said, Pull her up a bit will you, Mac, I want to unload there.
Said, Pull her up my rear end, first come first serve.
Said, Give her the gun, Bud, he needs a taste of his own bumper.
Then the usher came out and got into the act:

Said, Pull her up, pull her up a bit, we need this space, sir.   5
Said, For God's sake, is this still a free country or what?
You go back and take care of Gary Cooper's horse
And leave me handle my own car.

Saw them unloading the lame old lady,
Ducked out under the wheel and gave her an elbow,   10
Said, All you needed to do was just explain;
Reason, Reason is my middle name.

Aside from the introductory word *said* the only clues we have about the speakers are their words and the dramatic action of the situation. What does the last line mean?

Sometimes the poet uses other clues to indicate that the speaking voice has changed. At times the language and attitude will be supported by the rhetorical arrangement of the words in the stanza. Different voices may occupy the same position in each stanza, or the poet may provide a further clue by changing the typeface or punctuation to indicate either a different speaker or two attitudes of the same speaker as in Berryman's "Dream Song #4" where Mr. Bones's words are preceded by a dash. Notice that in the following poem the different speakers are identified by the details, words and attitudes of their utterances, but that these differences are supported by placing the speaker's words in the same position in each stanza.

HENRY REED (b. 1914)

Naming of Parts

Today we have naming of parts. Yesterday,
We had daily cleaning. And tomorrow morning,
We shall have what to do after firing. But today,
Today we have naming of parts. Japonica
Glistens like coral in all of the neighboring gardens,⠀⠀⠀⠀⠀⠀⠀⠀⠀5
⠀⠀⠀And today we have naming of parts.

This is the lower sling swivel. And this
Is the upper sling swivel, whose use you will see,
When you are given your slings. And this is the piling swivel,
Which in your case you have not got. The branches⠀⠀⠀⠀⠀⠀10
Hold in the gardens their silent, eloquent gestures,
⠀⠀⠀Which in our case we have not got.

This is the safety-catch, which is always released
With an easy flick of the thumb. And please to not let me
See anyone using his finger. You can do it quite easy⠀⠀⠀⠀15
If you have any strength in your thumb. The blossoms
Are fragile and motionless, never letting anyone see
⠀⠀⠀Any of them using their finger.

And this you can see is the bolt. The purpose of this
Is to open the breech, as you see. We can slide it⠀⠀⠀⠀⠀⠀20
Rapidly backwards and forwards: we call this
Easing the spring. And rapidly backwards and forwards
The early bees are assaulting and fumbling the flowers:
⠀⠀⠀They call it easing the Spring.

They call it easing the Spring: it is perfectly easy 25
If you have any strength in your thumb: like the bolt,
And the breech, and the cocking-piece, and the point of balance,
Which in our case we have not got; and the almond-blossom
Silent in all of the gardens and the bees going backwards and forwards,
  For today we have naming of parts. 30

What is the occupation of the first speaker? We can tell from the details of his speech he is explaining the functions of the parts of something: "sling swivel," "safety catch," "bolt," "breech," etc. How do these references clarify his role? Where do the second speaker's words begin? They are in approximately the same place in each stanza. Does the second voice speak out loud? How can you tell? Specific contrasting details serve to characterize him in relation to the first voice. How are the obvious differences in the two speakers' outlooks underscored by the rhetorical arrangement of the two utterances?

The dramatic counterpoint of the two voices in "Naming of Parts" works effectively because of the ironic inappropriateness of the setting which the poet takes full advantage of in the contrapuntal second voice's descriptions. All of the dramatic potential is captured in the poem's actions, words, characters and setting. Robert Frost once observed, "Everything written is as good as it is dramatic, [that is] a person in a scene—in character, in a setting." What Frost was suggesting is that, like plays, poems present us with slices of life, fragments of time that involve character, conflict and a setting. Here is a miniature play, a dramatic poem, by Frost in which the voice of the poem, like the voice of the playwright, is offstage and comments in the first person only once to express a wish. The time and place of the setting are given in line 6 of the poem, and the conflict of youthful innocence and adult cynicism builds to its climax in the last lines of the poem. There are abundant details, but also many unanswered questions. Why was the boy given "a man's job"? Did the father insist? Was economic necessity responsible? Is fate to blame?

ROBERT FROST (1874–1963)

"Out, Out . . ."

The buzz saw snarled and rattled in the yard
And made dust and dropped stove-length sticks of wood,
Sweet-scented stuff when the breeze drew across it.
And from there those that lifted eyes could count
Five mountain ranges one behind the other 5

Under the sunset far into Vermont.
And the saw snarled and rattled, snarled and rattled,
As it ran light, or had to bear a load.
And nothing happened: day was all but done.
Call it a day, I wish they might have said   10
To please the boy by giving him the half hour
That a boy counts so much when saved from work.
His sister stood beside them in her apron
To tell them "Supper." At the word, the saw,
As if to prove saws knew what supper meant,   15
Leaped out at the boy's hand, or seemed to leap—
He must have given the hand. However it was,
Neither refused the meeting. But the hand!
The boy's first outcry was a rueful laugh,
As he swung toward them holding up the hand,   20
Half in appeal, but half as if to keep
The life from spilling. Then the boy saw all—
Since he was old enough to know, big boy
Doing a man's work, though a child at heart—
He saw all spoiled. "Don't let him cut my hand off—   25
The doctor, when he comes. Don't let him, sister!"
So. But the hand was gone already.
The doctor put him in the dark of ether.
He lay and puffed his lips out with his breath.
And then—the watcher at his pulse took fright.   30
No one believed. They listened at his heart.
Little—less—nothing!—and that ended it.
No more to build on there. And they, since they
Were not the one dead, turned to their affairs.

The complete quotation from Shakespeare's *Macbeth* alluded to in the
title reflects the speaker's predominant pessimistic attitude.

> . . . Out, out brief candle!
> Life's but a walking shadow, a poor player,
> that struts and frets his hour upon the stage
> and then is heard no more. It is a tale
> Told by an idiot, full of sound and fury,
> Signifying nothing.

The passage emphasizes the brevity and the senselessness of life, both of
which are emphasized in the dramatic situation of Frost's poem. However,
some lines suggest the speaker's attitude is somewhat softer than the
harsh, stoical tone that seems to dominate the drama—for example "big
boy/Doing a man's work, though a child at heart." How old does the boy

seem in the poem? Is this important in establishing the dramatic conflict of the poem? Notice how the verbs *snarled* and *rattled* describe the buzz saw's actions and help foreshadow the climax of the poem. What is the effect of the last two lines on the reader?

The drama may not always be presented as directly as in Frost's poem. We may need to put together what we know about the speaker and the auditor with what we know about the setting in order to grasp the implications of the drama or to actually understand the conflict. In Gerard Manley Hopkins' "Spring and Fall: To a Young Child," the title and the first word of the poem tell us that Margaret, a young girl, is being addressed by an older person. Here the setting—the fall of the year—and Margaret's reactions to it are important. The full implications of the connection between what Frost called **character in setting** are revealed as the speaker predicts Margaret's subsequent reactions to the death of the year and to her growing understanding of *why* she weeps.

GERARD MANLEY HOPKINS (1844–1889)

Spring and Fall

to a young child

Márgarét, áre you grieving
Over Goldengrove unleaving?
Leáves, líke the things of man, you
With your fresh thoughts care for, can you?
Áh! ás the heart grows older   5
It will come to such sights colder
By and by, nor spare a sigh
Though worlds of wanwood leafmeal lie;
And yet you *will* weep and know why.
Now no matter, child, the name: 10
Sórrow's spríngs áre the same.
Nor mouth had, no nor mind expressed
What heart heard of, ghost guessed:
It ís the blight man was born for,
It is Margaret you mourn for.   15

The drama of Hopkins's poem is more subtle than that of Frost's; nevertheless, the conflict between heart and head, youth and age, is no less significant. Does the speaker seem to contradict himself in lines 6 and 9? Do lines 12 and 13 reconcile the contradiction? What does the speaker mean by "mind expressing" and "ghost guessing"? By weeping now, which one of these activities is Margaret performing?

One of the more intricate tasks for the reader is to discern the **tone** or attitude of the voices in the poem. How often have you mistaken what someone has said because you failed to catch the tone of voice? Suppose you're leaving what you regarded as a bad movie when your date says to you, "That's one movie I won't forget for a long time!" At first you're puzzled by the disparity in your tastes, just when you thought you had so much in common, until you realize from subsequent remarks that your date, too, thought the movie was awful. We convey our attitudes toward many things by changes in the tone of our voice. Tone in poetry means approximately the same thing: the attitude of the speaker toward the subject and the audience. However, the matter of tone is somewhat more complicated in poetry than it is in ordinary speech.

First, we are reading the *printed* poem, so we must imagine the *oral* tone of voice of the speaker. The poet, however, gives us clues to assist our imagination in recreating the tone of voice the speaker was intended to have. The range of possible tones is enormous, but it could include matter-of-factness, irony, amusement, anger, smoldering hatred, deep-seated bitterness, uninhibited joy, tranquility, playfulness, shock, pained or delighted surprise, and so on. The intended tone is indicated by the choice of words, their arrangement, and by the details selected. Notice in the earlier poem by Henry Reed that the words of the first speaker, their rhetorical pattern, and the details selected differ markedly from those of the second speaker. The harsh, matter-of-fact authoritative tone of the drill sergeant's speech differs from the meditatively sad tone of the more sensitive recruit's thoughts. Read carefully the following poem by Theodore Roethke to determine the tone of the speaker's voice. Is he angry with his father for excessive drinking and for carelessly scraping his ear, or is he expressing nostalgia for a scene out of his childhood? How can you tell which is the correct tone? Which words and which details help you answer the questions?

THEODORE ROETHKE (1908–1963)

My Papa's Waltz

The whiskey on your breath
Could make a small boy dizzy;
But I hung on like death:
Such waltzing was not easy.

We romped until the pans 5
Slid from the kitchen shelf;
My mother's countenance
Could not unfrown itself.

The hand that held my wrist
Was battered on one knuckle;   10
At every step you missed
My right ear scraped a buckle.

You beat time on my head
With a palm caked hard by dirt,
Then waltzed me off to bed   15
Still clinging to your shirt.

The tone is clarified by details that help characterize the father as someone who works with his hands: "battered on one knuckle," "Palm caked
hand by dirt." What tempers his roughness? How do the words chosen in
lines 3 and 15 help establish the tone of the poem? How does line 12 add
further support to the true tone of the poem? The phrase "beat time" is
deliberately ambiguous. Referring to more than waltz time, it reminds us
that the speaker of the poem is no longer a boy and is looking back in time
from the perspective of an adult. The second stanza presents a picture of
the mother. Is her disapproval genuine? What is it that she disapproves of?

A second problem in hearing the tone of a poem arises from the presence of more than one tone. This may be due to mixed tones or attitudes
of the persona—that is, the voice of the poem may express either an ambiguous or confused attitude, or the poem may be a "growth poem" in which
the speaker grows out of one mood into another. Notice that in the following poem by W. D. Snodgrass, the poet, taking stock of his life, assumes a
self-deprecating tone, demeaning his present position. He's grown middle-
aged and has little to show for his accomplishments. Assuming the world's
standards as a measure of his success, he deems himself a failure. He's in
debt. He seems irresponsible. He's no longer attractive to his younger students. He hasn't gotten an advanced degree or published a scholarly work,
hence he's been passed over for promotion. The tone, however, begins to
shift with the inventory of his small accomplishments in stanza 6, so that
by the time we reach the final two stanzas, the tone of the poem has
changed to one of celebration at having chosen a different and more fulfilling standard of success.

W. D. SNODGRASS (b. 1926)

April Inventory

The green catalpa tree has turned
All white; the cherry blooms once more.
In one whole year I haven't learned

A blessed thing they pay you for.
The blossoms snow down in my hair; 5
The trees and I will soon be bare.

The trees have more than I to spare.
The sleek, expensive girls I teach,
Younger and pinker every year,
Bloom gradually out of reach. 10
The pear tree lets its petals drop
Like dandruff on a tabletop.

The girls have grown so young by now
I have to nudge myself to stare.
This year they smile and mind me how 15
My teeth are falling with my hair.
In thirty years I may not get
Younger, shrewder, or out of debt.

The tenth time, just a year ago,
I made myself a little list 20
Of all the things I'd ought to know,
Then told my parents, analyst,
And everyone who's trusted me
I'd be substantial, presently.

I haven't read one book about 25
A book or memorized one plot.
Or found a mind I did not doubt.
I learned one date. And then forgot.
And one by one the solid scholars
Get the degrees, the jobs, the dollars. 30

And smile above their starchy collars.
I taught my classes Whitehead's notions;
One lovely girl, a song of Mahler's.
Lacking a source-book or promotions,
I showed one child the colors of 35
A luna moth and how to love.

I taught myself to name my name,
To bark back, loosen love and crying;
To ease my woman so she came,
To ease an old man who was dying. 40
I have not learned how often I
Can win, can love, but choose to die.

I have not learned there is a lie
Love shall be blonder, slimmer, younger;
That my equivocating eye   45
Loves only by my body's hunger;
That I have forces, true to feel,
Or that the lovely world is real.

While scholars speak authority
And wear their ulcers on their sleeves,   50
My eyes in spectacles shall see
These trees procure and spend their leaves.
There is a value underneath
The gold and silver in my teeth.

Though trees turn bare and girls turn wives,   55
We shall afford our costly seasons;
There is a gentleness survives
That will outspeak and has its reasons.
There is a loveliness exists,
Preserves us, not for specialists.   60

Multiple tones may also result when the persona and a character in the poem hold different attitudes. The voice of the poet, or some aspect of the poet's persona may interpret events in the miniature drama of the poem differently from one of the poet's characters. In the following poem by Randall Jarrell, for instance, there are three distinct voices: that of the girl asleep in the library, that of the poet (the "I" of the poem), and that of Tatyana Larina, a character in one of the books in the library, who according to Jarrell's note to the poem "looks out of Pushkin's *Eugene Onegin* at the girl." Each voice represents a different tone or attitude.

RANDALL JARRELL (1914–1965)

A Girl in a Library

An object among dreams, you sit here with your shoes off
And curl your legs up under you; your eyes
Close for a moment, your face moves toward sleep . . .
You are very human.
            But my mind, gone out in tenderness,   5
Shrinks from its object with a thoughtful sigh.
This is a waist the spirit breaks its arm on.
The gods themselves, against you, struggle in vain.

This broad low strong-boned brow; these heavy eyes;
These calves, grown muscular with certainties;   10
This nose, three medium-sized pink strawberries
—But I exaggerate. In a little you will leave:
I'll hear, half squeal, half shriek, your laugh of greeting—
Then, *decrescendo*, bars of that strange speech
In which each sound sets out to seek each other,   15
Murders its own father, marries its own mother,
And ends as one grand transcendental vowel.

(Yet for all I know, the Egyptian Helen spoke so.)
As I look, the world contracts around you:
I see Brünnhilde had brown braids and glasses   20
She used for studying; Salome straight brown bangs,
A calf's brown eyes, and sturdy light-brown limbs
Dusted with cinnamon, an apple-dumpling's . . .
Many a beast has gnawn a leg off and got free,
Many a dolphin curved up from Necessity—   25
The trap has closed about you, and you sleep.
If someone questioned you, *What doest thou here?*
You'd knit your brows like an orangoutang
(But not so sadly; not so thoughtfully)
And answer with a pure heart, guilelessly: 30
I'm studying . . . .
                        If only you were not!

Assignments,
          recipes,
                    the *Official Rulebook*   35
Of Basketball—ah, let them go; you needn't mind.
The soul has no assignments, neither cooks
Nor referees: it wastes its time.
                                    It wastes its time.
Here in this enclave there are centuries   40
For you to waste: the short and narrow stream
Of Life meanders into a thousand valleys
Of all that was, or might have been, or is to be.
The books, just leafed through, whisper endlessly . . .
Yet it is hard. One sees in your blurred eyes   45
The "uneasy half-soul" Kipling saw in dogs'.
One sees it, in the glass, in one's own eyes.
In rooms alone, in galleries, in libraries,
In tears, in searchings of the heart, in staggering joys
We memorize once more our old creation,   50
Humanity: with what yawns the unwilling
Flesh puts on its spirit, O my sister!

So many dreams! And not one troubles
Your sleep of life? no self stares shadowily
From these worn hexahedrons, beckoning   55
With false smiles, tears? . . .

                  Meanwhile Tatyana
Larina (gray eyes nickel with the moonlight
That falls through the willows onto Lensky's tomb;
Now young and shy, now old and cold and sure)   60
Asks, smiling: "But what is she dreaming of, fat thing?"
I answer: She's not fat. She isn't dreaming.
She purrs or laps or runs, all in her sleep;
Believes, awake, that she is beautiful;
She never dreams.

               Those sunrise-colored clouds   65
Around man's head—that inconceivable enchantment
From which, at sunset, we come back to life
To find our graves dug, families dead, selves dying:
Of all this, Tanya, she is innocent.   70
For nineteen years she's faced reality:
They look alike already.

              They say, man wouldn't be
The best thing in this world—and isn't he?—
If he were not good for it. But she   75
—She's good enough for it.

                And yet sometimes
Her sturdy form, in its pink strapless formal,
Is as if bathed in moonlight-modulated
Into a form of joy, a Lydian mode;   80
This Wooden Mean's a kind, furred animal
That speaks, in the Wild of things, delighting riddles
To the soul that listens, trusting . . .

                Poor senseless Life:
When, in the last light sleep of dawn, the messenger   85
Comes with his message, you will not awake.
He'll give his feathery whistle, shake you hard,
You'll look with wide eyes at the dewy yard
And dream, with calm slow factuality:
"Today's Commencement. My bachelor's degree   90
In Home Ec., my doctorate of philosophy
In Phys. Ed.

        [Tanya, they won't even *scan*]
Are waiting for me. . . ."

                Oh, Tatyana,   95
The Angel comes: better to squawk like a chicken
Than to say with truth, "But I'm a *good* girl,"
And Meet his Challenge with a last firm strange

Uncomprehending smile; and—then, then!—see
The blind date that has stood you up: your life.   100
(For all this, if it isn't, perhaps, life,
Has yet, at least, a language of its own
Different from the books'; worse than the books'.)
And yet, the ways we miss our lives are life.
Yet . . . yet . . .
                    to have one's life add up to *yet!*   105

You sigh a shuddering sigh. Tatyana murmurs,
"Don't cry, little peasant"; leaves us with a swift
"Good-bye, good-bye . . . Ah, don't think ill of me . . ."
Your eyes open: you sit here thoughtlessly.   110

I love you—and yet—and yet—I love you.

Don't cry, little peasant. Sit and dream.
One comes, a finger's width beneath your skin,
To the braided maidens singing as they spin;
There sound the shepherd's pipe, the watchman's rattle   115
Across the short dark distance of the years.
I am a thought of yours: and yet, you do not think . . .
The firelight of a long, blind, dreaming story
Lingers upon your lips; and I have seen
Firm, fixed forever in your closing eyes,   120
The Corn King beckoning to his Spring Queen.

    Jarrell gives us clues to help identify each of the three speakers in the poem. The remarks of the "I," the poet, studded with allusions to Oedipus, Helen of Troy, Kipling, and the operas of Strauss and Wagner establish him as the voice of culture. The implications of the girl's majoring in home economics and physical education establish her voice as somewhat philistine. What does the poet mean by "She isn't dreaming," (line 55) and "the ways we miss our lives are life." (line 91)? The poet responds to the girl's assertion, "I'm studying. . ." with the ironical remark, "if only you were not!" (lines 29–30)? Does this mean he's angry with her, or in love with her? Significantly, most of the poet's remarks are addressed to Tatyana Larina, the heroine of Alexander Pushkin's *Eugene Onegin*, with whom he has more in common. Why does the poet say that life has "a language of its own/Different from the books'; worse than the books'" (lines 89–90)? What is the tone of this remark? Explain the significance of the allusion in the last line to the Corn King and his Spring Queen.

    The dramatic situation of poems like Jarrell's requires us to respond to the "facts" of the poem. Who is speaking to whom? In what tone of voice? Is there a conflict? Lying midway between simple paraphrase of the literal meaning of the poem and detailed interpretation of the poem's figures of speech, analysis of a poem's dramatic situation, persona, and tone requires attention to detail and sensitivity to nuances. Just as careful listening during a conversation is essential for full participation; careful listening with what Robert Frost called "the ear of the imagination" can open the door to the experience the poet intended you to have in reading a poem.

ROBERT BROWNING (1812–1889)

My Last Duchess

Ferrara

That's my last duchess painted on the wall,
Looking as if she were alive. I call
That piece a wonder, now: Frà Pandolf's hands
Worked busily a day, and there she stands.
Will't please you sit and look at her? I said   5
"Frà Pandolf" by design, for never read
Strangers like you that pictured countenance,
The depth and passion of its earnest glance,
But to myself they turned (since none puts by
The curtain I have drawn for you, but I)   10
And seemed as they would ask me, if they durst,
How such a glance came there; so, not the first
Are you to turn and ask thus. Sir, 'twas not
Her husband's presence only, called that spot
Of joy into the Duchess' cheek: perhaps   15
Frà Pandolf chanced to say "Her mantle laps
Over my lady's wrist too much," or "Paint
Must never hope to reproduce the faint
Half-flush that dies along her throat": such stuff
Was courtesy, she thought, and cause enough   20
For calling up that spot of joy. She had
A heart—how shall I say?—too soon made glad,
Too easily impressed; she liked whate'er
She looked on, and her looks went everywhere.
Sir, 'twas all one! My favor at her breast,   25
The dropping of the daylight in the West,
The bough of cherries some officious fool
Broke in the orchard for her, the white mule
She rode with round the terrace—all and each
Would draw from her alike the approving speech,   30
Or blush, at least. She thanked men—good! but thanked
Somehow—I know not how—as if she ranked
My gift of a nine-hundred-years-old name

With anybody's gift. Who'd stoop to blame
This sort of trifling? Even had you skill   35
In speech—which I have not—to make your will
Quite clear to such an one, and say, "Just this
Or that in you disgusts me; here you miss,
Or there exceed the mark"—and if she let
Herself be lessoned so, nor plainly set   40
Her wits to yours, forsooth, and made excuse,
—E'en then would be some stooping; and I choose
Never to stoop. Oh sir, she smiled, no doubt,
Whene'er I passed her; but who passed without
Much the same smile? This grew; I gave commands;   45
Then all smiles stopped together. There she stands
As if alive. Will't please you rise? We'll meet
The company below, then. I repeat,
The Count your master's known munificence
Is ample warrant that no just pretense   50
Of mine for dowry will be disallowed;
Though his fair daughter's self, as I avowed
At starting, is my object. Nay, we'll go
Together down, sir. Notice Neptune, though,
Taming a sea-horse, thought a rarity,   55
Which Claus of Innsbruck cast in bronze for me!

1. A dramatic monologue is a poem in which a speaker, while addressing a
   silent listener, unintentionally reveals hidden things about himself. What
   character traits does the Duke reveal about himself?
2. Who is the listener? Why is he there?
3. Why does the Duke usually keep the portrait of the Duchess covered?
   Why does he draw back the curtain now?
4. What do you surmise happened to the Duchess? What evidence do you
   have? Of what significance is the sculpture ("Neptune . . . taming a sea
   horse") mentioned at the end of the peom? Why does the Duke give the
   sculptor's name?

e. e. cummings (1894–1962)

a salesman is an it that stinks Excuse

a salesman is an it that stinks Excuse

Me whether it's president of the you were say
or a jennelman name misder finger isn't
important whether it's millions of other punks

or just a handful absolutely doesn't   5
matter and whether it's in lonjewray

or shrouds is immaterial it stinks

a salesman is an it that stinks to please

but whether to please itself or someone else
makes no more difference than if it sells   10
hate condoms education snakeoil vac
uumcleaners terror strawberries democ
ra (caveat emptor) cy superfluous hair

or Think We've Met subhuman rights Before

1. Is there more than one voice in the poem? How do we know? Does
   Cummings' capitalizing words in the opening and closing of the poem
   help us hear another voice? Whose?
2. What is the attitude of the persona toward salesmen? Why does he call
   them "it"? Is the speaker just talking about people who sell products?
   Who else does he have in mind?
3. Why does Cummings use phonetical spelling (jennelman for gentleman,
   lonjewray for lingerie) in the poem? What sort of tone is established
   through its use?

JOHN DONNE (1572–1631)

The Flea

Mark but this flea, and mark in this
How little that which thou deny'st me is;
It sucked me first, and now sucks thee,
And in this flea our two bloods mingled be;
Thou know'st that this cannot be said   5
A sin, nor shame, nor loss of maidenhead,
    Yet this enjoys before it woo,
    And pampered swells with one blood made of two,
    And this, alas, is more than we would do.

Oh stay, three lives in one flea spare,   10
Where we almost, yea more than, married are.
This flea is you and I, and this
Our marriage bed, and marriage temple is;

Though parents grudge, and you, we're met
And cloistered in these living walls of jet.   15
   Though use make you apt to kill me,
   Let not to that, self-murder added be,
   And sacrilege, three sins in killing three.

Cruel and sudden, hast thou since
Purpled thy nail in blood of innocence?   20
Wherein could this flea guilty be,
Except in that drop which it sucked from thee?
Yet thou triumph'st, and say'st that thou
Find'st not thyself, nor me, the weaker now;
   'Tis true; then learn how false, fears be;   25
   Just so much honor, when thou yield'st to me,
   Will waste, as this flea's death took life from thee.

ALAN DUGAN (b. 1923)

Love Song: I and Thou

Nothing is plumb, level or square:
   the studs are bowed, the joists
are shaky by nature, no piece fits
   any other piece without a gap
or pinch, and bent nails   5
   dance all over the surfacing
like maggots. By Christ
   I am no carpenter. I built
the roof for myself, the walls
   for myself, the floors   10
for myself, and got
   hung up in it myself. I
danced with a purple thumb
   at this house-warming, drunk
with my prime whiskey: rage.   15
   Oh I spat rage's nails
into the frame-up of my work:
   it held. It settled plumb,
level, solid, square and true
   for that great moment. Then   20
it screamed and went on through,
   skewing as wrong the other way.
God damned it. This is hell,
   but I planned it, I sawed it,

I nailed it, and I
   will live in it until it kills me.   25
I can nail my left palm
   to the left-hand cross-piece but
I can't do everything myself.
   I need a hand to nail the right,   30
a help, a love, a you, a wife.

T. S. ELIOT (1888–1965)

The Love Song of J. Alfred Prufrock

> *S'io credessi che mia risposta fosse a persona*
> *che mai tornasse al mondo, questa fiamma*
> *staria senza più scosse. Ma per ciò che giam-*
> *mai di questo fondo non tornò vivo alcun, s'i'*
> *odo il vero, senza terma d'infamia ti rispondo.*

Let us go then, you and I,
When the evening is spread out against the sky
Like a patient etherised upon a table;
Let us go, through certain half-deserted streets,
The muttering retreats   5
Of restless nights in one-night cheap hotels
And sawdust restaurants with oyster-shells:
Streets that follow like a tedious argument
Of insidious intent
To lead you to an overwhelming question   10
Oh, do not ask, 'What is it?'
Let us go and make our visit.

In the room the women come and go
Talking of Michelangelo.

The yellow fog that rubs its back upon the window-panes,   15
The yellow smoke that rubs its muzzle on the window-panes,
Licked its tongue into the corners of the evening,
Lingered upon the pools that stand in drains,
Let fall upon its back the soot that falls from chimneys.

Slipped by the terrace, made a sudden leap,   20
And seeing that it was a soft October night,
Curled once about the house, and fell asleep.

And indeed there will be time
For the yellow smoke that slides along the street
Rubbing its back upon the window-panes;   25
There will be time, there will be time
To prepare a face to meet the faces that you meet;
There will be time to murder and create,
And time for all the works and days of hands
That lift and drop a question on your plate;   30
Time for you and time for me,
And time yet for a hundred indecisions,
And for a hundred visions and revisions,
Before the taking of a toast tea.

In the room the women come and go   35
Talking of Michelangelo.

And indeed there will be time
To wonder, 'Do I dare?' and, 'Do I dare?'
Time to turn back and descend the stair,
With a bald spot in the middle of my hair—   40
(They will say: 'How his hair is growing thin!')
My morning coat, my collar mounting firmly to the chin,
My necktie rich and modest, but asserted by a simple pin—
(They will say: "But how his arms and legs are thin!")
Do I dare   45
Disturb the universe?
In a minute there is time
For decisions and revisions which a minute will reverse.

For I have known them all already, known them all—
Have known the evenings, mornings, afternoons,   50
I have measured out my life with coffee spoons;
I know the voices dying with a dying fall
Beneath the music from a farther room.
   So how should I presume?

And I have known the eyes already, known them all—   55
The eyes that fix you in a formulated phrase,
And when I am formulated, sprawling on a pin,
When I am pinned and wriggling on the wall,
Then how should I begin
To spit out all the butt-ends of my days and ways?   60
  And how should I presume?

And I have known the arms already, known them all—
Arms that are braceleted and white and bare

(But in the lamplight, downed with light brown hair!)
Is it perfume from a dress   65
That makes me so digress?
Arms that lie along a table, or wrap about a shawl.
   And should I then presume?
   And how should I begin?
   . . . . .

Shall I say, I have gone at dusk through narrow streets   70
And watched the smoke that rises from the pipes
Of lonely men in shirt-sleeves, leaning out of windows? . . .

I should have been a pair of ragged claws
Scuttling across the floors of silent seas.
   . . . . .

And the afternoon, the evening, sleeps so peacefully!   75
Smoothed by long fingers,
Asleep . . . tired . . . or it malingers,
Stretched on the floor, here beside you and me.
Should I, after tea and cakes and ices,
Have the strength to force the moment to its crisis?   80
But though I have wept and fasted, wept and prayed,
Though I have seen my head (grown slightly bald) brought in upon a
   platter,
I am no prophet—and here's no great matter;
I have seen the moment of my greatness flicker,
And I have seen the eternal Footman hold my coat, and snicker,   85
And in short, I was afraid.

And would it have been worth it, after all,
After the cups, the marmalade, the tea,
Among the porcelain, among some talk of you and me,
Would it have been worth while,   90
To have bitten off the matter with a smile,
To have squeezed the universe into a ball
To roll it towards some overwhelming question,
To say: 'I Lazarus, come from the dead,
Come back to tell you all, I shall tell you all'—   95
If one, settling a pillow by her head,
   Should say: 'That is not what I meant at all.
   That is not it, at all.'

And would it have been worth it, after all,
Would it have been worth while,   100
After the sunsets and the dooryards and the sprinkled streets,

After the novels, after the teacups, after the skirts that trail along
   the floor—

And this, and so much more?—
It is impossible to say just what I mean!
But as if a magic lantern threw the nerves in patterns on a screen: 105
Would it have been worth while
If one, settling a pillow or throwing off a shawl,
And turning toward the window, should say:
   'That is not it at all,
   That is not what I meant, at all.'   110
  . . . . .

No! I am not Prince Hamlet, nor was meant to be;
Am an attendant lord, one that will do
To swell a progress, start a scene or two,
Advise the prince; no doubt, an easy tool,
Deferential, glad to be of use,   115
Politic, cautious, and meticulous;
Full of high sentence, but a bit obtuse;
At times, indeed, almost ridiculous—
Almost, at times, the Fool.

I grow old . . . I grow old . . .   120
I shall wear the bottoms of my trousers rolled.

Shall I part my hair behind? Do I dare to eat a peach?
I shall wear white flannel trousers, and walk upon the beach.
I have heard the mermaids singing, each to each.

I do not think that they will sing to me.   125

   I have seen them riding seaward on the waves
Combing the white hair of the waves blown back
When the wind blows the water white and black.

We have lingered in the chambers of the sea
By sea-girls wreathed with seaweed red and brown   130
Till human voices wake us, and we drown.

ROBERT FROST (1874–1963)

Stopping by Woods on a Snowy Evening

Whose woods these are I think I know
His house is in the village though;
He will not see me stopping here
To watch his woods fill up with snow.

My little horse must think it queer   5
To stop without a farmhouse near
Between the woods and frozen lake
The darkest evening of the year.

He gives his harness bells a shake
To ask if there is some mistake.   10
The only other sound's the sweep
Of easy wind and downy flake.

The woods are lovely, dark and deep.
But I have promises to keep,
And miles to go before I sleep,   15
And miles to go before I sleep.

1. Why does the speaker stop to "watch the woods fill up with snow"?
   What kind of person would you say he is?
2. To whom do the woods belong? Why does the speaker introduce this
   idea?
3. Why does his horse think stopping is "queer"? Does this comment on
   the speaker's actions?
4. What are the "promises" and "miles" mentioned in the last stanza? Why
   is the final line repeated?

THOMAS HARDY (1840–1928)

Channel Firing

That night your great guns, unawares,
Shook all our coffins as we lay,
And broke the chancel window-squares,
We thought it was the Judgment-day

And sat upright. While drearisome   5
Arose the howl of wakened hounds:

The mouse let fall the altar-crumb,
The worms drew back into the mounds,

The glebe cow drooled. Till God called, "No;   10
It's gunnery practice out at sea
Just as before you went below;
The world is as it used to be:

"All nations striving strong to make
Red war yet redder. Mad as hatters
They do no more for Christés sake   15
Than you who are helpless in such matters.

"That this is not the judgment-hour
For some of them's a blessed thing,
For if it were they'd have to scour
Hell's floor for so much threatening. . . .   20

"Ha, ha. It will be warmer when
I blow the trumpet (if indeed
I ever do; for you are men,
And rest eternal sorely need)."

So down we lay again. "I wonder,   25
Will the world ever saner be,"
Said one, "than when He sent us under
In our indifferent century!"

And many a skeleton shook his head.
"Instead of preaching forty year,"   30
My neighbor Parson Thirdly said,
"I wish I had stuck to pipes and beer."

Again the guns disturbed the hour,
Roaring their readiness to avenge,
As far inland as Stourton Tower,   35
And Camelot, and starlit Stonehenge.

             April 1914

1. Who are the speakers in the opening two stanzas? Why are they awakened? What do they think is happening? What has actually awakened them?
2. What speaker is introduced in the third stanza? What is the tone of lines 17–24? What do the words of the parson (lines 30–32) tell us about Hardy's attitude toward organized religion and its influence on human conduct?

PHILIP LARKIN (1922–1985)

Vers de Societé

My wife and I have asked a crowd of craps
To come and waste their time and ours: perhaps
You'd care to join us? In a pig's arse, friend.
Day comes to an end.
The gas fire breathes, the trees are darkly swayed.   5
And so *Dear Warlock-Williams: I'm afraid*—

Funny how hard it is to be alone.
I could spend half my evenings, if I wanted,
Holding a glass of washing sherry, canted
Over to catch the drivel of some bitch   10
Who's read nothing but *Which*;
Just think of all the spare time that has flown

Straight into nothingness by being filled
With forks and faces, rather than repaid
Under a lamp, hearing the noise of wind,   15
And looking out to see the moon thinned
To an air-sharpened blade.
A life, and yet how sternly it's instilled

All solitude is selfish. No one now
Believes the hermit with his gown and dish   20
Talking to God (who's gone too); the big wish
Is to have people nice to you, which means
Doing it back somehow.
Virtue is social. Are, then, these routines

Playing at goodness, like going to church?   25
Something that bores us, something we don't do well
(Asking that ass about his fool research)
But try to feel, because, however crudely,
It shows us what should be?
Too subtle, that. Too decent, too. Oh hell,   30

Only the young can be alone freely.
The time is shorter now for company,
And sitting by a lamp more often brings
Not peace, but other things.
Beyond the light stand failure and remorse   35
Whispering *Dear Warlock-Williams: Why, of course*—

1. Are the opening lines actually spoken by someone? Who has recon-structed them? What is he parodying? What tone are the lines spoken in?
2. What is the conflict in the poem? Does the speaker believe "All solitude is selfish," and "Virtue is social"? What would he rather be doing?
3. What are the "other things" mentioned in line 34? How is the conflict resolved? Why does the speaker change his mind?

ANDREW MARVELL (1621–1678)

To His Coy Mistress

Had we but world enough, and time,
This coyness, lady, were no crime.
We would sit down, and think which way
To walk, and pass our long love's day.
Thou by the Indian Ganges' side   5
Shouldst rubies find; I by the tide
of Humber would complain. I would
Love you ten years before the Flood,
And you should, if you please, refuse
Till the conversion of the Jews.   10
My vegetable love should grow
Vaster than empires, and more slow;
An hundred years should go to praise
Thine eyes and on thy forehead gaze,
Two hundred to adore each breast,   15
But thirty thousand to the rest:
An age at least to every part,
And the last age should show your heart.
For, lady, you deserve this state,
Nor would I love at lower rate.   20
   But at my back I always hear
Time's wingèd chariot hurrying near;
And yonder all before us lie
Deserts of vast eternity.
Thy beauty shall no more be found,   25
Nor in thy marble vault shall sound
My echoing song; then worms shall try
That long preserved virginity,
And your quaint honor turn to dust,
And into ashes all my lust.   30
The grave's a fine and private place,

But none, I think, do there embrace.
  Now, therefore, while the youthful hue
Sits on thy skin like morning dew,
And while thy willing soul transpires   35
At every pore with instant fires,
Now let us sport us while we may,
Rather at once our time devour
Than languish in his slow-chapped power.
Let us roll all our strength and all   40
Our sweetness up into one ball,
And tear our pleasures with rough strife
Thorough the iron gates of life.
Thus, though we cannot make our sun
Stand still, yet we will make him run.   45

EDWIN ARLINGTON ROBINSON (1869–1935)

Richard Cory

Whenever Richard Cory went down town,
We people on the pavement looked at him:
He was a gentleman from sole to crown,
Clean favored, and imperially slim.

And he was always quietly arrayed,   5
And he was always human when he talked;
But still he fluttered pulses when he said,
"Good-morning," and he glittered when he walked.

And he was rich—yes, richer than a king—
And admirably schooled in every grace: 10
In fine, we thought that he was everything
To make us wish that we were in his place.

So on we worked, and waited for the light,
And went without the meat, and cursed the bread;
And Richard Cory, one calm summer night,   15
Went home and put a bullet through his head.

1. Who is the speaker of the poem? What do we know about him? What is
   the attitude of the speaker toward Richard Cory?
2. Is he surprised by Richard Cory's suicide? Why or why not?
3. What does "waited for the light" mean?

WILLIAM STAFFORD (b. 1914)

Traveling Through the Dark

Traveling through the dark I found a deer
dead on the edge of the Wilson River road.
It is usually best to roll them into the canyon:
that road is narrow; to swerve might make more dead.

By glow of the tail-light I stumbled back of the car   5
and stood by the heap, a doe, a recent killing;
she had stiffened already, almost cold.
I dragged her off; she was large in the belly.

My fingers touching her side brought me the reason—
her side was warm; her fawn lay there waiting,   10
alive, still, never to be born.
Beside that mountain road I hesitated.

The car aimed ahead its lowered parking lights;
under the hood purred the steady engine.
I stood in the glare of the warm exhaust turning red;   15
around our group I could hear the wilderness listen.

I thought hard for us all—my only swerving—
then pushed her over the edge into river.

1. What are the details of the dramatic scene presented in the poem? What
   reason does the speaker give for stopping?
2. What is the function of the references to the speaker's car in the third
   stanza? What has this to do with the conflict?
3. When the speaker examines the dead doe what does he discover? What
   does he do? Why does he call his act "My only swerving"?

ALFRED, LORD TENNYSON (1809–1892)

Ulysses

It little profits that an idle king,
By this still hearth, among these barren crags,
Matched with an agèd wife, I mete and dole
Unequal laws unto a savage race,
That hoard, and sleep, and feed, and know not me.   5

I cannot rest from travel; I will drink
Life to the lees. All times I have enjoyed
Greatly, have suffered greatly, both with those
That loved me, and alone; on shore, and when
Through scudding drifts the rainy Hyades   10
Vext the dim sea. I am become a name;
For always roaming with a hungry heart
Much have I seen and known—cities of men
And manners, climates, councils, governments,
Myself not least, but honored of them all,—   15
And drunk delight of battle with my peers,
Far on the ringing plains of windy Troy.
I am a part of all that I have met;
Yet all experience is an arch wherethrough
Gleams that untraveled world whose margin fades   20
For ever and for ever when I move.
How dull it is to pause, to make an end,
To rust unburnished, not to shine in use!
As though to breathe were life! Life piled on life
Were all too little, and of one to me   25
Little remains; but every hour is saved
From that eternal silence, something more,
A bringer of new things; and vile it were
For some three suns to store and hoard myself,
And this gray spirit yearning in desire   30
To follow knowledge like a sinking star,
Beyond the utmost bound of human thought.
　　This is my son, mine own Telemachus,
To whom I leave the scepter and the isle,
Well-loved of me, discerning to fulfill   35
This labor, by slow prudence to make mild
A rugged people, and through soft degrees
Subdue them to the useful and the good.
Most blameless is he, centered in the sphere
Of common duties, decent not to fail   40
In offices of tenderness, and pay
Meet adoration to my household gods,
When I am gone. He works his work, I mine.
　　There lies the port; the vessel puffs her sail;
There gloom the dark, broad seas. My mariners,   45
Souls that have toiled, and wrought, and thought with me,
That ever with a frolic welcome took
The thunder and the sunshine, and opposed
Free hearts, free foreheads—you and I are old;
Old age hath yet his honor and his toil.   50

Death closes all; but something ere the end,
Some work of noble note, may yet be done,
Not unbecoming men that strove with gods.
The lights begin to twinkle from the rocks;
The long day wanes; the slow moon climbs; the deep   55
Moans round with many voices. Come, my friends,
'Tis not too late to seek a newer world.
Push off, and sitting well in order smite
The sounding furrows; for my purpose holds
To sail beyond the sunset, and the baths   60
Of all the western stars, until I die.
It may be that the gulfs will wash us down;
It may be we shall touch the Happy Isles,
and see the great Achilles, whom we knew.
Though much is taken, much abides; and though   65
We are not now that strength which in old days
Moved earth and heaven, that which we are, we are,
One equal temper of heroic hearts,
made weak by time and fate, but strong in will
To strive, to seek, to find, and not to yield.   70

WRITING ABOUT PERSONA, DRAMATIC SITUATION, AND TONE

Alexander Pope seemed to be paying a beautiful woman a compliment when he penned the couplet:

> Her lively looks a sprightly mind disclose,
> Quick as her eyes, and as unfixed as those.

But what he was actually suggesting, as his more astute readers were aware, was that the lady was not quick-witted but flirtatious and flighty. Pope's real meaning was evident to those who had paid attention to the tone of the lines and to the speaker's character. Furthermore, the lines occur in a longer poem whose dramatic context provides additional evidence for the speaker's attitude toward the lady.

Reading poetry involves attending to many literal details before we can begin to ask, "What do they all add up to?" Poems can be viewed as miniature dramas, much like the dramas we witness and overhear everyday: a conversation between two neighbors at a checkout stand, a woman in a restaurant pouring out her grief to a close friend who is a willing listener, a couple obviously fond of each other playfully pointing out sights as they stroll along a crowded city street. All of these are commonplaces that we tune in and out of our consciousnesses daily. When we read a poem, even a love lyric, we are in the presence of a similar experience—but one that places far greater demands on our attention and that contains far greater rewards than temporarily satisfying our curiosity.

Every poem has at least one speaker, voice, or *persona*. What do we know about the speaker? Is it a man or a woman? How old is he or she? Do we know the speaker's occupation? If there is also a listener, what do we know about the listener and the relationship to the speaker? Are we addressed as listeners, or are we overhearing a conversation? Is there conflict implied in what happens or in what the speaker says? Finally, what is the attitude of the speaker toward what has been described or said? What attitude do any other characters in the poem express?

Reading a poem in any complete sense usually involves taking some tentative stabs at one of these related areas and then qualifying that view with the answers to other questions. We cannot separate our response to the character of the speaker from the tone of the poem or from the situation which prompted the speaker to view things as he or she did. In short, while all these questions cannot be asked simultaneously, we must qualify our discoveries as each new piece of evidence presents itself. Reading a poem is, in a sense, an exercise in skepticism and discovery. Just as you might have done with an overheard conversation, your preliminary conclusions about the situation and the character of the speaker were qualified as you heard more and altered what you had earlier thought. Since poems are carefully constructed, the poet presents these bits of information in a patterned way that is quite different from the randomness of overheard conversations.

Take for instance "Love Song: I and Thou" by Alan Dugan on page 000. The poem might at first seem like the kind of angry tirade you might hear from someone completely disgusted with his life. The speaker blames himself for how badly his life (house) has turned out. No less than twenty first-person pronouns appear in the thirty-one lines. We seem to be overhearing his raging monologue. His language suggests that he is aware of the reasons for his twisted nature; verbs like *spat* and *screamed*, nouns like *maggots* and *hell*, and adjectives like *bowed* and *bent* are part of the self-characterization of his life. He seems determined on his course of angry self-destruction, and we realize the full irony when we discover the silent listener is the object of his "love song," the *thou* of the poem, his proposed future wife who he hopes will add to his self-crucifixion. The humor is black and bitter. The allusion to Martin Buber's *I and Thou*, a book which suggests the importance of forming human I–Thou relationships, is a final crowning irony. The view that such relationships will only increase our suffering and add to our martyrdom is another cruel joke the speaker has at his own expense. All of these aspects of the poem—the speaker's character, the tone, the situation the speaker finds himself in—are evident from the words chosen, and the details assembled to tell us about himself in his dramatic monologue. As we overhear his bitter monologue, we gain increasing insight into how he regards suffering as an endless cycle, one that will eventually embrace love as well.

Therefore, as you begin to prepare material for your paper on persona, dramatic situation, and tone, decide which one of these elements you will focus on, but recognize that they are woven together. As with Dugan's poem, be sure not to completely identify the persona with the poet. That peom's ironic title at once distances the poet from the persona whose rage stems from his solipsistic failure to build an "I-Thou" relationship in his life. The poet implies the persona will continue to "crucify" himself. If the utterance has a physical setting, note its relevance to the speaker's mood, and to any dramatic action in the poem. Finally, isolate the dominant tone of the poem, but be aware that there could be more than one tone if the persona and any characters hold different views, or if there is a shift in the persona's attitude in the course of the poem.

"Memories of the West Street and Lepke": Lowell's Agonizing Reappraisal

Robert Lowell's confessional poem "Memories of West Street and Lepke," which appeared in Life Studies (1959), is more than an autobiographical reminiscence of the poet's one-year jail term for conscientious objection in World War II. It is a dramatic flashback told by one aspect of Lowell's personality, the persona of the forty-year-old poet-professor, about another aspect of his personality, the "manic" twenty-year-old conscientious objector. The result of this double focus is an exploration of the conflicting claims of calm maturity and youthful idealism.

The persona of the opening stanza depicts himself as a man in tune with his times, "the tranquilized fifties." He is an establishment poet with an academic sinecure, "Only teaching on Tuesdays." In keeping with the dispassionate calm he attributes to being forty, he has chosen to live in the traditional city of Boston, specifically on what Henry James described with characteristic understatement as "hardly passionate Marlborough Street." Here even the deprived are conservative "young Republican(s)." However, the tone as revealed by the details selected and the language chosen by the forty-year-old poet is hardly one of smug satisfaction; rather, it is one of disbelief that he should have ventured so far from his youthful radicalism to have become one of the leisured class, lounging (bookworming) in pajamas and hogging a whole house. The language suggests excess (hog), a kind of intellectual effeteness (bookworm) and early retirement or rest (pajamas). The inappropriateness of his situation culminates in the allusion to his infant daughter who is "young enough to be my granddaughter." However, the allusion to the poet's daughter also marks a change in color and tone in the poem. Her "flame-flamingo infant's wear" is an appropriate transitional detail from the forty year old poet to the childish "fire-breathing Catholic C.O." that the poet was at twenty.

At first the tone of the flashback as told by the forty year old is critical. The twenty year old was a fool. His declaration of conscientious objection ("manic statement") gets him thrown into the "bull pen" with the other social outcasts ("a Negro boy with curlicues/of marijuana in his hair.") A hot young stud, he's put in a place to cool off, or as the baseball term suggests, a place where he has to wait to get in the game. Yet the question that the older persona asks in the second line of stanza two, "Ought I to regret my seedtime?", introduces a mixed tone as the double meaning of seedtime implies. Should the poet regret this sowing of "wild

oats" when he was younger, or ought he to regret having gone to seed at
forty?

On the surface, the final two stanzas are a <u>reductio ad absurdam</u> of the
experience in the West Street jail. The older man sees the young C.O.'s
principled stance as pointless. The twenty year old is thrown into jail with a
motley cast of characters—a vegetarian pacifist, two Hollywood pimps, a
Jehovah's Witness and the underworld head of the syndicate which killed
for hire, Murder Incorporated's Czar Lepke. The absurdity of this makes a
mockery of his pacifism. Here the setting is in sharp contrast of the poet's
present circumstances. Located in passionate New York, the jail is a kind of
school, the roof of which reminds him of his "school soccer court." No clean
clothes from washers grace this environment, but "sooty clothesline
entanglements and bleaching khaki tenements." The leisure class has
disappeared to be replaced by a fanatic even more fervent than the twenty
year old: Abramowitz "so vegetarian, /. he wore rope shoes and preferred
fallen fruit." The colors of reality are more deeply perceived here than in the
later Boston environment. Abramowitz's pacifism is put to the test at West
Street for he is beaten "black and blue" by the Hollywood pimps in their
"chocolate double breasted suits."

The language with which the speaker recalls the figure of Czar Lepke
and the details of the portrait at first seem a continuation of the mature
poet's bemused view of the absurdity of the twenty year old's situation and
his naivete ("I was so out of things"). Yet as the portrait progresses, the
issue raised by the question in stanza two is reintroduced: "Ought I to regret
my seedtime?" The imagined sinister figure of Lepke is in actuality a fat,
bald trustee shuffling about the halls, "piling towels on a rack, /or dawdling
off to his little segregated cell." He's a celebrity who has access to "things
forbidden the common man." The persona of the poem begins subtly to draw
parallels between himself, the celebrity poet who has accumulated the
objects approved by conservative society and who lives a comfortable life,
and Lepke. Lepke's toy American flags and Easter palm mock the totem
objects of the conservative forty-year-old poet. But the final parallel reveals
the depths of the forty year old's dissatisfaction. Lepke's lobotomy has
removed any sense of guilt, any connection between the murders he was
responsible for and the consequence of those murders: the electric chair.
Like a mirage the chair hangs "in his air of lost connections." The speaker
has shifted his tone in the course of his description of Lepke to see himself
as "lobotomized" drifting in a "sheepish calm." Yet unlike Lepke, his
monologue *is* an "agonizing reappraisal" of what twenty years have done to
him. Lepke's connections have been severed by his lobotomy, but the speaker
continues to agonize over the question of his present secure calm position
and his early idealistic passions.

"Memories of West Street and Lepke" asks a perennial question: Which
is the more accurate view of life, the passionate commitment to ideals
associated with youth, or the calmer reappraisal of maturity? Lowell's
sensitive persona rises above his early simplistic view of both youth and
maturity to see each stage as a loss and a gain; yearning for the passion of
youth, he feels lobotomized in his present "sheepish calm," but it is, after all,
the forty-year-old who has gained sufficient insight to examine his condition
with enough objectivity to regret the loss.

SUGGESTED TOPICS FOR WRITING

1. Write an essay on the problem of speaker and listener in Keats' "Ode on a Grecian Urn." Pay particular attention to the problems raised by the use of the pronouns *thou* and *ye* in the last stanza. Who is the speaker of "Beauty is truth, truth beauty"? How does this affect the meaning of the poem?
2. Write an essay on the persona of "Lapis Lazuli." How does the opening present a dramatic situation that the remainder of the poem resolves?
3. Explain the attitude toward the twentieth century of the persona of Robert Lowell's "For the Union Dead." What has Colonel Shaw to do with this attitude? What is the tone of most of the poem?
4. Investigate the tone of irony used by the speaker in Philip Larkin's "Vers de Societé."
5. Describe the function of the details mentioned in the setting of Robert Browning's "My Last Duchess." How do they serve to characterize the Duke?
6. Delineate the conflict of William Stafford's "Traveling Through the Dark," characterizing the speaker who feels the conflict.
7. Write an essay on the persona of the young wife in Ezra Pound's "The River-Merchant's Wife: A Letter."
8. Discuss the use of language to establish tone in E. E. Cummings's "a salesman is an it that stinks Excuse."

METER, RHYTHM, AND FREE VERSE

Because of nursery rhymes, greeting cards, television jingles, song lyrics, and popular or classical poetry from an earlier day, most of us grow up thinking that one of the distinguishing qualities of poetry is **meter** or "beat"—a theoretically regular, recurring pattern of stressed and unstressed syllables. Read aloud this stanza from A. E. Housman's "To an Athlete Dying Young" (page 701). Its "beat" is particularly noticeable.

> The time you won your town the race
> We chaired you through the market-place;
> Man and boy stood cheering by,
> And home we brought you shoulder high.

Notice that each line contains eight syllables, and that there is a pronounced alternation between relatively unstressed syllables (the odd-numbered ones) and relatively stressed syllables (the even-numbered ones). This regular alternation is *meter*. In Housman's poem, the presence of meter is reinforced by the obvious rhyme and by the use of four line stanzas or groups of lines.

Now read these lines from John Milton's "Description of Satan" (page 000) from *Paradise Lost*.

> High on a throne of royal state, which far
> Outshone the wealth of Ormus and of Ind,
> Or where the gorgeous East with richest hand
> Show'rs on her kings barbaric pearl and gold,
> Satan exalted sat, . . .

This verse also has meter: each line contains ten syllables, and, generally, there is an alternation between unstressed and stressed syllables. But these lines do not rhyme, and because the "beat" is not so regular, the meter of the passage seems less pronounced. Such unrhymed lines with ten syllables alternating between unstressed and stressed are called **blank verse**.

One last example will allow us to put meter in its proper perspective.

LAWRENCE FERLINGHETTI (b. 1919)

Constantly risking absurdity

```
Constantly risking absurdity
                        and death
        whenever he performs
                    above the heads
                            of his audience          5
The poet like an acrobat
            climbs on rime
                    to a high wire of his own making
and balancing on eyebeams
                    above a sea of faces             10
        paces his way
                to the other side of day
    performing entrechats
                    and sleight-of-foot tricks
and other high theatrics                             15
                    and all without mistaking
        any thing
                for what it may not be
```

For he's the super realist
                         who must perforce perceive   20
          taut truth
                         before the taking of each stance or step
   in his supposed advance
                         toward that still higher perch
where Beauty stands and waits   25
                         with gravity
                         to start her death-defying leap

   And he
          a little charleychaplin man
                         who may or may not catch   30
          her fair eternal form
                         spreadeagled in the empty air
          of existence

This poem has no meter, no regular line length, and no rhyme. Except for the line as a structural unit, we cannot immediately sense any pattern around which Ferlinghetti has organized his poem.

Each of these examples, including "Constantly risking absurdity," has **rhythm,** which we could define as the overall motion of a line (or lines) of poetry. Rhythm *includes* meter, but goes beyond it to encompass other aspects of motion such as *tempo, pauses, punctuation, line length,* and the *arrangement* of lines on the page. As readers of poetry, we must be able to detect meter and assess its importance, but we must also—particularly if we want to understand much modern poetry—be sensitive to the general rhythms of poems.

When we study meter and rhythm, as well as sound effects and versification (which will be taken up in subsequent chapters), we are studying **prosody.** The study of prosody usually begins with the study of meter, which is perhaps the single most obvious feature of conventional English verse. Reviewing some of the terms that poets and scholars use to describe meter will help us understand metered verse and will prepare us to appreciate some of the subtleties and complexities of poetry that relies on "extrametrical" factors to achieve its rhythm.

Historically, meter has been determined in one of four ways. **Quantitative meter** (in which classical Greek and Latin poems were generally written) is based on the length of syllables, which are considered short or long depending upon their duration in time. This kind of meter is rarely employed in poetry written in English.

In **accentual meter,** the number of stressed or accented syllables determines the line, which can contain any number of unstressed syllables. Such meter was used almost universally in Anglo-Saxon poetry (700–1100 A.D.), where it was accompanied by heavy alliteration on the stressed syllables. Richard Wilbur's "Junk" uses this kind of meter in describing modern subject matter.

RICHARD WILBUR (b. 1921)

Junk

> *Huru Welandes*
> > *worc ne geswiceð*
> *monna anigum*
> > *ðara ðe Mimming can*
> *heardne gehealdan.*
> > > > *—WALDERE*

An axe angles
> from my neighbor's ashcan;
It is hell's handiwork,
> the wood not hickory,
The flow of the grain
> not faithfully followed.
The shivered shaft
> rises from a shellheap
Of plastic playthings,
> paper plates,   5
And the sheer shards
> of shattered tumblers
That were not annealed
> for the time needful.
At the same curbside,
> a cast-off cabinet
Of wavily-warped
> unseasoned wood
Waits to be trundled
> in the trash-man's truck.   10
Haul them off! Hide them!
> The heart winces
For junk and gimcrack,
> for jerrybuilt things
And the men who make them
> for a little money,
Bartering pride
> like the bought boxer
Who pulls his punches,
> or the paid-off jockey   15

Who in the home stretch
            holds in his horse.
Yet the things themselves
            in thoughtless honor
Have kept composure,
            like captives who would not
Talk under torture.
            Tossed from a tailgate
Where the dump displays
            its random dolmens,   20
Its black barrows
            and blazing valleys,
They shall waste in the weather
            toward what they were.
The sun shall glory
            in the glitter of glass-chips,
Forseeing the salvage
            of the prisoned sand,
And the blistering paint
            peel off in patches,   25
That the good grain
            be discovered again.
Then burnt, bulldozed,
            they shall all be buried
To the depth of diamonds,
            in the making dark
Where halt Hephaestus
            keeps his hammer
And Wayland's work
            is worn away.   30

A third kind of meter, **syllabic meter,** uses the number of syllables to control the length of the line. This kind of meter, common in French poetry, is not used frequently in English-language verse. Notice, as you read the following poem by Thomas Campion, that the number of stressed and unstressed syllables varies from line to line, but that the lines in each stanza have 5, 8, 8, and 4 syllables respectively.

THOMAS CAMPION (1567–1620)

Rose-cheeked Laura

Rose-cheeked Laura, come,
Sing thou smoothly with thy beauty's
Silent music, either other
    Sweetly gracing.

Lovely forms do flow   5
from concent divinely framed;
Heav'n is music, and thy beauty's
    Birth is heavenly.

These dull notes we sing
Discords need for helps to grace them;   10
Only beauty purely loving
    Knows no discord,

But still moves delight,
Like clear springs renewed by flowing,
Ever perfect, ever in them-   15
    selves eternal.

Since the time of Geoffrey Chaucer (c. 1340–1400), author of *The Canterbury Tales*, metered poetry in English has generally been written in **accentual-syllabic** meter. That is, it has combined the accentual and syllabic systems and has used both numbers of stresses and numbers of syllables to determine the metrical lengths of lines. The Housman stanza with which this chapter began typifies this kind of meter. Each line contains eight syllables, four stressed and four unstressed.

If we isolate one line from this poem and mark its stressed and unstressed syllables, we perceive the following pattern.

$$\smile \; / \; \smile \; / \; \smile \; / \; \smile \; /$$
The time you won your town the race

We call this marking of stressed and unstressed syllables **scansion** (the verb is *to scan*). Any line of poetry, metered or unmetered, can be scanned; only metered verse will reveal, as this line does, a regular pattern. Scansion can be a subtle procedure subject to some interpretation because of context, emphasis, and meaning. When you scan a poem, try not to force the syllables into a pattern. Say them as naturally as possible, mark what you hear, and try to perceive the general pattern. There will usually be exceptions to the "ideal," regular patterns discussed here.

Note that there are four recurring units in the first line of the Housman poem:

⏑ / ⏑ / ⏑ / ⏑ /
The time / you won / your town / the race

These units, the smallest recurring metrical units in the line, are called **feet**. In English language poetry, six kinds of poetic feet are commonly used.

Foot	Adjective Form	Scansion	Example
iamb	iambic	./	Elaine
trochee	trochaic	/.	Joseph
anapest	anapestic	../	in the house
dactyl	dactylic	/..	edible
spondee	spondaic	//	Babe Ruth
pyrrhic	pyrrhic	..	(context required)

English poetry, for obvious reasons, is never really written in spondaic or pyrrhic meter. These kinds of feet are usually used as substitutions for others. In Emily Dickinson's poem "I like to see it lap the Miles" (page 721), Dickinson uses both a spondee and a pyrrhic foot in the following line:

⏑⏑ / / ⏑ /
at its / own sta / ble door

Meters whose feet end in a stressed syllable (iambic and anapestic) are generally called **rising meters;** meters ending in an unstressed syllable (trochaic and dactylic) are generally called **falling meters.** Samuel Taylor Coleridge uses a variety of poetic feet in the following clever poem.

SAMUEL TAYLOR COLERIDGE (1772–1834)

Metrical Feet

Lesson for a Boy

Trōchĕe trīps frŏm lōng tŏ shōrt;
From long to long in solemn sort
Slōw Spōndēe stālks; strōng fŏŏt! yet ill able
Ēvĕr tŏ cōme ŭp wĭth Dāctўl trĭsўllăblĕ.
Ĭāmbĭcs mārch frŏm shōrt tŏ lōng—   5
Wĭth ă lēap ănd ă bōŭnd thĕ swĭft Anăpĕsts thrōng;
One syllable long, with one short at each side,
Ămphībrăchўs hāstes wĭth ă stātelŷ stride—
Fīrst ănd lāst bēing lōng, mĭddlĕ shōrt, Ămphĭmācer
Strīkes hĭs thūndērĭng hōŏfs lĭke ă prōŭd hĭgh-brĕd Rācer.   10

If Derwent be innocent, steady, and wise,
And delight in the things of earth, water, and skies;
Tender warmth at his heart, with these meters to show it,
With sound sense in his brains, may make Derwent a poet—
May crown him with fame, and must win him the love   15
Of his father on earth and his Father above.
            My dear, dear child!
Could you stand upon Skiddaw, you would not from its whole ridge
See a man who so loves you as your fond S. T. Coleridge.

If you scan the first six lines of this poem, you will see that each line is written in the kind of meter named in it.

The full name of a meter in English combines the designation for the kind of foot with a word signalling the number of feet per line: *monometer* (1), *dimeter* (2), *trimeter* (3), *tetrameter* (4), *pentameter* (5), *hexameter* (6), and so forth. Here are some lines of poetry exemplifying frequently used English meters.

FREQUENTLY USED ENGLISH METERS

Iambic pentameter: And knaves and fools we both abhorred alike.
                       Dryden, "To the Memory of Mr. Oldham" (page 698), line 6

Iambic tetrameter   Had we but world enough and time
                       Marvell, "To His Coy Mistress" (page 670), line 1

Trochaic dimeter   Edward, Edward
                       Anonymous, "Edward" (page 800), line 2

Anapestic tetrameter With a leap and a bound the swift anapests throng
                       Coleridge, "Metrical Feet" (page 684), line 5

Dactylic tetrameter Or is it only the breeze, in its listlessness
                       Hardy, "The Voice" (page 699), line 9

Iambic trimeter   a spotted shaft is seen
                       Dickinson, "A narrow Fellow in the Grass" (page 561), line 1

Iambic hexameter   And consummation comes, and jars two hemispheres.
                       Hardy, "The Convergence of the Twain" (page 603), line 33

The exercises at the end of this section will give you more practice in scanning and labeling various meters.

Knowing what meter is, we might want to ask why poets, historically, have used it so frequently. Although English speech may tend to fall into a generally iambic pattern (iambic meter is by far the most common in English verse), regular meter still may strike us as artificial. One important function of meter in fact derives from this very artificiality. Meter in poetry reinforces our sense that we are reading something *made*, and made carefully. Only language that has been "worked over" will fall into a regular meter. Hence meter, like rhyme, serves to remove poetry from the everyday use of language and place it in a special sphere. Meter secures our attention and engages our interest. It is a way of saying "listen up!" The sense of formalism meter provides also makes poetry more memorizable, and more memorable. Read "To the Memory of Mr. Oldham" (page 698) and "The Dance" by William Carlos Williams (page 706), and then try memorizing them, even five lines of them. You will find that even though Williams' poem is written in a more modern idiom, it is much harder to memorize because it lacks meter.

Meter has other functions. It provides greater vividness to most writing, and can sometimes be used for mimetic effects; that is, it can be used to imitate the very subject it describes. Notice how, in the following poem by Emily Dickinson, the regularity of the meter, and the "speed" this produces in the reading of the lines, helps to support the idea of rapid motion that the poem takes up.

EMILY DICKINSON (1830–1886)

Because I could not stop for Death

Because I could not stop for Death—
He kindly stopped for me—
The Carriage held but just Ourselves—
And Immortality.

We slowly drove—He knew no haste   5
And I had put away
My labor and my leisure too,
For His Civility—

We passed the School, where Children strove
At Recess—in the Ring—   10
We passed the Fields of Gazing Grain—
We passed the Setting Sun—

Or rather—He passed Us—
The Dews drew quivering and chill—
For only Gossamer, my Gown—   15
My Tippet—only Tulle—

We paused before a House that seemed
A Swelling of the Ground—
The Roof was scarcely visible—
The Cornice—in the Ground—   20

Since then—'tis Centuries—and yet
Feels shorter than the Day
I first surmised the Horses' Heads
Were toward Eternity—

Meter, since it is a pattern used consistently, also gives unity to a poem. Moreover, because it provides a general unity of effect, poets are better able to create extraordinary emphasis by suddenly varying the meter. Notice how, at the beginning of the second stanza of "Meeting at Night," Robert Browning emphasizes the first words of lines seven and eight by using metrical substitutions.

ROBERT BROWNING (1812–1889)

Meeting at Night

I

The gray sea and the long black land;
And the yellow half-moon large and low;
And the startled little waves that leap
In fiery ringlets from their sleep,
As I gain the cove with pushing prow,   5
And quench its speed i' the slushy sand.

II

Then a mile of warm sea-scented beach;
Three fields to cross till a farm appears;
A tap at the pane, the quick sharp scratch
And blue spurt of a lighted match,   10
And a voice less loud, through its joys and fears,
Than the two hearts beating each to each!

Line six of this poem begins with the expected iamb; the use of a trochee at the beginning of line seven ("Then a") and a spondee at the beginning of line eight ("Three fields") make these lines stand out from the previously established pattern.

There are other ways besides variation in meter to alter a rhythmical pattern: **letter sounds, enjambment** and **caesura.** These devices will affect rhythm whether or not the passage in which they appear is metered. D. H. Lawrence's poem "Snake" exhibits all three.

D. H. LAWRENCE (1885–1930)

Snake

A snake came to my water-trough
On a hot, hot day, and I in pajamas for the heat,
To drink there.

In the deep, strange-scented shade of the great dark carob-tree
I came down the steps with my pitcher   5
And must wait, must stand and wait, for there he was at the trough
   before me.

He reached down from a fissure in the earth-wall in the gloom
And trailed his yellow-brown slackness soft-bellied down, over the
   edge of the stone trough
And rested his throat upon the stone bottom,
And where the water had dripped from the tap, in a small clearness,   10
He sipped with his straight mouth,
Softly drank through his straight gums, into his slack long body,
Silently.

Someone was before me at my water-trough,
And I, like a second comer, waiting.   15

He lifted his head from his drinking, as cattle do,
And looked at me vaguely, as drinking cattle do,
And flickered his two-forked tongue from his lips, and mused a
   moment,
And stooped and drank a little more,
Being earth-brown, earth-golden from the burning bowels of the earth   20
On the day of Sicilian July, with Etna smoking.

The voice of my education said to me
He must be killed,
For in Sicily the black, black snakes are innocent, the gold are
   venomous.

And voices in me said, If you were a man   25
You would take a stick and break him now, and finish him off.

But must I confess how I liked him,
How glad I was he had come like a guest in quiet, to drink at my
   water-trough

And depart peaceful, pacified, and thankless,
Into the burning bowels of this earth?   30

Was it cowardice, that I dared not kill him?
Was it perversity, that I longed to talk to him?
Was it humility, to feel so honored?
I felt so honored.

And yet those voices: 35
If you were not afraid, you would kill him!

And truly I was afraid, I was most afraid,
But even so, honored still more
That he should seek my hospitality
From out the dark door of the secret earth.   40

He drank enough
And lifted his head, dreamily, as one who has drunken,
And flickered his tongue like a forked night on the air, so black,
Seeming to lick his lips,
And looked around like a god, unseeing, into the air,   45
And slowly turned his head,
And slowly, very slowly, as if thrice adream,
Proceeded to draw his slow length curving round
And climb again the broken bank of my wall-face.

And as he put his head into that dreadful hole,   50
And as he slowly drew up, snake-easing his shoulders, and entered
    farther,
A sort of horror, a sort of protest against his withdrawing into that
    horrid black hole,
Deliberately going into the blackness, and slowly drawing himself after,
Overcame me now his back was turned.

I looked round, I put down my pitcher,   55
I picked up a clumsy log
And threw it at the water-trough with a clatter.

I think it did not hit him,
But suddenly that part of him that was left behind convulsed in
    undignified haste.
Writhed like lightning, and was gone   60
Into the black hole, the earth-lipped fissure in the wall-front,
At which, in the intense still noon, I stared with fascination.

And immediately I regretted it.
I thought how paltry, how vulgar, what a mean act!
I despised myself and the voices of my accursed human education.   65

And I thought of the albatross
And I wished he would come back, my snake.

For he seemed to me again like a king,
Like a king in exile, uncrowned in the underworld,
Now due to be crowned again.   70

And so, I missed my chance with one of the lords
Of life.
And I have something to expiate;
A pettiness.

                                                            Taormina.

Look again at line eight; it is an excellent example of how a poet can
use the sounds of letters to slow down the verse. The vowel sounds in
slackness and *trough* take a relatively long time to say. The *s* sounds in *slackness, soft,* and *stone* also slow the line down. Moreover, the repeated consonants at the end of one word and the beginning of the next, as in "slack-
nes*s s*oft-bellie*d d*own" slow the line still further. Conversely, of course,
poets can speed lines up by using sounds that are simple to articulate.

In lines seven and eight, Lawrence uses *enjambment,* the running on of
one line of poetry to the next without punctuation or pause, to approximate
the sinuous movement of the snake as it curls down to the trough. This
"wrap-around" effect forces us to pay careful attention to the sentence
structure Lawrence uses. In lines 31 to 33, Lawrence uses a *caesura* or distinct pause, usually but not always accompanied by punctuation, to slow
down the lines.

> Was it cowardice, // that I dared not kill him?
> Was it perversity, // that I longed to talk to him?
> Was it humility, // to feel so honored?

Double slashes are customarily used to mark caesuras. Note that these
heavy pauses help to emphasize the key nouns of the passage: *cowardice,
perversity,* and *humility.*

Lawrence's "Snake" is written in **free verse**—verse without rhyme and
without any consistent metrical patterns. When scanned, the verse is seen
to be generally iambic, but because Lawrence is not "required" to stick to
an exclusively iambic pattern, he is able to achieve, not a greater, but a
different variety of rhythmical effects (lines 41–49 will reveal this).

The tradition of free verse poetry in English begins, for all practical purposes, with the American poet Walt Whitman. He perceived the need for a more oracular, more spacious and less constrained form for the open-ended, spontaneous, colloquial, and "democratic" poems he included in his major work, *Leaves of Grass* (first edition, 1855). Whitman felt that America was too vast, too mercurial, too restless to be captured in tidy couplets, regular meters, and short, traditional forms. "Crossing Brooklyn Ferry," one of his masterworks, typifies the effects he was able to create using free verse. A look at this long poem will help to show us some of the properties of free verse, and, by implication, why poets would want to use it in the first place.

WALT WHITMAN (1819–1892)

Crossing Brooklyn Ferry

I

Flood-tide below me! I see you face to face!
Clouds of the west—sun there half an hour high—I see you also face to
    face.

Crowds of men and women attired in the usual costumes, how curious
    you are to me!
On the ferry-boats the hundreds and hundreds that cross, returning
    home, are more curious to me than you suppose,
And you that shall cross from shore to shore years hence are more to   5
    me, and more in my meditations, than you might suppose.

II

The impalpable sustenance of me from all things at all hours of
    the day,
The simple, compact, well-join'd scheme, myself disintegrated, every
    one disintegrated yet part of the scheme,
The similitudes of the past and those of the future,
The glories strung like beads on my smallest sights and hearings,
    on the walk in the street and the passage over the river,
The current rushing so swiftly and swimming with me far away,   10
The others that are to follow me, the ties between me and them,
The certainty of others, the life, love, sight, hearing of others.

Others will enter the gates of the ferry and cross from shore to shore,
Others will watch the run of the flood-tide,
Others will see the shipping of Manhattan north and west, and the   15
    heights of Brooklyn to the south and east,

Others will see the islands large and small;
Fifty years hence, others will see them as they cross, the sun half an
    hour high,
A hundred years hence, or ever so many hundred years hence, others
    will see them,
Will enjoy the sunset, the pouring-in of the flood-tide, the falling-back
    to the sea of the ebb-tide.

III

It avails not, time nor place—distance avails not,   20
I am with you, you men and women of generation, or ever so many
    generations hence,
Just as you feel when you look on the river and sky, so I felt,
Just as any of you is one of a living crowd, I was one of a crowd,
Just as you are refresh'd by the gladness of the river and the bright
    flow, I was refresh'd,
Just as you stand and lean on the rail, yet hurry with the swift current, 25
    I stood yet was hurried,
Just as you look on the numberless masts of ships and the
    thick-stemm'd pipes of steamboats, I look'd.

I too many and many a time cross'd the river of old,
Watched the Twelfth-month sea-gulls, saw them high in the air
    floating with motionless wings, oscillating their bodies,
Saw how the glistening yellow lit up parts of their bodies and left the
    rest in strong shadow,
Saw the slow-wheeling circles and the gradual edging toward the south, 30
Saw the reflection of the summer sky in the water,
Had my eyes dazzled by the shimmering track of beams,
Look'd at the fine centrifugal spokes of light round the shape of my
    head in the sunlit water,
Look'd on the haze on the hills southward and south-westward,
Look'd on the vapor as it flew in fleeces tinged with violet,   35
Look'd toward the lower bay to notice the vessels arriving,
Saw their approach, saw aboard those that were near me,
Saw the white sails of schooners and sloops, saw the ships at anchor,
The sailors at work in the rigging or out astride the spars,
The round masts, the swinging motion of the hulls, the slender   40
    serpentine pennants,
The large and small steamers in motion, the pilots in their pilot-houses,
The white wake left by the passage, the quick tremulous whirl of the
    wheels,
The flags of all nations, the falling of them at sunset,
The scallop-edged waves in the twilight, the ladled cups, the
    frolicsome crests and glistening,

The stretch afar growing dimmer and dimmer, the gray walls of the   45
    granite storehouses by the docks,
On the river the shadowy group, the big steam-tug closely flank'd on
    each side by the barges, the hay-boat, the belated lighter,
On the neighboring shore the fires from the foundry chimneys burning
    high and glaringly into the night,
Casting their flicker of black contrasted with wild red and yellow light
    over the tops of houses, and down into the clefts of streets.

IV

These and all else were to me the same as they are to you,
I loved well those cities, loved well the stately and rapid river,   50
The men and women I saw were all near to me,
Others the same—others who look back on me because I look'd
    forward to them,
(The time will come, though I stop here to-day and to-night.)

V

What is it then between us?
What is the count of the scores or hundreds of years between us?   55

Whatever it is, it avails not—distance avails not, and place avails not,
I too lived, Brooklyn of ample hills was mine,
I too walk'd the streets of Manhattan island, and bathed in the waters
    around it,
I too felt the curious abrupt questionings stir within me,
In the day among crowds of people sometimes they came upon me,   60
In my walks home late at night or as I lay in my bed they came upon
    me,
I too had been struck from the float forever held in solution,
I too had receiv'd identity by my body,
That I was I knew was of my body, and what I should be I knew I
    should be of my body.

VI

It is not upon you alone the dark patches fall,   65
The dark threw its patches down upon me also,
The best I had done seem'd to me blank and suspicious,
My great thoughts as I supposed them, were they not in reality
    meagre?
Nor is it you alone who know what it is to be evil,
I am he who knew what it was to be evil,   70
I too knitted the old knot of contrariety,

Blabb'd, blush'd, resented, lied, stole, grudg'd,
Had guile, anger, lust, hot wishes I dared not speak,
Was wayward, vain, greedy, shallow, sly, cowardly, malignant,
The wolf, the snake, the hog, not wanting in me,   75
The cheating look, the frivolous word, the adulterous wish, not
    wanting,
Refusals, hates, postponements, meanness, laziness, none of these
    wanting,
Was one with the rest, the days and haps of the rest,
Was call'd by my nighest name by clear loud voices of young men as
    they saw me approaching or passing,
Felt their arms on my neck as I stood, or the negligent leaning of their 80
    flesh against me as I sat,
Saw many I loved in the street or ferry-boat or public assembly, yet
    never told them a word,
Lived the same life with the rest, the same old laughing, gnawing,
    sleeping,
Play'd the part that still looks back on the actor or actress,
The same old role, the role that is what we make it, as great as
    we like,
Or as small as we like, or both great and small.   85

VII

Closer yet I approach you,
What thought you have of me now, I had as much of you—I laid in
    my stores in advance,
I consider'd long and seriously of you before you were born.

Who was to know what should come home to me?
Who knows but I am enjoying this?   90
Who knows, for all the distance, but I am as good as looking at you
    now, for all you cannot see me?

VIII

Ah, what can ever be more stately and admirable to me than mast-
    hemm'd Manhattan?
River and sunset and scallop-edg'd waves of flood-tide?
The sea-gulls oscillating their bodies, the hay-boat in the twilight, and
    the belated lighter?
What gods can exceed these that clasp me by the hand, and with   95
    voices I love call me promptly and loudly by my nighest name
    as I approach?
What is more subtle than this which ties me to the woman or man that
    looks in my face?
Which fuses me into you now, and pours my meaning into you?

We understand then do we not?
What I promis'd without mentioning it, have you not accepted?
What the study could not teach—what the preaching could not   100
    accomplish is accomplish'd, is it not?

IX

Flow on, river! flow with the flood-tide, and ebb with the ebb-tide!
Frolic on, crested and scallop-edg'd waves!
Gorgeous clouds of the sunset! drench with your splendor me,
    or the men and women generations after me!
Cross from shore to shore, countless crowds of passengers!
Stand up, tall masts of Mannahatta! stand up, beautiful hills of   105
    Brooklyn!
Throb, baffled and curious brain! throw out questions and answers!
Suspend here and everywhere, eternal float of solution!
Gaze, loving and thirsting eyes, in the house or street or public
    assembly!
Sound out, voices of young men! loudly and musically call me
    by my nighest name!
Live, old life! play the part that looks back on the actor or actress!   110
Play the old role, the role that is great or small according as one
    makes it!
Consider, you who peruse me, whether I may not in unknown ways
    be looking upon you;
Be firm, rail over the river, to support those who lean idly, yet haste
    with the hasting current;
Fly on, sea-birds! fly sideways, or wheel in large circles high
    in the air;
Receive the summer sky, you water, and faithfully hold it till all   115
    downcast eyes have time to take it from you!
Diverge, fine spokes of light, from the shape of my head, or any
    one's head, in the sunlit water!
Come on, ships from the lower bay! pass up or down, white-sail'd
    schooners, sloops, lighters!
Flaunt away, flags of all nations! be duly lower'd at sunset!
Burn high your fires, foundry chimneys! cast black shadows at
    nightfall! cast red and yellow light over the tops of the houses!
Appearances, now or henceforth, indicate what you are,   120
You necessary film, continue to envelop the soul,
About my body for me, and your body for you, be hung our
    divinest aromas,
Thrive, cities—bring your freight, bring your shows, ample
    and sufficient rivers,
Expand, being than which none else is perhaps more spiritual,
Keep your places, objects than which none else is more lasting.   125

You have waited, you always wait, you dumb, beautiful ministers,
We receive you with free sense at last, and are insatiate hence forward,
Not you any more shall be able to foil us, or withhold yourselves
    from us,
We use you, and do not cast you aside—we plant you permanently
    within us,
We fathom you not—we love you—there is perfection in you also,   130
You furnish your parts toward eternity,
Great or small, you furnish your parts toward the soul.

Before you even read this poem, you probably noticed one significant feature of free verse. Because of its lack of strict regularity, it permits and even invites a freer and more creative use of the space of the page. Free verse does not generally march symmetrically down the page; it can meander, turn suddenly, become narrow, become wide, and so forth. Some poets take advantage of this quality to reinforce the meaning of their work. For example, the long lines Whitman prefers suggest the flowing of the river.

The principal distinguishing quality of free verse and the one that gives it its name is its lack of a regular meter and the absence of rhyme. If you scan a few lines of the poem, you will notice that its predominant meter is iambic. This is true of the English language in general. But free verse permits the use of changing meters and sudden shifts from one to another. Thus a poet can, in one poem, use a more or less regular iambic meter to suggest orderliness, then shift to anapestic meter to suggest rapid motion. Free verse permits more rhythmical variety.

Free verse also presumes that, besides meter and rhyme, there are other significant ways of imparting order and organization to a poem. Line length is one of these, as in any poem. Free verse poems, by their nature, permit more flexibility in both the length of lines and the ways in which groups of lines can be arranged. Long lines can be used to pile up information or detail (one of Whitman's favorite techniques); short lines can be used to give sudden emphasis to images or ideas. Repetition of key words or phrases, often at the beginnings or ends of lines—as in the second section of Whitman's poem—permit still another kind of order or patterning. Moreover, it is possible that the unavailability of meter and rhyme as ordering devices forces the poet to search harder for ways of arranging and developing ideas.

Besides the freer use of the page, the possibility for rhythmic variety, and the invitation to search for new means of ordering poems, free verse also allows for subtle modulations of tempo. Without the need to adhere to a general metrical pattern, poets can adjust words and syllables to suggest almost any speed, many natural sounds, and many kinds of recurring patterns. Polysyllabic words can also be used more freely, as suggested by such words as *impalpable, sustenance,* and *disintegrated* at the beginning of the second section of Whitman's poem. Perhaps more than any other verse form, free verse allows a poet to approximate something like natural, colloquial, spontaneous speech.

Two other historical reasons can be cited which help to clarify why so many modern poets, beginning with British and American poets of the 1920s, have turned to free verse. One is the desire to rebel against the restraints of past poetic forms, to forge a new path, to get along without the sometimes ossified conventions of past generations. The other reason is that many poets, having witnessed the ravages of World War I and the Depression years, felt that they lived, in fact, in a world that *was* chaotic, formless, even (at times) senseless and absurd. Free verse helped to reflect this sense of chaos, of rootlessness, of disjunction from the past.

It would be erroneous, of course, to think that free verse presented unalloyed advantages to the poet. In fact, its use carries with it a whole set of significant possible disadvantages as well. Robert Frost, himself one of the most metrically regular of modern poets, said that writing poetry in free verse was like "playing tennis without the net." Free verse takes away some of the "rules" that help poets write more precisely and effectively. At worst, and in the worst hands, free verse permits anything to be said, in any way. It invites a formlessness that may attempt to pass itself off as spontaneous and modern. Furthermore, since free verse establishes no set patterns, poets cannot use variations from an established pattern for emphasis. Without regularity, that is, contrast becomes more difficult. At its worst, free verse handled without skill resembles bad prose chopped up into lines.

The debate about the merits of free verse continues. Like rock-and-roll music, it is the predominant mode of contemporary expression, and needs to be considered with the same critical eye as any other poetic mode. A modern poem is not good or bad because it is written in free verse any more than an older poem is good or bad because it uses rhyme and a regular meter. Modern poetry has extraordinary variety from the point of view of metrics. But it too is part of the long tradition of poetry in English. Free verse has helped modern poets to augment that tradition, not to transcend it.

QUESTIONS

1. Identify the predominant meters of the following lines:
    A . Woman much missed, how you call to me, call to me . . .
    B . I wander thro' each charter'd street . . .
    C . What men or gods are these? What maidens loath?
    D . Whose woods these are I think I know.
    E . A spotted shaft is seen.

2. Scan the following passages:

    A . All things counter, original, spare, strange;
        Whatever is fickle, freckled (who knows how?)

With swift, slow; sweet, sour; adazzle, dim;
He fathers-forth whose beauty is past change:
                              Praise him.

Hopkins, "Pied Beauty" (page 700), lines 7–11

B . Who are these coming to the sacrifice?
    To what green altar, O mysterious priest,
Lead'st thou that heifer lowing at the skies,
    And all her silken flanks with garlands dressed?

Keats, "Ode on a Grecian Urn" (page 559), lines 31–34

C . When I see birches bend to left and right
Across the lines of straighter darker trees,
I like to think some boy's been swinging them.
But swinging doesn't bend them down to stay.

Frost, "Birches" (page 615), lines 1–4

D . These and all else were to me the same as they are to you,
    I loved well those cities, loved well the stately and rapid
        river,
The men and women I saw were all near to me,
Others the same—others who look back on me because I
        look'd forward to them,
(The time will come, though I stop here to-day and to-night.)

Whitman, "Crossing Brooklyn Ferry" (page 691), lines 49–53

E . The old South Boston Aquarium stands
    in a Sahara of snow now. Its broken windows are boarded.
The bronze weathervane cod has lost half its scales.
The airy tanks are dry.

Lowell, "For the Union Dead" (page 566), lines 1–4.

JOHN DRYDEN (1631–1700)

To the Memory of Mr. Oldham

Farewell, too little and too lately known,
Whom I began to think and call my own:
For sure our souls were near allied, and thine
Cast in the same poetic mold with mine.
One common note on either lyre did strike,   5
And knaves and fools we both abhorred alike.

To the same goal did both our studies drive;
The last set out the soonest did arrive.
Thus Nisus fell upon the slippery place,
While his young friend performed and won the race.　　　10
O early ripe! to thy abundant store
What could advancing age have added more?
It might (what nature never gives the young)
Have taught the numbers of thy native tongue.
But satire needs not those, and wit will shine　　　15
Through the harsh cadence of a rugged line.
A noble error, and but seldom made,
When poets are by too much force betrayed.
Thy gen'rous fruits, though gathered ere their prime,
Still showed a quickness; and maturing time　　　20
But mellows what we write to the dull sweets of rime.
Once more, hail, and farewell! farewell, thou young
But ah! too short, Marcellus of our tongue!
Thy brows with ivy and with laurels bound;
But fate and gloomy night encompass thee around.　　　25

THOMAS HARDY (1840–1928)

The Voice

Woman much missed, how you call to me, call to me,
Saying that now you are not as you were
When you had changed from the one who was all to me,
But as at first, when our day was fair.

Can it be you that I hear? Let me view you, then,　　　5
Standing as when I drew near to the town
Where you would wait for me: yes, as I knew you then,
Even to the original air-blue gown!

Or is it only the breeze, in its listlessness
Travelling across the wet mead to me here,　　　10
You being ever dissolved to wan wistlessness,
Heard no more again far or near?

　　　Thus I; faltering forward,
Leaves around me falling,
Wind oozing thin through the thorn from norward,　　　15
　　　And the woman calling.

1. Why does Hardy employ a different metrical scheme in his last stanza?

GERARD MANLEY HOPKINS (1844–1889)

God's Grandeur

The world is charged with the grandeur of God.
  It will flame out, like shining from shook foil;
  It gathers to a greatness, like the ooze of oil
Crushed. Why do men then now not reck his rod?
Generations have trod, have trod, have trod;   5
  And all is seared with trade; bleared, smeared with toil;
  And wears man's smudge and shares man's smell: the soil
Is bare now, nor can foot feel, being shod.

And for all this, nature is never spent;
  There lives the dearest freshness deep down things;   10
And though the last lights off the black West went
  Oh, morning, at the brown brink eastward, springs—
Because the Holy Ghost over the bent
  World broods with warm breast and with ah! bright wings.

1. What does Hopkins' use of enjambment in lines 7, 11, and 13 add to
    the poem?
2. What effects are created by the internal caesuras of Hopkins' lines?

Pied Beauty

Glory be to God for dappled things—
  For skies of couple-colour as a brinded cow;
    For rose-moles all in stipple upon trout that swim;
Fresh-firecoal chestnut-falls; finches' wings;
  Landscape plotted and pieced—fold, fallow, and plough;   5
    And all trades, their gear and tackle and trim.
All things counter, original, spare, strange;
  Whatever is fickle, freckled (who knows how?)
    With swift, slow; sweet, sour; adazzle, dim;
He fathers-forth whose beauty is past change: 10
                        Praise him.

A. E. HOUSMAN (1859–1936)

To an Athlete Dying Young

The time you won your town the race
We chaired you through the market-place;
Man and boy stood cheering by,
And home we brought you shoulder-high.

Today, the road all runners come,   5
Shoulder-high we bring you home,
And set you at your threshold down,
Townsman of a stiller town.

Smart lad, to slip betimes away
From fields where glory does not stay   10
And early though the laurel grows
It withers quicker than the rose.

Eyes the shady night has shut
Cannot see the record cut,
And silence sounds no worse than cheers   15
After earth has stopped the ears:

Now you will not swell the rout
Of lads that wore their honors out,
Runners whom renown outran
And the name died before the man.   20

So set, before its echoes fade,
The fleet foot on the sill of shade,
And hold to the low lintel up
The still-defended challenge-cup.

And round that early-laureled head   25
Will flock to gaze the strengthless dead,
And find unwithered on its curls
The garland briefer than a girl's.

JOSEPH LANGLAND (b. 1917)

Fall of Icarus: Breughel

Flashing through falling sunlight
A frantic leg late plunging from its strange
Communicating moment
Flutters in shadowy waves.

Close by those shattered waters—   5
The spray, no doubt, struck shore—
One dreamless shepherd and his old sheep dog
Define outrageous patience
Propped on staff and haunches,
Intent on nothing, backs bowed against the sea,   10
While the slow flocks of sheep gnaw on the grass-thin coast.
Crouched in crimson homespun an indifferent peasant
Guides his blunt plow through gravelled ground,
Cutting flat furrows hugging this hump of land.
One partridge sits immobile on its bough   15
Watching a Flemish fisherman pursue
Fish in the darkening bay;
Their stillness mocks rude ripples rising and circling in.

Yet that was a stunning greeting
For any old angler, peasant, or the grand ship's captain,   20
Though sent by a mere boy
Bewildered in the gravitational air,
Flashing his wild white arms at the impassive sea-drowned sun.

Now only coastal winds
Ruffle the partridge feathers,   25
Muting the soft ripping of sheep cropping,
The heavy whisper
Of furrows falling, ship cleaving,
Water lapping.

Lulled in the loose furl and hum of infamous folly,   30
Darkly, how silently, the cold sea suckles him.

JOHN MILTON (1608–1674)

Description of Satan (from *Paradise Lost*)

High on a throne of royal state, which far
Outshone the wealth of Ormus and of Ind,
Or where the gorgeous East with richest hand
Show'rs on her kings barbaric pearl and gold,
Satan exalted sat, by merit raised   5
To that bad eminence; and, from despair
Thus high uplifted beyond hope, aspires
Beyond thus high, insatiate to pursue
Vain war with Heav'n, and by success untaught,
His proud imaginations thus displayed: 10
   "Powers and Dominions, Deities of Heav'n,
For since no deep within her gulf can hold
Immortal vigor, though oppressed and fall'n,
I give not Heav'n for lost. From this descent
Celestial virtues rising will appear   15
More glorious and more dread than from no fall,
And trust themselves to fear no second fate.
Me though just right and the fixed laws of Heav'n
Did first create your leader, next, free choice,
With what besides, in council or in fight,   20
Hath been achieved of merit, yet this loss,
Thus far at least recovered, hath much more
Established in a safe unenvied throne
Yielded with full consent. The happier state
In Heav'n, which follows dignity, might draw   25
Envy from each inferior; but who here
Will envy whom the highest place exposes
Foremost to stand against the Thunderer's aim
Your bulwark, and condemns to greatest share
Of endless pain? Where there is then no good   30
For which to strive, no strife can grow up there
From faction; for none sure will claim in hell
Precedence, none, whose portion is so small
Of present pain, that with ambitious mind
Will covet more. With this advantage then   35
To union, and firm faith, and firm accord,
More than can be in Heav'n, we now return
To claim our just inheritance of old,
Surer to prosper than prosperity
Could have assured us: and by what best way,   40
Whether of open war or covert guile,
We now debate; who can advise, may speak."

MARIANNE MOORE (1887–1972)

Poetry

I, too, dislike it: there are things that are important beyond all this
        fiddle.
Reading it, however, with a perfect contempt for it, one discovers in
it after all, a place for the genuine.
    Hands that can grasp, eyes
    that can dilate, hair that can rise   5
      if it must, these things are important not because a

high-sounding interpretation can be put upon them but because they
        are
useful. When they become so derivative as to become unintelligible,
the same thing may be said for all of us, that we
    do not admire what   10
    we cannot understand: the bat
      holding on upside down or in quest of something to

eat, elephants pushing, a wild horse taking a roll, a tireless wolf under
    a tree, the immovable critic twitching his skin like a horse that feels
        a flea, the base   15
ball fan, the statistician—
    nor is it valid
      to discriminate against "business documents and

school books"; all these phenomena are important. One must make a
        distinction
however: when dragged into prominence by half poets, the result is
        not poetry,   20
nor till the poets among us can be
    "literalists of
    the imagination"—above
      insolence and triviality and can present

for inspection, "imaginary gardens with real toads in them," shall we
        have   25
it. In the meantime, if you demand on the one hand,
the raw material of poetry in
    all its rawness and
    that which is on the other hand
      genuine, you are interested in poetry.

1. What commentary does this poem imply about the nature of free verse?
2. Moore's stanzas appear at first sight to be only loosely arranged. Can you find any consistency among them?

GARY SNYDER (b. 1930)

A heifer clambers up

```
a heifer clambers up
      nighthawk goes out
                  horses
trail back to the barn.
      spider gleams in his                          5
                  new web
dew on the shingles, on the car,
      on the mailbox—
the mole, the onion, and the beetle
      cease their wars.                             10
                  worlds tip
into the sunshine, men and women
      get up, babies crying
children grab their lunches
                  and leave for school.             15
the radio announces
      in the milking barn
                  in the car bound for work
"tonight all the countries
      will get drunk and have a party"              20
russia, america, china,
                  singing with their poets,
pregnant and gracious,
      sending flowers and dancing bears
                  to all the capitals               25
fat
      with the baby happy land
```

1. How does Snyder use the arrangement of his lines on the page to create emphasis?

WILLIAM CARLOS WILLIAMS (1883–1963)

The Dance

In Breughel's great picture, The Kermess,
the dancers go round, they go round and
around, the squeal and the blare and the
tweedle of bagpipes, a bugle and fiddles
tipping their bellies (round as the thick-   5
sided glasses whose wash they impound)
their hips and their bellies off balance
to turn them. Kicking and rolling about
the Fair Grounds, swinging their butts, those
shanks must be sound to bear up under such   10
rollicking measures, prance as they dance
in Breughel's great picture, The Kermess.

WRITING ABOUT METER, RHYTHM, AND FREE VERSE

There are several good reasons for writing about the rhythmic qualities of a poem, not the least of which is that all poems have rhythm—that is, they are made of sounds expressed in time. Analyzing rhythmical features gives us a chance to do some close reading, to get down into the nuts and bolts of a poem and see how it works. The analysis of rhythm and meter—two of the elements that help to distinguish most poetry from most prose—gives us special insight into the poet's craft. By understanding the technical features of a poem, we are better able to appreciate what is unique or unusual about it and about the poet who created it. Furthermore, we are able to see how the meaning of a poem, and the distinct impression it makes, arise out of the numerous small choices the poet makes in putting words onto the page. We thus come to grips with another aspect of poetic style.

From a practical standpoint, writing about rhythm and meter in a poem can be an important step toward writing a full-blown *explication*, an analysis attempting to tie together all the elements of a poem to show both the range of its effects and its fundamental unity. Because the quality of rhythm appears throughout the poem, we are forced to pay attention to how it develops, how it becomes a whole, and how its parts interact.

As you begin your analysis of the meter and rhythm of a poem, read the poem carefully several times. Read it aloud, naturally and expressively, as you would before a group of your fellow students. Then scan the poem; be as accurate as you can, but be flexible. Do not allow your perception of the general metrical pattern to force you into a strained reading. On the other hand, remember that some words will always be stressed or unstressed depending on form or part of speech. For example, one-syllable nouns will almost always be stressed; prepositions such as *in*, *on*, and *of* will almost always be unstressed; a word such as *sister* will always be scanned as a trochee (/.), and so forth. Watch for significant caesuras and for the use of enjambment. Try whenever possible to label the metrical and rhythmical features with appropriate technical names.

Pay particular attention to recurrent patterns, repetitions of any kind, significant variations in the metrical pattern, or any other feature you consider striking or characteristic. Reading the poem again after you have scanned it and noted some of its technical features will prepare you for the next step in your analysis: an evaluation of the function and significance of meter and rhythm.

Such an analysis might include three important topics: the *relationship* between meter and rhythm and another element of the poem; the general *character* of the poem and its relation to metrical tradition; and the *effect* of meter and rhythm upon the theme of the poem or on the main impression the poem makes. Meter and rhythm can have an important relationship to the structure of the poem, its sound, or its tone. The rhythm may correspond with important stanza divisions. The shape of the poem on the page may be significant. The rhythmic properties of the poem may develop or change in some way as the poem proceeds. Rhythmical patterns may recur or undergo transformation.

The relationship between sound and tone in a poem will often be suggested by its meter or rhythm. The poem may have a lilting, breezy sound, or a ponderous one; it may seem to start and stop, rush headlong down the page, or drag itself slowly from one long line to the next. Rhythm, as we have seen, can have a broadly imitative effect that can be used appropriately or inappropriately. Imagine a birthday greeting written in solemn blank verse, or a funeral elegy written in leaping anapests!

This last point suggests the potentially crucial connection among meter, rhythm, and theme. The meter or rhythm of a poem should support or suggest—or at least not contradict—its general meaning and tone. This suggestiveness will not always be blatant, or even obvious. Still, a sensitive and attentive reading of the poem should reveal instances where the poet has used meter and rhythm, either in general or at specific points, to create surprise, to highlight key ideas, or to imitate motions or sounds.

In addition to providing specific local effects, the meter and rhythm of a poem should tell you something about its general character or its place in the poetic tradition. Some kinds of poems—sonnets, odes, limericks, elegies—are associated with particular meters or configurations of lines. Sonnets in English will always consist of fourteen lines of iambic pentameter; limericks will always have five lines of mixed iambs and anapests. Eighteenth-century poetry usually employs rhymed couplets, whereas poetry written after 1920 will, more often than not, be written in free verse.

Of course, the beginning student of poetry cannot be expected to be conversant with the tradition of English-language poetry, with all of the numerous verse forms, genres, metrical patterns, and historical twists and turns. Such familiarity requires years of wide reading and close study. Nonetheless, the best analyses of rhythm and meter will reflect some general awareness of the chronology of the poem, its subject and how the rhythm is adapted to this subject, and its general form (free verse, blank verse, rhymed verse, and so forth).

How you organize and develop your essay about meter and rhythm will vary depending upon the poem you choose. A deeper understanding of the poem and how it works will be your goal in any case. You could proceed by citing examples of striking rhythmical features, and then by making appropriate generalizations about a poet's skill in using a particular verse form. Or you could move through the poem from beginning to end to show the cumulative effects of rhythm, how features develop, change, and repeat themselves. Your emphasis in this case would be upon the unity of the poem, not just on its most striking features. Finally, you could, in an attempt to combine the two methods, write an integrated analysis which shows how the rhythm and verse form of the poem suit, support, and contain its meaning. This kind of analysis would help to reveal the reciprocal nature of matter and method, form and content. The following essay on Lawrence Ferlinghetti's "Constantly risking absurdity" (page 679) reveals how the meter of the poem (the method) comments on the content of the poem (the matter). Writing in free verse, Ferlinghetti uses the comparison of a poet to a tightrope walker to show the dangers the poet encounters and the risks he takes when he puts his work before the public. The writing of free verse, we see, is a chancy business.

Risk and the Poet's Performance:
Ferlinghetti's "Constantly risking absurdity"

Even before we read Lawrence Ferlinghetti's "Constantly risking absurdity," we notice his unusual use of the space of the page. The lines dance up and down, skitter from side to side; phrases and clauses are arranged in uneven units of two to ten syllables. Although sporadic rhyme and regular alliteration contribute significantly to the poem, it is Ferlinghetti's use of a free verse form that imparts a special character to his lines. When we look more closely at the poem, we see that it is in fact about the perils of writing poetry, particularly poetry written in irregular, free verse form. The poem proves to be about itself.

Throughout the piece, Ferlinghetti develops an extended analogy between a poet and a tightrope walker. The form taken on by the lines of the poem reinforce this analogy. With their various indentations, uneven lengths, and sudden drops and turns, the lines cause our perception of the poem to shift back and forth suddenly from side to side, much as our eyes would if we were following the subtle, dangerous tricks of an aerial artist.

In addition to the horizontal placement of the lines, Ferlinghetti uses their vertical placement to suggest the relative positioning of the tightrope "poet" and his audience. We see the artist

> . . . balancing on eyebeams
>> above a sea of faces . . .

The lines are positioned to reinforce the relationship of the poet ("up there," for all to view) and his audience. Appropriately, the audience's sight sustains the artist. Both the horizontal and the vertical positioning of the lines serves to emphasize the precariousness of the artist's performance. Through a combination of his own skill and his audience's visual "endorsement," he is able to stay balanced on the wire.

Ferlinghetti also uses short, two-word lines to suggest both the danger and the purpose of the artist's "journey" across the wire. These short lines, such as "and death" and "with gravity," have a way of suddenly arresting our attention, much as the motion of our eyes would stop abruptly when the tightrope walker paused in equipoise upon his wire. When Ferlinghetti says

> For he's the super realist
>> who must perforce perceive
> taut truth
>> before the taking of each stance or step,

we perceive, with great emphasis, how the performer must know his medium--his words or his wire--very well before he takes each dangerous step.

The result of Ferlinghetti's acrobatic attempts to describe an acrobat is a poem whose form and content support one another closely. In describing a physical analogue for what the poet does, Ferlinghetti has emphasized three important elements. First, the poet must possess great technical skill. He must use all the tricks he knows to capture beauty, but he must avoid pretentiousness, obscurity, or inaccuracy. Second, his work presumes the presence of an audience, one waiting anxiously for him to succeed and thus sustaining him, but which will also notice failure. Third, the business of the poet, like that of the tightrope walker, is a risky one. He may not catch beauty; he may not be able to dazzle his audience. If each step or movement is not calculated with great precision, beauty may plummet past him and fall to her doom, and the poet may be condemned before the eyes of his audience. Ferlinghetti's free verse proves to be a fitting vehicle which links poet, performance, audience, and beauty.

SUGGESTIONS FOR WRITING

1. Show how the meter and rhythm of D. H. Lawrence's "Snake" (page 688) are appropriate to his subject.

2. Assess the ways that Whitman injects variety and repetition into "Crossing Brooklyn Ferry" (page 691).

3. Demonstrate how Milton uses enjambment, caesuras, and metrical substitutions to create metrical variety in his "Description of Satan from *Paradise Lost*" (page 703).

4. Compare and contrast the metrical features of Gerard Manley Hopkins's "God's Grandeur" (page 700) and "Pied Beauty" (page 700).
5. Evaluate the metrical appropriateness of Denise Levertov's "Merrit Parkway" (page 570).

RHYME AND OTHER SOUND DEVICES

Like meter, **rhyme** is one of the most conventionally distinctive features of poetry. Consider this poem published in 1928 by the American poet Robinson Jeffers.

ROBINSON JEFFERS (1887–1962)

Hurt Hawks

I

The broken pillar of the wing jags from the clotted shoulder,
The wing trails like a banner in defeat,
No more to use the sky forever but live with famine
And pain a few days: cat nor coyote
Will shorten the week of waiting for death, there is game without 5
    talons.
He stands under the oak-bush and waits
The lame feet of salvation; at night he remembers freedom
And flies in a dream, the dawns ruin it.
He is strong and pain is worse to the strong, incapacity is worse.
The curs of the day come and torment him 10
At distance, no one but death the redeemer will humble that head,
The intrepid readiness, the terrible eyes.
The wild God of the world is sometimes merciful to those
That ask mercy, not often to the arrogant.
You do not know him, you communal people, or you have forgotten 15
    him;
Intemperate and savage, the hawk remembers him;
Beautiful and wild, the hawks, and men that are dying, remember him.

II

I'd sooner, except the penalties, kill a man than a hawk; but the great
   redtail
Had nothing left but unable misery
From the bone too shattered for mending, the wing that trailed under   20
   his talons when he moved.
We had fed him six weeks, I gave him freedom,
He wandered over the foreland hill and returned in the evening, asking
   for death,
Not like a beggar, still eyed with the old
Implacable arrogance. I gave him the lead gift in the twilight.
   What fell was relaxed,
Owl-downy, soft feminine feathers; but what   25
Soared: the fierce rush: the night-herons by the flooded river cried fear
   at its rising
Before it was quite unsheathed from reality.

Many readers would say, "I like it, but where's the rhyme?" Still others
would say, "I'd like it better if it rhymed." A still more extreme reaction
might be: "It's not a poem because it doesn't rhyme. It's just prose chopped
up into lines." The range of these plausible responses—which imply that
rhyme is expected, preferred, or demanded—shows how closely this time-
honored device is associated, for most readers, with the very idea of poetry.

There is nothing wrong, of course, with taking pleasure in rhyme. That
is part of its purpose: the pure, simple pleasure of repeated sounds, as in
music. Poetry is after all an aural art, meant to be heard as well as seen and
read, and rhyme is an important aural feature of many poems. But rhyme
is only one of several important sound devices that poets use to get our
attention, to help organize their verse and make it memorable, and to enchant or disturb us with their verbal music. As students of poetry, and
particularly of modern poetry, we must be sensitive to all aspects of sound
in the poems we read. We do ourselves a disservice if we allow the need for
rhyme to cloud our understanding or judgment. Before we turn to rhyme,
then, we might do well to consider other, sometimes more subtle, aspects
of sound in poetry. Doing so will help us appreciate these other devices and
will help to clarify the reasons for rhyme.

The sounds that individual letters and words make have an immediate
and obvious importance for poets trying to give significance to everything
in their work. Sounds can be used to bind words and ideas to one another,
to imitate or suggest sounds heard in natural contexts, or to give an overall
timbre to a poem. They can be explosive (b,d,p,t); sibilant (soft c,s); resonant (m,n, and all vowels); guttural (q,k, and hard g); breathy (h); or
liquid (l,r) depending on the effects the poet wants to produce. For exam-

ple, in the first line of "Hurt Hawks" ("The broken pillar of the wing jags from the clotted shoulder"), the harsh sounds provided by the letters *b*, *p*, *g*, and hard *c* prepare us for the harsh subject matter: a man forced to destroy a wounded hawk. In the following poem, Thom Gunn uses many repeated letter sounds to help support his main ideas.

THOM GUNN (b. 1929)

The Byrnies

The heroes paused upon the plain.
When one of them but swayed, ring mashed on ring:
   Sound of the byrnie's knitted chain,
Vague evocations of the constant Thing.

They viewed beyond a salty hill   5
Barbaric forest, mesh of branch and root
   —A huge obstruction growing still,
Darkening the land, in quietness absolute.

That dark was fearful—lack of presence—
Unless some man could chance upon or win   10
   Magical signs to stay the essence
Of the broad light that they adventured in.

Elusive light of light that went
Flashing on water, edging round a mass,
   Inching across fat stems, or spent   15
Lay thin and shrunk among the bristling grass.

Creeping from sense to craftier sense,
Acquisitive, and loss their only fear,
   These men had fashioned a defence
Against the nicker's snap, and hostile spear.   20

Byrnie on byrnie! as they turned
They saw light trapped between the man-made joints,
   Central in every link it burned,
Reduced and steadied to a thousand points.

Thus for each blunt-faced ignorant one   25
The great grey rigid uniform combined
   Safety with virtue of the sun.
Thus concepts linked like chainmail in the mind.

Reminded, by the grinding sound,
Of what they sought, and partly understood,   30
They paused upon that open ground,
A little group above the foreign wood.

Notice that Gunn uses words like *mashed* (line 2), *chain* (line 3), and *mesh* and *branch* (line 6) to suggest the sounds made by the coats of mail, even in words that are not directly applied to the byrnies. In line 26, Gunn describes a byrnie as a "great grey rigid uniform"; to do so, he uses sounds which are themselves stiff, ponderous, and rigid. Also, in line 29, he uses the similar sounds in *reminded* and *grinding* to link these two important words.

In the following excerpt from Alexander Pope's "An Essay on Criticism," letter sounds are used along with other elements such as meter and tempo to exemplify the precepts Pope is advancing about the uses of sound in poetry.

ALEXANDER POPE (1688–1744)

[*Sound and Sense*]

But most by numbers judge a poet's song;
And smooth or rough, with them, is right or wrong:
In the bright muse though thousand charms conspire,
Her voice is all these tuneful fools admire;
Who haunt Parnassus but to please their ear,   5
Not mend their minds; as some to church repair,
Not for the doctrine, but the music there.
These equal syllables alone require,
Though oft the ear the open vowels tire;
While expletives their feeble aid do join;   10
And ten low words oft creep in one dull line:
While they ring round the same unvaried chimes,
With sure returns of still expected rhymes;
Where'er you find "the cooling western breeze,"
In the next line, it "whispers through the trees":   15
If crystal streams "with pleasing murmurs creep,"
The reader's threatened (not in vain) with "sleep":
Then, at the last and only couplet fraught
With some unmeaning thing they call a thought,
A needless Alexandrine ends the song,   20
That, like a wounded snake, drags its slow length along.
Leave such to tune their own dull rhymes, and know
What's roundly smooth, or languishingly slow;

And praise the easy vigor of a line,
Where Denham's strength, and Waller's sweetness join 25
True ease in writing comes from art, not chance,
As those move easiest who have learned to dance.
'Tis not enough no harshness gives offense,
The sound must seem an echo to the sense:
Soft is the strain when Zephyr gently blows, 30
And the smooth stream in smoother numbers flows;
But when loud surges lash the sounding shore,
The hoarse, rough verse should like the torrent roar:
When Ajax strives some rock's vast weight to throw,
The line too labors, and the words move slow; 35
Not so, when swift Camilla scours the plain,
Flies o'er th' unbending corn, and skims along the main.

Can you locate words whose letter sounds are clearly designed to support what Pope is saying? Can you find examples of lines which can be read quickly or slowly in a way that supports the meaning they convey? Also, what main idea does this passage attempt to teach us?

Letter sounds are of course present whenever a poet writes, and sometimes particular sounds will occur as if by chance. Poets' choices are governed by numerous considerations, many of which are more important than the sounds of individual letters. We should be cautious about overinterpreting what may be merely accidental effects.

Three other sound devices are specific and common enough to have been labelled by literary scholars: **alliteration**, **assonance**, and **onomatopoeia**. *Alliteration*, or the agreement of nearby consonant sounds, has a long history in English poetry. Anglo-Saxon poets (700–1100), along with many poets of the Middle English period (1100–1500), used it as a structural principle for each line, which generally contained three identical consonant sounds, as in this line translated from *Sir Gawain and the Green Knight*, a fourteenth century narrative poem: "After the siege and assault had *ceased* at Troy" (*Sir Gawain and the Green Knight*, line 1, translated by Marie Borroff). Although alliteration is not a central and distinguishing feature of English poetry since 1500, it does occur frequently in small doses, as in "The Man of Many L's" by Maxine Kumin.

MAXINE KUMIN (b. 1925)

The Man of Many L's

My whole childhood I feared cripples
and how they got that way: the one-
legged Lavender Man who sold
his sachets by St. Mary's steeple,
the blind who tapped past humming what they knew,   5
even the hunchback seamstress, a ragdoll
who further sagged to pin my mother's hems,
had once been sturdy, had once been whole.
Something entered people, something chopped,
pressed, punctured, had its way with them   10
and if you looked, bad child, it entered you.

When we found out what the disease would do,
lying, like any council's stalwarts,
all of us swore to play our parts
in the final act at your command.   15

The first was easy. You gave up your left hand
and the right grew wiser, a juggler for its king.
When the poor dumb leg began to falter
you took up an alpenstock for walking
once flourished Sundays by our dead father.   20
Month by month the battleground grew thinner.
When you could no longer swallow meat
we steamed and mashed your dinner
and bent your straw to chocolate soda treats.

And when you could not talk, still you could write   25
questions and answers on a magic slate,
then lift the page, like laundry to the wind.
I plucked the memory splinter from your spine
as we played at being normal, who
had eased each other in the cold zoo   30
of childhood. Three months before
you died I wheeled you through the streets
of placid Palo Alto to catch
spring in its flamboyant tracks.
You wrote the name of every idiot flower   35
I did not know. Yucca rained.
Mimosa shone. The bottlebrush took fire
as you fought to hold your great head on its stem.

Lillac, you wrote, *Magnollia. Lilly.*
And further, *olleander. Dellphinium.*   40

O man of many L's, brother, my wily
resident ghost, may I never spell
these crowfoot dogbane words again
these showy florid words again
except I name them under your spell.   45

Notice how Kumin anticipates the crippling of the brother with her reference to the "one- / legged Lavender Man" in lines 2 and 3. She uses the alliteration of *l* sounds here and elsewhere in the poem to foreshadow the brother's memorable and poignant inability to spell *l* words correctly. In the last stanza, the words *wily* (line 41), *spell* (line 42), and *spell* (line 45)—linked by alliteration—reinforce the strength of the dead brother's grip on the speaker's memory.

Assonance is the name given to the corresponding use of similar vowel sounds in nearby words. "The rain in Spain stays mainly in the plain" is a familiar example. Sometimes sound devices such as alliteration and assonance are used throughout a poem, as in Sylvia Plath's "Daddy" (page 726).

Alliteration and assonance of course produce significant aural effects (or even tactile effects) when we read poems aloud, thus contributing to the music that we hear. But they have more subtle uses too. They link key words to one another. They create emphasis. They provide pattern. They have an intangible effect on the memorability of poems. And they may even suggest theme or mood, as in the painful *oo* sounds of "Daddy."

Onomatopoeia is usually a more obvious and more self-consciously employed sound device. The word is difficult to spell, but its meaning is simple. Derived from a Greek word meaning "to coin names," it is applied to words that sound like what they mean. *Buzz, crackle, sizzle,* and *boom* are familiar examples. Poets use onomatopoetic words—sparingly in most cases—to imitate natural sounds directly, much as a composer might use a flute to imitate a bird call or a kettledrum to imitate a blacksmith pounding at his anvil. In "The Bells" (page 728), Edgar Allan Poe uses onomatopoeia (as well as other devices of sound and meter) to imitate the sound of bells.

Despite the prevalence and importance of the sound devices already mentioned, most readers still draw a close association between poetry and the presence of rhyme. The historical importance of rhyme, its continued presence in contemporary verse, and the significant functions it can serve make it a subject worthy of careful attention and appraisal. Though it is a simple aural phenomenon familiar to all of us from youth, poets are capable of employing it in some extraordinarily subtle and effective ways.

On the basis of the degree of similarity of the rhyming sounds employed, rhymes can divided into three types:

Rich rhyme: exhibits identical sounds in all parts of the rhyming words. *Air / heir* and *there / their* are examples. This kind of rhyme is used only incidentally, never consistently.

Conventional rhyme: the stressed vowel sounds and all subsequent sounds of the rhyming words are identical, but the initial sounds differ. *Smoke / stroke, here / clear, eye / sky,* and *suspend / contend* are examples. Such rhymes as the above are called *strong* rhymes because they end on a stressed syllable.

Conventional rhyme (weak): ends on an unstressed syllable. *Readily / steadily* is an example of weak rhyme (which tends to be used less frequently than strong rhyme). The following poem by John Donne typifies conventional rhyme.

JOHN DONNE (1572–1631)

Holy Sonnet 10: "Death be not Proud . . ."

Death, be not proud, though some have callèd thee
Mighty and dreadful, for thou art not so;
For those whom thou think'st thou dost overthrow
Die not, poor Death, nor yet canst thou kill me.
From rest and sleep, which but thy pictures be,   5
Much pleasure; then from thee much more must flow;
And soonest our best men with thee do go,
Rest of their bones and souls' delivery.
Thou'rt slave to fate, chance, kings, and desperate men,
And dost with poison, war, and sickness dwell;   10
And poppy or charms can make us sleep as well
And better than thy stroke. Why swell'st thou then?
One short sleep past, we wake eternally,
And Death shall be no more: Death, thou shalt die.

In **slant rhyme** (sometimes called "half," "off," or "oblique" rhyme) there is an approximate coincidence of sounds in the rhyming words, but not an exact one. Wilfred Owen's "Strange Meeting" uses slant rhyme exclusively.

WILFRED OWEN (1893–1918)

Strange Meeting

It seemed that out of battle I escaped
Down some profound dull tunnel, long since scooped
Through granites which titanic wars had groined.
Yet also there encumbered sleepers groaned,
Too fast in thought or death to be bestirred.   5
Then, as I probed them, one sprang up, and stared
With piteous recognition in fixed eyes,
Lifting distressful hands as if to bless.
And by his smile, I knew that sullen hall,
By his dead smile I knew we stood in Hell.   10
With a thousand pains that vision's face was grained;
Yet no blood reached there from the upper ground,
And no guns thumped, or down the flues made moan.
"Strange friend," I said, "here is no cause to mourn."
"None," said the other, "save the undone years,   15
The hopelessness. Whatever hope is yours,
Was my life also; I went hunting wild
After the wildest beauty in the world,
Which lies not calm in eyes, or braided hair,
But mocks the steady running of the hour,   20
And if it grieves, grieves richlier than here.
For of my glee might many men have laughed,
And of my weeping something had been left,
Which must die now. I mean the truth untold,
The pity of war, the pity war distilled.   25
Now men will go content with what we spoiled,
Or, discontent, boil bloody, and be spilled.
They will be swift with swiftness of the tigress.
None will break ranks, though nations trek from progress.
Courage was mine, and I had mystery,   30
Wisdom was mine, and I had mastery:
To miss the march of this retreating world
Into vain citadels that are not walled.
Then, when much blood had clogged their chariot-wheels,
I would go up and wash them from sweet wells,   35
Even with truths that lie too deep for taint.
I would have poured my spirit without stint
But not through wounds; not on the cess of war.
Foreheads of men have bled where no wounds were.
I am the enemy you killed, my friend.   40
I knew you in this dark: for so you frowned

Yesterday through me as you jabbed and killed.
I parried; but my hands were loath and cold.
Let us sleep now. . . . "

Notice that Owen uses several kinds of slant rhymes. Sometimes the rhyming words differ only in their stressed vowel sounds (*grained* / *ground*, lines 11–12); sometimes just the final sound will coincide (*taint* / *stint*, lines 36–37). In no cases, however, do the stressed vowels of the rhyming words coincide. This is typical, though not universal, in slant rhyme.

Slant rhyme has the virtue of being more subtle in most cases than conventional rhyme. It also increases the number of possible rhymes a poet can draw upon. Notice that Owen even employs an occasional *internal rhyme* (also slant) in lines 8 (*distressful . . . bless*), 11 (*pains . . . gained*), and 28 (*swiftness . . . tigress*). Slant rhyme should not be viewed as an inferior sort of rhyme, but one with different, less final effects than conventional rhyme permits.

That rhyme is so prevalent in poetry, and that it persists in much contemporary poetry, suggests that poets consider it important, effective, and even vital in their work. But what specific functions does rhyme serve?

First, like other artful uses of sound devices, or like rhythm and meter, rhyme serves an ornamental purpose; thus it removes the language of poetry from the language we use every day. If contemporary poetic practice is any indication—and of course it is—then we would have to conclude that many modern poets consider rhyme artificial and unnatural, or at least as standing in the way of simple, direct, speech-like utterance.

Also, like rhythm and meter, rhyme has an important mnemonic value. If you make the attempt, you will find that Robert Frost's poem "Design" (page 722) is much easier to memorize than, say, Robinson Jeffers's "Hurt Hawks" (page 710).

Rhyme also creates marked emphasis, particularly when it occurs, as it usually does, at the ends of lines. As a glance at Pope's "Sound and Sense" (page 713) will disclose, these terminal positions are usually occupied by nouns, verbs, or adjectives. Rhyme invests these words with still greater importance, thereby suggesting and reinforcing their centrality to the overall meaning of the poem.

Rhyme also enhances the musical quality of poetry. This musical effect derives not only from the chiming assonance of final, rhymed syllables, but also from the sense of closure or resolution that the rhymes create. This resolution is similar to that which occurs at the end of a phrase in music or the return to a dominant tonality in a musical passage. Pope's "Sound and Sense" also exemplifies this quality.

The patterns that rhyming words assume have an important effect on the structure of many poems. If you look again at Donne's "Death Be Not Proud," and if you mark each different rhyming sound with a different letter—this is called marking the **rhyme scheme**—you will find the following pattern:

a

b

b

a

a

b

b

a

c

d

d

c

e

e

These designations make the stanzas of the poem clearer. Stanzas are groups of related lines which are printed separately on the page and/or are held together by a consistent pattern of rhymes. Donne's rhyme scheme suggests either a two-part structure (lines 1–8, 9–14); a three-part structure (lines 1–4, 5–8, 9–14); or a four-part structure (lines 1–4, 5–8, 9–12, 13–14). Such stanzas or divisions serve to focus our attention on discrete aspects or stages of Donne's meaning. In this case, the four smaller rhyming patterns coincide with the four verse sentences of the poem.

When you read rhymed verse, then, mark the patterns and see whether the larger divisions thus created help you to perceive the overall organization of the poem. Paying attention to these divisions and seeing how they work together can be of much help when you try to write about a poem. (More about stanza forms will be found in the next chapter.)

Like the other sound devices mentioned previously, rhyme also serves to bind important ideas to each other. Notice how, in Donne's poem, the rhyme of the fourth line (*me*) is connected to the rhyme of the first (*thee*). The speaker is drawing a contrast between himself and death. The rhyme connects and reinforces the two contrasted ideas. The rhyme also connects important ideas in lines 6 and 7 (*flow* and *go*) and lines 13 and 14 (*eternally* and *die*).

Two other functions of rhyme should be noted. First, the need to find rhymes is a restriction that helps good poets write more carefully by making the search for the exact word that much more difficult. Unless poets are seduced by easy, predictable solutions to the problem of finding rhymes, this search will usually promote precision and exactness. Second, rhyme is one means of evoking the tradition that stands behind poetic practice in English. To write a Shakespearean sonnet is to evoke and participate in the Shakespearean tradition; to write in rhymed couplets is to invite comparison to the work of Alexander Pope and other British writers of the eighteenth century. The reverberations thus set in motion by the imitation of prior poetic styles and techniques can help enrich or extend any poem, and give it still another level of appeal.

As you read the following poems, pay careful attention to the rhyme and other sound devices they employ. Or, read other poems in this book from the point of view of the sound devices you find in them. Try to see how these sound devices function, what they contribute to the total effect and impressiveness of the poem.

EMILY DICKINSON (1830–1886)

I like to see it lap the Miles

I like to see it lap the Miles—
And lick the Valleys up—
And stop to feed itself at Tanks—
And then—prodigious step

Around a Pile of Mountains—   5
And supercilious peer
In Shanties—by the sides of Roads—
And then a Quarry pare

To fit its Ribs
And crawl between   10
Complaining all the while
In horrid—hooting stanza—
Then chase itself down Hill—

And neigh like Boanerges—
Then—punctual as a Star   15
Stop—docile and omnipotent
At its own stable door—

1. Find examples of slant rhyme in this poem. Why are they more effective than conventional rhyme would be?

ROBERT FROST (1874–1963)

Design

I found a dimpled spider, fat and white,
On a white heal-all, holding up a moth
Like a white piece of rigid satin cloth—
Assorted characters of death and blight
Mixed ready to begin the morning right,   5
Like the ingredients of a witches' broth—
A snow-drop spider, a flower like froth,
And dead wings carried like a paper kite.

What had that flower to do with being white,
The wayside blue and innocent heal-all?   10
What brought the kindred spider to that height,
Then steered the white moth thither in the night?
What but design of darkness to appall?—
If design govern in a thing so small.

1. Mark the rhyme scheme of Frost's poem.
2. What repeated words and letter sounds does Frost use to lend unity to
   the poem?

ROBERT HAYDEN (1913–1980)

Those Winter Sundays

Sundays too my father got up early
and put his clothes on in the blueblack cold,
then with cracked hands that ached
from labor in the weekday weather made
banked fires blaze. No one ever thanked him.   5

I'd wake and hear the cold splintering, breaking.
When the rooms were warm, he'd call,
and slowly I would rise and dress,
fearing the chronic angers of that house,

Speaking indifferently to him,   10
who had driven out the cold
and polished my good shoes as well.
What did I know, what did I know
of love's austere and lonely offices?

H. D. [HILDA DOOLITTLE] (1886–1961)

Stars Wheel in Purple

Stars wheel in purple, yours is not so rare
as Hesperus, nor yet so great a star
as bright Aldeboran or Sirius,
nor yet the stained and brilliant one of War;

stars turn in purple, glorious to the sight;   5
yours is not gracious as the Pleiads are
nor as Orion's sapphires, luminous;

yet disenchanted, cold, imperious face,
when all the others blighted, reel and fall,
your star, steel-set, keeps lone and frigid tryst   10
to freighted ships, baffled in wind and blast.

1. Find examples of alliteration and assonance in the poem. What important ideas do these devices help to emphasize?

KENNETH KOCH (b. 1925)

Hearing

Hear the beautiful tinny voices of the trumpets
Beside the rushing sound of the great blue waterfall;
See the guns fire, then hear the leaves drop to the ground;
Lie back in your chair—and now there is the clatter of
    pennies!
The familiar scraping noise of the chair feet on the   5
    ground,
As if a worm had grown six feet tall! And here is the
    worm,
And hear his softly scraping noise at the forest gate.
In the Bourse the diamonds clink and clank against each
    other,
And the violet airplane speaks to the farmland with its
    buzz
From high in the air, but you hear the slice   10
Of shears and watch the happy gardener's face whiten
As he hears the final throbs of his failing heart.
All is not stillness—far from it. The tinny
Trumpets renew their song among the eglantine's

Too speciously gracious brilliance, and a hen drops   15
An egg, with infinite gentleness, into the straw.

Who is this young man with the tremendous French horn
    in the garden
With a lady in lilac bending her head to catch each note
That flows, serene and unbidden, from the silvery throat?
I think they are strangers here. Stones fall in the pool.   20
She smiles; she is very witty, she bends too far, and now
    we hear
The sound of her lilac dress ripping in the soft summer
    air.

For it is summer! Hear the cool rush of the stream and
    the heavy black
Vocalism of leaves in the wind. A note then comes, arises
In the air, it is a glass in which a few warm drops of rain   25
Make music; there are roars and meows, turkeys and
    spaniels
Come running to the great piano, which, covered with
    pearls,
Gives extra, clinking sounds to your delighted ears;
And the dogs bark, and there is the little thrilled silence
    of snails. . . .
Above all else you hear the daisies being torn apart   30
By tremendous bumblebees who have come here from
    another Department!
"Wisteria tapping the house, so comes your blood. . . ."

Now rain, now this earth streams with water!
Hear the tooting of Triton among the clouds
And on the earth! See the trumpets of heaven floating   35
    toward us
Blaring among the wet masses of citron and vermilion
    wings!
They play "Put down the cushion on the chair,
Put down the cushion on the chair, put down
The cushion, put it down, put the cushion down on the
    chair,
Ra ta ta. . . ." The young man's French horn is wet, it   40
    makes a different noise,
The girl turns her face toward him and he hears strings
    (it is another tear in her dress!).
In the kitchen the sound of raspberries being mashed in
    the cream

Reminds you of your childhood and all the fantasies you
  had then!

In the highest part of an oak tree is a blue bird
Trilling. A drying friend reads *Orlando Furioso*   45
Sitting on a beach chair; then you hear awnings being
  stretched out!
A basso sings, and a soprano answers him.
Then there is thunder in a clear blue sky,
And, from the earth, a sigh: "This song is finished."

1. What verbs, nouns, and adjectives of Koch's poem reinforce the idea
    that it is a poem about hearing?
2. What examples of onomatopoeia can you find in the poem?

WILFRED OWEN (1893–1918)

Anthem for Doomed Youth

What passing-bells for these who die as cattle?
  Only the monstrous anger of the guns.
  Only the stuttering rifles' rapid rattle
Can patter out their hasty orisons.
No mockeries now for them; no prayers nor bells   5
  Nor any voice of mourning save the choirs,—
The shrill, demented choirs of wailing shells;
  And bugles calling for them from sad shires.

What candles may be held to speed them all?
  Not in the hands of boys, but in their eyes   10
Shall shine the holy glimmers of good-byes.
  The pallor of girls' brows shall be their pall;
Their flowers the tenderness of patient minds,
And each slow dusk a drawing-down of blinds.

1. What examples of onomatopoeia does Owen use in the first eight lines
    of the poem?
2. How does Owen use rhyme to link important ideas in the poem?

SYLVIA PLATH (1932–1963)

Daddy

You do not do, you do not do
Any more, black shoe
In which I have lived like a foot
For thirty years, poor and white,
Barely daring to breathe or Achoo.   5

Daddy, I have had to kill you.
You died before I had time—
Marble-heavy, a bag full of God,
Ghastly statue with one gray toe
Big as a Frisco seal   10

And a head in the freakish Atlantic
Where it pours bean green over blue
In the waters off beautiful Nauset.
I used to pray to recover you.
Ach, du.   15

In the German tongue, in the Polish town
Scraped flat by the roller
Of wars, wars, wars.
But the name of the town is common.
My Polack friend   20

Says there are a dozen or two.
So I never could tell where you
Put your foot, your root,
I never could talk to you.
The tongue stuck in my jaw.   25

It stuck in a barbwire snare.
Ich, ich, ich, ich,
I could hardly speak.
I thought every German was you.
And the language obscene   30

An engine, an engine
Chuffing me off like a Jew.
A Jew to Dachau, Auschwitz, Belsen.
I began to talk like a Jew.
I think I may well be a Jew.   35

The snows of the Tyrol, the clear beer of Vienna
Are not very pure or true.
With my gypsy ancestress and my weird luck
And my Taroc pack and my Taroc pack
I may be a bit of a Jew.   40

I have always been scared of *you*,
With your Luftwaffe, your gobbledygoo.
And your neat moustache
And your Aryan eye, bright blue.
Panzer-man, panzer-man, O You——   45

Bit my pretty red heart in two.
I was ten when they buried you.
At twenty I tried to die
And get back, back, back to you.
I thought even the bones would do.   50

But they pulled me out of the sack,
And they stuck me together with glue,
And then I knew what to do.
I made a model of you,
A man in black with a Meinkampf look   55

And a love of the rack and the screw.
And I said I do, I do.
So daddy, I'm finally through.
The black telephone's off at the root,
The voices just can't worm through.   60

If I've killed one man, I've killed two——
The vampire who said he was you
And drank my blood for a year,
Seven years, if you want to know.
Daddy, you can lie back now.   65

There's a stake in your fat black heart
And the villagers never liked you.
They are dancing and stamping on you.
They always *knew* it was you.
Daddy, daddy, you bastard, I'm through.   70

EDGAR ALLAN POE (1809–1849)

The Bells

I

Hear the sledges with the bells—
     Silver bells!
What a world of merriment their melody foretells!
     How they tinkle, tinkle, tinkle,
          In the icy air of night!   5
     While the stars that oversprinkle
     All the heavens, seem to twinkle
          With a crystalline delight;
          Keeping time, time, time,
          In a sort of Runic rhyme,   10
To the tintinnabulation that so musically wells
     From the bells, bells, bells, bells,
          Bells, bells, bells—
From the jingling and the tinkling of the bells.

II

Hear the mellow wedding bells—   15
     Golden Bells!
What a world of happiness their harmony foretells!
     Through the balmy air of night
     How they ring out their delight!—
          From the molten-golden notes,   20
          And all in tune,
          What a liquid ditty floats
To the turtle-dove that listens, while she gloats
          On the moon!
     Oh, from out the sounding cells,   25
What a gush of euphony voluminously wells!
          How it swells!
          How it dwells
     On the Future!—how it tells
     Of the rapture that impels   30
     To the swinging and the ringing
          Of the bells, bells, bells—
     Of the bells, bells, bells, bells,
          Bells, bells, bells—
To the rhyming and the chiming of the bells!   35

III

Hear the loud alarum bells—
Brazen bells!
What a tale of terror, now their turbulency tells!
In the startled ear of night
How they scream out their affright!   40
Too much horrified to speak,
They can only shriek, shriek,
Out of tune,
In a clamorous appealing to the mercy of the fire,
In a mad expostulation with the deaf and frantic fire,   45
Leaping higher, higher, higher,
With a desperate desire,
And a resolute endeavour
Now—now to sit, or never,
By the side of the pale-faced moon.   50
Oh, the bells, bells, bells!
What a tale their terror tells
Of Despair!
How they clang, and clash, and roar!
What a horror they outpour   55
On the bosom of the palpitating air!
Yet the ear, it fully knows,
By the twanging,
And the clanging,
How the danger ebbs and flows;   60
Yet the ear distinctly tells,
In the jangling,
And the wrangling,
How the danger sinks and swells,
By the sinking or the swelling in the anger of the bells—   65
Of the bells—
Of the bells, bells, bells, bells,
Bells, bells, bells—
In the clamor and the clanging of the bells!

IV

Hear the tolling of the bells—   70
Iron bells!
What a world of solemn thought their monody compels!
In the silence of the night,
How we shiver with affright

At the melancholy menace of their tone!   75
For every sound that floats
From the rust within their throats
Is a groan.
And the people—ah, the people—
They that dwell up in the steeple,   80
All alone,
And who, tolling, tolling, tolling,
In that muffled monotone,
Feel a glory in so rolling
On the human heart a stone—   85
They are neither man nor woman—
They are neither brute nor human—
They are Ghouls:—
And their king it is who tolls:—
And he rolls, rolls, rolls,   90
Rolls
A pæan from the bells!
And his merry bosom swells
With the pæan of the bells!
And he dances, and he yells;   95
Keeping time, time, time,
In a sort of Runic rhyme,
To the pæan of the bells;—
Of the bells:
Keeping time, time, time   100
In a sort of Runic rhyme,
To the throbbing of the bells—
Of the bells, bells, bells—
To the sobbing of the bells:—
Keeping time, time, time,   105
As he knells, knells, knells,
In a happy Runic rhyme,
To the rolling of the bells—
Of the bells, bells, bells:—
To the tolling of the bells—   110
Of the bells, bells, bells, bells,
Bells, bells, bells—
To the moaning and the groaning of the bells.

WRITING ABOUT RHYME AND OTHER SOUND DEVICES

Not all poems rhyme, but all poems have sound—and all poets use sound to help organize, clarify, and reinforce the meaning or the imagery of their work. Still, not all poems make suitable subjects for essays about rhyme and other sound devices. If you are assigned a poem to write about from this point of view, your instructor has probably selected one in which rhyme or other sound devices count in an evident way. If you are allowed to select your own poem, you have a similar right (and the same reasons) to pick a poem whose sound has a clear, though perhaps subtle, importance. If you compare Poe's "The Bells" (page 728) or Pope's "Sound and Sense" (page 731) with, say, Keats's "On First Looking Into Chapman's Homer" (page 557), you will readily note that both Poe and Pope exploit sound in a much more obvious way than Keats does. Such judgments, coupled with your own interests and abilities, should guide you toward a suitable choice of subject.

Though all poems have sound, it may be helpful to distinguish between its local effect and its overall effect. The alliteration in the last line of John Donne's "Holy Sonnet #10" (page 717)—"And Death shall be no more: Death, thou shalt die"—is a local effect. It serves to link key words in the line to one another, and to lend an air of appropriate finality to the poem. Donne does not use alliteration extensively in the poem. Furthermore (although this is arguable), the poem's sound is not its distinctive feature. The kind of significant local sound effect cited here might fittingly be mentioned in a thorough explication of the poem's total effect and meaning, but it is unlikely that alliteration in Donne's poem would present itself as an obviously workable subject.

Contrast this local effect with the overall effect of sound throughout Poe's "The Bells." Poe employs a variety of sound devices to imitate the sound of the bells. His use (some might say abuse) of a wide range of sound effects is clearly the central rationale for the poem. "The Bells" is a poem whose sound demands to be written about.

Most essays about sound in poetry are concerned with the functions of auditory devices—how they help the poem "work"—and with the skill with which poets employ them. These twin concerns of function and evaluation can, of course, be joined in the same essay; moreover, they both require that the writer exercise the ability to read closely and pay attention to the subtleties of the text.

No matter what poem you write about, and no matter what sound devices that poem may contain, you would do well to note the connections between sound devices and the *structure* of the poem; the *meaning* of the poem—the consistent sense it makes; the *rhetorical emphasis* of the poem; and the *musical*, *imitative*, or *ornamental qualities* of the poem. Considering each of these in turn may disclose some useful strategies and questions that should help you as you plan your essay.

To see how rhyme helps create structure in a poem, look once again at Emily Dickinson's "I like to see it lap the Miles" (page 721). Note that, as is frequently but not always the case, the rhyme coincides with the separately printed stanzas of the poem. This invites us to see four structural units in the poem, each with its own discrete bit of meaning or imagery.

The rhyme gives these units a sense of closure. Does this closure come at appropriate points? Is there, in fact, any real unity within each stanza? Why are there five lines, not the expected four, in the third stanza? If we re-examine the poem with these questions in mind, we begin to see a connection between the rhyme of the poem and its transitions, another important aspect of the structure. Are these transitions clear and fluent? If the stanzas close on a rhyme, how does Dickinson handle the grammatical shift to the next stanza? In Dickinson's poem, the sentence structure, as in *step/around*, pushes us onward even as the rhyme invites us to pause. This "herky-jerky" motion is appropriate to the subject of the poem and to our reading of it.

Rhyme, then, can affect structure. But sometimes sound devices have a still more important impact on the meaning or tone of a poem. In "Daddy" (page 726), Sylvia Plath uses assonance and other sound devices to create a tone which is at once mordantly playful, pained, and bitter, and which reinforces the meaning and imagery of her presentation of the speaker's relationship with her father and her husband. The repeated *oo* sounds, which appear dozens of times in the course of the poem, create a singsong, nursery rhyme effect, while at the same time sounding like intermittent cries of pain. This sense of pain is augmented by the rough, guttural qualities of the German used in the poem, the "barbed wire" sounds such as *Ach* and *Ich*. In writing about Plath's poem, you would want to ask yourself whether the dominant sounds create appropriate effects, given the rest of the poem. Do they link important ideas together? Do they conjure up fitting associations to bolster the sadistic imagery in the poem? Would other sounds have been more effective? Why is the nursery rhyme quality present? Thinking about questions such as these will help you see the unity of the poem, the consistent impression it tries to make, and how it uses sound along with other elements such as rhythm, imagery, and figurative language to create this impression.

Sound devices of various kinds are also used to create the important rhetorical feature of emphasis, a feature which allows us to assess what a poet considers important—the ideas that he or she especially wants us to notice. Rhyme does this not only by chiming but also by appearing at the most emphatic position of any line: its end. Robert Hayden achieves somewhat more subtle effects than this in the poem "Those Winter Sundays" (page 722), an unrhymed free verse poem. In the first stanza alone, Hayden uses internal rhyme (*banked*, *thanked*), alliteration (*clothes*, *cold*, and *cracked*) and assonance (*ached*, *labor*) to join important ideas and to create emphasis, a kind of doubling of the effects the words have when considered singly. The *clothes* protect Hayden's father from the *cold*; the *labor* makes his hands *ache*. The links of sound between these sets of words draw our attention to them, enriching the associations and the surface complexity of the poem. Of course when you locate such features in a poem you are writing about, you must ask yourself whether such connections should, in fact, be made. Are the words linked by sound closely associated with each other, or do they pull in inappropriately opposite directions? Are the linked ideas important enough to deserve emphasis? Never force connections between ideas merely because of their similarity in sound. Consider the entire context of the poem.

A fourth way of approaching an essay about rhyme and other sound devices in a poem is to describe and evaluate what might be called the musical, imitative, or ornamental qualities of the verse. Edgar Allan Poe's "The Bells" (page 728) offers an embarrassment of riches in this regard. Poe uses alliteration, assonance, rhyme, onomatopoeia, repetition, and rhythm to capture the musical qualities of the bells and to force their sound on our attention. He *does* make us hear the bells, but do the sounds they make begin to cloy or irritate? Do they indeed distract us from the meaning of the poem and its other features? Or is the poem just an ingenious exercise that exists for the sake of its sound? Is this a sufficient justification for a poem? Whatever your answers to these questions, a clear focus on the sound of the poem will take you right to its heart. Perhaps you will even notice that in the final line of each stanza Poe has used key sounds that reinforce the changing tone of the poem as he moves from wintertime merriment, to the joyous bells of a wedding day, to the frightful bells of alarm, to the droning, terrifying bells that announce someone's death. Sound in a poem presumes motion of some kind, so watch for progression and development.

The following essay on Thom Gunn's "The Byrnies" (page 712) attempts to show the importance of a variety of sound devices in a poem whose sound is one of its most significant features. Note that the essay treats a variety of sound devices used throughout the poem. It employs many examples, but it does not grasp at the insignificant or far-fetched. It avoids, that is, the common mistake of over-reading; it stays within the bounds of the thesis prescribed in the first paragraph. Moreover, it attempts to account for the patterns of sound in the poem, and to link these patterns to other concerns such as imagery, organization, and theme.

Concepts Linked Like Chainmail:
The Sound of Thom Gunn's "The Byrnies"

Thom Gunn's "The Byrnies" is an excellent example of a poem that achieves unity by having its method coincide ingeniously with its subject and theme. Gunn employs associated images of sound and light to show how the "heroes" of the poem have protected themselves against the "fearful" darkness and silence that threaten them as they prepare to fight. Just as the byrnies--or coats of linked chainmail--literally protect the men, the sound, light, and sense of union and security produced by the byrnies protect them symbolically. Gunn uses letter sounds, alliteration, assonance, and rhyme to provide a glittering texture for the poem and to show how the concepts of literal and symbolic protection are linked.

"The Byrnies" describes a group of armed medieval soldiers pausing on a plain before moving on into battle. They are headed toward a dark "Barbaric forest." Loss is "their only fear." They need some defense against the dark silence of the unknown. In fact, they are wearing this defense. Standing in the sunlight, "they saw light trapped between the man-made joints" of their byrnies. They literally dazzle. The sunlight, coupled with the sound the byrnies make as the men move ("ring mashed on ring"), makes them aware that "the great gray rigid uniform combined / Safety with virtue of the sun." They are thus doubly protected. Their byrnies, their literal defense, make a comforting sound; and the sun, with its radiant power to make all of them dazzle, unites them in a common purpose. The men may be "blunt-faced," "ignorant," and inarticulate, but the byrnies remind them "of what they sought, and partly understood."

Gunn accomplishes this union of concepts--sound, light, and defense--by a clever manipulation of the sound of the poem. One example of this is his use of letter sounds or clusters of consonants such as <u>r</u>, <u>sh</u>, <u>ch</u>, and j to suggest the sound the byrnies make. These sounds--which we hear in such words as <u>ring</u>, <u>mash</u>, <u>chain</u>, <u>mesh</u>, <u>chance</u>, <u>edging</u>, <u>inching</u>, <u>bristling</u>, and <u>joints</u>--link the parts of the poem together and help us "hear" the men as they stand in the sunlight.

The poem also contains significant examples of alliteration and assonance. In "elusive light of light" we can hear the dancing, shimmering effect of sunlight on water. In "great gray rigid uniform," we can hear the massive, grinding weight of the men's defense.

These imitative effects are less important, however, than the thematic connections Gunn brings about by using alliteration, assonance, and rhyme to link important ideas. The poem, we must remember, is <u>about</u> the linking of concepts by sound and sunlight. Hence it is not surprising that Gunn uses sound to effect these links. In the sixth stanza, for example, the words <u>byrnie</u>, <u>burned</u>, and <u>turned</u>--each containing <u>ur</u> sounds--are used because the turning causes the light to burn on the men's chests. When we hear <u>light</u>, <u>central</u>, and <u>link</u> in the same stanza, we are reminded by the l sounds that light causes the men to be linked together and that it is a central aspect of their unity. The assonance of the rhyme in stanza seven (<u>combined</u> . . . <u>mind</u>) is appropriate because it reinforces <u>where</u> the key concepts of the poem are linked, in the minds of the soldiers. Finally, the assonance in <u>reminded</u> . . . <u>grinding</u> in the last stanza shows how, for the men, sensory impressions (the sound of the byrnies) and ideas ("what they sought") are conjoined.

The end result of Gunn's use of sound in "The Byrnies" is a poem as carefully wrought, as dazzling, and as unified as the objects denoted by its title. Each coat of chainmail worn by the men is one thing made up of smaller linked units. So it is with the poem too. The "concepts linked like chainmail in the mind" find their fit expression in a poem whose diverse sounds are linked into a whole.

SUGGESTIONS FOR WRITING ABOUT RHYME AND OTHER SOUND DEVICES

1. Discuss the importance of alliteration in Maxine Kumin's "The Man of Many L's" (page 715).
2. Show the connection between the harsh sounds of Sylvia Plath's "Daddy" (page 726) and what you consider to be the theme of the poem.
3. Demonstrate how William Butler Yeats uses rhyme and repetition to unite the individual stanzas of "Sailing to Byzantium" (page 563) and to effect transitions between these stanzas.
4. Analyze how Poe uses changing sounds in the four parts of the "The Bells" (page 728) to suggest the different kinds of bells he is writing about.
5. Select a poem whose sound does not at first seem to be a striking feature, such as Denise Levertov's "An English Field in the Nuclear Age" (page 571) or Seamus Heaney's "Mid-Term Break" (page 573). Then write an essay about the importance of sound in the poem you select.

COMMON STANZA FORMS, THE SONNET, AND OPEN FORMS

Would we be disappointed in a birthday without a cake, Thanksgiving without a turkey, or Christmas without a tree? Do we expect baseball to have innings, symphonies to have movements, and operas to have overtures? If the answer to all these questions is "yes," it is because these activities follow conventions. Conventions are set ways of doing things and their absence would critically alter the form of the activity. So it is with poetry. We have grown accustomed to seeing poems appear in certain forms, conventional shapes on a page, usually some kind of symmetrical box surrounded by the white space of the unprinted portion of the page. In fact, however, such conventional forms are not the only kinds of poems. Some contemporary poetry is much more asymmetrical and sprawls all over the page.

We call the form of a poem, the traditional box within which the poem is enclosed, a **stanza,** from the Italian meaning a "room" or "stopping place." Like paragraphs in prose, stanzas are stopping or resting places, or they might be compared to rooms within the house of the poem. A stanza might be defined more precisely as a unit within the structure of a poem, consisting of two or more lines arranged in a regular pattern of meter and (sometimes) rhyme. Like those familiar with the conventions of holidays, sports, or other art forms, readers of poetry derive a certain satisfaction from seeing how poets use or adapt the conventional form for their own purposes. Experienced readers of poetry have something of an advantage for they bring traditional associations to the form along with a knowledge of how other poets have previously used the form. For example, there is often something ironic in Emily Dickinson's use of the four line *hymnal stanza*, traditionally associated in America with the Puritan *Bay Psalm Book*, when she uses it in such poems as "Because I could not stop for Death" (page 686). The irony comes from Dickinson's use of the stanza employed in many Protestant hymns for a poem depicting death as a suitor who comes to call on the female speaker of the poem. Or, reading Alexander Pope's incisively witty couplets in "An Essay on Man," we may know what to look for in the rhetorical play of ideas and form if we are already familiar with Dryden's use of the same couplet some fifty years before.

Some knowledge of the more commonly used stanza forms will increase our appreciation of the craft of poetry, but will also assist us in understanding what the poem is communicating. Certain forms have traditionally been associated with particular emotions or experiences.

The shortest stanza form possible is the **couplet**, which consists of two usually rhyming lines. The octosyllabic couplet with its frequency of chiming rhymes is usually associated with comic effects, as in Samuel Butler's satiric seventeenth-century poem *Hudibras* with its unvarying jog-trot meter and its comic rhymes:

> Besides, 'tis known he could speak Greek
> As naturally as pigs squeak;
> That Latin was no more difficile
> Than to a blackbird 'tis to whistle.

> (Part I, Canto 1, lines 51–54)

But the octosyllabic couplet has also been used for serious poems such as Marvell's "To His Coy Mistress" (page 670), and Milton's paired poems "L'Allegro" and "Il Pensoroso." A more common form of the couplet is the pentameter couplet, also known as the **heroic couplet** from its frequent use in the seventeenth and eighteenth centuries in translations of heroic poems (such as Dryden's translation of Virgil's *Aeneid* and Pope's translations of Homer's *Iliad* and *Odyssey*). In its *enjambed* or *open form*, as used by Dryden in the opening of "Absalom and Achitophel," the sense of the passage runs past the completion of the rhyming couplet into the third line or beyond.

> Then Isreal's monarch after Heaven's own heart,
> His vigorous warmth did variously impart

To wives and slaves: and, wide as his command,
Scattered his Maker's image through the land.

(lines 7–10)

In its *closed form*, the sense of the passage is completed with the rhyme and the line is usually marked with some form of terminal punctuation. Dryden's "To the Memory of Mr. Oldham" (page 698) is written wholly in closed couplets, as is most of Pope's "An Essay on Man" (page 760) from which the following closed couplet is taken:

Know then thyself, presume not God to scan;
The proper study of mankind is Man.

(II, lines 1–2)

Since the couplet has a pithy epigrammatic quality (two rhyming lines are easily remembered), it has often been used in long philosophical poems, or as a summary statement in the conclusion of shorter poems.

Two variations on the heroic couplet are the introduction of a third rhyming line called a **triplet**, illustrated by these lines from "An Essay on Criticism":

But as the slightest sketch, if justly traced,
Is by ill coloring but the more disgraced,
So by false learning is good sense defaced.

(I, lines 23–25)

The second variation is the use of a twelve syllable line called an **alexandrine** (after a romance about Alexander the Great) which Dryden uses as the closing line of "To the Memory of Mr. Oldham" (page 698):

But fate and gloomy night encompass thee around.

Another use of the triplet is illustrated by Herrick's "Upon Julia's Clothes" (page 757) which consists entirely of two triplets.

The usual form for a three line stanza or **tercet** is that used by Dante in *The Divine Comedy*. **Terza rima** uses an interlocking rhyme scheme. The first and third lines of the stanza rhyme while the unrhymed word in the second line rhymes with the first and third lines of the following stanza. The rhyme scheme is therefore *a b a, b c b, c d c,* and so on. See Frost's use of terza rima in "Acquainted with the Night" (page 841), and Shelley's use of the same form in "Ode to the West Wind" (page 764). Both Frost's and Shelley's poems follow every four tercets with a couplet. It is important to note that each of these basic stanza forms can be combined with one another to form more elaborate patterns.

The **quatrain,** or four-line stanza rhymed or unrhymed, is the most frequently used stanza form in English, and the **common meter** or **ballad stanza,** appears more often than any other form of quatrain. The ballad (also known as the hymnal) stanza rhymes the second and fourth lines (*a b x b, x* standing for the uncompleted rhyme), and uses iambic tetrameter as the meter for lines one and three, and iambic trimeter for lines two and four. (See "The Wife of Usher's Well," page 802 and Emily Dickinson's poems on pages 832/833 and 686.) Another quatrain, the **heroic quatrain** (or **elegiac stanza** from its use in eighteenth- and nineteenth-century elegies such as Thomas Gray's "Elegy Written in a Country Churchyard") uses iambic pentameter and an *a b a b* rhyme scheme:

> Full many a gem of purest ray serene,
>> The dark unfathomed caves of ocean bear:
> Full many a flower is born to blush unseen,
> And waste its sweetness on the desert air.
>
> (lines 53–56)

The **"In Memoriam" stanza** derives its name from Tennyson's use of the form in his long elegy "In Memoriam." It consists of four iambic tetrameter lines rhyming *a b b a,* as in the following passage:

> There rolls the deep where grew the tree.
>> O earth, what changes thou hast seen!
>> There where the long sea roars hath been
> The stillness of the central sea.
>
> (123, lines 1–4)

See also Yeats' use of the quatrain with varying line lengths in "The Lake Isle of Innisfree," page 922.

Five line stanzas (**quintains**) are uncommon in English, but are usually formed by adding an *a* or *b* rhyme to a quatrain. The six line stanza has a variety of forms. The **"Venus and Adonis" stanza** (deriving its name from Shakespeare's use of the stanza in his poem of the same name), consists of a quatrain and a concluding couplet (*a b a b c c*) in iambic pentameter. This same configuration in iambic tetrameter is used by W. D. Snodgrass in "April Inventory" (page 653). Robert Burns popularized a six-line stanza known as **rime coueé** (tail rhyme), now more often referred to as **Burns stanza,** in which a short "tail" of iambic dimeter in lines four and six completes the other four lines of iambic tetrameter. The rhyme scheme employs only two rhymes (*a a a b a b*), as the following stanza from Burns' "To a Mouse" illustrates:

> But Mousie, thou art no thy lane,
> In proving foresight may be vain:
> The best laid schemes o' mice an' men

> Gang aft a-gley,
> An' lea'e us nought but grief an' pain,
> For promised joy.
>
> (lines 37–42)

John Berryman employs a similar stanza in his "Dream Songs" (page 641) with the third and last lines forming the shorter tail, and with eye rhyme or no rhyme completing the pattern. Thomas Gray's "Ode On the Death of a Favorite Cat" (page 756) lengthens the same verse form in the shorter third and sixth lines to six syllables.

A seven-line stanza of iambic pentameter rhyming *a b a b b c c* (the "Venus and Adonis" stanza with an extra *b* rhyme inserted after the quatrain) is called **rhyme royal** because it was used by James I of Scotland in *The Kingis Quair* (*The King's Book*, 1423–24). Sometimes known as **Chaucerian stanza**, it was first used by Chaucer in his long poems *The Parliament of Foules* and *Troilus and Criseyde* and also in "Complaint to His Purse" (page 818).

The most frequently used eight line stanza is **ottava rima** (rhyme in eights) consisting of eight lines of iambic pentameter rhyming *a b a b a b c c*. The comic turn provided by the final rhyming couplet was exploited by Lord Byron in his comic epic *Don Juan*:

> Man, being reasonable, must get drunk;
>   The best of life is but intoxication:
> Glory, the grape, love, gold, in these are sunk
>   The hopes of all men, and of every nation;
> Without their sap, how branchless were the trunk
>   Of life's strange tree, so fruitful on occasion:
> But to return—Get very drunk; and when
> You wake with headache, you shall see what then.
>
> (Canto II, 179)

The witty return from the digression to the final rhyming couplet made the ottava rima an admirable vehicle for Byron's witty thrusts in *Don Juan* (see also page 753). The ottava rima is, however, a versatile form which can be turned to serious purposes, as Yeats demonstrates in "Sailing to Byzantium" (page 563) where the new rhyme serves to bring to a clarifying climax the thought of each stanza.

The nine-line stanza known as **Spenserian stanza** was first used by Spenser in *The Faerie Queen* (1590). It consists of eight lines of iambic pentameter with a concluding alexandrine. The rhyme scheme (*a b a b b c b c c*) allowed Spenser the flexibility of two interlocking quatrains and the power of the concluding couplet with its long last line.

> A Gentle Knight was pricking on the plaine,
>   Ycladd in mightie armes and silver shielde,

Wherein old dints of deepe wounds did remaine,
The cruell markes of many a bloudy fielde;
Yet armes till that time did he never wield:
His angry steed did chide his foming bitt,
As much disdayning to the curbe to yield:
Full jolly knight he seemd, and faire did sitt,
As one for knightly giusts and fierce encounters fitt.

(Canto I, 1, lines 1–9)

In general, stanzas longer than nine lines are composed by combining shorter stanza forms. The **sonnet** (from the Italian *sonetto*, "a little sound") is a fourteen-line poem in iambic pentameter. Most major English poets have tried their hands at the challenging form of the sonnet. In one form, the **Italian** or **Petrarchan** (after Francesco Petrarch, an Italian poet of the fourteenth century), the sonnet consists of an eight-line section known as the **octave**, rhyming *a b b a a b b a* and a six-line section known as the **sestet**, rhyming *c d e c d e*, (or *c d c d c d*, or some other variation which does not usually include a closing couplet). Usually, in the Italian sonnet, the octave introduces a problem, a situation, or an issue which is then explored and occasionally resolved in the sestet. Some sort of terminal punctuation separates the two sections of the poem, and often editors will reprint the poem with space between its two movements. The following sonnet by Wordsworth uses a variant rhyme scheme in the sestet, but does not adhere to the problem-solution pattern. Instead, the sestet takes the description of the city's beauty to its source—not just the early morning light illuminating the naked beauties of the city, but the human power of the city at rest.

WILLIAM WORDSWORTH (1770–1850)

Composed Upon Westminster Bridge, September 3, 1802

Earth has not anything to show more fair:
Dull would he be of soul who could pass by
A sight so touching in its majesty;
This City now doth, like a garment, wear
The beauty of the morning; silent, bare,   5
Ships, towers, domes, theaters, and temples lie
Open unto the fields, and to the sky;
All bright and glittering in the smokeless air.
Never did sun more beautifully steep
In his first splendor, valley, rock, or hill;   10
Ne'er saw I, never felt, a calm so deep!
The river glideth at his own sweet will:

Dear God! the very houses seem asleep;
And all that mighty heart is lying still!

Does Wordsworth gain anything from the tighter rhyme scheme of the variant sestet which allows only four instead of five rhymes? Note that these two rhymes culminate in auditory images: "asleep" and "still." What point is Wordsworth making about the city's beauty and its silence? How is lack of motion and activity a part of this beauty? Notice also how the imagery of the octave and the sestet effects a transition by reminding the reader of nature outside the city, and yet how the rhyme scheme and the punctuation separate the two halves of the poem to illustrate the difference between the urban and the rural. (For other examples of the Italian sonnet see: Keats, page 557; Owen, page 725; Donne, page 717; Frost, page 722; and Shelley, page 767.)

The **English** or **Shakespearean sonnet**, rhyming *a b a b c d c d e f e f g g*, is composed of three quatrains and a concluding couplet. Not as discursive as the sestet of the Italian sonnet, the couplet provides an emotional punch line to the three quatrains, each of which is usually controlled by a single metaphor. In Shakespeare's *Sonnet 73*, the imagery shifts every four lines beginning with a comparison of the speaker to autumn (and, by implication, his death to winter), moving on to a comparison of his age to twilight, and finally to the diminishing light of glowing coals in a dying fire. Each image intensifies the focus: the dwindling of light and heat.

WILLIAM SHAKESPEARE (1564–1616)

Sonnet 73

That time of year thou mayst in me behold
When yellow leaves, or none, or few, do hang
Upon those boughs which shake against the cold,
Bare ruined choirs, where late the sweet birds sang.
In me thou see'st the twilight of such day   5
As after sunset fadeth in the west;
Which by and by black night doth take away,
Death's second self, that seals up all in rest.
In me thou see'st the glowing of such fire,
That on the ashes of his youth doth lie,   10
As the deathbed whereon it must expire,
Consumed with that which it was nourished by.
This thou perceiv'st, which makes thy love more strong,
To love that well which thou must leave ere long.

The rhymes add an intensity to the point of the poem (*behold / cold, west / rest, fire / expire*), which continues to build until the release of the final couplet. What is the function of the rhetorical repetitiveness of the phrase "in me"? How does the clustering of other images support the connection between the sonnet's form and its meaning? Is the paradox of the conclusion—love becoming stronger while the lover's body becomes weaker—prepared for by other images earlier in the poem? (For other English sonnets see pages 758 and 763.)

Another set stanza assembled out of shorter forms is the **villanelle**, a French stanza form meaning a country song. The villanelle is a nineteen-line poem using only two rhymes. It is assembled out of five tercets rhyming *a b a* and a concluding quatrain. The distinctive feature of the villanelle is its use of two alternating refrains, or repeated lines, which appear in the first tercet as the first and third lines and then reappear alternately as the third line of tercets 2, 3, 4, and 5. In the final quatrain of the villanelle, they appear together as the concluding couplet. The use of the alternating refrain gives the villanelle great dramatic power while avoiding the monotonous chiming quality of a single repeated refrain. Yet at the same time the villanelle has great climactic force when the two refrains join in the last lines of the poem. Dylan Thomas' "Do Not Go Gentle Into That Good Night," the most famous villanelle in English, was written on the occasion of his father's death. Each stanza presents a different way of living which, when examined at the moment of death, proves inadequate. The frustration of having many lives to live and not enough time to live them is caught by the anger and rage of the returning alternate refrain.

DYLAN THOMAS (1914–1953)

Do Not Go Gentle Into That Good Night

Do not go gentle into that good night,
Old age should burn and rave at close of day;
Rage, rage against the dying of the light.

Though wise men at their end know dark is right,
Because their words had forked no lightning they   5
Do not go gentle into that good night.

Good men, the last wave by, crying how bright
Their frail deeds might have danced in a green bay,
Rage, rage against the dying of the light.

Wild men who caught and sang the sun in flight,   10
And learn, too late, they grieved it on its way,
Do not go gentle into that good night.

Grave men, near death, who see with blinding sight
Blind eyes could blaze like meteors and be gay,
Rage, rage against the dying of the light.   15

And you, my father, there on the sad height,
Curse, bless, me now with your fierce tears, I pray.
Do not go gentle into that good night.
Rage, rage against the dying of the light.

The French philosopher and novelist Albert Camus once observed that the thought of his own death brought "angry blood beating to my brain." A similar thought lies behind Thomas' poem as he vicariously feels his father's emotions facing death. How does the recurring rhyme of the refrains (*night*, *light*) reinforce the pattern of imagery within each stanza and support the central idea of the poem? What does Thomas mean by the regrets of the wise men whose words "forked no lightning," or by good men's "frail deeds"? See if you can find a phrase in each tercet that captures the frustration of that particular life's choice. Does the final quatrain serve Thomas' purpose, or does it seem an inappropriately abrupt shift?

The challenge of a still more complex form, the **sestina**, has been taken up by a number of contemporary poets. The sestina consists of six stanzas of six lines each, followed by a three line conclusion (envoy). Instead of rhyme, six key words are repeated systematically as the last word of each line. If we represent the order of the words in the first stanza by numbers— 1, 2, 3, 4, 5, 6—then the second stanza begins with the last word and weaves back and forth from last to first. Thus, the order of the second stanza is 6, 1, 5, 2, 4, 3; the third stanza 3, 6, 4, 1, 2, 5; the fourth 5, 3, 2, 6, 1, 4; the fifth 4, 5, 1, 3, 6, 2; the sixth 2, 4, 6, 5, 3, 1. The six key words are repeated again in the envoy, three within the lines and three at the ends.

If the sestina seems an unnecessarily complex form, we need to remember that poetry is, in part, a game played with words. While a great many poems do more than play with the potential arrangements of sounds, lines, and configurations of words, a few great poems focus on the difficulties of the medium—those formal features that give the poem an intractability like the immalleability of marble or some metals. Few would object to a sculptor's demonstrating skill by producing an aesthetically pleasing object from a difficult medium, yet some readers insist that poems must do more than demonstrate the poet's virtuosity. Archibald Macleish's famous line "A poem should not mean/But be" argues against this insistence, as does the skill demonstrated by Diane Wakoski in the following sestina—which not only meets the formal demands of the sestina, but does so with functional ease and grace.

DIANE WAKOSKI (b. 1937)

Sestina for the Home Gardener

These dried-out paint brushes which fell from my lips have been
    removed
with your departure; they are such minute losses
compared with the light bulb gone from my brain, the sections
of chicken wire from my liver, the precise
silver hammers in my ankles which delicately banged and pointed   5
magnetically to you. Love has become unfamiliar

and plenty of time to tend the paint brushes now. Once unfamiliar
with my processes. Once removed
from that sizzling sun, the ego, to burn my poet shadow to the wall, I
    pointed,
I suppose, only to your own losses   10
which made you hate that 200 pound fish called marriage. Precise
ly, I hate my life, hate its freedom, hate the sections

of fence stripped away, hate the time for endless painting, hate the
    sections
of my darkened brain that wait for children to snap on the light, the
    unfamiliar
corridors of my heart with strangers running in them, shouting. The   15
    precise
incisions in my hip to extract an image, a dripping pickaxe or palmtree
    removed
and each day my paint brushes get softer and cleaner—better tools,
    and losses
cease to mean loss. Beauty, to each eye, differently pointed.

I admire sign painters and carpenters. I like that black hand pointed
up a drive-way whispering to me, "The Washingtons live in those   20
    sections"
and I explain autobiographically that George Washington is sympa-
    thetic to my losses;
His face or name is everywhere. No one is unfamiliar
with the American dollar, and since you've been removed
from my life I can think of nothing else. A precise

replacement for love can't be found. But art and money are precise   25
ly for distraction. The stars popping out of my blood are pointed
nowhere. I have removed
my ankles so that I cannot travel. There are sections

of my brain growing teeth and unfamiliar
hands tie strings through my eyes. But there are losses 30

Of the spirit like vanished bicycle tires and losses
of the body, like the whole bike, every precise
bearing, spoke, gear, even the unfamiliar
handbrakes vanished. I have pointed
myself in every direction, tried sections 35
of every map. It's no use. The real body has been removed.

Removed by the ice tongs. If a puddle remains what losses
can those sections of glacier be? Perhaps a precise
count of drops will substitute the pointed mountain, far away, unfamiliar?

It is clear from many of the lines and images, but chiefly from the key words repeated throughout the poem, that it is about the loss of a lover and the devastating aftermath of that loss. Three of the key words (*removed, losses, unfamiliar*) deal with the lover's departure and its effect on the speaker of the poem. Many of the images suggest a home garden (*tools, chicken wire, sections*) and the poet's return to her art which had formerly, like the "dried-out paint brushes," been set aside. Even though her "paint brushes get softer and cleaner—better tools, and losses/cease to mean loss," she can find no "precise/replacement for love." What makes Wakoski's sestina interesting is the way she makes the seemingly accidental confluence of the six repeated words work for her, suggesting new possibilities of connection and thought. But like some of the poem's surrealistic imagery ("that 200 pound fish called marriage," "I have removed my ankles"), the connections are not arbitrary but lie just below the level of our consciousness in our dreams, in what Wakoski calls the "deep image." Does the loss of love itself serve as a metaphor for other subjects: the connection between the body and the spirit, pain as a prerequisite for creativity?

Not all forms are as restrictive as the sestina or the villanelle. We have already seen that poems can be written in stanzas of varying length, rhymed or unrhymed. The lines of unrhymed iambic pentameter that are blank verse, (page 679) join together in blocks like prose paragraphs to form *verse paragraphs* that divide the poem into sections (Frost's "Mending Wall," page 783). Another form, the **ode**, a stately poem on a dignified subject, in some versions does not use regularly repeated stanza forms. While Shelley (page 764), Keats (pages 557, 558), and Gray (page 756) do use the regularly recurring stanzaic patterns of the **Horatian Ode** named after the Latin poet Horace (65–68 B.C.), Allen Tate uses the more open form of the **Pindaric Ode** named after the Greek poet Pindar (*c.* 522–443 B.C.). The Pindaric Ode allows for flexibility in combining stanzas of varying length (see page 895).

The form of a poem can employ visual aids as well. As far back as the medieval period copyists would illuminate manuscripts with elaborate graphic designs. In the eighteenth century, William Blake, an engraver by training, etched the plates from which his *Songs of Innocence and Experience* (1794) were printed; then, before the pages were bound, he painted with watercolors scenes in the margins of the page relating to the text. A century before Blake, some poets arranged the lines of their poems to form the shape of the object the poem was about. While later critics sometimes attacked these *shaped poems* for their forced ingenuity, those which have survived testify to the visual possibilities of the printed word on the page. Consider the following shaped poem by George Herbert:

GEORGE HERBERT (1593–1633)

Easter Wings

Lord, who createdst man in wealth and store,
  Though foolishly he lost the same,
    Decaying more and more,
      Till he became
        Most poor: 5
        With thee
      O let me rise
    As larks, harmoniously,
  And sing this day thy victories:
Then shall the fall further the flight in me.   10

My tender age in sorrow did begin:
  And still with sicknesses and shame
    Thou didst so punish sin,
      That I became
        Most thin.   15
        With thee
      Let me combine,
    And feel this day thy victory:
  For if I imp my wing on thine,
Affliction shall advance the flight in me.   20

The poem goes beyond mere typographical replication of the shape of Easter wings when the page is turned sideways; the movement in each stanza is toward depletion ("Most poor," "Most thin") in the center of each stanza, and then expansion as the stanza moves toward its completion. Similarly, the content suggests the death-and-resurrection theme of Easter as the poem's persona rises beyond the consequences of original sin (*decaying, sorrow, sickness, shame*) through redemption. How does the rhyme scheme of each stanza add a further correspondence to the theme of redemption? (For a contemporary variation on the shaped poem, see Roger McGough's "40–Love," page 758.)

We have already seen that much contemporary poetry is written in free verse (page 690); that is, lines that have no fixed meter or rhyme. *Vers Libre*, or free verse, is written in stanzaic patterns that do not follow traditional rules of recurring line length, stanza length, or rhyming pattern. These **open forms** are what T. S. Eliot called a "revolt against dead form"; like the music of Stravinsky and Copland, they are not unstructured but merely reflect the more complex structure of twentieth century society. Analogous to contemporary music, the openness to possibilities of these freer stanzaic patterns suggests less patience with confinement, more interest in individual expression, and greater leeway for an introspective democratic voice. Like the shaped poems, open forms take advantage of the space of the whole page and use the eye's movement across the line and down the page to set the appropriate rhythms for the subject. In the following poem by e. e. cummings, the typographic arrangement of words and lines complements the shifts in rhythm, line length, and line placement to recreate the action of Buffalo Bill riding his horse and shooting clay pigeons in a Wild West show, as well as his defeat at the hands of death.

e. e. cummings (1897–1962)

[*Portrait*]

Buffalo Bill's
defunct
      who used to
      ride a watersmooth-silver
                 stallion
and break onetwothreefourfive pigeonsjustlikethat
                       Jesus

he was a handsome man
            and what i want to know is
how do you like your blueeyed boy
Mister Death

There are many ways to describe open form. Allen Ginsberg has described the line lengths as "breath pauses" and, like his predecessor Walt Whitman, he clusters lines in groups with similar cadences using parallel structures to bind them together. Compare, for example, the opening lines from Ginsberg's "Last Night in Calcutta" (page 755) with those of Whitman's "A Noiseless Patient Spider" (page 773).

Another practitioner of open form, Charles Olson, has used the terms *projective verse* and *open field composition* to describe the way the line should project the individual's private vision of the world and the manner in which ideas should be freely explored on the page. If stanzaic form is an aid to the poet in discovering thought, then—paradoxically—open form has seemed to remove that aid and yet has liberated poets to discover new forms compatible to their own unique visions. Olson's theories are put to practice by A. R. Ammons in "Corsons Inlet" (below), ostensibly a poem about walking along the shore of an inlet, but actually a poem celebrating, via the metaphor of a liberating stroll through the inlet's varied topography, the freedom of his poetry's open form.

Whether poets follow one of the traditional forms or invent their own forms, the stanzaic pattern, the use of line length and line placement, and the presence or absence of rhyming patterns all contribute in a worthwhile poem to the complete experience of the poem. This experience is at once aesthetic, emotional, and intellectual. Like the pleasure we derive from merging sound and sense, the complete meshing of form and meaning or experience is one of the pleasures we expect from poetry. While the convention of stanza form aids us in coming to terms with the experience of poetry, it also fulfills some basic human need for a human construct to order the world—which far too often seems disordered.

A. R. AMMONS (b. 1926)

Corson's Inlet

I went for a walk over the dunes again this morning
to the sea,
then turned right along
    the surf

                  rounded a naked headland   5
                  and returned

  along the inlet shore:

it was muggy sunny, the wind from the sea steady and high,
crisp in the running sand,
    some breakthroughs of sun   10
  but after a bit

continuous overcast:

the walk liberating, I was released from forms,
from the perpendiculars,

straight lines, blocks, boxes, binds   15
of thought
into the hues, shadings, rises, flowing bends and blends
        of sight:

                I allow myself eddies of meaning:
yield to a direction of significance   20
running
like a stream through the geography of my work:
    you can find
in my sayings
                swerves of action   25
                like the inlet's cutting edge:
        there are dunes of motion,
organizations of grass, white sandy paths of remembrance
in the overall wandering of mirroring mind:

but Overall is beyond me: is the sum of these events   30
I cannot draw, the ledger I cannot keep, the accounting
beyond the account:

in nature there are few sharp lines: there are areas of
primrose
        more or less dispersed;   35
disorderly orders of bayberry; between the rows
of dunes,
irregular swamps of reeds,
though not reeds alone, but grass, bayberry, yarrow, all . . .
predominantly reeds: 40

I have reached no conclusions, have erected no boundaries,
shutting out and shutting in, separating inside

        from outside: I have
        drawn no lines:
        as   45

manifold events of sand
change the dune's shape that will not be the same shape
tomorrow,

so I am willing to go along, to accept
the becoming   50
thought, to stake off no beginnings or ends, establish
        no walls:

by transitions the land falls from grassy dunes to creek
to undercreek: but there are no lines, though
    change in that transition is clear   55
    as any sharpness: but "sharpness" spread out,
allowed to occur over a wider range
than mental lines can keep:

the moon was full last night: today, low tide was low:
black shoals of mussels exposed to the risk   60
of air
and, earlier, of sun,
waved in and out with the waterline, waterline inexact,
caught always in the event of change:
    a young mottled gull stood free on the shoals   65
    and ate
to vomiting: another gull, squawking possession, cracked a crab,
picked out the entrails, swallowed the soft-shelled legs, a ruddy
turnstone running in to snatch leftover bits:

risk is full: every living thing in   70
siege: the demand is life, to keep life: the small
white blacklegged egret, how beautiful, quietly stalks and spears
    the shallows, darts to shore
            to stab—what? I couldn't
see against the black mudflats—a frightened   75
fiddler crab?

        the news to my left over the dunes and
reeds and bayberry clumps was

        fall: thousands of tree swallows
        gathering for flight: 80
        an order held
        in constant change: a congregation
rich with entropy: nevertheless, separable, noticeable
    as one event
           not chaos: preparations for   85
flight from winter,
cheet, cheet, cheet, cheet, wings rifling the green clumps,
beaks
at the bayberries
    a perception full of wind, flight, curve,   90
sound:

the possibility of rule as the sum of rulelessness:

the "field" of action
with moving, incalculable center:

in the smaller view, order tight with shape: 95
blue tiny flowers on a leafless weed: carapace of crab:
snail shell:
      pulsations of order
      in the bellies of minnows: orders swallowed,
broken down, transferred through membranes   100
to strengthen larger orders: but in the large view, no
lines or changeless shapes: the working in and out, together
      and against, of millions of events: this,
            so that I make
            no form   105
            formlessness:

orders as summaries, as outcomes of actions override
or in some way result, not predictably (seeing me gain
the top of a dune,
the swallows   110
could take flight—some other fields of bayberry
      could enter fall
      berryless) and there is serenity:

      no arranged terror: no forcing of image, plan,
or thought: 115
no propaganda, no humbling of reality to precept:

terror pervades but is not arranged, all possibilities
of escape open: no route shut, except in
  the sudden loss of all routes:

      I see narrow orders, limited tightness, but will   120
not run to that easy victory:
      still around the looser, wider forces work:
      I will try
    to fasten into order enlarging grasps of disorder, widening
scope, but enjoying the freedom that   125
Scope eludes my grasp, that there is no finality of vision,
that I have perceived nothing completely,
      that tomorrow a new walk is a new walk.

1. Cite several examples of where Ammons uses the open form of his verse
   to illustrate the concept he is discussing. For instance, in lines 43–48

the length of the lines shifts as Ammons speaks of the changing shapes of sand dunes.

2. What topographical features does Ammons observe on his walk around the inlet that serve as metaphors for his own poetic practices?

ANONYMOUS (15TH CENTURY)

The Unquiet Grave

"The wind doth blow today, my love,
    And a few small drops of rain;
I never had but one true-love,
    In cold grave she was lain.

"I'll do as much for my true-love   5
    As any young man may;
I'll sit and mourn all at her grave
    For a twelvemonth and a day."

The twelvemonth and a day being up,
    The dead began to speak: 10
"Oh who sits weeping on my grave,
    And will not let me sleep?"

"'Tis I, my love, sits on your grave,
    And will not let you sleep;
For I crave one kiss of your clay-cold lips,   15
    And that is all I seek."

"You crave one kiss of my clay-cold lips;
    But my breath smells earthy strong;
If you have one kiss of my clay-cold lips,
    Your time will not be long.   20

"'Tis down in yonder garden green,
    Love, where we used to walk,
The finest flower that e'er was seen
    Is withered to a stalk.

"The stalk is withered dry, my love,   25
    So will our hearts decay;
So make yourself content, my love,
    Till God calls you away."

GEORGE GORDON, LORD BYRON (1788–1824)

Don Juan, Canto I, Sections 6–13

VI

Most epic poets plunge *"in medias res"*
  (Horace makes this the heroic turnpike road),
And then your hero tells, when'er you please,
  What went before—by way of episode,
While seated after dinner at his ease,   5
  Beside his mistress in some soft abode,
Palace, or garden, paradise, or cavern,
Which serves the happy couple for a tavern.

VII

That is the usual method, but not mine—
  My way is to begin with the beginning;   10
The regularity of my design
  Forbids all wandering as the worst of sinning,
And therefore I shall open with a line
  (Although it cost me half an hour in spinning),
Narrating somewhat of Don Juan's father,   15
And also of his mother, if you'd rather.

VIII

In Seville was he born, a pleasant city,
  Famous for oranges and women—he
Who has not seen it will be much to pity,
  So says the proverb—and I quite agree;   20
Of all the Spanish towns is none more pretty,
  Cadiz perhaps—but that you soon may see;
Don Juan's parents lived beside the river,
A noble stream, and called the Guadalquivir.

IX

His father's name was José—*Don*, of course,—   25
  A true Hidalgo, free from every stain
Of Moor or Hebrew blood, he traced his source
  Through the most Gothic gentlemen of Spain;
A better cavalier ne'er mounted horse,
  Or, being mounted, e'er got down again,   30

Than José, who begot our hero, who
Begot—but that's to come—Well, to renew:

X

His mother was a learnéd lady, famed
    For every branch of every science known—
In every Christain language ever named,   35
    With virtues equaled by her wit alone:
She made the cleverest people quite ashamed,
    And even the good with inward envy groan,
Finding themselves so very much exceeded,
In their own way, by all the things that she did.   40

XI

Her memory was a mine: she knew by heart
    All Calderon and greater part of Lopé,
So, that if any actor missed his part,
    She could have served him for the prompter's copy;
For her Feinagle's were an useless art,   45
    And he himself obliged to shut up shop—he
Could never make a memory so fine as
That which adorned the brain of Donna Inez.

XII

Her favorite science was the mathematical,
    Her noblest virtue was her magnanimity,   50
Her wit (she sometimes tried at wit) was Attic all,
    Her serious sayings darkened to sublimity;
In short, in all things she was fairly what I call
    A prodigy—her morning dress was dimity,
Her evening silk, or, in the summer, muslin,   55
And other stuffs, with which I won't stay puzzling.

XIII

She knew the Latin—that is, "the Lord's prayer,"
    And Greek—the alphabet—I'm nearly sure;
She read some French romances here and there,
    Although her mode of speaking was not pure;   60
For native Spanish she had no great care,
    At least her conversation was obscure;
Her thoughts were theorems, her words a problem,
As if she deemed that mystery would ennoble 'em.

1. What examples can you find of Byron's use of comic rhymes in the final couplet of the ottava rima stanza? Does he use comic rhyme elsewhere in the stanza? Where?
2. What variations in the ten-syllable line occur? What is their function?
3. How does Byron show his irreverence for convention in these lines?

ALLEN GINSBERG (b. 1926)

Last Night in Calcutta

Still night. The old clock Ticks,
half past two. A ringing of crickets
awake in the ceiling. The gate is locked
on the street outside—sleepers, mustaches,
nakedness, but no desire. A few mosquitos   5
waken the itch, the fan turns slowly—
a car thunders along the black asphalt,
a bull snorts, something is expected—
Time sits solid in the four yellow walls.
No one is here, emptiness filled with train   10
whistles & dog barks, answered a block away.
Pushkin sits on the bookshelf, Shakespeare's
complete works as well as Blake's unread—
O Spirit of Poetry, no use calling on you
babbling in this emptiness furnished with beds   15
under the bright oval mirror—perfect
night for sleepers to dissolve in tranquil
blackness, and rest there eight hours
—Waking to stained fingers, bitter mouth
and lung gripped by cigarette hunger,   20
what to do with this big toe, this arm
this eye in the starving skeleton-filled
sore horse tramcar-heated Calcutta in
Eternity—sweating and teeth rotted away—
Rilke at least could dream about lovers,   25
the old breast excitement and trembling belly,
is that it? And the vast starry space—
If the brain changes matter breathes
fearfully back on man—But now
the great crash of buildings and planets   30
breaks thru the walls of language and drowns
me under its Ganges heaviness forever.
No escape but thru Bangkok and New York death.
Skin is sufficient to be skin, that's all
it ever could be, tho screams of pain in the kidney   35

make it sick of itself, a wavy dream
dying to finish its all too famous misery
—Leave immortality for another to suffer like a fool,
not get stuck in the corner of the universe
sticking morphine in the arm and eating meat.   40

1. What is the function of the allusions to time and poetry in Ginsberg's
   poem?
2. How do the parallel structures in lines 5–9 convey the sense of timelessness? Why does Ginsberg use so many participial constructions (lines 14,
   15, 19, 24)?

THOMAS GRAY (1716–1771)

Ode

On the death of a favorite cat,
drowned in a tub of goldfishes

"Twas on a lofty vase's side,
Where China's gayest art had dyed
　　The azure flowers that blow;
Demurest of the tabby kind,
The pensive Selima, reclined,   5
　　Gazed on the lake below.

Her conscious tail her joy declared;
The fair round face, the snowy beard,
　　The velvet of her paws,
Her coat, that with the tortoise vies,   10
Her ears of jet, and emerald eyes,
　　She saw; and purred applause.

Still had she gazed; but 'midst the tide
Two angel forms were seen to glide,
　　The genii of the stream: 15
Their scaly armor's Tyrian hue
Through richest purple to the view
　　Betrayed a golden gleam.

The hapless nymph with wonder saw:
A whisker first and then a claw,   20
　　With many an ardent wish,
She stretched in vain to reach the prize.

What female heart can gold despise?
   What cat's averse to fish?

Presumptuous maid! with looks intent   25
Again she stretched, again she bent,
   Nor knew the gulf between.
(Malignant Fate sat by and smiled)
The slippery verge her feet beguiled,
   She tumbled headlong in.   30

Eight times emerging from the flood
She mewed to every watery god,
   Some speedy aid to send.
No dolphin came, no Nereid stirred;
Nor cruel Tom, nor Susan heard;   35
   A favorite has no friend!

From hence, ye beauties, undeceived,
Know, one false step is ne'er retrieved,
   And be with caution bold.
Not all that tempts your wandering eyes   40
And heedless hearts, is lawful prize;
   Nor all that glisters, gold.

ROBERT HERRICK (1591–1674)

Upon Julia's Clothes

Whenas in silks my Julia goes
Then, then, methinks, how sweetly flows
That liquefaction of her clothes.

Next, when I cast mine eyes, and see
That brave vibration, each way free,   5
O, how that glittering taketh me!

X. J. KENNEDY (b. 1929)

Nude Descending a Staircase

Toe upon toe, a snowing flesh,
A gold of lemon, root and rind,

She sifts in sunlight down the stairs
With nothing on. Nor on her mind.

We spy beneath the banister   5
A constant thresh of thigh on thigh—
Her lips imprint the swinging air
That parts to let her parts go by.

One-woman waterfall, she wears
Her slow descent like a long cape   10
And pausing, on the final stair
Collects her motions into shape.

ROGER MCGOUGH (b. 1937)

40–Love

middle	aged
couple	playing
ten	nis
when	the
game	ends 5
and	they
go	home
the	net
will	still
be	be 10
tween	them

CLAUDE MCKAY (1890–1948)

If We Must Die

If we must die, let it not be like hogs
Hunted and penned in an inglorious spot,
While round us bark the mad and hungry dogs,
Making their mock at our accursed lot.
If we must die, O let us nobly die,   5
So that our precious blood may not be shed
In vain; then even the monsters we defy
Shall be constrained to honor us though dead!
O kinsmen! we must meet the common foe!
Though far outnumbered let us show us brave,   10

And for their thousand blows deal one deathblow!
What though before us lies the open grave?
Like men we'll face the murderous, cowardly pack,
Pressed to the wall, dying, but fighting back!

1. What kind of sonnet has McKay written? Does the final couplet sum up
   the emotional thrust of the poem? Why?
2. If McKay rejects the simile of the opening line, what is the implied
   metaphor of the final line?

SYLVIA PLATH (1932–1963)

The Eye-Mote

Blameless as daylight I stood looking
At a field of horses, necks bent, manes blown,
Tails streaming against the green
Backdrop of sycamores. Sun was striking
While chapel pinnacles over the roofs,   5
Holding the horses, the clouds, the leaves

Steadily rooted though they were all flowing
Away to the left like reeds in a sea
When the splinter flew in and stuck my eye,
Needling it dark. Then I was seeing   10
A melding of shapes in a hot rain:
Horses warped on the altering green,

Outlandish as double-humped camels or unicorns,
Grazing at the margins of a bad monochrome,
Beasts of oasis, a better time.   15
Abrading my lid, the small grain burns:
Red cinder around which I myself,
Horses, planets and spires revolve.

Neither tears nor the easing flush
Of eyebaths can unseat the speck: 20
It sticks, and it has stuck a week.
I wear the present itch for flesh,
Blind to what will be and what was.
I dream that I am Oedipus.

What I want back is what I was   25
Before the bed, before the knife,
Before the brooch-pin and the salve

Fixed me in this parenthesis;
Horses fluent in the wind,
A place, a time gone out of mind.   30

1. What kind of stanza does Plath employ?
2. Is the rhyme scheme consistent? Note in the first stanza the rhyme
   scheme is a b b a c c. What kind of rhyme does Plath use? Why?
3. Explain the allusion to Oedipus. How does it fit the theme of the poem?
   Why is she fixed in "this parenthesis"?

ALEXANDER POPE (1688–1744)

From *An Essay on Man, Epistle II*

Know then thyself, presume not God to scan;
The proper study of Mankind is Man.
Plac'd on this isthmus of a middle state,
A being darkly wise, and rudely great:
With too much knowledge for the Sceptic side,   5
With too much weakness for the Stoic's pride,
He hangs between; in doubt to act, or rest,
In doubt to deem himself a God, or Beast;
In doubt his Mind or Body to prefer,
Born but to die, and reas'ning but to err;   10
Alike in ignorance, his reason such,
Whether he thinks too little, or too much:
Chaos of Thought and Passion, all confus'd;
Still by himself abus'd, or disabus'd;
Created half to rise, and half to fall;   15
Great lord of all things, yet a prey to all;
Sole judge of Truth, in endless Error hurl'd:
The glory, jest, and riddle of the world!

ADRIENNE RICH (b. 1929)

Necessities of Life

Piece by piece I seem
to re-enter the world: I first began

a small, fixed dot, still see
that old myself, a dark-blue thumbtack

pushed into the scene,
a hard little head protruding

from the pointillist's buzz and bloom.
After a time the dot

begins to ooze. Certain heats
melt it.
          Now I was hurriedly

blurring into ranges
of burnt red, burning green,

whole biographies swam up and
swallowed me like Jonah.

Jonah! I was Wittgenstein,
Mary Wollstonecraft, the soul

of Louis Jouvet, dead
in a blown-up photograph.

Till, wolfed almost to shreds,
I learned to make myself

unappetizing. Scaly as a dry bulb
thrown into a cellar

I used myself, let nothing use me.
Like being on a private dole,

sometimes more like kneading bricks in Egypt.
What life was there, was mine,

now and again to lay
one hand on a warm brick

and touch the sun's ghost
with economical joy,

now and again to name
over the bare necessities.

So much for those days. Soon
practice may make me middling-perfect, I'll

5

10

15

20

25

30

35

dare inhabit the world
trenchant in motion as an eel, solid

as a cabbage-head. I have invitations:
a curl of mist steams upward

from a field, visible as my breath,   40
houses along a road stand waiting

like old women knitting, breathless
to tell their tales.

1. How is the spareness of the couplets an appropriate form for the ideas
   Rich expresses?
2. What does she mean by the lines "I used myself, let nothing use me. /
   Like being on a private dole"? What are the bare necessities she refers
   to in line 33?
3. Why does the stanza form change between lines 9 and 15?

THEODORE ROETHKE (1908–1963)

The Waking

I wake to sleep, and take my waking slow.
I feel my fate in what I cannot fear.
I learn by going where I have to go.

We think by feeling. What is there to know?
I hear my being dance from ear to ear.   5
I wake to sleep, and take my waking slow.

Of those so close beside me, which are you?
God bless the Ground! I shall walk softly there,
And learn by going where I have to go.

Light takes the Tree; but who can tell us how?   10
The lowly worm climbs up a winding stair;
I wake to sleep, and take my waking slow.

Great Nature has another thing to do
To you and me; so take the lively air,
And, lovely, learn by going where to go.   15

This shaking keeps me steady. I should know.
What falls away is always. And is near.
I wake to sleep, and take my waking slow.
I learn by going where I have to go.

1. The poem presents a number of paradoxes: waking to sleep, going to discover the goal, thinking by feeling, shaking to keep steady. How does the form of the villanelle with its double refrain help resolve these paradoxes?
2. In what sense is Roethke's poem about life and death? What images support this idea?

WILLIAM SHAKESPEARE (1564–1616)

Sonnet 55

Not marble, nor the gilded monuments
Of princes, shall outlive this powerful rhyme;
But you shall shine more bright in these conténts
Than unswept stone, besmeared with sluttish time.
When wasteful war shall statues overturn,   5
And broils root out the work of masonry,
Nor Mars his sword nor war's quick fire shall burn
The living record of your memory.
'Gainst death and all-oblivious enmity
Shall you pace forth; your praise shall still find room   10
Even in the eyes of all posterity
That wear this world out to the ending doom.
So, till the judgment that yourself arise,
You live in this, and dwell in lovers' eyes.

Sonnet 116

Let me not to the marriage of true minds
Admit impediments. Love is not love
Which alters when it alteration finds,
Or bends with the remover to remove:
Oh, no! it is an ever-fixéd mark,   5
That looks on tempests and is never shaken;
It is the star to every wandering bark,
Whose worth's unknown, although his height be taken.
Love's not Time's fool, though rosy lips and cheeks

Within his bending sickle's compass come;   10
Love alters not with his brief hours and weeks,
But bears it out even to the edge of doom.
If this be error and upon me proved,
I never writ, nor no man ever loved.

1. Shakespeare's sonnet about the constancy of true love uses imagery from
   navigation in the second quatrain (lines 5–8). How does this imagery
   serve as a metaphor for love's constancy?
2. What image is suggested in lines 9 and 10? How are Shakespeare's as-
   sertions strengthened by the boldness of the concluding couplet?

PERCY BYSSHE SHELLEY (1792–1822)

Ode to the West Wind

I

O wild West Wind, thou breath of Autumn's being,
Thou, from whose unseen presence the leaves dead
Are driven, like ghosts from an enchanter fleeing,

Yellow, and black, and pale, and hectic red,
Pestilence-stricken multitudes: O thou,   5
Who chariotest to their dark wintry bed

The wingéd seeds, where they lie cold and low,
Each like a corpse within its grave, until
Thine azure sister of the Spring shall blow

Her clarion o'er the dreaming earth, and fill   10
(Driving sweet buds like flocks to feed in air)
With living hues and odors plain and hill:

Wild Spirit, which art moving everywhere;
Destroyer and preserver; hear, oh, hear!

II

Thou on whose stream, mid the steep sky's commotion,   15
Loose clouds like earth's decaying leaves are shed,
Shook from the tangled boughs of Heaven and Ocean,

Angels of rain and lightning: there are spread
On the blue surface of thine aëry surge,
Like the bright hair uplifted from the head   20

Of some fierce Maenad, even from the dim verge
Of the horizon to the zenith's height,
The locks of the approaching storm. Thou dirge

Of the dying year, to which this closing night
Will be the dome of a vast sepulcher,   25
Vaulted with all thy congregated might

Of vapors, from whose solid atmosphere
Black rain, and fire, and hail will burst: oh, hear!

III

Thou who didst waken from his summer dreams
The blue Mediterranean, where he lay,   30
Lulled by the coil of his crystálline streams,

Beside a pumice isle in Baiae's bay,
And saw in sleep old palaces and towers
Quivering within the wave's intenser day,

All overgrown with azure moss and flowers   35
So sweet, the sense faints picturing them! Thou
For whose path the Atlantic's level powers

Cleave themselves into chasms, while far below
The sea-blooms and the oozy woods which wear
The sapless foliage of the ocean, know   40

Thy voice, and suddenly grow gray with fear,
And tremble and despoil themselves: oh, hear!

IV

If I were a dead leaf thou mightest bear;
If I were a swift cloud to fly with thee;
A wave to pant beneath thy power, and share   45

The impulse of thy strength, only less free
Than thou, O uncontrollable! If even
I were as in my boyhood, and could be

The comrade of thy wanderings over Heaven,
As then, when to outstrip thy skyey speed 50
Scarce seemed a vision; I would ne'er have striven

As thus with thee in prayer in my sore need.
Oh, lift me as a wave, a leaf, a cloud!
I fall upon the thorns of life! I bleed!

A heavy weight of hours has chained and bowed 55
One too like thee: tameless, and swift, and proud.

V

Make me thy lyre, even as the forest is:
What if my leaves are falling like its own!
The tumult of thy mighty harmonies

Will take from both a deep, autumnal tone, 60
Sweet though in sadness. Be thou, Spirit fierce,
My spirit! Be thou me, impetuous one!

Drive my dead thoughts over the universe
Like withered leaves to quicken a new birth!
And, by the incantation of this verse, 65

Scatter, as from an unextinguished hearth
Ashes and sparks, my words among mankind!
Be through my lips to unawakened earth

The trumpet of a prophecy! O Wind,
If Winter comes, can Spring be far behind? 70

1. Shelley's ode uses the interlocking stanza of terza rima with a couplet
   following the fourth tercet. How does Shelley use the stanza to develop
   the idea of the wind being a destroyer and a preserver?
2. Each of the first three sections of the ode describes the effects of the
   wind on one or more of the elements of earth, air, fire and water. How
   is this development continued in sections four and five of the ode? How
   does the final couplet represent a return to the original paradox of the
   wind being a destroyer and a preserver?

Ozymandias

I met a traveler from an antique land
Who said: Two vast and trunkless legs of stone
Stand in the desert . . . Near them, on the sand,
Half sunk, a shattered visage lies, whose frown,
And wrinkled lip, and sneer of cold command,   5
Tell that its sculptor well those passions read
Which yet survive, stamped on these lifeless things,
The hand that mocked them, and the heart that fed:
And on the pedestal these words appear:
"My name is Ozymandias, king of kings: 10
Look on my works, ye Mighty, and despair!"
Nothing beside remains. Round the decay
Of that colossal wreck, boundless and bare
The lone and level sands stretch far away.

1. What is unconventional about the rhyming pattern of Shelley's sonnet?
   Does the poem divide after line 8 into an octave and a sestet?
2. How are lines 6 and 7 ambiguous? How does this ambiguity anticipate
   the irony of the inscription on the pedestal?

WILLIAM WORDSWORTH (1770–1850)

Nuns Fret Not

Nuns fret not at their convent's narrow room;
And hermits are contented with their cells;
And students with their pensive citadels;
Maids at the wheel, the weaver at his loom,
Sit blithe and happy; bees that soar for bloom,   5
High as the highest Peak of Furness-fells,
Will murmur by the hour in foxglove bells:
In truth the prison, unto which we doom
Ourselves, no prison is: and hence for me,
In sundry moods, 'twas pastime to be bound   10
Within the sonnet's scanty plot of ground;
Pleased if some souls (for such there needs must be)
Who have felt the weight of too much liberty,
Should find brief solace there, as I have found.

1. In what sense is this sonnet about writing a sonnet?
2. Is the rhyme scheme typical of a Petrarchan sonnet? Why has Wordsworth run the sense past line 8 into line 9?

WRITING ABOUT COMMON STANZA FORMS, THE SONNET, AND OPEN FORMS

The human mind delights in forms. If you recall the first time you tried to draw a picture of a house, you probably remember that the house was a perfect square surmounted by a perfect triangle to represent the slant of the roof. Above the house was a perfectly round sun. In front of the house were flowers, all carefully formed with round centers and petals in the shape of tear drops.

Poets, too, take delight in form: in the shape and sound of a line, the turn of one line into the next, the closure provided by a carefully rhymed stanza, the openness that results from a series of free verse lines squirming down the page in defiance of any obvious attempt to order them. As readers of poetry, particularly as readers concerned with writing about poetry, we must learn to notice poetic forms, to show how they work in poems, to learn the traditions associated with them, and to evaluate how skillfully the poet has used them. These abilities to perceive, interpret, and evaluate form—and to write about the discoveries—are signs of a reader's maturity in the study of poetry.

As a preliminary to writing about the form of the poem you have selected, get a sense of its most obvious formal features. How is it laid out on the page? What is its shape? How many lines does it have? How many stanzas? How many lines per stanza? Check the meter or rhythm of the poem, and its rhyme scheme. Get a feel for any significant repetitions. Whether it is a rhymed and metered poem or a free verse poem, note whether it has stanzas (a **strophic** poem) or a series of continuous lines (a **stichic** poem). If it is strophic, there should be some common principle that unifies each stanza and marks it off from the next, some rhyme scheme or metrical pattern that you should note. If it is a stichic poem, you may have to look harder to discover its divisions. Some poets, as we have seen, divide stichic poems into verse paragraphs. Such preliminaries will help you invent ideas for your essay and may suggest ways of organizing it.

Your next task is to see how the *form* of the poem contains the *matter* of the poem. Here you must try to see the rhetorical principles that underlie the poem. Does it use contrast? Does it move from examples to a generalization about them? Or does it move from a generalization to examples? If it is a narrative or a descriptive poem, what can you discern about the plot of the narrative or the arrangement of the descriptive details? Furthermore, how does the parcelling out of the poem into stanzas or groups of lines help to capture these rhetorical principles? Shakespeare's "Sonnet 73" (page 741) is a good example of a poem that leads from a series of images to a conclusion about them. In the first stanza (in this case a group of four lines with an *a b a b* rhyme scheme), the speaker of the poem compares himself to autumn. In the second, he compares himself to nightfall, and in the third to a dying fire. Each of these comparisons is expressed in four lines comprising one sentence. The last stanza of the poem is a couplet whose sentiment follows logically from the three preceding images. The person addressed in the poem, since he is about to lose the speaker, should love the speaker more strongly.

Your awareness of this four part structure, of course, would be helped along by the knowledge that it is common to most Shakespearean sonnets. Similarly, the Italian sonnet, like Wordsworth's "Nuns Fret Not" (page 769), is more commonly divided into two parts, one corresponding to the octave, one to the sestet. Other conventional forms will display other means of organizing material. Knowing these traditions (a matter, finally, of experience in reading poetry) is helpful, but not vital for the beginner. You should look at what you see and try to make sense of it. As you read more and more poetry, your sense of poetic tradition will ripen along with your understanding of individual poems.

Whether it is closed or open, form will always, if the poem is a good one, contain meaning. In many instances—and in some of the most brilliant poems in our language—it will also reflect or embody meaning. You have already seen (page 679) how Lawrence Ferlinghetti uses the arrangement of the lines on the page to reflect the precariousness of the tightrope walker's act. Note too that in the selection from Pope's "Essay on Man" (page 760) the closed form of Pope's couplets embodies the logical progression of his thoughts. Pairs of half-lines, couplets, or pairs of couplets are used to embody the contrasts of Pope's thinking, or to reflect the addition of one logical unit to the next. Similarly, in the open form of A. R. Ammons "Corson's Inlet" (page 748), the arrangement of free verse lines on the page reflects or imitates the coastline he walks along and the digressive, erratic quality of his thinking. Such happy conjunctions between form and content are relatively rare, and are always a delightful surprise. They provide us with the pleasure of perceiving that the poet has found the best means to a good end.

A written analysis of form can be valuable in its own right, or it can be used to support a different kind of analysis (one of imagery or meter, for example), or a full-blown explication of a poem. In any event, your essay will probably be organized either stanzaically or on the basis of a relationship between generalizations about the form of the poem and particulars to support those generalizations. The benefit of this kind of analysis, and of the study of form in general, is that it forces you to see the poem whole, whether as an organism or a mechanism. It allows you to perceive and evaluate how the parts of the poem shape and constitute the whole—and to see how these parts work together to deliver the entirety of the poem's statement. The essay which follows, on X. J. Kennedy's "Nude Descending a

Staircase" (page 757) attempts to show how the form of the poem reflects the form of the painting it describes. Care is taken in the essay to show how each stanza delivers a portion of the content, and how each, while having its own integrity, connects with the other stanzas.

Words Sliding into Place: Form in X. J. Kennedy's
"Nude Descending a Staircase"

X. J. Kennedy's "Nude Descending a Staircase" is a poetic description of the Cubist painting of the same title by the French painter Marcel Duchamp. In the poem, Kennedy uses three iambic tetrameter quatrains rhymed a b a b to convey the impression of the nude's movement down the staircase. The form of the poem brilliantly recaptures the sense of repetition and motion in the painting; furthermore, the way the parts of the poem slide into place at the end accurately reflects their unity. The closure at the end of Kennedy's poem exactly recreates the arrival of the nude at the bottom of the staircase.

Duchamp's painting, in fact, shows many apparent nudes descending one staircase, all of them captured as in a series of photographic stills. Kennedy's first stanza gives us our initial sense of this repeated motion. "Toe upon toe" is the first of several repetitions in the poem. Lines six and eight also contain key repetitions. Moreover, Kennedy uses alliteration ("thigh on thigh") and assonance ("Toe upon toe, a snowing flesh") to reinforce our sense that many parts are being replicated throughout the poem. The first stanza also shows us the color of the nude ("A gold of lemon, root and rind"--note the additional alliteration) and presents us with the first verb of motion, sifts.

We should also note the rhyme scheme of the stanza. With the exception of the first line, lines one and three of each stanza use the air rhyme. This is another significant repetition that helps to suggest downward motion. The rhymes, too, move down the page as we read the poem. The closure suggested by the full rhymes of lines two and four in each stanza prepares us for the closure of the conclusion, where the nude gathers into herself at the bottom of the steps.

The second stanza, beginning with "We spy," reinforces the idea that we are watching the nude as she descends. Thresh again augments our sense of repeated motion, as sifts did in the first stanza. We see her thighs moving past us in a blur; the very air seems to divide to admit her progress. The repetition of thigh and parts suggests the notion that fragments are moving past us on their way toward wholeness. It should be pointed out that this is exactly what the poem itself is doing--line follows line as it gathers toward a completed statement.

In the final stanza, Kennedy again uses alliteration ("One-woman waterfall") to suggest diversity in unity--multiple w sounds associated with one person. The long vowels of line 10 (slow and cape) slow us down as we read--giving us time, so to speak, to review the protracted shapes (repetitions of herself) that are spread out behind the nude. The heavy caesuras of line 11 ("And pausing, on the final stair--") force us to pause as we read, as though we are collecting ourselves for the end of the poem, just as the nude seems to collect herself at the bottom of the stairs. The word shape at the end of the poem (and we should remember that the entire poem, and the painting, is about a shape), chimes precisely with cape, thus giving us a complete sense of closure, of words sliding into place, as the nude completes her descent. This full rhyme, a rhyme of both sight and sound, resembles that in the first stanza of the poem (rind and mind).

"Nude Descending a Staircase" is a *tour de force*, a brilliant illustration of the resemblance between two arts: as with painting, so with poetry. The form of the poem, parts gathered into a whole, accurately reflects the process of perceiving repeated motions and watching those motions become one completed object.

SUGGESTIONS FOR WRITING ABOUT FORM

1. Write an analysis of W. B. Yeats "Sailing to Byzantium" (page 563) that shows the individual integrity of its four parts and the means Yeats uses to effect transitions between them.
2. Show the unity of each of the numbered sections of Keats's "Ode on a Grecian Urn" (page 558).
3. Analyze the stichic form of Ginsberg's "Last Night in Calcutta" (page 755), and write an essay that reveals the sequence of the speaker's reflections.
4. Discuss the relationship between form and imagery in Shelley's "Ode to the West Wind" (page 764).
5. Demonstrate how the free verse form and the line arrangements of Levertov's "Merrit Parkway" (page 570) reflect the content of the poem.
6. Select a smaller poem such as Lowell's "Children of Light" (page 569) or Levertov's "The Ache of Marriage" (page 571) and write an essay about its form.

THEME AND MEANING

When we read a poem it is natural to want to know what it means, and a good deal of our initial interest in poetry centers on discovering the theme or meaning of poems. However, such an approach not only oversimplifies the act of reading poetry, but what is worse, the search for the "hidden meaning" in poetry often distorts the nature of the poem itself. T. S. Eliot once observed that poetry "communicates before it is understood," by which he meant that there are many complicated factors contributing to our total response to the poem's meaning, several of which work on an unconscious level. Diane Wakoski, echoing Eliot's observation, cautions listeners of poetry to let the sounds break over them initially rather than to try piecing together the suggestions of all the words on first hearing (or reading) a poem. There are many kinds of poems, not all of them with "grand ideas" at their core.

There are also a number of ways in which **theme** can be oversimplified, resulting in a misreading or at least a misplaced emphasis on one aspect of a poem. Three common ways in which theme is oversimplified:

1. *Theme means the moral of the poem.* While some poetry may be morally uplifting, there is no inherent connection between poetry and morality. In fact, poems and poets, going back to ancient Greece, have often been charged with encouraging immorality by celebrating the pleasurable and sensual in life. William Blake mocked the use of poetry for pious purposes in his poem from *Songs of Innocence*, "The Chimney Sweeper," an exposé of the evils of eighteenth century child labor, which concludes with the ironically pious injunction, "So if all do their duty, they need not fear harm." This is not to say that poems may not be religious. Note the religious fervor expressed by two priests, John Donne and Gerard Manley Hopkins (pages 717 and 700). Nor does it mean that if the poem has a religious subject that we need agree with the poet's theology.

2. *Theme is the poet's stated purpose.* Ordinarily, when the poet tells us why a poem was written, we can be reasonably certain that the poet's statement is a fairly accurate expression of the poem's theme. But such a view fails to take into account the subconscious meaning *posited* in the poem. Not all writing is on a conscious level, and frequently meaningful material will be included in a poem without the poet's complete awareness. The "intentional fallacy," as it is called by critics William Wimsatt and Monroe Beardsley, fails to account for such subconscious meanings. Several years ago W. D. Snodgrass told the story of a student approaching him after he had read from his poems at a midwestern university. What the student wanted to know was why Snodgrass had so many references to "wrists" in his poetry. "Where?" asked Snodgrass, unaware that he had referred to wrists at all. "Here, and here, and here . . ." The student went on documenting the presence of wrists as an important image in Snodgrass' poetry—to the poet's astonishment. Poets are usually highly conscious of how they use their craft to convey exactly what they mean, but at times secondary themes appear without a poet's full awareness.

3. *Theme is a prose paraphrase of the main idea of the poem.* Confronted with a prose summary of the main idea of a poem, you may have often thought, "If that's all it means, why didn't the poet say so in the first place?" The fact remains that the prose statement will never equal all of the poem and that an abstract of the intellectual content of the poem is not the same as the experience of the poem. This experience (and a prose statement of the theme would only approximately capture it) would include the effect of all the elements of the poem working together on the reader. To say that the meaning of e. e. cummings' "pity this busy mon-

ster, manunkind" (page 774), is summed up in the lines "A world of made/ is not a world of born," is to ignore the complexity of language, form, sound and idea in the poem.

If theme is not any of these things alone, then what is it? How do we know when we have found it? Theme is, in fact, all of these things—and more. Theme is not only the poet's purpose and the main ideas of the poem, but the combination of what poet-critic John Ciardi has called the *what* and *how* of the poem, not only *what* the poem means, but *how* it means: the qualifications and amplifications of meaning through the technique of the poet's craft. While technique is a dull and inadequate word to describe the language, form, and sound of the poem, it does serve to remind us that the *how* and *what* are, at least in poetry, inseparable, and that a full statement of the theme would take into account all of these elements. But such a statement would perhaps fill a small volume. We frequently have to rely on merely suggesting how these other elements are part of the experience of what the poet is communicating.

THEME AND FIGURES OF SPEECH

Confronted with the complexity of *what* and *how* of a poem, where do we begin to experience the poem's theme? Often, the way into a poem's theme is through its figurative language for, as Robert Frost has pointed out, poetry is "metaphor, saying one thing and meaning another, saying one thing in terms of another, the pleasure of ulteriority." If the poet has ulterior motives, then how do we know we have arrived at the same motives or meaning? Often the poem will have a focal or dominant figure of speech, such as the figure of kingship or royalty in "Richard Cory" (page 671), around which the other images gather. For instance, consider Whitman's use of the figure of the spider as a metaphor for the human soul in isolation in the following poem.

WALT WHITMAN (1819–1892)

A Noiseless Patient Spider

A noiseless patient spider,
I mark'd where on a little promontory it stood isolated,
Mark'd how to explore the vacant vast surrounding,
It launch'd forth filament, filament, filament, out of itself,
Ever unreeling down, ever tirelessly speeding them.   5

And you O my soul where you stand,
Surrounded, detached, in measureless oceans of space,

Ceaselessly musing, venturing, throwing, seeking the spheres to con-
nect them,
Till the bridge you will need be form'd, till the ductile anchor hold,
Till the gossamer thread you fling catch somewhere, O my soul.   10

A prose summary of the main idea of Whitman's poem might state that it is about the essential isolation of each person's soul in the world and about the search for relations in the form of a "soul mate," or of ideas that one immediately recognizes as expressing our innermost, deepest thoughts and desires, or of things with which we can develop connections; or of friends and acquaintances who fulfill parts of ourselves. A fuller statement of the theme would recognize the parallels between the isolated spider and the detached human soul. The dominant metaphor gathers the descriptions of the parallel actions into units. For example, the spider exploring "the vacant vast surrounding" becomes the "musing, venturing, throwing, seek-ing" soul; the filaments of the spider become the "gossamer threads" by which the soul hopes to anchor itself to surrounding reality. An even more complete statement of the theme would recognize how the rhetorical paral-lels of Whitman's catalogues and repetitions describing the respective ac-tions of the spider and human soul loosely match each other: the repetition of *filament* is matched in the second stanza by the series of participles in line 8.

At times the theme of a poem is revealed through several related **image clusters**. Groups of images cluster together to form sets of ideas and our response to the meaning of the poem involves our seeing the interrelation-ship among them. In the following poem by e. e. cummings, the persona of the poem is a doctor diagnosing the disease mankind (here *manunkind*) is suffering from: progress.

e.e. cummings (1894–1962)

pity this busy monster,manunkind

pity this busy monster,manunkind,

not. Progress is a comfortable disease:
your victim(death and life safely beyond)

plays with the bigness of his littleness
—electrons deify one razorblade   5
into a mountainrange;lenses extend

unwish through curving wherewhen till unwish
returns on its unself.

> A world of made
> is not a world of born—pity poor flesh 10
>
> and trees,poor stars and stones,but never this
> fine specimen of hypermagical
>
> ultraomnipotence. We doctors know
>
> a hopeless case if—listen:there's a hell
> of a good universe next door;let's go 15

The images cluster around sickness (*disease, victim, hopeless case*) and unnaturalness, primarily distortion of size (*monster, bigness of . . . littleness, razorblade into a mountain range*). Putting these clusters together, we can restate the point or key idea of the poem, bearing in mind that is is only a *partial* account of the poem's theme. The poet is lamenting human arrogance, which has cut us off from the real universe of *flesh and trees, stars and stones,* and has substituted a manufactured world which we believe is progress, the terminal illness that has made him into a busy monster. While his microscopes can see electrons comprising matter, and his telescopes can explore the universe of stars, he has not come to terms with himself or the real desires in his nature that need fulfillment. There is one hope for man, and that is offered as a cure in the final line. He needs to get out of his manufactured world to the universe of *born* things that is just next door. The dominant tone of e. e. cummings' poem is sarcasm. What is sarcastic about calling mankind a *fine specimen of hypermagical ultraomnipotence?* What does the choice of the word *deify* add to the theme of the poem? Why are razorblades *deified*, and why into a *mountainrange"?* What is the function of the image of refraction (*through curving*) and of time/place (*wherewhen*)? The answers to all of these questions would add even more detail to the theme of cummings' poem.

THEME AND SOUND

There are occasions when the focus of a poem is not conceptual but sonic. The theme or meaning of a poem may not be something primarily paraphrasable but may lie instead in the play of its sounds, just as children's nursery rhymes delight our sense of linguistic sound-play but defy conceptualization. Often, the emphasis on message hunting leaves us with the impression that poems are more difficult ways of saying something simple. The antidote to this view is to examine a poem whose primary meaning lies not in any intellectual statement but, as in the nursery rhymes, in the way we respond to its sounds. Unfortunately, such poems are not emphasized often enough beyond the primary grades because poetry is viewed as serious and not as playful.

Notice in the "The Dance" by William Carlos Williams (page 706), how the playfulness of sounds is the reason for the poem's existence. Words not only refer to things but are also melodic, and the human vocal apparatus can reconstruct the sounds of a thing the words describe just as the words themselves can be used conceptually. Williams' poem appeared in a volume entitled *Pictures from Brueghel,* a series of poems describing the paintings of the Dutch master. "The Dance" is both an attempt to recreate the visual geometry of Brueghel's painting, *The Kermess,* and also an attempt to create the imagined sounds of the original scene that inspired the painter. While the poem appears to be free verse, it is actually a series of anapestic feet alternating with iambic feet that sometimes extend beyond the line's end. The effect of the meter is to capture the circular dance rhythm of the people in the foreground of the Brueghel painting. One person in the painting is playing a bagpipe, the musical accompaniment of the dancers. In Williams' poem, not only does the rhythm recreate a jig-like movement, but the clustering of alliterative *r*'s and *b*'s effectively imitates the sound of a bagpipe. If you expect a grand idea from the Williams' poem, you will be sadly disappointed. It is not that kind of poem. Yet, like the painting, it recreates an aspect of life, and for those familiar with the painting, Williams' translation of the experience from a static, silent, spatial medium to a dynamic sound medium is a *tour de force.* Stating the theme of such a poem is not easy because it has nothing in the way of a recognizable idea. It is the experience of the poem that needs to be described rather than any abstract set of ideas derived from it. Most poem will have a balance between what Alexander Pope called "the sound" and "the sense." Examine Gary Snyder's "Steak" to see how the sounds of the poem are actually part of the statement that the poem is making.

GARY SYNDER (b. 1930)

Steak

Up on the bluff, the steak houses
called "The Embers"—called
"Fireside"
with a smiling disney cow on the sign
or a stockman's pride—huge   5
full-color photo of standing Hereford stud
above the very booth
his bloody sliced muscle is
    served in;
      "rare"   10

The Chamber of Commerce eats there,
the visiting lecturer,

stockmen in Denver suits,
Japanese-American animal nutrition experts
    from Kansas,   15
    with Buddhist beads;

And down by the tracks
in frozen mud, in the feed lots,
fed surplus grain
(the ripped-off land)   20
the beeves are standing round—
bred heavy.
Steaming, stamping,
long-lashed, slowly thinking
with the rhythm of their   25
breathing,
frosty—breezy—
early morning prairie sky.

"Steak" is one of a number of poems in *Turtle Island* that are critical of waste in western culture. Here Snyder indicts a wasteful culture that feeds itself on meat when it would be more efficient for people to consume grain directly. The poem's theme, however, is conveyed partly through the sounds, especially the *r* sound that imitates a carnivore eating meat. Why does Snyder have *rare* and *there* rhyme? Are there any other kinds of rhyme in the poem? How do they affect the poem's theme? What are the rhythms of the final four lines? Why does the poem assume a somewhat more regular rhythm at this point?

THEME AND FORM

Another element of poetry that has a bearing on theme is the form in which a poem is written. Like any other convention, form carries with it certain expectations on the part of the audience familiar with the traditions that lie behind the convention. Take for instance the convention of the sonnet, which follows either the English pattern of three quatrains (four line sections) and a couplet, or the Italian pattern of an octave (an eight-line section) followed by a sestet (a six-line section). Each convention has its traditional uses determining what type of situation and theme can be dealt with. The English sonnet lends itself well to the slow exposition of an idea through three figures of speech followed by an intense summation in the final couplet. The Italian sonnet, however, usually presents a problematical situation in the octave and attempts to solve it in the sestet. Of course, poets are free to defy convention and put the form to other uses— but they do so at the risk of being misunderstood. The reader familiar with the convention recognizes the form and expects a certain pattern of thematic development before even reading a word.

Examine the following poem by John Donne. What is the problematic situation he is examining? What is the primary figure of speech through which the situation is described? How is the conflict resolved in the sestet?

JOHN DONNE (1572–1631)

Holy Sonnet #14

Batter my heart, three-personed God; for You
As yet but knock, breathe, shine, and seek to mend;
That I may rise and stand, o'erthrow me, and bend
Your force, to break, blow, burn, and make me new.
I, like an usurped town, to another due,   5
Labor to admit You, but Oh, to no end!
Reason, Your viceroy in me, me should defend,
But is captived, and proves weak or untrue.
Yet dearly I love You, and would be loved fain.
But am betrothed unto Your enemy: 10
Divorce me, untie, or break that knot again,
Take me to You, imprison me, for I,
Except You enthrall me, never shall be free,
Nor ever chaste, except You ravish me.

The poem deals with the conflict between man's free will and God's laws. Donne works this idea into the form of a town (man's soul) under siege by the three-personed God who is attempting to capture it from the devil ("your enemy"). The sestet suggests that the soul will, paradoxically, be free only if it is imprisoned by God—that is, only if God has his will of the soul ("ravish me"). The function of the violent imagery is to suggest that man's weakness stems from choice and only by removing choice will man remain faithful to God. Whether or not we agree with Donne's theology is immaterial to our evaluation of the theme of the poem. The dominant figure of a town under siege meshes well with the formal demands of the Italian sonnet, and the powerful expression of violently denying free will works as a resolution within the framework of the sonnet. Form, then, is inherently a part of the thematic statement a poem is making. Examine Donne's "Death Be Not Proud" (page 717), to see how form and theme unite in that sonnet.

THEME AND TRADITION

One popular definition of *theme* is a recurring idea or pattern in life. The more you read poetry, the more you will become aware of the repetition of themes by poets. The same subject can produce the same theme. Since poets draw from the same cultural stock, it is not surprising that they often refer to one another's work in their poems, especially those dealing with the same theme. When T. S. Eliot has his character J. Alfred Prufrock (page 663) say of himself, "I am not Prince Hamlet, nor was meant to be," he is using an **allusion** to Shakespeare's play and drawing on a common theme of indecision that tenuously links the two characters. Sometimes poets demand that their readers be familiar with the rich literary tradition that precedes them in order to understand the poem. While not all poems are richly allusive and place theme demands on the reader, those that do will not pose as great a threat the more you read and become familiar with poetry.

One popular theme in poetry is that of transiency, the passing of time, and the desire to make the most of youth while you still have it. Frequently the theme takes the form of a complaint about the swift passage of time; the *carpe diem* theme means to seize the day. Consider how Robert Herrick handles the *carpe diem* theme in "To the Virgins."

ROBERT HERRICK (1591–1674)

To the Virgins, to Make Much of Time

Gather ye rosebuds while ye may:
   Old Time is still a-flying;
And this same flower that smiles today,
   Tomorrow will be dying.

The glorious lamp of heaven, the sun,   5
   The higher he's a-getting,
The sooner will his race be run,
   And nearer he's to setting.

That age is best which is the first,
   When youth and blood are warmer;   10
But being spent, the worse, and worst
   Times, still succeed the former.

Then be not coy, but use your time;
   And while ye may, go marry:
For, having lost but once your prime,   15
   You may for ever tarry.

Each stanza either directly or indirectly refers to the passage of time. The image of the sun in a race across the heavens suggests the speed with which time and youth can be wasted. The injunction to marry links the virgins' "prime" with the early morning, and the season of spring when rosebuds may be gathered; similarly, the poet extends the warm season to the youthful passions. The rosebuds are associated not only with gathering pleasure but, by extension, with the maidens themselves. Like the rosebuds, the maidens have but a short time. Each quatrain ends with a negative consequence of failing to *seize the day*, or to *seize the time*.

Compare Herrick's poem with Andrew Marvell's "To His Coy Mistress" (page 670), and with Richard Wilbur's "Late Aubade" (page 913). Does Wilbur's poem contain any illusions to Herrick's? Where? Why does Wilbur use the image in the first stanza of a "liver-spotted page"? Do you think he refers just to a page? The last line of the poem should help you answer this question. The same argument is used by Marvell in his seduction poem. What is the function of the reference to his lady's skin in lines 33 and 34 of "To His Coy Mistress"? How does his macabre observation in lines 31 and 32 underlie all these *carpe diem* poems?

While it may seem that there is little in poetry that does not pertain to theme, and that the task of fully trying to state a poem's theme is as futile as trying to rewrite the poem itself, nevertheless the process of trying to restate the primary meaning of a poem gives us a focus in dealing with what at times may seem a labyrinth of meaning in some poems. Keeping in mind that each poem is a unique experience, but one in which the poet takes into account the tradition in which he or she is working, each poem represents a unique challenge to share a living moment. While our prose summary may lack the power of the original, it nevertheless affords us the opportunity to stand back and attempt to express the power of an experience that defies paraphrase.

W. H. AUDEN (1907–1973)

Musée des Beaux Arts

About suffering they were never wrong,
The Old Masters: how well they understood
Its human position; how it takes place
While someone else is eating or opening a window or just walking
    dully along;
How, when the aged are reverently, passionately waiting   5
For the miraculous birth, there always must be
Children who did not specially want it to happen, skating
On a pond at the edge of the wood:
They never forgot
That even the dreadful martyrdom must run its course   10
Anyhow in a corner, some untidy spot
Where the dogs go on with their doggy life and the torturer's horse
Scratches its innocent behind on a tree.

In Brueghel's *Icarus,* for instance: how everything turns away
Quite leisurely from the disaster; the plowman may   15
Have heard the splash, the forsaken cry,
But for him it was not an important failure; the sun shone
As it had to on the white legs disappearing into the green
Water; and the expensive delicate ship that must have seen
Something amazing, a boy falling out of the sky,   20
Had somewhere to get to and sailed calmly on.

1. Auden's poem presents an argument about human suffering. What is his
   basic premise about this aspect of life? How do the paintings of the Old
   Masters illustrate his point? What does he mean by *position* in line 3?
   Does he mean only location on the painter's canvas?
2. Look up the myth of Icarus and Daedalus. What does the second stanza
   suggest about the meaning of the myth? Is the stanza an accurate representation of Brueghel's painting? Compare the details of Joseph Lang-
   land's poem (page 702). Which poet has described the painting more
   accurately? What are the different themes of the two poems?
3. Why does Auden use the adjectives *innocent* (line 14), *important* (line 17),
   and *expensive delicate* (line 19)? What does each contribute to the theme
   of the poem?

JOHN DRYDEN (1631–1700)

"Why should a foolish marriage vow"

Why should a foolish marriage vow,
   Which long ago was made,
Oblige us to each other now
   When passion is decayed?
We loved, and we loved, as long as we could,   5
   Till our love was loved out in us both;
But our marriage is dead when the pleasure is fled:
   'Twas pleasure first made it an oath.

If I have pleasures for a friend,
   And farther love in store,   10
What wrong has he whose joys did end,
   And who could give no more?
'Tis a madness that he should be jealous of me,
   Or that I should bar him of another:
For all we can gain is to give ourselves pain,   15
   When neither can hinder the other.

1. What is the speaker's tone? How does his tone indicate the poem's theme? What is the sex of the speaker? How do you know?
2. How does the repetition of *love* and *pleasure* in the first stanza reveal the theme of the poem? Does the second stanza present a depressing view of love? Why or why not?

PAUL LAURENCE DUNBAR (1872–1906)

We Wear the Mask

We wear the mask that grins and lies,
It hides our cheeks and shades our eyes,—
This debt we pay to human guile;
With torn and bleeding hearts we smile,
And mouth with myriad subtleties.   5

Why should the world be over-wise,
In counting all our tears and sighs?
Nay, let them only see us, while
    We wear the mask.

We smile, but, O great Christ, our cries   10
To thee from tortured souls arise.
We sing, but oh the clay is vile
Beneath our feet, and long the mile;
But let the world dream otherwise,
    We wear the mask!   15

1. What is the mask a metaphor for? What lines in the poem explain its meaning? What is the underlying tone of the poem? Would you have guessed that Dunbar is a black poet? Why?
2. What activities are represented by the mask? What activities does it hide? Who is the "world"? What is the effect of the repetition of the phrase "We wear the mask"?

ROBERT FROST (1874–1963)

Desert Places

Snow falling and night falling fast, oh fast
In a field I looked into going past,
And the ground almost covered smooth in snow,
But a few weeds and stubble showing last.

The woods around it have it—it is theirs.   5
All animals are smothered in their lairs.
I am too absent-spirited to count;
The loneliness includes me unawares.

And lonely as it is, that loneliness
Will be more lonely ere it will be less—   10
A blanker whiteness of benighted snow
With no expression, nothing to express.

They cannot scare me with their empty spaces
Between stars—on stars where no human race is.
I have it in me so much nearer home   15
To scare myself with my own desert places.

1. What is the function of the bleak winter setting? What does the speaker
   mean when he says, "The loneliness includes me unawares"?
2. In line 10, is the speaker talking only about the setting when he says,
   "A blanker whiteness of benighted snow/With no expression, nothing to
   express"? What else might he be referring to?
3. What are the desert places the speaker refers to in the last line? How
   does the feminine (weak) rhyme enhance the point of the last stanza?

ROBERT FROST (1874–1963)

Mending Wall

Something there is that doesn't love a wall,
That sends the frozen-ground-swell under it,
And spills the upper boulders in the sun;
And makes gaps even two can pass abreast.
The work of hunters is another thing: 5
I have come after them and made repair
Where they have left not one stone on a stone,
But they would have the rabbit out of hiding,
To please the yelping dogs. The gaps I mean,
No one has seen them made or heard them made,   10
But at spring mending-time we find them there.
I let my neighbor know beyond the hill;
And on a day we meet to walk the line
And set the wall between us once again.
We keep the wall between us as we go.   15
To each the boulders that have fallen to each.
And some are loaves and some so nearly balls

We have to use a spell to make them balance:
'Stay where you are until our backs are turned!'
We wear our fingers rough with handling them.   20
Oh, just another kind of outdoor game,
One on a side. It comes to little more:
There where it is we do not need the wall:
He is all pine and I am apple orchard.
My apple trees will never get across   25
And eat the cones under his pines, I tell him.
He only says, 'Good fences make good neighbors.'
Spring is the mischief in me, and I wonder
If I could put a notion in his head:
'*Why* do they make good neighbors? Isn't it   30
Where there are cows? But here there are no cows.
Before I built a wall I'd ask to know
What I was walling in or walling out,
And to whom I was like to give offense.
Something there is that doesn't love a wall,   35
That wants it down.' I could say 'Elves' to him,
But it's not elves exactly, and I'd rather
He said it for himself. I see him there
Bringing a stone grasped firmly by the top
In each hand, like an old-stone savage armed.   40
He moves in darkness as it seems to me,
Not of woods only and the shade of trees.
He will not go behind his father's saying,
And he likes having thought of it so well
He says again, 'Good fences make good neighbors.'   45

1. Frost's poem is in the form of a debate. Which lines express each character's position in the debate? What do walls symbolize in the poem?
2. Why does the speaker compare his neighbor to "an old stone savage armed"? What is the *darkness* of line 41?
3. Is there any evidence in the poem suggesting that the speaker has created a more formidable barrier than his neighbor's stone wall?

GERARD MANLEY HOPKINS (1844–1889)

The Caged Skylark

As a dare-gale skylark scanted in a dull cage
   Man's mounting spirit in his bone-house, mean house,
      dwells—
   That bird beyond the remembering his free fells,
This in drudgery, day-labouring-out life's age.

Though aloft on turf or perch or poor low stage,   5
  Both sing sometímes the sweetest, sweetest spells,
  Yet both droop deadly sómetimes in their cells
Or wring their barriers in bursts of fear or rage.

Not that the sweet-fowl, song-fowl, needs no rest—
Why, hear him, hear him babble and drop down to his nest,   10
  But his own nest, wild nest, no prison.

Man's spirit will be flesh-bound when found at best,
But uncumberéd: meadow-down is not distressed
  For a rainbow footing it nor he for his bónes rísen.

1. A common subject in medieval literature is the debate between body and
   soul. Even though written in the nineteenth century, how does Hopkins'
   poem use this subject to express its theme?
2. What is the opening simile? How is the simile developed in the octave
   of the sonnet?
3. How is the simile resolved in the sestet? What parallel does Hopkins
   draw between the skylark's nest and man's body? How does the dominant figure of speech shift in the final couplet? What does the rainbow
   stand for?
4. Does Hopkins' Catholic belief in the resurrection of the body on Judgment Day make the poem inaccessible to non-believers?

A. E. HOUSMAN (1859–1936)

When I Was One-and-Twenty

When I was one-and-twenty
  I heard a wise man say,
"Give crowns and pounds and guineas
  But not your heart away;
Give pearls away and rubies   5
  But keep your fancy free."
But I was one-and-twenty,
  No use to talk to me.

When I was one-and-twenty
  I heard him say again,   10
"The heart out of the bosom
  Was never given in vain;
'Tis paid with sighs a plenty
  And sold for endless rue."

And I am two-and-twenty,   15
  And oh, 'tis true, 'tis true.

1. What implied event has preceded the speaker's statements? How do you
   know as early as the first stanza?
2. Why does the speaker use commercial imagery ("crowns and pounds and
   guineas") when he is giving his heart away freely? What do "paid for"
   and "sold" imply? Are they merely part of an honest bargain?
3. How do the final lines of the two stanzas sum up the theme?

ROBINSON JEFFERS (1887–1962)

Shine, Perishing Republic

While this America settles in the mold of its vulgarity, heavily
  thickening to empire,
And protest, only a bubble in the molten mass, pops and sighs
  out, and the mass hardens,

I sadly smiling remember that the flower fades to make fruit,
  the fruit rots to make earth.
Out of the mother; and through the spring exultances, ripeness and
  decadence; and home to the mother.

You making haste haste on decay: not blameworthy; life is
  good, be it stubbornly long or suddenly   5
A mortal splendor: meteors are not needed less than mountains:
  shine, perishing republic.

But for my children, I would have them keep their distance
  from the thickening center; corruption
Never has been compulsory, when the cities lie at the monster's
  feet there are left the mountains.

And boys, be in nothing so moderate as in love of man, a clever
  servant, insufferable master.
There is the trap that catches noblest spirits, that caught—
  they say—God, when he walked on earth.   10

1. What is the dominant image of the early part of the poem? Is America
   as a melting pot being alluded to? What does the line "meteors are not
   needed less than mountains" mean?
2. What does Jeffers mean by "home to the mother"? Does the direction
   of the poem shift with the line "corruption has never been compulsory"?

3. What is the monster at whose feet the cities lie? Who are the boys addressed in the final lines? What is Jeffers saying about idealistic reformers?

LINDA PASTAN (b. 1932)

A Symposium: Apples

Eve: Remember a season
of apples, the orchard
full of them, my apron
full of them. One day
we wandered from tree   5
to tree, sharing a basket
feeling the weight of apples
increase between us.
And how your muscles ripened
with all that lifting.   10
I felt them round and hard
under my teeth; white
and sweet the flesh
of men and apples.

Gabriel: Nameless in Eden,   15
the apple itself
was innocent—an ordinary
lunchpail fruit.
Still it reddened
for the way it was used.   20
Afterward the apple
chose for itself
names untrusting
on the tongue: stayman,
gravenstein,   25
northern spy.

The Serpent: Ordinary, innocent
yes. But deep
in each center of whiteness
one dark star . . .   30

Adam: In the icebox
an apple
will keep

for weeks.
Then its skin   35
wrinkles up
like the skin of the old man
I have become,
from a single
bite.   40

1. Why is the poem called a *symposium?* What does each speaker focus on?
   Why?
2. To what does Eve transfer the apple? What does this say about women?
   What does Adam think about? What does this say about men? How are
   both their reactions a consequence of the fall?
3. What is untrusting about the names of apples? According to the arch-
   angel Gabriel, where did apples get their red color? What feature of
   apples does the serpent notice? How does it fit Lucifer's name?

WALLACE STEVENS (1879–1955)

The Emporer of Ice-Cream

Call the roller of big cigars,
The muscular one, and bid him whip
In kitchen cups concupiscent curds.
Let the wenches dawdle in such dress
As they are used to wear, and let the boys   5
Bring flowers in last month's newspapers.
Let be be finale of seem.
The only emperor is the emperor of ice-cream.

Take from the dresser of deal.
Lacking the three glass knobs, the sheet   10
On which she embroidered fantails once
And spread it so as to cover her face.
If her horny feet protrude, they come
To show how cold she is, and dumb.
Let the lamp affix its beam.   15
The only emperor is the emperor of ice-cream.

1. What is the scene of the first stanza? How do the characters, "the roller
   of big cigars" and the "wenches" help you to determine the context?
2. What is the function of the corpse in stanza 2? Why does Stevens emphasize "how cold she is, and dumb"? Are there any qualities that are
   common to ice cream and the corpse?

3. How are the statements "Let be be finale of seem" and "Let the lamp affix its beam" the most explicit statements of the poem's theme? How would you paraphrase the first statement? Who is the Emperor of Ice Cream?

WILLIAM BUTLER YEATS (1865–1939)

The Second Coming

Turning and turning in the widening gyre
The falcon cannot hear the falconer;
Things fall apart; the centre cannot hold;
Mere anarchy is loosed upon the world,
The blood-dimmed tide is loosed, and everywhere   5
The ceremony of innocence is drowned;
The best lack all conviction, while the worst
Are full of passionate intensity.

Surely some revelation is at hand;
Surely the Second Coming is at hand.   10
The Second Coming! Hardly are those words out
When a vast image out of *Spiritus Mundi*
Troubles my sight: somewhere in sands of the desert
A shape with lion body and the head of a man,
A gaze blank and pitiless as the sun,   15
Is moving its slow thighs, while all about it
Reel shadows of the indignant desert birds.
The darkness drops again; but now I know
That twenty centuries of stony sleep
Were vexed to nightmare by a rocking cradle,   20
And what rough beast, its hour come round at last,
Slouches towards Bethlehem to be born?

1. Yeats' conception of history was derived from an Italian historian, Giovanni Baptista Vico, who believed that history moved in 2000-year cycles, called *gyres* by Yeats. What metaphor does Yeats use in the opening stanza to visually embody his theme? How does the metaphor change in the second stanza? To what does the Second Coming refer?
2. What new image emerges out of the desert? To what does the "shape with lion body and head of man" refer? How does the word *slouches* convey the new era of history about to be born?

WRITING ABOUT THEME AND MEANING

Undoubtedly, the most frequently assigned papers in literature classes are **explications of text,** papers explaining the theme of a piece of literature. Because of the great compression of language in poetry, explications of poetic texts are particularly demanding assignments. However, if the task is divided into two stages—the explication of the text and the writing of the explication—you will have an easier time with this assignment.

Because you are primarily concerned with the meaning of the poem (although other elements of poetry like rhythm and form embody and qualify meaning) you will want to get to the starting point by the most direct means. The following steps should help get to the central meaning of the poem, but bear in mind that, for the moment in the initial three steps, you are ignoring what John Ciardi calls *how* the poem means in order to concentrate on *what* it means.

Paraphrase the poem. A paraphrase is a prose summary, written in our own words, of the literal meaning of the poem. You may not actually use material from the paraphrase in the written explication, but paraphrasing is a useful exercise that insures you do not misconstrue some important fact in the poem and thus misinterpret the theme. If the poem contains a dramatic situation, a paraphrase will tell you who is speaking (the persona), who is listening (the auditor), where the action is taking place, what the conflict is, and how it is resolved. The paraphrase does not interpret these details; it merely presents the bare facts. Unfamiliar words and allusions should be looked up in a dictionary or other reference book. The following paragraph is a brief paraphrase of John Keats' "On First Looking into Chapman's Homer" (page 557):

> The speaker of the poem has read widely in Western literature and has discovered the worlds created by many different writers. He had heard about Homer but had yet to read him. When finally he read George Chapman's vigorous translation, he knew the excitement an astronomer must feel when discovering a new planet, or the silent wonder felt by the Spanish explorer and his men when they stood on a peak overlooking the Pacific Ocean. (Keats mistakenly attributed the discovery of the Pacific to Cortez rather than Balboa.)

Locate and explain the poem's dominant figure of speech, if there is one. Because poems are often built around a central metaphor, simile, symbol, or other figure of speech, coming to terms with its meaning is often the most direct way of getting into the poem. Other figurative language may change the initial dominant figure, but it is usually the key to the poem's meaning.

> The dominant figures of speech in Keats' poem are the pair of similes that accompany the implied metaphor of discovery. Keats compares discovering Homer's world to discovering a planet or an ocean: the same sense of excitement and wonder accompanies each discovery.

Explain how other secondary images relate to the theme. What does each image contribute to your understanding of the central meaning emerging out of the dominant figure of speech? Do these images add nuances or qualify the first impression of the theme?

> The emphasis on sight and speech qualifies the metaphor of discovery and suggests that there are various kinds of seeing and different ways of conveying one's discoveries. The speaker, like Chapman, seems to be someone who would "speak out loud and bold." Saying what the experience of discovery is like seems a necessary part of completing it.

Explain what contribution the form makes to the poem's meaning. The form is not an arbitrary "box" containing the poem's statement, but a "shape" growing organically out of the nature of the experience recorded in the poem. Another way to view this relationship between form and meaning is to see the stanza pattern as an organizational unit of meaning.

> Keats' use of the Italian sonnet matches the "problem" he has set for himself: to convey the excitement of discovery. The octave contains the situation of having discovered Homer's poetry, while the sestet offers two analogies to resolve the idea of discovery.

Explain what contribution sound effects make to the poem's meaning. A shift in accent, the yoking together of two words in rhyme, the echoic qualities of consonance, assonance, or onomatopoeia are some of the ways in which the sound of a poem can echo its sense. The relationship between sound and meaning was succinctly put by Robert Frost when he observed, "The sound is the gold in the ore."

> Keats' rhyming pattern supports the conceptual idea of discovery by linking together in rhyme what might seem like disparate observations. For example, by rhyming *ken* with *men*, Keats suggests that the understanding of the astronomer is akin to the "wild surmise," the speechless wonder of Cortez's men. Similarly, the need to communicate discovery is implicit in the rhyme which links *told* with "speak out loud and *bold*."

The steps through which we come to terms with a poem's theme may not follow this particular order, but usually responding to words on the conceptual level occurs prior to responding to their sounds and the shape of the poem. However, some poems—like William Carlos Williams' "The Dance" (page 706) and William Butler Yeats' "Lapis Lazuli" (page 564)—are best approached through their sound or their stanza pattern.

One final word needs to be said about the distinction between the subject of a poem and its theme. We can speak of traditional themes such as the *carpe diem* theme, or humanity's indifference to suffering, or the frustrations of unrequited love, or loneliness, but we are using the term "theme" loosely here. These "themes" are actually subjects, starting points for the treatment of a theme. Two poems may have the same broad subject—racial strife as in Claude McKay's "If We Must Die" (page 758), and Paul Laurence Dunbar's "We Wear the Mask" (782)—but each embodies a very different theme.

Once you are satisfied that you have established the poem's meaning, it is time to start the second step: writing the explication. Since you cannot possibly deal with all the sub-themes a poem may have, nor all the elements that embody those themes, it is best to begin by finding a focus. Assuming the poem has several themes, which one will you write about? What element led you to the poem's theme? Perhaps you might wish to write about how the dominant figure of speech clarifies the poem's major theme. Or perhaps your topic might be how several less important images qualified your view of the theme. Perhaps the poet's technique and how it contributes to the theme might be a suitable topic.

Go through the poem several times, noting how the element you are examining embodies the theme. Find as many examples as possible in the poem. Rather than discussing the poem in the order in which the lines were written, go to the heart of the poem. After all, the casual reader is not as familiar with the poem as you are. You need to remember that, essentially, you are *teaching* the poem and have studied it in more detail than the casual reader. Once the major evidence for a reading of the theme is cited, find other supporting evidence. Organize the material so that it can be discussed in terms of the concepts the poet is presenting. For instance, in Keats' poem, discuss all the sight images and their contributions to the theme. Gathering together evidence into similar categories will give you the paragraph structure and logical organization needed in the paper.

Whatever thematic exploration you choose, explicating a poem's theme can be a rewarding experience. Coming to terms with the poet's experience, perhaps recognizing a parallel experience in your own life, can produce a shock of recognition that makes all the effort of explication worthwhile.

Discovering New Worlds:
Keats' "On First Looking into Chapman's Homer"

On an evening in October 1816, John Keats and his former teacher, Charles Cowden Clarke, stayed up all night reading the Elizabethan poet George Chapman's translation of Homer. When Keats reached home that morning, he wrote his first major sonnet, "On First Looking into Chapman's Homer." While the sonnet seems to be about the experience of reading the Greek epic poet, Keats, like Chapman before him, took the occasion to translate the immediate experience into a larger subject; the excitement of discovery and the need to communicate it.

From the beginning of the poem, Keats translates his personal excitement into tangible form by linking Homer's imagined world with real lands: realms, states, kingdoms, islands, demesnes. The images have an antique, legendary quality about them, as the allusions to fealty and Apollo suggest. The last two lines of the sonnet's octave imply that this ancient land was always there awaiting discovery but it wasn't until Chapman spoke about it (in his translation) that legend ("oft had I been told") became reality.

Keats weaves three other motifs into the octave, each of which is developed in the sonnet's sestet. The first motif is that of seeing. Homer was a blind poet, hence he is given the Homeric epithet, "deep-browed." The adjective connotes, as well, wisdom or seeing with an inward eye. The speaker has seen many kingdoms, but had only been told about Homer's demesne until he "heard Chapman speak out." The second motif, that of telling, is an implicit part of the act of discovery without which the experience is incomplete. The third motif is one of expansiveness, of freedom from confinement denoted by the reference to travelling in line 1, the phrase "wide expanse" in line 5, and the clarity and freshness of the air, "pure serene" in line 7. All three of these motifs are developed in the sestet in which Keats, following the convention of the Italian sonnet, uses two similes, two tangible parallels--the astronomer and the explorer--to communicate the excitement of discovery.

The first simile--comparing the speaker to an astronomer who has discovered a new planet--is the shorter of the two and develops the ideas of seeing and expansiveness. The elation of discovery is given tangible form through the comparison with the astronomer, who is called a "Watcher of the skies." His discovery of the "new planet" is fortuitous, for even though he has been watching, the planet "swims into his ken." Swims develops the implicit ocean image associated with Homer's Aegean Sea between Greece and Turkey, and anticipates the final ocean image of the geographic simile that concludes the poem. All of these images have an expansiveness about them, especially the astronomer's looking heavenward to the home of Apollo. By far the more interesting word, however, is ken, a Scottish archaic term which means both sight and knowledge or understanding, something akin to vision. Like "deep-browed Homer," the astronomer has seen not merely a new thing, but has come to understand the universe in a more comprehensive way.

The second simile brings the theme of the poem to a culmination for all three motifs are contained in the portrait of the explorer standing on the heights of Darien in the isthmus of Panama, seeing the Pacific Ocean from the Americas for the first time. Imagery of sight and wonder dominate the simile: Cortez has "eagle eyes"; from above he stares down at the Pacific; and his men look at each other. Legend becomes reality and the men are speechless, confronted with what is before them. All they can do is communicate through looks their guesses, "wild surmise," about what this means.

There is a reverence for the previously undiscovered in the silence on that peak in Darien; yet Keats the poet, like his predecessors Homer and Chapman, feels impelled to translate into words the wonder of the experience. The sonnet is the poet's attempt to communicate the excitement of discovery, to publish to the world not only the wonder of discovering Homer, but of discovering his own poetic voice and his link with other explorers and discoverers of an expansive world. The chain of discovery continues, for like Cortez, who had stared at the Pacific, Keats had looked into Chapman's Homer. And reading Keats, we, too, share in the wonder of discovery.

SUGGESTIONS FOR WRITING ABOUT THEME

1. The pursuit of an unrealizable ideal is a traditional subject in many romantic poems. Show how Keats develops this subject in "La Belle Dame Sans Merci" (p. 559).
2. Discuss the connection between the theme of unconventionality and the imagery of Emily Dickinson's "Much Madness is divinest Sense" (p. 562).
3. Explore the connections between the mythological allusions and theme in William Butler Yeats' "Leda and the Swan" (p. 563).
4. Discuss the subject of cycles of history and the stanza pattern used in William Butler Yeats' "Lapis Lazuli" (p. 564). How does the organization embody the theme?
5. Write an essay discussing the dominant light and dark imagery and the theme of Robert Lowell's "Children of Light" (p. 569).
6. Investigate how the imagery and parenthetical structure of Denise Levertov's "The Ache of Marriage" (p. 571)
7. Write an essay on Wallace Stevens' "Sunday Morning" (p. 889) as an expression of the philosophy of hedonism, a philosophy that contends that the only way we can know things is through sensual pleasure.
8. Discuss the connection among patterns of imagery, structure and theme in Robert Frost's "To Earthward" (p. 839).
9. Compare and contrast the theme of fatherhood in Sylvia Plath's "Daddy" (p. 726) and Diane Wakoski's "The Father of Our Country" (p. 898).
10. Compare the imagery and the theme of seduction in Richard Wilbur's "Late Aubade" (p. 913) and Andrew Marvell's "To His Coy Mistress" (p. 670).
11. Write an essay explaining how the structure and patterns of imagery in Shakespeare's Sonnet 73 (p. 741) embody the poem's theme.

INTEGRATION AND EVALUATION

AN ANALYSIS OF EMILY DICKINSON'S "A NARROW FELLOW IN THE GRASS"

As we have seen throughout these chapters on poetry, a poem is an intricate verbal pattern that often contains or reflects on a powerful emotional state or situation. As such, good poems present us with both intellectual and emotional challenges when we read them or write about them. If they seem simple, we learn to appreciate their complexity. If they seem complex, we learn to appreciate their simplicity, the way they speak the same words to all of us. We let them live and be themselves, no matter how obscure, variegated, or obvious they may be. So when we analyze them, we must be sure to vivisect them, not dissect. After we have picked it apart, the subject of our analysis should in fact be more alive for us than before we started. Analysis and evaluation should add to, not diminish, the delight we take in a poem.

We can help ourselves toward this increased pleasure by a careful integration of the many kinds of impressions a poem makes. When we read any poem carefully, we are likely to notice at least three kinds of effects simultaneously. First are those individual effects—such as rhyme, meter, sound devices, striking images—which stand out or arrest our attention as we read. Second come the effects that arise from the nature of the poem's persona and the dramatic situation in which he or she has been placed. These unfold over the course of the poem, so we must pay careful attention to accumulation of meaning, change, and development if we are to fully understand them. A third kind of effect is the one we perceive after we finish the poem, its overall effect. This is difficult to define, but it obviously includes what we customarily call the theme of the poem or its meaning. This theme, which is usually governed or supported by the tone of the poem, will often seem to waver between the universal and the particular. A poem, by attempting to tell us something in a new *way*, tells us something *new*.

A carefully integrated explication of a poem will show us the interrelationships among all these effects; will show, that is, the connections between the means and the ends of the poem. An explication is an explanation that shows how the whole of a poem exceeds the sum of its parts. To better understand this apparent paradox, think of floor tiles, each of which contains part of a design that only emerges when the tiles are laid in their proper order. This design exceeds any arrangement of the parts except itself.

A careful explication will put the writer in a position to begin to make tentative judgments of the quality of the work. Judging quality is of course difficult. What kinds of questions can we ask, what kinds of criteria can we apply, that will cut through the defenses that individual tastes, predispositions, and prejudices have set up? Though perhaps no answers to this question can be final, we might suggest the following as tentative criteria.

1. The poem must have unity. That is, it should be a single rhetorical "performance" that all of the parts support and to which all of the parts are subordinate.
2. The poem must be coherent. It must have a principle of order, even if this principle is apparent disorderliness. It must be designed.
3. The poem must be inevitable. That is, nothing in it should be insignificant or expendable.
4. The poem must exhibit appropriate technical effects. These effects

should not contradict the unity of the poem. Furthermore, one kind of effect should not cancel out another. A somber poem, for instance, should not be written in a singsong meter unless the writer is being ironic or creating surprise through the use of an apparently contradictory rhythm.

5. The poem should have both emotive and rational impact, ideally at the same time and for the same reasons. Poems need not make profound philosophical statements, but they should provide both sudden and durable insights about some aspect of human experience.

6. The poem should extend beyond itself. That is, it should activate our sense of the potentiality of language in general and of the traditions which it either follows or augments.

Predictably, these may seem like difficult criteria to apply. But they all concern aspects of a somewhat complex common sense. They concern what the poem is and what it does. Most explications will touch on ideas related to all six of these points. We can show how this is the case by explaining how one might undertake an explication of Emily Dickinson's short poem "A narrow Fellow in the Grass." See page 561.

Your first task of course is to read and reread the poem, look up any unfamiliar words, and get a general sense of the subject, the situation, and, so far as possible, the tone and meaning of the poem. You may also want to try to paraphrase the poem, put it into your own words to get a solid grasp of the sensible statements it makes. Read the poem again in light of what you have discovered through the paraphrase.

All of these tasks are preliminary to your actual analysis. First, get a sense of the natural parts into which the poem divides. This will tell you something about the rhetorical principles underlying the poem and will be your first step toward appreciating its unity. In the case of Dickinson's poem, you might notice that the first two stanzas make general statements concerning the presence and movements of the snake in the grass. Notice that Dickinson uses the pronoun "you" to show that anyone, not just the speaker of the poem, could readily have seen such a sight as the snake. The middle, longer stanza of the poem concerns the speaker's familiarity with the snake from his own boyhood. (Uncustomarily, Dickinson has used a male persona.)

The last two stanzas concern the speaker's feelings for "Nature's People." But note the contrast between the two stanzas: the first shows the cordiality with which he views most animals, but the second shows that he finds the snake threatening. The five stanzas could be outlined this way:

1. general familiarity with snake
2. description of snake's movements
3. speaker's boyhood familiarity with snakes
4. speaker's cordiality with most animals
5. threatening aspect of snake

Viewed in this way, the poem moves from the general to the particular—that is, from experiences anyone might have to experiences the speaker has had. Furthermore, the poem relies on the contrast between the benign and the threatening aspects of nature. Discovering these two rhetorical principles will help you make more sense of the poem as you continue to analyze it and may well suggest a way in which you can organize this analysis. The 2–1–2 organization of the stanzas might suggest three parts to your analysis.

Just as importantly, your discovery of the rhetorical principles of the poem will help you appreciate its unity and coherence. Its unity revolves around the threatening aspect of the "snake in the grass," a hidden danger that surprises us. Its coherence arises from an increasingly sharp focus on a particular snake and the speaker's feelings about it.

Once these general features of the poem are clearly understood (and most poems will have a similar unity and direction of movement), the details will often fall into place. At this point you might move onto considerations of rhythm, language, imagery, and sound which help to support Dickinson's general meaning. Take still another look at the poem and decide which features seem in any way remarkable. Chances are that doing so will help provide the additional data you need to substantiate your general description of the poem.

But what features of Dickinson's poem could be considered striking? Do these features in any way support our general findings about it? Among those you might have noticed are its rhythm, its sentence structure, its imagery, and its sound. The rhythm of the poem, including Dickinson's frequent use of enjambment, give the poem a fluid motion similar to the snake's. Moreover, the changes in the number of syllables from stanza to stanza serve to reinforce the differences between the first two stanzas (made up of alternating lines of 8 and 6 syllables) and the last three (made up of alternating lines of 7 and 6 syllables). This shift accompanies the change from the *you* stanzas of the poem to the *I* stanzas and serves to intensify the speaker's concentration on his own experiences.

Dickinson also uses internal punctuation to vary both the rhythm and the patterns of her sentences. This again suggests the fluid, side-to-side, but occasionally erratic motion of the snake. The grammatical inversion in line four ("His notice sudden is") serves to achieve emphasis and bring us up short, just as though we had suddenly seen a snake while walking through tall grass.

You might also see, as you continue to consider the parts of the poem in light of the general features and meaning you noticed originally, that although the imagery of the poem is somewhat spare, it develops in a way that supports the increasingly threatening view of the snake. In the second stanza it is merely a "spotted shaft." In the third stanza the coldness of the snake is emphasized by reference to the ground it prefers. Moreover, it is now compared to a whip, a more sinister image than the spotted shaft. The final images of the snake in the last stanza concern the effect that seeing it has on the speaker. These effects are decidedly negative. "Tighter breathing," with its suggestion of choking or constriction, shows the immediate physical impact the snake has on the speaker. "Zero at the Bone," however, suggests a far more fundamental fearsomeness. It is as though the speaker, in the presence of the snake, feels a sense of annihilation. This sense of foreboding and emptiness—the real subjects of the poem—is underscored by the long, somber syllables of *zero* and *bone*.

So far, then, you as the analyst of Dickinson's poem would have gathered both general and specific information about the structure and theme of the poem and about its technical details. You need not have written a word of your analysis, although you may have taken some notes on your discoveries. These must now be conveyed in a suitable form. Each poem will suggest a different form for the essay that analyzes it, so be flexible and pay attention to what you have actually found out. In the case of Dickinson's poem, two possible methods of organizing your paper seem to have been suggested by the discoveries made about it.

First you could organize your analysis, so to speak, "stem to stern"; that is, you could divide your written analysis into sections that correspond to the "natural" divisions of the poem mentioned above, then work through the poem chronologically, explaining the fine points of your analysis along the way. Or you could organize your analysis on the basis of the poem's components—organization, rhetoric, rhythm, imagery, sound—and use your perception of the theme of the poem as something like a thesis statement to give your paper unity. Either way, you are proceeding to an integrated analysis that accounts for much that is important in the poem and which has sufficient evidence to support your generalizations about it.

As you can perhaps sense, the process of analyzing the poem contains, though latently, your first tentative judgments about it. The process of evaluating the poem should ideally occur simultaneously with the analysis. This will lend conviction to your evaluation and insure that you have as much information to support your judgments as you do your description of the poem. As we have seen in the analytical remarks above, Dickinson's poem displays a wealth of technical features (rhythm, grammar, imagery) that all work to support the poem and make it a unified whole. The poem is a single coherent performance whose parts work together to establish in our minds a meaning or a situation to which we respond both rationally and emotionally. Moreover, the poem as a whole, and particularly the last stanza, activates our sense of the powerful emotional impact of the natural world upon the human mind. The conventional associations of the snake with Satan, and the Biblical precedents investing the snake with a kind of evil significance, only serve to heighten the power of this impact. Dickinson is writing about the effect of a snake upon a single individual, but her powerful description reminds us of the forces of malevolence loose in the world, and how they can present themselves to us with frightful suddenness.

The foregoing has not been intended to imply that Dickinson's performance is perfect. One of your tasks as a critical reader is to point out the faults or weakness of the poem you are analyzing, not just its strengths or beauties. For instance, is the lilting, "greeting card" rhythm consistent with the threatening subject, or is Dickinson possibly using it for ironic effect? Is there occasional coyness of expression, as in "Nature's People"? Does the relative neutrality of some of the language (*unbraiding* for instance) seem to contradict the sinister impression or tone of the poem by distracting the reader from the threatening nature of the snake?

Your answers to these questions may support a positive or a negative judgment of the poem. That, fortunately, is up to you to decide. That there can be disagreements about both the details of a poem and its overall meaning remains one of the principal pleasures and challenges of reading poetry in the first place. Your attempts to describe, analyze, interpret, and evaluate the poems you read, and to state your findings in an organized and integrated way, should only serve to enhance the pleasures and address the challenges.

SECTION

4

Poems for Further Reading

ANONYMOUS (15TH CENTURY)

Edward

I

"Why does your brand sae drap wi' bluid,
    Edward, Edward,
Why does your brand sae drap wi' bluid,
  And why sae sad gang ye, O?"
"O I ha'e killed my hawk sae guid,   5
    Mither, mither,
O I ha'e killed my hawk sae guid,
  And I had nae mair but he, O."

II

"Your hawke's bluid was never sae reid,
    Edward, Edward,   10
Your hawke's bluid was never sae reid,
  My dear son I tell thee, O."
"O I ha'e killed my reid-roan steed,
    Mither, mither,
O I ha'e killed my reid-roan steed,   15
  That erst was sae fair and free, O."

III

"Your steed was auld, and ye ha'e gat mair,
    Edward, Edward,

Your steed was auld, and ye ha'e gat mair,
   Some other dule ye drie, O." 20
"O I ha'e killed my fader dear,
   Mither, mither,
O I ha'e killed my fader dear,
   Alas, and wae is me, O!"

IV

"And whatten penance wul ye drie for that, 25
   Edward, Edward?
And whatten penance wul ye dree for that,
   My dear son, now tell me O?"
"I'll set my feet in yonder boat,
   Mither, mither, 30
I'll set my feet in yonder boat,
   And I'll fare over the sea, O."

V

"And what wul ye do wi' your towers and your ha',
   Edward, Edward?
And what wul ye do wi' your towers and your ha', 35
   That were sae fair to see, O?"
"I'll let them stand tul they down fa',
   Mither, mither,
I'll let them stand tul they down fa',
   For here never mair maun I be, O." 40

VI

"And what wul ye leave to your bairns and your wife,
   Edward, Edward?
And what wul ye leave to your bairns and your wife,
   Whan ye gang over the sea, O?"
"The warlde's room, let them beg thrae life, 45
   Mither, mither,
The warlde's room, let them beg thrae life,
   For them never mair wul I see, O."

VII

"And what wul ye leave to your ain mither dear,
   Edward, Edward? 50
And what wul ye leave to your ain mither dear,

My dear son, now tell me, O?"
"The curse of hell frae me sall ye bear,
    Mither, mither,
The curse of hell frae me sall ye bear,   55
    Sic counsels ye gave to me, O."

ANONYMOUS (15TH CENTURY)

The Wife of Usher's Well

I

There lived a wife at Usher's Well,
    And a wealthy wife was she;
She had three stout and stalwart sons,
    And sent them o'er the sea.

II

They hadna been a week from her,   5
    A week but barely ane,
Whan word came to the carlin wife
    That her three sons were gane.

III

They hadna been a week from her,
    A week but barely three,   10
Whan word came to the carlin wife
    That her sons she'd never see.

IV

"I wish the wind may never cease,
    Nor fashes in the flood,
Till my three sons come hame to me,   15
    In earthly flesh and blood."

V

It fell about the martinmass,
    When nights are lang and mirk,
The carlin wife's three sons came hame,
    And their hats were o' the birk.   20

VI

It neither grew in syke nor ditch,
   Nor yet in any sheugh;
But at the gates o' paradise,
   That birk grew fair eneugh.

VII

"Blow up the fire, my maidens,   25
   Bring water from the well;
For a' my house shall feast this night,
   Since my three sons are well."

VIII

And she has made to them a bed,
   She's made it large and wide,   30
And she's ta'en her mantle her about,
   Sat down at the bed-side.

IX

Up then crew the red, red cock,
   And up and crew the gray;
The eldest to the youngest said,   35
   " 'T is time we were away."

X

The cock he hadna crawed but once,
   And clapped his wings at a',
When the youngest to the eldest said,
   "Brother, we must awa'.   40

XI

"The cock doth craw, the day doth daw,
   The channerin' worm doth chide;
Gin we be missed out o' our place,
   A sair pain we maun bide.

XII

"Fare ye weel, my mother dear!   45
   Fareweel to barn and byre!

And fare ye weel, the bonny lass,
  That kindles my mother's fire!"

JOHN ASHBERY (b. 1927)

Pyrography

Out here on Cottage Grove it matters. The galloping
Wind balks at its shadow. The carriages
Are drawn forward under a sky of fumed oak.
This is America calling:
The mirroring of state to state, 5
Of voice to voice on the wires,
The force of colloquial greetings like golden
Pollen sinking on the afternoon breeze.
In service stairs the sweet corruption thrives;
The page of dusk turns like a creaking revolving stage in 10
  Warren, Ohio.

If this is the way it is let's leave,
They agree, and soon the slow boxcar journey begins,
Gradually accelerating until the gyrating fans of suburbs
Enfolding the darkness of cities are remembered
Only as a recurring tic. And midway 15
We meet the disappointed, returning ones, without its
Being able to stop us in the headlong night
Toward the nothing of the coast. At Bolinas
The houses doze and seem to wonder why through the
Pacific haze, and the dreams alternately glow and grow dull. 20
Why be hanging on here? Like kites, circling,
Slipping on a ramp of air, but always circling?
But the variable cloudiness is pouring it on,
Flooding back to you like the meaning of a joke.
The land wasn't immediately appealing; we built it 25
Partly over with fake ruins, in the image of ourselves:
An arch that terminates in mid-keystone, a crumbling stone
  pier
For laundresses, an open-air theater, never completed
And only partially designed. How are we to inhabit
This space from which the fourth wall is invariably missing, 30
As in a stage-set or dollhouse, except by staying as we are,
In lost profile, facing the stars, with dozens of as yet
Unrealized projects, and a strict sense
Of time running out, of evening presenting

The tactfully folded-over bill? And we fit   35
Rather too easily into it, become transparent,
Almost ghosts. One day
The birds and animals in the pasture have absorbed
The color, the density of the surroundings,
The leaves are alive, and too heavy with life.   40

A long period of adjustment followed.
In the cities at the turn of the century they knew about it
But were careful not to let on as the iceman and the milkman
Disappeared down the block and the postman shouted
His daily rounds. The children under the trees knew it   45
But all the fathers returning home
On streetcars after a satisfying day at the office undid it:
The climate was still floral and all the wallpaper
In a million homes all over the land conspired to hide it.
One day we thought of painted furniture, of how   50
It just slightly changes everything in the room
And in the yard outside, and how, if we were going
To be able to write the history of our time, starting with
        today,
It would be necessary to model all these unimportant details
So as to be able to include them; otherwise the narrative   55
Would have that flat, sandpapered look the sky gets
Out in the middle west toward the end of summer,
The look of wanting to back out before the argument
Has been resolved, and at the same time to save appearances
So that tomorrow will be pure. Therefore, since we have to   60
    do our business
In spite of things, why not make it in spite of everything?
That way, maybe the feeble lakes and swamps
Of the back country will get plugged into the circuit
And not just the major events but the whole incredible
Mass of everything happening simultaneously and pairing   65
    off,
Channeling itself into history, will unroll
As carefully and as casually as a conversation in the next
    room,
And the purity of today will invest us like a breeze,
Only be hard, spare, ironical: something one can
Tip one's hat to and still get some use out of.   70

The parade is turning into our street.
My stars, the burnished uniforms and prismatic
Features of this instant belong here. The land

Is pulling away from the magic, glittering coastal towns
To an aforementioned rendezvous with August and   75
  December.
The hunch is it will always be this way,
The look, the way things first scared you
In the night light, and later turned out to be,
Yet still capable, all the same, of a narrow fidelity
To what you and they wanted to become;   80
No sighs like Russian music, only a vast unravelling
Out toward the junctions and to the darkness beyond
To these bare fields, built at today's expense.

MARGARET ATWOOD (b. 1939)

The Animals in That Country

In that country the animals
have the faces of people:
the ceremonial
cats possessing the streets

the fox run   5
politely to earth, the huntsmen
standing around him, fixed
in the tapestry of manners

the bull, embroidered
with blood and given   10
an elegant death, trumpets, his name
stamped on him, heraldic brand
because

(when he rolled
on the sand, sword in his heart, the teeth   15
in his blue mouth were human)

he is really a man

even the wolves, holding resonant
conversations in their
forests thickened with legend.   20

          In this country the animals
          have the faces of
          animals.

Their eyes
flash once in car headlights   25
and are gone.

Their deaths are not elegant.

They have the faces of
no-one.

W. H. AUDEN (1902–1973)

The Unknown Citizen

(To JS/07/M378
This Marble Monument
Is Erected by the State)

He was found by the Bureau of Statistics to be
One against whom there was no official complaint,
And all the reports on his conduct agree
That, in the modern sense of an old-fashioned world, he was a saint,
For in everything he did he served the Greater Community.   5
Except for the War till the day he retired
He worked in a factory and never got fired,
But satisfied his employers, Fudge Motors Inc.
Yet he wasn't a scab or odd in his views,
For his Union reports that he paid his dues,   10
(Our report on his Union shows it was sound)
And our Social Psychology workers found
That he was popular with his mates and liked a drink.
The Press are convinced that he bought a paper every day
And that his reactions to advertisements were normal in every way. 15
Policies taken out in his name prove that he was fully insured,
And his Heatlh-card shows he was once in hospital but left it cured.
Both Producers Research and High-Grade Living declare
He was fully sensible to the advantages of the Installment Plan
And had everything necessary to the Modern man,   20
A phonograph, a radio, a car and a frigidaire.
Our researchers into Public Opinion are content
That he held the proper opinions for the time of year;
When there was peace, he was for peace, when there was war, he
     went.
He was married and added five children to the population,   25
Which our Eugenist says was the right number for a parent of his
     generation,

And our teachers report that he never interfered with their education.
Was he free? Was he happy? The question is absurd:
Had anything been wrong, we should certainly have heard.

The Fall of Rome

For Cyril Connolly

The piers are pummelled by the waves;
In a lonely field the rain
Lashes an abandoned train;
Outlaws fill the mountain caves.

Fantastic grow the evening gowns;   5
Agents of the Fisc pursue
Absconding tax-defaulters through
The sewers of provincial towns.

Private rites of magic send
The temple prostitutes to sleep;   10
All the literati keep
An imaginary friend.

Cerebrotonic Catos may
Extol the Ancient Disciplines,
But the muscle-bound Marines   15
Mutiny for food and pay.

Caesar's double-bed is warm
As an unimportant clerk
Writes I DO NOT LIKE MY WORK
On a pink official form.   20

Unendowed with wealth or pity,
Little birds with scarlet legs,
Sitting on their speckled eggs,
Eye each flu-infected city.

Altogether elsewhere, vast   25
Herds of reindeer move across
Miles and miles of golden moss,
Silently and very fast.

AMIRI BARAKA [LEROI JONES] (b. 1934)

Black Art

Poems are bullshit unless they are
teeth or trees or lemons piled
on a step. Or black ladies dying
of men leaving nickel hearts
beating them down. Fuck poems   5
and they are useful, they shoot
come at you, love what you are,
breathe like wrestlers, or shudder
strangely after pissing. We want live
words of the hip world live flesh &   10
coursing blood. Hearts Brains
Souls splintering fire. We want poems
like fists beating niggers out of Jocks
or dagger poems in the slimy bellies
of the owner-jews. Black poems to   15
smear on girdlemamma mulatto bitches
whose brains are red jelly stuck
between 'lizabeth taylor's toes. Stinking
Whores! We want "poems that kill."
Assassin poems, Poems that shoot   20
guns. Poems that wrestle cops into alleys
and take their weapons leaving them dead
with tongues pulled out and sent to Ireland. Knockoff
poems for dope selling wops or slick half white
politicians. Airplane poems. rrrrrrrrrrrrrrrrrrrr   25
rrrrrrrrrrr. . . .tuhtuhtuhtuhtuhtuhtuhtuhtuh. . . .
rrrrrrrrrrrrrrr . . .Setting fire and death to
whities ass. Look at the Liberal
Spokesman for the jews clutch his throat
& puke himself into eternity . . . rrrrrrrrrr   30
There's a negroleader pinned to
a bar stool in Sardi's eyeballs melting
in hot flame. Another negroleader
on the steps of the white house one
kneeling between the sheriff's thighs   35
negotiating cooly for his people.
Aggh . . . stumbles across the room . . .
Put it on him, poem. Strip him naked
to the world! Another bad poem cracking
steel knuckles in a jewlady's mouth   40

Poem scream poison gas on beasts in green berets
Clean out the world of virtue and love,
Let there be no love poems written
until love can exist freely and
cleanly. Let Black People understand   45
that they are the lovers and the sons
of lovers and warriors and sons
of warriors Are poems & poets &
all the loveliness here in the world.

We want a black poem. And a   50
Black World.
Let the world be a Black Poem
And Let All Black People Speak This Poem
Silently

or LOUD   55

WENDELL BERRY (b. 1934)

The Man Born to Farming

The grower of trees, the gardener, the man born to farming,
whose hands reach into the ground and sprout,
to him the soil is a divine drug. He enters into death
yearly, and comes back rejoicing. He has seen the light lie down
in the dung heap, and rise again in the corn.   5
His thought passes along the row ends like a mole.
What miraculous seed has he swallowed
that the unending sentence of his love flows out of his mouth
like a vine clinging in the sunlight, and like water
descending in the dark?   10

ELIZABETH BISHOP (1911–1979)

The Map

Land lies in water; it is shadowed green.
Shadows, or are they shallows, at its edges
showing the line of long sea-weeded ledges
where weeds hang to the simple blue from green.
Or does the land lean down to lift the sea from under,   5
drawing it unperturbed around itself?

Along the fine tan sandy shelf
is the land tugging at the sea from under?

The shadow of Newfoundland lies flat and still.
Labrador's yellow, where the moony Eskimo   10
has oiled it. We can stroke these lovely bays,
under a glass as if they were expected to blossom,
or as if to provide a clean cage for invisible fish.
The names of seashore towns run out to sea,
the names of cities cross the neighboring mountains   15
—the printer here experiencing the same excitement
as when emotion too far exceeds its cause.
These peninsulas take the water between thumb and finger
like women feeling for the smoothness of yard-goods.

Mapped waters are more quiet than the land is,   20
lending the land their waves' own conformation:
and Norway's hare runs south in agitation,
profiles investigate the sea, where land is.
Are they assigned, or can the countries pick their colors?
—What suits the character or the native waters best.   25
Topography displays no favorites; North's as near as West.
More delicate than the historians' are the map-makers' colors.

ROBERT BLY (b. 1926)

Mourning Pablo Neruda

Water is practical,
especially in
August.
Faucet water
that drops   5
into the buckets
I carry
to the young
willow trees
whose leaves have been eaten   10
off by grasshoppers.
Or this jar of water
that lies next to me
on the carseat
as I drive to my shack.   15
When I look down,

the seat all
around the jar
is dark,
for water doesn't intend   20
to give, it gives
anyway,
and the jar of water
lies
there quivering   25
as I drive
through a countryside
of granite quarries,
stones
soon to be shaped   30
into blocks for the dead,
the only
thing they have
left that is theirs.
For the dead remain inside   35
us, as water
remains
inside granite—
hardly at all—
for their job is to   40
go
away,
and not come back,
even when we ask them,
but water   45
comes to us—
it doesn't care
about us, on the way
to the Minnesota River,
to the Mississippi River,   50
to the Gulf,
always closer
to where
it has to be.
No one lays flowers   55
on the grave
of water,
for it is not
here,
it is   60
gone.

EMILY BRONTË (1818–1848)

Remembrance

Cold in the earth—and the deep snow piled above thee,
Far, far removed, cold in the dreary grave!
Have I forgot, my only Love, to love thee,
Severed at last by Time's all-severing wave?

Now, when alone, do my thoughts no longer hover   5
Over the mountains, on that northern shore,
Resting their wings where heath and fern leaves cover
Thy noble heart forever, ever more?

Cold in the earth—and fifteen wild Decembers,
From those brown hills, have melted into spring;   10
Faithful, indeed, is the spirit that remembers
After such years of change and suffering!

Sweet Love of youth, forgive, if I forget thee,
While the world's tide is bearing me along;
Other desires and other hopes beset me,   15
Hopes which obscure, but cannot do thee wrong!

No later light has lightened up my heaven,
No second morn has ever shone for me;
All my life's bliss from thy dear life was given,
All my life's bliss is in the grave with thee.   20

But, when the days of golden dreams had perished,
And even Despair was powerless to destroy,
Then did I learn how existence could be cherished,
Strengthened, and fed without the aid of joy.

Then did I check the tears of useless passion—   25
Weaned my young soul from yearning after thine;
Sternly denied its burning wish to hasten
Down to that tomb already more than mine.

And, even yet, I dare not let it languish,
Dare not indulge in memory's rapturous pain;   30
Once drinking deep of that divinest anguish,
How could I seek the empty world again?

GWENDOLYN BROOKS (b. 1917)

First Fight. Then Fiddle.

First fight. Then fiddle. Ply the slipping string
With feathery sorcery; muzzle the note
With hurting love; the music that they wrote
Bewitch, bewilder. Qualify to sing
Threadwise. Devise no salt, no hempen thing   5
For the dear instrument to bear. Devote
The bow to silks and honey. Be remote
A while from malice and from murdering.
But first to arms, to armor. Carry hate
In front of you and harmony behind.   10
Be deaf to music and to beauty blind.
Win war. Rise bloody, maybe not too late
For having first to civilize a space
Wherein to play your violin with grace.

We Real Cool

The Pool Players.
Seven at the Golden Shovel.

We real cool. We
Left school. We

Lurk late. We
Strike straight. We

Sing sin. We   5
Thin gin. We

Jazz June. We
Die soon.

ROBERT BROWNING (1812–1889)

The Bishop Orders His Tomb at St. Praxed's Church

Rome, 15–

Vanity, saith the preacher, vanity!
Draw round my bed; is Anselm keeping back?
Nephews—sons mine . . . ah God, I know not! Well—
She, men would have to be your mother once,
Old Gandolf envied me, so fair she was!   5
What's done is done, and she is dead beside,
Dead long ago, and I am Bishop since,
And as she died so must we die ourselves,
And thence ye may perceive the world's a dream.
Life, how and what is it? As here I lie   10
In this state-chamber, dying by degrees,
Hours and long hours in the dead night, I ask
"Do I live, am I dead?" peace, peace seems all.
Saint Praxed's ever was the church for peace;
And so, about this tomb of mine. I fought   15
With tooth and nail to save my niche, ye know:
—Old Gandolf cozened me, despite my care;
Shrewd was that snatch from out of the corner south
He graced his carrion with, God curse the same!
Yet still my niche is not so cramped but thence   20
One sees the pulpit o' the epistle-side,
And somewhat of the choir, those silent seats,
And up into the aery dome where live
The angels, and a sunbeam's sure to lurk:
And I shall fill my slab of basalt there,   25
And 'neath my tabernacle take my rest,
With those nine columns round me, two and two,
The odd one at my feet where Anselm stands:
Peach-blossom marble all, the rare, the ripe
As fresh-poured red wine of a mighty pulse.   30
—Old Gandolf with his paltry onion-stone,
Put me where I may look at him! True peach,
Rosy and flawless: how I earned the prize!
Draw close: that conflagration of my church
—What then? So much was saved if aught were missed!   35
My sons, ye would not be my death? Go dig
The white-grape vineyard where the oil-press stood,

Drop water gently till the surface sink,
And if ye find . . . Ah God, I know not, I! . . .
Bedded in store of rotten fig-leaves soft, 40
And corded up in a tight olive-frail,
Some lump, ah God, of *lapis lazuli*,
Big as a Jew's head cut off at the nape,
Blue as a vein o'er the Madonna's breast . . .
Sons, all have I bequeathed you, villas, all, 45
That brave Frascati villa with its bath,
So, let the blue lump poise between my knees,
Like God the Father's globe on both his hands
Ye worship in the Jesu Church so gay,
For Gandolf shall not choose but see and burst! 50
Swift as a weaver's shuttle fleet our years:
Man goeth to the grave, and where is he?
Did I say basalt for my slab, sons? Black—
'Twas ever antique-black I meant! How else
Shall ye contrast my frieze to come beneath? 55
The bas-relief in bronze ye promised me,
Those Pans and Nymphs ye wot of, and perchance
Some tripod, thyrsus, with a vase or so,
The Savior at his sermon on the mount,
Saint Praxed in a glory, and one Pan 60
Ready to twitch the Nymph's last garment off,
And Moses with the tables . . . but I know
Ye mark me not! What do they whisper thee,
Child of my bowels, Anselm? Ah, ye hope
To revel down my villas while I gasp 65
Bricked o'er with beggar's moldy travertine
Which Gandolf from his tomb-top chuckles at!
Nay, boys, ye love me—all of jasper, then!
'T is jasper ye stand pledged to, lest I grieve
My bath must needs be left behind, alas! 70
One block, pure green as a pistachio-nut,
There's plenty jasper somewhere in the world—
And have I not Saint Praxed's ears to pray
Horses for ye, and brown Greek manuscripts,
And mistresses with great smooth marbly limbs? 75
—That's if ye carve my epitaph aright,
Choice Latin, picked phrase, Tully's every word,
No gaudy ware like Gandolf's second line—
Tully, my masters? Ulpian serves his need!
And then how I shall lie through centuries, 80
And hear the blessed mutter of the mass,

And see God made and eaten all day long,
And feel the steady candle-flame, and taste
Good strong thick stupefying incense-smoke!
For as I lie here, hours of the dead night, 85
Dying in state and by such slow degrees,
I fold my arms as if they clasped a crook,
And stretch my feet forth straight as stone can point,
And let the bedclothes, for a mortcloth, drop
Into great laps and folds of sculptor's-work: 90
And as yon tapers dwindle, and strange thoughts
Grow, with a certain humming in my ears,
About the life before I lived this life,
And this life too, popes, cardinals and priests,
Saint Praxed at his sermon on the mount, 95
Your tall pale mother with her talking eyes,
And new-found agate urns as fresh as day,
And marble's language, Latin pure, discreet,
—Aha, ELUCESCEBAT quoth our friend?
No Tully, said I, Ulpian at the best! 100
Evil and brief hath been my pilgrimage.
All *lapis*, all, son! Else I give the Pope
My villas! Will ye ever eat my heart?
Ever your eyes were as a lizard's quick,
They glitter like your mother's for my soul, 105
Or ye would heighten my impoverished frieze,
Piece out its starved design, and fill my vase
With grapes, and add a vizor and a Term,
And to the tripod ye would tie a lynx
That in his struggle throws the thyrsus down, 110
To comfort me on my entablature
Whereon I am to lie till I must ask
"Do I live, am I dead?" There, leave me, there!
For ye have stabbed me with ingratitude
To death—ye wish it—God, ye wish it! Stone— 115
Gritstone, a-crumble! Clammy squares which sweat
As if the corpse they keep were oozing through—
And no more *lapis* to delight the world!
Well, go! I bless ye. Fewer tapers there,
But in a row: and, going, turn your backs 120
—Ay, like departing altar-ministrants,
And leave me in my church, the church for peace,
That I may watch at leisure if he leers—
Old Gandolf, at me, from his onion-stone,
As still he envied me, so fair she was! 125

GEOFFREY CHAUCER (1340?–1400?)

Complaint to His Purse

To you, my purs, and to noon other wight,
Complaine I, for ye be my lady dere.
I am so sory, now that ye be light,
For certes, but if ye make me hevy cheere,
Me were as lief be laid upon my beere;   5
For which unto youre mercy thus I crye:
Beeth hevy again, or elles moot I die.

Now voucheth sauf this day er it be night
That I of you the blisful soun may heere,
Or see youre colour, lik the sonne bright,   10
That of yelownesse hadde nevere peere.
Ye be my life, ye be myn hertes steere,
Queene of confort and of good compaignye:
Beeth hevy again, or elles moot I die.

Ye purs, that been to me my lives light   15
And saviour, as in this world down here,
Out of this tonne helpe me thurgh your might,
Sith that ye wol nat be my tresorere;
For I am shave as neigh as any frere.
But yit I praye unto youre curteisye: 20
Beeth hevy again, or elles moot I die.

Envoy to Henry IV

O conquerour of Brutus Albioun,
Which that by line and free eleccioun
Been verray king, this song to you I sende:
And ye, that mowen alle oure harmes amende,   25
have minde upon my supplicacioun.

AMY CLAMPITT (b. 1920)

Or Consider Prometheus

In 1859 petroleum was discovered in Pennsylvania. Kerosene, petroleum, and paraffin
began rapidly to replace whale oil, sperm oil, and spermaceti wax. . . . Consider
whaling as FRONTIER, *and* INDUSTRY. *A product wanted, men got it: big business.*
The Pacific as sweatshop . . . the whaleship as factory, the whaleboat the preci-
sion instrument. . . .

—CHARLES OLSON, *Call Me Ishmael*

I

Would Prometheus, cursing on his rock
as he considered fire, the smuggled gem
inside the weed stem, and the excesses
since his protracted punishment began,

have cursed the ocean's copious antidote,   5
its lapping, cold, incessant undulance
plowed to shards by wheeling porpoises,
hydrogen-cum-oxygen fanned up in mimicries

of hard carbon, diamond of purest water,
the unforbidden element crosscut by fire,   10
its breakup the absolving smile of rainbows?
Or, considering leviathan, whose blameless

progenitors turned from the shore, from its
seducing orchards, renouncing the prehensile
dangle of a brain all eyes and claws,   15
twittering fishhook strategies of grasp

and mastery, for immersion among moving
declivities, have envied the passivity
whose massive ease is not more than his own
tormented rectitude, immune from drowning?   20

II

How would the great cetaceans, Houyhnhnm
intelligences sans limbs, ungoaded by
the Promethean monkeyshines that gave us
haute cuisine, autos-da-fé and fireworks,

dining al fresco off cuttlefish and krill, 25
serving up baleen-strained plankton, whose
unmanipulative ears explore Olympian parterres
of sonar, devise the ringing calculus

of icebergs, compute the density of ships
as pure experience of hearing—how 30
would these basking reservoirs of fuel,
wax and glycerine have read the trypots

readied for their rendering into tallow
for a thousand candles? How, astronomers
of the invisible, would they have tracked 35
the roaring nimbus of that thieving

appetite, our hunger for the sun, or
charted the harrowing of jet and piston
pterodactyls, robots fed on their successor,
fire-drinking vampires of hydrocarbon? 40

SAMUEL TAYLOR COLERIDGE (1772–1834)

Kubla Khan

Or a Vision in a Dream. A Fragment

In Xanadu did Kubla Khan
A stately pleasure dome decree:
Where Alph, the sacred river, ran
Through caverns measureless to man
   Down to a sunless sea. 5
So twice five miles of fertile ground
With walls and towers were girdled round;
And there were gardens bright with sinuous rills,
Where blossomed many an incense-bearing tree;
And here were forests ancient as the hills, 10
Enfolding sunny spots of greenery.

But oh! that deep romantic chasm which slanted
Down the green hill athwart a cedarn cover!
A savage place! as holy and enchanted
As e'er beneath a waning moon was haunted 15
By woman wailing for her demon lover!
And from this chasm, with ceaseless turmoil seething,

As if this earth in fast thick pants were breathing,
A mighty fountain momently was forced:
Amid whose swift half-intermitted burst   20
Huge fragments vaulted like rebounding hail,
Or chaffy grain beneath the thresher's flail:
And 'mid these dancing rocks at once and ever
It flung up momently the sacred river.
Five miles meandering with a mazy motion   25
Through wood and dale the sacred river ran,
Then reached the caverns measureless to man,
And sank in tumult to a lifeless ocean:
And 'mid this tumult Kubla heard from far
Ancestral voices prophesying war!   30

   The shadow of the dome of pleasure
   Floated midway on the waves;
   Where was heard the mingled measure
   From the fountain and the caves.
It was a miracle of rare device,   35
A sunny pleasure dome with caves of ice!

   A damsel with a dulcimer
   In a vision once I saw:
   It was an Abyssinian maid,
   And on her dulcimer she played,   40
   Singing of Mount Abora.
   Could I revive within me
   Her symphony and song,
   To such a deep delight 'twould win me,
That with music loud and long,   45
I would build that dome in air,
That sunny dome! those caves of ice!
And all who heard should see them there,
And all should cry, Beware! Beware!
His flashing eyes, his floating hair!   50
Weave a circle round him thrice,
And close your eyes with holy dread,
For he on honey-dew hath fed,
And drunk the milk of Paradise.

GREGORY CORSO (b. 1930)

Dream of a Baseball Star

I dreamed Ted Williams
leaning at night
against the Eiffel Tower, weeping.

He was in uniform
and his bat lay at his feet   5
—knotted and twiggy.

'Randall Jarrell says you're a poet!' I cried.
'So do I! I say you're a poet!'

He picked up his bat with blown hands;
stood there astraddle as he would in the batter's box,   10
and laughed! flinging his schoolboy wrath
toward some invisible pitcher's mound
—waiting the pitch all the way from heaven.

It came; hundreds came! all afire!
He swung and swung and swung and connected not one   15
sinker curve hook or right-down-the-middle.
A hundred strikes!
The umpire dressed in strange attire
thundered his judgement: YOU'RE OUT!
And the phantom crowd's horrific boo   20
dispersed the gargoyles from Notre Dame.

And I screamed in my dream:
God! throw thy merciful pitch!
Herald the crack of bats!
Hooray the sharp liner to left!   25
Yea the double, the triple!
Hosannah the home run!

ROBERT CREELEY (b. 1926)

For My Mother: Genevieve Jules Creeley

April 8, 1887–October 7, 1972

Tender, semi-
articulate flickers
of your

presence, all
those years   5
past

now, eighty-
five, impossible to
count them

one by one, like   10
addition, sub-
traction, missing

not one. The last
curled up, in
on yourself,   15

position you take
in the bed, hair
wisped up

on your head, a
top knot, body   20
skeletal, eyes

closed against,
it must be,
further disturbance—

breathing a skim   25
of time, lightly
kicks the intervals—

days, days and
years of it,
work, changes,   30

sweet flesh caught
at the edges,
dignity's faded

dilemma. It
is *your* life, oh   35
no one's

forgotten anything
ever. They want
to make you

happy when   40
they remember. Walk
a little, get

up, now, die
safely,
easily, into   45

singleness, too
tired with it
to keep

on and on.
Waves break at   50
the darkness

under the road, sounds
in the faint
night's softness. Look

at them, catching   55
the light, white
edge as they turn—

always again
and again. Dead
one, two,   60

three hours—
all these minutes
pass. Is it,

was it, ever
you alone
again, how   65

long you kept
at it, your
pride, your

lovely, confusing   70
discretion. Mother, I
love you—for

whatever that
means,
meant—more   75

than I know, body
gave me my
own, generous,

inexorable place
of you. I feel   80
the mouth's sluggish-

ness, slips on
turns of things
said, to you,

too soon, too late,   85
wants to
go back to beginning,

smells of the hospital
room, the doctor
she responds   90

to now, the
order—get me
there. "Death's

let you out—"
comes true,   95
this, that,

endlessly circular
life, and we
came back

to see you one   100
last
time, this

time? Your head
shuddered,
it seemed, your   105

eyes wanted,
I thought,
to see

who it was.
I am here,   110
and will follow.

COUNTEE CULLEN (1903–1946)

Heritage

For Harold Jackman

What is Africa to me:
Copper sun or scarlet sea,
Jungle star or jungle track,
Strong bronzed men, or regal black
Women from whose loins I sprang   5
When the birds of Eden sang?
One three centuries removed
From the scenes his fathers loved,
Spicy grove, cinnamon tree,
What is Africa to me?   10

So I lie, who all day long
Want no sound except the song
Sung by wild barbaric birds
Goading massive jungle herds,
Juggernauts of flesh that pass   15
Trampling tall defiant grass
Where young forest lovers lie,

Plighting troth beneath the sky.
So I lie, who always hear,
Though I cram against my ear   20
Both my thumbs, and keep them there,
Great drums throbbing through the air.
So I lie, whose fount of pride,
Dear distress, and joy allied,
Is my somber flesh and skin,   25
With the dark blood dammed within
Like great pulsing tides of wine
That, I fear, must burst the fine
Channels of the chafing net
Where they surge and foam and fret.   30

Africa? A book one thumbs
Listlessly, till slumber comes.
Unremembered are her bats
Circling through the night, her cats
Crouching in the river reeds,   35
Stalking gentle flesh that feeds
By the river brink; no more
Does the bugle-throated roar
Cry that monarch claws have leapt
From the scabbards where they slept.   40
Silver snakes that once a year
Doff the lovely coats you wear,
Seek no covert in your fear
Lest a mortal eye should see;
What's your nakedness to me?   45
Here no leprous flowers rear
Fierce corollas in the air;
Here no bodies sleek and wet,
Dripping mingled rain and sweat,
Tread the savage measures of   50
Jungle boys and girls in love.
What is last year's snow to me,
Last year's anything? The tree
Budding yearly must forget
How its past arose or set—   55
Bough and blossom, flower, fruit,
Even what shy bird with mute
Wonder at her travail there,
Meekly labored in its hair.
One three centuries removed   60
From the scenes his fathers loved,

Spicy grove, cinnamon tree,
What is Africa to me?

So I lie, who find no peace
Night or day, no slight release   65
From the unremitten beat
Made by cruel padded feet
Walking through my body's street.
Up and down they go, and back,
Treading out a jungle track.   70
So I lie, who never quite
Safely sleep from rain at night—
I can never rest at all
When the rain begins to fall;
Like a soul gone mad with pain   75
I must match its weird refrain;
Ever must I twist and squirm,
Writhing like a baited worm,
While its primal measures drip
Through my body, crying, "Strip!   80
Doff this new exuberance.
Come and dance the Lover's Dance!"
In an old remembered way
Rain works on me night and day.

Quaint, outlandish heathen gods   85
Black men fashion out of rods,
Clay, and brittle bits of stone,
In a likeness like their own,
my conversion came high-priced;
I belong to Jesus Christ,   90
Preacher of humility;
Heathen gods are naught to me.

Father, Son, and Holy Ghost,
So I make an idle boast;
Jesus of the twice-turned cheek,   95
Lamb of God, although I speak
With my mouth thus, in my heart
Do I play a double part.
Ever at Thy glowing altar
Must my heart grow sick and falter,   100
Wishing He I served were black,
thinking then it would not lack
Precedent of pain to guide it,

Let who would or might deride it;
Surely then this flesh would know   105
Yours had borne a kindred woe.
Lord, I fashion dark gods, too,
Daring even to give You
Dark despairing features where,
Crowned with dark rebellious hair,   110
Patience wavers just so much as
Mortal grief compels, while touches
Quick and hot, of anger, rise
To smitten cheek and weary eyes.
Lord, forgive me if my need   115
Sometimes shapes a human creed.
All day long and all night through,
One thing only must I do:
Quench my pride and cool my blood,
Lest I perish in the flood.   120
Lest a hidden ember set
Timber that I thought was wet
Burning like the dryest flax,
Melting like the merest wax,
Lest the grave restore its dead.   125
Not yet has my heart or head
In the least way realized
They and I are civilized.

JAMES DICKEY (b. 1923)

Cherrylog Road

Off highway 106
At Cherrylog Road I entered
The '34 Ford without wheels,
Smothered in kudzu,
With a seat pulled out to run   5
Corn whiskey down from the hills,

And then from the other side
Crept into an Essex
With a rumble seat of red leather
And then out again, aboard   10
A blue Chevrolet, releasing
The rust from its other color,

Reared up on three building blocks.
None had the same body heat;
I changed with them inward, toward   15
The weedy heart of the junkyard,
For I knew that Doris Holbrook
Would escape from her father at noon

And would come from the farm
To seek parts owned by the sun   20
Among the abandoned chassis,
Sitting in each in turn
As I did, leaning forward
As in a wild stock-car race

In the parking lot of the dead.   25
Time after time, I climbed in
And out the other side, like
An envoy or movie star
Met at the station by crickets.
A radiator cap raised its head,   30

Become a real toad or a kingsnake
As I neared the hub of the yard,
Passing through many states,
Many lives, to reach
Some grandmother's long Pierce-Arrow   35
Sending platters of blindness forth

From its nickel hubcaps
And spilling its tender upholstery
On sleepy roaches,
The glass panel in between   40
Lady and colored driver
Not all the way broken out,

The back-seat phone
Still on its hook.
I got in as though to exclaim,   45
"Let us go to the orphan asylum,
John; I have some old toys
For children who say their prayers."

I popped with sweat as I thought
I heard Doris Holbrook scrape   50
Like a mouse in the southern-state sun

That was eating the paint in blisters
From a hundred car tops and hoods.
She was tapping like code,

Loosening the screws,   55
Carrying off headlights,
Sparkplugs, bumpers,
Cracked mirrors and gear-knobs,
Getting ready, already,
To go back with something to show   60

Other than her lips' new trembling
I would hold to me soon, soon,
Where I sat in the ripped back seat
Talking over the interphone,
Praying for Doris Holbrook   65
To come from her father's farm

And to get back there
With no trace of me on her face
To be seen by her red-haired father
Who would change, in the squalling barn,   70
Her back's pale skin with a strop,
Then lay for me

In a bootlegger's roasting car
With a string-triggered 12-gauge shotgun
To blast the breath from the air.   75
Not cut by the jagged windshields,
Through the acres of wrecks she came
With a wrench in her hand,

Through dust where the blacksnake dies
Of boredom, and the beetle knows   80
The compost has no more life.
Someone outside would have seen
The oldest car's door inexplicably
Close from within:

I held her and held her and held her   85
Convoyed at terrific speed
By the stalled, dreaming traffic around us,
So the blacksnake, stiff
With inaction, curved back
Into life, and hunted the mouse   90

With deadly overexcitement,
The beetles reclaimed their field
As we clung, glued together,
With the hooks of the seat springs
Working through to catch us red-handed   95
Amidst the gray breathless batting

That burst from the seat at our backs.
We left by separate doors
Into the changed, other bodies
Of cars, she down Cherrylog Road   100
And I to my motorcycle
Parked like the soul of the junkyard

Restored, a bicycle fleshed
With power, and tore off
Up Highway 106, continually   105
Drunk on the wind in my mouth,
Wringing the handle bar for speed,
Wild to be wreckage forever.

EMILY DICKINSON (1830–1886)

"I died for Beauty"

I died for Beauty—but was scarce
Adjusted in the Tomb
When One who died for Truth, was lain
In an adjoining Room—

He questioned softly "Why I failed"?   5
"For Beauty", I replied—
"And I—for Truth—Themself are One—
We Brethren, are", He said—

And so, as Kinsmen, met a Night—
We talked between the Rooms—   10
Until the Moss had reached our lips—
And covered up—our names—

"I heard a Fly buzz—when I died"

I heard a Fly buzz—when I died—
The Stillness in the Room
Was like the Stillness in the Air—
Between the Heaves of Storm—

The Eyes around—had wrung them dry—   5
And Breaths were gathering firm
For that last Onset—when the King
Be witnessed—in the Room—

I willed my Keepsakes—Signed away
What portion of me be   10
Assignable—and then it was
There interposed a Fly—

With Blue—uncertain stumbling Buzz—
Between the light—and me—
And then the Windows failed—and then   15
I could not see to see—

"The Soul selects her own Society"

The Soul selects her own Society—
Then—shuts the Door—
To her divine Majority—
Present no more—

Unmoved—she notes the Chariots—pausing—   5
At her low Gate—
Unmoved—an Emperor be kneeling
Upon her Mat—

I've known her—from an ample nation—
Choose One—   10
Then—close the Valves of her attention—
Like Stone—

ALAN DUGAN (b. 1923)

Fabrication of Ancestors

*For Old Billy Dugan, Shot in the ass in the
Civil War, My father said.*

The old wound in my ass
has opened up again, but I
am past the prodigies
of youth's campaigns, and weep
where I used to laugh   5
in war's red humors, half
in love with silly-assed pains
and half not feeling them.
I have to sit up with
an indoor unsittable itch   10
before I go down late
and weeping to the storm-
cellar on a dirty night
and go to bed with the worms.
So pull the dirt up over me   15
and make a family joke
for Old Billy Blue Balls,
the oldest private in the world
with two ass-holes and no
place more to go to for a laugh   20
except the last one. Say:
The North won the Civil War
without much help from me
although I wear a proof
of the war's obscenity.   25

RICHARD EBERHART (b. 1904)

The Fury of Aerial Bombardment

You would think the fury of aerial bombardment
Would rouse God to relent; the infinite spaces
Are still silent. He looks on shock-pried faces.
History, even, does not know what is meant.

You would feel that after so many centuries   5
God would give man to repent; yet he can kill

As Cain could, but with multitudinous will,
No farther advanced than in his ancient furies.

Was man made stupid to see his own stupidity?
Is God by definition indifferent, beyond us all?   10
Is the eternal truth man's fighting soul
Wherein the Beast ravens in its own avidity?

Of Van Wettering I speak, and Averill,
Names on a list, whose faces I do not recall
But they are gone to early death, who late in school   15
Distinguished the belt feed lever from the belt holding pawl.

The Groundhog

In June, amid the golden fields,
I saw a groundhog lying dead.
Dead lay he; my senses shook,
And mind outshot our naked frailty.
There lowly in the vigorous summer   5
His form began its senseless change,
And made my senses waver dim
Seeing nature ferocious in him.
Inspecting close his maggots' might
And seething cauldron of his being,   10
Half with loathing, half with a strange love,
I poked him with an angry stick.
The fever arose, became a flame
And Vigour circumscribed the skies,
Immense energy in the sun,   15
And through my frame a sunless trembling.
My stick had done nor good nor harm.
Then stood I silent in the day
Watching the object, as before;
And kept my reverence for knowledge   20
Trying for control, to be still,
To quell the passion of the blood;
Until I had bent down on my knees
Praying for joy in the sight of decay.
And so I left; and I returned   25
In Autumn strict of eye, to see
The sap gone out of the groundhog,
But the bony sodden hulk remained.
But the year had lost its meaning,
And in intellectual chains   30

I lost both love and loathing,
Mured up in the wall of wisdom.
Another summer took the fields again
Massive and burning, full of life,
But when I chanced upon the spot   35
There was only a little hair left,
And bones bleaching in the sunlight
Beautiful as architecture;
I watched them like a geometer,
And cut a walking stick from a birch.   40
It has been three years, now.
There is no sign of the groundhog.
I stood there in the whirling summer,
My hand capped a withered heart,
And thought of China and of Greece,   45
Of Alexander in his tent;
Of Montaigne in his tower,
Of Saint Theresa in her wild lament.

KENNETH FEARING (1902–1961)

Dirge

1–2–3 was the number he played but today the number came 3–2–1;
Bought his Carbide at 30 and it went to 29; had the favorite at
    Bowie but the track was slow—

O executive type, would you like to drive a floating-power, knee-
    action, silk-upholstered six? Wed a Hollywood star? Shoot the   5
    course in 58? Draw to the ace, king, jack?

O fellow with a will who won't take no, watch out for three ciga-
    rettes on the same, single match; O democratic voter born in
    August under Mars, beware of liquidated rails—

Denouement to denouement, he took a personal pride in the certain,   10
    certain way he lived his own, private life,
But nevertheless, they shut off his gas; nevertheless, the bank fore-
    closed; nevertheless, the landlord called; nevertheless, the radio
    broke,

And twelve o'clock arrived just once too often,   15
Just the same he wore one gray tweed suit, bought one straw hat,
    drank one straight Scotch, walked one short step, took one long

look, drew one deep breath,
Just one too many,

And wow he died as wow he lived,   20
Going whop to the office and blooie home to sleep and biff got mar-
    ried and bam had children and oof got fired,
Zowie did he live and zowie did he die,

With who the hell are you at the corner of his casket, and where the
    hell're we going on the right-hand silver knob, and who the hell   25
    cares walking second from the end with an American Beauty
    wreath from why the hell not,

Very much missed by the circulation staff of the New York Evening
    Post; deeply, deeply mourned by the B.M.T.
Wham, Mr. Roosevelt; pow, Sears Roebuck; awk, big dipper; bop,   30
    summer rain;
Bong, Mr., bong, Mr., bong, Mr., bong.

CAROLYN FORCHÉ (b. 1950)

The Memory of Elena

We spend our morning
in the flower stalls counting
the dark tongues of bells
that hang from ropes waiting
for the silence of an hour.   5
We find a table, ask for *paella*,
cold soup and wine, where a calm
light trembles years behind us.

In Buenos Aires only three
years ago, it was the last time his hand   10
slipped into her dress, with pearls
cooling her throat and bells like
these, chipping at the night—

As she talks, the hollow
clopping of a horse, the sound   15
of bones touched together.
The *paella* comes, a bed of rice
and *camarones*, fingers and shells,
the lips of those whose lips

have been removed, mussels   20
the soft blue of a leg socket.

This is not *paella*, this is what
has become of those who remained
in Buenos Aires. This is the ring
of a rifle report on the stones,   25
her hand over her mouth,
her husband falling against her.

These are the flowers we bought
this morning, the dahlias tossed
on his grave and bells   30
waiting with their tongues cut out
for this particular silence.

ROBERT FROST (1874–1963)

Tree at My Window

Tree at my window, window tree,
My sash is lowered when night comes on;
But let there never be curtain drawn
Between you and me.

Vague dream-head lifted out of the ground,   5
And thing next most diffuse to cloud,
Not all your light tongues talking aloud
Could be profound.

But, tree, I have seen you taken and tossed,
And if you have seen me when I slept,   10
You have seen me when I was taken and swept
And all but lost.

That day she put our heads together,
Fate had her imagination about her,
Your head so much concerned with outer,   15
Mine with inner, weather.

To Earthward

Love at the lips was touch
As sweet as I could bear;

And once that seemed too much;
I lived on air

That crossed me from sweet things,   5
The flow of—was it musk
From hidden grapevine springs
Downhill at dusk?

I had the swirl and ache
From sprays of honeysuckle   10
That when they're gathered shake
Dew on the knuckle.

I craved strong sweets, but those
Seemed strong when I was young;
The petal of the rose   15
It was that stung.

Now no joy but lacks salt,
That is not dashed with pain
And weariness and fault;
I crave the stain   20

Of tears, the aftermark
Of almost too much love,
The sweet of bitter bark
And burning clove.

When stiff and sore and scarred   25
I take away my hand
From leaning on it hard
In grass and sand,

The hurt is not enough:
I long for weight and strength   30
To feel the earth as rough
To all my length.

Two Tramps in Mud Time

Out of the mud two strangers came
And caught me splitting wood in the yard.
And one of them put me off my aim
By hailing cheerily "Hit them hard!"
I knew pretty well why he dropped behind   5

And let the other go on a way.
I knew pretty well what he had in mind:
He wanted to take my job for pay.

Good blocks of oak it was I split,
As large around as the chopping block;   10
And every piece I squarely hit
Fell splinterless as a cloven rock.
The blows that a life of self-control
Spares to strike for the common good,
That day, giving a loose to my soul,   15
I spent on the unimportant wood.

The sun was warm but the wind was chill.
You know how it is with an April day
When the sun is out and the wind is still,
You're one month on in the middle of May.   20
But if you so much as dare to speak,
A cloud comes over the sunlit arch,
A wind comes off a frozen peak,
And you're two months back in the middle of March.

A bluebird comes tenderly up to alight   25
And turns to the wind to unruffle a plume,
His song so pitched as not to excite
A single flower as yet to bloom.
It is snowing a flake: and he half knew
Winter was only playing possum.   30
Except in color he isn't blue,
But he wouldn't advise a thing to blossom.

The water for which we may have to look
In summertime with a witching wand,
In every wheelrut's now a brook,   35
In every print of a hoof a pond.
Be glad of water, but don't forget
The lurking frost in the earth beneath
That will steal forth after the sun is set
And show on the water its crystal teeth.   40

The time when most I loved my task
These two must make me love it more
By coming with what they came to ask.
You'd think I never had felt before
The weight of an ax-head poised aloft,   45

The grip on earth of outspread feet,
The life of muscles rocking soft
And smooth and moist in vernal heat.

Out of the woods two hulking tramps
(From sleeping God knows where last night,   50
But not long since in the lumber camps).
They thought all chopping was theirs of right.
Men of the woods and lumberjacks,
They judged me by their appropriate tool.
Except as a fellow handled an ax   55
They had no way of knowing a fool.

Nothing on either side was said.
They knew they had but to stay their stay
And all their logic would fill my head:
As that I had no right to play   60
With what was another man's work for gain.
My right might be love but their was need.
And where the two exist in twain
Theirs was the better right—agreed.

But yield who will to their separation,   65
My object in living is to unite
My avocation and my vocation
As my two eyes make one in sight.
Only where love and need are one,
And the work is play for mortal stakes,   70
Is the deed ever really done
For Heaven and the future's sakes.

Acquainted With the Night

I have been one acquainted with the night.
I have walked out in rain—and back in rain.
I have outwalked the furthest city light.

I have looked down the saddest city lane.
I have passed by the watchman on his beat   5
And dropped my eyes, unwilling to explain.

I have stood still and stopped the sound of feet
When far away an interrupted cry
Came over houses from another street,

But not to call me back or say good-by;   10
And further still at an unearthly height
One luminary clock against the sky

Proclaimed the time was neither wrong nor right.
I have been one acquainted with the night.

NIKKI GIOVANNI (b. 1943)

Nikki–Rosa

childhood   remembrances are always a drag
if you're Black
you always remember things like living in Woodlawn
with no inside toilet
and if you become famous or something   5
they never talk about how happy you were to have your mother
all to yourself and
how good the water felt when you got your bath from one of those
big tubs that folk in chicago barbecue in
and somehow when you talk about home   10
it never gets across how much you
understood their feelings
as the whole family attended meetings about Hollydale
and even though you remember
your biographers never understand   15
your father's pain as he sells his stock
and another dream goes
and though you're poor it isn't poverty that
concerns you
and though they fought a lot   20
it isn't your father's drinking that makes any difference
but only that everybody is together and you
and your sister have happy birthdays and very good christmasses
and I really hope no white person ever has cause to write about me
because they never understand Black love is Black wealth and they'll   25
probably talk about my hard childhood and never understand that
all the while I was quite happy

LOUISE GLÜCK (b. 1943)

Horse

What does the horse give you
that I cannot give you?

I watch you when you are alone,
when you ride into the field behind the dairy,
your hands buried in the mare's   5
dark mane.

Then I know what lies behind your silence:
scorn, hatred of me, of marriage. Still,
you want me to touch you; you cry out
as brides cry, but when I look at you I see   10
there are no children in your body.
Then what is there?

Nothing, I think. Only haste
to die before I die.

In a dream, I watched you ride the horse   15
over the dry fields and then
dismount; you two walked together;
in the dark, you had no shadows.
But I felt them coming toward me
since at night they go anywhere,   20
they are their own masters.

Look at me. You think I don't understand?
What is the animal
if not passage out of this life?

ROBERT GRAVES (1895–1985)

Down, Wanton, Down!

Down, wanton, down! Have you no shame
That at the whisper of Love's name,
Or Beauty's, presto! up you raise
Your angry head and stand at gaze?

Poor bombard-captain, sworn to reach   5
The ravelin and effect a breach—
Indifferent what you storm or why,
So be that in the breach you die!

Love may be blind, but Love at least
Knows what is man and what mere beast;   10
Or Beauty wayward, but requires
More delicacy from her squires.

Tell me, my witless, whose one boast
Could be your staunchness at the post,
When were you made a man of parts   15
To think fine and profess the arts?

Will many-gifted Beauty come
Bowing to your bald rule of thumb,
Or Love swear loyalty to your crown?
Be gone, have done! Down, wanton, down!   20

THOMAS HARDY (1840–1928)

The Man He Killed

"Had he and I but met
    By some old ancient inn,
We should have sat us down to wet
    Right many a nipperkin!

"But ranged as infantry,   5
    And staring face to face,
I shot at him as he at me,
    And killed him in his place.

"I shot him dead because—
    Because he was my foe,   10
Just so: my foe of course he was;
    That's clear enough; although

"He thought he'd 'list, perhaps
    Off-hand like—just as I—
Was out of work—had sold his traps—   15
    No other reason why.

"Yes; quaint and curious war is!
   You shoot a fellow down
You'd treat if met where any bar is,
   Or help to half-a-crown."   20

The Darkling Thrush

I leant upon a coppice gate
   When Frost was specter-gray,
And Winter's dregs made desolate
   The weakening eye of day.
The tangled bine-stems scored the sky   5
   Like strings of broken lyres,
And all mankind that haunted nigh
   Had sought their household fires.

The land's sharp features seemed to be
   The Century's corpse outleant,   10
His crypt the cloudy canopy,
   The wind his death-lament.
The ancient pulse of germ and birth
   Was shrunken hard and dry,
And every spirit upon earth   15
   Seemed fervorless as I.

At once a voice arose among
   The bleak twigs overhead
In a full-hearted evensong
   Of joy illimited;   20
An aged thrush, frail, gaunt, and small,
   In blast-beruffled plume,
Had chosen thus to fling his soul
   Upon the growing gloom.

So little cause for carolings   25
   Of such ecstatic sound
Was written on terrestrial things
   Afar or nigh around,
That I could think there trembled through
   His happy good-night air   30
Some blessed Hope, whereof he knew
   And I was unaware.
                   December 31, 1900

ANTHONY HECHT (b. 1923)

The Grapes

At five o'clock of a summer afternoon
We are already shadowed by the mountain
On whose lower slopes we perch, all of us here
At the *Hôtel de l'Univers et Déjeuner*.
The fruit trees and the stone lions out front   5
In deepening purple silhouette themselves
Against the bright green fields across the valley
Where, at the *Beau Rivage*, patrons are laved
In generous tides of gold. At cocktail time
Their glasses glint like gems, while we're eclipsed.   10
Which may explain
Why the younger set, which likes to get up late,
Assess its members over aperitifs,
Prefers that western slope, while we attract
A somewhat older, quieter clientele,   15
Americans mostly, though they seem to come
From everywhere, and are usually good tippers.
Still, it is strange and sad, at cocktail time,
To look across the valley from our shade,
As if from premature death, at all that brilliance   20
Across which silently on certain days
Shadows of clouds slide past in smooth parade,
While even our daisies and white irises
Are filled with blues and darkened premonitions.
Yet for our patrons, who are on holiday,   25
Questions of time are largely set aside.
They are indulgently amused to find
All the news magazines on the wicker table
In the lobby are outrageously outdated.
But Madame likes to keep them on display;   30
They add a touch of color, and a note
Of home and habit for many, and it's surprising
How thoroughly they are read on rainy days.
And I myself have smuggled one or two
Up to my bedroom, there to browse upon   35
Arrested time in *Time, Incorporated*.
There it is always 1954,
And Marlon Brando, perfectly preserved,
Sullen and brutal and desirable,
Avoids my eyes with a scowl; the record mile   40
Always belongs to Roger Bannister;

The rich and sleek of the international set
Are robbed of their furs and diamonds, get divorced
In a world so far removed from the rest of us
It almost seems arranged for our amusement   45
As they pose for pictures, perfectly made-up,
Coiffeured by Mr. Charles, languid, serene.
They never show up here—our little resort
Is far too mean for them—except in my daydreams.
My dreams at night are reserved for Marc-Antoine,   50
One of the bellboys at the *Beau Rivage*.
In his striped vest with flat buttons of brass
He comes to me every night after my prayers,
In fantasy, of course; in actual fact
He's taken no notice of me whatsoever.   55
Quite understandable, for I must be
Easily ten years older than he, and only
A chambermaid. As with all the very young,
To him the future's limitless and bright,
Anything's possible, one has but to wait.   60
No doubt he dreams of a young millionairess,
Beautiful, spoiled and ardent, at his feet.
Perhaps it shall come to pass. Such things have happened.
Even barmaids and pantry girls have been seen   65
Translated into starlets tanning themselves
At the end of a diving board. But just this morning
Something came over me like the discovery
Of a deep secret of the universe.
It was early. I was in the dining room   70
Long before breakfast was served. I was alone.
Mornings, of course, it's we who get the light,
An especially tender light, hopeful and soft.
I stood beside a table near a window,
Gazing down at a crystal bowl of grapes   75
In ice-water. They were green grapes, or, rather,
They were a sort of pure, unblemished jade,
Like turbulent ocean water, with misted skins,
Their own pale, smoky sweat, or tiny frost.
I leaned over the table, letting the sun   80
Fall on my forearm, contemplating them.
Reflections of the water dodged and swam
In nervous incandescent filaments
Over my blouse and up along the ceiling.
And all those little bags of glassiness,   85
Those clustered planets, leaned their eastern cheeks
Into the sunlight, each one showing a soft

Meridian swelling where the thinning light
Mysteriously tapered into shadow,
To cool recesses, to the tranquil blues 90
That then were pillowing the *Beau Rivage*.
And watching I could almost see the light
Edge slowly over their simple surfaces,
And feel the sunlight moving on my skin
Like a warm glacier. And I seemed to know 95
In my blood the meaning of sidereal time
And know my little life had somehow crested.
There was nothing left for me now, nothing but years.
My destiny was cast and Marc-Antoine
Would not be called to play a part in it. 100
His passion, his Dark Queen, he'd meet elsewhere.
And I knew at last, with a faint, visceral twitch,
A flood of weakness that comes to the resigned,
What it must have felt like in that rubber boat
In mid-Pacific, to be the sole survivor 105
Of a crash, idly dandled on that blank
Untroubled waste, and see the light decline,
Taper and fade in graduated shades
Behind the International Date Line—
An accident I read about in *Time*. 110

A. D. HOPE (b. 1907)

Imperial Adam

Imperial Adam, naked in the dew,
Felt his brown flanks and found the rib was gone.
Puzzled he turned and saw where, two and two,
The mighty spoor of Jahweh marked the lawn.

Then he remembered through mysterious sleep 5
The surgeon fingers probing at the bone,
The voice so far away, so rich and deep:
"It is not good for him to live alone."

Turning once more he found Man's counterpart
In tender parody breathing at his side. 10
He knew her at first sight, he knew by heart
Her allegory of sense unsatisfied.

The pawpaw drooped its golden breasts above
Less generous than the honey of her flesh,
The innocent sunlight showed the place of love;   15
The dew on its dark hairs winked crisp and fresh.

This plump gourd severed from his virile root,
She promised on the turf of Paradise
Delicious pulp of the forbidden fruit;
Sly as the snake she loosed her sinuous thighs,   20

And waking, smiled up at him from the grass;
Her breasts rose softly and he heard her sigh—
From all the beasts whose pleasant task it was
In Eden to increase and multiply

Adam had learned the jolly deed of kind;   25
He took her in his arms and there and then,
Like the clean beasts, embracing from behind,
Began in joy to found the breed of men.

Then from the spurt of seed within her broke
Her terrible and triumphant female cry,   30
Split upward by the sexual lightning stroke.
It was the beasts now who stood watching by:

The gravid elephant, the calving hind,
The breeding bitch, the she-ape big with young
Were the first gentle midwives of mankind;   35
The teeming lioness rasped her with her tongue;

The proud vicuña nuzzled her as she slept
Lax on the grass; and Adam watching too
Saw how her dumb breasts at their ripening wept,
The great pod of her belly swelled and grew,   40

And saw its water break, and saw, in fear,
Its quaking muscles in the act of birth,
Between her legs a pigmy face appear,
And the first murderer lay upon the earth.

LANGSTON HUGHES (1902–1967)

Jazzonia

Oh, silver tree!
Oh, shining rivers of the soul!

In a Harlem cabaret
Six long-headed jazzers play.
A dancing girl whose eyes are bold   5
Lifts high a dress of silken gold.

Oh, singing tree!
Oh, shining rivers of the soul!

Were Eve's eyes
In the first garden   10
Just a bit too bold?
Was Cleopatra gorgeous
In a gown of gold?

Oh, shining tree!
Oh, silver rivers of the soul!   15

In a whirling cabaret
Six long-headed jazzers play.

TED HUGHES (b. 1930)

Crow's First Lesson

God tried to teach Crow how to talk.
"Love," said God. "Say Love."
Crow gaped, and the white shark crashed into the sea
And went rolling downwards, discovering its own depth.

"No, no," said God, "Say Love. Now try it. LOVE."   5
Crow gaped, and a bluefly, a tsetse, a mosquito
Zoomed out and down
To their sundry flesh-pots.

"A final try," said God. "Now, LOVE"
Crow convulsed, gaped, retched and   10
Man's bodiless prodigious head

Bulbed out onto the earth, with swiveling eyes,
Jabbering protest—

And Crow retched again, before God could stop him.
And woman's vulva dropped over man's neck and tightened.   15
The two struggled together on the grass.
God struggled to part them, cursed, wept—

Crow flew guiltily off.

BEN JONSON (1573–1637)

On My First Son

Farewell, thou child of my right hand, and joy;
My sin was too much hope of thee, loved boy,
Seven years thou wert lent to me, and I thee pay,
Exacted by thy fate, on the just day.
O, could I lose all father now. For why   5
Will man lament the state he should envy?
To have so soon 'scaped world's and flesh's rage,
And, if no other misery, yet age?
Rest in soft peace, and asked, say, "Here doth lie
Ben Jonson his best piece of poetry."   10
For whose sake henceforth all his vows be such,
As what he loves may never like too much.

RODNEY JONES (b. 1950)

For the Eating of Swine

I have learned sloppiness from an old sow
wallowing her ennui in the stinking lot,
a slow vessel filled with a thousand candles,
her whiskers matted with creek mud,
her body helpless to sweat the dull spirit.   5
I have wrestled the hindquarters of a young boar
while my father clipped each testicle
with a sharpened Barlow knife, returning him,
good fish, to his wastery, changed life.
And I have learned pleasure from a gilt   10
as she lay on her back, offering her soft belly
like a dog, the loose bowel of her throat

opening to warble the consonants of her joy.
I have learned lassitude, pride, stubbornness,
and greed from my many neighbors, the pigs.   15
I have gone with low head and slanted blue eyes
through the filthy streets, wary of the blade,
my whole life, a toilet or a kitchen,
the rotting rinds, the wreaths of flies.
For the chicken, the cow, forgetfulness. Mindlessness   20
blesses their meat. Only the pigs are holy,
the rings in their snouts, their fierce, motherly indignation,
and their need always to fill themselves.
I remember a photograph. A sheriff had demolished
a still, spilling a hundred gallons of moonshine.   25
Nine pigs passed out in the shade of a mulberry tree.
We know pigs will accommodate demons,
run into rivers, drowning of madness.
They will devour drunks who fall in their ways.
Like Christ, they will befriend their destroyers.   30
In the middle of winter I have cupped my hands
and held the large and pliable brain of a pig.
As the fires were heating the black kettles,
I have scrupulously placed my rifle between pigs' eyes
and with one clean shot, loosened the slabs   35
of side-meat, the sausages that begin
with the last spasms of the trotters.
O dolphins of the barnyard, frolickers
in the gray and eternal muck, in all your parts
useful, because I have known you, this is the sage,   40
and salt, the sacrificial markers of pepper.
What pity should I feel, or gratitude, raising you
on my fork as all the dead shall be risen?

DONALD JUSTICE (b. 1925)

Counting the Mad

This one was put in a jacket,
This one was sent home,
This one was given bread and meat
But would eat none,
And this one cried No No No No   5
All day long.

This one looked at the window
As though it were a wall,

This one saw things that were not there,
This one things that were,   10
And this one cried No No No No
All day long.

This one thought himself a bird,
This one a dog,
And this one thought himself a man,   15
An ordinary man,
And cried and cried No No No No
All day long.

In Bertram's Garden

Jane looks down at her organdy skirt
As if *it* somehow were the thing disgraced,
For being there, on the floor, in the dirt,
And she catches it up about her waist,
Smooths it out along one hip,   5
And pulls it over the crumpled slip.

On the porch, green-shuttered, cool,
Asleep is Bertram, that bronze boy,
Who, having wound her around a spool,
Sends her spinning like a toy   10
Out to the garden, all alone,
To sit and weep on a bench of stone.

Soon the purple dark will bruise
Lily and bleeding heart and rose,
And the little Cupid lose   15
Eyes and ears and chin and nose,
And Jane lie down with others soon
Naked to the naked moon.

PATRICK KAVANAGH (1904–1967)

Inniskeen Road: July Evening

The bicycles go by in twos and threes—
There's a dance in Billy Brennan's barn to-night,
And there's the half-talk code of mysteries
And the wink-and-elbow language of delight.
Half-past eight and there is not a spot   5
Upon a mile of road, no shadow thrown

That might turn out a man or woman, not
A footfall tapping secrecies of stone.

I have what every poet hates in spite
Of all the solemn talk of contemplation.　　　　　　　10
Oh, Alexander Selkirk knew the plight
Of being king and government and nation.
A road, a mile of kingdom, I am king
Of banks and stones and every blooming thing.

JOHN KEATS (1795–1821)

Ode to a Nightingale

I

My heart aches, and a drowsy numbness pains
　　My sense, as though of hemlock I had drunk,
Or emptied some dull opiate to the drains
　　One minute past, and Lethe-wards had sunk:
'Tis not through envy of thy happy lot,　　　　　　　5
　　But being too happy in thine happiness—
　　　　That thou, light-wingéd Dryad of the trees,
　　　　　　In some melodious plot
　　Of beechen green, and shadows numberless,
　　　　Singest of summer in full-throated ease.　　　　10

II

O, for a draught of vintage! that hath been
　　Cooled a long age in the deep-delvéd earth,
Tasting of Flora and the country green,
　　Dance, and Provençal song, and sunburnt mirth!
O for a beaker full of the warm South,　　　　　　　15
　　Full of the true, the blushful Hippocrene,
　　　　With beaded bubbles winking at the brim,
　　　　　　And purple-stainéd mouth;
　　That I might drink, and leave the world unseen,
　　　　And with thee fade away into the forest dim:　　20

III

Fade far away, dissolve, and quite forget
　　What thou among the leaves hast never known,
The weariness, the fever, and the fret

Here, where men sit and hear each other groan;
Where palsy shakes a few, sad, last gray hairs,   25
  Where youth grows pale, and specter-thin, and dies,
    Where but to think is to be full of sorrow
      And leaden-eyed despairs,
  Where Beauty cannot keep her lustrous eyes,
    Or new Love pine at them beyond tomorrow.   30

IV

Away! away! for I will fly to thee,
  Not charioted by Bacchus and his pards,
But on the viewless wings of Poesy,
  Though the dull brain perplexes and retards:
Already with thee! tender is the night,   35
  And haply the Queen-Moon is on her throne,
    Clustered around by all her starry Fays;
      But here there is no light,
  Save what from heaven is with the breezes blown
    Through verdurous glooms and winding mossy ways.   40

V

I cannot see what flowers are at my feet,
  Nor what soft incense hangs upon the boughs,
But, in embalméd darkness, guess each sweet
  Wherewith the seasonable month endows
The grass, the thicket, and the fruit tree wild;   45
  White hawthorn, and the pastoral eglantine;
    Fast fading violets covered up in leaves;
      And mid-May's eldest child,
The coming musk-rose, full of dewy wine,
    The murmurous haunt of flies on summer eves.   50

VI

Darkling I listen; and for many a time
I have been half in love with easeful Death,
Called him soft names in many a muséd rhyme,
  To take into the air my quiet breath;
Now more than ever seems it rich to die,   55
  To cease upon the midnight with no pain,
    While thou art pouring forth thy soul abroad
      In such an ecstasy!
  Still wouldst thou sing, and I have ears in vain—
    To thy high requiem become a sod.   60

VII

Thou wast not born for death, immortal Bird!
    No hungry generations tread thee down;
The voice I hear this passing night was heard
    In ancient days by emperor and clown:
Perhaps the selfsame song that found a path   65
    Through the sad heart of Ruth, when, sick for home,
        She stood in tears amid the alien corn;
            The same that ofttimes hath
Charmed magic casements, opening on the foam
    Of perilous seas, in faery lands forlorn.   70

VIII

Forlorn! the very word is like a bell
    To toll me back from thee to my sole self!
Adieu! the fancy cannot cheat so well
    As she is famed to do, deceiving elf.
Adieu! adieu! thy plaintive anthem fades   75
    Past the near meadows, over the still stream,
        Up the hill side; and now 'tis buried deep
            In the next valley-glades:
Was it a vision, or a waking dream?
    Fled is that music:—Do I wake or sleep?   80

GALWAY KINNELL (b. 1927)

The Correspondence School Instructor
Says Goodbye to His Poetry Students

Goodbye, lady in Bangor, who sent me
snapshots of yourself, after definitely hinting
you were beautiful; goodbye,
Miami Beach urologist, who enclosed plain
brown envelopes for the return of your *very*   5
"Clinical Sonnets"; goodbye, manufacturer
of brassieres on the Coast, whose eclogues
give the fullest treatment in literature yet
to the sagging breast motif; goodbye, you in San Quentin,
who wrote, "Being German my hero is Hitler,"   10
instead of "Sincerely yours," at the end of long,
neat-scripted letters demolishing
the pre-Raphaelites:

I swear to you, it was just my way
of cheering myself up, as I licked   15
the stamped, self-addressed envelopes,
the game I had
of trying to guess which one of you, this time,
had poisoned his glue. I did care.
I did read each poem entire.   20
I did say what I thought was the truth
in the mildest words I knew. And now,
in this poem, or chopped prose, not any better,
I realize, than those troubled lines
I kept sending back to you,   25
I have to say I am relieved it is over:
at the end I could feel only pity
for that urge toward more life
your poems kept smothering in words, the smell
of which, days later, would tingle   30
in your nostrils as new, God-given impulses
to write.

Goodbye,
you who are, for me, the postmarks again
of shattered towns—Xenia, Burnt Cabins, Hornell—   35
their loneliness
given away in poems, only their solitude kept.

Vapor Trail Reflected in a Frog Pond

I

The old watch: their
thick eyes
puff and foreclose by the moon. The young, heads
trailed by the beginning of necks,
shiver,   5
in the guarantee they shall be bodies.

In the frog pond
the vapor trail of a SAC bomber creeps,

I hear its drone, drifting, high up
in immaculate ozone.   10

II

And I hear,
coming over the hills, America singing,
her varied carols I hear:
crack of deputies' rifles practicing their aim on stray dogs
    at night,
sput of cattleprod,   15
TV groaning at the smells of the human body,
curses of the soldiers as he poisons, burns, grinds, and stabs
the rice of the world,
with open mouth, crying strong, hysterical curses.

III

And by rice paddies in Asia   20
bones
wearing a few shadows
walk down a dirt road, smashed
bloodsuckers on their heels, knowing
the flesh a man throws down in the sunshine   25
dogs shall eat
and the flesh that is up thrown in the air
shall be seized by birds,
shoulder blades smooth, unmarked by old feather-holes,
hands rivered   30
by blue, erratic wanderings of the blood,
eyes crinkled up
as they gaze up at the drifing sun that gives us our lives,
seed dazzled over the foot battered blaze of the earth.

TED KOOSER (b. 1939)

A Fencerow in Early March

The last snowdrifts
have drawn themselves up
out of the light,
clinging to winter.
Beyond them,   5
a muddy stubble field
has sponged up
all the darkness—

the February nights,
the iron stoves,
the ink of every letter
written in longing.
And the fencerow
goes on, up and over
the next low rise
and the next, casting
its cold, white shadow,
its gate still closed
on spring.   20

GREG KUZMA (b. 1944)

To My Sons, Unborn

No one prepared me for you.
Perhaps you will not occur.
Is it wrong to talk of occurrence,
My father used to hold my hand
in the dark, and it grew lighter   5
when he did. My mother
used to say
I should be a good boy and not
stay out too late. I
remember I learned to take my   10
stiff iced dungarees off
on the cellar floor.
My legs were flaming red
like a girl's.

I have made a list of the things   15
I will want you to try.
I will take you out
into the middle of fields
and then lose you.
I will give you heavy wrenches   20
to hold.
You will think back on those days
as genuine experiences.
You will not see my magic hands
lifting the wounded birds   25
and placing them in front of you.

I fool myself. I do
not know how I will occur to you
or you to me.
I do not know who will get lost   30
in the dark
who will be holding whose hand.
But I have my hand out anyway.
I look forward to your coming.
It is almost necessary to me.   35
I do not know what I will do without you.

PHILLIP LAMANTIA (b. 1927)

Celestial Estrangement

We have been carried here against our will

Burnt stars
Oceanic gardens
where the clouds are soaked into my eyes

How much sand floats in the teacup of your dreams   5
The rivers you perceive are those of horses
they carry red water
the odor of imperishable sweat
putrescent human bellies stuffed with revolvers and nuns

At the top of the tower   10
where hounds part with a pool of water
where one comes only with a flaming lance
where there is no escaping the pain of a horse's kick
where toy dolls are nailed to the beds
where lovers suck their bodies dry   15
as harp strings are plucked away
in this hermit world of old gunny sacks and broken heads

we encounter tons of wingless birds

PHILIP LARKIN (1922–1985)

Talking in Bed

Talking in bed ought to be easiest,
Lying together there goes back so far,
An emblem of two people being honest.

Yet more and more time passes silently.
Outside, the wind's incomplete unrest   5
Builds and disperses clouds about the sky,

And dark towns heap up on the horizon.
None of this cares for us. Nothing shows why
At this unique distance from isolation

It becomes still more difficult to find   10
Words at once true and kind,
Or not untrue and not unkind.

DON L. LEE (b. 1942)

Man Thinking About Woman

some thing is lost in me,
like
the way you lose old thoughts   that
somehow seemed unlost at the right time.

i've not known it or you many days;   5
we met as friends with an absence of strangeness.
it was the month
that my lines got longer & my metaphors softer.

it was the week   that
i felt the city's narrow breezes rush about   10
me
looking for a place to disappear
as   i walked the clearway,
sure footed in used sandals screaming to be replaced

your empty shoes (except for used stockings)   15
partially hidden beneath the dresser

looked at me,
as i sat thoughtlessly   waiting
for your touch.

that day,   20
as your body rested upon my chest
i saw the shadow of the
window blinds   beam
across the unpainted ceiling
going somewhere   25
like the somewhere i was going
when
the clearness of yr/teeth,
& the scars on yr/legs stopped me.

your beauty;   un-noticed by regular eyes   is   30
like   a blackbird resting
on a telephone wire   that moves
quietly with the wind.

a southwind.

PHILIP LEVINE (b. 1928)

The Survivors

in memory of my cousin,
David Ber Prishkulnick

Nîmes, August, 1966, and I
am going home. Home is here,
you say; your hand reaches
out and touches nothing.
Russia, New York, back,   5
that was your father; you
took up the road, moving
at dawn or after dusk
in the corrugated Citroen
loaded with shirts and ties.   10
Light broke in the fields
of poplars and up ahead
was one more village fair
and the peddling.

Once upon a day in 1940   15
a little man had to leave
his dinner and save his life
and go with his house
on his back, sleeping nowhere,
eating nothing, a shadow   20
running, a dark stop. That's
how grandpa told the story.
Waking, I found you waiting,
your feet crossed and swinging,
like a child on the bench   25
outside the window, holding
a sack of warm rolls
for breakfast.

Gray suit, woolen vest,
collar, tie. Now you are   30
dispersed into the atoms
of gasoline and air
that explode an instant
and are always, dispersed
to the earth that never   35
warmed you and the rain
drumming down on the hoods
of trucks stalled on the bridge
to Arles. You stop a moment
in my hand that cannot   40
stop and rise and stumble
onward toward the heart
where there is no rest.

LARRY LEVIS (b. 1946)

Whitman

> "I say we had better look our nation search-
> ingly in the face, like a physician diagnosing
> some deep disease."
>
> Democratic Vistas
>
> "Look for me under your bootsoles."

On Long Island, they moved my clapboard house
Across a turnpike, & then felt so guilty they

Named a shopping center after me!
Now that I'm required reading in your high schools,
Teen-agers call me a fool.   5
Now what I sang stops breathing.

And yet
It was only when everyone stopped believing in me
That I began to live, again—
First in the thin whine of Montana fence wire,   10
Then in the transparent, cast off garments hung
In the windows of the poorest families,
Then in the glad music of Charlie Parker.
At times now,
I even come back to watch you   15
From the eyes of a taciturn boy at Malibu.
Across the counter at the beach concession stand,
I sell you hot dogs, Pepsis, cigarettes—
My blond hair long, greasy, & swept back
In a vain old ducktail, deliciously   20
Out of style.
And no one notices.
Once, I even came back as *me*,
An aging homosexual who ran the Tilt-a-Whirl
At county fairs, the chilled paint on each gondola   25
Changing color as it picked up speed,
And a Mardi Gras tattoo on my left shoulder.
A few of you must have seen my photographs,
For when you looked back,
I thought you caught the meaning of my stare: 30
Still water,
Merciless.

A Kosmos. One of the roughs.

Leave me alone.
A father who's outlived his only child.   35
To find me now will cost you everything.

AUDRE LORD (b. 1934)

Hanging Fire

I am fourteen
and my skin has betrayed me

the boy I cannot live without
still sucks his thumb
in secret
how come my knees are   5
always so ashy
what if I die
before morning
and momma's in the bedroom   10
with the door closed.

I have to learn how to dance
in time for the next party
my room is too small for me
suppose I die before graduation   15
they will sing sad melodies
but finally
tell the truth about me
There is nothing I want to do
and too much   20
that has to be done
and momma's in the bedroom
with the door closed.

Nobody even stops to think
about my side of it   25
I should have been on Math Team
my marks were better than his
why do I have to be
the one
wearing braces   30
I have nothing to wear tomorrow
will I live long enough
to grow up
and momma's in the bedroom
with the door closed.   35

RICHARD LOVELACE (1618–1658)

To Lucasta, Going to the Wars

Tell me not, sweet, I am unkind,
  That from the nunnery
Of thy chaste breast and quiet mind
  To war and arms I fly.

True, a new mistress now I chase,
   The first foe in the field;
And with a stronger faith embrace
   A sword, a horse, a shield.

Yet this inconstancy is such
   As you too shall adore;
I could not love thee, dear, so much,
   Loved I not honor more.

GEORGE MACBETH (b. 1932)

Bats

have no accidents. They loop
their incredible horse-shoe
loops, dead-stop

on air-brakes,
road-safe on
squeaks: racketeering

their SOS noise in a
jai-alai
bat-jam

of collapsed umbrellas, a
Chancery Lane
of avoided

collisions, all in a
cave without lights: then
hung

happy, a snore
of strap-hangers
undergrounding

without an *Evening*
Standard between them
to the common Waterloo

that awaits bats, like
all beasts, then
off now, zoom!,

Man, you can't even
hear them; bats,
are they?

25

ARCHIBALD MACLEISH (1892–1982)

You, Andrew Marvell

And here face down beneath the sun
And here upon earth's noonward height
To feel the always coming on
The always rising of the night

To feel creep up the curving east   5
The earthy chill of dusk and slow
Upon those under lands the vast
And ever climbing shadow grow

And strange at Ecbatan the trees
Take leaf by leaf the evening strange   10
The flooding dark about their knees
The mountains over Persia change

And now at Kermanshah the gate
Dark empty and the withered grass
And through the twilight now the late   15
Few travelers in the westward pass

And Baghdad darken and the bridge
Across the silent river gone
And through Arabia the edge
Of evening widen and steal on   20

And deepen on Palmyra's street
The wheel rut in the ruined stone
And Lebanon fade out and Crete
High through the clouds and overblown

And over Sicily the air   25
Still flashing with the landward gulls
And loom and slowly disappear
The sails above the shadowy hulls

And Spain go under and the shore
Of Africa the gilded sand   30

And evening vanish and no more
The low pale light across that land

Nor now the long light on the sea
And here face downward in the sun
To feel how swift how secretly   35
The shadow of the night comes on. . . .

PAUL MARIANI (b. 1940)

The Lesson

Silent, my jaws working, I knew
as we drove home from Mass he'd learn
his lesson, get it right this time.

I knew it when I pulled him
from the back seat by the scruff   5
of his neck, squeezing till his shoulders

scrunched, knew it when I half flung him
up the porch steps, through the cold
kitchen and up the stairs. And when I

turned and faltered for a moment to hear   10
him mutter, I knew that that was that.
I must have taken those goddamned

steps by threes, slamming that bent body,
that cowering shape against the wall. He
set his face hard to meet my shouts—   15

give him credit—but his eyes
were somewhere else. Glazed, dreamy,
they floated in that round face

of his, they. . . . I can't remember now
just what it was I nailed him for, or   20
what it was I said or what he said. Let's

call it part of growing up. Once, when I
was ten, an altarboy in that old converted
hangar back in Levittown, I got it

into me to act the clown and fool around   25
communion time. I slapped my head a dozen times
in wonder at those queuing sheep,

fiddled with my shoes, kept gaping
at my watch. Another Charlie Chaplin.
Except my father saw it different.   30

He was silent going home, though his jaws
kept working, and that was bad. Once we were
safe inside, though, he rammed me up against

the kitchen wall and held me rigid there,
my neck between his outstretched thumb   35
and forefinger to show me how to stand

in church. Some lessons you just can't
forget. So with my own son here in this ritual
re-enactment, this nailing to the wall,

for dark motives one calls "exercise"   40
of virtue, righteous anger, discipline. Yet
for all that, one thing only keeps playing

back: that slight shaking of the rigid
head, the eyes turning as the
fingers tighten on the scrawny neck.   45

ANDREW MARVELL (1621–1678)

The Garden

 How vainly men themselves amaze
To win the palm, the oak, or bays,
And their incessant labors see
Crowned from some single herb, or tree,
Whose short and narrow-vergéd shade   5
Does prudently their toils upbraid;
While all flowers and all trees do close
To weave the garlands of repose!

 Fair Quiet, have I found thee here,
And Innocence, thy sister dear?   10
Mistaken long, I sought you then

In busy companies of men.
Your sacred plants, if here below,
Only among the plants will grow;
Society is all but rude
To this delicious solitude.   15

   No white nor red was ever seen
So amorous as this lovely green.
Fond lovers, cruel as their flame,
Cut in these trees their mistress' name: 20
Little, alas, they know or heed
How far these beauties hers exceed!
Fair trees, wheresoe'er your barks I wound,
No name shall but your own be found.

   When we have run our passion's heat,   25
Love hither makes his best retreat.
The gods, that mortal beauty chase,
Still in a tree did end their race:
Apollo hunted Daphne so,
Only that she might laurel grow;   30
And Pan did after Syrinx speed,
Not as a nymph, but for a reed.

   What wondrous life is this I lead!
Ripe apples drop about my head;
The luscious clusters of the vine   35
Upon my mouth do crush their wine;
The nectarine and curious peach
Into my hands themselves do reach;
Stumbling on melons, as I pass,
Insnared with flowers, I fall on grass.   40

   Meanwhile the mind, from pleasures less,
Withdraws into its happiness;
The mind, that ocean where each kind
Does straight its own resemblance find;
Yet it creates, transcending these,   45
Far other worlds and other seas,
Annihilating all that's made
To a green thought in a green shade.

   Here at the fountain's sliding foot,
Or at some fruit tree's mossy root,   50
Casting the body's vest aside,

My soul into the boughs does glide:
There, like a bird, it sits and sings,
Then whets and combs its silver wings,
And, till prepared for longer flight,   55
Waves in its plumes the various light.

   Such was that happy garden-state
While man there walked without a mate:
After a place so pure and sweet,
What other help could yet be meet!   60
But 'twas beyond a mortal's share
To wander solitary there:
Two paradises 'twere in one
To live in paradise alone.

   How well the skillful gardener drew   65
Of flowers and herbs this dial new,
Where, from above, the milder sun
Does through a fragrant zodiac run;
And as it works, th' industrious bee
Computes its time as well as we!   70
How could such sweet and wholesome hours
Be reckoned but with herbs and flowers?

WILLIAM MATTHEWS (b. 1942)

Charming

Because language dreams in metaphors,
charm is always like something else,
like luck, or wealth, or like a tune
to whistle while coaxing soup
from chicken bones and two turnips.   5

Because ice is like stone, though once
it was water, and because kissed ice
means blue lips, charm needs to know
the names of distress and remedy,
and what words are not spoken, and when.   10

Because charm is an argument
about politics, that it works best
for the rich, and about magic,

that it works best for those who recant
politics, charm is warily polite.   15

And because charm is like love,
the way ice is like water, charm
tends its investment and dreams
when it sleeps, and wakes hungry,
as if from exacting work.   20

And because to fly in a dream is fierce
pleasure, charm wakes with a kind word.
It's important to start in the right place,
like a child possessed of a story.
First the witch, then the snow, and then   25

the starling-throng like a blizzard
of shameful thoughts, and then winter:
ice to kiss and the right names
in the right order, the sexual secret
of spring's coming back at all.   30

Though spring is all burgeon and broadcast,
a tosspurse, survival's brash manners,
because charm dwindles and hoards,
because charm repeats, because charm
will save itself before it remembers us.   35

HERMAN MELVILLE (1819–1891)

The Berg

(A Dream.)

I saw a ship of martial build
(Her standards set, her brave apparel on)
Directed as by madness mere
Against a stolid iceberg steer,
Nor budge it, though the infatuate ship went down.   5
The impact made huge ice-cubes fall
Sullen, in tons that crashed the deck;
But that one avalanche was all—
No other movement save the foundering wreck.

Along the spurs of ridges pale,   10
Not any slenderest shaft and frail,

A prism over glass-green gorges lone,
Toppled; nor lace of traceries fine,
Nor pendant drops in grot or mine
Were jarred, when the stunned ship went down.   15
Nor sole the gulls in cloud that wheeled
Circling one snow-flanked peak afar,
But nearer fowl the floes that skimmed
And crystal beaches, felt no jar.
No thrill transmitted stirred the lock   20
Of jack-straw needle-ice at base;
Towers undermined by waves—the block
Atilt impending—kept their place.
Seals, dozing sleek on sliddery ledges
Slipt never, when by loftier edges   25
Through very inertia overthrown,
The impetuous ship in bafflement went down.

Hard Berg (methought), so cold, so vast,
With mortal damps self-overcast;
Exhaling still thy dankish breath—   30
Adrift dissolving, bound for death;
Though lumpish thou, a lumbering one—
A lumbering lubbard loitering slow,
Impingers rue thee and go down
Sounding thy precipice below,   35
Nor stir the slimy slug that sprawls
Along thy dead indifference of walls.

JAMES MERRILL (b. 1926)

The Mad Scene

Again last night I dreamed the dream called Laundry.
In it, the sheets and towels of a life we were going to share,
The milk-stiff bibs, the shroud, each rag to be ever
Trampled or soiled, bled on or groped for blindly,
Came swooning out of an enormous willow hamper   5
Onto moon-marbly boards. We had just met. I watched
From outer darkness. I had dressed myself in clothes
Of a new fiber that never stains or wrinkles, never
Wears thin. The opera house sparkled with tiers
And tiers of eyes, like mine enlarged by belladonna,   10
Trained inward. There I saw the cloud-clot, gust by gust,
Form, and the lightning bite, and the roan mane unloosen.
Fingers were running in panic over the flute's nine gates.

Why did I flinch? I loved you. And in the downpour laughed
To have us wrung white, gnarled together, one   15
Topmost mordent of wisteria,
As the lean tree burst into grief.

W. S. MERWIN (b. 1927)

The Drunk in the Furnace

   For a good decade
The furnace stood in the naked gully, fireless
And vacant as any hat. Then when it was
No more to them than a hulking black fossil
To erode unnoticed with the rest of the junk-hill   5
By the poisonous creek, and rapidly to be added
   To their ignorance.

   They were afterwards astonished
To confirm, one morning, a twist of smoke like a pale
Resurrection, staggering out of its chewed hole,   10
And to remark then other tokens that someone,
Cozily bolted behind the eye-holed iron
Door of the drafty burner, had there established
   His bad castle.

   Where he gets his spirits   15
It's a mystery. But the stuff keeps him musical:
Hammer-and-anviling with poker and bottle
To his jugged bellowings, till the last groaning clang
As he collapses onto the rioting
Springs of a litter of car-seats ranged on the grates,   20
   To sleep like an iron pig.

   In their tar-paper church
On a text about stoke-holes that are sated never
Their Reverend lingers. They nod and hate trespassers.
When the furnace wakes, though, all afternoon   25
Their witless offspring flock like piped rats to its siren
Crescendo, and agape on the crumbling ridge
   Stand in a row and learn.

OGDEN NASH (1902–1971)

Columbus

Once upon a time there was an Italian,
And some people thought he was a rapscallion,
But he wasn't offended,
Because other people thought he was splendid,
And he said the world was round,   5
And everybody made an uncomplimentary sound,
But he went and tried to borrow some money from
    Ferdinand
But Ferdinand said America was a bird in the bush
    and he'd rather have a berdinand,
But Columbus' brain was fertile, it wasn't arid,
And he remembered the Ferdinand was married,   10
And he thought, there is no wife like a misunderstood one,
Because if her husband thinks something is a terrible
    idea she is bound to think it a good one,
So he perfumed his handkerchief with bay rum and citronella,
And he went to see Isabella,
And he looked wonderful but he had never felt sillier,   15
And she said, I can't place the face but the aroma is familiar,
And Columbus didn't say a word,
All he said was, I am Columbus, the fifteenth-century
    Admiral Byrd,
And, just as he thought, her disposition was very malleable,
And she said, Here are my jewels, and she wasn't   20
    penurious like Cornelia the mother of the Gracchi, she
    wasn't referring to her children, no, she was referring
    to her jewels, which were very very valuable,
So Columbus said, Somebody show me the sunset
    and somebody did and he set sail for it,
And he discovered America and they put him in jail for it,
And the fetters gave him welts,
And they named America after somebody else,
So the sad fate of Columbus ought to be pointed out to
    every child and every voter,   25
Because it has a very important moral, which is, Don't
    be a discoverer, be a promoter.

SHARON OLDS (b. 1942)

Rite of Passage

As the guests arrive at my son's party
they gather in the living room—
short men, men in first grade
with smooth jaws and chins.
Hands in pockets, they stand around   5
jostling, jockeying for place, small fights
breaking out and calming. One says to another
How old are you? Six. I'm seven. So?
They eye each other, seeing themselves
tiny in the other's pupils. They clear their   10
throats a lot, a room of small bankers,
they fold their arms and frown. *I could beat you
up,* a seven says to a six,
the dark cake, round and heavy as a
turret, behind them on the table. My son,   15
freckles like specks of nutmeg on his cheeks,
chest narrow as the balsa keel of a
model boat, long hands
cool and thin as the day they guided him
out of me, speaks up as a host   20
for the sake of the group.
We could easily kill a two-year-old,
he says in his clear voice. The other
men agree, they clear their throats
like Generals, they relax and get down to   25
playing war, celebrating my son's life.

MICHAEL ONDAATJE (b. 1943)

Gold and Black

At night the gold and black slashed bees come
pluck my head away. Vague thousands drift
leave brain naked stark as liver
each one carries atoms of flesh, they
walk my body in their fingers.   5
The mind stinks out.

In the black Kim is turning

a geiger counter to this pillow.
She cracks me open like a lightbulb.

Love, the real,   10
terrifies
the dreamer in his riot cell.

EZRA POUND (1885–1972)

Canto 45

With *Usura*
With usura hath no man a house of good stone
each block cut smooth and well fitting
that design might cover their face,
with usura   5
hath no man a painted paradise on his church wall
harpes et luthes
or where virgin receiveth message
and halo projects from incision,
with usura   10
seeth no man Gonzaga his heirs and his concubines
no picture is made to endure nor to live with
but it is made to sell and sell quickly
with usura, sin against nature,
is thy bread ever more of stale rags   15
is thy bread dry as paper,
with no mountain wheat, no strong flour
with usura the line grows thick
with usura is no clear demarcation
and no man can find site for his dwelling.   20
Stone cutter is kept from his loom
WITH USURA
wool comes not to market
sheep bringeth no gain with usura   25
Usura is a murrain, usura
blunteth the needle in the maid's hand
and stoppeth the spinner's cunning. Pietro Lombardo
came not by usura
Duccio came not by usura   30
nor Pier della Francesca; Zuan Bellin' not by usura
nor was 'La Calunnia' painted.
Came not by usura Angelico; came not Ambrogio Praedis,
Came no church of cut stone signed: *Adamo me fecit.*

Not by usura St Trophime   35
Not by usura Saint Hilaire,
Usura rusteth the chisel
It rusteth the craft and the craftsman
It gnaweth the thread in the loom
None learneth to weave gold in her pattern;   40
Azure hath a canker by usura; cramoisi is unbroidered
Emerald findeth no Memling
Usura slayeth the child in the womb
It stayeth the young man's courting
It hath brought palsey to bed, lyeth   45
between the young bride and her bridegroom
                    CONTRA NATURAM
They have brought whores for Eleusis
Corpses are set to banquet
at behest of usura.   50

MARGE PIERCY (b. 1936)

The Love of Lettuce

With a pale green curly
lust I gloat over it nestled
there on the wet earth
(oakleaf, buttercrunch, ruby, cos)
like so many nests   5
waiting for birds
who lay hard boiled eggs.

The first green eyes
of the mustard, the frail
wands of carrots, the fat   10
thrust of the peas: all
are precious as I kneel
in the mud weeding
and the thinnings go into the salad.

The garden with crooked   15
wandering rows dug
by the three of us
drunk with sunshine has
an intricate pattern emerging
like the back of a rug.   20

The tender seedlings
raise their pinheads
with the cap of seed stuck on.
Cruel and smiling with sharp
teeth is the love of lettuce.   25
You grow out of last year's
composted dinner and you
will end in my hot mouth.

ISHMAEL REED (b. 1938)

beware: do not read this poem

tonite   ,   thriller was
abt an ol woman   , so vain she
surrounded herself w/
            many mirrors

it got so bad that finally she   5
locked herself indoors & her
whole life became the
            mirrors

one day the villagers broke
into her house   ,   but she was too   10
swift for them   .   she disappeared
            into a mirror

each tenant who bought the house
after that   ,   lost a loved one to
            the ol woman in the mirror   :   15
            first a little girl
            then a young woman
            then the young woman/s husband

the hunger of this poem is legendary
it has taken in many victims   20
back off from this poem
it has drawn in yr feet
back off from this poem
it has drawn in yr legs

back off from this poem   25
it is a greedy mirror

you are into this poem . from
  the waist down
nobody can hear you can they ?
this poem has had you up to here   30
  belch
this poem aint got no manners
you cant call out frm this poem
relax now & go w/ this poem
move & roll on to this poem   35
do not resist this poem
this poem has yr eyes
this poem has his head
this poem has his arms
this poem has his fingers   40
this poem has his fingertips

this poem is the reader & the
reader this poem

statistic :   the us bureau of missing persons reports
                 that in 1968 over 100,000 people disappeared   45
                 leaving no solid clues
                        nor trace   only
     a space   in the lives of their friends

KENNETH REXROTH (b. 1905)

Sorrow (translated from the Chinese)

Heaven took my wife. Now it
Has also taken my son.
My eyes are not allowed a
Dry season. It is too much
For my heart. I long for death.   5
When the rain falls and enters
The earth, when a pearl drops into
The depth of the sea, you can
Dive in the sea and find the
Pearl, you can dig in the earth   10
And find the water. But no one
Has ever come back from the
Underground Springs. Once gone, life
Is over for good. My chest
Tightens against me. I have   15

No one to turn to. Nothing,
Not even a shadow in a mirror.

MEI YAO CH'EN

ADRIENNE RICH (b. 1929)

Diving Into the Wreck

First having read the book of myths,
and loaded the camera,
and checked the edge of the knife-blade,
I put on
the body-armor of black rubber   5
the absurd flippers
the grave and awkward mask.
I am having to do this
not like Cousteau with his
assiduous team   10
aboard the sun-flooded schooner
but here alone.

There is a ladder.
The ladder is always there
hanging innocently   15
close to the side of the schooner.
We know what it is for,
we who have used it.
otherwise
it is a piece of maritime floss   20
some sundry equipment.

I go down.
Rung after rung and still
the oxygen immerses me
the blue light   25
the clear atoms
of our human air.
I go down.
My flippers cripple me,
I crawl like an insect down the ladder   30
and there is no one
to tell me when the ocean
will begin.

First the air is blue and then
it is bluer and then green and then
black I am blacking out and yet   35
my mask is powerful
it pumps my blood with power
the sea is another story
the sea is not a question of power   40
I have to learn alone
to turn my body without force
in the deep element.

And now; it is easy to forget
what I came for   45
among so many who have always
lived here
swaying their crenellated fans
between the reefs
and besides   50
you breathe differently down here.

I came to explore the wreck.
The words are purposes.
The words are maps.
I came to see the damage that was done   55
and the treasures that prevail.
I stroke the beam of my lamp
slowly along the flank
of something more permanent
than fish or weed   60

the thing I came for:
the wreck and not the story of the wreck
the thing itself and not the myth
the drowned face always staring
toward the sun   65
the evidence of damage
worn by salt and sway into this thread-bare beauty
the ribs of the disaster
curving their assertion
among the tentative haunters.   70

This is the place.
And I am here, the mermaid whose dark hair
streams black, the merman in his armored body.
We circle silently

about the wreck   75
we dive into the hold.
I am she: I am he

whose drowned face sleeps with open eyes
whose breasts still bear the stress
whose silver, copper, vermeil cargo lies   80
obscurely inside barrels
half-wedged and left to rot
we are the half-destroyed instruments
that once held to a course
the water-eaten log   85
the fouled compass

We are, I am, you are
by cowardice or courage
the one who find our way
back to this scene   90
carrying a knife, a camera
a book of myths
in which
our names do not appear.

EDWIN ARLINGTON ROBINSON (1869–1935)

Mr. Flood's Party

Old Eben Flood, climbing alone one night
Over the hill between the town below
And the forsaken upland hermitage
That held as much as he should ever know
On earth again of home, paused warily.   5
The road was his with not a native near;
And Eben, having leisure, said aloud,
For no man else in Tilbury Town to hear:

"Well, Mr. Flood, we have the harvest moon
Again, and we may not have many more;   10
The bird is on the wing, the poet says,
And you and I have said it here before.
Drink to the bird." He raised up to the light
The jug that he had gone so far to fill,
And answered huskily: "Well, Mr. Flood   15
Since you propose it, I believe I will."

Alone, as if enduring to the end
A valiant armor of scarred hopes outworn,
He stood there in the middle of the road
Like Roland's ghost winding a silent horn.   20
Below him, in the town among the trees,
Where friends of other days had honored him,
A phantom salutation of the dead
Rang thinly till old Eben's eyes were dim.

Then, as a mother lays her sleeping child   25
Down tenderly, fearing it may awake,
He set the jug down slowly at his feet
With trembling care, knowing that most things break;
And only when assured that on firm earth
It stood, and the uncertain lives of men   30
Assuredly did not, he paced away,
And with his hand extended paused again:

"Well, Mr. Flood, we have not met like this
In a long time; and many a change has come
To both of us, I fear, since last it was   35
We had a drop together. Welcome home!"
Convivially returning with himself,
Again he raised the jug up to the light;
And with an acquiescent quaver said:
"Well, Mr. Flood, if you insist, I might.   40

"Only a very little, Mr. Flood—
For auld lang syne. No more, sir; that will do."
So, for the time, apparently it did,
And Eben evidently thought so too;
For soon amid the silver loneliness   45
Of night he lifted up his voice and sang,
Secure, with only two moons listening,
Until the whole harmonious landscape rang—

"For auld lang syne." The weary throat gave out,
The last word wavered; and the song being done,   50
He raised again the jug regretfully
And shook his head, and was again alone.
There was not much that was ahead of him,
And there was nothing in the town below—
Where strangers would have shut the many doors   55
That many friends had opened long ago.

Eros Turannos

She fears him, and will always ask
  What fated her to choose him;
She meets in his engaging mask
  All reasons to refuse him;
But what she meets and what she fears   5
Are less than are the downward years,
Drawn slowly to the foamless weirs
  Of age, were she to lose him.

Between a blurred sagacity
  That once had power to sound him,   10
And Love, that will not let him be
  The Judas that she found him,
Her pride assuages her almost,
As if it were alone the cost.
He sees that he will not be lost,   15
  And waits and looks around him.

A sense of ocean and old trees
  Envelopes and allures him;
Tradition, touching all he sees,
  Beguiles and reassures him;   20
And all her doubts of what he says
Are dimmed with what she knows of days—
Till even prejudice delays
  And fades, and she secures him.

The falling leaf inaugurates   25
  The reign of her confusion;
The pounding wave reverberates
  The dirge of her illusion;
And home, where passion lived and died,
Becomes a place where she can hide,   30
While all the town and harbor side
  Vibrate with her seclusion.

We tell you, tapping on our brows,
  The story as it should be,
As if the story of a house   35
  Were told, or ever could be;
We'll have no kindly veil between
Her visions and those we have seen,

As if we guessed what hers have been,
  Or what they are or would be.   40

Meanwhile we do no harm; for they
  That with a god have striven,
Not hearing much of what we say,
  Take what the god has given;
Though like waves breaking it may be,   45
Or like a changed familiar tree,
Or like a stairway to the sea
  Where down the blind are driven.

KARL SHAPIRO (b. 1913)

Auto Wreck

Its quick soft silver bell beating, beating
And down the dark one ruby flare
Pulsing out red light like an artery,
The ambulance at top speed floating down
Past beacons and illuminated clocks   5
Wings in a heavy curve, dips down,
And brakes speed, entering the crowd.
The doors leap open, emptying the light;
Stretchers are laid out, the mangled lifted
And stowed into the little hospital.   10
Then the bell, breaking the hush, tolls once,
And the ambulance with its terrible cargo
Rocking, slightly rocking, moves away,
As the doors, an afterthought, are closed.

We are deranged, walking among the cops   15
Who sweep glass and are large and composed.
One is still making notes under the light.
One with a bucket douches ponds of blood
Into the street and gutter.
One hangs lanterns on the wrecks that cling,   20
Empty husks of locusts, to iron poles.

Our throats were tight as tourniquets,
Our feet were bound with splints, but now,
Like convalescents intimate and gauche,
We speak through sickly smiles and warn   25
With the stubborn saw of common sense,

The grim joke and the banal resolution.
The traffic moves around with care,
But we remain, touching a wound
That opens to our richest horror.   30
Already old, the question Who shall die?
Becomes unspoken Who is innocent?

For death in war is done by hands;
Suicide has cause and stillbirth, logic;
And cancer, simple as a flower, blooms.   35
But this invites the occult mind,
Cancels our physics with a sneer,
And spatters all we knew of denouement
Across the expedient and wicked stones.

CHARLES SIMIC (b. 1938)

Dismantling the Silence

Take down its ears first
Carefully so they don't spill over.
With a sharp whistle slit its belly open.
If there are ashes in it, close your eyes
And blow them whichever way the wind is pointing.   5
If there's water, sleeping water,
Bring the root of a plant that hasn't drunk for a month.

When you reach the bones,
And you haven't got a pack of dogs with you,
And you haven't got a pine coffin   10
And a wagon pulled by oxen to make them rattle,
Slip them quickly under your skin,
Next time you pick up your sack,
You'll hear them setting your teeth on edge. . .

It is now completely dark.   15
Slowly and with patience
Feel its heart. You will need to haul
A heavy chest of drawers
Into its emptiness
To make it creak   20
On its wheel.

WILLIAM JAY SMITH (b. 1918)

American Primitive

Look at him there in his stovepipe hat,
His high-top shoes, and his handsome collar;
Only my Daddy could look like that,
And I love my Daddy like he loves his Dollar.

The screen door bangs, and it sounds so funny—   5
There he is in a shower of gold;
His pockets are stuffed with folding money,
His lips are blue, and his hands feel cold.

He hangs in the hall by his black cravat,
The ladies faint, and the children holler: 10
Only my Daddy could look like that,
And I love my Daddy like he loves his Dollar.

WALLACE STEVENS (1879–1955)

A Study of Two Pears

I

Opusculum paedagogum.
The pears are not viols,
Nudes or bottles.
They resemble nothing else.

II

They are yellow forms   5
Composed of curves
Bulging toward the base,
They are touched red.

III

They are not flat surfaces
Having curved outlines.   10
They are round
Tapering toward the top.

IV

In the way they are modelled
There are bits of blue.
A hard dry leaf hangs   15
From the stem.

V

The yellow glistens.
It glistens with various yellows,
Citrons, oranges and greens
Flowering over the skin.   20

VI

The shadows of the pears
Are blobs on the green cloth.
The pears are not seen
As the observer wills.

Sunday Morning

I

Complacencies of the peignoir, and late
Coffee and oranges in a sunny chair,
And the green freedom of a cockatoo
Upon a rug mingle to dissipate
The holy hush of ancient sacrifice.   5
She dreams a little, and she feels the dark
Encroachment of that old catastrophe,
As a calm darkens among water-lights.
The pungent oranges and bright, green wings
Seem things in some procession of the dead,   10
Winding across wide water, without sound.
The day is like wide water, without sound,
Stilled for the passing of her dreaming feet
Over the seas, to silent Palestine,
Dominion of the blood and sepulchre.   15

II

Why should she give her bounty to the dead?
What is divinity if it can come
Only in silent shadows and in dreams?
Shall she not find in comforts of the sun,
In pungent fruit and bright, green wings, or else 20
In any balm or beauty of the earth,
Things to be cherished like the thought of heaven?
Divinity must live within herself:
Passions of rain, or moods in falling snow;
Grievings in loneliness, or unsubdued 25
Elations when the forest blooms; gusty
Emotions on wet roads on autumn nights;
All pleasures and all pains, remembering
The bough of summer and the winter branch.
These are the measures destined for her soul. 30

III

Jove in the clouds had his inhuman birth.
No mother suckled him, no sweet land gave
Large-mannered motions to his mythy mind
He moved among us, as a muttering king,
Magnificent, would move among his hinds, 35
Until our blood, commingling, virginal,
With heaven, brought such requital to desire
The very hinds discerned it, in a star.
Shall our blood fail? Or shall it come to be
The blood of paradise? And shall the earth 40
Seem all of paradise that we shall know?
The sky will be much friendlier then than now,
A part of labor and a part of pain,
And next in glory to enduring love,
Not this dividing and indifferent blue. 45

IV

She says, "I am content when wakened birds,
Before they fly, test the reality
Of misty fields, by their sweet questionings;
But when the birds are gone, and their warm fields
Return no more, where, then, is paradise?" 50
There is not any haunt of prophecy,
Nor any old chimera of the grave,

Neither the golden underground, nor isle
Melodious, where spirits gat them home,
Nor visionary south, nor cloudy palm   55
Remote on heaven's hill, that has endured
As April's green endures; or will endure
Like her remembrance of awakened birds,
Or her desire for June and evening, tipped
By the consummation of the swallow's wings.   60

V

She says, "But in contentment I still feel
The need of some imperishable bliss."
Death is the mother of beauty; hence from her,
Alone, shall come fulfilment to our dreams
And our desires. Although she strews the leaves   65
Of sure obliteration on our paths,
The path sick sorrow took, the many paths
Where triumph rang its brassy phrase, or love
Whispered a little out of tenderness,
She makes the willow shiver in the sun   70
For maidens who were wont to sit and gaze
Upon the grass, relinquished to their feet.
She causes boys to pile new plums and pears
On disregarded plate. The maidens taste
And stray impassioned in the littering leaves.   75

VI

Is there no change of death in paradise?
Does ripe fruit never fall? Or do the boughs
Hang always heavy in that perfect sky,
Unchanging, yet so like our perishing earth,
With rivers like our own that seek for seas   80
They never find, the same receding shores
That never touch with inarticulate pang?
Why set the pear upon those river-banks
Or spice the shores with odors of the plum?
Alas, that they should wear our colors there,   85
The silken weavings of our afternoons,
And pick the strings of our insipid lutes!
Death is the mother of beauty, mystical,
Within whose burning bosom we devise
Our earthly mothers waiting, sleeplessly.   90

VII

Supple and turbulent, a ring of men
Shall chant in orgy on a summer morn
Their boisterous devotion to the sun,
Not as a god, but as a god might be,
Naked among them, like a savage source.   95
Their chant shall be a chant of paradise,
Out of their blood, returning to the sky;
And in their chant shall enter, voice by voice,
The windy lake wherein their lord delights,
The trees, like serafin, and echoing hills,   100
That choir among themselves long afterward.
They shall know well the heavenly fellowship
Of men that perish and of summer morn.
And whence they came and whither they shall go
The dew upon their feet shall manifest.   105

VIII

She hears, upon that water without sound,
A voice that cries, "The tomb in Palestine
Is not the porch of spirits lingering.
It is the grave of Jesus, where he lay."
We live in an old chaos of the sun,   110
Or old dependency of day and night,
Or island solitude, unsponsored, free,
Of that wide water, inescapable.
Deer walk upon our mountains, and the quail
Whistle about us their spontaneous cries;   115
Sweet berries ripen in the wilderness;
And, in the isolation of the sky,
At evening, casual flocks of pigeons make
Ambiguous undulations as they sink,
Downward to darkness, on extended wings.   120

Peter Quince at the Clavier

I

Just as my fingers on these keys
Make music, so the selfsame sounds
On my spirit make a music, too.

Music is feeling, then, not sound;

And thus it us that what I feel,   5
Here in this room, desiring you,

Thinking of your blue-shadowed silk,
Is music. It is like the strain
Waked in the elders by Susanna.

Of a green evening, clear and warm,   10
She bathed in her still garden, while
The red-eyed elders watching, felt

The basses of their beings throb
In witching chords, and their thin blood
Pulse pizzicati of Hosanna.   15

II

In the green water, clear and warm,
Susanna lay.
She searched
The touch of springs,
And found   20
Concealed imaginings.
She sighed,
For so much melody.

Upon the bank, she stood
In the cool   25
Of spent emotions.
She felt, among the leaves,
The dew
Of old devotions.

She walked upon the grass,   30
Still quavering.
The winds were like her maids,
On timid feet,
Fetching her woven scarves,
Yet wavering.   35

A breath upon her hand
Muted the night.
She turned—
A cymbal crashed,
And roaring horns.   40

III

Soon, with a noise like tambourines,
Came her attendant Byzantines.

They wondered why Susanna cried
Against the elders by her side;

And as they whispered, the refrain   45
Was like a willow swept by rain.

Anon, their lamps' uplifted flame
Revealed Susanna and her shame.

And then, the simpering Byzantines
Fled, with a noise like tambourines.   50

IV

Beauty is momentary in the mind—
the fitful tracing of a portal;
But in the flesh it is immortal.
The body dies; the body's beauty lives.
So evenings die, in their green going,   55
A wave, interminably flowing.
So gardens die, their meek breath scenting
The cowl of winter, done repenting.
So maidens die, to the auroral
Celebration of a maiden's choral.   60
Susanna's music touched the bawdy strings
Of those white elders; but, escaping,
Left only Death's ironic scraping.
Now, in its immortality, it plays
On the clear viol of her memory,   65
And makes a constant sacrament of praise.

MARK STRAND (b. 1934)

Eating Poetry

Ink runs from the corners of my mouth.
There is no happiness like mine.
I have been eating poetry.

The librarian does not believe what she sees.
Her eyes are sad   5
and she walks with her hands in her dress.

The poems are gone.
The light is dim.
The dogs are on the basement stairs and coming up.

Their eyeballs roll,   10
their blond legs burn like brush.
The poor librarian begins to stamp her feet and weep.

She does not understand.
When I get on my knees and lick her hand,
she screams.   15

I am a new man.
I snarl at her and bark,
I romp with joy in the bookish dark.

ALLEN TATE (b. 1899)

Ode to the Confederate Dead

Row after row with strict impunity
The headstones yield their names to the element,
The wind whirrs without recollection:
In the riven troughs the splayed leaves
Pile up, of nature the casual sacrament   5
To the seasonal eternity of death;
Then driven by the fierce scrutiny
Of heaven to their election in the vast breath,
They sough the rumour of mortality.

Autumn is desolation in the plot   10
Of a thousand acres where these memories grow
From the inexhaustible bodies that are not
Dead, but feed the grass row after rich row.
Think of the autumns that have come and gone!—
Ambitious November with the humors of the year,   15
With a particular zeal for every slab,
Staining the uncomfortable angels that rot

On the slabs, a wing chipped here, an arm there:
The brute curiosity of an angel's stare
Turns you, like them, to stone, 20
Transforms the heaving air
Till plunged to a heavier world below
You shift your sea-space blindly
Heaving, turning like the blind crab.

    Dazed by the wind, only the wind 25
    The leaves flying, plunge

You know who have waited by the wall
The twilight certainty of an animal,
Those midnight restitutions of the blood
You know—the immitigable pines, the smoky frieze 30
Of the sky, the sudden call: you know the rage,
The cold pool left by the mounting flood,
Of muted Zeno and Parmenides.
You who have waited for the angry resolution
Of those desires that should be yours tomorrow, 35
You know the unimportant shrift of death
And praise the vision
And praise the arrogant circumstance
Of those who fall
Rank upon rank, hurried beyond decision— 40
Here by the sagging gate, stopped by the wall.

    Seeing, seeing only the leaves
    Flying, plunge and expire

Turn your eyes to the immoderate past,
Turn to the inscrutable infantry rising 45
Demons out of the earth—they will not last.
Stonewall, Stonewall, and the sunken fields of hemp,
Shiloh, Antietam, Malvern Hill, Bull Run.
Lost in that orient of the thick-and-fast
You will curse the setting sun. 50

    Cursing only the leaves crying
    Like an old man in a storm

You hear the shout, the crazy hemlocks point
With troubled fingers to the silence which
Smothers you, a mummy, in time. 55

The hound bitch
Toothless and dying, in a musty cellar
Hears the wind only.

Now that the salt of their blood
Stiffens the saltier oblivion of the sea,   60
Seals the malignant purity of the flood,
What shall we who count our days and bow
Our heads with a commemorial woe
In the ribboned coats of grim felicity,
What shall we say of the bones, unclean,   65
Whose verdurous anonymity will grow?
The ragged arms, the ragged heads and eyes
Lost in these acres of the insane green?
The gray lean spiders come, they come and go;
In a tangle of willows without light   70
The singular screech-owl's tight
Invisible lyric seeds the mind
With the furious murmur of their chivalry.

We shall say only the leaves
Flying, plunge and expire   75

We shall say only the leaves whispering
In the improbable mist of nightfall
That flies on multiple wing;
Night is the beginning and the end
And in between the ends of distraction   80
Waits mute speculation, the patient curse
That stones the eyes, or like the jaguar leaps
For his own image in a jungle pool, his victim.

What shall we say who have knowledge
Carried to the heart? Shall we take the act   85
To the grave? Shall we, more hopeful, set up the grave
In the house? The ravenous grave?

Leave now
The shut gate and the decomposing wall: 90
The gentle serpent, green in the mulberry bush,
Riots with his tongue through the hush—
Sentinel of the grave who counts us all!

DIANE WAKOSKI (b. 1937)

The Father of Our Country

All fathers in Western civilization must have
a military origin. The
ruler,
governor,
yes,   5
he is
was the
general at one time or other.
And George Washington
won the hearts   10
of his country—the rough military man
with awkward
sincere
drawing-room manners.

My father;   15
have you ever heard me speak of him? I seldom
do. But I had a father,
and he had military origins—or my origins from
him
are military,   20
militant. That is, I remember him only in uniform. But of the navy,
30 years a chief petty officer,
Always away from home.

It is rough/hard for me to
speak now.   25
I'm not used to talking
about him.
Not used to
naming his objects/
objects   30
that never surrounded me.

A woodpecker with fresh bloody crest
knocks
at my mouth. Father, for the first
time I say   35
your name. Name rolled in thick Polish parchment scrolls,
name of Roman candle drippings when I sit at my table
alone, each night,

name of naval uniforms and name of
telegrams, name of   40
coming home from your aircraft carrier,
name of shiny shoes,
name of Hawaiian dolls, name
of mess spoons, name of greasy machinery, and name of
stencilled names.   45
Is it your blood I carry in a test tube,
my arm,
to let fall, crack, and spill on the sidewalk
in front of the men
I know,   50
I love,
I know, and
want? So you left my house when I was under two,
being replaced by other machinery, and
I didn't believe you left me.   55

    This scene: the trunk yielding treasures of
    a green fountain pen, heart-shaped mirror,
    amber beads, old letters with brown ink, and
    the gopher snake stretched across the palm tree
    in the front yard with woody trunk like monkey skins,   60
    and a sunset through the skinny persimmon trees. You
    came walking, not even a telegram or post card from
    Tahiti. Love, love, through my heart like ink in
    the thickest nubbed pen, black and flowing into words.
    You came to me, and I at least six. Six doilies   65
    of lace, six battleship cannon, six old beerbottles,
    six thick steaks, six love letters, six clocks running
    backwards, six watermelons, and six baby teeth, a six
    cornered hat on six men's heads, six lovers at once
    or one lover at sixes and sevens; how I confuse   70
    all this with my
    dream
    walking the tightrope bridge
    with gold knots
    over   75
    the mouth of an anemone/tissue spiral lips
    and holding on so that the ropes burned
    as if my wrist had been tied

If George Washington
had not   80
been the Father

of my Country,
it is doubtful that I would ever have
found
a father. Father in my mouth, on my lips, in my   85
tongue, out of all my womanly fire,
Father I have left in my steel filing cabinet as a name on my birth
certificate, Father, I have left in the teeth pulled out at
dentists' offices and thrown into their garbage cans,
Father living in my wide cheekbones and short feet,   90
Father in my Polish tantrums and my American speech, Father, not a
holy name, not a name I cherish but the name I bear, the name
that makes me one of a kind in any phone book because
you changed it, and nobody
but us   95
has it,
Father who makes me dream in the dead of night of the falling cherry
blossoms, Father who make me know all men will leave me
if I love them
Father who made me a maverick,   100
a writer
a namer,
name/father, sun/father, moon/father, bloody mars/father,

other children said, "My father is a doctor,"
or   105
"My father gave me this camera,"
or
"My father took me to
the movies,"
or   110
"My father and I went swimming,"
but
my father is coming in a letter
once a month
for a while,   115
and my father
sometimes came in a telegram
but
mostly
my father came to me   120
in sleep, my father because I dreamed in one night that I dug through
the ash heap in back of the pepper tree and found a diamond shaped
like a dog and my father called the dog and it came leaping over to
him and he walked away out of the yard down the road with the dog
jumping and yipping at his heels,   125

my father was not in the telephone book
in my city;
my father was not sleeping with my mother
at home;
my father did not care if I studied the   130
piano;
my father did not care what
I did;
and I thought my father was handsome and I loved him and I wondered
why   135
he left me alone so much,
so many years
in fact, but
my father
made me what I am   140
a lonely woman
without a purpose, just as I was
a lonely child
without any father. I walked with words, words, and names,
names, Father was not   145
one of my words.
Father was not
one of my names. But now I say, George you have become my father,
in his 20th century naval uniform. George Washington, I need your
love; George, I want to call you Father, Father, my Father,   150
Father of my country,
that is
me. And I say the name to chant it. To sing it. To lace it around me
like weaving cloth. Like a happy child on that shining afternoon in
the palmtree sunset with her mother's trunk yielding treasures,   155
I cry and
cry,
Father,
Father,
Father,   160
have you really come home?

DEREK WALCOTT (b. 1930)

A Far Cry From Africa

A wind is ruffling the tawny pelt
Of Africa. Kikuyu, quick as flies,
Batten down the bloodstreams of the veldt.

Corpses are scattered through a paradise.
Only the worm, colonel of carrion, cries: 5
'Waste no compassion on these separate dead!'
Statistics justify and scholars seize
The salients of colonial policy.
What is that to the white child hacked in bed?
To savages, expendable as Jews?   10

Threshed out by beaters, the long rushes break
In a white dust of ibises whose cries
Have wheeled since civilization's dawn
From the perched river or beast-teeming plain.
The violence of beast on beast is read   15
As natural law, but upright man
Seeks his divinity by inflicting pain.
Delirious as these worried beasts, his wars
Dance to the tightened carcass of a drum,
While he calls courage still that native dread   20
Of the white peace contracted by the dead.

Again brutish necessity wipes its hands
Upon the napkin of a dirty cause, again
A waste of our compassion, as with Spain,
The gorilla wrestles with the superman.   25

I who am poisoned with the blood of both,
Where shall I turn, divided to the vein?
I who have cursed
The drunken officer of British rule, how choose
Between this Africa and the English tongue I love?   30
Betray them both, or give back what they give?
How can I face such slaughter and be cool?
How can I turn from Africa and live?

ROBERT PENN WARREN (b. 1905)

Bearded Oaks

The oaks, how subtle and marine,
Bearded, and all the layered light
Above them swims; and thus the scene,
Recessed, awaits the positive night.

So, waiting, we in the grass now lie   5
Beneath the languorous tread of light:
The grasses, kelp-like, satisfy
The nameless motions of the air.

Upon the floor of light, and time,
Unmurmuring, of polyp made,   10
We rest; we are, as light withdraws,
Twin atolls on a shelf of shade.

Ages to our construction went,
Dim architecture, hour by hour:
And violence, forgot now, lent   15
The present stillness all its power.

The storm of noon above us rolled,
Of light the fury, furious gold,
The long drag troubling us, the depth:
Dark is unrocking, unrippling, still.   20

Passion and slaughter, ruth, decay
Descend, minutely whispering down,
Silted down swaying streams, to lay
Foundation for our voicelessness.

All our debate is voiceless here,   25
As all our rage, the rage of stone;
If hope is hopeless, then fearless is fear,
And history is thus undone.

Our feet once wrought the hollow street
With echo when the lamps were dead   30
At windows, once our headlight glare
Disturbed the doe that, leaping, fled.

I do not love you less that now
The caged heart makes iron stroke,
Or less that all that light once gave   35
The graduate dark should now revoke.

We live in time so little time
And we learn all so painfully,
That we may spare this hour's term
To practice for eternity.   40

TOM WAYMAN (b. 1945)

What Good Poems Are For

To sit on a shelf in the cabin across the lake
where the young man and the young woman
have come to live—there are only a few books
in this dwelling, and one of them
is this book of poems. 5

           To be like plants
on a sunlit windowsill
of a city apartment—all the hours of care
that go into them, the tending and watering,
and yet to the casual eye they are just present 10
—a brief moment of enjoyment.
Only those who work on the plant
know how slowly it grows
and changes, almost dies from its own causes
or neglect, or how other plants 15
can be started from this one
and used elsewhere in the house
or given to friends.
But everyone notices the absence of plants
in a residence 20
even those who don't have plants themselves.

There is also (though this is more rare)
Bob Smith's story about the man in the bar up north,
a man in his 50s, taking a poem from a new book Bob showed him
around from table to table, reading it aloud 25
to each group of drinkers because, he kept saying,
the poem was about work he did, what he knew about,
written by somebody like himself.
But where could he take it
except from table to table, past the *Fuck offs* 30
and the *Hey, that's pretty goods?* Over the noise
of the jukebox and the bar's TV,
past the silence of the lake,
a person is speaking
in a world full of people talking. 35
Out of all that is said, these particular words
put down roots in someone's mind
so that he or she likes to have them here—

these words no one was paid to write
that live with us for a while   40
in a small container
on the ledge where the light enters

WALT WHITMAN (1819–1892)

When Lilacs Last in the Dooryard Bloom'd

I

When lilacs last in the dooryard bloom'd,
And the great star early droop'd in the western sky in the night,
I mourn'd, and yet shall mourn with ever-returning spring.
Ever-returning spring, trinity sure to me you bring,
Lilac blooming perennial and drooping star in the west,   5
And thought of him I love.

II

O powerful western fallen star!
O shades of night—O moody, tearful night!
O great star disappear'd—O the black murk that hides the star!
O cruel hands that hold me powerless—O helpless soul of me!   10
O harsh surrounding cloud that will not free my soul.

III

In the dooryard fronting an old farm-house near the white-wash'd
    palings,
Stands the lilac-bush tall-growing with heart-shaped leaves of rich
    green,
With many a pointed blossom rising delicate, with the perfume
    strong I love,
With every leaf a miracle—and from this bush in the dooryard,   15
With delicate-color'd blossoms and heart-shaped leaves of rich green,
A sprig with its flower I break.

IV

In the swamp in secluded recesses,
A shy and hidden bird is warbling a song.

Solitary the thrush, 20
The hermit withdrawn to himself, avoiding the settlements,
Sings by himself a song.

Song of the bleeding throat,
Death's outlet song of life, (for well dear brother I know,
If thou wast not granted to sing thou would'st surely die.) 25

V

Over the breast of the spring the land, amid cities,
Amid lanes and through old woods, where lately the violets
    peep'd from the ground, spotting the gray debris,
Amid the grass in the fields each side of the lanes, passing the
    endless grass,
Passing the yellow-spear'd wheat, every grain from its shroud in the
    dark-brown fields uprisen,
Passing the apple-tree blows of white and pink in the orchards, 30
Carrying a corpse to where it shall rest in the grave,
Night and day journeys a coffin.

VI

Coffin that passes through lanes and streets,
Through day and night with the great cloud darkening the land,
With the pomp of the inloop'd flags with the cities draped in black, 35
With the show of the States themselves as of crape-veil'd women
    standing,
With processions long and winding and the flambeaus of the night,
With the countless torches lit, with the silent sea of faces and the
    unbared heads,
With the waiting depot, the arriving coffin, and the sombre faces,
With dirges through the night, with the thousand voices rising strong
    and solemn, 40
With all the mournful voices of the dirges pour'd around the coffin,
The dim-lit churches and the shuddering organs—where amid these you
    journey,
With the tolling bells' perpetual clang,
Here, coffin that slowly passes,
I give you my sprig of lilac. 45

VII

(Nor for you, for one alone,
Blossoms and branches green to coffins all I bring,

For fresh as the morning, thus would I chant a song for you
    O sane and sacred death.

All over bouquets of roses,
O death, I cover you over with roses and early lilies,   50
But mostly and now the lilac that blooms the first,
Copious I break, I break the sprigs from the bushes,
With loaded arms I come, pouring for you,
For you and the coffins all of you O death.)

VIII

O western orb sailing the heaven,   55
Now I know what you must have meant as a month since I walk'd,
As I walk'd in silence the transparent shadowy night,
As I saw you had something to tell as you bent to me night after night,
As you droop'd from the sky low down as if to my side, (while the
    other stars all look'd on,)
As we wander'd together the solemn night, (for something I know not
    what kept me from sleep,)   60
As the night advanced, and I saw on the rim of the west how full you
    were of woe,
As I stood on the rising ground in the breeze in the cool
    transparent night,
As I watch'd where you passed and was lost in the netherward black of
    the night,
As my soul in its trouble dissatisfied sank, as where you sad orb,
Concluded, dropt in the night, and was gone.   65

IX

Sing on there in the swamp,
O singer bashful and tender, I hear your notes, I hear your call,
I hear, I come presently, I understand you,
But a moment I linger, for the lustrous star has detain'd me,
The star my departing comrade holds and detains me.   70

X

O how shall I warble myself for the dead one there I loved?
And how shall I deck my song for the large sweet soul that has gone?
And what shall my perfume be for the grave of him I love?

Sea-winds blown from east and west,
Blown from the Eastern sea and blown from the Western sea, till
    there on the prairies meeting,   75

These and with these and the breath of my chant,
I'll perfume the grave of him I love.

XI

O what shall I hang on the chamber walls?
And what shall the pictures be that I hang on the walls,
To adorn the burial-house of him I love?   80

Pictures of growing spring and farms and homes,
With the Fourth-month eve at sundown, and the gray smoke lucid and
    bright,
With floods of the yellow gold of the gorgeous, indolent, sinking sun,
    burning, expanding the air,
With the fresh sweet herbage under foot, and the pale green leaves
    of the trees prolific,
In the distance the flowing glaze, the breast of the river, with a wind-
    dapple here and there,   85
With ranging hills on the banks, with many a line against the sky, and
    shadows,
And the city at hand with dwellings so dense, and stacks of chimneys,
And all the scenes of life and the workshops, and the workmen
    homeward returning.

XII

Lo, body and soul—this land,
My own Manhattan with spires, and the sparkling and hurrying
    tides, and the ships.   90
The varied and ample land, the South and the North in the light,
    Ohio's shores and flashing Missouri,
And ever the far-spreading prairies cover'd with grass and corn.

Lo, the most excellent sun so calm and haughty,
The violet and purple morn with just-felt breezes,
The gentle soft-born measureless light,   95
The miracle spreading bathing all, the fulfill'd noon,
The coming eve delicious, the welcome night and the stars,
Over my cities shining all, enveloping man and land.

XIII

Sing on, sing on you gray-brown bird,
Sing from the swamps, the recesses, pour your chant from the
    bushes,   100

Limitless out of the dusk, out of the cedars and pines.

Sing on dearest brother, warble your reedy song,
Loud human song, with voice of uttermost woe.

O liquid and free and tender!
O wild and loose to my soul—O wondrous singer!   105
You only I hear—yet the star holds me, (but will soon depart,)
Yet the lilac with mastering odor holds me.

XIV

Now while I sat in the day and look'd forth,
In the close of the day with its light and the fields of spring, and the
     farmers preparing their crops,
In the large unconscious scenery of my land with its lakes and forests, 110
In the heavenly aerial beauty, (after the perturb'd winds and
     the storms,)
Under the arching heavens of the afternoon swift passing, and the voices
     of children and women.
The many-moving sea-tides, and I saw the ships how they sail'd,
And the summer approaching with richness, and the fields all busy with
     labor,
And the infinite separate houses, how they all went on, each with
     its meals and minutia of daily usages,   115
And the streets how their throbbings throbb'd, and the cities pent—lo,
     then and there,
Falling upon them all and among them all, enveloping me with the rest,
Appear'd the cloud, appear'd the long black trail,
And I knew death, its thought, and the sacred knowledge of death.

Then with the knowledge of death as walking one side of me,   120
And the thought of death close-walking the other side of me,
And I in the middle as with companions, and as holding the hands of
     companions,
I fled forth to the hiding receiving night that talks not,
Down to the shores of the water, the path by the swamp in the
     dimness,
To the solemn shadowy cedars and ghostly pines so still.   125

And the singer so shy to the rest receiv'd me,
The gray-brown bird I know receiv'd us comrades three,
And he sang the carol of death, and a verse for him I love.

From deep secluded recesses,

From the fragrant cedars and the ghostly pines so still,   130
Came the carol of the bird.

And the charm of the carol rapt me,
As I held as if by their hands my comrades in the night,
And the voice of my spirit tallied the song of the bird.

Come lovely and soothing death,   135
Undulate round the world, serenely arriving, arriving,
In the day, in the night, to all, to each,
Sooner or later delicate death.

Prais'd be the fathomless universe,
For life and joy, and for objects and knowledge curious,   140
And for love, sweet love—but praise! praise! praise!
For the sure-enwinding arms of cool-enfolding death.

Dark mother always gliding near with soft feet,
Have none chanted for thee a chant of fullest welcome?
Then I chant it for thee, I glorify thee above all,   145
I bring thee a song that when thou must indeed come, come
    unfalteringly.

Approach strong deliveress,
When it is so, when thou has taken them I joyously sing the dead,
Lost in the loving floating ocean of thee,
Loved in the flood of thy bliss O death.   150

From me to thee glad serenades,
Dances for thee I propose saluting thee, adornments and feastings for
    thee,
And the sights of the open landscape and the high-spread sky
    are fitting,
And life and the fields, and the huge and thoughtful night.

The night in silence under many a star,   155
The ocean shore and the husky whispering wave whose voice I know,
And the soul turning to thee O vast and well-veil'd death,
And the body gratefuly nestling close to thee.

Over the tree-tops I float thee a song,
Over the rising and sinking waves, over the myriad fields and
    the prairies wide,   160
Over the dense-pack'd cities all and the teeming wharves and ways,
I float this carol with joy, with joy to thee O death.

XV

To the tally of my soul,
Loud and strong kept up the gray-brown bird,
With pure deliberate notes spreading filling the night.   165

Loud in the pines and cedars dim,
Clear in the freshness moist and the swamp-perfume
And I with my comrades there in the night.

While my sight that was bound in my eyes unclosed,
As to long panoramas of visions.   170

And I saw askant the armies,
I saw as in noiseless dreams hundreds of battle-flags,
Borne through the smoke of the battles and pierc'd with missiles I saw
        them,
And carried hither and yon through the smoke, and torn and bloody,
And at last but a few shreds left on the staffs, (and all in silence,)   175
And the staffs all splinter'd and broken.

I saw battle-corpses, myriads of them,
And the white skeletons of young men, I saw them,
I saw the debris and debris of all the slain soldiers of the war,
But I saw they were not as was thought,   180
They themselves were fully at rest, they suffer'd not,
The living remain'd and suffer'd, the mother suffer'd,
And the wife and the child and the musing comrade suffer'd,
And the armies that remain'd suffer'd.

XVI

Passing the visions, passing the night,   185
Passing, unloosing the hold of my comrades' hands,
Passing the song of the hermit bird and the tallying song of my soul,
Victorious song, death's outlet song, yet varying ever-altering song,
As low and wailing, yet clear the notes, rising and falling flooding the
        night,
Sadly sinking and fainting, as warning and warning, and yet again
        bursting with joy,   190
Covering the earth and filling the spread of the heaven,
As that powerful psalm in the night I heard from recesses,
Passing, I leave thee lilac with heart-shaped leaves,
I leave thee there in the door-yard, blooming, returning with spring.

I cease from my song for thee,   195
From my gaze on thee in the west, fronting the west, communing
    with thee,
O comrade lustrous with silver face in the night.

Yet each to keep and all, retrievements out of the night,
The song, the wondrous chant of the gray-brown bird,
And the tallying chant, the echo arous'd in my soul,   200
With the lustrous and drooping star with the countenance full of woe,
With the holders holding my hand nearing the call of the bird,
Comrades mine and I in the midst, and their memory ever to keep,
    for the dead I love so well,
For the sweetest, wisest soul of all my days and lands—and this for his
    dear sake,
Lilac and star and bird twined with the chant of my soul,   205
There in the fragrant pines and the cedars dusk and dim.

I Saw in Lousiana a Live-oak Growing

I saw in Lousiana a live-oak growing,
All alone stood it and the moss hung down from the branches,
Without any companion it grew there uttering joyous leaves of dark
    green,
And its look, rude, unbending, lusty, made me think of myself,
But I wonder'd how it could utter joyous leaves standing alone there   5
    without its friend near, for I knew I could not,
And I broke off a twig with a certain number of leaves upon it, and
    twined around it a little moss,
And brought it away, and I have placed it in sight in my room,
It is not needed to remind me as of my own dear friends,
(For I believe lately I think of little else than of them,)
Yet it remains to me a curious token, it makes me think of manly love; 10
For all that, and though the live-oak glistens there in Louisiana solitary
    in a wide flat space,
Uttering joyous leaves all its life without a friend a lover near,
I know very well I could not.

RICHARD WILBUR (b. 1921)

Love Calls Us to the Things of this World

The eyes open to a cry of pulleys,
And spirited from sleep, the astounded soul

Hangs for a moment bodiless and simple
As false dawn.
                  Outside the open window   5
The morning air is all awash with angels.

Some are in bed-sheets, some are in blouses,
Some are in smocks: but truly there they are.
Now they are rising together in calm swells
Of halcyon feeling, filling whatever they wear   10
With the deep joy of their impersonal breathing;

Now they are flying in place, conveying
The terrible speed of their omnipresence, moving
And staying like white water; and now of a sudden
They swoon down into so rapt a quiet   15
That nobody seems to be there.
                     The soul shrinks

From all that it is about to remember,
From the punctual rape of every blessèd day,
And cries,   20
          "Oh, let there be nothing on earth but laundry,
Nothing but rosy hands in the rising steam
And clear dances done in the sight of heaven."

Yet, as the sun acknowledges
With a warm look the world's hunks and colors,   25
The soul descends once more in bitter love
To accept the waking body, saying now
In a changed voice as the man yawns and rises,

"Bring them down from their ruddy gallows;
Let there be clean linen for the backs of thieves,   30
Let lovers go fresh and sweet to be undone,
And the heaviest nuns walk in a pure floating
Of dark habits,
                  keeping their difficult balance."

Late Aubade

You could be sitting now in a carrel
Turning some liver-spotted page,
Or rising in an elevator-cage
Toward Ladies' Apparel.

You could be planting a raucous bed   5
Of salvia, in rubber gloves,
Or lunching through a screed of someone's loves
With pitying head,

Or making some unhappy setter
Heel, or listening to a bleak   10
Lecture on Schoenberg's serial technique.
Isn't this better?

Think of the time you are not
Wasting, and would not care to waste,
Such thing, thank God, not being to your taste,   15
Think what a lot

Of time, by woman's reckoning,
You've saved, and so may spend on this,
You who had rather lie in bed and kiss
Than anything.   20

It's almost noon, you say? If so,
Time flies, and I need not rehearse
The rosebuds-theme of centuries of verse.
If you *must* go,

Wait for a while, then slip downstairs   25
And bring us up some chilled white wine,
And some blue cheese, and crackers, and some fine
Ruddy-skinned pears.

WILLIAM CARLOS WILLIAMS (1883–1963)

Landscape with the Fall of Icarus

According to Brueghel
when Icarus fell
it was spring

a farmer was ploughing
his field   5
the whole pageantry

of the year was
awake tingling
near

the edge of the sea   10
concerned
with itself

sweating in the sun
that melted
the wings' wax   15

unsignificantly
off the coast
there was

a splash quite unnoticed
this was   20
Icarus drowning

Spring and All

By the road to the contagious hospital
under the surge of the blue
mottled clouds driven from the
northeast—a cold wind. Beyond, the
waste of broad, muddy fields   5
brown with dried weeds, standing and fallen

patches of standing water
the scattering of tall trees

All along the road the reddish
purplish, forked, upstanding, twiggy   10
stuff of bushes and small trees
with dead, brown leaves under them
leafless vines—

Lifeless in appearance, sluggish
dazed spring approaches—   15

They enter the new world naked,
cold, uncertain of all
save that they enter. All about them
the cold, familiar wind—

Now the grass, tomorrow   20
the stiff curl of wildcarrot leaf
One by one objects are defined—
It quickens: clarity, outline of leaf

But now the stark dignity of
entrance—Still, the profound change   25
has come upon them: rooted, they
grip down and begin to awaken

WILLIAM WORDSWORTH (1770–1850)

ODE: Intimations of Immortality from Recollections of Early Childhood

> *The Child is father of the Man;*
> *And I could wish my days to be*
> *Bound each to each by natural piety.*

I

There was a time when meadow, grove, and stream,
The earth, and every common sight,
     To me did seem
     Appareled in celestial light,
The glory and the freshness of a dream.   5
It is not now as it hath been of yore—
     Turn whereso'er I may,
     By night or day,
The things which I have seen I now can see no more.

II

     The Rainbow comes and goes,   10
     And lovely is the Rose,
     The Moon doth with delight
Look round her when the heavens are bare,
     Waters on a starry night
     Are beautiful and fair;   15
  The sunshine is a glorious birth;
  But yet I know, where'er I go,
That there hath passed away a glory from the earth.

III

Now, while the birds thus sing a joyous song,
     And while the young lambs bound   20
     As to the tabor's sound,
To me alone there came a thought of grief:

A timely utterance gave that thought relief,
 And I again am strong:
The cataracts blow their trumpets from the steep;   25
No more shall grief of mine the season wrong;
I hear the Echoes through the mountains throng,
The Winds come to me from the fields of sleep,
 And all the earth is gay;
  Land and sea   30
 Give themselves up to jollity,
  And with the heart of May
Doth every Beast keep holiday—
 Thou Child of Joy,
Shout round me, let me hear thy shouts, thou happy Shepherd-boy! 35

IV

Ye blesséd Creatures, I have heard the call
 Ye to each other make; I see
The heavens laugh with you in your jubilee;
 My heart is at your festival,
  My head hath its coronal,   40
The fullness of your bliss, I feel—I feel it all.
  Oh, evil day! if I were sullen
  While Earth herself is adorning,
   This sweet May morning,
  And the Children are culling   45
   On every side,
  In a thousand valleys far and wide,
  Fresh flowers; while the sun shines warm,
And the Babe leaps up on his Mother's arm—
  I hear, I hear, with joy I hear!   50
  —But there's a Tree, of many, one,
A single Field which I have looked upon,
Both of them speak of something that is gone:
  The Pansy at my feet
  Doth the same tale repeat: 55
Whither is fled the visionary gleam?
Where is it now, the glory and the dream?

V

Our birth is but a sleep and a forgetting:
The Soul that rises with us, our life's Star,
  Hath had elsewhere its setting,   60
  And cometh from afar:

Not in entire forgetfulness,
And not in utter nakedness,
But trailing clouds of glory do we come
    From God, who is our home: 65
Heaven lies about us in our infancy!
Shades of the prison-house begin to close
    Upon the growing Boy
        But he
Beholds the light, and whence it flows, 70
    He sees it in his joy;
The Youth, who daily farther from the east
    Must travel, still is Nature's Priest,
    And by the vision splendid
    Is on his way attended; 75
At length the Man perceives it die away,
And fade into the light of common day.

VI

Earth fills her lap with pleasures of her own;
Yearnings she hath in her own natural kind,
And, even with something of a Mother's mind, 80
    And no unworthy aim,
    The homely Nurse doth all she can
To make her foster child, her Inmate Man,
    Forget the glories he hath known,
And that imperial palace whence he came. 85

VII

Behold the Child among his newborn blisses,
A six-years' Darling of a pygmy size!
See, where 'mid work of his own hand he lies,
Fretted by sallies of his mother's kisses,
With light upon him from his father's eyes! 90
See, at his feet, some little plan or chart,
Some fragment from his dream of human life,
Shaped by himself with newly-learnéd art;
    A wedding or a festival,
    A mourning or a funeral; 95
        And this hath now his heart,
    And unto this he frames his song;
        Then will he fit his tongue
To dialogues of business, love, or strife;
        But it will not be long 100

Ere this be thrown aside,
And with new joy and pride
The little Actor cons another part;
Filling from time to time his "humorous stage"
With all the Persons, down to palsied Age, 105
That Life brings with her in her equipage;
　　As if his whole vocation
　　Were endless imitation.

VIII

Thou, whose exterior semblance doth belie
　　Thy Soul's immensity; 110
Thou best Philosopher, who yet dost keep
Thy heritage, thou Eye among the blind,
That, deaf and silent, read'st the eternal deep,
Haunted forever by the eternal mind—
　　Mighty Prophet! Seer blest! 115
　　On whom those truths do rest,
Which we are toiling all our lives to find,
In darkness lost, the darkness of the grave;
Thou, over whom thy Immortality
Broods like the Day, a Master o'er a Slave, 120
A Presence which is not to be put by;
Thou little Child, yet glorious in the might
Of heaven-born freedom on thy being's height,
Why with such earnest pains dost thou provoke
The years to bring the inevitable yoke, 125
Thus blindly with thy blessedness at strife?
Full soon thy Soul shall have her earthly freight,
And custom lie upon thee with a weight,
Heavy as frost, and deep almost as life!

IX

　　O joy! that in our embers 130
　　Is something that doth live,
　　That nature yet remembers
　　What was so fugitive!
The thought of our past years in me doth breed
Perpetual benediction: not indeed 135
For that which is most worthy to be blest;
Delight and liberty, the simple creed
Of Childhood, whether busy or at rest,
With new-fledged hope still fluttering in his breast—

Not for these I raise   140
The song of thanks and praise;
But for those obstinate questionings
Of sense and outward things,
Fallings from us, vanishings;
Blank misgivings of a Creature   145
Moving about in worlds not realized,
High instincts before which our mortal Nature
Did tremble like a guilty Thing surprised;
But for those first affections,
Those shadowy recollections,   150
Which, be they what they may,
Are yet the fountain light of all our day,
Are yet a master light of all our seeing;
Uphold us, cherish, and have power to make
Our noisy years seem moments in the being   155
Of the eternal Silence: truths that wake,
To perish never;
Which neither listlessness, nor mad endeavor,
Nor Man nor Boy,
Nor all that is at enmity with joy,   160
Can utterly abolish or destroy!
Hence in a season of calm weather
Though inland far we be,
Our Souls have sight of that immortal sea
Which brought us hither,   165
Can in a moment travel thither,
And see the Children sport upon the shore,
And hear the mighty waters rolling evermore.

X

Then sing, ye Birds, sing, sing a joyous song!
And let the young Lambs bound   170
As to the tabor's sound!
We in thought will join your throng,
Ye that pipe and ye that play,
Ye that through your hearts today
Feel the gladness of the May!   175
What though the radiance which was once so bright
Be now forever taken from my sight,
Though nothing can bring back the hour
Of splendor in the grass, of glory in the flower;
We will grieve not, rather find   180
Strength in what remains behind;

In the primal sympathy
Which having been must ever be;
In the soothing thoughts that spring
Out of human suffering;   185
In the faith that looks through death,
In years that bring the philosophic mind.

XI

And O, ye Fountains, Meadows, Hills, and Groves,
Forebode not any severing of our loves!
Yet in my heart of hearts I feel your might;   190
I only have relinquished one delight
To live beneath your more habitual sway.
I love the Brooks which down their channels fret,
Even more than when I tripped lightly as they;
The innocent brightness of a newborn Day   195
    Is lovely yet;
The clouds that gather round the setting sun
Do take a sober coloring from an eye
That hath kept watch o'er man's mortality;
Another race hath been, and other palms are won.   200
Thanks to the human heart by which we live,
Thanks to its tenderness, its joys, and fears,
To me the meanest flower that blows can give
Thoughts that do often lie too deep for tears.

CHARLES WRIGHT (b. 1935)

Photographs

One of my father; he stands
In hunting clothes in front
Of our house; two dogs
Nuzzle the fingers of
His outstretched hand;   5
Under his right arm
The shotgun that now is mine
Gleams in the sunlight—
I cannot tell if he leaves
Or if he is just returned.   10

One of my mother, and blurred;
Sunday; the afternoon
Is smoky and overcast;
Standing beside the lake,
She balances on a rock   15
At the waterline, gazing out;
Someone is in a boat
Taking her picture; she
Is waiting for them to land.
The water . . . The shoreline . . .   20

  . . .

This one of me at six
At play in the backyard—
Marbles of some sort;
The ring is quite visible
In the August dust;   25
I have Ups, and am fudging;
Off to one side,
A group of three boys:
One is my brother and one
Is someone I do not know.   30

  . . .

I shut the album hard.
What good are these now?
They do not answer *What next?*
Or *What was I trying to prove?*
They do not explain us: 35
Such poses are unrecorded—
They lurk like money, just
Out of reach, shining
And unredeemed:
And we hold such poses forever.   40

WILLIAM BUTLER YEATS (1865–1939)

The Lake Isle of Innisfree

I will arise and go now, and go to Innisfree,
And a small cabin build there, of clay and wattles made:
Nine bean-rows will I have there, a hive for the honey-bee,
And live alone in the bee-loud glade.

And I shall have some peace there, for peace comes dropping slow,   5
Dropping from the veils of the morning to where the cricket sings;

There midnight's all a glimmer, and noon a purple glow,
And evening full of the linnet's wings.

I will arise and go now, for always night and day
I hear lake water lapping with low sounds by the shore;   10
While I stand on the roadway, or on the pavements gray,
I hear it in the deep heart's core.

The Circus Animals Desertion

I

I sought a theme and sought for it in vain,
I sought it daily for six weeks or so.
Maybe at last, being but a broken man,
I must be satisfied with my heart, although
Winter and summer till old age began   5
My circus animals were all on show,
Those stilted boys, that burnished chariot,
Lion and woman and the Lord knows what.

II

What can I but enumerate old themes?
First that sea-rider Oisin led by the nose   10
Through three enchanted islands, allegorical dreams,
Vain gaiety, vain battle, vain repose,
Themes of the embittered heart, or so it seems,
That might adorn old songs or courtly shows;
But what cared I that set him on to ride,   15
I, starved for the bosom of his faery bride?

And then a counter-truth filled out its play,
The Countess Cathleen was the name I gave it;
She, pity-crazed, had given her soul away,
But masterful Heaven had intervened to save it.   20
I thought my dear must her own soul destroy,
So did fanaticism and hate enslave it,
And this brought forth a dream and soon enough
This dream itself had all my thought and love.

And when the Fool and Blind Man stole the bread   25
Cuchulain fought the ungovernable sea;
Heart-mysteries there, and yet when all is said
It was the dream itself enchanted me:
Character isolated by a deed

To engross the present and dominate memory.   30
Players and painted stage took all my love,
And not those things that they were emblems of.

III

Those masterful images because complete
Grew in pure mind, but out of what began?
A mound of refuse or the sweepings of a street,   35
Old kettles, old bottles, and a broken can,
Old iron, old bones, old rags, that raving slut
Who keeps the till. Now that my ladder's gone,
I must lie down where all the ladders start,
In the foul rag-and-bone shop of the heart.   40

Critical Touchstones

ROBERT FROST (1874–1963)

[The Figure a Poem Makes]

Robert Frost, perhaps America's best-loved and best-known poet of the twentieth century, was born in San Francisco but spent most of his life in New Hampshire and Vermont. His first book of poems, *A Boy's Will,* appeared first in London in 1913. He won the Pulitzer Prize for Poetry in 1924, 1931, 1937, and 1943. His *Collected Poems,* including the following essay, appeared in 1939, his *Complete Poems* in 1949. In "The Figure a Poem Makes," Frost argues for the importance of theme and subject matter in poetry, disclaiming the notion that technique alone can create sufficient variety among poems. He also emphasizes the apparent inevitability of most good poems, how a poem "like a piece of ice on a hot stove. . .must ride on its own melting." A good poem must lead its writer, and its reader, "from delight to wisdom."

Abstraction is an old story with the philosophers, but it has been like a new toy in the hands of the artists of our day. Why can't we have any one quality of poetry we choose by itself? We can have in thought. Then it will go hard if we can't in practice. Our lives for it.

Granted no one but a humanist much cares how sound a poem is if it is only *a* sound. The sound is the gold in the ore. Then we will have the sound out alone and dispense with the inessential. We do till we make the discovery that the object in writing poetry is to make all poems sound as different as possible from each other, and the resources for that of vowels, consonants, punctuation, syntax, words, sentences, meter are not enough. We need the help of context—meaning—subject matter. That is the greatest help towards variety. All that can be done with words is soon told. So also with meters—particularly in our language where there are virtually but two, strict iambic and loose iambic. The ancients with many were still poor if they depended on meters for all tune. It is painful to watch our sprung-rhythmists straining at the point of omitting one short from a foot for relief from monotony. The possiblities for tune from the dramatic tones of meaning struck across the rigidity of a limited meter are endless. And we are back in poetry as merely one more art of having something to say, sound or unsound. Probably better if sound, because deeper and from wider experience.

Then there is this wildness whereof it is spoken. Granted again that it has an equal claim with sound to being a poem's better half. If it is a wild tune, it is a poem. Our problem then is, as modern abstractionists, to have the wildness pure; to be wild with nothing to be wild about. We bring up as aberrationists, giving way to undirected associations and kicking ourselves for one chance suggestion to another in all directions as of a hot afternoon in the life of a grasshopper. Theme alone can steady us down. Just as the first mystery was how a poem could have a tune in such a straightness as meter, so the second mystery is how a poem can have wildness and at the same time a subject that shall be fulfilled.

It should be of the pleasure of a poem itself to tell how it can. The figure a poem makes. It begins in delight and ends in wisdom. The figure is the same as for love. No one can really hold that the ecstasy should be static and stand still in one place. It begins in delight, it inclines to the impulse, it assumes direction with the first line laid down, it runs a course of lucky events, and ends in a clarification of life—not necessarily a great clarification, such as sects and cults are founded on, but in a momentary stay against confusion. It has denouement. It has an outcome that though unforseen was predestined from the first image of the original mood—and indeed from the very mood. It is but a trick poem and no poem at all if the best of it was thought of first and saved for the last. It finds its own name as it goes and discovers the best waiting for it in some final phrase at once wise and sad—the happy-sad blend of the drinking song.

No tears in the writer, no tears in the reader. No surprise for the writer, no surpirse for the reader. For me the initial delight is in the surprise of remembering something I didn't know I knew. I am in a place, in a situation, as if I had materialized from a cloud or risen out of the ground. There is a glad recognition of the long lost and the rest follows. Step by step the wonder of unexpected supply keeps growing. The impressions most useful to my purpose seem always those I was unaware of and so made no note of at the time when taken, and the conclusion is come to that like giants we are always hurling experience ahead of us to pave the future with against the day when we may want to strike a line of purpose across it for somewhere. The line will have the more charm for not being mechanically straight. We enjoy the straight crookedness of a good walking stick. Modern instruments of precision are being used to make things crooked as if by eye and hand in the old days.

I tell how there may be a better wildness of logic than of inconsequence. But the logic is backward, in retrospect, after the act. It must be more felt than seen ahead like prophecy. It must be a revelation, or a series of revelations, as much for the poet as for the reader. For it to be that there must have been the greatest freedom of the material to move about in it and to establish relations in it regardless of time and space, previous relation, and everything but affinity. We prate of freedom. We call our schools free because we are not free to stay away from them till we are sixteen years of age. I have given up my democratic prejudices and now willingly set the lower classes free to be completely taken care of by the upper classes. Political freedom is nothing to me. I bestow it right and left. All I would keep for myself is the freedom of my material—the condition of body and mind now and then to summons aptly from the vast chaos of all I have lived through.

Scholars and artists thrown together are often annoyed at the puzzle of where they differ. Both work from knowledge; but I suspect they differ most importantly in the way their knowledge is come by. Scholars get theirs with conscientious thoroughness along projected lines of logic; poets theirs cavalierly and as it happens in and out of books. They stick to nothing deliberately, but let what will stick to them like burrs where they walk in the fields. No acquirement is on assignment, or even self-assignment. Knowledge of the second kind is much more available in the wild free ways of wit and art. A schoolboy may be defined as one who can tell you what he knows in the order in which he learned it. The artist must value himself as he snatches a thing from some previous order in time and space into a new order with not so much as a ligature clinging to it of the old place where it was organic.

More than once I should have lost my soul to radicalism if it had been the originality it was mistaken for by its young converts. Originality and initiative are what I ask for my country. For myself the originality need be no more than the freshness of a poem run in the way I have described: from delight to wisdom. The figure is the same as for love. Like a piece of ice on a hot stove the poem must ride on its own melting. A poem may be worked over once it is in being, but may not be worried into being. Its most precious quality will remain its having run itself and carried away the poet with it. Read it a hundred times: it will forever keep its freshness as a metal keeps it fragrance. It can never lose its sense of a meaning that once unfolded by surprise as it went.

PAUL FUSSELL (b. 1924)

[*The Meaning of Meter*]

Paul Fussell received his Ph.D. from Harvard and now teaches at Rutgers University in New Jersey. Among his books are *The Rhetorical World of Augustan Humanism* (1965) and *The Great War and Modern Memory,* which won the 1976 National Book Award for Arts and Letters. In the following selection from *Poetic Meter and Poetic Form* (1965), Fussell describes how meter can "mean" by removing language from everyday usage, by varying from itself, and by its association with certain conventional subjects. The passage reminds us that meter is more than merely decorative: each meter has its own properties and usefulness, and poets must select or create or adapt meters with care and appropriateness to convey the subjects they treat.

Meter, one of the primary correlatives of meaning in a poem, can "mean" in at least three ways. First, all meter, by distinguishing rhythmic from ordinary statement, objectifies that statement and impels it toward a significant formality and even ritualism. This ritual "frame" in which meter encloses experience is like the artificial border of a painting: like a picture frame, meter reminds the apprehender unremittingly that he is not experiencing the real object of the "imitation" (in the Aristotelian sense) but is experiencing instead that object transmuted into symbolic form. Meter is thus a primary convention of artifice in poetry, like similar indispensable conventions (the palpably artificial stone flesh of statues, for example) in the other arts. The second way a meter can "mean" is by varying from itself: as we shall see, departures from metrical norms powerfully reinforce emotional effects. And third, meters can mean by association and convention. Because of its associations with certain kinds of statements and feelings, a given meter tends to maintain a portion of its meaning, whether symbolic sounds are attached to it or not. In the limerick, for example, the very pattern of short anapestic lines is so firmly associated with light impudence or indecency that a poet can hardly write in anything resembling this measure without evoking smiles. To "translate" a limerick into, say, iambic tetrameter, is to drain off the comedy: we must conclude that a great deal of the comedy inheres by now in the meter alone.

Similarly, triple meters (based on anapestic or dactylic feet) seem inevitably to have something vaguely joyous, comical, light, or superficial about them. In "Retaliation," Oliver Goldsmith makes the whimsical associations of triple meter work for him:

To make out the dinner full certain I am
That Ridge is anchovy, and Reynolds is lamb;
That Hickey's a capon, and by the same rule,
Magnanimous Goldsmith a gooseberry fool.

In "The Poplar-Field," on the other hand, William Cowper, like Longfellow in "Evangeline," unwittingly allows the whimsical associations of triple meter to work against him:

> My fugitive years are all hasting away,
> And I must ere long lie as lowly as they,
> With a turf on my breast, and a stone at my head,
> Ere another such grove shall arrive in its stead.

On the other hand, William Carlos Williams happily exploits the associations of triple meter in "The Dance":

> In Breughel's great picture, The Kermess,
> the dancers go round, they go round and
> around, the squeal and the blare and the
> tweedle of bagpipes. . . .

So, with an impressive delicacy and fineness, does Henry Reed in "Naming of Parts," where a fatuous military instructor delivers his lesson in rifle nomenclature:

> To-day we have naming of parts. Yesterday,
> We had daily cleaning. And to-morrow morning,
> We shall have what to to after firing. But to-day,
> To-day we have naming of parts. . . .

Since ordinary people, and least of all noncommisioned officers, do not speak metrically, to present them speaking metrically is to transform them from creatures of nature into creatures of art. And when it is the poet's voice that we hear speaking metrically, the meter announces or implies his vatic role, just as meter tends to invest with a mysterious air of authority and permanence the words that assume its patterns. The strange power of meter to burnish the commonplace has tempted some people to regard metrical patterns as Platonic forms, themselves inherently and permanently beautiful, forms which the poet perceives as if by special illumination and toward which he constantly urges the rhythms of his own utterance.

If, like some Platonists, one regards regular meter as a kind of ideal, then one becomes extraordinarily sensitive to those places in the poem where the "sense" pattern of the language rhythm lies at some distance from the normal or "base" abstract rhythm of the metrical scheme. Prosodists and critics who have attended closely to this frequent distance between a poem's ideal and real meter have promulgated a theory of prosodic "tension": these theorists hold that one of the important sources of metrical power and pleasure is this perpetual tension between perfect and imperfect, or between general and particular, metrical patterns. The perpetual tension between the theoretical meter and the actual rhythms in a poem constitutes a sort of play or suspension between opposites, which may remind us of the aesthetics of Coleridge.

One complication to be kept in mind when we are dealing with meter is this: different kinds of poems use meter in different ways. Except for some of its most obvious offices, for example, it is apparent that meter does not do the same things in lyric that it does in poetic drama, where it helps actors memorize lines; nor does it do the same things in narrative poetry that it does in satiric. In "Thirty Days Hath September" and in the metered genealogies of epic, the function of meter is largely mnemonic; in a poem like "Kubla Khan" its function is musical and hypnotic; in something like the "Essay on Man" it is oratorical and analytically pedagogic. Different metrical values attach not only to the several modes of poetry (lyric, narrative, dramatic, satiric) but also to the several kinds (elegy, song, sonnet, ode). Thus what is merit in a limerick is a disaster in a sonnet. The kind of meter which sustains a long performance like "The Prelude" is likely to be too diffuse for a short one like "The World is Too Much with Us." There is one perfect meter for "The Love Song of J. Alfred Prufrock" and another for "Mauberley": they should not be the same. We could do worse than agree with Pound when he says, "I believe in an absolute rhythm, a rhythm, that is, in poetry which corresponds exactly with the emotion or shade of emotion to be expressed."

John Hollander has spoken of "the metrical contract" which every poet undertakes with his reader from the first few words of a poem. Given the nature of each metrical contract, the reader tends to do certain things and not others as he reads. I. A. Richards has emphasized likewise the way the reader's response is determined and governed by the first lines of any poem. He says: "Just as the eye reading print unconsciously expects the spelling to be as usual, the fount of type to remain the same, so the mind after reading a line or two of verse . . . prepares itself ahead for any one of a number of possible sequences, at the same time negatively incapacitating itself for others." And emphasizing that meter is illusion, and often illusion created more by the mind of the reader than by the pen of the writer, Richards concludes: "The effect produced by what actually follows [in the poem] depends very closely upon this unconscious preparation and consists largely of the further twist which it gives to expectancy."

What Richards is implying is that the reader's experience of meter is a phenomenon of which only the hints and promptings are provided by the actual rhythm of the poetic words. That is, the apprehender's mind and psyche and even physique tend to read meter into language in order to achieve their own organizational satisfactions. It is easy to test this premise by our own experience. The ticking of a clock constitutes an unvaried succession of regular sounds: when no one is listening, the clock goes *tick, tick, tick, tick* all day long. But let a human ear approach, and the clock goes *tick, tock, tick, tock,* and the ticking now "becomes" rhythmical because the listening ear wants it to be.

Consider now the following lines from the beginning of William Blake's "The Chimney Sweeper" (*Songs of Innocence*):

When my mother died I was very young,
And my father sold me while yet my tongue
Could scarcely cry, "'weep! 'weep! 'weep! 'weep!"

Here the poet has so contracted that the reader refuses to consider the four 'weep's as a series of sounds equally stressed (contrast the reader's very different treatment of King Lear's "Then kill, kill, kill, kill, kill, kill!"); instead, the reader shapes the four 'weep's into two iambic groups and pauses between the two groups. But if the 'weep's were removed from their context, the metrical contract would be abrogated, and the reader would give them equal stress as he does Lear's kill's. Such is the authority of the reader's lust for rhythm, once the poet who is in charge has indicated that it is time for it to be unleashed and satisfied.

SEAMUS HEANEY (b. 1939)

[Finding a Voice]

In 1980, the Irish poet Seamus Heaney published a collection of essays and reviews entitled *Preoccupations*. In the following selection from one essay, "Feeling Into Words," Heaney describes how he first found his own poetic voice in his poem "Digging" (page 572). He compares poems to archeological artifacts, "elements of continuity" dug up from the poet's literal voice, each having its own distinctive sound, as unique as a signature or a fingerprint. (For further details on Heaney, see 572).

I intend to retrace some paths into what William Wordsworth called in *The Prelude* 'the hiding places'.

The hiding places of my power
Seem open; I approach, and then they close;
I see by glimpses now; when age comes on,
May scarcely see at all, and I would give,
While yet we may, as far as words can give,
A substance and a life to what I feel:
I would enshrine the spirit of the past
For future restoration.

Implicit in those lines is a view of poetry which I think is implicit in the few poems I have written that give me any right to speak: poetry as divination, poetry as revelation of the self to the self, as restoration of the culture to itself; poems as elements of continuity, with the aura and authenticity of archaeological finds, where the buried shard has an importance that is not diminished by the importance of the buried city; poetry as a dig, a dig for finds that end up being plants.

'Digging', in fact, was the name of the first poem I wrote where I thought my feelings had got into words, or to put it more accurately, where I thought my *feel* had got into words. Its rhythms and noises still please me, although there are a couple of lines in it that have more of the theatricality of the gunslinger than the self-absorption of the digger. I wrote it in the summer of 1964, almost two years after I had begun to 'dabble in verses'. This was the first place where I felt I had done more than make an arrangement of words: I felt that I had let down a shaft into real life. The facts and surfaces of the thing were true, but more important, the excitement that came from naming them gave me a kind of insouciance and a kind of confidence. I didn't care who thought what about it: somehow, it had surprised me by coming out with a stance and an idea that I would stand over:

> The cold smell of potato mould, the squelch and slap
> Of soggy peat, the curt cuts of an edge
> Through living roots awaken in my head.
> But I've no spade to follow men like them.

> Between my finger and my thumb
> The squat pen rests.
> I'll dig with it.

As I say, I wrote it down years ago; yet perhaps I should say that I dug it up, because I have come to realize that it was laid down in me years before that even. The pen/spade analogy was the simple heart of the matter and *that* was simply a matter of almost proverbial common sense. As a child on the road to and from school, people used to ask you what class you were in and how many slaps you'd got that day and invariably they ended up with an exhortation to keep studying because 'learning's easy carried' and 'the pen's lighter than the spade'. And the poem does no more than allow that bud of wisdom to exfoliate, although the significant point in this context is that at the time of writing I was not aware of the proverbial structure at the back of my mind. Nor was I aware that the poem was an enactment of yet another digging metaphor that came back to me years later. This was the rhyme we used to chant on the road to school, though, as I have said before, we were not fully aware of what we were dealing with:

> 'Are your praties dry
> And are they fit for digging?'
> 'Put in your spade and try,'
> Says Dirty-Faced McGuigan.

There digging becomes a sexual metaphor, an emblem of initiation, like putting your hand into the bush or robbing the nest, one of the various natural analogies for uncovering and touching the hidden thing. I now believe that the 'Digging' poem had for me the force of an initiation: the confidence I mentioned arose from a sense that perhaps I could do this poetry thing too, and having experienced the excitement and release of it once, I was doomed to look for it again and again.

I don't want to overload 'Digging' with too much significance. It is a big coarse-grained navvy of a poem, but it is interesting as an example— and not just as an example of what one reviewer called 'mud-caked fingers in Russell Square', for I don't think that the subject-matter has any particular virtue in itself—it is interesting as an example of what we call 'finding a voice'.

Finding a voice means that you can get your own feeling into your own words and that your words have the feel of you about them; and I believe that it may not even be a metaphor, for a poetic voice is probably very intimately connected with the poet's natural voice, the voice that he hears as the ideal speaker of the lines he is making up.

In his novel *The First Circle*, Solzhenitzyn sets the action in a prison camp on the outskirts of Moscow where the inmates are all highly skilled technicians forced to labour at projects dreamed up by Stalin. The most important of these is an attempt to devise a mechanism to bug a phone. But what is to be special about this particular bugging device is that it will not simply record the voice and the message but that it will identify the essential sound patterns of the speaker's voice; it will discover, in the words of the narrative, 'what it is that makes every human voice unique', so that no matter how the speaker disguises his accent or changes his language, the fundamental structure of his voice will be caught. The idea was that a voice is like a finger-print, possessing a constant and unique signature that can, like a fingerprint, be recorded and employed for identification.

Now one of the purposes of a literary education as I experienced it was to turn the student's ear into a poetic bugging device, so that a piece of verse denuded of name and date could be identified by its diction, tropes and cadences. And this secret policing of English verse was also based on the idea of a style as a signature. But what I wish to suggest is that there is a connection between the core of a poet's speaking voice and the core of his poetic voice, between his original accent and his discovered style. I think that the discovery of a way of writing that is natural and adequate to your sensibility depends on the recovery of that essential quick which Solzhenitzyn's technicians were trying to pin down. This is the absolute register to which your proper music has to be tuned.

How, then, do you find it? In practice, you hear it coming from somebody else, you hear something in another writer's sounds that flows in through your ear and enters the echo-chamber of your head and delights your whole nervous system in such a way that your reaction will be, 'Ah, I wish I had said that, in that particular way.' This other writer, in fact, has spoken something essential to you, something you recognize instinctively as a true sounding of aspects of yourself and your experience. And your first steps as a writer will be to imitate, consciously or unconsciously, those sounds that flowed in, that in-fluence.

JOHN KEATS (1795–1821)

[*Negative Capability*]

The letters of John Keats are among the most sensitive and informative of those written by any English poet. With their shifting, informal tone and their wealth of circumstantial detail, they provide important insights into Keat's life and times and into his growth and development as a lyric poet. In the following famous letter to his brothers, he defines, with a fitting lack of precision, what he calls "negative capability," the ability of the poet to leave doubts unresolved in the belief that "Beauty overcomes every other consideration." (For further details on Keats, see page 557.)

[21, 27 (?) December 1817
Hampstead Sunday

My dear Brothers
   I must crave your pardon for not having written ere this. * * * I saw Kean return to the public in Richard III, & finely he did it, & at the request of Reynolds I went to criticise his Luke in Riches—the critique is in todays champion, which I send you with the Examiner in which you will find very proper lamentation on the obsoletion of christmas Gambols & pastimes: but it was mixed up with so much egotism of that drivelling nature that pleasure is entirely lost. Hone the publisher's trial, you must find very amusing; & as Englishmen very (amusing) encouraging—his *Not Guilty* is a thing, which not to have been, would have dulled still more Liberty's Emblazoning—Lord Ellenborough has been paid in his own coin—Wooler & Hone have done us an essential service—I have had two very pleasant evenings with Dilke yesterday & today; & am at this moment just come from him & feel in the humour to go on with this, began in the morning, & from which he came to fetch me. I spent Friday evening with Wells & went the next morning to see *Death on the Pale horse*. It is a wonderful picture, when West's age is considered; But there is nothing to be intense upon; no women one feels mad to kiss; no face swelling into reality. the excellence of every Art is its intensity, capable of making all disagreeables evaporate, from their being in close relationship with Beauty & Truth—Examine King Lear & you will find this examplified throughout; but in this picture we have unpleasantness without any momentous depth of speculation excited, in which to bury its repulsiveness—The picture is larger than Christ rejected—I dined with

Haydon the sunday after you left, & had a very pleasant day, I dined too
(for I have been out too much lately) with Horace Smith & met his two
Brothers with Hill & Kingston & one Du Bois, they only served to
convince me, how superior humour is to wit in respect to enjoyment—
These men say things which make one start, without making one feel,
they are all alike; their manners are alike; they all know fashionables; they
have a mannerism in their very eating & drinking, in their mere handling
a Decanter—They talked of Kean & his low company—Would I were
with that company instead of yours said I to myself! I know such like
acquaintance will never do for me & yet I am going to Reynolds, on
wednesday—Brown & Dilke walked with me & back from the Christmas
pantomime. I had not a dispute but a disquisition with Dilke, on various
subjects; several things dovetailed in my mind, & at once it struck me,
what quality went to form a Man of Achievement especially in Literature
& which Shakespeare possessed so enormously—I mean *Negative
Capability,* that is when man is capable of being in uncertainties,
Mysteries, doubts, without any irritable reaching after fact & reason—
Coleridge, for instance, would let go by a fine isolated verisimilitude
caught from the Penetralium of mystery, from being incapable of
remaining content with half knowledge. This pursued through Volumes
would perhaps take us no further than this, that with a great poet the
sense of Beauty overcomes every other consideration, or rather obliterates
all consideration.

Shelley's poem is out, & there are words about its being objected too,
as much as Queen Mab was. Poor Shelley I think he has his Quota of
good qualities, in sooth la!! Write soon to your most sincere friend &
affectionate Brother.

John

EZRA POUND (1885–1972)

[Charged Language]

Ezra Pound was born in Idaho but brought up in the East. For most
of his life he was an expatriate, living primarily in England and Italy. He
became perhaps the most influential of all modern poets, giving advice and
encouragement to such notable writers as William Butler Yeats, T. S.
Eliot, James Joyce, and Hilda (H. D.) Doolittle. His most famous poems
are the one hundred and twenty *Cantos,* written and published between
1925 and 1971. Pound was also an important literary critic. His work in
this vein is erratic and eccentric, but always provocative. In the following
excerpt from *The A B C of Reading* (1934), Pound begins with the notion
that to write (*Dichten,* from German) is to condense (*condensare,* from
Italian). Condensed language is charged with meaning by its images, its
sound, and its context.

'Great literature is simply charged with meaning to the utmost possible degree.'

Dichten = condensare.

I begin with poetry because it is the most concentrated form of verbal expression. Basil Bunting, fumbling about with a German-Italian dictionary, found that this idea of poetry as concentration is as old almost as the German language. 'Dichten' is the German verb corresponding to the noun 'Dichtung' meaning poetry, and the lexicographer has rendered it by the Italian verb meaning 'to condense.'

The charging of language is done in three principal ways: You receive the language as your race has left it, the words have meanings which have 'grown into the race's skin'; the Germans say 'wie einem der Schnabel gewachsen ist', as his beak grows. And the good writer chooses his words for their 'meaning', but that meaning is not a set, cut-off thing like the move of knight or pawn on a chess-board. It comes up with roots, with associations, with how and where the word is familiarly used, or where it has been used brilliantly or memorably.

You can hardly say 'incarnadine' without one or more of your auditors thinking of a particular line of verse.

Numerals and words referring to human inventions have hard, cut-off meanings. That is, meanings which are more obtrusive than a word's 'associations'.

Bicycle now has a cut-off meaning.

But tandem, or 'bicycle built for two', will probably throw the image of a past decade upon the reader's mental screen.

There is no end to the number of qualities which some people can associate with a given word or kind of word, and most of these vary with the individual.

You have to go almost exclusively to Dante's criticism to find a set of OBJECTIVE categories for words. Dante called words 'buttered' and 'shaggy' because of the different NOISES they make. Or *pexa et hirsuta*, combed and unkempt.

He also divided them by their different associations.

NEVERTHELESS you still charge words with meaning mainly in three ways, called phanopoeia, melopoeia, logopoeia. You use a word to throw a visual image onto the reader's imagination or you charge it by sound, or you use groups of words to do this.

Thirdly, you take the greater risk of using the word in some special relation to 'usage', that is, to the kind of context in which the reader expects, or is accustomed, to find it.

This is the last means to develop, it can only be used by the sophisticated.

ADRIENNE RICH (b. 1929)

[*Integrating Poetry and Life*]

Adrienne Rich was born in Baltimore and graduated from Radcliffe College in 1951. Her first book of poems, *A Change of World* (1951), won the Yale Younger Poets Award. Her other books of poetry include *Necessities of Life* (1966), *Diving Into the Wreck* (1973), which won a National Book Award, and *A Wild Patience Has Taken Me This Far* (1981). The following excerpt is part of an interview between Rich and Barbara and Albert Gelpi of Stanford University. In the interview, Rich discusses the relationship between women poets and the predominantly male poetic tradition they are working within or against. She advocates a poetry in which artists, female or male, have "their work and their lives integrated."

AR: What in the past did we go to poetry for—I'm speaking now as a woman—specifically what did we go to men's poetry for? Or even to women's poetry? Wasn't it for those unconscious perceptions, if anything, that seemed to be speaking to something in our own unconscious? Now that thing in our own unconscious has become more conscious. We are aware of a lot of hungers and longings and denials and frustrations that we were only unconsciously aware of in the past. What does this do to the way we now read the poetry of the past, especially by men—since that is the major tradition? And how is it going to affect the way we read poetry written in the future? Many women are saying that much of this art has never really talked about us in our deepest mode of being as opposed to what we had laid on us. The great silence in poems about lesbians and all women who are not defined by the men in their lives. Which is one reason why women's poetry is important to women now.

BCG: Do you think there are dangers in becoming too conscious? If you start consciously trying to come to these perceptions, are the perceptions going to change into dogmas, party slogans?

AR: Well, I still believe that the energy of poetry comes from the unconscious and always will. So a poetry which could affirm woman or the female, which could affirm a bisexual vision, or which could affirm a whole other way of being male and female as part of its consciousness, as part of its tradition, such a poetry of the future would still, it seems to me, be churning up new unconscious material, which we would be fascinated and influenced by. If it's not doing that, then it's not poetry as far as I'm concerned. Then it is slogans and pamphlets, which are valuable—those things can be useful—but it's not poetry.

BCG: You're thinking that the slogans and pamphlets can then finally affect the unconscious so that the images that would come from the unconscious and thereby revivify and renew the world would be reacting to a greater conscious understanding of male-female relationships, of what the feminine really is. Is that what you're thinking?

AG: Not only that, but the range of perceptions and responses that the unconscious might churn up or tap could be broadened if we acknowledged the bisexual nature of the psyche. Then instead of thinking of the unconscious as tapping the female aspects of the psyche or the masculine, there would be a much broader range of possibilities and responses. . . . One of the things that you insist on in your poetry is both a psychological and a political dimension and on making the connection between the psychological and the political. But that seems to me uncharacteristic of most politically active people, especially radicals.

AR: It's not uncharacteristic, though, of feminists. I think that feminism is the place where in the most natural, organic way subjectivity and politics have to come together. For instance, Phyllis Chesler's book. It's not a very political book, but it does try to attack the ways in which women are labeled as crazy to prevent them from having access to their own powers. The mental asylum as a prison for women. Even on that level, the psychological becomes political. More lobotomies and more electro-shock therapy and more psycho-surgery are performed on women than on men by far; the margin is incredible. So madness, i.e., eruptions, disturbances of the unconscious, have had a very political meaning for women all along.

AG: But it seems to me that the response of a lot of feminists would be to say: since we're really threatened politically in society, we can't get distracted into talking about subjective psychological factors; we've got to go out and change conditions.

AR: I think you're really talking about women who are, quite correctly, but narrowly, into equal pay for equal work, more women's appointments, and so on. Academic and professional women often have had to deny their own subjectivity in order to survive in the patriarchy. They have learned to play the game like a man and seek power on male terms. If they are trying to get more power for other women, that's fine. But I don't see a radical feminism as proceeding from anything but a connection between inner and outer. We are attempting, in fact, to break down that fragmentation of inner and outer in every possible realm. The psyche and the world out there are being acted on and interacting intensely all the time. There is no such thing as the private psyche, whether you're a woman—or a man, for that matter. Nor do I see anything but reformism in a politics that denies the unconscious life and the need for transcendence. A lot of women, both in and out of universities, are trying to think about what it means to be female in and of itself, outside of stereotypes and roles, and about the potential of femaleness as a positive value. And about the reversals that have been practiced on women so that it becomes hard to think about ourselves at all. Mary Daly's very good on that: patriarchy calls something by a pejorative name, and you start thinking of it as a negative value. It may be a positive strength to you as a woman, but it's always been named pejoratively. A nice example: there is an article in *Women, Culture, and Society* about the so-called "weak ego boundaries" of women—which might be a negative way of describing the fact that women have tremendous powers of intuitive identification and sympathy with other people. And, yes, a woman could get totally lost in that—she can lose all sense of her own ego, but that is not necessary—it might be a source of power.

BCG: John Keats had weak ego boundaries.

AR: Negative capability. Exactly. Any artist has to have it to some extent.

BCG: Well, again, Jung thinks weak ego boundaries are absolutely necessary.

AR: The male ego, which is described as the strong ego, could really be the weak ego, because it encapsulates itself and will not let itself be threatened or vulnerable to other people.

BCG: And becomes then destructive.

AR: What I really love in Daly is her constant insistence that the people who name things have the power and that everything has been named by men, and the questions have been framed by men, and so women's questions are nonquestions. Given that, you have to be constantly critiquing even the tools that you use to explore and define what it is to be female.

BCG: I wanted to bring you back to poetry. Are you thinking: what good does it do women to have poets writing poems about how great women are, since the really great thing is to write poems?

AR: Well, that's going even further than I was going, but *yes!* In fact, that was something I was toying around with in that poem "The Demon Lover," although I hadn't really zeroed in on it. That question was very much afflicting me at the time: do you, as a woman poet, really want to be Ronsard writing the sonnet to Hélène, or do you want to be Hélène, immortalized so that when she's old and gray and nodding by the fire, they'll point to her and say, that's the woman Ronsard sang about? But again, you put it very neatly, what good does it do to be the woman that the poems are written about, and beyond that, what good does it do women to have these poems about women exist? Poems in which women are all beautiful, and preferably asleep. Of course, others are full of unconscious material which says that the female principle is the source of life, of power, of energy, etc., etc., etc. You can really wire into that kind of poem as a woman, but you don't quite know why. You feel very attracted to it; it does something for you, more than those sonnets about how beautiful or unaccommodating some woman is. But what difference, finally, has it made in women's lives that those poems existed? When I read "The Idea of Order at Key West" for the first time, I really felt wired into that poem because it's about a woman whose singing was establishing the order of things—the order of the universe. I identified with her, not the men in the poem.

AG: But it's in Wallace Stevens' mind.

AR: Yes. If a woman had written that poem, my God!

AG: But it seems to me we're coming back to the same questions. I thought you were making a political statement saying that poems can't be validated unless they are changing the conditions which keep women in servitude or relative servitude. Then I thought Barbara was translating that political statement into a psychological statement about women writing the poems.

AR: Certainly when women are not in a state of utter servitude—one of the things we do is write poems. We do a lot of other things, but one of the things we do is write poems. I am made uneasy by the notion that one would dictate *a priori* what kind of poetry should be written. But what I am asking myself is not, if we had a political program what kind of poems would poets by taught to write, but if we were in an altered state of consciousness, if we were free of the dreck of the past, of the stereotypes, of the projections, of all the ways in which women have been used as esthetic objects, what kind of poetry would we have then? It's not like wanting to lay out a program and saying that this is what we should have and this is what poets had better be writing about. I really want to dream about what poems could be written in the future.

BCG: Shelley wrote about Intellectual Beauty as woman, and yet he used his women. . . .

AR: Yes, and suppose we no longer had that split even, because I cannot think of a single male poet, however marvelously he has written about the female principle or intellectual beauty, who hasn't misused and abused actual women. It's just appallingly true. I am saying that politically and psychically and in every way it would be better if artists had their work and their lives integrated. I would want to try to do that for myself. I think that a lot of women are trying to do that. That doesn't mean that there wouldn't be a lot of unconscious images coming up in your work. But consciously you try to integrate as much as possible. I think it would make a difference in the world.

AG: Sure. But I would think that a woman poet would write some poems for the short run—it may not be so short—to shock people into recognizing and changing external social and political conditions. And there would be other kinds of poems you might write which draw on the unconscious and on psychological resources, the anxieties and myths which would carry you really further into the possibility of the future. And I was wondering whether those two impulses are consonant in the writing of the poems you've been writing in the last few years.

AR: I think that we acknowledge that there are different kinds of poems, that in one's complex life there are moments when you use certain types of poems and other moments when you use other kinds of poems. Some fairly uncomplicated poems hit you at a certain point, when that is exactly what you need. They can make an immense psychic difference— open windows of consciousness—yet lack a certain kind of density. Maybe the poetry that you go on reading over and over all your life, getting more and more out of it, would be a much more complex, dense kind of poetry. But I think there's room for both. Also, a lot of women are now writing poems out of their experience, who have never written poetry before. What might sound like something very simplistic and propagandistic in a poem by such a woman, for *her* might represent a very radical, dangerous exploration. And that's important, too; I'm not about to write that off. I think that it's too easy to see that kind of poem in the context of the whole long complicated male tradition with its baroque, in-group quality and not realize that that woman might have gone out on a limb and taken a risk every bit as painful as D. H. Lawrence was taking when he wrote as a man out of consciousness that was very radical for his time and place. One honors the risk, maybe. And it can speak to others who are taking it.

AG: What you say makes sense; what I might read as sloganizing in a poem may be a very deep thrust.

AR: I still think you can say that something is a good poem or not. That's different, because there are so many things that happen in a good poem. There's sound and rhythm and language being used in an original way. And finally, I would think that a really good poem opens up a possibility for other poems, rather than being the end of a succession of things. Instead of wrapping something up it explodes the possibilities.

WALLACE STEVENS (1879–1955)

[Poetry and the Gods]

Wallace Stevens represents an anomaly in modern poetry. He was not a member of any "school" of verse, was not closely associated with any of the other great figures of modern poetry, and lived a "double life" as an executive for the Hartford Accident and Indemnity Company. Still, his reputation for lyric poetry of great power and beauty has grown during the twentieth century so that he now occupies a place as lofty as that of Yeats, Frost, Pound, or Eliot. Among his most famous volumes of poetry are *Harmonium* (1923), *The Man with the Blue Guitar* (1937), and *Transport to Summer* (1947). His *Collected Poems* appeared in 1954. In the following excerpt from *Opus Posthumous* (1957), Stevens stresses the importance of style in poetry. He also advances the notion that the gods are human creations, specifically the creations of poets, who endow them with voices, character, and style. The glory of the gods, therefore, is "the fundamental glory of men and women."

My first proposition is that the style of a poem and the poem itself are one.

One of the better known poems in *Fleurs du Mal* is the one (XII) entitled "La Vie Antérieure" or "Former Life." It begins with the line

J'ai longtemps habité sous de vastes portiques

or

> A long time I lived beneath tremendous porches.

It continues:

> Which the salt-sea suns tinged with a thousand fires
> And which great columns, upright and majestic,
> At evening, made resemble basalt grottoes.

The poem concerns the life among the images, sounds and colors of those calm, sensual presences.

> At the center of azure, of waves, of brilliances,

and so on. I have chosen this poem to illustrate my first proposition, because it happens to be a poem in which the poem itself is immediately recognizable without reference to the manner in which it is rendered. If the style and the poem are one, one ought to choose, for the purpose of illustration, a poem that illustrates this as, for example, Yeat's *Lake-Isle of Innisfree*. To choose a French poem which has to be translated is to choose an example in which the style is lost in the paraphrase of translation. On the other hand, Baudelaire's poem is useful because it identifies what is meant by the poem itself. The idea of an earlier life is like the idea of a later life, or like the idea of a different life, part of the classic repertory of poetic ideas. It is part of one's inherited store of poetic subjects. Precisely, then, because it is traditional and because we understand its romantic nature and know what to expect from it, we are suddenly and profoundly touched when we hear it declaimed by a voice that says:

> I lived, for long, under huge porticoes.

It is as if we had stepped into a ruin and were startled by a flight of birds that rose as we entered. The familiar experience is made unfamiliar and from that time on, whenever we think of that particular scene, we remember how we held our breath and how the hungry doves of another world rose out of nothingness and whistled away. We stand looking at a remembered habitation. All old dwelling-places are subject to these transmogrifications and the experience of all of us includes a succession of old dwelling-places: abodes of the imagination, ancestral or memories of places that never existed. It is plain that when, in this world of weak feeling and blank thinking, in which we are face to face with the poem every moment of time, we encounter some integration of the poem that pierces and dazzles us, the effect is an effect of style and not of the poem itself or at least not of the poem alone. The effective integration is not a disengaging of the subject. It is a question of the style in which the subject is presented.

Although I have limited myself to an instance of the relation between style and the familiar, one gets the same result in considering the relation between style and its own creations, that is between style and the unfamiliar. What we are really considering here are the creations of modern art and modern literature. If one keeps in mind the fact that most poets who have something to say are content with what they say and that most poets who have little or nothing to say are concerned primarily with the way in which they say it, the importance of this discussion becomes clear. I do not mean to imply that the poets who have something to say are the poets that matter; for obviously if it is true that the style of a poem and the poem itself are one, it follows that, in considering style and its own creations, that is to say, the relation between style and the unfamiliar it may be, or become, that the poets who have little or nothing to say are, or will be, the poets that matter. Today, painters who have something to say are less admired than painters who seem to have little or nothing to say but who do at least believe that style and the painting are one. The inclination toward arbitrary or schematic constructions in poetry is, from the point of view of style, very strong; and certainly if these constructions were effective it would be true that style and the poem were one.

In the light of this first idea the prejudice in favor of plain English, for instance, comes to nothing. I have never been able to see why what is called Anglo-Saxon should have the right to higgle and haggle all over the page, contesting the right of other words. If a poem seems to require a hierophantic phrase, the phrase should pass. This is a way of saying that one of the consequences of the ordination of style is not to limit it, but to enlarge it, not to impoverish it, but to enrich and liberate it.

The second idea relates to poetry and the gods, both ancient and modern, both foreign and domestic. To simplify, I shall speak only of the ancient and foreign gods. I do not mean to refer to them in their religious aspects but as creations of the imagination; and I suppose that as with all creations of the imagination I have been thinking of them from the point of view of style, that is to say of their style. When we think of Jove, while we take him for granted as the symbol of omnipotence, the ruler of mankind, we do not fear him. He does have a superhuman size, but at least not so superhuman as to amaze and intimidate us. He has a large head and a beard and is a relic, a relic that makes a kindly impression on us and reminds us of stories that we have heard about him. All of the noble images of all of the gods have been profound and most of them have been forgotten. To speak of the origin and end of gods is not a light matter. It is to speak of the origin and end of years of human belief. And while it is easy to look back on those that have disappeared as if they were the playthings of cosmic make-believe, and on those that made petitions to them and honored them and received their benefits as legendary innocents, we are bound, nevetheless, to concede that the gods were personae of a peremptory elevation and glory. It would be wrong to look back to them as if they had existed in some indigence of the spirit. They were in fact, as we see them now, the clear giants of a vivid time, who in the style of their beings made the style of the gods and the gods themselves one.

This brings me to the third idea, which is this: In an age of disbelief, or, what is the same thing, in a time that is largely humanistic, in one sense or another, it is for the poet to supply the satisfactions of belief, in his measure and in his style. I say in his measure to indicate that the figures of the philosopher, the artist, the teacher, the moralist and other figures, including the poet, find themselves, in such a time, to be figures of an importance greatly enhanced by the requirements both of the individual and of society; and I say in his style by way of confining the poet to his role and thereby of intensifying that role. It is this that I want to talk about today. I want to try to formulate a conception of perfection in poetry with reference to the present time and the near future and to speculate on the activities possible to it as it deploys itself throughout the lives of men and women. I think of it as a role of the utmost seriousness. It is, for one thing, a spiritual role. One might stop to draw an ideal portrait of the poet. But that would be parenthetical. In any case, we do not say that the philosopher, the artist or the teacher is to take the place of the gods. Just so, we do not say that the poet is to take the place of the gods.

To see the gods dispelled in mid-air and dissolve like clouds is one of the great human experiences. It is not as if they had gone over the horizon to disappear for a time; nor as if they had been overcome by other gods of greater power and profounder knowledge. It is simply that they came to nothing. Since we have always shared all things with them and have always had a part of their strength and, certainly, all of their knowledge, we shared likewise this experience of annihilation. It was their annihilation, not ours, and yet it left us feeling that in a measure, we, too, had been annihilated. It left us feeling dispossessed and alone in a solitude, like children without parents, in a home that seemed deserted, in which the amical rooms and halls had taken on a look of hardness and emptiness. What was most extraordinary is that they left no momentoes behind, no thrones, no mystic rings, no texts either of the soil or of the soul. It was as if they had never inhabited the earth. There was no crying out for their return. They were not forgotten because they had been a part of the glory of the earth. At the same time, no man ever muttered a petition in his heart for the restoration of those unreal shapes. There was always in every man the increasingly human self, which instead of remaining the observer, the nonparticipant, the delinquent, became constantly more and more all there was or so it seemed, and whether it was so or merely seemed so still left it for him to resolve life and the world in his own terms.

Thinking about the end of the gods creates singular attitudes in the mind of the thinker. One attitude is that the gods of classical mythology were merely aesthetic projections. They were not the objects of belief. They were expressions of delight. Perhaps delight is too active a word. It is true that they were engaged with the future world and the immortality of the soul. It is true, also, that they were the objects of veneration and therefore of religious dignity and sanctity. But in the blue air of the Mediterranean these white and a little colossal figures had a special propriety, a special felicity. Could they have been created for that propriety, that felicity? Notwithstanding their divinity, they were close to the people among whom they moved. Is it one of the normal activities of humanity, in the solitude of reality and in the unworthy treatment of solitude, to create companions, a little colossal as I have said, who, if not superficially explicative, are, at least, assumed to be full of the secret of things and who in any event bear in themselves even, if they do not always wear it, the peculiar majesty of mankind's sense of worth, neither too much nor too little? To a people of high intelligence, whose gods have benefited by having been accepted and addressed by the superior minds of a superior world, the symbolic paraphernalia of the very great becomes unnecessary and the very great become the very natural. However all that may be the celestial atmosphere of these deities, their ultimate remote celestial residences are not matters of chance. Their fundamental glory is the fundamental glory of men and women, who being in need of it create it, elevate it, without too much searching of its identity.

The people, not the priests, made the gods. The personages of immortality were something more than the conceptions of priests, although they may have picked up many of the conceits of priests. Who were the priests? Who have always been the high priests of any of the gods? Certainly not those officials or generations of officials who administered rites and observed rituals. The great and true priest of Apollo was he that composed the most moving of Apollo's hymns. The really illustrious archimandrite of Zeus was the one that made the being of Zeus people the whole of Olympus and the Olympian land, just as the only marvelous bishops of heaven have always been those that made it seem like heaven. I said a moment ago that we had not forgotten the gods. What is it that we remember of them? In the case of those masculine do we remember their ethics or is it their port and mien, their size, their color, not to speak of their adventures, that we remember? In the case of those feminine do we remember, as in the case of Diana, their fabulous chastity or their beauty? Do we remember those masculine in any way differently from the way in which we remember Ulysses and other men of supreme interest and excellence? In the case of those feminine do we remember Venus in any way differently from the way in which we remember Penelope and other women of much mark and feeling? In short, while the priests helped to realize the gods, it was the people that spoke of them and to them and heard their replies.

DIANE WAKOSKI (b. 1937)

[*How Not to Treat a Poet*]

Diane Wakoski was born in Whittier, California, and received her B.A. from the University of California at Berkeley in 1960. Among her best-known books of poems are *Discrepancies and Apparitions* (1966), *The George Washington Poems* (1967), and *The Motorcycle Betrayal Poems* (1971). In the following excerpt from *Toward a New Poetry* (1980), she comments on a phenomenon associated with the latter half of the twentieth century—the public poetry reading. While stressing the potential benefits of such readings (she is, in fact, widely known for her readings), Wakoski laments the lack of preparation among the students and teachers who invite her to read. One risk of the poorly prepared reading, she claims, is that everyone's time will be wasted.

I recently went to a college to give a reading and to spend a day being available to people who really wanted to talk to me about poetry. The reading was just fine; but that day seemed typical of how both students' time and my time is often wasted. Remember, now, I am a *resource* when I come to a college campus. That should mean that students and teachers have already studied about me, my poetry, and/or modern poetry before I've come. I do not come to give a basic or beginning course in poetry. I come to read my poetry, to talk about it a bit, and to *extend* the already existing discussion of modern poetry as much as I can.

On the particular day in question, I went to a class in the morning. It was a poetry class of about five serious students. But it had been augmented with a class of special studies high school students who were bright but really knew nothing about poetry. I had prepared to read a long and difficult poem (which I would not ordinarily read in a public reading) and to talk about some of my concerns now as a poet. I went ahead and did this, but did not realize (yes, this was my fault, but none of us is perfect) that only the five students from the special class who had been to my public reading the night before, knew or cared about the concerns I was discussing. Those high school students simply were not advanced enough. Had I realized that, I would have asked that the groups be separated, or what I simply would have done if that was not possible would have been to give another public poetry reading—i.e., a wide range of poetry, little talk, mostly reading, no attempt to focus on technique or professional concerns of writing. *And* if I had not been an experienced teacher and talker, I would have been stunned by the blank looks on most of those high school students' faces. They were not *prepared* to see me. As a resource, I was wasted.

The next thing I did that day was to be "at home" or "available" to students in the coffee shop from 12 to 1 P.M. Fine. I had to eat lunch. The coffee shop was pleasant. I am happy to talk to people who really want to talk to me, or just sit in friendly company while eating and drinking, even if there is no talk. But what happened was that the students who had not been to my poetry reading the night before (and needless to say, had not read my poetry at all) were the ones to come and sit in the coffee house with the visiting poet. And, you know, we have encouraged two very debased phenomena in our culture. One is that we cannot tolerate silence; and consequently people talk just to prevent silence. Not necessarily because they have anything to say. Silence means something to me. When there is silence, it means that no one is ready to talk. The other phenomenon is that we encourage people to be "spontaneous." To say whatever comes to their heads. This produces so much bullshit in talk that I wonder we listen, but alas we do. If I had not been the sort of prickly person I am, who despises verbal bullshit, the whole noon conversation would have been conducted by a boy who had never read my poetry, who knew nothing about contemporary poetry, who (naturally, narcissist that he was) claimed he wanted to write poetry but was locked by having learned haiku. Now, what this had to do with me or *anything* I can think of in the whole world of my concerns, I don't know. All I know is that he came because he saw a chance for a forum. I told him to fuck off. A more polite poet wouldn't have. And a hypersensitive poet like Anne Sexton would have gone home with a headache and another argument about why she shouldn't have to be exposed to those philistines on campus. And many poets would have tried to relate to the student, only to find themselves dragged into his idea of an encounter session. Everybody's time could have been wasted because, again, no preparations were made; and when you count on spontaneous meetings, you are sitting ducks for all the "quacks," student or other-wise, just waiting to use another person's forum for their troubles.

The third thing I did was go to a class in Art in Contemporary America. Yes, to speak about my poetry. This class was supposed to be studying all the arts—painting, poetry, theatre, etc.—and I don't know what this teacher's other qualifications were but one thing she *didn't* know about was contemporary poetry. That's why I was there, I guess. To give a crash course in contemporary poetry.

Now, isn't that unfair. To me, the poet, and to those students?

What I discovered was that with a little conscientious teaching I still could have been used as an enriching resource. Maybe even *especially* as an enriching resource, simply because I was going to be the only contact with poetry the class had all semester. Just the materials at hand could have been used with a little preparation. Here's what I mean: the students all had available a mimeographed sheet of about five page of my poetry. Theoretically their teacher told them to read it, and theoretically they had also gone to my poetry reading the night before. However, these students had not ever really been taught to study poetry and therefore to tell them to read the worksheet for homework meant that they spent four or five minutes (however fast you can speed-read five pages of poetry) and then come to class to "discuss." Needless to say, they were victims of the modern educational concept that the student spends five minutes reading and three hours discussing something. After half an hour of bullshit and my trying to make sense out of their talk, I realized they were simply talking because they were supposed to. And nothing of substance was being said. I wound up giving them a lecture on what was wrong with contemporary education. And telling them that no visiting writer or scholar expects to be asked and certainly will not answer many questions about his personal life—wife, children, job, love affairs, bank account, etc. We didn't come there to be psychoanalysed, nor to be interviewed for a job. We came to talk about our poetry. But these students (most students) were not prepared to talk about poetry and so in desperation they asked me to be personal instead. Not fair to anybody. Not fair to poetry.

Well, you say, what could they do? Answer: lots and lots of things. Let me give you a for-instance. For instance, their teacher who knew nothing about poetry *should* have known something about studying. She could have asked them (and done it herself as homework) to go home the night before with only that five-page worksheet. To spend half an hour reading, making notes in the margins, looking for common themes and ideas, noting image, metaphor, symbol, trying to describe the kind of language used, writing perhaps a paragraph on what the poet seems to be trying to do in those five pages of poetry, then jotting down the questions the reader might have as a result of these observations, etc. Couldn't any serious student do this with any five pages of material? And then the next day wouldn't it make more sense for him to meet the writer and ask him or her to speak further about the ideas the student found there? Couldn't any class do this?

In lieu of it, the poet either has to give a critical lecture on his own work or answer questions about his love affairs. Is it fair to ask any of us to do either? I think not.

So you see, the poet comes wanting to talk about his work, wanting to leave you understanding more about it, but he often isn't given the chance. Don't invite a poet to your campus unless you're willing to spend half an hour thinking about his poetry in advance. Is that so much to ask?

WALT WHITMAN (1819–1892)

[*The Democratic Poet*]

Whether as the "great, gray poet," "the father of modern poetry," or "the father of free verse," Walt Whitman has exerted an enormous influence on modern poetry, which can safely be said to begin with the publication of his monumental *Leaves of Grass* in 1855. Whitman opened up new vistas of form and subject matter for the American poet and gave this country its first authentic national (and international) voice. In the following excerpt from the Preface to *Leaves of Grass*, Whitman expounds, in typically rhapsodic fashion, upon the idea of the democratic American poet, who "hardly knows pettiness or triviality" and who is "hungry for equals night and day."

The greatest poet hardly knows pettiness or triviality. If he breathes into any thing that was before thought small it dilates with the grandeur and life of the universe. He is a seer . . . he is individual . . . he is complete in himself . . . the others are as good as he, only he sees it and they do not. He is not one of the chorus . . . he does not stop for any regulations . . . he is the president of regulation. What the eyesight does to the rest he does to the rest. Who knows the curious mystery of the eyesight? The other senses corroborate themselves, but this is removed from any proof but its own and foreruns the identities of the spiritual world. A single glance of it mocks all the investigations of man and all the instruments and books of the earth and all reasoning. What is marvelous? what is unlikely? what is impossible or baseless or vague? after you have once just opened the space of a peachpit and given audience to far and near and to the sunset and had all things enter with electric swiftness softly and duly without confusion or jostling or jam.

The land and sea, the animals fishes and birds, the sky of heaven and the orbs, the forests mountains and rivers, are not small themes . . . but folks expect of the poet to indicate more than the beauty and dignity which always attach to dumb real objects . . . they expect him to indicate the path between reality and their souls. Men and women perceive the beauty well enough . . . probably as well as he. The passionate tenacity hunters, woodmen, early risers, cultivators of gardens and orchards and fields, the love of healthy women for the manly form, seafaring persons, drivers of horses, the passion for light and the open air, all is an old varied sign of the unfailing perception of beauty and of a residence of the poetic in outdoor people. They can never be assisted by poets to perceive . . . some may but they never can. The poetic quality is not marshalled in rhyme or uniformity or abstract addresses to things nor in melancholy complaints or good precepts, but is the life of these and much else and is in the soul. The profit of rhyme is that it drops seeds of a sweeter and more luxuriant rhyme, and of uniformity that it conveys itself into its own roots in the ground out of sight. The rhyme and uniformity of perfect poems show the free growth of metrical laws and bud from them as unerringly and loosely as lilacs or roses on a bush, and take shapes as compact as the shapes of chestnuts and oranges and melons and pears, and shed the perfume impalpable to form. The fluency and ornaments of the finest poems or music or orations or recitations are not independent but dependent. All beauty comes from beautiful blood and a beautiful brain. If the greatnesses are in conjunction in a man or woman it is enough . . . the fact will prevail through the universe . . . but the gaggery and gilt of a million years will not prevail. Who troubles himself about his ornaments or fluency is lost. This is what you shall do: Love the earth and sun and the animals, despise riches, give alms to every one that asks, stand up for the stupid and crazy, devote your income and labor to others, hate tyrants, argue not concerning God, have patience and indulgence toward the people, take off your hat to nothing known or unknown or to any man or number of men, go freely with powerful uneducated persons and with the young and with the mothers of families, read these leaves in the open air every season of every year of your life, re-examine all you have been told at school or church or in any book, dismiss whatever insults your own soul, and your very flesh shall be a great poem and have the richest fluency not only in its words but in the silent lines of its lips and face and between the lashes of your eyes and in every motion and joint of your body. . . . The poet shall not spend his time in unneeded work. He shall know that the ground is always ready plowed and manured . . . others may not know it but he shall. He shall go directly to the creation. His trust shall master the trust of everything he touches . . . and shall master all attachment.

The known universe has one complete lover and that is the greatest poet. He consumes an eternal passion and is indifferent which chance happens and which possible contingency of fortune or misfortune and persuades daily and hourly his delicious pay. What balks or breaks others is fuel for his burning progress to contact and amorous joy. Other proportions of the reception of pleasure dwindle to nothing to his proportions. All expected from heaven or from the highest he is rapport with in the sight of the day-break or a scene of the winterwoods or the presence of children playing or with his arm round the neck of a man or woman. His love above all love has leisure and expanse . . . he leaves room ahead of himself. He is no irresolute or suspicious lover . . . he is sure . . . he scorns intervals. His experience and the showers and thrills are not for nothing. Nothing can jar him . . . suffering and darkness cannot—death and fear cannot. To him complaint and jealousy and envy are corpses buried and rotten in the earth . . . he saw them buried. The sea is not surer of the shore or the shore of the sea than he is of the fruition of his love and of all perfection and beauty.

The fruition of beauty is no chance of hit or miss . . . it is inevitable as life . . . it is exact and plumb as gravitation. From the eyesight proceeds another eyesight and from the hearing proceeds another hearing and from the voice proceeds another voice eternally curious of the harmony of things with man. To these respond perfections not only in the committees that were supposed to stand for the rest but in the rest themselves just the same. These understand the law of perfection in masses and floods . . . that its finish is to each for itself and onward from itself . . . that it is profuse and impartial . . . that there is not a minute of the light or dark nor an acre of the earth or sea without it—nor any direction of the sky nor any trade or employment nor any turn of events. This is the reason that about the proper expression of beauty there is precision and balance . . . one part does not need to be thrust above another. The best singer is not the one who has the most lithe and powerful organ . . . the pleasure of poems is not in them that take the handsomest measure and similes and sound.

Without effort and without exposing in the least how it is done the greatest poet brings the spirit of any or all events and passions and scenes and persons some more and some less to bear on your individual character as you hear or read. To do this well is to compete with the laws that pursue and follow time. What is the purpose must surely be there and the clue of it must be there . . . and the faintest indication is the indication of the best and then becomes the clearest indication. Past and present and future are not disjoined but joined. The greatest poet forms the consistence of what is to be from what has been and is. He drags the dead out of their coffins and stands them again on their feet . . . he says to the past, Rise and walk before me that I may realize you. He learns the lesson . . . he places himself where the future becomes present. The greatest poet does not only dazzle his rays over character and scenes and passions . . . he finally ascends and finishes all . . . he exhibits the pinnacles that no man can tell what they are for or what is beyond . . . he glows a moment on the extremest verge. He is most wonderful in his last half-hidden smile or frown . . . by that flash of the moment of parting the one that sees it shall be encouraged or terrified afterwards for many years. The greatest poet does not moralize or make applications of morals . . . he knows the soul. The soul has that measureless pride which consists in never acknowledging any lessons but its own. But it has sympathy as measureless as its pride and the one balances the other and neither can stretch too far while it stretches in company with the other. The inmost secrets of art sleep with the twain. The greatest poet has lain close betwixt both and they are vital in his style and thoughts.

The art of art, the glory of expression and the sunshine of the light of letters is simplicity. Nothing is better than simplicity . . . nothing can make up for excess or for the lack of definiteness. To carry on the heave of impulse and pierce intellectual depths and give all subjects their articulations are powers neither common nor very uncommon. But to speak in literature with the perfect rectitude and insousiance of the movements of animals and the unimpeachableness of the sentiment of trees in the woods and grass by the roadside is the flawless triumph of art. If you have looked on him who has achieved it you have looked on one of the masters of the artists of all nations and times. You shall not contemplate the flight of the gray gull over the bay or the mettlesome action of the blood horse or the tall leaning of sunflowers on their stalk or the appearance of the sun journeying through heaven or the appearance of the moon afterward with any more satisfaction than you shall contemplate him. The greatest poet has less a marked style and is more the channel of thoughts and things without increase or diminution, and is the free channel of himself. He swears to his art, I will not be meddlesome, I will not have in my writing any elegance or effect or originality to hang in the way between me and the rest like curtains. I will have nothing hang in the way, not the richest curtains. What I tell I tell for precisely what it is. Let who may exalt or startle or fascinate or sooth I will have purposes as health or heat or snow has and be as regardless of observation. What I experience or portray shall go from my composition without a shred of my composition. You shall stand by my side and look in the mirror with me.

The old red blood and stainless gentility of great poets will be proved by their unconstraint. A heroic person walks at his ease through and out of that custom or precedent or authority that suits him not. Of the traits of the brotherhood of writers savans musicians inventors and artists nothing is finer than silent defiance advancing from new free forms. In the need of poems philosophy politics mechanism science behaviour, the craft of art, an appropriate native grand-opera, shipcraft, or any craft, he is greatest forever and forever who contributes the greatest original practical example. The cleanest expression is that which finds no sphere worthy of itself and makes one.

The messages of great poets to each man and woman are, Come to us on equal terms, Only then can you understand us, We are no better than you, What we enclose you enclose, What we enjoy you may enjoy. Did you suppose there could be only one Supreme? We affirm there can be unnumbered Supremes, and that one does not countervail another any more than one eyesight countervails another . . . and that men can be good or grand only of the consciousness of their supremacy within them. What do you think is the grandeur of storms and dismemberments and the deadliest battles and wrecks and the wildest fury of the elements and the power of the sea and the motion of nature and of the throes of human desires and dignity and hate and love? It is that something in the soul which says, Rage on, Whirl on, I tread master here and everywhere, Master of the spasms of the sky and of the shatter of the sea, Master of nature and passion and death, And of all terror and all pain.

The American bards shall be marked for generosity and affection and for encouraging competitors. . . . They shall be kosmos . . . without monopoly or secresy . . . glad to pass any thing to any one . . . hungry for equals night and day. They shall not be careful of riches and privilege they shall be riches and privilege . . . they shall perceive who the most affluent man is. The most affluent man is he that confronts all the shows he sees by equivalents out of the stronger wealth of himself. The American bard shall delineate no class of persons nor one or two out of the strata of interests nor love most nor truth most nor the soul most nor the body most . . . and not be for the eastern states more than the western or the northern states more than the southern.

Exact science and its practical movements are no checks on the greatest poet but always his encouragement and support. The outset and remembrance are there . . . there are the arms that lifted him first and brace him best . . . there he returns after all his goings and comings. The sailor and traveler . . . the atomist chemist astronomer geologist phrenologist spiritualist mathematician historian and lexicographer are not poets, but they are the lawgivers of poets and their construction underlies the structure of every perfect poem. No matter what rises or is uttered they sent the seed of the conception of it . . . of them and by them stand the visible proofs of souls . . . always of their fatherstuff must be begotten the sinewy races of bards. If there shall be love and content between the father and the son and if the greatness of the son is the exuding of the greatness of the father there shall be love between the poet and the man of demonstrable science. In the beauty of poems are the tuft and final applause of science.

Great is the faith of the flush of knowledge and of the investigation of the depths of qualities and things. Cleaving and circling here swells the soul of the poet yet is president of itself always. The depths and fathomless and therefore calm. The innocence and nakedness are resumed . . . they are neither modest nor immodest. The whole theory of the special and supernatural and all that was twined with it or educed out of it departs as a dream. What has ever happened . . . what happens and whatever may or shall happen, the vital laws enclose all . . . they are sufficient for any case and for all cases . . . none to be hurried or retarded . . . any miracle of affairs or persons inadmissible in the vast clear scheme where every motion and every spear of grass and the frames and spirits of men and women and all that concerns them are unspeakably perfect miracles all referring to all and each distinct and in its place. It is also not consistent with the reality of the soul to admit that there is anything in the known universe more divine than men and women.

WILLIAM WORDSWORTH (1770–1850)
[*Feeling, Thought, and Language in Poetry*]

Wordsworth is the dominant figure of the Romantic period of English poetry (1798–1832). His *Lyrical Ballads* (1798), written with Samuel Taylor Coleridge, ushered in a new poetic era, and his Preface to that volume became a manifesto for a generation of English poets. In the following excerpt from this Preface, Wordsworth announces his famous dictum that "good poetry is the spontaneous overflow of powerful feelings." He goes on to qualify this statement by emphasizing the need for thought and reflection in poetry and concludes with remarks about the similarities between poetic language and that of prose.

I cannot, however, be insensible of the present outcry against the triviality and meanness both of thought and language, which some of my contemporaries have occasionally introduced into their metrical compositions; and I acknowledge, that this defect, where it exists, is more dishonorable to the Writer's own character than false refinement or arbitrary innovation, though I should contend at the same time that it is far less pernicious in the sum of its consequences. From such verses the Poems in these volumes will be found distinguished at least by one mark of difference, that each of them has a worthy *purpose*. Not that I mean to say, that I always began to write with a distinct purpose formally conceived; but I believe that my habits of meditation have so formed my feelings, as that my descriptions of such objects as strongly excite those feelings, will be found to carry along with them a *purpose*. If in this opinion I am mistaken, I can have little right to the name of Poet. For all good poetry is the spontaneous overflow of powerful feelings: but though this be true, Poems to which any value can be attached were never produced on any variety of subjects but by a man, who being possessed of more than usual organic sensibility, had also thought long and deeply. For our continued influxes of feeling are modified and directed by our thoughts, which are indeed the representatives of all our past feelings; and, as by contemplating the relation of these general representatives to each other we discover what is really important to men, so, by the repetition and continuance of this act, our feelings will be connected with important subjects, till at length, if we be originally possessed of much sensibility, such habits of mind will be produced, that, by obeying blindly and mechanically the impulses of those habits, we shall describe objects, and utter sentiments, of such a nature and in such connection with each other, that the understanding of the being to whom we address ourselves, if he be in a healthful state of association, must necessarily be in some degree enlightened, and his affections ameliorated.

I have said that each of these poems has a purpose. I have also informed my Reader what this purpose will be found principally to be: namely to illustrate the manner in which our feelings and ideas are associated in a state of excitement. But, speaking in language somewhat more appropriate, it is to follow the fluxes and refluxes of the mind when agitated by the great and simple affections of our nature. This object I have endeavoured in these short essays to attain by various means; by tracing the maternal passion through many of its more subtle windings . . . ; by accompanying the last struggles of a human being, at the approach of death, cleaving in solitude to life and society . . . ; by shewing . . . the perplexity and obscurity which in childhood attend our notion of death, or rather our utter inability to admit that notion; or by displaying the strength of fraternal, or to speak more philosophically, of moral attachment when early associated with the great and beautiful objects of nature . . . ; or by placing my Reader in the way of receiving from ordinary moral sensations another and more salutary impression than we are accustomed to receive from them. It has also been part of my general purpose to attempt to sketch characters under the influence of less impassioned feelings . . . characters of which the elements are simple, belonging rather to nature than to manners, such as exist now, and will probably always exist, and which from their constitution may be distinctly and profitably comtemplated. I will not abuse the indulgence of my Reader by dwelling longer upon this subject; but it is proper that I should mention one other circumstance which distinguishes these Poems from the popular Poetry of the day; it is this, that the feeling therein developed gives importance to the action and situation, and not the action and situation to the feeling. . . .

I will not suffer a sense of false modesty to prevent me from asserting, that I point my Reader's attention to this mark of distinction, far less for the sake of these particular Poems than from the general importance of the subject. The subject is indeed important! For the human mind is capable of being excited without the application of gross and violent stimulants; and he must have a very faint perception of its beauty and dignity who does not know this, and who does not further know, that one being is elevated above another, in proportion as he possesses this capability. It has therefore appeared to me, that to endeavour to produce or enlarge this capability is one of the best services in which, at any period, a Writer can be engaged; but this service, excellent at all times, is especially so at the present day. For a multitude of causes, unknown to former times, are now acting with a combined force to blunt the discriminating powers of the mind, and unfitting it for all voluntary exertion to reduce it to a state of almost savage torpor. The most effective of these causes are the great national events which are daily taking place, and the encreasing accumulation of men in cities, where the uniformity of their occupations produces a craving for extraordinary incident, which the rapid communication of intelligence hourly gratifies. To this tendency of life and manners the literature and theatrical exhibitions of the country have conformed themselves. The invaluable works of our elder writers, I had almost said the works of Shakespear and Milton, are driven into neglect by frantic novels, sickly and stupid German Tragedies, and deluges of idle and extravagant stories in verse.— When I think upon this degrading thirst after outrageous stimulation, I am almost ashamed to have spoken of the feeble effort with which I have endeavoured to counteract it; and, reflecting upon the magnitude of the general evil, I should be oppressed with no dishonorable melancholy, had I not a deep impression of certain inherent and indestructible qualities of the human mind, and likewise of certain powers in the great and permanent objects that act upon it which are equally inherent and indestructible; and did I not further add to this impression a belief, that the time is approaching when the evil will be systematically opposed, by men of greater powers, and with far more distinguished success.

Having dwelt thus long on the subjects and aim of these Poems, I shall request the Reader's permission to apprize him of a few circumstances relating to their *style*, in order, among other reasons, that I may not be censured for not having performed what I never attempted. The Reader will find that personifications of abstract ideas rarely occur in these volumes; and, I hope, are utterly rejected as an ordinary device to elevate the style, and raise it above prose. I have proposed to myself to imitate, and, as far as is possible, to adopt the very language of men; and assuredly such personifications do not make any natural or regular part of that language. They are, indeed, a figure of speech occasionally prompted by passion, and I have made use of them as such; but I have endeavoured utterly to reject them as a mechanical device of style, or as a family language which Writers in metre seem to lay claim to by prescription. I have wished to keep my Reader in the company of flesh and blood, persuaded that by so doing I shall interest him. I am, however, well aware that others who pursue a different track may interest him likewise; I do not interfere with their claim, I only wish to prefer a different claim of my own. There will also be found in these volumes little of what is usually called poetic diction; I have taken as much pains to avoid it as others ordinarily take to produce it; this I have done for the reason already alleged, to bring my language near to the language of men, and further, because the pleasure which I have proposed to myself to impart is of a kind very different from that which is supposed by many persons to be the proper object of poetry. I do not know how without being culpably particular I can give my Reader a more exact notion of the style in which I wished these poems to be written than by informing him that I have at all times endeavoured to look steadily at my subject, consequently, I hope that there is in these Poems little falsehood of description, and that my ideas are expressed in language fitted to their respective importance. Something I must have gained by this practice, as it is friendly to one property of all good poetry, namely, good sense; but it has necessarily cut me off from a large portion of phrases and figures of speech which from father to son have long been regarded as the common inheritance of Poets. I have also thought it expedient to restrict myself still further, having abstained from the use of many expressions, in themselves proper and beautiful, but which have been foolishly repeated by bad Poets, till such feelings of disgust are connected with them as it is scarcely possible by any art of association to overpower.

If in a Poem there should be found a series of lines, or even a single line, in which the language, though naturally arranged and according to the strict laws of metre, does not differ from that of prose, there is a numerous class of critics, who, when they stumble upon these prosaisms as they call them, imagine that they have made a notable discovery, and exult over the Poet as over a man ignorant of his own profession. Now these men would establish a canon of criticism which the Reader will conclude he must utterly reject, if he wishes to be pleased with these volumes. And it would be a most easy task to prove to him, that not only the language of a large portion of every good poem, even of the most elevated character, must necessarily, except with reference to the metre, in no respect differ from that of good prose, but likewise that some of the most interesting parts of the best poems will be found to be strictly the language of prose, when prose is well written. The truth of this assertion might be demonstrated by innumerable passages from almost all the poetical writings, even of Milton himself. I have not space for much quotation; but, to illustrate the subject in a general manner, I will here adduce a short composition of Gray, who was at the head of those who by their reasonings have attempted to widen the space of separation betwixt Prose and Metrical composition, and was more than any other man curiously elaborate in the structure of his own poetic diction.

In vain to me the smiling mornings shine,
And reddening Phoebus lifts his golden fire:
The birds in vain their amorous descant join,
Or chearful fields resume their green attire:
These ears alas! for other notes repine;
A different object do these eyes require;
My lonely anguish melts no heart but mine;
And in my breast the imperfect joys expire;
Yet Morning smiles the busy race to cheer,
And new-born pleasure brings to happier men;
The fields to all their wonted tribute bear;
To warm their little loves the birds complain.
I fruitless mourn to him that cannot hear
And weep the more because I weep in vain.

It will easily be perceived that the only part of this Sonnet which is of any value is the lines printed in Italics: it is equally obvious, that, except in the rhyme, and in the use of the single word "fruitless" for fruitlessly, which is so far a defect, the language of these lines does in no respect differ from that of prose.

By the foregoing quotation I have shewn that the language of Prose may yet be well adapted to Poetry; and I have previously asserted that a large portion of the language of every good poem can in no respect differ from that of good Prose. I will go further. I do not doubt that it may be safely affirmed, that there neither is, nor can be, any essential difference between the language of prose and metrical composition. We are fond of tracing the resemblance between Poetry and Painting, and, accordingly, we call them Sisters: but where shall we find bonds of connection sufficiently strict to typify the affinity betwixt metrical and prose composition? They both speak by and to the same organs; the bodies in which both of them are clothed may be said to be of the same substance, their affections are kindred and almost identical, not necessarily differing even in degree; Poetry sheds no tears "such as Angels weep," but natural and human tears; she can boast of no celestial Ichor that distinguishes her vital juices from those of prose; the same human blood circulates through the veins of them both.

If it be affirmed that rhyme and metrical arrangement of themselves constitute a distinction which overturns what I have been saying on the strict affinity of metrical language with that of prose, and paves the way for other artificial distinctions which the mind voluntarily admits, I answer that the language of such Poetry as I am recommending is, as far as is possible, a selection of the language really spoken by men; that this selection, wherever it is made with true taste and feeling, will of itself form a distinction far greater than would at first be imagined and will entirely separate the composition from the vulgarity and meanness of ordinary life; and, if metre be superadded thereto, I believe that a dissimilitude will be produced altogether sufficient from the gratification of a rational mind. What other distinction would we have? Whence is it to come? And where is it to exist? Not, surely, where the Poet speaks through the mouths of his characters: it cannot be necessary here, either for elevation of style, or any of its supposed ornaments: for, if the Poet's subject be judiciously chosen, it will naturally, and upon fit occasion, lead him to passions the language of which, if selected truly and judiciously, must necessarily be dignified and variegated, and alive with metaphors and figures. I forbear to speak of an incongruity which would shock the intelligent Reader, should the Poet interweave any foreign splendour of his own with that which the passion naturally suggests: it is sufficient to say that such addition is unnecessary. And, surely, it is more probable that those passages, which with propriety abound with metaphors and figures, will have their due effect, if, upon other occasions where the passions are of a milder character, the style also be subdued and temperate.

But, as the pleasure which I hope to give by the Poems I now present to the Reader must depend entirely on just notions upon this subject, and, as it is in itself of the highest importance to our taste and moral feelings, I cannot content myself with these detached remarks. And if, in what I am about to say, it shall appear to some that my labour is unnecessary, and that I am like a man fighting a battle without enemies, I would remind such persons, that, whatever may be the language outwardly holden by men, a practical faith in the opinions which I am wishing to establish is almost unknown. If my conclusions are admitted, and carried as far as they must be carried if admitted at all, our judgments concerning the works of the greatest Poets both ancient and modern will be far different from what they are at present, both when we praise, and when we censure: and our moral feelings influencing, and influenced by these judgments will, I believe, be corrected and purified.

III

DRAMA

SECTION

1

How to Read Drama

HOW TO READ DRAMA

Taken in its literal sense as something *done* or performed on the stage (from the Greek *dran,* a deed or action), drama is not literature. There are many significant differences between the printed script of a play and the production of that script by actors in costume performing on a stage before a live audience. The characters are not seen on the printed page as they are seen by an audience in a live production. The stage directions (usually written in italics) and the **dramatis personae,** or list of characters, sometimes provide a brief description of a character before he or she makes an entrance on the stage.

Consider Arthur Miller's stage directions for *Death of a Salesman* (page 973). Written primarily for the actor, director, and producer of the play, nonetheless they help the reader envision the appearance of the characters. Miller describes Willie Loman as "past sixty years of age, dressed quietly. Even as he crosses the stage to the doorway of the house, his exhaustion is apparent." Not only has Miller described Willie's general appearance, he has also provided one of Willie's essential characteristics: after a lifetime of working to support his family and having little to show for it, he is mentally and physically exhausted. Later in the first act his neighbor Charley is described in more detail as "a large man, slow of speech, laconic, immovable. In all he says, despite what he says, there is pity, and, now, trepidation. He has a robe over pajamas, slippers on his feet." This is an even fuller description than the one for Willie, and it also contains Miller's intentions about how the actor should deliver Charley's lines. Still, we have no idea, in the kind of defining particularities we expect in life, how either Willie or Charlie looks. We might have trouble identifying either of them in a crowd. Unlike the writer of fiction, the playwright does not interrupt the action to tell us what the characters look like. Does Willie have a prominent nose? Is his face wrinkled? Is he stocky or of slight build? It is up to the director to cast an actor in the role who will be consistent with the character Miller has created.

Sometimes an actor's portrayal of a character becomes so closely identified with the playwright's creation that he or she becomes inseparable from the character. Such is the case with Yul Brynner's portrayal of the King of Siam in *The King and I*, of Laurette Taylor's Amanda Wingfield in Tennessee Williams's *The Glass Menagerie*, and of Lee J. Cobb's Willie Loman in the initial production of *Death of a Salesman*. Arthur Miller has said that for him Cobb would always be Willie Loman. Yet a very different Willie Loman was embodied by Dustin Hoffman in a 1984 Broadway production of the play (also filmed for television), for which Miller had to approve a change in the dialogue. A physical description of the stockily built Cobb was inappropriate for the slightly built Hoffman. In the original production, Cobb says, "I'm fat. I'm very—foolish to look at, Linda. I didn't tell you, but Christmas time I happened to be calling on F. N. Stewarts, and a salesman I know, as I was going in to see the buyer I heard him say something about—Walrus. And I—I cracked him right across the face." To accommodate Hoffman, "fat" was changed to "short," and "walrus" was altered to "shrimp."

The only other clue a reader of a play has about the appearance of a character is the **dialogue,** the words spoken by one character to another. Through dialogue a playwright expects the audience to see with an inward eye the essential nature of the characters. When in *Death of a Salesman* Willie tries to understand why his neighbor Charley's son is successful while his own sons have failed, he asks Charley, "And you never told him what to do, did you? You never took any interest in him." And Charley replies, "My salvation is that I never took any interest in anything." In that exchange lies the essential nature of the two characters: Willie wondering what he did wrong, Charley not really caring what he did right. Yet, the reader of *Death of a Salesman* is no more enlightened by dialogue than by stage directions about the external appearance of these characters.

Another difference between watching a production of a play and reading the script is the absence of tone in the printed dialogue and other clarifying visual hints such as gestures and movement. Often the playwright will provide clues to tone, as in the opening lines of *Death of a Salesman* where the stage directions indicate that Linda should call Willie's name "with some trepidation," and that Willie should respond to her questions "with casual irritation." But no stage directions can substitute for a skilled actor's complete absorption in a role—what Truman Capote called the actor's "salamander guile," which does for the live audience what the reader must do for himself through imagination. Readers of drama must, therefore, do the work of director *and* actor, imagining the character in outline form at first, tentatively filling in the outline as the play unfolds, perhaps imagining themselves as casting director and envisioning which actor would ideally be cast in the role.

Neither the playwrights of the classical Greek theater of the fifth century B.C., nor the playwrights of Shakespeare's theater in the late sixteenth and early seventeenth centuries provided stage directions for their plays. Neither stage had painted scenery or many props. The building that provided the background against which the Greek plays were set was called the **skene,** from which we get the modern word *scene* or *scenery,* but it would hardly qualify as scenery by today's elaborate standards. And the Elizabethan stage's elaborate architecture, while serving the basic need for scenery (see "Stagecraft and Spectacle," p. 1161), depended on the actors' speeches to establish whether it and the stage apron were meant to represent the interior of a castle or a battlefield. For radio listeners of a generation ago, the spoken word carried the substance out of which the audience's imagination constructed the details of the setting. In the modern period, playwrights customarily provide details in the stage directions from which the actual physical set will be elaborated.

Miller's own stage directions for *Death of a Salesman* include a detailed description of the single set for the entire play (in many plays sets are changed between scenes or acts), and also Miller's directions about how the set is to be used by the actors. (Turn to the directions Miller gives at the beginning of Act One of *Death of a Salesman,* p. 974).

Even with these directions, a novice reader may become confused and have trouble distinguishing between the times Willie is hallucinating or retreating into the past and when Willie is actually in present time talking with people who are now physically before him. No such difficulty exists for the audience viewing the play. While there is an aura of unreality about the play (and the set reflects this), there are at the same time real chairs, a real kitchen table and refrigerator, and real beds in the bedroom. In a purely realistic play, stage props might be even more numerous, but the point is that even in an imaginative set, such as Jo Mielziner's for the original production of *Death of a Salesman,* there is a recreation of a physical world that no amount of verbal description can equal.

Music is another feature of a performance not available to the reader of a play. While for the most part music may seem an ancillary element of drama, it can sometimes be essential. In ancient Greek plays, the **chorus,** a group of actors who chanted their lines and collectively represented a public voice commenting on the action, originally sang and danced as part of the drama. *Death of a Salesman* uses music as an essential commentary on the action. In the opening stage directions, Miller describes an overture and actually introduces an instrument which not only becomes a symbol in the play, but whose sound also serves as one of the clues that Willie is slipping into the past and out of his present world: "A melody is heard, played upon a flute. It is small and fine, telling of grass and trees and the horizon." Thus the flute music symbolizes the lost rural America that Biff is in search of and that runs counter to the modern urban world. Significantly, Willie's father was a travelling salesman, but unlike Willie he sold the product of his labors, the handcarved flutes he made.

Finally, in addition to costumes, set, actors, tonally colored dialogue, and music, the printed version of a play lacks the sense of audience participation that comes with viewing a play. It was not by accident that when drama emerged in the western world, first among the Greeks and later in the medieval Christian world, it originated from religious ceremonies. That ceremonial aspect is still present in the theater when an audience assembles to witness actors on a stage portraying familiar human traits and behavior. The electric quality of a performance is an experience we achieve only as members of an audience.

This sense of shared participation extends to the actors as well, affecting them as they are caught up and encouraged by a sympathetic audience, or discouraged into giving a lackluster performance by an unresponsive audience. The same 1984 revival of Miller's *Death of a Salesman* is an illustration. In the explosive scene in Act Two, Biff whips out the rubber hose that Willie has secretly fitted to the gas water heater thinking to kill himself, lays it on the kitchen table, and says to his father, "All right, phony! Then let's lay it on the line." The audience was stunned into silence and later moved to tears when Biff shouts, "We never told the truth for ten minutes in this house." The impact was a result not only of Miller's lines, but of the complete connection between actors and members of the audience. Not only did the audience weep at the end of the performance; during the curtain calls the actors wept as well.

But reading a play has its advantages—and not many people have the money or the opportunity to see as many plays as they can read. Since many of the elements of drama are similar to those of fiction—characters, plot, conflict, dialogue, symbols, setting—drama can be studied profitably as literature. As we will see, these elements, although they may differ slightly when written for the stage, retain a basic similarity to fiction. Furthermore, readers of a play have an advantage over the viewer: they may reread a passage that seems complex or rich with meaning, whereas in the theater, as in life, when a line of dialogue is uttered, the audience cannot ask for an instant replay. Like a reader of poetry, the reader of a play can study the use of language, the patterns of images that convey the theme, the nuances of speech that reveal character, and the shifts in diction that heighten or reduce emotion. When, in the "Requiem" section of *Death of a Salesman*, Charley delivers what amounts to Willie's funeral oration, he takes on the function of the ancient Greek chorus, explaining to the audience the significance of the actions they have just witnessed. He does so in a mixture of colloquial, poetic, and archaic diction.

Nobody dast blame this man. You don't understand: Willie was a salesman. And for a salesman, there is no rock bottom to the life. He don't put a bolt to a nut, he don't tell you the law or give you medicine. He's a man way out there in the blue, riding on a smile and a shoeshine. And when they start not smiling back—that's an earthquake. And then you get yourself a couple of spots on your hat, and you're finished. Nobody dast blame this man. A salesman is got to dream, boy. It comes with the territory.

The speech repays careful study with its images of law, insubstantiality, smiles, and territory, and with its mixture of diction—"dast," "He don't," "A salesman is got"—but such a pause for study is impossible for the theater-goer. Readers can make up their own minds about a character while reading a play, and not be swayed by an actor's or director's interpretation of a role. George C. Scott gave such a powerfully sympathetic portrayal of the villain Shylock in Shakespeare's *The Merchant of Venice*, that Shylock's vengeance seemed justified in view of the anti-Semitism to which he had been subjected earlier in the play. An unusual interpretation by an actor may take you away from the playwright's intentions.

In addition to being aware of the relative merits of watching a production and reading a play, the student of drama should have some idea of its forms and elements. The elements of drama most often cited are those listed by Aristotle in his *Poetics*, a treatise based on his observations of fifth century B.C. Greek tragedies. Aristotle found six elements in drama: plot, character, thought, diction, song, and spectacle. The list is in order of importance.

Plot, the first element, bears a resemblance to plot in fiction: it is the story of what happens to the characters. However, drama presents the action directly rather than narrating it from an observor's point of view. The point of view of drama is always objective; the events are portrayed directly for the audience's benefit. Aristotle, therefore, defined the essential nature of drama as "an imitation of an action," *imitation* because the actors are *portraying* real people. The space in which the action takes place is meant to represent a real place, and the action is meant to reproduce what actually happened. Like plots in fiction, dramatic plots are often divided into five parts.

Exposition. This is the background information necessary to understand the drama. Usually this information is presented at the beginning of the play. In the first act of *Death of a Salesman,* for example, within the first few minutes we learn from the conversation between Willie and Linda that Willie is a travelling salesman who covers the New England territory, that he is physically and mentally exhausted, and that his 34-year-old son Biff, in whom Willie is disappointed, has just returned home after a long absence spent working as a farmhand. Other information about Willie's older brother, Ben, and their father is provided later in the play.

Rising action. At the beginning of a play, the forces of conflict that drive the action to its conclusion are latent, at rest. An incident spurs the conflict on, bringing it into the open. Willie has almost hit someone with his car; he can't keep his mind on his driving and is disturbed by "strange thoughts." Willie's failure in business and with his sons, especially Biff, who showed such promise in high school ("like a young god, Hercules"), is revealed in the dialogue between the two brothers, and the extent of Willie's "illness" is clear from his hallucinations in the first act, a train of memories of happier times. The action continues to rise with the promise of better times and dreams of success. Willie's unrealistic expectations are raised to their highest point at the beginning of Act Two when he exclaims to Linda, "I'm gonna knock Howard for a loop, kid. I'll get an advance, and I'll come home with a New York job. Goddammit, now I'm gonna do it!" Caught up in his enthusiasm, Linda responds, "It's changing, Willie, I can feel it changing!"

Turning point. This is a reversal, a discovery that marks a victory or a defeat for the main character. Often the turning point will occur near the middle of the play. It does not mark the end of the action, or the utter victory or defeat of the main character. Rather, it is an indicator of the direction the action is taking and a predictor of its final result. In *Death of a Salesman* the turning point occurs when Willie is fired from his job by Howard, the son of the firm's original owner. Willie's final defeat at the hands of the business world is justified by Howard, who tells Willie, "business is business," and who rejects Willie's desperate plea: "I put thirty-four years into this firm, Howard, and now I can't pay my insurance! You can't eat the orange and throw the peel away—a man is not a piece of fruit!"

Falling action. This completes the defeat or reversal marked by the turning point. In subsequent scenes, Willie must humble himself by borrowing money from his neighbor Charlie, see what a successful lawyer Charlie's son Bernard has become, and suffer a denial of his paternity by his sons: "No that's not my father. He's just a guy." The penultimate scene in Act II (Willie's planting seeds in the garden at night) brings together the double defeat by the urban-business world and his offspring. Willie's suicide is the only logical outcome of the action.

Denouement. This explains the action. Miller's requiem section explains the nature of Willie's life and death, while the two sons represent the sides of Willie's character that were at war: urban-business success based on such intangibles as "being well-liked," and the nostalgia for a rural America of tangible accomplishments. Linda's final speech sums up the futility of the life lived by the "little man."

The second most important element listed by Aristotle, **character** can be viewed in much the same way as character in fiction, with one important exception. A reader depends on dialogue and actions to infer the personality of the characters. Except for stage directions, there is no narrative voice interpreting the stage directions and the action for us. Repeated phrases, like Willie's use of the expression "being well-liked," and Ben's "When I walked into the jungle, I was seventeen. When I walked out I was twenty-one. And, by God, I was rich!'' are a means of establishing character, as are repeated actions or associations with objects, such as Willie's interest in rebuilding things.

As in fiction, plays have fully developed individuated characters as well as **stock characters** who serve their purpose as stereotypes, but who fail to reflect the multi-dimensionality of real people. Thus we don't find Ben, the stereotypic turn-of-the-century robber baron, or Bernard, the quintessential unathletic intellectual who succeeds in his profession, as interesting as either Willie or Biff. Even the main characters may have some traits of a flat character about them—that is, until the playwright fills in the outline motivating the character to behavior not covered by the stereotype. Thus Biff may seem like the dumb high school football star who couldn't make it in life—until Miller explores the complex reasons for his failure. He also gives Biff a sensitivity stemming from another system of values alien to the ethos of the business world. Linda may seem like the saintly housewife, oblivious to conflict, who quietly assumes responsibility for the running of the home—until her speech to her sons when she criticizes them for their treatment of Willie: "He's a human being and a terrible thing is happening to him. So attention must be paid. He's not to be allowed to fall into his grave like an old dog. Attention, attention must finally be paid to such a person." Linda emerges as one of the strong figures in the play who maintains her dignity and gains the audience's sympathy in the end.

Aristotle's third most important element, **thought,** might be taken up together with **diction;** it is through diction that thought, or theme—the main idea, purpose, or significance of a play—is revealed to the reader. A simple statement of the play's theme will not adequately sum up all that the playwright has implied; nevertheless, any attempt to articulate the theme may help clarify some of the play's complex meaning. For example, to say that *Death of a Salesman* is an indictment of America's emphasis on defining success in materialistic terms, or that parents should not force their dreams of success on their children, or that the American Dream is an ill-defined amalgamation of rural simplicity and urban materialism, is in each case to state *part* of what the play is about.

How are these partial statements of the thought of a play arrived at? The meaning of a play is often to be found in objects repeatedly associated with a character or an idea throughout the play. Repeated relationships in *Death of a Salesman*—father to sons, brother to brother, husband to wife, employer to employee, neighbor to neighbor—define some of the strength and weaknesses of modern America and American family life. As in fiction or poetry, the language of drama can be studied to reveal the playwright's intentions. The constant undercurrent of references to grass and trees in both Willie's and Biff's speeches tells of a yearning for a pastoral America obliterated by the menace of urbanization. Together father and son express—vaguely and obliquely, never adequately enough to communicate with one another—their unrealizable dreams. Thus the frustration and anger felt by the characters in *Death of a Salesman* are understood by the reader of the play, but *not* by the characters, who remain prisoners of their half-articulated dreams.

The remaining elements—**song** (or music) and **spectacle**—have already been dealt with earlier in this chapter. Spectacle, Aristotle felt, was the least artistic of the elements and depended more "on the stage machinist" for its effect than upon the playwright. Like music, spectacle—the use of scenery, costumes, and special lightings effects—can enhance a performance, but anyone who has watched an effective reader's theater can attest to the power of the spoken word by itself. However, the stark power of a play like Sophocles' *Oedipus the King* is made visible, and the performance becomes a riveting experience, when set and costume design are combined with music and with the movements of the actors on the stage. This kind of effect may not occur when a play is read; still, the study of drama as literature gives us access to a number of plays that would otherwise be unavailable.

If we are to understand the plays we read, we must be familiar with the conventions of drama. Like other forms of literature, plays can be divided into types, or **genres,** each with its own conventions. While every play might not fit neatly into any of the genres of drama, an understanding of the general conventions of each type is useful; it would be unfair to expect a play to fulfill requirements outside its conventions. More detailed explanations of the characteristics and origins of each type of play will follow in subsequent chapters. For now it is enough to say that plays can be divided according to two criteria: how the play ends and how realistic it is.

In the simplest sense, plays that end unhappily with the death or suffering of the main character are **tragedies,** and plays which end happily, usually with couples being reunited or married, are **comedies.** Both tragedy and comedy have taken on a host of associations which should be clarified. Since Aristotle, tragedy has come to mean a play about a great man or woman who falls from some high station, status, or condition. In earlier societies (Greek and Elizabethan) this station was aristocratic, that of royalty: a king, queen, prince, or princess. The issue of whether we can have tragedies in egalitarian societies has been discussed by Arthur Miller in connection with *Death of a Salesman* (p. 973).

The tragic hero fails as a result of what the Greeks called **hamartia**—a transgression, a mistake, but sometimes translated as "tragic flaw," a character trait causing the hero's downfall. At some point in the action the fortunes of the hero are reversed. As we have seen, Willie Loman's reversal begins with his visit to Howard's office to request a job in New York, a visit that ends instead with Willie's being fired. According to the Greeks, recognition must occur as an outcome of the hero's suffering. The suffering must not remain meaningless, but lead to insight for the tragic hero or for the audience. In *Death of a Salesman,* the meaning of Willie's suffering is not perceived by Willie himself, but by the audience through Charlie.

Finally, Aristotle called attention to the effect on the audience of watching the hero's suffering. The audience underwent a **katharsis,** or a purging of pity and fear. Exactly what Aristotle meant by *katharsis* has been argued by modern scholars, but all agree that some element of empathy for the hero as a suffering fellow human being is felt by the audience. The stirring of pity for his suffering is accompanied by a concomitant fear that the same kind of tragic outcome is possible for any member of the audience. The raising of these emotions has a cathartic effect; that is, the audience's emotions are raised and then, when the action is over and the routine of everyday life resumed, there is relief in having escaped the fate of the hero. This purgation is not a feeling of moral superiority, but a sharing in the precariousness of human existence.

If tragedies make us weep, then comedies make us laugh, if not out loud, then at least inwardly. The antics of human beings—their pretensions, their weaknesses, their absurdities—are the stuff of which comedies are made. Unlike the fear we feel over the outcome of a tragedy, the threats to the well-being of the characters in the world of comedy are temporary obstacles soon to be overcome. In Shakespeare's *A Midsummer Night's Dream,* we laugh at Bottom the weaver with his ass's ears and braying talk, but we know that he will soon return to human form. **Romantic comedies** present a world of improbabilities: mistaken identities, disguises, lovers separated, and treacherous villains; identities clarified, lovers united, and villains defeated at the conclusion. Romantic comedies such as Shakespeare's *Much Ado About Nothing* present a world of life-affirming forces where even the gods smile on human life. **Social comedies,** while they end happily with the vindication of the virtuous characters, expose various human flaws from slight foibles to serious vices. The satiric aim of such comedies is the correction and improvement of society. Because social fashions and humor change, social comedy needs to be placed in its historical context if it is to be understood. Reading the bitter, self-mocking humor of Samuel Beckett's *Krapp's Last Tape* is far different from reading the amusing comedy of Molière's *Misanthrope.* In short, it is important to adjust your expectations of the genre to the play's historical and cultural milieu.

Since the middle of the nineteenth century, it has been common to find plays which are a mixture of tragedy and comedy, so-called **tragicomedies.** Even the comedies of Shapespeare's final period, while they end happily, have a dark tonality about them. Thus they are often called the "dark comedies." Tragedies may have comic scenes in them, such as the gravedigger's scene in *Hamlet,* or comedies may have dark, nihilistic implications.

Finally, plays may be more or less realistic. **Realistic drama** strives to recreate an appearance of life on the stage through sets, costume, props, dialogue, characters, and action. Henrik Ibsen's earlier plays (*A Doll's*

House and *Ghosts*) tried to create the impression for the audience that they were looking on domestic scenes of everyday life through the invisible fourth wall of a room. American drama of the 1930s and 40s, in which the characters were often working class people—plays like Clifford Odet's *Waiting for Lefty* or Elmer Rice's *Street Scene*—tried to give the audience a *slice of life,* that is, the impression that this was a segment taken from real life.

At the opposite end of the spectrum, playwrights began to experiment with subject matter and devices that were not objective and realistic, but subjective and mental. Some playwrights extended their subject matter to include fantasies, dreams, memories, and psychological states. Such plays fall under the heading of **expressionistic drama** from the art movement of Expressionism which began in Germany after World War I. American plays such as Eugene O'Neill's *The Emperor Jones,* Tennessee Williams's *The Glass Menagerie,* and Arthur Miller's *Death of a Salesman,* combine both the modes of expressionistic and realistic drama; their characters speak realistic dialogue, and deal with real social concerns in real settings, but as the plays unfold, those worlds dissolve into memory or nightmare. It is therefore important in reading a play to determine in what mode it is written, for it would be inappropriate to apply realistic standards to an expressionistic play.

With all that has been said about drama's ambiguous status as both live performance and literary text, one final question should be raised: Why read drama at all? First, reading enables the student of drama to participate imaginatively in the recreation of a living artwork. The script of a play, like an architect's blueprint, provides the outline, but leaves open to the reader the actual imaginative reconstruction of the drama. Perhaps the pleasure of reading a play is more like that of a musician giving life to a score by playing it on an instrument. Second, in a world of increasing isolation and fragmentation, of gated communities isolating people by economics and age, drama offers an opportunity for sharing some of the most important moments of what it means to be human. Through drama we can directly touch the lives of people who, like Sophocles, lived twenty-five centuries ago.

Exemplary Text

ARTHUR MILLER (b. 1915)

Death of a Salesman

Arthur Miller was born in New York City and attended the University
of Michigan. Along with Tennessee Williams, he is generally considered
the greatest American dramatist of the period following World War II.
Among his most famous plays are the Pulitzer Prize-winning *Death of a
Salesman* (1949), *The Crucible* (1953), *A View from the Bridge* (1955), and
After the Fall (1964). He has also written a novel, *Focus* (1945) and an
important essay about the possibilities for tragic drama in the modern
theatre (see "Tragedy and the Common Man," page 1598).

CHARACTERS

WILLY LOMAN	UNCLE BEN
LINDA	HOWARD WAGNER
BIFF	JENNY
HAPPY	STANLEY
BERNARD	MISS FORSYTHE
THE WOMAN	LETTA
CHARLEY	

*The action takes place in Willy Loman's house and yard and in various places
he visits in the New York and Boston of today.*

Throughout the play, in the stage directions, left and right mean stage left and stage right.

ACT ONE

A melody is heard, played upon a flute. It is small and fine, telling of grass and trees and the horizon. The curtain rises.

Before us is the Salesman's house. We are aware of towering, angular shapes behind it, surrounding it on all sides. Only the blue light of the sky falls upon the house and forestage; the surrounding area shows an angry glow of orange. As more light appears, we see a solid vault of apartment houses around the small, fragile-seeming home. An air of the dream clings to the place, a dream rising out of reality. The kitchen at center seems actual enough, for there is a kitchen table with three chairs, and a refrigerator. But no other fixtures are seen. At the back of the kitchen there is a draped entrance, which leads to the living-room. To the right of the kitchen, on a level raised two feet, is a bedroom furnished only with a brass bedstead and a straight chair. On a shelf over the bed a silver athletic trophy stands. A window opens onto the apartment house at the side.

Behind the kitchen, on a level raised six and a half feet, is the boys' bedroom, at present barely visible. Two beds are dimly seen, and at the back of the room a dormer window. (This bedroom is above the unseen living-room.) At the left a stairway curves up to it from the kitchen.

The entire setting is wholly, or, in some places, partially transparent. The roof-line of the house is one-dimensional; under and over it we see the apartment buildings. Before the house lies an apron, curving beyond the forestage into the orchestra. This forward area serves as the back yard as well as the locale of all Willy's imaginings and of his city scenes. Whenever the action is in the present the actors observe the imaginary wall-lines, entering the house only through its door at the left. But in the scenes of the past these boundaries are broken, and characters enter or leave a room by stepping "through" a wall onto the forestage.

From the right, Willy Loman, the Salesman, enters, carrying two large sample cases. The flute plays on. He hears but is not aware of it. He is past sixty years of age, dressed quietly. Even as he crosses the stage to the doorway of the house, his exhaustion is apparent. He unlocks the door, comes into the kitchen, and thankfully lets his burden down, feeling the soreness of his palms. A word-sigh escapes his lips—it might be "Oh, boy, oh, boy." He closes the door, then carries his cases out into the living-room, through the draped kitchen doorway.

Linda, his wife, has stirred in her bed at the right. She gets out and puts on a robe, listening. Most often jovial, she has developed an iron repression of her exceptions to Willy's behavior—she more than loves him, she admires him, as though his mercurial nature, his temper, his massive dreams and little cruelties, served her only as sharp reminders of the turbulent longings within him, longings which she shares but lacks the temperament to utter and follow to their end.

LINDA, *hearing Willy outside the bedroom, calls with some trepidation:*   Willy!

WILLY: It's all right. I came back.

LINDA: Why? What happened? *Slight pause.* Did something happen, Willy?

WILLY: No, nothing happened.

LINDA: You didn't smash the car, did you?

WILLY, *with casual irritation:*   I said nothing happened. Didn't you hear me?

LINDA: Don't you feel well?

WILLY: I'm tired to the death. *The flute has faded away. He sits on the bed beside her, a little numb.* I couldn't make it. I just couldn't make it, Linda.

LINDA, *very carefully, delicately:*   Where were you all day? You look terrible.

WILLY: I got as far as a little above Yonkers. I stopped for a cup of coffee. Maybe it was the coffee.

LINDA: What?

WILLY, *after a pause.:*   I suddenly couldn't drive any more. The car kept going off onto the shoulder, y'know?

LINDA, *helpfully:*   Oh, Maybe it was the steering again. I don't think Angelo knows the Studebaker.

WILLY: No, it's me, it's me. Suddenly I realize I'm goin' sixty miles an hour and I don't remember the last five minutes. I'm—I can't seem to—keep my mind to it.

LINDA: Maybe it's your glasses. You never went for your new glasses.

WILLY: No, I see everything. I came back ten miles an hour. It took me nearly four hours from Yonkers.

LINDA, *resigned:*   Well, you'll just have to take a rest, Willy, you can't continue this way.

WILLY: I just got back from Florida.

LINDA: But you didn't rest your mind. Your mind is overactive, and the mind is what counts, dear.

WILLY: I'll start out in the morning. Maybe I'll feel better in the morning. *She is taking off his shoes.* These goddam arch supports are killing me.

LINDA: Take an aspirin. Should I get you an aspirin? It'll soothe you.

WILLY, *with wonder:*   I was driving along, you understand? And I was fine. I was even observing the scenery. You can imagine, me looking at scenery, on the road every week of my life. But it's so beautiful up there. Linda, the trees are so thick, and the sun is warm. I opened the windshield and just let the warm air bathe over me. And then all of a sudden I'm goin' off the road! I'm tellin' ya, I absolutely forgot I was driving. If I'd've gone the other way over the white line I might've killed somebody. So I went on again—and five minutes later I'm dreamin' again, and I nearly— *He presses two fingers against his eyes.* I have such thoughts, I have such strange thoughts.

LINDA: Willy, dear. Talk to them again. There's no reason why you can't work in New York.

WILLY: They don't need me in New York. I'm the New England man. I'm vital in New England.

LINDA: But you're sixty years old. They can't expect you to keep traveling every week.

WILLY: I'll have to send a wire to Portland. I'm supposed to see Brown and Morrison tomorrow morning at ten o'clock to show the line. Goddammit, I could sell them! *He starts putting on his jacket.*

LINDA, *taking the jacket from him:*   Why don't you go down to the place tomorrow and tell Howard you've simply got to work in New York? You're too accommodating, dear.

WILLY: If old man Wagner was alive I'd a been in charge of New York now! That man was a prince, he was a masterful man. But that boy of his, that Howard, he don't appreciate. When I went north the first time, the Wagner Company didn't know where New England was!

LINDA: Why don't you tell those things to Howard, dear?

WILLY, *encouraged:*   I will, I definitely will. Is there any cheese?

LINDA::   I'll make you a sandwich.

WILLY: No, go to sleep. I'll take some milk. I'll be up right away. The boys in?

LINDA: They're sleeping. Happy took Biff on a date tonight.

WILLY, *interested:*   That so?

LINDA: It was so nice to see them shaving together, one behind the other, in the bathroom. And going out together. You notice? The whole house smells of shaving lotion.

WILLY: Figure it out. Work a lifetime to pay off a house. You finally own it, and there's nobody to live in it.

LINDA: Well, dear, life is a casting off. It's always that way.

WILLY: No, no, some people—some people accomplish something. Did Biff say anything after I went this morning?

LINDA: You shouldn't have criticized him, Willy, especially after he just got off the train. You mustn't lose your temper with him.

WILLY: When the hell did I lose my temper? I simply asked him if he was making any money. Is that a criticism?

LINDA: But, dear, how could he make any money?

WILLY, *worried and angered:*   There's such an undercurrent in him. He became a moody man. Did he apologize when I left this morning?

LINDA: He was crestfallen, Willy. You know how he admires you. I think if he finds himself, then you'll both be happier and not fight any more.

WILLY: How can he find himself on a farm? Is that a life? A farmhand? In the beginning, when he was young, I thought, well, a young man, it's good for him to tramp around, take a lot of different jobs. but it's more than ten years now and he has yet to make thirty-five dollars a week!

LINDA: He's finding himself, Willy.

WILLY: Not finding yourself at the age of thirty-four is a disgrace!

LINDA: Shh!

WILLY: The trouble is he's lazy, goddammit!

LINDA: Willy, please!

WILLY: Biff is a lazy bum!

LINDA: They're sleeping. Get something to eat. Go on down.

WILLY: Why did he come home? I would like to know what brought him home.

LINDA: I don't know. I think he's still lost, Willy. I think he's very lost.

WILLY: Biff Loman is lost. In the greatest country in the world a young man with such—personal attractiveness, gets lost. And such a hard worker. There's one thing about Biff—he's not lazy.

LINDA: Never.

WILLY, *with pity and resolve:*   I'll see him in the morning; I'll have a nice talk with him. I'll get him a job selling. He could be big in no time. My God! Remember how they used to follow him around in high school? When he smiled at one of them their faces lit up. When he walked down the street—*He loses himself in reminiscences.*

LINDA, *trying to bring him out of it:*   Willy, dear, I got a new kind of American-type cheese today. It's whipped.

WILLY: Why do you get American when I like Swiss?

LINDA: I just thought you'd like a change—

WILLY: I don't want a change! I want Swiss cheese. Why am I always being contradicted?

LINDA, *with a covering laugh:*   I thought it would be a surprise.

WILLY: Why don't you open a window in here, for God's sake?

LINDA, *with infinite patience:*   They're all open, dear.

WILLY: The way they boxed us in here. Bricks and windows, windows and bricks.

LINDA: We should've bought the land next door.

WILLY: The street is lined with cars. There's not a breath of fresh air in the neighborhood. The grass don't grow any more, you can't raise a carrot in the back yard. They should've had a law against apartment houses. Remember those two beautiful elm trees out there? When I and Biff hung the swing between them?

LINDA: Yeah, like being a million miles from the city.

WILLY: They should've arrested the builder for cutting those down. They massacred the neighborhood. *Lost:* More and more I think of those days, Linda. This time of year it was lilac and wisteria. And then the peonies would come out, and the daffodils. What fragrance in this room!

LINDA: Well, after all, people had to move somewhere.

WILLY: No, there's more people now.

LINDA: I don't think there's more people. I think—

WILLY: There's more people! That's what's ruining this country! Population is getting out of control. The competition is maddening! Smell the stink from that apartment house! And another one on the other side . . . How can they whip cheese?

On Willy's last line, Biff and Happy raise themselves up in their beds, listening.

LINDA: Go down, try it. And be quiet.

WILLY, *turning to Linda, guiltily:* You're not worried about me, are you, sweetheart?

BIFF: What's the matter?

HAPPY: Listen!

LINDA: You've got too much on the ball to worry about.

WILLY: You're my foundation and my support, Linda

LINDA: Just try to relax, dear. You make mountains out of molehills.

WILLY: I won't fight with him any more. If he wants to go back to Texas, let him go.

LINDA: He'll find his way.

WILLY: Sure. Certain men just don't get started till later in life. Like Thomas Edison, I think. Or B. F. Goodrich. One of them was deaf. *He starts for the bedroom doorway.* I'll put my money on Biff.

LINDA: And Willy—if it's warm Sunday we'll drive in the country. And we'll open the windshield, and take lunch.

WILLY: No, the windshields don't open on the new cars.

LINDA: But you opened it today.

WILLY: Me? I didn't. *He stops.* Now isn't that peculiar! Isn't that a remarkable— *He breaks off in amazement and fright as the flute is heard distantly.*

LINDA: What, darling?

WILLY: That is the most remarkable thing.

LINDA: What, dear?

WILLY: I was thinking of the Chevvy. *Slight pause.* Nineteen twenty-eight . . . when I had that red Chevvy— Breaks off. That funny? I coulda sworn I was driving that Chevvy today.

LINDA: Well, that's nothing. Something must've reminded you.

WILLY: Remarkable. Ts. Remember those days? The way Biff used to simonize that car? The dealer refused to believe there was eighty thousand miles on it. *He shakes his head.* Heh! *To Linda:* Close your eyes, I'll be right up. *He walks out of the bedroom.*

HAPPY, *to Biff:* Jesus, maybe he smashed up the car again!

LINDA, *calling after Willy:* Be careful on the stairs, dear! The cheese is on the middle shelf! *She turns, goes over to the bed, takes his jacket, and goes out of the bedroom.*

Light has risen on the boys' room. Unseen, Willy is heard talking to himself, "Eighty thousand miles," and a little laugh. Biff gets out of bed, comes downstage a bit, and stands attentively. Biff is two years older than his brother Happy, well built, but in these days bears a worn air and seems less self-assured. He has succeeded less, and his dreams are stronger and less acceptable than Happy's. Happy is tall, powerfully made. Sexuality is like a visible color on him, or a scent that many women have discovered. He, like his brother, is lost, but in a different way, for he had never allowed himself to turn his face toward defeat and is thus more confused and hard-skinned, although seemingly more content.

HAPPY, *getting out of bed:* He's going to get his license taken away if he keeps that up. I'm getting nervous about him, y'know, Biff?

BIFF: His eyes are going.

HAPPY: No, I've driven with him. He sees all right. He just doesn't keep his mind on it. I drove into the city with him last week. He stops at a green light and then it turns red and he goes. *He laughs.*

BIFF: Maybe he's color-blind.

HAPPY: Pop? Why he's got the finest eye for color in the business. You know that.

BIFF, *sitting down on his bed:* I'm going to sleep.

HAPPY: You're not still sour on Dad, are you, Biff?

BIFF: He's all right, I guess.

WILLY, *underneath them, in the living-room:* Yes, sir, eighty thousand miles—eighty-two thousand!

BIFF: You smoking?

HAPPY, *holding out a pack of cigarettes:* Want one?

BIFF, *taking a cigarette:* I can never sleep when I smell it.

WILLY: What a simonizing job, heh!

HAPPY, *with deep sentiment:* Funny, Biff, y'know? Us sleeping in here again? The old beds. *He pats his bed affectionately.* All the talk that went across those two beds, huh? Our whole lives.

BIFF: Yeah. Lotta dreams and plans.

HAPPY, *with a deep and masculine laugh:* About five hundred women would like to know what was said in this room.

They share a soft laugh.

BIFF: Remember that big Betsy something—what the hell was her name—over on Bushwick Avenue?

HAPPY, *combing his hair:* With the collie dog!

BIFF: That's the one. I got you in there, remember?

HAPPY: Yeah, that was my first time—I think. Boy, there was a pig! *They laugh, almost crudely.* You taught me everything I know about women. Don't forget that.

BIFF: I bet you forgot how bashful you used to be. Especially with girls.

HAPPY: Oh, I still am, Biff.

BIFF: Oh, go on.

HAPPY: I just control it, that's all. I think I got less bashful and you got more so. What happened, Biff? Where's the old humor, the old confidence? *He shakes Biff's knee Biff gets up and moves restlessly about the room.* What's the matter?

BIFF: Why does Dad mock me all the time?

HAPPY: He's not mocking you, he—

BIFF: Everything I say there's a twist of mockery on his face. I can't get near him.

HAPPY: He just wants you to make good, that's all. I wanted to talk to you about Dad for a long time, Biff. Something's—happening to him. He—talks to himself.

BIFF: I noticed that this morning. But he always mumbled.

HAPPY: But not so noticeable. It got so embarrassing I sent him to Florida. And you know something? Most of the time he's talking to you.

BIFF: What's he say about me?

HAPPY: I can't make it out.

BIFF: What's he say about me?

HAPPY: I think the fact that you're not settled, that you're still kind of up in the air . . .

BIFF: There's one or two other things depressing him, Happy.

HAPPY: What do you mean?

BIFF: Never mind. Just don't lay it all to me.

HAPPY: But I think if you just got started—I mean—is there any future for you out there?

BIFF: I tell ya. Hap, I don't know what the future is. I don't know—what I'm supposed to want.

HAPPY: What do you mean?

BIFF: Well, I spent six or seven years after high school trying to work myself up. Shipping clerk, salesman, business of one kind or another. And it's a measly manner of existence. To get on that subway on the hot mornings in summer. To devote your whole life to keeping stock, or making phone calls, or selling or buying. To suffer fifty weeks of the year for the sake of a two-week vacation, when all you really desire is to be outdoors, with your shirt off. And always to have to get ahead of the next fella. And still—that's how you build a future.

HAPPY: Well, you really enjoy it on a farm? Are you content out there?

BIFF, *with rising agitation:*   Hap, I've had twenty or thirty different kinds of jobs since I left home before the war, and it always turns out the same. I just realized it lately. In Nebraska when I herded cattle, and the Dakotas, and Arizona, and now in Texas. It's why I came home now, I guess, because I realized it. This farm I work on, it's spring there now, see? And they've got about fifteen new colts. There's nothing more inspiring or—beautiful than the sight of a mare and a new colt. And it's cool there now, see? Texas is cool now, and it's spring. And whenever spring comes to where I am, I suddenly get the feeling, my God, I'm not getting anywhere! What the hell am I doing, playing around with horses, twenty-eight dollars a week! I'm thirty-four years old, I oughta be makin' my future. That's when I come running home. And now, I get here, and I don't know what to do with myself. *After a pause:* I've always made a point of not wasting my life, and everytime I come back here I know that all I've done is to waste my life.

HAPPY: You're a poet, you know that, Biff? You're a—you're an idealist!

BIFF: No, I'm mixed up very bad. Maybe I oughta get married. Maybe I oughta get stuck into something. Maybe that's my trouble. I'm like a boy. I'm not married, I'm not in business, I just—I'm like a boy. Are you content, Hap? You're a success, aren't you? Are you content?

HAPPY: Hell, no!

BIFF: Why? You're making money, aren't you?

HAPPY, *moving about with energy, expressiveness:*   All I can do now is wait for the merchandise manager to die. And suppose I get to be merchandise manager? He's a good friend of mine, and he just built a terrific estate on Long Island. And he lived there about two months and sold it, and now he's building another one. He can't enjoy it once it's finished. And I know that's just what I would do. I don't know what the hell I'm workin' for. Sometimes I sit in my apartment—all alone. And I think of the rent I'm paying. And it's crazy. But then, it's what I always wanted. My own apartment, a car, and plenty of women. And still, goddammit, I'm lonely.

BIFF, *with enthusiasm:*   Listen, why don't you come out West with me?

HAPPY: You and I, heh?

BIFF: Sure, maybe we could buy a ranch. Raise cattle, use our muscles. Men built like we are should be working out in the open.

HAPPY, *avidly:*   The Loman Brothers, heh?

BIFF, *with vast affection:*   Sure, we'd be known all over the counties!

HAPPY, *enthralled:*   That's what I dream about, Biff. Sometimes I want to just rip my clothes off in the middle of the store and outbox that goddam merchandise manager. I mean I can outbox, outrun, and outlift anybody in that store, and I have to take orders from those common, petty sons-of-bitches till I can't stand it any more.

BIFF: I'm tellin' you, kid, if you were with me I'd be happy out there.

HAPPY, *enthused:*   See, Biff, everybody around me is so false that I'm constantly lowering my ideals . . .

BIFF: Baby, together we'd stand up for one another, we'd have someone to trust.

HAPPY: If I were around you—

BIFF: Hap, the trouble is we weren't brought up to grub for money. I don't know how to do it.

HAPPY: Neither can I!

BIFF: Then let's go!

HAPPY: The only thing is—what can you make out there?

BIFF: But look at your friend. Builds an estate and then hasn't the peace of mind to live in it.

HAPPY: Yeah, but when he walks into the store the waves part in front of him. That's fifty-two thousand dollars a year coming through the revolving door, and I got more in my pinky finger than he's got in his head.

BIFF: Yeah, but you just said—

HAPPY: I gotta show some of those pompous, self-important executives over there that Hap Loman can make the grade. I want to walk into the store the way he walks in. Then I'll go with you, Biff. We'll be together yet, I swear. But take those two we had tonight. Now weren't they gorgeous creatures?

BIFF: Yeah, yeah, most gorgeous I've had in years.

HAPPY: I get that anytime I want, Biff. Whenever I feel disgusted. The only trouble is, it gets like bowling or something. I just keep knockin' them over and it doesn't mean anything. You still run around a lot?

BIFF: Naa. I'd like to find a girl—steady, somebody with substance.

HAPPY: That's what I long for.

BIFF: Go on! You'd never come home.

HAPPY: I would! Somebody with character, with resistance! Like Mom, y'know? You're gonna call me a bastard when I tell you this. That girl Charlotte I was with tonight is engaged to be married in five weeks. *He tries on his new hat.*

BIFF: No kiddin'!

HAPPY: Sure, the guy's in line for the vice-presidency of the store. I don't know what gets into me, maybe I just have an overdeveloped sense of competition or something, but I went and ruined her, and furthermore I can't get rid of her. And he's the third executive I've done that to. Isn't that a crummy characteristic? And to top it all, I go to their weddings! *Indignantly, but laughing:* Like I'm not supposed to take bribes. Manufacturers offer me a hundred-dollar bill now and then to throw an order their way. You know how honest I am, but it's like this girl, see. I hate myself for it. Because I don't want the girl, and, still, I take it and—I love it!

BIFF: Let's go to sleep.

HAPPY: I guess we didn't settle anything, heh?

BIFF: I just got one idea that I think I'm going to try.

HAPPY: What's that?

BIFF: Remember Bill Oliver?

HAPPY: Sure, Oliver is very big now. You want to work for him again?

BIFF: No, but when I quit he said something to me. He put his arm on my shoulder, and he said, "Biff, if you ever need anything, come to me."

HAPPY: I remember that. That sounds good.

BIFF: I think I'll go to see him. If I could get ten thousand or even seven or eight thousand dollars I could buy a beautiful ranch.

HAPPY: I bet he'd back you. 'Cause he thought highly of you, Biff, I mean, they all do. You're well liked, Biff. That's why I say to come back here, and we both have the apartment. And I'm tellin' you, Biff, any babe you want . . .

BIFF: No, with a ranch I could do the work I like and still be something. I just wonder though. I wonder if Oliver still thinks I stole that carton of basketballs.

HAPPY: Oh, he probably forgot that long ago. It's almost ten years. You're too sensitive. Anyway, he didn't really fire you.

BIFF: Well, I think he was going to. I think that's why I quit. I was never sure whether he knew or not. I know he thought the world of me, though. I was the only one he'd let lock up the place.

WILLY, *below:* You gonna wash the engine, Biff?

HAPPY: Shh!

Biff looks at Happy, who is gazing down, listening. Willy is mumbling in the parlor.

HAPPY: You hear that?

They listen. Willy laughs warmly.

BIFF, *growing angry:*   Doesn't he know Mom can hear that?
WILLY: Don't get your sweater dirty, Biff!

A look of pain crosses Biff's face.

HAPPY: Isn't that terrible? Don't leave again, will you? You'll find a job
    here. You gotta stick around. I don't know what to do about him, it's
    getting embarrassing.
WILLY: What a simonizing job!
BIFF: Mom's hearing that!
WILLY: No kiddin', Biff, you got a date? Wonderful!
HAPPY: Go on to sleep. But talk to him in the morning, will you?
BIFF, *reluctantly getting into bed:*   With her in the house. Brother!
HAPPY, *getting into bed:*   I wish you'd have a good talk with him.

The light on their room begins to fade.

BIFF, *to himself in bed:*   That selfish, stupid . . .

HAPPY: Sh . . . Sleep, Biff.

*Their light is out. Well before they have finished speaking, Willy's form is dimly
seen below in the darkened kitchen. He opens the refrigerator, searches in there,
and takes out a bottle of milk. The apartment houses are fading out, and the
entire house and surroundings become covered with leaves. Music insinuates itself
as the leaves appear.*

WILLY: Just wanna be careful with those girls, Biff, that's all. Don't make
    any promises. No promises of any kind. Because a girl, y'know, they
    always believe what you tell 'em and you're very young, Biff, you're
    too young to be talking seriously to girls.

*Light rises on the kitchen. Willy, talking, shuts the refrigerator door and comes
downstage to the kitchen table. He pours milk into a glass. He is totally immersed
in himself, smiling faintly.*

WILLY: Too young entirely, Biff. You want to watch your schooling first.
    Then when you're all set, there'll be plenty of girls for a boy like you.
    He smiles broadly at a kitchen chair. That so? The girls pay for you? *He
    laughs.* Boy, you must really be makin' a hit.

*Willy is gradually addressing—physically—a point offstage, speaking through
the wall of the kitchen, and his voice has been rising in volume to that of a
normal conversation.*

WILLY: I been wondering why you polish your car so careful. Ha! Don't
    leave the hubcaps, boys. Get the chamois to the hubcaps. Happy, use

newspaper on the windows, it's the easiest thing. Show him how to do it, Biff! You see, Happy? Pad it up, use it like a pad. That's it, that's it, good work. You're doin' all right, Hap. *He pauses, then nods in approbation for a few seconds, then looks upward.* Biff, first thing we gotta do when we get time is clip that big branch over the house. Afraid it's gonna fall in a storm and hit the roof. Tell you what. We get a rope and sling her around, and then we climb up there with a couple of saws and take her down. Soon as you finish the car, boys, I wanna see ya. I got a surprise for you, boys.

BIFF, *offstage:*   —Whatta ya got, Dad?

WILLY: No, you finish first. Never leave a job till you're finished—remember that. *Looking toward the "big trees":* Biff, up in Albany I saw a beautiful hammock. I think I'll buy it next trip, and we'll hang it right between those two elms. Wouldn't that be something? Just swingin' there under those branches. Boy, that would be . . .

Young Biff and Young Happy appear from the direction Willy was addressing. Happy carries rags and a pail of water. Biff, wearing a sweater with a block "S," carries a football.

BIFF, *pointing in the direction of the car offstage:*   How's that, Pop, professional?

WILLY: Terrific. Terrific job, boys. Good work, Biff.

HAPPY: Where's the surprise, Pop?

WILLY: In the back seat of the car.

HAPPY: Boy! *He runs off.*

BIFF: What is it, Dad? Tell me, what'd you buy?

WILLY, *laughing, cuffs him:*   Never mind, something I want you to have.

BIFF, *turns and starts off:*   What is it, Hap?

HAPPY, *offstage:*   It's a punching bag!

BIFF: Oh, Pop!

WILLY: It's got Gene Tunney's signature on it!

Happy runs onstage with a punching bag.

BIFF: Gee, how'd you know we wanted a punching bag?

WILLY: Well, it's the finest thing for the timing.

HAPPY, *lies down on his back and pedals with his feet:*   I'm losing weight, you notice, Pop?

WILLY, *to Happy:*   Jumping rope is good too.

BIFF: Did you see the new football I got?

WILLY, *examining the ball:*   Where'd you get a new ball?

BIFF: The coach told me to practice passing.

WILLY: That so? And he gave you the ball, heh?

BIFF: Well, I borrowed it from the locker room. *He laughs confidentially.*

WILLY, *laughing with him at the theft:*   I want you to return that.

HAPPY: I told you he wouldn't like it!

BIFF, *angrily:*   Well, I'm bringing it back!

WILLY, *stopping the incipient argument, to Happy:*   Sure, he's gotta practice

with a regulation ball, doesn't he? *To Biff:* Coach'll probably congratulate you on your initiative!

BIFF: Oh, he keeps congratulating my initiative all the time, Pop.

WILLY: That's because he likes you. If somebody else took that ball
there'd be an uproar. So what's the report, boys, what's the report?

BIFF: Where'd you go this time, Dad? Gee we were lonesome for you.

WILLY, *pleased, puts an arm around each boy and they come down to the
apron:*   Lonesome, heh?

BIFF: Missed you every minute.

WILLY: Don't say? Tell you a secret, boys. Don't breathe it to a soul.
Someday I'll have my own business, and I'll never have to leave home
any more.

HAPPY: Like Uncle Charley, heh?

WILLY: Bigger than Uncle Charley! Because Charley is not—liked. He's
liked, but he's not—well liked.

BIFF: Where'd you go this time, Dad?

WILLY: Well, I got on the road, and I went north to Providence. Met the
Mayor.

BIFF: The Mayor of Providence!

WILLY: He was sitting in the hotel lobby.

BIFF: What'd he say?

WILLY: He said, "Morning!" And I said, "You got a fine city here,
Mayor." And then he had coffee with me. And then I went to Waterbury. Waterbury is a fine city. Big clock city, the famous Waterbury
clock. Sold a nice bill there. And then Boston—Boston is the cradle of
the Revolution. A fine city. And a couple of other towns in Mass., and
on to Portland and Bangor and straight home!

BIFF: Gee, I'd love to go with you sometime, Dad.

WILLY: Soon as summer comes.

HAPPY: Promise?

WILLY: You and Hap and I, and I'll show you all the towns. America is
full of beautiful towns and fine, upstanding people. And they know me,
boys, they know me up and down New England. The finest people.
And when I bring you fellas up, there'll be open sesame for all of us,
'cause one thing, boys: I have friends. I can park my car in any street
in New England, and the cops protect it like their own. This summer,
heh?

BIFF and HAPPY, *together:*   Yeah! You bet!

WILLY: We'll take our bathing suits.

HAPPY: We'll carry your bags, Pop!

WILLY: Oh, won't that be somthing! Me comin' into the Boston stores
with you boys carryin' my bags. What a sensation!

Biff is prancing around, practicing passing the ball.

WILLY: You nervous, Biff, about the game?

BIFF: Not if you're gonna be there.

WILLY: What do they say about you in school, now that they made you
captain?

HAPPY: There's a crowd of girls behind him everytime the classes change.

BIFF, *taking Willy's hand:*   This Saturday, Pop, this Saturday—just for you, I'm going to break through for a touchdown.

HAPPY: You're supposed to pass.

BIFF: I'm takin' one play for Pop. You watch me, Pop, and when I take off my helmet, that means I'm breakin' out. Then you watch me crash through that line!

WILLY, *kisses Biff:*   Oh, wait'll I tell this in Boston!

Bernard enters in knickers. He is younger than Biff, earnest and loyal, a worried boy.

BERNARD: Biff, where are you? You're supposed to study with me today.

WILLY: Hey, looka Bernard. What're you lookin' so anemic about, Bernard?

BERNARD: He's gotta study, Uncle Willy. He's got Regents next week.

HAPPY, *tauntingly, spinning Bernard around:*   Let's box, Bernard!

BERNARD: Biff! *He gets away from Happy.* Listen, Biff, I heard Mr. Birnbaum say that if you don't start studyin' math he's gonna flunk you, and you won't graduate. I heard him!

WILLY: You better study with him, Biff. Go ahead now.

BERNARD: I heard him!

BIFF: Oh, Pop, you didn't see my sneakers! *He holds up a foot for Willy to look at.*

WILLY: Hey, that's a beautiful job of printing!

BERNARD, *wiping his glasses:*   Just because he printed University of Virginia on his sneakers doesn't mean they've got to graduate him, Uncle Willy!

WILLY, *angrily:*   What're you talking about? With scholarships to three universities they're gonna flunk him?

BERNARD: But I heard Mr. Birnbaum say—

WILLY: Don't be a pest, Bernard! *To his boys:* What an anemic!

BERNARD: Okay, I'm waiting for you in my house, Biff.

Bernard goes off. The Lomans laugh.

WILLY: Bernard is not well liked, is he?

BIFF: He's liked, but he's not well liked.

HAPPY: That's right, Pop.

WILLY: That's just what I mean. Bernard can get the best marks in school, y'understand, but when he gets out in the business world, y'understand, you are going to be five times ahead of him. That's why I thank Almighty God you're both built like Adonises. Because the man who makes an appearance in the business world, the man who creates personal interest, is the man who gets ahead. Be liked and you will never want. You take me, for instance. I never have to wait in line to see a buyer. "Willy Loman is here!" That's all they have to know, and I go right through.

BIFF: Did you knock them dead, Pop?

WILLY: Knocked 'em cold in Providence, slaughtered 'em in Boston.

HAPPY, *on his back, pedaling again::*   I'm losing weight, you notice, Pop?

Linda enters, as of old, a ribbon in her hair, carrying a basket of washing.

LINDA, *with youthful energy:*   Hello, dear!

WILLY: Sweetheart!

LINDA: How'd the Chevvy run?

WILLY: Chevrolet, Linda, is the greatest car ever built. *To the boys:* Since when do you let your mother carry wash up the stairs?

BIFF: Grab hold there, boy!

HAPPY: Where to, Mom?

LINDA: Hang them up on the line. And you better go down to your friends, Biff. The cellar is full of boys. They don't know what to do with themselves.

BIFF: Ah, when Pop comes home they can wait!

WILLY, *laughs appreciatively:*   You better go down and tell them what to do, Biff.

BIFF: I think I'll have them sweep out the furnace room.

WILLY: Good work, Biff.

BIFF, *goes through wall-line of kitchen to doorway at back and calls down:*   Fellas! Everybody sweep out the furnace room! I'll be right down!

VOICES: All right! Okay, Biff.

BIFF: George and Sam and Frank, come out back! We're hangin' up the wash! Come on, Hap, on the double! *He and Happy carry out the basket.*

LINDA: The way they obey him!

WILLY: Well, that's training, the training. I'm tellin' you, I was sellin' thousands and thousands, but I had to come home.

LINDA: Oh, the whole block'll be at that game. Did you sell anything?

WILLY: I did five hundred gross in Providence and seven hundred gross in Boston.

LINDA: No! Wait a minute, I've got a pencil. *She pulls pencil and paper out of her apron pocket.* That makes your commission . . . Two hundred—my God! Two hundred and twelve dollars!

WILLY: Well, I didn't figure it yet, but . . .

LINDA: How much did you do?

WILLY: Well, I—I did—about a hundred and eighty gross in Providence. Well, no—it came to—roughly two hundred gross on the whole trip.

LINDA, *without hesitation:*   Two hundred gross. That's . . . *She figures.*

WILLY: The trouble was that three of the stores were half closed for inventory in Boston. Otherwise I woulda broke records.

LINDA: Well, it makes seventy dollars and some pennies. That's very good.

WILLY: What do we owe?

LINDA: Well, on the first there's sixteen dollars on the refrigerator—

WILLY: Why sixteen?

LINDA: Well, the fan belt broke, so it was a dollar eighty.

WILLY: But it's brand new.

LINDA: Well, the man said that's the way it is. Till they work themselves in, y'know.

They move through the wall-line into the kitchen.

WILLY: I hope we didn't get stuck on that machine.

LINDA: They got the biggest ads of any of them!

WILLY: I know, it's a fine machine. What else?

LINDA: Well, there's nine-sixty for the washing machine. And for the vacuum cleaner there's three and a half due on the fifteenth. Then the roof, you got twenty-one dollars remaining.

WILLY: It don't leak, does it?

LINDA: No, they did a wonderful job. Then you owe Frank for the carburetor.

WILLY: I'm not going to pay that man! That goddam Chevrolet, they ought to prohibit the manufacture of that car!

LINDA: Well, you owe him three and a half. And odds and ends, comes to around a hundred and twenty dollars by the fifteenth.

WILLY: A hundred and twenty dollars! My God, if business don't pick up I don't know what I'm gonna do!

LINDA: Well, next week you'll do better.

WILLY: Oh, I'll knock 'em dead next week. I'll go to Hartford. I'm very well liked in Hartford. You know, the trouble is, Linda, people don't seem to take to me.

They move on to the forestage.

LINDA: Oh, don't be foolish.

WILLY: I know it when I walk in. They seem to laugh at me.

LINDA: Why? Why would they laugh at you? Don't talk that way, Willy.

Willy moves to the edge of the stage. Linda goes into the kitchen and starts to darn stockings.

WILLY: I don't know the reason for it, but they just pass me by. I'm not noticed.

LINDA: But you're doing wonderful, dear. You're making seventy to a hundred dollars a week.

WILLY: But I gotta be at it ten, twelve hours a day. Other men—I don't know—they do it easier. I don't know why—I can't stop myself—I talk too much. A man oughta come in with a few words. One thing about Charley. He's a man of few words, and they respect him.

LINDA: You don't talk too much, you're just lively.

WILLY, *smiling:* Well, I figure, what the hell, life is short, a couple of jokes. *To himself:* I joke too much! *The smile goes.*

LINDA: Why? You're—

WILLY: I'm fat. I'm very—foolish to look at, Linda. I didn't tell you, but Christmas time I happened to be calling on F. H. Stewarts, and a salesman I know, as I was going in to see the buyer I heard him say something about—walrus. And I—I cracked him right across the face. I won't take that. I simply will not take that. But they do laugh at me. I know that.

LINDA: Darling . . .

WILLY: I gotta overcome it. I know I gotta overcome it. I'm not dressing to advantage, maybe.

LINDA: Willy, darling, you're the handsomest man in the world—

WILLY: Oh, no, Linda.

LINDA: To me you are. *Slight pause.* The handsomest.

From the darkness is heard the laughter of a woman. Willy doesn't turn to it, but it continues through Linda's lines.

LINDA: And the boys, Willy. Few men are idolized by their children the way you are.

Music is heard as behind a scrim, to the left of the house, The Woman, dimly seen, is dressing.

WILLY, *with great feeling:*   You're the best there is, Linda, you're a pal, you know that? On the road—on the road I want to grab you sometimes and just kiss the life outa you.

The laughter is loud now, and he moves into a brightening area at the left, where The Woman has come from behind the scrim and is standing, putting on her hat, looking into a "mirror" and laughing.

WILLY: 'Cause I get so lonely—especially when business is bad and there's nobody to talk to. I get the feeling that I'll never sell anything again, that I won't make a living for you, or a business, a business for the boys. *He talks through The Woman's subsiding laughter; The Woman primps at the "mirror."* There's so much I want to make for—

THE WOMAN: Me? You didn't make me, Willy. I picked you.

WILLY, *pleased:*   You picked me?

THE WOMAN, *who is quite proper-looking, Willy's age:*   I did. I've been sitting at that desk watching all the salesmen go by, day in, day out. But you've got such a sense of humor, and we do have such a good time together, don't we?

WILLY: Sure, sure. *He takes her in his arms.* Why do you have to go now?

THE WOMAN: It's two o'clock . . .

WILLY: No, come on in! *He pulls her.*

THE WOMAN: . . . my sisters'll be scandalized. When'll you be back?

WILLY: Oh, two weeks about. Will you come up again?

THE WOMAN: Sure thing. You do make me laugh. It's good for me. *She squeezes his arm, kisses him.* And I think you're a wonderful man.

WILLY: You picked me, heh?

THE WOMAN: Sure. Because you're so sweet. And such a kidder.

WILLY: Well, I'll see you next time I'm in Boston.

THE WOMAN: I'll put you right through to the buyers.

WILLY, *slapping her bottom:* Right. Well, bottoms up!

THE WOMAN, *slaps him gently and laughs:* You just kill me, Willy. *He suddenly grabs her and kisses her roughly.* You kill me. And thanks for the stockings. I love a lot of stockings. Well, good night.

WILLY: Good night. And keep your pores open!

THE WOMAN: Oh, Willy!

The Woman bursts out laughing, and Linda's laughter blends in. The Woman disappears into the dark. Now the area at the kitchen table brightens. Linda is sitting where she was at the kitchen table, but now is mending a pair of her silk stockings.

LINDA: You are, Willy. The handsomest man. You've got no reason to feel that—

WILLY, *coming out of The Woman's dimming area and going over to Linda:* I'll make it all up to you, Linda, I'll—

LINDA: There's nothing to make up, dear. You're doing fine, better than—

WILLY, *noticing her mending:* What's that?

LINDA: Just mending my stockings. They're so expensive—

WILLY, *angrily, taking them from her:* I won't have you mending stockings in this house! Now throw them out!

Linda puts the stockings in her pocket.

BERNARD, *entering on the run:* Where is he? If he doesn't study!

WILLY, *moving to the forestage, with great agitation:* You'll give him the answers!

BERNARD: I do, but I can't on a Regents! That's a state exam! They're liable to arrest me!

WILLY: Where is he? I'll whip him, I'll whip him!

LINDA: And he'd better give back that football, Willy, it's not nice.

WILLY: Biff! Where is he? Why is he taking everything?

LINDA: He's too rough with the girls, Willy. All the mothers are afraid of him!

WILLY: I'll whip him!

BERNARD: He's driving the car without a license!

The Woman's laugh is heard.

WILLY: Shut up!

LINDA: All the mothers—

WILLY: Shut up!

BERNARD, *backing quietly away and out:* Mr. Birnbaum says he's stuck up.

WILLY: Get outa here!

BERNARD: If he doesn't buckle down he'll flunk math! *He goes off.*

LINDA: He's right, Willy, you've gotta—

WILLY, *exploding at her:*   There's nothing the matter with him! You want him to be a worm like Bernard? He's got spirit, personality . . .

As he speaks, Linda, almost in tears, exits into the living-room. Willy is alone in the kitchen, wilting and staring. The leaves are gone. It is night again, and the apartment houses look down from behind.

WILLY: Loaded with it. Loaded! What is he stealing? He's giving it back, isn't he? Why is he stealing? What did I tell him? I never in my life told him anything but decent things.

Happy in pajamas has come down the stairs; Willy suddenly becomes aware of Happy's presence.

HAPPY: Let's go now, come on.

WILLY, *sitting down at the kitchen table:*   Huh! Why did she have to wax the floors herself? Everytime she waxes the floors she keels over. She knows that!

HAPPY: Shh! Take it easy. What brought you back tonight?

WILLY: I got an awful scare. Nearly hit a kid in Yonkers. God! Why didn't I go to Alaska with my brother Ben that time! Ben! That man was a genius, that man was success incarnate! What a mistake! He begged me to go.

HAPPY: Well, there's no use in—

WILLY: You guys! There was a man started with the clothes on his back and ended up with diamond mines!

HAPPY: Boy, someday I'd like to know how he did it.

WILLY: What's the mystery? The man knew what he wanted and went out and got it! Walked into a jungle, and comes out, the age of twenty-one, and he's rich! The world is an oyster, but you don't crack it open on a mattress!

HAPPY: Pop, I told you I'm gonna retire you for life.

WILLY: You'll retire me for life on seventy goddam dollars a week? And your women and your car and your apartment, and you'll retire me for life! Christ's sake, I couldn't get past Yonkers today! Where are you guys, where are you? The woods are burning! I can't drive a car!

Charley has appeared in the doorway. He is a large man, slow of speech, laconic, immovable. In all he says, despite what he says, there is pity, and, now, trepidation. He has a robe over pajamas, slippers on his feet. He enters the kitchen.

CHARLEY: Everything all right?

HAPPY: Yeah, Charley, everything's . . .

WILLY: What's the matter?

CHARLEY: I heard some noise. I thought something happened. Can't we do something about the walls? You sneeze in here, and in my house hats blow off.

HAPPY: Let's go to bed, Dad. Come on.

Charley signals to Happy to go.

WILLY: You go ahead, I'm not tired at the moment.

HAPPY, *to Willy:*   Take it easy, huh? *He exits.*

WILLY: What're you doin' up?

CHARLEY, *sitting down at the kitchen table opposite Willy:*   Couldn't sleep good. I had a heartburn.

WILLY: Well, you don't know how to eat.

CHARLEY: I eat with my mouth.

WILLY: No, you're ignorant. You gotta know about vitamins and things like that.

CHARLEY: Come on, let's shoot. Tire you out a little.

WILLY, *hesitantly:*   All right. You got cards?

CHARLEY, *taking a deck from his pocket:*   Yeah, I got them. Someplace. What is it with those vitamins?

WILLY, *dealing:*   They build up your bones. Chemistry.

CHARLEY: Yeah, but there's no bones in a heartburn.

WILLY: What are you talkin' about? Do you know the first thing about it?

CHARLEY: Don't get insulted.

WILLY: Don't talk about something you don't know anything about.

They are playing. Pause.

CHARLEY: What're you doin' home?

WILLY: A little trouble with the car.

CHARLEY: Oh. *Pause.* I'd like to take a trip to California.

WILLY: Don't say.

CHARLEY: You want a job?

WILLY: I got a job, I told you that. *After slight pause:* What the hell are you offering me a job for?

CHARLY: Don't get insulted.

WILLY: Don't insult me.

CHARLEY: I don't see no sense in it. You don't have to go on this way.

WILLY: I got a good job. *Slight pause.* What do you keep comin' in here for?

CHARLEY: You want me to go?

WILLY, *after a pause, withering:*   I can't understand it. He's going back to Texas again. What the hell is that?

CHARLEY: Let him go.

WILLY: I got nothin' to give him, Charley, I'm clean, I'm clean.

CHARLEY: He won't starve. None of them starve. Forget about him.

WILLY: Then what have I got to remember?

CHARLEY: You take it too hard. To hell with it. When a deposit bottle is broken you don't get your nickel back.

WILLY: That's easy enough for you to say.

CHARLEY: That ain't easy for me to say.

WILLY: Did you see the ceiling I put up in the living-room?

CHARLEY: Yeah, that's a piece of work. To put up a ceiling is a mystery to me. How do you do it?

WILLY: What's the difference?

CHARLEY: Well, talk about it.

WILLY: You gonna put up a ceiling?

CHARLEY: How could I put up a ceiling?

WILLY: Then what the hell are you bothering me for?

CHARLEY: You're insulted again.

WILLY: A man who can't handle tools is not a man. You're disgusting.

CHARLEY: Don't call me disgusting, Willy.

Uncle Ben, carrying a valise and an umbrella, enters the forestage from around the right corner of the house. He is a stolid man, in his sixties, with a mustache and an authoritative air. He is utterly certain of his destiny, and there is an aura of far places about him. He enters exactly as Willy speaks.

WILLY: I'm getting awfully tired, Ben.

Ben's music is heard. Ben looks around at everything.

CHARLEY: Good, keep playing; you'll sleep better. Did you call me Ben?

Ben looks at his watch.

WILLY: That's funny. For a second there you reminded me of my brother Ben.

BEN: I only have a few minutes. *He strolls, inspecting the place. Willy and Charley continue playing.*

CHARLEY: You never heard from him again, heh? Since that time?

WILLY: Didn't Linda tell you? Couple of weeks ago we got a letter from his wife in Africa. He died.

CHARLEY: That so.

BEN, *chuckling:*   So this is Brooklyn, eh?

CHARLEY: Maybe you're in for some of his money.

WILLY: Naa, he had seven sons. There's just one opportunity I had with that man . . .

BEN: I must make a train, William. There are several properties I'm looking at in Alaska.

WILLY: Sure, sure! If I'd gone with him to Alaska that time, everything would've been totally different.

CHARLEY: Go on, you'd froze to death up there.

WILLY: What're you talking about?

BEN: Opportunity is tremendous in Alaska, William. Surprised you're not up there.

WILLLY: Sure, tremendous.

CHARLEY: Heh?

WILLY: There was the only man I ever met who knew the answers.

CHARLEY: Who?

BEN: How are you all?

WILLY, *taking a pot, smiling:*   Fine, fine.

CHARLEY: Pretty sharp tonight.

BEN: Is Mother living with you?

WILLY: No, she died a long time ago.

CHARLEY: Who?

BEN: That's too bad. Fine specimen of a lady, Mother.

WILLY, *to Charley:*   Heh?

BEN: I'd hoped to see the old girl.

CHARLEY: Who died?

BEN: Heard anything from Father, have you?

WILLY, *unnerved:*   What do you mean, who died?

CHARLEY, *taking a pot:*   What're you talkin' about?

BEN, *looking at his watch:*   William, it's half-past eight!

WILLY, *as though to dispel his confusion he angrily stops Charley's hand:*   That's my build!

CHARLEY: I put the ace—

WILLY: If you don't know how to play the game I'm not gonna throw my money away on you!

CHARLEY, *rising:*   It was my ace, for God's sake!

WILLY: I'm through, I'm through!

BEN: When did Mother die?

WILLY: Long ago. Since the beginning you never knew how to play cards.

CHARLEY, *picks up the cards and goes to the door:*   All right! Next time I'll bring a deck with five aces.

WILLY: I don't play that kind of game!

CHARLEY, *turning to him:*   You ought to be ashamed of yourself!

WILLY: Yeah?

CHARLEY: Yeah! *He goes out.*

WILLY, *slamming the door after him:*   Ignoramus!

BEN, *as Willy comes toward him through the wall-line of the kitchen:*   So you're William.

WILLY, *shaking Ben's hand:*   Ben! I've been waiting for you so long! What's the answer? How did you do it?

BEN: Oh, there's a story in that.

Linda enters the forestage, as of old, carrying the wash basket.

LINDA: Is this Ben?

BEN, *gallantly:*   How do you do, my dear.

LINDA: Where've you been all these years? Willy's always wondered why you—

WILLY, *pulling Ben away from her impatiently:*   Where is Dad? Didn't you follow him? How did you get started?

BEN: Well, I don't know how much you remember.

WILLY: Well, I was just a baby, of course, only three or four years old—

BEN: Three years and eleven months.

WILLY: What a memory, Ben!

BEN: I have many enterprises, William, and I have never kept books.

WILLY: I remember I was sitting under the wagon in—was it Nebraska?

BEN: It was South Dakota, and I gave you a bunch of wild flowers.

WILLY: I remember you walking away down some open road.

BEN, *laughing:*   I was going to find Father in Alaska.

WILLY: Where is he?

BEN: At that age I had a very faulty view of geography, William. I discovered after a few days that I was heading due south, so instead of Alaska, I ended up in Africa.

LINDA: Africa!

WILLY: The Gold Coast!

BEN: Principally diamond mines.

LINDA: Diamond mines!

BEN: Yes, my dear. But I've only a few minutes—

WILLY: No! Boys! Boys! *Young Biff and Happy appear.* Listen to this. This is your Uncle Ben, a great man! Tell my boys, Ben!

BEN: Why, boys, when I was seventeen I walked into the jungle, and when I was twenty-one I walked out. *He laughs.* And by God I was rich.

WILLY, *to the boys:*   You see what I been talking about? The greatest things can happen!

BEN, *glancing at his watch:*   I have an appointment in Ketchikan Tuesday week.

WILLY: No, Ben! Please tell about Dad. I want my boys to hear. I want them to know the kind of stock they spring from. All I remember is a man with a big beard, and I was in Mamma's lap, sitting around a fire, and some kind of high music.

BEN: His flute. He played the flute.

WILLY: Sure, the flute, that's right!

New music is heard, a high, rollicking tune.

BEN: Father was a very great and a very wild-hearted man. We would start in Boston, and he'd toss the whole family into the wagon, and then he'd drive the team right across the country; through Ohio, and Indiana, Michigan, Illinois, and all the Western states. And we'd stop in the towns and sell the flutes that he'd made on the way. Great inventor, Father. With one gadget he made more in a week than a man like you could make in a lifetime.

WILLY: That's just the way I'm bringing them up, Ben—rugged, well liked, all-around.

BEN: Yeah? *To Biff:* Hit that, boy—hard as you can. *He pounds his stomach.*

BIFF: Oh, no, sir!

BEN, *taking boxing stance:* Come on, get to me! *He laughs.*

WILLY: Go to it, Biff! Go ahead, show him!

BIFF: Okay! *He cocks his fists and starts in.*

LINDA, *to Willy:* Why must he fight, dear?

BEN, *sparring with Biff:* Good boy! Good boy!

WILLY: How's that, Ben, heh?

HAPPY: Give him the left, Biff!

LINDA: Why are you fighting?

BEN: Good boy! *Suddenly comes in, trips Biff, and stands over him, the point of his umbrella poised over Biff's eye.*

LINDA: Lookout, Biff!

BIFF: Gee!

BEN, *patting Biff's knee:* Never fight fair with a stranger, boy. You'll never get out of the jungle that way. *Taking Linda's hand and bowing:* It was an honor and a pleasure to meet you, Linda.

LINDA, *withdrawing her hand coldly, frightened:* Have a nice—trip.

BEN, *to Willy:* And good luck with your—what do you do?

WILLY: Selling.

BEN: Yes. Well . . . *He raises his hand in farewell to all.*

WILLY: No, Ben, I don't want you to think . . . *He takes Ben's arm to show him.* It's Brooklyn, I know, but we hunt too.

BEN: Really, now.

WILLY: Oh, sure, there's snakes and rabbits and—that's why I moved out here. Why, Biff can fell any one of these trees in no time! Boys! Go right over to where they're building the apartment house and get some sand. We're gonna rebuild the entire front stoop right now! Watch this, Ben!

BIFF: Yes, sir! On the double, Hap!

HAPPY, *as he and Biff run off:* I lost weight, Pop, you notice?

Charley enters in knickers, even before the boys are gone.

CHARLEY: Listen, if they steal any more from that building the watchman'll put the cops on them!

LINDA, *to Willy:* Don't let Biff . . .

Ben laughs lustily.

WILLY: You shoulda seen the lumber they brought home last week. At least a dozen six-by-tens worth all kinds a money.

CHARLEY: Listen, if that watchman—

WILLY: I gave them hell, understand. But I got a couple of fearless characters there.

CHARLEY: Willy, the jails are full of fearless characters.

BEN, *clapping Willy on the back, with a laugh at Charley:* And the stock exchange, friend!

WILLY, *joining in Ben's laughter:* Where are the rest of your pants?

CHARLEY: My wife bought them.

WILLY: Now all you need is a golf club and you can go upstairs and go to sleep. *To Ben:* Great athlete! Between him and his son Bernard they can't hammer a nail!

BERNARD, *rushing in:*   The watchman's chasing Biff!

WILLY, *angrily:*   Shut up! He's not stealing anything!

LINDA, *alarmed, hurrying off left:*   Where is he? Biff, dear! *She exits.*

WILLY, *moving toward the left, away from Ben:*   There's nothing wrong. What's the matter with you?

BEN: Nervy boy. Good!

WILLY, *laughing:*   Oh, nerves of iron, that Biff!

CHARLEY: Don't know what it is. My New England man comes back and he's bleedin', they murdered him up there.

WILLY: It's contacts, Charley, I got important contacts!

CHARLEY, *sarcastically:*   Glad to hear it, Willy. Come in later, we'll shoot a little casino. I'll take some of your Portland money. *He laughs at Willy and exits.*

WILLY, *turning to Ben:*   Business is bad, it's murderous. But not for me, of course.

BEN: I'll stop by on my way back to Africa.

WILLY, *longingly:*   Can't you stay a few days? You're just what I need, Ben, because I—I have a fine position here, but I—well, Dad left when I was such a baby and I never had a chance to talk to him and I still feel—kind of temporary about myself.

BEN: I'll be late for my train.

They are at opposite ends of the stage.

WILLY: Ben, my boys—can't we talk? They'd go into the jaws of hell for me, see, but I—

BEN: William, you're being first-rate with your boys. Outstanding, manly chaps!

WILLY, *hanging onto his words:*   Oh, Ben, that's good to hear! Because sometimes I'm afraid that I'm not teaching them the right kind of— Ben, how should I teach them?

BEN, *giving great weight to each word, and with a certain vicious audacity:* William, when I walked into the jungle, I was seventeen. When I walked out I was twenty-one. And, by God, I was rich! *He goes off into the darkness around the right corner of the house.*

WILLY: . . . was rich! That's just the spirit I want to imbue them with! To walk into a jungle! I was right! I was right! I was right!

Ben is gone, but Willy is still speaking to him as Linda, in nightgown and robe, enters the kitchen, glances around for Willy, then goes to the door of the house, looks out and sees him. Comes down to his left. He looks at her.

LINDA: Willy, dear? Willy?

WILLY: I was right!

LINDA: Did you have some cheese? *He can't answer.* It's very late, darling. Come to bed, heh?

WILLY, *looking straight up:*   Gotta break your neck to see a star in this yard.

LINDA: You coming in?

WILLY: Whatever happened to that diamond watch fob? Remember? When Ben came from Africa that time? Didn't he give me a watch fob with a diamond in it?

LINDA: You pawned it, dear. Twelve, thirteen years ago. For Biff's radio correspondence course.

WILLY: Gee, that was a beautiful thing. I'll take a walk.

LINDA: But you're in your slippers.

WILLY, *starting to go around the house at the left:*   I was right! I was! *Half to Linda, as he goes, shaking his head:* What a man! There was a man worth talking to. I was right!

LINDA, *calling after Willy:*   But in your slippers, Willy!

Willy is almost gone when Biff, in his pajamas, comes down the stairs and enters the kitchen.

BIFF: What is he doing out there?

LINDA: Sh!

BIFF: God Almighty, Mom, how long has he been doing this?

LINDA: Don't, he'll hear you.

BIFF: What the hell is the matter with him?

LINDA: It'll pass by morning.

BIFF: Shouldn't we do anything?

LINDA: Oh, my dear, you should do a lot of things, but there's nothing to do, so go to sleep.

Happy comes down the stair and sits on the steps.

HAPPY: I never heard him so loud, Mom.

LINDA: Well, come around more often; you'll hear him. *She sits down at the table and mends the lining of Willy's jacket.*

BIFF: Why didn't you ever write me about this, Mom?

LINDA: How would I write to you? For over three months you had no address.

BIFF: I was on the move. But you know I thought of you all the time. You know that, don't you, pal?

LINDA: I know, dear, I know. But he likes to have a letter. Just to know that there's still a possibility for better things.

BIFF: He's not like this all the time, is he?

LINDA: It's when you come home he's always the worst.

BIFF: When I come home?

LINDA: When you write you're coming, he's all smiles, and talks about the future, and—he's just wonderful. And then the closer you seem to come, the more shaky he gets, and then, by the time you get here, he's arguing, and he seems angry at you. I think it's just that maybe he can't bring himself to—to open up to you. Why are you so hateful to each other? Why is that?

BIFF, *evasively:*   I'm not hateful, Mom.

LINDA: But you no sooner come in the door than you're fighting!

BIFF: I don't know why. I mean to change. I'm tryin', Mom, you understand?

LINDA: Are you home to stay now?

BIFF: I don't know. I want to look around, see what's doin'.

LINDA: Biff, you can't look around all your life, can you?

BIFF: I just can't take hold, Mom. I can't take hold of some kind of a life.

LINDA: Biff, a man is not a bird, to come and go with the springtime.

BIFF: Your hair . . . *He touches her hair.* Your hair got so gray.

LINDA: Oh, it's been gray since you were in high school. I just stopped dyeing it, that's all.

BIFF: Dye it again, will ya? I don't want my pal looking old. *He smiles.*

LINDA: You're such a boy! You think you can go away for a year and . . . You've got to get it into your head now that one day you'll knock on this door and there'll be strange people here—

BIFF: What are you talking about? You're not even sixty, Mom.

LINDA: But what about your father?

BIFF, *lamely:*   Well, I meant him too.

HAPPY: He admires Pop.

LINDA: Biff, dear, if you don't have any feeling for him, then you can't have any feeling for me.

BIFF: Sure I can, Mom.

LINDA: No, You can't just come to see me, because I love him. *With a threat, but only a threat, of tears:* He's the dearest man in the world to me, and I won't have anyone making him feel unwanted and low and blue. You've got to make up your mind now, darling, there's no leeway any more. Either he's your father and you pay him that respect, or else you're not to come here. I know he's not easy to get along with— nobody knows that better than me—but . . .

WILLY, *from the left, with a laugh:*   Hey, hey, Biffo!

BIFF, *starting to go out after Willy:*   What the hell is the matter with him? *Happy stops him.*

LINDA: Don't—don't go near him!

BIFF: Stop making excuses for him! He always, always wiped the floor with you. Never had an ounce of respect for you.

HAPPY: He's always had respect for—

BIFF: What the hell do you know about it?

HAPPY, *surlily:*   Just don't call him crazy!

BIFF: He's got no character—Charley wouldn't do this. Not in his own house—spewing out that vomit from his mind.

HAPPY: Charley never had to cope with what he's got to.

BIFF: People are worse off than Willy Loman. Believe me, I've seen them!

LINDA: Then make Charley your father, Biff. You can't do that, can you? I don't say he's a great man. Willy Loman never made a lot of money. His name was never in the paper. He's not the finest character that ever lived. But he's a human being, and a terrible thing is happening to him. So attention must be paid. He's not to be allowed to fall into his grave like an old dog. Attention, attention must be finally paid to such a person. You called him crazy—

BIFF: I didn't mean—

LINDA: No, a lot of people think he's lost his—balance. But you don't have to be very smart to know what his trouble is. The man is exhausted.

HAPPY: Sure!

LINDA: A small man can be just as exhausted as a great man. He works for a company thirty-six years this March, opens up unheard-of territories to their trademark, and now in his old age they take his salary away.

HAPPY, *indignantly:* I didn't know that, Mom.

LINDA: You never asked, my dear! Now that you get your spending money someplace else you don't trouble your mind with him.

HAPPY: But I gave you money last—

LINDA: Christmas time, fifty dollars! To fix the hot water it cost ninety-seven fifty! For five weeks he's been on straight commission, like a beginner, an unknown!

BIFF: Those ungrateful bastards!

LINDA: Are they any worse than his sons? When he brought them business, when he was young, they were glad to see him. But now his old friends, the old buyers that loved him so and always found some order to hand him in a pinch—they're all dead, retired. He used to be able to make six, seven calls a day in Boston. Now he takes his valises out of the car and puts them back and takes them out again and he's exhausted. Instead of walking he talks now. He drives seven hundred miles, and when he gets there no one knows him any more, no one welcomes him. And what goes through a man's mind, driving seven hundred miles home without having earned a cent? Why shouldn't he talk to himself? Why? When he has to go to Charley and borrow fifty dollars a week and pretend to me that it's his pay? How long can that go on? How long? You see what I'm sitting here and waiting for? And you tell me he has no character? The man who never worked a day but for your benefit? When does he get the medal for that? Is this his reward—to turn around at the age of sixty-three and find his sons, who he loved better than his life, one a philandering bum—

HAPPY: Mom!

LINDA: That's all you are, my baby! *To Biff:* And you! What happened to the love you had for him? You were such pals! How you used to talk to him on the phone every night! How lonely he was till he could come home to you!

BIFF: All right, Mom. I'll live here in my room, and I'll get a job. I'll keep away from him, that's all.

LINDA: No, Biff. You can't stay here and fight all the time.

BIFF: He threw me out of this house, remember that.

LINDA: Why did he do that? I never knew why.

BIFF: Because I know he's a fake and he doesn't like anybody around who knows!

LINDA: Why a fake? In what way? What do you mean?

BIFF: Just don't lay it all at my feet. It's between me and him—that's all I have to say. I'll chip in from now on. He'll settle for my pay check. He'll be all right. I'm going to bed. *He starts for the stairs.*

LINDA: He won't be all right.

BIFF, *turning on the stairs, furiously:* I hate this city and I'll stay here. Now what do you want?

LINDA: He's dying, Biff.

Happy turns quickly to her, shocked.

BIFF, *after a pause:* Why is he dying?

LINDA: He's been trying to kill himself.

BIFF, *with great horror:* How?

LINDA: Remember I wrote you that he smashed up the car again? In February?

BIFF: Well?

LINDA: The insurance inspector came. He said that they have evidence. That all these accidents in the last year—weren't—weren't—accidents.

HAPPY: How can they tell that? That's a lie.

LINDA: It seems there's a woman . . . *She takes a breath as*

BIFF, *sharply but contained:* What woman?

LINDA, *simultaneously:* . . . and this woman . . .

LINDA: What?

BIFF: Nothing. Go ahead.

LINDA: What did you say?

BIFF: Nothing. I just said what woman?

HAPPY: What about her?

LINDA: Well, it seems she was walking down the road and saw his car. She says that he wasn't driving fast at all, and that he didn't skid. She says he came to that little bridge, and then deliberately smashed into the railing, and it was only the shallowness of the water that saved him.

BIFF: Oh, no, he probably just fell asleep again.

LINDA: I don't think he fell alseep.

BIFF: Why not?

LINDA: Last month . . . *With great difficulty:* Oh, boys, it's so hard to say a thing like this! He's just a big stupid man to you, but I tell you there's more good in him than in many other people. *She chokes, wipes her eyes.* I was looking for a fuse. The lights blew out, and I went down the cellar. And behind the fuse box—it happened to fall out—was a length of rubber pipe—just short.

HAPPY: No kidding?

LINDA: There's a little attachment on the end of it. I knew right away. And sure enough, on the bottom of the water heater there's a new little nipple on the gas pipe.

HAPPY, *angrily:* That—jerk.

BIFF: Did you have it taken off?

LINDA: I'm—I'm ashamed to. How can I mention it to him? Every day I go down and take away that little rubber pipe. But, when he comes home, I put it back where it was. How can I insult him that way? I don't know what to do. I live from day to day, boys. I tell you, I know every thought in his mind. It sounds so old-fashioned and silly, but I tell you he put his whole life into you and you've turned your backs on him. *She is bent over in the chair, weeping, her face in her hands.* Biff, I swear to God! Biff, his life is in your hands!

HAPPY, *to Biff:* How do you like that damned fool!

BIFF, *kissing her:* All right, pal, all right. It's all settled now. I've been remiss. I know that, Mom. But now I'll stay, and I swear to you, I'll apply myself. *Kneeling in front of her, in a fever of self-reproach:* It's just—you see, Mom, I don't fit in business. Not that I won't try. I'll try, and I'll make good.

HAPPY: Sure you will. The trouble with you in business was you never tried to please people.

BIFF: I know, I—

HAPPY: Like when you worked for Harrison's. Bob Harrison said you were tops, and then you go and do some damn fool thing like whistling whole songs in the elevator like a comedian.

BIFF, *against Happy:* So what? I like to whistle sometimes.

HAPPY: You don't raise a guy to a responsible job who whistles in the elevator!

LINDA: Well, don't argue about it now.

HAPPY: Like when you'd go off and swim in the middle of the day instead of taking the line around.

BIFF, *his resentment rising:* Well, don't you run off? You take off sometimes, don't you? On a nice summer day?

HAPPY: Yeah, but I cover myself!

LINDA: Boys!

HAPPY: If I'm going to take a fade the boss can call any number where I'm supposed to be and they'll swear to him that I just left. I'll tell you something that I hate to say, Biff, but in the business world some of them think you're crazy.

BIFF, *angered:* Screw the business world!

HAPPY: All right, screw it! Great, but cover yourself!

LINDA: Hap, Hap!

BIFF: I don't care what they think! They've laughed at Dad for years, and you know why? Because we don't belong in this nuthouse of a city! We should be mixing cement on some open plain, or—or carpenters. A carpenter is allowed to whistle!

Willy walks in from the entrance of the house, at left.

WILLY: Even your grandfather was better than a carpenter. *Pause. They watch him.* You never grew up. Bernard does not whistle in the elevator, I assure you.

BIFF, *as though to laugh Willy out of it:* Yeah, but you do, Pop.

WILLY: I never in my life whistled in an elevator! And who in the business world thinks I'm crazy?

BIFF: I didn't mean it like that, Pop. Now don't make a whole thing out of it, will ya?

WILLY: Go back to the West! Be a carpenter, a cowboy, enjoy yourself!

LINDA: Willy, he was just saying—

WILLY: I heard what he said!

HAPPY, *trying to quiet Willy:*   Hey, Pop, come on now . . .

WILLY, *continuing over Happy's line:*   They laugh at me, heh? Go to Filene's, go to the Hub, go to Slattery's, Boston. Call out the name Willy Loman and see what happens! Big shot!

BIFF: All right, Pop.

WILLY: Big!

BIFF: All right!

WILLY: Why do you always insult me?

BIFF: I didn't say a word. *To Linda:* Did I say a word?

LINDA: He didn't say anything, Willy.

WILLY, *going to the door-way of the living-room:*   All right, good night, good night.

LINDA: Willy, dear, he just decided . . .

WILLY, *to Biff:*   If you get tired hanging around tomorrow, paint the ceiling I put up in the living-room.

BIFF: I'm leaving early tomorrow.

HAPPY: He's going to see Bill Oliver, Pop.

WILLY, *interestedly:*   Oliver? For what?

BIFF, *with reserve, but trying, trying:*   He always said he'd stake me. I'd like to go into business, so maybe I can take him up on it.

LINDA: Isn't that wonderful?

WILLY: Don't interrupt. What's wonderful about it? There's fifty men in the City of New York who'd stake him. *To Biff:* Sporting goods?

BIFF: I guess so. I know something about it and—

WILLY: He knows something about it! You know sporting goods better than Spalding, for God's sake! How much is he giving you?

BIFF: I don't know, I didn't even see him yet, but—

WILLY: Then what're you talking about?

BIFF, *getting angry:*   Well, all I said was I'm gonna see him, that's all!

WILLY, *turning away:*   Ah, you're counting your chickens again.

BIFF, *starting left for the stairs:*   Oh, Jesus, I'm going to sleep!

WILLY, *calling after him:*   Don't curse in this house!

BIFF, *trying to stop them:*   Wait a . . .

WILLY: Don't use that language to me! I won't have it!

HAPPY, *grabbing Biff, shouts:*   Wait a minute! I got an idea. I got a feasible idea. Come here, Biff, let's talk this over now, let's talk some sense here. When I was down in Florida last time, I thought of a great idea to sell sporting goods. It just came back to me. You and I, Biff—we have a line, the Loman Line. We train a couple of weeks, and put on a couple of exhibitions, see?

WILLY: That's an idea!

HAPPY: Wait! We form two basketball teams, see? Two water-polo teams. We play each other. It's a million dollars' worth of publicity. Two brothers, see? The Loman Brothers. Displays in the Royal Palms—all the hotels. And banners over the ring and the basketball court: "Loman Brothers." Baby, we could sell sporting goods!

WILLY: That is a one-million-dollar idea!

LINDA: Marvelous!

BIFF: I'm in great shape as far as that's concerned.

HAPPY: And the beauty of it is, Biff, it wouldn't be like a business. We'd be out playin' ball again . . .

BIFF, *enthused:*   Yeah, that's . . .

WILLY: Million-dollar . . .

HAPPY: And you wouldn't get fed up with it, Biff. It'd be the family again. There'd be the old honor, and comradeship, and if you wanted to go off for a swim or somethin'—well, you'd do it! Without some smart cooky gettin' up ahead of you!

WILLY: Lick the world! You guys together could absolutely lick the civilized world.

BIFF: I'll see Oliver tomorrow. Hap, if we could work that out . . .

LINDA: Maybe things are beginning to—

WILLY, *wildly enthused, to Linda:*   Stop interrupting! *To Biff:* But don't wear sport jacket and slacks when you see Oliver.

BIFF: No, I'll—

WILLY: A business suit, and talk as little as possible, and don't crack any jokes.

BIFF: He did like me. Always liked me.

LINDA: He loved you!

WILLY, *to Linda:*   Will you stop! *To Biff:* Walk in very serious. You are not applying for a boy's job. Money is to pass. Be quiet, fine, and serious. Everybody likes a kidder, but nobody lends him money.

HAPPY: I'll try to get some myself, Biff. I'm sure I can.

WILLY: I see great things for you kids, I think your troubles are over. But remember, start big and you'll end big. Ask for fifteen. How much you gonna ask for?

BIFF: Gee, I don't know—

WILLY: And don't say "Gee." "Gee" is a boy's word. A man walking in for fifteen thousand dollars does not say "Gee!"

BIFF: Ten, I think, would be top though.

WILLY: Don't be so modest. You always started too low. Walk in with a big laugh. Don't look worried. Start off with a couple of your good stories to lighten things up. It's not what you say, it's how you say it— because personality always wins the day.

LINDA: Oliver always thought the highest of him—

WILLY: Will you let me talk?

BIFF: Don't yell at her, Pop, will ya?

WILLY, *angrily:*   I was talking, wasn't I?

BIFF: I don't like you yelling at her all the time, and I'm tellin' you, that's all.

WILLY: What're you, takin' over this house?

LINDA: Willy—

WILLY, *turning on her:*   Don't take his side all the time, goddammit!

BIFF, *furiously:*   Stop yelling at her!

WILLY, *suddenly pulling on his cheek, beaten down, guilt ridden:*   Give my best to Bill Oliver—he may remember me. *He exits through the living-room doorway.*

LINDA, *her voice subdued:* What'd you have to start that for? *Biff turns away.* You see how sweet he was as soon as you talked hopefully? *She goes over to Biff.* Come up and say good night to him. Don't let him go to bed that way.

HAPPY: Come on, Biff, let's buck him up.

LINDA: Please, dear. Just say good night. It takes so little to make him happy. Come. *She goes through the living-room doorway, calling upstairs from within the living room:* Your pajamas are hanging in the bathroom, Willy!

HAPPY, *looking toward where Linda went out:* What a woman! They broke the mold when they made her. You know that, Biff?

BIFF: He's off salary. My God, working on commission!

HAPPY: Well, let's face it: he's no hot-shot selling man. Except that sometimes, you have to admit, he's a sweet personality.

BIFF, *deciding:* Lend me ten bucks, will ya? I want to buy some new ties.

HAPPY: I'll take you to a place I know. Beautiful stuff. Wear one of my striped shirts tomorrow.

BIFF: She got gray. Mom got awful old. Gee, I'm gonna go into Oliver tomorrow and knock him for a—

HAPPY: Come on up. Tell that to Dad. Let's give him a whirl. Come on.

BIFF, *steamed up:* You know, with ten thousand bucks, boy!

HAPPY, *as they go into the living room:* That's the talk, Biff, that's the first time I've heard the old confidence out of you! *From within the living-room, fading off:* You're gonna live with me, kid, and any babe you want just say the word . . . *The last lines are hardly heard. They are mounting the stairs to their parents' bedroom.*

LINDA, *entering her bedroom and addressing Willy, who is in the bathroom. She is straightening the bed for him:* Can you do anything about the shower? It drips.

WILLY, *from the bathroom:* All of a sudden everything falls to pieces! Goddam plumbing, oughta be sued, those people. I hardly finished putting it in and the thing . . . *His words rumble off.*

LINDA: I'm just wondering if Oliver will remember him. You think he might?

WILLY, *coming out of the bathroom in his pajamas:* Remember him? What's the matter with you, you crazy? If he'd've stayed with Oliver he'd be on top by now! Wait'll Oliver gets a look at him. You don't know the average caliber any more. The average young man today—*he is getting into bed*—is got a caliber of zero. Greatest thing in the world for him was to bum around.

Biff and Happy enter the bedroom. Slight pause.

WILLY, *stops short, looking at Biff:* Glad to hear it boy.

HAPPY: He wanted to say good night to you, sport.

WILLY, *to Biff:* Yeah. Knock him dead, boy. What'd you want to tell me?

BIFF: Just take it easy, Pop. Goodnight. *He turns to go.*

WILLY, *unable to resist:* And if anything falls off the desk while you're talking to him—like a package or something—don't pick it up. They have office boys for that.

LINDA: I'll make a big breakfast—

WILLY: Will you let me finish? *To Biff:* Tell him you were in the business in the West. Not farm work.

BIFF: All right, Dad.

LINDA: I think everything—

WILLY, *going right through her speech:* And don't undersell yourself. No less than fifteen thousand dollars.

BIFF, *unable to bear him:* Okay. Good night, Mom. *He starts moving.*

WILLY: Because you got a greatness in you, Biff, remember that. You got all kinds of greatness . . . *He lies back, exhausted. Biff walks out.*

LINDA, *calling after Biff:* Sleep well, darling!

HAPPY: I'm gonna get married, Mom. I wanted to tell you.

LINDA: Go to sleep, dear.

HAPPY, *going:* I just wanted to tell you.

WILLY: Keep up the good work. *Happy exits.* God . . . remember that Ebbets Field game? The championship of the city?

LINDA: Just rest. Should I sing to you?

WILLY: Yeah. Sing to me. *Linda hums a soft lullaby.* When that team came out—he was the tallest, remember?

LINDA: Oh, yes. And in gold.

Biff enters the darkened kitchen, takes a cigarette, and leaves the house. He comes downstage into a golden pool of light. He smokes, staring at the night.

WILLY: Like a young god. Hercules—something like that. And the sun, the sun all around him. Remember how he waved to me? Right up from the field, with the representatives of three colleges standing by? And the buyers I brought, and the cheers when he came out—Loman, Loman, Loman! God Almighty, he'll be great yet. A star like that, magnificent, can never really fade away!

The light on Willy is fading. The gas heater begins to glow through the kitchen wall, near the stairs, a blue flame beneath red coils.

LINDA, *timidly:* Willy dear, what has he got against you?

WILLY: I'm so tired. Don't talk any more.

Biff slowly returns to the kitchen. He stops, stares toward the heater.

LINDA: Will you ask Howard to let you work in New York?

WILLY: First thing in the morning. Everything'll be all right.

Biff reaches behind the heater and draws out a length of rubber tubing. He is horrified and turns his head toward Willy's room, still dimly lit, from which the strains of Linda's desperate but monotonous humming rise.

WILLY, *staring through the window into the moonlight:* Gee, look at the moon moving between the buildings!

Biff wraps the tubing around his hand and quickly goes up the stairs.

Curtain

ACT TWO

Music is heard, gay and bright. The curtain rises as the music fades away. Willy, in shirt sleeves, is sitting at the kitchen table, sipping coffee, his hat in his lap. Linda is filling his cup when she can.

WILLY: Wonderful coffee. Meal in itself.

LINDA: Can I make you some eggs?

WILLY: No. Take a breath.

LINDA: You look so rested, dear.

WILLY: I slept like a dead one. First time in months. Imagine, sleeping till ten on a Tuesday morning. Boys left nice and early, heh?

LINDA: They were out of here by eight o'clock.

WILLY: Good work!

LINDA: It was so thrilling to see them leaving together. I can't get over the shaving lotion in this house!

WILLY, *smiling:* Mmm—

LINDA: Biff was very changed this morning. His whole attitude seemed to be hopeful. He couldn't wait to get downtown to see Oliver.

WILLY: He's heading for a change. There's no question, there simply are certain men that take longer to get—solidified. How did he dress?

LINDA: His blue suit. He's so handsome in that suit. He could be a— anything in that suit!

Willy gets up from the table. Linda holds his jacket for him.

WILLY: There's no question, no question at all. Gee, on the way home tonight I'd like to buy some seeds.

LINDA, *laughing:* That'd be wonderful. But not enough sun gets back there. Nothing'll grow any more.

WILLY: You wait, kid, before it's all over we're gonna get a little place out in the country, and I'll raise some vegetables, a couple of chickens. . .

LINDA: You'll do it yet, dear.

Willy walks out of his jacket. Linda follows him.

WILLY: And they'll get married, and come for a weekend. I'd build a little guest house. 'Cause I got so many fine tools, all I'd need would be a little lumber and some peace of mind.

LINDA, *joyfully:* I sewed the lining . . .

WILLY: I could build two guest houses, so they'd both come. Did he decide how much he's going to ask Oliver for?

LINDA, *getting him into the jacket:* He didn't mention it, but I imagine ten or fifteen thousand. You going to talk to Howard today?

WILLY: Yeah. I'll put it to him straight and simple. He'll just have to take me off the road.

LINDA: And Willy, don't forget to ask for a little advance, because we've got the insurance premium. It's the grace period now.

WILLY: That's a hundred . . . ?

LINDA: A hundred and eight, sixty-eight. Because we're a little short again.

WILLY: Why are we short?

LINDA: Well, you had the motor job on the car . . .

WILLY: That goddam Studebaker!

LINDA: And you got one more payment on the refrigerator . . .

WILLY: But it just broke again!

LINDA: Well, it's old, dear.

WILLY: I told you we should've bought a well-advertised machine. Charley bought a General Electric and it's twenty years old and it's still good, that son-of-a-bitch.

LINDA: But, Willy—

WILLY: Whoever heard of a Hastings refrigerator? Once in my life I would like to own something outright before it's broken! I'm always in a race with the junkyard! I just finished paying for the car and it's on its last legs. The refrigerator consumes belts like a goddam maniac. They time those things. They time them so when you finally paid for them, they're used up.

LINDA, *buttoning up his jacket as he unbuttons it:* All told, about two hundred dollars would carry us, dear. But that includes the last payment on the mortgage. After this payment, Willy, the house belongs to us.

WILLY: It's twenty-five years!

LINDA: Biff was nine years old when we bought it.

WILLY: Well, that's a great thing. To weather a twenty-five year mortgage is—

LINDA: It's an accomplishment.

WILLY: All the cement, the lumber, the reconstruction I put in this house! There ain't a crack to be found in it any more.

LINDA: Well, it served its purpose.

WILLY: What purpose? Some stranger'll come along, move in, and that's that. If only Biff would take this house, and raise a family . . . *he starts to go.* Good-by, I'm late.

LINDA, *suddenly remembering:* Oh, I forgot! You're supposed to meet them for dinner.

WILLY: Me?

LINDA: At Frank's Chop House on Forty-eighth near Sixth Avenue.

WILLY: Is that so! How about you?

LINDA: No, just the three of you. They're gonna blow you to a big meal!

WILLY: Don't say! Who thought of that?

LINDA: Biff came to me this morning, Willy, and he said, "Tell Dad, we want to blow him to a big meal." Be there six o'clock. You and your two boys are going to have dinner.

WILLY: Gee whiz! That's really somethin'. I'm gonna knock Howard for a loop, kid. I'll get an advance, and I'll come home with a New York job. Goddammit, now I'm gonna do it!

LINDA: Oh, that's the spirit, Willy!

WILLY: I will never get behind a wheel the rest of my life!

LINDA: It's changing, Willy, I can feel it changing!

WILLY: Beyond a question. G'by, I'm late. *He starts to go again.*

LINDA, *calling after him as she runs to the kitchen table for a handkerchief:* You got your glasses?

WILLY, *feels for them, then comes back in:*   Yeah, yeah, got my glasses.

LINDA, *giving him the handkerchief:*   And a handkerchief.

WILLY: Yeah, handkerchief.

LINDA: And your saccharine?

WILLY: Yeah, my saccharine.

LINDA: Be careful on the subway stairs.

She kisses him, and a silk stocking is seen hanging from her hand. Willy notices it.

WILLY: Will you stop mending stockings? At least while I'm in the house. It gets me nervous. I can't tell you. Please.

Linda hides the stocking in her hand as she follows Willy across the forestage in front of the house.

LINDA: Remember, Frank's Chop House.

WILLY, *passing the apron:*   Maybe beets would grow out there.

LINDA, *laughing:*   But you tried so many times.

WILLY: Yeah. Well, don't work hard today. *He disappears around the right corner of the house.*

LINDA: Be careful!

As Willy vanishes, Linda waves to him. Suddenly the phone rings. She runs across the stage and into the kitchen and lifts it.

LINDA: Hello? Oh, Biff! I'm so glad you called, I just . . . . Yes, sure, I just told him. Yes, he'll be there for dinner at six o'clock, I didn't forget. Listen, I was just dying to tell you. You know that little rubber pipe I told you about? That he connected to the gas heater? I finally decided to go down the cellar this morning and take it away and destroy it. But it's gone! Imagine? He took it away himself, it isn't there! *She listens.* When? Oh, then you took it. Oh—nothing, it's just that I'd hoped he'd taken it away himself. Oh, I'm not worried, darling, because this morning he left in such high spirits, it was like the old days! I'm not afraid any more. Did Mr. Oliver see you? . . . Well, you wait there then. And make a nice impression on him, darling. Just don't perspire too much before you see him. And have a nice time with Dad. He may have big news too! . . . That's right, a New York job. And be sweet to him tonight, dear. Be loving to him. Because he's only a little boat looking for a harbor. *She is trembling with sorrow and joy.* Oh, that's wonderful, Biff, you'll save his life. Thanks, darling. Just put your arm around him when he comes into the restaurant. Give him a smile. That's the boy . . . Good-by, dear. . . . You got your comb? . . . That's fine. Good-by, Biff dear.

In the middle of her speech, Howard Wagner, thirty-six, wheels on a small typewriter table on which is a wire recording machine and proceeds to plug it in. This is on the left forestage. Light slowly fades on Linda as it rises on Howard. Howard is intent on threading the machine and only glances over his shoulder as Willy appears.

WILLY: Pst! Pst!
HOWARD: Hello, Willy, come in.
WILLY: Like to have a little talk with you, Howard.
HOWARD: Sorry to keep you waiting. I'll be with you in a minute.
WILLY: What's that, Howard?
HOWARD: Didn't you ever see one of these? Wire recorder.
WILLY: Oh. Can we talk a minute?
HOWARD: Records things. Just got delivery yesterday. Been driving me crazy, the most terrific machine I ever saw in my life. I was up all night with it.
WILLY: What do you do with it?
HOWARD: I bought it for dictation, but you can do anything with it. Listen to this. I had it home last night. Listen to what I picked up. The first one is my daughter. Get this. *He flicks the switch and "Roll out the Barrel" is heard being whistled.* Listen to that kid whistle.
WILLY: That is lifelike, isn't it?
HOWARD: Seven years old. Get that tone.
WILLY: Ts, ts. Like to ask a little favor if you . . .

The whistling breaks off, and the voice of Howard's daughter is heard.

HIS DAUGHTER: "Now you, Daddy."
HOWARD: She's crazy for me! *Again the same song is whistled.* That's me! Ha! *He winks.*
WILLY: You're very good!

The whistling breaks off again. The machine runs silent for a moment.

HOWARD: Sh! Get this now, this is my son.

HIS SON: "The capital of Alabama is Montgomery; the capital of Arizona is Phoenix; the capital of Arkansas is Little Rock; the capital of California is Sacramento . . ." *and on, and on.*

HOWARD, *holding up five fingers:*   Five years old, Willy!

WILLY: He'll make an announcer some day!

HIS SON, *continuing:*   "The capital . . ."

HOWARD: Get that—alphabetical order! *The machine breaks off suddenly.* Wait a minute. The maid kicked the plug out.

WILLY: It certainly is a—

HOWARD: Sh, for God's sake!

HIS SON: "It's nine o'clock, Bulova watch time. So I have to go to sleep."

WILLY: That really is—

HOWARD: Wait a minute! The next is my wife.

They wait.

HOWARD'S VOICE: "Go on, say something." *Pause.* "Well, you gonna talk?"

HIS WIFE: "I can't think of anything."

HOWARD'S VOICE: "Well, talk—it's turning."

HIS WIFE, *shyly beaten:*   "Hello." *Silence.* "Oh, Howard, I can't talk into this . . ."

HOWARD, *snapping the machine off:*   That was my wife.

WILLY: That is a wonderful machine. Can we—

HOWARD: I tell you, Willy, I'm gonna take my camera, and my bandsaw, and all my hobbies, and out they go. This is the most fascinating relaxation I ever found.

WILLY: I think I'll get one myself.

HOWARD: Sure, they're only a hundred and a half. You can't do without it. Supposing you wanna hear Jack Benny, see? But you can't be at home at that hour. So you tell the maid to turn the radio on when Jack Benny comes on, and this automatically goes on with the radio . . .

WILLY: And when you come home you . . .

HOWARD: You can come home twelve o'clock, one o'clock, any time you like, and you get yourself a Coke and sit yourself down, throw the switch, and there's Jack Benny's program in the middle of the night!

WILLY: I'm definitely going to get one. Because lots of time I'm on the road, and I think to myself, what I must be missing on the radio!

HOWARD: Don't you have a radio in the car?

WILLY: Well, yeah, but who ever thinks of turning it on?

HOWARD: Say, aren't you supposed to be in Boston?

WILLY: That's what I want to talk to you about, Howard. You got a minute? *He draws a chair in from the wing.*

HOWARD: What happened? What're you doing here?

WILLY: Well . . .

HOWARD: You didn't crack up again, did you?

WILLY: Oh, no. No . . .

HOWARD: Geez, you had me worried there for a minute. What's the trouble?

WILLY: Well, tell you the truth, Howard. I've come to the decision that I'd rather not travel any more.

HOWARD: Not travel! Well, what'll you do?

WILLY: Remember, Christmas time, when you had the party here? You said you'd try to think of some spot for me here in town.

HOWARD: With us?

WILLY: Well, sure.

HOWARD: Oh, yeah, yeah. I remember. Well, I couldn't think of anything for you, Willy.

WILLY: I tell ya, Howard. The kids are all grown up, y'know. I don't need much any more. If I could take home—well, sixty-five dollars a week, I could swing it.

HOWARD: Yeah, but Willy, see I—

WILLY: I tell ya why, Howard. Speaking frankly and between the two of us, y'know—I'm just a little tired.

HOWARD: Oh, I could understand that, Willy. But you're a road man, Willy, and we do a road business. We've only got a half-dozen salesmen on the floor here.

WILLY: God knows, Howard, I never asked a favor of any man. But I was with the firm when your father used to carry you in here in his arms.

HOWARD: I know that, Willy, but—

WILLY: Your father came to me the day you were born and asked me what I thought of the name of Howard, may he rest in peace.

HOWARD: I appreciate that, Willy, but there just is no spot here for you. If I had a spot I'd slam you right in, but I just don't have a single solitary spot.

He looks for his lighter. Willy has picked it up and gives it to him. Pause.

WILLY, *with increasing anger*: Howard, all I need to set my table is fifty dollars a week.

HOWARD: But where am I going to put you, kid?

WILLY: Look, it isn't a question of whether I can sell merchandise, is it?

HOWARD: No, but it's a business, kid, and everybody's gotta pull his own weight.

WILLY, *desperately*: Just let me tell you a story, Howard—

HOWARD: 'Cause you gotta admit, business is business.

WILLY, *angrily*: Business is definitely business, but just listen for a minute. You don't understand this. When I was a boy—eighteen, nineteen—I was already on the road. And there was a question in my mind as to whether selling had a future for me. Because in those days I had a yearning to go to Alaska. See, there were three gold strikes in one month in Alaska, and I felt like going out. Just for the ride, you might say.

HOWARD, *barely interested*: Don't say.

WILLY: Oh, yeah, my father lived many years in Alaska. He was an adventurous man. We've got quite a little streak of self-reliance in our family. I thought I'd go out with my older brother and try to locate him, and maybe settle in the North with the old man. And I was almost decided to go, when I met a salesman in the Parker House. His name was Dave Singleman. And he was eighty-four years old, and he'd drummed merchandise in thirty-one states. And old Dave, he'd go up to his room, y'understand, put on his green velvet slippers—I'll never forget—and pick up his phone and call the buyers, and without ever leaving his room, at the age of eighty-four, he made his living. And when I saw that, I realized that selling was the greatest career a man could want. 'Cause what could be more satisfying than to be able to go, at the age of eighty-four, into twenty or thirty different cities, and pick up a phone, and be remembered and loved and helped by so many different people? Do you know? when he died—and by the way he died the death of a salesman, in his green velvet slippers in the smoker of the New York, New Haven and Hartford, going into Boston—when he died, hundreds of salesmen and buyers were at his funeral. Things were sad on a lotta trains for months after that. *He stands up. Howard has not looked at him.* In those days there was personality in it, Howard. There was respect, and comradeship, and gratitude in it. Today, it's all cut and dried, and there's no chance for bringing friendship to bear— or personality. You see what I mean? They don't know me any more.

HOWARD, *moving away, to the right*:   That's just the thing, Willy.

WILLY: If I had forty dollars a week—that's all I'd need. Forty dollars, Howard.

HOWARD: Kid, I can't take blood from a stone, I—

WILLY, *desperation is on him now*:   Howard, the year Al Smith was nominated, your father came to me and—

HOWARD, *starting to go off*:   I've got to see some people, kid.

WILLY, *stopping him*:   I'm talking about your father! There were promises made across this desk! You mustn't tell me you've got people to see— I put thirty-four years into this firm, Howard, and now I can't pay my insurance! You can't eat the orange and throw the peel away—a man is not a piece of fruit! *After a pause*: Now pay attention. Your father— in 1928 I had a big year. I averaged a hundred and seventy dollars a week in commissions.

HOWARD, *impatiently*:   Now, Willy, you never averaged—

WILLY, *banging his hand on the desk*:   I averaged a hundred and seventy dollars a week in the year of 1928! And your father came to me—or rather, I was in the office here—it was right over this desk—and he put his hand on my shoulder—

HOWARD, *getting up*:   You'll have to excuse me, Willy, I gotta see some people. Pull yourself together. *Going out*: I'll be back in a little while.

On Howard's exit, the light on his chair grows very bright and strange.

WILLY: Pull myself together! What the hell did I say to him? My God, I was yelling at him! How could I! *Willy breaks off, staring at the light,*

*which occupies the chair, animating it. He approaches this chair, standing
across the desk from it.* Frank, Frank, don't you remember what you
told me that time? How you put your hand on my shoulder, and Frank
. . . *He leans on the desk and as he speaks the dead man's name he accidentally switches on the recorder, and instantly*

HOWARD'S SON: " . . . of New York is Albany. The capital of Ohio is
Cincinnati, the capital of Rhode Island is . . . " *The recitation continues.*

WILLY, *leaping away with fright, shouting*:   Ha! Howard! Howard! Howard!

HOWARD, *rushing in*:   What happened?

WILLY, *pointing at the machine, which continues nasally, childishly, with the
capital cities*:   Shut it off! Shut it off!

HOWARD, *pulling the plug out*:   Look, Willy . . .

WILLY, *pressing his hands to his eyes*:   I gotta get myself some coffee. I'll
get some coffee . . .

Willy starts to walk out. Howard stops him.

HOWARD, *rolling up the cord*:   Willy, look . . .

WILLY: I'll go to Boston.

HOWARD: Willy, you can't go to Boston for us.

WILLY: Why can't I go?

HOWARD: I don't want you to represent us. I've been meaning to tell you
for a long time now.

WILLY: Howard, are you firing me?

HOWARD: I think you need a good long rest, Willy.

WILLY: Howard—

HOWARD: And when you feel better, come back, and we'll see if we can
work something out.

WILLY: But I gotta earn money, Howard. I'm in no position to—

HOWARD: Where are your sons? Why don't your sons give you a hand?

WILLY: They're working on a very big deal.

HOWARD: This is no time for false pride, Willy. You go to your sons and
you tell them that you're tired. You've got two great boys, haven't you?

WILLY: Oh, no question, no question, but in the meantime . . .

HOWARD: Then that's that, heh?

WILLY: All right, I'll go to Boston tomorrow.

HOWARD: No, no.

WILLY: I can't throw myself on my sons. I'm not a cripple!

HOWARD: Look, kid, I'm busy this morning.

WILLY, *grasping Howard's arm*:   Howard, you've got to let me go to Boston!

HOWARD, *hard, keeping himself under control*:   I've got a line of people to
see this morning. Sit down, take five minutes, and pull yourself together, and then go home, will ya? I need the office, Willy. *He starts to
go, turns, remembering the recorder, starts to push off the table holding the
recorder.* Oh, yeah, Whenever you can this week, stop by and drop off

the samples. You'll feel better, Willy, and then come back and we'll talk. Pull yourself together, kid, there's people outside.

Howard exits, pushing the table off left. Willy stares into space, exhausted. Now the music is heard—Ben's music—first distantly, then closer, closer. As Willy speaks, Ben enters from the right. He carries valise and umbrella.

WILLY: Oh, Ben, how did you do it? What is the answer? Did you wind up the Alaska deal already?

BEN: Doesn't take much time if you know what you're doing. Just a short business trip. Boarding ship in an hour. Wanted to say good-by.

WILLY: Ben, I've got to talk to you.

BEN, *glancing at his watch*:   Haven't the time, William.

WILLY, *crossing the apron to Ben*:   Ben, nothing's working out. I don't know what to do.

BEN: Now, look here, William. I've bought timberland in Alaska and I need a man to look after things for me.

WILLY: God, timberland! Me and my boys in those grand outdoors!

BEN: You've a new continent at your doorstep, William. Get out of these cities, they're full of talk and time payments and courts of law. Screw on your fists and you can fight for a fortune up there.

WILLY: Yes, yes! Linda, Linda!

Linda enters as of old, with the wash.

LINDA: Oh, you're back?

BEN: I haven't much time.

WILLY: No, wait! Linda, he's got a proposition for me in Alaska.

LINDA: But you've got— *To Ben:* He's got a beautiful job here.

WILLY: But in Alaska, kid, I could—

LINDA: You're doing well enough, Willy!

BEN, *to Linda*:   Enough for what, my dear?

LINDA, *frightened of Ben and angry at him*:   Don't say those things to him! Enough to be happy right here, right now. *To Willy, while Ben laughs:* Why must everybody conquer the world? You're well liked, and the boys love you, and someday—*to Ben*—why, old man Wagner told him just the other day that if he keeps it up he'll be a member of the firm, didn't he, Willy?

WILLY: Sure, sure. I am building something with this firm, Ben, and if a man is building something he must be on the right track, mustn't he?

BEN: What are you building? Lay your hand on it. Where is it?

WILLY, *hesitantly*:   That's true, Linda, there's nothing.

LINDA: Why? *To Ben:* There's a man eighty-four years old—

WILLY: That's right, Ben, that's right. When I look at that man I say, what is there to worry about?

BEN: Bah!

WILLY: It's true, Ben. All he has to do is go into any city, pick up the phone, and he's making his living and you know why?

BEN, *picking up his valise*: I've got to go.
WILLY, *holding Ben back*: Look at this boy!

Biff, in his high school sweater, enters carrying suitcase. Happy carries Biff's shoulder guards, gold helmet, and football pants.

WILLY: Without a penny to his name, three great universities are begging for him, and from there the sky's the limit, because it's not what you do, Ben. It's who you know and the smile on your face! It's contacts, Ben, contacts! The whole wealth of Alaska passes over the lunch table at the Commodore Hotel, and that's the wonder, the wonder of this country, that a man can end with diamonds here on the basis of being liked! *He turns to Biff.* And that's why when you get out on that field today it's important. Because thousands of people will be rooting for you and loving you. *To Ben, who has again begun to leave*: And Ben! when he walks into a business office his name will sound out like a bell and all the doors will open to him! I've seen it, Ben, I've seen it a thousand times! You can't feel it with your hand like timber, but it's there!
BEN: Good-by, William.
WILLY: Ben, am I right? Don't you think I'm right? I value your advice.
BEN: There's a new continent at your doorstep, William. You could walk out rich. Rich! *He is gone.*
WILLY: We'll do it here, Ben! You hear me? We're gonna do it here!

Young Bernard rushes in. The gay music of the Boys is heard.

BERNARD: Oh, gee, I was afraid you left already!
WILLY: Why? What time is it?
BERNARD: It's half-past one!
WILLY: Well, come on, everybody! Ebbets Field next stop! Where's the pennants? *He rushes through the wall-line of the kitchen and out into the living-room.*
LINDA, *to Biff*: Did you pack fresh underwear?
BIFF, *who has been limbering up*: I want to go!
BERNARD: Biff, I'm carrying your helmet, ain't I?
HAPPY: No, I'm carrying the helmet.
BERNARD: Oh, Biff, you promised me.
HAPPY: I'm carrying the helmet.
BERNARD: How am I going to get in the locker room?
LINDA: Let him carry the shoulder guards. *She puts her coat and hat on in the kitchen.*
BERNARD: Can I, Biff? 'Cause I told everybody I'm going to be in the locker room.
HAPPY: In Ebbets Field it's the clubhouse.
BERNARD: I meant the clubhouse. Biff!
HAPPY: Biff!
BIFF, *grandly, after a slight pause*: Let him carry the shoulder guards.
HAPPY, *as he gives Bernard the shoulder guards*: Stay close to us now.

Willy rushes in with the pennants.

WILLY, *handing them out*:   Everybody wave when Biff comes out on the field. *Happy and Bernard run off.* You set now, boy?

The music has died away.

BIFF: Ready to go, Pop. Every muscle is ready.

WILLY, *at the edge of the apron*:   You realize what this means?

BIFF: That's right, Pop.

WILLY, *feeling Biff's muscles*:   You're comin' home this afternoon captain of the All-Scholastic Championship Team of the City of New York.

BIFF: I got it, Pop. And remember, pal, when I take off my helmet, that touchdown is for you.

WILLY: Let's go! *He is starting out, with his arm around Biff, when Charley enters, as of old, in knickers.* I got no room for you, Charley.

CHARLEY: Room? For what?

WILLY: In the car.

CHARLEY: You goin' for a ride? I wanted to shoot some casino.

WILLY, *furiously*:   Casino! *Incredulously*: Don't you realize what today is?

LINDA: Oh, he knows, Willy. He's just kidding you.

WILLY: That's nothing to kid about!

CHARLEY: No. Linda, what's goin' on?

LINDA: He's playing in Ebbets Field.

CHARLEY: Baseball in this weather?

WILLY: Don't talk to him. Come on, come on! *He is pushing them out.*

CHARLEY: Wait a minute, didn't you hear the news?

WILLY: What?

CHARLEY: Don't you listen to the radio? Ebbets Field just blew up.

WILLY: You go to hell! *Charley laughs. Pushing them out:* Come on, come on! We're late.

CHARLEY, *as they go*:   Knock a homer, Biff, knock a homer!

WILLY, *the last to leave, turning to Charley*:   I don't think that was funny, Charley. This is the greatest day of his life.

CHARLEY: Willy, when are you going to grow up?

WILLY: Yeah, heh? When this game is over, Charley, you'll be laughing out of the other side of your face. They'll be calling him another Red Grange. Twenty-five thousand a year.

CHARLEY, *kidding*:   Is that so?

WILLY: Yeah, that's so.

CHARLEY: Well, then, I'm sorry, Willy. But tell me something.

WILLY: What?

CHARLEY: Who is Red Grange?

WILLY: Put up your hands. Goddam you, put up your hands!

Charley, chuckling, shakes his head and walks away, around the left corner of the stage. Willy follows him. The music rises to a mocking frenzy.

WILLY: Who the hell do you think you are, better than everybody else? You don't know everything, you big, ignorant, stupid . . . Put up your hands!

Light rises, on the right side of the forestage, on a small table in the reception room of Charley's office. Traffic sounds are heard. Bernard, now mature, sits whistling to himself. A pair of tennis rackets and an overnight bag are on the floor beside him.

WILLY, *offstage*: What are you walking away for? Don't walk away! If you're going to say something say it to my face! I know you laugh at me behind my back. You'll laugh out of the other side of your goddam face after this game. Touchdown! Touchdown! Eighty thousand people! Touchdown! Right between the goal posts.

Bernard is a quiet, earnest, but self-assured young man. Willy's voice is coming from right upstage now. Bernard lowers his feet off the table and listens. Jenny, his father's secretary, enters.

JENNY, *distressed*: Say, Bernard, will you go out in the hall?

BERNARD: What is that noise? Who is it?

JENNY: Mr. Loman. He just got off the elevator.

BERNARD, *getting up*: Who's he arguing with?

JENNY: Nobody. There's nobody with him. I can't deal with him any more, and your father gets all upset everytime he comes. I've got a lot of typing to do, and your father's waiting to sign it. Will you see him?

WILLY, *entering*: Touchdown! Touch— *He sees Jenny.* Jenny, Jenny, good to see you. How're ya? Workin'? Or still honest?

JENNY: Fine. How've you been feeling?

WILLY: Not much any more, Jenny. Ha, ha! *He is surprised to see the rackets.*

BERNARD: Hello, Uncle Willy.

WILLY, *almost shocked*: Bernard! Well, look who's here! *He comes quickly, guiltily, to Bernard and warmly shakes his hand.*

BERNARD: How are you? Good to see you.

WILLY: What are you doing here?

BERNARD: Oh, just stopped by to see Pop. Get off my feet till my train leaves. I'm going to Washington in a few minutes.

WILLY: Is he in?

BERNARD: Yes, he's in his office with the accountant. Sit down.

WILLY, *sitting down*: What're you going to do in Washington?

BERNARD: Oh, just a case I've got there, Willy.

WILLY: That so? *Indicating the rackets:* You going to play tennis there?

BERNARD: I'm staying with a friend who's got a court.

WILLY: Don't say. His own tennis court. Must be fine people, I bet.

BERNARD: They are, very nice. Dad tells me Biff's in town.

WILLY, *with a big smile*: Yeah, Biff's in. Working on a very big deal, Bernard.

BERNARD: What's Biff doing?

WILLY: Well, he's been doing very big things in the West. But he decided to establish himself here. Very big. We're having dinner. Did I hear your wife had a boy?

BERNARD: That's right. Our second.

WILLY: Two boys! What do you know!

BERNARD: What kind of a deal has Biff got?

WILLY: Well, Bill Oliver—very big sporting-goods man—he wants Biff very badly. Called him in from the West. Long distance, carte blanche, special deliveries. Your friends have their own private tennis court?

BERNARD: You still with the old firm, Willy?

WILLY, *after a pause*:   I'm—I'm overjoyed to see how you made the grade, Bernard, overjoyed. It's an encouraging thing to see a young man really—really—Looks very good for Biff—very—*He breaks off, then:* Bernard— *He is so full of emotion, he breaks off again.*

BERNARD: What is it, Willy?

WILLY, *small and alone*:   What—what's the secret?

BERNARD: What secret?

WILLY: How—how did you? Why didn't he ever catch on?

BERNARD: I wouldn't know that, Willy.

WILLY, *confidentially, desperately*:   You were his friend, his boyhood friend. There's something I don't understand about it. His life ended after that Ebbets Field game. From the age of seventeen nothing good ever happened to him.

BERNARD: He never trained himself for anything.

WILLY: But he did, he did. After high school he took so many correspondence courses. Radio mechanics; television; God knows what, and never made the slightest mark.

BERNARD, *taking off his glasses*:   Willy, do you want to talk candidly?

WILLY, *rising, faces Bernard*:   I regard you as a very brilliant man, Bernard. I value your advice.

BERNARD: Oh, the hell with the advice, Willy. I couldn't advise you. There's just one thing I've always wanted to ask you. When he was supposed to graduate, and the math teacher flunked him—

WILLY: Oh, that son-of-a-bitch ruined his life.

BERNARD: Yeah, but, Willy, all he had to do was go to summer school and make up that subject.

WILLY: That's right, that's right.

BERNARD: Did you tell him not to go to summer school?

WILLY: Me? I begged him to go. I ordered him to go!

BERNARD: Then why wouldn't he go?

WILLY: Why? Why! Bernard, that question has been trailing me like a ghost for the last fifteen years. He flunked the subject, and laid down and died like a hammer hit him!

BERNARD: Take it easy, kid.

WILLY: Let me talk to you—I got nobody to talk to. Bernard, Bernard, was it my fault? Y'see? It keeps going around in my mind, maybe I did something to him. I got nothing to give him.

BERNARD: Don't take it so hard.

WILLY: Why did he lay down? What is the story there? You were his friend!

BERNARD: Willy, I remember, it was June, and our grades came out. And he'd flunked math.

WILLY: That son-of-a-bitch!

BERNARD: No, it wasn't right then. Biff just got very angry, I remember, and he was ready to enroll in summer school.

WILLY, *surprised*:   He was?

BERNARD: He wasn't beaten by it at all. But then, Willy, he disappeared from the block for almost a month. And I got the idea that he'd gone up to New England to see you. Did he have a talk with you then?

Willy stares in silence.

BERNARD: Willy?

WILLY, *with a strong edge of resentment in his voice*:   Yeah, he came to Boston. What about it?

BERNARD: Well, just that when he came back—I'll never forget this, it always mystifies me. Because I'd thought so well of Biff, even though he'd always taken advantage of me. I loved him, Willy, y'know? And he came back after that month and took his sneakers—remember those sneakers with "University of Virginia" printed on them? He was so proud of those, wore them every day. And he took them down in the cellar, and burned them up in the furnace. We had a fist fight. It lasted at least half an hour. Just the two of us, punching each other down the cellar, and crying right through it. I've often thought of how strange it was that I knew he'd given up his life. What happened in Boston, Willy?

Willy looks at him as at an intruder.

BERNARD: I just bring it up because you asked me.

WILLY, *angrily*:   Nothing. What do you mean, "What happened?" What's that got to do with anything?

BERNARD: Well, don't get sore.

WILLY: What are you trying to do, blame it on me? If a boy lays down is that my fault?

BERNARD: Now, Willy, don't get—

WILLY: Well, don't—don't talk to me that way! What does that mean, "What happened?"

Charley enters. He is in his vest, and he carries a bottle of bourbon.

CHARLEY: Hey, you're going to miss that train. *He waves the bottle.*

BERNARD: Yeah, I'm going. *He takes the bottle.* Thanks, Pop. *He picks up his rackets and bag.* Good-by, Willy, and don't worry about it. You know, "If at first you don't succeed . . . ."

WILLY: Yes, I believe in that.

BERNARD: But sometimes, Willy, it's better for a man just to walk away.

WILLY: Walk away?

BERNARD: That's right.

WILLY: But if you can't walk away?

BERNARD, *after a slight pause*: I guess that's when it's tough. *Extending his hand:* Good-by, Willy.

WILLY, *shaking Bernard's hand*: Good-by, boy.

CHARLEY, *an arm on Bernard's shoulder*: How do you like this kid? Gonna argue a case in front of the Supreme Court.

BERNARD, *protesting*: Pop!

WILLY, *genuinely shocked, pained, and happy*: No! The Supreme Court!

BERNARD: I gotta run. 'By, Dad!

CHARLEY: Knock 'em dead, Bernard!

Bernard goes off.

WILLY, *as Charley takes out his wallet*: The Supreme Court! And he didn't even mention it!

CHARLEY, *counting out money on the desk*: He don't have to—he's gonna do it.

WILLY: And you never told him what to do, did you? You never took any interest in him.

CHARLEY: My salvation is that I never took any interest in anything. There's some money—fifty dollars. I got an accountant inside.

WILLY: Charley, look . . . *With difficulty:* I got my insurance to pay. If you can manage it—I need a hundred and ten dollars.

Charley doesn't reply for a moment; merely stops moving.

WILLY: I'd draw it from my bank but Linda would know, and I . . .

CHARLEY: Sit down, Willy.

WILLY, *moving toward the chair*: I'm keeping an account of everything, remember. I'll pay every penny back. *He sits.*

CHARLEY: Now listen to me, Willy.

WILLY: I want you to know I appreciate . . .

CHARLEY, *sitting down on the table*: Willy, what're you doin'? What the hell is goin' on in your head?

WILLY: Why? I'm simply . . .

CHARLEY: I offered you a job. You can make fifty dollars a week. And I won't send you on the road.

WILLY: I've got a job.

CHARLEY: Without pay? What kind of a job is a job without pay? *He rises.* Now, look, kid, enough is enough. I'm no genius but I know when I'm being insulted.

WILLY: Insulted!

CHARLEY: Why don't you want to work for me?

WILLY: What's the matter with you? I've got a job.

CHARLEY: Then what're you walkin' in here every week for?

WILLY, *getting up*: Well, if you don't want me to walk in here—

CHARLEY: I am offering you a job.

WILLY: I don't want your goddam job!

CHARLEY: When the hell are you going to grow up?

WILLY, *furiously*: You big ignoramus, if you say that to me again I'll rap you one! I don't care how big you are! *He's ready to fight.*

Pause.

CHARLEY, *kindly, going to him*: How much do you need, Willy?

WILLY: Charley, I'm strapped, I'm strapped. I don't know what to do. I was just fired.

CHARLEY: Howard fired you?

WILLY: That snotnose. Imagine that? I named him. I named him Howard.

CHARLEY: Willy, when're you gonna realize that them things don't mean anything? You named him Howard, but you can't sell that. The only thing you got in this world is what you can sell. And the funny thing is that you're a salesman, and you don't know that.

WILLY: I've always tried to think otherwise, I guess. I always felt that if a man was impressive, and well liked, that nothing—

CHARLEY: Why must everybody like you? Who liked J. P. Morgan? Was he impressive? In a Turkish bath he'd look like a butcher. But with his pockets on he was very well liked. Now listen, Willy, I know you don't like me, and nobody can say I'm in love with you, but I'll give you a job because—just for the hell of it, put it that way. Now what do you say?

WILLY: I—I just can't work for you, Charley.

CHARLEY: What're you, jealous of me?

WILLY: I can't work for you, that's all, don't ask me why.

CHARLEY, *angered, takes out more bills*: You been jealous of me all your life, you damned fool! Here, pay your insurance. *He puts the money in Willy's hand.*

WILLY: I'm keeping strict accounts.

CHARLEY: I've got some work to do. Take care of yourself. And pay your insurance.

WILLY, *moving to the right*: Funny, y'know? After all the highways, and the trains, and the appointments, and the years, you end up worth more dead than alive.

CHARLEY: Willy, nobody's worth nothin' dead. *After a slight pause:* Did you hear what I said?

Willy stands still, dreaming.

CHARLEY: Willy!

WILLY: Apologize to Bernard for me when you see him. I didn't mean to argue with him. He's a fine boy. They're all fine boys, and they'll end up big—all of them. Someday they'll all play tennis together. Wish me luck, Charley. He saw Bill Oliver today.

CHARLEY: Good luck.

WILLY, *on the verge of tears*:   Charley, you're the only friend I got. Isn't that a remarkable thing? *He goes out.*

CHARLEY: Jesus!

Charley stares after him a moment and follows. All light blacks out. Suddenly raucous music is heard, and a red glow rises behind the screen at right. Stanley, a young waiter, appears, carrying a table, followed by Happy, who is carrying two chairs.

STANLEY, *putting the table down*:   That's all right, Mr. Loman, I can handle it myself. *He turns and takes the chairs from Happy and places them at the table.*

HAPPY, *glancing around*:   Oh, this is better.

STANLEY: Sure, in the front there you're in the middle of all kinds a noise. Whenever you got a party, Mr. Loman, you just tell me and I'll put you back here. Y'know, there's a lotta people they don't like it private, because when they go out they like to see a lotta action around them because they're sick and tired to stay in the house by theirself. But I know you, you ain't from Hackensack. You know what I mean?

HAPPY, *sitting down*:   So how's it coming, Stanley?

STANLEY: Ah, it's a dog's life. I only wish during the war they'd a took me in the Army. I coulda been dead by now.

HAPPY: My brother's back, Stanley.

STANLEY: Oh, he come back, heh? From the Far West.

HAPPY: Yeah, big cattle man, my brother, so treat him right. And my father's coming too.

STANLEY: Oh, your father too!

HAPPY: You got a couple of nice lobsters?

STANLEY: Hundred per cent, big.

HAPPY: I want them with the claws.

STANLEY: Don't worry, I don't give you no mice. *Happy laughs.* How about some wine? It'll put a head on the meal.

HAPPY: No. You remember, Stanley, that recipe I brought you from overseas? With the champagne in it?

STANLEY: Oh, yeah, sure. I still got it tacked up yet in the kitchen. But that'll have to cost a buck apiece anyways.

HAPPY: That's all right.

STANLEY: What'd you, hit a number or somethin'?

HAPPY: No, it's a little celebration. My brother is—I think he pulled off a big deal today. I think we're going into business together.

STANLEY: Great! That's the best for you. Because a family business, you know what I mean?—that's the best.

HAPPY: That's what I think.

STANLEY: 'Cause what's the difference? Somebody steals? It's in the family. Know what I mean? *Sotto voce:* Like this bartender here. The boss is goin' crazy what kinda leak he's got in the cash register. You put it in but it don't come out.

HAPPY, *raising his head*:   Sh!
STANLEY: What?
HAPPY: You notice I wasn't lookin' right or left, was I?
STANLEY: No.
HAPPY: And my eyes are closed.
STANLEY: So what's the—?
HAPPY: Strudel's comin'.
STANLEY, *catching on, looks around*:   Ah, no, there's no—

He breaks off as a furred, lavishly dressed girl enters and sits at the next table. Both follow her with their eyes.

STANLEY: Geez, how'd ya know?
HAPPY: I got radar or something. *Staring directly at her profile:* Oooooooo . . . Stanley.
STANLEY: I think that's for you, Mr. Loman.
HAPPY: Look at that mouth. Oh, God. And the binoculars.
STANLEY: Geez, you got a life, Mr. Loman.
HAPPY: Wait on her.
STANLEY, *going to the girl's table*:   Would you like a menu, ma'am?
GIRL: I'm expecting someone, but I'd like a—
HAPPY: Why don't you bring her—excuse me, miss, do you mind? I sell champagne, and I'd like you to try my brand. Bring her a champagne, Stanley.
GIRL: That's awfully nice of you.
HAPPY: Don't mention it. It's all company money. *He laughs.*
GIRL: That's a charming product to be selling, isn't it?
HAPPY: Oh, gets to be like everything else. Selling is selling, y'know.
GIRL: I suppose.
HAPPY: You don't happen to sell, do you?
GIRL: No, I don't sell.
HAPPY: Would you object to a compliment from a stranger? You ought to be on a magazine cover.
GIRL, *looking at him a little archly*:   I have been.

Stanley comes in with a glass of champagne.

HAPPY: What'd I say before, Stanley? You see? She's a cover girl.
STANLEY: Oh, I could see, I could see.
HAPPY, *to the Girl*:   What magazine?
GIRL: Oh, a lot of them. *She takes the drink.* Thank you.
HAPPY: You know what they say in France, don't you? "Champagne is the drink of the complexion"—Hya, Biff!

Biff has entered and sits with Happy.

BIFF: Hello, kid. Sorry I'm late.
HAPPY: I just got here. Uh, Miss—?

GIRL: Forsythe.

HAPPY: Miss Forsythe, this is my brother.

BIFF: Is Dad here?

HAPPY: His name is Biff. You might've heard of him. Great football player.

GIRL: Really? What team?

HAPPY: Are you familiar with football?

GIRL: No, I'm afraid I'm not.

HAPPY: Biff is quarterback with the New York Giants.

GIRL: Well, that is nice, isn't it? *She drinks.*

HAPPY: Good health.

GIRL: I'm happy to meet you.

HAPPY: That's my name. Hap. It's really Harold, but at West Point they called me Happy.

GIRL, *now really impressed*:   Oh, I see. How do you do? *She turns her profile.*

BIFF: Isn't Dad coming?

HAPPY: You want her?

BIFF: Oh, I could never make that.

HAPPY: I remember the time that idea would never come into your head. Where's the old confidence, Biff?

BIFF: I just saw Oliver—

HAPPY: Wait a minute. I've got to see that old confidence again. Do you want her? She's on call.

BIFF: Oh, no. *He turns to look at the Girl.*

HAPPY: I'm telling you. Watch this. *Turning to the Girl:* Honey? *She turns to him.* Are you busy?

GIRL: Well, I am . . . but I could make a phone call.

HAPPY: Do that, will you, honey? And see if you can get a friend. We'll be here for a while. Biff is one of the greatest football players in the country.

GIRL, *standing up*:   Well, I'm certainly happy to meet you.

HAPPY: Come back soon.

GIRL: I'll try.

HAPPY: Don't try, honey, try hard.

The Girl exits. Stanley follows, shaking his head in bewildered admiration.

HAPPY: Isn't that a shame now? A beautiful girl like that? That's why I can't get married. There's not a good woman in a thousand. New York is loaded with them, kid!

BIFF: Hap, look—

HAPPY: I told you she was on call!

BIFF, *strangely unnerved*:   Cut it out, will ya? I want to say something to you.

HAPPY: Did you see Oliver?

BIFF: I saw him all right. Now look, I want to tell Dad a couple of things and I want you to help me.

HAPPY: What? Is he going to back you?

BIFF: Are you crazy? You're out of your goddam head, you know that?

HAPPY: Why? What happened?

BIFF, *breathlessly*:   I did a terrible thing today, Hap. It's been the strangest day I ever went through. I'm all numb, I swear.

HAPPY: You mean he wouldn't see you?

BIFF: Well, I waited six hours for him, see? All day. Kept sending my name in. Even tried to date his secretary so she'd get me to him, but no soap.

HAPPY: Because you're not showin' the old confidence, Biff. He remembered you, didn't he?

BIFF, *stopping Happy with a gesture*:   Finally, about five o'clock, he comes out. Didn't remember who I was or anything. I felt like such an idiot, Hap.

HAPPY: Did you tell him my Florida idea?

BIFF: He walked away. I saw him for one minute. I got so mad I could've torn the walls down! How the hell did I ever get the idea I was a salesman there? I even believed myself that I'd been a salesman for him! And then he gave me one look and—I realized what a ridiculous lie my whole life has been! We've been talking in a dream for fifteen years. I was a shipping clerk.

HAPPY: What'd you do?

BIFF, *with great tension and wonder*:   Well, he left, see. And the secretary went out. I was all alone in the waiting-room. I don't know what came over me, Hap. The next thing I know I'm in his office—paneled walls, everything. I can't explain it. I—Hap, I took his fountain pen.

HAPPY: Geez, did he catch you?

BIFF: I ran out. I ran down all eleven flights. I ran and ran and ran.

HAPPY: That was an awful dumb—what'd you do that for?

BIFF, *agonized*:   I don't know, I just—wanted to take something, I don't know. You gotta help me, Hap, I'm gonna tell Pop.

HAPPY: You crazy? What for?

BIFF: Hap, he's got to understand that I'm not the man somebody lends that kind of money to. He thinks I've been spiting him all these years and it's eating him up.

HAPPY: That's just it. You tell him something nice.

BIFF: I can't.

HAPPY: Say you got a lunch date with Oliver tomorrow.

BIFF: So what do I do tomorrow?

HAPPY: You leave the house tomorrow and come back at night and say Oliver is thinking it over. And he thinks it over for a couple of weeks, and gradually it fades away and nobody's the worse.

BIFF: But it'll go on forever!

HAPPY: Dad is never so happy as when he's looking forward to something!

Willy enters.

HAPPY: Hello, scout!

WILLY: Gee, I haven't been here in years!

Stanley has followed Willy in and sets a chair for him. Stanley starts off but Happy stops him.

HAPPY: Stanley!

Stanley stands by, waiting for an order.

BIFF, *going to Willy, with guilt, as to an invalid*:   Sit down, Pop. You want a drink?

WILLY: Sure, I don't mind.

BIFF: Let's get a load on.

WILLY: You look worried.

BIFF: N-no. *To Stanley:* Scotch all around. Make it doubles.

STANLEY: Doubles, right. *He goes.*

WILLY: You had a couple already, didn't you?

BIFF: Just a couple, yeah.

WILLY: Well, what happened, boy? *Nodding affirmatively, with a smile:* Everything go all right?

BIFF, *takes a breath, then reaches out and grasps Willy's hand*:   Pal . . . *He is smiling bravely, and Willy is smiling too.* I had an experience today.

HAPPY: Terrific, Pop.

WILLY: That so? What happened?

BIFF, *high, slightly alcoholic, above the earth*:   I'm going to tell you everything from first to last. It's been a strange day. *Silence. He looks around, composes himself as best he can, but his breath keeps breaking the rhythm of his voice.* I had to wait quite a while for him, and—

WILLY: Oliver?

BIFF: Yeah, Oliver. All day, as a matter of cold fact. And a lot of—instances—facts, Pop, facts about my life came back to me. Who was it, Pop? Who ever said I was a salesman with Oliver?

WILLY: Well, you were.

BIFF: No, Dad, I was a shipping clerk.

WILLY: But you were practically—

BIFF, *with determination*:   Dad, I don't know who said it first, but I was never a salesman for Bill Oliver.

WILLY: What're you talking about?

BIFF: Let's hold on to the facts tonight, Pop. We're not going to get anywhere bullin' around. I was a shipping clerk.

WILLY, *angrily*:   All right, now listen to me—

BIFF: Why don't you let me finish?

WILLY: I'm not interested in stories about the past or any crap of that kind because the woods are burning, boys, you understand? There's a big blaze going on all around. I was fired today.

BIFF, *shocked*:   How could you be?

WILLY: I was fired, and I'm looking for a little good news to tell your mother, because the woman has waited and the woman has suffered. The gist of it is that I haven't got a story left in my head, Biff. So don't give me a lecture about facts and aspects. I am not interested. Now what've you got to say to me?

Stanley enters with three drinks. They wait until he leaves.

WILLY: Did you see Oliver?

BIFF: Jesus, Dad!

WILLY: You mean you didn't go up there?

HAPPY: Sure he went up there.

BIFF: I did. I—saw him. How could they fire you?

WILLY, *on the edge of his chair*: What kind of a welcome did he give you?

BIFF: He won't even let you work on commission?

WILLY: I'm out! *Driving:* So tell me, he gave you a warm welcome?

HAPPY: Sure, Pop, sure!

BIFF, *driven*: Well, it was kind of—

WILLY: I was wondering if he'd remember you. *To Happy:* Imagine, man doesn't see him for ten, twelve years and gives him that kind of welcome!

HAPPY: Damn right!

BIFF, *trying to return to the offensive*: Pop, look—

WILLY: You know why he remembered you, don't you? Because you impressed him in those days.

BIFF: Let's talk quietly and get this down to the facts, huh?

WILLY, *as though Biff had been interrupting*: Well, what happened? It's great news, Biff. Did he take you into his office or'd you talk in the waiting-room?

BIFF: Well, he came in, see, and—

WILLY, *with a big smile*: What'd he say? Betcha he threw his arm around you.

BIFF: Well, he kinda—

WILLY: He's a fine man. *To Happy:* Very hard man to see, y'know.

HAPPY, *agreeing*: Oh, I know.

WILLY, *to Biff*: Is that where you had the drinks?

BIFF: Yeah, he gave me a couple of—no, no!

HAPPY, *cutting in*: He told him my Florida idea.

WILLY: Don't interrupt. *To Biff:* How'd he react to the Florida idea?

BIFF: Dad, will you give me a minute to explain?

WILLY: I've been waiting for you to explain since I sat down here! What happened? He took you into his office and what?

BIFF: Well—I talked. And—and he listened, see.

WILLY: Famous for the way he listens, y'know. What was his answer?

BIFF: His answer was— *He breaks off, suddenly angry.* Dad, you're not letting me tell you what I want to tell you!

WILLY, *accusing, angered*: You didn't see him, did you?

BIFF: I did see him!

WILLY: What'd you insult him or something? You insulted him, didn't you?

BIFF: Listen, will you let me out of it, will you just let me out of it!

HAPPY: What the hell!

WILLY: Tell me what happened!

BIFF, *to Happy*: I can't talk to him!

A single trumpet note jars the ear. The light of green leaves stains the house, which holds the air of night and a dream. Young Bernard enters and knocks on the door of the house.

YOUNG BERNARD, *frantically*:   Mrs. Loman, Mrs. Loman!
HAPPY: Tell him what happened!
BIFF, *to Happy*:   Shut up and leave me alone!
WILLY: No, no! You had to go and flunk math!
BIFF: What math? What're you talking about?
YOUNG BERNARD: Mrs. Loman, Mrs. Loman!

Linda appears in the house, as of old.

WILLY, *wildly*:   Math, math, math!
BIFF: Take it easy, Pop!
YOUNG BERNARD: Mrs. Loman!
WILLY, *furiously*:   If you hadn't flunked you'd've been set by now!
BIFF: Now, look, I'm gonna tell you what happened, and you're going to listen to me.
YOUNG BERNARD: Mrs. Loman!
BIFF: I waited six hours—
HAPPY: What the hell are you saying?
BIFF: I kept sending in my name but he wouldn't see me. So finally he . . . *He continues unheard as light fades low on the restaurant.*
YOUNG BERNARD: Biff flunked math!
LINDA: No!
YOUNG BERNARD: Birnbaum flunked him! They won't graduate him!
LINDA: But they have to. He's gotta go to the university. Where is he? Biff! Biff!
YOUNG BERNARD: No, he left. He went to Grand Central.
LINDA: Grand—You mean he went to Boston!
YOUNG BERNARD: Is Uncle Willy in Boston?
LINDA: Oh, maybe Willy can talk to the teacher. Oh, the poor, poor boy!

Light on house area snaps out.

BIFF, *at the table, now audible, holding up a gold fountain pen*:   . . . so I'm washed up with Oliver, you understand? Are you listening to me?
WILLY, *at a loss*:   Yeah, sure. If you hadn't flunked—
BIFF: Flunked what? What're you talking about?
WILLY: Don't blame everything on me! I didn't flunk math—you did! What pen?
HAPPY: That was awful dumb, Biff, a pen like that is worth—
WILLY, *seeing the pen for the first time*:   You took Oliver's pen?
BIFF, *weakening*:   Dad, I just explained it to you.
WILLY: You stole Bill Oliver's fountain pen!
BIFF: I didn't exactly steal it! That's just what I've been explaining to you!
HAPPY: He had it in his hand and just then Oliver walked in, so he got nervous and stuck it in his pocket!

WILLY: My God, Biff!

BIFF: I never intended to do it, Dad!

OPERATOR'S VOICE: Standish Arms, good evening!

WILLY, *shouting*:   I'm not in my room!

BIFF, *frightened*:   Dad, what's the matter? *He and Happy stand up.*

OPERATOR: Ringing Mr. Loman for you!

WILLY: I'm not there, stop it!

BIFF, *horrified, gets down on one knee before Willy*:   Dad, I'll make good, I'll make good. *Willy tries to get to his feet. Biff holds him down.* Sit down now.

WILLY: No, you're no good, you're no good for anything.

BIFF: I am, Dad, I'll find something else, you understand? Now don't worry about anything. *He holds up Willy's face:* Talk to me, Dad.

OPERATOR: Mr. Loman does not answer. Shall I page him?

WILLY, *attempting to stand, as though to rush and silence the Operator*:   No, no, no!

HAPPY: He'll strike something, Pop.

WILLY: No, no . . .

BIFF, *desperately, standing over Willy*:   Pop, listen! Listen to me! I'm telling you something good. Oliver talked to his partner about the Florida idea. You listening? He—he talked to his partner, and he came to me . . . I'm going to be all right, you hear? Dad, listen to me, he said it was just a question of the amount!

WILLY: Then you . . . got it?

HAPPY: He's gonna be terrific, Pop!

WILLY, *trying to stand*:   Then you got it, haven't you? You got it! You got it!

BIFF, *agonized, holds Willy down*:   No, no. Look, Pop. I'm supposed to have lunch with them tomorrow. I'm just telling you this so you'll know that I can still make an impression, Pop. And I'll make good somewhere, but I can't go tomorrow, see?

WILLY: Why not? You simply—

BIFF: But the pen, Pop!

WILLY: You give it to him and tell him it was an oversight!

HAPPY: Sure, have lunch tomorrow!

BIFF: I can't say that—

WILLY: You were doing a crossword puzzle and accidentally used his pen!

BIFF: Listen, kid, I took those balls years ago, now I walk in with his fountain pen? That clinches it, don't you see? I can't face him like that! I'll try elsewhere.

PAGE'S VOICE: Paging Mr. Loman!

WILLY: Don't you want to be anything?

BIFF: Pop, how can I go back?

WILLY: You don't want to be anything, is that what's behind it?

BIFF, *now angry at Willy for not crediting his sympathy*:   Don't take it that way! You think it was easy walking into that office after what I'd done to him? A team of horses couldn't have dragged me back to Bill Oliver!

WILLY: Then why'd you go?

BIFF: Why did I go? Why did I go! Look at you! Look at what's become of you!

Off left, The Woman laughs.

WILLY: Biff, you're going to go to that lunch tomorrow, or—
BIFF: I can't go. I've got no appointment!
HAPPY: Biff, for . . . !
WILLY: Are you spiting me?
BIFF: Don't take it that way! Goddammit!
WILLY, *strikes Biff and falters away from the table*:   You rotten little louse!
    Are you spiting me?
THE WOMAN: Someone's at the door, Willy!
BIFF: I'm no good, can't you see what I am?
HAPPY, *separating them*:   Hey, you're in a restaurant! Now cut it out, both
    of you! *The girls enter.* Hello, girls, sit down.

The Woman laughs, off left.

MISS FORSYTHE: I guess we might as well. This is Letta.
THE WOMAN: Willy, are you going to wake up?
BIFF, *ignoring Willy*:   How're ya, miss, sit down. What do you drink?
MISS FORSYTHE: Letta might not be able to stay long.
LETTA: I gotta get up very early tomorrow. I got jury duty. I'm so ex-
    cited! Were you fellows ever on a jury?
BIFF: No, but I been in front of them! *The girls laugh.* This is my father.
LETTA: Isn't he cute? Sit down with us, Pop.
HAPPY: Sit him down, Biff!
BIFF, *going to him*:   Come on, slugger, drink us under the table. To hell
    with it! Come on, sit down, pal.

On Biff's last insistence, Willy is about to sit.

THE WOMAN, *now urgently*:   Willy, are you going to answer the door!

The Woman's call pulls Willy back. He starts right, befuddled.

BIFF: Hey, where are you going?
WILLY: Open the door.
BIFF: The door?
WILLY: The washroom . . . the door . . . where's the door?
BIFF, *leading Willy to the left:* Just go straight down.

Willy moves left.

THE WOMAN: Willy, Willy, are you going to get up, get up, get up, get
    up?

Willy exits left.

LETTA: I think it's sweet you bring your daddy along.
MISS FORSYTHE: Oh, he isn't really your father!

BIFF, *at left, turning to her resentfully*: Miss Forsythe, you've just seen a prince walk by. A fine, troubled prince. A hardworking, unappreciated prince. A pal, you understand? A good companion. Always for his boys.

LETTA: That's so sweet.

HAPPY: Well, girls, what's the program? We're wasting time. Come on, Biff. Gather round. Where would you like to go?

BIFF: Why don't you do something for him?

HAPPY: Me!

BIFF: Don't you give a damn for him, Hap?

HAPPY: What're you talking about? I'm the one who—

BIFF: I sense it, you don't give a good goddam about him. *He takes the rolled-up hose from his pocket and puts it on the table in front of Happy.* Look what I found in the cellar, for Christ's sake. How can you bear to let it go on?

HAPPY: Me? Who goes away? Who runs off and—

BIFF: Yeah, but he doesn't mean anything to you. You could help him— I can't! Don't you understand what I'm talking about? He's going to kill himself, don't you know that?

HAPPY: Don't I know it! Me!

BIFF: Hap, help him! Jesus . . . help him . . . Help me, help me, I can't bear to look at his face! *Ready to weep, he hurries out, up right.*

HAPPY, *starting after him*: Where are you going?

MISS FORSYTHE: What's he so mad about?

HAPPY: Come on, girls, we'll catch up with him.

MISS FORSYTHE, *as Happy pushes her out*: Say, I don't like that temper of his!

HAPPY: He's just a little overstrung, he'll be all right!

WILLY, *off left, as The Woman laughs*: Don't answer! Don't answer!

LETTA: Don't you want to tell your father—

HAPPY: No, that's not my father. He's just a guy. Come on, we'll catch Biff, and, honey, we're going to paint this town! Stanley, where's the check! Hey, Stanley!

They exit. Stanley looks toward left.

STANLEY, *calling to Happy indignantly*: Mr. Loman! Mr. Loman!

Stanley picks up a chair and follows them off. Knocking is heard off left. The Woman enters, laughing. Willy follows her. She is in a black slip; he is buttoning his shirt. Raw, sensuous music accompanies their speech.

WILLY: Will you stop laughing? Will you stop?

THE WOMAN: Aren't you going to answer the door? He'll wake the whole hotel.

WILLY: I'm not expecting anybody.

THE WOMAN: Whyn't you have another drink, honey, and stop being so damn self-centered?

WILLY: I'm so lonely.

THE WOMAN: You know you ruined me, Willy? From now on, whenever you come to the office, I'll see that you go right through to the buyers. No waiting at my desk any more, Willy. You ruined me.

WILLY: That's nice of you to say that.

THE WOMAN: Gee, you are self-centered! Why so sad? You are the saddest, self-centeredest soul I ever did see-saw. *She laughs. He kisses her.* Come on inside, drummer boy. It's silly to be dressing in the middle of the night. *As knocking is heard:* Aren't you going to answer the door?

WILLY: They're knocking on the wrong door.

THE WOMAN: But I felt the knocking. And he heard us talking in here. Maybe the hotel's on fire!

WILLY, *his terror rising*: It's a mistake.

THE WOMAN: Then tell him to go away!

WILLY: There's nobody there.

THE WOMAN: It's getting on my nerves, Willy. There's somebody standing out there and it's getting on my nerves!

WILLY, *pushing her away from him*: All right, stay in the bathroom here, and don't come out. I think there's a law in Massachusetts about it, so don't come out. It may be that new room clerk. He looked very mean. So don't come out. It's a mistake, there's no fire.

The knocking is heard again. He takes a few steps away from her, and she vanishes into the wing. The light follows him, and now he is facing Young Biff, who carries a suitcase. Biff steps toward him. The music is gone.

BIFF: Why didn't you answer?

WILLY: Biff! What are you doing in Boston?

BIFF: Why didn't you answer? I've been knocking for five minutes, I called you on the phone—

WILLY: I just heard you. I was in the bathroom and had the door shut. Did anything happen home?

BIFF: Dad—I let you down.

WILLY: What do you mean?

BIFF: Dad . . .

WILLY: Biffo, what's this about? *Putting his arm around Biff:* Come on, let's go downstairs and get you a malted.

BIFF: Dad, I flunked math.

WILLY: Not for the term?

BIFF: The term. I haven't got enough credits to graduate.

WILLY: You mean to say Bernard wouldn't give you the answers?

BIFF: He did, he tried, but I only got a sixty-one.

WILLY: And they wouldn't give you four points?

BIFF: Birnbaum refused absolutely. I begged him, Pop, but he won't give me those points. You gotta talk to him before they close the school. Because if he saw the kind of man you are, and you just talked to him in your way, I'm sure he'd come through for me. The class came right before practice, see, and I didn't go enough. Would you talk to him? He'd like you, Pop. You know the way you could talk.

WILLY: You're on. We'll drive right back.

BIFF: Oh, Dad, good work! I'm sure he'll change it for you!

WILLY: Go downstairs and tell the clerk I'm checkin' out. Go right down.

BIFF: Yes, sir! See, the reason he hates me, Pop—one day he was late for class so I got up at the blackboard and imitated him. I crossed my eyes and talked with a lithp.

WILLY, *laughing*:   You did? The kids like it?

BIFF: They nearly died laughing!

WILLY: Yeah? What'd you do?

BIFF: The thquare root of thixthy twee is . . . *Willy bursts out laughing; Biff joins him.* And in the middle of it he walked in!

Willy laughs and The Woman joins in offstage.

WILLY, *without hesitation*:   Hurry downstairs and—

BIFF: Somebody in there?

WILLY: No, that was next door.

The Woman laughs offstage.

BIFF: Somebody got in your bathroom!

WILLY: No, it's the next room, there's a party—

THE WOMAN, *enters, laughing. She lisps this*:   Can I come in? There's something in the bathtub, Willy, and it's moving!

Willy looks at Biff, who is staring open-mouthed and horrified at The Woman.

WILLY: Ah—you better go back to your room. They must be finished painting by now. They're painting her room so I let her take a shower here. Go back, go back . . . *He pushes her.*

THE WOMAN, *resisting*:   But I've got to get dressed, Willy, I can't—

WILLY: Get out of here! Go back, go back . . . *Suddenly striving for the ordinary:* This is Miss Francis, Biff, she's a buyer. They're painting her room. Go back, Miss Francis, go back . . .

THE WOMAN: But my clothes, I can't go out naked in the hall!

WILLY, *pushing her offstage*:   Get outa here! Go back, go back!

Biff slowly sits down on his suitcase as the argument continues offstage.

THE WOMAN: Where's my stockings? You promised me stockings, Willy!

WILLY: I have no stockings here!

THE WOMAN: You had two boxes of size nine sheers for me, and I want them!

WILLY: Here, for God's sake, will you get outa here!

THE WOMAN, *enters holding a box of stockings*:   I just hope there's nobody in the hall. That's all I hope. *To Biff:* Are you football or baseball?

BIFF: Football.

THE WOMAN, *angry, humiliated*:   That's me too. G'night. *She snatches her clothes from Willy, and walks out.*

WILLY, *after a pause*:   Well, better get going. I want to get to the school first thing in the morning. Get my suits out of the closet. I'll get my valise. *Biff doesn't move.* What's the matter? *Biff remains motionless, tears falling.* She's a buyer. Buys for J. H. Simmons. She lives down the hall—they're painting. You don't imagine— *He breaks off. After a pause:* Now listen, pal, she's just a buyer. She sees merchandise in her room and they have to keep it looking just so . . . *Pause. Assuming command:* All right, get my suits. *Biff doesn't move.* Now stop crying and do as I say. I gave you an order. Biff, I gave you an order! Is that what you do when I give you an order? How dare you cry! *Putting his arm around Biff:* Now look, Biff, when you grow up you'll understand about these things. You mustn't—you mustn't overemphasize a thing like this. I'll see Birnbaum first thing in the morning.

BIFF: Never mind.

WILLY, *getting down beside Biff*:   Never mind! He's going to give you those points. I'll see to it.

BIFF: He wouldn't listen to you.

WILLY: He certainly will listen to me. You need those points for the U. of Virginia.

BIFF: I'm not going there.

WILLY: Heh? If I can't get him to change that mark you'll make it up in summer school. You've got all summer to—

BIFF, *his weeping breaking from him*:   Dad . . .

WILLY, *infected by it*:   Oh, my boy . . .

BIFF: Dad . . .

WILLY: She's nothing to me, Biff. I was lonely, I was terribly lonely.

BIFF: You—you gave her Mama's stockings! *His tears break through and he rises to go.*

WILLY, *grabbing for Biff*:   I gave you an order!

BIFF: Don't touch me, you—liar!

WILLY: Apologize for that!

BIFF: You fake! You phony little fake! You fake! *Overcome, he turns quickly and weeping fully goes out with his suitcase. Willy is left on the floor on his knees.*

WILLY: I gave you an order! Biff, come back here or I'll beat you! Come back here! I'll whip you!

Stanley comes quickly in from the right and stands in front of Willy.

WILLY, *shouts at Stanley*:   I gave you an order . . .

STANLEY: Hey, let's pick it up, pick it up, Mr. Loman. *He helps Willy to his feet.* Your boys left with the chippies. They said they'll see you home.

A second waiter watches some distance away.

WILLY: But we were supposed to have dinner together.

Music is heard, Willy's theme.

STANLEY: Can you make it?

WILLY: I'll—sure, I can make it. *Suddenly concerned about his clothes:* Do I—I look all right?

STANLEY: Sure, you look all right. *He flicks a speck off Willy's lapel.*

WILLY: Here—here's a dollar.

STANLEY: Oh, your son paid me. It's all right.

WILLY, *putting it in Stanley's hand:*   No, take it. You're a good boy.

STANLEY: Oh, no, you don't have to . . .

WILLY: Here—here's some more, I don't need it any more. *After a slight pause:* Tell me—is there a seed store in the neighborhood?

STANLEY: Seeds? You mean like to plant?

As Willy turns, Stanley slips the money back into his jacket pocket.

WILLY: Yes. Carrots, peas . . .

STANLEY: Well, there's hardware stores on Sixth Avenue, but it may be too late now.

WILLY, *anxiously:*   Oh, I'd better hurry. I've got to get some seeds. *He starts off to the right.* I've got to get some seeds, right away. Nothing's planted. I don't have a thing in the ground.

Willy hurries out as the light goes down. Stanley moves over to the right after him, watches him off. The other waiter has been staring at Willy.

STANLEY, *to the waiter:*   Well, whatta you looking at?

The waiter picks up the chairs and moves off right. Stanley takes the table and follows him. The light fades on this area. There is a long pause, the sound of the flute coming over. The light gradually rises on the kitchen, which is empty. Happy appears at the door of the house, followed by Biff. Happy is carrying a large bunch of long-stemmed roses. He enters the kitchen, looks around for Linda. Not seeing her, he turns to Biff, who is just outside the house door, and makes a gesture with his hands, indicating "Not here, I guess." He looks into the living-room and freezes. Inside, Linda, unseen, is seated, Willy's coat on her lap. She rises ominously and quietly and moves toward Happy, who backs up into the kitchen, afraid.

HAPPY: Hey, what're you doing up? *Linda says nothing but moves toward him implacably.* Where's Pop? *He keeps backing to the right, and now Linda is in full view in the doorway to the living-room.* Is he sleeping?

LINDA: Where were you?

HAPPY, *trying to laugh it off:*   We met two girls, Mom, very fine types. Here, we brought you some flowers. *Offering them to her:* Put them in your room, Ma.

She knocks them to the floor at Biff's feet. He has now come inside and closed the door behind him. She stares at Biff, silent.

HAPPY: Now what'd you do that for? Mom, I want you to have some flowers—

LINDA, *cutting Happy off, violently to Biff*:   Don't you care whether he lives or dies?

HAPPY, *going to the stairs*:   Come upstairs, Biff.

BIFF, *with a flare of disgust, to Happy*:   Go away from me! *To Linda:* What do you mean, lives or dies? Nobody's dying around here, pal.

LINDA: Get out of my sight! Get out of here!

BIFF: I wanna see the boss.

LINDA: You're not going near him!

BIFF: Where is he? *He moves into the living-room and Linda follows.*

LINDA, *shouting after Biff*:   You invite him for dinner. He looks forward to it all day—*Biff appears in his parents' bedroom, looks around, and exits*—and then you desert him there. There's no stranger you'd do that to!

HAPPY: Why? He had a swell time with us. Listen, when I—*Linda comes back into the kitchen*—desert him I hope I don't outlive the day!

LINDA: Get out of here!

HAPPY: Now look, Mom . . .

LINDA: Did you have to go to women tonight? You and your lousy rotten whores!

Biff re-enters the kitchen.

HAPPY: Mom, all we did was follow Biff around trying to cheer him up! *To Biff:* Boy, what a night you gave me!

LINDA: Get out of here, both of you, and don't come back! I don't want you tormenting him any more. Go on now, get your things together! *To Biff:* You can sleep in his apartment. *She starts to pick up the flowers and stops herself.* Pick up this stuff, I'm not your maid any more. Pick it up, you bum, you!

Happy turns his back to her in refusal. Biff slowly moves over and gets down on his knees, picking up the flowers.

LINDA: You're a pair of animals! Not one, not another living soul would have had the cruelty to walk out on that man in a restaurant!

BIFF, *not looking at her*:   Is that what he said?

LINDA: He didn't have to say anything. He was so humiliated he nearly limped when he came in.

HAPPY: But, Mom, he had a great time with us—

BIFF, *cutting him off violently*:   Shut up!

Without another word, Happy goes upstairs.

LINDA: You! You didn't even go in to see if he was all right!

BIFF, *still on the floor in front of Linda, the flowers in his hand; with self-loathing*: No. Didn't. Didn't do a damned thing. How do you like that, heh? Left him babbling in a toilet.

LINDA: You louse, You . . .

BIFF: Now you hit it on the nose! *He gets up, throws the flowers in the wastebasket.* The scum of the earth, and you're looking at him!

LINDA: Get out of here!

BIFF: I gotta talk to the boss, Mom. Where is he?

LINDA: You're not going near him. Get out of this house!

BIFF, *with absolute assurance, determination*: No. We're gonna have an abrupt conversation, him and me.

LINDA: You're not talking to him!

Hammering is heard from outside the house, off right. Biff turns toward the noise.

LINDA, *suddenly pleading*: Will you please leave him alone?

BIFF: What's he doing out there?

LINDA: He's planting the garden!

BIFF, *quietly*: Now? Oh, my God!

Biff moves outside, Linda following. The light dies down on them and comes up on the center of the apron as Willy walks into it. He is carrying a flashlight, a hoe, and a handful of seed packets. He raps the top of the hoe sharply to fix it firmly, and then moves to the left, measuring off the distance with his foot. He holds the flashlight to look at the seed packets, reading off the instructions. He is in the blue of night.

WILLY: Carrots . . . quarter-inch apart. Rows . . . one-foot rows. *He measures it off.* One foot. *He puts down a package and measures off.* Beets. *He puts down another package and measures again.* Lettuce. *He reads the package, puts it down.* One foot—*He breaks off as Ben appears at the right and moves slowly down to him.* What a proposition, ts, ts. Terrific, terrific. 'Cause she's suffered, Ben, the woman has suffered. You understand me? A man can't go out the way he came in, Ben, a man has got to add up to something. You can't, you can't—*Ben moves toward him as though to interrupt.* You gotta consider, now. Don't answer so quick. Remember, it's a guaranteed twenty-thousand-dollar proposition. Now look, Ben, I want you to go through the ins and outs of this thing with me. I've got nobody to talk to, Ben, and the woman has suffered, you hear me?

BEN, *standing still, considering*: What's the proposition?

WILLY: It's twenty thousand dollars on the barrelhead. Guaranteed, gilt-edged, you understand?

BEN: You don't want to make a fool of yourself. They might not honor the policy.

WILLY: How can they dare refuse? Didn't I work like a coolie to meet every premium on the nose? And now they don't pay off? Impossible!

BEN: It's called a cowardly thing, William.

WILLY: Why? Does it take more guts to stand here the rest of my life ringing up a zero?

BEN, *yielding*:   That's a point, William. *He moves, thinking, turns.* And twenty thousand—that *is* something one can feel with the hand, it is there.

WILLY, *now assured, with rising power*:   Oh, Ben, that's the whole beauty of it! I see it like a diamond, shining in the dark, hard and rough, that I can pick up and touch in my hand. Not like—like an appointment! This would not be another damned-fool appointment, Ben, and it changes all the aspects. Because he thinks I'm nothing, see, and so he spites me. But the funeral— *Straightening up:* Ben, that funeral will be massive! They'll come from Maine, Massachusetts, Vermont, New Hampshire! All the old-timers with the strange license plates—that boy will be thunder-struck, Ben, because he never realized—I am known! Rhode Island, New York, New Jersey—I am known, Ben, and he'll see it with his eyes once and for all. He'll see what I am, Ben! He's in for a shock, that boy!

BEN, *coming down to the edge of the garden*:   He'll call you a coward.

WILLY, *suddenly fearful*:   No, that would be terrible.

BEN: Yes. And a damned fool.

WILLY: No, no, he mustn't, I won't have that! *He is broken and desperate.*

BEN: He'll hate you, William.

The gay music of the Boys is heard.

WILLY: Oh, Ben, how do we get back to all the great times? Used to be so full of light, and comradeship, the sleigh-riding in winter, and the ruddiness on his cheeks. And always some kind of good news coming up, always something nice coming up ahead. And never even let me carry the valises in the house, and simonizing, simonizing that little red car! Why, why can't I give him something and not have him hate me?

BEN: Let me think about it. *He glances at his watch.* I still have a little time. Remarkable proposition, but you've got to be sure you're not making a fool of yourself.

Ben drifts off upstage and goes out of sight. Biff comes down from the left.

WILLY, *suddenly conscious of Biff, turns and looks up at him, then begins picking up the packages of seeds in confusion*:   Where the hell is that seed? *Indignantly:* You can't see nothing out here! They boxed in the whole goddam neighborhood!

BIFF: There are people all around here. Don't you realize that?

WILLY: I'm busy. Don't bother me.

BIFF, *taking the hoe from Willy*:   I'm saying good-by to you, Pop. *Willy looks at him, silent, unable to move.* I'm not coming back any more.

WILLY: You're not going to see Oliver tomorrow?

BIFF: I've got no appointment, Dad.

WILLY: He put his arm around you, and you've got no appointment?

BIFF: Pop, get this now, will you? Everytime I've left it's been a fight that sent me out of here. Today I realized something about myself and I tried to explain it to you and I—I think I'm just not smart enough to make any sense out of it for you. To hell with whose fault it is or anything like that. *He takes Willy's arm.* Let's just wrap it up, heh? Come on in, we'll tell Mom. *He gently tries to pull Willy to left.*

WILLY, *frozen, immobile, with guilt in his voice*: No, I don't want to see her.

BIFF: Come on! *He pulls again, and Willy tries to pull away.*

WILLY, *highly nervous*: No, no, I don't want to see her.

BIFF, *tries to look into Willy's face, as if to find the answer there*: Why don't you want to see her?

WILLY, *more harshly now*: Don't bother me, will you?

BIFF: What do you mean, you don't want to see her? You don't want them calling you yellow, do you? This isn't your fault; it's me, I'm a bum. Now come inside! *Willy strains to get away.* Did you hear what I said to you?

Willy pulls away and quickly goes by himself into the house. Biff follows.

LINDA, *to Willy*: Did you plant, dear?

BIFF, *at the door, to Linda*: All right, we had it out. I'm going and I'm not writing any more.

LINDA, *going to Willy in the kitchen*: I think that's the best way, dear. 'Cause there's no use drawing it out, you'll just never get along.

Willy doesn't respond.

BIFF: People ask where I am and what I'm doing, you don't know, and you don't care. That way it'll be off your mind and you can start brightening up again. All right? That clears it, doesn't it? *Willy is silent, and Biff goes to him.* You gonna wish me luck, scout? *He extends his hand.* What do you say?

LINDA: Shake his hand, Willy.

WILLY, *turning to her, seething with hurt*: There's no necessity to mention the pen at all, y'know.

BIFF, *gently*: I've got no appointment, Dad.

WILLY, *erupting fiercely*: He put his arm around . . . ?

BIFF: Dad, you're never going to see what I am, so what's the use of arguing? If I strike oil I'll send you a check. Meantime forget I'm alive.

WILLY, *to Linda*: Spite, see?

BIFF: Shake hands, Dad.

WILLY: Not my hand.

BIFF: I was hoping not to go this way.

WILLY: Well, this is the way you're going. Good-by.

Biff looks at him a moment, then turns sharply and goes to the stairs.

WILLY, *stops him with*: May you rot in hell if you leave this house!

BIFF, *turning*: Exactly what is it that you want from me?

WILLY: I want you to know, on the train, in the mountains, in the valleys, wherever you go, that you cut down your life for spite!

BIFF: No, no.

WILLY: Spite, spite, is the word of your undoing! And when you're down and out, remember what did it. When you're rotting somewhere beside the railroad tracks, remember, and don't you dare blame it on me!

BIFF: I'm not blaming it on you!

WILLY: I won't take the rap for this, you hear?

Happy comes down the stairs and stands on the bottom step, watching.

BIFF: That's just what I'm telling you!

WILLY, *sinking into a chair at the table, with full accusation*: You're trying to put a knife in me—don't think I don't know what you're doing!

BIFF: All right, phony! Then let's lay it on the line. *He whips the rubber tube out of his pocket and puts it on the table.*

HAPPY: You crazy—

LINDA: Biff! *She moves to grab the hose, but Biff holds it down with his hand.*

BIFF: Leave it there! Don't move it!

WILLY, *not looking at it*: What is that?

BIFF: You know goddam well what that is.

WILLY, *caged, wanting to escape*: I never saw that.

BIFF: You saw it. The mice didn't bring it into the cellar! What is this supposed to do, make a hero out of you? This supposed to make me sorry for you?

WILLY: Never heard of it.

BIFF: There'll be no pity for you, you hear it? No pity!

WILLY, *to Linda*: You hear the spite!

BIFF: No, you're going to hear the truth—what you are and what I am!

LINDA: Stop it!

WILLY: Spite!

HAPPY, *coming down toward Biff*: You cut it now!

BIFF, *to Happy*: The man don't know who we are! The man is gonna know! *To Willy:* We never told the truth for ten minutes in this house!

HAPPY: We always told the truth!

BIFF, *turning on him*: You big blow, are you the assistant buyer? You're one of the two assistants to the assistant, aren't you?

HAPPY: Well, I'm practically—

BIFF: You're practically full of it! We all are! And I'm through with it. *To Willy:* Now hear this, Willy, this is me.

WILLY: I know you!

BIFF: You know why I had no address for three months? I stole a suit in Kansas City and I was in jail. *To Linda, who is sobbing:* Stop crying. I'm through with it.

Linda turns away from them, her hands covering her face.

WILLY: I suppose that's my fault!

BIFF: I stole myself out of every good job since high school!

WILLY: And whose fault is that?

BIFF: And I never got anywhere because you blew me so full of hot air I could never stand taking orders from anybody! That's whose fault it is!

WILLY: I hear that!

LINDA: Don't, Biff!

BIFF: It's goddam time you heard that! I had to be boss big shot in two weeks, and I'm through with it!

WILLY: Then hang yourself! For spite, hang yourself!

BIFF: No! Nobody's hanging himself, Willy! I ran down eleven flights with a pen in my hand today. And suddenly I stopped, you hear me? And in the middle of that office building, do you hear this? I stopped in the middle of that building and I saw—the sky. I saw the things that I love in this world. The work and the food and time to sit and smoke. And I looked at the pen and said to myself, what the hell am I grabbing this for? Why am I trying to become what I don't want to be? What am I doing in an office, making a contemptuous, begging fool of myself, when all I want is out there, waiting for me the minute I say I know who I am! Why can't I say that, Willy? *He tries to make Willy face him, but Willy pulls away and moves to the left.*

WILLY, *with hatred, threateningly*:   The door of your life is wide open!

BIFF: Pop! I'm a dime a dozen, and so are you!

WILLY, *turning on him now in an uncontrolled outburst*:   I am not a dime a dozen! I am Willy Loman, and you are Biff Loman!

Biff starts for Willy, but is blocked by Happy. In his fury, Biff seems on the verge of attacking his father.

BIFF: I am not a leader of men, Willy, and neither are you. You were never anything but a hard-working drummer who landed in the ash can like all the rest of them! I'm one dollar an hour, Willy! I tried seven states and couldn't raise it. A buck an hour! Do you gather my meaning? I'm not bringing home any prizes any more, and you're going to stop waiting for me to bring them home!

WILLY, *directly to Biff*:   You vengeful, spiteful mut!

Biff breaks from Happy. Willy, in fright, starts up the stairs. Biff grabs him.

BIFF, *at the peak of his fury*:   Pop, I'm nothing! I'm nothing, Pop. Can't you understand that? There's no spite in it any more. I'm just what I am, that's all.

Biff's fury has spent itself, and he breaks down, sobbing, holding on to Willy, who dumbly fumbles for Biff's face.

WILLY, *astonished*:   What're you doing? What're you doing? *To Linda:* Why is he crying?

BIFF, *crying broken*:   Will you let me go, for Christ's sake? Will you take that phony dream and burn it before something happens? *Struggling to contain himself, he pulls away and moves to the stairs.* I'll go in the morning. Put him—put him to bed. *Exhausted, Biff moves up the stairs to his room.*

WILLY, *after a long pause, astonished, elevated*:   Isn't that—isn't that remarkable? Biff—he likes me!

LINDA: He loves you, Willy!

HAPPY, *deeply moved*:   Always did, Pop.

WILLY: Oh, Biff! *Staring wildly:* He cried! Cried to me. *He is choking with his love, and now cries out his promise:* That boy—that boy is going to be magnificent!

Ben appears in the light just outside the kitchen.

BEN: Yes, outstanding, with twenty thousand behind him.

LINDA, *sensing the racing of his mind, fearfully, carefully*:   Now come to bed, Willy. It's all settled now.

WILLY, *finding it difficult not to rush out of the house*:   Yes, we'll sleep. Come on. Go to sleep, Hap.

BEN: And it does take a great kind of a man to crack the jungle.

In accents of dread, Ben's idyllic music starts up.

HAPPY, *his arm around Linda*:   I'm getting married, Pop, don't forget it. I'm changing everything. I'm gonna run that department before the year is up. You'll see, Mom. *He kisses her.*

BEN: The jungle is dark but full of diamonds, Willy.

Willy turns, moves, listening to Ben.

LINDA: Be good. You're both good boys, just act that way, that's all.

HAPPY: 'Night, Pop. *He goes upstairs.*

LINDA, *to Willy*:   Come, dear.

BEN, *with greater force*:   One must go in to fetch a diamond out.

WILLY, *to Linda, as he moves slowly along the edge of the kitchen, toward the door*:   I just want to get settled down, Linda. Let me sit alone for a little.

LINDA, *almost uttering her fear*:   I want you upstairs.

WILLY, *taking her in his arms*:   In a few minutes, Linda. I couldn't sleep right now. Go on, you look awful tired. *He kisses her.*

BEN: Not like an appointment at all. A diamond is rough and hard to the touch.

WILLY: Go on now. I'll be right up.

LINDA: I think this is the only way, Willy.

WILLY: Sure, it's the best thing.

BEN: Best thing!

WILLY: The only way. Everything is gonna be—go on, kid, get to bed. You look so tired.

LINDA: Come right up.

WILLY: Two minutes.

Linda goes into the living-room, then reappears in her bedroom. Willy moves just outside the kitchen door.

WILLY: Loves me. *Wonderingly:* Always loved me. Isn't that a remarkable thing? Ben, he'll worship me for it!

BEN, *with promise:* It's dark there, but full of diamonds.

WILLY: Can you imagine that magnificence with twenty thousand dollars in his pocket?

LINDA, *calling from her room:* Willy! Come up!

WILLY, *calling into the kitchen:* Yes! Yes. Coming! It's very smart, you realize that, don't you, sweetheart? Even Ben sees it. I gotta go, baby. 'By! 'By! *Going over to Ben, almost dancing:* Imagine? When the mail comes he'll be ahead of Bernard again!

BEN: A perfect proposition all around.

WILLY: Did you see how he cried to me? Oh, if I could kiss him, Ben!

BEN: Time, William, time!

WILLY: Oh, Ben, I always knew one way or another we were gonna make it, Biff and I!

BEN, *looking at his watch:* The boat. We'll be late. *He moves slowly off into the darkness.*

WILLY, *elegiacally, turning to the house:* Now when you kick off, boy, I want a seventy-yard boot, and get right down the field under the ball, and when you hit, hit low and hit hard, because it's important, boy. *He swings around and faces the audience.* There's all kinds of important people in the stands, and the first thing you know . . . *Suddenly realizing he is alone:* Ben! Ben, where do I . . . ? *He makes a sudden movement of search.* Ben, how do I . . . ?

LINDA, *calling:* Willy, you coming up?

WILLY, *uttering a gasp of fear, whirling about as if to quiet her:* Sh! *He turns around as if to find his way; sounds, faces, voices, seem to be swarming in upon him and he flicks at them, crying, Sh! Sh! Suddenly music, faint and high, stops him. It rises in intensity, almost to an unbearable scream. He goes up and down on his toes, and rushes off around the house.* Shhh!

LINDA: Willy?

There is no answer. Linda waits. Biff gets up off his bed. He is still in his clothes. Happy sits up. Biff stands listening.

LINDA, *with real fear:* Willy, answer me! Willy!

There is the sound of a car starting and moving away at full speed.

LINDA: No!

BIFF, *rushing down the stairs*:   Pop!

As the car speeds off, the music crashes down in a frenzy of sound, which becomes the soft pulsation of a single cello string. Biff slowly returns to his bedroom. He and Happy gravely don their jackets. Linda slowly walks out of her room. The music has developed into a dead march. The leaves of day are appearing over everything. Charley and Bernard, somberly dressed, appear and knock on the kitchen door. Biff and Happy slowly descend the stairs to the kitchen as Charley and Bernard enter. All stop a moment when Linda, in clothes of mourning, bearing a little bunch of roses, comes through the draped doorway into the kitchen. She goes to Charley and takes his arm. Now all move toward the audience, through the wall-line of the kitchen. At the limit of the apron, Linda lays down the flowers, kneels, and sits back on her heels. All stare down at the grave.

REQUIEM

CHARLEY: It's getting dark, Linda.

Linda doesn't react. She stares at the grave.

BIFF: How about it, Mom? Better get some rest, heh? They'll be closing the gate soon.

Linda makes no move. Pause.

HAPPY, *deeply angered*:   He had no right to do that. There was no necessity for it. We would've helped him.

CHARLEY, *grunting*:   Hmmm.

BIFF: Come along, Mom.

LINDA: Why didn't anybody come?

CHARLEY: It was a very nice funeral.

LINDA: But where are all the people he knew? Maybe they blame him.

CHARLEY: Naa. It's a rough world, Linda. They wouldn't blame him.

LINDA: I can't understand it. At this time especially. First time in thirty-five years we were just about free and clear. He only needed a little salary. He was even finished with the dentist.

CHARLEY: No man only needs a little salary.

LINDA: I can't understand it.

BIFF: There were a lot of nice days. When he'd come home from a trip; or on Sundays, making the stoop; finishing the cellar; putting on the new porch; when he built the extra bathroom; and put up the garage. You know something, Charley, there's more of him in that front stoop than in all the sales he ever made.

CHARLEY: Yeah. He was a happy man with a batch of cement.

LINDA: He was so wonderful with his hands.

BIFF: He had the wrong dreams. All, all, wrong.

HAPPY, *almost ready to fight Biff*:   Don't say that!

BIFF: He never knew who he was.

CHARLEY, *stopping Happy's movement and reply. To Biff*:   Nobody dast blame this man. You don't understand: Willy was a salesman. And for a salesman, there is no rock bottom to the life. He don't put a bolt to a nut, he don't tell you the law or give you medicine. He's a man way out there in the blue, riding on a smile and a shoeshine. And when they start not smiling back—that's an earthquake. And then you get yourself a couple of spots on your hat, and you're finished. Nobody dast blame this man. A salesman is got to dream, boy. It comes with the territory.

BIFF: Charley, the man didn't know who he was.

HAPPY, *infuriated*:   Don't say that!

BIFF: Why don't you come with me, Happy?

HAPPY: I'm not licked that easily. I'm staying right in this city, and I'm gonna beat this racket! *He looks at Biff, his chin set.* The Loman Brothers!

BIFF: I know who I am, kid.

HAPPY: All right, boy. I'm gonna show you and everybody else that Willy Loman did not die in vain. He had a good dream. It's the only dream you can have—to come out number-one man. He fought it out here, and this is where I'm gonna win it for him.

BIFF, *with a hopeless glance at Happy, bends toward his mother*:   Let's go, Mom.

LINDA: I'll be with you in a minute. Go on, Charley. *He hesitates.* I want to, just for a minute. I never had a chance to say good-by.

Charley moves away, followed by Happy. Biff remains a slight distance up and left of Linda. She sits there, summoning herself. The flute begins, not far away, playing behind her speech.

LINDA: Forgive me, dear. I can't cry. I don't know what it is, but I can't cry. I don't understand it. Why did you ever do that? Help me, Willy, I can't cry. It seems to me that you're just on another trip. I keep expecting you. Willy, dear, I can't cry. Why did you do it? I search and search and I search, and I can't understand it, Willy. I made the last payment on the house today. Today, dear. And there'll be nobody home. *A sob rises in her throat.* We're free and clear. *Sobbing more fully, released:* We're free. *Biff comes slowly toward her.* We're free . . . We're free . . .

Biff lifts her to her feet and moves out up right with her in his arms. Linda sobs quietly. Bernard and Charley come together and follow them, followed by Happy. Only the music of the flute is left on the darkening stage as over the house the hard towers of the apartment buildings rise into sharp focus, and

The Curtain Falls

SECTION
3

The Elements of Drama

PLOT AND CHARACTER

In many ways, plot and character in drama resemble their counterparts in fiction. In most plays we find some kind of conflict with a background, a rising intensity, and a conclusion (either tragic or comic) that restores order. Similarly, we find characters caught up in conflict, either causing it or being affected by it. These characters are developed in accordance with their roles in the play, and are revealed to us by their appearance, their speech, and their actions.

What we know about fiction, then, will help us in our study of drama. However, as discussed in the previous chapter, there are fundamental differences between fiction read in a book and drama seen or heard upon a stage. Remember that even though we can read the texts of plays, we must treat them as words and deeds that are meant to be acted out in front of us. The key differences between fiction and drama as they handle plot and character lie in point of view and how it is constricted by a dramatic performance.

Space is the first constriction. Plays are meant to be acted out on a stage whose size and shape are limited so that the action can be seen by an audience. The stage as a defined space limits the number of characters a playwright can use, the kinds of actions they can perform, and the kind of world they can inhabit. One cannot literally portray a tired salesman driving a car upon a stage. A short story writer could display this event vividly to our imaginations; a playwright can only suggest it to our sight.

Time is a second constriction. Plots and characters develop and change in time. But a playwright is usually limited to less than three hours (though there have been some exceptions to this) to present the action. The time of the play's action may coincide with "real" time; or the passage of time can be suggested by changes of scenery, changes of costume, or, most importantly, through what the characters say. In any event, time governs the playwright in a different way than it does the writer of fiction.

A third constriction in the playwright's point of view lies in the **fact of performance,** the effects of which, though in some ways predictable and obvious, create difficulties as well as possibilities unique to playwrights. The presence of the actors, the visibility of the play's pageantry, and the audibility of the speeches lend an immediacy to a dramatic performance that poems, stories, or novels cannot really approximate. This immediacy, however, is tempered by two considerations caused by the fact of performance, which significantly influence the elements of plot and character in a drama.

First, because the action is presented to us as immediate scene, not something told to us by a narrator (as in a short story), the playwright must rely heavily on the speeches and the visible actions of the characters to convey information to us. Almost all we know of plot and character—including significant prior or future events, the characters' backgrounds, and what they are thinking and feeling—must be delivered to us by the characters themselves, through their deeds and speeches. No narrator is there to fill us in about past events or to dip inside a character's mind and tell us how he or she is feeling.

Second, audiences are affected by time no less than by space. Plays must be performed continuously in time. We cannot stop them to have a character repeat lines; we cannot go back to scene one to see how a theme was introduced; we cannot jump ahead to see how the play ends. Moreover, because of the waywardness of human memory and attentiveness, the playwright must allow for our limited ability to retain what we have seen or heard. These considerations affect the complexity of plots, the images or motifs that a playwright may employ, the ways the characters are grouped and balanced, and how long the play itself can last. If these are limitations (and in one sense, of course, they are), they tend to disappear when we read a play and are able to stop the time of the play at will. But we must remember that plays are meant to be performed and that their plotting and characterization are unique because of this fact.

Since the birth of drama in ancient Greece, dramatists have struggled to accommodate, and to exploit, these constrictions or limitations. Their attempts have resulted in two broad types of drama which are customarily called the **theater of convention** and the **theater of illusion.** Both of these terms apply to the play as a performance to be seen and heard. In either kind of theater an audience tactitly agrees that what it is seeing and hearing is not real life, but something acted out. The two kinds of theater represent differences in the degree of realism expended on the attempt to make theatrical performances look and sound like real life.

Plays of the theater of convention are, in general, less insistent on strict realism. Characters may wear masks (as in Greek tragedy) which prohibit facial expressions, but which express agony, for example, with great power.

Or characters may, as in Elizabethan drama, deliver asides which only the audience can hear. Or the dramatic performance itself can take on an aura of ritual or pageant that is almost religious in its impact.

In plays of the theater of illusion, on the other hand, the playwright attempts to make what is happening on the stage look and sound as much like real life as possible. The characters will wear clothes appropriate to the period in which the play is set. The settings will contain real chairs for the characters to sit in and real teacups for them to drink from. At the extreme, plays of this type will use only one setting (so the illusion will not be broken by the changing of scenes) and will take up only as much time as the actions would in real life. During the Renaissance, such "unity of space" and "unity of time" were considered essential (along with the "unity of action" first named by Aristotle) to the well-made play. These have since been called the **three dramatic unities.** Like any other critical prescription, they have by turns been slavishly adhered to, modified, or ignored by playwrights.

No matter how the playwright handles dramatic illusion, conflict is central to the plot. From conflict the plot arises; conflict moves the plot; and, with the cessation of conflict, the plot ends. The conflict can be within a character's mind, between two characters (or among several), or between a character and his entire conception of the world. Shakespeare's *Hamlet* richly illustrates the possibilities for conflict in a drama. Hamlet struggles mightily to decide whether, and how, and when, he should take revenge upon his murderous Uncle Claudius. This internal struggle is augmented— and in part caused by—Hamlet's conflicts with other characters in the play. He is in conflict with Claudius in that they are both trying to outwit each other. He is in conflict with his mother because of her hasty decision to marry a lesser man after her husband's death. He is in conflict with Polonius, whom he knows to be in league with Claudius. And he is in conflict with Laertes upon a point of honor. These conflicts, and the deceit and disillusionment which accompany them, infect Hamlet's entire view of the world, which he sees as a rank, unweeded garden populated by traitors.

Such conflicts, no matter what their kind or number, produce the basis for the action of most plays. This action is usually accompanied by, and productive of, tension of some kind. The tension can range anywhere from simple suspense about what is going to happen next to a richly complicated fabric of emotions woven slowly throughout the play and then displayed in the fullness of resolution, or "untying," at the end. Like the tension of the plot of a short story, the shape of the tension of a play commonly follows the triangular pattern cited under the discussion of plot in fiction (page 31). There will be **exposition** giving information about the background of the play (the talks on the ramparts at the beginning of *Hamlet*). Conflict will be introduced (the ghost) so that the **rising action** may begin (Hamlet's efforts to establish Claudius's guilt and to overcome his own irresolution). The action will rise toward a **climax** (the catastrophe of Hamlet's death). After this peak of emotional intensity, the **falling action** ensues, tension is released, and the plot is resolved in the **denouement** (from the French *denouer*, "to untie"). In *Hamlet* the denouement occurs with the arrival of Fortinbras at the end. The tension has dissipated, and the situation returns to a state of equilibrium.

As with fiction, the characters of a play cannot really be separated from the plot. Actions make the plot, and characters perform the actions. As we have seen, the physical restrictions of the stage limit the number of characters which can reasonably be used or which can be present on the stage at once. Samuel Beckett's *Krapp's Last Tape* (page 1359) uses only one named character on the stage; Miller's *Death of a Salesman* uses thirteen; *Hamlet* uses twenty-five, plus some unnamed characters who are part of processions and scenes at the court of Denmark. Usually, the number of significant speaking characters on the stage at one time will not exceed five. Following the Greeks, we customarily give the name **protagonist** to the main actor (Hamlet, for example). **Antagonist** is used for the character whose conflict with the protagonist provides the principal tension of the plot.

These terms, and considerations about the number of actors in a play, should not cloud our awareness of a more important feature: the ways characters are grouped or patterned in a play. We should be attentive to how playwrights use pairs of characters, triangles, and contrasts to advance character portrayal and enrich conflict. In *Death of a Salesman*, Willy, a father who clings to illusions, and his disillusioned son Biff provide the contrasts—and the painful similarities—that make the action of the play so intense. In *Hamlet*, Shakespeare uses the triangle of Hamlet, Claudius, and Gertrude (or a quartet if we include the ghost of Hamlet's father) to probe the motivations, causes, conflict, and outcome of the action. Each character provides a kind of mirror in which the others see a projection, or a distortion, of themselves. Sometimes playwrights use paired characters who resemble each other in some respects, but differ significantly in others. We call such characters **foils.** Laertes is a foil to Hamlet. He is a young courtier whose father has been killed, but his reactions to this death differ markedly from Hamlet's reactions to his own father's death. In Laertes we see a possible Hamlet, a Hamlet who might have been. The differences between the two provide important insights into Hamlet's character.

The means through which characters are revealed in plays resemble the corresponding means that we have seen in fiction (page 53). Their speech and the images it contains are of course vital, as is what other characters say about them. For example, Hamlet asks literally dozens of questions; these questions are an index of both his uncertainty and of his intellectual cast of mind. He is a man obsessed with knowing—how to act, how to react, how to be. Also, he repeatedly employs images of disease or disguise in his speeches, and these repeated references tell us much about his concerns: the kingdom is diseased, and controlled by a deceiver. Hamlet himself must adopt a disguise to help set things right again. We should, as careful readers of drama, be attuned to recurrent patterns of images and ideas.

The physical actions and apprearance (physique, age, dress) of the characters are also important. Action reflects motivation and in turn causes reaction. Willie's attempted suicide in *Death of a Salesman* reflects his own beleagured state of mind, and also causes an important reaction on the part of his son Biff. Because we cannot literally see what characters do when we read plays, we must, just as when we read fiction, make every effort to visualize their actions and to see how these actions are affirmed or contradicted by their speech.

The fact that a drama is a staged production, visible and audible to an audience, permits and necessitates some means of characterization which are specific to the theater. For example, a character's dress may have greater impact because we can literally see it. Hamlet's "inky cloak" of black may strike us with a more tangible mournfulness than a written description of his dark clothes might. The setting of the stage and the stage properties— Mr. Oliver's fountain pen in *Death of a Salesman* comes to mind—take on, because of their visibility and manipulability, a keen symbolic significance which can greatly enhance the revelation of character.

Two other means of characterization specific to drama (one particular to stage productions and one to the printed text) deserve special mention. Some playwrights use a **soliloquy** to reveal a character's thoughts to us. *Hamlet* is perhaps the most famous example. In a true soliloquy a character alone on the stage unburdens himself or herself in front of us, so that we can hear what is being thought or felt. When the words are spoken in the presence of others (who do not "hear" the words in spite of their proximity to the speaker), we call these speeches **asides.** Both soliloquies and asides are acceptable dramatic conventions which, while breaking the dramatic illusion, can provide us with important insights that otherwise would be unavailable. They also serve to draw us into collusion with the actors and thus can intensify whatever emotions attend our presence at the performance.

Many playwrights, particularly modern ones, use **stage directions** in the printed version of a play. Such directions provide information for actors, directors, and readers and can even include judgments about the characters. As we have seen, Arthur Miller uses stage directions skillfully to set the scene before the reader's mind, to reveal character, and to provide clues for the production of the play. Though such directions are *extra-theatrical* (for they are not actually spoken in front of the audience), they can still add another dimension to the portrayal of character for readers and actors alike.

As you read Shakespeare's *Hamlet* and attempt to understand its plot and its characters, try to visualize the action. Remember that any speech can help to characterize not only the speaker but also other characters in the play. Try to get a sense of the plot's outline by writing a brief statement about the major occurrences within each act. Pay particular attention to how character is revealed and developed.

WILLIAM SHAKESPEARE (1564–1616)

Hamlet

William Shakespeare is commonly considered to be England's—and the world's—greatest dramatist. Born in Stratford-upon-Avon, he began his theatrical career in London around 1592. From around 1590 until his death, he wrote thirty-eight plays, one hundred and fifty-four sonnets, and several longer poems. His brilliant command of dramatic poetry and his penetrating insights into the human character are matched by his extraordinary versatility as a dramatist. His tragedies, comedies, histories, and romances constitute an unparalleled achievement in the theater. His major plays include *Romeo and Juliet* (1595), *Twelfth Night* (1600), *Othello* (1605), *King Lear* (1606), *Macbeth* (1606), *The Tempest* (1612), and *Hamlet*, which was probably completed around 1601.

CHARACTERS

CLAUDIUS, *King of Denmark*

HAMLET, *son to the late, and nephew to the present, king*

POLONIUS, *Lord Chamberlain*

HORATIO, *friend to Hamlet*

LAERTES, *son to Polonius*

VOLTEMAND
CORNELIUS
ROSENCRANTZ
GUILDENSTERN } *courtiers*
OSRIC
A GENTLEMAN

A PRIEST

MARCELLUS
BARNARDO } *officers*

FRANCISCO, *a soldier*

REYNALDO, *servant to Polonius*

PLAYERS

TWO CLOWNS, *gravediggers*

FORTINBRAS, *Prince of Norway*

A NORWEGIAN CAPTAIN

ENGLISH AMBASSADORS

GERTRUDE, *Queen of Denmark, mother to Hamlet*

OPHELIA, *daughter to Polonius*

GHOST *of Hamlet's father*

LORDS, LADIES, OFFICERS, SOLDIERS, SAILORS, MESSENGERS, ATTENDANTS

SCENE: *Elsinore*

ACT I

SCENE I. *A guard platform of the castle.*

Enter BARNARDO *and* FRANCISCO, *two sentinels.*

BARNARDO: Who's there?

FRANCISCO: Nay, answer me. Stand and unfold° yourself.

2 unfold disclose

BARNARDO: Long live the king!°
FRANCISCO: Barnardo?
BARNARDO: He.   5
FRANCISCO: You come most carefully upon your hour.
BARNARDO: 'Tis now struck twelve. Get thee to bed, Francisco.
FRANCISCO: For this relief much thanks. 'Tis bitter cold,
And I am sick at heart.
BARNARDO: Have you had a quiet guard?
FRANCISCO: Not a mouse stirring.   10
BARNARDO: Well, good night.
If you do meet Horatio and Marcellus,
The rivals° of my watch, bid them make haste.

Enter HORATIO *and* MARCELLUS.

FRANCISCO: I think I hear them. Stand, ho! Who is there?
HORATIO: Friends to this ground.
MARCELLUS: And liegemen to the Dane.°   15
FRANCISCO: Give you° good night.
MARCELLUS: O, farewell, honest soldier.
Who hath relieved you?
FRANCISCO: Barnardo hath my place.
Give you good night.   *Exit* FRANCISCO.
MARCELLUS: Holla, Barnardo!
BARNARDO: Say—
What, is Horatio there?
HORATIO: A piece of him.
BARNARDO: Welcome, Horatio. Welcome, good Marcellus.   20
MARCELLUS: What, has this thing appeared again tonight?
BARNARDO: I have seen nothing.
MARCELLUS: Horatio says 'tis but our fantasy,
And will not let belief take hold of him
Touching this dreaded sight twice seen of us;   25
Therefore I have entreated him along
With us to watch the minutes of this night,
That, if again this apparition come,
He may approve° our eyes and speak to it.
HORATIO: Tush, tush, 'twill not appear.
BARNARDO: Sit down awhile,   30
And let us once again assail your ears,
That are so fortified against our story,
What we have two nights seen.
HORATIO: Well, sit we down,
And let us hear Barnardo speak of this.
BARNARDO: Last night of all,   35
When yond same star that's westward from the pole°

3 **Long . . . king** perhaps a password, perhaps a greeting   13 **rivals** partners
15 **liegeman . . . Dane** loyal subjects to the King of Denmark   16 **Give you** God
give you   29 **approve** confirm   36 **pole** polestar

Had made his course t' illume that part of heaven
Where now it burns, Marcellus and myself,
The bell then beating one—

Enter GHOST.

MARCELLUS:	Peace, break thee off. Look where it comes again.	40
BARNARDO:	In the same figure like the king that's dead.	
MARCELLUS:	Thou art a scholar; speak to it, Horatio.	
BARNARDO:	Looks 'a not like the king? Mark it, Horatio.	
HORATIO:	Most like: it harrows me with fear and wonder.	
BARNARDO:	It would be spoke to.	
MARCELLUS:	Speak to it, Horatio.	45
HORATIO:	What art thou that usurp'st this time of night,	

Together with that fair and warlike form
In which the majesty of buried Denmark°
Did sometimes march? By heaven I charge thee, speak.

MARCELLUS: It is offended.
BARNARDO: See, it stalks away.   50
HORATIO: Stay! Speak, speak. I charge thee, speak.   *Exit* GHOST.
MARCELLUS: 'Tis gone and will not answer.
BARNARDO: How now, Horatio? You tremble and look pale.

Is not this something more than fantasy?
What think you on't?   55

HORATIO: Before my God, I might not this believe

Without the sensible and true avouch°
Of mine own eyes.

MARCELLUS: Is it not like the king?
HORATIO: As thou art to thyself.

Such was the very armor he had on   60
When he the ambitious Norway° combated:
So frowned he once, when, in an angry parle,°
He smote the sledded Polacks° on the ice.
'Tis strange.

MARCELLUS: Thus twice before, and jump° at this dead hour,   65

With martial stalk hath he gone by our watch.

HORATIO: In what particular thought to work I know not;

But, in the gross and scope° of my opinion,
This bodes some strange eruption to our state.

MARCELLUS: Good now, sit down, and tell me he that knows,   70

Why this same strict and most observant watch
So nightly toils the subject° of the land,
And why such daily cast of brazen cannon
And foreign mart° for implements of war,

48 buried Denmark the buried King of Denmark   **57 sensible . . . avouch** sensory and true proof   **61 Norway** King of Norway   **62 parle** parley   **63 sledded Polacks** Poles in sledges   **65 jump** just   **68 gross and scope** general drift **72 toils the subject** makes the subjects toil   **74 mart** trading

Why such impress° of shipwrights, whose sore task   75
Does not divide the Sunday from the week,
What might be toward° that this sweaty haste
Doth make the night joint-laborer with the day?
Who is't that can inform me?

HORATIO: That can I.
   At least the whisper goes so: our last king,   80
   Whose image even but now appeared to us,
   Was, as you know, by Fortinbras of Norway,
   Thereto pricked on by a most emulate pride,
   Dared to the combat; in which our valiant Hamlet
   (For so this side of our known world esteemed him)   85
   Did slay this Fortinbras, who, by a sealed compact
   Well ratified by law and heraldry,°
   Did forfeit, with his life, all those his lands
   Which he stood seized° of, to the conqueror;
   Against the which a moiety competent°   90
   Was gagèd° by our king, which had returned
   To the inheritance of Fortinbras,
   Had he been vanquisher, as, by the same comart°
   And carriage of the article designed,°
   His fell to Hamlet. Now, sir, young Fortinbras,   95
   Of unimprovèd° mettle hot and full,
   Hath in the skirts° of Norway here and there
   Sharked up° a list of lawless resolutes,°
   For food and diet, to some enterprise
   That hath a stomach in't;° which is no other,   100
   As it doth well appear unto our state,
   But to recover of us by strong hand
   And terms compulsatory, those foresaid lands
   So by his father lost; and this, I take it,
   Is the main motive of our preparations,   105
   The source of this our watch, and the chief head°
   Of this posthaste and romage° in the land.

BARNARDO: I think it be no other but e'en so;
   Well may it sort° that this portentous figure
   Comes armèd through our watch so like the king   110
   That was and is the question of these wars.

HORATIO: A mote it is to trouble the mind's eye:
   In the most high and palmy state of Rome,
   A little ere the mightiest Julius fell,

---

75 impress forced service   **77 toward** in preparation   **87 law and heraldry** heraldic law (governing the combat)   **89 seized** possessed   **90 moiety competent** equal portion   **91 gagèd**   engaged, pledged   **3 comart** agreement   **94 carriage . . . designed** import of the agreement drawn up   **96 unimprovèd** untried   **97 skirts** borders   **98 Sharked up** collected indiscriminately (as a shark gulps its prey); **resolutes** desperadoes   **100 hath . . . in't** requires courage   **106 head** fountainhead, origin   **107 romage** bustle   **109 sort** befit

The graves stood tenantless, and the sheeted dead   115
Did squeak and gibber in the Roman streets;°
As stars with trains of fire and dews of blood,
Disasters° in the sun; and the moist star,°
Upon whose influence Neptune's empire stands,
Was sick almost to doomsday with eclipse.   120
And even the like precurse° of feared events,
As harbingers° preceding still° the fates
And prologue to the omen° coming on,
Have heaven and earth together demonstrated
Unto our climatures° and countrymen.   125

Enter GHOST.

But soft, behold, lo where it comes again!
I'll cross it,° though it blast me.—Stay, illusion.

It spread his° arms.

It thou hast any sound or use of voice,
Speak to me.
If there be any good thing to be done   130
That may to thee do ease and grace to me,
Speak to me.
If thou art privy to thy country's fate,
Which happily° foreknowing may avoid,
O, speak!   135
Or if thou hast uphoarded in thy life
Extorted° treasure in the womb of earth,
For which, they say, you spirits oft walk in death,

The cock crows.

Speak of it. Stay and speak. Stop it, Marcellus.
MARCELLUS: Shall I strike at it with my partisan?°   140
HORATIO: Do, if it will not stand.
BARNARDO: 'Tis here.
HORATIO: 'Tis here.
MARCELLUS: 'Tis gone.   *Exit* GHOST.
          We do it wrong, being so majestical,

116 **Did . . . streets** the break in the sense which follows this line suggests that a line has dropped out   118 **Disasters** threatening signs;   **moist star** moon 121 **precurse** precursor, foreshadowing   122 **harbingers** forerunners;   **still** always   123 **omen** calamity   125 **climatures** regions   127 **cross it** (1) cross its path, confront it (2) make the sign of the cross in front of it   127 **s.d. his** its, the Ghost's (though possibly what is meant is that Horatio spreads his own arms, making a cross of himself)   134 **happily** haply, perhaps   137 **Extorted** ill-won 140 **partisan** pike (a long-handled weapon)

To offer it the show of violence,
For it is as the air, invulnerable,   145
And our vain blows malicious mockery.
BARNARDO: It was about to speak when the cock crew.
HORATIO: And then it started, like a guilty thing
Upon a fearful summons. I have heard,
The cock, that is the trumpet to the morn,   150
Doth with his lofty and shrill-sounding throat
Awake the god of day, and at his warning,
Whether in sea or fire, in earth or air,
Th' extravagant and erring° spirit hies
To his confine; and of the truth herein   155
This present object made probation.°
MARCELLUS: It faded on the crowing of the cock.
Some say that ever 'gainst° that season comes
Wherein our Savior's birth is celebrated,
This bird of dawning singeth all night long,   160
And then, they say, no spirit dare stir abroad,
The nights are wholesome, then no planets strike,°
No fairy takes,° nor witch hath power to charm:
So hallowed and so gracious is that time.
HORATIO: So have I heard and do in part believe it.   165
But look, the morn in russet mantle clad
Walks o'er the dew of yon high eastward hill.
Break we our watch up, and by my advice
Let us impart what we have seen tonight
Unto young Hamlet, for upon my life   170
This spirit, dumb to us, will speak to him.
Do you consent we shall acquaint him with it,
As needful in our loves, fitting our duty?
MARCELLUS: Let's do't, I pray, and I this morning know
Where we shall find him most convenient.   *Exeunt.*   175

SCENE II. The castle.

Flourish.° Enter Claudius, KING *of Denmark, Gertrude the* QUEEN, COUNCI-
LORS, POLONIUS *and his son* LAERTES, HAMLET, *cum aliis° (including* VOL-
TEMAND *and* CORNELIUS).

KING: Though yet of Hamlet our dear brother's death
The memory be green, and that it us befitted
To bear our hearts in grief, and our whole kingdom
To be contracted in one brow of woe,
Yet so far hath discretion fought with nature   5
That we with wisest sorrow think on him

154 **extravagant and erring** out of bounds and wandering   156 **probation** proof
158 **'gainst** just before   162 **strike** exert an evil influence   163 **takes** bewitches
I.ii.s.d. Flourish fanfare of trumpets;   **cum aliis** with others (Latin)

Together with remembrance of ourselves.
Therefore our sometime sister,° now our queen,
Th' imperial jointress° to this warlike state,
Have we, as 'twere, with a defeated joy, 10
With an auspicious° and a dropping eye,
With mirth in funeral, and with dirge in marriage,
In equal scale weighing delight and dole,
Taken to wife. Nor have we herein barred
Your better wisdoms, which have freely gone 15
With this affair along. For all, our thanks.
Now follows that you know young Fortinbras,
Holding a weak supposal of our worth,
Or thinking by our late dear brother's death
Our state to be disjoint and out of frame,° 20
Colleaguèd with this dream of his advantage,°
He hath not failed to pester us with message,
Importing the surrender of those lands
Lost by his father, with all bands of law,
To our most valiant brother. So much for him. 25
Now for ourself and for this time of meeting.
Thus much the business is: we have here writ
To Norway, uncle of young Fortinbras—
Who, impotent and bedrid, scarcely hears
Of this his nephew's purpose—to suppress 30
His further gait° herein, in that the levies,
The lists, and full proportions° are all made
Out of his subject;° and we here dispatch
You, good Cornelius, and you, Voltemand,
For bearers of this greeting to old Norway, 35
Giving to you no further personal power
To business with the king, more than the scope
Of these delated articles° allow.
Farewell, and let your haste commend your duty.
CORNELIUS, VOLTEMAND: In that, and all things, will we
show our duty. 40
KING: We doubt it nothing. Heartily farewell.

Exit VOLTEMAND *and* CORNELIUS.

And now, Laertes, what's the news with you?
You told us of some suit. What is't, Laertes?
You cannot speak of reason to the Dane
And lose your voice.° What wouldst thou beg, Laertes, 45

---

8 our sometime sister my (the royal "we") former sister-in-law   **9 jointress** joint tenant, partner   **11 auspicious** joyful   **20 frame** order   **21 advantage** superiority   **31 gait** proceeding   **32 proportions** supplies for war   **33 Out . . . subject** out of old Norway's subjects and realm   **38 delated articles** detailed documents

And lose your voice.° What wouldst thou beg, Laertes,   45
That shall not be my offer, not thy asking?
The head is not more native° to the heart,
The hand more instrumental to the mouth,
Than is the throne of Denmark to thy father.
What wouldst thou have, Laertes?

LAERTES: My dread lord,   50
Your leave and favor to return to France,
From whence, though willingly I came to Denmark
To show my duty in your coronation,
Yet now I must confess, that duty done,
My thoughts and wishes bend again toward France   55
    And bow them to your gracious leave and pardon.

KING: Have you your father's leave? What says Polonius?
POLONIUS: He hath, my lord, wrung from me my slow leave
By laborsome petition, and at last
Upon his will I sealed my hard consent.°   60
I do beseech you give him leave to go.

KING: Take thy fair hour, Laertes. Time be thine,
And thy best graces spend it at thy will.
But now, my cousin° Hamlet, and my son—
HAMLET *aside:*   A little more than kin, and less than kind!°   65
KING: How is it that the clouds still hang on you?
HAMLET: Not so, my lord. I am too much in the sun.°
QUEEN: Good Hamlet, cast thy nighted color off,
And let thine eye look like a friend on Denmark.
Do not forever with thy vailèd° lids   70
Seek for thy noble father in the dust.
Thou know'st 'tis common; all that lives must die,
Passing through nature to eternity.
HAMLET: Ay, madam, it is common.°
QUEEN: If it be,
Why seems it so particular with thee?   75
HAMLET: Seems, madam? Nay, it is. I know not "seems."
'Tis not alone my inky cloak, good mother,
Nor customary suits of solemn black,
Nor windy suspiration° of forced breath,
No, nor the fruitful river in the eye,   80
Nor the dejected havior of the visage,
Together with all forms, moods, shapes of grief,
That can denote me truly. These indeed seem,
For they are actions that a man might play,

45 lose your voice waste your breath   **47 native** related   **60 Upon . . . consent**
To his desire I gave my reluctant consent   **64 cousin** kinsman   **65 kind** pun on
the meanings "kindly" and "natural"; though doubly related—"more than kin"—
Hamlet asserts that he neither resembles Claudius in nature nor feels kindly toward
him   **67 sun** sunshine of royal favor (with a pun on *son*)   **70 vailèd** lowered
74 common (1) universal (2) vulgar   **79 windy suspiration** heavy sighing

But I have that within which passes show;   85
These but the trappings and the suits of woe.
KING: 'Tis sweet and commendable in your nature, Hamlet,
    To give these mourning duties to your father,
    But you must know your father lost a father,
    That father lost, lost his, and the survivor bound   90
    In filial obligation for some term
    To do obsequious° sorrow. But to persever
    In obstinate condolement° is a course
    Of impious stubbornness. 'Tis unmanly grief.
    It shows a will most incorrect to heaven,   95
    A heart unfortified, a mind impatient,
    An understanding simple and unschooled.
    For what we know must be and is as common
    As any the most vulgar° thing to sense,
    Why should we in our peevish opposition   100
    Take it to heart? Fie, 'tis a fault to heaven,
    A fault against the dead, a fault to nature,
    To reason most absurd, whose common theme
    Is death of fathers, and who still hath cried,
    From the first corse° till he that died today,   105
    "This must be so." We pray you throw to earth
    This unprevailing° woe, and think of us
    As of a father, for let the world take note
    You are the most immediate to our throne,
    And with no less nobility of love   110
    Than that which dearest father bears his son
    Do I impart toward you. For your intent
    In going back to school in Wittenberg,
    It is most retrograde° to our desire,
    And we beseech you, bend you° to remain   115
    Here in the cheer and comfort of our eye,
    Our chiefest courtier, cousin, and our son.
QUEEN: Let not thy mother lose her prayers, Hamlet.
    I pray thee stay with us, go not to Wittenberg.
HAMLET: I shall in all my best obey you, madam.   120
KING: Why, 'tis a loving and a fair reply.
    Be as ourself in Denmark. Madam, come.
    This gentle and unforced accord of Hamlet
    Sits smiling to my heart, in grace whereof
    No jocund health that Denmark drinks today,   125
    But the great cannon to the clouds shall tell,
    And the king's rouse° the heaven shall bruit° again,
    Respeaking earthly thunder. Come away.

92 obsequious suitable to obsequies (funerals) **93 condolement** mourning
99 vulgar common **105 corse** corpse **107 unprevailing** unavailing **114 retrograde** contrary **115 bend you** incline **127 rouse** deep drink; **bruit** announce noisily

Flourish. Exeunt all but HAMLET.

HAMLET: O that this too too sullied° flesh would melt,
Thaw, and resolve itself into a dew,   130
Or that the Everlasting had not fixed
His canon° 'gainst self-slaughter. O God, God,
How weary, stale, flat, and unprofitable
Seem to me all the uses of this world!
Fie on't, ah, fie, 'tis an unweeded garden   135
That grows to seed. Things rank and gross in nature
Possess it merely.° That it should come to this:
But two months dead, nay, not so much, not two,
So excellent a king, that was to this
Hyperion° to a satyr, so loving to my mother   140
That he might not beteem° the winds of heaven
Visit her face too roughly. Heaven and earth,
Must I remember? Why, she would hang on him
As if increase of appetite had grown
By what it fed on; and yet within a month—   145
Let me not think on't; frailty, thy name is woman—
A little month, or ere those shoes were old
With which she followed my poor father's body
Like Niobe,° all tears, why she, even she—
O God, a beast that wants discourse of reason°   150
Would have mourned longer—married with my uncle,
My father's brother, but no more like my father
Than I to Hercules. Within a month,
Ere yet the salt of most unrighteous tears
Had left the flushing° in her gallèd eyes,   155
She married. O, most wicked speed, to post°
With such dexterity to incestuous° sheets!
It is not, nor it cannot come to good.
But break my heart, for I must hold my tongue.

Enter HORATIO, MARCELLUS, *and* BARNARDO.

HORATIO: Hail to your lordship!
HAMLET: I am glad to see you well.   160
Horatio—or I do forget myself.
HORATIO: The same, my lord, and your poor servant ever.

---

129 sullied Q₂ has "sallied," here modernized to "sullied," which makes sense and is therefore given; but the Folio reading, "solid," which fits better with "melt," is quite possibly correct   **132 canon** law   **137 merely** entirely   **140 Hyperion** the sun god and a model of beauty   **141 beteem** allow   **149 Niobe** a mother who wept profusely at the death of her children   **150 wants . . . reason** lacks reasoning power   **155 left the flushing** stopped reddening   **156 post** hasten **157 incestuous** canon law considered marriage with a deceased brother's widow to be incestuous

HAMLET: Sir, my good friend, I'll change° that name with you.
And what make you from Wittenberg, Horatio?
Marcellus.   165
MARCELLUS: My good lord!
HAMLET: I am very glad to see you. *To* BARNARDO. Good even, sir.
But what, in faith, make you from Wittenberg?
HORATIO: A truant disposition, good my lord.
HAMLET: I would not hear your enemy say so,   170
Nor shall you do my ear that violence
To make it truster° of your own report
Against yourself. I know you are no truant.
But what is your affair in Elsinore?
We'll teach you to drink deep ere you depart.   175
HORATIO: My lord, I came to see your father's funeral.
HAMLET: I prithee do not mock me, fellow student.
I think it was to see my mother's wedding.
HORATIO: Indeed, my lord, it followed hard upon.
HAMLET: Thrift, thrift, Horatio. The funeral baked meats   180
Did coldly furnish forth the marriage tables.
Would I had met my dearest° foe in heaven
Or ever I had seen that day, Horatio!
My father, methinks I see my father.
HORATIO: Where, my lord?
HAMLET: In my mind's eye, Horatio.   185
HORATIO: I saw him once. 'A° was a goodly king.
HAMLET: 'A was a man, take him for all in all,
I shall not look upon his like again.
HORATIO: My lord, I think I saw him yesternight.
HAMLET: Saw? Who?   190
HORATIO: My lord, the king your father.
HAMLET: The king my father?
HORATIO: Season your admiration° for a while
With an attent ear till I may deliver
Upon the witness of these gentlemen
This marvel to you.
HAMLET: For God's love let me hear!   195
HORATIO: Two nights together had these gentlemen,
Marcellus and Barnardo, on their watch
In the dead waste and middle of the night
Been thus encountered. A figure like your father,
Armèd at point exactly, cap-a-pe,°   200
Appears before them, and with solemn march
Goes slow and stately by them. Thrice he walked
By their oppressed and fear-surprisèd eyes,

163 **change** exchange   172 **truster** believer   182 **dearest** most intensely felt
186 **'A** he   192 **Season your admiration** control your wonder   200 **cap-a-pe**
head to foot

Within his truncheon's length,° whilst they, distilled°
Almost to jelly with the act° of fear, 205
Stand dumb and speak not to him. This to me
In dreadful° secrecy impart they did,
And I with them the third night kept the watch,
Where, as they had delivered, both in time,
Form of the thing, each word made true and good, 210
The apparition comes. I knew your father.
These hands are not more like.

HAMLET: But where was this?
MARCELLUS: My lord, upon the platform where we watched.
HAMLET: Did you not speak to it?
HORATIO: My lord, I did;
But answer made it none. Yet once methought 215
It lifted up it° head and did address
Itself to motion like as it would speak:
But even then the morning cock crew loud,
And at the sound it shrunk in haste away
And vanished from our sight.

HAMLET: 'Tis very strange. 220
HORATIO: As I do live, my honored lord, 'tis true,
And we did think it writ down in our duty
To let you know of it.
HAMLET: Indeed, indeed, sirs, but this troubles me.
Hold you the watch tonight?

ALL: We do, my lord. 225
HAMLET: Armed, say you?
ALL: Armed, my lord.
HAMLET: From top to toe?
ALL: My lord, from head to foot.
HAMLET: Then saw you not his face.
HORATIO: O, yes, my lord. He wore his beaver° up. 230
HAMLET: What, looked he frowningly?
HORATIO: A countenance more in sorrow than in anger.
HAMLET: Pale or red?
HORATIO: Nay, very pale.
HAMLET: And fixed his eyes upon you?
HORATIO: Most constantly.
HAMLET: I would I had been there. 235
HORATIO: It would have much amazed you.
HAMLET: Very like, very like. Stayed it long?
HORATIO: While one with moderate haste might tell° a hundred.
BOTH: Longer, longer.
HORATIO: Not when I saw't.

---

204 truncheon's length space of a short staff;   **distilled** reduced   **205 act** action
207 dreadful terrified   **216 it** its   **230 beaver** visor, face guard   **238 tell** count

HAMLET: His beard was grizzled,° no?   240
HORATIO: It was as I have seen it in his life,
   A sable silvered.°
HAMLET: I will watch tonight.
   Perchance 'twill walk again.
HORATIO: I warr'nt it will.
HAMLET: If it assume my noble father's person,
   I'll speak to it though hell itself should gape   245
   And bid me hold my peace. I pray you all,
   If you have hitherto concealed this sight,
   Let it be tenable° in your silence still,
   And whatsomever else shall hap tonight,
   Give it an understanding but no tongue;   250
   I will requite your loves. So fare you well.
   Upon the platform 'twixt eleven and twelve
   I'll visit you.
ALL: Our duty to your honor.
HAMLET: Your loves, as mine to you. Farewell.

                              Exeunt all but HAMLET.

My father's spirit—in arms? All is not well.   255
I doubt° some foul play. Would the night were come!
Till then sit still, my soul. Foul deeds will rise,
Though all the earth o'erwhelm them, to men's eyes.

                                                    Exit.

SCENE III. A room.

Enter LAERTES *and* OPHELIA, *his sister.*

LAERTES: My necessaries are embarked. Farewell.
   And, sister, as the winds give benefit
   And convoy° is assistant, do not sleep,
   But let me hear from you.
OPHELIA: Do you doubt that?
LAERTES: For Hamlet, and the trifling of his favor,   5
   Hold it a fashion and a toy° in blood,
   A violet in the youth of primy° nature,
   Forward,° not permanent, sweet, not lasting,
   The perfume and suppliance° of a minute,
   No more.
OPHELIA: No more but so?
LAERTES: Think it no more.   10

---

240 grizzled gray   **242 sable silvered** black mingled with white   **248 tenable**
held   **256 doubt** suspect   **I.iii.3 convoy** conveyance   **6 toy** idle fancy
7 primy springlike   **8 Forward** premature   **9 suppliance** diversion

For nature crescent° does not grow alone
In thews° and bulk, but as this temple° waxes,
The inward service of the mind and soul
Grows wide withal. Perhaps he loves you now,
And now no soil nor cautel° doth besmirch   15
The virtue of his will; but you must fear,
His greatness weighed,° his will is not his own.
For he himself is subject to his birth.
He may not, as unvalued° persons do,
Carve for himself; for on his choice depends   20
The safety and health of this whole state;
And therefore must his choice be circumscribed
Unto the voice and yielding of that body
Whereof he is the head. Then if he says he loves you,
It fits your wisdom so far to believe it   25
As he in his particular act and place
May give his saying deed, which is no further
Than the main voice of Denmark goes withal.
Then weigh what loss your honor may sustain
If with too credent° ear you list his songs,   30
Or lose your heart, or your chaste treasure open
To his unmastered importunity.
Fear it, Ophelia, fear it, my dear sister,
And keep you in the rear of your affection,
Out of the shot and danger of desire.   35
The chariest maid is prodigal enough
If she unmask her beauty to the moon.
Virtue itself scapes not calumnious strokes.
The canker° galls the infants of the spring
Too oft before their buttons° be disclosed,   40
And in the morn and liquid dew of youth
Contagious blastments are most imminent.
Be wary then; best safety lies in fear;
Youth to itself rebels, though none else near.
OPHELIA: I shall the effect of this good lesson keep   45
As watchman to my heart, but, good my brother,
Do not, as some ungracious° pastors do,
Show me the steep and thorny way to heaven,
Whiles, like a puffed and reckless libertine,
Himself the primrose path of dalliance treads   50
And recks not his own rede.°

Enter POLONIUS.

---

11 cresent growing   **12 thews** muscles and sinews;   **temple** the body
15 cautel deceit   **17 greatness weighed** high rank considered   **19 unvalued** of
low rank   **30 credent** credulous   **39 canker** cankerworm   **40 buttons** buds
47 ungracious lacking grace   **51 recks . . . rede** does not heed his own advice

LAERTES: O, fear me not.
    I stay too long. But there my father comes.
    A double blessing is a double grace;
    Occasion smiles upon a second leave.
POLONIUS: Yet here, Laertes? Aboard, aboard, for shame!   55
    The wind sits in the shoulder of your sail,
    And you are stayed for. There—my blessing with thee,
    And these few precepts in thy memory
    Look thou character.° Give thy thoughts no tongue,
    Nor any unproportioned° thought his act.   60
    Be thou familiar, but by no means vulgar.
    Those friends thou hast, and their adoption tried,
    Grapple them unto thy soul with hoops of steel,
    But do not dull thy palm with entertainment
    Of each new-hatched, unfledged courage.° Beware   65
    Of entrance to a quarrel; but being in,
    Bear't that th' opposèd may beware of thee.
    Give every man thine ear, but few thy voice;
    Take each man's censure,° but reserve thy judgment.
    Costly thy habit as thy purse can buy,   70
    But not expressed in fancy; rich, not gaudy,
    For the apparel oft proclaims the man,
    And they in France of the best rank and station
    Are of a most select and generous, chief in that.°
    Neither a borrower nor a lender be,   75
    For loan oft loses both itself and friend,
    And borrowing dulleth edge of husbandry.°
    This above all, to thine own self be true,
    And it must follow, as the night the day,
    Thou canst not then be false to any man.   80
    Farewell. My blessing season this° in thee!
LAERTES: Most humbly do I take my leave, my lord.
POLONIUS: The time invites you. Go, your servants tend.°
LAERTES: Farewell, Ophelia, and remember well
    What I have said to you.
OPHELIA: 'Tis in my memory locked,   85
    And you yourself shall keep the key of it.
LAERTES: Farewell.   *Exit* LAERTES.
POLONIUS: What is't, Ophelia, he hath said to you?
OPHELIA: So please you, something touching the Lord Hamlet.
POLONIUS: Marry,° well bethought.   90
    'Tis told me he hath very oft of late
    Given private time to you, and you yourself

59 character inscribe   **60 unproportioned** unbalanced   **65 courage** gallant youth
69 censure opinion   **74 Are . . . that** show their fine taste and their gentlemanly
instincts more in that than in any other point of manners (Kittredge)   **77 husban-
dry** thrift   **81 season this** make fruitful this (advice)   **83 tend** attend   **90 Marry**
a light oath, from "By the Virgin Mary"

Have of your audience been most free and bounteous.
If it be so—as so 'tis put on me,
And that in way of caution—I must tell you   95
You do not understand yourself so clearly
As it behooves my daughter and your honor.
What is between you? Give me up the truth.

OPHELIA: He hath, my lord, of late made many tenders°
Of his affection to me.   100

POLONIUS: Affection pooh! You speak like a green girl,
Unsifted° in such perilous circumstance.
Do you believe his tenders, as you call them?

OPHELIA: I do not know, my lord, what I should think.

POLONIUS: Marry, I will teach you. Think yourself a baby   105
That you have ta'en these tenders for true pay
Which are not sterling. Tender yourself more dearly,
Or (not to crack the wind of the poor phrase)
Tend'ring it thus you'll tender me a fool.°

OPHELIA: My lord, he hath importuned me with love   110
In honorable fashion.

POLONIUS: Ay, fashion you may call it. Go to, go to.

OPHELIA: And hath given countenance to his speech, my lord,
With almost all the holy vows of heaven.

POLONIUS: Ay, springes to catch woodcocks.° I do know,   115
When the blood burns, how prodigal the soul
Lends the tongue vows. These blazes, daughter,
Giving more light than heat, extinct in both,
Even in their promise, as it is a-making,
You must not take for fire. From this time   120
Be something scanter of your maiden presence.
Set your entreatments° at a higher rate
Than a command to parley. For Lord Hamlet,
Believe so much in him that he is young,
And with a larger tether may he walk   125
Than may be given you. In few, Ophelia,
Do not believe his vows, for they are brokers,°
Not of that dye° which their investments° show,
But mere implorators° of unholy suits,
Breathing like sanctified and pious bonds,°   130
The better to beguile. This is for all:
I would not, in plain terms, from this time forth
Have you so slander° any moment leisure

---

99 tenders offers (in line 103 it has the same meaning, but in line 106 Polonius
speaks of "tenders" in the sense of counters or chips; in line 109 "Tend'ring" means
"holding," and "tender" means "give," "present")   **102 Unsifted** untried
109 tender . . . fool (1) present me with a fool (2) present me with a baby
115 springes . . . woodcocks snares to catch stupid birds   **122 entreat-
ments** interviews   **127 brokers** procurers   **128 dye** i.e., kind;   **investments** garments   **129 implorators** solicitors   **130 bonds** pledges   **133 slander** disgrace

As to give words or talk with the Lord Hamlet.
Look to't, I charge you. Come your ways.   135
OPHELIA: I shall obey, my lord.   *Exeunt.*

SCENE IV. A guard platform.

Enter HAMLET, HORATIO, *and* MARCELLUS.

HAMLET: The air bites shewdly;° it is very cold
HORATIO: It is a nipping and an eager° air.
HAMLET: What hour now?
HORATIO: I think it lacks of twelve.
MARCELLUS: No, it is struck.
HORATIO: Indeed? I heard it not. It then draws near the season   5
Wherein the spirit held his wont to walk.

A flourish of trumpets, and two pieces go off.

What does this mean, my lord?
HAMLET: The king doth wake° tonight and takes his rouse,°
Keeps wassail, and the swagg'ring upspring° reels,
And as he drains his draughts of Rhenish° down   10
The kettledrum and trumpet thus bray out
The triumph of his pledge.°
HORATIO: Is it a custom?
HAMLET: Ay, marry, is't,
But to my mind, though I am native here
And to the manner born, it is a custom   15
More honored in the breach than the observance.
This heavy-headed revel east and west
Makes us traduced and taxed of ° other nations.
They clepe° us drunkards and with swinish phrase
Soil our addition,° and indeed it takes   20
From our achievements, though performed at height,
The pith and marrow of our attribute.°
So oft it chances in particular men
That for some vicious mole° of nature in them,
As in their birth, wherein they are not guilty,   25
(Since nature cannot choose his origin)
By the o'ergrowth of some complexion,°
Oft breaking down the pales° and forts of reason,

I.iv.1 **shrewdly** bitterly   2 **eager** sharp   8 **wake** hold a revel by night;   **takes
his rouse** carouses   9 **upspring** a dance   10 **Rhenish** Rhine wine   12 **triumph
. . . pledge**   achievement (of drinking a wine cup in one draught) of his toast
18 **taxed of** blamed by   19 **clepe** call   20 **addition** reputation (literally, "title of
honor")   22 **attribute** reputation   24 **mole** blemish   27 **complexion** natural
disposition   28 **pales** enclosures

Or by some habit that too much o'erleavens°
The form of plausive° manners, that (these men,   30
Carrying, I say, the stamp of one defect,
Being nature's livery, or fortune's star°)
Their virtues else, be they as pure as grace,
As infinite as man may undergo,
Shall in the general censure° take corruption   35
From that particular fault. The dram of evil
Doth all the noble substance of a doubt,
To his own scandal.°

Enter GHOST.

HORATIO: Look, my lord, it comes.
HAMLET: Angels and ministers of grace defend us!
    Be thou a spirit of health° or goblin damned,   40
    Bring with thee airs from heaven or blasts from hell,
    Be thy intents wicked or charitable,
    Thou com'st in such a questionable° shape
    That I will speak to thee. I'll call thee Hamlet,
    King, father, royal Dane. O, answer me!   45
    Let me not burst in ignorance, but tell
    Why thy canonized° bones, hearsèd in death,
    Have burst their cerements,° why the sepulcher
    Wherein we saw thee quietly interred
    Hath oped his ponderous and marble jaws   50
    To cast thee up again. What may this mean
    That thou, dead corse, again in complete steel,
    Revisits thus the glimpses of the moon,
    Making night hideous, and we fools of nature
    So horridly to shake our disposition°   55
    With thoughts beyond the reaches of our souls?
    Say, why is this? Wherefore? What should we do?

GHOST *beckons* HAMLET.

HORATIO: It beckons you to go away with it,
    As if some impartment° did desire
    To you alone.
MARCELLUS: Look with what courteous action   60

29 **o'erleavens** mixes with, corrupts   30 **plausive** pleasing   32 **nature's** . . .
star nature's equipment (i.e., "innate"), or a person's destiny determined by the
stars   35 **general censure** popular judgment   36–38 **The dram . . . scandal**
though the drift is clear, there is no agreement as to the exact meaning of these lines
40 **spirit of health** good spirit   43 **questionable** (1) capable of discourse (2)
dubious   47 **canonized** buried according to the canon or ordinance of the church
48 **cerements** waxed linen shroud   55 **shake our disposition** disturb us
59 **impartment** communication

It waves you to a more removèd ground.
But do not go with it.
HORATIO: No, by no means.
HAMLET: It will not speak. Then I will follow it.
HORATIO: Do not, my lord.
HAMLET: Why, what should be the fear?
I do not set my life at a pin's fee,   65
And for my soul, what can it do to that,
Being a thing immortal as itself?
It waves me forth again. I'll follow it.
HORATIO: What if it tempt you toward the flood, my lord,
Or to the dreadful summit of the cliff   70
That beetles° o'er his base into the sea,
And there assume some other horrible form,
Which might deprive your sovereignty of reason°
And draw you into madness? Think of it.
The very place puts toys° of desperation,   75
Without more motive, into every brain
That looks so many fathoms to the sea
And hears it roar beneath.
HAMLET: It waves me still.
Go on; I'll follow thee.
MARCELLUS: You shall not go, my lord.
HAMLET: Hold off your hands.   80
HORATIO: Be ruled. You shall not go.
HAMLET: My fate cries out
And makes each petty artere° in this body
    As hardy as the Nemean lion's nerve.°
Still am I called! Unhand me, gentlemen.
By heaven, I'll make a ghost of him that lets° me!   85
    I say, away! Go on. I'll follow thee.

                       Exit GHOST, *and* HAMLET.

HORATIO: He waxes desperate with imagination.
MARCELLUS: Let's follow. 'Tis not fit thus to obey him.
HORATIO: Have after! To what issue will this come?
MARCELLUS: Something is rotten in the state of Denmark.   90
HORATIO: Heaven will direct it.
MARCELLUS: Nay, let's follow him.   *Exeunt.*

SCENE V. The battlements.

Enter GHOST *and* HAMLET.

71 beetles juts our   **73 deprive . . . reason** destroy the sovereignty of your reason   **75 toys** whims, fancies   **82 artere** artery   **83 Nemean lion's nerve** sinews of the mythical lion slain by Hercules   **85 lets** (1) allows (2) hinders

HAMLET: Whither wilt thou lead me? Speak; I'll go no further.
GHOST: Mark me.
HAMLET: I will.
GHOST: My hour is almost come,
    When I to sulf'rous and tormenting flames
    Must render up myself.
HAMLET: Alas, poor ghost.
GHOST: Pity me not, but lend thy serious hearing   5
    To what I shall unfold.
HAMLET: Speak, I am bound to hear.
GHOST: So art thou to revenge, when thou shalt hear.
HAMLET: What?
GHOST: I am thy father's spirit,
    Doomed for a certain term to walk the night,   10
    And for the day confined to fast in fires,
    Till the foul crimes° done in my days of nature
    Are burnt and purged away. But that I am forbid
    To tell the secrets of my prison house,
    I could a tale unfold whose lightest word   15
    Would harrow up thy soul, freeze thy young blood,
    Make thy two eyes like stars start from their spheres,°
    Thy knotted and combinèd locks to part,
    And each particular hair to stand an° end
    Like quills upon the fearful porpentine.°   20
    But this eternal blazon° must not be
    To ears of flesh and blood. List, list, O, list!
    If thou didst ever thy dear father love—
HAMLET: O God!
GHOST: Revenge his foul and most unnatural murder.   25
HAMLET: Murder?
GHOST: Murder most foul, as in the best it is,
    But this most foul, strange, and unnatural.
HAMLET: Haste me to know't, that I, with wings as swift
    As meditation° or the thoughts of love,   30
    May sweep to my revenge.
GHOST: I find thee apt,
    And duller shouldst thou be than the fat weed
    That roots itself in ease on Lethe wharf,°
    Wouldst thou not stir in this. Now, Hamlet, hear.
    'Tis given out that, sleeping in my orchard,   35
    A serpent stung me. So the whole ear of Denmark
    Is by a forgèd process° of my death
    Rankly abused. But know, thou noble youth,

I.v.12 **crimes** sins   17 **spheres** in Ptolemaic astronomy, each planet was fixed in
a hollow transparent shell concentric with the earth   19 **an** on   20 **fearful por-
pentine** timid porcupine   21 **eternal blazon** revelation of eternity   30 **meditation** thought   33 **Lethe wharf** bank of the river of forgetfulness in Hades
37 **forgèd process** false account

The serpent that did sting thy father's life
Now wears his crown.
HAMLET: O my prophetic soul!   40
My uncle?
GHOST: Ay, that incestuous, that adulterate° beast,
With witchcraft of his wits, with traitorous gifts—
O wicked wit and gifts, that have the power
So to seduce!—won to his shameful lust   45
The will of my most seeming-virtuous queen.
O Hamlet, what a falling-off was there,
From me, whose love was of that dignity
That it went hand in hand even with the vow
I made to her in marriage, and to decline   50
Upon a wretch whose natural gifts were poor
To those of mine.
But virtue, as it never will be moved,
Though lewdness° court it in a shape of heaven,
So lust, though to a radiant angel linked,   55
Will sate itself in a celestial bed
And prey on garbage.
But soft, methinks I scent the morning air;
Brief let me be. Sleeping within my orchard,
My custom always of the afternoon,   60
Upon my secure° hour thy uncle stole
With juice of cursed hebona° in a vial,
And in the porches of my ears did pour
The leperous distillment, whose effect
Holds such an enmity with blood of man   65
That swift as quicksilver it courses through
The natural gates and alleys of the body,
And with a sudden vigor it doth posset°
And curd, like eager° droppings into milk,
The thin and wholesome blood. So did it mine,   70
And a most instant tetter° barked about
Most lazarlike° with vile and loathsome crust
All my smooth body.
Thus was I, sleeping, by a brother's hand
Of life, of crown, of queen at once dispatched,   75
Cut off even in the blossoms of my sin,
Unhouseled, disappointed, unaneled,°
No reck'ning made, but sent to my account
With all my imperfections on my head.
O, horrible! O, horrible! Most horrible!   80
If thou hast nature in thee, bear it not.

---

42 adulterate adulterous   **54 lewdness** lust   **61 secure** unsuspecting   **62 hebona** a poisonous plant   **68 posset** curdle   **69 eager** acid   **71 tetter** scab
72 lazarlike leperlike   **77 Unhouseled, disappointed, unaneled** without the sacrament of communion, unabsolved, without extreme unction

Let not the royal bed of Denmark be
A couch for luxury° and damnèd incest.
But howsomever thou pursues this act,
Taint not thy mind, nor let thy soul contrive
Against thy mother aught. Leave her to heaven   85
And to those thorns that in her bosom lodge
To prick and sting her. Fare thee well at once.
The glowworm shows the matin° to be near
And 'gins to pale his uneffectual fire.   90
Adieu, adieu, adieu. Remember me.   *Exit.*
HAMLET: O all you host of heaven! O earth! What else?
And shall I couple hell? O fi! Hold, hold, my heart,
And you, my sinews, grow not instant old,
But bear me stiffly up. Remember thee?   95
Ay, thou poor ghost, whiles memory holds a seat
In this distracted globe.° Remember thee?
Yea, from the table° of my memory
I'll wipe away all trivial fond° records,
All saws° of books, all forms, all pressures° past   100
That youth and observation copied there,
And thy commandment all alone shall live
Within the book and volume of my brain,
Unmixed with baser matter. Yes, by heaven!
O most pernicious woman!   105
O villain, villain, smiling, damnèd villain!
My tables—meet it is I set it down
That one may smile, and smile, and be a villain.
At least I am sure it may be so in Denmark.

Writes.

So, uncle, there you are. Now to my word: 110
It is "Adieu, adieu, remember me."
I have sworn't.
HORATIO *and* MARCELLUS *within:* My lord, my lord!

Enter HORATIO *and* MARCELLUS.

MARCELLUS: Lord Hamlet!
HORATIO: Heavens secure him!
HAMLET: So be it!
MARCELLUS: Illo, ho, ho,° my lord!   115
HAMLET: Hillo, ho, ho, boy! Come, bird, come.
MARCELLUS: How is't, my noble lord?

83 luxury lust   **89 matin** morning   **97 globe** i.e., his head   **98 table** tablet,
notebook **99 fond** foolish **100 saws** maxims; **pressures** impressions
115 Illo, ho, ho falconer's call to his hawk

HORATIO: What news, my lord?
HAMLET: O, wonderful!
HORATIO: Good my lord, tell it.
HAMLET: No, you will reveal it.
HORATIO: Not I, my lord, by heaven.
MARCELLUS: Nor I, my lord.   120
HAMLET: How say you then? Would heart of man once think it?
  But you'll be secret?
BOTH: Ay, by heaven, my lord.
HAMLET: There's never a villain dwelling in all Denmark
  But he's an arrant knave.
HORATIO: There needs no ghost, my lord, come from the grave   125
  To tell us this.
HAMLET: Why, right, you are in the right;
  And so, without more circumstance° at all,
  I hold it fit that we shake hands and part:
  You, as your business and desire shall point you,
  For every man hath business and desire   130
  Such as it is, and for my own poor part,
  Look you, I'll go pray.
HORATIO: These are but wild and whirling words my lord.
HAMLET: I am sorry they offend you, heartily;
  Yes, faith, heartily.
HORATIO: There's no offense, my lord.   135
HAMLET: Yes, by Saint Patrick, but there is, Horatio,
  And much offense too. Touching this vision here,
  It is an honest ghost,° that let me tell you.
  For your desire to know what is between us,
  O'ermaster't as you may. And now, good friends,   140
  As you are friends, scholars, and soldiers,
  Give me one poor request.
HORATIO: What is't, my lord? We will.
HAMLET: Never make known what you have seen tonight.
BOTH: My lord, we will not.
HAMLET: Nay, but swear't.   145
HORATIO: In faith,
  My lord, not I.
MARCELLUS: Nor I, my lord—in faith.
HAMLET: Upon my sword.
MARCELLUS: We have sworn, my lord, already.
  HAMLET: Indeed, upon my sword, indeed.

GHOST *cries under the stage.*

GHOST: Swear.

127 circumstance details   **138 honest ghost** not a demon in his father's shape

HAMLET: Ha, ha, boy, say'st thou so? Art thou there, 150
truepenny?°
Come on. You hear this fellow in the cellarage.
Consent to swear.
HORATIO: Propose the oath, my lord.
HAMLET: Never to speak of this that you have seen.
Swear by my sword.
GHOST *beneath:*   Swear. 155
HAMLET: Hic et ubique?° Then we'll shift our ground;
Come hither, gentlemen,
And lay your hands again upon my sword.
Swear by my sword
Never to speak of this that you have heard. 160
GHOST *beneath:*   Swear by his sword.
HAMLET: Well said, old mole! Canst work i' th' earth so fast?
A worthy pioner!° Once more remove, good friends.
HORATIO: O day and night, but this is wondrous strange!
HAMLET: And therefore as a stranger give it welcome. 165
There are more things in heaven and earth, Horatio,
Than are dreamt of in your philosophy.
But come:
Here as before, never, so help you mercy,
How strange or odd some'er I bear myself 170
(As I perchance hereafter shall think meet
To put an antic disposition° on),
That you, at such times seeing me, never shall
With arms encumb'red° thus, or this headshake,
Or by pronouncing of some doubtful phrase, 175
As "Well, well, we know," or "We could, an if we would,"
Of "If we list to speak," or "There be, an if they might,"
Or such ambiguous giving out, to note
That you know aught of me—this do swear,
So grace and mercy at your most need help you. 180
GHOST *beneath:*   Swear.

They swear.

HAMLET: Rest, rest, perturbèd spirit. So, gentlemen,
With all my love I do commend me° to you,
And what so poor a man as Hamlet is
May do t' express his love and friending to you, 185
God willing, shall not lack. Let us go in together,
And still your fingers on your lips, I pray.

---

150 truepenny honest fellow   **156 Hic et ubique** here and everywhere (Latin)
163 pioner digger of mines   **172 antic disposition** fantastic behavior   **174 encumb'red** folded   **183 commend me** entrust myself

The time is out of joint. O cursèd spite,
That ever I was born to set it right!
Nay, come, let's go together.   *Exeunt.*   190

ACT II

SCENE I. A room.

Enter old POLONIUS, *with his man* REYNALDO.

POLONIUS: Give him this money and these notes, Reynaldo.
REYNALDO: I will, my lord.
POLONIUS: You shall do marvell's° wisely, good Reynaldo,
    Before you visit him, to make inquire
    Of his behavior.
REYNALDO: My lord, I did intend it.   5
POLONIUS: Marry, well said, very well said. Look you sir,
    Inquire me first what Danskers° are in Paris,
    And how, and who, what means, and where they keep,°
    What company, at what expense; and finding
    By this encompassment° and drift of question   10
    That they do know my son, come you more nearer
    Than your particular demands° will touch it.
    Take you as 'twere some distant knowledge of him,
    As thus, "I know his father and his friends,
    And in part him." Do you mark this, Reynaldo?   15
REYNALDO: Ay, very well, my lord.
POLONIUS: "And in part him, but," you may say, "not well,
    But if't be he I mean, he's very wild,
    Addicted so and so." And there put on him
    What forgeries° you please; marry, none so rank   20
    As may dishonor him—take heed of that—
    But, sir, such wanton, wild, and usual slips
    As are companions noted and most known
    To youth and liberty.
REYNALDO: As gaming, my lord.
POLONIUS: Ay, or drinking, fencing, swearing, quarreling,   25
    Drabbing.° You may go so far.
REYNALDO: My lord, that would dishonor him.
POLONIUS: Faith, no, as you may season it in the charge.
    You must not put another scandal on him,

II.i.3 marvell's marvelous(ly)   **7 Danskers** Danes   **8 keep** dwell   **10 encompassment** circling   **12 demands** questions   **20 forgeries** inventions   **26 Drabbing** wenching

That he is open to incontinency.° 30
That's not my meaning. But breathe his faults so quaintly°
That they may seem the taints of liberty,
The flash and outbreak of a fiery mind,
A savageness in unreclaimèd blood,
Of general assault.°
REYNALDO: But, my good lord— 35
POLONIUS: Wherefore should you do this?
REYNALDO: Ay, my lord,
I would know that.
POLONIUS: Marry, sir, here's my drift,
And I believe it is a fetch of warrant.°
You laying these slight sullies on my son
As 'twere a thing a little soiled i' th' working, 40
Mark you,
Your party in converse, him you would sound,
Having ever seen in the prenominate crimes°
The youth you breathe of guilty, be assured
He closes with you in this consequence:° 45
"Good sir," or so, or "friend," or "gentleman"—
According to the phrase or the addition°
Of man and country—
REYNALDO: Very good, my lord.
POLONIUS: And then, sir, does 'a° this—'a does—
What was I about to say? By the mass, I was about 50
to say something! Where did I leave?
REYNALDO: At "closes in the consequence," at "friend
or so," and "gentleman."
POLONIUS: At "closes in the consequence"—Ay, marry!
He closes thus: "I know the gentleman; 55
I saw him yesterday, or t'other day,
Or then, or then, with such or such, and, as you say,
There was 'a gaming, there o'ertook in's rouse,
There falling out at tennis"; or perchance,
"I saw him enter such a house of sale," 60
Videlicet,° a brothel, or so forth.
See you now—
Your bait of falsehood take this carp of truth,
And thus do we of wisdom and of reach,°
With windlasses° and with assays of bias,° 65
By indirections find directions out.

---

30 incontinency habitual licentiousness   **31 quaintly** ingeniously, delicately   **35 Of general assault** common to all men   **38 fetch of warrant** justifiable device   **43 Having . . . crimes** if he has ever seen in the aforementioned crimes   **45 He . . . consequence** he falls in with you in this conclusion   **47 addition** title   **49 'a** he   **61 Videlicet** namely   **64 reach** far-reaching awareness (?)   **65 windlasses** circuitous courses;   **assays of bias** indirect attempts (metaphor from bowling; "bias" = curved course)

So, by my former lecture and advice,
Shall you my son. You have me, have you not?
REYNALDO: My lord, I have.
POLONIUS: God bye ye, fare ye well.
REYNALDO: Good my lord. 70
POLONIUS: Observe his inclination in yourself.°
REYNALDO: I shall, my lord.
POLONIUS: And let him ply his music.
REYNALDO: Well, my lord.
POLONIUS: Farewell. *Exit* REYNALDO.

Enter OPHELIA.

How now, Ophelia, what's the matter?
OPHELIA: O my lord, my lord, I have been so affrighted! 75
POLONIUS: With what, i' th' name of God?
OPHELIA: My lord, as I was sewing in my closet,°
Lord Hamlet, with his doublet all unbraced,°
No hat upon his head, his stockings fouled,
Ungartered, and down-gyvèd° to his ankle, 80
Pale as his shirt, his knees knocking each other,
And with a look so piteous in purport,°
As if he had been loosèd out of hell
To speak of horrors—he comes before me.
POLONIUS: Mad for thy love?
OPHELIA: My lord, I do not know, 85
But truly I do fear it.
POLONIUS: What said he?
OPHELIA: He took me by the wrist and held me hard;
Then goes he to the length of all his arm,
And with his other hand thus o'er his brow
He falls to such perusal of my face 90
As 'a would draw it. Long stayed he so.
At last, a little shaking of mine arm,
And thrice his head thus waving up and down,
He raised a sigh so piteous and profound
As it did seem to shatter all his bulk 95
And end his being. That done, he lets me go,
And, with his head over his shoulder turned,
He seemed to find his way without his eyes,
For out o'doors he went without their helps,
And to the last bended their light on me. 100
POLONIUS: Come, go with me. I will go seek the king.
This is the very ecstasy° of love,

---

71 in yourself for yourself **77 closet** private room **78 doublet all unbraced**
jacket entirely unlaced **80 down-gyvèd** hanging down like fetters **82 purport**
expression **102 ecstasy** madness

Whose violent property fordoes° itself
And leads the will to desperate undertakings
As oft as any passions under heaven   105
That does afflict our natures. I am sorry.
What, have you given him any hard words of late?
OPHELIA: No, my good lord; but as you did command,
I did repel his letters and denied
His access to me.
POLONIUS: That hath made him mad.   110
I am sorry that with better heed and judgment
I had not quoted° him. I feared he did but trifle
And meant to wrack thee; but beshrew my jealousy.°
By heaven, it is as proper° to our age
To cast beyond ourselves° in our opinions   115
As it is common for the younger sort
To lack discretion. Come, go we to the king.
This must be known, which, being kept close, might move
More grief to hide than hate to utter love.°
Come.   *Exeunt.*   120

SCENE II. *The castle.*

Flourish. Enter KING *and* QUEEN, ROSENCRANTZ, *and* GUILDENSTERN, *with others.*

KING: Welcome, dear Rosencrantz and Guildenstern.
Moreover that° we much did long to see you,
The need we have to use you did provoke
Our hasty sending. Something have you heard
Of Hamlet's transformation: so call it,   5
Sith° nor th' exterior nor the inward man
Resembles that it was. What it should be,
More than his father's death, that thus hath put him
So much from th' understanding of himself,
I cannot dream of. I entreat you both   10
That, being of so° young days brought up with him,
And sith so neighbored to his youth and havior,°
That you vouchsafe your rest° here in our court
Some little time, so by your companies

---

103 property fordoes quality destroys   **112 quoted** noted   **113 beshrew my jealousy** curse my suspicions   **114 proper** natural   **115 To . . . ourselves** to be overcalculating   **117–19 Come . . . love** the general meaning is that while telling the king of Hamlet's love may anger the king, more grief would come from keeping it secret   **II.ii.2 Moreover that** besides the fact that   **6 Sith** since   **11 of so** from such   **12 youth and havior** behavior in his youth   **13 vouchsafe your rest** consent to remain

To draw him on to pleasures, and to gather   15
So much as from occasion you may glean,
Whether aught to us unknown afflicts him thus,
That opened° lies within our remedy.

QUEEN: Good gentlemen, he hath much talked of you,
And sure I am, two men there is not living   20
To whom he more adheres. If it will please you
To show us so much gentry° and good will
As to expend your time with us awhile
For the supply and profit of our hope,
Your visitation shall receive such thanks   25
As fits a king's remembrance.

ROSENCRANTZ: Both your majesties
Might, by the sovereign power you have of us,
Put your dread pleasures more into command
Than to entreaty.

GUILDENSTERN: But we both obey,
And here give up ourselves in the full bent°   30
To lay our service freely at your feet,
To be commanded.

KING: Thanks, Rosencrantz and gentle Guildenstern.
QUEEN: Thanks, Guildenstern and gentle Rosencrantz.
And I beseech you instantly to visit   35
My too much changèd son. Go, some of you,
And bring these gentlemen where Hamlet is.

GUILDENSTERN: Heavens make our presence and our practices
Pleasant and helpful to him!

QUEEN: Ay, amen!

Exeunt ROSENCRANTZ *and* GUILDENSTERN
with some ATTENDANTS.

Enter POLONIUS.

POLONIUS: Th' ambassadors from Norway, my good lord,   40
Are joyfully returned.
KING: Thou still° hast been the father of good news.
POLONIUS: Have I, my lord? Assure you, my good liege,
I hold my duty, as I hold my soul,
Both to my God and to my gracious king;   45
And I do think, or else this brain of mine
Hunts not the trail of policy so sure°
As it hath used to do, that I have found
The very cause of Hamlet's lunacy.

18 **opened** revealed   22 **gentry** courtesy   30 **in . . . bent** entirely (the figure is of
a bow bent to its capacity)   42 **still** always   47 **Hunts . . . sure** does not follow clues of political doings with such sureness

KING: O, speak of that! That do I long to hear.   50
POLONIUS: Give first admittance to th' ambassadors.
     My news shall be the fruit to that great feast.
KING: Thyself do grace to them and bring them in.

                                             Exit POLONIUS.

     He tells me, my dear Gertrude, he hath found
     The head and source of all your son's distemper.   55
QUEEN: I doubt° it is no other but the main,°
     His father's death and our o'erhasty marriage.
KING: Well, we shall sift him.

Enter POLONIUS, VOLTEMAND, *and* CORNELIUS.

                              Welcome, my good friends.
     Say, Voltemand, what from our brother Norway?
VOLTEMAND: Most fair return of greetings and desires.   60
     Upon our first,° he sent out to suppress
     His nephew's levies, which to him appeared
     To be a preparation 'gainst the Polack;
     But better looked into, he truly found
     It was against your highness, whereat grieved,   65
     That so his sickness, age, and impotence
     Was falsely borne in hand,° sends out arrests
     On Fortinbras; which he, in brief, obeys,
     Receives rebuke from Norway, and in fine,°
     Makes vow before his uncle never more   70
     To give th' assay° of arms against your majesty.
     Whereon old Norway, overcome with joy,
     Gives him threescore thousand crowns in annual fee
     And his commission to employ those soldiers,
     So levied as before, against the Polack,   75
     With an entreaty, herein further shown,

Gives a paper.

     That it might please you to give quiet pass
     Through your dominions for this enterprise,
     On such regards of safety and allowance°
     As therein are set down.
KING: It likes us well;   80
     And at our more considered time° we'll read,
     Answer, and think upon this business.

---

56 doubt suspect;   **main** principal point   **61 first** first audience   **67 borne in
hand** deceived   **69 in fine** finally   **71 assay** trial   **79 regards . . . allowance** i.e.,
conditions   **81 considered time** time proper for considering

Meantime, we thank you for your well-took labor.
Go to your rest; at night we'll feast together.
Most welcome home!

Exeunt ambassadors VOLTEMAND *and* CORNELIUS.

POLONIUS: This business is well ended.   85
My liege and madam, to expostulate°
What majesty should be, what duty is,
Why day is day, night night, and time is time,
Were nothing but to waste night, day, and time.
Therefore, since brevity is the soul of wit,°   90
And tediousness the limbs and outward flourishes,
I will be brief. Your noble son is mad.
Mad call I it, for, to define true madness,
What is't but to be nothing else but mad?
But let that go.
QUEEN: More matter, with less art.   95
POLONIUS: Madam, I swear I use no art at all.
That he's mad, 'tis true: 'tis true 'tis pity,
And pity 'tis 'tis true—a foolish figure,°
But farewell it, for I will use no art.
Mad let us grant him then; and now remains   100
That we find out the cause of this effect,
Or rather say, the cause of this defect,
For this effect defective comes by cause.
Thus it remains, and the remainder thus.
Perpend.°   105
I have a daughter: have, while she is mine,
Who in her duty and obedience, mark,
Hath given me this. Now gather, and surmise.

Reads the letter.

"To the celestial, and my soul's idol, the most
beautified Ophelia"—   110
That's an ill phrase, a vile phrase; "beautified" is a vile
phrase. But you shall hear. Thus:
"In her excellent white bosom, these, &c."
QUEEN: Came this from Hamlet to her?
POLONIUS: Good madam, stay awhile, I will be faithful.   115
        "Doubt thou the stars are fire,
            Doubt that the sun doth move;
        Doubt° truth to be a liar,
            But never doubt I love.

86 **expostulate** discuss   90 **wit** wisdom, understanding   98 **figure** figure of rhetoric   105 **Perpend** consider carefully   118 **Doubt** suspect

O dear Ophelia, I am ill at these numbers.° I have not   120
art to reckon my groans; but that I love thee best, O
most best, believe it. Adieu.
     Thine evermore, most dear lady,
     whilst this machine° is to him, Hamlet."
This in obedience hath my daughter shown me,   125
And more above° hath his solicitings,
As they fell out by time, by means, and place,
All given to mine ear.
KING: But how hath she
Received his love?
POLONIUS: What do you think of me?
KING: As of a man faithful and honorable.   130
POLONIUS: I would fain prove so. But what might you think,
When I had seen this hot love on the wing
(As I perceived it, I must tell you that,
Before my daughter told me), what might you,
Or my dear majesty your queen here, think,   135
If I had played the desk or table book,°
Or given my heart a winking,° mute and dumb,
Or looked upon this love with idle sight?
What might you think? No, I went round to work
And my young mistress thus I did bespeak: 140
"Lord Hamlet is a prince, out of thy star.°
This must not be." And then I prescripts gave her,
That she should lock herself from his resort,
Admit no messengers, receive no tokens.
Which done, she took the fruits of my advice,   145
And he, repellèd, a short tale to make,
Fell into a sadness, then into a fast,
Thence to a watch,° thence into a weakness,
Thence to a lightness,° and, by this declension,
Into the madness wherein now he raves,   150
And all we mourn for.
KING: Do you think 'tis this?
QUEEN: It may be, very like.
POLONIUS: Hath there been such a time, I would fain know that,
That I have positively said, " 'Tis so,"
When it provèd otherwise?
KING: Not that I know.   155
POLONIUS *pointing to his head and shoulder:*
Take this from this, if this be otherwise.
If circumstances lead me, I will find

120 **ill . . . numbers** unskilled in verses   124 **machine** complex device (here, his body)   126 **more above** in addition   136 **played . . . book** i.e., been a passive recipient of secrets   137 **winking** closing of the eyes   141 **star** sphere   148 **watch** wakefulness   149 **lightness** mental derangement

Where truth is hid, though it were hid indeed
Within the center.°

KING: How may we try it further?

POLONIUS: You know sometimes he walks four hours together   160
Here in the lobby.

QUEEN: So he does indeed.

POLONIUS: At such a time I'll loose my daughter to him.
Be you and I behind an arras° then.
Mark the encounter. If he love her not,
And be not from his reason fall'n thereon,   165
Let me be no assistant for a state
But keep a farm and carters.

KING: We will try it.

Enter HAMLET *reading on a book.*

QUEEN: But look where sadly the poor wretch comes reading.

POLONIUS: Away, I do beseech you both, away.

                                        Exit KING *and* QUEEN.

I'll board him presently.° O, give me leave. How does my good   170
Lord Hamlet?

HAMLET: Well, God-a-mercy.

POLONIUS: Do you know me, my lord?

HAMLET: Excellent well. You are a fishmonger.°

POLONIUS: Not I, my lord.   175

HAMLET: Then I would you were so honest a man.

POLONIUS: Honest, my lord?

HAMLET: Ay, sir. To be honest, as this world goes, is to be one
man picked out of ten thousand.

POLONIUS: That's very true, my lord.   180

HAMLET: For if the sun breed maggots in a dead dog, being a good
kissing carrion°—have you a daughter?

POLONIUS: I have, my lord.

HAMLET: Let her not walk i' th' sun. Conception° is a blessing, but
as your daughter may conceive, friend, look to't.   185

POLONIUS *aside:* How say you by that? Still harping on my daughter. Yet he knew me not at first. 'A said I was a fishmonger. 'A
is far gone, far gone. And truly in my youth I suffered much
extremity for love, very near this. I'll speak to him
again.—What do you read, my lord?   190

HAMLET: Words, words, words.

POLONIUS: What is the matter, my lord?

HAMLET: Between who?

159 center center of the earth   **163 arras** tapestry hanging in front of a wall
170 board him presently accost him at once   **174 fishmonger** dealer in fish (slang
for a procurer)   **182 a good . . . carrion** perhaps the meaning is "a good piece of
flesh to kiss," but many editors emend "good" to "god," taking the word to refer
to the sun   **184 Conception** (1) understanding (2) becoming pregnant

POLONIUS: I mean the matter° that you read, my lord.

HAMLET: Slanders, sir; for the satirical rogue says here that old men 195
have gray beards, that their faces are wrinkled, their eyes purging
thick amber and plumtree gum, and that they have a plentiful
lack of wit, together with most weak hams. All which, sir, though
I most powerfully and potently believe, yet I hold it not honesty°
to have it thus set down; for you yourself, sir, should be old as I 200
am if, like a crab, you could go backward.

POLONIUS *aside:* Though this be madness, yet there is method in't.
Will you walk out of the air, my lord?

HAMLET: Into my grave.

POLONIUS: Indeed, that's out of the air. *Aside.* How pregnant° 205
sometimes his replies are! A happiness° that often madness hits
on, which reason and sanity could not so prosperously be delivered of. I will leave him and suddenly contrive the means of meeting between him and my daughter.—My lord, I will take my
leave of you. 210

HAMLET: You cannot take from me anything that I will more willingly part withal—except my life, except my life, except my life.

Enter GUILDENSTERN *and* ROSENCRANTZ.

POLONIUS: Fare you well, my lord.

HAMLET: These tedious old fools!

POLONIUS: You go to seek the Lord Hamlet? There he is. 215

ROSENCRANTZ *to* POLONIUS: God save you, sir!

Exit POLONIUS.

GUILDENSTERN: My honored lord!

ROSENCRANTZ: My most dear lord!

HAMLET: My excellent good friends! How dost thou,
Guildenstern? Ah, Rosencrantz! Good lads, how do you both? 220

ROSENCRANTZ: As the indifferent° children of the earth.

GUILDENSTERN: Happy in that we are not overhappy.
On Fortune's cap we are not the very button.

HAMLET: Nor the soles of her shoe?

ROSENCRANTZ: Neither, my lord. 225

HAMLET: Then you live about her waist, or in the middle of her
favors?

GUILDENSTERN: Faith, her privates° we.

HAMLET: In the secret parts of Fortune? O, most true! She is a
strumpet. What news? 230

---

194 matter Polonius means "subject matter," but Hamlet pretends to take the word
in the sense of "quarrel" **199 honesty** decency **205 pregnant** meaningful
206 happiness apt turn of phrase **221 indifferent** ordinary **228 privates** ordinary men (with a pun on *private parts*)

ROSENCRANTZ: None, my lord, but that the world's grown honest.

HAMLET: Then is doomsday near. But your news is not true. Let me question more in particular. What have you, my good friends, deserved at the hands of Fortune that she sends you to prison hither? 235

GUILDENSTERN: Prison, my lord?

HAMLET: Denmark's a prison.

ROSENCRANTZ: Then is the world one.

HAMLET: A goodly one, in which there are many confines, wards,° and dungeons, Denmark being one o' th' worst. 240

ROSENCRANTZ: We think not so, my lord.

HAMLET: Why, then 'tis none to you, for there is nothing either good or bad but thinking makes it so. To me it is a prison.

ROSENCRANTZ: Why then your ambition makes it one. 'Tis too narrow for your mind. 245

HAMLET: O God, I could be bounded in a nutshell and count myself a king of infinite space, were it not that I have bad dreams.

GUILDENSTERN: Which dreams indeed are ambition, for the very substance of the ambitious is merely the shadow of a dream.

HAMLET: A dream itself is but a shadow. 250

ROSENCRANTZ: Truly, and I hold ambition of so airy and light a quality that it is but a shadow's shadow.

HAMLET: Then are our beggars bodies, and our monarchs and outstretched heroes the beggars' shadows.° Shall we to th' court? For, by my fay,° I cannot reason. 255

BOTH: We'll wait upon you.

HAMLET: No such matter. I will not sort you with the rest of my servants, for, to speak to you like an honest man, I am most dreadfully attended. But in the beaten way of friendship, what make you at Elsinore? 260

ROSENCRANTZ: To visit you, my lord; no other occasion.

HAMLET: Beggar that I am, I am even poor in thanks, but I thank you; and sure, dear friends, my thanks are too dear a halfpenny.° Were you not sent for? Is it your own inclining? Is it a free visitation? Come, come, deal justly with me. Come, come; nay, 265 speak.

GUILDENSTERN: What should we say, my lord?

HAMLET: Why anything—but to th' purpose. You were sent for, and there is a kind of confession in your looks, which your modesties have not craft enough to color. I know the good king and 270 queen have sent for you.

ROSENCRANTZ: To what end, my lord?

HAMLET: That you must teach me. But let me conjure you by the rights of your fellowship, by the consonancy of our youth, by the

---

239 wards cells **254 Then . . . shadows** By your logic, beggars (lacking ambition) are substantial, and great men are elongated shadows **255 fay** faith **263 too . . . halfpenny** not worth a halfpenny

obligation of our ever-preserved love, and by what more dear a   275
better proposer can charge you withal, be even and direct with
me, whether you were sent for or no.

ROSENCRANTZ *aside to* GUILDENSTERN: What say you?

HAMLET *aside:*   Nay then, I have an eye of you.—If you love me,
hold not off.   280

GUILDENSTERN: My lord, we were sent for.

HAMLET: I will tell you why; so shall my anticipation prevent your
discovery,° and your secrecy to the king and queen molt no
feather. I have of late, but wherefore I know not, lost all my
mirth, forgone all custom of exercises; and indeed, it goes so   285
heavily with my disposition that this goodly frame, the earth,
seems to me a sterile promontory; this most excellent canopy, the
air, look you, this brave o'erhanging firmament, this majestical
roof fretted° with golden fire: why, it appeareth nothing to me
but a foul and pestilent congregation of vapors. What a piece of   290
work is a man, how noble in reason, how infinite in faculties, in
form and moving how express° and admirable, in action how like
an angel, in apprehension how like a god: the beauty of the world,
the paragon of animals; and yet to me, what is this quintessence
of dust? Man delights not me; nor woman neither, though by   295
your smiling you seem to say so.

ROSENCRANTZ: My lord, there was no such stuff in my thoughts.

HAMLET: Why did ye laugh then, when I said, "Man delights not
me"?

ROSENCRANTZ: To think, my lord, if you delight not in man, what   300
lenten° entertainment the players shall receive from you. We
coted° them on the way, and hither are they coming to offer you
service.

HAMLET: He that plays the king shall be welcome; his majesty shall
have tribute of me; the adventurous knight shall use his foil and   305
target;° the lover shall not sigh gratis; the humorous man° shall
end his part in peace; the clown shall make those laugh whose
lungs are tickle o' th' sere;° and the lady shall say her mind freely,
or° the blank verse shall halt° for't. What players are they?

ROSENCRANTZ: Even those you were wont to take such delight in,   310
the tragedians of the city.

HAMLET: How chances it they travel? Their residence, both in reputation and profit, was better both ways.

ROSENCRANTZ: I think their inhibition° comes by the means of the
late innovation.°   315

283 prevent your discovery forestall your disclosure   **289 fretted** adorned
292 express exact   **301 lenten** meager   **302 coted** overtook   **306 target** shield;
humorous man i.e., eccentric man (among stock characters in dramas were men
dominated by a "humor" or odd trait)   **308 tickle . . . sere** on hair trigger
("sere" = part of the gunlock)   **309 or** else;   **halt** limp   **314 inhibition** hindrance
315 innovation probably an allusion to the companies of child actors that had become popular and were offering serious competition to the adult actors

HAMLET: Do they hold the same estimation they did when I was in
the city? Are they so followed?

ROSENCRANTZ: No indeed, are they not.

HAMLET: How comes it? Do they grow rusty?

ROSENCRANTZ: Nay, their endeavor keeps in the wonted pace, but   320
there is, sir, an eyrie° of children, little eyases, that cry out on the
top of question° and are most tyrannically° clapped for't. These
are now the fashion, and so berattle the common stages° (so they
call them) that many wearing rapiers are afraid of goosequills° and
dare scarce come thither.   325

HAMLET: What, are they children? Who maintains 'em? How are
they escoted?° Will they pursue the quality° no longer than they
can sing? Will they not say afterwards, if they should grow themselves to common players (as it is most like, if their means are no
better), their writers do them wrong to make them exclaim   330
against their own succession?°

ROSENCRANTZ: Faith, there has been much to-do on both sides, and
the nation holds it no sin to tarre° them to controversy. There
was, for a while, no money bid for argument° unless the poet and
the player went to cuffs in the question.   335

HAMLET: Is't possible?

GUILDENSTERN: O, there has been much throwing about of brains.

HAMLET: Do the boys carry it away?

ROSENCRANTZ: Ay, that they do, my lord—Hercules and his load°
too.   340

HAMLET: It is not very strange, for my uncle is King of Denmark,
and those that would make mouths at him while my father lived
give twenty, forty, fifty, a hundred ducats apiece for his picture
in little. 'Sblood,° there is something in this more than natural, if
philosophy could find it out.   345

A flourish.

GUILDENSTERN: There are the players.

HAMLET: Gentlemen, you are welcome to Elsinore. Your hands,
come then. Th' appurtenance of welcome is fashion and ceremony. Let me comply° with you in this garb,° lest my extent° to
the players (which I tell you must show fairly outwards) should   350

---

321 eyrie nest   **322 eyases . . . question** unfledged hawks that cry shrilly above
others in matters of debate;   **tyrannically** violently   **323 berattle . . . stages** cry
down the public theaters (with the adult acting companies)   **324 goosequills** pens
(of satirists who ridicule the public theaters and their audiences)   **327 escoted** financially supported;   **quality** profession of acting   **331 succession** future
333 tarre incite   **334 argument** plot of a play   **339 Hercules . . . load** i.e., the
whole world (with a reference to the Globe Theatre, which had a sign that represented Hercules bearing the globe)   **334 'Sblood** by God's blood   **349 comply** be
courteous;   **garb** outward show;   **extent** behavior

more appear like entertainment than yours. You are welcome. But
my uncle-father and aunt-mother are deceived.

GUILDENSTERN: In what, my dear lord?

HAMLET: I am but mad north-northwest:° when the wind is south-
erly I know a hawk from a handsaw.°   355

Enter POLONIUS.

POLONIUS: Well be with you, gentlemen.

HAMLET: Hark you, Guildenstern, and you too; at each ear a
hearer. That great baby you see there is not yet out of his swad-
dling clouts.

ROSENCRANTZ: Happily° he is the second time come to them, for   360
they say an old man is twice a child.

HAMLET: I will prophesy he comes to tell me of the players. Mark
it.—You say right, sir; a Monday morning, 'twas then indeed.

POLONIUS: My lord, I have news to tell you.

HAMLET: My lord, I have news to tell you. When Roscius° was an   365
actor in Rome—

POLONIUS: The actors are come hither, my lord.

HAMLET: Buzz, buzz,°

POLONIUS: Upon my honor—

HAMLET: Then came each actor on his ass—   370

POLONIUS: The best actors in the world, either for tragedy, comedy,
history, pastoral, pastoral-comical, historical-pastoral, tragical-his-
torical, tragical-comical-historical-pastoral; scene individable,° or
poem unlimited.° Seneca° cannot be too heavy, nor Plautus° too
light. For the law of writ and the liberty,° these are the only men.   375

HAMLET: O Jeptha, judge of Israel,° what a treasure hadst thou!

POLONIUS: What a treasure had he, my lord?

HAMLET: Why,
      "One fair daughter, and no more,
      The which he lovèd passing well."   380

POLONIUS *aside:*   Still on my daughter.

HAMLET: Am I not i' th' right, old Jeptha?

354 north-northwest i.e., on one point of the compass only   **355 hawk from a
handsaw** "hawk" can refer not only to a bird but to a kind of pickax; "handsaw"—
a carpenter's tool—may involve a similar pun on *hernshaw,* a heron)
360 Happily perhaps   **365 Roscius** a famous Roman comic actor   **368 Buzz,
buzz** an interjection, perhaps indicating that the news is old   **373 scene individable** plays observing the unities of time, place, and action   **374 poem unlimited**
plays not restricted by the tenets of criticism; **Seneca** Roman tragic dramatist;
Plautus Roman comic dramatist   **375 For . . . liberty** perhaps "for sticking to
the text and improvising"; perhaps "for classical plays and for modern loosely written plays"   **376 Jeptha . . . Israel** the title of a ballad on the Hebrew judge who
sacrificed his daughter; see Judges 11

POLONIUS: If you call me Jeptha, my lord, I have a daughter that I
love passing well.

HAMLET: Nay, that follows not.   385

POLONIUS: What follows then, my lord?

HAMLET: Why,
           "As by lot, God wot,"
and then, you know,
           "It came to pass, as most like it was."   390
The first row of the pious chanson° will show you more, for look
where my abridgment° comes.

Enter the PLAYERS.

You are welcome, masters, welcome, all. I am glad to see thee
well. Welcome, good friends. O, old friend, why, thy face is val-
anced° since I saw thee last. Com'st thou to beard me in Den-   395
mark? What, my young lady° and mistress? By'r Lady, your
ladyship is nearer to heaven than when I saw you last by the alti-
tude of a chopine.° Pray God your voice, like a piece of uncurrent
gold, be not cracked within the ring.°—Masters, you are all welcome. We'll e'en to't like French falconers, fly at anything we see.   400
We'll have a speech straight. Come, give us a taste of your
quality. Come, a passionate speech.

PLAYER: What speech, my good lord?

HAMLET: I heard thee speak me a speech once, but it was never
acted, or if it was, not above once, for the play, I remember,   405
pleased not the million; 'twas caviary to the general,° but it was
(as I received it, and others, whose judgments in such matters
cried in the top of ° mine) an excellent play, well digested in the
scenes, set down with as much modesty as cunning.° I remember
one said there were no sallets° in the lines to make the matter   410
savory; nor no matter in the phrase that might indict the author
of affectation, but called it an honest method, as wholesome as
sweet, and by very much more handsome than fine.° One speech
in't I chiefly loved. 'Twas Aeneas' tale to Dido, and thereabout of
it especially when he speaks of Priam's slaughter. If it live in your   415
memory, begin at this line—let me see, let me see:

391 **row . . . chanson** stanza of the scriptural song   392 **abridgment** (1) i.e., en-
tertainers, who abridge the time (2) interrupters   395 **valanced** fringed (with a
beard)   396 **young lady** i.e., boy for female roles   398 **chopine** thick-soled shoe
398–99 **like . . . ring** a coin was unfit for legal tender if a crack extended from the
edge through the ring enclosing the monarch's head; Hamlet, punning on *ring*,
refers to the change of voice that the boy actor will undergo   406 **caviary . . .
general** i.e., too choice for the multitude   408 **in the top of** overtopping'
409 **modesty as cunning** restraint as art   410 **sallets** salads, spicy jests   413 **more
. . . fine** well-proportioned rather than ornamented

"The rugged Pyrrhus, like th' Hyrcanian beast°—"
'Tis not so; it begins with Pyrrhus:
"The rugged Pyrrhus, he whose sable° arms,
Black as his purpose, did the night resemble   420
When he lay couchèd in th' ominous horse,°
Hath now this dread and black complexion smeared
With heraldry more dismal.° Head to foot
Now is he total gules, horridly tricked°
With blood of fathers, mothers, daughters, sons,   425
Baked and impasted° with the parching streets,
That lend a tyrannous and a damnèd light
To their lord's murder. Roasted in wrath and fire,
And thus o'ersizèd° with coagulate gore,
With eyes like carbuncles, the hellish Pyrrhus   430
Old grandsire Priam seeks."
  So, proceed you.
POLONIUS: Fore God, my lord, well spoken, with good accent and
  good discretion.
PLAYER: "Anon he finds him,   435
Striking too short at Greeks. His antique sword,
Rebellious to his arm, lies where it falls,
Repugnant to command.° Unequal matched,
Pyrrhus at Priam drives, in rage strikes wide,
But with the whiff and wind of his fell sword   440
Th' unnervèd father falls. Then senseless Ilium,°
Seeming to feel this blow, with flaming top
Stoops to his base,° and with a hideous crash
Takes prisoner Pyrrhus' ear. For lo, his sword,
Which was declining on the milky head   445
Of reverend Priam, seemed i' th' air to stick.
So as a painted tyrant° Pyrrhus stood,
And like a neutral to his will and matter°
Did nothing.
But as we often see, against° some storm,   450
A silence in the heavens, the rack° stand still,
The bold winds speechless, and the orb below
As hush as death, anon the dreadful thunder
Doth rend the region, so after Pyrrhus' pause,
A rousèd vengeance sets him new awork,   455
And never did the Cyclops' hammers fall
On Mars's armor, forged for proof eterne,°

---

417 Hyrcanian beast tiger (Hyrcania was in Asia)   **419 sable** black   **421 ominous horse** wooden horse at the siege of Troy   **423 dismal** ill-omened   **424 total . . . tricked** all red, horridly adorned   **426 impasted** encrusted   **429 o'ersizèd** smeared over   **438 Repugnant to command** disobedient   **441 senseless Ilium** insensate Troy   **443 Stoops . . . base** collapses ("his" = its)   **447 painted tyrant** tyrant in a picture   **448 matter** task   **450 against** just before   **451 rack** clouds   **457 proof eterne** eternal endurance

With less remorse than Pyrrhus' bleeding sword
Now falls on Priam.
Out, out, thou strumpet Fortune! All you gods,   460
In general synod° take away her power,
Break all the spokes and fellies° from her wheel,
And bowl the round nave° down the hill of heaven,
As low as to the fiends."

POLONIUS: This is too long.   465

HAMLET: It shall to the barber's, with your beard.—Prithee say on.
He's for a jig or a tale of bawdry, or he sleeps. Say on; come to
Hecuba.

PLAYER: "But who (ah woe!) had seen the mobled° queen—"

HAMLET: "The mobled queen"?   470

POLONIUS: That's good. "Mobled queen" is good.

PLAYER: "Run barefoot up and down, threat'ning the flames
With bisson rheum;° a clout° upon that head
Where late the diadem stood, and for a robe,
About her lank and all o'erteemèd° lions,   475
A blanket in the alarm of fear caught up—
Who this had seen, with tongue in venom steeped
'Gainst Fortune's state would treason have pronounced.
But if the gods themselves did see her then,
When she saw Pyrrhus make malicious sport   480
In mincing with his sword her husband's limbs,
The instant burst of clamor that she made
(Unless things mortal move them not at all)
Would have made milch° the burning eyes of heaven
And passion in the gods."   485

POLONIUS: Look, whe'r° he has not turned his color, and has tears
in's eyes. Prithee no more.

HAMLET: 'Tis well. I'll have thee speak out the rest of this soon.
Good my lord, will you see the players well bestowed?° Do you
hear? Let them be well used, for they are the abstract and brief   490
chronicles of the time. After your death you were better have a
bad epitaph than their ill report while you live.

POLONIUS: My lord, I will use them according to their desert.

HAMLET: God's bodkin,° man, much better! Use every man after his
desert, and who shall scape whipping? Use them after your own   495
honor and dignity. The less they deserve, the more merit is in your
bounty. Take them in.

POLONIUS: Come, sirs.

HAMLET: Follow him, friends. We'll hear a play tomorrow. *Aside to*
PLAYER. Dost thou hear me, old friend? Can you play *The Murder*   500
of Gonzago?

461 **synod** council   462 **fellies** rims   463 **nave** hub   469 **mobled** muffled
473 **bisson rheum** blinding tears;   **clout** rag   475 **o'erteemèd** exhausted with
childbearing   484 **milch** moist (literally "milk-giving")   486 **whe'r** whether
489 **bestowed** housed   494 **God's bodkin** by God's little body

PLAYER: Ay, my lord.

HAMLET: We'll ha't tomorrow night. You could for a need study a speech of some dozen or sixteen lines which I would set down and insert in't, could you not? 505

PLAYER: Ay, my lord.

HAMLET: Very well. Follow that lord, and look you mock him not. My good friends, I'll leave you till night. You are welcome to Elsinore.

Exeunt POLONIUS *and* PLAYERS.

ROSENCRANTZ: Good my lord. 510

Exeunt ROSENCRANTZ *and* GUILDENSTERN.

HAMLET: Ay, so, God bye to you.—Now I am alone.
O, what a rogue and peasant slave am I!
Is it not monstrous that this player here,
But in a fiction, in a dream of passion,°
Could force his soul so to his own conceit° 515
That from her working all his visage wanned,
Tears in his eyes, distraction in his aspect,
A broken voice, and his whole function° suiting
With forms° to his conceit? And all for nothing!
For Hecuba! 520
What's Hecuba to him, or he to Hecuba,
That he should weep for her? What would he do
Had he the motive and the cue for passion
That I have? He would drown the stage with tears
And cleave the general ear with horrid speech, 525
Make mad the guilty and appall the free,°
Confound the ignorant, and amaze indeed
The very faculties of eyes and ears.
Yet I,
A dull and muddy-mettled° rascal, peak 530
Like John-a-dreams,° unpregnant of ° my cause,
And can say nothing. No, not for a king,
Upon whose property and most dear life
A damned defeat was made. Am I a coward?
Who calls me villain? Breaks my pate across? 535
Plucks off my beard and blows it in my face?
Tweaks me by the nose? Gives me the lie i' th' throat
As deep as to the lungs? Who does me this?

514 dream of passion imaginary emotion   **515 conceit** imagination   **518 function** action   **519 forms** bodily expressions   **526 appall the free** terrify (make pale?) the guiltless   **530 muddy-mettled** weak-spirited; **peak Like John-a-dreams** mope like a dreamer   **531 unpregnant of** unquickened by

Ha, 'swounds,° I should take it, for it cannot be
But I am pigeon-livered° and lack gall   540
To make oppression bitter, or ere this
I should ha' fatted all the region kites°
With this slave's offal. Bloody, bawdy villain!
Remorseless, treacherous, lecherous, kindless° villain!
O, vengeance!   545
Why, what an ass am I! This is most brave,°
That I, the son of a dear father murdered,
Prompted to my revenge by heaven and hell,
Must, like a whore, unpack my heart with words
And fall a-cursing like a very drab,°   550
A stallion!° Fie upon't, foh! About,° my brains.
Hum—
I have heard that guilty creatures sitting at a play
Have by the very cunning of the scene
Been struck so to the soul that presently°   555
They have proclaimed their malefactions.
For murder, though it have no tongue, will speak
With most miraculous organ. I'll have these players
Play something like the murder of my father
Before mine uncle. I'll observe his looks,   560
I'll tent° him to the quick. If 'a do blench,°
I know my course. The spirit that I have seen
May be a devil, and the devil hath power
T 'assume a pleasing shape, yea, and perhaps
Out of my weakness and my melancholy,   565
As he is very potent with such spirits,
Abuses me to damn me. I'll have grounds
More relative° than this. The play's the thing
Wherein I'll catch the conscience of the king.   *Exit.*

ACT III

SCENE I. The castle.

Enter KING, QUEEN, POLONIUS, OPHELIA, ROSENCRANTZ, GUILDENSTERN,
LORDS.

KING: And can you by no drift of conference°
    Get from him why he puts on this confusion,

---

539 'swounds by God's wounds   **540 pigeon-livered** gentle as a dove   **542 region
kites** kites (scavenger birds) of the sky   **544 kindless** unnatural   **546 brave** fine
550 drab prostitute   **551 stallion** male prostitue (perhaps one should adopt the
Folio reading, "scullion" = kitchen wench);   **About** to work   **555 presently**
immediately   **561 tent** probe;   **blench** flinch   **568 relative** probably "pertinent,"
but possibly "able to be related plausibly"   **III.i.1 drift of conference** management
of conversation

Grating so harshly all his days of quiet
With turbulent and dangerous lunacy?
ROSENCRANTZ: He does confess he feels himself distracted,   5
But from what cause 'a will by no means speak.
GUILDENSTERN: Nor do we find him forward to be sounded,°
But with a crafty madness keeps aloof
When we could bring him on to some confession
Of his true state.
QUEEN: Did he receive you well?   10
ROSENCRANTZ: Most like a gentleman.
GUILDENSTERN: But with much forcing of his disposition.°
ROSENCRANTZ: Niggard of question,° but of our demands
Most free in his reply.
QUEEN: Did you assay° him
To any pastime?   15
ROSENCRANTZ: Madame, it so fell out that certain players
We o'erraught° on the way; of these we told him,
And there did seem in him a kind of joy
To hear of it. They are here about the court,
And, as I think, they have already order   20
This night to play before him.
POLONIUS: 'Tis most true,
And he beseeched me to entreat your majesties
To hear and see the matter.
KING: With all my heart, and it doth much content me
To hear him so inclined.   25
Good gentlemen, give him a further edge
And drive his purpose into these delights.
ROSENCRANTZ: We shall, my lord.

Exeunt ROSENCRANTZ *and* GUILDENSTERN.

KING: Sweet Gertrude, leave us too,
For we have closely° sent for Hamlet hither,
That he, as 'twere by accident, may here   30
Affront° Ophelia.
Her father and myself (lawful espials°)
Will so bestow ourselves that, seeing unseen,
We may of their encounter frankly judge
And gather by him, as he is behaved,   35
If 't be th' affliction of his love or no
That thus he suffers for.
QUEEN: I shall obey you.
And for your part, Ophelia, I do wish

---

7 forward . . . sounded willing to be questioned   **12 forcing . . . disposition**
effort   **13 Niggard of question** uninclined to talk   **14 assay** tempt   **17 o'er-**
raught overtook   **29 closely** secretly   **31 Affront** meet face to face   **32 espials**
spies

That your good beauties be the happy cause
Of Hamlet's wildness. So shall I hope your virtues   40
Will bring him to his wonted way again,
To both your honors.
OPHELIA: Madam, I wish it may.

Exit QUEEN.

POLONIUS: Ophelia, walk you here.—Gracious, so please you,
   We will bestow ourselves. *To* OPHELIA. Read on this book,
   That show of such an exercise may color°   45
   Your loneliness. We are oft to blame in this,
   'Tis too much proved, that with devotion's visage
   And pious action we do sugar o'er
   The devil himself.
KING *aside:*   O, 'tis too true.
   How smart a lash that speech doth give my conscience!   50
   The harlot's cheek, beautied with plast'ring art,
   Is not more ugly to the thing that helps it
   Than is my deed to my most painted word.
   O heavy burden!
POLONIUS: I hear him coming. Let's withdraw, my lord.   55

Exeunt KING *and* POLONIUS.

Enter HAMLET.

HAMLET: To be, or not to be: that is the question:
   Whether 'tis nobler in the mind to suffer
   The slings and arrows of outrageous fortune,
   Or to take arms against a sea of troubles,
   And by opposing end them. To die, to sleep—   60
   No more—and by a sleep to say we end
   The heartache, and the thousand natural shocks
   That flesh is heir to! 'Tis a consummation
   Devoutly to be wished. To die, to sleep—
   To sleep—perchance to dream: ay, there's the rub,°   65
   For in that sleep of death what dreams may come
   When we have shuffled off this mortal coil,°
   Must give us pause. There's the respect°
   That makes calamity of so long life:°
   For who would bear the whips and scorns of time,   70
   Th' oppressor's wrong, the proud man's contumely,

45 exercise may color act of devotion may give a plausible hue to (the book is one
of devotion)   **65 rub** impediment (obstruction to a bowler's ball)   **67 coil** (1) turmoil (2) a ring of rope (here the flesh encircling the soul)   **68 respect**
consideration   **69 makes . . . life** (1) makes calamity so long-lived (2) makes living
so long a calamity

The pangs of despised love, the law's delay,
The insolence of office, and the spurns
That patient merit of th' unworthy takes,
When he himself might his quietus° make   75
With a bare bodkin?° Who would fardels° bear,
To grunt and sweat under a weary life,
But that the dread of something after death,
The undiscovered country, from whose bourn°
No traveler returns, puzzles the will,   80
And makes us rather bear those ills we have,
Than fly to others that we know not of?
Thus conscience° does make cowards of us all,
And thus the native hue of resolution
Is sicklied o'er with the pale cast° of thought,   85
And enterprises of great pitch° and moment,
With this regard° their currents turn awry,
And lose the name of action.—Soft you now,
The fair Ophelia!—Nymph, in thy orisons°
Be all my sins remembered.

OPHELIA: Good my lord,   90
How does your honor for this many a day?

HAMLET: I humbly thank you; well, well, well.

OPHELIA: My lord, I have remembrances of yours
That I have longèd long to redeliver.
I pray you now, receive them.

HAMLET: No, not I,   95
I never gave you aught.

OPHELIA: My honored lord, you know right well you did, And with
them words of so sweet breath composed as made
these things more rich. Their perfume lost,
Take these again, for to the noble mind   100
Rich gifts wax poor when givers prove unkind.
There, my lord.

HAMLET: Ha, ha! Are you honest?°

OPHELIA: My lord?

HAMLET: Are you fair?   105

OPHELIA: What means your lordship?

HAMLET: That if you be honest and fair, your honesty should admit
no discourse to your beauty.°

OPHELIA: Could beauty, my lord, have better commerce than with
honesty?   110

HAMLET: Ay, truly; for the power of beauty will sooner transform

---

75 quietus full discharge (a legal term)   **76 bodkin** dagger;   **fardels** burdens
79 bourn region   **83 conscience** self-consciousness, introspection   **85 cast** color
86 pitch height (a term from falconry)   **87 regard** consideration   **89 orisons**
prayers   **103 Are you honest** (1) Are you modest? (2) Are you chaste (3) Have you
integrity?   **107–08 your honesty . . . beauty** your modesty should permit no approach to your beauty

honesty from what it is to a bawd° than the force of honesty can
translate beauty into his likeness. This was sometime a paradox,
but now the time gives it proof. I did love you once.

OPHELIA: Indeed, my lord, you made me believe so.   115

HAMLET: You should not have believed me, for virtue
cannot so inoculate° our old stock but we shall relish of it.° I loved
you not.

OPHELIA: I was the more deceived.

HAMLET: Get thee to a nunnery. Why wouldst thou be a breeder of   120
sinners? I am myself indifferent honest,° but yet I could accuse
me of such things that it were better my mother had not borne
me: I am very proud, revengeful, ambitious, with more offenses
at my beck° than I have thoughts to put them in, imagination to
give them shape, or time to act them in. What should such fellows   125
as I do crawling between earth and heaven? We are arrant knaves
all; believe none of us. Go thy ways to a nunnery. Where's your
father?

OPHELIA: At home, my lord.

HAMLET: Let the doors be shut upon him, that he may play the fool   130
nowhere but in's own house. Farewell.

OPHELIA: O help him, you sweet heavens!

HAMLET: If thou dost marry, I'll give thee this plague for thy
dowry: be thou as chaste as ice, as pure as snow, thou shalt not
escape calumny. Get thee to a nunnery. Go, farewell. Or if thou   135
wilt needs marry, marry a fool, for wise men know well enough
what monsters° you make of them. To a nunnery, go, and quickly
too. Farewell.

OPHELIA: Heavenly powers, restore him!

HAMLET: I have heard of your paintings, well enough. God hath   140
given you one face, and you make yourselves another. You jig and
amble, and you lisp; you nickname God's creatures and make
your wantonness your ignorance.° Go to, I'll no more on't; it hath
made me mad. I say we will have no moe° marriage. Those that
are married already—all but one—shall live. The rest shall keep   145
as they are. To a nunnery, go.   *Exit*.

OPHELIA: O what a noble mind is here o'erthrown!
The courtier's, soldier's, scholar's, eye, tongue, sword,
Th' expectancy and rose° of the fair state,
The glass of fashion, and the mold of form,°   150
Th' observed of all observers, quite, quite down!
And I, of ladies most deject and wretched,
That sucked the honey of his musicked vows,
Now see that noble and most sovereign reason

---

112 bawd procurer   **117 inoculate** graft; **relish of it** smack of it (our old sinful
nature)   **121 indifferent honest** moderately virtuous   **124 beck** call   **137 monsters** horned beasts, cuckolds   **142–43 make . . . ignorance** excuse your wanton
speech by pretending ignorance   **144 moe** more   **149 expectancy and rose** i.e.,
fair hope   **150 The glass . . . form** the mirror of fashion, and the pattern of
excellent behavior

Like sweet bells jangled, out of time and harsh,   155
That unmatched form and feature of blown° youth
Blasted with ecstasy.° O, woe is me
T' have seen what I have seen, see what I see!

Enter KING *and* POLONIUS.

KING: Love? His affections° do not that way tend,
    Nor what he spake, though it lacked form a little,   160
    Was not like madness. There's something in his soul
    O'er which his melancholy sits on brood,
    And I do doubt° the hatch and the disclose
    Will be some danger; which for to prevent,
    I have in quick determination   165
    Thus set it down: he shall with speed to England
    For the demand of our neglected tribute.
    Haply the seas, and countries different,
    With variable objects, shall expel
    This something-settled° matter in his heart,   170
    Whereon his brains still beating puts him thus
    From fashion of himself. What think you on't?
POLONIUS: It shall do well. But yet do I believe
    The origin and commencement of his grief
    Sprung from neglected love. How now, Ophelia?   175
    You need not tell us what Lord Hamlet said;
    We heard it all. My lord, do as you please,
    But if you hold it fit, after the play,
    Let his queen mother all alone entreat him
    To show his grief. Let her be round° with him,   180
    And I'll be placed, so please you, in the ear
    Of all their conference. If she find him not,°
    To England send him, or confine him where
    Your wisdom best shall think.
KING: It shall be so.
    Madness in great ones must not unwatched go.   185
                                Exeunt.

SCENE II. The castle

Enter HAMLET *and three of the* PLAYERS.

HAMLET: Speak the speech, I pray you, as I pronounced it to you,
    trippingly on the tongue. But if you mouth it, as many of our
    players do, I had as lief the town crier spoke my lines. Nor do

156 **blown** blooming   157 **esctasy** madness   159 **affections** inclinations
163 **doubt** fear   170 **something-settled** somewhat settled   180 **round** blunt
182 **find him not** does not find him out

not saw the air too much with your hand, thus, but use all gently,
for in the very torrent, tempest, and (as I may say) whirlwind of   5
your passion, you must acquire and beget a temperance that may
give it smoothness. O, it offends me to the soul to hear a robustious periwig-pated° fellow tear a passion to tatters, to very rags,
to split the ears of the groundlings,° who for the most part are
capable of ° nothing but inexplicable dumb shows° and noise. I   10
would have such a fellow whipped for o'erdoing Termagant. It
out-herods Herod.° Pray you avoid it.

PLAYER: I warrant your honor.

HAMLET: Be not too tame neither, but let your own discretion be
your tutor. Suit the action to the word, the word to the action,   15
with this special observance, that you o'erstep not the modesty of
nature. For anything so o'erdone is from° the purpose of playing,
whose end, both at the first and now, was and is, to hold, as
'twere, the mirror up to nature; to show virtue her own feature,
scorn her own image, and the very age and body of the time his   20
form and pressure.° Now, this overdone, or come tardy off,
though it makes the unskillful laugh, cannot but make the judicious grieve, the censure of the which one must in your allowance
o'erweigh a whole theater of others. O, there be players that I
have seen play, and heard others praise, and that highly (not to   25
speak it profanely), that neither having th' accent of Christians,
nor the gait of Christian, pagan, nor man, have so strutted and
bellowed that I have thought some of Nature's journeymen° had
made men, and not made them well, they imitated humanity so
abominably.   30

PLAYER: I hope we have reformed that indifferently° with us, sir.

HAMLET: O, reform it altogether! And let those that play your
clowns speak no more than is set down for them, for there be of
them that will themselves laugh, to set on some quantity of barren
spectators to laugh too, though in the meantime some necessary   35
question of the play be then to be considered. That's villainous
and shows a most pitiful ambition in the fool that uses it. Go
make you ready.   *Exit* PLAYERS.

Enter POLONIUS, GUILDENSTERN, *and* ROSENCRANTZ.

How now, my lord? Will the king hear this piece of work?

POLONIUS: And the queen too, and that presently.   40

HAMLET: Bid the players make haste.

III.ii.8 robustious periwig-pated boisterous wig-headed   **9 groundlings** those who
stood in the pit of the theater (the poorest and presumably most ignorant of the
audience)   **10 are capable of** are able to understand;   **dumb shows** it had been
the fashion for actors to preface plays or parts of plays with silent mime   **11–12**
Termagant . . . Herod boisterious characters in the old mystery plays   **17 from**
contrary to   **21 pressure** image, impress   **28 journeymen** workers not yet masters of their craft   **31 indifferently** tolerable

Exit POLONIUS.

Will you two help to hasten them?
ROSENCRANTZ: Ay, my lord.   *Exeunt they two.*
HAMLET: What, ho, Horatio!

Enter HORATIO.

HORATIO: Here, sweet lord, at your service.   45
HAMLET: Horatio, thou art e'en as just a man
  As e'er my conversation coped withal.°
HORATIO: O, my dear lord—
HAMLET: Nay, do not think I flatter.
  For what advancement° may I hope from thee,
  That no revenue hast but thy good spirits   50
  To feed and clothe thee? Why should the poor be flattered?
  No, let the candied° tongue lick absurd pomp,
  And crook the pregnant° hinges of the knee
  Where thrift° may follow fawning. Dost thou hear?
  Since my dear soul was mistress of her choice   55
  And could of men distinguish her election,
  S' hath sealed thee° for herself, for thou hast been
  As one, in suff'ring all, that suffers nothing,
  A man that Fortune's buffets and rewards
  Hast ta'en with equal thanks; and blest are those   60
  Whose blood° and judgment are so well commeddled°
  That they are not a pipe for Fortune's finger
  To sound what stop she please. Give me that man
  That is not passion's slave, and I will wear him
  In my heart's core, ay, in my heart of heart,   65
  As I do thee. Something too much of this—
  There is a play tonight before the king.
  One scene of it comes near the circumstance
  Which I have told thee, of my father's death.
  I prithee, when thou see'st that act afoot,   70
  Even with the very comment° of thy soul
  Observe my uncle. If his occulted° guilt
  Do not itself unkennel in one speech,
  It is a damnèd ghost that we have seen,
  And my imaginations are as foul   75
  As Vulcan's stithy.° Give him heedful note,
  For I mine eyes will rivet to his face,

---

47 coped withal met with   **49 advancement** promotion   **52 candied** sugared,
flattering   **53 pregnant** (1) pliant (2) full of promise of good fortune   **54 thrift**
profit   **57 S' . . . thee** she (the soul) has set a mark on you   **61 blood** passion;
commeddled blended   **71 very comment** deepest wisdom   **72 occulted** hidden
76 stithy forge, smithy

And after we will both our judgments join
In censure of his seeming.°
HORATIO: Well, my lord.
    If 'a steal aught the whilst this play is playing,   80
    And scape detecting, I will pay the theft.

Enter trumpets and kettleddrums, KING, QUEEN, POLONIUS, OPHELIA, RO-
SENCRANTZ, GUILDENSTERN, *and other* LORDS *attendant, with his* GUARD
carrying torches. Danish march. Sound a flourish.

HAMLET: They are coming to the play: I must be idle;° Get you a
    place.
KING: How fares our cousin Hamlet?
HAMLET: Excellent, i' faith, of the chameleon's dish;° I eat the air,   85
    promise-crammed; you cannot feed capons so.
KING: I have nothing with this answer, Hamlet; these words are not
    mine.
HAMLET: No, nor mine now. *To* POLONIUS. My lord, you played
    once i' th' university, you say?   90
POLONIUS: That did I, my lord, and was accounted a good actor.
HAMLET: What did you enact?
POLONIUS: I did enact Julius Caesar. I was killed i' th' Capitol; Bru-
    tus killed me.
HAMLET: It was a brute part of him to kill so capital a calf there.   95
    Be the players ready?
ROSENCRANTZ: Ay, my lord. They stay upon your patience.
QUEEN: Come hither, my dear Hamlet, sit by me.
HAMLET: No, good mother. Here's metal more attractive.°
POLONIUS *to the* KING: O ho! Do you mark that?   100
HAMLET: Lady, shall I lie in your lap?

He lies at Ophelia's feet.

OPHELIA: No, my lord.
HAMLET: I mean, my head upon your lap?
OPHELIA: Ay, my lord.
HAMLET: Do you think I meant country matters?°   105
OPHELIA: I think nothing, my lord.
HAMLET: That's a fair thought to lie between maids' legs.
OPHELIA: What is, my lord?
HAMLET: Nothing.
OPHILIA: You are merry, my lord.   110
HAMLET: Who, I?

79 censure . . . seeming judgment on his looks   **83 be idle** play the fool
85 the chamelon's dish air (on which chameleons were thought to live)   **99 attractive** magnetic   **105 country matters** rustic doings (with a pun on the vulgar word
for the pudendum)

OPHELIA: Ay, my lord.

HAMLET: O God, your only jig-maker!° What should a man do but be merry? For look you how cheerfully my mother looks, and my father died within's two hours. 115

OPHELIA: Nay, 'tis twice two months, my lord.

HAMLET: So long? Nay then, let the devil wear black, for I'll have a suit of sables.° O heavens! Die two months ago, and not forgotten yet? Then there's hope a great man's memory may outlive his life half a year. But, by'r Lady, 'a must build churches then, or 120 else shall 'a suffer not thinking on, with the hobbyhorse,° whose epitaph is "For O, for O, the hobbyhorse is forgot!"

The trumpets sound. Dumb show follows:

Enter a KING *and a* QUEEN *very lovingly, the* QUEEN *embracing him, and he her. She kneels; and makes show of protestation unto him. He takes her up, and declines his head upon her neck. He lies him down upon a bank of flowers. She, seeing him asleep, leaves him. Anon come in another man: takes off his crown, kisses it, pours poison in the sleeper's ears, and leaves him. The* QUEEN *returns, finds the* KING *dead, makes passionate action. The* POISONER, *with some three or four, come in again, seem to condole with her. The dead body is carried away. The* POISONER *woos the* QUEEN *with gifts; she seems harsh awhile, but in the end accepts love.* Exeunt.

OPHELIA: What means this, my lord?

HAMLET: Marry, this is miching mallecho;° it means mischief.

OPHELIA: Belike this show imports the argument° of the play. 125

Enter PROLOGUE.

HAMLET: We shall know by this fellow. The players cannot keep counsel; they'll tell all.

OPHELIA: Will 'a tell us what this show meant?

HAMLET: Ay, or any show that you will show him. Be not you ashamed to show, he'll not shame to tell you what it means. 130

OPHELIA: You are naught,° you are naught; I'll mark the play.

PROLOGUE:

> For us, and for our tragedy,
> Here stooping to your clemency,
> We beg your hearing patiently. *Exit.*

HAMLET: Is this a prologue, or the posy of a ring?° 135

OPHELIA: 'Tis brief, my lord.

HAMLET: As woman's love.

113 jig-maker composer of songs and dances (often a fool, who performed them) **118 sables** pun on the meanings "black" and "luxurious furs" **121 hobbyhorse** mock horse worn by a performer in the morris dance **124 miching mallecho** sneaking mischief **125 argument** plot **131 naught** wicked, improper **135 posy . . . ring** motto inscribed in a ring

Enter two PLAYERS *as king and queen.*

PLAYER KING: Full thirty times hath Phoebus' cart° gone round
Neptune's salt wash° and Tellus'° orbèd ground,
And thirty dozen moons with borrowed sheen   140
About the world have times twelve thirties been,
Since love our hearts, and Hymen did our hands,
Unite commutual in most sacred bands.
PLAYER QUEEN: So many journeys may the sun and moon
Make us again count o'er ere love be done!   145
But woe is me, you are so sick of late,
So far from cheer and from your former state,
That I distrust° you. Yet, though I distrust,
Discomfort you, my lord, it nothing must.
For women fear too much, even as they love,   150
And women's fear and love hold quantity,
In neither aught, or in extremity.°
Now what my love is, proof° hath made you know,
And as my love is sized, my fear is so.
Where love is great, the littlest doubts are fear;   155
Where little fears grow great, great love grows there.
PLAYER KING: Faith, I must leave thee, love, and shortly too;
My operant° powers their functions leave to do;
And thou shalt live in this fair world behind,
Honored, beloved, and haply one as kind   160
For husband shalt thou—
PLAYER QUEEN: O, confound the rest!
Such love must needs be treason in my breast.
In second husband let me be accurst!
None wed the second but who killed the first.
HAMLET *Aside*:   That's wormwood.°   165
PLAYER QUEEN: The instances° that second marriage move°
Are base respects of thrift,° but none of love.
A second time I kill my husband dead.
When second husband kisses me in bed.
PLAYER KING: I do believe you think what now you speak,   170
But what we do determine oft we break.
Purpose is but the slave to memory,
Of violent birth, but poor validity,°
Which now like fruit unripe sticks on the tree,
But fall unshaken when they mellow be.   175

---

138 Phoebus' cart the sun's chariot   **139 Neptune's salt wash** the sea;   **Tellus**
Roman goddess of the earth   **148 distrust** am anxious about   **151–52 And . . .
extremity** perhaps the idea is that women's anxiety is great or little in proportion to
their love; the previous line, unrhymed, may be a false start that Shakespeare neglected to delete   **153 proof** experience   **158 operant** active   **165 wormwood** a
bitter herb   **166 instances** motives;   **move** induce   **167 respects of thrift** considerations of profit   **173 validity** strength

Most necessary 'tis that we forget
To pay ourselves what to ourselves is debt.
What to ourselves in passion we propose,
The passion ending, doth the purpose lose.
The violence of either grief or joy   180
Their own enactures° with themselves destroy:
Where joy most revels, grief doth most lament;
Grief joys, joy grieves, on slender accident.
This world is not for aye, nor 'tis not strange
That even our loves should with our fortunes change,   185
For 'tis a question left us yet to prove,
Whether love lead fortune, or else fortune love.
The great man down, you mark his favorite flies;
The poor advanced makes friends of enemies;
And hitherto doth love on fortune tend,   190
For who not needs shall never lack a friend;
And who in want a hollow friend doth try,
Directly seasons him° his enemy.
But, orderly to end where I begun,
Our wills and fates do so contrary run   195
That our devices still are overthrown;
Our thoughts are ours, their ends none of our own.
So think thou wilt no second husband wed,
But die thy thoughts when thy first lord is dead.
PLAYER QUEEN: Nor earth to me give food, nor heaven light,   200
  Sport and repose lock from me day and night,
  To desperation turn my trust and hope,
  An anchor's° cheer in prison be my scope,
  Each opposite that blanks° the face of joy
  Meet what I would have well, and it destroy: 205
  Both here and hence pursue me lasting strife,
  If, once a widow, ever I be wife!
HAMLET: If she should break it now!
PLAYER KING: 'Tis deeply sworn. Sweet, leave me here awhile;
  My spirits grow dull, and fain I would beguile   210
  The tedious day with sleep.
PLAYER QUEEN: Sleep rock thy brain,

He sleeps.

  And never come mischance between us twain!   *Exit.*
HAMLET: Madam, how like you this play?
QUEEN: The lady doth protest too much, methinks.
HAMLET: O, but she'll keep her word.   215
KING: Have you heard the argument?° Is there no offense in't?

181 enactures acts   **193 seasons him** ripens him into   **203 anchor's** anchorite's,
hermit's   **204 opposite that blanks** adverse thing that blanches   **216 argument**
plot

HAMLET: No, no, they do but jest, poison in jest; no offense i' th'
world.
KING: What do you call the play?
HAMLET: *The Mousetrap.* Marry, how? Tropically.° The play is the   220
image of a murder done in Vienna: Gonzago is the duke's name;
his wife, Baptista. You shall see anon. 'Tis a knavish piece of
work, but what of that? Your majesty, and we that have free°
souls, it touches us not. Let the galled jade winch;° our withers
are unwrung.   225

Enter LUCIANUS.

This is one Lucianus, nephew to the king.
OPHELIA: You are as good as a chorus, my lord.
HAMLET: I could interpret° between you and your love, if I could
see the puppets dallying.
OPHELIA: You are keen° my lord, you are keen.   230
HAMLET: It would cost you a groaning to take off mine edge.
OPHELIA: Still better, and worse.
HAMLET: So you mistake° your husbands.—Begin, murderer.
Leave thy damnable faces and begin. Come, the croaking raven
doth bellow for revenge.   235
LUCIANUS: Thoughts black, hands apt, drugs fit, and time agreeing,
Confederate season,° else no creature seeing,
Thou mixture rank, of midnight weeds collected,
With Hecate's ban° thrice blasted, thrice infected,
Thy natural magic and dire property°   240
On wholesome life usurps immediately.

Pours the poison in his ears.

HAMLET: 'A poisons him i' th' garden for his estate. His name's
Gonzago. The story is extant, and written in very choice Italian.
You shall see anon how the murderer gets the love of Gonzago's
wife.   245
OPHELIA: The king rises.
HAMLET: What, frighted with false fire?°
QUEEN: How fares my lord?
POLONIUS: Give o'er the play.
KING: Give me some light. Away!   250
POLONIUS: Lights, lights, lights!

220 Tropically figuratively (with a pun on *trap*)   **223 free** innocent   **224 galled
jade winch** chafed horse wince   **228 interpret** like a showman explaining the action
of puppets   **230 keen** (1) sharp (2) sexually aroused   **233 mistake** err in taking
237 Confederate season the opportunity allied with me   **239 Hecate's ban** the
curse of the goddess of sorcery   **240 property** nature   **247 false fire** blank discharge of firearms

Exeunt all but HAMLET *and* HORATIO.

HAMLET:
      Why, let the strucken deer go weep,
        The hart ungallèd play:
      For some must watch, while some must sleep;
        Thus runs the world away.   255
    Would not this, sir, and a forest of feathers°—if the rest of my
fortunes turn Turk° with me—with two Provincial roses° on my
razed° shoes, get me a fellowship in a cry° of players?
HORATIO: Half a share.
HAMLET: A whole one, I.   260
      For thou dost know, O Damon dear,
        This realm dismantled was
      Of Jove himself; and now reigns here.
        A very, very—pajock.°
HORATIO: You might have rhymed.°   265
HAMLET: O good Horatio, I'll take the ghost's word for a thousand
    pound. Didst perceive?
HORATIO: Very well, my lord.
HAMLET: Upon the talk of poisoning?
HORATIO: I did very well note him.   270
HAMLET: Ah ha! Come, some music! Come, the recorders!°
      For if the king like not the comedy,
      Why then, belike he likes it not, perdy.°
    Come, some music!

Enter ROSENCRANTZ *and* GUILDENSTERN.

GUILDENSTERN: Good my lord, vouchsafe me a word with you.   275
HAMLET: Sir, a whole history.
GUILDENSTERN: The king, sir—
HAMLET: Ay, sir, what of him?
GUILDENSTERN: Is in his retirement marvelous distemp'red.
HAMLET: With drink, sir?   280
GUILDENSTERN: No, my lord, with choler.°
HAMLET: Your wisdom should show itself more richer to signify
    this to the doctor, for for me to put him to his purgation would
    perhaps plunge him into more choler.
GUILDENSTERN: Good my lord, put your discourse into some   285
    frame,° and start not so wildly from my affair.

---

256 feathers plumes were sometimes part of a costume   **257 turn Turk** go bad, treat me badly; **Provincial roses** rosettes like the roses of Provence (?)   **258 razed** ornamented with slashes;   **cry** pack, company   **264 pajock** peacock   **265 You . . . rhymed** i.e., rhymed "was" with "ass"   **271 recorders** flutelike instruments **273 perdy** by God (French *par dieu*)   **281 choler** anger (but Hamlet pretends to take the word in its sense of "biliousness")   **286 frame** order, control

HAMLET: I am tame, sir; pronounce.

GUILDENSTERN: The queen, your mother, in most great affliction
of spirit hath sent me to you.

HAMLET: You are welcome.   290

GUILDENSTERN: Nay, good my lord, this courtesy is not of the right
breed. If it shall please you to make me a wholesome answer, I
will do your mother's commandment: if not, your pardon and my
return shall be the end of my business.

HAMLET: Sir, I cannot.   295

ROSENCRANTZ: What, my lord?

HAMLET: Make you a wholesome° answer; my wit's diseased. But,
sir, such answer as I can make you shall command, or rather, as
you say, my mother. Therefore no more, but to the matter. My
mother, you say—   300

ROSENCRANTZ: Then thus she says: your behavior hath struck her
into amazement and admiration.°

HAMLET: O wonderful son, that can so stonish a mother! But is
there no sequel at the heels of this mother's admiration? Impart.

ROSENCRANTZ: She desires to speak with you in her closet° ere you   305
go to bed.

HAMLET: We shall obey, were she ten times our mother. Have you
any further trade with us?

ROSENCRANTZ: My lord, you once did love me.

HAMLET: And do still, by these pickers and stealers.°   310

ROSENCRANTZ: Good my lord, what is your cause of distemper?
You do surely bar the door upon your own liberty, if you deny
your griefs to your friend.

HAMLET: Sir, I lack advancement.°

ROSENCRANTZ: How can that be, when you have the voice of the   315
king himself for your succession in Denmark?

Enter the PLAYERS *with recorders.*

HAMLET: Ay, sir, but "while the grass grows"—the proverb° is
something musty. O, the recorders. Let me see one. To with-
draw° with you—why do you go about to recover the wind° of me
as if you would drive me into a toil?°   320

GUILDENSTERN: O my lord, if my duty be too bold, my love is too
unmannerly.°

HAMLET: I do not well understand that. Will you play upon this
pipe?

297 wholesome sane   **302 admiration** wonder   **305 closet** private room
310 pickers and stealers i.e., hands (with reference to the prayer, "Keep my hands
from picking and stealing")   **314 advancement** promotion   **317 proverb** "While
the grass groweth, the horse starveth"   **319 withdraw** speak in private; **recover
the wind** get on the windward side (as in hunting)   **320 toil** snare   **321–22 if
. . . unmannerly** if these questions seem rude, it is because my love for you leads
me beyond good manners

GUILDENSTERN: My lord, I cannot.   325
HAMLET: I pray you.
GUILDENSTERN: Believe me, I cannot.
HAMLET: I pray you.
GUILDENSTERN: Believe me, I cannot.
HAMLET: I do beseech you.   330
GUILDENSTERN: I know no touch of it, my lord.
HAMLET: It is as easy as lying. Govern these ventages° with your
fingers and thumb, give it breath with your mouth, and it will
discourse most eloquent music. Look you, these are the stops.
GUILDENSTERN: But these cannot I command to any utt'rance of   335
harmony; I have not the skill.
HAMLET: Why, look you now, how unworthy a thing you make of
me! You would play upon me; you would seem to know my stops;
you would pluck out the heart of my mystery; you would sound
me from my lowest note to the top of my compass;° and there is   340
much music, excellent voice, in this little organ,° yet cannot you
make it speak. 'Sblood, do you think I am easier to be played on
than a pipe? Call me what instrument you will, though you can
fret° me, you cannot play upon me.

Enter POLONIUS.

God bless you, sir!   345
POLONIUS: My lord, the queen would speak with you, and pres-
ently.
HAMLET: Do you see yonder cloud that's almost in shape of a
camel?
POLONIUS: By th' mass and 'tis, like a camel indeed.   350
HAMLET: Methinks it is like a weasel.
POLONIUS: It is backed like a weasel.
HAMLET: Or like a whale.
POLONIUS: Very like a whale.
HAMLET: Then I will come to my mother by and by. *Aside.* They   355
fool me to the top of my bent.°—I will come by and by.°
POLONIUS: I will say so.   *Exit.*
HAMLET: "By and by" is easily said. Leave me, friends.

Exeunt all but HAMLET.

'Tis now the very witching time of night,
When churchyards yawn, and hell itself breathes out   360
Contagion to this world. Now could I drink hot blood

---

332 ventages vents, stops on a recorder   **340 compass** range of voice   **341 organ**
the recorder   **344 fret** vex (with a pun alluding to the frets, or ridges, that guide
the fingering on some instruments)   **356 They . . . bent** They compel me to play
the fool to the limit of my capacity; **by and by** very soon

And do such bitter business as the day
Would quake to look on. Soft, now to my mother.
O heart, lose not thy nature; let not ever
The soul of Nero° enter this firm bosom.   365
Let me be cruel, not unnatural;
I will speak daggers to her, but use none.
My tongue and soul in this be hypocrites:
How in my words somever she be shent,°
To give them seals° never, my soul, consent!   *Exit.*   370

SCENE III. The castle.

Enter KING, ROSENCRANTZ, *and* GUILDENSTERN.

KING: I like him not, nor stands it safe with us
To let his madness range. Therefore prepare you.
I your commission will forthwith dispatch,
And he to England shall along with you.
The terms° of our estate may not endure   5
Hazard so near's° as doth hourly grow
Out of his brows.
GUILDENSTERN: We will ourselves provide.
Most holy and religious fear it is
To keep those many many bodies safe
That live and feed upon your majesty.   10
ROSENCRANTZ: The single and peculiar° life is bound
With all the strength and armor of the mind
To keep itself from noyance,° but much more
That spirit upon whose weal depends and rests
The lives of many. The cess of majesty°   15
Dies not alone, but like a gulf° doth draw
What's near it with it; or it is a massy wheel
Fixed on the summit of the highest mount,
To whose huge spokes ten thousand lesser things
Are mortised and adjoined, which when it falls,   20
Each small annexment, petty consequence,
Attends° the boist'rous ruin. Never alone
Did the king sigh, but with a general groan.
KING: Arm° you, I pray you, to this speedy voyage,
For we will fetters put about this fear,   25
Which now goes too free-footed.

---

365 Nero Roman emperor who had his mother murdered   **369 shent** rebuked
370 give them seals confirm them with deeds   **III.iii.5 terms** conditions
6 near's near us   **11 peculiar** individual, private   **13 noyance** injury   **15 cess
of majesty** cessation (death) of a king   **16 gulf** whirlpool   **22 Attends** waits on,
participates in   **24 Arm** prepare

ROSENCRANTZ: We will haste us.

Exeunt gentlemen ROSENCRANTZ *and*
GUILDENSTERN.

Enter POLONIUS.

POLONIUS: My lord, he's going to his mother's closet.
Behind the arras I'll convey myself
To hear the process.° I'll warrant she'll tax him home,°
And, as you said, and wisely was it said,   30
'Tis meet that some more audience than a mother,
Since nature makes them partial, should o'erhear
The speech of vantage.° Fare you well, my liege.
I'll call upon you ere you go to bed
And tell you what I know.
KING: Thanks, dear my lord.   35

Exit POLONIUS.

O, my offense is rank, it smells to heaven;
It hath the primal eldest curse° upon't,
A brother's murder. Pray can I not,
Though inclination be as sharp as will.
My stronger guilt defeats my strong intent,   40
And like a man to double business bound
I stand in pause where I shall first begin,
And both neglect. What if this cursèd hand
Were thicker than itself with brother's blood,
Is there not rain enough in the sweet heavens   45
To wash it white as snow? Whereto serves mercy
But to confront° the visage of offense?
And what's in prayer but this twofold force,
To be forestallèd ere we come to fall,
Or pardoned being down? Then I'll look up.   50
My fault is past. But, O, what form of prayer
Can serve my turn? "Forgive me my foul murder"?
That cannot be, since I am still possessed
Of those effects° for which I did the murder,
My crown, mine own ambition, and my queen.   55
May one be pardoned and retain th' offense?
In the corrupted currents of this world
Offense's gilded hand may shove by justice,
And oft 'tis seen the wicked prize itself

---

29 process proceedings;   **tax him home** censure him sharply   **33 of vantage**
from an advantageous place   **37 primal eldest curse** curse of Cain, who killed
Abel   **47 confront** oppose   **54 effects** things gained

Buys out the law. But 'tis not so above. 60
There is no shuffling;° there the action lies
In his true nature, and we ourselves compelled,
Even to the teeth and forehead of our faults,
To give in evidence. What then? What rests?°
Try what repentance can. What can it not? 65
Yet what can it when one cannot repent?
O wretched state! O bosom black as death!
O limèd° soul, that struggling to be free
Art more engaged!° Help, angels! Make assay.°
Bow, stubborn knees, and, heart with strings of steel, 70
Be soft as sinews of the newborn babe.
All may be well.

He kneels.

Enter HAMLET.

HAMLET: Now might I do it pat, now 'a is a-praying,
And now I'll do't. And so 'a goes to heaven,
And so am I revenged. That would be scanned.° 75
A villain kills my father, and for that
I, his sole son, do this same villain send
To heaven.
Why, this is hire and salary, not revenge.
'A took my father grossly, full of bread,° 80
With all his crimes broad blown,° as flush° as May;
And how his audit° stands, who knows save heaven?
But in our circumstance and course of thought,
'Tis heavy with him; and am I then revenged,
To take him in the purging of his soul, 85
When he is fit and seasoned for his passage?
No.
Up, sword, and know thou a more horrid hent.°
When he is drunk asleep, or in his rage,
Or in th' incestuous pleasure of his bed, 90
At game a-swearing, or about some act
That has no relish° of salvation in't—
Then trip him, that his heels may kick at heaven,
And that his soul may be as damned and black
As hell, whereto it goes. My mother stays. 95

---

61 shuffling trickery   **64 rests** remains   **68 limèd** caught (as with bird lime, a
sticky substance spread on boughs to snare birds)   **69 engaged** ensnared;   **assay**
an attempt   **75 would be scanned** ought to be looked into   **80 bread** i.e.,
wordly gratification   **81 crimes broad blown** sins in full bloom;   **flush**
vigorous   **82 audit** account   **88 hent** grasp (here, occasion for seizing)
92 relish flavor

This physic° but prolongs thy sickly days.   *Exit.*
KING *rises:*   My words fly up, my thoughts remain below.
Words without thoughts never to heaven go.   *Exit.*

SCENE IV. The queen's closet.

Enter QUEEN *Gertrude and* POLONIUS.

POLONIUS: 'A will come straight. Look you lay home° to him.
 Tell him his pranks have been too broad° to bear with,
 And that your grace hath screened and stood between
 Much heat and him. I'll silence me even here.
 Pray you be round with him.   5
HAMLET *within:*   Mother, Mother, Mother!
QUEEN: I'll warrant you; fear me not. Withdraw; I hear him com-
ing.   POLONIUS *hides behind the arras.*

Enter HAMLET.

HAMLET: Now, Mother, what's the matter?
QUEEN: Hamlet, thou hast thy father much offended.   10
HAMLET: Mother, you have my father much offended.
QUEEN: Come, come, you answer with an idle° tongue.
HAMLET: Go, go, you question with a wicked tongue.
QUEEN: Why, how now, Hamlet?
HAMLET: What's the matter now?
QUEEN: Have you forgot me?
HAMLET: No, by the rood,° not so!   15
 You are the queen, your husband's brother's wife,
 And, would it were not so, you are my mother.
QUEEN: Nay, then I'll set those to you that can speak.
HAMLET: Come, come, and sit you down. You shall not budge.
 You go not till I set you up a glass°   20
 Where you may see the inmost part of you!
QUEEN: What wilt thou do? Thou wilt not murder me?
 Help, ho!
POLONIUS *behind:*   What, ho! Help!
HAMLET *draws:*   How now? A rat? Dead for a ducat, dead!   25

Makes a pass through the arras and kills POLONIUS.

POLONIUS *behind:*   O, I am slain!
QUEEN: O me, what has thou done?

96 physic Claudius' purgation by prayer, as Hamlet thinks in line 85   **III.iv.1 lay**
home thrust (rebuke) him sharply   **2 broad** unrestrained   **12 idle** foolish
15 rood cross   **20 glass** mirror

HAMLET: Nay, I know not. Is it the king?

QUEEN: O, what a rash and bloody deed is this!

HAMLET: A bloody deed—almost as bad, good Mother,
    As kill a king, and marry with his brother. 30

QUEEN: As kill a king?

HAMLET: Ay, lady, it was my word.

Lifts up the arras and sees POLONIUS.

    Thou wretched, rash, intruding fool, farewell!
    I took thee for thy better. Take thy fortune.
    Thou find'st to be too busy is some danger.—
    Leave wringing of your hands. Peace, sit you down 35
    And let me wring your heart, for so I shall
    If it be made of penetrable stuff,
    If damnèd custom have not brazed° it so
    That it be proof ° and bulwark against sense.°

QUEEN: What have I done that thou dar'st wag thy tongue 40
    In noise so rude against me?

HAMLET: Such an act
    That blurs the grace and blush of modesty,
    Calls virtue hypocrite, takes off the rose
    From the fair forehead of an innocent love,
    And sets a blister° there, makes marriage vows 45
    As false as dicers' oaths. O, such a deed
    As from the body of contraction° plucks
    The very soul, and sweet religion makes
    A rhapsody° of words! Heaven's face does glow
    O'er this solidity and compound mass 50
    With heated visage, as against the doom
    Is thoughtsick at the act.°

QUEEN: Ay me, what act,
    That roars so loud and thunders in the index?°

HAMLET: Look here upon this picture, and on this,
    The counterfeit presentment° of two brothers. 55
    See what a grace was seated on this brow:
    Hyperion's curls, the front° of Jove himself,
    An eye like Mars, to threaten and command,
    A station° like the herald Mercury
    New lighted on a heaven-kissing hill— 60
    A combination and a form indeed
    Where every god did seem to set his seal
    To give the world assurance of a man.

---

38 brazed hardened like brass   **39 proof** armor;   **sense** feeling   **45 sets a
blister** brands (as a harlot)   **47 contraction** marriage contract   **49 rhapsody**
senseless string   **49–52 Heaven's . . . act** The face of heaven blushes over this
earth (compounded of four elements), the face hot, as if Judgment Day were near,
and it is thoughtsick at the act   **53 index** prologue   **55 counterfeit presentment**
represented image   **57 front** forehead   **59 station** bearing

This was your husband. Look you now what follows.
Here is your husband, like a mildewed ear 65
Blasting his wholesome brother. Have you eyes?
Could you on this fair mountain leave to feed,
And batten° on this moor? Ha! Have you eyes?
You cannot call it love, for at your age
The heyday° in the blood is tame, it's humble, 70
And waits upon the judgment, and what judgment
Would step from this to this? Sense° sure you have,
Else could you not have motion, but sure that sense
Is apoplexed,° for madness would not err,
Nor sense to ecstasy° was ne'er so thralled 75
But it reserved some quantity of choice
To serve in such a difference. What devil was't
That thus hath cozened you at hoodman-blind?°
Eyes without feeling, feeling without sight,
Ears without hands or eyes, smelling sans° all, 80
Or but a sickly part of one true sense
Could not so mope.°
O shame, where is thy blush? Rebellious hell,
If thou canst mutine in a matron's bones,
To flaming youth let virtue be as wax 85
And melt in her own fire. Proclaim no shame
When the compulsive ardor° gives the charge,
Since frost itself as actively doth burn,
And reason panders will.°
QUEEN: O Hamlet, speak no more.
Thou turn'st mine eyes into my very soul, 90
And there I see such black and grainèd° spots
As will not leave their tinct.°
HAMLET: Nay, but to live
In the rank sweat of an enseamèd° bed,
Stewed in corruption, honeying and making love
Over the nasty sty—
QUEEN: O, speak to me no more. 95
These words like daggers enter in my ears.
No more, sweet Hamlet.
HAMLET: A murderer and a villain,
A slave that is not twentieth part the tithe°
Of your precedent lord, a vice° of kings,
A cutpurse of the empire and the rule, 100

---

68 batten feed gluttonously   **70 heyday** excitement   **72 Sense** feeling   **74 apoplexed** paralyzed   **75 ecstasy** madness   **78 cozened . . . hoodman-blind**
cheated you at blindman's buff   **80 sans** without   **82 mope** be stupid
87 compulsive ardor compelling passion   **89 reason panders will** reason acts as a
procurer for desire   **91 grainèd** dyed in grain (fast dyed)   **92 tinct** color
93 enseamèd perhaps "soaked in grease,"i.e., sweaty; perhaps "much wrinkled"
98 tithe tenth part   **99 vice** like the Vice, a fool and mischief-maker in the old
morality plays

That from a shelf the precious diadem stole
And put it in his pocket—
QUEEN: No more.

Enter GHOST.

HAMLET: A king of shreds and patches—
Save me and hover o'er me with your wings,
You heavenly guards! What would your gracious figure?   105
QUEEN:
Alas, he's mad.
HAMLET: Do you not come your tardy son to chide,
That, lapsed in time and passion, lets go by
Th' important acting of your dread command?
O, say!   110
GHOST: Do not forget. This visitation
Is but to whet thy almost blunted purpose.
But look, amazement on thy mother sits.
O, step between her and her fighting soul!
Conceit° in weakest bodies strongest works.   115
Speak to her, Hamlet.
HAMLET: How is it with you, lady?
QUEEN: Alas, how is't with you,
That you do bend your eye on vacancy,
And with th' incorporal° air do hold discourse?
Forth at your eyes your spirits wildly peep,   120
And as the sleeping soldiers in th' alarm
Your bedded hair° like life in excrements°
Start up and stand an end.° O gentle son,
Upon the heat and flame of thy distemper
Sprinkle cool patience. Whereon do you look?   125
HAMLET: On him, on him! Look you, how pale he glares!
His form and cause conjoined, preaching to stones,
Would make them capable.°—Do not look upon me,
Lest with this piteous action you convert
My stern effects.° Then what I have to do   130
Will want true color; tears perchance for blood.
QUEEN: To whom do you speak this?
HAMLET: Do you see nothing there?
QUEEN: Nothing at all; yet all that is I see.
HAMLET: Nor did you nothing hear?
QUEEN: No, nothing but ourselves.
HAMLET: Why, look you there! Look how it steals away!   135

---

115 Conceit imagination   **119 incorporal** bodiless   **122 bedded hair** hairs laid
flat;   **excrements** outgrowths (here, the hair)   **123 an end** on end   **128 ca-**
pable receptive   **129–30 convert . . . effects** divert my stern deeds

My father, in his habit° as he lived!
Look where he goes even now out at the portal!

Exit GHOST.

QUEEN: This is the very coinage of your brain.
   This bodiless creation ecstasy
   Is very cunning in.
HAMLET: Ecstasy?   140
   My pulse as yours doth temperately keep time
   And makes as healthful music. It is not madness
   That I have uttered. Bring me to the test,
   And I the matter will reword, which madness
   Would gambol° from. Mother, for love of grace,   145
   Lay not that flattering unction° to your soul,
   That not your trespass but my madness speaks.
   It will but skin and film the ulcerous place
   Whiles rank corruption, mining° all within,
   Infects unseen. Confess yourself to heaven,   150
   Repent what's past, avoid what is to come,
   And do not spread the compost° on the weeds
   To make them ranker. Forgive me this my virtue.
   For in the fatness of these pursy° times
   Virtue itself of vice must pardon beg,   155
   Yea curb° and woo for leave to do him good.
QUEEN: O Hamlet, thou hast cleft my heart in twain.
HAMLET: O, throw away the worser part of it,
   And live the purer with the other half.
   Good night—but go not to my uncle's bed.   160
   Assume a virtue, if you have it not.
   That monster custom, who all sense doth eat,
   Of habits devil, is angel yet in this,
   That to the use° of actions fair and good
   He likewise gives a frock or livery°   165
   That aptly is put on. Refrain tonight,
   And that shall lend a kind of easiness
   To the next abstinence; the next more easy;
   For use almost can change the stamp of nature,
   And either° the devil, or throw him out   170
   With wondrous potency. Once more, good night,
   And when you are desirous to be blest,

---

136 habit garment (Q1, though a "bad" quarto, is probably correct in saying that at line 102 the Ghost enters "in his night gown," i.e., dressing gown)   **145 gambol** start away   **146 unction** ointment   **149 mining** undermining   **152 compost** fertilizing substance   **154 pursy** bloated   **156 curb** bow low   **164 use** practice **165 livery** characteristic garment (punning on "habits" in line 163)   **170 either** probably a word is missing after "either"; among suggestions are *master, curb,* and *house;* but possibly "either" is a verb meaning "make easier"

I'll blessing beg of you.—For this same lord,
I do repent; but heaven hath pleased it so,
To punish me with this, and this with me,   175
That I must be their° scourge and minister.
I will bestow° him and will answer well
The death I gave him. So again, good night.
I must be cruel only to be kind.
Thus bad begins, and worse remains behind.   180
One word more, good lady.
QUEEN: What shall I do?
HAMLET: Not this, by no means, that I bid you do:
Let the bloat king tempt you again to bed,
Pinch wanton on your cheek, call you his mouse,
And let him, for a pair of reechy° kisses,   185
Or paddling in your neck with his damned fingers,
Make you to ravel° all this matter out,
That I essentially am not in madness,
But mad in craft. 'Twere good you let him know,
For who that's but a queen, fair, sober, wise,   190
Would from a paddock,° from a bat, a gib,°
Such dear concernings hide? Who would do so?
No, in despite of sense and secrecy,
Unpeg the basket on the house's top,
Let the birds fly, and like the famous ape,   195
To try conclusions,° in the basket creep
And break your own neck down.
QUEEN: Be thou assured, if words be made of breath,
And breath of life, I have no life to breathe
What thou hast said to me.   200
HAMLET: I must to England; you know that?
QUEEN: Alack,
I had forgot. 'Tis so concluded on.
HAMLET: There's letters sealed, and my two schoolfellows,
Whom I will trust as I will adders fanged,
They bear the mandate,° they must sweep my way   205
And marshal me to knavery. Let it work;
For 'tis the sport to have the enginer°
Hoist with his own petar,° and't shall go hard
But I will delve one yard below their mines
And blow them at the moon. O, 'tis most sweet   210
When in one line two crafts° directly meet.
This man shall set me packing:
I'll lug the guts into the neighbor room.

---

176 **their** the heavens'   177 **bestow** stow, lodge   185 **reechy** foul (literally
"smoky")   187 **ravel** unravel, reveal   191 **paddock** toad;   **gib** tomcat
196 **To try conclusions** to make experiments   205 **mandate** command   207 **enginer** (1) demolition expert (2) contriver   208 **petar** bomb   211 **crafts** (1) boats
(2) acts of guile, crafty schemes

Mother, good night. Indeed, this counselor
Is now most still, most secret, and most grave,   215
Who was in life a foolish prating knave.
Come, sir, to draw toward an end with you.
Good night, Mother.

Exit the QUEEN. *Then exit* HAMLET, *tugging in Polonius.*

ACT IV

SCENE I. The castle.

Enter KING *and* QUEEN, *with* ROSENCRANTZ *and* GUILDENSTERN.

KING: There's matter in these sighs. These profound heaves
You must translate; 'tis fit we understand them.
Where is your son?
QUEEN: Bestow this place on us a little while.

Exeunt ROSENCRANTZ *and* GUILDENSTERN.

Ah, mine own lord, what have I seen tonight!   5
KING: What, Gertrude? How does Hamlet?
QUEEN: Mad as the sea and wind when both contend
Which is the mightier. In his lawless fit,
Behind the arras hearing something stir,
Whips out his rapier, cries, "A rat, a rat!"   10
And in this brainish apprehension° kills
The unseen good old man.
KING: O heavy deed!
It had been so with us, had we been there.
His liberty is full of threats to all,
To you yourself, to us, to everyone.   15
Alas, how shall this bloody deed be answered?
It will be laid to us, whose providence°
Should have kept short, restrained, and out of haunt°
This mad young man. But so much was our love
We would not understand what was most fit,   20
But, like the owner of a foul disease,
To keep it from divulging, let it feed
Even on the pith of life. Where is he gone?
QUEEN: To draw apart the body he hath killed;
O'er whom his very madness, like some ore   25

IV.i.11 brainish apprehension mad imagination   **17 providence** foresight   **18 out
of haunt** away from association

Among a mineral° of metals base,
Shows itself pure. 'A weeps for what is done.
KING: O Gertrude, come away!
The sun no sooner shall the mountains touch
But we will ship him hence, and this vile deed   30
We must with all our majesty and skill
Both countenance and excuse. Ho, Guildenstern!

Enter ROSENCRANTZ *and* GUILDENSTERN.

Friends both, go join you with some further aid:
Hamlet in madness hath Polonius slain,
And from his mother's closet hath he dragged him.   35
Go seek him out; speak fair, and bring the body
Into the chapel. I pray you haste in this.

Exeunt ROSENCRANTZ *and* GUILDENSTERN.

Come, Gertrude, we'll call up our wisest friends
And let them know both what we mean to do
And what's untimely done . . .°   40
Whose whisper o'er the world's diameter,
As level as the cannon to his blank°
Transports his poisoned shot, may miss our name
And hit the woundless° air. O, come away!
My soul is full of discord and dismay.   *Exeunt.*   45

SCENE II. The castle.

Enter HAMLET.

HAMLET: Safely stowed.
GENTLEMEN *Within:*   Hamlet! Lord Hamlet!
HAMLET: But soft, what noise? Who calls on Hamlet?
O, here they come.

Enter ROSENCRANTZ *and* GUILDENSTERN.

ROSENCRANTZ: What have you done, my lord, with the dead body?   5
HAMLET: Compounded it with dust, whereto 'tis kin.
ROSENCRANTZ: Tell us where 'tis, that we may take it thence
And bear it to the chapel.
HAMLET: Do not believe it.

25–26 ore . . . mineral vein of gold in a mine   40 done . . . evidently something
has dropped out of the text; Capell's conjecture, "So, haply slander," is usually
printed   42 blank white center of a target   44 woundless invulnerable

ROSENCRANTZ: Believe what?   10

HAMLET: That I can keep your counsel and not mine own. Besides, to be demanded of ° a sponge, what replication° should be made by the son of a king?

ROSENCRANTZ: Take you me for a sponge, my lord?

HAMLET: Ay, sir, that soaks up the king's countenance,° his re-   15
wards, his authorities. But such officers do the king best service in the end. He keeps them, like an ape, in the corner of his jaw, first mouthed, to be last swallowed. When he needs what you have gleaned, it is but squeezing you and, sponge, you shall be dry again.   20

ROSENCRANTZ: I understand you not, my lord.

HAMLET: I am glad of it: a knavish speech sleeps in a foolish ear.

ROSENCRANTZ: My lord, you must tell us where the body is and go with us to the king.

HAMLET: The body is with the king, but the king is not with the   25
body. The king is a thing—

GUILDENSTERN: A thing, my lord?

HAMLET: Of nothing. Bring me to him. Hide fox, and all after.°

Exeunt.

SCENE III. *The castle.*

Enter KING, *and two or three.*

KING: I have sent to seek him and to find the body:
How dangerous is it that this man goes loose!
Yet must not we put the strong law on him:
He's loved of the distracted° multitude,
Who like not in their judgment, but their eyes,   5
And where 'tis so, th' offender's scourge is weighted,
But never the offense. To bear° all smooth and even,
This sudden sending him away must seem
Deliberate pause.° Diseases desperate grown
By desperate appliance are relieved,   10
Or not at all.

Enter ROSENCRANTZ, GUILDENSTERN, *and all the rest.*

         How now? What hath befall'n?

ROSENCRANTZ: Where the dead body is bestowed, my lord,
We cannot get from him.

KING: But where is he?

ROSENCRANTZ: Without, my lord; guarded, to know your pleasure.

IV.ii.12 demanded of questioned by; **replication** reply   **15 countenance** favor
28 Hide . . . after a cry in a game such as hide-and-seek; Hamlet runs from the
stage   **IV.iii.4 distracted** bewildered, senseless   **7 bear** carry out   **9 pause**
planning

KING: Bring him before us.
ROSENCRANTZ: Ho! Bring in the lord. 15

They enter.

KING: Now, Hamlet, where's Polonius?
HAMLET: At supper.
KING: At supper? Where?
HAMLET: Not where he eats, but where 'a is eaten. A certain convocation of politic° worms are e'en at him. Your worm is your 20
only emperor for diet. We fat all creatures else to fat us, and we
fat ourselves for maggots. Your fat king and your lean beggar is
but variable service°—two dishes, but to one table. That's the
end.
KING: Alas, alas!
HAMLET: A man may fish with the worm that hath eat of a king, 25
and eat of the fish that hath fed of that worm.
KING: What does thou mean by this?
HAMLET: Nothing but to show you how a king may go to progress°
through the guts of a beggar.
KING: Where is Polonius? 30
HAMLET: In heaven. Send thither to see. If your messenger find him
not there, seek him i' th' other place yourself. But if indeed you
find him not within this month, you shall nose him as you go up
the stairs into the lobby.
KING *to* ATTENDANTS: Go seek him there. 35
HAMLET: 'A will stay till you come.

Exeunt ATTENDANTS.

KING: Hamlet, this deed, for thine especial safety,
Which we do tender° as we dearly grieve
For that which thou hast done, must send thee hence
With fiery quickness. Therefore prepare thyself. 40
The bark is ready and the wind at help,
Th' associates tend,° and everything is bent
For England.
HAMLET: For England?
KING: Ay, Hamlet.
HAMLET: Good.
KING: So is it, if thou knew'st our purposes.
HAMLET: I see a cherub° that sees them. But come, for England! 45
Farewell, dear Mother.
KING: Thy loving father, Hamlet.

---

20 politic statesmanlike, shrewd   **23 variable service** different courses   **28 progress** royal journey   **38 tender** hold dear   **42 tend** wait   **45 cherub** angel of knowledge

HAMLET: My mother—father and mother is man and wife, man and
    wife is one flesh, and so, my mother. Come, for England! *Exit.*
KING: Follow him at foot;° tempt him with speed aboard. 50
    Delay it not; I'll have him hence tonight.
    Away! For everything is sealed and done
    That else leans° on th' affair. Pray you make haste.

                           Exeunt all but the KING.

    And, England, if my love thou hold'st at aught—
    As my great power thereof may give thee sense, 55
    Since yet thy cicatrice° looks raw and red
    After the Danish sword, and thy free awe°
    Pays homage to us—thou mayst not coldly set
    Our sovereign process,° which imports at full
    By letters congruing to that effect 60
    The present° death of Hamlet. Do it, England,
    For like the hectic° in my blood he rages,
    And thou must cure me. Till I know 'tis done,
    Howe'er my haps,° my joys were ne'er begun.   *Exit.*

SCENE IV. *A plain in Denmark.*

Enter FORTINBRRAS *with his* ARMY *over the stage.*

FORTINBRAS: Go, captain, from me greet the Danish king,
    Tell him that by his license Fortinbras
    Craves the conveyance of ° a promised march
    Over his kingdom. You know the rendezvous.
    If that his majesty would aught with us, 5
    We shall express our duty in his eye;°
    And let him know so.
CAPTAIN: I will do't, my lord.
FORTINBRAS: Go softly° on.

                         Exeunt all but the CAPTAIN.

Enter HAMLET, ROSENCRANTZ, &c.

HAMLET: Good sir, whose powers° are these?
CAPTAIN: They are of Norway, sir. 10
HAMLET: How purposed, sir, I pray you?
CAPTAIN: Against some part of Poland.

---

50 at foot closely   **53 leans** depends   **56 cicatrice** scar   **57 free awe** uncompelled submission   **58–59 coldly . . . process** regard slightly our royal command   **61 present** instant   **62 hectic** fever   **64 haps** chances, fortunes **IV.iv.3 conveyance of** escort for   **6 in his eye** before his eyes (i.e., in his presence)   **8 softly** slowly   **9 powers** forces

HAMLET: Who commands them, sir?
CAPTAIN: The nephew of old Norway, Fortinbras.
HAMLET: Goes it against the main° of Poland, sir,   15
Or for some frontier?
CAPTAIN: Truly to speak, and with no addition,°
We go to gain a little patch of ground
That hath in it no profit but the name.
To pay five ducats, five, I would not farm it,   20
Nor will it yield to Norway or the Pole
A ranker° rate, should it be sold in fee.°
HAMLET: Why, then the Polack never will defend it.
CAPTAIN: Yes, it is already garrisoned.
HAMLET: Two thousand souls and twenty thousand ducats   25
Will not debate° the question of this straw.
This is th' imposthume° of much wealth and peace,
That inward breaks, and shows no cause without
Why the man dies. I humbly thank you, sir.
CAPTAIN: God by you, sir.   *Exit.*
ROSENCRANTZ: Will't please you go, my lord?   30
HAMLET: I'll be with you straight. Go a little before.

                              Exeunt all but HAMLET.

How all occasions do inform against me
And spur my dull revenge! What is a man,
If his chief good and market° of his time
Be but to sleep and feed? A beast, no more.   35
Sure he that make us with such large discourse,°
Looking before and after, gave us not
That capability and godlike reason
To fust° in us unused. Now, whether it be
Bestial oblivion,° or some craven scruple   40
Of thinking too precisely on th' event°—
A thought which, quartered, hath but one part wisdom
And ever three parts coward—I do not know
Why yet I live to say, "This thing's to do,"
Sith I have cause, and will, and strength, and means   45
To do't. Examples gross° as earth exhort me.
Witness this army of such mass and charge,°
Led by a delicate and tender prince,
Whose spirit, with divine ambition puffed,
Makes mouths at the invisible event,°   50

15 main main part   **17 with no addition** plainly   **22 ranker** higher;   **in fee**
outright   **26 debate** settle   **27 imposthume** abscess, ulcer   **34 market** profit
36 discourse understanding   **39 fust** grow moldy   **40 oblivion** forgetfulness
41 event outcome   **46 gross** large obvious   **47 charge** expense   **50 Makes . . .**
event makes scornful faces (is contemptuous of) the unseen outcome

Exposing what is mortal and unsure
To all that fortune, death, and danger dare,
Even for an eggshell. Rightly to be great
Is not° to stir without great argument,°
But greatly° to find quarrel in a straw   55
When honor's at the stake. How stand I then,
That have a father killed, a mother stained,
Excitements° of my reason and my blood,
And let all sleep, while to my shame I see
The imminent death of twenty thousand men   60
That for a fantasy and trick of fame°
Go to their graves like beds, fight for a plot
Whereon the numbers cannot try the cause,
Which is not tomb enough and continent°
To hide the slain? O, from this time forth,   65
My thoughts be bloody, or be nothing worth!   *Exit.*

SCENE V. The castle.

Enter HORATIO, QUEEN *Gertrude, and a* GENTLEMAN.

QUEEN: I will not speak with her.
GENTLEMAN: She is importunate, indeed distract.
   Her mood will needs be pitied.
QUEEN: What would she have?
GENTLEMEN: She speaks much of her father, says she hears
   There's tricks i' th' world, and hems, and beats her heart,   5
   Spurns enviously at straws,° speaks things in doubt°
   That carry but half sense. Her speech is nothing,
   Yet the unshaped use of it doth move
   The hearers to collection;° they yawn° at it,
   And botch the words up fit to their own thoughts,   10
   Which, as her winks and nods and gestures yield them,
   Indeed would make one think there might be thought,
   Though nothing sure, yet much unhappily.
HORATIO: 'Twere good she were spoken with, for she may strew
   Dangerous conjectures in ill-breeding minds.   15
QUEEN: Let her come in.   *Exit* GENTLEMAN.

Aside.

---

54 not the sense seems to require "not not"; **argument** reason   **55 greatly**
nobly   **58 Excitements** incentives   **61 fantasy . . . fame** illusion and trifle of
reputation   **64 continent** receptacle, container   **IV.v.6 Spurns . . . straws** objects spitefully to insignificant matters;   **in doubt** uncertainly   **8–9 Yet . . .**
collection yet the formless manner of it moves her listeners to gather up some sort
of meaning   **9 yawn** gape (?)

To my sick soul (as sin's true nature is).
Each toy seems prologue to some great amiss;°
So full of artless jealousy° to guilt
It spills° itself in fearing to be spilt.   20

Enter OPHELIA *distracted.*

OPHELIA: Where is the beauteous majesty of Denmark?
QUEEN: How now, Ophelia?
OPHELIA *She sings:*
          How should I your truelove know
              From another one?
          By his cockle hat° and staff   25
          And his sandal shoon.°
QUEEN: Alas, sweet lady, what imports this song?
OPHELIA: Say you? Nay, pray you mark.
                              Song.
          He is dead and gone, lady,
              He is dead and gone;   30
          At his head a grass-green turf,
              At his heels a stone.
     Oh, ho!
QUEEN: Nay, but Ophelia—
OPHELIA: Pray you mark. *Sings.*   35
     White his shroud as the mountain snow—

Enter KING.

QUEEN: Alas, look here, my lord.
OPHELIA:
                              Song.
          Larded° all with sweet flowers
          Which bewept to the grave did not go
              With truelove showers.   40
KING: How do you, pretty lady?
OPHELIA: Well, God dild° you! They say the owl was a baker's
     daughter.° Lord, we know what we are, but know not what we
     may be. God be at your table!
KING: Conceit° upon her father.   45
OPHELIA: Pray let's have no words of this, but when they ask you
     what it means, say you this:
                              Song.

18 amiss misfortune   **19 artless jealousy** crude suspicion   **20 spills** destroys
25 cockle hat a cockleshell on the hat was the sign of a pilgrim who had journeyed
to shrines overseas; the association of lovers and pilgrims was a common one
26 shoon shoes   **38 Larded** decorated   **42 dild** yield, i.e., reward   **43 baker's
daughter** an allusion to a tale of a baker's daughter who begrudged bread to Christ
and was turned into an owl   **45 Conceit** brooding

> Tomorrow is Saint Valentine's day.°
>   All in the morning betime,
> And I a maid at your window,   50
>   To be your Valentine.
>
> Then up he rose and donned his clothes
>   And dupped° the chamber door,
> Let in the maid, that out a maid
>   Never departed more.   55

KING: Pretty Ophelia.

OPHELIA: Indeed, la, without an oath, I'll make an end on't: *Sings.*
>   By Gis° and by Saint Charity,
>   Alack, and fie for shame!
>   Young men will do't if they come to't,   60
>   By Cock,° they are to blame.
>   Quoth she, "Before you tumbled me,
>   You promised me to wed."

He answers:
>   "So would I 'a' done, by yonder sun,
>   An thou hadst not come to my bed."

KING: How long hath she been thus?

OPHELIA: I hope all will be well. We must be patient, but I cannot choose but weep to think they would lay him i' th' cold ground. My brother shall know of it; and so I thank you for your good counsel. Come, my coach! Good night, ladies, good night. Sweet ladies, good night, good night.   *Exit.*

KING: Follow her close; give her good watch, I pray you.

> *Exit* HORATIO.

> O, this is the poison of deep grief; it springs
> All from her father's death—and now behold!   75
> O Gertrude, Gertrude,
> When sorrows come, they come not single spies,
> But in battalions: first, her father slain;
> Next, your son gone, and he most violent author
> Of his own just remove; the people muddied,°   80
> Thick and unwholesome in their thoughts and whispers
> For good Polonius' death, and we have done but greenly°
> In huggermugger° to inter him; poor Ophelia
> Divided from herself and her fair judgment,
> Without the which we are pictures or mere beasts;   85
> Last, and as much containing as all these,
> Her brother is in secret come from France,

---

48 Saint Valentine's day February 14 (the notion was that a bachelor would become the truelove of the first girl he saw on this day)   **53 dupped** opened (did up)   **58 Gis** (contraction of *Jesus*)   **61 Cock** (1) God (2) phallus   **80 muddied** muddled   **82 greenly** foolishly   **83 huggermugger** secret haste

Feeds on his wonder,° keeps himself in clouds,
And wants not buzzers° to infect his ear
With pestilent speeches of his father's death,   90
Wherein necessity, of matter beggared,°
Will nothing stick° our person to arraign
In ear and ear. O my dear Gertrude, this,
Like to a murd'ring piece,° in many places
Gives me superfluous death. *A noise within.*

Enter a MESSENGER.

QUEEN: Alack, what noise is this?   95
KING: Attend, where are my Switzers?° Let them guard the door.
    What is the matter?
MESSENGER: Save yourself, my lord
    The ocean, overpeering of his list,°
    Eats not the flats with more impiteous haste
    Than young Laertes, in a riotous head,°   100
    O'erbears your officers. The rabble call him lord,
    And, as the world were now but to begin,
    Antiquity forgot, customs not known,
    The ratifiers and props of every word,
    They cry, "Choose we! Laertes shall be king!"   105
    Caps, hands, and tongues applaud it to the clouds,
    "Laertes shall be king! Laertes king!"

A noise within.

QUEEN: How cheerfully on the false trail they cry!
    O, this is counter,° you false Danish dogs!

Enter LAERTES, *with others.*

KING: The doors are broke.   110
LAERTES: Where is this king?—Sirs, stand you all without.
ALL: No, let's come in.
LAERTES: I pray you give me leave.
ALL: We will, we will.
LAERTES: I thank you. Keep the door.   *Exeunt his* FOLLOWERS.
    O thou vile king,   115
    Give me my father.
QUEEN: Calmly, good Laertes.
LAERTES: That drop of blood that's calm proclaims me bastard,

---

88 wonder suspicion   **89 wants not buzzers** does not lack talebearers   **91 of matter beggared** unprovided with facts   **92 Will nothing stick** will not hesitate   **94 murd'ring piece** a cannon that shot a kind of shrapnel   **96 Switzers** Swiss guards   **98 list** shore   **100 in . . . head** with a rebellious force   **109 counter** a hound runs counter when he follows the scent backward from the prey

Cries cuckold° to my father, brands the harlot
Even here between the chaste unsmirchèd brow
Of my true mother.

KING: What is the cause, Laertes,   120
That thy rebellion looks so giantlike?
Let him go, Gertrude. Do not fear° our person.
There's such divinity doth hedge a king
That treason can but peep to° what it would,
Acts little of his will. Tell me, Laertes,   125
Why thou art thus incensed. Let him go, Gertrude.
Speak, man.

LAERTES: Where is my father?

KING::   Dead.

QUEEN: But not by him.

KING: Let him demand his fill.

LAERTES: How came he dead? I'll not be juggled with.
To hell allegiance, vows to the blackest devil,   130
Conscience and grace to the profoundest pit!
I dare damnation. To this point I stand,
That both the worlds I give to negligence,°
Let come what comes, only I'll be revenged
Most throughly for my father.

KING: Who shall stay you?   135

LAERTES: My will, not all the world's.
And for my means, I'll husband them° so well
They shall go far with little.

KING: Good Laertes,
If you desire to know the certainty
Of your dear father, is't writ in your revenge   140
That swoopstake° you will draw both friend and foe,
Winner and loser?

LAERTES: None but his enemies.

KING: Will you know them then?

LAERTES: To his good friends thus wide I'll ope my arms
And like the kind life-rend'ring pelican°   145
Repast° them with my blood.

KING: Why, now you speak
Like a good child and a true gentleman.
That I am guiltless of your father's death,
And am most sensibly° in grief for it,
It shall as level to your judgment 'pear
As day does to your eye.

A noise within: "Let her come in."

---

118 cuckold man whose wife is unfaithful   **122 fear** fear for   **124 peep to** i.e., look at from a distance   **133 That . . . negligence** i.e., I care not what may happen (to me) in this world or the next   **137 husband them** use them economically   **141 swoopstake** in a clean sweep   **145 pelican** thought to feed its young with its own blood   **146 Repast** feed   **149 sensibly**

LAERTES: How now? What noise is that?

Enter OPHELIA.

O heat, dry up my brains; tears seven times salt
Burn out the sense and virtue° of mine eye!
By heaven, thy madness shall be paid with weight   155
Till our scale turn the beam.° O rose of May,
Dear maid, kind sister, sweet Ophelia!
O heavens, is't possible a yound maid's wits
Should be as mortal as an old man's life?
Nature is fine° in love, and where 'tis fine,   160
It sends some precious instance° of itself
After the thing it loves.

OPHELIA: *Song.*
        They bore him barefaced on the bier
            Hey non nony, nony, hey nony
        And in his grave rained many a tear—   165
Fare you well, my dove!

LAERTES: Hadst thou thy wits, and didst persuade revenge,
It could not move thus.

OPHELIA: You must sing "A-down a-down, and you call him a-
down-a." O, how the wheel° becomes it! It is the false steward,   170
that stole his master's daughter.

LAERTES: This nothing's more than matter.°

OPHELIA: There's rosemary, that's for remembrance. Pray you,
love, remember. And there is pansies, that's for thoughts.

LAERTES: A document° in madness, thoughts and remembrance fit-   175
ted.

OPHELIA: There's fennel° for you, and columbines.There's rue for
you, and here's some for me. We may call it herb of grace o' Sundays. O, you must wear your rue with a difference. There's a
daisy. I would give you some violets, but they withered all when
my father died. They say 'a made a good end.   180
Sings.
        For bonny sweet Robin is all my joy.

LAERTES: Thought and affliction, passion, hell itself,
She turns to favor° and to prettiness.

---

154 **virtue** power   156 **turn the beam** weigh down the bar (of the balance)
160 **fine** refined, delicate   161 **instance** sample   170 **wheel** of uncertain meaning, but probably a turn or dance of Ophelia's, rather than Fortune's wheel
172 **This . . . matter** This nonsense has more meaning than matters of
consequence   175 **document** lesson   176 **fennel** the distribution of flowers in
the ensuing lines has symbolic meaning, but the meaning is disputed; perhaps "fennel" = flattery, "columbines" = cuckoldry, "rue" = sorrow for Ophelia and repentance for the queen, "daisy" = dissembling, "violets" = faithfulness.   183
favor charm, beauty

OPHELIA: *Song.*
    And will 'a not come again?
    And will 'a not come again?   185
      No, no, he is dead,
      Go to thy deathbed,
    He never will come again.

    His beard was as white as snow,
    All flaxen was his poll.°   190
      He is gone, he is gone,
      And we cast away moan.
    God 'a' mercy on his soul!
And of all Christian souls, I pray God. God bye you.

                                          Exit.
                                          195

LAERTES: Do you see this, O God?
KING: Laertes, I must commune with your grief,
Or you deny me right. Go but apart,
Make choice of whom your wisest friends you will,
And they shall hear and judge 'twixt you and me.
If by direct or by collateral° hand   200
They find us touched,° we will our kingdom, give
Our crown, our life, and all that we call ours,
To you in satisfaction; but if not,
Be you content to lend your patience to us,
And we shall jointly labor with your soul   205
To give it due content.
LAERTES: Let this be so.
His means of death, his obscure funeral—
No trophy, sword, nor hatchment° o'er his bones,
No noble rite nor formal ostentation°—
Cry to be heard, as 'twere from heaven to earth,   210
That I must call't in question.
KING: So you shall;
And where th' offense is, let the great ax fall.
I pray you go with me.   *Exeunt.*

SCENE VI. The castle.

Enter HORATIO *and others.*

HORATIO: What are they that would speak with me?
GENTLEMAN: Seafaring men, sir. They say they have letters for you.

---

190 All . . . poll white as flax was his head   **200 collateral** indirect
201 touched implicated   **208 hatchment** tablet bearing the coat of arms of the
dead   **209 ostentation** ceremony

HORATIO: Let them come in.   *Exit* GENTLEMAN.
  I do not know from what part of the world
  I should be greeted, if not from Lord Hamlet.   5

Enter SAILORS.
SAILOR: God bless you, sir.
HORATIO: Let Him bless thee too.
SAILOR: 'A shall, sir, an't please Him. There's a letter for you, sir—
  it came from th' ambassador that was bound for England—if your
  name be Horatio, as I am let to know it is.   10
HORATIO *Reads the letter:*   "Horatio, when thou shalt have over-
  looked° this, give these fellows some means to the king. They
  have letters for him. Ere we were two days old at sea, a pirate of
  very warlike appointment° gave us chase. Finding ourselves too
  slow of sail, we put on a compelled valor, and in the grapple I   15
  boarded them. On the instant they got clear of our ship; so I alone
  became their prisoner. They have dealt with me like thieves of
  mercy, but they knew what they did; I am to do a good turn for
  them. Let the king have the letters I have sent, and repair thou
  to me with as much speed as thou wouldest fly death. I have   20
  words to speak in thine ear will make thee dumb; yet are they
  much too light for the bore° of the matter. These good fellows
  will bring thee where I am. Rosencrantz and Guildenstern hold
  their course for England. Of them I have much to tell thee. Farewell.
                                   He that thou knowest thine, Hamlet."   25
  Come, I will give you way for these your letters,
  And do't the speedier that you may direct me
  To him from whom you brought them.   *Exeunt.*

SCENE VII. The castle.

KING: Now must your conscience my acquittance seal,
  And you must put me in your heart for friend,
  Sith you have heard, and with a knowing ear,
  That he which hath your noble father slain
  Pursued my life.
LAERTES: It well appears. But tell me   5
  Why you proceeded not against these feats
  So criminal and so capital° in nature,
  As by your safety, greatness, wisdom, all things else,
  You mainly° were stirred up.
KING: O, for two special reasons,

IV.vi.12 **overlooked** surveyed   14 **appointment** equipment   22 **bore** caliber
(here, "importance")   IV.vii.7 **capital** deserving death   9 **mainly** powerfully

Which may to you perhaps seem much unsinewed,° 10
But yet to me they're strong. The queen his mother
Lives almost by his looks, and for myself—
My virtue or my plague, be it either which—
She is so conjunctive° to my life and soul,
That, as the star moves not but in his sphere, 15
I could not but by her. The other motive
Why to a public count° I might not go
Is the great love the general gender° bear him,
Who, dipping all his faults in their affection,
Would, like the spring that turneth wood to stone,° 20
Convert his gyves° to graces; so that my arrows,
Too slightly timbered° for so loud a wind,
Would have reverted to my bow again,
And not where I had aimed them.

LAERTES: And so have I a noble father lost, 25
A sister driven into desp'rate terms,°
Whose worth, if praises may go back again,°
Stood challenger on mount of all the age
For her perfections. But my revenge will come.

KING: Break not your sleeps for that. You must think
That we are made of stuff so flat and dull
That we can let our beard be shook with danger,
And think it pastime. You shortly shall hear more.
I loved your father, and we love ourself,
And that, I hope, will teach you to imagine— 35

Enter a MESSENGER *with letters.*

How now? What news?
MESSENGER: Letters, my lord, from Hamlet:
These to your majesty; this to the queen.
KING: From Hamlet? Who brought them?
MESSENGER: Sailors, my lord, they say; I saw them not.
They were given me by Claudio; he received them 40
Of him that brought them.
KING: Laertes, you shall hear them.—
Leave us.   *Exit* MESSENGER.
Reads. "High and mighty, you shall know I am set naked° on
your kingdom. Tomorrow shall I beg leave to see your kingly
eyes; when I shall (first asking your pardon thereunto) recount 45

---

10 unsinewed weak   **14 conjunctive** closely united   **17 count** reckoning
18 general gender common people   **20 spring . . . stone** a spring in Shakespeare's county was so charged with lime that it would petrify wood placed in it
21 gyves fetters   **22 timbered** shafted   **26 terms** conditions   **27 go back again**
revert to what is past   **43 naked** destitute

the occasion of my sudden and more strange return.
Hamlet."
What should this mean? Are all the rest come back?
Or is it some abuse, ° and no such thing?

LAERTES: Know you the hand?

KING: 'Tis Hamlet's character.° "Naked"!   50
And in a postscript here, he says "alone."
Can you devise° me?

LAERTES: I am lost in it, my lord. But let him come.
It warms the very sickness in my heart
That I shall live and tell him to his teeth,   55
"Thus didst thou."

KING: If it be so, Laertes
(As how should it be so? How otherwise?),
Will you be ruled by me?

LAERTES: Ay, my lord,
So you will not o'errule me to a peace.

KING: To thine own peace. If he be now returned,   60
As checking at° his voyage, and that he means
No more to undertake it, I will work him
To an exploit now ripe in my device,
Under the which he shall not choose but fall;
And for his death no wind of blame shall breathe,   65
But even his mother shall uncharge the practice°
And call it accident.

LAERTES: My lord, I will be ruled;
The rather if you could devise it so
That I might be the organ.

KING: It falls right.
You have been talked of since your travel much,   70
And that in Hamlet's hearing, for a quality
Wherein they say you shine. Your sum of parts
Did not together pluck such envy from him
As did that one, and that, in my regard,
Of the unworthiest siege.°

LAERTES: What part is that, my lord?   75

KING: A very riband in the cap of youth,
Yet needful too, for youth no less becomes
The light and careless livery that it wears
Than settled age his sables and his weeds,°
Importing health and graveness. Two months since   80
Here was a gentleman of Normandy.
I have seen myself, and served against, the French,
And they can° well on horseback, but this gallant

49 **abuse** deception   50 **character** handwriting   52 **devise** advise   61 **check-ing at** turning away from (a term in falconry)   66 **uncharge the practice** not charge the device with treachery   75 **siege** rank   79 **sables . . . weeds** i.e., sober attire   83 **can** do

Had witchcraft in't. He grew unto his seat,
And to such wondrous doing brought his horse   85
As had he been incorpsed and deminatured
With the brave beast. So far he topped my thought
That I, in forgery° of shapes and tricks,
Come short of what he did.
LAERTES: A Norman was't?
KING: A Norman.
LAERTES: Upon my life, Lamord.
KING: The very same.   90
LAERTES: I know him well. He is the brooch° indeed
And gem of all the nation.
KING: He made confession° of you,
And gave you such a masterly report,
For art and exercise in your defense,
And for your rapier most especial,
That he cried out 'twould be a sight indeed
If one could match you. The scrimers° of their nation
He swore had neither motion, guard, nor eye,
If you opposed them. Sir, this report of his
Did Hamlet so envenom with his envy
That he could nothing do but wish and beg
Your sudden coming o'er to play with you.
Now, out of this—
LAERTES: What out of his, my lord?
KING: Laertes, was your father dear to you?   105
Or are you like the painting of a sorrow,
A face without a heart?
LAERTES: Why ask you this?
KING: Not that I think you did not love your father,
But that I know love is begun by time,
And that I see, in passages of proof,°   110
Time qualifies° the spark and fire of it.
There lives within the very flame of love,
A kind of wick or snuff° that will abate it,
And nothing is at a like goodness still,°
For goodness, growing to a plurisy,°   115
Dies in his own too-much. That we would do
We should do when we would, for this "would" changes,
And hath abatements and delays as many
As there are tongues, are hands, are accidents,
And then this "should" is like a spendthrift sigh,°   120

---

88 forgery invention   **91 brooch** ornament   **93 confession** report   **98 scrimers** fencers   **110 passages of proof** proved cases   **111 qualifies** diminishes   **113 snuff** residue of burnt wick (which dims the light)   **114 still** always   **115 plurisy** fullness, excess   **120 spendthrift sigh** sighing provides ease, but because it was thought to thin the blood and so shorten life it was spendthrift

That hurts by easing. But to the quick° of th' ulcer—
Hamlet comes back; what would you undertake
To show yourself in deed your father's son
More than in words?

LAERTES: To cut his throat i' th' church!

KING: No place indeed should murder sanctuarize;°   125
Revenge should have no bounds. But, good Laertes,
Will you do this? Keep close within your chamber.
Hamlet returned shall know you are come home.
We'll put on those° shall praise your excellence
And set a double varnish on the fame   130
The Frenchman gave you, bring you in fine° together
And wager on your heads. He, being remiss,
Most generous, and free from all contriving,
Will not peruse the foils, so that with ease,
Or with a little shuffling, you may choose   135
A sword unbated,° and, in a pass of practice,°
Requite him for your father.

LAERTES: I will do 't,
And for that purpose I'll anoint my sword.
I bought an unction of a mountebank,°
So mortal that, but dip a knife in it,   140
Where it draws blood, no cataplasm° so rare,
Collected from all simples° that have virtue°
Under the moon, can save the thing from death
That is but scratched withal. I'll touch my point
With this contagion, that, if I gall him slightly,   145
It may be death.

KING: Let's further think of this,
Weigh what convenience both of time and means
May fit us to our shape.° If this should fail,
And that our drift look through° our bad performance,
'Twere better not assayed. Therefore this project   150
Should have a back or second, that might hold
If this did blast in proof.° Soft, let me see.
We'll make a solemn wager on your cunnings—
I ha 't!
When in your motion you are hot and dry—   155
As make your bouts more violent to that end—
And that he calls for drink, I'll have prepared him
A chalice for the nonce,° whereon but sipping,
If he by chance escape your venomed stuck,°
Our purpose may hold there.—But stay, what noise?   160

---

121 **quick** sensitive flesh   125 **sanctuarize** protect   129 **We'll . . . those** we'll
incite persons who   131 **in fine** finally   136 **unbated** not blunted;   **pass of
practice** treacherous thrust   139 **mountebank** quack   141 **cataplasm** poultice
142 **simples** medicinal herbs;   **virtue** power (to heal)   148 **shape** role
149 **drift look through** purpose show through   152 **blast in proof** burst (fail) in
performance   158 **nonce** occasion   159 **stuck** thrust

Enter QUEEN.

QUEEN: One woe doth tread upon another's heel,
　　So fast they follow. Your sister's drowned, Laertes.
LAERTES: Drowned! O, where?
QUEEN: There is a willow grows askant° the brook,
　　That shows his hoar° leaves in the glassy stream:　　　　　　165
　　Therewith° fantastic garlands did she make
　　Of crowflowers, nettles, daisies, and long purples,
　　That liberal° shepherds give a grosser name,
　　But our cold maids do dead men's fingers call them.
　　There on the pendent boughs her crownet° weeds　　　　　170
　　Clamb'ring to hang, an envious sliver° broke,
　　When down her weedy trophies and herself
　　Fell in the weeping brook. Her clothes spread wide,
　　And mermaidlike awhile they bore her up,
　　Which time she chanted snatches of old lauds,°　　　　　175
　　As one incapable° of her own distress,
　　Or like a creature native and indued°
　　Unto that element. But long it could not be
　　Till that her garments, heavy with their drink,
　　Pulled the poor wretch from her melodious lay　　　　　180
　　To muddy death.
LAERTES:　　　　　　　Alas, then she is drowned?
QUEEN: Drowned, drowned.
LAERTES: Too much of water hast thou, poor Ophelia,
　　And therefore I forbid my tears; but yet
　　It is our trick;° nature her custom holds,　　　　　　185
　　Let shame say what it will: when these are gone,
　　The woman° will be out. Adieu, my lord.
　　I have a speech o' fire, that fain would blaze,
　　But that this folly drowns it.　　　　　　　　　*Exit.*
KING:　　　　　　　　　Let's follow, Gertrude.
　　How much I had to do to calm his rage!　　　　　　190
　　Now fear I this will give it start again;
　　Therefore let's follow.　　　　　　　　　　*Exeunt.*

ACT V

SCENE I. A churchyard.

Enter two CLOWNS.°

---

164 askant aslant　　**165 hoar** silver-gray　　**166 Therewith** i.e., with willow twigs
168 liberal free-spoken, coarse-mouthed　　**170 crownet** coronet　　**171 envious
sliver** malicious branch　　**175 lauds** hymns　　**176 incapable** unaware　　**177 in-
dued** in harmony with　　**185 trick** trait, why　　**187 woman** i.e., womanly part of
me　　**V.i.s.d. clowns** rustics

CLOWN: Is she to be buried in Christian burial when she willfully
seeks her own salvation?

OTHER: I tell thee she is. Therefore make her grave straight.° The
crowner° hath sate on her, and finds it Christian burial.

CLOWN: How can that be, unless she drowned herself in her own   5
defense?

OTHER: Why, 'tis found so.

CLOWN: It must be se offendendo;° it cannot be else. For here lies
the point: if I drown myself wittingly, it argues an act, and an act
hath three branches—it is to act, to do, to perform. Argal,° she   10
drowned herself wittingly.

OTHER: Nay, but hear you, Goodman Delver.

CLOWN: Give me leave. Here lies the water—good. Here stands the
man—good. If the man go to this water and drown himself, it is,
will he nill he,° he goes; mark you that. But if the water come to   15
him and drown him, he drowns not himself. Argal, he that is not
guilty of his own death, shortens not his own life.

OTHER: But is this law?

CLOWN: Ay marry, is't—crowner's quest° law.

OTHER: Will you ha' the truth on't? If this had not been a gentle-   20
woman, she should have been buried out o' Christian burial.

CLOWN: Why, there thou say'st. And the more pity that great folk
should have count'nance° in this world to drown or hang themselves more than their even-Christen.° Come, my spade. There is
no ancient gentlemen but gard'ners, ditchers, and gravemakers.   25
They hold up° Adam's profession.

OTHER: Was he a gentleman?

CLOWN: 'A was the first that ever bore arms.°

OTHER: Why, he had none.

CLOWN: What, art a heathen? How doest thou understand the   30
Scripture? The Scripture says Adam digged. Could he dig without
arms? I'll put another question to thee. If thou answerest me not
to the purpose, confess thyself—

OTHER: Go to.

CLOWN: What is he that builds stronger then either the mason, the   35
shipwright, or the carpenter?

OTHER: The gallowsmaker, for that frame outlives a thousand tenants.

CLOWN: I like thy wit well, in good faith. The gallows does well.
But how does it well? It does well to those that do ill. Now thou   40
dost ill to say the gallows is built stronger than the church. Argal,
the gallows may do well to thee. To't again, come.

---

3 straight straightway   **4 crowner** coroner   **8 se offendendo** blunder for *se de-
fendendo*, a legal term meaning "in self-defense"   **10 Argal** blunder for Latin *ergo*,
"therefore"   **15 will he . . . he** will he or will he not (whether he will or will
not)   **19 quest** inquest   **23 count'nance** privilege   **24 even-Christen** fellow
Christian   **26 hold up** keep up   **28 bore arms** had a coat of arms (the sign of a
gentleman)

OTHER: Who builds stronger than a mason, a ship-wright, or a car-
penter?
CLOWN: Ay, tell me that, and unyoke.°   45
OTHER: Marry, now I can tell.
CLOWN: To't.
OTHER: Mass,° I cannot tell.

Enter HAMLET *and* HORATIO *afar off.*

CLOWN: Cudgel thy brains no more about it, for your dull ass will
not mend his pace with beating. And when you are asked this   50
question next, say "a gravemaker." The houses he makes lasts till
doomsday. Go, get thee in, and fetch me a stoup° of liquor.

Exit OTHER CLOWN.

Song.
In youth when I did love, did love,
Methought it was very sweet
To contract—O—the time for—a—my behove,°   55
O, methought there—a—was nothing—a—meet.
HAMLET: Has this fellow no feeling of his business? 'A sings in
gravemaking.
HORATIO: Custom hath made it in him a property of easiness.°
HAMLET: 'Tis e'en so. The hand of little employment hath the dain- 60
tier sense.°
CLOWN: *Song.*
But age with his stealing steps
Hath clawed me in his clutch,
And hath shipped me into the land,
As if I had never been such.   65

Throws up a skull.

HAMLET: That skull had a tongue in it, and could sing once. How
the knave jowls° it to the ground, as if 'twere Cain's jawbone, that
did the first murder! This might be the pate of a politician, which
this ass now o'erreaches,° one that would circumvent God, might
it not?   70
HORATIO: It might, my lord.
HAMLET: Or of a courtier, which could say "Good morrow, sweet
lord! How dost thou, sweet lord?" This might be my Lord Such-

---

45 unyoke i.e., stop work for the day   **48 Mass** by the mass   **52 stoup** tankard
55 behove advantage   **59 in . . . easiness** easy for him   **60–1 hath . . . sense**
is more sensitive (because it is not calloused)   **67 jowls** hurls   **69 o'erreaches**
(1) reaches over (2) has the advantage over

a-one, that praised my Lord Such-a-one's horse when 'a went to
beg it, might it not? 75
HORATIO: Ay, my lord.
HAMLET: Why, e'en so, and now my Lady Worm's, chapless,° and
knocked about the mazzard° with a sexton's spade. Here's fine
revolution, as we had the trick to see't. Did these bones cost no
more the breeding but to play at loggets° with them? Mine ache 80
to think on't.
CLOWN: *Song.*
   A pickax and a spade, a spade,
     For and a shrouding sheet;
   O, a pit of clay for to be made
     For such a guest is meet. 85

Throws up another skull.

HAMLET: There's another. Why may not that be the skull of a lawyer? Where be his quiddities° now, his quillities,° his cases, his
tenures,° and his tricks? Why does he suffer this mad knave now
to knock him about the sconce° with a dirty shovel, and will not
tell him of his action of battery? Hum! This fellow might be in's 90
time a great buyer of land, with his statutes, his recognizances,
his fines,° his double vouchers, his recoveries. Is this the fine° of
his fines, and the recovery of his recoveries, to have his fine pate
full of fine dirt? Will his vouchers vouch him no more of his purchases, and double ones too, than the length and breadth of a pair 95
of indentures?° The very conveyances° of his lands will scarcely
lie in this box, and must th' inheritor himself have no more, ha?
HORATIO: Not a jot more, my lord.
HAMLET: Is not parchment made of sheepskins?
HORATIO: Ay, my lord, and of calveskins too. 100
HAMLET: They are sheep and calves which seek out assurance° in
that. I will speak to this fellow. Whose grave's this, sirrah?
CLOWN: Mine, sir. *Sings.*
   O, a pit of clay for to be made
     For such a guest is meet. 105
HAMLET: I think it be thine indeed, for thou liest in't.
CLOWN: You lie out on't, sir, and therefore 'tis not yours. For my
part, I do not lie in't, yet it is mine.

---

77 chapless lacking the lower jaw   **78 mazzard** head   **80 loggets** a game in
which small pieces of wood were thrown at an object;   **87 quiddities** subtle arguments (from Latin *quidditas* = whatness);   **quillities** fine distinctions   **88 tenures** legal means of holding land   **89 sconce** head   **91–92 his statutes . . .
fines** his documents giving a creditor control of a debtor's land, his bonds of surety,
his documents changing an entailed estate into fee simple (unrestricted ownership);
fine end   **96 indentures** contracts;   **conveyances** legal documents for the trans-
ference of land   **101 assurance** safety

HAMLET: Thou dost lie in't, to be in't and say it is thine. 'Tis for
   the dead, not for the quick;° therefore thou liest.   110
CLOWN: 'Tis a quick lie, sir; 'twill away again from me to you.
HAMLET: What man dost thou dig it for?
CLOWN: For no man, sir.
HAMLET: What woman then?
CLOWN: For none neither.   115
HAMLET: Who is to be buried in't?
CLOWN: One that was a woman, sir; but, rest her soul, she's dead.
HAMLET: How absolute° the knave is! We must speak by the card,°
   or equivocation° will undo us. By the Lord, Horatio, this three
   years I have took note of it, the age is grown so picked° that the   120
   toe of the peasant comes so near the heel of the courtier he galls
   his kibe.° How long hast thou been a gravemaker?
CLOWN: Of all the days i' th' year, I came to't that day that our last
   king Hamlet overcame Fortinbras.
HAMLET: How long is that since?   125
CLOWN: Cannot you tell that? Every fool can tell that. It was that
   very day that young Hamlet was born—he that is mad, and sent
   into England.
HAMLET: Ay, marry, why was he sent into England?
CLOWN: Why, because 'a was mad. 'A shall recover his wits there;   130
   or, if 'a do not, 'tis no great matter there.
HAMLET: Why?
CLOWN: 'Twill not be seen in him there. There the men are as mad
   as he.
HAMLET: How came he mad?   135
CLOWN: Very strangely, they say.
HAMLET: How strangely?
CLOWN: Faith, e'en with losing his wits.
HAMLET: Upon what ground?
CLOWN: Why, here in Denmark. I have been sexton here, man and   140
   boy, thirty years.
HAMLET: How long will a man lie i' th' earth ere he rot?
CLOWN: Faith, if 'a be not rotten before 'a die (as we have many
   pocky corses° nowadays that will scarce hold the laying in), 'a will
   last you some eight year or nine year. A tanner will last you nine   145
   year.
HAMLET: Why he more than another?
CLOWN: Why, sir, his hide is so tanned with his trade that 'a will
   keep out water a great while, and your water is a sore decayer of
   your whoreson dead body. Here's a skull now hath lien you i' th'   150
   earth three and twenty years.
HAMLET: Whose was it?

110 quick living   **118 absolute** positive, decided;   **by the card** by the compass
card, i.e., exactly   **119 equivocation** ambiguity   **120 picked** refined   **122 kibe**
sore on the back of the heel   **144 pocky corses** bodies of persons who had been
infected with the pox (syphilis)

CLOWN: A whoreson mad fellow's it was. Whose do you think it was?

HAMLET: Nay, I know not. 155

CLOWN: A pestilence on him for a mad rogue! 'A poured a flagon of Rhenish on my head once. This same skull, sir, was, sir, Yorick's skull, the king's jester.

HAMLET: This?

CLOWN: E'en that. 160

HAMLET: Let me see. *Takes the skull.* Alas, poor Yorick! I knew him, Horatio, a fellow of infinite jest, of most excellent fancy. He hath borne me on his back a thousand times. And now how abhorred in my imagination it is! My gorge rises at it. Here hung those lips that I have kissed I know not how oft. Where be your 165 gibes now? Your gambols, your songs, your flashes of merriment that were wont to set the table on a roar? Not one now to mock your own grinning? Quite chapfall'n°? Now get you to my lady's chamber, and tell her, let her paint an inch thick, to this favor° she must come. Make her laugh at that. Prithee, Horatio, tell me 170 one thing.

HORATIO: What's that, my lord?

HAMLET: Dost thou think Alexander looked o' this fashion i' th' earth?

HORATIO: E'en so. 175

HAMLET: And smelt so? Pah!

Puts down the skull.

HORATIO: E'en so, my lord.

HAMLET: To what base uses we may return, Horatio! Why may not imagination trace the noble dust of Alexander till 'a find it stopping a bunghole? 180

HORATIO: 'Twere to consider too curiously,° to consider so.

HAMLET: No, faith, not a jot, but to follow him thither with modesty enough,° and likelihood to lead it; as thus: Alexander died, Alexander was buried, Alexander returneth to dust; the dust is earth; of earth we make loam; and why of that loam whereto he 185 was converted might they not stop a beer barrel?
Imperious Caesar, dead and turned to clay,
Might stop a hole to keep the wind away.
O, that that earth which kept the world in awe
Should patch a wall t' expel the winter's flaw!° 190
But soft, but soft awhile! Here comes the king.

Enter KING, QUEEN, LAERTES, *and a coffin, with* LORDS *attendant and a* DOCTOR *of Divinity.*

168 **chapfall'n** (1) down in the mouth (2) jawless   169 **favor** facial appearance
181 **curiously** minutely   183 **with modesty enough** without exaggeration.
190 **flaw** gust

The queen, the courtiers. Who is this they follow?
And with such maimèd° rites? This doth betoken
The corse they follow did with desp'rate hand
Fordo it° own life. 'Twas of some estate.°   195
Couch° we awhile, and mark. *Retires with* HORATIO.

LAERTES: What ceremony else?
HAMLET: That is Laertes,
A very noble youth. Mark.
LAERTES: What ceremony else?
DOCTOR: Her obsequies have been as far enlarged   200
As we have warranty. Her death was doubtful,°
And, but that great command o'ersways the order,
She should in ground unsanctified been lodged
Till the last trumpet. For charitable prayers,
Shards,° flints, and pebbles should be thrown on her.   205
Yet here she is allowed her virgin crants,°
Her maiden strewments,° and the bringing home
Of bell and burial.
LAERTES: Must there no more be done?
DOCTOR: No more be done.
We should profane the service of the dead   210
To sing a requiem and such rest to her
As to peace-parted souls.
LAERTES: Lay her i' th' earth,
And from her fair and unpolluted flesh
May violets spring! I tell thee, churlish priest,
A minist'ring angel shall my sister be   215
When thou liest howling!
HAMLET: What, the fair Ophelia?
QUEEN: Sweets to the sweet! Farewell.

Scatters flowers.

I hoped thou shouldst have been my Hamlet's wife.
I thought thy bride bed to have decked, sweet maid,
And not have strewed thy grave.
LAERTES: O, treble woe   220
Fall ten times treble on that cursèd head
Whose wicked deed thy most ingenious sense°
Deprived thee of! Hold off the earth awhile,
Till I have caught her once more in mine arms.

Leaps in the grave.

193 **maimèd** incomplete   195 **Fordo it** destroy its;   **estate** high rank
196 **Couch** hide   201 **doubtful** suspicious   205 **Shards** broken pieces of pottery
206 **crants** garlands   207 **strewments** i.e., of flowers   222 **most ingenious sense**
finely endowed mind

Now pile your dust upon the quick and dead 225
Till of this flat a mountain you have made
T' o'ertop old Pelion° or the skyish head
Of blue Olympus.
HAMLET *Coming forward:*   What is he whose grief
Bears such an emphasis, whose phrase of sorrow 230
Conjures the wand'ring stars,° and makes them stand
Like wonder-wounded hearers? This is I,
Hamlet the Dane.
LAERTES: The devil take thy soul!

Grapples with him.°

HAMLET: Thou pray'st not well.
I prithee take thy fingers from my throat, 235
For, though I am not splentive° and rash,
Yet have I in me something dangerous,
Which let thy wisdom fear. Hold off thy hand.
KING: Pluck them asunder.
QUEEN: Hamlet, Hamlet!
ALL: Gentlemen!
HORATIO: Good my lord, be quiet. 240

ATTENDANTS *part them.*

HAMLET: Why, I will fight with him upon this theme
Until my eyelids will no longer wag.
QUEEN: O my son, what theme?
HAMLET: I loved Ophelia. Forty thousand brothers
Could not with all their quantity of love 245
Make up my sum. What wilt thou do for her?
KING: O, he is mad, Laertes.
QUEEN: For love of God forbear him.
HAMLET: 'Swounds, show me what thou't do.
Woo't weep? Woo't fight? Woo't fast? Woo't tear thyself? 250
Woo't drink up eisel?° Eat a crocodile?
I'll do't. Dost thou come here to whine?
To outface me with leaping in her grave?
Be buried quick with her, and so will I.

---

227 Pelion according to classical legend, giants in their fight with the gods sought to reach heaven by piling Mount Pelion and Mount Ossa on Mount Olympus **231 wand'ring stars** planets   **233 s.d. Grapples with him** Q1, a bad quarto, presumably reporting a version that toured, has a previous direction saying "Hamlet leaps in after Laertes"; possibly he does so, somewhat hysterically, but such a direction—absent from the two good texts. Q2 and F—makes Hamlet the aggressor, somewhat contradicting his next speech; perhaps Laertes leaps out of the grave to attack Hamlet   **236 splenitive** fiery (the spleen was thought to be the seat of anger)   **251 eisel** vinegar

And if thou prate of mountains, let them throw   255
Millions of acres on us, till our ground,
Singeing his pate against the burning zone,°
Make Ossa like a wart! Nay, an thou'lt mouth,
I'll rant as well as thou.
QUEEN: This is mere madness;
And thus a while the fit will work on him.   260
Anon, as patient as the female dove
When that her golden couplets are disclosed,°
His silence will sit drooping.
HAMLET: Hear you, sir.
What is the reason that you use me thus?
I loved you ever. But it is no matter.   265
Let Hercules himself do what he may,
The cat will new, and dog will have his day.
KING: I pray thee, good Horatio, wait upon him.

> *Exit* HAMLET *and* HORATIO.

To LAERTES.

Strengthen your patience in our last night's speech.
We'll put the matter to the present push.°   270
Good Gertrude, set some watch over your son.
This grave shall have a living° monument.
An hour of quiet shortly shall we see;
Till then in patience our proceeding be.   *Exeunt.*

SCENE II. The castle.

Enter HAMLET *and* HORATIO.

HAMLET: So much for this, sir; now shall you see the other.
You do remember all the circumstance?
HORATIO: Remember it, my lord!
HAMLET: Sir, in my heart there was a kind of fighting
That would not let me sleep. Methought I lay   5
Worse than the mutines in the bilboes.° Rashly
(And praised be rashness for it) let us know,
Our indiscretion sometime serves us well
When our deep plots do pall,° and that should learn us

---

257 burning zone sun's orbit   **262 golden . . . disclosed** the dove lays two eggs,
and the newly hatched ("disclosed") young are covered with golden down
270 present push immediate test   **272 living** lasting (with perhaps also a reference
to the plot against Hamlet's life)   **V.ii.6 mutines . . . bilboes** mutineers in
fetters   **9 pall** fail

There's a divinity that shapes our ends,   10
Rough-hew them how we will.

HORATIO: That is most certain.

HAMLET: Up from my cabin,
My sea gown scarfed about me, in the dark
Groped I to find out them, had my desire,
Fingered° their packet, and in fine° withdrew   15
To mine own room again, making so bold,
My fears forgetting manners, to unseal
Their grand commission; where I found, Horatio—
Ah, royal knavery!—an exact command,
Larded° with many several sorts of reasons,   20
Importing Denmark's health, and England's too,
With, ho, such bugs and goblins in my life,°
That on the supervise,° no leisure bated,°
No, not to stay the grinding of the ax,
My head should be struck off.

HORATIO: Is't possible?   25

HAMLET: Here's the commission; read it at more leisure.
But wilt thou hear now how I did proceed?

HORATIO: I beseech you.

HAMLET: Being thus benetted round with villains,
Or° I could make a prologue to my brains,   30
They had begun the play. I sat me down,
Devised a new commission, wrote it fair.
I once did hold it, as our statists° do,
A baseness to write fair,° and labored much
How to forget that learning, but, sir, now   35
It did me yeoman's service. Wilt thou know
Th' effect° of what I wrote?

HORATIO: Ay, good my lord.

HAMLET: An earnest conjuration from the king,
As England was his faithful tributary,
As love between them like the palm might flourish,   40
As peace should still her wheaten garland wear
And stand a comma° 'tween their amities,
And many suchlike as's of great charge,°
That on the view and knowing of these contents,
Without debatement further, more or less,   45
He should those bearers put to sudden death,
Not shriving° time allowed.

HORATIO: How was this sealed?

---

15 Fingered stole;   **in fine** finally   **20 Larded** enriched   **22 such . . . life**
such bugbears and imagined terrors if I were allowed to live   **23 supervise**
reading;   **leisure bated** delay allowed   **30 Or** ere   **33 statists** statesmen
34 fair clearly   **37 effect** purport   **42 comma** link   **43 great charge** (1) serious
exhortation (2) heavy burden (punning on *as's* and *asses*)   **47 shriving** absolution

HAMLET: Why, even in that was heaven ordinant.°
I had my father's signet in my purse,
Which was the model° of that Danish seal,   50
Folded the writ up in the form of th' other,
Subscribed it, gave't th' impression, placed it safely,
The changeling never known. Now, the next day
Was our sea fight, and what to this was sequent
Thou knowest already.   55
HORATIO: So Guildenstern and Rosencrantz go to't.
HAMLET: Why, man, they did make love to this employment.
They are not near my conscience; their defeat
Does by their own insinuation° grow.
'Tis dangerous when the baser nature comes   60
Between the pass° and fell° incensèd points
Of mighty opposites.
HORATIO: Why, what a king is this!
HAMLET: Does it not, think thee, stand me now upon°—
He that hath killed my king, and whored my mother,
Popped in between th' election° and my hopes,   65
Thrown out his angle° for my proper life,°
And with such coz'nage°—is't not perfect conscience
To quit° him with this arm? And is't not to be damned
To let this canker of our nature come
In further evil?   70
HORATIO: It must be shortly known to him from England
What is the issue of the business there.
HAMLET: It will be short; the interim's mine,
And a man's life's no more than to say "one."
But I am very sorry, good Horatio,   75
That to Laertes I forgot myself,
For by the image of my cause I see
The portraiture of his. I'll court his favors.
But sure the bravery° of his grief did put me
Into a tow'ring passion.
HORATIO: Peace, who comes here?   80

Enter young OSRIC, *a courtier.*

OSRIC: Your lordship is right welcome back to Denmark.
HAMLET: I humbly thank you, sir. *Aside to* HORATIO. Dost know
this waterfly?
HORATIO *aside to* HAMLET: No, my good lord.
HAMLET *aside to* HORATIO: Thy state is the more gracious, for 'tis a

---

48 ordinant ruling   **50 model** counterpart   **59 insinuation** meddling   **61 pass**
thrust;   **fell** cruel   **63 stand . . . upon** become incumbent upon me   **65 election**
the Danish monarchy was elective   **66 angle** fishing line;   **my proper life** my
own life   **67 coz'nage** trickery   **68 quit** pay back   **79 bravery** bravado

vice to know him. He hath much land, and fertile. Let a beast be   85
lord of beasts, and his crib shall stand at the king's mess.° 'Tis a
chough,° but, as I say, spacious° in the possession of dirt.

OSRIC: Sweet lord, if your lordship were at leisure, I should impart
a thing to you from his majesty.

HAMLET: I will receive it, sir, with all diligence of spirit. Put your   90
bonnet to his right use. 'Tis for the head.

OSRIC: I thank your lordship, it is very hot.

HAMLET: No, believe me, 'tis very cold; the wind is northerly.

OSRIC: It is indifferent cold, my lord, indeed.

HAMLET: But yet methinks it is very sultry and hot for my com-   95
plexion.°

OSRIC: Exceedingly, my lord; it is very sultry, as 'twere—I cannot
tell how. But, my lord, his majesty bade me signify to you that 'a
has laid a great wager on your head. Sir, this is the matter—

HAMLET: I beseech you remember.   100

HAMLET *moves him to put on his hat.*

OSRIC: Nay, good my lord; for my ease, in good faith. Sir, here is
newly come to court Laertes—believe me, an absolute gentleman,
full of most excellent differences,° of very soft society and great
showing. Indeed, to speak feelingly° of him, he is the card° or
calendar of gentry; for you shall find in him the continent° of   105
what part a gentleman would see.

HAMLET: Sir, his definement° suffers no perdition° in you, though,
I know, to divide him inventorially would dozy° th' arithmetic of
memory, and yet but yaw neither in respect of his quick sail.°
But, in the verity of extolment, I take him to be a soul of great   110
article,° and his infusion° of such dearth and rareness as, to make
true diction° of him, his semblable° is his mirror, and who else
would trace him, his umbrage,° nothing more.

OSRIC: Your lordship speaks most infallibly of him.

HAMLET: The concernancy,° sir? Why do we wrap the gentleman in   115
our more rawer breath?

OSRIC: Sir?

HORATIO: Is't not possible to understand in another tongue? You
will to't,° sir, really.

HAMLET: What imports the nomination of this gentleman?   120

OSRIC: Of Laertes?

86 mess table   **87 chough** jackdaw (here, chatterer);   **spacious** well off
96 complexion temperament   **103 differences** distinguishing characteristics
104 feelingly justly;   **card** chart   **105 continent** summary   **107 definement**
description;   **perdition** loss   **108 dozy** dizzy   **109 and yet . . . sail** and yet
only stagger despite all ("yaw neither") in trying to overtake his virtues   **111 article** literally, "item," but here perhaps "traits" or "importance";   **infusion** essential quality   **112 diction** description;   **semblable** likeness   **113 umbrage**
shadow   **115 concernancy** meaning   **119 will to't** will get there

HORATIO *aside to* HAMLET: His purse is empty already. All's golden
words are spent.

HAMLET: Of him, sir.

OSRIC: I now you are not ignorant—   125

HAMLET: I would you did, sir; yet, in faith, if you did, it would not
much approve° me. Well, sir?

OSRIC: You are not ignorant of what excellence Laertes is—

HAMLET: I dare not confess that, lest I should compare with him in
excellence; but to know a man well were to know himself.   130

OSRIC: I mean, sir, for his weapon; but in the imputation° laid on
him by them, in his meed° he's unfellowed.

HAMLET: What's his weapon?

OSRIC: Rapier and dagger.

HAMLET: That's two of his weapons—but well.   135

OSRIC: The king, sir, hath wagered with him six Barbary horses,
against the which he has impawned,° as I take it, six French rapiers and poniards, with their assigns,° as girdle, hangers,° and
so. Three of the carriages,° in faith, are very dear to fancy, very
responsive° to the hilts, most delicate carriages, and of very liberal   140
conceit.°

HAMLET: What call you the carriages?

HORATIO *aside to* HAMLET: I knew you must be edified by the mar-
gent° ere you had done.

OSRIC: The carriages, sir, are the hangers.   145

HAMLET: The phrase would be more germane to the matter if we
could carry a cannon by our sides. I would it might be hangers
till then. But on! Six Barbary horses against six French swords,
their assigns, and three liberal-conceited carriages—that's the
French bet against the Danish. Why is this all impawned, as you   150
call it?

OSRIC: The king, sir, hath laid, sir, that in a dozen passes between
yourself and him he shall not exceed you three hits; he hath laid
on twelve for nine, and it would come to immediate trial if your
lordship would vouchsafe the answer.   155

HAMLET: How if I answer no?

OSRIC: I mean, my lord, the opposition of your person in trial.

HAMLET: Sir, I will walk here in the hall. If it please his majesty, it
is the breathing time of day with me.° Let the foils be brought,
the gentleman willing, and the king hold his purpose, I will win   160
for him an I can; if not, I will gain nothing but my shame and
the odd hits.

OSRIC: Shall I deliver you e'en so?

---

127 approve commend   **131 imputation** reputation   **132 meed** merit   **137 impawned** wagered   **138 assigns** accompaniments;   **hangers** straps hanging the
sword to the belt   **139 carriages** an affected word for hangers   **140 responsive**
corresponding   **141 liberal conceit** elaborate design   **144 margent** i.e., marginal
(explanatory) comment   **159 breathing . . . me** time when I take exercise

HAMLET: To this effect, sir, after what flourish your nature will.
OSRIC: I commend my duty to your lordship.   165
HAMLET: Yours, yours. *Exit* OSRIC. He does well to commend it
   himself; there are no tongues else for's turn.
HORATIO: This lapwing° runs away with the shell on his head.
HAMLET: 'A did comply, sir, with his dug° before 'a sucked it. Thus
   has he, and many more of the same breed that I know the drossy   170
   age dotes on, only got the tune of the time and, out of an habit
   of encounter,° a kind of yeasty° collection, which carries them
   through and through the most fanned and winnowed opinions;
   and do but blow them to their trial, the bubbles are out.°

Enter a LORD.

LORD: My lord, his majesty commended him to you by young Os-   175
   ric, who brings back to him that you attend him in the hall. He
   sends to know if your pleasure hold to play with Laertes, or that
   you will take longer time.
HAMLET: I am constant to my purposes; they follow the king's plea-
   sure. If his fitness speaks, mine is ready; now or whensoever,   180
   provided I be so able as now.
LORD: The king and queen and all are coming down.
HAMLET: In happy time.
LORD: The queen desires you to use some gentle entertainment° to
   Laertes before you fall to play.   185
HAMLET: She well instructs me.   *Exit* LORD.
HORATIO: You will lose this wager, my lord.
HAMLET: I do not think so. Since he went into France I have been
   in continual practice. I shall win at the odds. But thou wouldst
   not think how ill all's here about my heart. But it is no matter.   190
HORATIO: Nay, good my lord—
HAMLET: It is but foolery, but it is such a kind of gaingiving° as
   would perhaps trouble a woman.
HORATIO: If your mind dislike anything, obey it. I will forestall
   their repair hither and say you are not fit.   195
HAMLET: Not a whit, we defy augury. There is special providence
   in the fall of a sparrow.° If it be now, 'tis not to come; if it be not
   to come, it will be now; if it be not now, yet it will come. The
   readiness is all. Since no man of aught he leaves knows, what is't
   to leave betimes?° Let be.   200

168 lapwing the new-hatched lapwing was thought to run around with half its shell
on its head   **169 'A . . . dug** he was ceremoniously polite to his mother's breast
171–2 out . . . encounter out of his own superficial way of meeting and conversing
with people   **172 yeasty** frothy   **174 the . . . out** i.e., they are blown away
(the reference is to the "yeasty collection")   **184 to . . . entertainment** to be
courteous   **192 gaingiving** misgiving   **197 the . . . sparrow** cf. Matthew 10:29,
"Are not two sparrows sold for a farthing? and one of them shall not fall on the
ground without your Father"   **200 betimes** early

A table prepared. Enter TRUMPETS, DRUMS, *and* OFFICERS *with cushions;* KING, QUEEN, OSRIC, *and all the* STATE, *with foils, daggers, and stoups of wine borne in; and* LAERTES.

KING: Come, Hamlet, come, and take this hand from me.

The KING *puts Laertes' hand into Hamlet's.*

HAMLET: Give me your pardon, sir. I have done you wrong,
But pardon't, as you are a gentleman.
This presence° knows, and you must needs have heard,
How I am punished with a sore distraction.   205
What I have done
That might your nature, honor, and exception°
Roughly awake, I here proclaim was madness.
Was't Hamlet wronged Laertes? Never Hamlet.
If Hamlet from himself be ta'en away,   210
And when he's not himself does wrong Laertes,
Then Hamlet does it not, Hamlet denies it.
Who does it then? His madness. If't be so,
Hamlet is of the faction° that is wronged;
His madness is poor Hamlet's enemy.   215
Sir, in this audience,
Let my disclaiming from a purposed evil
Free me so far in your most generous thoughts
That I have shot my arrow o'er the house
And hurt my brother.
LAERTES: I am satisfied in nature,   220
Whose motive in this case should stir me most
To my revenge. But in my terms of honor
I stand aloof, and will no reconcilement
Till by some elder masters of known honor
I have a voice and precedent° of peace   225
To keep my name ungored. But till that time
I do receive your offered love like love,
And will not wrong it.
HAMLET: I embrace it freely,
And will this brother's wager frankly play.
Give us the foils, Come on.
LAERTES: Come, one for me.   230
HAMLET: I'll be your foil,° Laertes. In mine ignorance
Your skill shall, like a star i' th' darkest night,
Stick fiery off° indeed.

---

204 presence royal assembly   **207 exception** disapproval   **214 faction** party, side   **225 voice and precedent** authoritative opinion justified by precedent **231 foil** (1) blunt sword (2) background (of metallic leaf) for a jewel   **233 Stick fiery off** stand out brilliantly

LAERTES: You mock me, sir.
HAMLET: No, by this hand.
KING: Give them the foils, young Osric. Cousin Hamlet,   235
  You know the wager?
HAMLET: Very well, my lord
  Your grace has laid the odds o' th' weaker side.
KING: I do not fear it, I have seen you both;
  But since he is bettered,° we have therefore odds.
LAERTES: This is too heavy; let me see another.   240
HAMLET: This likes me well. These foils have all a length?

Prepare to play.

OSRIC: Ay, my good lord.
KING: Set me the stoups of wine upon that table.
  If Hamlet give the first or second hit,
  Or quit° in answer of the third exchange,   245
  Let all the battlements their ordnance fire.
  The king shall drink to Hamlet's better breath,
  And in the cup an union° shall he throw
  Richer than that which four successive kings
  In Denmark's crown have worn. Give me the cups,   250
  And let the kettle° to the trumpet speak,
  The trumpet to the cannoneer without,
  The cannons to the heavens, the heaven to earth,
  "Now the king drinks to Hamlet." Come, begin.

Trumpets the while.

  And you, the judges, bear a wary eye.   255
HAMLET: Come on, sir.
LAERTES: Come, my lord. *They play.*
HAMLET: One.
LAERTES: No.
HAMLET: Judgement?
OSRIC: A hit, a very palpable hit.

Drum, trumpets, and shot. Flourish; a piece goes off.

LAERTES: Well, again.
KING: Stay, give me drink. Hamlet, this pearl is thine.   260
  Here's to thy health. Give him the cup.
HAMLET: I'll play this bout first; set it by awhile.
  Come. *They play.* Another hit. What say you?
LAERTES: A touch, a touch; I do confess't.

239 **bettered** has improved (in France)   245 **quit** repay, hit back   248 **union**
pearl   251 **kettle** kettle-drum

KING: Our son shall win.
QUEEN: He's fat,° and scant of breath.   265
   Here, Hamlet, take my napkin, rub thy brows.
   The queen carouses to thy fortune, Hamlet.
HAMLET: Good madam!
KING: Gertrude, do not drink.
QUEEN: I will, my lord; I pray you pardon me.

Drinks.

KING *aside*:   It is the poisoned cup; it is too late.   270
HAMLET: I dare not drink yet, madam—by and by.
QUEEN: Come, let me wipe thy face.
LAERTES: My lord, I'll hit him now.
KING: I do not think't.
LAERTES *aside*:   And yet it is almost against my conscience.
HAMLET: Come for the third, Laertes. You do but dally.   275
   I pray you pass with your best violence;
   I am sure you make a wanton° of me.
LAERTES: Say you so? Come on.

They play.

OSRIC: Nothing neither way.
LAERTES: Have at you now!   280

In scuffling they change rapiers, and both are wounded.

KING: Part them. They are incensed.
HAMLET: Nay, come—again! *The* QUEEN *falls.*
OSRIC: Look to the queen there, ho!
HORATIO: They bleed on both sides. How is it, my lord?
OSRIC: How is't, Laertes?   285
LAERTES: Why, as a woodcock to mine own springe,° Osric.
   I am justly killed with mine own treachery.
HAMLET: How does the queen?
KING: She sounds° to see them bleed.
QUEEN: No, no, the drink, the drink! O my dear Hamlet!
   The drink, the drink! I am poisoned.   *Dies.* 290
HAMLET: O villainy! Ho! Let the door be locked.
   Treachery! Seek it out.

LAERTES *falls.*

LAERTES: It is here, Hamlet. Hamlet, thou art slain;

265 fat (1) sweaty (2) out of training   **277 wanton** spoiled child   **286 springe**
snare   **288 sounds** swoons

No med'cine in the world can do thee good.
In thee there is not half an hour's life.   295
The treacherous instrument is in thy hand,
Unbated and envenomed. The foul practice°
Hath turned itself on me. Lo, here I lie,
Never to rise again. Thy mother's poisoned.
I can no more. The king, the king's to blame.   300
HAMLET: The point envenomed too?
Then, venom, to thy work.

Hurts the KING.

ALL: Treason! Treason!
KING: O, yet defend me, friends. I am but hurt.
HAMLET: Here, thou incestuous, murd'rous, damnèd Dane,   305
Drink off this potion. Is thy union here?
Follow my mother.   KING *dies*.
LAERTES: He is justly served.
It is a poison tempered° by himself.
Exchange forgiveness with me, noble Hamlet.
Mine and my father's death come not upon thee,   310
Nor thine on me!   *Dies*.
HAMLET: Heaven make thee free of it! I follow thee.
I am dead, Horatio. Wretched queen, adieu!
You that look pale and tremble at this chance,
That are but mutes° or audience to this act,   315
Had I but time (as this fell sergeant,° Death,
Is strict in his arrest) O, I could tell you—
But let it be. Horatio, I am dead;
Thou livest; report me and my cause aright
To the unsatisfied.°
HORATIO: Never believe it.   320
I am more an antique Roman° than a Dane.
Here's yet some liquor left.
HAMLET: As th' art a man,
Give me the cup. Let go. By heaven, I'll ha't!
O God, Horatio, what a wounded name,
Things standing thus unknown, shall live behind me!   325
If thou didst ever hold me in thy heart,
Absent thee from felicity° awhile,
And in this harsh world draw thy breath in pain,
To tell my story.   *A march afar off. Exit* OSRIC.
What warlike noise is this?

297 practice deception   **308 tempered** mixed   **315 mutes** performers who have
no words to speak   **316 fell sergeant** dread sheriff's officer   **320 unsatisfied**
uninformed   **321 antique Roman** with reference to the old Roman fashion of
suicide   **327 felicity** i.e., the felicity of death

Enter OSRIC.

OSRIC: Young Fortinbras, with conquest come from Poland,   330
  To th' ambassadors of England gives
  This warlike volley.
HAMLET: O, I die, Horatio!
  The potent poison quite o'ercrows° my spirit.
  I cannot live to hear the news from England,
  But I do prophesy th' election lights   335
  On Fortinbras. He has my dying voice.
  So tell him, with th' occurrents,° more and less,
  Which have solicited°—the rest is silence.   *Dies.*
HORATIO: Now cracks a noble heart. Good night, sweet prince,
  And flights of angels sing thee to thy rest.   340

March within.

  Why does the drum come hither?

Enter FORTINBRAS, *with the* AMBASSADORS *with drum, colors, and* ATTEN-
DANTS.

FORTINBRAS: Where is this sight?
HORATIO: What is it you would see?
  If aught of woe or wonder, cease your search.
FORTINBRAS: This quarry° cries on havoc.° O proud Death,
  What feast is toward° in thine eternal cell   345
  That thou so many princes at a shot
  So bloodily hast struck?
AMBASSADOR: The sight is dismal;
  And our affairs from England come too late.
  The ears are senseless that should give us hearing
  To tell him his commandment is fulfilled,   350
  That Rosencrantz and Guildenstern are dead.
  Where should we have our thanks?
HORATIO: Not from his° mouth,
  Had it th' ability of life to thank you.
  He never gave commandment for their death.
  But since, so jump° upon this bloody question,   355
  You from the Polack wars, and you from England,
  Are here arrived, give order that these bodies
  High on a stage° be placèd to the view,
  And let me speak to th' yet unknowing world

333 o'ercrows overpowers (as a triumphant cock crows over its weak opponent)
337 occurrents occurrences   **338 solicited** incited   **344 quarry** heap of slain
bodies;   **cries on havoc** proclaims general slaughter   **345 toward** in
preparation   **352 his** Claudius'   **355 jump** precisely   **358 stage** platform

How these things came about. So shall you hear   360
Of carnal, bloody, and unnatural acts,
Of accidental judgments, casual° slaughters,
Of deaths put on by cunning and forced cause,
And, in this upshot, purposes mistook
Fall'n on th' inventors' heads. All this can I   365
Truly deliver.
FORTINBRAS: Let us haste to hear it.
And call the noblest to the audience.
For me, with sorrow I embrace my fortune.
I have some rights of memory° in this kingdom,
Which now to claim my vantage doth invite me.   370
HORATIO: Of that I shall have also cause to speak,
And from his mouth whose voice will draw on° more.
But let this same be presently performed,
Even while men's minds are wild, lest more mischance
On° plots and errors happen.
FORTINBRAS: Let four captains   375
Bear Hamlet like a soldier to the stage,
For he was likely, had he been put on,°
To have proved most royal; and for his passage°
The soldiers' music and the rite of war
Speak loudly for him.   380
Take up the bodies. Such a sight as this
Becomes the field,° but here shows much amiss.
Go, bid the soldiers shoot.

Exeunt marching; after the which a peal of ordnance are shot off.

QUESTIONS

1. Describe the "state of Denmark" at the beginning of *Hamlet*. What
   social and political developments mentioned in the first act affect the
   action of the play as it unfolds? Pay particular attention to Horatio's
   speech at I, i, 79–108.
2. Reread Hamlet's first soliloquy (I, ii, 129–159). What does this speech
   reveal about his internal conflicts?
3. What changes take place in Hamlet's character after his first confrontation with the ghost (I, v)?
4. In II, i, Polonius instructs Reynaldo to spy upon Laertes. Find other
   instances in the play where the characters resort to "covert observation"
   to find out what other characters are doing or thinking. What do these
   instances tell us about humanity as it is portrayed in *Hamlet?*
5. Analyze Hamlet's soliloquy at the end of the second act (II, ii, 559–

---

362 **casual** not humanly planned, chance   369 **rights of memory** remembered
claims   372 **voice . . . on** vote will influence   375 **On** on top of   377 **put on**
advanced (to the throne)   378 **passage** death   382 **field** battlefield

617). Examine the contrast between acting and reality which he cites, and explain what this contrast tells us about his self-conception at this point in the play.

6. Explain the irony of the ending of III, ii, when Hamlet comes upon the praying Claudius. Why doesn't Hamlet kill Claudius at this point?

7. In III, iv, what contrasts does Hamlet draw between his father and Claudius? How does he want his mother, Gertrude, to alter her behavior toward Claudius?

8. Why does Ophelia go insane and commit suicide? Can you locate any parallels between her situation and Hamlet's?

9. What virtues or complexities of character (if any) does Claudius possess which allow us to see him as something other than a villain?

10. What is the effect of the gravedigger scene (V, i) within the overall plot of *Hamlet?* How is it a fitting introduction to the final unfolding of the tragedy?

11. How does the appearance of Fortinbras at the end of the play signal the restoration of order in the Danish kingdom?

WRITING ABOUT PLOT AND CHARACTER IN DRAMA

Exposition and argumentation are the rhetorical modes employed when writing about plot and character in drama. We attempt to explain, for example, the primary and secondary conflicts of a play and to show how they are developed within the classic "triangular" shape of a plot. Or we attempt to persuade the reader that the playwright has embodied, through characterization, a given theme. We have already noted—in "Plot in Fiction," "Character in Fiction," and "Plot and Character in Drama"—many techniques for analyzing and writing about plot and character. We will concentrate here on several kinds of essays and methods which critics employ when writing about plot and character in drama. These essays fall into five broad categories: plot summaries, essays about plot, essays about character, essays that show the relationship between plot or character and other elements, and essays that consider plot or character in light of other works of literary criticism.

Plot summaries: A plot summary is not an essay, but a description of the "skeleton" of a play. There can be many kinds of plot summaries, and their form will depend on the formal divisions into which a play is divided (if any), changes in scene, or the "stages" into which the action can be divided. For *Hamlet,* you might use a form like this:

I. Act One
   a. scene one
   b. scene two
   c. scene three (and so forth)

Follow a similar pattern for the other four acts. Now write out a one- or two-sentence description of each scene's principal action, including notes about setting and characters. Now give labels (a sentence or key phrase should suffice) to the act divisions of the play. You should have a clearer idea of how *Hamlet* develops, of how the settings change, and how the principal characters are disposed throughout the play. Plot summaries of this kind reveal the gross structure or "shape" of a play and the complexities of the plot's design as well as its recurrent ideas, images, or situations. They help to reveal how subplots and minor characters are treated. Finally, they provide important information which can be useful when writing other kinds of papers about the play.

Essays about plot: Critics use many different kinds of approaches when they write about the plot of a play. Most such essays will focus in some way upon the principal conflict which the plot contains: in *Hamlet*, the conflict between Hamlet and Claudius; in *Death of a Salesman*, the conflict between Willy Loman and his son Biff. Your paper might consider just the central conflict of the play, or it might emphasize the general construction of the plot and how it compares with the classic plot "triangle"; the function of a particular scene, act, or section and its relationship to the whole plot; or the function of a subplot and its connection with the main plot. Whatever form your paper takes, avoid a simple recounting of the incidents of the play. Your task as a critic should be to analyze, evaluate, and show significance—not merely to describe what happens.

Essays about character: Papers about character in a play should do more than just tell what happens to a particular character or what he or she does to warrant our interest. Give your paper a sharper focus by moving in one of the following five directions.

Analyze key character relationships in the play. Showing how Hamlet's actions and character affect or are affected by Claudius, Gertrude, or Laertes will reveal much about the motives of his behavior.

Analyze how characters are grouped or patterned. Are there significant relationships between families, or between factions, or between men and women? Does the playwright use a foil? Remember that any character's or group's significance in the play may go beyond the extent of its direct interaction with another character or group. Shakespeare's use of Laertes as a foil to Hamlet, for example, goes far beyond the extent of their direct interaction with each other.

Analyze a major or minor character. Comment on that character's function or personality, his or her development throughout the play and connections with the principal themes.

Analyze a single speech. Show the importance of its imagery, its place in the context of the plot, and its importance in portraying a stage of character development.

Analyze the means of characterization. Are there soliloquies? Do the actors talk about each other? Are gestures or actions employed significantly?

Essays concerning other elements: A potentially more complex kind of analysis results from examining the relationship between plot or character and some other element in the play such as staging or theme. *Death of a Salesman* provides an excellent example of how a playwright uses the physical space of the stage to control or suggest time in the development of his plot.

Essays concerning other critical texts: Much can be learned from attempting to show whether a play (or an element of it) conforms to theories of classical or contemporary dramatic criticism. Does Hamlet have a tragic flaw in the sense that Aristotle describes? Does the plot of *Death of a Salesman* resemble the "triangular" shape mentioned earlier? How does Molière's *Misanthrope* fit into the range of comic plays described by Northrop Frye in *The Anatomy of Criticism* (see "Critical Touchstones: Drama," page 1581)? Such essays will help show you the value of literary criticism, and will demonstrate the need to reevaluate and extend the applicability of critical documents.

You will find suggestions for most of these kinds of essays under "Suggestions for Writing about Plot and Character" at the end of this chapter. Remember that comparison and classification are useful ways to extend the range of any kind of essay about plot and character.

As you begin working up a topic about plot and character in drama, try to visualize the actions and characters. Pay scrupulous attention to the need for evidence, and support what you say with appropriate quotations from the text. The following sample essay about Shakespeare's *Hamlet* attempts to show how Laertes serves as a foil to Hamlet. Note how the essay is organized, and how, without undue recounting of the plot, it draws evidence from the entire play to show the main points of comparison and contrast between the two characters.

"And Hurt My Brother": Laertes as a Foil to Hamlet

Throughout <u>Hamlet</u>, Shakespeare establishes points of comparison between Hamlet, the Danish prince, and Laertes, the man who might, if things had turned out differently, have been Hamlet's brother-in-law. In their outward circumstances, their relationship to Ophelia, their dilemmas, and their fates, these two men share strong bonds. But because of chance and because of the machinations of Claudius, the bonds become webs entangling them as enemies. Laertes's presence in the play helps to define Hamlet's character.

Like Hamlet, Laertes is a model courtier. Both are young, vigorous, intelligent, and skilled. Their personal and political futures seem bright. But, because of the actions of Claudius and Gertrude, Hamlet has become disillusioned with his world, a world in which Ophelia, Laertes's sister, occupies a central place. Even before his departure for France, Laertes warns Ophelia not to take Hamlet's show of affection too seriously:

> Fear it, Ophelia, fear it, my dear sister,
> And keep you in the rear of your affection,
> Out of the shot and danger of desire.

(I, iii, 33-35)

But Hamlet's world has already started to come undone. Hamlet's disillusionment, and his subsequent need to put on an "antic disposition" to outwit Claudius, causes a radical change in his relationship with Ophelia, who becomes a victim of Hamlet's attempt to find out more about Claudius's crime.

As the play proceeds, and while Laertes is in France, their circumstances become more closely intertwined. Hamlet, whose father has been murdered by Claudius, inadvertently kills Polonius, Claudius's spy and Laertes's father. Thus Hamlet's desire to avenge his dead father, which causes Polonius to die, causes Laertes to want to avenge <u>his</u> dead father. Hamlet's subtlety, his need for assurance, and his slowness in taking revenge contrast starkly with Laertes's rashness and decisiveness upon learning of Polonius's death. He says:

> How came he dead? I'll not be juggled with.
> To hell allegiance, vows to the blackest devil,
> Conscience and grace to the profoundest pit!
> I dare damnation. To this point I stand,
> That both the worlds I give to negligence,
> Let come what comes, only I'll be revenged
> Most throughly for my father.
>
> (IV, v, 130-136)

Ironically, Hamlet's procrastination, which has in part been prolonged by his desire to prove beyond a doubt that Claudius is guilty, is finally ended by Laertes's need to avenge his father's death quickly. And, whereas Hamlet has been able to see through Claudius's veil of deceit, Laertes is quickly duped by the wicked king, who takes advantage of Laertes's hot-headedness and persuades him to duel with Hamlet. Thus Laertes can take his revenge, and Claudius will be free of the one man who knows of his heinous crime.

Before the duel in which Laertes and Hamlet kill each other, the two men become, except for the point of honor involved, reconciled with each other:

> Hamlet: Sir, in this audience,
> Let my disclaiming from a purposed evil
> Free me so far in your most generous thoughts
> That I have shot my arrow o'er the house
> And hurt my brother.
>
> Laertes: I am satisfied in nature,
> Whose motive in this case should stir me most
> To my revenge. But in my terms of honor
> I stand aloof, and will no reconcilement
> Till by some elder masters of known honor
> I have a voice and precedent of peace
> To keep my name ungored. But till that time
> I do receive your offered love like love,
> And will not wrong it.
>
> (V, ii, 246-254)

They are kindred spirits, brothers even, who have become entangled in fatal events through a combination of chance and choice. Their choices are predicated upon identical motives, but the ways these choices are manifested are entirely different. Having taken his revenge on Claudius, Hamlet dies, partly because of his own procrastination, at Laertes's hand. Laertes, Hamlet's foil, because he has rashly taken part in Claudius's ruse, gains his revenge also, but dies at the hand of his "brother."

SUGGESTIONS FOR WRITING ABOUT PLOT AND CHARACTER IN DRAMA

1. Write an essay about the principal subplots of *Hamlet*, that is, those involving Laertes and Rosencrantz and Guildenstern. What importance do these subplots have to the main action of the play?
2. Contrast the two appearances of the ghost in *Hamlet*. Specifically, how do these two appearances affect the plot of the play, and how might the ghost be symbolic of the state of Hamlet's mind?
3. Assess the conflicts Gertrude undergoes in *Hamlet*.
4. Imagine that you are a director who, because of the length of the play, must cut 750–1000 lines from *Hamlet*. Which lines would you cut? Write an essay which justifies your choices.
5. Write an essay about the significance of Charley and Bernard to Miller's *Death of a Salesman*.
6. Contrast the personalities of Biff and Happy in *Death of a Salesman*.
7. Describe and assess what you consider to be the key turning point (for Willy Loman and his son Biff) in *Death of a Salesman*.
8. How does Miller use objects (such as Willy's garden or Mr. Oliver's fountain pen) to develop character?
9. Show how Miller makes his transitions between past and present scenes.

STAGECRAFT AND SPECTACLE

In the *Poetics*, even through Aristotle is more concerned with language, plot construction, and character delineation, he nevertheless concedes that **spectacle,** the details of production—music, costumes, scenery, and the gestures of the actors—have "an emotional attraction of [their] own." While he calls these elements "embellishments," Aristotle admits that the playwright must keep the scene "before his eyes," and "work out his play, to the best of his powers, with appropriate gestures." If we add to these traditional elements two more not covered by Aristotle—lighting and stage architecture—we can see that these "embellishments" are essential to give physical form to the playwright's words.

But what precisely does each of these elements add to the drama?

Song or music, one of the elements associated with dialogue, emotionally enhances or heightens the play's language. *Music* sometimes accompanies the words spoken by the actor, the added melody helping to create an appropriate mood. Such is the case in *Death of a Salesman* when flute music is heard, "telling of grass and trees." This music accompanies Willie's reveries about the past and adds to the nostalgic mood of longing for a lost pastoral America. But music can be understood in a broader sense as referring to *speech rhythms,* the cadences with which the actors deliver their lines. In the theater of classical Greece, the chorus chanted its lines, and these speech rhythms enhanced the emotions generated by the words, much as background music sometimes does in today's plays.

It is well to keep in mind that a play is a collaborative effort, that what we see and hear on the stage is the result of the work of many people. It takes not only the work of actors to translate the words of the playwright into physical action, but the imaginative collaboration of producer, director, costume and scene designer, lighting engineer, and numerous other technicians and craftspeople to bring the playwright's words to life on the stage. This may be why some of the most successful playwrights—Shakespeare, Molière, Fugard, and Shepard—have themselves been actors familiar with the details of production. It is the job of the director to correlate the efforts of many people so that the final product, the drama on the stage, represents a coherent vision. Mindful of this, a playwright will sometimes give the director great latitude in the stage directions that determine what *actions* and *gestures* should accompany the dialogue. At other times, a playwright concerned that physical action and gesture match his or her conception of the play will dictate specifically what the actor should do on the stage. For example, in the stage directions for *Krapp's Last Tape,* Samuel Beckett delineates the pantomime with which the play opens in great detail, leaving actor and director little leeway for interpretation:

> Krapp remains a moment motionless, heaves a great sigh, looks at his watch, fumbles in his pockets, takes out an envelope, puts it back, fumbles, takes out a small bunch of keys, raises it to his eyes, chooses a key, gets up and moves to front of table. He stoops, unlocks first drawer, peers into it, feels about inside it, takes out a reel of tape, peers at it, puts it back, locks drawer, unlocks second drawer, peers into it, feels about inside it, takes out a large banana, peers at it, locks drawer, puts keys back in his pocket.

Clearly, Beckett has determined that this sequence of actions is essential to his purpose.

Just as the playwright sometimes suggests gestures to accompany dialogue, his stage directions often include descriptions of the *costumes* to be worn by the actors. Even as long ago as the fifth century B.C., costume played a part in the spectacle of classical Greek drama, helping the audience identify the historical or mythic figures the actors were meant to represent. The clothing and masks characterized the figures on the stage and in the case of the masks also amplified the actors' voices so they could be heard in an outdoor amphitheater holding as many as 15,000 spectators. The actors wore high platformed shoes which may have given the characters larger-than-life stature and made them more visible to the audience. Costumes in the sense that we have come to know them—historically authentic wardrobes meant to enhance the realism of the play—did not exist until the nineteenth century. Before then, in the Elizabethan theater for instance, the actors drew their costumes from a stock wardrobe that, except in elegance, were little different from the everyday clothing worn by members of the audience. In Restoration and eighteenth-century plays, however, more money often was spent on an elaborate costume for a leading actress than for the playwright's manuscript, and the action was sometimes even stopped to give the audience an opportunity to applaud the costume.

Today, to add to the authenticity of the drama, a great deal of research goes into insuring that the costume accurately reflects the period of the play or the psychological makeup of the character. A costume designer, for instance, might design a slovenly periwig and a somewhat old-fashioned costume for the character of Alceste in Molière's *The Misanthrope* to show his contempt for current fashions. This is precisely what Ibsen has done in *The Wild Duck* with the costume of Old Ekdal, whose wig is "a dirty, reddish-brown," and whose overcoat is "shabby."

Stage sets and all the associated machinery such as lighting and special effects help, of course, to sustain the illusion created by the writer's words and the actors' performances. While no amount of realistic scenery or special effects can substitute for the plausibility of a play, for what Samuel Taylor Coleridge called the "willing suspension of disbelief" in an audience, nevertheless scenery can help transform the same limited space from a kitchen in Brooklyn to a castle in Denmark, from a mountain trail in Jamaica to a fashionable restaurant in London.

Scenery was relatively unimportant in the Greek theater, and still less important in the Elizabethan theater, which relied on the playwright's words to recreate the setting for the action. Since the seventeenth century (when stock painted sets as a backdrop began to be used), scenery has increased in importance. Whether a broken front door tells of family violence in Sam Shepard's *Curse of the Starving Class*, or a dimly lit attic reveals a world of illusion in Ibsen's *The Wild Duck*, scenery is now rarely ancillary to the action, theme, and characters of a play. The bifurcated set in *The Wild Duck*, separating the living quarters from the attic, is merely one way of visibly establishing Ibsen's intentions.

Lighting is another way in which stage machinery can act as a visual metaphor. Until the advent of gas lighting in the nineteenth century, plays were performed during daylight hours or under poor artificial lighting, but Ibsen took full advantage of the possibilities of the new lighting. The very first action of his play is symbolic: the lighting (and shading) of a lamp. Each subsequent act of his play modulates the lighting, making it appropriate to the mood, and establishing emotional and thematic contrasts between the acts. In Act 3, "Daylight streams through the large window in the sloping roof," while in Act 5, "A cold, gray morning light filters in."

As we read plays from different historical periods, we need to keep in mind that playwrights wrote for audiences familiar with the conventions of their times, some of which were determined by the architectural structure, the stage on which the play was first performed. For example, to understand the many conventions of classical Greek drama it is important to be familiar with the conditions of the immense open–aired Greek amphitheaters. (See "Tragedy and Irony," pages 1246–1248.) Similarly, if we are to understand a convention of the Elizabethan theater such as the soliloquy (page 1051), we need to know about the *thrust stage*. The Elizabethan theaters derived their architectural style from the open yards of inns which served as early improvised theaters. In 1576, the first permanent theater in England was built outside of London, and was simply called The Theatre. The Globe, where many of Shakespeare's plays were first performed, was built in 1599. Typical of many Elizabethan theaters, The Globe was a three-storied polygonal building with an open central space called the yard or pit where the groundlings or lower-class patrons stood. The stage itself was a platform that "thrust" into the audience so that spectators stood or sat in covered galleries, surrounding the stage on three sides. Hence the intimacy between the audience and actor established by the thrust stage lent itself well to soliloquies, like those in *Hamlet*, which seem less artificial when spoken under these conditions than when an actor must walk forward to the apron of the stage to address an audience gathered in front of him. Because there was little scenery other than a few stage props, frequent scene changes were possible in Elizabethan plays, and because the playwright's words established the setting, the audience was accustomed to listen carefully to dialogue which helped locate the place and the roles of the characters as in the opening scene of *Hamlet:*

BERNARDO: 'Tis now struck twelve. Get thee to bed, Francisco.
FRANCISCO: For this relief much thanks. 'Tis bitter cold,
    and I am sick at heart.
BERNARDO: Have you had quiet guard?
FRANCISCO: Not a mouse stirring.
BERNARDO: Well, good night.
    If you do meet Horatio and Marcellus,
    The rivals of my watch, bid them make haste.   (I, i, 7–13)

Clearly, the dialogue establishes the setting as a sentry post and the two characters as soldiers. Subsequent dialogue reveals the necessity of the watch: young Fortinbras of Norway is attempting to recover lands his father had lost to the former Danish king. The hour is midnight, the witching hour, and the ghost of that same Danish king, young Hamlet's father, has appeared at this same sentry post twice before.

In the Elizabethan theater, the stage itself was a *neutral space*, one "colored in" by the words of the playwright, and a fast-paced action was possible since the architecture of the stage itself was used to accomplish what in today's theater might be accomplished by a change of set. At the rear of the stage was a three-storied tower. On the stage level, an enclosed room, separated from the main stage by a curtain, was the *discovery space*, no doubt the curtained arras behind which Polonius is discovered hiding in *Hamlet*. The second level of this tower (supported by pillars which could serve to represent trees in a forest scene or objects to hide behind and overhear conversations) held another acting area, or it could be used as a balcony as in the famous scene from *Romeo and Juliet*. The third story was an area sometimes used to house musicians. Below the stage of the Elizabethan theater was a space with access from the stage through a trap door. From this lower area demons emerged from hell to carry off Doctor Faustus in Christopher Marlowe's *The Tragical History of the Life and Death of Doctor Faustus*, or the space could be used to represent a grave, as in the gravedigger's scene from *Hamlet*. Since he wrote for a particular company of actors (Shakespeare's company was the Chamberlain's Men), and the company performed regularly in the same theater, the playwright was familiar with the resources of his theater and tailored his play accordingly.

With the closing of the English theaters in 1642 shortly after the outbreak of the Civil War, the creative dramatic genius of the Elizabethan and Jacobean theaters came to an end. When the theaters reopened at the Restoration in 1660, not only had the content of the drama changed, but so had the very appearance of the theater. King Charles II had brought back from his years of exile in France a taste for things French, including a taste for French drama. Molière's plays were the rage in France, and they were performed in a theater more recognizably like our own. It had a "picture frame" stage, a stage framed by a *proscenium arch*. The spectators sat in front watching the actors perform like moving figures in a framed painting. The action was highly stylized, the language elegant, witty, and polished, and life was generally an idealization of the social life of the upper classes much like that of neoclassical portraiture. Lost was the Elizabethan earthiness, the rough-textured language, the rapid scene changes, the broad philosophic sweep. Scenes in the new theater tended to be prolonged, the action based on verbal repartee, and the human activity reduced to the subjects of love or characters' reactions to social norms. The action followed the neoclassical notions of the *three unities* of time, place, and action falsely derived from Aristotle: plays were to be set in a single city, the action covering no more than 24 hours, and a mixture of comedy and tragedy was proscribed. However, just as the dynamism of the Elizabethan era tells us something of the tenor of the age, so too the importance of man as a social animal with reason and moderation guiding his actions is reflected in such French neoclassical comedies as Molière's *The Misanthrope*. The separation of spectator and actor by the picture frame stage lent distance and objectivity to the spectacle of human foibles and social norms which the audience could contemplate and criticize.

The nineteenth century retained the picture frame stage, but elaborated the realism of the setting. So realistic were the sets and props on the stage that the audience began to view the action on the stage as through an imaginary *fourth wall*. After 1870, Ibsen wrote plays so lifelike that the living rooms and studies were furnished with the paraphernalia of everyday life: chairs, tables, lamps, bookcases filled with real books, articles of clothing draped over sofas, pictures decorating the walls, fireplaces and stoves to keep people warm. The drama framed by the fourth wall was the drama of *domestic tragedy*, the lives of ordinary people caught in the everyday conflicts of middle-class life. Gone were the tragic kings and the elegant aristocrats, and in their place were the new professional people; yet the turbulence of human life and the conflict of moral dilemma were still there, reaching a new audience able to identify with the dilemmas of Ibsen's middle-class characters.

In our own century two changes have taken place in the theater which have deliberately dispelled the illusion that what is happening on the stage is "real." A more critical approach is demanded of the audience. The props have become fewer and the scenery sparer and more suggestive. Samuel Beckett's *Krapp's Last Tape* uses only a two-drawered desk, a tape recorder, and boxes of tapes. The audience is jarred out of its complacency as a result of reduced illusion and is introduced into a world without specific time or place, possibly without meaning. During the 1950s such drama came to be called *Theater of the Absurd*, after the philosopher Albert Camus' "absurd dilemma," the conditions in which man is alienated in a world where the old answers to his questions about existence no longer seem to make sense. The other development in the contemporary theater has been the increased use of the *arena stage*, or theater in the round, where the audience completely encloses the stage. The curtain has disappeared; entrances and exits are made using the aisles, and set changes are made in full view of the audience.

All of these developments, like the changes in theater architecture throughout the centuries, continue to affect in a dynamic way how drama is written. Technical developments in lighting and acoustics, makeup and costume, have made possible dramatic effects that would have been inconceivable for playwrights a century ago. As in the past, dramatists use the resources at their disposal, and innovations soon become conventions accepted by audiences.

While drama is action—what can be seen and heard on the stage—as readers of plays we have an opportunity to use our imaginations to recreate from the stage directions those features of stagecraft and spectacle usually witnessed only in a live performance. In a sense this recreative act puts us in the position of being collaborators with the playwright. Like directors we get to flesh out the play: not only choosing the appropriate actors but also costuming them, selecting complementary lighting, music, and sets, as well as helping the actors interpret their lines by matching dialogue with gesture. We take our clues as directors from the words of the playwright contained in the play's stage directions.

In the following play by Henrik Ibsen, the playwright is breaking new ground. Previously, Ibsen had been best known for his realistic plays dealing with controversial social issues, plays that insisted that people tell the truth to one another and stop hiding behind illusions. In *The Wild Duck*, Isben departs from the straightforward realism of his previous plays, *Ghosts* and *A Doll's House*, to brilliantly voice his concern that people had misunderstood him, had exposed at a terrible price destructive truths that had best been left unstated. Ibsen combines this idea with a new mode of drama, embarking on a theater of symbolism and illusion that was to carry him forward to the elusive drama of his final decade.

HENRIK IBSEN (1828–1906)

The Wild Duck

Henrik Ibsen was Norway's greatest writer and one of Europe's greatest dramatists. A master of dramatic construction and dialogue, he is particularly well known for the uncompromising manner in which he probed the major social and psychological issues of his day. His earlier plays, the greatest of which is probably *Peer Gynt* (1867), draw heavily on Scandanavian history and folklore. His major plays of the 1870s and 1880s—including *A Doll's House* (1879), *Ghosts* (1881), *An Enemy of the People* (1882), and *The Wild Duck* (1884)—have had such far-reaching influence that Ibsen is often called the "father" of modern realistic drama.

CHARACTERS

HAAKON WERLE, wholesale merchant and millowner	GRAABERG, a bookkeeper
GREGERS WERLE, his son	PETTERSEN, manservant to the elder Werle
OLD EKDAL	JENSEN, a hired waiter
HJALMAR EKDAL, his son, a photographer	A FAT MAN
	A BALD-HEADED MAN
GINA EKDAL, Hjalmar's wife	A NEARSIGHTED MAN
HEDVIG, their daughter, aged fourteen	SIX OTHER MEN, dinner guests at Werle's
MRS. SØRBY, housekeeper for the elder Werle	OTHER HIRED SERVANTS
	MOLVIK, a former divinity student
RELLING, a doctor	

The first act takes place in WERLE's *house; the following four acts in* HJALMAR EKDAL's *studio.*

ACT ONE

At WERLE'S *house. A richly and comfortably furnished study, with bookcases and upholstered furniture, a writing table, with papers and reports, in the middle of the floor, and green-shaded lamps softly illuminating the room. In the rear wall, open folding doors with curtains drawn back disclose a large, fashionable room, brightly lit by lamps and candelabra. In the right foreground of the study, a small private door leads to the offices. In the left foreground, a fireplace filled with glowing coals, and further back a double door to the dining room.*

WERLE'S manservant, PETTERSEN, *in livery, and* JENSEN, *a hired waiter, in black, are straightening up the study. In the larger room two or three other hired waiters are moving about, putting things in order and lighting more candles. In from the dining room come laughter and the hum of many voices in conversation; a knife clinks upon a glass; silence; a toast is made; cries of "Bravo," and the hum of conversation resumes.*

PETTERSEN *lighting a lamp by the fireplace and putting on the shade:*   Ah, you hear that, Jensen. Now the old boy's up on his feet, proposing a long toast to Mrs. Sørby.

JENSEN *moving an armchair forward:*   Is it really true what people say, that there's something between them?

PETTERSEN: Lord knows.

JENSEN: I've heard he was a real goat in his day.

PETTERSEN: Could be.

JENSEN: But they say it's his son he's throwing this party for.

PETTERSEN: Yes. His son came home yesterday.

JENSEN: I never knew before that old Werle had any son.

PETTERSEN: Oh yes, he's got a son. But he spends all his time up at the works in Hoidal. He hasn't been in town all the years I've served in this house.

A HIRED WAITER *in the door to the other room:*   Say, Pettersen, there's an old guy here who—

PETTERSEN *muttering:*   What the hell—somebody coming now!

Old EKDAL *appears from the right through the inner room. He is dressed in a shabby overcoat with a high collar, woolen gloves, and in his hand, a cane and a fur cap; under his arm is a bundle wrapped in brown paper. He has a dirty, reddish-brown wig and a little gray moustache.*

PETTERSEN *going toward him:*   Good Lord, what do *you* want in here?

EKDAL *at the door:*   Just have to get into the office, Pettersen.

PETTERSEN: The office closed an hour ago, and—

EKDAL: Heard that one at the door, boy. But Graaberg's still in there. Be nice, Pettersen, and let me slip in that way. *Pointing toward the private entrance.* I've gone that way before.

PETTERSEN: All right, go ahead, then. *Opens the door.* But don't forget now—take the other way out; we have guests.

EKDAL: Got you—hmm! Thanks, Pettersen, good old pal! Thanks. *To himself*. Bonehead! *He goes into the office;* PETTERSEN *shuts the door after him*.

JENSEN: Is *he* on the office staff too?

PETTERSEN: No, he's just someone who does copying on the outside when it's needed. Still, in his time he was well up in the world, old Ekdal.

JENSEN: Yes, he looks like he's been a little of everything.

PETTERSEN: Oh yes. He was a lieutenant once, if you can imagine.

JENSEN: Good Lord—him a lieutenant!

PETTERSEN: So help me, he was. But then he went into the lumber business or something. They say he must have pulled some kind of dirty deal on the old man once, for the two of them were running the Hoidal works together then. Oh, I know good old Ekdal, all right. We've drunk many a schnapps and bottle of beer together over at Eriksen's.

JENSEN: He can't have much money for standing drinks.

PETTERSEN: My Lord, Jensen, you can bet it's me that stands the drinks. I always say a person ought to act refined toward quality that's come down in life.

JENSEN: Did he go bankrupt, then?

PETTERSEN: No, worse than that. He was sent to jail.

JENSEN: To jail!

PETTERSEN: Or maybe it was the penitentiary. *Laughter from the dining room*. Hist! They're leaving the table.

The dining room door is opened by a pair of servants inside. MRS. SØRBY, *in conversation with two gentlemen, comes out. A moment later the rest of the guests follow, among them* WERLE. *Last of all come* HJALMAR EKDAL *and* GREGERS WERLE.

MRS. SØRBY *to the servant, in passing:* Pettersen, will you have coffee served in the music room.

PETTERSEN: Yes, Mrs. Sørby.

She and the two gentlemen go into the inner room and exit to the right. PETTERSEN *and* JENSEN *leave in the same way.*

A FAT GUEST *to a balding man:* Phew! That dinner—that was a steep bit of work!

THE BALD-HEADED GUEST: Oh, with a little good will a man can do wonders in three hours.

THE FAT GUEST: Yes, but afterward, my dear fellow, afterward.

A THIRD GUEST: I hear we can sample coffee and liqueur in the music room.

THE FAT GUEST: Fine! Then perhaps Mrs. Sørby will play us a piece.

THE BALD-HEADED GUEST *in an undertone:* Just so Mrs. Sørby doesn't play us to pieces.

THE FAT GUEST: Oh, now really, Berta wouldn't punish her old friends, would she? *They laugh and enter the inner room.*

WERLE *in a low, depressed tone:* I don't think anyone noticed it, Gregers.

GREGERS: What?

WERLE: Didn't you notice it either?

GREGERS: What should I have noticed?

WERLE: We were thirteen at the table.

GREGERS: Really? Were we thirteen?

WERLE *with a glance at* HJALMAR EKDAL: Yes—our usual number is twelve. *To the others.* Be so kind, gentlemen.

He and those remaining, except HJALMAR *and* GREGERS, *go out to the rear and right.*

HJALMAR *who has heard the conversation:* You shouldn't have sent me the invitation, Gregers.

GREGERS: What! The party's supposed to be for *me*. And then I'm not supposed to have my best and only friend—

HJALMAR: But I don't think your father likes it. Ordinarily I never come to this house.

GREGERS: So I hear. But I had to see you and talk with you, for I'm sure to be leaving soon again. Yes, we two old classmates, we've certainly drifted a long way apart. You know, we haven't seen each other now in sixteen—seventeen years.

HJALMAR: Has it been so long?

GREGERS: Yes, all of that. Well, how have you been? You look well. You're almost becoming stout.

HJALMAR: Hm, stout is hardly the word, though I probably look more of a man than I did then.

GREGERS: Yes, you do. The outer man hasn't suffered.

HJALMAR *in a gloomier tone:* Ah, but the inner man! Believe me, he has a different look. You know, of course how everything went to pieces for me and my family since you and I last saw each other.

GREGERS *dropping his voice:* How's it going for your father now?

HJALMAR: Oh, Gregers, let's not talk about that. My poor, unhappy father naturally lives at home with me. He's got no one else in the whole world to turn to. But this all is so terribly hard for me to talk about, you know. Tell me, instead, how you've found life up at the mine.

GREGERS: Marvelously solitary, that's what—with a good chance to mull over a great many things. Come on, let's be comfortable.

He sits in an armchair by the fire and urges HJALMAR *down into another by its side.*

HJALMAR *emotionally:* In any case, I'm grateful that you asked me here, Gregers, because it proves you no longer have anything against me.

GREGERS *astonished:* How could you think that I had anything against you?

HJALMAR: In those first years you did.

GREGERS: Which first years?

HJALMAR: Right after that awful misfortune. And it was only natural you should. It was just by a hair that your own father escaped being dragged into this—oh, this loathsome business.

GREGERS: And that's why I had it in for you? Whoever gave you that idea?

HJALMAR: I know you did, Gregers; it was your father himself who told me.

GREGERS *startled:*   Father! I see. Hm—is that why I never heard from you—not a single word?

HJALMAR: Yes.

GREGERS: Not even when you went out and became a photographer.

HJALMAR: Your father said it wasn't worth writing you—about anything.

GREGERS *looking fixedly ahead:*   No, no, maybe he was right there— But tell me, Hjalmar—do you find yourself reasonably content with things as they are?

HJALMAR *with a small sigh:*   Oh, I suppose I do. What else can I say? At first, you can imagine, it was all rather strange for me. They were such completely different expectations that I came into. But then everything was so different. That immense, shattering misfortune for Father—the shame and the scandal, Gregers—

GREGERS *shaken:*   Yes, yes. Of course.

HJALMAR: I couldn't dream of going on with my studies; there wasn't a penny to spare. On the contrary, debts instead—mainly to your father, I think—

GREGERS: Hm—

HJALMAR: Anyway, I thought it was best to make a clean break—and cut all the old connections. It was your father especially who advised me to; and since he'd already been so helpful to me—

GREGERS: He had?

HJALMAR: Yes, you knew that, didn't you? Where could *I* get the money to learn photography and fit out a studio and establish myself? I can tell you, that all adds up.

GREGERS: And all that Father paid for?

HJALMAR: Yes, Gregers, didn't you know? I understood him to say that he'd written you about it.

GREGERS: Not a word saying *he* was the one. Maybe he forgot. We've never exchanged anything but business letters. So that was Father, too—!

HJALMAR: That's right. He never wanted people to know, but he was the one. And he was also the one who put me in a position to get married. Or perhaps—didn't you know that either?

GREGERS: No, not at all. *Takes him by the arm.* But Hjalmar, I can't tell you how all this delights me—and disturbs me. Perhaps I've been unfair to my father—in certain ways. Yes, for all this does show good-heartedness, doesn't it? It's almost a kind of conscience—

HJALMAR: Conscience?

GREGERS: Yes, or whatever you want to call it. No, I can't tell you how glad I am to hear this about my father. So you're married, then, Hjalmar. That's further than I'll ever go. Well, I hope you're happy as a married man?

HJALMAR: Oh, absolutely. She's as capable and fine a wife as any man could wish for. And she's not entirely without culture, either.

GREGERS *a bit surprised:* No, I'm sure she's not.

HJALMAR: No. Life is a teacher, you see. Associating with me every day—and then there are one or two gifted people who visit us regularly. I can tell you, you wouldn't recognize Gina now.

GREGERS: Gina?

HJALMAR: Yes, Gregers, have you forgotten her name is Gina?

GREGERS: Whose name is Gina? I haven't the faintest idea—

HJALMAR: But don't you remember, she was here in this very house a while—in service?

GREGERS *looking at him:* You mean Gina Hansen—?

HJALMAR: Yes, of course. Gina Hansen.

GREGERS: Who was housekeeper for us that last year of Mother's illness?

HJALMAR: Exactly. But my dear Gregers, I know for sure that your father wrote you about my marriage.

GREGERS *who has gotten up:* Yes, of course he did. But not that— *Walks about the floor.* Yes, wait a minute—it may well be, now that I think of it. My father's letters are always so brief. *Sits on chair arm.* Listen, tell me, Hjalmar—this is interesting—how did you come to know Gina?—your wife, I mean.

HJALMAR: Oh, it was all very simple. Gina didn't stay long here in the house; there was so much confusion—your mother's sickness and all. Gina couldn't stand it, so she just up and left. That was the year before your mother died—or maybe it was the same year.

GREGERS: It was the same year. And I was up at the works at the time. But what then?

HJALMAR: Well, then Gina lived at home with her mother, a Mrs. Hansen, a very capable, hardworking woman who ran a little restaurant. She also had a room for rent, a very pleasant, comfortable room.

GREGERS: And you were lucky enough to find it?

HJALMAR: Yes. Actually it was your father who suggested it to me. And it was there, you see—there that I really got to know Gina.

GREGERS: And then your engagement followed?

HJALMAR: Yes. Young people fall in love so easily—hm—

GREGERS *getting up and pacing about a little:* Tell me—when you became engaged—was it *then* that my father got you to—I mean, was it then that you started in learning photography?

HJALMAR: That's right. I wanted to get on and set up a home as soon as possible, and both your father and I decided that this photography idea was the most feasible one. And Gina thought so too. Yes, and you see, there was another inducement, a lucky break, in that Gina had already taken up retouching.

GREGERS: That worked out wonderfully all around.

HJALMAR *pleased, getting up:* Yes, isn't that so? Don't you think it's worked out wonderfully all around?

GREGERS: Yes, I must say. My father has almost been a kind of providence to you.

HJALMAR *with feeling:* He didn't abandon his old friend's son in a time of need. You see, he does have a heart.

MRS. SØRBY *entering with* WERLE *on her arm:* No more nonsense, my dear Mr. Werle. You mustn't stay in there any longer, staring at all those lights; it's doing you no good.

WERLE *freeing his arm from hers and passing his hand over his eyes:* Yes, I guess you're right about that.

PETTERSEN *and* JENSEN *enter with trays.*

MRS. SØRBY *to the guests in the other room:* Gentlemen, please—if anyone wants a glass of punch, he must take the trouble to come in here.

THE FAT GUEST *comes over to* MRS. SØRBY: But really, is it true you've abolished our precious smoking privilege?

MRS. SØRBY: Yes. Here in Mr. Werle's sanctum, it's forbidden.

THE BALD-HEADED GUEST: When did you pass these drastic amendments to the cigar laws, Mrs. Sørby?

MRS. SØRBY: After the last dinner—when there were certain persons here who let themselves exceed all limits.

THE BALD-HEADED GUEST: And my dear Berta, one isn't permitted to exceed the limits, even a little bit?

MRS. SØRBY: Not in any instance, Mr. Balle.

Most of the guests have gathered in the study; the waiters are proffering glasses of punch.

WERLE *to* HJALMAR, *over by a table:* What is it you're poring over, Ekdal?

HJALMAR: It's only an album, Mr. Werle.

THE BALD-HEADED GUEST *who is wandering about:* Ah, photographs! Yes, of course, that's just the thing for you.

THE FAT GUEST *seated in an armchair:* Haven't you brought along some of your own?

HJALMAR: No, I haven't.

THE FAT GUEST: You really should have. It's so good for the digestion to sit and look at pictures.

THE BALD-HEADED GUEST: And then it always adds a morsel to the entertainment, you know.

A NEARSIGHTED GUEST: And all contributions are gratefully received.

MRS. SØRBY: These gentlemen mean that if one's invited for dinner, one must also work for the food, Mr. Ekdal.

THE FAT GUEST: Where the larder's superior, *that* is pure joy.

THE BALD-HEADED GUEST: My Lord, it's all in the struggle for existence—

MRS. SØRBY: How right you are! *They continue laughing and joking.*

GREGERS *quietly:* You should talk with them, Hjalmar.

HJALMAR *with a shrug:* What could I talk about?

THE FAT GUEST: Don't you think, Mr. Werle, that Tokay compares favorably as a healthful drink for the stomach?

WERLE *by the fireplace:*   The Tokay you had today I can vouch for in any case; it's one of the very, very finest years. But you recognized that well enough.

THE FAT GUEST: Yes, it had a remarkably delicate flavor.

HJALMAR *tentatively:*   Is there some difference between the years?

THE FAT GUEST *laughing:*   Oh, that's rich!

WERLE *smiling:*   It certainly doesn't pay to offer you a noble wine.

THE BALD-HEADED GUEST: Tokay wines are like photographs, Mr. Ekdal—sunshine is of the essence. Isn't that true?

HJALMAR: Oh yes, light is very important.

MRS. SØRBY: Exactly the same as with court officials—who push for their place in the sun too, I hear.

THE BALD-HEADED GUEST: Ouch! That was a tired quip.

THE NEARSIGHTED GUEST: The lady's performing—

THE FAT GUEST: And at our expense. *Frowning.* Mrs. Sørby, Mrs. Sørby!

MRS. SØRBY: Yes, but it certainly is true now that the years can vary enormously. The old vintages are the finest.

THE NEARSIGHTED GUEST: Do you count me among the old ones?

MRS. SØRBY: Oh, far from it.

THE BALD-HEADED GUEST: Ha, you see! But what about *me*, Mrs. Sørby—?

THE FAT GUEST: Yes, and me! What years would you put us among?

MRS. SØRBY: I would put you all among the sweet years, gentlemen. *She sips a glass of punch; the guests laugh and banter with her.*

WERLE: Mrs. Sørby always finds a way out—when she wants to. Pass your glasses, gentlemen. Pettersen, take care of them. Gregers, I think we'll have a glass together. GREGERS *does not stir.* Won't you join us, Ekdal? I had no chance to remember you at the table.

GRAABERG, *the bookkeeper, peers out from the door to the offices.*

GRAABERG: Beg pardon, Mr. Werle, but I can't get out.

WERLE: What, are you locked in again?

GRAABERG: Yes, and Flakstad's left with the keys—

WERLE: Well, then, go through here.

GRAABERG: But there's someone else—

WERLE: All right, all right, both of you. Don't be shy.

GRAABERG *and old* EKDAL *come out from the office.*

WERLE *involuntarily:*   Oh no!

The laughter and small talk die among the guests. HJALMAR *starts at the sight of his father, sets down his glass, and turns away toward the fireplace.*

EKDAL *without looking up, but bowing slightly to each side and mumbling:*

Beg your pardon. It's the wrong way. Door locked—door locked. Beg pardon. *He and* GRAABERG *exit in back to the right.*

WERLE *between his teeth:* That damned Graaberg!

GREGERS *with open mouth, staring at* HJALMAR: But it couldn't have been—!

THE FAT GUEST: What's going on? Who was that?

GREGERS: Oh, no one. Only the bookkeeper and somebody else.

THE NEARSIGHTED GUEST *to* HJALMAR: Did *you* know him?

HJALMAR: I don't know—I didn't notice—

THE FAT GUEST *getting up:* What in thunder's wrong?

He goes over to some others, who are talking.

MRS. SØRBY *whispering to the waiter:* Slip something to him outside, something really fine.

PETTERSEN *nodding:* I'll see to it. *He goes out.*

GREGERS *in a shocked undertone:* Then it really was him!

HJALMAR: Yes.

GREGERS: And yet you stood here and denied you knew him!

HJALMAR *whispering fiercely:* But how could I—!

GREGERS: Be recognized by your father?

HJALMAR *painfully:* Oh, if you were in my place, then—

The hushed conversations among the guests now mount into a forced joviality.

THE BALD-HEADED GUEST *approaching* HJALMAR *and* GREGERS *amiably:* Ah ha! You over here, polishing up old memories from your student years? Well? Won't you smoke, Mr. Ekdal? Have a light? Oh, that's right, we're not supposed to—

HJALMAR: Thanks, I couldn't—

THE FAT GUEST: Haven't you got a neat little poem to recite for us, Mr. Ekdal? In times past you did that so nicely.

HJALMAR: I'm afraid I can't remember any.

THE FAT GUEST: Oh, that's a shame. Well, Balle, what can we find to do? *The two men cross the floor into the other room and go out.*

HJALMAR *somberly:* Gregers—I'm going! When a man's had a hammer blow from fate on his head—you understand. Say good night to your father for me.

GREGERS: Yes, of course. Are you going straight home?

HJALMAR: Yes, why?

GREGERS: Well, I may pay you a visit later.

HJALMAR: No, you mustn't. Not to my home. My house is a sad one, Gregers—especially after a brilliant occasion like this. We can always meet somewhere in town.

MRS. SØRBY *who has approached; in a low voice:* Are you going, Ekdal?

HJALMAR: Yes.

MRS. SØRBY: Greet Gina.

HJALMAR: Thank you.

MRS. SØRBY: And tell her I'll stop by to see her one day soon.

HJALMAR: Yes, Thanks. *To* GREGERS. Stay here. I'd rather disappear without any fuss. *He strolls around the floor, then into the other room and out to the right.*

MRS. SØRBY *quietly to the waiter, who has returned:* Well, did the old man get something to take home?

PETTERSEN: Sure. I slipped him a bottle of cognac.

MRS. SØRBY: Oh, you could have found something better.

PETTERSEN: Not at all, Mrs. Sørby. He knows nothing better than cognac.

THE FAT GUEST *in the doorway, holding a score of music:* How about the two of us playing something, Mrs. Sørby?

MRS. SØRBY: All right. Let's.

The guests shout approval. MRS. SØRBY *and the others exit right, through the inner room.* GREGERS *remains standing by the fireplace.* WERLE *looks for something on the writing table, seeming to wish that* GREGERS *would leave; when he fails to stir,* WERLE *crosses toward the door.*

GREGERS: Father, won't you wait a moment?

WERLE *pausing:* What is it?

GREGERS: I must have a word with you.

WERLE: Can't it wait till we're alone?

GREGERS: No, it can't, because it just might occur that we never are alone.

WERLE *coming closer:* What does *that* mean?

Distant piano music is heard from the music room during the following conversation.

GREGERS: How could anyone here let that family decay so pitifully?

WERLE: You're referring to the Ekdals, no doubt.

GREGERS: Yes, I mean the Ekdals. Lieutenant Ekdal was once so close to you.

WERLE: Yes, worse luck, he was all too close; and for that I've paid a price these many years. He's the one I can thank for putting something of a blot on my good name and reputation.

GREGERS *quietly:* Was *he* really the only guilty one?

WERLE: Who else do you mean!

GREGERS: You and he were both in on buying that big stand of timber—

WERLE: But it was Ekdal, wasn't it, who made the survey of the sections—that incompetent survey? He was the one who carried out all the illegal logging on state property. In fact, he was in charge of the whole operation up there. I had no idea of what Lieutenant Ekdal was getting into.

GREGERS: Lieutenant Ekdal himself had no idea of what he was getting into.

WERLE: Very likely. But the fact remains that he was convicted and I was acquitted.

GREGERS: Yes, I'm aware that no proof was found.

WERLE: Acquittal is acquittal. Why do you rake up this ugly old story that's given me gray hair before my time? Is this what you've been brooding about all those years up there? I can assure you, Gregers— here in town the whole business has been forgotten long ago—as far as I'm concerned.

GREGERS: But that miserable Ekdal family!

WERLE: Seriously, what would you have me do for these people? When Ekdal was let out, he was a broken man, beyond any help. There are people in this world who plunge to the bottom when they've hardly been winged, and they never come up again. Take my word for it, Gregers; I've done everything I could, short of absolutely compromising myself and arousing all kinds of suspicion and gossip—

GREGERS: Suspicion—? So that's it.

WERLE: I've gotten Ekdal copying jobs from the office, and I pay him much, much more than his work is worth—

GREGERS *without looking at him:* Hm. No doubt.

WERLE: You're laughing? Maybe you think what I'm saying isn't true? There's certainly nothing to show in my books; I don't record such payments.

GREGERS *with a cold smile:* No. I'm sure that certain payments are best left unrecorded.

WERLE *surprised:* What do you mean by *that?*

GREGERS *plucking up his courage:* Did you record what it cost you to have Hjalmar Ekdal study photography?

WERLE: I? Why should I?

GREGERS: I know now it was you who paid for that. And now I know, too, that it was you who set him up so comfortably in business.

WERLE: Well, and I suppose this still means that I've done nothing for the Ekdals! I can assure you, those people have already cost me enough expense.

GREGERS: Have you recorded any of the expenses?

WERLE: Why do you ask that?

GREGERS: Oh, there are reasons. Listen, tell me—the time when you developed such warmth for your old friend's son—wasn't that just when he was planning to marry?

WERLE: How the devil—how, after so many years, do you expect me—?

GREGERS: You wrote me a letter then—a business letter, naturally; and in a postscript it said, brief as could be, that Hjalmar Ekdal had gotten married to a Miss Hansen.

WERLE: Yes, that's right; that was her name.

GREGERS: But you never said that this Miss Hansen was Gina Hansen— our former housekeeper.

WERLE *with a derisive, yet uneasy laugh:* No, it just never occurred to me that you'd be so very interested in our former housekeeper.

GREGERS: I wasn't. But—*Dropping his voice.* there were others in the house who were quite interested in her.

WERLE: What do you mean by that? *Storming at him.* You're not referring to me!

GREGERS *quietly but firmly:* Yes, I'm referring to you.

WERLE: And you dare—! You have the insolence—! How could he, that ungrateful dog, that—photographer; how could he have the gall to make such insinuations?

GREGERS: Hjalmar hasn't breathed a word of it. I don't think he has the shadow of a doubt about all this.

WERLE: Then where did you get it from? Who could have said such a thing?

GREGERS: My poor, unhappy mother said it—the last time I saw her.

WERLE: Your mother! Yes, I might have guessed. She and you—you always stuck together. It was she who, right from the start, turned your mind against me.

GREGERS: No. It was everything she had to suffer and endure until she broke down and died so miserably.

WERLE: Oh, she had nothing to suffer and endure—no more, at least, than so many others. But you can't get anywhere with sick, high-strung people. I've certainly learned that. Now you're going around suspecting that sort of thing, digging up all manner of old rumors and slanders against your own father. Now listen, Gregers, I really think that at your age you could occupy yourself more usefully.

GREGERS: Yes, all in due time.

WERLE: Then your mind might be clearer than it seems to be now. What can it lead to, you up there at the works, slaving away year in and year out like a common clerk, never taking a penny over your month's salary. It's pure stupidity.

GREGERS: Yes, if only I were so sure of that.

WERLE: I understand you well enough. You want to be independent, without obligation to me. But here's the very opportunity for you to become independent, your own man in every way.

GREGERS: So? And by what means—?

WERLE: When I wrote you that it was essential you come to town now, immediately—hmm—

GREGERS: Yes. What is it you really want of me? I've been waiting all day to find out.

WERLE: I'm suggesting that you come into the firm as a partner.

GREGERS: I! In your firm? As a partner?

WERLE: Yes. It wouldn't mean we'd need to be together much. You could take over the offices here in town, and then I'd move up to the mill.

GREGERS: You *would?*

WERLE: Yes. You see, I can't take on work now the way I once could. I have to spare my eyes, Gregers; they're beginning to fail.

GREGERS: They've always been weak.

WERLE: Not like this. Besides—circumstances may make it desirable for me to live up there—at least for a while.

GREGERS: I never dreamed of anything like this.

WERLE: Listen, Gregers, there are so very many things that keep us apart, and yet, you know—we're father and son still. I think we should be able to reach some kind of understanding.

GREGERS: Just on the surface, is that what you mean?

WERLE: Well, at least that would be something. Think it over, Gregers. Don't you think it ought to be possible? Eh?

GREGERS *looking at him coldly:*   There's something behind all this.

WERLE: How so?

GREGERS: It might be that somehow you're using me.

WERLE: In a relationship as close as ours, one can always be of use to the other.

GREGERS: Yes, so they say.

WERLE: I'd like to have you home with me now for a while. I'm a lonely man, Gregers; I've always felt lonely—all my life through, but particularly now when the years are beginning to press me. I need to have someone around—

GREGERS: You have Mrs. Sørby.

WERLE: Yes, I do—and she's become, you might say, almost indispensable. She's witty, even-tempered; she livens up the house—and that's what I need so badly.

GREGERS: Well, then, you've got everything the way you want it.

WERLE: Yes, but I'm afraid it can't go on. The world is quick to make inferences about a woman in her position. Yes, I was going to say, a man doesn't gain by it either.

GREGERS: Oh, when a man gives dinner parties like yours, he can certainly take a few risks.

WERLE: Yes, Gregers, but what about her? I'm afraid she won't put up with it much longer. And even if she did—even if, out of her feeling for me, she ignored the gossip and the backbiting and so on—do you still think, Gregers, you with your sharp sense of justice—

GREGERS *cutting him off:*   Tell me short and sweet just one thing. Are you planning to marry her?

WERLE: And if I *were* planning such a thing—what then?

GREGERS: Yes, that's what I'm asking. What then?

WERLE: Would you be so irreconcilably set against it?

GREGERS: No, not at all. Not in any way.

WERLE: Well, I really didn't know whether, perhaps out of regard for your dead mother's memory—

GREGERS: I am not high-strung.

WERLE: Well, you may or may not be, but in any case you've taken a great load off my mind. I'm really very happy that I can count on your support in this.

GREGERS *staring intently at him:*   Now I see how you want to use me.

WERLE: Use you! That's no way to talk!

GREGERS: Oh, let's not be squeamish in our choice of words. At least, not when it's man to man. *He laughs brusquely.* So that's it! That's why I— damn it all!—had to make my personal appearance in town. On account of Mrs. Sørby, family life is in order in this house. Tableau of father with son! That's something new, all right!

WERLE: How dare you speak in that tone!

GREGERS: When has there ever been family life here? Never, as long as I can remember. But *now,* of course, there's need for a little of that. For who could deny what a fine impression it would make to hear that the son—on the wings of piety—came flying home to the aging father's wedding feast. What's left then of all the stories about what the poor dead woman suffered and endured? Not a scrap. Her own son ground them to dust.

WERLE: Gregers—I don't think there's a man in this world you hate as much as me.

GREGERS: I've seen you at too close quarters.

WERLE: You've seen me with your mother's eyes. *Dropping his voice.* But you should remember that those eyes were—clouded at times.

GREGERS *faltering:*   I know what you mean. But who bears the guilt for Mother's fatal weakness? You, and all those—! The last of them was that female that Hjalmar Ekdal was fixed up with when you had no more—ugh!

WERLE *shrugs:*   Word for word, as if I were hearing your mother.

GREGERS *paying no attention to him:*   . . . and there he sits right now, he with his great, guileless, childlike mind plunged in deception—living under the same roof with that creature, not knowing that what he calls his home is built on a lie. *Coming a step closer.* When I look back on all you've done, it's as if I looked out over a battlefield with broken human beings on every side.

WERLE: I almost think the gulf is too great between us.

GREGERS *bows stiffly:*   So I've observed; therefore I'll take my hat and go.

WERLE: You're going? Out of this house?

GREGERS: Yes. Because now at last I can see a mission to live for.

WERLE: What mission is that?

GREGERS: You'd only laugh if you heard it.

WERLE: A lonely man doesn't laugh so easily, Gregers.

GREGERS *pointing toward the inner room:*   Look—your gentleman friends are playing blindman's bluff with Mrs. Sørby. Good night and good-bye.

He goes out at the right rear. Laughter and joking from the company, which moves into view in the inner room.

WERLE *muttering contemptuously after* GREGERS: Huh! Poor fool—and he says he's not high-strung!

ACT TWO

HJALMAR EKDAL's *studio. The room, which is fairly spacious, appears to be a loft. To the right is a sloping roof with great panes of glass, half hidden by a blue curtain. In the far right corner is the entrance; nearer on the same side, a door to the living room. Similarly, at the left there are two doors, and between these an iron stove. At the back is a wide double door, designed to slide back to the sides. The studio is simply but comfortably furnished and decorated. Between the right-hand doors, slightly away from the wall, stands a sofa beside a table and some chairs; on the table is a lighted lamp with a shade; by the stove an old armchair. Photographic apparatus and equipment of various sorts are set up here and there in the room. At the left of the double doors stands a bookcase containing a few books, small boxes and flasks of chemicals, various tools, implements, and other objects. Photographs and such small articles as brushes, paper, and the like lie on the table.*

GINA EKDAL *sits on a chair by the table, sewing.* HEDVIG *sits on the sofa, hands shading her eyes, thumbs in her ears, reading a book.*

GINA *having glanced over several times at* HEDVIG, *as if with anxiety:*   Hedvig! HEDVIG *does not hear.*

GINA *louder:*   Hedvig!

HEDVIG *removing her hands and looking up:*   Yes, Mother?

GINA: Hedvig dear, you mustn't sit and read anymore.

HEDVIG: Oh, but Mother, can't I please read a little longer? Just a little!

GINA: No, no—you must set the book down. Your father doesn't like it; *he* never reads in the evening.

HEDVIG *closing the book:*   No, Daddy's no great one for reading.

GINA *lays her sewing aside and takes a pencil and a small notebook from the table:*   Do you remember how much we spent for butter today?

HEDVIG: It was one sixty-five.

GINA: That's right. *Making a note.* It's awful how much butter gets used in this house. And then so much for smoked sausage, and for cheese— let me see—*Making more notes.* and so much for ham—hmm. *Adds.* Yes, that adds right up to—

HEDVIG: And then there's the beer.

GINA: Yes, of course. *Makes another note.* It mounts up—but it can't be helped.

HEDVIG: Oh, but you and I had no hot food for dinner, 'cause Daddy was out.

GINA: No, and that's to the good. What's more, I also took in eight crowns fifty for photographs.

HEDVIG: No! Was it that much?

GINA: Exactly eight crowns fifty.

Silence. GINA *again picks up her sewing.* HEDVIG *takes paper and pencil and starts to draw, shading her eyes with her left hand.*

HEDVIG: Isn't it something to think that Daddy's at a big dinner party at old Mr. Werle's?

GINA: You can't really say that he's at old Mr. Werle's. It was his son who sent him the invitation. *After a pause.* We have nothing to do with old Mr. Werle.

HEDVIG: I can hardly wait for Daddy to come home. He promised he'd ask Mrs. Sørby about bringing me a treat.

GINA: Yes, you can bet there are lots of treats to be had in *that* house.

HEDVIG *again drawing:*   Besides, I'm a little hungry, too.

Old EKDAL, *with a bundle of papers under his arm and another bundle in his coat pocket, comes in through the hall door.*

GINA: My, but you're late today, Grandfather.

EKDAL: They'd locked the office. Had to wait for Graaberg. And then I had to go through—uhh.

GINA: Did they give you something new to copy, Grandfather?

EKDAL: This whole pile. Just look.

GINA: That's fine.

HEDVIG: And you've got a bundle in your pocket, too.

EKDAL: Oh? Nonsense; that's nothing. *Puts his cane away in the corner.* Here's work for a good spell, Gina, this here. *Pulls one of the double doors slightly open.* Shh! *Peers into the room a moment, then carefully closes the door again.* He, he! They're sound asleep, the lot of them. And she's bedded down in the basket all on her own. He, he!

HEDVIG: Are you sure she won't be cold in the basket, Grandpa?

EKDAL: What a thought! Cold? In all that straw? *Goes toward the farther door on the left.* I'll find some matches in here, eh?

GINA: The matches are on the bureau.

EKDAL *goes into his room.*

HEDVIG: It's wonderful that Grandpa got all that copying to do.

GINA: Yes, poor old Father; he'll earn himself a little pocket money.

HEDVIG: And he also won't be able to sit the whole morning down in that horrid Mrs. Eriksen's café.

GINA: That too, yes. *A short silence.*

HEDVIG: Do you think they're still at the dinner table?

GINA: Lord only knows; it may well be.

HEDVIG: Just think, all the lovely food Daddy's eaten! I'm sure he'll be happy and content when he comes. Don't you think so, Mother?

GINA: Of course. Imagine if we could tell him now that we'd rented out the room.

HEDVIG: But that's not necessary tonight.

GINA: Oh, it could well come in handy, you know. It's no good to us as it is.

HEDVIG: No, I mean it's not necessary because tonight Daddy's feeling good. It's better we have news about the room some other time.

GINA *looking over at her:* Are you glad when you have something nice to tell your father when he comes home at night?

HEDVIG: Yes, for things here are pleasanter then.

GINA *reflecting:* Well, there's something to that.

Old EKDAL *comes in again and starts out through the nearer door to the left.*

GINA *half turning in her chair:* Does Grandfather want something from the kitchen?

EKDAL: I do, yes. Don't stir. *He goes out.*

GINA: He never fusses with the fire out there. *After a moment.* Hedvig, go see what he's doing.

EKDAL *reenters with a small jug of steaming water.*

HEDVIG: Are you after hot water, Grandpa?
EKDAL: Yes, I am. Need it for something. Have to write, and the ink is caked thick as porridge—hmm.
GINA: But you ought to have supper first, Grandfather. It's all set and waiting in there.
EKDAL: Never mind about the supper, Gina. Terribly busy, I tell you. I don't want anybody coming into my room—nobody. Hmm. *He goes into his room.* GINA *and* HEDVIG *exchange glances.*
GINA *lowering her voice:*   Where do you figure he's gotten money?
HEDVIG: He must have got it from Graaberg.
GINA: Not a chance. Graaberg always sends the pay to me.
HEDVIG: Maybe he got a bottle somewhere on credit.
GINA: Poor Grandpa, no one'll give him credit.

HJALMAR EKDAL, *wearing an overcoat and a gray felt hat, enters from the right.*

GINA *dropping her sewing and getting up:*   Ah, Hjalmar, here you are!
HEDVIG *jumping up at the same time:*   At last you're home, Daddy!
HJALMAR *putting his hat down:*   Yes, most of them were leaving.
HEDVIG: So early?
HJALMAR: Yes, it was only a dinner party. *Starts to remove his overcoat.*
GINA: Let me help you.
HEDVIG: Me too.

They take off his coat; GINA *hangs it up on the rear wall.*

HEDVIG: Were there many there, Daddy?
HJALMAR: Oh no, not many. We were some twelve, fourteen people at the table.
GINA: And you got to talk with every one of them?
HJALMAR: Oh yes, a little, though Gregers rather monopolized me.
GINA: Is Gregers ugly as ever?
HJALMAR: Well, he doesn't look any better. Isn't the old man home?
HEDVIG: Yes, Grandpa's inside, writing.
HJALMAR: Did he say anything?
GINA: No, what should he say?
HJALMAR: Didn't he mention anything of—I thought I heard that he'd been with Graaberg. I'll go in and have a word with him.
GINA: No, no, don't bother.
HJALMAR: Why not? Did he say he wouldn't see me?
GINA: He doesn't want anyone in there this evening.
HEDVIG *making signals:*   Uh—uh!

GINA *not noticing:*   He's already been out here and gotten hot water.

HJALMAR: Aha! Is he—?

GINA: Yes, exactly.

HJALMAR: Good Lord, my poor old white-haired father! Well, let him be, enjoying life's pleasures as he may.

Old EKDAL *in a bathrobe, smoking a pipe, enters from his room.*

EKDAL: Home, eh? Thought it was your voice I heard.

HJALMAR: I just arrived.

EKDAL: You didn't see me at all, did you?

HJALMAR: No, but they said you'd been through—so I thought I'd follow after.

EKDAL: Hm, good of you, Hjalmar. Who were they, all those people?

HJALMAR: Oh, different sorts. There was Flor—he's at the court—and Balle and Kaspersen and, uh—I forget his name, but people at court, all of them—

EKDAL *nodding:*   Listen to that, Gina! He travels only in the best circles.

GINA: Yes, it's real elegant in that house now.

HEDVIG: Did the court people sing, Daddy? Or give readings?

HJALMAR: No, they just babbled away. Of course they wanted *me* to recite for them, but I couldn't see that.

EKDAL: You couldn't see that, eh?

GINA: That you could easily have done.

HJALMAR: Never. One mustn't be a doormat for every passing foot. *Walking about the room.* At least, that's not my way.

EKDAL: No, no, that's not for Hjalmar.

HJALMAR: I don't know why I should always provide the entertainment, when I'm out in society so rarely. Let the others make an effort. There those fellows go from one banquet to the next, eating and drinking day in and day out. So let them do their tricks in return for all the good food they get.

GINA: But you didn't say that there?

HJALMAR *humming:*   Um—um—um—they were told a thing or two.

EKDAL: Right to the nobility!

HJALMAR: I don't see why not. *Casually.* Later we had a little quibble about Tokay.

EKDAL: Tokay, you mean? That's a fine wine, that.

HJALMAR *coming to a halt:*   On occasion. But I must tell you that not all years are equally good. Everything depends strictly on how much sun the grapes have had.

GINA: Really? Oh, Hjalmar, you know everything.

EKDAL: And they could argue about that?

HJALMAR: They tried to. But then they were informed that it's exactly the same with court officials. Among them as well, all years are not equally fine—it was said.

GINA: The things you think of!

EKDAL: He—he! So you served that up to them, eh?

HJALMAR: Smack between the eyes they got it.

EKDAL: Hear, Gina! He laid that one smack between the eyes of the nobility.

GINA: Just think, smack between the eyes.

HJALMAR: That's right. But I don't want a lot of talk about this. One doesn't speak of such things. Everything really went off in the most friendly spirit, naturally. They're all pleasant, genial people. How could I hurt their feelings? Never!

EKDAL: But smack between the eyes—

HEDVIG *ingratiatingly:* How nice to see you in evening clothes, Daddy. You look so well in them.

HJALMAR: Yes, don't you think so? And this one here really fits very well. It's almost as if it were made for me. A bit snug under the arms, maybe—help me, Hedvig. *Takes off the coat.* I'd rather wear my jacket. What did you do with my jacket, Gina.

GINA: Here it is. *Brings the jacket and helps him into it.*

HJALMAR: There! Now don't forget to give Molvik his coat back first thing in the morning.

GINA *putting it away:* I'll take care of it.

HJALMAR *stretching:* Ah, but this feels much more comfortable. This kind of free and easy dress suits my whole personality better. Don't you think so, Hedvig?

HEDVIG: Yes, Daddy.

HJALMAR: And when I pull my necktie out into a pair of flowing ends— so! Look! What then?

HEDVIG: Yes, it goes so well with your moustache and your long, curly hair.

HJALMAR: Curly? I wouldn't say it's that. I'd call it wavy.

HEDVIG: Yes, but it *is* so curly.

HJALMAR: No—wavy.

HEDVIG *after a moment, tugs at his sleeve:* Daddy!

HJALMAR: What is it?

HEDVIG: Oh, you know what.

HJALMAR: No, I don't. Honestly.

HEDVIG *laughing fretfully:* Come on, Daddy, don't tease me any longer.

HJALMAR: But what is it, then?

HEDVIG *shaking him:* Silly! Out with it, Daddy. You know—all the treats you promised me.

HJALMAR: Oh—no! How did I ever forget that?

HEDVIG: No, you can't fool me. Shame on you! Where have you hidden it?

HJALMAR: So help me if I didn't forget. But wait a minute! I've got something else for you, Hedvig. *Goes over and rummages in his coat pockets.*

HEDVIG *jumping and clapping her hands:* Oh, Mother, Mother!

GINA: You see, if you're only patient enough, then—

HJALMAR *returning with a piece of paper:* See, here we have it.

HEDVIG: That? But that's just a piece of paper.

HJALMAR: It's the bill of fare, the complete bill of fare. Here it says "menu"; that means "bill of fare."

HEDVIG: Don't you have anything else?

HJALMAR: I forgot to bring anything else, I tell you. But take my word for it; it's bad business, this doting on sugar candy. Now, if you'll sit down at the table and read the menu aloud, I'll describe for you just how each dish tasted. How's that, Hedvig?

HEDVIG *swallowing her tears:* Thanks. *She sits, but does not read.* GINA *makes gestures at her, which* HJALMAR *notices.*

HJALMAR *pacing about the floor:* What incredible things a family breadwinner is asked to remember; and if he forgets even the tiniest detail—immediately he's met with sour faces. Well, he has to get used to that, too. *Pauses at the stove beside* EKDAL. Have you looked inside this evening, Father?

EKDAL: Oh, that you can be sure of. She's gone into the basket.

HJALMAR: No! Into the basket? Then she's begun to get used to it.

EKDAL: Yes. You see, it was just as I predicted. But now there are some little things to do—

HJALMAR: Some improvements, eh?

EKDAL: But they've got to be done, you know.

HJALMAR: All right, let's talk a bit about the improvements, Father. Come, we'll sit here on the sofa.

EKDAL: Very good. Umm—think I'll fill my pipe first. Needs cleaning, too. Hmm. *He goes into his room.*

GINA *smiling at* HJALMAR: Clean his pipe!

HJALMAR: Ah, now, Gina, let him be. Poor shipwrecked old man. Yes, the improvements—it's best we get those off our hands tomorrow.

GINA: Tommorow you won't have time, Hjalmar—

HEDVIG *interrupting:* Oh yes, he will, Mother!

GINA: Remember those prints that need retouching. They've been called for so many times already.

HJALMAR: Oh yes, those prints again. They'll be finished in no time. Did any new orders come in?

GINA: No such luck. For tomorrow, I have nothing except those two portrait sittings you know about.

HJALMAR: Nothing else? Ah, well, if people won't even try, then naturally—

GINA: But what else can I do? I've put ads in the papers time and again.

HJALMAR: Yes, ads, ads—you see what a help they are. And of course nobody's been to look at the spare room either?

GINA: No, not yet.

HJALMAR: That was to be expected. If one doesn't keep wide awake—Gina, you've simply got to pull yourself together.

HEDVIG *going to him:* Let me bring you your flute, Daddy.

HJALMAR: No, no flute. I want no pleasures in this world. *Pacing about.* Ah, yes, work—I'll be deep in work tomorrow; there'll be no lack of *that.* I'll sweat and slave as long as my strength holds out—

GINA: But Hjalmar dear, I didn't mean it that way.

HEDVIG: Can't I get you a bottle of beer, then?

HJALMAR: Absolutely not. There's nothing I need. *Stopping.* Beer? Did you say beer?

HEDVIG *vivaciously:*   Yes, Daddy, lovely cool beer.

HJALMAR: Well—if you really insist, I suppose you could bring in a bottle.

GINA: Yes, do that. Then we'll have it cozy.

HEDVIG *runs toward the kitchen door.* HJALMAR *by the stove stops her, gazes at her, clasps her about the head and hugs her to him.*

HJALMAR: Hedvig! Hedvig!

HEDVIG *with tears of joy:*   Oh, my dearest Daddy!

HJALMAR: No, don't call me that. There I sat, helping myself at a rich man's table, gorging myself with all good things—! I could at least have remembered—

GINA *sitting at the table:*   Oh, nonsense, Hjalmar.

HJALMAR: Yes, I could! But you mustn't be too hard on me. You both know I love you anyway.

HEDVIG *throwing her arms around him:*   And we love you too, so much!

HJALMAR: And if I should seem unreasonable at times, then—good Lord—remember that I am a man assailed by a host of cares. Ah, yes! *Drying his eyes.* No beer at a time like this. Bring me my flute. HEDVIG *runs to the bookcase and fetches it.* Thank you. There—so. With flute in hand, and you two close by me—ah!

HEDVIG *sits at the table by* GINA, HJALMAR *walks back and forth, then forcefully begins to play a Bohemian folk dance, but in a slow elegiac tempo with sentimental intonation. After a moment he breaks off the melody and extends his left hand to* GINA.

HJALMAR *with feeling:*   So what if we skimp and scrape along under this roof, Gina—it's still our home. And I'll say this: it's good to be here. *He starts playing again; immediately there comes a knock on the hall door.*

GINA *getting up:*   Shh, Hjalmar. I think someone's there.

HJALMAR *returning the flute to the bookcase:*   What, again! GINA *goes over and opens the door.*

GREGERS WERLE *out in the hallway:*   Excuse me—

GINA *drawing back slightly:*   Oh!

GREGERS: But doesn't Mr. Ekdal, the photographer, live here?

GINA: Yes, that's right.

HJALMAR *going toward the door:*   Gregers! Is it really you? Well, come right in.

GREGERS *entering:*   I said I was going to drop in on you.

HJALMAR: But tonight? Have you left the party?

GREGERS: Left both party and family home. Good evening, Mrs. Ekdal. I don't know whether you recognize me?

GINA: Oh yes. Young Mr. Werle is not so hard to recognize.

GREGERS: No. I look like my mother, and you remember her, no doubt.

HJALMAR: Did you say you'd left your home?

GREGERS: Yes, I've moved into a hotel.

HJALMAR: I see. Well, now that you've come, take off your things and sit down.

GREGERS: Thank you. *Removes his overcoat. He is dressed now in a simple grey suit of somewhat rustic cut.*

HJALMAR: Here, on the sofa. Make yourself at home.

GREGERS *sits on the sofa,* HJALMAR *on a chair at the table.*

GREGERS *looking around:*   So this is where you work, then, Hjalmar. And you live here as well.

HJALMAR: This is the studio, as you can see—

GINA: There's more room in here, so we like it better.

HJALMAR: We had a better place before; but this apartment has one great advantage: it has such wonderful adjoining rooms—

GINA: And so we have a room on the other side of the hall that we can rent out.

GREGERS *to* HJALMAR: Ah, then you have lodgers, too.

HJALMAR: No, not yet. It's not that easy, you know. One has to keep wide awake. *To* HEDVIG. But how about that beer?

HEDVIG *nods and goes into the kitchen.*

GREGERS: So that's your daughter, then?

HJALMAR: Yes, that's Hedvig.

GREGERS: An only child?

HJALMAR: She's the only one, yes. She's the greatest joy of our lives, and—*Lowering his voice*—also our deepest sorrow, Gregers.

GREGERS: What do you mean?

HJALMAR: Yes. You see, there's the gravest imminent danger of her losing her sight.

GREGERS: Going blind!

HJALMAR: Yes. So far only the first signs are present, and things may go well for a while. All the same, the doctor has warned us. It will come inevitably.

GREGERS: What a dreadful misfortune! How did this happen?

HJALMAR *sighing:*   Heredity, most likely.

GREGERS *startled:*   Heredity?

GINA: Hjalmar's mother also had bad eyes.

HJALMAR: Yes, so my father says. I don't remember her.

GREGERS: Poor child. And how is she taking it?

HJALMAR: Oh, you can well imagine, we haven't the heart to tell her. She suspects nothing. She's carefree, gay, and singing like a tiny bird, she's fluttering into life's eternal night. *Overcome.* Oh, it's a brutal blow for me, Gregers.

HEDVIG *brings in beer and glasses on a tray, which she sets down on the table.*

HJALMAR *stroking her head:*   Thanks. Thanks, Hedvig.

HEDVIG *puts her arms around his neck and whispers in his ear.*

HJALMAR: No. No bread and butter now. *Looking over.* Or maybe Gregers will have a piece?

GREGERS *making a gesture of refusal:*   No. No, thanks.

HJALMAR *his tone still mournful:*   Well, you can bring in a little anyway. If you have a crust, that would be fine. And please, put enough butter on, too.

HEDVIG *nods contentedly and returns to the kitchen.*

GREGERS *after following her with his eyes:*   In every other respect she looks so strong and healthy.

GINA: Yes, thank God, she's got nothing else wrong with her.

GREGERS: She'll certainly look like you when she grows up, Mrs. Ekdal. How old is she now?

GINA: Hedvig is almost fourteen exactly; her birthday's the day after tomorrow.

GREGERS: Rather tall for her age.

GINA: Yes, she's shot right up this past year.

GREGERS: Nothing like the growth of a child to show us how old we're getting. How long is it you've been married now?

GINA: We've been married now for—yes, near fifteen years.

GREGERS: No, truly! Has it been that long?

GINA *looking at him, becoming wary:*   Yes, no doubt about it.

HJALMAR: That's right. Fifteen years, short a few months. *Changing the subject.* They must have been long years for you, Gregers, up there at the works.

GREGERS: They were long while I was living them—but now I scarcely know what became of the time.

Old EKDAL *enters from his room, without his pipe, but with his old military cap on his head; his walk is a bit unsteady.*

EKDAL: There, now, Hjalmar. Now we can settle down and talk about that—umm. What was it again?

HJALMAR *going toward him:*   Father, someone is here. Gregers Werle. I don't know if you remember him.

EKDAL *regarding GREGERS, who has gotten up:*   Werle? That's the son, isn't it? What does he want with me?

HJALMAR: Nothing; it's me he's come to see.

EKDAL: Well, then nothing's up, eh?

HJALMAR: No, of course not.

EKDAL *swinging his arms:*   It's not that I'm scared of anything, you know, but—

GREGERS *going over to him:*   I just want to greet you from your old hunting grounds, Lieutenant Ekdal.

EKDAL: Hunting grounds?

GREGERS: Yes, up there around the Hoidal works.

EKDAL: Oh, up there. Yes, I was well known there once.

GREGERS: In those days you were a tremendous hunter.

EKDAL: So I was. Still am, maybe. You're looking at my uniform. I ask nobody permission to wear it in here. As long as I don't walk in the streets with it—HEDVIG *brings a plate of buttered bread, which she places on the table.*

HJALMAR: Sit down, Father, and have a glass of beer. Help yourself, Gregers.

EKDAL *stumbles, muttering, over to the sofa.* GREGERS *sits on the chair nearest him,* HJALMAR *on the other side of* GREGERS. GINA *sits near the table and sews;* HEDVIG *stands beside her father.*

GREGERS: Do you remember, Lieutenant Ekdal, when Hjalmar and I would come up to visit you summers and at Christmas?

EKDAL: Did you? No, no, no, I don't recall. But I'll tell you something: I've been a first-rate hunter. Bear— I've shot them, too. Shot nine in all.

GREGERS *looking sympathetically at him:*   And now you hunt no more.

EKDAL: Oh, I wouldn't say *that*, boy. Get some hunting in now and then. Yes, but not that kind there. The woods, you see—the woods, the woods— *Drinks.* How do the woods look up there?

GREGERS: Not so fine as in your time. They've been cut into heavily.

EKDAL: Cut into? *More quietly, as if in fear.* It's a dangerous business, that. It catches up with you. The woods take revenge.

HJALMAR *filling his glass:*   Here, a little more, Father.

GREGERS: How can a man like you—such an outdoorsman—live in the middle of a stuffy city, cooped up in these four walls?

EKDAL *half laughs and glances at* HJALMAR: Oh, it's not so bad here. Not bad at all.

GREGERS: But all those other things, the very roots of your soul—that cool, sweeping breeze, that free life of the moors and forests, among the animals and birds—?

EKDAL *smiling:*   Hjalmar, should we show him?

HJALMAR *quickly and a bit embarrassed:*   No, no, Father, not tonight.

GREGERS: What's that he wants to show me?

HJALMAR: Oh, it's only a sort of—you can see it some other time.

GREGERS *speaking again to* EKDAL: Yes, my point was this, Lieutenant Ekdal, that now you might as well return with me to the works, for I'm sure to be leaving very soon. Without a doubt, you could get some copying to do up there; and here you've nothing in the world to stir your blood and make you happy.

EKDAL *staring at him, astonished:*   I have nothing, nothing at all—!

GREGERS: Of course you have Hjalmar, but then again, he has his own. And a man like you, who's always felt himself so drawn to whatever is free and wild—

EKDAL *striking the table:*   Hjalmar, now he's *got* to see it!

HJALMAR: But Father, is it worth it now? It's dark, you know—

EKDAL: Nonsense! There's moonlight. *Getting up.* I say he's got to see it. Let me by. Come and help me, Hjalmar!

HEDVIG: Oh yes, do that, Father!

HJALMAR *getting up:*   Well—all right.

GREGERS *to* GINA: What's this all about?

GINA: Oh, you really mustn't expect anything special.

EKDAL *and* HJALMAR *have gone to the back wall to push aside the two halves of the double door;* HEDVIG *helps her grandfather, while* GREGERS *remains standing by the sofa and* GINA *sits, imperturbably sewing. The doorway opens on an extensive, irregular loft room with many nooks and corners, and two separate chimney shafts ascending through it. Clear moonlight streams through skylights into certain parts of the large room; others lie in deep shadow.*

EKDAL *to* GREGERS: All the way over here, please.

GREGERS *going over to them:*   What *is* it, then?

EKDAL: See for yourself—hmm.

HJALMAR *somewhat self-conscious:*   All this belongs to Father, you understand.

GREGERS *peering in at the doorway:*   So you keep poultry, Lieutenant Ekdal!

EKDAL: I'll say we keep poultry! They're roosting now; but you just ought to see our poultry by daylight!

HEDVIG: And then there's a—

EKDAL: Shh, shh—don't say anything yet.

GREGERS: And you've got pigeons too, I see.

EKDAL: Oh yes, it might just be we've got some pigeons. They have their nesting boxes up there under the eaves; pigeons like to perch high, you know.

HJALMAR: They're not ordinary pigeons, all of them.

EKDAL: Ordinary! No, I should say not! We have tumblers, and we have a couple of pouters also. But look here! Can you see that hutch over there by the wall?

GREGERS: Yes. What do you use that for?

EKDAL: The rabbits sleep there at night, boy.

GREGERS: Well, so you have rabbits too?

EKDAL: Yes, what the devil do you think we have but rabbits! He asks if we have rabbits, Hjalmar! Hmm! But now listen, this is really something! This is it! Out of the way, Hedvig. Stand right here—that's it— and look straight down there. Do you see a basket there with straw in it?

GREGERS: Yes, and there's a bird nesting in the basket.

EKDAL: Hmm! "A bird"—

GREGERS: Isn't it a duck?

EKDAL *hurt:*   Yes, of course it's a duck.

HJALMAR: But what *kind* of duck?

HEDVIG: It's not just any old duck—

EKDAL: Shh!

GREGERS: And it's no exotic breed, either.

EKDAL: No, Mr.—Werle, it's not any exotic breed—because it's a wild duck.

GREGERS: No, is it really? A wild duck?

EKDAL: Oh yes, that's what it is. That "bird" as you said—that's a wild duck. That's our wild duck, boy.

HEDVIG: *My* wild duck—I own it.

GREGERS: And it can survive up here indoors? And do well?

EKDAL: You've got to understand, she's got a trough of water to splash around in.

HJALMAR: Fresh water every other day.

GINA *turning to* HJALMAR: Hjalmar dear, it's freezing cold in here now.

EKDAL: Hmm, let's close up, then. Doesn't pay to disturb their rest either. Lend a hand, Hedvig dear. HJALMAR *and* HEDVIG *push the double doors together.* Another time you can get a proper look at her. *Sits in the armchair by the stove.* Oh, they're most curious, the wild ducks, you know.

GREGERS: But how did you capture it, Lieutenant Ekdal?

EKDAL: Didn't capture it myself. There's a certain man here in town we can thank for it.

GREGERS *starts slightly:*   That man—it wouldn't be my father?

EKDAL: Exactly right—your father. Hmm.

HJALMAR: It was odd you were able to guess that, Gregers.

GREGERS: Well, you said before that you owed Father for so many different things, so I thought here too—

GINA: But we didn't get the duck from Mr. Werle himself—

EKDAL: We might just as well thank Haakon Werle for her anyhow, Gina. *To* GREGERS. He was out in his boat—follow me?—and he shot for her, but he sees so bad now, your father, that—hm—he only winged her.

GREGERS: I see. She took some shot in her body.

HJALMAR: Yes, some one, two—three pieces.

HEDVIG: She got it under the wing, and so she couldn't fly.

GREGERS: Ah, so she dived right for the bottom, eh?

EKDAL *sleepily, with a thick voice:*   You can bet on that. They always do, the wild ducks—streak for the bottom, deep as they can get, boy—bite right into the weeds and sea moss—and all that devil's beard that grows down there. And then they never come up again.

GREGERS: But Lieutenant Ekdal, *your* wild duck came up again.

EKDAL: He had such a remarkably clever dog, your father. And that dog—he dove down and brought her up.

GREGERS *turning to* HJALMAR: And then you got her here.

HJALMAR: Not directly. First she went home to your father's, but there she didn't do well, so Pettersen got his orders to put an end to her—

EKDAL *half asleep:*   Hm—yes, Pettersen—that bonehead—

HJALMAR *speaking more softly:*   That's the way we got her, you see. Father knows Pettersen a bit and when he heard all this about the wild duck, he arranged to have her handed over to us.

GREGERS: And now she's absolutely thriving in that attic room.

HJALMAR: Yes, it's incredible. She's gotten fat. I think she's been in there so long, too, that she's forgotten her old wild life, and that's what it all comes down to.

GREGERS: You're certainly right there, Hjalmar. Just don't let her ever catch sight of the sea and the sky— But I mustn't stay any longer, for I think your father's asleep.

HJALMAR: Oh, don't bother about that.

GREGERS: But incidentally—you said you had a room for rent, a free room?

HJALMAR: Yes. Why? Do you know someone, perhaps—?

GREGERS: Could I take that room?

HJALMAR: You?

GINA: No, not *you*, Mr. Werle—

GREGERS: Could I take the room? If so, I'll move in first thing in the morning.

HJALMAR: By all means, with the greatest pleasure—

GINA: No, but Mr. Werle, it's not at all the room for *you*.

HJALMAR: But Gina, how can you say that?

GINA: Oh, the room isn't large enough, or light enough, and—

GREGERS: That really doesn't matter, Mrs. Ekdal.

HJALMAR: I think it's a very pleasant room, and it's not badly furnished, either.

GINA: But remember those two who live right below.

GREGERS: What two are those?

GINA: Oh, one of them's been a private tutor—

HJALMAR: That's Molvik, from the university.

GINA: And then there's a doctor named Relling.

GREGERS: Relling? I know him somewhat. He practiced a while up in Hoidal.

GINA: They're a pretty wild pair, those fellows. They go out on the town evenings and then come home in the dead of night, and they're not always so—

GREGERS: One gets used to that soon enough. I'm hoping things will go for me the same as with the wild duck—

GINA: Well, I think you ought to sleep on it first, anyway.

GREGERS: You're not very anxious to have me in the house, Mrs. Ekdal.

GINA: Goodness, what makes you think that?

HJALMAR: Yes, Gina, this is really peculiar of you. *To* GREGERS. But tell me, do you expect to stay here in town for a while?

GREGERS *putting on his overcoat:* Yes, now I expect to stay on.

HJALMAR: But not at home with your father? What do you plan to do with yourself?

GREGERS: Yes, if I only knew that—then I'd be doing all right. But when one carries the cross of a name like Gregers—"Gregers"—and then "Werle" coming after—have you ever heard anything so disgusting?

HJALMAR: Oh, I don't agree at all.

GREGERS: Ugh! Phew! I feel I'd like to spit on any man with a name like that. But once you have to bear that cross of being Gregers—Werle in this world, as I do—

HJALMAR *laughing:* If you weren't Gregers Werle, who would you want to be?

GREGERS: If I could choose, above all else I'd like to be a clever dog.

GINA: A dog!

HEDVIG *involuntarily:* Oh no!

GREGERS: Yes. A really fantastic, clever dog, the kind that goes to the bottom after wild ducks when they dive under and bite fast into the weeds down in the mire.

HJALMAR: You know, Gregers—I can't follow a word you're saying.

GREGERS: Never mind. There's really nothing very remarkable in it. But tomorrow morning, early, I'll be moving in. *To* GINA. I won't be any trouble to you; I do everything for myself. *To* HJALMAR. The rest we can talk over tomorrow. Good night, Mrs. Ekdal. *Nods to* HEDVIG. Good night.

GINA: Good night, Mr. Werle.

HEDVIG: Good night.

HJALMAR *who has lit a lamp:* Just a minute. I'd better light your way; it's quite dark on the stairs.

GREGERS *and* HJALMAR *go out through the hall.*

GINA *gazing into space, her sewing in her lap:* Wasn't that a queer business, his wanting to be a dog?

HEDVIG: I'll tell you something, Mother—it seemed to me he meant something else by that.

GINA: What else could he mean?

HEDVIG: I don't know—but it was just as if he meant something else from what he said, all the time.

GINA: Do you think so? It was strange, all right.

HJALMAR *coming back:* The light was still lit. *Putting out the lamp and setting it down.* Ah, at last one can get a bite to eat. *Beginning on the bread and butter.* Well, now you see, Gina—if you simply keep wide awake, then—

GINA: What do you mean, wide awake?

HJALMAR: Well, it was lucky, then, that we got the room rented out for a while at last. And think—to a person like Gregers—a good old friend.

GINA: Yes. I don't know what to say. I don't.

HEDVIG: Oh, Mother, you'll see. It'll be fun.

HJALMAR: You really are peculiar. Before you were so eager to rent, and now you don't like it.

GINA: Yes, Hjalmar, if it could only have been somebody else. What do you think the old man will say?

HJALMAR: Old Werle? This doesn't concern him.

GINA: But you can sure bet that something has come up between them,

since the son is moving out. You know how those two get along together.

HJALMAR: Yes, that may well be, but—

GINA: And now maybe the old man thinks it's you that's behind—

HJALMAR: He can think that as much as he likes! Old Werle has done a
tremendous amount for me. God knows, I'm aware of that. But even
so, I can't make myself eternally dependent on him.

GINA: But Hjalmar dear, that can have its effect on Grandfather. He may
now lose that miserable little income he gets from Graaberg.

HJALMAR: I could almost say, so much the better! Isn't it rather humiliating for a man like me to see his gray-haired father go around like an
outcast? But now time is gathering to a ripeness, I think. *Takes another
piece of bread and butter.* Just as sure as I've got a mission in life, I'm
going to carry it out!

HEDVIG: Oh yes, Daddy! Do!

GINA: Shh! Don't wake him up.

HJALMAR *more quietly:* I *will* carry it out, I tell you. There will come a
day when— And that's why it's good we got the room rented out, for
now I'm more independently fixed. Any man *must* be that, who's got a
mission in life. *Over by the armchair; emotionally.* Poor old white-haired
Father—lean on your Hjalmar. He has broad shoulders—powerful
shoulders, in any case. One fine day you'll wake up and—*To* GINA.
You do believe that, don't you?

GINA *getting up:* Yes, of course I do. But first let's see about getting him
to bed.

HJALMAR: Yes, let's do that.

Gently they lift up the old man.

ACT THREE

HJALMAR EKDAL's *studio. It is morning. Daylight streams through the large
window in the sloping roof; the curtain is drawn back.*

HJALMAR *is sitting at the table, busy retouching a photograph; many other pictures lie in front of him. After a moment* GINA, *wearing a hat and coat, enters
by the hall door; she has a covered basket on her arm.*

HJALMAR: Back so soon, Gina?

GINA: Oh yes. Got to keep moving. *She sets the basket on a chair and takes
her coat off.*

HJALMAR: Did you look in on Gregers?

GINA: Um-hm, I certainly did. Looks real nice in there. The moment he
came, he got his room in beautiful shape.

HJALMAR: Oh?

GINA: Yes. He wanted to do everything himself, he said. So he starts
building a fire in the stove, and the next thing he's closed down the
damper so the whole room is full of smoke. Phew! What a stink,
enough to—

HJALMAR: Oh no!

GINA: But that's not the best part! So then he wants to put it out, so he empties his whole water pitcher into the stove and now the floor's swimming in the worst muck.

HJALMAR: That's a nuisance.

GINA: I got the janitor's wife to come and scrub up after him, the pig; but it'll be unfit to live in till afternoon.

HJALMAR: What's he doing with himself in the meantime?

GINA: Thought he'd take a little walk, he said.

HJALMAR: I was in to see him for a moment too—after you left.

GINA: I heard that. You asked him for lunch.

HJALMAR: Just the tiniest little midday snack, you understand. It's the very first day—we could hardly avoid it. You always have something in the house.

GINA: I'll see what I can find.

HJALMAR: But now don't make it too skimpy. Because Relling and Molvik are dropping in too, I think. I just met Relling on the stairs, you see, so of course I had to—

GINA: Oh? Must we have those two also?

HJALMAR: Good Lord, a couple of sandwiches more or less; what's the difference?

EKDAL *opening his door and looking in:*   Say, listen, Hjalmar—*Noticing* GINA. Oh, well.

GINA: Is there something Grandfather wants?

EKDAL: Oh no. Let it be. Hmm. *Goes in again.*

GINA *picking up the basket:*   Keep a sharp eye on him so he doesn't go out.

HJALMAR: Oh yes, I'll do that. Listen, Gina, a little herring salad would be awfully good—because Relling and Molvik were out on a binge last night.

GINA: Just so they don't come before I'm ready—

HJALMAR: Not a chance. Take your time.

GINA: That's fine, then—and meanwhile you can get a little work done.

HJALMAR: Can't you see how I'm working! I'm working for all I'm worth!

GINA: Because then you'll have *those* off your hands, you know. *She carries the basket out to the kitchen.* HJALMAR *sits for a while, tinting the photograph in a glum and listless manner.*

EKDAL *peeks in, peers about the studio, and whispers:*   Are you busy, boy?

HJALMAR: Of course. I'm sitting here struggling with these pictures—

EKDAL: Oh well, don't bother. If you're so busy, then—Hm! *He reenters his room, leaving the door ajar.*

HJALMAR *continues a moment in silence, then puts down the brush and goes over to the door:*   Father, are *you* busy?

EKDAL *grumbling from within:*   When you're busy—I'm busy too. Huh!

HJALMAR: Yes, of course. *Returns to his work.*

EKDAL *a moment later, coming in again:*   Hm. Well, now, Hjalmar, I'm really not *that* busy.

HJALMAR: I thought you had copying to do.

EKDAL: Oh, the devil! Can't he, Graaberg, wait a day or two? I'm sure it's no matter of life or death.

HJALMAR: No, and you're no slave, either.

EKDAL: And then there was that other business inside—

HJALMAR: Yes, that's just it. Maybe you want to go in? Shall I open it up for you?

EKDAL: Wouldn't be a bad idea, really?

HJALMAR *getting up:*   And then we'd have *that* off our hands.

EDKAL: Yes, exactly. And it has to be ready first thing tomorrow. But it *is* tomorrow, isn't it?

HJALMAR: It certainly is tomorrow.

HJALMAR *and* EKDAL *each push back one of the double doors. Within, morning sunlight shines through the skylights. A few doves fly back and forth; others perch, cooing, on the rafters. Chickens cackle now and then from back in the loft.*

HJALMAR: There, now you can get in, Father.

EKDAL *going in:*   Aren't you coming along?

HJALMAR: Well, you know what—I almost think—*Sees* GINA *in the kitchen doorway.* I? No, I haven't the time; I've got to work. But that means our new mechanism—

He pulls a cord; inside a curtain descends, its lower portion composed of a strip of old sailcloth, the upper part being a piece of worn-out fishnetting. By this means, the floor of the loft is rendered invisible.

HJALMAR *returning to the table:*   That's that. Now at last I can work in peace for a while.

GINA: Is he in there, romping around again?

HJALMAR: Isn't that better than having him run down to Mrs. Eriksen's? *Sitting.* Is there anything you want? You look so—

GINA: I only wanted to ask, do you think we can set the lunch table in here?

HJALMAR: Well, we haven't any portraits scheduled that early, have we?

GINA: No. I don't expect anybody except that couple who want to be taken together.

HJALMAR: Why the devil can't they be taken together some other day?

GINA: Now, Hjalmar dear, I've got them booked for during your midday nap.

HJALMAR: Well, that's fine, then. So we'll eat in here.

GINA: All right. But there's no hurry about setting the table; you can certainly use it a while longer.

HJALMAR: Oh, it's obvious I'm using the table as much as I can!

GINA: Because then you'll be free later on, you know. *She goes back into the kitchen. A short pause.*

EKDAL *at the door to the loft, behind the net:*   Hjalmar!

HJALMAR: Well?

EKDAL: 'Fraid we'll have to move the water trough after all.

HJALMAR: Yes, that's what I've been saying all along.

EKDAL: Hm—hm—hm. *Disappears from the doorway.*

HJALMAR *works a bit, glances toward the loft, and half rises.* HEDVIG *enters from the kitchen.*

HJALMAR *hurriedly sitting again:* What do you want?

HEDVIG: I was just coming in to you, Father.

HJALMAR *after a moment:* You seem to be kind of snooping around. Are you checking up, maybe?

HEDVIG: No, not at all.

HJALMAR: What's Mother doing out there now?

HEDVIG: Oh, she's half through the herring salad. *Going over to the table.* Don't you have some little thing I could help you with, Daddy?

HJALMAR: Oh no. It's better just to leave me alone with all this—so long as my strength holds out. Nothing to worry about, Hedvig—if only your father can keep his health—

HEDVIG: Oh, Daddy, no. That's horrid; you mustn't talk like that. *She wanders about a little, stops by the loft doorway, and looks in.*

HJALMAR: What's he trying to do now?

HEDVIG: It must be a new pathway up to the water trough.

HJALMAR: He can't possibly rig that up on his own! And I'm condemned to sit here—!

HEDVIG *going to him:* Let *me* take the brush, Daddy. I know I can.

HJALMAR: Oh, nonsense, you'll only ruin your eyes.

HEDVIG: No such thing. Give me the brush.

HJALMAR *getting up:* Well, it'll only be for a minute or two.

HEDVIG: Pooh! How could that hurt me? *Takes the brush.* There now. *Sitting.* And here's one to go by.

HJALMAR: But don't ruin your eyes! Hear me? I won't take the blame; you can take the blame yourself—you hear me?

HEDVIG *at work retouching:* Yes, yes, sure I will.

HJALMAR: You're wonderfully clever, Hedvig. Just for a couple of minutes now.

He slips around the edge of the curtain into the loft. HEDVIG *sits at her work.* HJALMAR *and* EKDAL *are heard arguing inside.*

HJALMAR *appearing behind the net:* Hedvig, just hand me the pliers from the shelf. And the chisel, please. *Turning over his shoulder.* Yes, now you'll see, Father. Will you give me a chance to show you the way I mean! HEDVIG *fetches the desired tools from the bookcase and passes them in to him.* Ah, thanks. See, dear, it was a good thing I came. *He vanishes from the doorway; sounds of carpentry and bantering are heard.* HEDVIG *remains, looking in at them. A moment later, a knock at the hall door; she fails to notice it.*

GREGERS *bareheaded, and without his overcoat, enters, hesitating slightly at the door:* Hm—

HEDVIG *turning and going toward him:* Good morning. Please come in.

GREGERS: Thanks. *Looking at the loft.* You seem to have workmen in the house.

HEDVIG: No, that's only Father and Grandfather. I'll go tell them.

GREGERS: No, no, don't bother. I'd rather wait a bit. *He sits on the sofa.*

HEDVIG: It's so messy here—*Starts to remove the photographs.*

GREGERS: Oh, they can stay. Are those some pictures that have to be finished?

HEDVIG: Yes, it's a little job I'm helping Daddy with.

GREGERS: Please don't let me disturb you.

HEDVIG: All right. *She gathers her materials around her and sets to work again;* GREGERS *meanwhile regards her in silence.*

GREGERS: Did the wild duck sleep well last night?

HEDVIG: Yes, I'm sure she did, thanks.

GREGERS *turning toward the loft:*   It looks so very different by daylight than it did by moonlight.

HEDVIG: Yes, it can change so completely. In the morning it looks different from in the afternoon; and when it rains it's different from when it's clear.

GREGERS: Have you noticed that?

HEDVIG: Sure. You can't help it.

GREGERS: And do you like it in there with the wild duck, too?

HEDVIG: Yes, whenever I can be there—

GREGERS: But of course you don't have much free time; you do go to school, don't you?

HEDVIG: No, not anymore. Daddy's afraid I'll hurt my eyes.

GREGERS: Oh. Then he tutors you himself.

HEDVIG: Daddy's promised to, but he hasn't found time for that yet.

GREGERS: But isn't there anyone else to help you a little?

HEDVIG: Sure, there's Mr. Molvik, but he isn't always exactly, really— well—

GREGERS: He gets drunk, eh?

HEDVIG: He *certainly* does.

GREGERS: Well, then you do have time to yourself. And inside—I'll bet in there it's just like a world of its own—am I right?

HEDVIG: Oh, completely! And then there are so many wonderful things.

GREGERS: Really?

HEDVIG: Yes, big cupboards with books in them; and lots of the books have pictures.

GREGERS: Ah!

HEDVIG: And then there's an old cabinet with drawers and compartments, and a huge clock with figures that are supposed to come out. But the clock doesn't go anymore.

GREGERS: Even time doesn't exist in there—with the wild duck.

HEDVIG: Yes. And then there's an old watercolor set and things like that. And then all the books.

GREGERS: And of course you read the books?

HEDVIG: Oh yes, whenever I can. But they're mostly in English, and I don't understand that. But then I look at the pictures. There's one just enormous book called *Harryson's History of London;* it must be a hundred years old, and it's got ever so many pictures in it. At the front there's a picture of Death with an hourglass and a girl. I think that's horrible. But then there are all the other pictures of churches and castles and streets and great ships sailing on the ocean.

GREGERS: But tell me, where did all these rare things come from!

HEDVIG: Oh, an old sea captain lived here once, and he brought them home. They called him "the flying Dutchman"—and that's the strangest thing, because he wasn't a Dutchman at all.

GREGERS: No?

HEDVIG: No. But then he didn't come back finally, and he left all these things behind.

GREGERS: Listen, tell me—when you sit in there and look at pictures, don't you ever want to go out and see the real world all for yourself?

HEDVIG: No, never! I'm going to stay at home always and help Daddy and Mother.

GREGERS: You mean finishing photographs?

HEDVIG: No, not just that. Most of all, I'd like to learn how to engrave pictures like those in the English books.

GREGERS: Hm. What does your father say to that?

HEDVIG: I don't think he likes it. Daddy's so funny about such things. Just think, he talks about me learning basketmaking and wickerwork! But I don't see anything in *that*.

GREGERS: Oh no, I don't either.

HEDVIG: But Daddy's right when he says that if I'd learned how to make baskets, I could have made the new basket for the wild duck.

GREGERS: You could have, yes—and that really was up to you.

HEDVIG: Yes, because it's *my* wild duck.

GREGERS: Yes, of course it is.

HEDVIG: Uh-huh, I own it. But Daddy and Grandpa can borrow it as much as they want.

GREGERS: Oh? What do they do with it?

HEDVIG: Oh, they look after it and build things for it and so on.

GREGERS: I can well imagine. The wild duck rules supreme in there, doesn't she?

HEDVIG: Yes, she does, and that's because she's a *real* wild bird. And then it's so sad for her; the poor thing has no one to turn to.

GREGERS: No family, like the rabbits—

HEDVIG: No. Even the chickens have all the others that they were baby chicks with, but she's so completely apart from any of her own. So you see, everything is so really mysterious about the wild duck. There's no one who knows her, and no one who knows where she's come from, either.

GREGERS: And actually, she's been in the depths of the sea.

HEDVIG *glances at him, suppresses a smile, and asks:*   Why did you say "depths of the sea"?

GREGERS: What else should I say?

HEDVIG: You could have said "bottom of the sea"—or "the ocean's bottom"?

GREGERS: But couldn't I just as well say "depths of the sea"?

HEDVIG: Sure. But to me it sounds so strange when someone else says "depths of the sea."
GREGERS: But why? Tell me why?
HEDVIG: No, I won't. It's something so stupid.
GREGERS: It couldn't be. Now tell me why you smiled.
HEDVIG: That was because always, when all of a sudden—in a flash—I happen to think of that in there, it always seems to me that the whole room and everything in it is called "the depths of the sea"! But that's all so stupid.
GREGERS: Don't you dare say that.
HEDVIG: Oh yes, because it's only an attic.
GREGERS: Are you so sure of that?
HEDVIG *astonished:* That it's an attic!
GREGERS: Yes. Do you know that for certain?

HEDVIG, *speechless, stares at him open-mouthed.* GINA *enters from the kitchen with a tablecloth.*

GREGERS *getting up:* I'm afraid I've come too early for you.
GINA: Oh, you can find yourself a spot; it's almost ready now. Clear the table, Hedvig.

HEDVIG *puts away the materials; during the following dialogue, she and* GINA *set the table.* GREGERS *settles in the armchair and pages through an album.*

GREGERS: I hear you do retouching, Mrs. Ekdal.
GINA *with a side-glance:* Um, yes, I do that.
GREGERS: That's really very lucky.
GINA: Why "lucky"?
GREGERS: With Hjalmar a photographer, I mean.
HEDVIG: Mother does photography, too.
GINA: Oh yes, I even got taught in *that* art.
GREGERS: So we might say it's you who runs the business.
GINA: Yes, when my husband hasn't the time himself—
GREGERS: He finds himself so taken up with his old father, I suppose.
GINA: Yes, and then it's no kind of thing for a man like Hjalmar to go taking portraits of your common average.
GREGERS: I agree; but once he's chosen this line of work, then—
GINA: Mr. Werle, you must realize that my husband is not just any old photographer.
GREGERS: Well, naturally; but even so—

A shot is fired in the loft.

GREGERS *jumping up:* What's that!
GINA: Uff, now they're shooting again.
GREGERS: They shoot, also?
HEDVIG: They go hunting.

GREGERS: What! *Going to the loft doorway.* Have you gone hunting, Hjalmar?

HJALMAR *behind the net:* Are you here? I didn't realize; I was so occupied— *To* HEDVIG. And you, you didn't tell us. *Comes into the studio.*

GREGERS: Do you go shooting in the loft?

HJALMAR *producing a double-barreled pistol:* Oh, only with this here.

GINA: Yes, some day you and Grandfather'll have an accident with that there gun.

HJALMAR *annoyed:* I believe I've remarked that this type of firearm is called a pistol.

GINA: I don't see that that makes it any better.

GREGERS: So you've turned out a "hunter" as well. Hjalmar?

HJALMAR: Just a little rabbit hunt, now and then. It's mainly for Father's sake, you understand.

GINA: Men are so funny, really; they've always got to have their little diversities.

HJALMAR *angrily:* That's right, yes—they always have to have their little diversions.

GINA: Yes, that's just what I was saying.

HJALMAR: Oh, well! *To* GREGERS. So that's it, and then we're very lucky in the way the loft is placed—nobody can hear us when we're shooting. *Puts the pistol on the highest bookshelf.* Don't touch the pistol, Hedvig! One barrel's still loaded, don't forget.

GREGERS *peering through the netting:* You've got a hunting rifle too, I see.

HJALMAR: Yes, that's Father's old rifle. It won't shoot anymore; something's gone wrong with the lock. But it's a lot of fun to have anyway, because we can take it all apart and clean it and grease it and put it together again—Of course, it's mostly Father who fools around with that sort of thing.

HEDVIG *crossing to* GREGERS: Now you can really see the wild duck.

GREGERS: I was just now looking at her. She seems to drag one wing a little.

HJALMAR: Well, no wonder; she took a bad wound.

GREGERS: And then she limps a little. Isn't that so?

HJALMAR: Maybe just a tiny bit.

HEDVIG: Yes, that was the foot the dog bit her in.

HJALMAR: But she hasn't a thing wrong with her otherwise; and that's simply remarkable when you think that she's had a charge of shot in her body and been held by the teeth of a dog—

GREGERS *with a glance at* HEDVIG: And been in the depths of the sea—so long.

HEDVIG *smiling:* Yes.

GINA *arranging the table:* Oh, that sacred duck—there's been crucifixes enough made for her.

HJALMAR: Hm. Are you nearly ready?

GINA: Yes, right away. Hedvig, now you can come and help me.

GINA *and* HEDVIG *exit into the kitchen.*

HJALMAR *in an undertone:* I don't think it's so good that you stand there, watching my father. He doesn't like it. GREGERS *comes away from the loft doorway.* And it's better, too, that I close up before the others come. *Shooing away the menagerie with his hands.* Hssh! Hssh! Go 'way now! *With this he raises the curtain and draws the double doors together.* I invented these contraptions myself. It's really great fun to have such things around to take care of and fix when they get out of whack. And besides, it's absolutely necessary, you know; Gina doesn't go for rabbits and chickens out here in the studio.

GREGERS: Of course not. And I suppose it *is* your wife who manages here?

HJALMAR: My general rule is to delegate the routine matters to her, and that leaves me free to retire to the living room to think over more important things.

GREGERS: And what sort of things are these, Hjalmar?

HJALMAR: I've been wondering why you haven't asked me that before. Or maybe you haven't heard about my invention.

GREGERS: Invention? No.

HJALMAR: Oh? Then you haven't? Well, no, up there in that waste and wilderness—

GREGERS: Then you've really invented something!

HJALMAR: Not completely invented it yet, but I'm getting very close. You must realize that when I decided to dedicate my life to photography, it wasn't my idea to spend time taking pictures of a lot of nobodies.

GREGERS: Yes, that's what your wife was just now saying.

HJALMAR: I swore that if I devoted my powers to the craft, I would then exalt it to such heights that it would become both an art and a science. That's when I decided on this amazing invention.

GREGERS: And what does this invention consist of? What's its purpose?

HJALMAR: Yes, Gregers, you mustn't ask for details like that yet. It takes time, you know. And you mustn't think it's vanity that's driving me, either. I'm certainly not working for myself. Oh no, it's my life's mission that stands before me day and night.

GREGERS: What life's mission is that?

HJALMAR: Remember the silver-haired old man?

GREGERS: Your poor father. Yes, but actually what can you do for him?

HJALMAR: I can raise his self-respect from the dead—by restoring the Ekdal name to dignity and honor.

GREGERS: So that's your life's work.

HJALMAR: Yes. I am going to rescue that shipwrecked man. That's just what he suffered—shipwreck—when the storm broke over him. When all those harrowing investigations took place, he wasn't himself anymore. That pistol, there—the one we use to shoot rabbits with—it's played a part in the tragedy of the Ekdals.

GREGERS: Pistol! Oh?

HJALMAR: When he was sentenced and facing prison, he had that pistol in his hand—

GREGERS: You mean he—

HJALMAR: Yes. But he didn't dare. He was a coward. That shows how broken and degraded he'd become by then. Can you picture it? He, a soldier, a man who'd shot nine bears and was directly descended from two lieutenant colonels—I mean, one after the other, of course. Can you picture it, Gregers?

GREGERS: Yes, I can picture it very well.

HJALMAR: Well, I can't. And then that pistol intruded on our family history once again. When he was under lock and key, dressed like a common prisoner—oh, those were agonizing times for me, you can imagine. I kept the shades of both my windows drawn. When I looked out, I saw the sun shining the same as ever. I couldn't understand it. I saw the people going along the street, laughing and talking of trivial things. I couldn't understand it. I felt all creation should be standing still, like during an eclipse.

GREGERS: I felt that way when my mother died.

HJALMAR: During one of those times Hjalmar Ekdal put a pistol to his own breast.

GREGERS: You were thinking of—

HJALMAR: Yes.

GREGERS: But you didn't shoot?

HJALMAR: No. In that critical moment I won a victory over myself. I stayed alive. But you can bet it takes courage to choose life in those circumstances.

GREGERS: Well, that depends on your point of view.

HJALMAR: Oh, absolutely. But it was all for the best, because now I've nearly finished my invention; and then Dr. Relling thinks, just as I do, that they'll let Father wear his uniform again. I want only that one reward.

GREGERS: So it's really the uniform that he—?

HJALMAR: Yes, that's what he really hungers and craves for. You've no idea how that makes my heart ache. Every time we throw a little family party—like my birthday, or Gina's, or whatever—then the old man comes in, wearing that uniform from his happier days. But if there's even a knock at the door, he goes scuttering back in his room fast as the old legs will carry him. You see, he doesn't dare show himself to strangers. What a heartrending spectacle for a son!

GREGERS: Approximately when do you think the invention will be finished?

HJALMAR: Oh, good Lord, don't hold me to a timetable. An invention, that's something you can hardly dictate to. It depends a great deal on inspiration, on a sudden insight—and it's nearly impossible to say in advance when that will occur.

GREGERS: But it *is* making progress?

HJALMAR: Of course it's making progress. Every single day I think about my invention. I'm brimming with it. Every afternoon, right after lunch, I lock myself in the living room where I can meditate in peace. But it's no use driving me; it simply won't work. Relling says so too.

GREGERS: And you don't think all those contraptions in the loft distract you and scatter your talents?

HJALMAR: No, no, no, on the contrary. You mustn't say that. I can't always go around here, brooding over the same nerve-racking problems. I need some diversion to fill in the time. You see, inspiration, the moment of insight—when that comes, nothing can stop it.

GREGERS: My dear Hjalmar, I suspect you've got a bit of the wild duck in you.

HJALMAR: Of the wild duck? What do you mean?

GREGERS: You've plunged to the bottom and clamped hold of the seaweed.

HJALMAR: I suppose you mean that near-fatal shot that brought down Father—and me as well?

GREGERS: Not quite that. I wouldn't say you're wounded; but you're wandering in a poisonous swamp, Hjalmar. You've got an insidious disease in your system, and so you've gone to the bottom to die in the dark.

HJALMAR: Me? Die in the dark! You know what, Gregers—you'll really have to stop that talk.

GREGERS: But never mind, I'm going to raise you up again. You know, I've found my mission in life, too. I found it yesterday.

HJALMAR: Yes, that may well be; but you can just leave me out of it. I can assure you that—apart from my quite understandable melancholy—I'm as well off as any man could wish to be.

GREGERS: And your thinking so is part of the sickness.

HJALMAR: Gregers, you're my old friend—please—don't talk any more about sickness and poison. I'm not used to that kind of conversation. In my house nobody talks to me about ugly things.

GREGERS: That's not hard to believe.

HJALMAR: Yes, because it isn't good for me. And there's no swamp air here, as you put it. In a poor photographer's house, life is cramped; I know that. My lot is a poor one—but, you know, I'm an inventor. And I'm the family breadwinner, too. *That's* what sustains me through all the pettiness. Ah, here they come with the lunch.

GINA *and* HEDVIG *bring in bottles of beer, a decanter of brandy, glasses, and the like. At the same time,* RELLING *and* MOLVIK *enter from the hall. Neither wears a hat or overcoat;* MOLVIK *is dressed in black.*

GINA *setting things down on the table:* Well, the two of them—right on time.

RELLING: Molvik was positive he could smell that herring salad, and there was just no holding him back. 'Morning for the second time, Ekdal.

HJALMAR: Gregers, I'd like you to meet Mr. Molvik. And Dr.—ah, but don't you know Relling?

GREGERS: Yes, slightly.

RELLING: Well, Mr. Werle junior. Yes, we've had a few run-ins together up at the Hoidal works. You've just moved in, haven't you?

GREGERS: I moved in this morning.

RELLING: And Molvik and I live downstairs; so you're not very far from a doctor and a priest, if you ever have need of such.

GREGERS: Thanks; that could happen. After all, we had thirteen at the table last night.

HJALMAR: Oh, don't start in on ugly subjects again!

RELLING: You don't have to worry, Hjalmar; Lord knows this doesn't involve you.

HJALMAR: I hope not, for my family's sake. But let's sit down and eat and drink and be merry.

GREGERS: Shouldn't we wait for your father?

HJALMAR: No, he'll have his lunch sent in to him later. Come now!

The men sit at the table, eating and drinking. GINA *and* HEDVIG *go in and out, serving the food.*

RELLING: Last night Molvik was tight as a tick, Mrs. Ekdal.

GINA: Oh? Last night again?

RELLING: Didn't you hear him when I finally brought him home?

GINA: No, can't say I did.

RELLING: That's lucky—because Molvik was revolting last night.

GINA: Is that so, Molvik?

MOLVIK: Let's draw a veil over last night's activities. Thay have no bearing on my better self.

RELLING *to* GREGERS: All of a sudden he's possessed by an impulse; and then I have to take him out on a bat. You see, Mr. Molvik is demonic.

GREGERS: Demonic?

RELLING: Molvik is demonic, yes.

GREGERS: Hm.

RELLING: And demonic natures aren't made to go through life on the straight and narrow; they've got to take detours every so often. Well— and you're still sticking it out there at that dark, hideous mill.

GREGERS: I've stuck it out till now.

RELLING: And did you ever serve that "summons" you were going around with?

GREGERS: Summons? *Understanding him.* Oh, that.

HJALMAR: Were you serving summonses, Gregers?

GREGERS: Nonsense.

RELLING: Oh, but he was, definitely. He went around to all the cotters' cabins and tendered something he called "Summons to the Ideal."

GREGERS: I was young then.

RELLING: You're right, there. You were very young. And that summons to the ideal—it wasn't ever honored during my time up there.

GREGERS: Nor later, either.

RELLING: Well, I guess you've learned enough to cut down your expectations a bit.

GREGERS: Never—when I meet a man who's a real man.

HJALMAR: Yes, that seems quite reasonable to me. A little butter, Gina.

RELLING: And then a piece of pork for Molvik.
MOLVIK: Ugh, no pork!

There is a knock on the loft door.

HJALMAR: Open it, Hedvig; Father wants to get out.

HEDVIG *goes to open the door a little; old* EKDAL *enters with a fresh rabbit skin. He closes the door after him.*

EKDAL: Good morning, gentlemen. Good hunting today. Shot a big one.
HJALMAR: And you went ahead and skinned it without waiting for me!
EKDAL: Salted it, too. It's nice tender meat, this rabbit meat. And it's so sweet. Tastes like sugar. Enjoy your food, gentlemen! *He goes into his room.*
MOLVIK *getting up:*   Pardon—I, I can't—got to go downstairs right—
RELLING: Drink soda water, man!
MOLVIK *rushing out the hall door:*   Ugh—ugh!
RELLING *to* HJALMAR: Let's empty a glass to the old hunter.
HJALMAR *clinking glasses with him:*   Yes, to the gallant sportsman on the brink of the grave.
RELLING: To the old, gray-haired—*Drinks.* Tell me something, is it gray hair he's got, or is it white?
HJALMAR: It's really a little of both. But as a matter of fact, he's scarcely got a hair on his head.
RELLING: Well, fake hair will take you through life, good as any. You know, Ekdal, you're really a very lucky man. You have your high mission in life to fight for—
HJALMAR: And I am fighting for it, too.
RELLING: And then you've got this clever wife of yours, padding around in her slippers and waggling her hips and keeping you neat and cozy.
HJALMAR: Yes, Gina—*Nodding at her*—you're a good companion for life's journey, you are.
GINA: Oh, don't sit there deprecating me.
RELLING: And what about your Hedvig, Ekdal?
HJALMAR *stirred:*   My child, yes! My child above all. Hedvig, come here to me. *Caresses her head.* What day is tomorrow, dear?
HEDVIG *shaking him:*   Oh, don't talk about it, Daddy!
HJALMAR: It's like a knife turning in my heart when I think how bare it's all going to be, just the tiniest celebration out in the loft—
HEDVIG: Oh, but that will be just wonderful!
RELLING: And wait till that marvelous invention comes to the world, Hedvig!
HJALMAR: Ah, yes—then you'll see! Hedvig, I've resolved to make your future secure. As long as you live, you'll live in style. I'll assure you of something, one way or another. That will be the poor inventor's sole reward.

HEDVIG *whispering, with her arms around his neck:*   Oh, you dear, dear Daddy!

RELLING *to* GREGERS: Well, now, isn't it good for a change to be sitting around a well-spread table in a happy family circle?

HJALMAR: Yes, I really prize these hours around the table.

GREGERS: I, for my part, don't thrive in marsh gas.

RELLING: Marsh gas?

HJALMAR: Oh, don't start that rubbish again!

GINA: Lord knows there isn't any marsh gas here, Mr. Werle; every blessed day I air the place out.

GREGERS *leaving the table:*   You can't air out the stench I mean.

HJALMAR: Stench!

GINA: What about that, Hjalmar!

RELLING: Beg pardon—but it wouldn't be you who brought that stench in with you from the mines up there?

GREGERS: It's just like you to call what I'm bringing into this house a stench.

RELLING *crossing over to him:*   Listen, Mr. Werle junior, I've got a strong suspicion that you're still going around with the uncut version of that "Summons to the Ideal" in your back pocket.

GREGERS: I've got it written in my heart.

RELLING: I don't care where the devil you've got it; I wouldn't advise you to play process-server here as long as I'm around.

GREGERS: And what if I do anyway?

RELLING: Then you'll go head first down the stairs, that's what.

HJALMAR *getting up:*   Come, now, Relling!

GREGERS: Yes, just throw me out—

GINA *coming between them:*   You can't do that, Relling. But I'll tell you this, Mr. Werle—that you, who made all that mess with your stove, have no right to come to me talking about smells.

A knock at the hall door.

HEDVIG: Mother, somebody's knocking.

HJALMAR: Wouldn't you know, it's open house!

GINA: I'll go—*She crosses and opens the door, gives a start, shudders and shrinks back.* Uff! Oh no!

Old WERLE, *in a fur coat, steps into the room.*

WERLE: Excuse me, but I think my son is living in this house.

GINA *catching her breath:*   Yes.

HJALMAR *coming closer:*   If Mr. Werle will be so good as to—

WERLE: Thanks, I'd just like to talk with my son.

GREGERS: Yes, why not? Here I am.

WERLE: I'd like to talk with you in your room.

GREGERS: In my room—fine—*Starts in.*

GINA: No. Good Lord, that's in no condition for—

WERLE: Well, out in the hall, then. This is just between us.

HJALMAR: You can talk here, Mr. Werle. Come into the living room, Relling.

HJALMAR *and* RELLING *go out to the right;* GINA *takes* HEDVIG *with her into the kitchen.*

GREGERS *after a brief interval:* Well, now it's just the two of us.

WERLE: You dropped a few remarks last night— And since you've now taken a room with the Ekdals, I must assume that you're planning something or other against me.

GREGERS: I'm planning to open Hjalmar Ekdal's eyes. He's going to see his situation just as it is—that's all.

WERLE: Is *that* the mission in life you talked about yesterday?

GREGERS: Yes. You haven't left me any other.

WERLE: Am I the one that spoiled your mind, Gregers?

GREGERS: You've spoiled my entire life. I'm not thinking of all that with Mother. But you're the one I can thank for my going around, whipped and driven by this guilt-ridden conscience.

WERLE: Ah, it's your conscience that's gone bad.

GREGERS: I should have taken a stand against you when the trap was laid for Lieutenant Ekdal. I should have warned him, for I had a pretty good idea what was coming off.

WERLE: Yes, you really should have spoken up then.

GREGERS: I didn't dare; I was so cowed and frightened. I was unspeakably afraid of you—both then and for a long time after.

WERLE: That fright seems to be over now.

GREGERS: It is, luckily. The harm done to old Ekdal, both by me and—others, can never be undone; but Hjalmar I can free from all the lies and evasions that are smothering him here.

WERLE: You believe you'd be doing him good by that?

GREGERS: That's what I believe.

WERLE: Maybe you think Ekdal's the kind of man who'll thank you for that friendly service?

GREGERS: Yes! He *is* that kind of man.

WERLE: Hmm—we'll see.

GREGERS: And besides—if I'm ever to go on living, I'll have to find a cure for my sick conscience.

WERLE: It'll never be sound. Your conscience has been sickly from childhood. It's an inheritance from your mother, Gregers—the only inheritance she left you.

GREGERS *with a wry half-smile:* You've never been able to accept the fact, have you, that you calculated wrong when you thought she'd bring you a fortune?

WERLE: Let's not get lost in irrelevancies. Then you're still intent on this goal of putting Ekdal on what you suppose is the right track?

GREGERS: Yes, I'm intent on that.

WERLE: Well, then I could have saved myself the walk up here. For there's no point in asking if you'll move back home with me?

GREGERS: No.

WERLE: And you won't come into the business either?

GREGERS: No.

WERLE: Very well. But since I'm now planning a second marriage, the estate, of course, will be divided between us.

GREGERS *quickly:* No, I don't want that.

WERLE: You don't want it?

GREGERS: No, I wouldn't dare, for the sake of my conscience.

WERLE *after a pause:* You going back to the works again?

GREGERS: No. I consider that I've retired from your service.

WERLE: But what are you going to do, then?

GREGERS: Simply carry out my life's mission; nothing else.

WERLE: Yes, but afterwards? What will you live on?

GREGERS: I have some of my salary put aside.

WERLE: Yes, that won't last long!

GREGERS: I think it will last my time.

WERLE: What do you mean by that?

GREGERS: I'm not answering any more.

WERLE: Good-bye then, Gregers.

GREGERS: Good-bye.

Old WERLE *goes out.*

HJALMAR *peering out:* Has he gone?

GREGERS: Yes.

HJALMAR *and* RELLING *come in.* GINA *and* HEDVIG *also return from the kitchen.*

RELLING: There's one lunch gone to the dogs.

GREGERS: Put your things on, Hjalmar; you've got to take a long walk with me.

HJALMAR: Yes, gladly. What did your father want? Was it anything to do with me?

GREGERS: Just come. We have some things to talk over. I'll go and get my coat. *He leaves by the hall door.*

GINA: You mustn't go out with him, Hjalmar.

RELLING: No, don't go. Stay where you are.

HJALMAR *getting his hat and overcoat:* But why? When a childhood friend feels a need to open his mind to me in private—

RELLING: But damn it all! Can't you see the man's mad, crazy, out of his skull!

GINA: Yes, that's the truth, if you'd listen. His mother, off and on, had those same conniption fits.

HJALMAR: That's just why he needs a friend's watchful eye on him. *To* GINA. Be sure dinner's ready in plenty of time. See you later. *Goes out the hall door.*

RELLING: It's really a shame that fellow didn't go straight to hell down one of the Hoidal mines.

GINA: Mercy—why do you say that?

RELLING *muttering:* Oh, I've got my reasons.

GINA: Do you think Gregers Werle is really crazy?

RELLING: No, worse luck. He's no crazier than most people. But he's got a disease in his system all the same.

GINA: What is it that's wrong with him?

RELLING: All right, I'll tell you, Mrs. Ekdal. He's suffering from an acute case of moralistic fever.

GINA: Moralistic fever?

HEDVIG: Is that a kind of disease?

RELLING: Oh yes, it's a national disease, but it only breaks out now and then. *Nodding to* GINA. Thanks for lunch. *He goes out through the hall door.*

GINA *walking restlessly around the room:* Ugh, that Gregers Werle—he was always a cold fish.

HEDVIG *standing by the table, looking searchingly at her:* This is all so strange to me.

ACT FOUR

HJALMAR EKDAL's *studio. A photograph has just been taken; a portrait camera covered with a cloth, a stand, a couple of chairs, a console table, among other things, stand well out in the room. Late afternoon light; it is near sunset; somewhat later it begins to grow dark.*

GINA is standing in the hall doorway with a plate-holder and a wet photographic plate in her hand, talking with someone outside.

GINA: Yes, that's definite. When I promise something, I keep my word. On Monday the first dozen will be ready. Good-bye. Good-bye. *Footsteps are heard descending the stairs.* GINA *closes the door, puts the plate into the holder, and slips both back into the covered camera.*

HEDVIG *coming in from the kitchen:* Are they gone?

GINA *tidying up:* Yes, thank goodness, at last I'm rid of them.

HEDVIG: But why do you suppose Daddy isn't home yet?

GINA: Are you sure he's not below with Relling?

HEDVIG: No, he's not there. I ran down the back stairs just now and asked.

GINA: And his dinner's standing and getting cold, too.

HEDVIG: Just imagine—Daddy's always sure to be on time for dinner.

GINA: Oh, he'll be right along, you'll see.

HEDVIG: Oh, I wish he would come! Everything's so funny around here.

GINA *calling out:* There he is!

HJALMAR *comes in by the hall door.*

HEDVIG *running toward him:* Daddy! Oh, we've waited ages for you!

GINA *eyeing him:* You've been out pretty long, Hjalmar.

HJALMAR *without looking at her:* I've been a while, yes.

He takes off his overcoat. GINA *and* HEDVIG *start to help him; he waves them away.*

GINA: Did you eat with Werle, maybe?

HJALMAR *hanging his coat up:*   No.

GINA *going toward the kitchen:*   I'll bring your dinner in, then.

HJALMAR: No, the dinner can wait. I don't want to eat now.

HEDVIG *coming closer:*   Don't you feel well, Daddy?

HJALMAR: Well? Oh yes, well enough. We had an exhausting walk, Gregers and I.

GINA: You shouldn't do that, Hjalmar; you're not used to it.

HJALMAR: Hm. There are a lot of things a man's got to get used to in this world. *Walking about the room a bit.* Did anyone come while I was out?

GINA: No one but that engaged couple.

HJALMAR: No new orders?

GINA: No, not today.

HEDVIG: You'll see, there'll be some tomorrow, Daddy.

HJALMAR: I certainly hope so, because tomorrow I'm going to throw myself into my work—completely.

HEDVIG: Tomorrow! But don't you remember what day tomorrow is?

HJALMAR: Oh yes, that's right. Well, the day after tomorrow, then. From now on, I'm doing everything myself; I just want to be left alone with all the work.

GINA: But Hjalmar, what's the point of that? It'll only make your life miserable. Let me handle the photographing, and then you'll be free to work on the invention.

HEDVIG: And free for the wild duck, Daddy—and for all the chickens and rabbits—

HJALMAR: Don't talk to me about that rubbish! Starting tomorrow I shall never again set foot in that loft.

HEDVIG: Yes, but Daddy, you promised me tomorrow there'd be a celebration.

HJALMAR: Hm, that's true. Well, the day after, then. That infernal wild duck—I'd almost like to wring its neck!

HEDVIG *crying out:*   The wild duck!

GINA: What an idea!

HEDVIG *shaking him:*   Yes, but Daddy—it's my wild duck!

HJALMAR: That's why I won't do it. I haven't the heart—for your sake, Hedvig, I haven't the heart. But deep inside me I feel I ought to. I shouldn't tolerate under my roof a creature that's been in that man's hand.

GINA: My goodness, just because Grandfather got her from that worthless Pettersen—

HJALMAR *pacing the floor:*   There are certain claims—what should I call them—ideal claims, let's say—a kind of summons that a man can't put aside without damaging his soul.

HEDVIG *following him:*   But think—the wild duck—the poor wild duck!

HJALMAR *stopping:*   You heard me say I'd spare it—for your sake. It won't be hurt, not a hair on its—well, anyway, I'll spare it. After all, there are greater missions than that to take on. But now, Hedvig, you ought to go out for your walk; the light's about right for your eyes.

HEDVIG: No, I don't want to go out now.

HJALMAR: Yes, go on. You seem to be blinking your eyes so. All these fumes in here aren't good for you; the air here under this roof is bad.

HEDVIG: All right, then, I'll run down the back stairs and take a little walk. My coat and hat? Oh, they're in my room. Daddy—promise you won't hurt the wild duck while I'm out.

HJALMAR: There won't be a feather ruffled on its head. *Drawing her to him.* You and I, Hedvig—we two! Now run along, dear.

HEDVIG *nods to her parents and goes out through the kitchen.*

HJALMAR *walking around without looking up:*   Gina.

GINA: Yes?

HJALMAR: From tomorrow on—or let's say the day after tomorrow—I'd prefer to keep the household accounts myself.

GINA: You want to keep the household accounts, too?

HJALMAR: Yes, or budget the income, in any case.

GINA: Lord love us, there's nothing to that.

HJALMAR: One wouldn't think so. It seems to me you can make our money stretch remarkably far. *Stopping and looking at her.* How *is* that?

GINA: Hedvig and I, we don't need much.

HJALMAR: Is it true that Father gets such good pay for the copying he does for Werle?

GINA: I don't know how good it is. I don't know rates for such things.

HJALMAR: Well, what does he get, just roughly? Tell me!

GINA: It's never the same. I suppose it's roughly what he costs us, with a little pocket money thrown in.

HJALMAR: What he costs us! That's something you've never told me before!

GINA: No, I never could. You were always so happy thinking he got everything from you.

HJALMAR: And instead it comes from Mr. Werle.

GINA: Oh, but he's got plenty to spare, that one.

HJALMAR: Let's have the lamp lit!

GINA *lighting it:*   And then we can't know if it really is the old man; it could well be Graaberg—

HJALMAR: Why try to put me off with Graaberg?

GINA: No, I don't know. I just thought—

HJALMAR: Hm!

GINA: You know it wasn't me that got Grandfather the copying. It was Berta, that time she came here.

HJALMAR: Your voice sounds so shaky.

GINA *putting the shade on the lamp:*   It does?

HJALMAR: And then your hands are trembling. Or aren't they?

GINA *firmly:*   Say it straight out, Hjalmar. What is it he's gone and said about me?

HJALMAR: Is it true—can it possibly be that—that there was some kind of involvement between you and Mr. Werle while you were in service there?

GINA: That's not true. Not then, there wasn't. Werle was after me, all right. And his wife thought there was something to it, and she made a big fuss and bother, and she roasted me coming and going, she did— so I quit.

HJALMAR: But then what!

GINA: Yes, so then I went home. And Mother—well, she wasn't all you took her to be, Hjalmar; she ran on telling me one thing and another, because Werle was a widower by then.

HJALMAR: Yes. And then!

GINA: Well, you might as well know it all. He didn't give up till he had his way.

HJALMAR *with a clap of his hands:*   And this is the mother of my child! How could you keep that hidden from me!

GINA: Yes, I did the wrong thing; I really should have told you long ago.

HJALMAR: Right at the start, you mean—so I could have known what sort you are.

GINA: But would you have married me anyway?

HJALMAR: How can you think that?

GINA: No. But that's why I didn't dare say anything then. Because I'd come to be so terribly in love with you, as you know. And then how could I make myself utterly miserable—

HJALMAR *walking about:*   And this is my Hedvig's mother! And then to know that everything I see around me—*Kicking at a table*—my whole home—I owe to a favored predecessor. Ah, that charmer Werle!

GINA: Do you regret the fourteen, fifteen years we've lived together?

HJALMAR *stopping in front of her:*   Tell me—don't you every day, every hour, regret this spider web of deception you've spun around me? Answer me that! Don't you really go around in a torment of remorse?

GINA: Hjalmar dear, I've got so much to think about just with the housework and the day's routine—

HJALMAR: Than you never turn a critical eye on your past!

GINA: No. Good Lord, I'd almost forgotten that old affair.

HJALMAR: Oh, this dull, unfeeling content! To me there's something outrageous about it. Just think—not one regret!

GINA: But Hjalmar, tell me now—what would have happened to you if you hadn't found a wife like me?

HJALMAR: Like you—!

GINA: Yes, because I've always been a bit more hardheaded and resourceful than you. Well, of course I'm a couple of years older.

HJALMAR: What would have happened to me?

GINA: You were pretty bad off at the time you met me; you can't deny that.

HJALMAR: "Pretty bad off" you call it. Oh, you have no idea what a man goes through when he's deep in misery and despair—especially a man of my fiery temperament.

GINA: No, that may be. And I shouldn't say nothing about it, either, because you turned out such a good-hearted husband as soon as you got a house and home—and now we've made it so snug and cozy here, and pretty soon both Hedvig and I could begin spending a little on food and clothes.

HJALMAR: In the swamp of deception, yes.

GINA: Ugh, that disgusting creature, tracking his way through our house!

HJALMAR: I also thought this home was a good place to be. That was a pipe dream. Now where can I find the buoyancy I need to carry my invention into reality? Maybe it'll die with me; and then it'll be your past, Gina, that killed it.

GINA *close to tears:*   No, you mustn't ever say such things, Hjalmar. All my days I've only wanted to do what's best for you!

HAJLMAR: I wonder—what happens now to the breadwinner's dream? When I lay in there on the sofa pondering my invention, I had a hunch it would drain my last bit of strength. I sensed that the day I took the patent in my hand—that would be the day of—departure. And it was my dream that then *you* would go on as the departed inventor's prosperous widow.

GINA *drying her eyes:*   No, don't say that, Hjalmar. Lord knows I never want to see the day I'm a widow.

HJALMAR: Oh, what does it matter? Everything's over and done with now. Everything!

GREGERS *cautiously opens the hall door and looks in.*

GREGERS: May I come in?

HJALMAR: Yes, do.

GREGERS *advancing with a beaming countenance, hands outstretched as if to take theirs:*   Now, you dear people—! *Looks from one to the other, then whispers to* HJALMAR. But isn't it done, then?

HJALMAR *resoundingly:*   It's done.

GREGERS: It is?

HJALMAR: I've just known the bitterest hour of my life.

GREGERS: But also the most exalted, I think.

HJALMAR: Well, anyway, it's off our hands for the moment.

GINA: God forgive you, Mr. Werle.

GREGERS *with great surprise:*   But I don't understand this.

HJALMAR: What don't you understand?

GREGERS: With this great rapport—the kind that forges a whole new way of life—a life, a companionship in truth with no more deception—

HJALMAR: Yes, I know, I know all that.

GREGERS: I was really positive that when I came through that door I'd be met by a transfigured light in both your faces. And what do I see instead but this gloomy, heavy, dismal—

GINA: How true. *She removes the lampshade.*

GREGERS: You don't want to understand me, Mrs. Ekdal. No, no, you'll need time— But you yourself, Hjalmar? You must have gained a sense of high purpose out of this great unburdening.

HJALMAR: Yes, naturally. That is—more or less.

GREGERS: Because there's nothing in the world that compares with showing mercy to a sinner and lifting her up in the arms of love.

HJALMAR: Do you think a man can recover so easily from the bitter cup I've just emptied!

GREGERS: Not an ordinary man, no. But a man like you—!

HJALMAR: Good Lord, yes, I know that. But you mustn't be driving me, Gregers. You see, these things take time.

GREGERS: You've *lots* of the wild duck in you, Hjalmar.

RELLING *has entered through the hall door.*

RELLING: Aha! The wild duck's flying again, eh?

HJALMAR: Yes, the wounded trophy of old Werle's hunt.

RELLING: Old Werle? Is it him you're talking about?

HJALMAR: Him and—all of us.

RELLING *under his breath to* GREGERS: The devil take you!

HJALMAR: What'd you say?

RELLING: I merely expressed my heartfelt desire that this quack would cut out for home. If he stays here, he's just the man to ruin you both.

GREGERS: They won't be ruined, Mr. Relling. Regarding Hjalmar, I'll say nothing. We know him. But she, too, surely, in the depths of her being, has something authentic, something sincere.

GINA *near tears:* Well, if I *was* that, why didn't you leave me alone?

RELLING *to* GREGERS: Would it be nosy to ask what you're really trying to do in this house?

GREGERS: I want to establish a true marriage.

RELLING: Then don't you think Ekdal's marriage is good enough as it is?

GREGERS: It's about as good a marriage as most, unfortunately. But it isn't yet a *true* marriage.

HJALMAR: You don't believe in ideals in life, Relling.

RELLING: Nonsense, sonny boy! Excuse me, Mr. Werle, but how many— in round numbers—how many "true marriages" have you seen in your time?

GREGERS: I believe I've hardly seen a single one.

RELLING: And I likewise.

GREGERS: But I've seen innumerable marriages of the opposite kind. And I've had a chance to see at close range what such a marriage can destroy in two people.

HJALMAR: A man's whole moral foundation can crumble under his feet; that's the dreadful thing.

RELLING: Well, I've never really exactly been married, so I'm no judge of these things. But I do know this, that the child is part of the marriage too. And you've got to leave the child in peace.

HJALMAR: Ah, Hedvig! My poor Hedvig!

RELLING: Yes, you'll please see that Hedvig's left out of it. You're both grown people; you're free, God knows, to slop up your private lives all you want. But I tell you, you've got to be careful with Hedvig, or else you might do her some serious harm.

HJALMAR: Harm!

RELLING: Yes, or she could do harm to herself—and possibly others as well.

GINA: But how can you know that, Relling?

HJALMAR: There's no immediate threat to her eyes, is there?

RELLING: This has nothing to do with her eyes. Hedvig's arrived at a difficult age. She's open to all kinds of erratic ideas.

GINA: You know—she is at that! She's begun to fool around something awful with the fire in the kitchen stove. She calls it playing house afire. I'm often scared she *will* set the house on fire.

RELLING: See what I mean? I knew it.

GREGERS *to* RELLING: But how do you explain something like that?

RELLING *brusquely:* Her voice is changing, junior.

HJALMAR: As long as the child has *me!* As long as I'm above the sod.

A knock is heard at the door.

GINA: Shh, Hjalmar, someone's in the hall. *Calling out.* Come on in!

MRS. SØRBY, *wearing street clothes, enters.*

MRS. SØRBY: Good evening!

GINA *going toward her:* Is it you, Berta!

MRS. SØRBY: Oh yes, it's me. But perhaps I came at an awkward time?

HJALMAR: Oh, not at all; a messenger from *that* house—

MRS. SØRBY *to* GINA: As a matter of fact, I'd hoped that I wouldn't find your menfolk in at this hour, so I ran over just to have a word with you and say good-bye.

GINA: Oh? Are you going away?

MRS. SØRBY: Yes, tomorrow, early—up to Hoidal. Mr. Werle left this afternoon. *Casually to* GREGERS. He sends his regards.

GINA: Just think!

HJALMAR: So Mr. Werle has left? And you're following him?

MRS. SØRBY: Yes, what do you say to that, Ekdal?

HJALMAR: I say watch out.

GREGERS: Let me explain. My father is marrying Mrs. Sørby.

HJALMAR: He's marrying her!

GINA: Oh, Berta, it's come at last!

RELLING *his voice quavering slightly:* This really can't be true.

MRS. SØRBY: Yes, my dear Relling, it's completely true.

RELLING: You want to marry again?

MRS. SØRBY: Yes, so it seems. Werle has gotten a special license, and we're going to have a very quiet wedding up at the works.

GREGERS: So I ought to wish you happiness, like a good stepson.

MRS. SØRBY: Thank you, if you really mean it. I'm hoping it will bring us happiness, both Werle and me.

RELLING: That's a reasonable hope. Mr. Werle never gets drunk—as far as *I* know; and he's certainly not given to beating up his wives the way the late horse doctor did.

MRS. SØRBY: Oh, now let Sørby rest in peace. He did have some worthy traits, you know.

RELLING: Old Werle's traits are worth rather more, I'll bet.

MRS.SØRBY: At least he hasn't wasted the best that's in him. Any man who does *that* has to take the consequences.

RELLING: Tonight I'm going out with Molvik.

MRS. SØRBY: You shouldn't, Relling. Don't do it—for my sake.

RELLING: What else is left? *To* HJALMAR. If you'd care to, you could come too.

GINA: No, thanks. Hjalmar never goes dissipating.

HJALMAR *in an angry undertone:*   Can't you keep quiet!

RELLING: Good-bye, Mrs.—Werle. *He goes out the hall door.*

GREGERS *to* MRS. SØRBY: It would seem that you and Dr. Relling know each other quite intimately.

MRS. SØRBY: Yes, we've known each other for many years. At one time something might have developed between us.

GREGERS: It was certainly lucky for you that it didn't.

MRS. SØRBY: Yes, that's true enough. But I've always been wary of following my impulses. After all, a woman can't just throw herself away.

GREGERS: Aren't you even a little bit afraid that I'll drop my father a hint about this old friendship?

MRS. SØRBY: You can be sure I've told him myself.

GREGERS: Oh?

MRS. SØRBY: Your father knows every last scrap of gossip that holds any grain of truth about me. I told him all of those things; it was the first thing I did when he made his intentions clear.

GREGERS: Then I think you're more frank than most people.

MRS. SØRBY: I've always been frank. In the long run, it's the best thing for us women to be.

HJALMAR: What do you say to that, Gina?

GINA: Oh, women are all so different. Some live one way and some live another.

MRS. SØRBY: Well, Gina, I do think it's wisest to handle things as I have. And Werle, for his part, hasn't held back anything either. Really, it's this that's brought us so close together. Now he can sit and talk to me as freely as a child. He's never had that chance before. He, a healthy, vigorous man, had to spend his whole youth and all his best years hearing nothing but sermons on his sins. And generally those sermons were aimed at the most imaginary failings—at least from what *I* could see.

GINA: Yes, that's just as true as you say.

GREGERS: If you women are going to explore this subject, I'd better leave.

MRS. SØRBY: You can just as well stay, for that matter; I won't say another word. But I did want you to understand that I haven't done anything sly or in any way underhanded. I suppose it looks like I've had quite a nice piece of luck, and that's true enough, up to a point. But, anyway, what I mean is that I'll not be taking any more than I give.

One thing I'll never do is desert him. And I can be useful to him and care for him now better than anyone else after he's helpless.

HJALMAR: After he's helpless?

GREGERS *to* MRS. SØRBY: All right, don't talk about that here.

MRS. SØRBY: No need to hide it any longer, much as he'd like to. He's going blind.

HJALMAR *astounded:* He's going blind? But that's peculiar. Is he going blind too?

GINA: Lots of people do.

MRS. SØRBY: And you can imagine what that means for a businessman. Well, I'll try to make my eyes do for his as well as I can. But I mustn't stay any longer; I've so much to take care of now. Oh yes, I was supposed to tell you this, Ekdal—that if there's anything Werle can do for you, please just get in touch with Graaberg.

GREGERS: That offer Hjalmar Ekdal will certainly decline.

MRS. SØRBY: Come, now, I don't think that in the past he's—

GINA: No, Berta, Hjalmar doesn't need to take anything from Mr. Werle now.

HJALMAR *slowly and ponderously:* Would you greet your future husband from me and say that I intend very shortly to call on his bookkeeper, Graaberg—

GREGERS: What! Is that what you want?

HJALMAR: To call on his bookkeeper Graaberg, as I said, to request an itemized account of what I owe his employer. I shall repay this debt of honor— *Laughs.* That's a good name for it, "debt of honor"! But never mind. I shall repay every penny of it, with five percent interest.

GINA: But Hjalmar dear, God knows we don't have the money for that.

HJALMAR: Will you tell your husband-to-be that I'm working away relentlessly at my invention. Would you tell him that what keeps my spirits up through this grueling ordeal is the desire to be quit of a painful burden of debt. That's why I'm making my invention. The entire proceeds will be devoted to shedding my monetary ties with your imminent partner.

MRS. SØRBY: Something has really happened in this house.

HJALMAR: Yes, it certainly has.

MRS. SØRBY: Well, good-bye, then. I still have a little more to talk about with you, Gina, but that can keep till another time. Good-bye.

HJALMAR *and* GREGERS *silently nod;* GINA *accompanies* MRS. SØRBY *to the door.*

HJALMAR: Not across the threshold, Gina!

MRS. SØRBY *leaves;* GINA *closes the door behind her.*

HJALMAR: There, now, Gregers—now I've got that pressing debt off my hands.

GREGERS: You will soon, anyway.

HJALMAR: I believe my attitude could be called correct.

GREGERS: You're the man I always thought you were.

HJALMAR: In certain circumstances it's impossible not to feel the summons of the ideal. As the family provider, you know, I've got to writhe and groan beneath it. Believe you me, it's really no joke for a man without means to try and pay off a long-standing debt over which the dust of oblivion, so to speak, had fallen. But it's got to be, all the same; my human self demands its rights.

GREGERS *laying one hand on his shoulder:*   Ah, Hjalmar—wasn't it a good thing I came?

HJALMAR: Yes.

GREGERS: Getting a clear picture of the whole situation—wasn't that a good thing?

HJALMAR *a bit impatiently:*   Of course it was good. But there's one thing that irks my sense of justice.

GREGERS: What's that?

HJALMAR: It's the fact that—oh, I don't know if I dare speak so freely about your father.

GREGERS: Don't hold back on my account.

HJALMAR: Well, uh—you see, I find something so irritating in the idea that I'm not the one, he's the one who's going to have the true marriage.

GREGERS: How can you say such a thing!

HJALMAR: But it's true. Your father and Mrs. Sørby are entering a marriage based on complete trust, one that's wholehearted and open on both sides. They haven't bottled up any secrets from each other; there isn't any reticence between them; they've declared—if you'll permit me—a mutual forgiveness of sins.

GREGERS: All right. So what?

HJALMAR: Yes, but that's the whole thing, then. You said yourself that the reason for all these difficulties was the founding of a true marriage.

GREGERS: But that marriage is a very different sort, Hjalmar. You certainly wouldn't compare either you or her with those two—well, you know what I mean.

HJALMAR: Still, I can't get over the idea that there's something in all this that violates my sense of justice. It really seems as if there's no just order to the universe.

GINA: Good Lord, Hjalmar, you mustn't say such things.

GREGERS: Hm, let's not start on that question.

HJALMAR: But then, on the other hand, I can definitely make out what seems to be the meticulous hand of fate. He's going blind.

GINA: Oh, that's not for sure.

HJALMAR: That is indisputable. Anyway, we oughtn't to doubt it, because it's precisely this fact that reveals the just retribution. Years back he abused the blind faith of a fellow human being—

GREGERS: I'm afraid he's done that to many others.

HJALMAR: And now a pitiless, mysterious something comes and claims the old man's eyes in return.

GINA: What a horrible thing to say! It really frightens me.

HJALMAR: It's useful sometimes to go down deep into the night side of existence.

HEDVIG, *in her hat and coat, comes in, happy and breathless, through the hall door.*

GINA: Back so soon?

HEDVIG: Yes, I got tired of walking, and it was just as well, 'cause then I met someone down at the door.

HJALMAR: That must have been Mrs. Sørby.

HEDVIG: Yes.

HJALMAR *pacing back and forth:*   I hope that's the last time you'll see her.

Silence. HEDVIG *glances timidly from one to the other, as if trying to read their feelings.*

HEDVIG *coaxingly, as she approaches:*   Daddy.

HJALMAR: Well—what is it, Hedvig?

HEDVIG: Mrs. Sørby brought along something for me.

HJALMAR *stopping:*   For you?

HEDVIG: Yes. It's something meant for tomorrow.

GINA: Berta's always brought some little gift for your birthday.

HJALMAR: What it it?

HEDVIG: No, you can't know that yet, because Mother has to bring it to me in bed first thing in the morning.

HJALMAR: Oh, all this conspiracy that I'm left out of!

HEDVIG *hurriedly:*   Oh, you can see it all right. It's a big letter. *She takes the letter out of her coat pocket.*

HJALMAR: A letter, too?

HEDVIG: Well, it's only the letter. I guess the rest will come later. But just think—a letter! I've never gotten a real letter before. And on the outside there, it says "Miss." *She reads.* "Miss Hedvig Ekdal." Just think—that's me.

HJALMAR: Let me see the letter.

HEDVIG *handing it over:*   See, there.

HJALMAR: That's old Werle's writing.

GINA: Are you positive, Hjalmar?

HJALMAR: See for yourself.

GINA: Oh, how would I know?

HJALMAR: Hedvig, mind if I open the letter—and read it?

HEDVIG: Sure. If you want to, go right ahead.

GINA: No, not tonight, Hjalmar. It's meant for tomorrow.

HEDVIG *softly:*   Oh, won't you let him read it! It's got to be something good, and then Daddy'll be happy and things will be pleasant again.

HJALMAR: May I open it, then?

HEDVIG: Yes, please do, Daddy. It'll be fun to find out what it is.

HJALMAR: Good. *He opens the envelope, takes out a sheet of paper, and reads it through with growing bewilderment.* Now what's this all about?

GINA: But what does it say?

HEDVIG: Oh yes, Daddy—tell us!

HJALMAR: Be quiet. *He reads it through once more, turns pale, then speaks with evident restraint.* This is a deed of gift, Hedvig.

HEDVIG: Honestly? What am I getting?

HJALMAR: Read for yourself.

HEDVIG *goes over to the lamp and reads for a moment.*

HJALMAR *clenching his fists, in almost a whisper:*   The eyes! The eyes—and now that letter!

HEDVIG *interrupting her reading:*   Yes, but I think the gift is for Grandfather.

HJALMAR *taking the letter from her:*   Gina—do you understand this?

GINA: I know nothing at all about it. Just tell me.

HJALMAR: Mr. Werle writes Hedvig to say that her old grandfather needn't trouble himself any longer with copying work, but that henceforth he can draw one hundred crowns a month from the office—

GREGERS: Aha!

HEDVIG: One hundred crowns, Mother! I read that.

GINA: That'll be nice for Grandfather.

HJALMAR: One hundred crowns, as long as he needs it. That means till death, of course.

GINA: Well, then he's provided for, poor dear.

HJALMAR: But there's more. You didn't read far enough, Hedvig. Afterwards this gift passes over to you.

HEDVIG: To me! All of it?

HJALMAR: You're assured the same income for the rest of your life, he writes. Hear that, Gina?

GINA: Yes, of course I heard.

HEDVIG: Imagine me getting all that money! *Shaking* HJALMAR. Daddy, Daddy, aren't you glad?

HJALMAR *disengaging himself:*   Glad! *Walking about the room.* Ah, what vistas—what perspectives it offers me. Hedvig is the one, she's the one he remembers so bountifully.

GINA: Of course, because it's Hedvig's birthday.

HEDVIG: And anyway, you'll have it, Daddy. You know that I'll give all the money to you and Mother.

HJALMAR: To Mother, yes! There we have it.

GREGERS: Hjalmar, this is a trap that's been set for you.

HJALMAR: You think it could be another trap?

GREGERS: When he was here this morning, he said, "Hjalmar Ekdal is not the man you think he is."

HJALMAR: Not the man—!

GREGERS: "You'll find that out," he said.

HJALMAR: Find out if I could be bought off for a price, eh—!

HEDVIG: But Mother, what's this all about?

GINA: Go and take your things off.

HEDVIG, *close to tears, goes out the kitchen door.*

GREGERS: Yes, Hjalmar—now we'll see who's right, he or I.

HJALMAR *slowly tearing the paper in half and putting both pieces on the table:* That is my answer.

GREGERS: What I expected.

HJALMAR *going over to* GINA, *who is standing by the stove, and speaking quietly:* And now no more pretenses. If that thing between you and him was all over when you—came to be so terribly in love with me, as you put it—then why did he give us the means to get married?

GINA: Maybe he thought he could come and go here.

HJALMAR: Is that all? Wasn't he afraid of a certain possibility?

GINA: I don't know what you mean.

HJALMAR: I want to know if—your child has the right to live under my roof.

GINA *draws herself up, her eyes flashing:*   And you can ask that?

HJALMAR: Just answer me this: does Hedvig belong to me—or? Well!

GINA *regarding him with chill defiance:*   I don't know.

HJALMAR *with a slight quaver:*   You don't know!

GINA: How would *I* know that? A woman of my sort—

HJALMAR *softly, turning from her:*   Then I have nothing more to do in this house.

GREGERS: You must think about this, Hjalmar.

HJALMAR *putting on his overcoat:*   There's nothing to think about for a man like me.

GREGERS: Oh, there's so very much to think about. You three have got to stay together if you're ever going to win through to a self-sacrificial, forgiving spirit.

HJALMAR: I don't want that. Never, never! My hat! *Takes his hat.* My home is down in ruins around me. *Breaks into tears.* Gregers, I have no child!

HEDVIG *who has opened the kitchen door:*   What are you saying! *Running toward him.* Daddy, Daddy!

GINA: Now look!

HJALMAR: Don't come near me, Hedvig! Keep away. I can't bear seeing you. Oh, the eyes! Goodbye. *Starts for the door.*

HEDVIG *clinging fast to him and shrieking:*   Oh no! Oh no! Don't leave me.

GINA *crying out:*   Look out for the child, Hjalmar! Look out for the child!

HJALMAR: I won't. I can't. I've got to get out—away from all this! *He tears himself loose from* HEDVIG *and goes out through the hall door.*

HEDVIG *with desperate eyes:*   He's left us, Mother! He's left us! He'll never come back again!

GINA: Now don't cry, Hedvig. Daddy's coming back.

HEDVIG *throws herself, sobbing, on the sofa:*   No, no, he'll never come home to us again.

GREGERS: Will you believe I've wanted everything for the best, Mrs. Ekdal?

GINA: Yes, I think I believe that—but God have mercy on you all the same.

HEDVIG *lying on the sofa:*   I think I'll die from all this. What did I do to him? Mother, you've got to make him come home!

GINA: Yes, yes, yes, just be calm, and I'll step out and look for him. *Putting on her coat.* Maybe he's gone down to Relling's. But now don't you lie there, wailing away. Will you promise?

HEDVIG *sobbing convulsively:*   Yes, I'll be all right—if only Daddy comes back.

GREGERS *to* GINA, *about to leave:*   Wouldn't it be better, though, to let him fight through his painful battle first?

GINA: Oh, he can do that later. First of all, we've got to comfort the child. *She goes out the hall door.*

HEDVIG *sitting up and drying her tears:*   Now you have to tell me what it's all about. Why does Daddy not want to see me anymore?

GREGERS: That's something you mustn't ask until you're big and grown-up

HEDVIG *catching her breath:*   But I can't go on being so horribly unhappy till I'm big and grown-up. I bet I know what it is. Perhaps I'm really not Daddy's child.

GREGERS *disturbed:*   How could that ever be?

HEDVIG: Mother could have found me. And now maybe Daddy's found out. I've read about these things.

GREGERS: Well, but if that was the—

HEDVIG: Yes, I think he could love me even so. Or maybe more. The wild duck was sent us as a present too, and I'm terribly fond of it, all the same.

GREGERS *divertingly:*   Of course, the wild duck, that's true. Let's talk a bit about the wild duck, Hedvig.

HEDVIG: The poor wild duck. He can't bear to see her again, either. Imagine, he wanted to wring her neck!

GREGERS: Oh, he certainly wouldn't do that.

HEDVIG: No, but that's what he said. And I think it was awful for Daddy to say, because each night I make a prayer for the wild duck and ask that she be delivered from death and everything evil.

GREGERS *looking at her:*   Do you always say your prayers at night?

HEDVIG: Uh-huh.

GREGERS: Who taught you that?

HEDVIG: I taught myself, and that was once when Daddy was so sick and had leeches on his neck, and then he said he was in the jaws of death.

GREGERS: Oh yes?

HEDVIG: So I said a prayer for him when I went to bed. And I've kept it up ever since.

GREGERS: And now you pray for the wild duck, too?

HEDVIG: I thought it was best to put the wild duck in, because she was ailing so at the start.

GREGERS: Do you say morning prayers, too?

HEDVIG: No, not at all.

GREGERS: Why not morning prayers as well?

HEDVIG: In the morning it's light, and so there's nothing more to be afraid of.

GREGERS: And the wild duck you love so much—your father wants to wring her neck.

HEDVIG: No. He said it would be the best thing for him if he did, but for my sake he would spare her; and that was good of Daddy.

GREGERS *coming closer:* But what if you now, of your own free will, sacrificed the wild duck for *his* sake.

HEDVIG *springing up:* The wild duck!

GREGERS: What if you, in a sacrificing spirit, gave up the dearest thing you own and know in the whole world?

HEDVIG: Do you think that would help?

GREGERS: Try it, Hedvig.

HEDVIG *softly, with shining eyes:* Yes, I'll try it.

GREGERS: And the strength of mind, do you think you have it?

HEDVIG: I'll ask Grandpa to shoot the wild duck for me.

GREGERS: Yes, do that. But not a word to your mother about all this!

HEDVIG: Why not?

GREGERS: She doesn't understand us.

HEDVIG: The wild duck? I'll try it tomorrow, early.

GINA *comes in through the hall door.*

HEDVIG *going toward her:* Did you find him, Mother?

GINA: No. But I heard he'd looked in downstairs and gotten Relling along.

GREGERS: Are you sure of that?

GINA: Yes, I asked the janitor's wife. And Molvik was with them, she said.

GREGERS: And this, right when his mind needs nothing so much as to wrestle in solitude—!

GINA *taking off her coat:* Oh, men are strange ones, they are. God knows where Relling has led him! I ran over to Mrs. Eriksen's café, but they weren't there.

HEDVIG *struggling with her tears:* Oh, what if he never comes back again!

GREGERS: He *will* come back. I'll get a message to him tomorrow, and then you'll see just how quick he comes. Believe that, Hedvig, and sleep well. Good night. *He goes out the hall door.*

HEDVIG *throwing herself, sobbing, into* GINA's *arms:* Mother, Mother!

GINA *pats her on the back and sighs:* Ah, me, Relling was right. That's the way it goes when these crazy people come around, summoning up their ideals.

ACT FIVE

HJALMAR EKDAL's *studio. A cold, gray morning light filters in; wet snow lies on the huge panes of the skylight.* GINA, *wearing a pinafore, comes in from the kitchen, carrying a feather duster and a cleaning cloth, and makes for the living room door. At the same moment* HEDVIG *rushes in from the hallway.*

GINA *stopping:*   Well?

HEDVIG: You know, Mother, I'm pretty sure he's down at Relling's—

GINA: There, you see!

HEDVIG: 'Cause the janitor's wife said she heard Relling had two others with him when he came in last night.

GINA: That's about what I thought.

HEDVIG: But it's still no good if he won't come up to us.

GINA: At least I can go down there and talk with him.

EKDAL, *in dressing gown and slippers, smoking a pipe, appears in the doorway to his room.*

EKDAL: Say, Hjalmar—Isn't Hjalmar home?

GINA: No, he's gone out, I guess.

EKDAL: So early? In a raging blizzard like this? Oh, well, never mind; I'll take my morning walk alone, that's all

He pulls the loft door ajar, HEDVIG *helping him. He goes in; she closes up after him.*

HEDVIG *lowering her voice:*   Just think, Mother, when Grandpa finds out that Daddy's leaving us.

GINA: Go on, Grandpa won't hear anything of the kind. It was a real stroke of providence he wasn't here yesterday in all that racket.

HEDVIG: Yes, but—

GREGERS *comes in the hall entrance.*

GREGERS: Well? Had any reports on him?

GINA: He should be down at Relling's, they tell me.

GREGERS: With Relling! Did he really go out with those fellows?

GINA: Apparently.

GREGERS: Yes, but he who needed so much to be alone to pull himself together—!

GINA: Yes, just as you say.

RELLING *enters from the hall.*

HEDVIG *going toward him:*   Is Daddy with you?

GINA *simultaneously:*   Is he there?

RELLING: Yes, of course he is.

HEDVIG: And you never told us!

RELLING: Oh, I'm a beast. But first of all, I had that other beast to manage—you know, the demonic one, him—and then, next, I fell so sound asleep that—

GINA: What's Hjalmar been saying today?

RELLING: He's said absolutely nothing.

HEDVIG: Hasn't he talked at all?

RELLING: Not a blessed word.

GREGERS: No, no, I can well understand that.

GINA: But what's he doing, then?

RELLING: He's laid out on the sofa, snoring.

GINA: Oh? Yes, Hjalmar's great at snoring.

HEDVIG: He's asleep? Can he sleep?

RELLING: Well, so it seems.

GREGERS: It's conceivable—when all that strife of spirit has torn him.

GINA: And then he's never been used to roaming around the streets at night.

HEDVIG: Maybe it's a good thing that he's getting some sleep, Mother.

GINA: I think so too. But then it's just as well we don't rouse him too soon. Thanks a lot, Relling. Now I've got to clean and straighten up here a bit, and then—Come and help me, Hedvig.

GINA *and* HEDVIG *disappear into the living room.*

GREGERS *turning to* RELLING: Have you an explanation for the spiritual upheaval taking place within Hjalmar Ekdal?

RELLING: For the life of me, I can't remember any spiritual upheaval in him.

GREGERS: Wait! At a time of crisis like this, when his life has been recast? How can you believe that a rare personality like Hjalmar—?

RELLING: Pah! Personality—him! If he's ever had a tendency toward anything so abnormal as what you call personality, it was ripped up, root and vine, by the time he was grown, and that's a fact.

GREGERS: That's rather surprising—with all the loving care he had as a child.

RELLING: From those two warped, hysterical maiden aunts, you mean?

GREGERS: I want to tell you they were women who always summoned themselves to the highest ideals—yes, now of course you'll start mocking me again.

RELLING: No, I'm hardly in a mood for that. Besides, I'm well informed here; he's regurgitated any amount of rhetoric about his "twin soul-mothers." I really don't believe he has much to thank them for. Ekdal's misfortune is that in his circle he's always been taken for a shining light—

GREGERS: And isn't he, perhaps, exactly that? In his heart's core, I mean?

RELLING: I've never noticed anything of the kind. His father thinks so—but that's nothing; the old lieutenant's been a fool all his life.

GREGERS: He has, all his life, been a man with a childlike awareness; and that's something you just don't understand.

RELLING: Oh, sure! But back when our dear, sweet Hjalmar became a student of sorts, right away he got taken up by his classmates as the great beacon of the future. Oh, he was good-looking, the lout—pink and white—just the way little moon-eyed girls like boys. And then he had that excitable manner and that heart-winning tremor in his voice, and he was so cute and clever at declaiming other people's poems and ideas—

GREGERS *indignantly:* Is it Hjalmar Ekdal you're speaking of that way?

RELLING: Yes, with your permission. That's an inside look at him, this idol you're groveling in front of.

GREGERS: I really didn't think I was utterly blind.

RELLING: Well, you're not far from it. Because you're a sick man, you are. You know that.

GREGERS: There you're right.

RELLING: Oh yes. Your case has complications. First there's this virulent moralistic fever; and then something worse—you keep going off in deliriums of hero worship; you always have to have something to admire that's outside of yourself.

GREGERS: Yes, I certainly have to look for it outside myself.

RELLING: But you're so woefully wrong about these great miraculous beings you think you see and hear around you. You've simply come back to a cotter's cabin with your summons to the ideal; there's no one but fugitives here.

GREGERS: If you've got no higher estimate of Hjalmar Ekdal than this, how can you ever enjoy seeing him day after day?

RELLING: Good Lord, I *am* supposed to be some kind of doctor, I'm ashamed to say. Well, then I ought to look after the poor sick people I live with.

GREGERS: Oh, come! Is Hjalmar Ekdal sick, too?

RELLING: Most of the world is sick, I'm afraid.

GREGERS: And what's your prescription for Hjalmar?

RELLING: My standard one. I try to keep up the life-lie in him.

GREGERS: The life-lie? I don't think I heard—

RELLING: Oh yes, I said the life-lie. The life-lie, don't you see—that's the animating principle of life.

GREGERS: May I ask what kind of lie has infected Hjalmar?

RELLING: No, thanks. I don't betray secrets like that to quacks. You'd just be able to damage him all the more for me. My method is tested, though. I've also used it on Molvik. I made him "demonic." That was my remedy for him.

GREGERS: Then he isn't demonic?

RELLING: What the devil does it mean to be demonic? That's just some hogwash I thought up to keep life going in him. If I hadn't done that, the poor innocent mutt would have given in years ago to self-contempt and despair. And then take the old lieutenant! But he really discovered his own cure himself.

GREGERS: Lieutenant Ekdal? How so?

RELLING: Well, what do you think of this bear hunter going into a dark loft to stalk rabbits? There isn't a happier sportsman in the world than the old man when he's prowling around in that junkyard. Those four or five dried-out Christmas trees he's got—to him they're like all the green forests of Hoidal; the hens and the rooster—they're the game birds up in the fir tops; and the rabbits hopping across the floor—they're the bears that call up his youth again, out in the mountain air.

GREGERS: Poor, unhappy old Ekdal, yes. He certainly had to pare down his early ideals.

RELLING: While I remember it, Mr. Werle junior—don't use that exotic word *ideals*. Not when we've got a fine native word—*lies*.

GREGERS: You're implying the two have something in common?

RELLING: Yes, about like tetanus and lockjaw.

GREGERS: Dr. Relling, I won't rest till I've gotten Hjalmar out of your clutches.

RELLING: So much the worse for him. Deprive the average man of his life-lie and you've robbed him of happiness as well. *To* HEDVIG, *entering from the living room*. Well, little wild-duck mother, now I'll go down and see if Papa's still lying and pondering his marvelous invention. *He goes out the hall door.*

GREGERS *approaching* HEDVIG: I can see by your face that it's not fulfilled.

HEDVIG: What? Oh, about the wild duck. No.

GREGERS: Your courage failed you when the time came to act, I suppose.

HEDVIG: No, it's not exactly that. But when I woke up this morning early and thought of what we talked about, then it seemed so strange to me.

GREGERS: Strange?

HEDVIG: Yes, I don't know—Last night, right at the time, there was something so beautiful about it, but after I'd slept and then thought it over, it didn't seem like so much.

GREGERS: Ah, no, you couldn't grow up here without some taint in you.

HEDVIG: I don't care about that; if only Daddy would come up, then—

GREGERS: Oh, if only your eyes were really open to what makes life worth living—if only you had the true, joyful, courageous spirit of self-sacrifice, *then* you'd see him coming up to you. But I still have faith in you. *He goes out the hall door.*

HEDVIG *wanders across the room, then starts into the kitchen. At that moment a knock comes on the loft door,* HEDVIG *goes over and opens it a space;* EKDAL *slips out, and she slides it shut again.*

EKDAL: Hm, a morning walk alone is no fun at all.

HEDVIG: Don't you want to go hunting, Grandpa?

EKDAL: The weather's no good for hunting. Awfully dark in there; you can hardly see ahead of you.

HEDVIG: Don't you ever want to shoot at anything but rabbits?

EKDAL: Aren't rabbits good enough, eh?

HEDVIG: Yes, but the wild duck, say?

EKDAL: Ha, ha! You're afraid I'll shoot the wild duck for you? Never in this world, dear. Never!

HEDVIG: No, you couldn't do that. It must be hard to shoot wild ducks.

EKDAL: Couldn't? I certainly could!

HEDVIG: How would you go about it, Grandpa?—I don't mean with *my* wild duck, but with others.

EKDAL: I'd be sure to shoot them in the breast, understand; that's the safest. And then they've got to be shot *against* the feathers, you see— not *with* the feathers.

HEDVIG: They die then, Grandpa?

EKDAL: Oh yes, they do indeed—if you shoot them right. Well, got to go in and clean up. Hm—you understand—hm. *He goes into his room.*

HEDVIG *waits a moment, glances at the living room door, goes to the bookcase, stands on tip-toe, takes down the double-barreled pistol from the shelf and looks at it.* GINA, *with duster and cloth, comes in from the living room.* HEDVIG *hastily sets down the pistol, unnoticed.*

GINA: Don't mess with your father's things, Hedvig.
HEDVIG *leaving the bookcase:*   I was just straightening up a little.
GINA: Go out in the kitchen instead and make sure the coffee's still hot; I'll take a tray along to him when I go down.

HEDVIG *goes out;* GINA *begins to dust and clean up the studio. After a moment the hall door is cautiously opened, and* HJALMAR *peers in. He wears his overcoat, but no hat. He is unwashed, with tousled, unruly hair; his eyes are dull and inert.*

GINA *standing rooted with duster in hand, looking at him:*   Don't tell me, Hjalmar—are you back after all?
HJALMAR *steps in and answers in a thick voice:*   I'm back—but only for one moment.
GINA: Oh yes, I'm sure of that. But my goodness—what a sight you are!
HJALMAR: Sight?
GINA: And then your good winter coat! Well, it's done for.
HEDVIG *at the kitchen door:*   Mother, should I— *Seeing* HJALMAR, *giving a squeal of delight, and running toward him.* Oh, Daddy, Daddy!
HJALMAR *turning from her and waving her off:*   Get away! Get away! *To* GINA. Make her get away from me, will you!
GINA *in an undertone:*   Go in the living room, Hedvig.

HEDVIG *silently goes out.*

HJALMAR *with a busy air, pulling out the table drawer:*   I must have my books along. Where are my books?
GINA: What books?
HJALMAR: My scientific works, of course—the technical journals I use for my invention.
GINA *looking over the bookshelves:*   Are these them, the ones without covers?
HJALMAR: Yes, exactly.
GINA *putting a stack of booklets on the table:*   Could I get Hedvig to cut the pages for you?
HJALMAR: Nobody has to cut pages for me. *A short silence.*
GINA: Then it's definite that you're moving out, Hjalmar?
HJALMAR *rummaging among the books:*   Yes, that would seem to me self-evident.
GINA: I see.

HJALMAR: How could I go on here and have my heart shattered every hour of the day!

GINA: God forgive you for thinking so badly of me.

HJALMAR: Show me proof—

GINA: I think *you're* the one to show proof.

HJALMAR: After your kind of past? There are certain claims—I'd like to call them ideal claims—

GINA: But Grandfather? What'll happen to him, poor dear?

HJALMAR: I know my duty; that helpless old soul leaves with me. I'm going downtown and make arrangements—hm— *Hesitantly.* Did anybody find my hat on the stairs?

GINA: No. Have you lost your hat?

HJALMAR: I had it on, naturally, when I came in last night; I'm positive of that. But today I couldn't find it.

GINA: My Lord, where did you go with those two stumblebums?

HJALMAR: Oh, don't bother me with petty questions. Do you think I'm in a mood to remember details?

GINA: I just hope you didn't catch cold, Hjalmar. *She goes out into the kitchen.*

HJALMAR *muttering to himself in exasperation, as he empties the table drawer:* You're a sneak, Relling! A barbarian, that's what! Oh, snake in the grass! If I could just get someone to strangle you! *He puts some old letters to one side, discovers the torn deed of the day before, picks it up and examines the pieces. He hurriedly puts them down as* GINA *enters.*

GINA *setting a breakfast tray on the table:* Here's a drop of something hot, if you care for it. And there's some bread and butter and a little salt meat.

HJALMAR *glancing at the tray:* Salt meat? Never under this roof! Of course I haven't enjoyed going without food for nearly twenty-four hours; but that doesn't matter—My notes! My unfinished memoirs! Where can I find my journal and my important papers? *Opens the living room door, then draws back.* There she is again!

GINA: Well, goodness, the child has to be somewhere.

HJALMAR: Come out. *He stands aside, and* HEDVIG, *terrified, comes into the studio.*

HJALMAR *with his hands on the doorknob, says to* GINA: These last moments I'm spending in my former home, I'd like to be free from intruders—*Goes into the living room.*

HEDVIG *rushing to her mother, her voice hushed and trembling:* Does he mean me?

GINA: Stay in the kitchen, Hedvig. Or, no—go into your own room instead. *Speaking to* HJALMAR *as she goes in to him.* Just a minute, Hjalmar. Don't muss up the bureau like that; I know where everything is. HEDVIG *stands for a moment as if frozen by fright and bewilderment, biting her lips to keep the tears back; then she clenches her fists convulsively.*

HEDVIG *softly:* The wild duck. *She steals over and takes the pistol from the the shelf, sets the loft door ajar, slips in and draws the door shut after her.* HJALMAR *and* GINA *start arguing in the living room.*

HJALMAR *reenters with some notebooks and old loose papers, which he lays on the table:*   Oh, what good is that traveling bag! I've got a thousand things to take with me.

GINA *following with the traveling bag:*   So leave everything else for the time being, and just take a shirt and a pair of shorts with you.

HJALMAR: Phew! These agonizing preparations! *Takes off his overcoat and throws it on the sofa.*

GINA: And there's your coffee getting cold, too.

HJALMAR: Hm. *Unthinkingly takes a sip and then another.*

GINA: The hardest thing for you will be to find another room like that, big enough for all the rabbits.

HJALMAR: What! Do I have to take all the rabbits with me, too?

GINA: Yes, Grandfather couldn't live without the rabbits, I'm sure.

HJALMAR: He's simply got to get used to it. The joys of life *I* have to renounce are higher than rabbits.

GINA *dusting the bookcase:*   Should I put your flute in the traveling bag?

HJALMAR: No. No flute for me. But give me the pistol!

GINA: You want your pistol along?

HJALMAR: Yes. My loaded pistol.

GINA *looking for it:*   It's gone. He must have taken it inside.

HJALMAR: Is he in the loft?

GINA: Of course he's in the loft.

HJALMAR: Hm—lonely old man. *He takes a piece of bread and butter, eats it, and finishes the cup of coffee.*

GINA: Now if we only hadn't rented the room, you could have moved in there.

HJALMAR: I should stay on under the same roof as—! Never! Never!

GINA: But couldn't you put up in the living room just for a day or two? You've got everything you need in there.

HJALMAR: Never within these walls!

GINA: Well, how about down with Relling and Molvik?

HJALMAR: Don't mention those barbarians' names! I can almost lose my appetite just thinking about them. Oh no, I've got to go out in sleet and snow—tramp from house to house and seek shelter for Father and me.

GINA: But you haven't any hat, Hjalmar! You've lost your hat.

HJALMAR: Oh, those two vermin, wallowing in sin! The hat will have to be bought. *Taking another piece of bread and butter.* Someone's got to make arrangements. I certainly don't intend to risk my life. *Looking for something on the tray.*

GINA: What are you looking for?

HJALMAR: Butter.

GINA: Butter's coming right up. *Goes into the kitchen.*

HJALMAR *calling after her:*   Oh, never mind; I can just as easily eat dry bread.

GINA *bringing in a butter dish:*   Look. It's fresh today. *She passes him another cup of coffee. He sits on the sofa, spreads more butter on the bread, eats and drinks a moment in silence.*

HJALMAR: Could I—without being annoyed by anybody—anybody at all—put up in the living room just for a day or two?

GINA: Yes, of course you could, if you want to.

HJALMAR: Because I can't see any possibility of getting all Father's things out in one trip.

GINA: And then there's this, too, that you've first got to tell him you're not living with us any longer.

HJALMAR *pushing the coffee cup away:* That too, yes. All these intricate affairs to unravel. I've got to clear my thinking; I need a breathing spell; I can't shoulder all these burdens in one day.

GINA: No, and not when the weather's like it is out.

HJALMAR *picking up* WERLE's *letter:* I see this letter's still kicking around.

GINA: Yes, *I* haven't touched it.

HJALMAR: This trash is nothing to me—

GINA: Well, I'm not going to use it for anything.

HJALMAR: All the same, there's no point in throwing it around helter-skelter. In all the confusion of my moving, it could easily—

GINA: I'll take good care of it, Hjalmar.

HJALMAR: First and foremost, the deed of gift is Father's; it's really his affair whether or not he wants to use it.

GINA *sighing:* Yes, poor old Father—

HJALMAR: Just for safety's sake—where would I find some paste?

GINA *going to the bookcase:* Here's the pastepot.

HJALMAR: And then a brush.

GINA: Here's a brush, too. *Bringing both.*

HJALMAR *taking a pair of scissors:* A strip of paper down the back, that's all. *Cutting and pasting.* Far be it from me to take liberties with another's property—least of all, a penniless old man's. No, nor with—the other person's. There, now. Let it lie a while. And when it's dry, then take it away. I don't want to set eyes on that document again. Ever!

GREGERS *enters from the hall.*

GREGERS *somewhat surprised:* What? You're sitting here, Hjalmar?

HJALMAR *springing up:* I was overcome by fatigue.

GREGERS: Still, you've had breakfast, I see.

HJALMAR: The body asserts its claims now and then.

GREGERS: What have you decided to do?

HJALMAR: For a man like me there's only one way open. I'm in the process of assembling my most important things. But that takes time, don't you know.

GINA *a bit impatient:* Should I get the room ready for you, or should I pack your bag?

HJALMAR *after a vexed glance at* GREGERS: Pack—and get the room ready!

GINA *taking the traveling bag:* All right, then I'll put in the shirt and the rest. *She goes into the living room, shutting the door behind her.*

GREGERS *after a short silence:* I never dreamed that things would end like this. Is it really necessary for you to leave house and home?

HJALMAR *pacing restlessly about:* What would you have me do? I wasn't made to be unhappy, Gregers. I've got to have it snug and secure and peaceful around me.

GREGERS: But why can't you, then? Give it a try. Now I'd say you have solid ground to build on—so make a fresh start. And don't forget you have your invention to live for, too.

HJALMAR: Oh, don't talk about the invention. That seems such a long way off.

GREGERS: Oh?

HJALMAR: Good Lord, yes. What would you really have me invent? Other people have invented so much already. It gets more difficult every day—

GREGERS: And you've put so much work in it.

HJALMAR: It was that dissolute Relling who got me started.

GREGERS: Relling?

HJALMAR: Yes, he was the one who first made me aware that I had a real talent for inventing something in photography.

GREGERS: Aha—that was Relling!

HJALMAR: Oh, I was so blissfully happy as a result. Not so much from the invention itself, but because Hedvig believed in it—believed in it with all the power and force of a child's mind. Yes, in other words, fool that I am, I've gone around imagining that she believed in it.

GREGERS: You can't really think that Hedvig could lie to you!

HJALMAR: Now I can think anything. It's Hedvig that ruins it all. She's managed to blot the sun right out of my life.

GREGERS: Hedvig! You mean Hedvig? How could she ever do that?

HJALMAR *without answering:*   How inexpressibly I loved that child! How inexpressibly happy I was whenever I came home to my poor rooms and she came flying to meet me with those sweet, fluttering eyes. I was so unspeakably fond of her—and so I dreamed and deluded myself into thinking that she, too, was fond of me beyond words.

GREGERS: Can you call *that* just a delusion?

HJALMAR: How can I tell? I can't get anything out of Gina; and besides, she has no feeling at all for the ideal phase of these complications. But with you, Gregers, I feel impelled to open my mind. There's this horrible doubt—maybe Hedvig never really, truly has loved me.

GREGERS: She may perhaps give you proof that she has. *Listening.* What's that? I thought I heard the wild duck cry.

HJALMAR: The duck's quacking. Father's in the loft.

GREGERS: Is he? *His face radiates joy.* I tell you, you may yet have proof that your poor, misjudged Hedvig loves you!

HJALMAR: Oh, what proof could she give me? I don't dare hope to be reassured from that quarter.

GREGERS: Hedvig's completely free of deceit.

HJALMAR: Oh, Gregers, that's just what I can't be sure of. Who knows what Gina and this Mrs. Sørby have whispered and gossiped about in all the times they've sat here? And Hedvig uses her ears, you know. Maybe the deed of gift wasn't such a surprise, after all. In fact, I seemed to get that impression.

GREGERS: What is this spirit that's gotten into you?

HJALMAR: I've had my eyes opened. Just wait—you'll see; the deed of gift is only the beginning. Mrs. Sørby has always cared a lot for Hedvig, and now she has the power to do what she wants for the child. They can take her away from me any time they like.

GREGERS: You're the last person in the world Hedvig would leave.

HJALMAR: Don't be too sure of that. If they stand beckoning her with all they have—? Oh, I who've loved her so inexpressibly! I who'd find my highest joy in taking her tenderly by the hand and leading her as one leads a child terrified of the dark through a huge, empty room! I can feel it now with such gnawing certainty; the poor photographer up in this attic has never meant much to her. She's merely been clever to keep on a good footing with him till the right time came.

GREGERS: You really don't believe that, Hjalmar.

HJALMAR: The worst thing is precisely that I don't know what to believe—that I'll never know. But can you honestly doubt that it's just what I'm saying? *With a bitter laugh.* Oh, you trust too much in the power of ideals, my dear Gregers! Suppose the others come with their hands full of riches and call out to the child: Leave him. Life waits for you here with us—

GREGERS *quickly:* Yes, then what?

HJALMAR: If I asked her then: Hedvig, are you willing to give up life for me? *Laughs derisively.* Yes, thanks—you'd hear all right what answer I'd get!

A pistol shot is heard in the loft.

GREGERS *with a shout of joy:* Hjalmar!

HJALMAR: Hear that. He's got to go hunting as well.

GINA *coming in:* Oh, Hjalmar, it sounds like Grandfather's shooting up the loft by himself.

HJALMAR: I'll take a look—

GREGERS *animated and exalted:* Wait now! Do you know what that was?

HJALMAR: Of course I know.

GREGERS: No, you don't know. But *I* do. That was the proof.

HJALMAR: What proof?

GREGERS: That was a child's sacrifice. She's had your father shoot the wild duck.

HJALMAR: Shoot the wild duck!

GINA: No, really—

HJALMAR: What for?

GREGERS: She wanted to sacrifice to you the best thing she had in the world, because she thought then you'd have to love her again.

HJALMAR *stirred, gently:* Ah, that child!

GINA: Yes, the things she thinks of!

GREGERS: She only wants your love again, Hjalmar; she felt she couldn't live without it.

GINA *struggling with tears:* There you are, Hjalmar.

HJALMAR: Gina, where's she gone?

GINA *sniffling:* Poor thing. I guess she's out in the kitchen.

HJALMAR *going over and flinging the kitchen door open:*   Hedvig, come! Come here to me! *Looking about.* No, she's not there.

GINA: Then she's in her own little room.

HJALMAR *out of sight:*   No, she's not there either. *Coming back in.* She may have gone out.

GINA: Yes, you didn't want her around anywhere in the house.

HJALMAR: Oh, if only she comes home soon—so I can just let her know—! Things will work out now, Gregers—for now I really believe we can start life over again.

GREGERS *quietly:*   I knew it; through the child everything rights itself.

EKDAL *appears at the door to his room; he is in full uniform, absorbed in buckling his sword.*

HJALMAR *astonished:*   Father! Are you there?

GINA: Were you out gunning in your room?

EKDAL *approaching angrily:*   So you've been hunting alone, eh, Hjalmar?

HJALMAR *baffled and anxious:*   Then it wasn't you who fired a shot in the loft?

EKDAL: Me, shoot? Hm!

GREGERS *shouting to* HJALMAR: She's shot the wild duck herself!

HJALMAR: What is all this! *Rushes to the loft doors, throws them open, looks in and cries:* Hedvig!

GINA *running to the door:*   Lord, what now!

HJALMAR *going in:*   She's lying on the floor!

GREGERS: Hedvig, on the floor! *Follows* HJALMAR *in.*

GINA *simultaneously:*   Hedvig! *Going into the loft.* No, no, no!

EKDAL: Ha, ha! So she's a hunter, too.

HJALMAR, GINA, *and* GREGERS *drag* HEDVIG *into the studio; her right hand hangs down and her fingers curve tightly around the pistol.*

HJALMAR *distraught:*   The pistol's gone off. She's wounded herself. Call for help! Help!

GINA *running into the hall and calling downstairs:*   Relling! Relling! Dr. Relling, come up as quick as you can!

HJALMAR *and* GREGERS *lay* HEDVIG *down on the sofa.*

EKDAL *hushed:*   The woods take revenge.

HJALMAR *on his knees by her:*   She's just coming to now. She's coming to now—oh yes, yes.

GINA *who has returned:*   Where is she wounded? I can't see anything—

RELLING *hurries in, and right after him,* MOLVIK, *who is without vest or tie, his dress coat open.*

RELLING: What's going on here?

GINA: They say Hedvig shot herself.

HJALMAR: Come here and help.

RELLING: Shot herself! *He shoves the table to one side and begins to examine her.*

HJALMAR *kneeling still, looking anxiously up at him:* It can't be serious? Huh, Relling? She's hardly bleeding. It can't be serious?

RELLING: How did this happen?

HJALMAR: Oh, how do I know—

GINA: She wanted to shoot the wild duck.

RELLING: The wild duck?

HJALMAR: The pistol must have gone off.

RELLING: Hm. I see.

EKDAL: The woods take revenge. But I'm not scared, even so. *He goes into the loft, shutting the door after him.*

HJALMAR: But Relling—why don't you say something?

RELLING: The bullet's entered her breast.

HJALMAR: Yes, but she's coming to!

RELLING: You can see for yourself that Hedvig is dead.

GINA *breaking into tears:* Oh, my child, my child!

GREGERS *hoarsely:* In the depths of the sea—

HJALMAR *jumping up:* No, no she *must* live! Oh, in God's name, Relling—just for a moment—just enough so I can tell her how inexpressibly I loved her all the time!

RELLING: It's reached the heart. Internal hemorrhage. She died on the spot.

HJALMAR: And I drove her from me like an animal! And she crept terrified into the loft and died out of love for me. *Sobbing.* Never to make it right again! Never to let her know—! *Clenching his fists and crying to heaven.* Oh, you up there—if you *do* exist. Why have you done this to me!

GINA: Hush, hush, you mustn't say those terrible things. We just didn't deserve to keep her, I guess.

MOLVIK: The child isn't dead; she sleepeth.

RELLING: Rubbish!

HJALMAR *becoming calm, going over to the sofa to stand, arms folded, looking at* HEDVIG: There she lies, so stiff and still.

RELLING *trying to remove the pistol:* She holds it so tight, so tight.

GINA: No, no, Relling, don't break her fingers. Let the gun be.

HJALMAR: She should have it with her.

GINA: Yes, let her. But the child shouldn't lie displayed out here. She ought to go into her own little room, she should. Give me a hand, Hjalmar.

HJALMAR *and* GINA *lift* HEDVIG *between them.*

HJALMAR *as they carry her off:* Oh, Gina, Gina, how can you bear it!

GINA: We must try to help each other. For now she belongs to us both, you know.

MOLVIK *outstretching his arms and mumbling:*   Praise be to God. Dust to dust, dust to dust—

RELLING *in a whisper:*   Shut up, you fool; you're drunk.

HJALMAR *and* GINA *carry the body out through the kitchen door.* RELLING *closes it after them.* MOLVIK *steals out the hall door.*

RELLING *going over to* GREGERS: Nobody's ever going to sell me the idea that this was an accident.

GREGERS *who has stood in a convulsive fit of horror:*   Who can say how this awful thing happened?

RELLING: There are powder burns on her blouse. She must have held the pistol right at her breast and fired.

GREGERS: Hedvig did not die in vain. Did you notice how grief freed the greatness in him?

RELLING: The grief of death brings out greatness in almost everyone. But how long do you think this glory will last with *him?*

GREGERS: I should think it would last and grow all his life.

RELLING: In less than a year little Hedvig will be nothing more to him than a pretty theme for recitations.

GREGERS: You dare say that about Hjalmar Ekdal!

RELLING: We'll be lectured on this when the first grass shows on her grave. Then you can hear him spewing out phrases about "the child torn too soon from her father's heart," and you'll have your chance to watch him souse himself in conceit and self-pity. Wait and see.

GREGERS: If you're right, and I'm wrong, then life isn't worth living.

RELLING: Oh, life would be good in spite of all, if we only could have some peace from these damned shysters who come badgering us poor people with their "summons to the ideal."

GREGERS *staring straight ahead:*   In that case, I'm glad my destiny is what it is.

RELLING: Beg pardon—but what *is* your destiny?

GREGERS *about to leave:*   To be the thirteenth man at the table.

RELLING: Oh, go to hell.

QUESTIONS

1. Describe the mood of the Werle's dinner party in the opening scene of *The Wild Duck.* How does it contrast with the mood of the Ekdal household in Act 2? How does music help establish this contrast?

2. Why does Ibsen have Hjalmar speak in so many clichés? How do Hjalmar's actions contradict his words? In what ways is this disparity an index to his character?

3. Why does Gina take people's figurative statements literally? How is this tendency consistent with her character? Why does Ibsen reveal part of her history in Act 1 before we actually meet her? What actions of Gina's in Acts 2 and 3 contradict the impression Gregers has of her?

4. In exposing Gina's past and Hedvig's paternity, is Gregers motivated by a desire to help the couple establish a marriage based on truth, or is he motivated by something else? Why does he call himself "the thirteenth man at the table"?
5. What is Doctor Relling's function in the play? Why does he conflict so openly with Gregers? Why is Werle reintroduced at the end of Act 3 and Mrs. Sørby at the end of Act 4? How do these scenes precipitate the climax?
6. In his working notes to *The Wild Duck,* Ibsen wrote, "Man undergoes the same change as when a child grows up. Instinct weakens, but the powers of logical thought are developed. Adults have lost the ability to play with dolls." How does the transformed attic represent a reversion to childhood for some of the characters? Which ones? Which characters have few childlike traits? What is Ibsen's purpose in establishing this contrast?
7. What does the wild duck symbolize? What details of the duck's capture fit Old Ekdal? Is the duck associated with Hedvig? How? Which character is the dog? Are there ironies in this identification?
8. Is *The Wild Duck* a tragedy? Why or why not?

WRITING ABOUT STAGECRAFT AND SPECTACLE

Because stagecraft and spectacle are not, strictly speaking, part of the dialogue of the play, they are the most elusive of the play's elements to define and write about. In a sense, analyzing and writing about them places you in the role of director of the play. You need to visualize the function and relative importance of those features not found exclusively in the printed dialogue: the actors' gestures or actions accompanying the dialogue; props associated with action and character development; stage sets and how they relate to the play's characters and theme; lighting and how it defines mood, and character developement; costumes as they clarify the play's historical setting or define character; and, finally, music as an enhancer of mood, a clarifier of theme, or an index to character. Music may even include a sense of the rhythm or pace of the dialogue. In short, stagecraft and spectacle have to do with all those elements found in the stage directions, or even in between the lines, what actors and directors sometimes refer to as the *subtext* of the play. While the actors never get to deliver the subtext as actual lines in the play, as part of their speeches, its presence nevertheless needs to be felt, for it crucially affects how the lines are delivered since it often explains *why* characters say what they say. Writing about stagecraft and spectacle exposes these elusive elements to the kind of scrutiny that clarifies their function in the play.

To write an analysis of the stagecraft and spectacle in a play, you should first read the play carefully, concentrating particularly on the characters and theme. While this concentration may seem to shift your focus away from stagecraft and spectacle, the function of these elements will not be clear unless the major features of the play are first understood. Then, reread the play and concentrate on stage directions and set descriptions, particularly at the beginning of each act. The following list of questions may prove helpful in analyzing each of the elements of stagecraft and spectacle.

SET

1. Are the sets the same or different for each act or scene?
2. What does each set contribute to the development of the action, theme, or character?
3. If the setting is historical, how is it appropriate or inappropriate to the action?
4. Are the sets meant to be realistic or expressionistic? Are they elaborate or minimal? Why?
5. What props are part of the setting? Do they help define character or elaborate on the theme?
6. Is a prop's significance developed through action and/or dialogue as the play unfolds?
7. How does the set reflect the kind of theatrical architecture customary during the playwright's time? What might be different in the action and dialogue if the play were staged in a different kind of theater?

LIGHTING

1. Are there special lighting effects indicated in the stage direction? If so, what is their function?
2. Is any character associated with one kind of light?
3. Does the lighting change in the play to indicate mood, character alteration, or theme?

GESTURES

1. Do the stage directions call for the actors to perform specified gestures to accompany the dialogue? If so, what is the intended effect?
2. Are any gestures repeated by a character? Are these defining gestures?
3. Does a gesture reveal how a character has reacted to what someone has said or done?

COSTUMES

1. Are the costumes described in the stage directions? How?
2. Are the costumes historical or contemporary?
3. How do the costumes define the characters' inner natures? Is there a contrast between the outer and inner character?

4. How would you costume the characters to reveal their social or professional status?

MUSIC

1. Is music used in the play? Do the stage directions explain its significance?
2. How would you use music to enhance the mood of a scene? Does a type of music or instrument suggest a particular mood?
3. Are the lyrics of any song passages connected to character, theme, or action?

STAGE

1. How does the theatrical architecture of the playwright's time influence the stage set?
2. Are the dialogue, actions, and scene affected by the type of stage on which the play was first performed?

The answers to these questions should provide sufficient material to write on a variety of topics. Because so much is encompassed by stagecraft and spectacle, it is advisable to limit your approach to one or a few related subtopics—set, lighting, gestures, costumes, music, stage—and to trace its contributions to one of the play's major elements: character, theme, or action. The approach used in the following essay on Ibsen's *The Wild Duck* is to explore what sets and lighting contribute to our understanding of the characters and theme of the play. For example, Old Ekdal's "shabby overcoat" and "dirty, reddish-brown wig" by themselves as part of his costume may not seem meaningful unless they are seen in relationship to the prosperity of the setting of the Werle household. His shabbiness helps clarify Werle's statement that, "There are people in this world who plunge to the bottom when they've hardly been winged, and they never come up again." The statement foreshadows the action of the play and helps establish the connection between Old Ekdal and the "winged" wild duck.

Your task, therefore, will be made a good deal easier if you decide at the outset what element or elements you will write about and what their primary function is: whether to clarify character or to help visualize theme. You may wish to concentrate on some bit of visual action, some foolish gesture that provides a comic insight into human nature: Hjalmar's lying down on the couch to work on his inventions or Krapp's methodicalness in *Krapp's Last Tape*. Whichever element or function you choose to write about, your analysis should demonstrate the contribution stagecraft and spectacle make to the performance of a play. Working as a hypothetical director you have an opportunity to demonstrate the truly collaborative nature of the drama.

The Boundaries of Reality: Visual Stagecraft in Ibsen's The Wild Duck

In The Wild Duck, Ibsen employs several devices as part of the play's stagecraft and spectacle to create a visual metaphor for his characters and theme. In fact, Ibsen emphasizes the very act of "seeing" as a motif in The Wild Duck to explore the elusive boundary between illusion and reality.

The boundary between illusion and reality is most clearly illustrated in Ibsen's stage directions for the sets of The Wild Duck. Ibsen sets his first act in the home of the financially successful merchant and mill-owner Haakon Werle. The set is divided with "a richly comfortably furnished study" in the foreground and "a large fashionable room" in the background separated from the study by "open folding doors" and a drawn curtain. The drawing room and its adjacent dining room are "brightly lit," while the study is softly illuminated by "green-shaded lamps." This same pattern of bifurcated set and contrasted lighting is employed in the set used for the remaining four acts. At first, economic differences between the Werles and the Ekdals seem to overshadow the similarities in the two sets: the luxury and spaciousness of Werle's socially respectable circumstances and the clutter and shabby gentility in the household of the socially disgraced Ekdals. Despite the differences, the Werle set is also divided into two halves: the dimly lit study where the truth is hidden, where sharp business practices took place that made such luxury possible, and the brightly lit drawing room where luxurious but empty dinners, the rewards of wealth, entertain guests who pretend to enjoy themselves and keep up a front only for the food and wine. Keeping up a front is what Werle is interested in, and he tries to use his son, Gregers, to create a family portrait, a "tableau of father and son," to gain public approval for his impending marriage to his housekeeper, Mrs. Sørby. Ironically, the first act closes with Mrs. Sørby leading the guests in a game of blindman's bluff.

While Hjalmar Ekdal sees only the differences between his home and that of the Werles--"My house is a sad one, Gregers--especially after a brilliant occasion like this"--the similarities are apparent to the audience through the stage set, Ekdal's studio. Here the bifurcation between the worlds of illusion and reality is clearer, with props and lighting assisting the contrast. In the foreground is Ekdal's living area and studio replete with photographic equipment, a visual metaphor for seeming truth or reality.

> Photographic apparatus and equipment of various sorts are set up here and there in the room. At the left of the double doors stands a bookcase containing a few books, small boxes and flasks of chemicals, various tools, implements, and other objects. Photographs and such small articles as brushes, paper, and the like lie on the table.

Depending on the mood, Ibsen varies the lighting in this portion of the set with sunlight emerging from the ceiling through a giant skylight. In contrast to the studio is the loft, or attic, the habitat of the wild duck, the world of illusion. It is separated from the studio proper by a sliding double door, and it is dimly lit by moonlight.

> The doorway opens on an extensive, irregular loft room with many nooks and corners, and two separate chimney shafts ascending through it. Clear moonlight streams through skylights into certain parts of the large room; others lie in deep shadow.

Later, in Act 2, Ibsen introduces a curtain composed of net and sailcloth which separates the attic room from the studio: "Inside a curtain descends, its lower portion composed of a strip of old sailcloth, the upper part being a piece of worn-out fishnetting." The curtain's sea imagery connects directly with the wild duck and Hedvig's subsequent allusion to the "Flying Dutchman, a legendary mariner condemned to sail the seas until Judgment Day." There is, therefore, something magical and childlike about the attic where the two Ekdal men and the child Hedvig "play" with a series of props that suggest illusion and dreams, what Doctor Relling plainly calls "lies." The significance of the attic is explained by Relling, who invented it for old Ekdal, as he has invented other illusions for Molvik and Hjalmar, to help them cope, to distract them from realities they could not live with.

> Well, what do you think of this bear hunter going into a dark loft to stalk rabbits? There isn't a happier sportsman in the world than the old man when he's prowling around in the junkyard. Those four or five dried-out Christmas trees he's got--to him they're like all the green forests of Hoidal; the hens and the rooster--they're the game birds up in the fir tops; and the rabbits hopping across the floor-- they're the bears that call up his youth again, out in the mountain air.

The studio itself, which on the surface seems to be very real with its photographic equipment meant to document reality, is actually part of the web of lies spun by the older Werle. Ironically, Hjalmar the photographer does little work; it is chiefly Gina, who takes everyone's remarks literally and who demonstrates practicality and efficiency, who does most of the photographic work, keeps accounts and makes sure the household continues to stay afloat despite Hjalmar's extravagances and laziness. Gina must be not only realistic enough for all of the Ekdal household, but she must also "retouch" the family portrait to make it acceptable to Hjalmar. Interestingly, she never enters the attic.

Making photographs requires exposure to light, and Ibsen cleverly uses this fact to create several visual metaphors to demonstrate the boundary between illusion and reality. As Act 3 opens, Hjalmar is busy "retouching a photograph," and illusions remain intact as "daylight streams through the large window in the sloping roof"; however, the mood changes with the revelations in Act 4--the camera is covered, and the light fades as the mood darkens: "Late afternoon light; it is near sunset; somewhat later it begins to grow dark." Hjalmar, in his new mood, under the influence of Gregers, calls for light and Gina characteristically puts a shade on the lamp. Lighting is, therefore, used by Ibsen to support his purpose, namely to suggest that there are those, like Hjalmar, who are unable to stand the exposure to the bright light of facts, and who are better off living in the shadow of illusion. After his revelations, Gregers expects to be met "by a transfigured light in both [Hjalmar's and Gina's] faces," but instead unexpectedly sees something "gloomy, heavy, dismal." Ironically, it is old Werle's life that is transformed by complete disclosure of his and Mrs. Sørby's former lives. It is through a further irony that Hjalmar learns of Hedvig's true paternity. Werle's failing eyesight provides the final clue that he is Hedvig's father. Gregers believes he is opening Hjalmar's eyes; "He's going to see his situation just as it is-- that's all." Yet it is Gregers who is blind to the reality of Hjalmar's character and who has seen his own father through his mother's eyes, which were "clouded at times." Frequent allusions like these establish a connection between the lighting used in the play to define the boundaries between illusion and reality and sightlessness.

That Gregers is mistaken in his assumptions about Hjalmar is clear from Doctor Relling's remark: "Ekdal's misfortune is that in his circle he's always been taken for a shining light." Throughout the play not only in the clichés Hjalmar mouths, but also in his gestures which always take intention for deed, he shows himself weak, easily misled, vain, and unoriginal. His weakness for butter, cheese and beer, his substituting the menu for the actual treat he was supposed to bring Hedvig, his assertion about paying back Werle every penny, his vague invention, and his pasting the property deed back together indicate his true habitat is the world of illusion. Even in his delusions Hjalmar is mistaken, as when he asserts that Hedvig has "managed to blot the sun right out of my life."

In The Wild Duck Ibsen has managed to create a well-made play for which he is justly famous, not only in the complex structure of action and dialogue, but in stagecraft and spectacle. The use of visual devices such as scenery and lighting complements the theme of The Wild Duck and thus provides a visual metaphor consistent with the play's overall intention.

SUGGESTIONS FOR WRITING ABOUT STAGECRAFT AND SPECTACLE

1. Write an essay on *The Wild Duck* explaining the function of the stage properties in the studio and the attic. Connect them to different characters in the play, demonstrating how the prop is a visual metaphor for that character.
2. Analyze Ibsen's use of photographic equipment and photos as props in *The Wild Duck*. What do photos represent in this play? How is Ibsen contrasting illusion and reality?
3. Examine the stage props, costumes, and gestures associated with each of the characters in Sam Shepard's *Curse of the Starving Class*. Show how the theme of the play is given visual form through these production details.
4. Discuss the connection between character and theme, and props and gestures in Samuel Beckett's *Krapp's Last Tape*.
5. Write an essay discussing how the conventions of the Greek or Elizabethan stage affect the way action is presented in either *Oedipus the King* or *Hamlet*. Account for the pace of the action (whether events are narrated or shown dramatically), the number and juxtaposition of acts and scenes, and the kinds of dramatic speeches which are given the actors. How is the content of the dialogue affected by the limitations of stagecraft and spectacle?

TRAGEDY AND IRONY

We should distinguish from the outset between the everyday use of the term **tragedy** and its use to describe a kind of drama. We speak of the tragedy of a fatal automobile accident, or of hunger in an impoverished land, or the tragic injury which befalls a star football player. As unfortunate as these events may be, they do not exhibit the qualities of dramatic tragedy. First, they are not acted out upon a stage; that is, they are not products of an artist's attempt to construct an ordered vision of the world and to affect an audience with that vision. Second, these "tragedies" are motiveless occurrences. They have causes—a flat tire, economic exploitation, a hard tackle—but they do not necessarily arise from the motives and choices of the victims. They have a random quality that is not present in literary tragedy. Orderliness, and suffering caused by choice: we should remember these elements as we reconstruct the definition of tragic drama as it has come down to us from its birthplace in classical Greece.

The exact origin of tragedy is still shrouded in mystery. The songs that apparently evolved into tragic plays were originally hymns sung in honor of Dionysus, god of fertility and of the vine, to celebrate his yearly resurrection—and to mourn, in anticipation, his yearly death. The songs were sung by men dressed as satyrs: men from the waist up, goats (an animal commonly associated with fertility) from the waist down. The Greek word *tragoidea* means "goat-song." It is generally believed that a man named Thespis, around the year 534 B.C., isolated one satyr and engaged him in a dialogue with the group. Thus drama—an actor talking to a "chorus" upon a stage—was born.

Whatever the origin and early form of Greek tragedy, our attention must focus on the period between 534 B.C., when Thespis "created" drama, and 406 B.C., at the death of Euripides, the last of the three great tragic playwrights whose works have survived. Athens, the principal Greek city-state of the time, formed the geographical center for this unparalleled 125-year period of dramatic activity. In Athens, great dramatic festivals were held each spring. Audience attendance was subsidized by the government, and playwrights from throughout Greece competed for prizes. In Athens, the great works of Aeschylus, Sophocles, and Euripides (32 surviving plays in all) were first performed. Each competing playwright presented a trilogy of tragic plays (three related dramas) along with a satiric, often bawdy, "satyr-play" in honor of Dionysus.

Our knowledge of fifth-century Athenian theater comes from a variety of sources: the extant texts of the plays themselves, historical accounts and records of the contests, and the remains of outdoor theaters. Besides the plays, perhaps the most significant source of our knowledge is the *Poetics* of the Greek philosopher Aristotle. This text, composed around 336 B.C., is important not only because of the facts and judgments it contains, but also because it is the first attempt to codify the principles of drama. Aristotle examined the Greek tragedies known to him and set out to describe the general laws that govern tragic drama. The *Poetics* is the earliest surviving work of literary criticism in the Western world. Because its influence was both pervasive and profound—many critics would say it has never been improved upon—it deserves careful attention. (Five chapters from the *Poetics* appear under "Critical Touchstones: Drama," page 1561.)

Aristotle defines tragedy as:

> the imitation of an action that is serious and also, as having magnitude, complete in itself; in language with pleasurable accessories, each kind brought in separately in parts of the work; in a dramatic, not in a narrative form; with incidents arousing pity and fear wherewith to accomplish its catharsis of such emotions. (Richard McKeon, *Introduction to Aristotle*)

Implicit in this definition are the six elements of tragedy Aristotle goes on to describe and which have been outlined in "How to Read Drama" (page 967): plot, character, thought, diction, melody, and spectacle. The most famous portions of Aristotle's analysis of these elements are the sections concerning plot and character. Along with spectacle, these are the elements to be discussed here.

For Aristotle, the best tragic plots concern a single action. This action should be significant and should be presented to us as a whole, unclouded by subplots and not requiring any information outside of the text itself. This plot should contain both **peripety,** or the reversal of the main character's fortunes, and **anagnorisis,** the character's recognition of the causes and consequences of this reversal. Either of these without the other creates an incomplete effect that fails to arouse the full measure of pity and fear in the audience.

A glance at the text of Sophocles' *Oedipus the King,* which follows, reveals some other significant features of a tragic plot. The prologue of the play provides important expository material and is followed by the **parados,** the song sung by the chorus as it enters. After the parados are four scenes followed by **choral odes.** In the fourth of these scenes, Oedipus undergoes his reversal and recognition. Then comes an **exodos,** or "exit" scene, in which the action of the play is resolved. The structure of the play is thus as orderly as the progressive revelation of Oedipus's real identity.

But what of the characters whose fates are enacted within this neat, almost symmetrical, framework? First, they were limited in number. Aeschylus is usually credited with adding a second actor to Thespis's original "soloist." Sophocles is generally credited with adding a third. These numbers refer not to the number of parts in the play but to the number of actors upon the stage at any one time, not counting the chorus. For reasons of artistic restraint or simplicity of design, the Greek tragedians never went beyond three. This simplicity of outward display is central to the convention of the Greek theater and underscores the emphasis on actions and speeches as the main components of a tragic play.

Aristotle allots most of his remarks about character to defining the nature of the protagonist or tragic hero. According to Aristotle, the tragic hero in a Greek play will be a person, usually of noble lineage (as in the case of Oedipus), who is essentially moral and good. We would not pity or identify with a totally bad person, whether he or she suffered good fortune or ill. Oedipus, as we will see, has an acute sense of right and wrong, is a skillful leader of his people, and does his best to avoid doing wrong. But if a perfectly good person were to meet a tragic end, the emotions proper to tragedy would also not be aroused. These emotions are best expressed when the essentially good hero suffers from a fatal flaw or error, called by Aristotle the *hamartia* (usually translated as "tragic flaw"). Often in Greek plays, this flaw is excessive pride, called *hubris* by the Greeks, which leads the main character to act in a way that causes both his downfall and his recognition of the reasons for it. In Oedipus's case, he shows pride in killing King Laios at the crossroads; he shows pride by not fully believing the oracles when they implicate him; he shows pride when he accuses Creon of treason; and he shows pride when he berates and accuses the old seer, Teiresias. Reprehensible as it may be in the instances cited, Oedipus's pride also makes him a moral person and a just ruler. His story reminds us that there are few absolutes in Greek drama, and that we should always try to view the characters in tragic plays from a rounded perspective. For a modern view of the tragic hero and the tragic struggle, read Arthur Miller's "Tragedy and the Common Man" (under "Critical Touchstones: Drama," page 1578).

Another vital element of characterization in Greek drama is the *chorus*, a group of fifteen or so actors who persist in Greek drama as a vestige from the days when tragic hymns were sung to Dionysus by a chorus of satyrs. The chorus and its leader, the *choragos* (who was sometimes given his own lines to speak), entered during the parados and were on stage throughout the play. They spoke as a group at key points of the performance: after the prologue, between the scenes (their *odes*), and again at the play's conclusion. The sections marked *strophe* in their odes (page 1255) were presumably spoken after they had advanced toward the audience; the sections marked *antistrophe* were spoken after they had stepped back.

By their presence upon the stage and through the content of their speeches, the chorus contributed in numerous ways to the total effect of the play. They summarized and anticipated important parts of the action, often helping to create suspense. They acted as the conservative voice of public opinion about the events portrayed. They helped to create the structure of the play. They served as someone for the other characters to talk to. And their dancing and chanting added to the spectacle of the play.

This spectacle was probably restrained and spare. The Greeks show little inclination for realistic effect, and they never portrayed violent deeds upon the stage. The stage was nearly round, and was surrounded on two thirds of its circumference by tiered seats for the audience. The play was performed in the round space of the *orchestra*, in front of a building whose facade, called the *skene*, served as the backdrop for the action. The skene, usually representing a palace, had two large doors in the middle and possibly an altar in front or to one side.

The actors wore masks which could reflect, in a general way, the mood of the play, and which contained small megaphones. (The acoustics of Greek theaters was excellent.) The actors also wore tall shoes called *kothor-*

noi (perhaps something like modern-day platform shoes) to make them more visible. They probably moved around very little, but, along with the chorus and its strophic movements, they did present some physical action.

Two machines were used to facilitate the stage action. One, a large basket or platform at the end of a crane, was used to lower characters, often gods, onto the stage when they were needed to resolve the action. This device, usually called the **deus ex machina** (Latin for "god out of a machine"), was used by Euripides in several of his plays. The name has come to stand for any kind of miraculous occurrence which, plausibly or not, resolves a complex plot. The other machine Greek dramatists employed, the *eccyclema*, was a wheeled cart used to bring characters (usually dead ones!) on the stage for display. The still tableaux thus created were considered more effective than the direct portrayal of violent deeds. This point warrants emphasis because it typifies the Greek belief that the gist of a tragedy lay in the speeches, the personalities, and the deeds of characters—not in the spectacle of the performance.

No matter how gruesome the actions portrayed or mentioned in a Greek play might seem, and no matter how grievous the error of the protagonist might be, the total effect was stately, noble, and orderly. Though they suffered terribly, tragic heroes ultimately made sense of their world, saw their own behavior with excruciating clarity, and accepted, indeed were elevated by, their "punishment." It is perhaps this notion of imposing order on suffering that Aristotle expressed when he said that the audience, after they had seen a tragic performance, should undergo a *katharsis* of the emotions of pity and fear. Katharsis has been translated as "purgation," "cleansing," "refinement," and "expression." However Aritotle's usage is construed, he clearly meant it as a positive experience. The Greek audience, or modern play-goers and readers, should not leave the play feeling depressed or full of despair, but ennobled by the knowledge that humans can see order in suffering; ennobled by the pity which tragic heroes can evoke; ennobled, even, by the fear that in spite of their example and the warning they provide, we may follow them in misery.

One other important element of Greek tragedy remains to be mentioned: **irony.** The Greek word *eiron* meant someone who feigned ignorance (like the philosopher Socrates) or who spoke in a dissembling manner. As a literary term, irony refers to speeches or situations that mean or imply something different (often opposite) from what they appear to or are intended to mean. Although there are many kinds of irony, two are of particular importance to students of drama. In **verbal irony** there is an intentional discrepancy between a character's speech and his or her meaning. When a man dressed in a white tuxedo is forced to change a flat tire and says to his companion, "Oh, I just love manual labor in formal wear," he is using verbal irony because he means the opposite of what he says.

Dramatic irony (sometimes called *tragic irony* or *Sophoclean irony* after the playwright who perfected its use) is more complicated. In dramatic irony a character, while fully meaning to say what he says or do what he does, fails to comprehend the full significance of his speech or action. The playwright and the audience *do* realize this full significance. Oedipus, for example, intends to kill the man at the crossroad, but decidedly does *not* intend to kill his father. That the man he kills turns out to be his father makes his deed an example of dramatic irony. The playwright and the audience know who the dead stranger was.

Another famous example of dramatic irony occurs in scene one of *Oedipus the King*. Oedipus, speaking to the chorus about the horrible crime that is the cause of the plague in Thebes, says:

> As for the criminal, I pray to God—
> Whether it be a lurking thief, or one of a number—
> I pray that that man's life be consumed in evil and wretchedness.
> And as for me, this curse applies no less
> If it should turn out that the culprit is my guest here,
> Sharing my hearth.
>
> (lines 232–7)

Oedipus intends to carry out what he promises, and he does find and punish the criminal. What he does not know—and what the audience *does* know—is that the criminal is Oedipus himself.

Dramatic irony is indeed a powerful tool in Sophocles' hands, and his use of it reminds us of the importance the Greeks placed on self-knowledge and awareness of one's own behavior. The split perspective that irony affords also draws the audience into the action and challenges both its memory and its awareness of the play's language.

The above description of Greek tragedies—with their flawed characters, symmetrical design, chanting choruses, ubiquitous irony—may create an impression of predictability. This impression can only be furthered when we remember that Greek audiences knew the broad outlines of the plots even before they saw them performed! (For more on the plot of *Oedipus the King*, see below.) However, Greek tragedy was far from being a lifeless, ossified form. The few plays that have survived reveal the durability of the essentials of a tradition. Greek tragedy remains one of humankind's most ennobling efforts to give order and artistic form to human suffering. *Oedipus the King*, though it may not be a typical tragedy, perhaps represents the perfection of these efforts. Even after 2,300 years we can still be moved by the grace of its design and by the catastrophic passions it records.

THE PLOT OF *OEDIPUS THE KING*

To say that Greek audiences knew the broad outlines of tragic plots before they saw the dramatic performances does not mean that the plays were without suspense. Though many of these plots were taken from myths, legends, and other texts (the story of Oedipus and Jocasta, for example, is described in Homer's *Odyssey*), each playwright brought his own fresh insights and gave his own design to the story he was reworking. We offer this description of the plot of *Oedipus the King* so that the reader may have the same chance that Greek audiences had to appreciate the irony of the play.

King Laios and Queen Jocasta of Thebes, having heard a prophecy that their son would kill his father, instructed a shepherd to leave the infant on a mountainside to die. But, having bound Oedipus's ankles together (hence his name, which means "swollen foot"), the Theban shepherd presented him to a Corinthian shepherd. Oedipus was taken to the Corinthian court of King Polybus and Queen Merope and grew up thinking they were his parents.

When Oedipus was a grown man, a drunken reveler told him he was not his father's son. Oedipus consulted the Delphic oracle to find out if this was true; the oracle answered obscurely by prophesying that Oedipus would kill his father, marry his mother, and beget children by her. Shocked, Oedipus left Corinth—leaving behind, he thought, the possibility of killing his real father and marrying his real mother—and vowed never to return. In his subsequent travels he encountered, at a place where three roads met, a man in a chariot. They quarreled, and Oedipus killed the man and four of his attendants. Unbeknownst to Oedipus, this man was his real father, King Laios of Thebes.

As Oedipus approached Thebes, he encountered the Sphinx, a monster who terrorized Thebes by killing anyone who could not answer her riddle: "What goes on four legs in the morning, two legs at noon, and three legs in the evening?" When Oedipus answered the riddle correctly—"A man, for he crawls as an infant, walks erect as a man, and uses a staff in old age"—the Sphinx destroyed herself.

Thus relieved of their menace, the Theban citizens make Oedipus King of Thebes, to replace Laios, and give him Queen Jocasta (Iokastê in the following translation), his real mother, as a wife. Oedipus married his mother and had two sons and two daughters by her.

Because the murder of Laios has gone unavenged, a terrible plague afflicts Thebes. Oedipus, as king, is determined to put an end to it. At this point, the action of *Oedipus the King* begins.

SOPHOCLES (496 B.C.?–406 B.C.?)

Oedipus the King

Of the three Greek tragedians whose works have survived—the others are Aeschylus and Euripides—Sophocles is considered the greatest. Born at Colonus, he lived most of his life in Athens, where he was active in both the political and the cultural life of the city. He is thought to have written over one hundred plays; unfortunately, only seven have survived. Among the most famous of these are *Antigone* (442 B.C.) and *Oedipus at Colonus*, which was produced posthumously in 401 B.C. *Oedipus the King* (429 B.C.), generally considered his greatest play, is a masterpiece of dramatic construction and dramatic irony.

CHARACTERS

OEDIPUS, *King of Thebes, supposed son of Polybus and Meropê, King and Queen of Corinth*

IOKASTÊ, *wife of Oedipus and widow of the late King Laïos*

KREON, *brother of Iokastê, a prince of Thebes*

TEIRESIAS, *a blind seer who serves Apollo*

PRIEST

MESSENGER, *from Corinth*

SHEPHERD, *former servant of Laïos*

SECOND MESSENGER, *from the palace*

CHORUS OF THEBAN ELDERS

CHORAGOS, *leader of the Chorus*

ANTIGONE *and* ISMENE, *young daughters of Oedipus and Iokastê. They appear in the Exodos but do not speak.*

SUPPLIANTS, GUARDS, SERVANTS

THE SCENE. *Before the palace of* OEDIPUS, *King of Thebes. A central door and two lateral doors open onto a platform which runs the length of the façade. On the platform, right and left, are altars; and three steps lead down into the or-chêstra, or chorus-ground. At the beginning of the action these steps are crowded by suppliants who have brought branches and chaplets of olive leaves and who sit in various attitudes of despair.* OEDIPUS *enters.*

PROLOGUE

OEDIPUS: My children, generations of the living
    In the line of Kadmos, nursed at his ancient hearth:
    Why have you strewn yourselves before these altars
    In supplication, with your boughs and garlands?
    The breath of incense rises from the city   5
    With a sound of prayer and lamentation.
                        Children,
    I would not have you speak through messengers,
    And therefore I have come myself to hear you—
    I, Oedipus, who bear the famous name.
    To a PRIEST You, there, since you are eldest in the company,   10
    Speak for them all, tell me what preys upon you,
    Whether you come in dread, or crave some blessing:
    Tell me, and never doubt that I will help you
    In every way I can; I should be heartless
    Were I not moved to find you suppliant here.   15

PRIEST: Great Oedipus, O powerful king of Thebes!
    You see how all the ages of our people
    Cling to your altar steps: here are boys
    Who can barely stand alone, and here are priests
    By weight of age, as I am a priest of God,   20
    And young men chosen from those yet unmarried;

As for the others, all that multitude,
They wait with olive chaplets in the squares,
At the two shrines of Pallas, and where Apollo
Speaks in the glowing embers.
                                        Your own eyes   25
Must tell you: Thebes is tossed on a murdering sea
And can not lift her head from the death surge.
A rust consumes the buds and fruits of the earth;
The herds are sick; children die unborn,
And labor is vain. The god of plague and pyre   30
Raids like detestable lightning through the city,
And all the house of Kadmos is laid waste,
All emptied, and all darkened: Death alone
Battens upon the misery of Thebes.

You are not one of the immortal gods, we know;   35
Yet we have come to you to make our prayer
As to the man surest in mortal ways
And wisest in the ways of God. You saved us
From the Sphinx, that flinty singer, and the tribute
We paid to her so long; yet you were never   40
Better informed than we, nor could we teach you:
A god's touch, it seems, enabled you to help us.

Therefore, O mighty power, we turn to you:
Find us our safety, find us a remedy,
Whether by counsel of the gods or of men.   45
A king of wisdom tested in the past
Can act in a time of troubles, and act well.
Noblest of men, restore
Life to your city! Think how all men call you
Liberator for your boldness long ago;   50
Ah, when your years of kingship are remembered,
Let them not say *We rose, but later fell*—
Keep the State from going down in the storm!
Once, years ago, with happy augury,
You brought us fortune; be the same again!   55
No man questions your power to rule the land:
But rule over men, not over a dead city!
Ships are only hulls, high walls are nothing,
When no life moves in the empty passageways.
OEDIPUS: Poor children! You may be sure I know   60
All that you longed for in your coming here.
I know that you are deathly sick; and yet,
Sick as you are, not one is as sick as I.
Each of you suffers in himself alone
His anguish, not another's; but my spirit   65
Groans for the city, for myself, for you.

I was not sleeping, you are not waking me.
No, I have been in tears for a long while
And in my restless thought walked many ways.
In all my search I found one remedy,   70
And I have adopted it: I have sent Kreon,
Son of Menoikeus, brother of the queen,
To Delphi, Apollo's place of revelation,
To learn there, if he can,
What act or pledge of mine may save the city.   75
I have counted the days, and now, this very day,
I am troubled, for he has overstayed his time.
What is he doing? He has been gone too long.
Yet whenever he comes back, I should do ill
Not to take any action the god orders.   80

PRIEST: It is a timely promise. At this instant
They tell me Kreon is here.

OEDIPUS: O Lord Apollo!
May his news be fair as his face is radiant!

PRIEST: Good news, I gather! he is crowned with bay,
The chaplet is thick with berries.

OEDIPUS: We shall soon know;   85
He is near enough to hear us now.

Enter KREON.

O prince:
Brother: son of Menoikeus:
What answer do you bring us from the god?

KREON: A strong one. I can tell you, great afflictions
Will turn out well, if they are taken well.   90

OEDIPUS: What was the oracle? These vague words
Leave me still hanging between hope and fear.

KREON: Is it your pleasure to hear me with all these
Gathered around us? I am prepared to speak,
But should we not go in?

OEDIPUS: Speak to them all,   95
It is for them I suffer, more than for myself.

KREON: Then I will tell you what I heard at Delphi.
In plain words
The god commands us to expel from the land of Thebes
An old defilement we are sheltering.   100
It is a deathly thing, beyond cure;
We must not let it feed upon us longer.

OEDIPUS: What defilement? How shall we rid ourselves of it?

KREON: By exile or death, blood for blood. It was
Murder that brought the plague-wind on the city.   105

OEDIPUS: Murder of whom? Surely the god has named him?

KREON: My lord: Laïos once ruled this land,
Before you came to govern us.

OEDIPUS: I know;
    I learned of him from others; I never saw him.
KREON: He was murdered; and Apollo commands us now   110
    To take revenge upon whoever killed him.
OEDIPUS: Upon whom? Where are they? Where shall we find a clue
    To solve that crime, after so many years?
KREON: Here in this land, he said. Search reveals
    Things that escape an inattentive man.   115
OEDIPUS: Tell me: Was Laïos murdered in his house,
    Or in the fields, or in some foreign country?
KREON: He said he planned to make a pilgrimage.
    He did not come home again.
OEDIPUS: And was there no one,
    No witness, no companion, to tell what happened?   120
KREON: They were all killed but one, and he got away
    So frightened that he could remember one thing only.
OEDIPUS: What was that one thing? One may be the key
    To everything, if we resolve to use it.
KREON: He said that a band of highwaymen attacked them,   125
    Outnumbered them, and overwhelmed the king.
OEDIPUS: Strange, that a highwayman should be so daring—
    Unless some faction here bribed him to do it.
KREON: We thought of that. But after Laïos' death
    New troubles arose and we had no avenger.   130
OEDIPUS: What troubles could prevent your hunting down the killers?
KREON: The riddling Sphinx's song
    Made us deaf to all mysteries but her own.
OEDIPUS: Then once more I must bring what is dark to light.
    It is most fitting that Apollo shows,   135
    As you do, this compunction for the dead.
    You shall see how I stand by you, as I should,
    Avenging this country and the god as well,
    And not as though it were for some distant friend,
    But for my own sake, to be rid of evil.   140
    Whoever killed King Laïos might—who knows?—
    Lay violent hands even on me—and soon.
    I act for the murdered king in my own interest.

    Come, then, my children: leave the altar steps,
    Lift up your olive boughs!
                    One of you go   145
    And summon the people of Kadmos to gather here.
    I will do all that I can; you may tell them that.

Exit a PAGE.

    So, with the help of God,
    We shall be saved—or else indeed we are lost.
PRIEST: Let us rise, children. It was for this we came,   150
    And now the king has promised it.

Phoibos has sent us an oracle; may he descend
Himself to save us and drive out the plague.

Exeunt OEDIPUS *and* KREON *into the palace by the central door. The* PRIEST
and the SUPPLIANTS *disperse right and left. After a short pause the* CHORUS
enters the orchêstra.

PARODOS

STROPHE 1

CHORUS: What is God singing in his profound
Delphi of gold and shadow?   155
What oracle for Thebes, the sunwhipped city?
Fear unjoints me, the roots of my heart tremble.
Now I remember, O Healer, your power, and wonder:
Will you send doom like a sudden cloud, or weave it
Like nightfall of the past?   160
Speak to me, tell me, O
Child of golden Hope, immortal Voice.

ANTISTROPHE 1

Let me pray to Athenê, the immortal daughter of Zeus,
And to Artemis her sister
Who keeps her famous throne in the market ring,   165
And to Apollo, archer from distant heaven—
O gods, descend! Like three streams leap against
The fires of our grief, the fires of darkness;
Be swift to bring us rest!
As in the old time from the brilliant house   170
Of air you stepped to save us, come again!

STROPHE 2

Now our afflictions have no end,
Now all our stricken host lies down
And no man fights off death with his mind;
The noble plowland bears no grain,   175
And groaning mothers can not bear—
See, how our lives like birds take wing,
Like sparks that fly when a fire soars,
To the shore of the god of evening.

ANTISTROPHE 2

The plague burns on, it is pitiless,   180
Though pallid children laden with death
Lie unwept in the stony ways,

And old gray women by every path
Flock to the strand about the altars
There to strike their breasts and cry   185
Worship of Phoibos in wailing prayers:
Be kind, God's golden child!

STROPHE 3

There are no swords in this attack by fire,
No shields, but we are ringed with cries.
Send the besieger plunging from our homes   190
Into the vast sea-room of the Atlantic
Or into the waves that foam eastward of Thrace—
For the day ravages what the night spares—
Destroy our enemy, lord of the thunder!
Let him be riven by lightning from heaven!   195

ANTISTROPHE 3

Phoibos Apollo, stretch the sun's bowstring,
That golden cord, until it sing for us,
Flashing arrows in heaven!
                              Artemis, Huntress,
Race with flaring lights upon our mountains!
O scarlet god, O golden-banded brow,   200
O Theban Bacchos in a storm of Maenads,

Enter OEDIPUS, *center.*

Whirl upon Death, that all the Undying hate!
Come with blinding torches, come in joy!

SCENE I

OEDIPUS: Is this your prayer? It may be answered. Come,
    Listen to me, act as the crisis demands,   205
    And you shall have relief from all these evils.

    Until now I was a stranger to this tale,
    As I had been a stranger to the crime.
    Could I track down the murderer without a clue?
    But now, friends,   210
    As one who became a citizen after the murder,
    I make this proclamation to all Thebans:
    If any man knows by whose hand Laïos, son of Labdakos,
    Met his death, I direct that man to tell me everything,
    No matter what he fears for having so long withheld it.   215

Let it stand as promised that no further trouble
Will come to him, but he may leave the land in safety.
Moreover: If anyone knows the murderer to be foreign,
Let him not keep silent: he shall have his reward from me.
However, if he does conceal it; if any man   220
Fearing for his friend or for himself disobeys this edict,
Hear what I propose to do:

I solemnly forbid the people of this country,
Where power and throne are mine, ever to receive that man
Or speak to him, no matter who he is, or let him   225
Join in sacrifice, lustration, or in prayer.
I decree that he be driven from every house,
Being, as he is, corruption itself to us: the Delphic
Voice of Apollo has pronounced this revelation.
Thus I associate myself with the oracle   230
And take the side of the murdered king.

As for the criminal, I pray to God—
Whether it be a lurking thief, or one of a number—
I pray that that man's life be consumed in evil and wretchedness.
And as for me, this curse applies no less   235
If it should turn out that the culprit is my guest here,
Sharing my hearth.
                   You have heard the penalty.
I lay it on you now to attend to this
For my sake, for Apollo's, for the sick
Sterile city that heaven has abandoned.   240
Suppose the oracle had given you no command:
Should this defilement go uncleansed for ever?
You should have found the murderer: your king,
A noble king, had been destroyed!
                         Now I,
Having the power that he held before me,   245
Having his bed, begetting children there
Upon his wife, as he would have, had he lived—
Their son would have been my children's brother,
If Laïos had had luck in fatherhood!
(And now his bad fortune has struck him down)—   250
I say I take the son's part, just as though
I were his son, to press the fight for him
And see it won! I'll find the hand that brought
Death to Labdakos' and Polydoros' child,
Heir of Kadmos' and Agenor's line.   255
And as for those who fail me,
May the gods deny them the fruit of the earth,
Fruit of the womb, and may they rot utterly!
Let them be wretched as we are wretched, and worse!

For you, for loyal Thebans, and for all   260
Who find my actions right, I pray the favor
Of justice, and of all the immortal gods.
CHORAGOS: Since I am under oath, my lord, I swear
I did not do the murder, I can not name
The murderer. Phoibos ordained the search;   265
Why did he not say who the culprit was?
OEDIPUS: An honest question. But no man in the world
Can make the gods do more than the gods will.
CHORAGOS: There is an alternative, I think—
OEPIDUS: Tell me.
Any or all, you must not fail to tell me.   270
CHORAGOS: A lord clairvoyant to the lord Apollo,
As we all know, is the skilled Teiresias.
One might learn much about this from him, Oedipus.
OEDIPUS: I am not wasting time:
Kreon spoke of this, and I have sent for him—   275
Twice, in fact; it is strange that he is not here.
CHORAGOS: The other matter—that old report—seems useless.
OEDIPUS: What was that? I am interested in all reports.
CHORAGOS: The king was said to have been killed by highwaymen.
OEDIPUS: I know. But we have no witnesses to that.   280
CHORAGOS: If the killer can feel a particle of dread,
Your curse will bring him out of hiding!
OEDIPUS: No.
The man who dared that act will fear no curse.

Enter the blind seer TEIRESIAS, *led by a* PAGE.

CHORAGOS: But there is one man who may detect the criminal.
This is Teiresias, this is the holy prophet   285
In whom, alone of all men, truth was born.
OEDIPUS: Teiresias: seer: student of mysteries,
Of all that's taught and all that no man tells,
Secrets of Heaven and secrets of the earth:
Blind though you are, you know the city lies   290
Sick with plague; and from this plague, my lord,
We find that you alone can guard or save us.

Possibly you did not hear the messengers?
Apollo, when we sent to him,
Sent us back word that this great pestilence   295
Would lift, but only if we established clearly
The identity of those who murdered Laïos.
They must be killed or exiled.
                                                Can you use
Birdflight or any art of divination
To purify yourself, and Thebes, and me   300

From this contagion? We are in your hands.
There is no fairer duty
Than that of helping others in distress.

TEIRESIAS: How dreadful knowledge of the truth can be
When there's no help in truth! I knew this well,   305
But did not act on it: else I should not have come.

OEDIPUS: What is troubling you? Why are your eyes so cold?

TEIRESIAS: Let me go home. Bear your own fate, and I'll
Bear mine. It is better so: trust what I say.

OEDIPUS: What you say is ungracious and unhelpful   310
To your native country. Do not refuse to speak.

TEIRESIAS: When it comes to speech, your own is neither temperate
Nor opportune. I wish to be more prudent.

OEDIPUS: In God's name, we all beg you—

TEIRESIAS: You are all ignorant.
No; I will never tell you what I know.   315
Now it is my misery; then, it would be yours.

OEDIPUS: What! You do know something, and will not tell us?
You would betray us all and wreck the State?

TEIRESIAS: I do not intend to torture myself, or you.
Why persist in asking? You will not persuade me.   320

OEDIPUS: What a wicked old man you are! You'd try a stone's
Patience! Out with it! Have you no feeling at all?

TEIRESIAS: You call me unfeeling. If you could only see
The nature of your own feelings . . .

OEDIPUS: Why,
Who would not feel as I do? Who could endure   325
Your arrogance toward the city?

TEIRESIAS: What does it matter?
Whether I speak or not, it is bound to come.

OEDIPUS: Then, if "it" is bound to come, you are bound to tell me.

TEIRESIAS: No, I will not go on. Rage as you please.

OEDIPUS: Rage? Why not!
                          And I'll tell you what I think: 330
You planned it, you had it done, you all but
Killed him with your own hands: if you had eyes,
I'd say the crime was yours, and yours alone.

TEIRESIAS: So? I charge you, then,
Abide by the proclamation you have made: 335
From this day forth
Never speak again to these men or to me;
You yourself are the pollution of this country.

OEDIPUS: You dare say that! Can you possibly think you have
Some way of going free, after such insolence?   340

TEIRESIAS: I have gone free. It is the truth sustains me.

OEDIPUS: Who taught you shamelessness? It was not your craft.

TEIRESIAS: You did. You made me speak. I did not want to.

OEDIPUS: Speak what? Let me hear it again more clearly.

TEIRESIAS: Was it not clear before? Are you tempting me?   345

OEDIPUS: I did not understand it. Say it again.
TEIRESIAS: I say that you are the murderer whom you seek.
OEDIPUS: Now twice you have spat out infamy. You'll pay for it!
TEIRESIAS: Would you care for more? Do you wish to be really angry?
OEDIPUS: Say what you will. Whatever you say is worthless.   350
TEIRESIAS: I say you live in hideous shame with those
   Most dear to you. You can not see the evil.
OEDIPUS: Can you go on babbling like this for ever?
TEIRESIAS: I can, if there is power in truth.
OEDIPUS: There is:
   But not for you, not for you,   355
   You sightless, witless, senseless, mad old man!
TEIRESIAS: You are the madman. There is no one here
   Who will not curse you soon, as you curse me.
OEDIPUS: You child of total night! I would not touch you;
   Neither would any man who sees the sun.   360
TEIRESIAS: True: it is not from you my fate will come.
   That lies within Apollo's competence,
   As it is his concern.
OEDIPUS: Tell me, who made
   These fine discoveries? Kreon? or someone else?
TEIRESIAS: Kreon is no threat. You weave your own doom.   365
OEDIPUS: Wealth, power, craft of statemanship!
   Kingly position, everywhere admired!
   What savage envy is stored up against these,
   If Kreon, whom I trusted, Kreon my friend,
   For this great office which the city once   370
   Put in my hands unsought—if for this power
   Kreon desires in secret to destroy me!

   He has bought this decrepit fortune-teller, this
   Collecter of dirty pennies, this prophet fraud—
   Why, he is no more clairvoyant than I am!
                              Tell us: 375
   Has your mystic mummery ever approached the truth?
   When that hellcat the Sphinx was performing here,
   What help were you to these people?
   Her magic was not for the first man who came along:
   It demanded a real exorcist. Your birds—   380
   What good were they? or the gods, for the matter of that?
   But I came by,
   Oedipus, the simple man, who knows nothing—
   I thought it out for myself, no birds helped me!
   And this is the man you think you can destroy,   385
   That you may be close to Kreon when he's king!
   Well, you and your friend Kreon, it seems to me,
   Will suffer most. If you were not an old man,
   You would have paid already for your plot.
CHORAGOS: We can not see that his words or yours   390

Have been spoken except in anger, Oedipus,
And of anger we have no need. How to accomplish
The god's will best: that is what most concerns us.
TEIRESIAS: You are a king. But where argument's concerned
I am your man, as much a king as you.   395
I am not your servant, but Appollo's.
I have no need of Kreon or Kreon's name.

Listen to me. You mock my blindness, do you?
But I say that you, with both your eyes, are blind:
You can not see the wretchedness of your life,   400
Nor in whose house you live, no, nor with whom.
Who are your father and mother? Can you tell me?
You do not even know the blind wrongs
That you have done them, on earth and in the world below.
But the double lash of your parents' curse will whip you   405
Out of this land some day, with only night
Upon your precious eyes.
Your cries then—where will they not be heard?
What fastness of Kithairon will not echo them?
And that bridal-descant of yours—you'll know it then,   410
The song they sang when you came here to Thebes
And found your misguided berthing.
All this, and more, that you can not guess at now,
Will bring you to yourself among your children.

Be angry, then. Curse Kreon. Curse my words.   415
I tell you, no man that walks upon the earth
Shall be rooted out more horribly than you.
OEDIPUS: Am I to bear this from him?—Damnation
Take you! Out of this place! Out of my sight!
TEIRESIAS: I would not have come at all if you had not asked me.   420
OEDIPUS: Could I have told that you'd talk nonsense, that
You'd come here to make a fool of yourself, and of me?
TEIRESIAS: A fool? Your parents thought me sane enough.
OEDIPUS: My parents again!—Wait: who were my parents?
TEIRESIAS: This day will give you a father, and break your heart.   425
OEDIPUS: Your infantile riddles! Your damned abracadabra!
TEIRESIAS: You were a great man once at solving riddles.
OEDIPUS: Mock me with that if you like; you will find it true.
TEIRESIAS: It was true enough. It brought about your ruin.
OEDIPUS: But if it saved this town?
TEIRESIAS *to the* PAGE: Boy, give me your hand.   430
OEDIPUS: Yes, boy; lead him away.
                           —While you are here
We can do nothing. Go; leave us in peace.
TEIRESIAS: I will go when I have said what I have to say.
How can you hurt me? And I tell you again:
The man you have been looking for all this time,   435

The damned man, the murderer of Laïos,
That man is in Thebes. To your mind he is foreign-born,
But it will soon be shown that he is a Theban,
A revelation that will fail to please.
                                A blind man,
Who has his eyes now; a penniless man, who is rich now;   440
And he will go tapping the strange earth with his staff.
To the children with whom he lives now he will be
Brother and father—the very same; to her
Who bore him, son and husband—the very same
Who came to his father's bed, wet with his father's blood.   445

Enough. Go think that over.
If later you find error in what I have said,
You may say that I have no skill in prophecy.

Exit TEIRESIAS, *led by his* PAGE. OEDIPUS *goes into the palace.*

ODE 1

STROPHE 1

CHORUS: The Delphic stone of prophecies
        Remembers ancient regicide   450
        And a still bloody hand.
        That killer's hour of flight has come.
        He must be stronger than riderless
        Coursers of untiring wind,
        For the son of Zeus armed with his father's thunder   455
        Leaps in lightning after him;
        And the Furies hold his track, the sad Furies.

ANTISTROPHE 1

        Holy Parnassos' peak of snow
        Flashes and blinds that secret man,
        That all shall hunt him down: 460
        Though he may roam the forest shade
        Like a bull gone wild from pasture
        To rage through glooms of stone.
        Doom comes down on him; flight will not avail him;
        For the world's heart calls him desolate,   465
        And the immortal voices follow, for ever follow.

STROPHE 2

        But now a wilder thing is heard
        From the old man skilled at hearing Fate in the wing-beat of a bird.

Bewildered as a blown bird, my soul hovers and can not find
Foothold in this debate, or any reason or rest of mind.   470
But no man ever brought—none can bring
Proof of strife between Thebes' royal house,
Labdakos' line, and the son of Polybos;
And never until now has any man brought word
Of Laïos' dark death staining Oedipus the King.   475

ANTISTROPHE 2

Divine Zeus and Apollo hold
Perfect intelligence alone of all tales ever told;
And well though this diviner works, he works in his own night;
No man can judge that rough unknown or trust in second sight,
For wisdom changes hands among the wise.   480
Shall I believe my great lord criminal
At a raging word that a blind old man let fall?
I saw him, when the carrion woman faced him of old,
Prove his heroic mind. These evil words are lies.

SCENE II

KREON: Men of Thebes: 485
I am told that heavy accusations
Have been brought against me by King Oedipus.
I am not the kind of man to bear this tamely.

If in these present difficulties
He holds me accountable for any harm to him   490
Through anything I have said or done—why, then,
I do not value life in this dishonor.
It is not as though this rumor touched upon
Some private indiscretion. The matter is grave.
The fact is that I am being called disloyal   495
To the State, to my fellow citizens, to my friends.
CHORAGOS: He may have spoken in anger, not from his mind.
KREON: But did you not hear him say I was the one
Who seduced the old prophet into lying?
CHORAGOS: The thing was said; I do not know how seriously.   500
KREON: But you were watching him! Were his eyes steady?
Did he look like a man in his right mind?
CHORAGOS: I do not know.
I can not judge the behavior of great men.
But here is the king himself.

Enter OEDIPUS.

OEDIPUS: So you dared come back.
Why? How brazen of you to come to my house,   505

You murderer!
                    Do you think I do not know
That you plotted to kill me, plotted to steal my throne?
Tell me, in God's name: am I coward, a fool,
That you should dream you could accomplish this?
A fool who could not see your slippery game?   510
A coward, not to fight back when I saw it?
You are the fool, Kreon, are you not? hoping
Without support or friends to get a throne?
Thrones may be won or bought: you could do neither.

KREON: Now listen to me. You have talked; let me talk, too.   515
You can not judge unless you know the facts.

OEDIPUS: You speak well: there is one fact; but I find it hard
To learn from the deadliest enemy I have.

KREON: That above all I must dispute with you.

OEDIPUS: That above all I will not hear you deny.   520

KREON: If you think there is anything good in being stubborn
Against all reason, then I say you are wrong.

OEDIPUS: If you think a man can sin against his own kind
And not be punished for it, I say you are mad.

KREON: I agree. But tell me: what have I done to you?   525

OEDIPUS: You advised me to send for that wizard, did you not?

KREON: I did. I should do it again.

OEDIPUS: Very well. Now tell me:
How long has it been since Laïos—

KREON: What of Laïos?

OEDIPUS: Since he vanished in that onset by the road?

KREON: It was long ago, a long time.

OEDIPUS: And this prophet,   530
Was he practicing here then?

KREON: He was; and with honor, as now.

OEDIPUS: Did he speak of me at that time?

KREON: He never did,
At least, not when I was present.

OEDIPUS: But . . . the enquiry?
I suppose you held one?

KREON: We did, but we learned nothing.

OEDIPUS: Why did the prophet not speak against me then?   535

KREON: I do not know; and I am the kind of man
Who holds his tongue when he has no facts to go on.

OEDIPUS: There's one fact that you know, and you could tell it.

KREON: What fact is that? If I know it, you shall have it.

OEDIPUS: If he were not involved with you, he could not say   540
That it was I who murdered Laïos.

KREON: If he says that, you are the one that knows it!—
But now it is my turn to question you.

OEDIPUS: Put your questions. I am no murderer.

KREON: First, then: You married my sister?

OEDIPUS: I married your sister. 545

KREON: And you rule the kingdom equally with her?
OEDIPUS: Everything that she wants she has from me.
KREON: And I am the third, equal to both of you?
OEDIPUS: That is why I call you a bad friend.
KREON: No. Reason it out, as I have done.   550
    Think of this first: Would any sane man prefer
    Power, with all a king's anxieties,
    To that same power and the grace of sleep?
    Certainly not I.
    I have never longed for the king's power—only his rights.   555
    Would any wise man differ from me in this?
    As matters stand, I have my way in everything
    With your consent, and no responsibilities.
    If I were king, I should be a slave to policy.
    How could I desire a scepter more   560
    Than what is now mine—untroubled influence?
    No, I have not gone mad; I need no honors,
    Except those with the perquisites I have now.
    I am welcome everywhere; every man salutes me,
    And those who want your favor seek my ear,   565
    Since I know how to manage what they ask.
    Should I exchange this ease for that anxiety?
    Besides, no sober mind is treasonable.
    I hate anarchy
    And never would deal with any man who likes it.   570

    Test what I have said. Go to the priestess
    At Delphi, ask if I quoted her correctly.
    And as for this other thing: if I am found
    Guilty of treason with Teiresias,
    Then sentence me to death. You have my word   575
    It is a sentence I should cast my vote for—
    But not without evidence!
                    You do wrong
    When you take good men for bad, bad men for good.
    A true friend thrown aside—why, life itself
    Is not more precious!
                  In time you will know this well: 580
    For time, and time alone, will show the just man,
    Though scoundrels are discovered in a day.
CHORAGOS: This is well said, and a prudent man would ponder it.
    Judgments too quickly formed are dangerous.
OEDIPUS: But is he not quick in his duplicity?   585
    And shall I not be quick to parry him?
    Would you have me stand still, hold my peace, and let
    This man win everything, through my inaction?
KREON: And you want—what is it, then? To banish me?
OEDIPUS: No, not exile. It is your death I want,   590
    So that all the world may see what treason means.

KREON: You will persist, then? You will not believe me?
OEDIPUS: How can I believe you?
KREON: Then you are a fool.
OEDIPUS: To save myself?
KREON: In justice, think of me.
OEDIPUS: You are evil incarnate.
KREON: But suppose that you are wrong? 595
OEDIPUS: Still I must rule.
KREON: But not if you rule badly.
OEDIPUS: O city, city!
KREON: It is my city, too!
CHORAGOS: Now, my lords, be still. I see the queen,
    Iokastê, coming from her palace chambers;
    And it is time she came, for the sake of you both. 600
    This dreadful quarrel can be resolved through her.

Enter IOKASTÊ.

IOKASTÊ. Poor foolish men, what wicked din is this?
    With Thebes sick to death, is it not shameful
    That you should rake some private quarrel up?
    To OEDIPUS. Come into the house.
                                        —And you, Kreon, go now: 605
    Let us have no more of this tumult over nothing.
KREON: Nothing? No, sister: what your husband plans for me
    Is one of two great evils: exile or death.
OEDIPUS: He is right.
                            Why, woman I have caught him squarely
    Plotting against my life.
KREON: No! Let me die 610
    Accurst if ever I have wished you harm!
IOKASTÊ: Ah, believe it, Oedipus!
    In the name of the gods, respect this oath of his
    For my sake, for the sake of these people here!

STROPHE 1

CHORAGOS: Open your mind to her, my lord. Be ruled by her, I
    beg you! 615
OEDIPUS: What would you have me do?
CHORAGOS: Respect Kreon's word. He has never spoken like a fool,
    And now he has sworn on oath.
OEDIPUS: You know what you ask?
CHORAGOS: I do.
OEDIPUS: Speak on, then.
CHORAGOS: A friend so sworn should not be baited so,
    In blind malice, and without final proof. 620
OEDIPUS: You are aware, I hope, that what you say
    Means death for me, or exile at the least.

STROPHE 2

CHORAGOS: No, I swear by Helios, first in heaven!
        May I die friendless and accurst,
        The worst of deaths, if ever I meant that!   625
        It is the withering fields
        That hurt my sick heart:
        Must we bear all these ills,
        And now your bad blood as well?
OEDIPUS: Then let him go. And let me die, if I must,   630
Or be driven by him in shame from the land of Thebes.
It is your unhappiness, and not his talk,
That touches me.
            As for him—
Wherever he goes, hatred will follow him.
KREON: Ugly in yielding, as you were ugly in rage!   635
Natures like yours chiefly torment themselves.
OEDIPUS: Can you not go? Can you not leave me?
KREON: I can.
You do not know me; but the city knows me,
And in its eyes I am just, if not in yours. *Exit* KREON.

ANTISTROPHE 1

CHORAGOS: Lady Iokastê, did you not ask the King to go to his
  chambers?   640
IOKASTÊ: First tell me what has happened.
CHORAGOS: There was suspicion without evidence; yet it rankled
  As even false charges will.
IOKASTÊ: On both sides?
CHORAGOS: On both.
IOKASTÊ: But what was said?
CHORAGOS: Oh let it rest, let it be done with!
Have we not suffered enough?   645
OEDIPUS: You see to what your decency has brought you:
You have made difficulties where my heart saw none.

ANTISTROPHE 2

CHORAGOS: Oedipus, it is not once only I have told you—
        You must know I should count myself unwise
        To the point of madness, should I now forsake you—   650
        You, under whose hand,
        In the storm of another time,
        Our dear land sailed out free.
        But now stand fast at the helm!
IOKASTÊ: In God's name, Oedipus, inform your wife as well: 655
Why are you so set in this hard anger?

OEDIPUS: I will tell you, for none of these men deserves
    My confidence as you do. It is Kreon's work,
    His treachery, his plotting against me.
IOKASTÊ: Go on, if you can make this clear to me.   660
OEDIPUS: He charges me with the murder of Laïos.
IOKASTÊ: Has he some knowledge? Or does he speak from hearsay?
OEDIPUS: He would not commit himself to such a charge,
    But he has brought in that damnable soothsayer
    To tell his story.
IOKASTÊ: Set your mind at rest.   665
    If it is a question of soothsayers, I tell you
    That you will find no man whose craft gives knowledge
    Of the unknowable.
                Here is my proof:
    An oracle was reported to Laïos once
    (I will not say from Phoibos himself, but from   670
    His appointed ministers, at any rate)
    That his doom would be death at the hands of his own son—
    His son, born of his flesh and of mine!

    Now, you remember the story: Laïos was killed
    By marauding strangers where three highways meet;   675
    But his child had not been three days in this world
    Before the king had pierced the baby's ankles
    And left him to die on a lonely mountainside.

    Thus, Apollo never caused that child
    To kill his father, and it was not Laïos' fate   680
    To die at the hands of his son, as he had feared.
    This is what prophets and prophecies are worth!
    Have no dread of them.
               It is God himself
    Who can show us what he wills, in his own way.
OEDIPUS: How strange a shadowy memory crossed my mind,   685
    Just now while you were speaking; it chilled my heart.
IOKASTÊ: What do you mean? What memory do you speak of?
OEDIPUS: If I understand you, Laïos was killed
    At a place where three roads meet.
IOKASTÊ: So it was said;
    We have no later story.
OEDIPUS: Where did it happen?   690
IOKASTÊ: Phokis, it is called: at a place where the Theban Way
    Divides into the roads toward Delphi and Daulia.
OEDIPUS: When?
IOKASTÊ: We had the news not long before you came
    And proved the right to your succession here.
OEDIPUS: Ah, what net has God been weaving for me?   695
IOKASTÊ: Oedipus! Why does this trouble you?

OEDIPUS: Do not ask me yet.
First, tell me how Laïos looked, and tell me
How old he was.
IOKASTÊ: He was tall, his hair just touched
With white; his form was not unlike your own.
OEDIPUS: I think that I myself may be accurst   700
By my own ignorant edict.
IOKASTÊ: You speak strangely.
It makes me tremble to look at you, my king.
OEDIPUS: I am not sure that the blind man can not see.
But I should know better if you were to tell me—
IOKASTÊ: Anything—though I dread to hear you ask it.   705
OEDIPUS: Was the king lightly escorted, or did he ride
With a large company, as a ruler should?
IOKASTÊ: There were five men with him in all: one was a herald;
And a single chariot, which he was driving.
OEDIPUS: Alas, that makes it plain enough!
                                                But who—   710
Who told you how it happened?
IOKASTÊ: A household servant,
The only one to escape.
OEDIPUS: And is he still
A servant of ours?
IOKASTÊ: No; for when he came back at last
And found you enthroned in the place of the dead king,
He came to me, touched my hand with his, and begged   715
That I would send him away to the frontier district
Where only the shepherds go—
As far away from the city as I could send him.
I granted his prayer; for although the man was a slave,
He had earned more than this favor at my hands.   720
OEDIPUS: Can he be called back quickly?
IOKASTÊ: Easily.
But why?
OEDIPUS: I have taken too much upon myself
Without enquiry; therefore I wish to consult him.
IOKASTÊ: Then he shall come.
                                But am I not one also
To whom you might confide these fears of yours?   725
OEDIPUS: That is your right; it will not be denied you,
Now least of all; for I have reached a pitch
Of wild foreboding. Is there anyone
To whom I should sooner speak?

Polybos of Corinth is my father.   730
My mother is a Dorian: Meropê.
I grew up chief among the men of Corinth
Until a strange thing happened—

Not worth my passion, it may be, but strange.
At a feast, a drunken man maundering in his cups 735
Cries out that I am not my father's son!

I contained myself that night, though I felt anger
And a sinking heart. The next day I visited
My father and mother, and questioned them. They stormed,
Calling it all the slanderous rant of a fool; 740
And this relieved me. Yet the suspicion
Remained always aching in my mind;
I knew there was talk; I could not rest;
And finally, saying nothing to my parents,
I went to the shrine at Delphi. 745

The god dismissed my question without reply;
He spoke of other things.
                              Some were clear,
Full of wretchedness, dreadful, unbearable:
As, that I should lie with my own mother, breed
Children from whom all men would turn their eyes; 750
And that I should be my father's murderer.

I heard all this, and fled. And from that day
Corinth to me was only in the stars
Descending in that quarter of the sky,
As I wandered farther and farther on my way 755
To a land where I should never see the evil
Sung by the oracle. And I came to this country
Where, so you say, King Laïos was killed.

I will tell you all that happened there, my lady.

There were three highways 760
Coming together at a place I passed;
And there a herald came towards me, and a chariot
Drawn by horses, with a man such as you describe
Seated in it. The groom leading the horses
Forced me off the road at his lord's command; 765
But as this charioteer lurched over towards me
I struck him in my rage. The old man saw me
And brought his double goad down upon my head
As I came abreast.
                      He was paid back, and more! 770
Swinging my club in this right hand I knocked him
Out of his car, and he rolled on the ground.
                                              I killed him.

I killed them all.
Now if that stranger and Laïos were—kin,

Where is a man more miserable than I?
More hated by the gods? Citizen and alien alike   775
Must never shelter me or speak to me—
I must be shunned by all.
                  And I myself
Pronounced this malediction upon myself!

Think of it: I have touched you with these hands,
These hands that killed your husband. What defilement!   780

Am I all evil, then? It must be so,
Since I must flee from Thebes, yet never again
See my own countrymen, my own country,
For fear of joining my mother in marriage
And killing Polybos, my father.
                       Ah,   785
If I was created so, born to this fate,
Who could deny the savagery of God?

O holy majesty of heavenly powers!
May I never see that day! Never!
Rather let me vanish from the race of men   790
Than know the abomination destined me!
CHORAGOS: We too, my lord, have felt dismay at this.
    But there is hope: you have yet to hear the shepherd.
OEDIPUS: Indeed, I fear no other hope is left me.
IOKASTÊ: What do you hope from him when he comes?
OEDIPUS: This much: 795
    If his account of the murder tallies with yours,
    Then I am cleared.
IOKASTÊ: What was it that I said
    Of such importance?
OEDIPUS: Why, "marauders," you said,
    Killed the king, according to this man's story.
    If he maintains that still, if there were several,   800
    Clearly the guilt is not mine: I was alone.
    But if he says one man, singlehanded, did it,
    Then the evidence all points to me.
IOKASTÊ: You may be sure that he said there were several;
    And can he call back that story now? He can not.   805
    The whole city heard it as plainly as I.
    But suppose he alters some detail of it:
    He can not ever show that Laïos' death
    Fulfilled the oracle: for Apollo said
    My child was doomed to kill him; and my child—   810
    Poor baby!—it was my child that died first.

    No. From now on, where oracles are concerned,
    I would not waste a second thought on any.

OEDIPUS: You may be right.

But come: let someone go
For the shepherd at once. This matter must be settled. 815
IOKASTÊ: I will send for him.
I would not wish to cross you in anything,
And surely not in this.—Let us go in.

Exeunt into the palace.

ODE II

STROPHE 1

CHORUS: Let me be reverent in the ways of right,
Lowly the paths I journey on; 820
Let all my words and actions keep
The laws of the pure universe
From highest Heaven handed down.
For Heaven is their bright nurse,
Those generations of the realms of light; 825
Ah, never of mortal kind were they begot,
Nor are they slaves of memory, lost in sleep:
Their Father is greater than Time, and ages not.

ANTISTROPHE 1

The tyrant is a child of Pride
Who drinks from his great sickening cup 830
Recklessness and vanity,
Until from his high crest headlong
He plummets to the dust of hope.
That strong man is not strong.
But let no fair ambition be denied; 835
May God protect the wrestler for the State
In government, in comely policy,
Who will fear God, and on His ordinance wait.

STROPHE 2

Haughtiness and the high hand of disdain
Tempt and outrage God's holy law; 840
And any mortal who dares hold
No immortal Power in awe
Will be caught up in a net of pain:
The price for which his levity is sold.
Let each man take due earnings, then, 845
And keep his hands from holy things,
And from blasphemy stand apart—

Else the crackling blast of heaven
Blows on his head, and on his desperate heart.
Though fools will honor impious men,   850
In their cities no tragic poet sings.

ANTISTROPHE 2

Shall we lose faith in Delphi's obscurities,
We who have heard the world's core
Discredited, and the sacred wood
Of Zeus at Elis praised no more?   855
The deeds and the strange prophecies
Must make a pattern yet to be understood.
Zeus, if indeed you are lord of all,
Throned in light over night and day,
Mirror this in your endless mind: 860
Our masters call the oracle
Words on the wind, and the Delphic vision blind!
Their hearts no longer know Apollo,
And reverence for the gods has died away.

SCENE III

Enter IOKASTÊ.

IOKASTÊ: Princes of Thebes, it has occurred to me   865
To visit the altars of the gods, bearing
These branches as a suppliant, and this incense.
Our king is not himself: his noble soul
Is overwrought with fantasies of dread,
Else he would consider   870
The new prophecies in the light of the old.
He will listen to any voice that speaks disaster,
And my advice goes for nothing.

She approaches the altar, right.

                              To you, then, Apollo,
Lycéan lord, since you are nearest, I turn in prayer.
Receive these offerings, and grant us deliverance   875
From defilement. Our hearts are heavy with fear
When we see our leader distracted, as helpless sailors
Are terrified by the confusion of their helmsman.

Enter MESSENGER.

MESSENGER: Friends, no doubt you can direct me:
Where shall I find the house of Oedipus,   880
Or, better still, where is the king himself?

CHORAGOS: It is this very place, stranger; he is inside.
This is his wife and mother of his children.
MESSENGER: I wish her happiness in a happy house,
Blest in all the fulfillment of her marriage. 885
IOKASTÊ: I wish as much for you: your courtesy
Deserves a like good fortune. But now, tell me:
Why have you come? What have you to say to us?
MESSENGER: Good news, my lady, for your house and your husband.
IOKASTÊ: What news? Who sent you here?
MESSENGER: I am from Corinth. 890
The news I bring ought to mean joy for you,
Though it may be you will find some grief in it.
IOKASTÊ: What is it? How can it touch us in both ways?
MESSENGER: The word is that the people of the Isthmus
Intend to call Oedipus to be their king. 895
IOKASTÊ: But old King Polybos—is he not reigning still?
MESSENGER: No. Death holds him in his sepulchre.
IOKASTÊ: What are you saying? Polybos is dead?
MESSENGER: If I am not telling the truth, may I die myself.
IOKASTÊ to a MAIDSERVANT: Go in, go quickly; tell this to
your master. 900
O riddlers of God's will, where are you now!
This was the man whom Oedipus, long ago,
Feared so, fled so, in dread of destroying him—
But it was another fate by which he died.

Enter OEDIPUS, *center.*

OEDIPUS: Dearest Iokastê, why have you sent for me? 905
IOKASTÊ: Listen to what this man says, and then tell me
What has become of the solemn prophecies.
OEDIPUS: Who is this man? What is his news for me?
IOKASTÊ: He has come from Corinth to announce your father's death!
OEDIPUS: Is it true, stranger? Tell me in your own words. 910
MESSENGER: I can not say it more clearly: the king is dead.
OEDIPUS: Was it by treason? Or by an attack of illness?
MESSENGER: A little thing brings old men to their rest.
OEDIPUS: It was sickness, then?
MESSENGER: Yes, and his many years.
OEDIPUS: Ah! 915
Why should a man respect the Pythian hearth, or
Give heed to the birds that jangle above his head?
They prophesied that I should kill Polybos,
Kill my own father; but he is dead and buried,
And I am here—I never touched him, never, 920
Unless he died of grief for my departure,
And thus, in a sense, through me. No. Polybos
Has packed the oracles off with him underground.
They are empty words.

IOKASTÊ:	Had I not told you so?
OEDIPUS:	You had; it was my faint heart that betrayed me. 925
IOKASTÊ:	From now on never think of those things again.
OEDIPUS:	And yet—must I not fear my mother's bed?
IOKASTÊ:	Why should anyone in this world be afraid,

Since Fate rules us and nothing can be foreseen?
A man should live only for the present day. 930

Have no more fear of sleeping with your mother:
How many men, in dreams, have lain with their mothers!
No reasonable man is troubled by such things.

OEDIPUS:	That is true; only—

If only my mother were not still alive! 935
But she is alive. I can not help my dread.

IOKASTÊ:	Yet this news of your father's death is wonderful.
OEDIPUS:	Wonderful. But I fear the living woman.
MESSENGER:	Tell me, who is this woman that you fear?
OEDIPUS:	It is Meropê, man; the wife of King Polybos. 940
MESSENGER:	Meropê? Why should you be afraid of her?
OEDIPUS:	An oracle of the gods, a dreadful saying.
MESSENGER:	Can you tell me about it or are you sworn to silence?
OEDIPUS:	I can tell you, and I will.

Apollo said through his prophet that I was the man 945
Who should marry his own mother, shed his father's blood
With his own hands. And so, for all these years
I have kept clear of Corinth, and no harm has come—
Though it would have been sweet to see my parents again.

MESSENGER:	And is this the fear that drove you out of Corinth? 950
OEDIPUS:	Would you have me kill my father?
MESSENGER:	As for that

You must be reassured by the news I gave you.

OEDIPUS:	If you could reassure me, I would reward you.
MESSENGER:	I had that in mind, I will confess: I thought

I could count on you when you returned to Corinth. 955

OEDIPUS:	No: I will never go near my parents again.
MESSENGER:	Ah, son, you still do not know what you are doing—
OEDIPUS:	What do you mean? In the name of God tell me!
MESSENGER:	—If these are your reasons for not going home.
OEDIPUS:	I tell you, I fear the oracle may come true. 960
MESSENGER:	And guilt may come upon you through your parents?
OEDIPUS:	That is the dread that is always in my heart.
MESSENGER:	Can you not see that all your fears are groundless?
OEDIPUS:	Groundless? Am I not my parents' son?
MESSENGER:	Polybos was not your father.
OEDIPUS:	Not my father? 965
MESSENGER:	No more your father than the man speaking to you.
OEDIPUS:	But you are nothing to me!
MESSENGER:	Neither was he.
OEDIPUS:	Then why did he call me son?

MESSENGER: I will tell you:
　　Long ago he had you from my hands, as a gift.
OEDIPUS: Then how could he love me so, if I was not his?   970
MESSENGER: He had no children, and his heart turned to you.
OEDIPUS: What of you? Did you buy me? Did you find me by chance?
MESSENGER: I came upon you in the woody vales of Kithairon.
OEDIPUS: And what were you doing there?
MESSENGER: Tending my flocks.
OEDIPUS: A wandering sheperd?
MESSENGER: But your savior, son, that day.   975
OEDIPUS: From what did you save me?
MESSENGER: Your ankles should tell you that.
OEDIPUS: Ah, stranger, why do you speak of that childhood pain?
MESSENGER: I pulled the skewer that pinned your feet together.
OEDIPUS: I have had the mark as long as I can remember.
MESSENGER: That was why you were given the name you bear.   980
OEDIPUS: God! Was it my father or my mother who did it?
　　Tell me!
MESSENGER: I do not know. The man who gave you to me
　　Can tell you better than I.
OEDIPUS: It was not you that found me, but another?
MESSENGER: It was another shepherd gave you to me.   985
OEDIPUS: Who was he? Can you tell me who he was?
MESSENGER: I think he was said to be one of Laïos' people.
OEDIPUS: You mean the Laïos who was king here years ago?
MESSENGER: Yes; King Laïos; and the man was one of his herdsmen.
OEDIPUS: Is he still alive? Can I see him?
MESSENGER: These men here   990
　　Know best about such things.
OEDIPUS: Does anyone here
　　Know this shepherd that he is talking about?
　　Have you seen him in the fields, or in the town?
　　If you have, tell me. It is time things were made plain.
CHORAGOS: I think the man he means is that same shepherd   995
　　You have already asked to see. Iokastê perhaps
　　Could tell you something.
OEDIPUS: Do you know anything
　　About him, Lady? Is he the man we have summoned?
　　Is that the man this shepherd means?
IOKASTÊ: Why think of him?
　　Forget this herdsman. Forget it all.   1000
　　This talk is a waste of time.
OEDIPUS: How can you say that,
　　When the clues to my true birth are in my hands?
IOKASTÊ: For God's love, let us have no more questioning!
　　Is your life nothing to you?
　　My own is pain enough for me to bear.   1005
OEDIPUS: You need not worry. Suppose my mother a slave,
　　And born of slaves: no baseness can touch you.

IOKASTÊ:	Listen to me, I beg you: do not do this thing!
OEDIPUS:	I will not listen; the truth must be made known.
IOKASTÊ:	Everything that I say is for your own good!
OEDIPUS:	My own good 1010

Snaps my patience, then; I want none of it.

IOKASTÊ: You are fatally wrong! May you never learn who you are!

OEDIPUS: Go, one of you, and bring the shepherd here.

Let us leave this woman to brag of her royal name.

IOKASTÊ: Ah, miserable!   1015

That is the only word I have for you now.

That is the only word I can ever have. *Exit into the palace.*

CHORAGOS: Why has she left us, Oedipus? Why has she gone

In such a passion of sorrow? I fear this silence:

Something dreadful may come of it.

OEDIPUS: Let it come!   1020

However base my birth, I must know about it.

The Queen, like a woman, is perhaps ashamed

To think of my low origin. But I

Am a child of Luck; I can not be dishonored.

Luck is my mother; the passing months, my brothers,   1025

Have seen me rich and poor.

                                 If this is so,

How could I wish that I were someone else?

How could I not be glad to know my birth?

ODE III

STROPHE

CHORUS: If ever the coming time were known

To my heart's pondering,   1030

Kithairon, now by Heaven I see the torches

At the festival of the next full moon,

And see the dance, and hear the choir sing

A grace to your gentle shade.

Mountain where Oedipus was found,   1035

O mountain guard of a noble race!

May the god who heals us lend his aid,

And let that glory come to pass

For our king's cradling-ground.

ANTISTROPHE

Of the nymphs that flower beyond the years,   1040

Who bore you, royal child,

To Pan of the hills or the timberline Apollo,

Cold in delight where the upland clears,

Or Hermês for whom Kyllenê's heights are piled?

Or flushed as evening cloud,   1045
Great Dionysos, roamer of mountains,
He—was it he who found you there,
And caught you up in his own proud
Arms from the sweet god-ravisher
Who laughed by the Muses' fountains?   1050

SCENE IV

OEDIPUS: Sirs: though I do not know the man,
  I think I see him coming, this shepherd we want:
  He is old, like our friend here, and the men
  Bringing him seem to be servants of my house.
  But you can tell, if you have ever seen him.   1055

Enter SHEPHERD *escorted by* SERVANTS.

CHORAGOS: I know him, he was Laïos' man. You can trust him.
OEDIPUS: Tell me first, you from Corinth: is this the shepherd
  We were discussing?
MESSENGER: This is the very man.
OEDIPUS *to* SHEPHERD: Come here. No, look at me. You must answer
  Everything I ask.—You belonged to Laïos?   1060
SHEPHERD: Yes: born his slave, brought up in his house.
OEDIPUS: Tell me: what kind of work did you do for him?
SHEPHERD: I was a shepherd of his, most of my life.
OEDIPUS: Where mainly did you go for pasturage?
SHEPHERD: Sometimes Kithairon, sometimes the hills near-by.   1065
OEDIPUS: Do you remember ever seeing this man out there?
SHEPHERD: What would he be doing there? This man?
OEDIPUS: This man standing here. Have you ever seen him before?
SHEPHERD: No. At least, not to my recollection.
MESSENGER: And that is not strange, my lord. But I'll refresh   1070
  His memory: he must remember when we two
  Spent three whole seasons together, March to September,
  On Kithairon or thereabouts. He had two flocks;
  I had one. Each autumn I'd drive mine home
  And he would go back with his to Laïos' sheepfold.—   1075
  Is this not true, just as I have described it?
SHEPHERD: True, yes; but it was all so long ago.
MESSENGER: Well, then: do you remember, back in those days,
  That you gave me a baby boy to bring up as my own?
SHEPHERD: What if I did? What are you trying to say?   1080
MESSENGER: King Oedipus was once that little child.
SHEPHERD: Damn you, hold your tongue!
OEDIPUS: No more of that!
  It is your tongue needs watching, not this man's.
SHEPHERD: My king, my master, what is it I have done wrong?
OEDIPUS: You have not answered his question about the boy.   1085

SHEPHERD: He does not know . . . He is only making trouble . . .
OEDIPUS: Come, speak plainly, or it will go hard with you.
SHEPHERD: In God's name, do not torture an old man!
OEDIPUS: Come here, one of you; bind his arms behind him.
SHEPHERD: Unhappy king! What more do you wish to learn?   1090
OEDIPUS: Did you give this man the child he speaks of?
SHEPHERD: I did.

And I would to God I had died that very day.
OEDIPUS: You will die now unless you speak the truth.
SHEPHERD: Yet if I speak the truth, I am worse than dead.
OEDIPUS *to* ATTENDANT: He intends to draw it out, apparently—   1095
SHEPHERD: No! I have told you already that I gave him the boy.
OEDIPUS: Where did you get him? From your house? From somewhere
        else?
SHEPHERD: Not from mine, no. A man gave him to me.
OEDIPUS: Is that man here? Whose house did he belong to?
SHEPHERD: For God's love, my king, do not ask me any more!   1100
OEDIPUS: You are a dead man if I have to ask you again.
SHEPHERD: Then . . . Then the child was from the palace of Laïos.
OEDIPUS: A slave child? or a child of his own line?
SHEPHERD: Ah, I am on the brink of dreadful speech!
OEDIPUS: And I of dreadful hearing. Yet I must hear.   1105
SHEPHERD: If you must be told, then . . .

                                        They said it was Laïos' child;
        But it is your wife who can tell you about that.
OEDIPUS: My wife!—Did she give it to you?
SHEPHERD: My lord, she did.
OEDIPUS: Do you know why?
SHEPHERD: I was told to get rid of it.
OEDIPUS: Oh heartless mother!
SHEPHERD: But in dread of prophecies . . .   1110
OEDIPUS: Tell me.
SHEPHERD: It was said that the boy would kill his own father.
OEDIPUS: Then why did you give him over to this old man?
SHEPHERD: I pitied the baby, my king,
And I thought that this man would take him far away
To his own country.

                        He saved him—but for what a fate!   1115
For if you are what this man says you are,
No man living is more wretched than Oedipus.
OEDIPUS: Ah God!
It was true!
            All the prophecies!
                        —Now,
O Light, may I look on you for the last time!   1120
I, Oedipus,
Oedipus, damned in his birth, in his marriage damned,
Damned in the blood he shed with his own hand! *He rushes into the
palace.*

ODE IV

STROPHE 1

CHORUS: Alas for the seed of men.
    What measure shall I give these generations   1125
    That breathe on the void and are void
    And exist and do not exist?
    Who bears more weight of joy
    Than mass of sunlight shifting in images,
    Or who shall make his thought stay on   1130
    That down time drifts away?
    Your splendor is all fallen.
    O naked brow of wrath and tears,
    O change of Oedipus!
    I who saw your days call no man blest—   1135
    Your great days like ghósts góne.

ANTISTROPHE 1

    That mind was a strong bow.
    Deep, how deep you drew it then, hard archer,
    At a dim fearful range,
    And brought dear glory down!   1140
    You overcame the stranger—
    The virgin with her hooking lion claws—
    And though death sang, stood like a tower
    To make pale Thebes take heart.
    Fortress against our sorrow!   1145
    True king, giver of laws,
    Majestic Oedipus!
    No prince in Thebes had ever such renown,
    No prince won such grace of power.

STROPHE 2

    And now of all men ever known   1150
    Most pitiful is this man's story:
    His fortunes are most changed, his state
    Fallen to a low slave's
    Ground under bitter fate.
    O Oedipus, most royal one!   1155
    The great door that expelled you to the light
    Gave at night—ah, gave night to your glory:
    As to the father, to the fathering son.
    All understood too late.
    How could that queen whom Laïos won,   1160
    The garden that he harrowed at his height,
    Be silent when that act was done?

ANTISTROPHE 2

But all eyes fail before time's eye,
All actions come to justice there.
Though never willed, though far down the deep past,   1165
Your bed, your dread sirings,
Are brought to book at last.
Child by Laïos doomed to die,
Then doomed to lose that fortunate little death,
Would God you never took breath in this air   1170
That with my wailing lips I take to cry:
For I weep the world's outcast.
I was blind, and now I can tell why:
Asleep, for you had given ease of breath
To Thebes, while the false years went by.   1175

EXODOS

Enter, from the palace, SECOND MESSENGER.

SECOND MESSENGER: Elders of Thebes, most honored in this land,
What horrors are yours to see and hear, what weight
Of sorrow to be endured, if, true to your birth,
You venerate the line of Labdakos!
I think neither Istros nor Phasis, those great rivers,   1180
Could purify this place of all the evil
It shelters now, or soon must bring to light—
Evil not done unconsciously, but willed.

The greatest griefs are those we cause ourselves.
CHORAGOS: Surely, friend, we have grief enough already;   1185
What new sorrow do you mean?
SECOND MESSENGER: The queen is dead.
CHORAGOS: O miserable queen! But at whose hand?
SECOND MESSENGER: Her own.
The full horror of what happened you can not know,
For you did not see it; but I, who did, will tell you
As clearly as I can how she met her death.   1190

When she had left us,
In passionate silence, passing through the court,
She ran to her apartment in the house,
Her hair clutched by the fingers of both hands.
She closed the doors behind her; then, by that bed   1195
Where long ago the fatal son was conceived—
That son who should bring about his father's death—
We heard her call upon Laïos, dead so many years,
And heard her wail for the double fruit of her marriage,
A husband by her husband, children by her child.   1200

Exactly how she died I do not know:
For Oedipus burst in moaning and would not let us
Keep vigil to the end: it was by him
As he stormed about the room that our eyes were caught.
From one to another of us he went, begging a sword,   1205
Hunting the wife who was not his wife, the mother
Whose womb had carried his own children and himself.
I do not know: it was none of us aided him
But surely one of the gods was in control!
For with a dreadful cry   1210
He hurled his weight, as though wrenched out of himself,
At the twin doors: the bolts gave, and he rushed in.
And there we saw her hanging, her body swaying
From the cruel cord she had noosed about her neck
A great sob broke from him, heartbreaking to hear,   1215
As he loosed the rope and lowered her to the ground.

I would blot out from my mind what happened next!
For the king ripped from her gown the golden brooches
That were her ornament, and raised them, and plunged them down
Straight into his own eyeballs, crying, "No more,   1220
No more shall you look on the misery about me,
The horrors of my own doing! Too long you have known
The faces of those whom I should never have seen,
Too long been blind to those for whom I was searching!
From this hour, go in darkness!" And as he spoke,   1225
He struck at his eyes—not once, but many times;
And the blood spattered his beard,
Bursting from his ruined sockets like red hail.

So from the unhappiness of two this evil has sprung,
A curse on the man and woman alike. The old   1230
Happiness of the house of Labdakos
Was happiness enough: where is it today?
It is all wailing and ruin, disgrace, death—all
The misery of mankind that has a name—
And it is wholly and for ever theirs.   1235
CHORAGOS: Is he in agony still? Is there no rest for him?
SECOND MESSENGER: He is calling for someone to open the doors wide
So that all the children of Kadmos may look upon
His father's murderer, his mother's—no,
I can not say it!
                    And then he will leave Thebes,   1240
Self-exiled, in order that the curse
Which he himself pronounced may depart from the house.
He is weak, and there is none to lead him,
So terrible is his suffering.
                    But you will see:

Look, the doors are opening; in a moment   1245
You will see a thing that would crush a heart of stone.

The central door is opened; OEDIPUS, *blinded, is led in.*

CHORAGOS: Dreadful indeed for men to see.
    Never have my own eyes
    Looked on a sight so full of fear.

    Oedipus!   1250
    What madness came upon you, what daemon
    Leaped on your life with heavier
    Punishment than a mortal man can bear?
    No: I can not even
    Look at you, poor ruined one.   1255
    And I would speak, question, ponder,
    If I were able. No.
    You make me shudder.
OEDIPUS: God. God.
    Is there a sorrow greater?   1260
    Where shall I find harbor in this world?
    My voice is hurled far on a dark wind.
    What has God done to me?
CHORAGOS: Too terrible to think of, or to see.

STROPHE 1

OEDIPUS: O cloud of night,   1265
    Never to be turned away: night coming on,
    I can not tell how: night like a shroud!
    My fair winds brought me here.
                      O God. Again
    The pain of the spikes where I had sight,
    The flooding pain   1270
    Of memory, never to be gouged out.
CHORAGOS: This is not strange.
    You suffer it all twice over, remorse in pain,
    Pain in remorse.

ANTISTROPHE 1

OEDIPUS: Ah dear friend   1275
    Are you faithful even yet, you alone?
    Are you still standing near me, will you stay here,
    Patient, to care for the blind?
                     The blind man!
    Yet even blind I know who it is attends me,
    By the voice's tone—   1280
    Though my new darkness hide the comforter.

CHORAGOS: Oh fearful act!
       What god was it drove you to rake black
       Night across your eyes?

STROPHE 2

OEDIPUS: Apollo. Apollo. Dear   1285
       Children, the god was Apollo.
       He brought my sick, sick fate upon me.
       But the blinding hand was my own!
       How could I bear to see
       When all my sight was horror everywhere?   1290
CHORAGOS: Everywhere; that is true.
OEDIPUS: And now what is left?
       Images? Love? A greeting even,
       Sweet to the senses? Is there anything?
       Ah, no, friends: lead me away.   1295
       Lead me away from Thebes.
                                        Lead the great wreck
       And hell of Oedipus, whom the gods hate.
CHORAGOS: Your misery, you are not blind to that.
       Would God you had never found it out!

ANTISTROPHE 2

OEDIPUS: Death take the man who unbound   1300
       My feet on that hillside
       And delivered me from death to life! What life?
       If only I had died,
       This weight of monstrous doom
       Could not have dragged me and my darlings down.   1305
CHORAGOS: I would have wished the same.
OEDIPUS: Oh never to have come here
       With my father's blood upon me! Never
       To have been the man they call his mother's husband!
       Oh accurst! Oh child of evil,   1310
       To have entered that wretched bed—
                                        the selfsame one!
       More primal than sin itself, this fell to me.
CHORAGOS: I do not know what words to offer you.
       You were better dead than alive and blind.
OEDIPUS: Do not counsel me any more. This punishment   1315
       That I have laid upon myself is just.
       If I had eyes,
       I do not know how I could bear the sight
       Of my father, when I came to the house of Death,
       Or my mother: for I have sinned against them both   1320

So vilely that I could not make my peace
By strangling my own life.
                              Or do you think my children,
Born as they were born, would be sweet to my eyes?
Ah never, never! Nor this town with its high walls,
Nor the holy images of the gods.
                              For I,   1325
Thrice miserable!—Oedipus, noblest of all the line
Of Kadmos, have condemned myself to enjoy
These things no more, by my own malediction
Expelling that man whom the gods declared
To be a defilement in the house of Laïos.   1330
After exposing the rankness of my own guilt,
How could I look men frankly in the eyes?
No, I swear it,
If I could have stifled my hearing at its source,
I would have done it and made all this body   1335
A tight cell of misery, blank to light and sound:
So I should have been safe in my dark mind
Beyond external evil.
                   Ah Kithairon!
Why did you shelter me? When I was cast upon you,
Why did I not die? Then I should never   1340
Have shown the world my execrable birth.

Ah Polybos! Corinth, city that I believed
The ancient seat of my ancestors: how fair
I seemed, your child! And all the while this evil
Was cancerous within me!
                      For I am sick   1345
In my own being, sick in my origin.

O three roads, dark ravine, woodland and way
Where three roads met: you, drinking my father's blood,
My own blood, spilled by my own hand: can you remember
The unspeakable things I did there, and the things   1350
I went on from there to do?
                        O marriage, marriage!
The act that engendered me, and again the act
Performed by the son in the same bed—
                              Ah, the net
Of incest, mingling fathers, brothers, sons,
With brides, wives, mothers: the last evil   1355
That can be known by men: no tongue can say
How evil!
          No. For the love of God, conceal me
Somewhere far from Thebes; or kill me; or hurl me
Into the sea, away from men's eyes for ever.

Come, lead me. You need not fear to touch me.   1360
Of all men, I alone can bear this guilt.

Enter KREON.

CHORAGOS: Kreon is here now. As to what you ask,
He may decide the course to take. He only
Is left to protect the city in your place.
OEDIPUS: Alas, how can I speak to him? What right have I   1365
To beg his courtesy whom I have deeply wronged?
KREON: I have not come to mock you, Oedipus,
Or to reproach you, either.
                     To ATTENDANTS   —You, standing there:
If you have lost all respect for man's dignity,
At least respect the flame of Lord Helios: 1370
Do not allow this pollution to show itself
Openly here, an affront to the earth
And Heaven's rain and the light of day. No, take him
Into the house as quickly as you can.
For it is proper   1375
That only the close kindred see his grief.
OEDIPUS: I pray you in God's name, since your courtesy
Ignores my dark expectation, visiting
With mercy this man of all men most execrable:
Give me what I ask—for your good, not for mine.   1380
KREON: And what is it that you turn to me begging for?
OEDIPUS: Drive me out of this country as quickly as may be
To a place where no human voice can ever greet me.
KREON: I should have done that before now—only,
God's will had not been wholly revealed to me.   1385
OEDIPUS: But his command is plain: the parricide
Must be destroyed. I am that evil man.
KREON: That is the sense of it, yes; but as things are,
We had best discover clearly what is to be done.
OEDIPUS: You would learn more about a man like me?   1390
KREON: You are ready now to listen to the god.
OEDIPUS: I will listen. But it is to you
That I must turn for help. I beg you, hear me.

The woman in there—
Give her whatever funeral you think proper: 1395
She is your sister.
                     —But let me go, Kreon!
Let me purge my father's Thebes of the pollution
Of my living here, and go out to the wild hills,
To Kithairon, that has won such fame with me,
The tomb my mother and father appointed for me,   1400
And let me die there, as they willed I should.

And yet I know
Death will not ever come to me through sickness
Or in any natural way: I have been preserved
For some unthinkable fate. But let that be. 1405

As for my sons, you need not care for them.
They are men, they will find some way to live.
But my poor daughters, who have shared my table,
Who never before have been parted from their father—
Take care of them, Kreon; do this for me. 1410

And will you let me touch them with my hands
A last time, and let us weep together?
Be kind, my lord,
Great prince, be kind!
            Could I but touch them,
They would be mine again, as when I had my eyes. 1415

Enter ANTIGONE *and* ISMENE, *attended.*

Ah, God!
Is it my dearest children I hear weeping?
Has Kreon pitied me and sent my daughters?
KREON: Yes, Oedipus: I knew that they were dear to you
In the old days, and know you must love them still. 1420
OEDIPUS: May God bless you for this—and be a friendlier
Guardian to you than he has been to me!

Children, where are you?
Come quickly to my hands: they are your brother's—
Hands that have brought your father's once clear eyes 1425
To this way of seeing—
                Ah dearest ones,
I had neither sight nor knowledge then, your father
By the woman who was the source of his own life!
And I weep for you—having no strength to see you—,
I weep for you when I think of the bitterness 1430
That men will visit upon you all your lives.
What homes, what festivals can you attend
Without being forced to depart again in tears?
And when you come to marriageable age,
Where is the man, my daughters, who would dare 1435
Risk the bane that lies on all my children?
Is there any evil wanting? Your father killed
His father; sowed the womb of her who bore him;
Engendered you at the fount of his own existence!
That is what they will say of you.
               Then, whom 1440

Can you ever marry? There are no bridegrooms for you,
And your lives must wither away in sterile dreaming.

O Kreon, son of Menoikeus!
You are the only father my daughters have,
Since we, their parents, are both of us gone for ever. 1445
They are your own blood: you will not let them
Fall into beggary and loneliness;
You will keep them from the miseries that are mine!
Take pity on them; see, they are only children,
Friendless except for you. Promise me this, 1450
Great prince, and give me your hand in token of it.

KREON *clasps his right hand.*

Children:
I could say much, if you could understand me,
But as it is, I have only this prayer for you:
Live where you can, be as happy as you can— 1455
Happier, please God, than God has made your father.
KREON: Enough. You have wept enough. Now go within.
OEDIPUS: I must; but it is hard.
KREON: Time eases all things.
OEDIPUS: You know my mind, then?
KREON: Say what you desire.
OEDIPUS: Send me from Thebes!
KREON: God grant that I may! 1460
OEDIPUS: But since God hates me . . .
KREON: No, he will grant your wish.
OEDIPUS: You promise?
KREON: I can not speak beyond my knowledge.
OEDIPUS: Then lead me in.
KREON: Come now, and leave your children.
OEDIPUS: No! Do not take them from me!
KREON: Think no longer
That you are in command here, but rather think 1465
How, when you were, you served your own destruction.

Exeunt into the house all but the CHORUS; *the* CHORAGOS *chants directly to the audience.*

CHORAGOS: Men of Thebes: look upon Oedipus.

This is the king who solved the famous riddle
And towered up, most powerful of men.
No mortal eyes but looked on him with envy, 1470
Yet in the end ruin swept over him.

Let every man in mankind's frailty
Consider his last day; and let none
Presume on his good fortune until he find
Life, at his death, a memory without pain.   1475

QUESTIONS

1. What does the Prologue reveal about the relationship between Oedipus and the Theban citizens?
2. Discuss the importance of oracles in the play. What different attitudes are expressed toward them?
3. What examples of dramatic irony can you find in Oedipus's longer speeches at the beginning of the play?
4. The chorus in *Oedipus* provides a sounding board of public opinion. What major themes does this collective voice announce?
5. Examine the question of free will in *Oedipus*. To what extent does he choose to act as he does? To what extent are his actions fated to occur? How can we reconcile these opposed claims of fate and choice?
6. When does Jocasta realize what has happened? How does she react to the discovery? What are the effects of her reactions?
7. Why are blindness and exile appropriate forms of punishment for Oedipus?

WRITING ABOUT TRAGEDY AND IRONY

Tragedy and Comedy are not so much elements of drama as they are types. Though we say that *Hamlet* has comic "elements" (the gravedigger scene), we call it a tragedy because its spirit, its total effect, arises from a human confrontation with catastrophe.

When we write about tragedy we usually concentrate on one or more of the elements of drama: plot, character, or stagecraft and spectacle. But we approach these elements from a special angle when we consider the spirit that makes the play a tragedy. What *is* that spirit? How do we tell that a particular play is a tragedy?

To locate this spirit, we might begin by asking questions about qualities that acknowledged tragedies share. To illustrate this, we have posed five questions based on similarities among *Death of a Salesman, Hamlet,* and *Oedipus the King*. (The answer to all five questions is "yes." So much for suspense!) Probing these questions, their affirmative answers, and their applicability to other plays will help us determine whether a play is a tragedy, and will suggest ways to approach a paper about tragedy.

1. Does the main character of the play possess a "flawed virtue" that implies a shortcoming relative to a system of values extending beyond himself or herself?

This system could be the Greek world of gods and prophecies, the Renaissance world of Christianity and secular humanism, or the modern American world of the capitalist ideal of effort and success. This question implies that the world of tragedy has values, that no struggle is wholly private and no effort wholly successful. Residing within this question are the following subjects for papers about tragedy: (a) the flaw of the protagonist, (b) his or her essential goodness, (c) his or her aspirations and failures, with their attendant causes and consequences, and (d) the values embodied by the protagonist.

2. *Does the main character undergo an extreme reversal of fortune, and does he or she recognize the causes and consequences of this reversal?* The first question concerned the nature of the tragic character; this one concerns the dynamism of the tragic plot. Though it may be an oversimplification, one could say that a tragedy with no reversal would generate no fear in its audience, and that a tragedy without recognition would generate no pity. Suffering a horrible misfortune is one thing; identifying with it is quite another. The best tragic playwrights allow for both. Implicit in this question are the following subjects for papers about tragedy: (a) the nature of the reversal and the "states" or situations portrayed before and after it (Oedipus as powerful king versus Oedipus as abject wanderer—see the sample essay below, page 1291), (b) the irony surrounding the resemblances and differences between the two states (Oedipus as an ignorant man who can see, then Oedipus as a blind man who "sees" far more deeply into his own fate), and (c) the recognition as a recognition of values.

3. *Is there a causal connection between the "flawed virtue" of the protagonist and his or her recognition and reversal?* This question unites the elements of character and plot. The tragic protagonist will be flawed enough to behave in a way which leads to reversal, but virtuous enough to acknowledge the system of values that these actions violate. Possible subjects for papers here include: (a) the relationship between the protagonist's flaw and his or her virtue, (b) the ironic relationship between the protagonist's flaw and his or her recognition, (c) the ironic relationship between the protagonist's virtue and his or her reversal, and (d) the way other characters in the play define and counterbalance the protagonist's flaws, virtues, reversal, or recognition.

4. *Does the protagonist assert his or her ability to act independently while ironically being entrapped by the consequences of this assertion?* The best tragedies *seem* inevitable, and usually exhibit a contrast between appearance and reality. Hamlet, for example, in his attempt to verify the reality of the ghost, chooses to wait before killing Claudius and suffers from the consequences of his waiting. This question suggests the following subjects for papers: (a) the theme of appearance versus reality, (b) the way tragic action draws all the characters into its wake, and (c) the causal links of the actions of the play.

5. *Does the play affirm human potentiality while displaying the waste of this potentiality?* Tragedy does not show humankind as a debased species, but as

a species doomed to an incomplete realization of its potential. The following paper subjects arise from this question: (a) the human potential affirmed by the play, (b) the values implied by this potential, (c) the stature that the protagonist acquires despite falling short of realizing his or her potential.

The difficulty of these many questions and subjects reflects the complexity of tragedy as an artistic form. By addressing the "big" issues, they are designed to extend your awareness to the whole play and deepen your thinking about the truths and paradoxes of tragic drama. Any part of a tragedy—a scene, a minor character, a single speech—is connected to at least one of these questions. The following sample essay about *Oedipus the King* analyzes Oedipus's first and last major speeches to reveal the contrasting situations on either side of his reversal. It typifies one way that you can move from the "smaller" ideas of individual speeches to the major themes of a whole play.

Peripety in Oedipus the King

The utter reversal of Oedipus's fortunes in Oedipus the King becomes apparent when we compare his first major speeches to the Theban suppliants (lines 1-15 and 60-80) with his last speech to his children and to Kreon (lines 1421-56). The Oedipus of the final scene represents a grotesque contradiction of the earlier Oedipus. The tableaux that Sophocles present contrast Oedipus's sight, knowledge, bearing, and power. These four qualities reveal the extent of his transformation.

The Oedipus of the Prologue possesses his physical vision, but has only apparent knowledge of his situation. He proudly announces to the gathered elders:

> Poor children, you may be sure I know
> All that you longed for in your coming here.
> I know that you are deathly sick; and yet,
> Sick as you are, no one is as sick as I.
>
> (lines 60-63)

The irony here needs no explanation. At the end of the play, conversely, Oedipus exclaims to his real children, "I had neither sight nor knowledge then, your father/ By the woman who was the source of his own life" (lines 1427-28). His knowledge, as we know, concerns his real identity; this knowledge has profoundly altered his relationship with the very children to whom he speaks.

Oedipus's bearing at the beginning and at the end of the play also contrast starkly. In the Prologue he weeps tears of pity for his stricken Theban subjects. He tells them: "No, I have been in tears for a long while/ And in my restless thought walked many ways." (lines 68-69). But he is in command of the situation and has taken steps to remedy their misery by dispatching Kreon to Delphi. He treats the citizens as children he must help. At the end of the play he is a defeated man. The children he addresses are literally his, but with such a difference! They have become his siblings too. Now he weeps tears of bitterness for his forlorn kin:

> And I weep for you--having no strength to see you--,
> I weep for you when I think of the bitterness
> That men will visit upon you all yours lives.
>
> (lines 1429-31)

> Just as his pity rises from the past (he and the Theban citizens are mutually indebted to each other), so does his bitterness extend into the future.
>   The extent of Oedipus's power is also drastically diminished by the events of the play. In the beginning he is a powerful ruler whom his subjects respect. At the end of the play, he exiles himself from the city because of his unnatural crimes. In the beginning he bears a famous name, in the end an infamous one. His relationship with Kreon shows the extent of his downfall. Although he is a member of the triumvirate at the beginning of the play, Kreon is clearly subordinate to Oedipus. By the end of the play, Kreon has assumed sole power in the city. He becomes both Oedipus' scourge and the benefactor of his children, the literal ones and the figurative ones (the Theban citizens). He grants Oedipus the wish of ignominious exile.
>   The end of Oedipus the King, then, presents us with a mirror image of the Prologue. Some things, such as Oedipus's sight, are completely reversed. Others, such as his weeping, are seen in a new, ironic light. The high king has fallen; the noble husband has sunk into the incestuous son; the regal father has become the outcast brother.

SUGGESTIONS FOR WRITING ABOUT TRAGEDY AND IRONY

1. Read Arthur Miller's essay "Tragedy and the Common Man" (page 1578). Write an essay that shows how Willy Loman possesses the traits Miller finds requisite for the tragic hero.
2. Analyze the choral speeches in *Oedipus the King*. Assess the chorus's changing views of the action.
3. Compare the ways Shakespeare and Miller present the exposition of their plays.
4. Analyze the illusions of Willy Loman, Hamlet, and Oedipus.
5. Read Ernst Jones's "The Theme of Matricide" (page 1574) and use it as a source document in a short paper that shows how the key relationship in *Hamlet* is the one between Hamlet and Gertrude.

COMEDY

"Man is the only animal that laughs and weeps; for he is the only animal that is struck with the difference between what things are, and what they ought to be." Essayist William Hazlitt made this astute observation a century and a half ago. Hazlitt's comment reminds us that the line separating tragedy and comedy is often a slender one. The two faces of drama, represented by the traditional weeping tragic mask with its downturned mouth and the laughing comic mask with its upturned mouth, are more similar than they are different; as has often been noted, the laugh is more a grimace than an expression of joy.

When Nietzsche remarked in *The Birth of Tragedy* (page 1565), "From the smile of this Dionysus sprang the Olympian gods, from his tears sprang man," he was commenting on the essential place each of these types of drama held in the Greek mind and subsequently in Western theater. According to Nietzsche the tragic suffering of the hero is the result of "individuation," whereas comic joy results from restoration of oneness with the universe. If we apply this notion to Oedipus, it is clear that Oedipus' suffering is a result of his individualistic drive to resist the prophecy of the oracle. His *hubris* brings him into conflict with the most sacred bonds that tie an individual to society, the bonds of child to parent, subject to ruler. Both as child-subject and as parent-ruler Oedipus fails to see his proper place and his blindness to these relationships necessitates his punishment. In both tragedy and comedy individuality is a kind of evil, a deviation from the "oneness" that constitutes the desired order of things. In tragedy, the hero is defeated and punished for his transgression; in comedy, those who deviate are the butt of the jokes, but are often offered the opportunity to reform and join the fold.

Traditionally, tragedy ends unhappily with the defeat or death of the tragic hero, who has struggled unsuccessfully against an insurmountable obstacle. Comedy, on the other hand, traditionally ends happily with the hero overcoming some temporary obstacle, and in the process of reestablishing a desired order of things, correcting those obstructions which caused disunity. Lovers are united, social disruption cured, and hope is extended even to those who seem to lie beyond society's norms. But this is not always so. A dark comedy like Molière's *The Misanthrope* concludes with Alceste, the misanthrope, deciding he must live apart from other people; yet even here he is offered the possibility of reform and union within the human community.

In modern comedy, however, the traditional masks are blended into a sardonic grin; that is, some modern comedies neither end happily nor offer hope for establishing some sort of order. If we regard Samuel Beckett's *Krapp's Last Tape* as a representational comedy, the humor is dark (often at the expense of the comic protagonist); the ending unhappy or inconclusive (disillusionment); and belief in a social or moral order turns into a cosmic joke. The protagonist of Beckett's play, for instance, ironically named Krapp, is a sixty-nine-year-old man who listens to tapes of his own voice recorded thirty years ago and makes bitter comments about his younger self. At first, when he laughs at his own foolishness, the audience laughs with him. By the end of the play, however, the audience is no longer laughing at the pathetic spectacle of a bitter, lonely old man and we are reminded not of Dionysus' smiles but of his tears.

Still, we are left with the question, why do some things make us laugh while other things make us weep? Horace Walpole thought the difference lay not in the material of the play but in the spectator. "The world is a comedy to those that think, and a tragedy to those that feel." Walpole's words suggest that the difference lies in the superior perspective, the wise aloofness of comic vision. The tragic hero, like Oedipus or Hamlet, is an idealist, a man of feeling acting out of emotions which bring him into conflict with the established nature of things. We sometimes admire his pertinacity (although his strong emotions cause him to make mistakes, even commit crimes); we empathize with his suffering; yet the very nature of the human condition dooms him to defeat. His will is inevitably subject to the conditions of the universe, his aspirations tie him to failure, or as King Lear puts it in Shakespeare's tragedy, "I am bound upon a wheel of fire." The thinking hero of comedy, on the other hand, has more limited aims; he, too, may wish to change things, but in a more modest, social way. Unlike the idealistic tragic hero, he recognizes human nature's shortcomings and wishes to amend them. However, when the thinking man's intellect is clouded by his emotions (as in Molière's *The Misanthrope*) we may laugh at his inconsistencies, but he suffers an unhappy fate not unlike that of a tragic hero.

In traditional comedies which end happily, we often laugh because we know we are in a special world where threats prove to be harmless, and danger is only temporary. We laugh at the character dangling precariously from the hands of the giant clock atop a tall building because we know no harm will come to him. Charlie Chaplin, eating a boiled shoe with a knife and fork in *The Gold Rush*, has created one of the funniest pieces of business in that classic silent movie but only because we know that the character will not actually starve to death. That Chaplin later admitted he had gotten the idea for the comic scene from an account of the tragic Donner Party (whose members actually had to resort to cannibalism to survive) simply underscores the imperviousness of the comic world to permanent harm. We laugh because we really know the topsy-turvy world will return to order, normality will be restored and (temporarily at least) justice and decency will prevail. This has been the history of comedy for 2500 years, but to fully understand the nature of comedy, we should look to its origins and subsequent evolution.

Comedy comes from the greek word *komoidos*, a singer in the revels. Developing after tragedy, but from the same Dionysian rituals as tragedy, comedy can be traced back to the celebration of wine-drinking and mating by a chorus dressed in goat-like costumes who sang and danced animatedly and drunkenly about the stage. The function of the one-day *komos*, or revels, was also to provide comic relief from the three days of tragedies. Five writers competed for a prize, each represented by a comedy. The five comedies were presented in the same theater as the tragedies. Often the jokes in these comedies turned on the exaggerated phalluses worn by the actors as part of their costumes. Aristophanes (448?–380? B.C.) wrote the oldest extant comedies, but of his 40 or more plays, only 11 have survived. They deal with contemporary social issues—politics, war, literary rivalries and quarrels—and often attack specific individuals. Unlike tragedies, comedies did not usually rely on legends and myths for their plots but used original materials. Typical of Aristophanes' comedies is *Lysistrata* (411 B.C.), an attack on the Peloponnesian War, in which, to put an end to the fighting, the women stage a sex strike—which affords the playwright countless opportunities for phallic jokes. These early satiric comedies, often personal in nature, are called **Old Comedy,** and they are replaced in the 3rd century B.C. by **New Comedy** which uses stock romantic situations.

In new comedy, a young man and woman who wish to marry are opposed by the young man's father or a rival. At the end of the play, aided by a clever and manipulative servant, the couple are united, and a new society develops around the newly joined pair. Even the opposing character is invited to join in this affirmation of life.

Old and new comedy, therefore, lead to two of the broadest categories of comedy: **Satiric Comedy** and **Romantic Comedy.** Satiric comedy is corrective: it holds up to ridicule traits that represent deviations from some sort of moral, ethical, or social norms. Characters are absurd, morally inferior, or less attractive people than those found in romantic comedy. Satiric comedy exposes departures from the norm with the intent of correcting them. *Lysistrata* offers the spectacle of a male-dominated society caught in playing war games, unable to resume the normal roles of husbands and fathers. Sometimes society itself has moved from the norm and needs reform.

Finally, humor can at times be bitter and we are led to laugh *at* and not with the offending character. In romantic comedy we are presented with likeable characters, excepting the blocking or obstructing character. It is this person who has deviated from the social norm, and at the play's conclusion, we are invited to laugh *with* rather than *at* him. The obstructing character is often obsessed by a single trait, sometimes a dominant characteristic which dictates his behavior and sets him or her apart as an outsider. At the end of the play when the young couple are united, this character is invited to join the others and to participate in the new ideal world that is about to be created. In *Twelfth Night* Shakespeare has created such a character in Malvolio, a portrait of a self-righteous Puritan who is finally exposed as a hypocrite.

New comedy influenced Renaissance drama directly and through its popular adaptations in the Italian *commedia dell'arte* which developed stock characters such as the figures of Harlequin, the clown; Punchinello, a hook-nosed dwarf (the ancestor of Punch in Punch and Judy puppet shows); and

Miles Gloriosus, the braggart soldier who later appears as Falstaff in Shakespeare's *Henry IV* and *The Merry Wives of Windsor*. These stereotypes find their way into the plays of Ben Jonson in the late Renaissance where the stock characters are the source of traditional jokes. The cast of characters in *Volpone* (1606) includes a shyster lawyer named Voltore (the vulture), a jealous husband, Corvino (the crow), an old miser, Corbaccio (the raven), the wily confidence man of the title, Volpone (the fox), and his unscrupulous servant, Mosca (the fly). By the mid-seventeenth and early eighteenth centuries, the **Comedy of Manners** had succeeded as the lineal descendent of new comedy. Comedy of manners exploits the main character's misdirected attempt to adhere to a mistaken social code, usually some *fixed idea* that determines the protagonist's behavior. During this period, known as the Enlightenment or the Age of Reason, emphasis was placed on man as a social creature, and a good deal of importance attached to cooperation among members of society. All reasonable, right-thinking people would get along. Social frictions and political upheavals would be avoided if people practiced moderation, used their reason, and adhered to traditional norms which reflected accumulated social wisdom. In Molière's *The Misanthrope*, for example, Alceste refuses to do less than tell the absolute truth, even when such frankness will be harmful. While under normal circumstances honesty is a virtue, Alceste carries his policy too far and actually becomes an anti-social force.

Comedies of manners extol the social graces and hold the values of civilized society as a norm for human conduct. From the Restoration (1660) through the eighteenth century, it was the dominant dramatic genre in England and France. These plays were characterized by grace, wit, elegance, and verbal repartee. The plot lines developed from the marital intrigues of the aristocratic class. Double entendres and verbal irony characterize the clever dialogue of comedies of manners. In Molière's *The Misanthrope*, the characters often respond to an insult with sarcasm, saying the opposite of what they mean. When Alceste is convinced he has proof of Célimène's unfaithfulness he tells her angrily, "Nothing Hell's or Heaven's wrath could do/Ever produced so bad a thing as you." To which she replies, "Your compliments were always sweet and pretty." Oscar Wilde's *The Importance of Being Earnest* (1895) is sometimes cited as the final example of comedy of manners, its tongue-in-cheek improbabilities culminating in the verbal pun of the title. In the play, the obstructing force is the two heroines' refusal to marry anyone not named Ernest, which is resolved by the improbable discovery that both heroes are actually named Ernest.

Sometimes also called **High Comedy**, since such verbal wit appeals to the intellect, comedy of manners represents one line of development from new comedy; the other line of development, through *commedia dell'arte*, is farce, slapstick, or **Low Comedy**, which draws its humor from physical action. Often based on the physical discomfort or even abuse of one character to whom we feel superior, low comedy often appears as a comic interlude in a tragedy. The pope-baiting episode in Christopher Marlowe's *The Tragical History of the Life and Death of Dr. Faustus* (1604) involves invisible devils striking the pope and setting fireworks off among his clerical retinue. Such an episode, like the gravediggers' episode in *Hamlet,* provides the necessary psychological relief from the cumulative suffering of the tragic hero before he is led inexorably to his fall. On the other hand, sometimes low comedy is used to mock something regarded as important, reverent, or sanctimonious. The opera's popularity under George I in early eighteenth-century England was resented by many writers who saw in it a pretentious art form which deprived them of royal patronage. John Gay parodied such operas by setting the *Beggar's Opera* (1728) in Newgate Prison, making the hero a notorious highwayman and including in it a scene in which two rival sopranos pull each other's hair.

The ideal world predicated by romantic comedy, whether the green pastoral world of Shakespeare's *Tempest* or *Midsummer Night's Dream,* or the elegant embroidered world of William Congreve's *The Way of the World* (1700), each assumed in its own way a standard of behavior with which to hold people accountable. A world ruled over by a benevolent deity insured that the virtuous would be rewarded and the villainous would, in the end, prove to be ineffectual. No one would gainsay the improbabilities of plot, because in the world of comedy things *are* meant to turn out right. Since World War II, however, **Absurdist Drama** has turned increasingly toward **Black Comedy** as a way of expressing man's loneliness and alienation. Living in a post-atomic world, having witnessed the Holocaust, humanity no longer has the certainty of a smiling benevolent deity ordering the universe, nor the rational order of optimistic science. Unheroic characters move through plotless dramas without beginnings, middles, or ends in the plays of Samuel Beckett, Jean Genêt, and Eugène Ionesco, or the characters' helplessness and purposelessness are emphasized by the bizarre things they say and do, as in the plays of Bertolt Brecht, Edward Albee, Arthur Kopit, or Beth Henley.

There is also ample room in the modern theater for satiric comedy. Social criticism appears in the often revived *The Time of Your Life* (1940) by William Saroyan, *Travesties* (1975) by Tom Stoppard, and even in the comic scenes of essentially serious plays by Athol Fugard and Sam Shepard.

In many ways, comedy may be closer to the wisdom of human nature than tragedy. That wisdom which comes with seeing ourselves as foolish, as frequently not acting in accord with what is best in human nature, is essential to the comic spirit. Whether it is the slashingly satiric comedy of Aristophanes finding its modern equivalent in Samuel Beckett's biting irony in *Krapp's Last Tape,* or the escapist humor of Shakespeare's *A Midsummer Night's Dream* being captured in the fantasies of the heroes of Shepard's plays, humanity will always need to smile and laugh more often than it will need to weep.

MOLIÈRE (1622–1673)

The Misanthrope

Jean Baptiste Poquelin, whom the world knows as Molière, was a lifelong Parisian and is perhaps the only comic writer for the stage whose work can stand comparison with Shakespeare's. His comedies are distinguished by their often farcical plots, their brilliant repartee, and their trenchant satire. His major works include *Tartuffe* (1664), *The Imaginary Invalid* (1673), and *The Misanthrope* (1666), which is generally considered his greatest comedy.

CHARACTERS

ALCESTE, *in love with Célimène*
PHILINTE, *Alceste's friend*
ORONTE, *in love with Célimène*
CÉLIMÈNE, *Alceste's beloved*
ELIANTE, *Célimène's cousin*
ARSINOÉ, *a friend of Célimène's*
ACASTE ⎫
          ⎬ *marquesses*
CLITANDRE ⎭
BASQUE, *Célimène's servant*
A GUARD *of the Marshalsea*
DUBOIS, *Alceste's valet*

The scene throughout is in Célimène's house at Paris.

ACT I

SCENE I

PHILINTE: Now, what's got into you?
ALCESTE *seated:*   Kindly leave me alone.
PHILINTE: Come, come, what is it? This lugubrious tone. . .
ALCESTE: Leave me, I said; you spoil my solitude.
PHILINTE: Oh, listen to me, now, and don't be rude.
ALCESTE: I choose to be rude, Sir, and to be hard of hearing.   5
PHILINTE: These ugly moods of yours are not endearing;
    Friends though we are, I really must insist. . .
ALCESTE *abruptly rising:*   Friends? Friends, you say? Well, cross me off
        your list.
    I've been your friend till now, as you well know;
    But after what I saw a moment ago   10
    I tell you flatly that our ways must part.
    I wish no place in a dishonest heart.

PHILINTE: Why, what have I done, Alceste? Is this quite just?
ALCESTE: My God, you ought to die of self-disgust.
    I call your conduct inexcusable, Sir,   15
    And every man of honor will concur.
    I see you almost hug a man to death,
    Exclaim for joy until you're out of breath,
    And supplement these loving demonstrations
    With endless offers, vows, and protestations;   20
    Then when I ask you "Who was that?" I find
    That you can barely bring his name to mind!
    Once the man's back is turned, you cease to love him,
    And speak with absolute indifference of him!
    By God, I say it's base and scandalous   25
    To falsify the heart's affections thus;
    If I caught myself behaving in such a way,
    I'd hang myself for shame, without delay.
PHILINTE: It hardly seems a hanging matter to me;
    I hope that you will take it graciously   30
    If I extend myself a slight reprieve,
    And live a little longer, by your leave.
ALCESTE: How dare you joke about a crime so grave?
PHILINTE: What crime? How else are people to behave?
ALCESTE: I'd have them be sincere, and never part   35
    With any word that isn't from the heart.
PHILINTE: When someone greets us with a show of pleasure,
    It's but polite to give him equal measure,
    Return his love the best that we know how,
    And trade him offer for offer, vow for vow.   40
ALCESTE: No, no, this formula you'd have me follow,
    However fashionable, is false and hollow,
    And I despise the frenzied operations
    Of all these barterers of protestations,
    These lavishers of meaningless embraces,   45
    These utterers of obliging commonplaces,
    Who court and flatter everyone on earth
    And praise the fool no less than the man of worth.
    Should you rejoice that someone fondles you,
    Offers his love and service, swears to be true,   50
    And fills your ears with praises of your name,
    When to the first damned fop he'll say the same?
    No, no: no self-respecting heart would dream
    Of prizing so promiscuous an esteem;
    However high the praise, there's nothing worse   55
    Than sharing honors with the universe.
    Esteem is founded on comparison:
    To honor all men is to honor none.
    Since you embrace this indiscriminate vice,
    Your friendship comes at far too cheap a price;   60
    I spurn the easy tribute of a heart

Which will not set the worthy man apart:
I choose, Sir, to be chosen; and in fine,
The friend of mankind is no friend of mine.

PHILINTE: But in polite society, custom decrees 65
That we show certain outward courtesies. . .

ALCESTE: Ah, no! we should condemn with all our force
Such false and artificial intercourse.
Let men behave like men; let them display
Their inmost hearts in everything they say; 70
Let the heart speak, and let our sentiments
Not mask themselves in silly compliments.

PHILINTE: In certain cases it would be uncouth
And most absurd to speak the naked truth;
With all respect for your exalted notions, 75
It's often best to veil one's true emotions.
Wouldn't the social fabric come undone
If we were wholly frank with everyone?
Suppose you met with someone you couldn't bear;
Would you inform him of it then and there? 80

ALCESTE: Yes.

PHILINTE: Then you'd tell old Emilie it's pathetic
The way she daubs her features with cosmetic
And plays the gay coquette at sixty-four?

ALCESTE: I would.

PHILINTE: And you'd call Dorilas a bore,
And tell him every ear at court is lame 85
From hearing him brag about his noble name?

ALCESTE: Precisely.

PHILINTE: Ah, you're joking.

ALCESTE: *Au contraire:*
In this regard there's none I'd choose to spare.
All are corrupt; there's nothing to be seen
In court or town but aggravates my spleen. 90
I fall into deep gloom and melancholy
When I survey the scene of human folly,
Finding on every hand base flattery,
Injustice, fraud, self-interest, treachery. . .
Ah, it's too much; mankind has grown so base, 95
I mean to break with the whole human race.

PHILINTE: This philosophic rage is a bit extreme;
You've no idea how comical you seem;
Indeed, we're like those brothers in the play
Called *School for Husbands,* one of whom was prey. . . 100

ALCESTE: Enough, now! None of your stupid similes.

PHILINTE: Then let's have no more tirades, if you please.
The world won't change, whatever you say or do;
And since plain speaking means so much to you,
I'll tell you plainly that by being frank 105
You've earned the reputation of a crank,

And that you're thought ridiculous when you rage
And rant against the manners of the age.
ALCESTE: So much the better; just what I wish to hear.
No news could be more grateful to my ear.   110
All men are so detestable in my eyes,
I should be sorry if they thought me wise.
PHILINTE: Your hatred's very sweeping, is it not?
ALCESTE: Quite right: I hate the whole degraded lot.
PHILINTE: Must all poor human creatures be embraced,   115
Without distinction, by your vast distaste?
Even in these bad times, there are surely a few. . .
ALCESTE: No, I include all men in one dim view:
Some men I hate for being rogues; the others
I hate because they treat the rogues like brothers,   120
And, lacking a virtuous scorn for what is vile,
Receive the villain with a complaisant smile.
Notice how tolerant people choose to be
Toward that bold rascal who's at law with me.
His social polish can't conceal his nature;   125
One sees at once that he's a treacherous creature;
No one could possibly be taken in
By those soft speeches and that sugary grin.
The whole world knows the shady means by which
The low-brow's grown so powerful and rich,   130
And risen to a rank so bright and high
That virtue can but blush, and merit sigh.
Whenever his name comes up in conversation,
None will defend his wretched reputation;
Call him knave, liar, scoundrel, and all the rest,   135
Each head will nod, and no one will protest.
And yet his smirk is seen in every house,
He's greeted everywhere with smiles and bows,
And when there's any honor that can be got
By pulling strings, he'll get it, like as not.   140
My God! It chills my heart to see the ways
Men come to terms with evil nowadays;
Sometimes, I swear, I'm moved to flee and find
Some desert land unfouled by humankind.
PHILINTE: Come, let's forget the follies of the times   145
And pardon mankind for its petty crimes;
Let's have an end of rantings and of railings,
And show some leniency toward human failings.
This world requires a pliant rectitude;
Too stern a virtue makes one stiff and rude;   150
Good sense views all extremes with detestation,
And bids us to be noble in moderation.
The rigid virtues of the ancient days
Are not for us; they jar with all our ways
And ask of us too lofty a perfection.   155

Wise men accept their times without objection,
And there's no greater folly, if you ask me,
Than trying to reform society.
Like you, I see each day a hundred and one
Unhandsome deeds that might be better done, 160
But still, for all the faults that meet my view,
I'm never known to storm and rave like you.
I take men as they are, or let them be,
And teach my soul to bear their frailty;
And whether in court or town, whatever the scene, 165
My phlegm's as philosophic as your spleen.

ALCESTE: This phlegm which you so eloquently commend,
Does nothing ever rile it up, my friend?
Suppose some man you trust should treacherously
Conspire to rob you of your property, 170
And do his best to wreck your reputation?
Wouldn't you feel a certain indignation?

PHILINTE: Why, no. These faults of which you so complain
Are part of human nature, I maintain,
And it's no more a matter for disgust 175
That men are knavish, selfish and unjust,
Than that the vulture dines upon the dead,
And wolves are furious, and apes ill-bred.

ALCESTE: Shall I see myself betrayed, robbed, torn to bits,
And not . . . Oh, let's be still and rest our wits. 180
Enough of reasoning, now. I've had my fill.

PHILINTE: Indeed, you would do well, Sir, to be still.
Rage less at your opponent, and give some thought
To how you'll win this lawsuit that he's brought.

ALCESTE: I assure you I'll do nothing of the sort. 185

PHILINTE: Then who will plead your case before the court?

ALCESTE: Reason and right and justice will plead for me.

PHILINTE: Oh, Lord. What judges do you plan to see?

ALCESTE: Why, none. The justice of my cause is clear.

PHILINTE: Of course, man; but there's politics to fear. . . 190

ALCESTE: No, I refuse to lift a hand. That's flat.
I'm either right, or wrong.

PHILINTE: Don't count on that.

ALCESTE: No, I'll do nothing.

PHILINTE: Your enemy's influence
Is great, you know. . .

ALCESTE: That makes no difference.

PHILINTE: It will; you'll see.

ALCESTE: Must honor bow to guile? 195
If so, I shall be proud to lose the trial.

PHILINTE: Oh, really. . .

ALCESTE: I'll discover by this case
Whether or not men are sufficiently base

And impudent and villainous and perverse
To do me wrong before the universe. 200
PHILINTE: What a man!
ALCESTE: Oh, I could wish, whatever the cost,
Just for the beauty of it, that my trial were lost.
PHILINTE: If people heard you talking so, Alceste,
They'd split their sides. Your name would be a jest.
ALCESTE: So much the worse for jesters.
PHILINTE: May I enquire 205
Whether this rectitude you so admire,
And these hard virtues you're enamored of
Are qualities of the lady whom you love?
It much surprises me that you, who seem
To view mankind with furious disesteem, 210
Have yet found something to enchant your eyes
Amidst a species which you so despise.
And what is more amazing, I'm afraid,
Is the most curious choice your heart has made.
The honest Eliante is fond of you, 215
Arsinoé, the prude, admires you too;
And yet your spirit's been perversely led
To choose the flighty Célimène instead,
Whose brittle malice and coquettish ways
So typify the manners of our days. 220
How is it that the traits you most abhor
Are bearable in this lady you adore?
Are you so blind with love that you can't find them?
Or do you contrive, in her case, not to mind them?
ALCESTE: My love for that young widow's not the kind 225
That can't perceive defects; no, I'm not blind.
I see her faults, despite my ardent love,
And all I see I fervently reprove.
And yet I'm weak; for all her falsity,
That woman knows the art of pleasing me, 230
And though I never cease complaining of her,
I swear I cannot manage not to love her.
Her charm outweighs her faults; I can but aim
To cleanse her spirit in my love's pure flame.
PHILINTE: That's no small task; I wish you all success. 235
You think then that she loves you?
ALCESTE: Heavens, yes!
I wouldn't love her did she not love me.
PHILINTE: Well, if her taste for you is plain to see,
Why do these rivals cause you such despair?
ALCESTE: True love, Sir, is possessive, and cannot bear 240
To share with all the world. I'm here today
To tell her she must send that mob away.
PHILINTE: If I were you, and had your choice to make,

Eliante, her cousin, would be the one I'd take;
That honest heart, which cares for you alone, 245
Would harmonize far better with your own.
ALCESTE: True, true: each day my reason tells me so;
But reason doesn't rule in love, you know.
PHILINTE: I fear some bitter sorrow is in store;
This love. . .

SCENE II

ORONTE *to* ALCESTE: The servants told me at the door 250
That Eliante and Célimène were out,
But when I heard, dear Sir, that you were about,
I came to say, without exaggeration,
That I hold you in the vastest admiration,
And that it's always been my dearest desire 255
To be the friend of one I so admire.
I hope to see my love of merit requited,
And you and I in friendship's bond united.
I'm sure you won't refuse—if I may be frank—
A friend of my devotedness—and rank. 260

During this speech of ORONTE'S, ALCESTE *is abstracted, and seems unaware that he is being spoken to. He only breaks off his reverie when*
ORONTE *says.* . .

It was for you, if you please, that my words were intended.
ALCESTE: For me, Sir?
ORONTE: Yes, for you. You're not offended?
ALCESTE: By no means. But this much surprises me. . .
The honor comes most unexpectedly. . .
ORONTE: My high regard should not astonish you;
The whole world feels the same. It is your due. 265
ALCESTE: Sir. . .
ORONTE: Why, in all the State there isn't one
Can match your merits; they shine, Sir, like the sun.
ALCESTE: Sir. . .
ORONTE: You are higher in my estimation
Than all that's most illustrious in the nation. 270
ALCESTE: Sir. . .
ORONTE: If I lie, may heaven strike me dead!
To show you that I mean what I have said,
Permit me, Sir, to embrace you most sincerely,
And swear that I will prize our friendship dearly.
Give me your hand. And now, Sir, if you choose, 275
We'll make our vows.
ALCESTE: Sir. . .

ORONTE: What! You refuse?
ALCESTE: Sir, it's a very great honor you extend:
　　But friendship is a sacred thing, my friend;
　　It would be profanation to bestow
　　The name of friend on one you hardly know.   280
　　All parts are better played when well-rehearsed;
　　Let's put off friendship, and get acquainted first.
　　We may discover it would be unwise
　　To try to make our natures harmonize.
ORONTE: By heaven! You're sagacious to the core;   285
　　This speech has made me admire you even more.
　　Let time, then, bring us closer day by day;
　　Meanwhile, I shall be yours in every way.
　　If, for example, there should be anything
　　You wish at court, I'll mention it to the King.   290
　　I have his ear, of course; it's quite well known
　　That I am much in favor with the throne.
　　In short, I am your servant. And now, dear friend,
　　Since you have such fine judgment, I intend
　　To please you, if I can, with a small sonnet   295
　　I wrote not long ago. Please comment on it,
　　And tell me whether I ought to publish it.
ALCESTE: You must excuse me, Sir; I'm hardly fit
　　To judge such matters.
ORONTE: Why not?
ALCESTE: I am, I fear,
　　Inclined to be unfashionably sincere.   300
ORONTE: Just what I ask; I'd take no satisfaction
　　In anything but your sincere reaction.
　　I beg you not to dream of being kind.
ALCESTE: Since you desire it, Sir, I'll speak my mind.
ORONTE: *Sonnet.* It's a sonnet . . . *Hope* . . . The poem's
　　　　addressed   305
　　To a lady who wakened hopes within my breast.
　　Hope . . . this is not the pompous sort of thing,
　　Just modest little verses, with a tender ring.
ALCESTE: Well, we shall see.
ORONTE: *Hope* . . . I'm anxious to hear
　　Whether the style seems properly smooth and clear,   310
　　And whether the choice of words is good or bad.
ALCESTE: We'll see, we'll see.
ORONTE: Perhaps I ought to add
　　That it took me only a quarter-hour to write it.
ALCESTE: The time's irrelevant, Sir: kindly recite it.
ORONTE *reading:*   Hope comforts us awhile, t'is true,   315
　　Lulling our cares with careless laughter,
　　And yet such joy is full of rue,
　　My Phyllis, if nothing follows after.

PHILINTE: I'm charmed by this already; the style's delightful.

ALCESTE *sotto voce, to* PHILINTE: How can you say that? Why, the thing
    is frightful. 320

ORONTE: Your fair face smiled on me awhile,
    But was it kindness so to enchant me?
    'Twould have been fairer not to smile,
    If hope was all you meant to grant me.

PHILINTE: What a clever thought! How handsomely you phrase it! 325

ALCESTE *sotto voce, to* PHILINTE: You know the thing is trash.
    How dare you praise it?

ORONTE: If it's to be my passion's fate
    Thus everlastingly to wait,
    Then death will come to set me free:
    For death is fairer than the fair; 330
    Phyllis, to hope is to despair
    When one must hope eternally.

PHILINTE: The close is exquisite—full of feeling and grace.

ALCESTE *sotto voce, aside:* Oh, blast the close; you'd better close your face
Before you send your lying soul to hell. 335

PHILINTE: I can't remember a poem I've liked so well.

ALCESTE *sotto voce, aside:* Good Lord!

ORONTE *to* PHILINTE: I fear you're flattering me a bit.

PHILINTE: Oh, no!

ALCESTE *sotto voce, aside:* What else d'you call it, you hypocrite?

ORONTE *to* ALCESTE: But you, Sir, keep your promise now: don't shrink
    From telling me sincerely what you think. 340

ALCESTE: Sir, these are delicate matters; we all desire
    To be told that we've the true poetic fire.
    But once, to one whose name I shall not mention,
    I said, regarding some verse of his invention,
    That gentlemen should rigorously control 345
    That itch to write which often afflicts the soul;
    That one should curb the heady inclination
    To publicize one's little avocation;
    And that in showing off one's works of art
    One often plays a very clownish part. 350

ORONTE: Are you suggesting in a devious way
    That I ought not. . .

ALCESTE: Oh, that I do not say.
    Further, I told him that no fault is worse
    Than that of writing frigid, lifeless verse,
    And that the merest whisper of such a shame 355
    Suffices to destroy a man's good name.

ORONTE: D'you mean to say my sonnet's dull and trite?

ALCESTE: I don't say that. But I went on to cite
    Numerous cases of once-respected men
    Who came to grief by taking up the pen. 360

ORONTE: And am I like them? Do I write so poorly?

ALCESTE: I don't say that. But I told this person, "Surely

You're under no necessity to compose;
Why you should wish to publish, heaven knows.
There's no excuse for printing tedious rot   365
Unless one writes for bread, as you do not.
Resist temptation, then, I beg of you;
Conceal your pastimes from the public view;
And don't give up, on any provocation,
Your present high and courtly reputation,   370
To purchase at a greedy printer's shop
The name of silly author and scribbling fop."
These were the points I tried to make him see.
ORONTE: I sense that they are also aimed at me;
But now—about my sonnet—I'd like to be told. . .   375
ALCESTE: Frankly, that sonnet should be pigeonholed.
You've chosen the worst models to imitate.
The style's unnatural. Let me illustrate:

> For example, Your fair face smiled on me awhile,
> Followed by, 'Twould have been fairer not to smile!   380
> Or this: such joy if full of rue;
> Or this: For death is fairer than the fair;
> Or, Phyllis, to hope is to despair
>   When one must hope eternally!

This artificial style, that's all the fashion,   385
Has neither taste, nor honesty, nor passion;
It's nothing but a sort of wordy play,
And nature never spoke in such a way.
What, in this shallow age, is not debased?
Our fathers, though less refined, had better taste;   390
I'd barter all that men admire today
For one old love-song I shall try to say:

> If the King had given me for my own
> Paris, his citadel,
> And I for that must leave alone   395
> Her whom I love so well,
> I'd say then to the Crown,
> Take back your glittering town;
> My darling is more fair, I swear,
> My darling is more fair.   400

The rhyme's not rich, the style is rough and old,
But don't you see that it's the purest gold
Beside the tinsel nonsense now preferred,
And that there's passion in its every word?

> If the King had given me for my own   405
> Paris, his citadel,

And I for that must leave alone
Her whom I love so well,
I'd say then to the Crown,
Take back your glittering town;   410
My darling is more fair, I swear,
My darling is more fair.

There speaks a loving heart. *To* PHILINTE: You're laughing, eh?
Laugh on, my precious wit. Whatever you say,
I hold that song's worth all the bibelots   415
That people hail today with ah's and oh's.
ORONTE: And I maintain my sonnet's very good.
ALCESTE: It's not at all surprising that you should.
You have your reasons; permit me to have mine
For thinking that you cannot write a line.   420
ORONTE: Others have praised my sonnet to the skies.
ALCESTE: I lack their art of telling pleasant lies.
ORONTE: You seem to think you've got no end of wit.
ALCESTE: To praise your verse, I'd need still more of it.
ORONTE: I'm not in need of your approval, Sir.   425
ALCESTE: That's good; you couldn't have it if you were.
ORONTE: Come now, I'll lend you the subject of my sonnet;
I'd like to see you try to improve upon it.
ALCESTE: I might, by chance, write something just as shoddy;
But then I wouldn't show it to everybody.   430
ORONTE: You're most opinionated and conceited.
ALCESTE: Go find your flatterers, and be better treated.
ORONTE: Look here, my little fellow, pray watch your tone.
ALCESTE: My great big fellow, you'd better watch your own.
PHILINTE *stepping between them:*   Oh, please, please, gentlemen!
This will never do.   435
ORONTE: The fault is mine, and I leave the field to you.
I am your servant, Sir, in every way.
ALCESTE: And I, Sir, am your most abject valet.

SCENE III

PHILINTE: Well, as you see, sincerity in excess
Can get you into a very pretty mess;   440
Oronte was hungry for appreciation. . .
ALCESTE: Don't speak to me
PHILINTE: What?
ALCESTE: No more conversation.
PHILINTE: Really, now. . .
ALCESTE: Leave me alone.
PHILINTE: If I. . .
ALCESTE: Out of my sight!
PHILINTE: But what. . .

ALCESTE:　　　　　I won't listen.
PHILINTE:　　　　　　　　　　But. . .
ALCESTE:　　　　　　　　　　　　Silence!
PHILINTE:　　　　　　　　　　　　　　Now, is it polite. . .
ALCESTE:　By heaven, I've had enough. Don't follow me.　　445
PHILINTE:　Ah, you're just joking. I'll keep you company.

ACT II

SCENE I

ALCESTE:　Shall I speak plainly, Madam? I confess
　　Your conduct gives me infinite distress,
　　And my resentment's grown too hot to smother.
　　Soon, I foresee, we'll break with one another.
　　If I said otherwise, I should deceive you;　　　　　　5
　　Sooner or later, I shall be forced to leave you,
　　And if I swore that we shall never part,
　　I should misread the omens of my heart.
CÉLIMÈNE:　You kindly saw me home, it would appear,
　　So as to pour invectives in my ear.　　　　　　　　10
ALCESTE:　I've no desire to quarrel. But I deplore
　　Your inability to shut the door
　　On all these suitors who beset you so.
　　There's what annoys me, if you care to know.
CÉLIMÈNE:　Is it my fault that all these men pursue me?　　15
　　Am I to blame if they're attracted to me?
　　And when they gently beg an audience,
　　Ought I to take a stick and drive them hence?
ALCESTE:　Madam, there's no necessity for a stick;
　　A less responsive heart would do the trick.　　　　20
　　Of your attractiveness I don't complain;
　　But those your charms attract, you then detain
　　By a most melting and receptive manner,
　　And so enlist their hearts beneath your banner.
　　It's the agreeable hopes which you excite　　　　　25
　　That keep these lovers round you day and night;
　　Were they less liberally smiled upon,
　　That sighing troop would very soon be gone.
　　But tell me, Madam, why it is that lately
　　This man Clitandre interests you so greatly?　　　　30
　　Because of what high merits do you deem
　　Him worthy of the honor of your esteem?
　　Is it that your admiring glances linger
　　On the splendidly long nail of his little finger?
　　Or do you share the general deep respect　　　　　35
　　For the blond wig he chooses to affect?
　　Are you in love with his embroidered hose?

Do you adore his ribbons and his bows?
Or is it that this paragon bewitches
Your tasteful eye with his vast German breeches?   40
Perhaps his giggle, or his falsetto voice,
Makes him the latest gallant of your choice?

CÉLIMÈNE: You're much mistaken to resent him so.
Why I put up with him you surely know:
My lawsuit's very shortly to be tried,   45
And I must have his influence on my side.

ALCESTE: Then lose your lawsuit, Madam, or let it drop;
Don't torture me by humoring such a fop.

CÉLIMÈNE: You're jealous of the whole world, Sir.

ALCESTE: That's true,   50
Since the whole world is well-received by you.

CÉLIMÈNE: That my good nature is so unconfined
Should serve to pacify your jealous mind;
Were I to smile on one, and scorn the rest,
Then you might have some cause to be distressed.

ALCESTE: Well, if I mustn't be jealous, tell me, then,   55
Just how I'm better treated than other men.

CÉLIMÈNE: You know you have my love. Will that not do?

ALCESTE: What proof have I that what you say is true?

CÉLIMÈNE: I would expect, Sir, that my having said it
Might give the statement a sufficient credit.   60

ALCESTE: But how can I be sure that you don't tell
The selfsame thing to other men as well?

CÉLIMÈNE: What a gallant speech! How flattering to me!
What a sweet creature you make me out to be!
Well then, to save you from the pangs of doubt,   65
All that I've said I hereby cancel out;
Now, none but yourself shall make a monkey of you:
Are you content?

ALCESTE: Why, why am I doomed to love you?
I swear that I shall bless the blissful hour
When this poor heart's no longer in your power!   70
I make no secret of it: I've done my best
To exorcise this passion from my breast;
But thus far all in vain; it will not go;
It's for my sins that I must love you so.

CÉLIMÈNE: Your love for me is matchless, Sir; that's clear.   75

ALCESTE: Indeed, in all the world it has no peer;
Words can't describe the nature of my passion,
And no man ever loved in such a fashion.

CÉLIMÈNE: Yes, it's a brand-new fashion, I agree:
You show your love by castigating me,   80
And all your speeches are enraged and rude.
I've never been so furiously wooed.

ALCESTE: Yet you could calm that fury, if you chose.

Come, shall we bring our quarrels to a close?
Let's speak with open hearts, then, and begin . . .   85

SCENE II

CÉLIMÈNE: What is it?
BASQUE: Acaste is here.
CÉLIMÈNE: Well, send him in.

SCENE III

ALCESTE: What! Shall we never be alone at all?
You're always ready to receive a call,
And you can't bear, for ten ticks of the clock,
Not to keep open house for all who knock.   90
CÉLIMÈNE: I couldn't refuse him: he'd be most put out.
ALCESTE: Surely that's not worth worrying about.
CÉLIMÈNE: Acaste would never forgive me if he guessed
That I consider him a dreadful pest.
ALCESTE: If he's a pest, why bother with him then?   95
CÉLIMÈNE: Heavens! One can't antagonize such men;
Why, they're the chartered gossips of the court,
And have a say in things of every sort.
One must receive them, and be full of charm;
They're no great help, but they can do you harm,   100
And though your influence be ever so great,
They're hardly the best people to alienate.
ALCESTE: I see, dear lady, that you could make a case
For putting up with the whole human race;
These friendships that you calculate so nicely . . .   105

SCENE IV

BASQUE: Madam, Clitandre is here as well.
ALCESTE: Precisely.
CÉLIMÈNE: Where are you going?
ALCESTE: Elsewhere.
CÉLIMÈNE: Stay.
ALCESTE: No, no.
CÉLIMÈNE: Stay, Sir.
ALCESTE: I can't.
CÉLIMÈNE: I wish it.
ALCESTE: No, I must go.
I beg you, Madam, not to press the matter;
You know I have no taste for idle chatter.   110
CÉLIMÈNE: Stay: I command you.

ALCESTE: No, I cannot stay.
CÉLIMÈNE: Very well; you have my leave to go away.

SCENE V

ELIANTE *to* CÉLIMÈNE: The Marquesses have kindly come to call.
Were they announced?
CÉLIMÈNE: Yes. Basque, bring chairs for all. BASQUE
provides the chairs, and exits. To ALCESTE:
You haven't gone?
ALCESTE: No; and I shan't depart   115
Till you decide who's foremost in your heart.
CÉLIMÈNE: Oh, hush.
ALCESTE: It's time to choose; take them, or me.
CÉLIMÈNE: You're mad.
ALCESTE: I'm not, as you shall shortly see.
CÉLIMÈNE: Oh?
ALCESTE: You'll decide.
CÉLIMÈNE: You're joking now, dear friend.
ALCESTE: No, no; you'll choose; my patience is at an end.   120
CLITANDRE: Madam, I come from court, where poor Cléonte
Behaved like a perfect fool, as is his wont.
Has he no friend to counsel him, I wonder,
And teach him less unerringly to blunder?
CÉLIMÈNE: It's true, the man's a most accomplished dunce;   125
His gauche behavior charms the eye at once;
And every time one sees him, on my word,
His manner's grown a trifle more absurd.
ACASTE: Speaking of dunces, I've just now conversed
With old Damon, who's one of the very worst;   130
I stood a lifetime in the broiling sun
Before his dreary monologue was done.
CÉLIMÈNE: Oh, he's a wondrous talker, and has the power
To tell you nothing hour after hour:
If, by mistake, he ever came to the point,   135
The shock would put his jawbone out of joint.
ELIANTE *to* PHILINTE: The conversation takes its usual turn,
And all our dear friends' ears will shortly burn.
CLITANDRE: Timante's a character, Madam.
CÉLIMÈNE: Isn't he, though?
A man of mystery from top to toe,   140
Who moves about in a romantic mist
On secret missions which do not exist.
His talk is full of eyebrows and grimaces;
How tired one gets of his momentous faces;
He's always whispering something confidential   145
Which turns out to be quite inconsequential;

Nothing's too slight for him to mystify;
He even whispers when he says "good-by."

ACASTE: Tell us about Géralde.

CÉLIMÈNE: That tiresome ass.
He mixes only with the titled class,   150
And fawns on dukes and princes, and is bored
With anyone who's not at least a lord.
The man's obsessed with rank, and his discourses
Are all of hounds and carriages and horses;
He uses Christian names with all the great,   155
And the word Milord, with him, is out of date.

CLITANDRE: He's very taken with Bélise, I hear.

CÉLIMÈNE: She is the dreariest company, poor dear.
Whenever she comes to call, I grope about
To find some topic which will draw her out,   160
But, owing to her dry and faint replies,
The conversation wilts, and droops, and dies.
In vain one hopes to animate her face
By mentioning the ultimate commonplace;
But sun or shower, even hail or frost   165
Are matters she can instantly exhaust.
Meanwhile her visit, painful though it is,
Drags on and on through mute eternities,
And though you ask the time, and yawn, and yawn,
She sits there like a stone and won't be gone.   170

ACASTE: Now for Adraste.

CÉLIMÈNE: Oh, that conceited elf
Has a gigantic passion for himself;
He rails against the court, and cannot bear it
That none will recognize his hidden merit;
All honors given to others give offense   175
To his imaginary excellence.

CLITANDRE: What about young Cléon? His house, they say,
Is full of the best society, night and day.

CÉLIMÈNE: His cook has made him popular, not he:
It's Cléon's table that people come to see.   180

ELIANTE: He gives a splendid dinner, you must admit.

CÉLIMÈNE: But must he serve himself along with it?
For my taste, he's a most insipid dish
Whose presence sours the wine and spoils the fish.

PHILINTE: Damis, his uncle, is admired no end.   185
What's your opinion, Madam?

CÉLIMÈNE: Why, he's my friend.

PHILINTE: He seems a decent fellow, and rather clever.

CÉLIMÈNE: He works too hard at cleverness, however.
I hate to see him sweat and struggle so
To fill his conversation with bons mots.   190
Since he's decided to become a wit

His taste's so pure that nothing pleases it;
He scolds at all the latest books and plays,
Thinking that wit must never stoop to praise,
That finding fault's a sign of intellect,   195
That all appreciation is abject,
And that by damning everything in sight
One shows oneself in a distinguished light.
He's scornful even of our conversations:
Their trivial nature sorely tries his patience;   200
He folds his arms, and stands above the battle,
And listens sadly to our childish prattle.

ACASTE: Wonderful, Madam! You've hit him off precisely.

CLITANDRE: No one can sketch a character so nicely.

ALCESTE: How bravely, Sirs, you cut and thrust at all   205
These absent fools, till one by one they fall:
But let one come in sight, and you'll at once
Embrace the man you lately called a dunce,
Telling him in a tone sincere and fervent
How proud you are to be his humble servant.   210

CLITANDRE: Why pick on us? Madame's been speaking, Sir,
And you should quarrel, if you must, with her.

ALCESTE: No, no, by God, the fault is yours, because
You lead her on with laughter and applause,
And make her think that she's the more delightful   215
The more her talk is scandalous and spiteful.
Oh, she would stoop to malice far, far less
If no such claque approved her cleverness.
It's flatterers like you whose foolish praise
Nourishes all the vices of these days.   220

PHILINTE: But why protest when someone ridicules
Those you'd condemn, yourself, as knaves or fools?

CÉLIMÈNE: Why, Sir? Because he loves to make a fuss.
You don't expect him to agree with us,
When there's an opportunity to express   225
His heaven-sent spirit of contrariness?
What other people think, he can't abide;
Whatever they say, he's on the other side;
He lives in deadly terror of agreeing;
'Twould make him seem an ordinary being.   230
Indeed, he's so in love with contradiction,
He'll turn against his most profound conviction
And with a furious eloquence deplore it,
If only someone else is speaking for it.

ALCESTE: Go on, dear lady, mock me as you please;   235
You have your audience in ecstasies.

PHILINTE: But what she says is true: you have a way
Of bridling at whatever people say;
Whether they praise or blame, your angry spirit
Is equally unsatisfied to hear it.   240

ALCESTE: Men, Sir, are always wrong, and that's the reason
That righteous anger's never out of season;
All that I hear in all their conversation
Is flattering praise or reckless condemnation.
CÉLIMÈNE: But . . .
ALCESTE: No, no, Madam, I am forced to state   245
That you have pleasures which I deprecate,
And that these others, here, are much to blame
For nourishing the faults which are your shame.
CLITANDRE: I shan't defend myself, Sir; but I vow
I'd thought this lady faultless until now.   250
ACASTE: I see her charms and graces, which are many;
But as for faults, I've never noticed any.
ALCESTE: I see them, Sir; and rather than ignore them,
I strenuously criticize her for them.
The more one loves, the more one should object   255
To every blemish, every least defect.
Were I this lady, I would soon get rid
Of lovers who approved of all I did,
And by their slack indulgence and applause
Endorsed my follies and excused my flaws.   260
CÉLIMÈNE: If all hearts beat according to your measure,
The dawn of love would be the end of pleasure;
And love would find its perfect consummation
In ecstasies of rage and reprobation.
ELIANTE: Love, as a rule, affects men otherwise,   265
And lovers rarely love to criticize.
They see their lady as a charming blur,
And find all things commendable in her.
If she has any blemish, fault, or shame,
They will redeem it by a pleasing name.   270
The pale-faced lady's lily-white, perforce;
The swarthy one's a sweet brunette, of course;
The spindly lady has a slender grace;
The fat one has a most majestic pace;
The plain one, with her dress in disarray,   275
They classify as *beauté négligée;*
The hulking one's a goddess in their eyes,
The dwarf, a concentrate of Paradise;
The haughty lady has a noble mind;
The mean one's witty, and the dull one's kind;   280
The chatterbox has liveliness and verve,
The mute one has a virtuous reserve.
So lovers manage, in their passion's cause,
To love their ladies even for their flaws.
ALCESTE: But I still say . . .
CÉLIMÈNE: I think it would be nice   285
To stroll around the gallery once or twice.
What! You're not going, Sirs?

CLITANDRE and ACASTE: No, Madam, no.
ALCESTE: You seem to be in terror lest they go.
   Do what you will, Sirs; leave, or linger on,
   But I shan't go till after you are gone.   290
ACASTE: I'm free to linger, unless I should perceive
   Madame is tired, and wishes me to leave.
CLITANDRE: And as for me, I needn't go today
   Until the hour of the King's *coucher*.
CÉLIMÈNE *to* ALCESTE: You're joking, surely?
ALCESTE: Not in the least;
   We'll see   295
   Whether you'd rather part with them, or me.

SCENE VI

BASQUE *to* ALCESTE: Sir, there's a fellow here who bids me state
   That he must see you, and that it can't wait.
ALCESTE: Tell him that I have no such pressing affairs.
BASQUE: It's a long tailcoat that this fellow wears,   300
   With gold all over.
CÉLIMÈNE *to* ALCESTE: You'd best go down and see.
   Or—have him enter.

SCENE VII

ALCESTE *confronting the guard:*   Well, what do you want with me?
   Come in, Sir.
GUARD: I've a word, Sir, for your ear.
ALCESTE: Speak it aloud, Sir; I shall strive to hear.
GUARD: The Marshals have instructed me to say   305
   You must report to them without delay.
ALCESTE: Who? Me, Sir?
GUARD: Yes, Sir; you.
ALCESTE: But what do they want?
PHILINTE *to* ALCESTE: To scotch your silly quarrel with Oronte.
CÉLIMÈNE *to* PHILINTE: What quarrel?
PHILINTE: Oronte and he have fallen out
   Over some verse he spoke his mind about;   310
   The Marshals wish to arbitrate the matter.
ALCESTE: Never shall I equivocate or flatter!
PHILINTE: You'd best obey their summons; come, let's go.
ALCESTE: How can they mend our quarrel, I'd like to know?
   Am I to make a cowardly retraction,   315
   And praise those jingles to his satisfaction?
   I'll not recant; I've judged that sonnet rightly.
   It's bad.
PHILINTE: But you might say so more politely. . . .
ALCESTE: I'll not back down; his verses make me sick.
PHILINTE: If only you could be more politic!   320
   But come, let's go.

ALCESTE: I'll go, but I won't unsay
   A single word.
PHILINTE: Well, let's be on our way.
ALCESTE: Till I am ordered by my lord the King
   To praise that poem, I shall say the thing
   Is scandalous, by God, and that the poet   325
   Ought to be hanged for having the nerve to show it. *To* CLITANDRE
   and ACASTE, *who are laughing*:
   By heaven, Sirs, I really didn't know
   That I was being humorous.
CÉLIMÈNE: Go, Sir, go;
   Settle your business.
ALCESTE: I shall, and when I'm through,
   I shall return to settle things with you.   330

ACT III

SCENE I

CLITANDRE: Dear Marquess, how contented you appear;
   All things delight you, nothing mars your cheer.
   Can you, in perfect honesty, declare
   That you've a right to be so debonair?
ACASTE: By Jove, when I survey myself, I find   5
   No cause whatever for distress of mind.
   I'm young and rich; I can in modesty
   Lay claim to an exalted pedigree;
   And owing to my name and my condition
   I shall not want for honors and position.   10
   Then as to courage, that most precious trait,
   I seem to have it, as was proved of late
   Upon the field of honor, where my bearing,
   They say, was very cool and rather daring.
   I've wit, of course; and taste in such perfection   15
   That I can judge without the least reflection,
   And at the theater, which is my delight,
   Can make or break a play on opening night,
   And lead the crowd in hisses or bravos,
   And generally be known as one who knows.   20
   I'm clever, handsome, gracefully polite;
   My waist is small, my teeth are strong and white;
   As for my dress, the world's astonished eyes
   Assure me that I bear away the prize.
   I find myself in favor everywhere,   25
   Honored by men, and worshiped by the fair;
   And since these things are so, it seems to me
   I'm justified in my complacency.

CLITANDRE: Well, if so many ladies hold you dear,
Why do you press a hopeless courtship here?   30
ACASTE: Hopeless, you say? I'm not the sort of fool
That likes his ladies difficult and cool.
Men who are awkward, shy, and peasantish
May pine for heartless beauties, if they wish,
Grovel before them, bear their cruelties,   35
Woo them with tears and sighs and bended knees,
And hope by dogged faithfulness to gain
What their poor merits never could obtain.
For men like me, however, it makes no sense
To love on trust, and foot the whole expense.   40
Whatever any lady's merits be,
I think, thank God, that I'm as choice as she;
That if my heart is kind enough to burn
For her, she owes me something in return;
And that in any proper love affair   45
The partners must invest an equal share.
CLITANDRE: You think, then, that our hostess favors you?
ACASTE: I've reason to believe that that is true.
CLITANDRE: How did you come to such a mad conclusion?
You're blind, dear fellow. This is sheer delusion.   50
ACASTE: All right, then: I'm deluded and I'm blind.
CLITANDRE: Whatever put the notion in your mind?
ACASTE: Delusion.
CLITANDRE: What persuades you that you're right?
ACASTE: I'm blind.
CLITANDRE: But have you any proofs to cite?
ACASTE: I tell you I'm deluded.
CLITANDRE: Have you, then,   55
Received some secret pledge from Célimène?
ACASTE: Oh, no: she scorns me.
CLITANDRE: Tell me the truth, I beg.
ACASTE: She just can't bear me.
CLITANDRE: Ah, don't pull my leg.
Tell me what hope she's given you, I pray.
ACASTE: I'm hopeless, and it's you who win the day.   60
She hates me thoroughly, and I'm so vexed
I mean to hang myself on Tuesday next.
CLITANDRE: Dear Marquess, let us have an armistice
And make a treaty. What do you say to this?
If ever one of us can plainly prove   65
That Célimène encourages his love,
The other must abandon hope, and yield,
And leave him in possession of the field.
ACASTE: Now, there's a bargain that appeals to me;
With all my heart, dear Marquess, I agree.   70
But hush.

SCENE II

CÉLIMÈNE: Still here?
CLITANDRE: 'Twas love that stayed our feet.
CÉLIMÈNE: I think I heard a carriage in the street.
  Whose is it? D'you know?

SCENE III

BASQUE: Arsinoé is here,
  Madame.
CÉLIMÈNE: Arsinoé, you say? Oh, dear.
BASQUE: Eliante is entertaining her below. 75
CÉLIMÈNE: What brings the creature here, I'd like to know?
ACASTE: They say she's dreadfully prudish, but in fact
  I think her piety . . .
CÉLIMÈNE: It's all an act.
  At heart she's worldly, and her poor success
  In snaring men explains her prudishness. 80
  It breaks her heart to see the beaux and gallants
  Engrossed by other women's charms and talents,
  And so she's always in a jealous rage
  Against the faulty standards of the age.
  She lets the world believe that she's a prude 85
  To justify her loveless solitude,
  And strives to put a brand of moral shame
  On all the graces that she cannot claim.
  But still she'd love a lover; and Alceste
  Appears to be the one she'd love the best. 90
  His visits here are poison to her pride;
  She seems to think I've lured him from her side;
  And everywhere, at court or in the town,
  The spiteful, envious woman runs me down.
  In short, she's just as stupid as can be, 95
  Vicious and arrogant in the last degree,
  And . . .

SCENE IV

CÉLIMÈNE: Ah! What happy chance has brought you here?
  I've thought about you ever so much, my dear.
ARSINOÉ: I've come to tell you something you should know.
CÉLIMÈNE: How good of you to think of doing so! 100

CLITANDRE *and* ACASTE *go out, laughing.*

SCENE V

ARSINOÉ: It's just as well those gentlemen didn't tarry.
CÉLIMÈNE: Shall we sit down?
ARSINOÉ: That won't be necessary.
   Madam, the flame of friendship ought to burn
   Brightest in matters of the most concern,
   And as there's nothing which concerns us more   105
   Than honor, I have hastened to your door
   To bring you, as your friend, some information
   About the status of your reputation.
   I visited, last night, some virtuous folk,
   And, quite by chance, it was of you they spoke;   110
   There was, I fear, no tendency to praise
   Your light behavior and your dashing ways.
   The quantity of gentlemen you see
   And your by now notorious coquetry
   Were both so vehemently criticized   115
   By everyone, that I was much surprised.
   Of course, I needn't tell you where I stood;
   I came to your defense as best I could,
   Assured them you were harmless, and declared
   Your soul was absolutely unimpaired.   120
   But there are some things, you must realize,
   One can't excuse, however hard one tries,
   And I was forced at last into conceding
   That your behavior, Madam, is misleading,
   That it makes a bad impression, giving rise   125
   To ugly gossip and obscene surmise,
   And that if you were more *overtly* good,
   You wouldn't be so much misunderstood.
   Not that I think you've been unchaste—no! no!
   The saints preserve me from a thought so low!   130
   But mere good conscience never did suffice:
   One must avoid the outward show of vice.
   Madam, you're too intelligent, I'm sure,
   To think my motives anything but pure
   In offering you this counsel—which I do   135
   Out of a zealous interest in you.
CÉLIMÈNE: Madam, I haven't taken you amiss;
   I'm very much obliged to you for this;
   And I'll at once discharge the obligation
   By telling you about *your* reputation.   140
   You've been so friendly as to let me know
   What certain people say of me, and so
   I mean to follow your benign example
   By offering you a somewhat similar sample.
   The other day, I went to an affair   145

And found some most distinguished people there
Discussing piety, both false and true.
The conversation soon came round to you.
Alas! Your prudery and bustling zeal
Appeared to have a very slight appeal.   150
Your affectation of a grave demeanor,
Your endless talk of virtue and of honor,
The aptitude of your suspicious mind
For finding sin where there is none to find,
Your towering self-esteem, that pitying face   155
With which you contemplate the human race,
Your sermonizings and your sharp aspersions
On people's pure and innocent diversions—
All these were mentioned, Madam, and, in fact,
Were roundly and concertedly attacked.   160
"What good," they said, "are all these outward shows,
When everything belies her pious pose?
She prays incessantly; but then, they say,
She beats her maids and cheats them of their pay;
She shows her zeal in every holy place,   165
But still she's vain enough to paint her face;
She holds that naked statues are immoral,
But with a naked *man* she'd have no quarrel."
Of course, I said to everybody there
That they were being viciously unfair;   170
But still they were disposed to criticize you,
And all agreed that someone should advise you
To leave the morals of the world alone,
And worry rather more about your own.
They felt that one's self-knowledge should be great   175
Before one thinks of setting others straight;
That one should learn the art of living well
Before one threatens other men with hell,
And that the Church is best equipped, no doubt,
To guide our souls and root our vices out.   180
Madam, you're too intelligent, I'm sure,
To think my motives anything but pure
In offering you this counsel—which I do
Out of a zealous interest in you.
ARSINOÉ: I dared not hope for gratitude, but I   185
Did not expect so acid a reply;
I judge, since you've been so extremely tart,
That my good counsel pierced you to the heart.
CÉLIMÈNE: Far from it, Madam. Indeed, it seems to me
We ought to trade advice more frequently.   190
One's vision of oneself is so defective
That it would be an excellent corrective.
If you are willing, Madam, let's arrange

Shortly to have another frank exchange
In which we'll tell each other, *entre nous,* 195
What you've heard tell of me, and I of you.

ARSINOÉ: Oh, people never censure you, my dear;
It's me they criticize. Or so I hear.

CÉLIMÈNE: Madam, I think we either blame or praise
According to our taste and length of days. 200
There is a time of life for coquetry,
And there's a season, too, for prudery.
When all one's charms are gone, it is, I'm sure,
Good strategy to be devout and pure:
It makes one seem a little less forsaken. 205
Some day, perhaps, I'll take the road you've taken:
Time brings all things. But I have time aplenty,
And see no cause to be a prude at twenty.

ARSINOÉ: You give your age in such a gloating tone
That one would think I was an ancient crone; 210
We're not so far apart, in sober truth,
That you can mock me with a boast of youth!
Madam, you baffle me. I wish I knew
What moves you to provoke me as you do.

CÉLIMÈNE: For my part, Madam, I should like to know 215
Why you abuse me everywhere you go.
Is it my fault, dear lady, that your hand
Is not, alas, in very great demand?
If men admire me, if they pay me court
And daily make me offers of the sort 220
You'd dearly love to have them make to you,
How can I help it? What would you have me do?
If what you want is lovers, please feel free
To take as many as you can from me.

ARSINOÉ: Oh, come. D'you think the world is losing sleep 225
Over that flock of lovers which you keep,
Or that we find it difficult to guess
What price you pay for their devotedness?
Surely you don't expect us to suppose
Mere merit could attract so many beaux? 230
It's not your virtue that they're dazzled by;
Nor is it virtuous love for which they sigh.
You're fooling no one, Madam; the world's not blind;
There's many a lady heaven has designed
To call men's noblest, tenderest feelings out, 235
Who has no lovers dogging her about;
From which it's plain that lovers nowadays
Must be acquired in bold and shameless ways,
And only pay one court for such reward
As modesty and virtue can't afford. 240
Then don't be quite so puffed up, if you please,
About your tawdry little victories;

Try, if you can, to be a shade less vain,
And treat the world with somewhat less disdain.
If one were envious of your amours,   245
One soon could have a following like yours;
Lovers are no great trouble to collect
If one prefers them to one's self-respect.
CÉLIMÈNE: Collect them then, my dear; I'd love to see
You demonstrate that charming theory;   250
Who knows, you might . . .
ARSINOÉ: Now, Madam, that will do;
It's time to end this trying interview.
My coach is late in coming to your door,
Or I'd have taken leave of you before.
CÉLIMÈNE: Oh, please don't feel that you must rush away;   255
I'd be delighted, Madam, if you'd stay.
However, lest my conversation bore you,
Let me provide some better company for you;
This gentleman, who comes most apropos,
Will please you more than I could do, I know.   260

SCENE VI

CÉLIMÈNE: Alceste, I have a little note to write
Which simply must go out before tonight;
Please entertain *Madame;* I'm sure that she
Will overlook my incivility.

SCENE VII

ARSINOÉ: Well, Sir, our hostess graciously contrives   265
For us to chat until my coach arrives;
And I shall be forever in her debt
For granting me this little tête-à-tête.
We women very rightly give our hearts
To men of noble character and parts,   270
And your especial merits, dear Alceste,
Have roused the deepest sympathy in my breast.
Oh, how I wish they had sufficient sense
At court, to recognize your excellence!
They wrong you greatly, Sir. How it must hurt you   275
Never to be rewarded for your virtue!
ALCESTE: Why, Madam, what cause have I to feel aggrieved?
What great and brilliant thing have I achieved?
What service have I rendered to the King
That I should look to him for anything?   280
ARSINOÉ: Not everyone who's honored by the State
Has done great services. A man must wait
Till time and fortune offer him the chance.

Your merit, Sir, is obvious at a glance,
And . . .
ALCESTE: Ah, forget my merit; I'm not neglected.   285
The court, I think, can hardly be expected
To mine men's souls for merit, and unearth
Our hidden virtues and our secret worth.
ARSINOÉ: *Some* virtues, though, are far too bright to hide;
Yours are acknowledged, Sir, on every side.   290
Indeed, I've heard you warmly praised of late
By persons of considerable weight.
ALCESTE: This fawning age has praise for everyone,
And all distinctions, Madam, are undone.
All things have equal honor nowadays,   295
And no one should be gratified by praise.
To be admired, one only need exist,
And every lackey's on the honors list.
ARSINOÉ: I only wish, Sir, that you had your eye
On some position at court, however high;   300
You'd only have to hint at such a notion
For me to set the proper wheels in motion;
I've certain friendships I'd be glad to use
To get you any office you might choose.
ALCESTE: Madam, I fear that any such ambition   305
Is wholly foreign to my disposition.
The soul God gave me isn't of the sort
That prospers in the weather of a court.
It's all too obvious that I don't possess
The virtues necessary for success.   310
My one great talent is for speaking plain;
I've never learned to flatter or to feign;
And anyone so stupidly sincere
Had best not seek a courtier's career.
Outside the court, I know, one must dispense   315
With honors, privilege, and influence;
But still one gains the right, foregoing these,
Not to be tortured by the wish to please.
One needn't live in dread of snubs and slights,
Nor praise the verse that every idiot writes,   320
Nor humor silly Marquesses, nor bestow
Politic sighs on Madam So-and-So.
ARSINOÉ: Forget the court, then; let the matter rest.
But I've another cause to be distressed
About your present situation, Sir.   325
It's to your love affair that I refer.
She whom you love, and who pretends to love you,
Is, I regret to say, unworthy of you.
ALCESTE: Why, Madam! Can you seriously intend
To make so grave a charge against your friend?   330

ARSINOÉ: Alas, I must. I've stood aside too long
　　　And let that lady do you grievous wrong;
　　　But now my debt to conscience shall be paid:
　　　I tell you that your love has been betrayed.
ALCESTE: I thank you, Madam; you're extremely kind.　　　335
　　　Such words are soothing to a lover's mind.
ARSINOÉ: Yes, though she *is* my friend, I say again
　　　You're very much too good for Célimène.
　　　She's wantonly misled you from the start.
ALCESTE: You may be right; who knows another's heart?　　　340
　　　But ask yourself if it's the part of charity
　　　To shake my soul with doubts of her sincerity.
ARSINOÉ: Well, if you'd rather be a dupe than doubt her,
　　　That's your affair. I'll say no more about her.
ALCESTE: Madam, you know that doubt and vague suspicion　　　345
　　　Are painful to a man in my position;
　　　It's most unkind to worry me this way
　　　Unless you've some real proof of what you say.
ARSINOÉ: Sir, say no more: all doubt shall be removed,
　　　And all that I've been saying shall be proved.　　　350
　　　You've only to escort me home, and there
　　　We'll look into the heart of this affair.
　　　I've ocular evidence which will persuade you
　　　Beyond a doubt, that Célimène's betrayed you.
　　　Then, if you're saddened by that revelation,　　　355
　　　Perhaps I can provide some consolation.

ACT IV

SCENE I

PHILINTE: Madam, he acted like a stubborn child;
　　　I thought they never would be reconciled;
　　　In vain we reasoned, threatened, and appealed;
　　　He stood his ground and simply would not yield.
　　　The Marshals, I feel sure, have never heard　　　5
　　　An argument so splendidly absurd.
　　　"No, gentlemen," said he, "I'll not retract.
　　　His verse is bad: extremely bad, in fact.
　　　Surely it does the man no harm to know it.
　　　Does it disgrace him, not to be a poet?　　　10
　　　A gentleman may be respected still,
　　　Whether he writes a sonnet well or ill.
　　　That I dislike his verse should not offend him;
　　　In all that touches honor, I commend him;
　　　He's noble, brave, and virtuous—but I fear　　　15
　　　He can't in truth be called a sonneteer.

I'll gladly praise his wardrobe; I'll endorse
His dancing, or the way he sits a horse;
But, gentlemen, I cannot praise his rhyme.
In fact, it ought to be a capital crime   20
For anyone so sadly unendowed
To write a sonnet, and read the thing aloud."
At length he fell into a gentler mood
And, striking a concessive attitude,
He paid Oronte the following courtesies: 25
"Sir, I regret that I'm so hard to please,
And I'm profoundly sorry that your lyric
Failed to provoke me to a panegyric."
After these curious words, the two embraced,
And then the hearing was adjourned—in haste.   30

ELIANTE: His conduct has been very singular lately;
   Still, I confess that I respect him greatly.
   The honesty in which he takes such pride
   Has—to my mind—its noble, heroic side.
   In this false age, such candor seems outrageous;   35
   But I could wish that it were more contagious.

PHILINTE: What most intrigues me in our friend Alceste
   Is the grand passion that rages in his breast.
   The sullen humors he's compounded of
   Should not, I think, dispose his heart to love;   40
   But since they do, it puzzles me still more
   That he should choose your cousin to adore.

ELIANTE: It does, indeed, belie the theory
   That love is born of gentle sympathy,
   And that the tender passion must be based   45
   On sweet accords of temper and of taste.

PHILINTE: Does she return his love, do you suppose?

ELIANTE: Ah, that's a difficult question, Sir. Who knows?
   How can we judge the truth of her devotion?
   Her heart's a stranger to its own emotion.   50
   Sometimes it thinks it loves, when no love's there;
   At other times it loves quite unaware.

PHILINTE: I rather think Alceste is in for more
   Distress and sorrow than he's bargained for;
   Were he of my mind, Madam, his affection   55
   Would turn in quite a different direction,
   And we would see him more responsive to
   The kind regard which he receives from you.

ELIANTE: Sir, I believe in frankness, and I'm inclined,
   In matters of the heart, to speak my mind.   60
   I don't oppose his love for her; indeed,
   I hope with all my heart that he'll succeed,
   And were it in my power, I'd rejoice
   In giving him the lady of his choice.

But if, as happens frequently enough   65
In love affairs, he meets with a rebuff—
If Célimène should grant some rival's suit—
I'd gladly play the role of substitute;
Nor would his tender speeches please me less
Because they'd once been made without success.   70

PHILINTE: Well, Madam, as for me, I don't oppose
Your hopes in this affair; and heaven knows
That in my conversations with the man
I plead your cause as often as I can.
But if those two should marry, and so remove   75
All chance that he will offer you his love,
Then I'll declare my own, and hope to see
Your gracious favor pass from him to me.
In short, should you be cheated of Alceste,
I'd be most happy to be second best.   80

ELIANTE: Philinte, you're teasing.

PHILINTE: Ah, Madam, never fear;
No words of mine were ever so sincere,
And I shall live in fretful expectation
Till I can make a fuller declaration.

SCENE II

ALCESTE: Avenge me, Madam! I must have satisfaction,   85
Or this great wrong will drive me to distraction!

ELIANTE: Why, what's the matter? What's upset you so?

ALCESTE: Madam, I've had a mortal, mortal blow.
If Chaos repossessed the universe,
I swear I'd not be shaken any worse.   90
I'm ruined . . . I can say no more . . . My soul . . .

ELIANTE: Do try, sir, to regain your self-control.

ALCESTE: Just heaven! Why were so much beauty and grace
Bestowed on one so vicious and so base?

ELIANTE: Once more, Sir, tell us . . .

ALCESTE: My world has gone to wrack;   95
I'm—I'm betrayed; she's stabbed me in the back:
Yes, Célimène (who would have thought it of her?)
Is false to me, and has another lover.

ELIANTE: Are you quite certain? Can you prove these things?

PHILINTE: Lovers are prey to wild imaginings   100
And jealous fancies. No doubt there's some mistake . . .

ALCESTE: Mind your own business, Sir, for heaven's sake.
To ELIANTE Madam, I have the proof that you demand
Here in my pocket, penned by her own hand.
Yes, all the shameful evidence one could want   105
Lies in this letter written to Oronte—

Oronte! whom I felt sure she couldn't love,
And hardly bothered to be jealous of.
PHILINTE: Still, in a letter, appearances may deceive;
This may not be so bad as you believe.   110
ALCESTE: Once more I beg you, Sir, to let me be;
Tend to your own affairs; leave mine to me.
ELIANTE: Compose yourself; this anguish that you feel . . .
ALCESTE: Is something, Madam, you alone can heal.
My outraged heart, beside itself with grief,   115
Appeals to you for comfort and relief.
Avenge me on your cousin, whose unjust
And faithless nature has deceived my trust;
Avenge a crime your pure soul must detest.
ELIANTE: But how, Sir?
ALCESTE: Madam, this heart within my breast   120
Is yours; pray take it; redeem my heart from her,
And so avenge me on my torturer.
Let her be punished by the fond emotion,
The ardent love, the bottomless devotion,
The faithful worship which this heart of mine   125
Will offer up to yours as to a shrine.
ELIANTE: You have my sympathy, Sir, in all you suffer;
Nor do I scorn the noble heart you offer;
But I suspect you'll soon be mollified,
And this desire for vengeance will subside.   130
When some beloved hand has done us wrong
We thirst for retribution—but not for long;
However dark the deed that she's committed,
A lovely culprit's very soon acquitted.
Nothing's so stormy as an injured lover,   135
And yet no storm so quickly passes over.
ALCESTE: No, Madam, no—this is no lovers' spat;
I'll not forgive her; it's gone too far for that;
My mind's made up; I'll kill myself before
I waste my hopes upon her any more.   140
Ah, here she is. My wrath intensifies.
I shall confront her with her tricks and lies,
And crush her utterly, and bring you then
A heart no longer slave to Célimène.

SCENE III

ALCESTE *aside:*   Sweet heaven, help me to control my passion.   145
CÉLIMÈNE *aside, to* ALCESTE: Oh, Lord. Why stand there
    staring in that fashion?
And what d'you mean by those dramatic sighs,
And that malignant glitter in your eyes?

ALCESTE: I mean that sins which cause the blood to freeze
    Look innocent beside your treacheries;   150
    That nothing Hell's or Heaven's wrath could do
    Ever produced so bad a thing as you.
CÉLIMÈNE: Your compliments were always sweet and pretty.
ALCESTE: Madam, it's not the moment to be witty.
    No, blush and hang your head; you've ample reason,   155
    Since I've the fullest evidence of your treason.
    Ah, this is what my sad heart prophesied;
    Now all my anxious fears are verified;
    My dark suspicion and my gloomy doubt
    Divined the truth, and now the truth is out.   160
    For all your trickery, I was not deceived;
    It was my bitter stars that I believed.
    But don't imagine that you'll go scot-free;
    You shan't misuse me with impunity.
    I know that love's irrational and blind;   165
    I know the heart's not subject to the mind,
    And can't be reasoned into beating faster;
    I know each soul is free to choose its master;
    Therefore had you but spoken from the heart,
    Rejecting my attentions from the start,   170
    I'd have no grievance, or at any rate
    I could complain of nothing but my fate.
    Ah, but so falsely to encourage me—
    That was a treason and a treachery
    For which you cannot suffer too severely,   175
    And you shall pay for that behavior dearly.
    Yes, now I have no pity, not a shred;
    My temper's out of hand; I've lost my head;
    Shocked by the knowledge of your double-dealings,
    My reason can't restrain my savage feelings;   180
    A righteous wrath deprives me of my senses,
    And I won't answer for the consequences.
CÉLIMÈNE: What does this outburst mean? Will you please explain?
    Have you, by any chance, gone quite insane?
ALCESTE: Yes, yes, I went insane the day I fell   185
    A victim to your black and fatal spell,
    Thinking to meet with some sincerity
    Among the treacherous charms that beckoned me.
CÉLIMÈNE: Pooh. Of what treachery can you complain?
ALCESTE: How sly you are, how cleverly you feign!   190
    But you'll not victimize me any more.
    Look: here's a document you've seen before.
    This evidence, which I acquired today,
    Leaves you, I think, without a thing to say.
CÉLIMÈNE: Is this what sent you into such a fit?   195
ALCESTE: You should be blushing at the sight of it.

CÉLIMÈNE: Ought I to blush? I truly don't see why.
ALCESTE: Ah, now you're being bold as well as sly;
  Since there's no signature, perhaps you'll claim . . .
CÉLIMÈNE: I wrote it, whether or not it bears my name.   200
ALCESTE: And you can view with equanimity
  This proof of your disloyalty to me!
CÉLIMÈNE: Oh, don't be so outrageous and extreme.
ALCESTE: You take this matter lightly, it would seem.
  Was it no wrong to me, no shame to you,   205
  That you should send Oronte this billet-doux?
CÉLIMÈNE: Oronte! Who said it was for him?
ALCESTE: Why, those
  Who brought me this example of your prose.
  But what's the difference? If you wrote the letter
  To someone else, it pleases me no better.   210
  My grievance and your guilt remain the same.
CÉLIMÈNE: But need you rage, and need I blush for shame,
  If this was written to a *woman* friend?
ALCESTE: Ah! Most ingenious. I'm impressed no end;
  And after that incredible evasion   215
  Your guilt is clear. I need no more persuasion.
  How dare you try so clumsy a deception?
  D'you think I'm wholly wanting in perception?
  Come, come, let's see how brazenly you'll try
  To bolster up so palpable a lie: 220
  Kindly construe this ardent closing section
  As nothing more than sisterly affection!
  Here, let me read it. Tell me, if you dare to,
  That this is for a woman . . .
CÉLIMÈNE   I don't care to.
  What right have you to badger and berate me,   225
  And so highhandedly interrogate me?
ALCESTE: Now, don't be angry; all I ask of you
  Is that you justify a phrase or two . . .
CÉLIMÈNE: No, I shall not. I utterly refuse,
  And you may take those phrases as you choose.   230
ALCESTE: Just show me how this letter could be meant
  For a woman's eyes, and I shall be content.
CÉLIMÈNE: No, no, it's for Oronte; you're perfectly right.
  I welcome his attentions with delight,
  I prize his character and his intellect,   235
  And everything is just as you suspect.
  Come, do your worst now; give your rage free rein;
  But kindly cease to bicker and complain.
ALCESTE *aside:*   Good God! Could anything be more inhuman?
  Was ever a heart so mangled by a woman?   240
  When I complain of how she has betrayed me,
  She bridles, and commences to upbraid me!
  She tries my tortured patience to the limit;

She won't deny her guilt; she glories in it!
And yet my heart's too faint and cowardly   245
To break these chains of passion, and be free,
To scorn her as it should, and rise above
This unrewarded, mad, and bitter love.
To CÉLIMÈNE Ah, traitress, in how confident a fashion
You take advantage of my helpless passion,   250
And use my weakness for your faithless charms
To make me once again throw down my arms!
But do at least deny this black transgression;
Take back that mocking and perverse confession;
Defend this letter and your innocence,   255
And I, poor fool, will aid in your defense.
Pretend, pretend, that you are just and true,
And I shall make myself believe in you.

CÉLIMÈNE: Oh, stop it. Don't be such a jealous dunce,
Or I shall leave off loving you at once.   260
Just why should I *pretend?* What could impel me
To stoop so low as that? And kindly tell me
Why, if I loved another, I shouldn't merely
Inform you of it, simply and sincerely!
I've told you where you stand, and that admission   265
Should altogether clear me of suspicion;
After so generous a guarantee,
What right have you to harbor doubts of me?
Since women are (from natural reticence)
Reluctant to declare their sentiments,   270
And since the honor of our sex requires
That we conceal our amorous desires,
Ought any man for whom such laws are broken
To question what the oracle has spoken?
Should he not rather feel an obligation   275
To trust that most obliging declaration?
Enough, now. Your suspicions quite disgust me;
Why should I love a man who doesn't trust me?
I cannot understand why I continue,
Fool that I am, to take an interest in you.   280
I ought to choose a man less prone to doubt,
And give you something to be vexed about.

ALCESTE: Ah, what a poor enchanted fool I am;
These gentle words, no doubt, were all a sham;
But destiny requires me to entrust   285
My happiness to you, and so I must.
I'll love you to the bitter end, and see
How false and treacherous you dare to be.

CÉLIMÈNE: No, you don't really love me as you ought.

ALCESTE: I love you more than can be said or thought;   290
Indeed, I wish you were in such distress
That I might show my deep devotedness.

Yes, I could wish that you were wretchedly poor,
Unloved, uncherished, utterly obscure;
That fate had set you down upon the earth   295
Without possessions, rank, or gentle birth;
Then, by the offer of my heart, I might
Repair the great injustice of your plight;
I'd raise you from the dust, and proudly prove
The purity and vastness of my love.   300

CÉLIMÈNE: This is a strange benevolence indeed!
God grant that I may never be in need . . .
Ah, here's Monsieur Dubois, in quaint disguise

SCENE IV

ALCESTE: Well, why this costume? Why those frightened eyes?
What ails you?

DUBOIS: Well, Sir, things are most mysterious.   305

ALCESTE: What do you mean?

DUBOIS: I fear they're very serious.

ALCESTE: What?

DUBOIS: Shall I speak more loudly?

ALCESTE: Yes; speak out.

DUBOIS: Isn't there someone here, Sir?

ALCESTE: Speak, you lout!
Stop wasting time.

DUBOIS: Sir, we must slip away.

ALCESTE: How's that?

DUBOIS: We must decamp without delay.   310

ALCESTE: Explain yourself.

DUBOIS: I tell you we must fly.

ALCESTE: What for?

DUBOIS: We mustn't pause to say good-by.

ALCESTE: Now what d'you mean by all of this, you clown?

DUBOIS: I mean, Sir, that we've got to leave this town.

ALCESTE: I'll tear you limb from limb and joint from joint   315
If you don't come more quickly to the point.

DUBOIS: Well, Sir, today a man in a black suit,
Who wore a black and ugly scowl to boot,
Left us a document scrawled in such a hand
As even Satan couldn't understand.   320
It bears upon your lawsuit, I don't doubt;
But all hell's devils couldn't make it out.

ALCESTE: Well, well, go on. What then? I fail to see
How this event obliges us to flee.

DUBOIS: Well, Sir: an hour later, hardly more,   325
A gentleman who's often called before
Came looking for you in an anxious way.
Not finding you, he asked me to convey

(Knowing I could be trusted with the same)
The following message . . . Now, what *was* his name?   330
ALCESTE: Forget his name, you idiot. What did he say?
DUBOIS: Well, it was one of your friends, Sir, anyway.
He warned you to begone, and he suggested
That if you stay, you may well be arrested.
ALCESTE: What? Nothing more specific? Think, man, think!   335
DUBOIS: No, Sir. He had me bring him pen and ink,
And dashed you off a letter which, I'm sure,
Will render things distinctly less obscure.
ALCESTE: Well—let me have it!
CÉLIMÈNE: What *is* this all about?
ALCESTE: God knows; but I have hopes of finding out.   340
How long am I to wait, you blitherer?
DUBOIS *after a protracted search for the letter:*   I must have left it on
        your table, Sir.
ALCESTE: I ought to . . .
CÉLIMÈNE: No, no, keep your self-control;
Go find out what's behind his rigmarole.
ALCESTE: It seems that fate, no matter what I do,   345
Has sworn that I may not converse with you;
But, Madam, pray permit your faithful lover
To try once more before the day is over.

ACT V

SCENE I

ALCESTE: No, it's too much. My mind's made up, I tell you.
PHILINTE: Why should this blow, however hard, compel you . . .
ALCESTE: No, no, don't waste your breath in argument;
Nothing you say will alter my intent;
This age is vile, and I've made up my mind   5
To have no further commerce with mankind.
Did not truth, honor, decency, and the laws
Oppose my enemy and approve my cause?
My claims were justified in all men's sight;
I put my trust in equity and right;   10
Yet, to my horror and the world's disgrace,
Justice is mocked, and I have lost my case!
A scoundrel whose dishonesty is notorious
Emerges from another lie victorious!
Honor and right condone his brazen fraud,   15
While rectitude and decency applaud!
Before his smirking face, the truth stands charmed,
And virtue conquered, and the law disarmed!
His crime is sanctioned by a court decree!
And not content with what he's done to me,   20

The dog now seeks to ruin me by stating
That I composed a book now circulating,
A book so wholly criminal and vicious
That even to speak its title is seditious!
Meanwhile Oronte, my rival, lends his credit   25
To the same libelous tale, and helps to spread it!
Oronte! a man of honor and of rank,
With whom I've been entirely fair and frank;
Who sought me out and forced me, willy-nilly,
To judge some verse I found extremely silly;   30
And who, because I properly refused
To flatter him, or see the truth abused,
Abets my enemy in a rotten slander!
There's the reward of honesty and candor!
The man will hate me to the end of time   35
For failing to commend his wretched rhyme!
And not this man alone, but all humanity
Do what they do from interest and vanity;
They prate of honor, truth, and righteousness,
But lie, betray, and swindle nonetheless.   40
Come then: man's villainy is too much to bear;
Let's leave this jungle and this jackal's lair.
Yes! treacherous and savage race of men,
You shall not look upon my face again.
PHILINTE: Oh, don't rush into exile prematurely;   45
Things aren't as dreadful as you make them, surely.
It's rather obvious, since you're still at large,
That people don't believe your enemy's charge.
Indeed, his tale's so patently untrue
That it may do more harm to him than you.   50
ALCESTE: Nothing could do that scoundrel any harm:
His frank corruption is his greatest charm,
And, far from hurting him, a further shame
Would only serve to magnify his name.
PHILINTE: In any case, his bald prevarication   55
Has done no injury to your reputation,
And you may feel secure in that regard.
As for your lawsuit, it should not be hard
To have the case reopened, and contest
This judgment . . .
ALCESTE: No, no, let the verdict rest.   60
Whatever cruel penalty it may bring,
I wouldn't have it changed for anything.
It shows the times' injustice with such clarity
That I shall pass it down to our posterity
As a great proof and signal demonstration   65
Of the black wickedness of this generation.
It may cost twenty thousand francs; but I
Shall pay their twenty thousand, and gain thereby

The right to storm and rage at human evil,
And send the race of mankind to the devil. 70
PHILINTE: Listen to me . . .
ALCESTE: Why? What can you possibly say?
Don't argue, Sir; your labor's thrown away.
Do you propose to offer lame excuses
For men's behavior and the times' abuses?
PHILINTE: No, all you say I'll readily concede: 75
This is a low, dishonest age indeed;
Nothing but trickery prospers nowadays,
And people ought to mend their shabby ways.
Yes, man's a beastly creature; but must we then
Abandon the society of men? 80
Here in the world, each human frailty
Provides occasion for philosophy,
And that is virtue's noblest exercise;
If honesty shone forth from all men's eyes,
If every heart were frank and kind and just, 85
What could our virtues do but gather dust
(Since their employment is to help us bear
The villainies of men without despair)?
A heart well-armed with virtue can endure . . .
ALCESTE: Sir, you're a matchless reasoner, to be sure; 90
Your words are fine and full of cogency;
But don't waste time and eloquence on me.
My reason bids me go, for my own good.
My tongue won't lie and flatter as it should;
God knows what frankness it might next commit, 95
And what I'd suffer on account of it.
Pray let me wait for Célimène's return
In peace and quiet. I shall shortly learn,
By her response to what I have in view,
Whether her love for me is feigned or true. 100
PHILINTE: Till then, let's visit Eliante upstairs.
ALCESTE: No, I am too weighed down with somber cares.
Go to her, do; and leave me with my gloom
Here in the darkened corner of this room.
PHILINTE: Why, that's no sort of company, my friend; 105
I'll see if Eliante will not descend.

SCENE II

ORONTE: Yes, Madam, if you wish me to remain
Your true and ardent lover, you must deign
To give me some more positive assurance.
All this suspense is quite beyond endurance. 110
If your heart shares the sweet desires of mine,
Show me as much by some convincing sign;

And here's the sign I urgently suggest:
That you no longer tolerate Alceste,
But sacrifice him to my love, and sever   115
All your relations with the man forever.
CÉLIMÈNE: Why do you suddenly dislike him so?
    You praised him to the skies not long ago.
ORONTE: Madam, that's not the point. I'm here to find
    Which way your tender feelings are inclined.   120
    Choose, if you please, between Alceste and me,
    And I shall stay or go accordingly.
ALCESTE *emerging from the corner:*   Yes, Madam, choose; this gentleman's demand
    Is wholly just, and I support his stand.
    I too am true and ardent; I too am here   125
    To ask you that you make your feelings clear.
    No more delays, now; no equivocation;
    The time has come to make your declaration.
ORONTE: Sir, I've no wish in any way to be
    An obstacle to your felicity.   130
ALCESTE: Sir, I've no wish to share her heart with you;
    That may sound jealous, but at least it's true.
ORONTE: If, weighing us, she leans in your direction . . .
ALCESTE: If she regards you with the least affection . . .
ORONTE: I swear I'll yield her to you there and then.   135
ALCESTE: I swear I'll never see her face again.
ORONTE: Now, Madam, tell us what we've come to hear.
ALCESTE: Madam, speak openly and have no fear.
ORONTE: Just say which one is to remain your lover.
ALCESTE: Just name one name, and it will all be over.   140
ORONTE: What! Is it possible that you're undecided?
ALCESTE: What! Can your feelings possibly be divided?
CÉLIMÈNE: Enough: this inquisition's gone too far:
    How utterly unreasonable you are!
    Not that I couldn't make the choice with ease;   145
    My heart has no conflicting sympathies;
    I know full well which one of you I favor,
    And you'd not see me hesitate or waver.
    But how can you expect me to reveal
    So cruelly and bluntly what I feel?   150
    I think it altogether too unpleasant
    To choose between two men when both are present;
    One's heart has means more subtle and more kind
    Of letting its affections be divined,
    Nor need one be uncharitably plain   155
    To let a lover know he loves in vain.
ORONTE: No, no, speak plainly; I for one can stand it.
    I beg you to be frank.
ALCESTE: And I demand it.
    The simple truth is what I wish to know,

And there's no need for softening the blow.   160
You've made an art of pleasing everyone,
But now your days of coquetry are done:
You have no choice now, Madam, but to choose,
For I'll know what to think if you refuse;
I'll take your silence for a clear admission   165
That I'm entitled to my worst suspicion.
ORONTE: I thank you for this ultimatum, Sir,
And I may say I heartily concur.
CÉLIMÈNE: Really, this foolishness is very wearing:
Must you be so unjust and overbearing?   170
Haven't I told you why I must demur?
Ah, here's Eliante; I'll put the case to her.

SCENE III

CÉLIMÈNE: Cousin, I'm being persecuted here
By these two persons, who, it would appear,
Will not be satisfied till I confess   175
Which one I love the more, and which the less,
And tell the latter to his face that he
Is henceforth banished from my company.
Tell me, has ever such a thing been done?
ELIANTE: You'd best not turn to me; I'm not the one   180
To back you in a matter of this kind:
I'm all for those who frankly speak their mind.
ORONTE: Madam, you'll search in vain for a defender.
ALCESTE: You're beaten, Madam, and may as well surrender.
ORONTE: Speak, speak, you must; and end this awful strain.   185
ALCESTE: Or don't, and your position will be plain.
ORONTE: A single word will close this painful scene.
ALCESTE: But if you're silent, I'll know what you mean.

SCENE IV

ACASTE *to* CÉLIMÈNE: Madam, with all due deference, we two
Have come to pick a little bone with you.   190
CLITANDRE *to* ORONTE *and* ALCESTE: I'm glad you're present, Sirs;
    As you'll soon learn,
Our business here is also your concern.
ARSINOÉ *to* CÉLIMÈNE: Madam, I visit you so soon again
Only because of these two gentlemen,
Who came to me indignant and aggrieved   195
About a crime too base to be believed.
Knowing your virtue, having such confidence in it,
I couldn't think you guilty for a minute,
In spite of all their telling evidence;
And, rising above our little difference,   200

I've hastened here in friendship's name to see
You clear yourself of this great calumny.
ACASTE: Yes, Madam, let us see with what composure
You'll manage to respond to this disclosure.
You lately sent Clitandre this tender note. 205
CLITANDRE: And this one, for Acaste, you also wrote.
ACASTE *to* ORONTE *and* ALCESTE: You'll recognize this
writing Sirs, I think;
The lady is so free with pen and ink
That you must know it all too well, I fear.
But listen: this is something you should hear. 210

"How absurd you are to condemn my lightheartedness
in society, and to accuse me of being happiest in the company of
others. Nothing could be more unjust; and if you do not come
to me instantly and beg pardon for saying such a thing, I shall
never forgive you as long as I live. Our big bumbling friend 215
the Viscount . . ."

What a shame that he's not here.

"Our big bumbling friend the Viscount, whose name
stands first in your complaint, is hardly a man to my
taste; and ever since the day I watched him spend three- 220
quarters of an hour spitting into a well, so as to make
circles in the water, I have been unable to think highly
of him. As for the little Marquess . . ."

In all modesty, gentlemen, that is I.

"As for the little Marquess, who sat squeezing my 225
hand for such a long while yesterday, I find him in all
respects the most trifling creature alive; and the only
things of value about him are his cape and his sword.
As for the man with the green ribbons . . ."

To ALCESTE It's your turn now, Sir. 230

"As for the man with the green ribbons, he amuses
me now and then with his bluntness and his bearish ill-
humor; but there are many times indeed when I think
him the greatest bore in the world. And as for the
sonneteer . . ." 235

To ORONTE Here's your helping.

"And as for the sonneteer, who has taken it into his
head to be witty, and insists on being an author in the
teeth of opinion, I simply cannot be bothered to listen to

him, and his prose wearies me quite as much as his   240
poetry. Be assured that I am not always so well-enter-
tained as you suppose; that I long for your company,
more than I dare to say, at all these entertainments to
which people drag me; and that the presence of those
one loves is true and perfect seasoning to all one's   245
pleasures."

CLITANDRE: And now for me.

    "Clitandre, whom you mention, and who so pesters
me with his saccharine speeches, is the last man on earth
for whom I could feel any affection. He is quite mad to   250
suppose that I love him, and so are you, to doubt that
you are loved. Do come to your senses; exchange your
suppositions for his; and visit me as often as possible,
to help me bear the annoyance of his unwelcome atten-
tions."   255

It's a sweet character that these letters show,
And what to call it, Madam, you well know.
Enough. We're off to make the world acquainted
With this sublime self-portrait that you've painted.
ACASTE: Madam, I'll make you no farewell oration;   260
No, you're not worthy of my indignation.
Far choicer hearts than yours, as you'll discover,
Would like this little Marquess for a lover.

SCENE V

ORONTE: So! After all those loving letters you wrote,
You turn on me like this, and cut my throat!   265
And your dissembling, faithless heart, I find,
Has pledged itself by turns to all mankind!
How blind I've been! But now I clearly see;
I thank you, Madam, for enlightening me.
My heart is mine once more, and I'm content;   270
The loss of it shall be your punishment.
To ALCESTE Sir, she is yours; I'll seek no more to stand
Between your wishes and this lady's hand.

SCENE VI

ARSINOÉ *to* CÉLIMÈNE: Madam, I'm forced to speak. I'm far too stirred
To keep my counsel, after what I've heard.   275
I'm shocked and staggered by your want of morals.
It's not my way to mix in others' quarrels;
But really, when this fine and noble spirit,

This man of honor and surpassing merit,
Laid down the offering of his heart before you, 280
How *could* you . . .
ALCESTE: Madam, permit me, I implore you,
To represent myself in this debate.
Don't bother, please, to be my advocate.
My heart, in any case, could not afford
To give your services their due reward; 285
And if I chose, for consolation's sake,
Some other lady, t'would not be you I'd take.
ARSINOÉ: What makes you think you could, Sir? And how dare you
Imply that I've been trying to ensnare you?
If you can for a moment entertain 290
Such flattering fancies, you're extremely vain.
I'm not so interested as you suppose
In Célimène's discarded gigolos.
Get rid of that absurd illusion, do.
Women like me are not for such as you. 295
Stay with this creature, to whom you're so attached;
I've never seen two people better matched.

SCENE VII

ALCESTE *to* CÉLIMÈNE: Well, I've been still throughout this exposé,
Till everyone but me has said his say.
Come, have I shown sufficient self-restraint? 300
And may I now . . .
CÉLIMÈNE: Yes, make your just complaint.
Reproach me freely, call me what you will;
You've every right to say I've used you ill.
I've wronged you, I confess it; and in my shame
I'll make no effort to escape the blame. 305
The anger of those others I could despise;
My guilt toward you I sadly recognize.
Your wrath is wholly justified, I fear;
I know how culpable I must appear,
I know all things bespeak my treachery, 310
And that, in short, you've grounds for hating me.
Do so; I give you leave.
ALCESTE: Ah, traitress—how,
How should I cease to love you, even now?
Though mind and will were passionately bent
On hating you, my heart would not consent. 315
To ELIANTE *and* PHILINTE Be witness to my madness, both of you;
See what infatuation drives one to;
But wait; my folly's only just begun,
And I shall prove to you before I'm done
How strange the human heart is, and how far 320

From rational we sorry creatures are.
To CÉLIMÈNE Woman, I'm willing to forget your shame,
And clothe your treacheries in a sweeter name;
I'll call them youthful errors, instead of crimes,
And lay the blame on these corrupting times. 325
My one condition is that you agree
To share my chosen fate, and fly with me
To that wild, trackless solitary place
In which I shall forget the human race.
Only by such a course can you atone 330
For those atrocious letters; by that alone
Can you remove my present horror of you,
And make it possible for me to love you.
CÉLIMÈNE: What! *I* renounce the world at my young age,
And die of boredom in some hermitage? 335
ALCESTE: Ah, if you really loved me as you ought,
You wouldn't give the world a moment's thought;
Must you have me, and all the world beside?
CÉLIMÈNE: Alas, at twenty one is terrified
Of solitude. I fear I lack the force 340
And depth of soul to take so stern a course.
But if my hand in marriage will content you,
Why, there's a plan which I might well consent to,
And . . .
ALCESTE: No, I detest you now. I could excuse 345
Everything else, but since you thus refuse
To love me wholly, as a wife should do,
And see the world in me, as I in you,
Go! I reject your hand, and disenthrall
My heart from your enchantments, once for all. 350

SCENE VIII

ALCESTE *to* ELIANTE: Madam, your virtuous beauty has no peer,
Of all this world, you only are sincere;
I've long esteemed you highly, as you know;
Permit me ever to esteem you so,
And if I do not now request your hand, 355
Forgive me, Madam, and try to understand.
I feel unworthy of it; I sense that fate
Does not intend me for the married state,
That I should do you wrong by offering you
My shattered heart's unhappy residue, 360
And that in short . . .
ELIANTE: Your argument's well taken:
Nor need you fear that I shall feel forsaken.
Were I to offer him this hand of mine,
Your friend Philinte, I think, would not decline.

PHILINTE: Ah, Madam, that's my heart's most cherished goal, 365
  For which I'd gladly give my life and soul.
ALCESTE *to* ELIANTE *and* PHILINTE: May you be true to all you now
    profess,
  And so deserve unending happiness.
  Meanwhile, betrayed and wronged in everything,
  I'll flee this bitter world where vice is king, 370
  And seek some spot unpeopled and apart
  Where I'll be free to have an honest heart.
PHILINTE: Come, Madam, let's do everything we can
  To change the mind of this unhappy man.

QUESTIONS

1. What three conflicts, central to *The Misanthrope,* are announced in the opening dialogue between Alceste and Philinte?
2. Why does Alceste object to Oronte's sonnet (I, ii)? Why does he prefer older poetry to modern verse? Is this preference consistent with his character?
3. How is Alceste's reaction to Célimène's unsigned letter (IV, iii) consistent with his vision of humankind?
4. Assess the likelihood that Philinte and Eliante will, at the end of the play, "change the mind of this unhappy man," Alceste.
5. Bearing *The Misanthrope* in mind, discuss the sufficiency (or insufficiency) of sincerity as an ideal in social behavior. Discuss the inter-relationships among sincerity, hypocrisy, politeness, and rudeness.
6. What proof are we given that Célimène prefers Alceste to all the other men in the play? Why won't this proof satisfy Alceste?

WRITING ABOUT COMEDY

Comedy offers a wide range of possibilities for critical essays, and writing about comedy means keeping alert to these possibilities. A list of valid approaches to writing about comedy would include how the elements of drama interact with each other, how each contributes to the overall comic effect of a play, how the playwright uses the potential range of comic emotions, how the different kinds of comedy have unique conventions, and how the historical background of a comedy contributes to its humor. Being knowledgeable about all of these approaches would require the skill of an expert, but for the beginner some fundamental information about each of them can make writing about comedy much easier.

Merely knowing something of the historical background of Molière's *The Misanthrope*—that it was written in the second half of the seventeenth century in France at the dawn of the Age of Reason—reveals much about the sources of the humor, the social satire, and the views Molière expresses in the frequent comic verbal debates of the play. For instance, the play presents several extreme attitudes—heart versus head, flattery versus rail-lery, solitude versus complete sociability, and so on. Molière's position is that of an Age of Enlightenment intellectual, one of moderation. Therefore extremes are always tempered by moderation, and those who embrace ex-tremes are always somewhat foolish, especially when it damages themselves. In this way Molière allies himself with the philosophical and social positions of Philinte and Eliante and shows how foolish and self-destructive Alceste is. Supported by this kind of historical information, a beginner can write an insightful essay about Molière's comedy. Even contemporary comedies demand some knowledge of theater history: what the Theater of the Ab-sured is, for example, and why props and scenery are at a minimum, and the dialogue is so full of non-sequiturs. Since a joke often depends on con-text (and the humor of a play is no exception), writing intelligently about a comedy demands that we know about a play's historical context.

Another approach to writing about comedy involves analyzing how the elements of drama—plot, character, stagecraft, language, and so forth—contribute to the humor of a play. Humor may depend on how one portion of the plot contrasts with another, or on how one scene is ironically juxta-posed with another. For example, Molière in the first scene in Act I pre-sents the debate between Philinte and Alceste to express the rigidity of Al-ceste's ideas about being frank and always telling the truth regardless of the consequences. Molière juxtaposes this with Scene II in which Oronte asks for Alceste's frank opinion about his sonnet, all the while really hoping for the customary flattering evaluation. When he gets honesty instead of flat-tery, Oronte, who is ironically Alceste's rival, seeks to have him arrested and ultimately gives damaging evidence against him. This second scene has further comic implications when you consider that in Act V (Scenes ii and iii), both Alceste and Oronte beg the coquettish Célimène to tell which of the two rivals she prefers. Similarly, Beckett's dark humor in *Krapp's Last Tape* stems from the juxtaposition of fragments of the present with those of the past. When the scene entitled "the end of love" is repeated at the end of the play in the light of the bitter speculations of the sixty-nine-year-old Krapp, it gains in meaning the second time. Molière's play uses the same kinds of repetition for comic effect. For example, in *The Misanthrope* he repeats scenes in Acts I and II that deal with the indiscriminate choice of friends, or with lawsuits. These repetitions create incongruities on which the humor turns.

Writing about a comic character can take you to the heart of what is truly comic in human behavior. An essay on a comic character often takes the form of analyzing what makes the character funny. Is it what the char-acter says or what the character does? Put another way, such an essay will consider whether the humor is due primarily to the language (verbal hu-mor), or to the actions of the character (situational humor).

Verbal humor may depend on recognizing the double meaning of a pun, as in *Hamlet* when the gravedigger is told by Hamlet that the grave he is digging is his, for the gravedigger *lies* in it, Hamlet is punning on the meaning of "lie," to rest or recline, and "lie," to tell a falsehood. Verbal humor can also take the form of repartee, or witty answers to observations in a quick-moving dialogue as in the opening scene of *The Misanthrope:*

> ALCESTE: All men are so detestable in my eyes.
> I should be sorry if they thought me wise.
> PHILINTE: Your hatred's very sweeping is it not?
> ALCESTE: Quite right: I hate the whole degraded lot.
> PHILINTE: Must all poor human creatures be embraced,
> Without distinction, by your vast distaste?
> Even in these bad times surely there are a few . . .
> ALCESTE: No, I include all men in one dim view.   (I, i, 111–118)

Or it may take the form of ironic or sarcastic observations, as in the opening scene in which Alceste expresses his disgust with Philinte's behavior by saying that if he had done the same thing he'd hang himself "for shame," to which Philinte replies:

> It hardly seems a hanging matter to me;
> I hope that you will take it graciously
> If I extend myself a slight reprieve,
> And live a little longer, by your leave.
>
> (I, i, 29–32)

Situational humor stems from the playwright's having established expectations in the audience about a character's behavior. Much of the humor of Alceste stems from the consistency and inconsistency with which he acts. As in fiction, drama sometimes uses stock characters. Alceste is funny as a stock character, as a misanthrope who will suffer the loss of a lawsuit rather than be guilty of insincere flattery. Yet as the play unfolds he increasingly shows traces of inconsistency in his actions, especially in his love for Célimène. Identifying stock characters and their humorous consistencies or inconsistencies may be an important part of analyzing a comic character. In the case cited, the humor gains an additional dimension by the juxtaposition of the stock character with his foil or opposite. Philinte's commonsense moderation contrasts with Alceste's extremism much as Eliante's good sense contrasts with the flightiness of Célimène.

Essays on comedy can also analyze the genre of comedy the playwright is working in and/or the range of comic emotion. Plays not ostensibly comic, like *Hamlet,* may still have comic scenes. And it is possible for some comedies to end unhappily.

If a play is *not* a comedy, what is the effect of the inserted comic material on the play as a whole or on the scenes that precede or follow it? If the play is, indeed, easily recognizable as a comedy, is it a romantic comedy or a satiric comedy? If, like Molière's play, it is primarily a romantic comedy, does it follow the formula of affirming life by removing obstacles and joining the couple? Obviously, Molière departs form the formulaic plot. Therefore, we need to remain open to the possibility that the play may take an unexpected turn, and to ask ourselves what purpose the playwright had in disappointing our expectations. Like other comedies of manners, Molière's play has a certain cynicism despite the encouragement offered for reform by the play's final couplet. So an analysis of the play might focus on the extent to which Molière combines elements of social satire with the usual romantic comedy's plot lines.

Comic emotion can range from lighthearted foolery to serious social satire to bitter brooding comic despair. Shakespeare's *A Midsummer Night's Dream* with its lighthearted affirmation of life certainly differs from the bitter self-mockery of Beckett's *Krapp's Last Tape*. Most of the time, the range of comic emotion will appear as a subtopic in an essay on the genre of a play, or in a character analysis.

While it may seem at times that writing about comedy is like explaining the punch line of a joke (either the joke strikes you as funny or not, and any explanation is superfluous) comic drama can nevertheless be subtle, and without analysis the artistic facets of the playwright's work may often escape notice. To observe that an audience laughed, snickered, or smiled may tell you whether the play was successful, but it doesn't solve the riddle of why we laugh. Answering that riddle tells us a good deal about ourselves, and that is one reason we read literature.

Molière's The Misanthrope: A Dark Comedy of Incongruity

In his "Preface" to Joseph Andrews (1742) Henry Fielding wrote that there is nothing inherently funny about ugliness; however, when the ugly man incongruously sets himself up as handsome, he becomes comic. The comedy in Molière's The Misanthrope is based on a similar incongruity: Alceste, who professes to hate the superficiality and falsity of the society he lives in, has fallen passionately in love with Célimène, a superficial coquette whose falsity is the antithesis of Alceste's honesty. Through this incongruous relationship Molière exposes numerous moral, social, and psychological disparities so that in the final act of the play Alceste is brought to admit "How strange the human heart is, and how far/From rational we sorry creatures are."

The play's opening debate, between the extreme position of the misanthrope Alceste and his more moderate friend Philinte, establishes the basis for the humorous incongruity. Should one be sincere, frank, and honest, or polite, flattering, and gracious?

At first Alceste is seen solely as a cranky extremist who is indiscriminate in his hatred for mankind and who charges others with being insincere in their professions of friendship. In the first act, the humor is largely repartee in the style of a debate, the fun coming from the wittiest turn of phrase, the amusing verbal game of the couplets' closing rhymes, and the cleverest argument to support a position. Whatever incongruity appears is a result of the inconsistencies in Alceste's own argument.

The real comedy develops out of situational incongruity in the opening scene of Act 2, in which Alceste reappears as Célimène's lover; the humor develops from the inappropriateness of Célimène as the object of Alceste's love, for she is a woman who basks in flattery, relishes tearing down other people's reputations behind their backs, and revels in the ways of the world—qualities that make her the worst possible match for Alceste. It is, therefore, particularly ironic that after expressing his anger at the number of flatterers she keeps about, Alceste should, in a moment of wished-for reconciliation, beg her "to speak with an open heart." Célimène is incapable of speaking honestly except in a private letter revealed in the last act in which she secretly expresses her real feelings toward Alceste, whom she calls blunt and bearish.

Instead of expressing his love in flattering terms, Alceste continues to rail at the woman he hopes to marry. This incongruous style of lovemaking is summed up in his words: "The more one loves, the more one should object/To every blemish." Célimène's cousin, Eliante, is a foil to her, just as Philinte is a foil to Alceste. Eliante reminds Alceste that a lover's part is best expressed not through criticism but through perceiving the beloved's faults as virtues:

> . . . lovers rarely love to criticize.
> They see their lady as a charming blur,
> And find all things commendable in her.
> If she has any blemish, fault, or shame,
> They will redeem it by a pleasing name.
>
> (Act 2, Sc. 5, lines 266-270)

She seems to understand Alceste's dual nature, for behind his criticism is a nobility of spirit and a philosophical idealism, but one not controlled by the moderating force of reason. In Act 4 Eliante sums up his character's positive side: "The honesty in which he takes such pride,/Has—to my mind—its noble heroic side." (Act 4, Sc. 1, lines 33-34). However, the noble side of Alceste disappears under the weight of his passion when, discovering the unfaithfulness of Célimène, he complains that the very world he has professed to despise "has gone to wrack." With all the mean-spiritedness he laments in others, and with his aloof superiority gone, Alceste asks Eliante to avenge him on her cousin. That he does so without regard for Eliante's own feelings is an example of his colossal egotism and of his failure to perceive that allowances must be made for people's shortcomings, even his own.

> And so avenge me on my torturer.
> Let her be punished by the fond emotion,
> The ardent love, the bottomless devotion,
> The faithful worship which this heart of mine
> Will offer up to yours as to a shrine.
>
> (Act 4, Sc. 2, lines 122-126)

The ultimate incongruity in the play is the irrationality of the supposedly rational lover. Despite his customary passion for honesty and truth, as a lover Alceste wishes to be deluded rather than to know what Célimène has been up to. When he presents her with a letter she had written to another lover, Alceste asks her to "Defend this letter and your innocence,/And I, poor fool, will aid in your defense." Underlying his incongruous behavior is the defeat of the mind by the heart, of reason by passion; the audience witnesses the comic incongruity of the misanthrope

caught in the web of his own arguments as his passions force him to go
against his best judgment:

> And yet my heart's too faint and cowardly
> To break these chains of passion, and be free.
> To scorn her as it should, and rise above
> This unrewarded, mad, and bitter love.
>
> (Act 4, Sc. 3, lines 245-248)

Here Molière parallels the courses of Alceste's love affair and his lawsuit.
Alceste has every reformer's passion for self-justification even if it means
suffering to prove he's right. Preferring to lose his lawsuit rather than
flatter, he loses his case and claims "justice is mocked." Similarly, rather
than renounce the inappropriate love of Célimène for the more suitable love
of Eliante, he announces to Célimène, "I'll love you to the bitter end, and see/
How false and treacherous you dare to be." (Act 4, Sc. 3, lines 287-288)

The incongruity of the misanthropic lover reaches its climax in Act 5
when Alceste, determined to leave "this jungle and this jackal's lair," offers
to forgive Célimène if she will join him in exile.

> To share my chosen fate, and fly with me
> To that wild, trackless, solitary place
> In which I shall forget the human race.
>
> (Act 5, Sc. 7, lines 327-329)

But at twenty, Célimène is "terrified of solitude." Refusing to listen to her
alternative proposal, Alceste claims she does not love him "wholly, as a wife
should do,/And see the world in me, as I in you."

Unlike romantic comedies, Molière's comedy of manners ends darkly for
the protagonist, Alceste. He concludes "that fate/Does not intend me for the
married state," and decides to

> . . . flee this bitter world where vice is king,
> And seek some spot unpeopled and apart
> Where I'll be free to have an honest heart.
>
> (Act 5, Sc. 8, lines 370-372)

Yet the pattern of the joined lovers in romantic comedy persists in Philinte
and Eliante. Normalcy and balance, represented by the pairing of the
moderate characters, are suggested as antidotes to the passionate extremism
of the misanthrope. Philinte's speech closes the play and it offers a glimmer
of hopeful assurance that matrimony is possible, and that the cure for
society's ills lies not in fleeing to some desert isle as Alceste does but
persisting in society by following a moderate course toward life's richness:

> Come, Madam, let's do everything we can
> To change the mind of this unhappy man.
>
> (Act 5, Sc. 8, lines 373-374)

Molière's dark comedy ends with a glimmer of light by suggesting that
the example of the moderate couple possibly might lighten the darkness of
dishonest flattery and destructive honesty. And the contrariness of human
nature, represented by Molière's incongruous misanthrope, is invited back
into the human fold.

SUGGESTIONS FOR WRITING ABOUT COMEDY

1. Read the excerpt from Northrop Frye's *Anatomy of Criticism* (page 1581) and write an essay that shows whether *The Misanthrope* is, given Frye's theoretical remarks, a comedy.
2. Explain how a director could introduce non-verbal humor into a production of *The Misanthrope*.
3. Show how the impermanence of things, suggested by the tapes in Beckett's *Krapp's Last Tape,* is the source of much of the bitter humor.
4. Ibsen's *The Wild Duck* and Molière's *The Misanthrope* deal with the same topic, the value of truth and sincerity; yet one play ends as a tragedy, while the other is classified as a comedy. Write an essay explaining how the differences in handling the topic make the plays so different.

INTEGRATION AND EVALUATION

DEATH OF A SALESMAN

Watching or reading a play intelligently is like appreciating a beautiful building. The observer's appreciation lies not only in the aesthetic lines of the building or the architect's use of space and lighting, but in the completed building, in the difficulties overcome by the contractors and workmen who carried out the architect's plans. A good play is like that building. It has an aesthetic design, a purpose which determines the arrangement of its parts. But all this is to no avail if the theatrical workmen—the director, stage set and costume designers, lighting engineers, and actors—are unable to transform the playwright's conception into a reality. In no other form of literature is such integration so essential, and in no other is it so difficult to evaluate whether all the parts work together. Most things designed by committees do not work, but a play's success depends on a collaborative effort.

As one of the most successful collaborative efforts in the history of the American theater, Arthur Miller's *Death of a Salesman* integrates not only the elements of drama, but also, in its initial production, the talents of many people who brought Miller's concept of a worn-out, discarded salesman to life on the stage.

One of the reasons for the play's continued success, after almost forty years, is the way it still reaches modern audiences. To some extent everyone can identify with Willy Loman's plight. Reality fails to measure up to his dreams; his years of work for his sons seem to add up to naught; his human failings have alienated him from his son Biff. His secret burden of guilt, his contrariness and contradictions in his dealings with his wife, Linda—all of these shortcomings are simply an acknowledgment that Willy Loman, as his name implies, is a common, ordinary man. As he acknowledged in "Tragedy and the Common Man," (page 1578), Miller was striving to create a democratic tragedy, one in which the protagonist was not noble or an aristocrat but an ordinary citizen. When Biff calls Willy "A fine, troubled prince. A hard-working, unappreciated prince," the term is used figuratively. Unlike Hamlet, Willy is not literally a prince. Instead, he is what Miller intended, what Linda calls him: "only a little boat looking for a harbor." We need to ask ourselves whether tragedy is confined to the high-born, whose fall ends kingdoms, or whether the death of a common man, too, can be tragic. Willy's death is the death of *a* salesman whose funeral is attended not by the throngs he imagined, but only by his family and next door neighbor. This is one reason why Miller subtitled his play, "Certain *Private* Conversations in Two Acts and a Requiem," to emphasize the personal and private nature of this ordinary hidden tragedy that occurs every day within families. Such tragedy is, therefore, called **Domestic Tragedy** as opposed to the kind of **Classical Tragedy** we find in *Oedipus* and *Hamlet*.

Yet like Ibsen's domestic tragedies, which influenced Miller, *Death of a Salesman* does have a larger social dimension. Miller believes that the suffering of a small man can be just as important as the suffering of an aristocrat. Linda insists that "a small man can be just as exhausted as a great man," and Miller gives her one of the most poignant arguments in the play for the value of Willy's suffering:

> I don't say he's a great man. Willy Loman never made a lot of money. His name was never in the paper. He's not the finest character who ever lived. But he's a human being, and a terrible thing is happening to him. So attention must be paid. He's not to be allowed to fall into his grave like an old dog. Attention, attention must be finally paid to such a person.

Willy comes close to arguing his own case only once in the play. When Biff tries to explain to Willy that he won't be the success Willy has envisioned, "Pop! I'm a dime a dozen, and so are you!" Willy responds by asserting his uniqueness, "I am not a dime a dozen! I am Willy Loman, and you are Biff Loman!" Miller's conception is of a democratic tragedy with the common man as tragic hero set in the context, not of the royal family, but of the average modern family.

Another departure from tradition that makes *Death of a Salesman* difficult initially is the combined use of realism and expressionism. In many of its essential elements, *Death of a Salesman* is a realistic play. The characters are recognizable American types: an unsuccessful older salesman, a has-been athlete, a faithful devoted wife; the dialogue is a realistic representation of everyday speech, and much of the action consists of commonplace events: a prodigal son's return, an unsuccessful attempt to raise money, the loss of a job, and so on. What makes *Death of a Salesman* complicated to read is the mixture of these realistic elements with an expressionistic presentation of the interior of Willy's mind. Miller has said that his first image of the play was of looking inside a man's giant head, the top of which had been removed. The plot swings between a realistic presentation of events as they are occurring in the present, and Willy's thoughts (or, at times, hallucinations) that are set for the most part approximately 15 years earlier when Biff was a senior in high school. Willy's mind circles over and over again around seven key events from the past:

1. The boys simonizing the old Chevy after Willy has returned from a sales trip to New England.
2. The woman in the hotel in Boston.
3. The visit from Willy's brother, Ben, who is on his way to Alaska.
4. The second visit from Ben and Willy's refusal of an offered job in Alaska.
5. Biff's championship football game in Ebbets Field.
6. Biff's flunking math and not being able to graduate.
7. Biff's surprise visit to see Willy in Boston.

A typical transition occurs from present to past when Willie is under stress and associates something in his immediate environment with something from the past. A characteristic scene occurs in the first act when Willy and Charley play cards. Charley, a successful businessman, reminds Willy of his older brother Ben, and Willy keeps slipping in and out of his imaginings and the actual card game. To Charley there is a dialogue accompanying the card game, but to Willy, he is involved in a three-way discussion with Ben and Charley:

> CHARLEY: Pretty sharp tonight.
> BEN: Is mother living with you?
> WILLY: No, she died a long time ago.
> CHARLEY: Who?
> BEN: That's too bad. Fine specimen of a lady, Mother.
> WILLY *to* CHARLEY: Heh?
> CHARLEY: Who died?
> BEN: Heard anything from Father, have you?
> WILLY *Unnerved*: What do you mean, who died?
> CHARLEY *taking a pot*: What're you talking about?

Often Willy's hallucinations, like the first one of the woman in Boston, and like the visit from Biff and the discovery of the woman, are touched off by guilt: the first by Linda's expressions of love, the second by Willy's alternating belief in and denial of his responsibility for Biff's failure. The expressionistic form of the plot structure, delving into the irrational and memories, is supported by the stagecraft of the play. Set, music, and lighting all help the viewer (and through stage directions, the reader) to know whether an event is in the present or in the past.

The set, for example, is transparent in places. When the action is in the present, the wall-lines are observed by the actors in their movements about the stage. When the action is a scene from the past, the characters step through a wall. The forestage is the location of Willy's imaginings. Another aspect of the set, the giant apartment buildings which loom over the "small, fragile-seeming" Loman house and at times take on an angry orange glow, are an obvious symbol of the impersonal modern world where there are "more people" and "the competition is maddening." Music and lighting assist the transitions from present to past. For example, when Willy imagines the scene in which the boys are simonizing the car, the apartment houses fade and "the entire house and surroundings become covered with leaves." Flute music, associated with Willy's father who made and sold flutes, is used to evoke a variety of moods: nostalgia for a lost pastoral America in Act 1, hopefulness and promise in the opening of Act 2, and the mournfulness of a funeral march as a transition to the final "Requiem."

Like most classical tragedies, Miller's democratic tragedy ends with the death of the hero. But it is about more than the passing of one salesman. It is a play about the passing of compassionate individualism and of much that is hopeful in American life. It is a play about dreams and the frustrations of those dreams.

First, Miller's play is about the American family, about a belief in what sociologists call upward mobility, and parents' aspirations for their children. It is above all about a belief that things will get better. At the beginning of Act 2, Biff is no longer "a disgrace" for not having found himself at thirty-four; he is now optimistically one of those men who "take longer to get—solidified." Of course, things often do actually get better for children, and Miller offers the example of Bernard, the unathletic intellectual, who is about to argue a case before the Supreme Court and who now plays tennis. By reversing the usual victory of the athletic type over the intellectual type, Miller emphasizes that Bernard had prepared himself for life while Biff, in Bernard's words, "never trained for anything." The outcome of the careers of Biff and Bernard shows what Biff comes to understand at the play's conclusion: he had learned from Willy, and Willy "had the wrong dreams." No longer do contacts, being well-liked, and personality determine success, if they ever did. Instead, "screwing on your fists" in the old-fashioned manner of Ben, the prototypical robber baron, is the style of contemporary capitalism. This is the second major theme of Miller's play: the destruction of personality, charitableness, and individual handicraft, which are replaced by impersonality and a machine culture.

Prior to firing Willy, Howard Wagner, the head of the firm, explains to Willy that "everybody's got to pull his own weight," because "business is business." Willy tries to lay claim to some obligation on the firm's part by citing his thirty-four years with the firm and that he even helped to give Howard his name. But as Charley, a businessman with a conscience, tells him, "When're you gonna realize that them things don't mean anything?" Willy's angry response to being fired by Howard—"You can't eat the orange and throw the peel away—a man is not a piece of fruit!"—sums up the play's criticism of the callous business ethic. Howard, the modern businessman, is the antithesis of Willy's older salesman hero, a solitary named Dave Singleman, who at eighty-four sold merchandise on the basis of personality when "there was respect, and comradeship, and gratitude." Instead, the modern business world resembles Ben's jungle where it doesn't pay to fight fair.

The American fascination with machinery, devices, gadgets, and inventions is another part of Miller's criticism of capitalism. Devices wear out before they are paid for; Willy is virtually enslaved by consumerism and payments on cars and refrigerators, and ironically is treated to a lecture by Howard on the importance of having a recording machine that costs more money than Willy's life insurance payment. That Howard shows more interest in the machine than in Willy tells us how far machines have replaced human contact.

Opposed to the depersonalizing machines are the products of handicraft. Like his father who made and sold flutes, Willy is happiest doing something with his hands. Manliness is defined as athleticism and the ability to use tools. Unathletic Charley admits that putting up a ceiling "is a mystery to me," to which Willy angrily responds, "A man who can't handle tools is not a man." Biff observes with bitterness, "Charley, there's more of him in that front stoop than in all the sales he ever made." Individually handcrafted items, the products of working with one's hands, are also associated with the American myth of a country of farmers and craftsmen who live a rural life. When things are looking up, Willy tells Linda, "You wait, kid, before it's all over we're gonna get a little place out in the country, and I'll raise some vegetables, a couple of chickens . . ." His fantasy continues to include his sons, who will marry, and he will build "a little guest house. 'Cause I got so many fine tools." Here Miller has combined a number of motifs centering around self-sufficiency and pride in work. These include the idea of escaping the city to a rural environment, using tools, planting a garden, and continuing the family through many generations. These motifs have a special poignancy at the end when Willy tries planting a garden at night in his little postage-stamp of a backyard, having failed to plant the seeds of a continuing family in his two sons. The "Requiem" isolates the two contradictory sides of Willy's character in his sons: Biff, the Western man who rhapsodizes over spring in Texas and working outdoors, and Hap, who decides to fight it out in the city: "This is where I'm gonna win it for him."

Miller's characterizations range from the stereotypic selfless wife, ("They threw away the mold when they made her.") and ruthless robber baron ("When I walked into the jungle, I was seventeen. When I walked out I was twenty-one. And, by God, I was rich!") to richly complex characters like Biff and Willy. Although father and son may at first seem like stereotypes, they are developed with a psychological subtlety that raises them above the stereotypic high-school athlete who never made it in life and the self-conscious salesman who hides his inferiority complex with backslapping, jokes, and exaggeration.

After thirty-four years of struggling to support his family as a salesman, Willy Loman is exhausted. Feeling "kind of temporary" about himself, as he confesses to his older brother Ben, and never having had an older male to model himself after, Willy selected Dave Singleman (a singularly inappropriate role model for a family man) as his model for a career. Willy compensates for his inferiority complex, his belief that people are laughing at him behind his back, by filling the void of being away from his family with altered versions of events: "I went north to Providence. Met the Mayor. . . . He said, 'Morning!' And I said, 'You got a fine city, here, Mayor.' And then he had coffee with me. . . . And they know me, boys, they know me up and down New England." He also has a continuing affair with a woman buyer. But even that fails to bring him satisfaction. His guilt gnaws at him every time he sees Linda darning a pair of stockings. Like Biff, Willy is terribly lost, uncertain of himself (as his contradictions attest), and happy only when he has something to look forward to. Ironically his son Hap expresses both Willy's living for the future by exaggerating the present and Willy's lonely sensuality. But it is Biff who represents the restless, longing side of Willy, the side that is self-conscious in an office but at home in the outdoors. Like the father, who finds the flowers in Yonkers pretty and tries to grow a vegetable garden, the son would rather be "mixing cement on an open plain" than "making a contemptuous begging fool" of himself in an office. Father and son belong to that class of American boymen who do not live a life of consciousness, but who find satisfaction in hyperbole and physical activity. As a father Willy builds himself into a hero by exaggerating his exploits, emphasizing popularity, and by skirting the rules when it is convenient. Cheating and stealing are all right if you don't get caught; they can even be excused as initiative. Yet, for all his shortcomings Willy is a loveable man willing to sacrifice himself for his sons. Willy is a classical case of a parent living vicariously through his children and enjoying the accomplishments he himself could never attain. However, Biff stops bringing home medals after high school, and because Willy is convinced Biff's failure is his way of getting back at him ("I want you to know, on the train, in the mountains, in the valleys, wherever you go, that you cut down your life for spite!"), bitterness, rancor, and mutual guilt taint their relationship, replacing the love and affection they once knew. Biff's epiphany, which occurs after he steals Bill Oliver's fountain pen, is to see himself truly for the first time: "There's no spite in it any more. I'm just what I am, that's all."

Another father and son pair, Charley and Bernard, stand in stark contrast to Willy and Biff. Just as Willy asks Ben (and later Bernard) for the secret of business success, he asks Charley for the key to success as a parent. As usual, Charley tells the unvarnished truth, "My salvation is that I never took any interest in anything." Bernard became a successful attorney because he was unencumbered by Charley's dreams and therefore free to pursue his own. Even Willy sees this when he tells Charley, "You never told him what to do, did you?" Charley advises Willy to let Biff go: "When a deposit bottle is broken you don't get your nickel back."

One character easily overlooked in the play is Linda, the quintessential loving and dutiful mother/wife as suffering saint. As in the standard mythical version of the American family, the silent suffering wife bears such indignities as angry outbursts without comment while she buoys up her husband's flagging self-confidence. Linda's compliments to Willy are a litany of replies to the discouraging fears that Willy hides under a boastful exterior. To Willy's fears about his appearance, "I'm fat. I'm very foolish to look at," Linda replies, "Willy, darling, you're the handsomest man in the world." Believing that he's not noticed, Willy complains, "they just pass me by," but Linda reassures him, "You're doing wonderful, dear." She helps keep his dreams alive, but also introduces a measure of reality into the family by assuming responsibility for paying bills and keeping the family's credit in balance. Linda also keeps up an optimistic viewpoint on life, something Willy has difficulty sustaining for long. When Willy points out the irony of paying off a house in which there is no one left to live, Linda sees the pattern as one of growth: "Well, dear, life is a casting off. It's always that way." She also acts as a realistic brake on Willy's romantic impulses such as his desire to run off to Alaska. Willy is more suited to working on the house in Brooklyn with his tools. Yet, lest Linda seem too weak to be believable, too accommodating to be an admirable person, when Willy is deserted by his sons in Frank's Chop House, Linda's anger is terrible: "You're a pair of animals! Not one, not another living soul would have had the cruelty to walk out on that man in a restaurant!" Linda's unquestioning loyalty toward Willy extends so far that she would give up seeing her children rather than see Willy humiliated by them: "Either he's your father and you pay him that respect, or else you're not to come here." Linda also acts as mediator, a traditional female role, between the different factions in this contentious masculine household.

Like *Oedipus* and *Hamlet*, Miller's play is about contentions within a family. What makes *Death of a Salesman* such an impressive play is the way in which, like other great plays, it touches basic human traits. As in these other memorable plays, tragedy occurs as a result of dreams gone wrong, dreams of establishing a wished-for order of things. Like Oedipus and Hamlet, Willy finds himself moved by events rather than moving them. Yet, unlike the protagonists of these classical tragedies who gained insight into life as a result of their struggles, Willy goes to his death blindly believing in the wrong dreams.

But the final measure of the effectiveness of a play is the audience's reaction. Judged by the response to *Death of a Salesman*, Aristotle was right about *katharsis*, whether produced by a classical or a democratic tragedy. The audience is purged of pity and fear by watching the salesman go to his death, and even though Willy himself cannot articulate the meaning of his suffering, a choral figure—in this case Charley—does it for him: "Nobody dast blame this man. A salesman is got to dream, boy. It comes with the territory." Miller's *Death of a Salesman* is a timeless tragedy whose values extend beyond its topical concerns to capture one person's struggles to realize his dreams in the face of an unyielding universe.

QUESTIONS

1. Why does Willy feel "temporary" about himself? What in his background accounts for his insecurity?
2. What aspects of Willy's character appear in his sons? Are there different qualities in Hap than in Biff? How are all three men "boys" in some sense?
3. Why is Biff "lost"? What accounts for Biff's and Hap's stealing? Why does Biff steal Bill Oliver's pen?
4. Why does *Death of a Salesman* give so much attention to sons?
5. What symbolic value does the Loman house take on? Why is there so much of Willy in it? Why does Miller call it a "small, fragile-seeming home"?
6. How does Willy's meeting Bernard in Charley's office increase his sense of failure? In how many ways has Bernard succeeded? Why does Willy ask Bernard virtually the same question he had asked Ben, "What's the secret?"
7. In what ways does the "Requiem" sum up for each character the meaning of Willy's death?

Plays for Further Reading

SAMUEL BECKETT (b. 1906)

Krapp's Last Tape

Samuel Beckett is an unusual phenomenon: an Irishman who writes most of his work in French. Born in Dublin, he has lived principally in France since World War II. He has written novels and stories, but his plays have had the most significant impact on contemporary literature, particularly "absurd" drama. Beckett's major plays include *Waiting for Godot* (1953), *Endgame* (1957), and *Krapp's Last Tape* (1958). He received the Nobel Prize for Literature in 1969.

A late evening in the future.

Krapp's den.

Front centre a small table, the two drawers of which open towards audience.

Sitting at the table, facing front, i.e. across from the drawers, a wearish old man: Krapp.

Rusty black narrow trousers too short for him. Rusty black sleeveless waistcoat, four capacious pockets. Heavy silver watch and chain. Grimy white shirt open at neck, no collar. Surprising pair of dirty white boots, size ten at least, very narrow and pointed.

White face. Purple nose. Disordered grey hair. Unshaven.

Very near-sighted (but unspectacled). Hard of hearing.

Cracked voice. Distinctive intonation.

Laborious walk.

On the table a tape-recorder with microphone and a number of cardboard boxes containing reels of recorded tapes.

Table and immediately adjacent area in strong white light. Rest of stage in darkness.

Krapp remains a moment motionless, heaves a great sigh, looks at his watch, fumbles in his pockets, takes out an envelope, puts it back, fumbles, takes out a small bunch of keys, raises it to his eyes, chooses a key, gets up and moves to front of table. He stoops, unlocks first drawer, peers into it, feels about inside it, takes out a reel of tape, peers at it, puts it back, locks drawer, unlocks second drawer, peers into it, feels about inside it, takes out a large banana, peers at it, locks drawer, puts keys back in his pocket. He turns,

*advances to edge of stage, halts, strokes banana, peels it, drops skin at his
feet, puts end of banana in his mouth and remains motionless, staring
vacuously before him. Finally he bites off the end, turns aside and begins
pacing to and fro at edge of stage, in the light, i.e. not more than four or five
paces either way, meditatively eating banana. He treads on skin, slips, nearly
falls, recovers himself, stoops and peers at skin and finally pushes it, still
stooping, with his foot over the edge of stage into pit. He resumes his pacing,
finishes banana, returns to table, sits down, remains a moment motionless,
heaves a great sigh, takes keys from his pockets, raises them to his eyes,
chooses key, gets up and moves to front of table, unlocks second drawer, takes
out a second large banana, peers at it, locks drawer, puts back keys in his
pocket, turns, advances to edge of stage, halts, strokes banana, peels it, tosses
skin into pit, puts end of banana in his mouth and remains motionless, staring
vacuously before him. Finally he has an idea, puts banana in his waistcoat
pocket, the end emerging, and goes with all the speed he can muster backstage
into darkness. Ten seconds. Loud pop of cork. Fifteen seconds. He comes back
into light carrying an old ledger and sits down at table. He lays ledger on
table, wipes his mouth, wipes his hands on the front of his waistcoat, brings
them smartly together and rubs them.*

KRAPP *briskly:* Ah! *He bends over ledger, turns the pages, finds the entry he
wants, reads.* Box . . . thrree . . . spool . . . five. *He raises his head
and stares front. With relish.* Spool! *Pause.* Spooool! *Happy smile. Pause.
He bends over table, starts peering and poking at the boxes.* Box . . .
thrree . . . thrree . . . four . . . two . . . *with surprise* nine! good
God! . . . seven . . . ah! the little rascal! *He takes up box, peers at it.*
Box thrree. *He lays it on table, opens it and peers at spools inside.* Spool
. . . *he peers at ledger* . . . five . . . *he peers at spools* . . . five . . .
five . . . ah! the little scoundrel! *He takes out a spool, peers at it.* Spool
five. *He lays it on table, closes box three, puts it back with the others,
takes up the spool.* Box thrree, spool five. *He bends over the machine,
looks up. With relish.* Spooool! *Happy smile. He bends, loads spool on
machine, rubs his hands.* Ah! *He peers at ledger, reads entry at foot of
page.* Mother at rest at last . . . Hm . . . The black ball . . . *He raises
his head, stares blankly front. Puzzled.* Black ball?. . . *He peers again at
ledger, reads.* The dark nurse. . .*He raises his head, broods, peers again
at ledger, reads.* Slight improvement in bowel condition . . . Hm . . .
Memorable . . . what? *He peers closer.* Equinox, memorable equinox.
He raises his head, stares blankly front. Puzzled. Memorable equinox? . . . *Pause. He shrugs his shoulders, peers again at ledger, reads.*
Farewell to—*he turns the page*—love.

*He raises his head, broods, bends over machine, switches on and assumes listen-
ing posture, i.e., leaning forward, elbows on table, hand cupping ear towards
machine, face front.*

TAPE *strong voice, rather pompous, clearly Krapp's at a much earlier time:*
Thirty-nine today, sound as a—*Settling himself more comfortably he*

knocks one of the boxes off the table, curses, switches off, sweeps boxes and ledger violently to the ground, winds tape back to beginning, switches on, resumes posture. Thirty-nine today, sound as a bell, apart from my old weakness, and intellectually I have now every reason to suspect at the . . . *hesitates* . . . crest of the wave—or thereabouts. Celebrated the awful occasion, as in recent years, quietly at the Winehouse. Not a soul. Sat before the fire with closed eyes, separating the grain from the husks. Jotted down a few notes, on the back of an envelope. Good to be back in my den, in my old rags. Have just eaten I regret to say three bananas and only with difficulty refrained from a fourth. Fatal things for a man with my condition. *Vehemently.* Cut 'em out! *Pause.* The new light above my table is a great improvement. With all this darkness round me I feel less alone. *Pause.* In a way. *Pause.* I love to get up and move about in it, then back here to . . . *hesitates* . . . me. *Pause.* Krapp.

Pause.

The grain, now what I wonder do I mean by that, I mean . . . *hesitates* . . . I suppose I mean those things worth having when all the dust has—when all *my* dust has settled. I close my eyes and try and imagine them.

Pause. Krapp closes his eyes briefly.

Extraordinary silence this evening, I strain my ears and do not hear a sound. Old Miss McGlome always sings at this hour. But not tonight. Songs of her girlhood, she says. Hard to think of her as a girl. Wonderful woman though. Connaught, I fancy. *Pause.* Shall I sing when I am her age, if I ever am? No. *Pause.* Did I sing as a boy? No. *Pause.* Did I ever sing? No.

Pause.

Just been listening to an old year, passages at random. I did not check in the book, but it must be at least ten or twelve years ago. At that time I think I was still living on and off with Bianca in Kedar Street. Well out of that, Jesus yes! Hopeless business. *Pause.* Not much about her, apart from a tribute to her eyes. Very warm. I suddenly saw them again. *Pause.* Incomparable! *Pause.* Ah well . . . *Pause.* These old P.M.s are gruesome, but I often find them—*Krapp switches off, broods, switches on*—a help before embarking on a new . . . *hesitates* . . . retrospect. Hard to believe I was ever that young whelp. The voice! Jesus! And the aspirations! *Brief laugh in which Krapp joins.* And the resolutions! *Brief laugh in which Krapp joins.* To drink less, in particular. *Brief laugh of Krapp alone.* Statistics. Seventeen hundred hours, out of the preceding eight thousand odd, consumed on licensed premises alone. More than 20%, say 40% of his waking life. *Pause.* Plans for a less . . . *hesitates* . . . engrossing sexual life. Last illness of his father. Flagging pursuit of happiness. Unattainable laxation. Sneers at what he calls his youth and thanks to God that it's over. *Pause.* False ring there. *Pause.* Shadows of the opus . . . magnum. Closing with a—*brief laugh*—yelp to Providence. *Prolonged laugh in which Krapp joins.* What remains of all that misery? A girl in a shabby green coat, on a railway-station platform? No?

Pause

When I look—

Krapp switches off, broods, looks at his watch, gets up, goes backstage into darkness. Ten seconds. Pop of cork. Ten seconds. Second cork. Ten seconds. Third cork. Ten seconds. Brief burst of quavering song.

KRAPP *sings:*   Now the day is over,
      Night is drawing nigh-igh,
      Shadows—

Fit of coughing. He comes back into light, sits down, wipes his mouth, switches on, resumes his listening posture.

TAPE: —back on the year that is gone, with what I hope is perhaps a glint of the old eye to come, there is of course the house on the canal where mother lay a-dying, in the late autumn, after her long viduity *Krapp gives a start, and the—Krapp switches off, winds back tape a little, bends his ear closer to machine, switches on—*a-dying, after her long viduity, and the—

Krapp switches off, raises his head, stares blankly before him. His lips move in the syllables of "viduity." No sound. He gets up, goes backstage into darkness, comes back with an enormous dictionary, lays it on table, sits down and looks up the word.

KRAPP *reading from dictionary:*   State—or condition of being—or remaining—a widow—or widower. *Looks up. Puzzled.* Being—or remaining? . . . *Pause. He peers again at dictionary. Reading.* "Deep weeds of viduity" . . . Also of an animal, especially a bird . . . the vidua or weaver-bird . . . Black plumage of male . . . *He looks up. With relish.* The vidua-bird!

Pause. He closes dictionary, switches on, resumes listening posture.

TAPE: —bench by the weir from where I could see her window. There I sat, in the biting wind, wishing she were gone. *Pause.* Hardly a soul, just a few regulars, nursemaids, infants, old men, dogs. I got to know them quite well—oh by appearance of course I mean! One dark young beauty I recollect particularly, all white and starch, incomparable bosom, with a big black hooded perambulator, most funereal thing. Whenever I looked in her direction she had her eyes on me. And yet when I was bold enough to speak to her—not having been introduced—she threatened to call a policeman. As if I had designs on her virtue! *Laugh. Pause.* The face she had! The eyes! Like . . . *hestitates* . . . chrysolite! *Pause.* Ah well . . . *Pause.* I was there when—*Krapp switches off, broods, switches on again*—the blind went down, one of those dirty brown roller affairs, throwing a ball for a little white dog, as chance would have it. I happened to look up and there it was. All over and done with, at last. I sat on for a few moments with the ball in my hand and the dog yelping and pawing at me. *Pause.* Moments. Her moments, my moments. *Pause.* The dog's moments. *Pause.* In the end I held it out to him and he took it in his mouth, gently, gently. A small, old, black, hard, solid rubber ball. *Pause.* I shall feel it, in my hand, until my dying day. *Pause.* I might have kept it. *Pause.* But I gave it to the dog.

Pause.

Ah well . . .

Pause.

Spiritually a year of profound gloom and indigence until that memorable night in March, at the end of the jetty, in the howling wind, never to be forgotten, when suddenly I saw the whole thing. The vision, at last. This I fancy is what I have chiefly to record this evening, against the day when my work will be done and perhaps no place left in my memory, warm or cold, for the miracle that . . . *hesitates* . . . for the fire that set it alight. What I suddenly saw then was this, that the belief I had been going on all my life, namely—*Krapp switches off impatiently, winds tape forward, switches on again*—great granite rocks the foam flying up in the light of the lighthouse and the wind-gauge spinning like a propellor, clear to me at last that the dark I have always struggled to keep under is in reality my most—*Krapp curses, switches off, winds tape forward, switches on again*—unshatterable association until my dissolution of storm and night with the light of the understanding and the fire—*Krapp curses louder, switches off, winds tape forward, switches on again*—my face in her breasts and my hand on her. We lay there without moving. But under us all moved, and moved us, gently, up and down, and from side to side.
Past midnight. Never knew such silence. The earth might be uninhabited.

Pause.

Here I end—

Krapp switches off, winds tape back, switches on again.

—upper lake, with the punt, bathed off the bank, then pushed out into the stream and drifted. She lay stretched out on the floorboards with her hands under her head and her eyes closed. Sun blazing down, bit of a breeze, water nice and lively. I noticed a scratch on her thigh and asked her how she came by it. Picking gooseberries, she said. I said again I thought it was hopeless and no good going on, and she agreed, without opening her eyes. *Pause.* I asked her to look at me and after a few moments—*pause*—after a few moments she did, but the eyes just slits, because of the glare. I bent over her to get them in the shadow and they opened. *Pause. Low.* Let me in. *Pause.* We drifted in among the flags and stuck. The way they went down, sighing, before the stem! *Pause.* I lay down across her with my face in her breasts and my hand on her. We lay there without moving. But under us all moved, and moved us, gently, up and down, and from side to side.

Pause.

Past midnight. Never knew—:

Krapp switches off, broods. Finally he fumbles in his pockets, encounters the banana, takes it out, peers at it, puts it back, fumbles, brings out the envelope, fumbles, puts back envelope, looks at his watch, gets up and goes backstage into darkness. Ten seconds. Sound of bottle against glass, then brief siphon. Ten seconds. Bottle against glass alone. Ten seconds. He comes back a little unsteadily into light, goes to front of table, takes out keys, raises them to his eyes, chooses key. Unlocks first drawer, peers into it, feels about inside, takes out reel, peers at it, locks drawer, puts keys back in his pocket, goes and sits down, takes reel off machine, lays it on dictionary, loads virgin reel on machine, takes envelope from his pocket, consults back of it, lays it on table, switches on, clears his throat and begins to record.

KRAPP: Just been listening to that stupid bastard I took myself for thirty years ago, hard to believe I was ever as bad as that. Thank God that's all done with anyway. *Pause.* The eyes she had! *Broods, realizes he is recording silence, switches off, broods. Finally.* Everything there, everything, all the—*Realizes this is not being recorded, switches on.* Everything there, everything on this old muckball, all the light and dark and famine and feasting of . . . *hesitates* . . . the ages! *In a shout.* Yes! *Pause.* Let that go! Jesus! Take his mind off his homework! Jesus! *Pause. Weary.* Ah well, maybe he was right. *Pause.* Maybe he was right. *Broods. Realizes. Switches off. Consults envelope.* Pah! *Crumples it and throws it away. Broods. Switches on.* Nothing to say, not a squeak. What's a year now? The sour cud and the iron stool. *Pause.* Revelled in the word spool. *With relish.* Spooool! Happiest moment of the past half million. *Pause.* Seventeen copies sold, of which eleven at trade price to free circulating libraries beyond the seas. Getting known. *Pause.* One pound six and something, eight I have little doubt. *Pause.* Crawled out once or twice, before the summer was cold. Sat shivering in the park, drowned in dreams and burning to be gone. Not a soul. *Pause.* Last fancies. *Vehemently.* Keep 'em under! *Pause.* Scalded the eyes out of me reading *Effie* again, a page a day, with tears again. Effie . . . *Pause.* Could have been happy with her, up there on the Baltic, and the pines, and the dunes. *Pause.* Could I? *Pause.* And she? *Pause.* Pah! *Pause.* Fanny came in a couple of times. Bony old ghost of a whore. Couldn't do much, but I suppose better than a kick in the crutch. The last time wasn't so bad. How do you manage it, she said, at your age? I told her I'd been saving up for her all my life. *Pause.* Went to Vespers once, like when I was in short trousers. *Pause. Sings.*

> Now the day is over,
> Night is drawing nigh-igh,
> Shadows—*coughing, then almost inaudible*—of the evening
> Steal across the sky.

Gasping. Went to sleep and fell off the pew. *Pause.* Sometimes wondered in the night if a last effort mightn't—*Pause.* Ah finish your booze now and get to your bed. Go on with this drivel in the morning. Or leave it at that. *Pause.* Leave it at that. *Pause.* Lie propped up in the dark—and wander. Be again in the dingle on a Christmas Eve, gathering holly, the red-berried. *Pause.* Be again on Croghan on a Sunday morning, in the haze, with the bitch, stop and listen to the bells. *Pause.* And so on. *Pause.* Be again, be again. *Pause.* All that old misery. *Pause.* Once wasn't enough for you. *Pause.* Lie down across her.

Long pause. He suddenly bends over machine, switches off, wrenches off tape, throws it away, puts on the other, winds it forward to the passage he wants, switches on, listens staring front.

TAPE: —gooseberries, she said. I said again I thought it was hopeless and no good going on, and she agreed, without opening her eyes. *Pause.* I asked her to look at me and after a few moments—*pause*—after a few moments she did, but the eyes just slits, because of the glare. I bent over her to get them in the shadow and they opened. *Pause. Low.* Let me in. *Pause.* We drifted in among the flags and stuck. The way they went down, sighing, before the stem! *Pause.* I lay down across her with my face in her breasts and my hand on her. We lay there without moving. But under us all moved, and moved us, gently, up and down, and from side to side.

Pause. Krapp's lips move. No sound.

Past midnight. Never knew such silence. The earth might be un-inhabited.

Pause.

Here I end this reel. Box—*pause*—three, spool—*pause*—five. *Pause.* Perhaps my best years are gone. When there was a chance of happiness. But I wouldn't want them back. Not with the fire in me now. No, I wouldn't want them back.

Krapp motionless staring before him. The tape runs on in silence.

Curtain

ANTON CHEKHOV (1860–1904)

The Brute

Anton Chekhov was born at Tagnarog in southern Russia. He received a medical degree in 1884 and practiced medicine throughout his life. A key figure in early modern drama, he is equally famous as one of the great masters of the short story. His earlier plays, such as *The Brute*, were primarily comedies. Later his plays took on a darker, autumnal, understated quality as he expressed the "tiredness" and triviality of everyday existence in Czarist Russia. His major full-length dramas include *The Seagull* (1898), *Three Sisters* (1901), and *The Cherry Orchard* (1904).

A JOKE IN ONE ACT

CHARACTERS

MRS. POPOV, *widow and landowner, small, with dimpled cheeks.*
MR. GRIGORY S. SMIRNOV, *gentleman farmer, middle-aged.*
LUKA, *Mrs. Popov's footman, an old man.*
GARDENER
COACHMAN
HIRED MEN

The drawing room of a country house. MRS. POPOV, *in deep mourning, is staring hard at a photograph.* LUKA *is with her.*

LUKA: It's not right, ma'am, you're killing yourself. The cook has gone off with the maid to pick berries. The cat's having a high old time in the yard catching birds. Every living thing is happy. But you stay moping here in the house like it was a convent, taking no pleasure in nothing. I mean it, ma'am! It must be a full year since you set foot out of doors.

MRS. POPOV: I must never set foot out of doors again, Luka. Never! I have nothing to set foot out of doors *for*. My life is done. *He* is in his grave. I have buried myself alive in this house. We are *both* in our graves.

LUKA: You're off again, ma'am. I just won't listen to you no more. Mr. Popov is dead, but what can we do about that? It's God's doing. God's will be done. You've cried over him, you've done your share of mourning, haven't you? There's a limit to everything. You can't go on weeping and wailing forever. My old lady died, for that matter, and I wept and wailed over her a whole month long. Well, that was it. I couldn't weep and wail all my life, she just wasn't worth it. *He sighs.* As for the neighbours, you've forgotten all about them, ma'am. You don't visit them and you don't let them visit you. You and I are like a pair of spiders—excuse the expression, ma'am—here we are in this house like a pair of spiders, we never see the light of day. And it isn't like there was no nice people around either. The whole county's swarming with 'em. There's a regiment quartered at Riblov, and the officers are so good-looking! The girls can't take their eyes off them—There's a ball at the camp every Friday—The military band plays most every day of the week—What do you say, ma'am? You're young, you're pretty, you could enjoy yourself! Ten years from now you may want to strut and show your feathers to the officers, and it'll be too late.

MRS. POPOV *firmly:*   You must never bring this subject up again, Luka. Since Popov died, life has been an empty dream to me, you know that. *You* may think I am alive. Poor ignorant Luka! You are wrong. I am dead. I'm in my grave. Never more shall I see the light of day, never strip from my body this . . . raiment of death! Are you listening, Luka? Let his ghost learn how I love him! Yes, *I* know, and *you* know, he was often unfair to me, he was cruel to me, and he was unfaithful to me. What of it? *I* shall be faithful to *him,* that's all. I will show him how *I* can love. Hereafter, in a better world than this, he will welcome me back, the same loyal girl I always was—

LUKA: Instead of carrying on this way, ma'am, you should go out in the garden and take a bit of a walk, ma'am. Or why not harness Toby and take a drive? Call on a couple of the neighbours, ma'am?

MRS. POPOV *breaking down:*   Oh, Luka!

LUKA: Yes, ma'am? What have I said, ma'am? Oh, dear!

MRS. POPOV: Toby! You said Toby! He adored that horse. When he drove me out to the Korchagins and the Vlasovs, it was always with Toby! He was a wonderful driver, do you remember, Luka? So graceful! So strong! I can see him now, pulling at those reins with all his might and main! Toby! Luka, tell them to give Toby an extra portion of oats today.

LUKA: Yes, ma'am.

A bell rings.

MRS. POPOV: Who is that? Tell them I'm not at home.

LUKA: Very good ma'am. *Exit.*

MRS. POPOV *gazing again at the photograph:*   You shall see, my Popov, how a wife can love and forgive. Till death do us part. Longer than that. Till death re-unite us forever! *Suddenly a titter breaks through her tears.* Aren't you ashamed of yourself, Popov? Here's your little wife, being good, being faithful, so faithful she's locked up here waiting for her own funeral, while you—doesn't it make you ashamed, you naughty boy? You were terrible, you know. You were unfaithful, and you made those awful scenes about it, you stormed out and left me alone for weeks—

Enter LUKA.

LUKA *upset:*   There's someone asking for you, ma'am. Says he must—

MRS. POPOV: I suppose you told him that since my husband's death I see no one?

LUKA: Yes, ma'am. I did, ma'am. But he wouldn't listen, ma'am. He says it's urgent.

MRS. POPOV *shrilly:*   I see no one!!

LUKA: He won't take no for an answer, ma'am. He just curses and swears and comes in anyway. He's a perfect monster, ma'am. He's in the dining room right now.

MRS. POPOV: In the dining room, is he? I'll give him his come uppance. Bring him in here this minute.

Exit LUKA.

Suddenly sad again. Why do they do this to me? Why? Insulting my grief, intruding on my solitude? *She sighs.* I'm afraid I'll have to enter a convent. I will, I *must* enter a convent!

Enter MR. SMIRNOV *and* LUKA.

SMIRNOV *to* LUKA: Dolt! Idiot! You talk too much! *Seeing* MRS. POPOV. *With dignity.* May I have the honour of introducing myself, madam? Grigory S. Smirnov, landowner and lieutenant of artillery, retired. Forgive me, madam, if I disturb your peace and quiet, but my business is both urgent and weighty.

MRS. POPOV *declining to offer him her hand:*   What is it you wish, sir?

SMIRNOV: At the time of his death, your late husband—with whom I had the honour to be acquainted, ma'am—was in my debt to the tune of twelve hundred rubles. I have two notes to prove it. Tomorrow, ma'am, I must pay the interest on a bank loan. I have therefore no alternative, ma'am, but to ask you to pay me the money today.

MRS. POPOV: Twelve hundred rubles? But what did my husband owe it to you for?

SMIRNOV: He used to buy his oats from me, madam.

MRS. POPOV *to* LUKA, *with a sigh:*   Remember what I said, Luka: tell them to give Toby an extra portion of oats today!

Exit LUKA.

My dear Mr.—what was the name again?

SMIRNOV: Smirnov, ma'am.

MRS. POPOV: My dear Mr. Smirnov, if Mr. Popov owed you money, you shall be paid—to the last ruble, to the last kopeck. But today—you must excuse me, Mr.—what was it?

SMIRNOV: Smirnov, ma'am.

MRS. POPOV: Today, Mr. Smirnov, I have no ready cash in the house.

SMIRNOV *starts to speak.*

Tomorrow, Mr. Smirnov, no, the day after tomorrow, all will be well. My steward will be back from town. I shall see that he pays what is owing. Today, no. In any case, today is exactly seven months from Mr. Popov's death. On such a day you will understand that I am in no mood to think of money.

SMIRNOV: Madam, if you don't pay up now, you can carry me out feet foremost. They'll seize my estate.

MRS. POPOV: You can have your money.

He starts to thank her.

Tomorrow.

He again starts to speak.

That is: the day after tomorrow.

SMIRNOV: I don't need the money the day after tomorrow. I need it to-day.

MRS. POPOV: I'm sorry, Mr.—

SMIRNOV *shouting:*   Smirnov!

MRS. POPOV *sweetly:*   Yes, of course. But you can't have it today.

SMIRNOV: But I can't wait for it any longer!

MRS. POPOV: Be sensible, Mr. Smirnov. How can I pay you if I don't have it?

SMIRNOV: You don't have it?

MRS. POPOV: I don't have it.

SMIRNOV: Sure?

MRS. POPOV: Positive.

SMIRNOV: Very well. I'll make a note to that effect. *Shrugging*. And then they want me to keep cool. I meet the tax commissioner on the street, and he says, 'Why are you always in such a bad humour, Smirnov?' Bad humour! How can I help it, in God's name? I need money, I need it desperately. Take yesterday: I leave home at the crack of dawn, I call on all my debtors. Not a one of them pays up. Footsore and weary, I creep at midnight into some little dive, and try to snatch a few winks of sleep on the floor by the vodka barrel. Then today, I come here, fifty miles from home, saying to myself, 'At last, at last, I can be sure of something,' and you're not in the mood! You give me a mood! Christ, how can I help getting all worked up?

MRS. POPOV: I thought I'd made it clear, Mr. Smirnov, that you'll get your money the minute my steward is back from town?

SMIRNOV: What the hell do I care about your steward? Pardon the expression ma'am. But it was you I came to see.

MRS. POPOV: What language! What a tone to take to a lady! I refuse to hear another word. *Quickly, exit*.

SMIRNOV: Not in the mood, huh? 'Exactly seven months since Popov's death,' huh? How about me? *Shouting after her*. Is there this interest to pay, or isn't there? I'm asking you a question: is there this interest to pay, or isn't there? So your husband died, and you're not in the mood, and your steward's gone off some place, and so forth and so on, but what *I* can do about all that, huh? What do *you* think I should do? Take a running jump and shove my head through the wall? Take off in a balloon? You don't know my *other* debtors. I call on Gruzdeff. Not at home. I look for Yaroshevitch. He's hiding out. I find Kooritsin. He kicks up a row, and I have to throw him through the window. I work my way right down the list. Not a kopeck. Then I come to you, and God damn it to hell, if you'll pardon the expression, you're not in the mood! *Quietly, as he realizes he's talking to air*. I've spoiled them all, that's what, I've let them play me for a sucker. Well, I'll show them. I'll show this one. I'll stay right here till she pays up. Ugh! *He shudders with rage*. I'm in a rage! I'm in a positively towering rage! Every nerve in my body is trembling at forty to the dozen! I can't breathe, I feel ill, I think I'm going to faint, hey, you there!

Enter LUKA.

LUKA: Yes, sir? Is there anything you wish, sir?
SMIRNOV: Water! Water! No, make it vodka.

Exit LUKA.

Consider the logic of it. A fellow creature is desperately in need of cash, so desperately in need that he has to seriously contemplate hanging himself, and this woman, this mere chit of a girl, won't pay up, and why not? Because, forsooth, she isn't in the mood! Oh, the logic of women! Come to that, I never have liked them, I could do without the whole sex. Talk to a woman? I'd rather sit on a barrel of dynamite, the very thought gives me gooseflesh. Women! Creatures of poetry and romance! Just to see one in the distance gets me mad. My legs start twitching with rage. I feel like yelling for help.

Enter LUKA, *handing* SMIRNOV *a glass of water.*

LUKA: Mrs. Popov is indisposed, sir. She is seeing no one.
SMIRNOV: Get out.

Exit LUKA.

Indisposed, is she? Seeing no one, huh? Well, she can see me or not, but I'll be here, I'll be right here till she pays up. If you're sick for a week, I'll be here for a week. If you're sick for a year, I'll be here for a year. You won't get around *me* with your widow's weeds and your schoolgirl dimples. I know all about dimples. *Shouting through the window.* Semyon, let the horses out of those shafts, we're not leaving, we're staying, and tell them to give the horses some oats, yes, oats, you fool, what do you think? *Walking away from the window.* What a mess, what an unholy mess! I didn't sleep last night, the heat is terrific today, not a damn one of 'em has paid up, and here's this—this skirt in mourning that's not in the mood! My head aches, where's that— *He drinks from the glass.* Water, ugh! You there!

Enter LUKA.

LUKA: Yes, sir. You wish for something, sir?
SMIRNOV: Where's that confounded vodka I asked for?

Exit LUKA.

SMIRNOV *sits and looks himself over:* Oof! A fine figure of a man *I* am! Unwashed, uncombed, unshaven, straw on my vest, dust all over me. The little woman must've taken me for a highwayman. *Yawns.* I suppose it wouldn't be considered polite to barge into a drawing room in this state, but who cares? I'm not a visitor, I'm a creditor—most unwelcome of guests, second only to Death.

Enter LUKA.

LUKA *handing him the vodka:* If I may say so, sir, you take too many liberties, sir.
SMIRNOV: What?!
LUKA: Oh, nothing, sir, nothing.
SMIRNOV: Who in hell do you think you're talking to? Shut your mouth!
LUKA *aside:* There's an evil spirit abroad. The Devil must have sent him. Oh!

Exit LUKA.

SMIRNOV: What a rage I'm in! I'll grind the whole world to powder. Oh, I feel ill again. You there!

Enter MRS. POPOV.

MRS. POPOV *looking at the floor:* In the solitude of my rural retreat, Mr. Smirnov, I've long since grown unaccustomed to the sound of the human voice. Above all, I cannot bear shouting. I must beg you not to break the silence.

SMIRNOV: Very well. Pay me my money and I'll go.

MRS. POPOV: I told you before, and I tell you again, Mr. Smirnov. I have no cash, you'll have to wait till the day after tomorrow. Can I express myself more plainly?

SMIRNOV: And *I* told *you* before, and *I* tell *you* again, that I need the money today, that the day after tomorrow is too late, and that if you don't pay, and pay now, I'll have to hang myself in the morning!

MRS. POPOV: But I have no cash. This is quite a puzzle.

SMIRNOV: You won't pay, huh?

MRS. POPOV: I *can't* pay, Mr. Smirnov.

SMIRNOV: In that case, I'm going to sit here and wait. *Sits down.* You'll pay up the day after tomorrow? Very good. Till the day after tomorrow, here I sit. *Pause. He jumps up.* Now look, do I have to pay that interest tomorrow, or don't I? Or do you think I'm joking?

MRS. POPOV: I must ask you to not raise your voice, Mr. Smirnov. This is not a stable.

SMIRNOV: Who said it was? Do I have to pay the interest tomorrow or not?

MRS. POPOV: Mr. Smirnov, do you know how to behave in the presence of a lady?

SMIRNOV: No, madam, I do not know how to behave in the presence of a lady.

MRS. POPOV: Just what I thought. I look at you, and I say: ugh! I hear you talk, and I say to myself: 'That man doesn't know how to talk to a lady.'

SMIRNOV: You'd like me to come simpering to you in French, I suppose. '*Enchanté, madame! Merci beaucoup* for not paying zee money, *madame! Pardonnez-moi* if I 'ave disturbed you, *madame!* How *charmante* you look in mourning, *madame!*'

MRS POPOV: Now you're being silly, Mr. Smirnov.

SMIRNOV *mimicking:* 'Now you're being silly, Mr. Smirnov.' 'You don't know how to talk to a lady, Mr. Smirnov.' Look here, Mrs. Popov, I've known more women than you've known pussy cats. I've fought three duels on their account. I've jilted twelve, and been jilted by nine others. Oh, yes, Mrs. Popov, I've played the fool in my time, whispered sweet nothings, bowed and scraped and endeavoured to please. Don't tell me I don't know what it is to love, to pine away with longing, to have the blues, to melt like butter, to be weak as water. I was full of tender emotion. I was carried away with passion. I squandered half my fortune on the sex. I chattered about women's emancipation.

But there's an end to everything, dear madam. Burning eyes, dark eye-lashes, ripe, red lips, dimpled cheeks, heaving bosoms, soft whisper-ings, the moon above, the lake below—I don't give a rap for that sort of nonsense any more, Mrs. Popov. I've found out about women. Pres-ent company excepted, they're liars. Their behaviour is mere play act-ing; their conversation is sheer gossip. Yes, dear lady, women, young or old, are false, petty, vain, cruel, malicious, unreasonable. As for intelligence, any sparrow could give them points. Appearances, I ad-mit, can be deceptive. In appearance, a woman may be all poetry and romance, goddess and angel, muslin and fluff. To look at her exterior is to be transported to heaven. But I have looked at her interior, Mrs. Popov, and what did I find there—in her very soul? A crocodile. *He has gripped the back of the chair so firmly that it snaps.* And, what is more revolting, a crocodile with an illusion, a crocodile that imagines tender sentiments are its own special province, a crocodile that thinks itself queen of the realm of love! Whereas, in sober fact, dear madam, if a woman can love anything except a lapdog you can hang me by the feet on that nail. For a man, love is suffering, love is sacrifice. A woman just swishes her train around and tightens her grip on your nose. Now, you're a woman, aren't you, Mrs. Popov? You must be an expert on some of this. Tell me, quite frankly, did you ever know a woman to be—faithful, for instance? Or even sincere? Only old hags, huh? Though some women are old hags from birth. But as for the others? You're right: a faithful woman is a freak of nature—like a cat with horns.

MRS. POPOV: Who *is* faithful, then? Who *have* you cast for the faithful lover? Not man?

SMIRNOV: Right first time, Mrs. Popov: man.

MRS. POPOV *going off into a peal of bitter laughter*:   Man! Man is faithful! that's a new one! *Fiercely*. What right do you have to say this, Mr. Smirnov? Men faithful? Let me tell you something. Of all the men I have ever known my late husband Popov was the best. I loved him, and there are women who know how to love, Mr. Smirnov. I gave him my youth, my happiness, my life, my fortune. I worshipped the ground he trod on—and what happened? The best of men was unfaithful to me, Mr. Smirnov. Not once in a while. All the time. After he died, I found his desk drawer full of love letters. While he was alive, he was always going away for the week-end. He squandered my money. He made love to other women before my very eyes. But, in spite of all, Mr. Smirnov, *I* was faithful. Unto death. And beyond. I am *still* faith-ful, Mr. Smirnov! Buried alive in this house, I shall wear mourning till the day I, too, am called to my eternal rest.

SMIRNOV *laughing scornfully:*   Expect me to believe that? As if I couldn't see through all this hocus-pocus. Buried alive! Till you're called to your eternal rest! Till when? Till some little poet—or some little subaltern with his first moustache—comes riding by and asks: 'Can that be the house of the mysterious Tamara who for love of her late husband has buried herself alive, vowing to see no man?' Ha!

MRS. POPOV *flaring up:*   How dare you? How dare you insinuate—?

SMIRNOV: You may have buried yourself alive, Mrs. Popov, but you haven't forgotten to powder your nose.

MRS. POPOV *incoherent:* How dare you? How—?

SMIRNOV: Who's raising his voice now? Just because I call a spade a spade. Because I shoot straight from the shoulder. Well, don't shout at me, I'm not your steward.

MRS. POPOV: I'm not shouting, you're shouting! Oh, leave me alone!

SMIRNOV: Pay me the money, and I will.

MRS. POPOV: You'll get no money out of me!

SMIRNOV: Oh! so that's it!

MRS. POPOV: Not a ruble, not a kopeck. Get out! Leave me alone!

SMIRNOV: Not being your husband, I must ask you not to make scenes with me. *He sits.* I don't like scenes.

MRS. POPOV *choking with rage:* You're sitting down?

SMIRNOV: Correct, I'm sitting down.

MRS. POPOV: I asked you to leave!

SMIRNOV: Then give me the money. *Aside.* Oh, what a rage I'm in, what a rage!

MRS. POPOV: The impudence of the man! I won't talk to you a moment longer. Get out. *Pause.* Are you going?

SMIRNOV: No.

MRS. POPOV: No?!

SMIRNOV: No.

MRS. POPOV: On your head be it. Luka!

Enter LUKA.

Show the gentleman out, Luka.

LUKA *approaching:* I'm afraid, sir, I'll have to ask you, um, to leave, sir, now, um—

SMIRNOV *jumping up:* Shut your mouth, you old idiot! Who do you think you're talking to? I'll make mincemeat of you.

LUKA *clutching his heart:* Mercy on us! Holy saints above! *He falls into an armchair.* I'm taken sick! I can't breathe!!

MRS. POPOV: Then where's Dasha? Dasha! Dasha! Come here at once! *She rings.*

LUKA: They gone picking berries, ma'am, I'm alone here—Water, water, I'm taken sick!

MRS. POPOV *to* SMIRNOV: Get out, you!

SMIRNOV: Can't you even be polite with me, Mrs. Popov?

MRS. POPOV *clenching her fists and stamping her feet:* With you? You're a wild animal, you were never house-broken!

SMIRNOV: What? What did you say?

MRS. POPOV: I said you were a wild animal, you were never house-broken.

SMIRNOV *advancing upon her:* And what right do you have to talk to me like that?

MRS. POPOV: Like what?

SMIRNOV: You have insulted me, madam.

MRS. POPOV: What of it? Do you think I'm scared of you?

SMIRNOV: So you think you can get away with it because you're a woman.

A creature of poetry and romance, huh? Well, it doesn't go down with me. I hereby challenge you to a duel.

LUKA: Mercy on us! Holy saints alive! Water!

SMIRNOV: I propose we shoot it out.

MRS. POPOV: Trying to scare me again? Just because you have big fists and a voice like a bull? You're a brute.

SMIRNOV: No one insults Grigory S. Smirnov with impunity! And I don't care if you *are* a female.

MRS. POPOV *trying to outshout him:*   Brute, brute, brute!

SMIRNOV: The sexes are equal, are they? Fine: then it's just prejudice to expect men alone to pay for insults. I hereby challenge—

MRS. POPOV *screaming:*   All right! You want to shoot it out? All right! Let's shoot it out!

SMIRNOV: And let it be here and now!

MRS. POPOV: Here and now! All right! I'll have Popov's pistols here in one minute! *Walks away, then turns.* Putting one of Popov's bullets through your silly head will be a pleasure! Au revoir. *Exit.*

SMIRNOV: I'll bring her down like a duck, a sitting duck. I'm not one of your little poets, I'm no little subaltern with his first moustache. No, sir, there's no weaker sex where I'm concerned!

LUKA: Sir! Master! *He goes down on his knees.* Take pity on a poor old man, and do me a favour: go away. It was bad enough before, you nearly scared me to death. But a duel—!

SMIRNOV *ignoring him:*   A duel! That's equality of the sexes for you! That's women's emancipation! Just as a matter of principle I'll bring her down like a duck. But what a woman! 'Putting one of Popov's bullets through your silly head . . .' Her cheeks were flushed, her eyes were gleaming! And, by God, she's accepted the challenge! I never knew a woman like this before!

LUKA: Sir! Master! Please go away! I'll always pray for you!

SMIRNOV *again ignoring him:*   What a woman! Phew!! *She's* no sour puss, *she's* no cry baby. She's fire and brimstone. She's a human cannon ball. What a shame I have to kill her!

LUKA *weeping:*   Please, kind sir, please, go away!

SMIRNOV *as before:*   I like her, isn't that funny! With those dimples and all? I like her. I'm even prepared to consider letting her off that debt. And where's my rage? It's gone. I never knew a woman like this before. *Enter* MRS. POPOV *with pistols.*

MRS. POPOV *boldly:*   Pistols, Mr. Smirnov! *Matter of fact.* But before we start, you'd better show me how it's done, I'm not too familiar with these things. In fact I never gave a pistol a second look.

LUKA: Lord, have mercy on us, I must go hunt up the gardener and the coachman. Why has this catastrophe fallen upon us, O Lord? *Exit.*

SMIRNOV *examining the pistols:*   Well, it's like this. There are several makes: one is the Mortimer, with capsules, especially constructed for dueling. What you have here are Smith and Wesson triple-action revolvers, with extractor, first-rate job, worth ninety rubles at the very least. You hold it this way. *Aside.* My God, what eyes she has! They're setting me on fire.

MRS. POPOV: This way?

SMIRNOV: Yes, that's right. You cock the trigger, take aim like this, head up, arm out like this. Then you just press with this finger here, and it's all over. The main thing is, keep cool, take slow aim, and don't let your arm jump.

MRS. POPOV: I see. And if it's inconvenient to do the job here, we can go out in the garden.

SMIRNOV: Very good. Of course, I should warn you: I'll be firing in the air.

MRS. POPOV: What? This is the end. Why?

SMIRNOV: Oh, well—because—for private reasons.

MRS. POPOV: Scared, huh? *She laughs heartily.* Now don't you try to get out of it, Mr. Smirnov. My blood is up. I won't be happy till I've drilled a hole through that skull of yours. Follow me. What's the matter? Scared?

SMIRNOV: That's right. I'm scared.

MRS. POPOV: Oh, come on, what's the matter with you?

SMIRNOV: Well, um, Mrs. Popov, I, um, I like you.

MRS. POPOV *laughing bitterly:* Good God! He likes me, does he? The gall of the man. *Showing him the door.* You may leave, Mr. Smirnov.

SMIRNOV *quietly puts the gun down, takes his hat, and walks to the door. Then he stops and the pair look at each other without a word. Then, approaching gingerly:* Listen, Mrs. Popov. Are you still mad at me? I'm in the devil of a temper myself, of course. But then, you see—what I mean is—it's this way—the fact is—*Roaring.* Well, is it my fault, damn it, if I like you? *Clutches the back of a chair. It breaks.* Christ, what fragile furniture you have here. I like you. Know what I mean? I could fall in love with you.

MRS. POPOV: I hate you. Get out!

SMIRNOV: What a woman! I never saw anything like it. Oh, I'm lost, I'm done for, I'm a mouse in a trap.

MRS. POPOV: Leave this house, or I shoot!

SMIRNOV: Shoot away! What bliss to die of a shot that was fired by that little velvet hand! To die gazing into those enchanting eyes. I'm out of my mind. I know: you must decide at once. Think for one second, then decide. Because if I leave now, I'll never be back. Decide! I'm a pretty decent chap. Landed gentleman, I should say. Ten thousand a year. Good stable. Throw a kopeck up in the air, and I'll put a bullet through it. Will you marry me?

MRS. POPOV *indignant, brandishing the gun:* We'll shoot it out! Get going! Take your pistol!

SMIRNOV: I'm out of my mind. I don't understand anything any more. *Shouting.* You there! That vodka!

MRS. POPOV: No excuses! No delays! We'll shoot it out!

SMIRNOV: I'm out of my mind. I'm falling in love. I *have* fallen in love. *He takes her hand vigorously; she squeals.* I love you. *He goes down on his knees.* I love you as I've never loved before. I jilted twelve, and was jilted by nine others. But I didn't love a one of them as I love you. I'm full of tender emotion. I'm melting like butter. I'm weak as water. I'm on my knees like a fool, and I offer you my hand. It's a shame, it's a disgrace. I haven't been in love in five years. I took a vow against it. And now, all of a sudden, to be swept off my feet, it's a scandal. I offer you my hand, dear lady. Will you or won't you? You won't? Then don't! *He rises and walks toward the door*.

MRS. POPOV: I didn't say anything.

SMIRNOV *stopping:*   What?

MRS. POPOV: Oh, nothing, you can go. Well, no, just a minute. No, you can go. Go! I detest you! But, just a moment. Oh, if you knew how furious I feel! *Throws the gun on the table*. My fingers have gone to sleep holding that horrid thing. *She is tearing her handkerchief to shreds*. And what are you standing around for? Get out of here!

SMIRNOV: Goodbye.

MRS. POPOV: Go, go, go! *Shouting*. Where are you going? Wait a minute! No, no, it's all right, just go. I'm fighting mad. Don't come near me, don't come near me!

SMIRNOV *who is coming near her:*   I'm pretty disgusted with myself—falling in love like a kid, going down on my knees like some moongazing whippersnapper, the very thought gives me gooseflesh. *Rudely*. I love you. But it doesn't make sense. Tomorrow, I have to pay that interest, and we've already started mowing. *He puts his arm about her waist*. I shall never forgive myself for this.

MRS. POPOV: Take your hands off me, I hate you! Let's shoot it out!

A long kiss. Enter LUKA *with an axe, the* GARDENER *with a rake, the* COACH-MAN *with a pitchfork,* HIRED MEN *with sticks.*

LUKA *seeing the kiss:*   Mercy on us! Holy saints above!

MRS. POPOV *dropping her eyes:*   Luka, tell them in the stable that Toby is *not* to have any oats today.

Translated by Eric Bentley

BETH HENLEY (b. 1952)

Crimes of the Heart

Beth Henley was born in Jackson, Mississippi, and studied drama at Southern Methodist University. *Crimes of the Heart*, first performed in 1979, won the Pulitzer Prize for Drama and the Drama Critics Circle Award in 1981. Her other plays include *The Miss Firecracker Contest* (1979) and *The Wake of Jamey Foster* (1981). She lives in Los Angeles.

CHARACTERS

LENNY MAGRATH, *thirty, the oldest sister*
CHICK BOYLE, *twenty-nine, the sister's first cousin*

DOC PORTER, *thirty, Meg's old boyfriend*
MEG MAGRATH, *twenty-seven, the middle sister*
BABE BOTRELLE, *twenty-four, the youngest sister*
BARNETTE LLOYD, *twenty-six, Babe's lawyer*

THE SETTING

The setting of the entire play is the kitchen in the MaGrath sisters' house in Hazlehurst, Mississippi, a small Southern town. The old-fashioned kitchen is unusually spacious, but there is a lived-in, cluttered look about it. There are four different entrances and exits to the kitchen: the back door, the door leading to the dining room and the front of the house, a door leading to the downstairs bedroom, and a staircase leading to the upstairs room. There is a table near the center of the room, and a cot has been set up in one of the corners.

THE TIME

In the fall, five years after Hurricane Camille.

ACT I

The lights go up on the empty kitchen. It is late afternoon. LENNY MAGRATH, *a thirty-year-old woman with a round figure and face, enters from the back door carrying a white suitcase, a saxophone case, and a brown paper sack. She sets the suitcase and the sax case down and takes the brown sack to the kitchen table. After glancing quickly at the door, she gets the cookie jar from the kitchen counter, a box of matches from the stove, and then brings both objects back to the kitchen table. Excitedly, she reaches into the brown sack and pulls out a package of birthday candles. She quickly opens the package and removes a candle. She tries to stick the candle onto a cookie—it falls off. She sticks the candle in again, but the cookie is too hard and it crumbles. Frantically, she gets a second cookie from the jar. She strikes a match, lights the candle, and begins dripping wax onto the cookie. Just as she is beginning to smile we hear* CHICK'S *voice from offstage.*

CHICK'S VOICE: Lenny! Oh, Lenny! LENNY *quickly blows out the candle and stuffs the cookie and candle into her dress pocket.* CHICK, *twenty-nine, enters from the back door. She is a brightly dressed matron with yellow hair and shiny red lips.*
CHICK: Hi! I saw your car pull up.
LENNY: Hi.
CHICK: Well, did you see today's paper?

LENNY *nods.*

CHICK: It's just too awful! It's just way too awful! How I'm gonna continue holding my head up high in this community, I do not know. Did you remember to pick up those pantyhose for me?

LENNY: They're in the sack.

CHICK: Well, thank goodness, at least I'm not gonna have to go into town wearing holes in my stockings. *She gets the package, tears it open, and proceeds to take off one pair of stockings and put on another throughout the following scene. There should be something slightly grotesque about this woman changing her stockings in the kitchen.*

LENNY: Did Uncle Watson call?

CHICK: Yes, Daddy has called me twice already. He said Babe's ready to come home. We've got to get right over and pick her up before they change their simple minds.

LENNY, *hesitantly:* Oh, I know, of course, it's just—

CHICK: What?

LENNY: Well, I was hoping Meg would call.

CHICK: Meg?

LENNY: Yes, I sent her a telegram: about Babe, and—

CHICK: A telegram?! Couldn't you just phone her up?

LENNY: Well, no, 'cause her phone's . . . out of order.

CHICK: Out of order?

LENNY: Disconnected. I don't know what.

CHICK: Well, that sounds like Meg. My, these are snug. Are you sure you bought my right size?

LENNY, *looking at the box:* Size extra-petite.

CHICK: Well, they're skimping on the nylon material. *Struggling to pull up the stockings:* That's all there is to it. Skimping on the nylon. *She finishes one leg and starts the other.* Now, just what all did you say in this "telegram" to Meg?

LENNY: I don't recall exactly. I, well, I just told her to come on home.

CHICK: To come on home! Why, Lenora Josephine, have you lost your only brain, or what?

LENNY, *nervously, as she begins to pick up the mess of dirty stockings and plastic wrappings:* But Babe wants Meg home. She asked me to call her.

CHICK: I'm not talking about what Babe wants.

LENNY: Well, what then?

CHICK: Listen, Lenora, I think it's pretty accurate to assume that after this morning's paper, Babe's gonna be incurring some mighty negative publicity around this town. And Meg's appearance isn't gonna help out a bit.

LENNY: What's wrong with Meg?

CHICK: She had a loose reputation in high school.

LENNY, *weakly:* She was popular.

CHICK: She was known all over Copiah County as cheap Christmas trash, and that was the least of it. There was that whole sordid affair with Doc Porter, leaving him a cripple.

LENNY: A cripple—he's got a limp. Just kind of, barely a limp.

CHICK: Well, his mother was going to keep *me* out of the Ladies' Social League because of it.

LENNY: What?

CHICK: That's right. I never told you, but I had to go plead with that mean old woman and convinced her that I was just as appalled with what Meg had done as she was, and that I was only a first cousin anyway and I could hardly be blamed for all the skeletons in the MaGraths' closet. It was humiliating. I tell you, she even brought up your mother's death. And that poor cat.

LENNY: Oh! Oh! Oh, please, Chick! I'm sorry. But you're in the Ladies' League now.

CHICK: Yes. That's true, I am. But frankly, if Mrs. Porter hadn't developed that tumor in her bladder, I wouldn't be in the club today, much less a committee head. *As she brushes her hair:* Anyway, you be a sweet potato and wait right here for Meg to call, so's you can convince her not to come back home. It would make things a whole lot easier on everybody. Don't you think it really would?

LENNY: Probably.

CHICK: Good, then suit yourself. How's my hair?

LENNY: Fine.

CHICK: Not pooching out in the back, is it?

LENNY: No.

CHICK, *cleaning the hair from her brush:* All right then, I'm on my way. I've got Annie May over there keeping an eye on Peekay and Buck Jr., but I don't trust her with them for long periods of time. *Dropping the ball of hair onto the floor:* Her mind is like a loose sieve. Honestly it is. *As she puts the brush back into her purse:* Oh! Oh! Oh! I almost forgot. Here's a present for you. Happy birthday to Lenny, from the Buck Boyles! *She takes a wrapped package from her bag and hands it to* LENNY.

LENNY: Why, thank you, Chick. It's so nice to have you remember my birthday every year like you do.

CHICK, *modestly:* Oh, well, now, that's just the way I am, I suppose. That's just the way I was brought up to be. Well, why don't you go on and open up the present?

LENNY: All right. *She starts to unwrap the gift.*

CHICK: It's a box of candy—assorted crèmes.

LENNY: Candy—that's always a nice gift.

CHICK: And you have a sweet tooth, don't you?

LENNY: I guess.

CHICK: Well, I'm glad you like it.

LENNY: I do.

CHICK: Oh, speaking of which, remember that little polka-dot dress you got Peekay for her fifth birthday last month?

LENNY: The red-and-white one?

CHICK: Yes; well, the first time I put it in the washing machine, I mean the very first time, it fell all to pieces. Those little polka dots just dropped right off in the water.

LENNY, *crushed:* Oh, no. Well, I'll get something else for her, then—a little toy.

CHICK: Oh, no, no, no, no, no! We wouldn't hear of it! I just wanted to let you know so you wouldn't go and waste any more of your hard-earned money on that make of dress. Those inexpensive brands just don't hold up. I'm sorry, but not in these modern washing machines.

DOC PORTER'S VOICE: Hello! Hello, Lenny!

CHICK, *taking over:* Oh, look, it's Doc Porter! Come on in Doc! Please come right on in!

DOC PORTER *enters through the back door. He is carrying a large sack of pecans. DOC is an attractively worn man with a slight limp that adds rather than detracts from his quiet seductive quality. He is thirty years old, but appears slightly older.*

CHICK: Well, how are you doing? How in the world are you doing?

DOC: Just fine, Chick.

CHICK: And how are you liking it now that you're back in Hazlehurst?

DOC: Oh, I'm finding it somewhat enjoyable.

CHICK: Somewhat! Only somewhat! Will you listen to him! What a silly, silly, silly man! Well, I'm on my way. I've got some people waiting on me. *Whispering to* DOC: It's Babe. I'm on my way to pick her up.

DOC: Oh.

CHICK: Well, goodbye! Farewell and goodbye!

LENNY: 'Bye.

CHICK *exits.*

DOC: Hello.

LENNY: Hi. I guess you heard about the thing with Babe.

DOC: Yeah.

LENNY: It was in the newspaper.

DOC: Uh huh.

LENNY: What a mess.

DOC: Yeah.

LENNY: Well, come on and sit down. I'll heat us up some coffee.

DOC: That's okay. I can only stay a minute. I have to pick up Scott; he's at the dentist.

LENNY: Oh; well, I'll heat some up for myself. I'm kinda thirsty for a cup of hot coffee. *She puts the coffeepot on the burner.*

DOC: Lenny—

LENNY: What?

DOC, *not able to go on:* Ah . . .

LENNY: Yes?

DOC: Here, some pecans for you. *He hands her the sack.*

LENNY: Why, thank you, Doc. I love pecans.

DOC: My wife and Scott picked them up around the yard.

LENNY: Well, I can use them to make a pie. A pecan pie.

DOC: Yeah. Look, Lenny, I've got some bad news for you.

LENNY: What?

DOC: Well, you know, you've been keeping Billy Boy out on our farm; he's been grazing out there.

LENNY: Yes—

DOC: Well, last night, Billy Boy died.

LENNY: He died?

DOC: Yeah. I'm sorry to tell you when you've got all this on you, but I thought you'd want to know.

LENNY: Well, yeah. I do. He died?

DOC: Uh huh. He was struck by lightning.

LENNY: Struck by lightning? In that storm yesterday?

DOC: That's what we think.

LENNY: Gosh, struck by lightning. I've had Billy Boy so long. You know. Ever since I was ten years old.

DOC: Yeah. He was a mighty old horse.

LENNY, *stung:* Mighty old.

DOC: Almost twenty years old.

LENNY: That's right, twenty years. 'Cause; ah, I'm thirty years old today. Did you know that?

DOC: No, Lenny, I didn't know. Happy birthday.

LENNY: Thanks. *She begins to cry.*

DOC: Oh, come on now, Lenny. Come on. Hey, hey, now. You know I can't stand it when you MaGrath women start to cry. You know it just gets me.

LENNY: Oh ho! Sure! You mean when Meg cries! Meg's the one you could never stand to watch cry! Not me! I could fill up a pig's trough!

DOC: Now, Lenny . . . stop it. Come on. Jesus!

LENNY: Okay! Okay! I don't know what's wrong with me. I don't mean to make a scene. I've been on this crying jag. *She blows her nose.* All this stuff with Babe, and Old Granddaddy's gotten worse in the hospital, and I can't get in touch with Meg.

DOC: You tried calling Meggy?

LENNY: Yes.

DOC: Is she coming home?

LENNY: Who knows. She hasn't called me. That's what I'm waiting here for—hoping she'll call.

DOC: She still living in California?

LENNY: Yes; in Hollywood.

DOC: Well, give me a call if she gets in. I'd like to see her.

LENNY: Oh, you would, huh?

DOC: Yeah, Lenny, sad to say, but I would.

LENNY: It is sad. It's very sad indeed.

They stare at each other, then look away. There is a moment of tense silence.

DOC: Hey, Jell-O Face, your coffee's boiling.

LENNY, *going to check:* Oh, it is? Thanks. *After she checks the pot:* Look, you'd better go on and pick Scott up. You don't want him to have to wait for you.

DOC: Yeah, you're right. Poor kid. It's his first time at the dentist.

LENNY: Poor thing.

DOC: Well, 'bye. I'm sorry to have to tell you about your horse.

LENNY: Oh, I know. Tell Joan thanks for picking up the pecans.
DOC: I will. *He starts to leave.*
LENNY: Oh, how's the baby?
DOC: She's fine. Real pretty. She, ah, holds your finger in her hand; like this.
LENNY: Oh, that's cute.
DOC: Yeah. 'Bye, Lenny.
LENNY: 'Bye.

DOC *exits.* LENNY *stares after him for a moment, then goes and sits back down at the kitchen table. She reaches into her pocket and pulls out a somewhat crumbled cookie and a wax candle. She lights the candle again, lets the wax drip onto the cookie, then sticks the candle on top of the cookie. She begins to sing the "Happy Birthday" song to herself. At the end of the song she pauses, silently makes a wish, and blows out the candle. She waits a moment, then relights the candle, and repeats her actions, only this time making a different wish at the end of the song. She starts to repeat the procedure for the third time, as the phone rings. She goes to answer it.*

LENNY: Hello . . . Oh, hello, Lucille, how's Zackery? . . . Oh, no! . . . Oh, I'm so sorry. Of course, it must be grueling for you . . . Yes, I understand. Your only brother . . . No, she's not here yet. Chick just went to pick her up . . . Oh, now, Lucille, she's still his wife, I'm sure she'll be interested . . . Well, you can just tell me the information and I'll relate it all to her . . . Uh hum, his liver's saved. Oh, that's good news! . . . Well, of course, when you look at it like that . . . Breathing stabilized . . . Damage to the spinal column, not yet determined . . . Okay . . . Yes, Lucille, I've got it all down . . . Uh huh, I'll give her that message. 'Bye, 'bye.

LENNY *drops the pencil and paper. She sighs deeply, wipes her cheeks with the back of her hand, and goes to the stove to pour herself a cup of coffee. After a few moments, the front door is heard slamming.* LENNY *starts. A whistle is heard, then* MEG'S *voice.*

MEG'S VOICE: I'm home! *She whistles the family whistle.* Anybody home?
LENNY: Meg? Meg!

MEG, *twenty-seven, enters from the dining room. She has sad, magic eyes and wears a hat. She carries a worn-out suitcase.*

MEG, *dropping her suitcase, running to hug* LENNY: Lenny—
LENNY: Well, Meg! Why, Meg! Oh, Meggy! Why didn't you call? Did you fly in? You didn't take a cab, did you? Why didn't you give us a call?
MEG, *overlapping:* Oh, Lenny! Why, Lenny! Dear Lenny! *Then she looks at* LENNY's *face.* My God, we're getting so old! Oh, I called, for heaven's sake. Of course, I called!

LENNY: Well, I never talked to you—

MEG: Well, I know! I let the phone ring right off the hook!

LENNY: Well, as a matter of fact, I was out most of the morning seeing to Babe—

MEG: Now, just what's all this business about Babe? How could you send me such a telegram about Babe? And Zackery! You say somebody's shot Zackery?

LENNY: Yes, they have.

MEG: Well, good Lord! Is he dead?

LENNY: No. But he's in the hospital. He was shot in his stomach.

MEG: In his stomach! How awful! Do they know who shot him? LENNY *nods*. Well, who? Who was it? Who? Who?

LENNY: Babe! They're all saying Babe shot him! They took her to jail! And they're saying she shot him! They're all saying it! It's horrible! It's awful!

MEG, *overlapping*:   Jail! Good Lord, jail! Well, who? Who's saying it? Who?

LENNY: Everyone! The policemen, the sheriff, Zackery, even Babe's saying it! Even Babe herself!

MEG: Well, for God's sake. For God's sake.

LENNY, *overlapping as she falls apart*:   It's horrible! It's horrible! It's just horrible!

MEG: Now calm down, Lenny. Just calm down. Would you like a Coke? Here, I'll get you some Coke. *She gets a Coke from the refrigerator. She opens it and downs a large swig.* Why? Why would she shoot him? Why? *She hands the Coke bottle to* LENNY.

LENNY: I talked to her this morning and I asked her that very question. I said, "Babe, why would you shoot Zackery? He was your own husband. Why would you shoot him?" And do you know what she said? MEG *shakes her head.* She said, " 'Cause I didn't like his looks. I just didn't like his looks."

MEG, *after a pause*:   Well, I don't like his looks.

LENNY: But you didn't shoot him! You wouldn't shoot a person 'cause you didn't like their looks! You wouldn't do that! Oh, I hate to say this—I do hate to say this—but I believe Babe is ill. I mean in-her-head ill.

MEG: Oh, now, Lenny, don't you say that! There're plenty of good sane reasons to shoot another person, and I'm sure that Babe had one. Now, what we've got to do is get her the best lawyer in town. Do you have any ideas on who's the best lawyer in town?

LENNY: Well, Zackery is, of course; but he's been shot!

MEG: Well, count him out! Just count him and his whole firm out!

LENNY: Anyway, you don't have to worry, she's already got her lawyer.

MEG: She does? Who?

LENNY: Barnette Lloyd. Annie Lloyd's boy. He just opened his office here in town. And Uncle Watson said we'd be doing Annie a favor by hiring him up.

MEG: Doing Annie a favor? Doing Annie a favor! Well, what about Babe? Have you thought about Babe? Do we want to do her a favor of thirty or forty years in jail? Have you thought about that?

LENNY: Now, don't snap at me! Just don't snap at me! I try to do what's right! All this responsibility keeps falling on my shoulders, and I try to do what's right!

MEG: Well, boo hoo, hoo, hoo! And how in the hell could you send me such a telegram about Babe!

LENNY: Well, if you had a phone, or if you didn't live way out there in Hollywood and not even come home for Christmas, maybe I wouldn't have to pay all that money to send you a telegram!

MEG, *overlapping:* BABE'S IN TERRIBLE TROUBLE—STOP! ZACKERY'S BEEN SHOT—STOP! COME HOME IMMEDIATELY—STOP! STOP! STOP!

LENNY: And what was that you said about how old we're getting? When you looked at my face, you said, "My God, we're getting so old!" But you didn't mean we—you meant me! Didn't you? I'm thirty years old today and my face is getting all pinched up and my hair is falling out in the comb.

MEG: Why, Lenny! It's your birthday, October 23. How could I forget. Happy birthday!

LENNY: Well, it's not. I'm thirty years old and Billy Boy died last night. He was struck by lightning. He was struck dead.

MEG, *reaching for a cigarette:* Struck dead. Oh, what a mess. What a mess. Are you really thirty? Then I must be twenty-seven and Babe is twenty-four. My God, we're getting so old.

They are silent for several moments as MEG *drags off her cigarette and* LENNY *drinks her Coke.*

MEG: What's the cot doing in the kitchen?

LENNY: Well, I rolled it out when Old Granddaddy got sick. So I could be close and hear him at night if he needed something.

MEG, *glancing toward the door leading to the downstairs bedroom:* Is Old Granddaddy here?

LENNY: Why, no. Old Granddaddy's at the hospital.

MEG: Again?

LENNY: Meg!

MEG: What?

LENNY: I wrote you all about it. He's been in the hospital over three months straight.

MEG: He has?

LENNY: Don't you remember? I wrote you about all those blood vessels popping in his brain?

MEG: Popping—

LENNY: And how he was so anxious to hear from you and to find out about your singing career. I wrote it all to you. How they have to feed him through those tubes now. Didn't you get my letters?

MEG: Oh, I don't know, Lenny. I guess I did. To tell you the truth, sometimes I kinda don't read your letters.

LENNY: What?

MEG: I'm sorry. I used to read them. It's just, since Christmas reading them gives me these slicing pains right here in my chest.

LENNY: I see. I see. Is that why you didn't use that money Old Granddaddy sent you to come home Christmas; because you hate us so much? We never did all that much to make you hate us. We didn't!

MEG: Oh, Lenny! Do you think I'd be getting slicing pains in my chest if I didn't care about you? If I hated you? Honestly, now, do you think I would?

LENNY: No.

MEG: Okay, then. Let's drop it. I'm sorry I didn't read your letters. Okay?

LENNY: Okay.

MEG: Anyway, we've got this whole thing with Babe to deal with. The first thing is to get her a good lawyer and get her out of jail.

LENNY: Well, she's out of jail.

MEG: She is?

LENNY: That young lawyer, he's gotten her out.

MEG: Oh, he has?

LENNY: Yes, on bail. Uncle Watson's put it up. Chick's bringing her back right now—she's driving her home.

MEG: Oh; well, that's a relief.

LENNY: Yes, and they're due home any minute now; so we can just wait right here for 'em.

MEG: Well, good. That's good. *As she leans against the counter:* So, Babe shot Zackery Botrelle, the richest and most powerful man in all of Hazlehurst, slap in the gut. It's hard to believe.

LENNY: It certainly is. Little Babe—shooting off a gun.

MEG: Little Babe.

LENNY: She was always the prettiest and most perfect of the three of us. Old Granddaddy used to call her his Dancing Sugar Plum. Why, remember how proud and happy he was the day she married Zackery.

MEG: Yes, I remember. It was his finest hour.

LENNY: He remarked how Babe was gonna skyrocket right to the heights of Hazlehurst society. And how Zackery was just the right man for her whether she knew it now or not.

MEG: Oh, Lordy, Lordy. And what does Old Granddaddy say now?

LENNY: Well, I haven't had the courage to tell him all about this as yet. I thought maybe tonight we could go to visit him at the hospital, and you could talk to him and . . .

MEG: Yeah; well, we'll see. We'll see. Do we have anything to drink around here—to the tune of straight bourbon?

LENNY: No. There's no liquor.

MEG: Hell. *She gets a Coke from the refrigerator and opens it.*

LENNY: Then you *will* go with me to see Old Granddaddy at the hospital tonight?

MEG: Of course. *She goes to her purse and gets out a bottle of Empirin. She takes out a tablet and puts it on her tongue.* Brother, I know he's gonna go on about my singing career. Just like he always does.

LENNY: Well, how is your career going?

MEG: It's not.

LENNY: Why, aren't you still singing at that club down on Malibu beach?

MEG: No. Not since Christmas.

LENNY: Well, then, are you singing someplace new?

MEG: No, I'm not singing. I'm not singing at all.

LENNY: Oh. Well, what do you do then?

MEG: What I do is I pay cold-storage bills for a dog-food company. That's what I do.

LENNY, *trying to be helpful:*   Gosh, don't you think it'd be a good idea to stay in the show business field?

MEG: Oh, maybe.

LENNY: Like Old Granddaddy says, "With your talent, all you need is exposure. Then you can make your own breaks!" Did you hear his suggestion about getting your foot put in one of those blocks of cement they've got out there? He thinks that's real important.

MEG: Yeah. I think I've heard that. And I'll probably hear it again when I go to visit him at the hospital tonight; so let's just drop it. Okay? *She notices the sack of pecans.* What's this? Pecans? Great, I love pecans! *She takes out two pecans and tries to open them by cracking them together.* Come on . . . Crack, you demons! Crack!

LENNY: We have a nutcracker!

MEG, *trying with her teeth:*   Ah, where's the sport in a nutcracker? Where's the challenge?

LENNY, *getting the nutcracker:*   It's over here in the utensil drawer.

As LENNY *gets the nutcracker,* MEG *opens the pecan by stepping on it with her shoe.*

MEG: There! Open! *She picks up the crumbled pecan and eats it.* Mmmm, delicious. Delicious. Where'd you get the fresh pecans?

LENNY: Oh . . . I don't know.

MEG: They sure are tasty.

LENNY: Doc Porter brought them over.

MEG: Doc. What's Doc doing here in town?

LENNY: Well, his father died a couple of months ago. Now he's back home seeing to his property.

MEG: Gosh, the last I heard of Doc, he was up in the East painting the walls of houses to earn a living. *Amused:* Heard he was living with some Yankee woman who made clay pots.

LENNY: Joan.

MEG: What?

LENNY: Her name's Joan. She came down here with him. That's one of her pots. Doc's married to her.

MEG: Married—

LENNY: Uh huh.

MEG: Doc married a Yankee?

LENNY: That's right; and they've got two kids.

MEG: Kids—

LENNY: A boy and a girl.

MEG: God. Then his kids must be half Yankee.

LENNY: I suppose.

MEG: God. That really gets me. I don't know why, but somehow that really gets me.

LENNY: I don't know why it should.

MEG: And what a stupid-looking pot! Who'd buy it, anyway?
LENNY: Wait—I think that's them. Yeah, that's Chick's car! Oh, there's Babe! Hello, Babe! They're home, Meg! They're home.

MEG *hides.*

BABE'S VOICE: Lenny! I'm home! I'm free!

BABE, *twenty-four, enters exuberantly. She has an angelic face and fierce, volatile eyes. She carries a pink pocketbook.*

BABE: I'm home!

MEG *jumps out of hiding.*

BABE: Oh, Meg— Look, it's Meg! *Running to hug her:* Meg! When did you get home?
MEG: Just now!
BABE: Well, it's so good to see you! I'm so glad you're home! I'm so relieved.

CHICK *enters.*

MEG: Why, Chick; hello.
CHICK: Hello, Cousin Margaret. What brings you back to Hazlehurst?
MEG: Oh, I came on home . . . *Turning to* BABE: I came on home to see about Babe.
BABE, *running to hug* MEG: Oh, Meg—
MEG: How are things with you, Babe?
CHICK: Well, they are dismal, if you want my opinion. She is refusing to cooperate with her lawyer, that nice-looking young Lloyd boy. She won't tell any of us why she committed this heinous crime, except to say that she didn't like Zackery's looks—
BABE: Oh, look, Lenny brought my suitcase from home! And my saxophone! Thank you! *She runs over to the cot and gets out her saxophone.*
CHICK: Now, that young lawyer is coming over here this afternoon, and when he gets here he expects to get some concrete answers! That's what he expects! No more of this nonsense and stubbornness from you, Rebecca MaGrath, or they'll put you in jail and throw away the key!
BABE, *overlapping to* MEG: Meg, come look at my new saxophone. I went to Jackson and bought it used. Feel it. It's so heavy.
MEG, *overlapping* CHICK: It's beautiful.

The room goes silent.

CHICK: Isn't that right, won't they throw away the key?
LENNY: Well, honestly, I don't know about that—
CHICK: They will! And leave you there to rot. So, Rebecca, what are you going to tell Mr. Lloyd about shooting Zackery when he gets here?

What are your reasons going to be?

BABE, *glaring:* That I didn't like his looks! I just didn't like his stinking looks! And I don't like yours much, either, Chick the Stick! So just leave me alone! I mean it! Leave me alone! Oooh! *She exits up the stairs.*

There is a long moment of silence.

CHICK: Well, I was only trying to warn her that she's going to have to help herself. It's just that she doesn't understand how serious the situation is. Does she? She doesn't have the vaguest idea. Does she, now?

LENNY: Well, it's true, she does seem a little confused.

CHICK: And that's putting it mildly, Lenny honey. That's putting it mighty mild. So, Margaret, how's your singing career going? We keep looking for your picture in the movie magazines.

MEG *moves to light a cigarette.*

CHICK: You know, you shouldn't smoke. It causes cancer. Cancer of the lungs. They say each cigarette is just a little stick of cancer. A little death stick.

MEG: That's what I like about it, Chick—taking a drag off of death. *She takes a long, deep drag.* Mmm! Gives me a sense of controlling my own destiny. What power! What exhilaration! Want a drag?

LENNY, *trying to break the tension:* Ah, Zackery's liver's been saved! His sister called up and said his liver was saved. Isn't that good news?

MEG: Well, yes, that's fine news. Mighty fine news. Why, I've been told that the liver's a powerful important bodily organ. I believe it's used to absorb all of our excess bile.

LENNY: Yes—well—it's been saved.

The phone rings. LENNY *gets it.*

MEG: So! Did you hear all that good news about the liver, Little Chicken!

CHICK: I heard it. And don't you call me Chicken! MEG *clucks like a chicken.* I've told you a hundred times if I've told you once not to call me Chicken. You cannot call me Chicken.

LENNY: . . . Oh, no! . . . Of course, we'll be right over! 'Bye! *She hangs up the phone.* That was Annie May—Peekay and Buck Jr. have eaten paint!

CHICK: Oh, no! Are they all right? They're not sick? They're not sick, are they?

LENNY: I don't know. I don't know. Come on. We've got to run on next door.

CHICK, *overlapping:* Oh, God! Oh, please! Please let them be all right! Don't let them die! Please, don't let them die!

CHICK *runs off howling, with* LENNY *following after,* MEG *sits alone, finishing her cigarette. After a moment,* BABE'S *voice is heard.*

BABE'S VOICE: Pst—Psst!

MEG *looks around*. BABE *comes tiptoeing down the stairs*.

BABE: Has she gone?
MEG: She's gone. Peekay and Buck Jr. just ate their paints.
BABE: What idiots.
MEG: Yeah.
BABE: You know, Chick's hated us ever since we had to move here from Vicksburg to live with Old Grandmama and Old Granddaddy.
MEG: She's an idiot.
BABE: Yeah. Do you know what she told me this morning while I was still behind bars and couldn't get away?
MEG: What?
BABE: She told me how embarrassing it was for her all those years ago, you know, when Mama—
MEG: Yeah, down in the cellar.
BABE: She said our mama had shamed the entire family, and we were known notoriously all through Hazlehurst. *About to cry:* Then she went on to say how I would now be getting just as much bad publicity, and humiliating her and the family all over again.
MEG: Ah, forget it, Babe. Just forget it.
BABE: I told her, "Mama got national coverage! National!" And if Zackery wasn't a senator from Copiah County, I probably wouldn't even be getting statewide.
MEG: Of course you wouldn't.
BABE, *after a pause:*   Gosh, sometimes I wonder . . .
MEG: What?
BABE: Why she did it. Why Mama hung herself.
MEG: I don't know. She had a bad day. A real bad day. You know how it feels on a real bad day.
BABE: And that old yellow cat. It was sad about that old cat.
MEG: Yeah.
BABE: I bet if Daddy hadn't of left us, they'd still be alive.
MEG: Oh, I don't know.
BABE: 'Cause it was after he left that she started spending whole days just sitting there and smoking on the back porch steps. She'd sling her ashes down onto the different bugs and ants that'd be passing by.
MEG: Yeah. Well, I'm glad he left.
BABE: That old yellow cat'd stay back there with her. I thought if she felt something for anyone it woulda been that old cat. Guess I musta been mistaken.
MEG: God, he was a bastard. Really, with his white teeth. Daddy was such a bastard.
BABE: Was he? I don't remember?

MEG *blows out a mouthful of smoke*.

BABE, *after a moment, uneasily:* I think I'm gonna make some lemonade. You want some?

MEG: Sure.

BABE *cuts lemons, dumps sugar, stirs ice cubes, etc., throughout the following exchange.*

MEG: Babe. Why won't you talk? Why won't you tell anyone about shooting Zackery?

BABE: Oooh—

MEG: Why not? You must have had a good reason. Didn't you?

BABE: I guess I did.

MEG: Well, what was it?

BABE: I . . . I can't say.

MEG: Why not? *Pause.* Babe, why not? You can tell me.

BABE: 'Cause . . . I'm sort of . . . protecting someone.

MEG: Protecting someone? Oh, Babe, then you really didn't shoot him! I knew you couldn't have done it! I knew it!

BABE: No, I shot him. I shot him all right. I meant to kill him. I was aiming for his heart, but I guess my hands were shaking and I—just got him in the stomach.

MEG, *collapsing:* I see.

BABE, *stirring the lemonade:* So I'm guilty. And I'm just gonna have to take my punishment and go on to jail.

MEG: Oh, Babe—

BABE: Don't worry, Meg, jail's gonna be a relief to me. I can learn to play my new saxophone. I won't have to live with Zackery anymore. And I won't have his snoopy old sister, Lucille, coming over and pushing me around. Jail will be a relief. Here's your lemonade.

MEG: Thanks.

BABE: It taste okay?

MEG: Perfect.

BABE: I like a lot of sugar in mine. I'm gonna add some more sugar.

BABE *goes to add more sugar to her lemonade as* LENNY *bursts through the back door in a state of excitement and confusion.*

LENNY: Well, it looks like the paint is primarily on their arms and faces, but Chick wants me to drive them all over to Dr. Winn's just to make sure. *She grabs her car keys from the counter, and as she does so, she notices the mess of lemons and sugar.* Oh, now, Babe, try not to make a mess here; and be careful with this sharp knife. Honestly, all that sugar's gonna get you sick. Well, 'bye, 'bye. I'll be back soon as I can.

MEG: 'Bye, Lenny.

BABE: 'Bye.

LENNY *exits.*

BABE: Boy, I don't know what's happening to Lenny.

MEG: What do you mean?

BABE: "Don't make a mess; don't make yourself sick; don't cut yourself with that sharp knife." She's turning into Old Grandmama.

MEG: You think so?

BABE: More and more. Do you know she's taken to wearing Old Grandmama's torn sunhat and her green garden gloves?

MEG: Those old lime-green ones?

BABE: Yeah; she works out in the garden wearing the lime-green gloves of a dead woman. Imagine wearing those gloves on your hands.

MEG: Poor Lenny. She needs some love in her life. All she does is work out at that brick yard and take care of Old Granddaddy.

BABE: Yeah. But she's so shy with men.

MEG, *biting into an apple:*   Probably because of that *shrunken* ovary she has.

BABE, *slinging ice cubes:*   Yeah, that *deformed* ovary.

MEG: Old Granddaddy's the one who's made her feel self-conscious about it. It's his fault. The old fool.

BABE: It's so sad.

MEG: God—you know what?

BABE: What?

MEG: I bet Lenny's never even slept with a man. Just think, thirty years old and never even had it once.

BABE, *slyly:*   Oh, I don't know. Maybe she's . . . had it once.

MEG: She has?

BABE: Maybe. I think so.

MEG: When? When?

BABE: Well . . . maybe I shouldn't say—

MEG: Babe!

BABE, *rapidly telling the story:*   All right, then. It was after Old Granddaddy when back to the hospital this second time. Lenny was really in a state of deep depression, I could tell that she was. Then one day she calls me up and asks me to come over and bring along my Polaroid camera. Well, when I arrive she's waiting for me out there in the sun parlor wearing her powder-blue Sunday dress and this old curled-up wig. She confided that she was gonna try sending in her picture to one of those lonely-hearts clubs.

MEG: Oh, my God.

BABE: Lonely Hearts of the South. She'd seen their ad in a magazine.

MEG: Jesus.

BABE: Anyway, I take some snapshots and she sends them on in to the club, and about two weeks later she receives in the mail this whole load of pictures of available men, most of 'em fairly odd-looking. But of course she doesn't call any of 'em up 'cause she's real shy. But one of 'em, this Charlie Hill from Memphis, Tennessee, he calls her.

MEG: He does?

BABE: Yeah. And time goes on and she says he's real funny on the phone, so they decide to get together to meet.

MEG: Yeah?

BABE: Well, he drives down here to Hazlehurst 'bout three or four different times and has supper with her; then one weekend she goes up to Memphis to visit him, and I think that is where it happened.

MEG: What makes you think so?

BABE: Well, when I went to pick her up from the bus depot, she ran off the bus and threw her arms around me and started crying and sobbing as though she'd like to never stop. I asked her, I said, "Lenny, what's the matter?" And she said, "I've done it, Babe! Honey, I have done it!"

MEG, *whispering:*   And you think she meant that she'd done *it?*

BABE, *whispering back, slyly:*   I think so.

MEG: Well, goddamn!

They laugh.

BABE: But she didn't say anything else about it. She just went on to tell me about the boot factory where Charlie worked and what a nice city Memphis was.

MEG: So, what happened to this Charlie?

BABE: Well, he came to Hazlehurst just one more time. Lenny took him over to meet Old Granddaddy at the hospital, and after that they broke it off?

MEG: 'Cause of Old Granddaddy?

BABE: Well, she said it was on account of her missing ovary. That Charlie didn't want to marry her on account of it.

MEG: Ah, how mean. How hateful.

BABE: Oh, it was. He seemed like such a nice man, too—kinda chubby, with red hair and freckles, always telling these funny jokes.

MEG: Hmmm, that just doesn't seem right. Something about that doesn't seem exactly right. *She paces about the kitchen and comes across the box of candy* LENNY *got for her birthday.* Oh, God. "Happy birthday to Lenny, from the Buck Boyles."

BABE: Oh, no! Today's Lenny's birthday!

MEG: That's right.

BABE: I forgot all about it!

MEG: I know. I did, too.

BABE: Gosh, we'll have to order up a big cake for her. She always loves to make those wishes on her birthday cake.

MEG: Yeah, let's get her a big cake! A huge one! *Suddenly noticing the plastic wrapper on the candy box:* Oh, God, that Chick's so cheap!

BABE: What do you mean?

MEG: This plastic has poinsettias on it!

BABE, *running to see:*   Oh, let me see—*She looks at the package with disgust.* Boy, oh, boy! I'm calling that bakery and ordering the very largest size cake they have! That jumbo deluxe!

MEG: Good!

BABE: Why, I imagine they can make one up to be about—*this* big. *She demonstrates.*

MEG: Oh, at least; at least that big. Why, maybe it'll even be *this* big. *She makes a very, very, very large-size cake.*

BABE: You think it could be *that* big?

MEG: Sure!

BABE, *after a moment, getting the idea:*   Or, or what if it were *this* big? *She maps out a cake that covers the room.* What if we get the cake and it's *this* big? *She gulps down a fistful of cake.* Gulp! Gulp! Gulp! Tasty treat!

MEG: Hmmm—I'll have me some more! Give me some more of that birthday cake!

Suddenly there is a loud knock at the door.

BARNETTE'S VOICE: Hello . . . Hello! May I come in?

BABE, *to* MEG, *in a whisper, as she takes cover:*   Who's that?

MEG: I don't know.

BARNETTE'S VOICE: *He is still knocking.* Hello! Hello, Mrs. Botrelle!

BABE: Oh, shoot! It's that lawyer. I don't want to see him.

MEG: Oh, Babe, come on. You've got to see him sometime.

BABE: No, I don't! *She starts up the stairs.* Just tell him I died. I'm going upstairs.

MEG: Oh, Babe! Will you come back here!

BABE, *as she exits:*   You talk to him, please, Meg. Please! I just don't want to see him—

MEG: Babe—Babe! Oh, shit . . . Ah, come on in! Door's open!

BARNETTE LLOYD, *twenty-six, enters carrying a briefcase. He is a slender, intelligent young man with an almost fanatical intensity that he subdues by sheer will.*

BARNETTE: How do you do. I'm Barnette Lloyd.

MEG: Pleased to meet you. I'm Meg MaGrath, Babe's older sister.

BARNETTE: Yes, I know. You're the singer.

MEG: Well, yes . . .

BARNETTE: I came to hear you five different times when you were singing at that club in Biloxi. Greeny's I believe was the name of it.

MEG: Yes, Greeny's.

BARNETTE: You were very good. There was something sad and moving about how you sang those songs. It was like you had some sort of vision. Some special sort of vision.

MEG: Well, thank you. You're very kind. Now . . . about Babe's case—

BARNETTE: Yes?

MEG: We've just got to win it.

BARNETTE: I intend to.

MEG: Of course. But, ah . . . *She looks at him.* Ah, you know, you're very young.

BARNETTE: Yes. I am. I'm young.

MEG: It's just, I'm concerned, Mr. Lloyd—

BARNETTE: Barnette. Please.

MEG: Barnette; that, ah, just maybe we need someone with, well, with more experience. Someone totally familiar with all the ins and outs and the this and thats of the legal dealings and such. As that.

BARNETTE: Ah, you have reservations.

MEG, *relieved:* Reservations. Yes, I have . . . reservations.

BARNETTE: Well, possibly it would help you to know that I graduated first in my class from Ole Miss Law School. I also spent three different summers taking advanced courses in criminal law at Harvard Law School. I made A's in all the given courses. I was fascinated!

MEG: I'm sure.

BARNETTE: And even now, I've just completed one year working with Jackson's top criminal law firm, Manchester and Wayne. I was invaluable to them. Indispensable. They offered to double my percentage if I'd stay on; but I refused. I wanted to return to Hazlehurst and open my own office. The reason being, and this is a key point, that I have a personal vendetta to settle with one Zackery F. Botrelle.

MEG: A personal vendetta?

BARNETTE: Yes, ma'am. You are correct. Indeed, I do.

MEG: Hmmm. A personal vendetta . . . I think I like that. So you have some sort of a personal vendetta to settle with Zackery?

BARNETTE: Precisely. Just between the two of us, I not only intend to keep that sorry s.o.b. from ever being reelected to the state senate by exposing his shady, criminal dealings; but I also intend to decimate his personal credibility by exposing him as a bully, a brute, and a red-neck thug!

MEG: Well; I can see that you're—fanatical about this.

BARNETTE: Yes, I am. I'm sorry if I seem outspoken. But for some reason I feel I can talk to you . . . those songs you sang. Excuse me; I feel like a jackass.

MEG: It's all right. Relax. Relax, Barnette. Let me think this out a minute. *She takes out a cigarette. He lights it for her.* Now just exactly how do you intend to get Babe off? You know, keep her out of jail.

BARNETTE: It seems to me that we can get her off with a plea of self-defense, or possibly we could go with innocent by reason of temporary insanity. But basically I intend to prove that Zackery Botrelle brutalized and tormented this poor woman to such an extent that she had no recourse but to defend herself in the only way she knew how!

MEG: I like that!

BARNETTE: Then, of course, I'm hoping this will break the ice and we'll be able to go on to prove that the man's a total criminal, as well as an abusive bully and contemptible slob!

MEG: That sounds good! To me that sounds very good!

BARNETTE: It's just our basic game plan.

MEG: But now, how are you going to prove all this about Babe being brutalized? We don't want anyone perjured. I mean to commit perjury.

BARNETTE: Perjury? According to my sources, there'll be no need for perjury.

MEG: You mean it's the truth?

BARNETTE: This is a small town, Miss MaGrath. The word gets out.

MEG: It's really the truth?

BARNETTE, *opening his briefcase:*   Just look at this. It's a photostatic copy of Mrs. Botrelle's medical chart over the past four years. Take a good look at it, if you want your blood to boil!

MEG, *looking over the chart:*   What! What! This is maddening. This is madness! Did he do this to her? I'll kill him; I will—I'll fry his blood! Did he do this?

BARNETTE, *alarmed:*   To tell you the truth, I can't say for certain what was accidental and what was not. That's why I need to talk with Mrs. Botrelle. That's why it's very important that I see her!

MEG, *her eyes are wild, as she shoves him toward the door:*   Well, look, I've got to see her first. I've got to talk to her first. What I'll do is I'll give you a call. Maybe you can come back over later on—

BARNETTE: Well, then, here's my card—

MEG: Okay. Goodbye.

BARNETTE: 'Bye!

MEG: Oh, wait! Wait! There's one problem with you.

BARNETTE: What?

MEG: What if you get so fanatically obsessed with this vendetta thing that you forget about Babe? You forget about her and sell her down the river just to get at Zackery. What about that?

BARNETTE: I—wouldn't do that.

MEG: You wouldn't?

BARNETTE: No.

MEG: Why not?

BARNETTE: Because I'm—I'm fond of her.

MEG: What do you mean you're fond of her?

BARNETTE: Well, she . . . she sold me a pound cake at a bazaar once. And I'm fond of her.

MEG: All right; I believe you. Goodbye.

BARNETTE: Goodbye. *He exits.*

MEG: Babe! Babe, come down here! Babe.

BABE *comes hurrying down the stairs.*

BABE: What? What is it? I called about the cake—

MEG: What did Zackery do to you?

BABE: They can't have it for today.

MEG: Did he hurt you? Did he? Did he do that?

BABE: Oh, Meg, please—

MEG: Did he? Goddamnit, Babe—

BABE: Yes, he did.

MEG: Why? Why?

BABE: I don't know? He started hating me, 'cause I couldn't laugh at his jokes. I just started finding it impossible to laugh at his jokes the way I used to. And then the sound of his voice got to where it tired me out awful bad to hear it. I'd fall asleep just listening to him at the dinner table. He'd say, "Hand me some of that gravy!" Or, "This roast beef is too damn bloody." And suddenly I'd be out cold like a light.

MEG: Oh, Babe. Babe, this is very important. I want you to sit down here and tell me what all happened right before you shot Zackery. That's right, just sit down and tell me.

BABE, *after a pause:* I told you, I can't tell you on account of I'm protecting someone.

MEG: But, Babe, you've just got to talk to someone about all this. You just do.

BABE: Why?

MEG: Because it's a human need. To talk about our lives. It's an important human need.

BABE: Oh. Well, I do feel like I want to talk to someone. I do.

MEG: Then talk to me; please.

BABE, *making a decision:* All right. *After thinking a minute:* I don't know where to start.

MEG: Just start at the beginning. Just there at the beginning.

BABE, *after a moment:* Well, do you remember Willie Jay? MEG *shakes her head.* Cora's youngest boy?

MEG: Oh, yeah, that little kid we used to pay a nickel to, to run down to the drugstore and bring us back a cherry Coke.

BABE: Right. Well, Cora irons at my place on Wednesdays now, and she just happened to mention that Willie Jay'd picked up this old stray dog and that he'd gotten real fond of him. But now they couldn't afford to feed him anymore. So she was gonna have to tell Willie Jay to set him loose in the woods.

MEG, *trying to be patient:* Uh huh.

BABE: Well, I said I liked dogs, and if he wanted to bring the dog over here, I'd take care of him. You see, I was alone by myself most of the time 'cause the senate was in session and Zackery was up in Jackson.

MEG: Uh huh. *She reaches for* LENNY'S *box of birthday candy. She takes little nibbles out of each piece throughout the rest of the scene.*

BABE: So the next day, Willie Jay brings over his skinny old dog with these little crossed eyes. Well, I asked Willie Jay what his name was, and he said they called him Dog. Well, I liked the name, so I thought I'd keep it.

MEG, *getting up:* Uh huh. I'm listening. I'm just gonna get me a glass of cold water. Do you want one?

BABE: Okay.

MEG: So you kept the name—Dog.

BABE: Yeah. Anyway, when Willie Jay was leaving he gave Dog a hug and said, "Goodbye, Dog. You're a fine ole dog." Well, I felt something for him, so I told Willie Jay he could come back and visit with Dog any time he wanted, and his face just kinda lit right up.

MEG, *offering the candy:* Candy—

BABE: No, thanks. Anyhow, time goes on and Willie Jay keeps coming over and over. And we talk about Dog and how fat he's getting, and then, well, you know, things start up.

MEG: No, I don't know. What things start up?

BABE: Well, things start up. Like sex. Like that.

MEG: Babe, wait a minute—Willie Jay's a boy. A small boy, about this tall. He's about this tall!

BABE: No! Oh, no! He's taller now! He's fifteen now. When you knew him he was only about seven or eight.

MEG: But even so—fifteen. And he's a black boy; a colored boy; a Negro.

BABE, *flustered:* Well, I realize that, Meg. Why do you think I'm so worried about his getting public exposure? I don't want to ruin his reputation!

MEG: I'm amazed, Babe. I'm really completely amazed. I didn't even know you were a liberal.

BABE: Well, I'm not! I'm not a liberal! I'm a democratic! I was just lonely! I was so lonely. And he was good. Oh, he was so, so good. I'd never had it that good. We'd always go out into the garage and—

MEG: It's okay. I've got the picture; I've got the picture! Now, let's just get back to the story. To yesterday, when you shot Zackery.

BABE: All right, then. Let's see . . . Willie Jay was over. And it was after we'd—

MEG: Yeah! Yeah.

BABE: And we were just standing around on the back porch playing with Dog. Well, suddenly Zackery comes from around the side of the house. And he startled me 'cause he's supposed to be away at the office, and there he is coming from round the side of the house. Anyway, he says to Willie Jay, "Hey, boy, what are you doing back here?" And I say, "He's not doing anything. You just go on home, Willie Jay! You just run right on home." Well, before he can move, Zackery comes up and knocks him once right across the face and then shoves him down the porch steps, causing him to skin up his elbow real bad on that hard concrete. Then he says, "Don't you ever come around here again, or I'll have them cut out your gizzard!" Well, Willie Jay starts crying— these tears come streaming down his face—then he gets up real quick and runs away, with Dog following off after him. After that, I don't remember much too clearly; let's see . . . I went on into the living room, and I went right up to the davenport and opened the drawer where we keep the burglar gun . . . I took it out. Then I—I brought it up to my ear. That's right. I put it right inside my ear. Why, I was gonna shoot off my own head! That's what I was gonna do. Then I heard the back door slamming and suddenly, for some reason, I thought about Mama . . . how she'd hung herself. And here I was about ready to shoot myself. Then I realized—that's right, I realized how I didn't want to kill myself! And she—she probably didn't want to kill herself. She wanted to kill him, and I wanted to kill him, too. I wanted to kill Zackery, not myself. 'Cause I—I wanted to live! So I waited for him to come on into the living room. Then I held out the gun, and I pulled the trigger, aiming for his heart but getting him in the stomach. *After a pause:* It's funny that I really did that.

MEG: It's a good thing that you did. It's a damn good thing that you did.

BABE: It was.

MEG: Please, Babe, talk to Barnette Lloyd. Just talk to him and see if he can help.

BABE: But how about Willie Jay?

MEG, *starting toward the phone:* Oh, he'll be all right. You just talk to that lawyer like you did to me. *Looking at the number on the card, she begins dialing.* See, 'cause he's gonna be on your side.

BABE: No! Stop, Meg, stop! Don't call him up! Please don't call him up! You can't! It's too awful. *She runs over and jerks the bottom half of the phone away from* MEG.

MEG *stands, holding the receiver.*

MEG: Babe!

BABE *slams her half of the phone into the refrigerator.*

BABE: I just can't tell some stranger all about my personal life. I just can't.

MEG: Well, hell, Babe; you're the one who said you wanted to live.

BABE: That's right. I did. *She takes the phone out of the refrigerator and hands it to* MEG. Here's the other part of the phone. *She moves to sit at the kitchen table.*

MEG *takes the phone back to the counter.*

BABE, *as she fishes a piece of lemon out of her glass and begins sucking on it:* Meg.

MEG: What?

BABE: I called the bakery. They're gonna have Lenny's cake ready first thing tomorrow morning. That's the earliest they can get it.

MEG: All right.

BABE: I told them to write on it, *Happy Birthday, Lenny—A Day Late.* That sound okay?

MEG, *at the phone:* It sounds nice.

BABE: I ordered up the very largest size cake they have. I told them chocolate cake with white icing and red trim. Think she'll like that?

MEG, *dialing the phone:* Yeah, I'm sure she will. She'll like it.

BABE: I'm hoping.

Curtain

ACT II

The lights go up on the kitchen. It is evening of the same day. MEG'S *suitcase has been moved upstairs.* BABE'S *saxophone has been taken out of the case and put together.* BABE *and* BARNETTE *are sitting at the kitchen table.* BARNETTE *is writing and rechecking notes with explosive intensity.* BABE, *who has changed into a casual shift, sits eating a bowl of oatmeal, slowly.*

BARNETTE, *to himself:*   Mmm huh! Yes! I see, I see! Well, we can work on that! And of course, this is mere conjecture! Difficult, if not impossible, to prove. Ha! Yes. Yes, indeed. Indeed—

BABE: Sure you don't want any oatmeal?

BARNETTE: What? Oh, no. No, thank you. Let's see; ah, where were we?

BABE: I just shot Zackery.

BARNETTE, *looking at his notes:* Right. Correct. You've just pulled the trigger.

BABE: Tell me, do you think Willie Jay can stay out of all this?

BARNETTE: Believe me, it is in our interest to keep him as far out of this as possible.

BABE: Good.

BARNETTE, *throughout the following, Barnette stays glued to Babe's every word:* All right, you've just shot one Zackery Botrelle, as a result of his continual physical and mental abuse—what happens now?

BABE: Well, after I shot him, I put the gun down on the piano bench, and then I went out into the kitchen and made up a pitcher of lemonade.

BARNETTE: Lemonade?

BABE: Yes, I was dying of thirst. My mouth was just as dry as a bone.

BARNETTE: So in order to quench this raging thirst that was choking you dry and preventing any possibility of you uttering intelligible sounds or phrases, you went out to the kitchen and made up a pitcher of lemonade?

BABE: Right. I made it just the way I like it, with lots of sugar and lots of lemon—about ten lemons in all. Then I added two trays of ice and stirred it up with my wooden stirring spoon.

BARNETTE: Then what?

BABE: Then I drank three glasses, one right after the other. They were large glasses—about this tall. Then suddenly my stomach kind of swole all up. I guess what caused it was all that sour lemon.

BARNETTE: Could be.

BABE: Then what I did was . . . I wiped my mouth off with the back of my hand, like this . . . *She demonstrates.*

BARNETTE: Hmmm.

BABE: I did it to clear off all those little beads of water that had settled there.

BARNETTE: I see.

BABE: Then I called out to Zackery. I said, "Zackery, I've made some lemonade. Can you use a glass?"

BARNETTE: Did he answer? Did you hear an answer?

BABE: No. He didn't answer.

BARNETTE: So what'd you do?

BABE: I poured him a glass anyway and took it out to him.

BARNETTE: You took it out to the living room?

BABE: I did. And there he was, lying on the rug. He was looking up at me trying to speak words. I said, "What? . . . Lemonade? . . . You don't want it? Would you like a Coke instead?" Then I got the idea—he was telling me to call on the phone for medical help. So I got on the phone and called up the hospital. I gave my name and address, and I told them my husband was shot and he was lying on the rug and there was plenty of blood. *She pauses a minute, as Barnette works frantically on his notes.* I guess that's gonna look kinda bad.

BARNETTE: What?

BABE: Me fixing that lemonade before I called the hospital.

BARNETTE: Well, not . . . necessarily.

BABE: I tell you, I think the reason I made up the lemonade, I mean besides the fact that my mouth was bone dry, was that I was afraid to call the authorities. I was afraid. I—I really think I was afraid they would see that I had tried to shoot Zackery, in fact, that I *had* shot him, and they would accuse me of possible murder and send me away to jail.

BARNETTE: Well, that's understandable.

BABE: I think so. I mean, in fact, that's what did happen. That's what is happening—'cause here I am just about ready to go right off to the Parchment Prison Farm. Yes, here I am just practically on the brink of utter doom. Why, I feel so all alone.

BARNETTE: Now, now, look— Why, there's no reason for you to get yourself so all upset and worried. Please don't. Please.

They look at each other for a moment.

BARNETTE: You just keep filling in as much detailed information as you can about those incidents on the medical reports. That's all you need to think about. Don't you worry, Mrs. Botrelle, we're going to have a solid defense.

BABE: Please don't call me Mrs. Botrelle.

BARNETTE: All right.

BABE: My name's Becky. People in the family call me Babe, but my real name's Becky.

BARNETTE: All right, Becky.

BARNETTE *and* BABE *stare at each other for a long moment.*

BABE: Are you sure you didn't go to Hazlehurst High?

BARNETTE: No, I went away to a boarding school.

BABE: Gosh, you sure do look familiar. You sure do.

BARNETTE: Well, I—I doubt you'll remember, but I did meet you once.

BABE: You did? When?

BARNETTE: At the Christmas bazaar, year before last. You were selling cakes and cookies and . . . candy.

BABE: Oh, yes! You bought the orange pound cake!

BARNETTE: Right.

BABE: Of course, and then we talked for a while. We talked about the Christmas angel.

BARNETTE: You do remember.

BABE: I remember it very well. You were even thinner then than you are now.

BARNETTE: Well, I'm surprised. I'm certainly . . . surprised.

The phone rings.

BABE, *as she goes to answer the phone:*   This is quite a coincidence! Don't

you think it is? Why, it's almost a fluke. *She answers the phone.* Hello
. . . Oh, hello, Lucille . . . Oh, he is? . . . Oh, he does? . . . Okay.
Oh, Lucille, wait! Has Dog come back to the house? . . . Oh, I see
. . . Okay. Okay. *After a brief pause:* Hello, Zackery? How are you
doing? . . . Uh huh . . . uh huh . . . Oh, I'm sorry . . . Please don't
scream . . . Uh huh . . . uh huh . . . You want what? . . . No, I
can't come up there now . . . Well, for one thing, I don't even have
the car. Lenny and Meg are up at the hospital right now, visiting with
Old Granddaddy . . . What? . . . Oh, really? . . . Oh, really? . . .
Well, I've got me a lawyer that's over here right now, and he's building
me up a solid defense! . . . Wait just a minute, I'll see. *To Barnette:*
He wants to talk to you. He says he's got some blackening evidence
that's gonna convict me of attempting to murder him in the first degree!

BARNETTE, *disgustedly:* Oh, bluff! He's bluffing! Here, hand me the
phone. *He takes the phone and becomes suddenly cool and suave.* Hello,
this is Mr. Barnette Lloyd speaking. I'm Mrs. . . . ah, Becky's attorney . . . Why, certainly, Mr. Botrelle, I'd be more than glad to check
out any pertinent information that you may have . . . Fine, then I'll
be right on over. Goodbye. *He hangs up the phone.*

BABE: What did he say?

BARNETTE: He wants me to come see him at the hospital this evening.
Says he's got some sort of evidence. Sounds highly suspect to me.

BABE: Oooh! Didn't you just hate his voice? Doesn't he have the most
awful voice? I just hate—I can't bear to hear it!

BARNETTE: Well, now—now, wait. Wait just a minute.

BABE: What?

BARNETTE: I have a solution. From now on, I'll handle all communica-
tions between you two. You can simply refuse to speak with him.

BABE: All right—I will. I'll do that.

BARNETTE, *starting to pack his briefcase:* Well, I'd better get over there
and see just what he's got up his sleeve.

BABE, *after a pause:* Barnette.

BARNETTE: Yes?

BABE: What's the personal vendetta about? You know, the one you have
to settle with Zackery.

BARNETTE: Oh, it's—it's complicated. It's a very complicated matter.

BABE: I see.

BARNETTE: The major thing he did was to ruin my father's life. He took
away his job, his home, his health, his respectability. I don't like to
talk about it.

BABE: I'm sorry. I just wanted to say—I hope you win it. I hope you win
your vendetta.

BARNETTE: Thank you.

BABE: I think it's an important thing that a person could win a lifelong
vendetta.

BARNETTE: Yes. Well, I'd better be going.

BABE: All right. Let me know what happens.

BARNETTE: I will. I'll get back to you right away.

BABE: Thanks.
BARNETTE: Goodbye, Becky.
BABE: Goodbye, Barnette.

BARNETTE *exits.* BABE *looks around the room for a moment, then goes over to her white suitcase and opens it up. She takes out her pink hair curlers and a brush. She begins brushing her hair.*

BABE: Goodbye, Becky. Goodbye, Barnette. Goodbye, Becky. Oooh.

LENNY *enters. She is fuming.* BABE *is rolling her hair throughout most of the following scene.*

BABE: Lenny, hi!
LENNY: Hi.
BABE: Where's Meg?
LENNY: Oh, she had to go by the store and pick some things up. I don't know what.
BABE: Well, how's Old Granddaddy?
LENNY, *as she picks up* BABE'S *bowl of oatmeal:* He's fine. Wonderful! Never been better!
BABE: Lenny, what's wrong? What's the matter?
LENNY: It's Meg! I could just wring her neck! I could just wring it!
BABE: Why? Wha'd she do?
LENNY: She lied! She sat in that hospital room and shamelessly lied to Old Granddaddy. She went on and on telling such untrue stories and lies.
BABE: Well, what? What did she say?
LENNY: Well, for one thing, she said she was gonna have an RCA record coming out with her picture on the cover, eating pineapples under a palm tree.
BABE: Well, gosh, Lenny, maybe she is! Don't you think she really is?
LENNY: Babe, she sat here this very afternoon and told me how all that she's done this whole year is work as a clerk for a dog-food company.
BABE: Oh, shoot. I'm disappointed.
LENNY: And then she goes on to say that she'll be appearing on the Johnny Carson show in two weeks' time. Two weeks' time! Why, Old Granddaddy's got a TV set right in his room. Imagine what a letdown it's gonna be.
BABE: Why, mercy me.
LENNY, *slamming the coffeepot on:* Oh, and she told him the reason she didn't use the money he sent her to come home Christmas was that she was right in the middle of making a huge multimillion-dollar motion picture and was just under too much pressure.
BABE: My word!
LENNY: The movie's coming out this spring. It's called, *Singing in a Shoe Factory*. But she only has a small leading role—not a large leading role.
BABE, *laughing:* For heaven's sake—

LENNY: I'm sizzling. Oh, I just can't help it! I'm sizzling!

BABE: Sometimes Meg does such strange things.

LENNY, *slowly, as she picks up the opened box of birthday candy:* Who ate this candy?

BABE, *hesitantly:* Meg.

LENNY: My one birthday present, and look what she does! Why, she's taken one little bite out of each piece and then just put it back in! Ooh! That's just like her! That is just like her!

BABE: Lenny, please—

LENNY: I can't help it! It gets me mad! It gets me upset! Why, Meg's always run wild—she started smoking and drinking when she was fourteen years old; she never made good grades—never made her own bed! But somehow she always seemed to get what she wanted. She's the one who got singing and dancing lessons, and a storebought dress to wear to her senior prom. Why, do you remember how Meg always got to wear twelve jingle bells on her petticoats, while we were only allowed to wear three apiece? Why? Why should Old Grandmama let her sew twelve golden jingle bells on her petticoats and us only three!

BABE, *who has heard all this before:* I don't know! Maybe she didn't jingle them as much!

LENNY: I can't help it! It gets me mad! I resent it. I do.

BABE: Oh, don't resent Meg. Things have been hard for Meg. After all, she was the one who found Mama.

LENNY: Oh, I know; she's the one who found Mama. But that's always been the excuse.

BABE: But I tell you, Lenny, after it happened, Meg started doing all sorts of these strange things.

LENNY: She did? Like what?

BABE: Like things I never even wanted to tell you about.

LENNY: What sort of things?

BABE: Well, for instance, back when we used to go over to the library, Meg would spend all her time reading and looking through this old black book called *Diseases of the Skin.* It was full of the most sickening pictures you've ever seen. Things like rotting-away noses and eyeballs drooping off down the sides of people's faces, and scabs and sores and eaten-away places all over all parts of people's bodies.

LENNY, *trying to pour her coffee:* Babe, please! That's enough.

BABE: Anyway, she'd spend hours and hours just forcing herself to look through this book. Why, it was the same way she'd force herself to look at the poster of crippled children stuck up in the window at Dixieland Drugs. You know, that one where they want you to give a dime. Meg would stand there and stare at their eyes and look at the braces on their little crippled-up legs—then she'd purposely go and spend her dime on a doublescoop ice cream cone and eat it all down. She'd say to me, "See, I can stand it. I can stand it. Just look how I'm gonna be able to stand it."

LENNY: That's awful.

BABE: She said she was afraid of being a weak person. I guess 'cause she cried in bed every night for such a long time.

LENNY: Goodness mercy. *After a pause:* Well, I suppose you'd have to be a pretty hard person to be able to do what she did to Doc Porter.

BABE, *exasperated:* Oh, shoot! It wasn't Meg's fault that hurricane wiped Biloxi away. I never understood why people were blaming all that on Meg—just because that roof fell in and crunched Doc's leg. It wasn't her fault.

LENNY: Well, it was Meg who refused to evacuate. Jim Craig and some of Doc's other friends were all down there, and they kept trying to get everyone to evacuate. But Meg refused. She wanted to stay on because she thought a hurricane would be—oh, I don't know—a lot of fun. Then everyone says she baited Doc into staying there with her. She said she'd marry him if he'd stay.

BABE, *taken aback by this new information:* Well, he has a mind of his own. He could have gone.

LENNY: But he didn't. 'Cause . . . 'cause he loved her. And then, after the roof caved in and they got Doc to the high school gym, Meg just left. She just left him there to leave for California—'cause of her career, she says. I think it was a shameful thing to do. It took almost a year for his leg to heal, and after that he gave up his medical career altogether. He said he was tired of hospitals. It's such a sad thing. Everyone always knew he was gonna be a doctor. We've called him Doc for years.

BABE: I don't know. I guess I don't have any room to talk; 'cause I just don't know. *Pause.* Gosh, you look so tired.

LENNY: I feel tired.

BABE: They say women need a lot of iron . . . so they won't feel tired.

LENNY: What's got iron in it? Liver?

BABE: Yeah, liver's got it. And vitamin pills.

After a moment, MEG *enters. She carries a bottle of bourbon that is already minus a few slugs, and a newspaper. She is wearing black boots, a dark dress, and a hat. The room goes silent.*

MEG: Hello.

BABE, *fooling with her hair:* Hi, Meg.

LENNY *quietly sips her coffee.*

MEG, *handing the newspaper to* BABE: Here's your paper.

BABE: Thanks. *She opens it.* Oh, here it is, right on the front page.

MEG *lights a cigarette.*

BABE: Where're the scissors, Lenny?

LENNY: Look in there in the ribbon drawer.

BABE: Okay. *She gets the scissors and glue out of the drawer and slowly begins cutting out the newspaper article.*

MEG, *after a few moments, filled only with the snipping of scissors:* All right—I lied! I lied! I couldn't help it . . . these stories just came pouring out of my mouth! When I saw how tired and sick Old Grand-daddy'd gotten—they just flew out! All I wanted was to see him smiling and happy. I just wasn't going to sit there and look at him all miserable and sick and sad! I just wasn't!

BABE: Oh, Meg, he is sick, isn't he—

MEG: Why, he's gotten all white and milky—he's almost evaporated!

LENNY, *gasping and turning to* MEG: But still you shouldn't have lied! It just was wrong for you to tell such lies—

MEG: Well, I know that! Don't you think I know that? I hate myself when I lie for that old man. I do. I feel so weak. And then I have to go and do at least three or four things that I know he'd despise just to get even with that miserable, old, bossy man!

LENNY: Oh, Meg, please don't talk so about Old Granddaddy! It sounds so ungrateful. Why, he went out of his way to make a home for us, to treat us like we were his very own children. All he ever wanted was the best for us. That's all he ever wanted.

MEG: Well, I guess it was; but sometimes I wonder what we wanted.

BABE, *taking the newspaper article and glue over to her suitcase:*   Well, one thing I wanted was a team of white horses to ride Mama's coffin to her grave. That's one thing I wanted.

LENNY *and* MEG *exchange looks.*

BABE: Lenny, did you remember to pack my photo album?

LENNY: It's down there at the bottom, under all that night stuff.

BABE: Oh, I found it.

LENNY: Really, Babe, I don't understand why you have to put in the articles that are about the unhappy things in your life. Why would you want to remember them?

BABE, *pasting the article in:*   I don't know. I just like to keep an accurate record, I suppose. There. *She begins flipping through the book.* Look, here's a picture of me when I got married.

MEG: Let's see.

They all look at the photo album.

LENNY: My word, you look about twelve years old.

BABE: I was just eighteen.

MEG: You're smiling, Babe. Were you happy then?

BABE, *laughing:*   Well, I was drunk on champagne punch. I remember that!

They turn the page.

LENNY: Oh, there's Meg singing at Greeny's!

BABE: Oooh, I wish you were still singing at Greeny's! I wish you were!

LENNY: You're so beautiful!

BABE: Yes, you are. You're beautiful.

MEG: Oh, stop! I'm not—

LENNY: Look, Meg's starting to cry.

BABE: Oh, Meg—

MEG: I'm not—

BABE: Quick, better turn the page; we don't want Meg crying—*She flips the pages.*

LENNY: Why, it's Daddy.

MEG: Where'd you get that picture, Babe? I thought she burned them all.

BABE: Ah, I just found it around.

LENNY: What does it say here? What's that inscription?

BABE: It says "Jimmy—clowning at the beach—1952."

LENNY: Well, will you look at that smile.

MEG: Jesus, those white teeth—turn the page, will you; we can't do any worse than this!

They turn the page. The room goes silent.

BABE: It's Mama and the cat.

LENNY: Oh, turn the page—

BABE: That old yellow cat. You know, I bet if she hadn't of hung that old cat along with her, she wouldn't have gotten all that national coverage.

MEG, *after a moment, hopelessly:*   Why are we talking about this?

LENNY: Meg's right. It was so sad. It was awfully sad. I remember how we all three just sat up on that bed the day of the service all dressed up in our black velveteen suits crying the whole morning long.

BABE: We used up one whole big box of Kleenexes.

MEG: And then Old Granddaddy came in and said he was gonna take us out to breakfast. Remember, he told us not to cry anymore 'cause he was gonna take us out to get banana splits for breakfast.

BABE: That's right—banana splits for breakfast!

MEG: Why, Lenny was fourteen years old, and he thought that would make it all better—

BABE: Oh, I remember he said for us to eat all we wanted. I think I ate about five! He kept shoving them down us!

MEG: God, we were so sick!

LENNY: Oh, we were!

MEG, *laughing:*   Lenny's face turned green—

LENNY: I was just as sick as a dog!

BABE: Old Grandmama was furious!

LENNY: Oh, she was!

MEG: The thing about Old Granddaddy is, he keeps trying to make us happy, and we end up getting stomachaches and turning green and throwing up in the flower arrangements.

BABE: Oh, that was me! I threw up in the flowers! Oh, no! How embarrassing!

LENNY, *laughing:*   Oh, Babe—

BABE, *hugging her sisters:*   Oh, Lenny! Oh, Meg!

MEG: Oh, Babe! Oh, Lenny! It's so good to be home!

LENNY: Hey, I have an idea—

BABE: What?

LENNY: Let's play cards!!

BABE: Oh, let's do!

MEG: All right!

LENNY: Oh, good! It'll be just like when we used to sit around the table playing hearts all night long.

BABE: I know! *Getting up:* I'll fix us up some popcorn and hot chocolate—

MEG, *getting up:*   Here, let me get out that old black popcorn pot.

LENNY, *getting up:*   Oh, yes! Now, let's see, I think I have a deck of cards around here somewhere.

BABE: Gosh, I hope I remember all the rules— Are hearts good or bad?

MEG: Bad, I think. Aren't they, Lenny?

LENNY: That's right. Hearts are bad, but the Black Sister is the worst of all—

MEG: Oh, that's right! And the Black Sister is the Queen of Spades.

BABE, *figuring it out:*   And spades are the black cards that aren't the puppy dog feet?

MEG, *thinking a moment:*   Right. And she counts a lot of points.

BABE: And points are bad?

MEG: Right. Here, I'll get some paper so we can keep score.

The phone rings.

LENNY: Oh, here they are!

MEG: I'll get it—

LENNY: Why, look at these cards! They're years old!

BABE: Oh, let me see!

MEG: Hello . . . No, this is Meg MaGrath . . . Doc. How are you? . . . Well, good . . . You're where? . . . Well, sure. Come on over . . . Sure I'm sure . . . Yeah, come right on over . . . All right. 'Bye. *She hangs up.* That was Doc Porter. He's down the street at Al's Grill. He's gonna come on over.

LENNY: He is?

MEG: He said he wanted to come see me.

LENNY: Oh. *After a pause:* Well, do you still want to play?

MEG: No, I don't think so.

LENNY: All right. *She starts to shuffle the cards, as Meg brushes her hair.* You know, it's really not much fun playing hearts with only two people.

MEG: I'm sorry; maybe after Doc leaves I'll join you.

LENNY: I know; maybe Doc'll want to play. Then we can have a game of bridge.

MEG: I don't think so. Doc never liked cards. Maybe we'll just go out somewhere.

LENNY, *putting down the cards.* BABE *picks them up:*   Meg—

MEG: What?

LENNY: Well, Doc's married now.

MEG: I know. You told me.

LENNY: Oh. Well, as long as you know that. *Pause.* As long as you know that.

MEG, *still primping:*   Yes, I know. She made the pot.

BABE: How many cards do I deal out?

LENNY, *leaving the table:*   Excuse me.

BABE: All of 'em, or what?

LENNY: Ah, Meg, could I—could I ask you something?

BABE *proceeds to deal out all the cards.*

MEG: What?

LENNY: I just wanted to ask you—

MEG: What?

Unable to go on with what she really wants to say, LENNY *runs and picks up the box of candy.*

LENNY: Well, just why did you take one little bite out of each piece of candy in this box and then just put it back in?

MEG: Oh. Well, I was looking for the ones with nuts.

LENNY: The ones with nuts.

MEG: Yeah.

LENNY: But there are none with nuts. It's a box of assorted crèmes—all it has in it are crèmes!

MEG: Oh.

LENNY: Why couldn't you just read on the box? It says right here, *Assorted Crèmes,* not nuts! Besides, this was a birthday present to me! My one and only birthday present; my only one!

MEG: I'm sorry. I'll get you another box.

LENNY: I don't want another box. That's not the point!

MEG: What is the point?

LENNY: I don't know; it's—it's— You have no respect for other people's property! You just take whatever you want. You just take it! Why, remember how you had layers and layers of jingle bells sewed onto your petticoats while Babe and I only had three apiece?!

MEG: Oh, God! She starting up about those stupid jingle bells!

LENNY: Well, it's an example! A specific example of how you always got what you wanted!

MEG: Oh, come on, Lenny, you're just upset because Doc called.

LENNY: Who said anything about Doc? Do you think I'm upset about Doc? Why, I've long since given up worrying about you and all your men.

MEG, *turning in anger:*   Look, I know I've had too many men. Believe me, I've had way too many men. But it's not my fault you haven't had any—or maybe just that one from Memphis.

LENNY, *stopping:*   What one from Memphis?

MEG, *slowly:*   The one Babe told me about. From the—club.

LENNY: Babe!

BABE: Meg!

LENNY: How could you! I asked you not to tell anyone! I'm so ashamed! How could you? Who else have you told? Did you tell anyone else?

BABE, *overlapping, to* MEG: Why'd you have to open your big mouth?

MEG, *overlapping:* How am I supposed to know? You never said not to tell!

BABE: Can't you use your head just for once? *To* LENNY: No, I never told anyone else. Somehow it just slipped out to Meg. Really, it just flew out of my mouth—

LENNY: What do you two have—wings on your tongues?

BABE: I'm sorry, Lenny. Really sorry.

LENNY: I'll just never, never, never be able to trust you again—

MEG, *furiously coming to* BABE's *defense:* Oh, for heaven's sake, Lenny, we were just worried about you! We wanted to find a way to make you happy!

LENNY: Happy! Happy! I'll never be happy!

MEG: Well, not if you keep living your life as Old Granddaddy's nurse-maid—

BABE: Meg, shut up!

MEG: I can't help it! I just know that the reason you stopped seeing this man from Memphis was because of Old Granddaddy.

LENNY: What— Babe didn't tell you the rest of the story—

MEG: Oh, she said it was something about your shrunken ovary.

BABE: Meg!

LENNY: Babe!

BABE: I just mentioned it!

MEG: But I don't believe a word of that story!

LENNY: Oh, I don't care what you believe! It's so easy for you—you always have men falling in love with you! But I have this underdeveloped ovary and I can't have children and my hair is falling out in the comb—so what man can love me? What man's gonna love me?

MEG: A lot of men!

BABE: Yeah, a lot! A whole lot!

MEG: Old Granddaddy's the only one who seems to think otherwise.

LENNY: 'Cause he doesn't want to see me hurt! He doesn't want to see me rejected and humiliated.

MEG: Oh, come on now, Lenny, don't be so pathetic! God, you make me angry when you just stand there looking so pathetic! Just tell me, did you really ask the man from Memphis? Did you actually ask that man from Memphis all about it?

LENNY, *breaking apart:* No, I didn't. I didn't. Because I just didn't want him not to want me—

MEG: Lenny—

LENNY, *furious:* Don't talk to me anymore! Don't talk to me! I think I'm gonna vomit— I just hope all this doesn't cause me to vomit! *She exits up the stairs sobbing.*

MEG: See! See! She didn't even ask him about her stupid ovary! She just broke it all off 'cause of Old Granddaddy! What a jackass fool!

BABE: Oh, Meg, shut up! Why do you have to make Lenny cry? I just hate it when you make Lenny cry! *She runs up the stairs.* Lenny! Oh, Lenny—

MEG *gives a long sigh and goes to get a cigarette and a drink.*

MEG: I feel like hell. *She sits in despair, smoking and drinking bourbon. There is a knock at the back door. She starts. She brushes her hair out of her face and goes to answer the door. It is* DOC.

DOC: Hello, Meggy.

MEG: Well, Doc. Well, it's Doc.

DOC, *after a pause:* You're home, Meggy.

MEG: Yeah, I've come home. I've come on home to see about Babe.

DOC: And how's Babe?

MEG: Oh, fine. Well, fair. She's fair.

DOC *nods.*

MEG: Hey, do you want a drink?

DOC: Whatcha got?

MEG: Bourbon.

DOC: Oh, don't tell me Lenny's stocking bourbon.

MEG: Well, no. I've been to the store. *She gets him a glass and pours them each a drink. They click glasses.*

MEG: So, how's your wife?

DOC: She's fine.

MEG: I hear ya got two kids.

DOC: Yeah. Yeah, I got two kids.

MEG: A boy and a girl.

DOC: That's right, Meggy, a boy and a girl.

MEG: That's what you always said you wanted, wasn't it? A boy and a girl.

DOC: Is that what I said?

MEG: I don't know. I thought it's what you said.

They finish their drinks in silence.

DOC: Whose cot?

MEG: Lenny's. She's taken to sleeping in the kitchen.

DOC: Ah. Where is Lenny?

MEG: She's in the upstairs room. I made her cry. Babe's up there seeing to her.

DOC: How'd you make her cry?

MEG: I don't know. Eating her birthday candy; talking on about her boyfriend from Memphis. I don't know. I'm upset about it. She's got a lot on her. Why can't I keep my mouth shut?

DOC: I don't know, Meggy. Maybe it's because you don't want to.

MEG: Maybe.

They smile at each other. MEG *pours each of them another drink.*

DOC: Well, it's been a long time.

MEG: It has been a long time.

DOC: Let's see—when was the last time we saw each other?

MEG: I can't quite recall.

DOC: Wasn't it in Biloxi?

MEG: Ah, Biloxi. I believe so.

DOC: And wasn't there a—a hurricane going on at the time?

MEG: Was there?

DOC: Yes, there was; one hell of a hurricane. Camille, I believe they called it. Hurricane Camille.

MEG: Yes, now I remember. It was a beautiful hurricane.

DOC: We had a time down there. We had quite a time. Drinking vodka, eating oysters on the half shell, dancing all night long. And the wind was blowing.

MEG: Oh, God, was it blowing.

DOC: Goddamn, was it blowing.

MEG: There never has been such a wind blowing.

DOC: Oh, God, Meggy. Oh, God.

MEG: I know, Doc. It was my fault to leave you. I was crazy. I thought I was choking. I felt choked!

DOC: I felt like a fool.

MEG: No.

DOC: I just kept on wondering why.

MEG: I don't know why . . . 'Cause I didn't want to care. I don't know. I did care, though. I did.

DOC, *after a pause:*   Ah, hell—*He pours them both another drink.* Are you still singing those sad songs?

MEG: No.

DOC: Why not?

MEG: I don't know, Doc. Things got worse for me. After a while, I just couldn't sing anymore. I tell you, I had one hell of a time over Christmas.

DOC: What do you mean?

MEG: I went nuts. I went insane. Ended up in L.A. County Hospital. Psychiatric ward.

DOC: Hell. Ah, hell, Meggy. What happened?

MEG: I don't really know. I couldn't sing anymore, so I lost my job. And I had a bad toothache. I had this incredibly painful toothache. For days I had it, but I wouldn't do anything about it. I just stayed inside my apartment. All I could do was sit around in chairs, chewing on my fingers. Then one afternoon I ran screaming out of the apartment with all my money and jewelry and valuables, and tried to stuff it all into one of those March of Dimes collection boxes. That was when they nabbed me. Sad story. Meg goes mad.

DOC *stares at her for a long moment. He pours them both another drink.*

DOC, *after quite a pause:*   There's a moon out.

MEG: Is there?

DOC: Wanna go take a ride in my truck and look out at the moon?

MEG: I don't know, Doc. I don't wanna start up. It'll be too hard if we start up.

DOC: Who says we're gonna start up? We're just gonna look at the moon.

For one night just you and me are gonna go for a ride in the country and look out at the moon.

MEG: One night?

DOC: Right.

MEG: Look out at the moon?

DOC: You got it.

MEG: Well . . . all right. *She gets up.*

DOC: Better take your coat. *He helps her into her coat.* And the bottle—*He takes the bottle.* MEG *picks up the glasses.* Forget the glasses—

MEG, *laughing:*   Yeah—forget the glasses. Forget the goddamn glasses.

MEG *shuts off the kitchen lights, leaving the kitchen with only a dim light over the kitchen sink.* MEG *and* DOC *leave. After a moment,* BABE *comes down the stairs in her slip.*

BABE: Meg—Meg? *She stands for a moment in the moonlight wearing only a slip. She sees her saxophone, then moves to pick it up. She plays a few shrieking notes. There is a loud knock on the back door.*

BARNETTE'S VOICE: Becky! Becky, is that you?

BABE *puts down the saxophone.*

BABE: Just a minute. I'm coming. *She puts a raincoat on over her slip and goes to answer the door.* Hello, Barnette. Come on in.

BARNETTE *comes in. He is troubled but is making a great effort to hide the fact.*

BARNETTE: Thank you.

BABE: What is it?

BARNETTE: I've, ah, I've just come from seeing Zackery at the hospital.

BABE: Oh?

BARNETTE: It seems . . . Well, it seems his sister, Lucille, was somewhat suspicious.

BABE: Suspicious?

BARNETTE: About you.

BABE: Me?

BARNETTE: She hired a private detective: he took these pictures.

He hands BABE *a small envelope containing several photographs.* BABE *opens the envelope and begins looking at the pictures in stunned silence.*

BARNETTE: They were taken about two weeks ago. It seems she wasn't going to show them to Botrelle straightaway. She, ah, wanted to wait till the time was right.

The phone rings one and a half times. BARNETTE *glances uneasily toward the phone.*

BARNETTE: Becky?

The phone stops ringing.

BABE, *looking up at Barnette, slowly:* These are pictures of Willie Jay and me . . . out in the garage.

BARNETTE, *looking away:* I know.

BABE: You looked at these pictures?

BARNETTE: Yes—I —well . . . professionally, I looked at them.

BABE: Oh, mercy. Oh, mercy! We can burn them, can't we? Quick, we can burn them—

BARNETTE: It won't do any good. They have the negatives.

BABE, *Holding the pictures, as she bangs herself hopelessly into the stove, table, cabinets, etc.:* Oh, no; oh, no; oh, no! Oh, no—

BARNETTE: There—there, now—there—

LENNY'S VOICE: Babe? Are you all right? Babe—

BABE, *hiding the pictures:* What? I'm all right. Go on back to bed.

BABE *hides the pictures as* LENNY *comes down the stairs. She is wearing a coat and wiping white night cream off of her face with a washrag.*

LENNY: What's the matter? What's going on down here?

BABE: Nothing! *Then as she begins dancing ballet style around the room:* We're—we're just dancing. We were just dancing around down here. *Signaling to* BARNETTE *to dance.*

LENNY: Well, you'd better get your shoes on, 'cause we've got—

BABE: All right, I will! That's a good idea! *She goes to get her shoes.* Now, you go on back to bed. It's pretty late and—

LENNY: Babe, will you listen a minute—

BABE, *holding up her shoes:* I'm putting 'em on—

LENNY: That was the hospital that just called. We've got to get over there. Old Granddaddy's had himself another stroke.

BABE: Oh. All right. My shoes are on. *She stands.*

They all look at each other as the lights black out.

Curtain

ACT III

The lights go up on the empty kitchen. It is the following morning. After a few moments, BABE *enters from the back door. She is carrying her hair curlers in her hands. She lies down on the cot. A few moments later,* LENNY *enters. She is tired and weary.* CHICK'S *voice is heard.*

CHICK'S VOICE: Lenny! Oh, Lenny!

LENNY *turns to the door.* CHICK *enters energetically.*

CHICK: Well . . . how is he?

LENNY: He's stabilized; they say for now his functions are all stabilized.

CHICK: Well, is he still in the coma?

LENNY: Uh huh.

CHICK: Hmmm. So do they think he's gonna be . . . passing on?

LENNY: He may be. He doesn't look so good. They said they'd phone us if there were any sudden changes.

CHICK: Well, it seems to me we'd better get busy phoning on the phone ourselves. *Removing a list from her pocket:* Now, I've made out this list of all the people we need to notify about Old Granddaddy's predicament. I'll phone half, if you'll phone half.

LENNY: But—what would we say?

CHICK: Just tell them the facts: that Old Granddaddy's got himself in a coma, and it could be he doesn't have long for this world.

LENNY: I—I don't know. I don't feel like phoning.

CHICK: Why, Lenora, I'm surprised; how can you be this way? I went to all the trouble of making up the list. And I offered to phone half of the people on it, even though I'm only one-fourth of the granddaughters. I mean, I just get tired of doing more than my fair share, when people like Meg can suddenly just disappear to where they can't even be reached in case of emergency!

LENNY: All right; give me the list. I'll phone half.

CHICK: Well, don't do it just to suit me.

LENNY, *wearily tearing the list in half:*   I'll phone these here.

CHICK, *taking her half of the list:*   Fine then. Suit yourself. Oh, wait—let me call Sally Bell. I need to talk to her, anyway.

LENNY: All right.

CHICK: So you add Great-uncle Spark Dude to your list.

LENNY: Okay.

CHICK: Fine. Well, I've got to get on back home and see to the kids. It is gonna be an uphill struggle till I can find someone to replace that good-for-nothing Annie May Jenkins. Well, you let me know if you hear any more.

LENNY: All right.

CHICK: Goodbye, Rebecca. I said goodbye. BABE *blows her sax.* CHICK *starts to exit in a flurry, then pauses to add:* And you really ought to try to get that phoning done before twelve noon. *She exits.*

LENNY, *after a long pause:*   Babe, I feel bad. I feel real bad.

BABE: Why, Lenny?

LENNY: Because yesterday I—I wished it.

BABE: You wished what?

LENNY: I wished that Old Granddaddy would be put out of his pain. I wished it on one of my birthday candles. I did. And now he's in this coma, and they say he's feeling no pain.

BABE: Well, when did you have a cake yesterday? I don't remember you having any cake.

LENNY: Well, I didn't . . . have a cake. But I just blew out the candles, anyway.

BABE: Oh. Well, those birthday wishes don't count, unless you have a cake.

LENNY: They don't?

BABE: No. A lot of times they don't even count when you do have a cake. It just depends.

LENNY: Depends on what?

BABE: On how deep your wish is, I suppose.

LENNY: Still, I just wish I hadn't of wished it. Gosh, I wonder when Meg's coming home.

BABE: Should be soon.

LENNY: I just wish we wouldn't fight all the time. I don't like it when we do.

BABE: Me, neither.

LENNY: I guess it hurts my feelings, a little, the way Old Granddaddy's always put so much stock in Meg and all her singing talent. I think I've been, well, envious of her 'cause I can't seem to do too much.

BABE: Why, sure you can.

LENNY: I can?

BABE: Sure. You just have to put your mind to it, that's all. It's like how I went out and bought that saxophone, just hoping I'd be able to attend music school and start up my own career. I just went out and did it. Just on hope. Of course, now it looks like . . . Well, it just doesn't look like things are gonna work out for me. But I know they would for you.

LENNY: Well, they'll work out for you, too.

BABE: I doubt it.

LENNY: Listen, I heard up at the hospital that Zackery's already in fair condition. They say soon he'll probably be able to walk and everything.

BABE: Yeah. And life sure can be miserable.

LENNY: Well, I know, 'cause—day before yesterday, Billy Boy was struck down by lightning.

BABE: He was?

LENNY, *nearing sobs:* Yeah. He was struck dead.

BABE, *crushed:* Life sure can be miserable.

They sit together for several moments in morbid silence. MEG *is heard singing a loud happy song. She suddenly enters through the dining room door. She is exuberant! Her hair is a mess, and the heel of one shoe has broken off. She is laughing radiantly and limping as she sings into the broken heel.*

MEG, *spotting her sisters:* Good morning! Good morning! Oh, it's a wonderful morning! I tell you, I am surprised I feel this good. I should feel like hell. By all accounts, I should feel like utter hell! *She is looking for the glue.* Where's that glue? This damn heel has broken off my shoe. La, la, la, la, la! Ah, here it is! Now, let me just get these shoes off. Zip, zip, zip, zip, zip! Well, what's wrong with you two? My God, you look like doom!

BABE *and* LENNY *stare helplessly at* MEG.

MEG: Oh, I know, you're mad at me 'cause I stayed out all night long. Well, I did.

LENNY: No, we're—we're not mad at you. We're just . . . depressed. *She starts to sob.*

MEG: Oh, Lenny, listen to me, now; everything's all right with Doc. I mean, nothing happened. Well, actually a lot did happen, but it didn't come to anything. Not because of me, I'm afraid. *Smearing glue on her heel:* I mean, I was out there thinking, What will I say when he begs me to run away with him? Will I have pity on his wife and those two half-Yankee children? I mean, can I sacrifice their happiness for mine? Yes! Oh, yes! Yes, I can! But . . . he didn't ask me. He didn't even want to ask me. I could tell by this certain look in his eyes that he didn't even want to ask me. Why aren't I miserable! Why aren't I morbid! I should be humiliated! Devastated! Maybe these feelings are coming—I don't know. But for now it was . . . just such fun. I'm happy. I realized I could care about someone. I could want someone. And I sang! I sang all night long! I sang right up into the trees! But not for Old Granddaddy. None of it was to please Old Granddaddy!

LENNY *and* BABE *look at each other.*

BABE: Ah, Meg—

MEG: What—

BABE: Well, it's just— It's . . .

LENNY: It's about Old Granddaddy—

MEG: Oh, I know; I know. I told him all those stupid lies. Well, I'm gonna go right over there this morning and tell him the truth. I mean every horrible thing. I don't care if he wants to hear it or not. He's just gonna have to take me like I am. And if he can't take it, if it sends him into a coma, that's just too damm bad!

BABE *and* LENNY *look at each other.* BABE *cracks a smile.* LENNY *cracks a smile.*

BABE: You're too late— Ha, ha, ha!

They both break up laughing.

LENNY: Oh, stop! Please! Ha, ha, ha!

MEG: What is it? What's so funny?

BABE, *still laughing:*   It's not— It's not funny!

LENNY, *still laughing:*   No, it's not! It's not a bit funny!

MEG: Well, what is it, then? What?

BABE, *trying to calm down:*   Well, it's just—it's just—

MEG: What?

BABE: Well, Old Granddaddy—he—he's in a coma!

BABE *and* LENNY *break up again.*

MEG: He's what?

BABE, *shrieking:*   In a coma!

MEG: My God! That's not funny!

BABE, *calming down:*   I know. I know. For some reason, it just struck us as funny.

LENNY: I'm sorry. It's—it's not funny. It's sad. It's very sad. We've been up all night long.

BABE: We're really tired.

MEG: Well, my God. How is he? Is he gonna live?

BABE *and* LENNY *look at each other.*

BABE: They don't think so!

They both break up again.

LENNY: Oh, I don't know why we're laughing like this. We're just sick! We're just awful!

BABE: We are—we're awful!

LENNY, *as she collects herself:*   Oh, good; now I feel bad. Now I feel like crying. I do; I feel like crying.

BABE: Me, too. Me, too.

MEG: Well, you've gotten me depressed!

LENNY: I'm sorry. I'm sorry. It, ah, happened last night. He had another stroke.

They laugh again.

MEG: I see.

LENNY: But he's stabilized now. *She chokes up once more.*

MEG: That's good. You two okay?

BABE *and* LENNY *nod.*

MEG: You look like you need some rest.

BABE *and* LENNY *nod again.*

MEG, *going on, about her heel:*   I hope that'll stay. *She puts the top back on the glue. A realization:* Oh, of course, now I won't be able to tell him the truth about all those lies I told. I mean, finally I get my wits about me, and he conks out. It's just like him. Babe, can I wear your slippers till this glue dries?

BABE: Sure.

LENNY, *after a pause:*   Things sure are gonna be different around here . . . when Old Granddaddy dies. Well, not for you two really, but for me.

MEG: It'll work out.

BABE, *depressed:*   Yeah. It'll work out.

LENNY: I hope so. I'm just afraid of being here all by myself. All alone.

MEG: Well, you don't have to be alone. Maybe Babe'll move back in here.

LENNY *looks at* BABE *hopefully.*

BABE: No, I don't think I'll be livng here.

MEG, *realizing her mistake:*   Well, anyway, you're your own woman. Invite some people over. Have some parties. Go out with strange men.

LENNY: I don't know any strange men.

MEG: Well . . . you know that Charlie.

LENNY, *shaking her head:*   Not anymore.

MEG: Why not?

LENNY, *breaking down:*   I told him we should never see each other again.

MEG: Well, if you told him, you can just untell him.

LENNY: Oh, no, I couldn't. I'd feel like a fool.

MEG: Oh, that's not a good enough reason! All people in love feel like fools. Don't they, Babe?

BABE: Sure.

MEG: Look, why don't you give him a call right now? See how things stand.

LENNY: Oh, no! I'd be too scared—

MEG: But what harm could it possibly do? I mean, it's not gonna make things any worse than this never seeing him again, at all, forever.

LENNY: I suppose that's true—

MEG: Of course it is; so call him up! Take a chance, will you? Just take some sort of chance!

LENNY: You think I should?

MEG: Of course! You've got to try— You do!

LENNY *looks over at* BABE.

BABE: You do, Lenny— I think you do.

LENNY: Really? Really, really?

MEG: Yes! Yes!

BABE: You should!

LENNY: All right. I will! I will!

MEG: Oh, good!

BABE: Good!

LENNY: I'll call him right now, while I've got my confidence up!

MEG: Have you got the number?

LENNY: Uh huh. But, ah, I think I wanna call him upstairs. It'll be more private.

MEG: Ah, good idea.

LENNY: I'm just gonna go on and call him up and see what happens— *She has started up the stairs.* Wish me good luck!

MEG: Good luck!

BABE: Good luck, Lenny!

LENNY: Thanks.

LENNY *gets almost out of sight when the phone rings. She stops;* MEG *picks up the phone.*

MEG: Hello? *Then, in a whisper:* Oh, thank you very much . . . Yes, I will. 'Bye, 'bye.
LENNY: Who was it?
MEG: Wrong number. They wanted Weed's Body Shop.
LENNY: Oh. Well, I'll be right back down in a minute. *She exits.*
MEG, *after a moment, whispering to* BABE: That was the bakery; Lenny's cake is ready!
BABE, *who has become increasingly depressed:* Oh.
MEG: I think I'll sneak on down to the corner and pick it up. *She starts to leave.*
BABE: Meg—
MEG: What?
BABE: Nothing.
MEG: You okay?

BABE *shakes her head.*

MEG: What is it?
BABE: It's just—
MEG: What?

BABE *gets the envelope containing the photographs.*

BABE: Here. Take a look.
MEG, *taking the envelope:* What is it?
BABE: It's some evidence Zackery's collected against me. Looks like my goose is cooked.

MEG *opens the envelope and looks at the photographs.*

MEG: My God, it's—it's you and . . . is *that* Willie Jay?
BABE: Yah.
MEG: Well, he certainly *has* grown. You were right about that. My, oh, my.
BABE: Please don't tell Lenny. She'd hate me.
MEG: I won't. I won't tell Lenny. *Putting the pictures back into the envelope:* What are you gonna do?
BABE: What can I do?

There is a knock on the door. BABE *grabs the envelope and hides it.*

MEG: Who is it?
BARNETTE'S VOICE: It's Barnette Lloyd.

MEG: Oh. Come on in, Barnette.

BARNETTE *enters. His eyes are ablaze with excitement.*

BARNETTE, *as he paces around the room:*   Well, good morning! *Shaking* MEG'S *hand:* Good morning, Miss MaGrath. *Touching* BABE *on the shoulder:* Becky. *Moving away:* What I meant to say is, How are you doing this morning?

MEG: Ah—fine. Fine.

BARNETTE: Good. Good. I—I just had time to drop by for a minute.

MEG: Oh.

BARNETTE: So, ah, how's your granddad doing?

MEG: Well, not very, ah—ah, he's in this coma. *She breaks up laughing.*

BARNETTE: I see . . . I see. *To* BABE: Actually, the primary reason I came by was to pick up that—envelope. I left it here last night in all the confusion. *Pause.* You, ah, still do have it?

BABE *hands him the envelope.*

BARNETTE: Yes. *Taking the envelope:* That's the one. I'm sure it'll be much better off in my office safe. *He puts the envelope into his coat pocket.*

MEG: I'm sure it will.

BARNETTE: Beg your pardon?

BABE: It's all right. I showed her the pictures.

BARNETTE: Ah; I see.

MEG: So what's going to happen now, Barnette? What are those pictures gonna mean?

BARNETTE, *after pacing a moment:*   Hmmm. May I speak frankly and openly?

BABE: Uh huh.

MEG: Please do—

BARNETTE: Well, I tell you now, at first glance, I admit those pictures had me considerably perturbed and upset. Perturbed to the point that I spent most of last night going over certain suspect papers and reports that had fallen into my hands—rather recklessly.

BABE: What papers do you mean?

BARNETTE: Papers that, pending word from three varied and unbiased experts, could prove graft, fraud, forgery, as well as a history of unethical behavior.

MEG: You mean about Zackery?

BARNETTE: Exactly. You see, I now intend to make this matter just as sticky and gritty for one Z. Botrelle as it is for us. Why, with the amount of scandal I'll dig up, Botrelle will be forced to settle this affair on our own terms!

MEG: Oh, Babe! Did you hear that?

BABE: Yes! Oh, yes! So you've won it! You've won your lifelong vendetta!

BARNETTE: Well . . . well, now of course it's problematic in that, well, in that we won't be able to expose him openly in the courts. That was the original game plan.

BABE: But why not? Why?

BARNETTE: Well, it's only that if, well, if a jury were to—to get, say, a glance at these, ah, photographs, well . . . well, possibly . . .

BABE: We could be sunk.

BARNETTE: In a sense. But! On the other hand, if a newspaper were to get a hold of our little item, Mr. Zackery Botrelle could find himself boiling in some awfully hot water. So what I'm looking for, very simply, is—a deal.

BABE: A deal?

MEG: Thank you, Barnette. It's a sunny day, Babe. *Realizing she is in the way:* Ooh, where's that broken shoe? *She grabs her boots and runs upstairs.*

BABE: So, you're having to give up your vendetta?

BARNETTE: Well, in a way. For the time. It, ah, seems to me you shouldn't always let your life be ruled by such things as, ah, personal vendettas. *Looking at* BABE *with meaning:* Other things can be important.

BABE: I don't know, I don't exactly know. How 'bout Willie Jay? Will he be all right?

BARNETTE: Yes, it's all been taken care of. He'll be leaving incognito on the midnight bus—heading north.

BABE: North.

BARNETTE: I'm sorry, it seemed the only . . . way.

BARNETTE *moves to her; she moves away.*

BABE: Look, you'd better be getting on back to your work.

BARNETTE, *awkwardly:* Right—'cause I—I've got those important calls out. *Full of hope for her:* They'll be pouring in directly. *He starts to leave, then says to her with love:* We'll talk.

MEG, *reappearing in her boots:* Oh, Barnette—

BARNETTE: Yes?

MEG: Could you give me a ride just down to the corner? I need to stop at Helen's Bakery.

BARNETTE: Be glad to.

MEG: Thanks. Listen, Babe, I'll be right back with the cake. We're gonna have the best celebration! Now, ah, if Lenny asks where I've gone, just say I'm . . . Just say, I've gone out back to, ah, pick up some pawpaws! Okay?

BABE: Okay.

MEG: Fine; I'll be back in a bit. Goodbye.

BABE: 'Bye.

BARNETTE: Goodbye, Becky.

BABE: Goodbye, Barnette. Take care.

MEG *and* BARNETTE *exit.* BABE *sits staring ahead, in a state of deep despair.*

BABE: Goodbye, Becky. Goodbye, Barnette. Goodbye, Becky. *She stops when* LENNY *comes down the stairs in a fluster.*

LENNY: Oh! Oh! Oh! I'm so ashamed! I'm such a coward! I'm such a yellow-bellied chicken! I'm so ashamed! Where's Meg?

BABE, *suddenly bright:*   She's, ah—gone out back—to pick up some paw-paws.

LENNY: Oh. Well, at least I don't have to face her! I just couldn't do it! I couldn't make the call! My heart was pounding like a hammer. Pound! Pound! Pound! Why, I looked down and I could actually see my blouse moving back and forth! Oh, Babe, you look so disappointed. Are you?

BABE, *despondently:*   Uh huh.

LENNY: Oh, no! I've disappointed Babe! I can't stand it! I've gone and disappointed my little sister, Babe! Oh, no! I feel like howling like a dog!

CHICK'S VOICE: Oooh, Lenny! *She enters dramatically, dripping with sympathy.* Well, I just don't know what to say! I'm so sorry! I am so sorry for you! And for little Babe here, too. I mean, to have such a sister as that!

LENNY: What do you mean?

CHICK: Oh, you don't need to pretend with me. I saw it all from over there in my own back yard; I saw Meg stumbling out of Doc Porter's pickup truck, not fifteen minutes ago. And her looking such a disgusting mess. You must be so ashamed! You must just want to die! Why, I always said that girl was nothing but cheap Christmas trash!

LENNY: Don't talk that way about Meg.

CHICK: Oh, come on now, Lenny honey, I know exactly how you feel about Meg. Why, Meg's a low-class tramp and you need not have one more blessed thing to do with her and her disgusting behavior.

LENNY: I said, don't you ever talk that way about my sister Meg again.

CHICK: Well, my goodness gracious, Lenora, don't be such a noodle—it's the truth!

LENNY: I don't care if it's the Ten Commandments. I don't want to hear it in my home. Not ever again.

CHICK: In your home?! Why, I never in all my life—This is my grandfather's home! And you're just living here on his charity; so don't you get high-falutin' with me, Miss Lenora Josephine MaGrath!

LENNY: Get out of here—

CHICK: Don't you tell me to get out! What makes you think you can order me around? Why, I've had just about my fill of you trashy MaGraths and your trashy ways: hanging yourselves in cellars; carrying on with married men; shooting your own husbands!

LENNY: Get out!

CHICK, *to* BABE: And don't you think she's not gonna end up at the state prison farm or in some—mental institution. Why, it's a clear-cut case of manslaughter with intent to kill!

LENNY: Out! Get out!

CHICK, *running on:*   That's what everyone's saying, deliberate intent to kill! And you'll pay for that! Do you hear me? You'll pay!

LENNY, *picking up a broom and threatening* CHICK *with it:* And I'm telling you to get out!

CHICK: You—you put that down this minute— Are you a raving lunatic?

LENNY, *beating* CHICK *with the broom:* I said for you to get out! That means out! And never, never, never come back!

CHICK, *overlapping, as she runs around the room:* Oh! Oh! Oh! You're crazy! You're crazy!

LENNY, *chasing* CHICK *out the door:* Do you hear me, Chick the Stick! This is my home! This is my house! Get out! Out!

CHICK, *overlapping:* Oh! Oh! Police! Police! You're crazy! Help! Help!

LENNY *chases* CHICK *out of the house. They are both screaming. The phone rings.* BABE *goes and picks it up.*

BABE: Hello? . . . Oh, hello Zackery! . . . Yes, he showed them to me! . . . You're what! . . . What do you mean? . . . What! . . . You can't put me out to Whitfield . . . 'Cause I'm not crazy . . . I'm not! I'm not! . . . She wasn't crazy, either . . . Don't you call my mother crazy! . . . No, you're not! You're not gonna. You're not! *She slams the phone down and stares wildly ahead.* He's not. He's not. *As she walks over to the ribbon drawer:* I'll do it. I will. And he won't . . . *She opens the drawer, pulls out the rope, becomes terrified, throws the rope back in the drawer, and slams it shut.*

LENNY *enters from the back door swinging the broom and laughing.*

LENNY: Oh, my! Oh, my! You should have seen us! Why, I chased Chick the Stick right up the mimosa tree. I did! I left her right up there screaming in the tree!

BABE, *laughing; she is insanely delighted:* Oh, you did!

LENNY: Yes, I did! And I feel so good! I do! I feel good! I feel good!

BABE, *overlapping:* Good! Good, Lenny! Good for you!

They dance around the kitchen.

LENNY, *stopping:* You know what—

BABE: What?

LENNY: I'm gonna call Charlie! I'm gonna call him up right now!

BABE: You are?

LENNY: Yeah, I feel like I can really do it!

BABE: You do?

LENNY: My courage is up; my heart's in it; the time is right! No more beating around the bush! Let's strike while the iron is hot!

BABE: Right! Right! No more beating around the bush! Strike while the iron is hot!

LENNY *goes to the phone.* BABE *rushes over to the ribbon drawer. She begins tearing through it.*

LENNY, *with the receiver in her hand:* I'm calling him up, Babe— I'm really gonna do it!

BABE, *still tearing through the drawer:* Good! Do it! Good!

LENNY, *as she dials:* Look. My hands aren't even shaking.

BABE, *pulling out a red rope:* Don't we have any stronger rope than this?

LENNY: I guess not. All the rope we've got's in that drawer. *About her hands:* Now they're shaking a little.

BABE *takes the rope and goes up the stairs.* LENNY *finishes dialing the number. She waits for an answer.*

LENNY: Hello? . . . Hello, Charlie. This is Lenny MaGrath . . . Well, I'm fine. I'm just fine. *An awkward pause:* I was, ah, just calling to see—how you're getting on . . . Well, good. Good . . . Yes, I know I said that. Now I wish I didn't say it . . . Well, the reason I said that before, about not seeing each other again, was 'cause of me, not you . . . Well, it's just I—I can't have any children. I—have this ovary problem . . . Why, Charlie, what a thing to say! . . . Well, they're not all little snot-nosed pigs! . . . You think they are! . . . Oh, Charlie, stop, stop! You're making me laugh . . . Yes, I guess I was. I can see now that I was . . . You are? . . . Well, I'm dying to see you, too . . . Well, I don't know when, Charlie . . . soon. How about, well, how about tonight? . . . You will? . . . Oh, you will! . . . All right, I'll be here. I'll be right here . . . Goodbye, then, Charlie. Goodbye for now. *She hangs up the phone in a daze.* Babe. Oh, Babe! He's coming! He's coming! Babe! Oh, Babe, where are you? Meg! Oh . . . out back—picking up paw-paws. *As she exits through the back door:* And those paw-paws are just ripe for picking up!

There is a moment of silence; then a loud, horrible thud is heard coming from upstairs. The telephone begins ringing immediately. It rings five times before BABE *comes hurrying down the stairs with a broken piece of rope hanging around her neck. The phone continues to ring.*

BABE, *to the phone:* Will you shut up! *She is jerking the rope from around her neck. She grabs a knife to cut if off.* Cheap! Miserable! I hate you! I hate you! *She throws the rope violently across the room. The phone stops ringing.* Thank God. *She looks at the stove, goes over to it, and turns the gas on. The sound of gas escaping is heard. She sniffs at it.* Come on. Come on . . . Hurry up . . . I beg of you—hurry up! *Finally, she feels the oven is ready; she takes a deep breath and opens the oven door to stick her head into it. She spots the rack and furiously jerks it out. Taking another breath, she sticks her head into the oven. She stands for several moments tapping her fingers furiously on top of the stove. She speaks from inside the oven:* Oh, please. Please. *After a few moments, she reaches for the box of matches with her head still in the oven. She tries to strike a match. It doesn't catch.* Oh, Mama, please! *She throws the match away and is getting a second one.* Mama . . . Mama . . . So that's why you done it!

In her excitement she starts to get up, bangs her head, and falls back in the oven.

MEG *enters from the back door, carrying a birthday cake in a pink box.*

MEG: Babe! *She throws the box down and runs to pull Babe's head out of the oven.* Oh, my God! What are you doing? What the hell are you doing?
BABE, *dizzily:*   Nothing. I don't know. Nothing.

MEG *turns off the gas and moves* BABE *to a chair near the open door.*

MEG: Sit down. Sit down! Will you sit down!
BABE: I'm okay. I'm okay.
MEG: Put your head between your knees and breathe deep!
BABE: Meg—
MEG: Just do it! I'll get you some water. *She gets some water for* BABE. Here.
BABE: Thanks.
MEG: Are you okay?
BABE: Uh huh.
MEG: Are you sure?
BABE: Yeah, I'm sure. I'm okay.
MEG, *getting a damp rag and putting it over her own face:*   Well, good. That's good.
BABE: Meg—
MEG: Yes?
BABE: I know why she did it.
MEG: What? Why who did what?
BABE, *with joy:*   Mama. I know why she hung that cat along with her.
MEG: You do?
BABE, *with enlightenment:*   It's 'cause she was afraid of dying all alone.
MEG: Was she?
BABE: She felt so unsure, you know, as to what was coming. It seems the best thing coming up would be a lot of angels and all of them singing. But I imagine they have high, scary voices and little gold pointed fingers that are as sharp as blades and you don't want to meet 'em all alone. You'd be afraid to meet 'em all alone. So it wasn't like what people were saying about her hating that cat. Fact is, she loved that cat. She needed him with her 'cause she felt so all alone.
MEG: Oh, Babe . . . Babe. Why, Babe? Why?
BABE: Why what?
MEG: Why did you stick your head into the oven?!
BABE: I don't know, Meg. I'm having a bad day. It's been a real bad day; those pictures, and Barnette giving up his vendetta; then Willie Jay heading north; and—and Zackery called me up. *Trembling with terror:* He says he's gonna have me classified insane and then send me on out to the Whitfield asylum.
MEG: What! Why, he could never do that!
BABE: Why not?

MEG: 'Cause you're not insane.

BABE: I'm not?

MEG: No! He's trying to bluff you. Don't you see it? Barnette's got him running scared.

BABE: Really?

MEG: Sure. He's scared to death—calling you insane. Ha! Why, you're just as perfectly sane as anyone walking the streets of Hazlehurst, Mississippi.

BABE: I am?

MEG: More so! A lot more so!

BABE: Good!

MEG: But, Babe, we've just got to learn how to get through these real bad days here. I mean, it's getting to be a thing in our family. *Slight pause as she looks at Babe:* Come on, now. Look, we've got Lenny's cake right here. I mean, don't you wanna be around to give her her cake, watch her blow out the candles?

BABE, *realizing how much she wants to be here:* Yeah, I do, I do. 'Cause she always loves to make her birthday wishes on those candles.

MEG: Well, then we'll give her her cake and maybe you won't be so miserable.

BABE: Okay.

MEG: Good. Go on and take it out of the box.

BABE: Okay. *She takes the cake out of the box. It is a magical moment.* Gosh, it's a pretty cake.

MEG, *handing her some matches:* Here now. You can go on and light up the candles.

BABE: All right. *She starts to light the candles.* I love to light up candles. And there are so many here. Thirty pink ones in all, plus one green one to grow on.

MEG, *watching her light the candles:* They're pretty.

BABE: They are. *She stops lighting the candles.* And I'm not like Mama. I'm not so all alone.

MEG: You're not.

BABE, *as she goes back to lighting candles:* Well, you'd better keep an eye out for Lenny. She's supposed to be surprised.

MEG: All right. Do you know where she's gone?

BABE: Well, she's not here inside—so she must have gone on outside.

MEG: Oh, well, then I'd better run and find her.

BABE: Okay; 'cause these candles are gonna melt down.

MEG *starts out the door.*

MEG: Wait—there she is coming. Lenny! Oh, Lenny! Come on! Hurry up!

BABE, *overlapping and improvising as she finishes lighting candles:* Oh, no! No! Well, yes— Yes! No, wait! Wait! Okay! Hurry up!

LENNY *enters.* MEG *covers* LENNY'S *eyes with her hands.*

LENNY, *terrified:* What? What is it? What?

MEG *and* BABE: Surprise! Happy birthday! Happy birthday to Lenny!

LENNY: Oh, no! Oh, me! What a surprise! I could just cry! Oh, look: *Happy birthday, Lenny—A Day Late!* How cute! My! Will you look at all those candles—it's absolutely frightening.

BABE, *a spontaneous thought:* Oh, no, Lenny, it's good! 'Cause—'cause the more candles you have on your cake, the stronger your wish is.

LENNY: Really?

BABE: Sure!

LENNY: Mercy! MEG *and* BABE *start to sing.*

LENNY, *interrupting the song:* Oh, but wait! I—can't think of my wish! My body's gone all nervous inside.

MEG: For God's sake, Lenny—Come on!

BABE: The wax is all melting!

LENNY: My mind is just a blank, a total blank!

MEG: Will you please just—

BABE, *overlapping:* Lenny, hurry! Come on!

LENNY: Okay! Okay! Just go!

MEG *and* BABE *burst into the "Happy Birthday" song. As it ends, Lenny blows out all the candles on the cake.* MEG *and* BABE *applaud loudly.*

MEG: Oh, you made it!

BABE: Hurray!

LENNY: Oh, me! Oh, me! I hope that wish comes true! I hope it does!

BABE: Why? What did you wish for?

LENNY, *as she removes the candles from the cake:* Why, I can't tell you that.

BABE: Oh, sure you can—

LENNY: Oh, no! Then it won't come true.

BABE: Why, that's just superstition! Of course it will, if you made it deep enough.

MEG: Really? I didn't know that.

LENNY: Well, Babe's the regular expert on birthday wishes.

BABE: It's just I get these feelings. Now, come on and tell us. What was it you wished for?

MEG: Yes, tell us. What was it?

LENNY: Well, I guess it wasn't really a specific wish. This—this vision just sort of came into my mind.

BABE: A vision? What was it of?

LENNY: I don't know exactly. It was something about the three of us smiling and laughing together.

BABE: Well, when was it? Was it far away or near?

LENNY: I'm not sure; but it wasn't forever; it wasn't for every minute. Just this one moment and we were all laughing.

BABE: Then, what were we laughing about?

LENNY: I don't know. Just nothing, I guess.

MEG: Well, that's a nice wish to make.

LENNY *and* MEG *look at each other a moment.*

MEG: Here, now, I'll get a knife so we can go ahead and cut the cake in celebration of Lenny being born!

BABE: Oh, yes! And give each one of us a rose. A whole rose apiece!

LENNY, *cutting the cake nervously:*   Well, I'll try—I'll try!

MEG, *licking the icing off a candle:*   Mmmm—this icing is delicious! Here, try some!

BABE: Mmmm! It's wonderful! Here, Lenny!

LENNY, *laughing joyously as she licks icing from her fingers and cuts huge pieces of cake that her sisters bite into ravenously:*   Oh, how I do love having birthday cake for breakfast! How I do!

The sisters freeze for a moment laughing and catching cake. The lights change and frame them in a magical, golden, sparkling glimmer; saxophone music is heard. The lights dim to blackout, and the saxophone continues to play.

Curtain

SAM SHEPARD (b. 1943)

Curse of the Starving Class

Sam Shepard, one of the most brilliant and certainly one of the most prolific of the younger American playwrights, was born in Illinois. He has worked as a rock musician, an actor, and a screen writer. *Buried Child,* perhaps his most famous play, won the Pulitzer Prize for drama in 1979. His other major plays include *La Turista* (1968), *The Tooth of Crime* (1974), and *True West* (1981). *Curse of the Starving Class* was first performed at the New York Shakespeare Festival in 1978.

Curse of the Starving Class was first performed by the New York Shakespeare Festival on March 2, 1978, presented by Joseph Papp. The director was Robert Woodruff, and the cast was as follows:

CHARACTERS

WESLEY	Ebbe Roe Smith
ELLA	Olympia Dukakis
EMMA	Pamela Reed
TAYLOR	Kenneth Welsh
WESTON	James Gammon
ELLIS	Eddie Jones
MALCOLM	John Aquino

EMERSON   Michael J. Pollard
SLATER   Raymond J. Barry

ACT I

SCENE: *Upstage center is a very plain breakfast table with a red oilcloth covering it. Four mismatched metal chairs are set one at each side of the table. Suspended in midair to stage right and stage left are two ruffled, red-checked curtains, slightly faded. In the down left corner of the stage are a working refrigerator and a small gas stove, set right up next to each other. In the down right corner is a pile of wooden debris, torn screen, etc., which are the remains of a broken door. Lights come up on* WESLEY, *in sweatshirt, jeans and cowboy boots, who is picking up the pieces of the door and throwing them methodically into an old wheelbarrow. This goes on for a while. Then* WESLEY'S *mother,* ELLA, *enters slowly from down left. She is a small woman wearing a bathrobe, pink fuzzy slippers, hair in curlers. She is just waking up and winds an alarm clock in her hand as she watches* WESLEY *sleepily.* WESLEY *keeps cleaning up the debris, ignoring her.*

ELLA *after a while:*   You shouldn't be doing that.
WESLEY: I'm doing it.
ELLA: Yes, but you shouldn't be. He should be doing it. He's the one who broke it down.
WESLEY: He's not here.
ELLA: He's not back yet?
WESLEY: Nope.
ELLA: Well, just leave it until he gets back.
WESLEY: In the meantime we gotta' live in it.
ELLA: He'll be back. He can clean it up then.

WESLEY *goes on clearing the debris into the wheelbarrow.* ELLA *finishes winding the clock and then sets it on the stove.*

ELLA *looking at clock:*   I must've got to sleep at five in the morning.
WESLEY: Did you call the cops?
ELLA: Last night?
WESLEY: Yeah.
ELLA: Sure I called the cops. Are you kidding? I was in danger of my life. I was being threatened.
WESLEY: He wasn't threatening you.
ELLA: Are you kidding me? He broke the door down, didn't he?
WESLEY: He was just trying to get in.
ELLA: That's no way to get into a house. There's plenty of other ways to get into a house. He could've climbed through a window.
WESLEY: He was drunk.
ELLA: That's not my problem.
WESLEY: You locked the door.
ELLA: Sure I locked the door. I told him I was going to lock the door. I

told him the next time that happened I was locking the door and he could sleep in a hotel.

WESLEY: Is that where he is now?

ELLA: How should I know?

WESLEY: He took the Packard I guess.

ELLA: If that's the one that's missing I guess that's the one he took.

WESLEY: How come you called the cops?

ELLA: I was scared.

WESLEY: You thought he was going to kill you?

ELLA: I thought— I thought, "I don't know who this is. I don't know who this is trying to break in here. Who is this? It could be anyone."

WESLEY: I heard you screaming at each other.

ELLA: Yes.

WESLEY: So you must've known who it was.

ELLA: I wasn't sure. That was the frightening part. I could smell him right through the door.

WESLEY: He was drinking that much?

ELLA: Not that. His skin.

WESLEY: Oh.

ELLA *suddenly cheerful:* You want some breakfast?

WESLEY: No, thanks.

ELLA *going to refrigerator:* Well I'm going to have some.

WESLEY *still cleaning:* It's humiliating to have the cops come to your own house. Makes me feel like we're someone else.

ELLA *looking in refrigerator:* There's no eggs but there's bacon and bread.

WESLEY: Makes me feel lonely. Like we're in trouble or something.

ELLA *still looking in refrigerator:* We're not in trouble. He's in trouble, but we're not.

WESLEY: You didn't have to call the cops.

ELLA *slamming refrigerator door and holding bacon and bread:* I told you, he was trying to kill me!

They look at each other for a moment. ELLA *breaks it by putting the bacon and bread down on top of the stove.* WESLEY *goes back to cleaning up the debris. He keeps talking as* ELLA *looks through the lower drawers of the stove and pulls out a frying pan. She lights one of the burners on the stove and starts cooking the bacon.*

WESLEY *as he throws wood into wheelbarrow:* I was lying there on my back. I could smell the avocado blossoms. I could hear the coyotes. I could hear stock cars squealing down the street. I could feel myself in my bed in my room in this house in this town in this state in this country. I could feel this country close like it was part of my bones. I could feel the presence of all the people outside, at night, in the dark. Even sleeping people I could feel. Even all the sleeping animals. Dogs. Peacocks. Bulls. Even tractors sitting in the wetness, waiting for the sun to come up. I was looking straight up at the ceiling at all my model airplanes hanging by all their thin metal wires. Floating. Swaying very quietly like they were being blown by someone's breath. Cobwebs moving with them. Dust laying on their wings. Decals peeling off their wings. My P-39. My Messerschmitt. My Jap Zero. I could feel myself lying far below them on my bed like I was on the ocean and overhead they were on reconnaissance. Scouting me. Floating. Taking pictures of the enemy. Me, the enemy. I could feel the space around me like a big, black world. I listened like an animal. My listening was afraid. Afraid of sound. Tense. Like any second something could invade me. Some foreigner. Something undescribable. Then I heard the Packard coming up the hill. From a mile off I could tell it was the Packard by the sound of the valves. The lifters have a sound like nothing else. Then I could picture my Dad driving it. Shifting unconsciously. Downshifting into second for the last pull up the hill. I could feel the headlights closing in. Cutting through the orchard. I could see the trees being lit one after the other by the lights, then going back to black. My heart was pounding. Just from my Dad coming back. Then I heard him pull the brake. Lights go off. Key's turned off. Then a long silence. Him just sitting in the car. Just sitting. I picture him just sitting. What's he doing? Just sitting. Waiting to get out. Why's he waiting to get out? He's plastered and can't move. He's plastered and doesn't want to move. He's going to sleep there all night. He's slept there before. He's woken up with dew on the hood before. Freezing headache. Teeth covered with peanuts. Then I hear the door of the Packard open. A pop of metal. Dogs barking down the road. Door slams. Feet. Paper bag being tucked under one arm. Paper bag covering "Tiger Rose." Feet coming. Feet walking toward the door. Feet stopping. Heart pounding. Sound of door not opening. Foot kicking door. Man's voice. Dad's voice. Dad calling Mom. No answer. Foot kicking. Foot kicking harder. Wood splitting. Man's voice. In the night. Foot kicking hard through door. One foot right through door. Bottle crashing. Glass breaking. Fist through door. Man cursing. Man going insane. Feet and hands tearing. Head smashing. Man yelling. Shoulder smashing. Whole body crashing. Woman screaming. Mom screaming. Mom screaming for police. Man throwing wood. Man throwing up. Mom calling cops. Dad crashing away. Back down driveway. Car door slamming. Ignition grinding. Wheels screaming. First gear grinding. Wheels screaming off down hill. Packard disappearing. Sound disappearing. No sound. No sight. Planes still hanging. Heart still pounding. No sound. Mom crying soft. Soft crying. Then no sound. Then softly crying. Then moving around through house. Then no moving. Then crying softly. Then stopping. Then, far off the freeway could be heard.

WESLEY *picks up one end of the wheelbarrow. He makes the sound of a car and pushes it off right, leaving* ELLA *alone at the stove watching the bacon. She speaks alone.*

ELLA: Now I know the first thing you'll think is that you've hurt yourself. That's only natural. You'll think that something drastic has gone wrong with your insides and that's why you're bleeding. That's only a natural reaction. But I want you to know the truth. I want you to know all the facts before you go off and pick up a lot of lies. Now, the first thing is that you should never go swimming when that happens. It can cause you to bleed to death. The water draws it out of you.

WESLEY's *sister,* EMMA, *enters from right. She is younger and dressed in a white and green 4-H Club uniform. She carries several hand-painted charts on the correct way to cut up a frying chicken. She sets the charts down on the table upstage and arranges them as* ELLA *talks to her as though she's just continuing the conversation.*

EMMA: But what if I'm invited? The Thompsons have a new heated pool. You should see it, Ma. They even got blue lights around it at night. It's really beautiful. Like a fancy hotel.

ELLA *tending to the bacon:*   I said no swimming and that's what I meant! This thing is no joke. Your whole life is changing. You don't want to live in ignorance do you?

EMMA: No, Ma.

ELLA: All right then. The next thing is sanitary napkins. You don't want to buy them out of any old machine in any old gas station bathroom. I know they say "sanitized" on the package but they're a far cry from "sanitized." They're filthy in fact. They've been sitting around in those places for months. You don't know whose quarters go into those machines. Those quarters carry germs. Those innocent looking silver quarters with Washington's head staring straight ahead. His handsome jaw jutting out. Spewing germs all over those napkins.

EMMA *still arranging charts:*   How come they call them napkins?

ELLA *stopping for a second:*   What?

EMMA: How come they call them napkins?

ELLA *back to the bacon:*   Well, I don't know. I didn't make it up. Somebody called them napkins a long time ago and it just stuck.

EMMA: "Sanitary napkins."

ELLA: Yes.

EMMA: It's a funny sound. Like a hospital or something.

ELLA: Well that's what they should be like, but unfortunately they're not. They're not hospital clean that's for sure. And you should know that anything you stick up in there should be absolutely hospital clean.

EMMA: Stick up in where?

ELLA *turns upstage toward* EMMA, *then changes the subject.*

ELLA: What are those things?

EMMA: They're for my demonstration.

ELLA: What demonstration?

EMMA: How to cut up a frying chicken.

ELLA *back to bacon:*   Oh.

EMMA: For 4-H. You know. I'm giving a demonstration at the fair. I told you before. I hope you haven't used up my last chicken.

EMMA *goes to refrigerator and looks inside for a chicken.*

ELLA: I forgot you were doing that. I thought that wasn't for months yet.
EMMA: I told you it was this month. The fair's always this month. Every year it's this month.
ELLA: I forgot.
EMMA: Where's my chicken?
ELLA *innocently:*   What chicken?
EMMA: I had a fryer in here all ready to go. I killed it and dressed it and everything!
ELLA: It's not in there. All we got is bacon and bread.
EMMA: I just stuck it in here yesterday, Ma! You didn't use it did you?
ELLA: Why would I use it?
EMMA: For soup or something.
ELLA: Why would I use a fryer for soup. Don't be ridiculous.
EMMA *slamming refrigerator:*   It's not in there!
ELLA: Don't start screaming in here! Go outside and scream if you're going to scream!

EMMA *storms off stage right.* ELLA *takes the bacon off the stove. Slight pause, then* EMMA *can be heard yelling off stage.* ELLA *puts some bread in the frying pan and starts frying it.*

EMMA'S VOICE *off:*   That was my chicken and you fucking boiled it! YOU BOILED MY CHICKEN! I RAISED THAT CHICKEN FROM THE INCUBATOR TO THE GRAVE AND YOU BOILED IT LIKE IT WAS ANY OLD FROZEN HUNK OF FLESH! YOU USED IT WITH NO CONSIDERATION FOR THE LABOR IN-VOLVED! I HAD TO FEED THAT CHICKEN CRUSHED CORN EVERY MORNING FOR A YEAR! I HAD TO CHANGE ITS WA-TER! I HAD TO KILL IT WITH AN AX! I HAD TO SPILL ITS GUTS OUT! I HAD TO PLUCK EVERY FEATHER ON ITS BODY! I HAD TO DO ALL THAT WORK SO THAT YOU COULD TAKE IT AND BOIL IT!

WESLEY *enters from left and crosses to center.*

WESLEY: What's all the screaming?
ELLA: Somebody stole her chicken.
WESLEY: Stole it?
ELLA: Boiled it.
WESLEY: You boiled it.
ELLA: I didn't know it was hers.
WESLEY: Did it have her name on it?
ELLA: No, of course not.
WESLEY: Then she's got nothing to scream about. *Yelling off stage.* SHUT UP OUT THERE! YOU SHOULD'VE PUT YOUR NAME ON IT IF YOU DIDN'T WANT ANYBODY TO BOIL IT!

EMMA'S VOICE *off:*   EAT MY SOCKS!

WESLEY *crossing up to table:*   Great language. *Noticing charts on table.* What's all this stuff?

ELLA: Her charts. She's giving a demonstration.

WESLEY *holding one of the charts up:*   A demonstration? On what?

ELLA: How to cut up a chicken. What else.

ELLA *takes her bacon and bread on a plate and crosses up to table. She sits at the stage left end.*

WESLEY: Anybody knows how to cut up a chicken.

ELLA: Well, there's special bones you have to crack. Special ways of doing it evidently.

WESLEY *turning downstage with chart held out in front of him:*   What's so special about it.

ELLA *eating at table:*   The anatomy is what's special. The anatomy of a chicken. If you know the anatomy you're half-way home.

WESLEY *facing front, laying chart down on floor:*   It's just bones.

EMMA'S VOICE *off:*   THERE'S NO CONSIDERATION! IF I'D COME ACROSS A CHICKEN IN THE FREEZER I WOULD'VE ASKED SOMEONE FIRST BEFORE I BOILED IT!

ELLA *yelling, still eating:*   NOT IF YOU WERE STARVING!

WESLEY *unzips his fly, takes out his pecker, and starts pissing all over the chart on the floor.* ELLA *just keeps eating at the table, not noticing.*

EMMA'S VOICE *off:*   NO ONE'S STARVING IN THIS HOUSE! YOU'RE FEEDING YOUR FACE RIGHT NOW!

ELLA: So what!

EMMA'S VOICE *off:*   SO NO ONE'S STARVING! WE DON'T BELONG TO THE STARVING CLASS!

ELLA: Don't speak unless you know what you're speaking about! There's no such thing as a starving class!

EMMA'S VOICE *off:*   THERE IS SO! THERE'S A STARVING CLASS OF PEOPLE, AND WE'RE NOT PART OF IT!

ELLA: WE'RE HUNGRY, AND THAT'S STARVING ENOUGH FOR ME!

EMMA'S VOICE *off:*   YOU'RE A SPOILED BRAT!

ELLA *to* WESLEY: Did you hear what she called me? *She notices what he's doing, she yells to* EMMA. EMMA!

EMMA'S VOICE *off:*   WHAT!

ELLA: YOUR BROTHER'S PISSING ALL OVER YOUR CHARTS! *Goes back to eating.*

EMMA *enters fast from right and watches* WESLEY *put his joint back in his pants and zip up. They stare at each other as* ELLA *goes on eating at the table.*

EMMA: What kind of a family is this?

ELLA *not looking up:*   I tried to stop him but he wouldn't listen.

EMMA *to* WESLEY: Do you know how long I worked on those charts? I had to do research. I went to the library. I took out books. I spent hours.

WESLEY: It's a stupid thing to spend your time on.

EMMA: I'm leaving this house! *She exits right.*

ELLA *calling after her but staying at table:*   YOU'RE TOO YOUNG! *To* WESLEY. She's too young to leave. It's ridiculous. I can't say I blame her but she's way too young. She's only just now having her first period.

WESLEY *crossing to refrigerator:*   Swell.

ELLA: Well, you don't know what it's like. It's very tough. You don't have to make things worse for her.

WESLEY *opening refrigerator and staring into it:*   I'm not. I'm opening up new possibilities for her. Now she'll have to do something else. It could change her whole direction in life. She'll look back and remember the day her brother pissed all over her charts and see that day as a turning point in her life.

ELLA: How do you figure?

WESLEY: Well, she's already decided to leave home. That's a beginning.

ELLA *standing abruptly:*   She's too young to leave! And get out of that refrigerator!

She crosses to refrigerator and slams the door shut. WESLEY *crosses up to the table and sits at the stage right end.*

ELLA: You're always in the refrigerator!

WESLEY: I'm hungry.

ELLA: How can you be hungry all the time? We're not poor. We're not rich but we're not poor.

WESLEY: What are we then?

ELLA *crossing back to table and sitting opposite* WESLEY: We're somewhere in between. *Pause as* ELLA *starts to eat again;* WESLEY *watches her.* We're going to be rich though.

WESLEY: What do you mean?

ELLA: We're going to have some money real soon.

WESLEY: What're you talking about?

ELLA: Never mind. You just wait though. You'll be very surprised.

WESLEY: I thought Dad got fired.

ELLA: He did. This has nothing to do with your father.

WESLEY: Well, you're not working are you?

ELLA: Just never mind. I'll let you know when the time comes. And then we'll get out of this place, once and for all.

WESLEY: Where are we going?

ELLA: Europe maybe. Wouldn't you like to go to Europe?

WESLEY: No.

ELLA: Why not?

WESLEY: What's in Europe?

ELLA: They have everything in Europe. High art. Paintings. Castles. Buildings. Fancy food.

WESLEY: They got all that here.

ELLA: Why aren't you sensitive like your Grandfather was? I always thought you were just like him, but you're not, are you?

WESLEY: No.

ELLA: Why aren't you? You're circumcized just like him. It's almost identical in fact.

WESLEY: How do you know?

ELLA: I looked. I looked at them both and I could see the similarity.

WESLEY: He's dead.

ELLA: When he was alive is when I looked. Don't be ridiculous.

WESLEY: What'd you sneak into his room or something?

ELLA: We lived in a small house.

EMMA'S VOICE *off:*   WHERE'S MY JODHPURS!

ELLA *to* WESLEY: What's she yelling about?

WESLEY: Her jodhpurs.

ELLA *yelling to* EMMA: What do you need your jodhpurs for?

EMMA'S VOICE *off:*   I'M TAKING THE HORSE!

ELLA: DON'T BE RIDICULOUS! DO YOU KNOW HOW FAR YOU'LL GET ON THAT HORSE? NOT VERY FAR!

EMMA'S VOICE *off:*   FAR ENOUGH!

ELLA: YOU'RE NOT TAKING THE HORSE! *To* WESLEY. Go down and lock that horse in the stall.

WESLEY: Let her go.

ELLA: On a horse? Are you crazy? She'll get killed on the freeway.

WESLEY: She won't take him on the freeway.

ELLA: That horse spooks at its own shadow. *Yelling off to* EMMA. EMMA, YOU'RE NOT TAKING THAT HORSE! *No answering from* EMMA. EMMA! *To* WESLEY. Go see if she went down there. I don't want her taking off on that horse. It's dangerous.

WESLEY: She's a good rider.

ELLA: I don't care!

WESLEY: You go down there then.

Pause. She looks at him.

ELLA: Well, maybe she'll be all right.

WESLEY: Sure she will. She's been out on overnight trail rides before.

ELLA: What a temper she's got.

WESLEY: She's just spoiled.

ELLA: No, she's not. I never gave her a thing extra. Nothing. Bare minimums. That's all.

WESLEY: The old man spoils her.

ELLA: He's never around. How could he spoil her?

WESLEY: When he's around he spoils her.

ELLA: That horse is a killer. I wish you'd go down there and check.

WESLEY: She can handle him.

ELLA: I've seen that horse get a new set of shoes and he's an idiot! They have to throw him down every time.

WESLEY: Look, where's this money coming from?

ELLA: What money?
WESLEY: This money that's going to make us rich.
ELLA: I'm selling the house.

Long pause, as WESLEY *stares at her. She turns away from him.*

ELLA: I'm selling the house, the land, the orchard, the tractor, the stock. Everything. It all goes.
WESLEY: It's not yours.
ELLA: It's mine as much as his!
WESLEY: You're not telling him?
ELLA: No! I'm not telling him and I shouldn't have told you. So just keep it under your hat.
WESLEY: How can you sell the house? It's not legal even.
ELLA: I signed the deed, same as him. We both signed it.
WESLEY: Then he has to co-sign the sale. Fifty-fifty.
ELLA: I already checked with a lawyer, and it's legal.
WESLEY: What about the mortgages? It's not even paid off, and you've borrowed money on it.
ELLA: Don't start questioning me! I've gone through all the arrangements already.
WESLEY: With who!
ELLA: I HAVE A LAWYER FRIEND!
WESLEY: A lawyer friend?
ELLA: Yes. He's very successful. He's handling everything for me.
WESLEY: You hired a lawyer?
ELLA: I told you, he's a friend. He's doing it as a favor.
WESLEY: You're not paying him?
ELLA: He's taking a percentage. A small percentage.
WESLEY: And you're just going to split with the money without telling anybody?
ELLA: I told you. That's enough. You could come with me.
WESLEY: This is where I live.
ELLA: Some home. It doesn't even have a front door now. Rain's going to pour right through here.
WESLEY: You won't even make enough to take a trip to San Diego off this house. It's infested with termites.
ELLA: This land is valuable. Everybody wants a good lot these days.
WESLEY: A lot?
ELLA: This is wonderful property for development. Do you know what land is selling for these days? Have you got any idea?
WESLEY: No.
ELLA: A lot. Tons. Thousands and thousands are being spent every day by ordinary people just on this very thing. Banks are loaning money right and left. Small family loans. People are building. Everyone wants a piece of land. It's the only sure investment. It can never depreciate like a car or a washing machine. Land will double its value in ten years. In less than that. Land is going up every day.
WESLEY: You're crazy.

ELLA: Why? For not being a sucker? Who takes care of this place?
WESLEY: Me!
ELLA: Ha! Are you kidding? What do you do? Feed a few sheep. Disc the orchard once in a while. Irrigate. What else?
WESLEY: I take care of it.
ELLA: I'm not talking about maintenance. I'm talking about fixing it up. Making it look like somebody lives here. Do you do that?
WESLEY: Somebody does live here!
ELLA: Who! Not your father!
WESLEY: He works on it. He does the watering.
ELLA: When he can stand up. How often is that? He comes in here and passes out on the floor for three days then disappears for a week. You call that work? I can't run this place by myself.
WESLEY: Nobody's asking you to!
ELLA: Nobody's asking me period! I'm selling it, and that's all there is to it!

Long pause, as they sit there. WESLEY *gets up fast.*

ELLA: Where are you going?
WESLEY: I'm gonna' feed the sheep!

He exits left, ELLA *calls after him.*

ELLA: Check on Emma for me would you, Wesley? I don't like her being down there all alone. That horse is crazy.
WESLEY'S VOICE *off:*   HE'S GOING TO KILL YOU WHEN HE FINDS OUT!
ELLA, *standing, shouting off:*   HE'S NOT GOING TO FIND OUT! *pause, as she waits for a reply; nothing; she yells again* THE ONLY PERSON HE'S GOING TO KILL IS HIMSELF!

Another pause, as she stands there waiting for WESLEY *to reply. Nothing. She turns to the table and stares at the plate. She picks up the plate and carries it to the stove. She sets it on the stove. She stares at the stove. She turns toward refrigerator and looks at it. She crosses to refrigerator and opens it. She looks inside.*

ELLA: Nothing.

She closes refrigerator door. She stares at refrigerator. She talks to herself.

ELLA: He's not going to kill me. I have every right to sell. Every right. He doesn't have a leg to stand on.

She stares at refrigerator, then opens it again and looks inside. EMMA *enters from right, holding a rope halter in one hand, her white uniform covered in mud. She watches* ELLA *staring into refrigerator.*

EMMA: That bastard almost killed me.

ELLA *shuts refrigerator and turns toward* EMMA.

ELLA: What happened to you?
EMMA: He dragged me clear across the corral.
ELLA: I told you not to play around with that fool horse. He's insane, that horse.
EMMA: How am I ever going to get out of here?
ELLA: You're not going to get out of here. You're too young. Now go and change your clothes.
EMMA: I'm not too young to have babies, right?
ELLA: What do you mean?
EMMA: That's what bleeding is, right? That's what bleeding's for.
ELLA: Don't talk silly, and go change your uniform.
EMMA: This is the only one I've got.
ELLA: Well, change into something else then.
EMMA: I can't stay here forever.
ELLA: Nobody's staying here forever. We're all leaving.
EMMA: We are?
ELLA: Yes. We're going to Europe.
EMMA: Who is?
ELLA: All of us.
EMMA: Pop too?
ELLA: No. Probably not.
EMMA: How come? He'd like it in Europe wouldn't he?
ELLA: I don't know.
EMMA: You mean just you, me, and Wes are going to Europe? That sounds awful.
ELLA: Why? What's so awful about that? It could be a vacation.
EMMA: It'd be the same as it is here.
ELLA: No, it wouldn't! We'd be in Europe. A whole new place.
EMMA: But we'd all be the same people.
ELLA: What's the matter with you? Why do you say things like that?
EMMA: Well, we would be.
ELLA: I do my best to try to make things right. To try to change things. To bring a little adventure into our lives and you go and reduce the whole thing to smithereens.
EMMA: We don't have any money to go to Europe anyway.
ELLA: Go change your clothes!
EMMA: No. *She crosses to table and sits stage right end.*
ELLA: If your father was here you'd go change your clothes.
EMMA: He's not.
ELLA: Why can't you just cooperate?
EMMA: Because it's deadly. It leads to dying.
ELLA: You're not old enough to talk like that.
EMMA: I was down there in the mud being dragged along.
ELLA: It's your own fault. I told you not to go down there.

EMMA: Suddenly everything changed. I wasn't the same person anymore. I was just a hunk of meat tied to a big animal. Being pulled.

ELLA: Maybe you'll understand the danger now.

EMMA: I had the whole trip planned out in my head. I was going to head for Baja California.

ELLA: Mexico?

EMMA: I was going to work on fishing boats. Deep sea fishing. Helping businessmen haul in huge swordfish and barracuda. I was going to work my way along the coast, stopping at all the little towns, speaking Spanish. I was going to learn to be a mechanic and work on four-wheel-drive vehicles that broke down. Transmissions. I could've learned to fix anything. Then I'd learn how to be a short-order cook and write novels on the side. In the kitchen. Kitchen novels. Then I'd get published and disappear into the heart of Mexico. Just like that guy.

ELLA: What guy?

EMMA: That guy who wrote *Treasure of Sierra Madre*.

ELLA: When did you see that?

EMMA: He had initials for a name. And he disappeared. Nobody knew where to send his royalties. He escaped.

ELLA: Snap out of it, Emma. You don't have that kind of a background to do jobs like that. That's not for you, that stuff. You can do beautiful embroidery; why do you want to be a mechanic?

EMMA: I like cars. I like travel. I like the idea of people breaking down and I'm the only one who can help them get on the road again. It would be like being a magician. Just open up the hood and cast your magic spell.

ELLA: What are you dreaming for?

EMMA: I'm not dreaming now. I was dreaming then. Right up to the point when I got the halter on. Then as soon as he took off I stopped. I stopped dreaming and saw myself being dragged through the mud.

ELLA: Go change your clothes.

EMMA: Stop saying that over and over as though by saying it you relieve yourself of responsibility.

ELLA: I can't even follow the way you talk to me anymore.

EMMA: That's good.

ELLA: Why is that good?

EMMA: Because if you could then that would mean that you understood me.

Pause. ELLA *turns and opens the refrigerator again and stares into it.*

EMMA: Hungry?

ELLA: No.

EMMA: Just habit?

ELLA: What?

EMMA: Opening and closing?

ELLA *closes refrigerator and turns toward* EMMA.

ELLA: Christ, Emma, what am I going to do with you?
EMMA: Let me go.
ELLA, *after pause:* You're too young.

ELLA *exits left.* EMMA *stays sitting at table. She looks around the space, then gets up slowly and crosses to the refrigerator. She pauses in front of it, then opens the door slowly and looks in. She speaks into refrigerator.*

EMMA: Hello? Anything in there? We're not broke you know, so you don't have to hide! I don't know where the money goes to but we're not broke! We're not part of the starving class!

TAYLOR, *the lawyer, enters from down right and watches* EMMA *as she speaks into refrigerator. He is dressed in a smart suit, middle-aged, with a briefcase. He just stands there watching her.*

EMMA, *into refrigerator:* Any corn muffins in there? Hello! Any produce? Any rutabagas? Any root vegetables? Nothing? It's all right. You don't have to be ashamed. I've had worse. I've had to take my lunch to school wrapped up in a Weber's bread wrapper. That's the worst. Worse than no lunch. So don't feel bad! You'll get some company before you know it! You'll get some little eggs tucked into your sides and some yellow margarine tucked into your little drawers and some frozen chicken tucked into your—*Pauses.* You haven't seen my chicken have you? You motherfucker!

She slams the door to refrigerator and turns around. She sees TAYLOR *standing there. They stare at each other.* TAYLOR *smiles.*

TAYLOR: Your mother home?
EMMA: I don't know.
TAYLOR: I saw her car out there so I thought she might be.
EMMA: That's not her car.
TAYLOR: Oh. I thought it was.
EMMA: It's my Dad's car.
TAYLOR: She drives it, doesn't she?
EMMA: He bought it.
TAYLOR: Oh. I see.
EMMA: It's a Kaiser-Fraser.
TAYLOR: Oh.
EMMA: He goes in for odd-ball cars. He's got a Packard, too.
TAYLOR: I see.
EMMA: Says they're the only ones made out of steel.
TAYLOR: Oh.
EMMA: He totaled that car but you'd never know it.
TAYLOR: The Packard?
EMMA: No, the other one.
TAYLOR: I see.

EMMA: Who are you anyway?

TAYLOR: My name's Taylor. I'm your mother's lawyer.

EMMA: Is she in trouble or something?

TAYLOR: No. Not at all.

EMMA: Then what are you doing here?

TAYLOR: Well, I've got some business with your mother.

EMMA: You're creepy.

TAYLOR: Oh, really?

EMMA: Yeah, really. You give me the creeps. There's something about you that's weird.

TAYLOR: Well, I did come to speak to your mother.

EMMA: I know, but you're speaking to me now.

TAYLOR: Yes. *Pause, as he looks around awkwardly.* Did someone break your door down?

EMMA: My Dad.

TAYLOR: Accident?

EMMA: No, he did it on purpose. He was pissed off.

TAYLOR: I see. He must have a terrible temper.

EMMA: What do you want?

TAYLOR: I told you—

EMMA: Yeah, but what do you want my mother for?

TAYLOR: We have some business.

EMMA: She's not a business woman. She's terrible at business.

TAYLOR: Why is that?

EMMA: She's a sucker. She'll believe anything.

TAYLOR: She seems level-headed enough to me.

EMMA: Depends on what you're using her for.

Pause, as TAYLOR *looks at her.*

TAYLOR: You don't have to be insulting.

EMMA: I got nothing to lose.

TAYLOR: You *are* her daughter, aren't you?

EMMA: What line of business are you in?

TAYLOR: Do you mind if I sit down?

EMMA: I don't mind. My Dad might mind, though.

TAYLOR: He's not home, is he?

EMMA: He might come home any second now.

TAYLOR *crossing to chair at table:* Well, I'll just wait for your mother.

EMMA: He's got a terrible temper. He almost killed one guy he caught her with.

TAYLOR *sitting in stage right chair:* You misunderstand me. I'm here on business.

EMMA: A short fuse they call it. Runs in the family. His father was just like him. And his father before him. Wesley is just like Pop, too. Like liquid dynamite.

TAYLOR *setting attaché case on table:* Liquid dynamite?

EMMA: Yeah. What's that stuff called?

TAYLOR: I don't know.

EMMA: It's chemical. It's the same thing that makes him drink. Something in the blood. Hereditary. Highly explosive.

TAYLOR: Sounds dangerous.

EMMA: Yeah.

TAYLOR: Don't you get afraid living in an environment like this?

EMMA: No. The fear lies with the ones who carry the stuff in their blood, not the ones who don't. I don't have it in me.

TAYLOR: I see.

EMMA: Nitroglycerine. That's what it's called. Nitroglycerine.

TAYLOR: What do you mean?

EMMA: In the blood. Nitroglycerine.

TAYLOR: Do you think you could call your mother for me?

EMMA *yelling but looking straight at* TAYLOR: MOM!!!!

TAYLOR *after pause:*   Thank you.

EMMA: What do you want my mother for?

TAYLOR *getting irritated:*   I've already told you!

EMMA: Does she bleed?

TAYLOR: What?

EMMA: You know. Does she have blood coming out of her?

TAYLOR: I don't think I want to talk any more.

EMMA: All right.

EMMA *crosses to table and sits opposite* TAYLOR *at the stage left end. She stares at him. They sit silently for a while.* TAYLOR *squirms nervously, taps on his attaché case.* EMMA *just watches him.*

TAYLOR: Marvelous house this is. *Pause, as she just looks at him.* The location I mean. The land is full of potential. *Pause.* Of course it's a shame to see agriculture being slowly pushed into the background in deference to low-cost housing, but that's simply a product of the times we live in. There's simply more people on the planet these days. That's all there is to it. Simple mathematics. More people demand more shelter. More shelter demands more land. It's an equation. We have to provide for the people some way. The new people. We're lucky to live in a country where that provision is possible. In some countries, like India for instance, it's simply not possible. People live under banana leaves.

WESLEY *enters from right carrying a small collapsible fence structure. He sets it up center stage to form a small rectangular enclosure. He turns and looks at* TAYLOR, *then turns to* EMMA.

WESLEY *to* EMMA: Who's he?

EMMA: He's a lawyer.

TAYLOR *stands, smiling broadly at* WESLEY *and extending his hand.* WESLEY *doesn't shake but just looks at him.*

TAYLOR: Taylor. You must be the son.
WESLEY: Yeah, I'm the son.

WESLEY exits right. TAYLOR sits down again. He smiles nervously at EMMA, who just stares at him.

TAYLOR: It's a funny sensation.
EMMA: What?
TAYLOR: I feel like I'm on enemy territory.
EMMA: You are.
TAYLOR: I haven't felt this way since the war.
EMMA: What war?

TAYLOR just looks at her. WESLEY enters again from right carrying a small live lamb. He sets the lamb down inside the fenced area. He watches the lamb as it moves around inside the fence.

EMMA *to* WESLEY: What's the matter with him?
WESLEY *watching lamb:*   Maggots.
EMMA: Can't you keep him outside? He'll spread germs in here.
WESLEY *watching lamb:*   You picked that up from Mom.
EMMA: Picked what up?
WESLEY: Germs. The idea of germs. Invisible germs mysteriously floating around in the air. Anything's a potential carrier.
TAYLOR *to* WESLEY: Well, it does seem that if the animal has maggots it shouldn't be in the kitchen. Near the food.
WESLEY: We haven't got any food.
TAYLOR: Oh. Well, when you do have food you prepare it in here, don't you?
EMMA: That's nothing. My brother pisses on the floor in here.
TAYLOR: Do you always talk this way to strangers?
EMMA: Look, that's his piss right there on the floor. Right on my chart.
WESLEY *turning to* TAYLOR: What're you doing here anyway?
TAYLOR: I don't feel I have to keep justifying myself all the time. I'm here to meet your mother.
WESLEY: Are you the one who's trying to sell the house?
TAYLOR: We're negotiating, yes.
EMMA *standing:*   What? Trying to sell what house? This house?
TAYLOR *to* EMMA: Didn't she tell you?
WESLEY: She told me.
EMMA: Where are we going to live?
WESLEY *to* EMMA: You're leaving home anyway. What do you care?
EMMA *yelling off stage:*   MOM!!!
TAYLOR *to* WESLEY: I didn't mean to shock her or anything.
WESLEY *to* TAYLOR: Aren't you going to talk to my old man.
TAYLOR: That's not necessary right now.
WESLEY: He'll never sell you know.

TAYLOR: Well, he may have to. According to your mother he owes a great deal of money.

EMMA: To who? Who does he owe money to?

TAYLOR: To everyone. He's in hock up to his ears.

EMMA: He doesn't owe a cent! Everything's paid for!

WESLEY: Emma, shut up! Go change your clothes.

EMMA: You shut up! This guy's a creep, and he's trying to sell us all down the river. He's a total meatball!

WESLEY: I know he's a meatball! Just shut up, will you?

EMMA *to* TAYLOR: My Dad doesn't owe money to anyone!

TAYLOR *to* WESLEY: I'm really sorry. I thought your mother told her.

ELLA *enters from left in a dress and handbag with white gloves.* TAYLOR *stands when he sees her.*

ELLA: What's all the shouting going on for? Oh, Mr. Taylor. I wasn't expecting you for another half-hour.

TAYLOR: Yes, I know, I saw the car out in front so I thought I'd stop in early.

ELLA: Well, I'm glad you did. Did you meet everyone?

TAYLOR: Yes, I did.

ELLA *noticing lamb:* What's that animal doing in here, Wesley?

WESLEY: It's got maggots.

ELLA: Well, get him out of the kitchen.

WESLEY: It's the warmest part of the house.

ELLA: Get him out!

EMMA: Mom, are you selling this house?

ELLA: Who told her?

TAYLOR: Well, I'm afraid it slipped out.

ELLA: Emma, I'm not going to discuss it now. Go change your clothes.

EMMA *coldly:* If you sell this house, I'm never going to see you again.

EMMA *exits left.* TAYLOR *smiles, embarrassed.*

TAYLOR: I'm very sorry. I assumed that she knew.

ELLA: It doesn't matter. She's leaving anyway. Now, Wes, I'm going out with Mr. Taylor for a little lunch and to discuss our business. When I come back I want that lamb out of the kitchen.

TAYLOR *to* WESLEY, *extending his hand again:* It was very nice to have met you.

WESLEY *ignores the gesture and just stares at him.*

ELLA *to* TAYLOR: He's sullen by nature. Picks it up from his father.

TAYLOR: I see. *To* WESLEY. Nitroglycerine, too, I suppose? *Chuckles.*

ELLA *and* TAYLOR *start to exit off right.* ELLA *turns to* WESLEY.

ELLA: Keep an eye out for Emma, Wes. She's got the curse. You know what that's like for a girl, the first time around.

TAYLOR *and* ELLA *exit.* WESLEY *stands there for a while. He turns and looks at the lamb.*

WESLEY *staring at lamb:*   "Eat American Lamb. Twenty million coyotes can't be wrong."

He crosses to refrigerator and opens it. He stares into it.

WESLEY: You're out of luck. Santa Claus hasn't come yet.

He slams refrigerator door and turns to lamb. He stares at lamb.

WESLEY *to lamb:*   You're lucky I'm not really starving. You're lucky this is a civilized household. You're lucky it's not Korea and the rains are pouring through the cardboard walls and you're tied to a log in the mud and you're drenched to the bone and you're skinny and starving, but it makes no difference because someone's starving more than you. Someone's hungry. And his hunger takes him outside with a knife and slits your throat and eats you raw. His hunger eats you, and you're starving.

Loud crash of garbage cans being knocked over off stage right. Sound of WES-TON, WESLEY'S *father, off right.*

WESTON'S VOICE *off right:*   WHO PUT THE GODDAMN GARBAGE CANS RIGHT IN FRONT OF THE GODDAMN DOOR?

WESLEY *listens for a second, then bolts off stage left. More crashing is heard off right. General cursing from* WESTON, *then he enters from right with a large duffel bag full of laundry and a large bag full of groceries. He's a very big man, middle-aged, wearing a dark overcoat which looks like it's been slept in, a blue baseball cap, baggy pants, and tennis shoes. He's unshaven and slightly drunk. He takes a few steps and stops cold when he sees the lamb. He just stares at the lamb for a minute, then crosses to the table and sets the bag of groceries and the laundry on the table. He crosses back to center and looks at the lamb inside the fence.*

WESTON *to lamb:*   What in the hell are you doin' in here? *He looks around the space, to himself.* Is this inside or outside? This is inside, right? This is the inside of the house. Even with the door out it's still the inside. *To lamb.* Right? *To himself.* Right. *To lamb.* So what the hell are you doing in here if this is the inside? *He chuckles to himself.* That's not funny.

He crosses to the refrigerator and opens it.

WESTON: Perfect! ZERO! ABSOLUTELY ZERO! NADA! GOOSE EGGS! *He yells at the house in general.* WE'VE DONE IT AGAIN! WE'VE GONE AND LEFT EVERYTHING UP TO THE OLD MAN AGAIN! ALL THE UPKEEP! THE MAINTENANCE! PERFECT!

He slams the refrigerator door and crosses back to the table.

WESTON: I don't even know why we keep a refrigerator in this house. All it's good for is slamming.

He picks up the bag of groceries and crosses back to the refrigerator, talking to himself.

WESTON: Slams all day long and through the night. SLAM! SLAM! SLAM! What's everybody hoping for, a miracle! IS EVERYBODY HOPING FOR A MIRACLE?

He opens refrigerator as WESLEY *enters from stage right and stops.* WESTON'S back is to him. WESTON *starts taking artichokes out of the bag and putting them in the refrigerator.*

WESTON *to house:* THERE'S NO MORE MIRACLES! NO MIRACLES TODAY! THEY'VE BEEN ALL USED UP! IT'S ONLY ME! MR. SLAVE LABOR HIMSELF COME HOME TO REPLENISH THE EMPTY LARDER!
WESLEY: What're you yelling for? There's nobody here.

WESTON *wheels around facing* WESLEY. WESLEY *stays still.*

WESTON: What the hell are you sneakin' up like that for? You coulda' got yourself killed!
WESLEY: What's in the bag?
WESTON: Groceries! What else. Somebody's gotta' feed this house.

WESTON *turns back to refrigerator and goes on putting more artichokes into it.*

WESLEY: What kind of groceries?
WESTON: Artichokes! What do you think?
WESLEY *coming closer:* Artichokes?
WESTON: Yeah. Good desert artichokes. Picked 'em up for half-price out in Hot Springs.
WESLEY: You went all the way out there for artichokes?
WESTON: 'Course not! What do you think I am, an idiot or something? I went out there to check on my land.
WESLEY: What land?

WESTON: My desert land! Now stop talking! Everything was all right until you came in. I was talking to myself and everything was all right.

WESTON *empties the bag into the refrigerator, then slams the door shut. He crunches up the bag and crosses back to the table. He opens up his bag of laundry and starts taking dirty clothes out and stacking them in piles on the table.* WESLEY *crosses to refrigerator and opens it, looks in at artichokes. He takes one out and looks at it closely, then puts it back in. They keep talking through all this.*

WESLEY: I didn't know you had land in the desert.
WESTON: 'Course I do. I got an acre and a half out there.
WESLEY: You never told me.
WESTON: Why should I tell you? I told your mother.
WESLEY: She never told me.
WESTON: Aw, shut up, will ya'?
WESLEY: What kind of land is it?
WESTON: It's not what I expected, that's for sure.
WESLEY: What is it, then?
WESTON: It's just not what I expected. Some guy came to the door selling land. So I bought some.
WESLEY: What guy?
WESTON: Some guy. Looked respectable. Talked a real good line. Said it was an investment for the future. All kinds of great things were going to be developed. Golf courses, shopping centers, banks, sauna baths. All that kinda' stuff. So I bought it.
WESLEY: How much did you pay?
WESTON: Well, I didn't pay the whole thing. I put something down on it. I'm not stupid.
WESLEY: How much?
WESTON: Why should I tell you? I borrowed it, so it's none of your goddamn business how much it was!
WESLEY: But it turned out to be a hoax, huh?
WESTON: A real piece of shit. Just a bunch of strings on sticks, with the lizards blowing across it.
WESLEY: Nothing around it?
WESTON: Not a thing. Just desert. No way to even get water to the goddamn place. No way to even set a trailer on it.
WESLEY: Where's the guy now?
WESTON: How should I know! Where's your mother anyway?
WESLEY *shutting refrigerator:* She went out.
WESTON: Yeah, I know she went out. The car's gone. Where'd she go to?
WESLEY: Don't know.
WESTON *bundling up empty duffel bag under his arm:* Well, when she gets back tell her to do this laundry for me. Tell her not to put bleach in anything but the socks and no starch in the collars. Can you remember that?
WESLEY: Yeah, I think so. No bleach and no starch.
WESTON: That's it. You got it. Now don't forget. *He heads for stage right.*

WESLEY: Where are you going?

WESTON: Just never mind where I'm going! I can take care of myself. *He stops and looks at the lamb.* What's the matter with the lamb?

WESLEY: Maggots.

WESTON: Poor little bugger. Put some a' that blue shit on it. That'll fix him up. You know that blue stuff in the bottle?

WESLEY: Yeah.

WESTON: Put some a' that on it. *Pauses a second, looks around.* You know I was even thinkin' a' sellin' this place.

WESLEY: You were?

WESTON: Yeah. Don't tell your mother though.

WESLEY: I won't.

WESTON: Bank probably won't let me, but I was thinkin' I could sell it and buy some land down in Mexico.

WESLEY: Why down there?

WESTON: I like it down there. *Looks at lamb again.* Don't forget about that blue stuff. Can't afford to lose any lambs. Only had but two sets a' twins this year, didn't we?

WESLEY: Three.

WESTON: Well, three then. It's not much.

WESTON *exits stage right.* WESLEY *looks at lamb. Lights fade to black.*

ACT II

SCENE: *Same set. Loud hammering and sawing heard in darkness. Lights come up slowly on* WESLEY *building a new door center stage. Hammers, nails, saw, and wood lying around, sawdust on floor. The fence enclosure and the lamb are gone. A big pot of artichokes is boiling away on the stove.* WESTON'S *dirty laundry is still in piles on the table.* EMMA *sits at the stage left end of the table making a new set of charts for her demonstration with magic markers and big sheets of cardboard. She is dressed in jodhpurs, riding boots, and a western shirt. Lights up full. They each continue working at their separate tasks in silence, each of them totally concentrated.* WESLEY *measures wood with a tape measure and then cuts it on one of the chairs with the saw. He nails pieces together. After a while they begin talking but still concentrate on their work.*

EMMA: Do you think she's making it with that guy?

WESLEY: Who, Taylor? How should I know?

EMMA: I think she is. She's after him for his money.

WESLEY: He's after our money. Why should she be after his?

EMMA: What money?

WESLEY: Our potential money.

EMMA: This place couldn't be that valuable.

WESLEY: Not the way it is now, but they'll divide it up. Make lots out of it.

EMMA: She's after more than that.

WESLEY: More than what?

EMMA: Money. She's after esteem.

WESLEY: With Taylor?

EMMA: Yeah. She sees him as an easy ticket. She doesn't want to be stuck out here in the boonies all her life.

WESLEY: She shoulda' thought of that a long time ago.

EMMA: She couldn't. Not with Pop. He wouldn't let her think. She just went along with things.

WESLEY: She can't think. He can't either.

EMMA: Don't be too harsh.

WESLEY: How can they think when they're behind the eight ball all the time. They don't have time to think.

EMMA: How come you didn't tell me when Pop came in last night?

WESLEY: I don't know.

EMMA: You could've told me.

WESLEY: He just brought his dirty laundry and then left.

EMMA: He brought food, too.

WESLEY: Artichokes.

EMMA: Better than nothing. *Pause, as they work*. They're probably half way to Mexico by now.

WESLEY: Who?

EMMA: She's snuggling up to him and giggling and turning the dial on the radio. He's feeling proud of himself. He's buying her hot dogs and bragging about his business.

WESLEY: She'll be back.

EMMA: She's telling him all about us and about how Dad's crazy and trying to kill her all the time. She's happy to be on the road. To see new places go flashing by. They cross the border and gamble on the jai alai games. They head for Baja and swim along the beaches. They build campfires and roast fish at night. In the morning they take off again. But they break down somewhere outside a little place called Los Cerritos. They have to hike five miles into town. They come to a small beat-up gas station with one pump and a dog with three legs. There's only one mechanic in the whole town, and that's me. They don't recognize me though. They ask if I can fix their "carro," and I speak only Spanish. I've lost the knack for English by now. I understand them though and give them a lift back up the road in my rebuilt four-wheel-drive International. I jump out and look inside the hood. I see that it's only the rotor inside the distributor that's broken, but I tell them that it needs an entire new generator, a new coil, points and plugs, and some slight adjustments to the carburetor. It's an overnight job, and I'll have to charge them for labor. So I set a cot up for them in the garage, and after they've fallen asleep I take out the entire engine and put in a rebuilt Volkswagen block. In the morning I charge them double for labor, see them on their way, and then resell their engine for a small mint.

WESLEY: If you're not doing anything, would you check the artichokes?

EMMA: I am doing something.

WESLEY: What?

EMMA: I'm remaking my charts.

WESLEY: What do you spend your time on that stuff for? You should be doing more important stuff.

EMMA: Like checking artichokes?

WESLEY: Yeah!

EMMA: You check the artichokes. I'm busy.

WESLEY: You're on the rag.

EMMA: Don't get personal. It's not nice. You should have more consideration.

WESLEY: Just put some water in them, would you? Before they burn.

EMMA *throws down her magic marker and crosses to the pot of artichokes. She looks in the pot and then crosses back to her chair and goes on working on her charts.*

WESLEY: Are they all right?

EMMA: Perfect. Just like a little boiling paradise in a pot. What're you making anyway?

WESLEY: A new door. What's it look like?

EMMA: Looks like a bunch of sawed-up wood to me.

WESLEY: At least it's practical.

EMMA: We're doing okay without a front door. Besides it might turn off potential buyers. Makes the place look like a chicken shack. *Remembers her chicken.* Oh, my chicken! I could've killed her right then.

WESLEY: You don't understand what's happening yet, do you?

EMMA: With what?

WESLEY: The house. You think it's Mr. and Mrs. America who're gonna' buy this place, but it's not. It's Taylor.

EMMA: He's a lawyer.

WESLEY: He works for an agency. Land development.

EMMA: So what?

WESLEY: So it means more than losing a house. It means losing a country.

EMMA: You make it sound like an invasion.

WESLEY: It is. It's a zombie invasion. Taylor is the head zombie. He's the scout for the other zombies. He's only a sign that more zombies are on their way. They'll be filing through the door pretty soon.

EMMA: Once you get it built.

WESLEY: There'll be bulldozers crashing through the orchard. There'll be giant steel balls crashing through the walls. There'll be foremen with their sleeves rolled up and blueprints under their arms. There'll be steel girders spanning acres of land. Cement pilings. Prefab walls. Zombie architecture, owned by invisible zombies, built by zombies for the use and convenience of all other zombies. A zombie city! Right here! Right where we're living now.

EMMA: We could occupy it. Dad's got a gun.

WESLEY: It's a Jap gun.

EMMA: It works. I saw him shoot a peacock with it once.

WESLEY: A peacock?

EMMA: Blasted it to smithereens. It was sitting right out there in the sycamore tree. It was screaming all night long.

WESLEY: Probably mating season.
EMMA *after long pause:*   You think they'll come back?
WESLEY: Who?
EMMA: Our parents.
WESLEY: You mean ever?
EMMA: Yeah. Maybe they'll never come back, and we'll have the whole place to ourselves. We could do a lot with this place.
WESLEY: I'm not staying here forever.
EMMA: Where are you going?
WESLEY: I don't know. Alaska, maybe.
EMMA: Alaska?
WESLEY: Sure. Why not?
EMMA: What's in Alaska?
WESLEY: The frontier.
EMMA: Are you crazy? It's all frozen and full of rapers.
WESLEY: It's full of possibilities. It's undiscovered.
EMMA: Who wants to discover a bunch of ice?

WESTON *suddenly stumbles on from stage right. He's considerably drunker than the last time.* EMMA *stands at the table, not knowing whether to stay or leave.* WESTON *looks at her.*

WESTON *to* EMMA: Just relax. Relax! It's only your old man. Sit down!

EMMA *sits again.* WESLEY *stands by awkwardly.* WESTON *looks at the wood on the floor.*

WESTON *to* WESLEY: What the hell's all this? You building a barn in here or something?
WESLEY: New door.
WESTON: What! Don't talk with your voice in the back of your throat like a worm! Talk with your teeth! Talk!
WESLEY: I am talking.
WESTON: All right. Now I asked you what all this is. What is all this?
WESLEY: It's a new door.
WESTON: What's a new door? What's the matter with the old door?
WESLEY: It's gone.

WESTON *turns around, weaving slightly, and looks off stage right.*

WESTON: Oh. *He turns back to* WESLEY. Where'd it go?
WESLEY: You broke it down.
WESTON: Oh. *He looks toward table.* My laundry done yet?
EMMA: She didn't come back yet.
WESTON: Who didn't?
EMMA: Mom.
WESTON: She didn't come back yet? It's been all night. Hasn't it been all night?
EMMA: Yes.

WESTON: Hasn't the sun rised and falled on this miserable planet?
EMMA: Yes.
WESTON *turning to* WESLEY: So where's she been?
WESLEY: Don't know.
WESTON: Don't pull that one! Don't pull that one on me!

He starts to come after WESLEY. WESLEY *backs off fast.* WESTON *stops. He stands there weaving in place.*

WESLEY: I don't know. Really.
WESTON: Don't try protecting her! There's no protection! Understand! None! She's had it!
WESLEY: I don't know where she went.
EMMA: She went with a lawyer.

WESTON *turns to* EMMA *slowly.*

WESTON: A what?
EMMA: A lawyer.
WESTON: What's a lawyer? A law man? A person of the law? *Suddenly yelling.* WHAT'S A LAWYER?
EMMA: A guy named Taylor.

Long pause, as WESTON *stares at her drunkenly, trying to fathom it. Then he turns to* WESLEY.

WESTON *to* WESLEY: Taylor? You knew?
WESLEY: I thought she'd be back by now. She said she was going out for a business lunch.
WESTON: You knew!
EMMA: Maybe they had an accident.
WESTON *to* EMMA: In my car! In my Kaiser-Fraser! I'll break his fucking back!
WESLEY: Maybe they did have an accident. I'll call the hospitals.
WESTON: DON'T CALL ANYBODY! *Quieter.* Don't call anybody. *Pause.* That car was an antique. Worth a fortune.
EMMA *after long pause:* You wanna' sit down, Pop?
WESTON: I'm standing. What's that smell in here? What's that smell!
WESLEY: Artichokes.
WESTON: They smell like that?
WESLEY: They're boiling.
WESTON: Stop them from boiling! They might boil over.

WESLEY *goes to stove and turns it off.*

WESTON: Where's that goddamn sheep you had in here? Is that what you're building? A barn for that sheep?
WESLEY: A door.

WESTON *staggering:*   I gotta sit down.

He stumbles toward table and sits at stage right end. EMMA *stands.*

WESTON *to* EMMA: Sit down! Sit back down! Turn off those artichokes!

WESLEY: I did.

WESTON *pushing laundry to one side:*   She didn't do any of this. It's the same as when I brought it. None of it!

EMMA: I'll do it.

WESTON: No, you won't do it! You let her do it! It's her job! What does she do around here anyway? Do you know? What does she do all day long? What does a woman do?

EMMA: I don't know.

WESTON: You should be in school.

EMMA: It's all right if I do it. I don't mind doing it.

WESTON: YOU'RE NOT DOING IT! *Long silence.* What do you think of this place?

EMMA: The house?

WESTON: The whole thing. The whole fandango! The orchard! The air! The night sky!

EMMA: It's all right.

WESTON *to* WESLEY: What do you think of it?

WESLEY: I wouldn't sell it.

WESTON: You wouldn't sell it. You couldn't sell it! It's not yours!

WESLEY: I know. But I wouldn't if it was.

WESTON: How come? What good is it? What good's it doing?

WESLEY: It's just here. And we're on it. And we wouldn't be if it got sold.

WESTON: Very sound reasoning. Very sound. *Turns to* EMMA. Your brother never was much in the brain department, was he? You're the one who's such a smart-ass. You're the straight-A student, aren't you?

EMMA: Yes.

WESTON: Straight-A's and you're moldering around this dump. What're you going to do with yourself?

EMMA: I don't know.

WESTON: You don't know. Well you better think of something fast, because I've found a buyer. *Silence.* I've found someone to give me cash. Cash on the line! *He slams table with his hand. Long silence, then* EMMA *gets up and exits off left.*

WESTON: What's the matter with her?

WESLEY: I don't know. She's got her first period.

WESTON: Her what? She's too young for that. That's not supposed to happen when they're that age. It's premature.

WESLEY: She's got it.

WESTON: What happens when I'm gone, you all sit around and talk about your periods? You're not supposed to know when your sister has her period! That's confidential between women. They keep it a secret that means.

WESLEY: I know what "confidential" means.

WESTON: Good.

WESLEY: Why don't you go to bed or something, so I can finish this door.

WESTON: What for? I told ya' I'm selling the joint. Why build a new door? No point in putting money into it.

WESLEY: I'm still living here. I'm living here right up to the point when I leave.

WESTON: Very brave. Very courageous outlook. I envy it in fact.

WESLEY: You do?

WESTON: Sure! Of course! What else is there to envy but an outlook? Look at mine! Look at my outlook. You don't envy it, right?

WESLEY: No.

WESTON: That's because it's full of poison. Infected. And you recognize poison, right? You recognize it when you see it?

WESLEY: Yes.

WESTON: Yes, you do. I can see that you do. My poison scares you.

WESLEY: Doesn't scare me.

WESTON: No?

WESLEY: No.

WESTON: Good. You're growing up. I never saw my old man's poison until I was much older than you. Much older. And then you know how I recognized it?

WESLEY: How?

WESTON: Because I saw myself infected with it. That's how. I saw me carrying it around. His poison in my body. You think that's fair?

WESLEY: I don't know.

WESTON: Well, what do you think? You think I asked for it?

WESLEY: No.

WESTON: So it's unfair, right?

WESLEY: It's just the way it happened.

WESTON: I didn't ask for it, but I got it.

WESLEY: What is it anyway?

WESTON: What do you mean, what is it? You can see it for yourself!

WESLEY: I know it's there, but I don't know what it is.

WESTON: You'll find out.

WESLEY: How?

WESTON: How do you poison coyotes?

WESLEY: Strychnine.

WESTON: How! Not what!

WESLEY: You put it in the belly of a dead lamb.

WESTON: Right. Now do you see?

WESLEY *after pause:* No.

WESTON: You're thick! You're really thick. *Pause.* You know I watched my old man move around. I watched him move through rooms. I watched him drive tractors, watched him watching baseball, watched him keeping out of the way of things. Out of the way of my mother. Away from my brothers. Watched him on the sidelines. Nobody saw him but me. Everybody was right there, but nobody saw him but me. He lived apart. Right in the midst of things and he lived apart. Nobody saw that.

Long pause.

WESLEY: You want an artichoke?
WESTON: No.
WESLEY: Who's the buyer?
WESTON: Some guy. Owns the "Alibi Club" downtown. Said he'll give me cash.
WESLEY: How much?
WESTON: Enough to get to Mexico. They can't touch me down there.
WESLEY: Who?
WESTON: None of your goddamn business! Why is it you always drive yourself under my skin when I'm around? Why is that?
WESLEY: We don't get along.
WESTON: Very smart! Very observant! What's the matter with you anyway? What're you doing around here?
WESLEY: I'm part of your offspring.
WESTON: Jesus, you're enough to drive a sane man crazy! You're like having an espionage spy around. Why are you watching me all the time?

WESTON *looks at him. They stare at each other for a moment.*

WESTON: You can watch me all you want to. You won't find out a thing.
WESLEY: Mom's trying to sell the place, too.

WESTON *looks at him hard.*

WESLEY: That's who the lawyer guy was. She's selling it through him.

WESTON *stands and almost topples over.*

WESTON: I'LL KILL HER! I'LL KILL BOTH OF THEM! Where's my gun? I had a gun here! A captured gun!
WESLEY: Take it easy.
WESTON: No, you take it easy! This whole thing has gone far enough! It's like living in a den of vipers! Spies! Conspiracies behind my back! I'M BEING TAKEN FOR A RIDE BY EVERY ONE OF YOU! I'm the one who works! I'm the one who brings home food! THIS IS MY HOUSE! I BOUGHT THIS HOUSE! AND I'M SELLING THIS HOUSE! AND I'M TAKING ALL THE MONEY BECAUSE IT'S OWED ME! YOU ALL OWE IT TO ME! EVERY LAST ONE OF YOU! SHE CAN'T STEAL THIS HOUSE AWAY FROM ME! IT'S MINE!

He falls into table and collapses on it. He tries to keep himself from falling to the floor. WESLEY *moves toward him.*

WESTON: JUST KEEP BACK! I'M NOT DYING, SO JUST KEEP BACK!

He struggles to pull himself up on the table, knocking off dirty laundry and EMMA'S *charts.*

WESTON: I don't need a bed. I don't need anything from you! I'll stay right here. DON'T ANYONE TRY TO MOVE ME! NOBODY! I'm staying right here.

He finally gets on table so that he's lying flat out on it. He slowly goes unconscious. WESLEY *watches him from a safe distance.*

WESLEY *still standing there watching* WESTON: EMMA! *No answer.* Oh, shit. Don't go out on me, Pop?

He moves toward WESTON *cautiously.* WESTON *comes to suddenly. Still lying on table.*

WESTON: DON'T GET TOO CLOSE!

WESLEY *jumps back.*

WESLEY: Wouldn't you rather be on the bed?
WESTON: I'm all right here. I'm numb. Don't feel a thing. Feels good to be numb.
WESLEY: We don't have to sell, you know. We could fix the place up.
WESTON: It's too late for that. I owe money.
WESLEY: I could get a job.
WESTON: You're gonna' have to.
WESLEY: I will. We could work this place by ourselves.
WESTON: Don't be stupid. There's not enough trees to make a living.
WESLEY: We could join the California Avocado Association. We could make a living that way.
WESTON: Get out of here! Get away from me!
WESLEY: Taylor can't buy this place without your signature.
WESTON: I'll kill him! If I have to, I'll kill myself along with him. I'll crash into him. I'll crash the Packard right into him. What's he look like? *No answer from* WESLEY. WHAT'S HE LOOK LIKE?
WESLEY: Ordinary. Like a crook.
WESTON *still lying on table:* I'll find him. Then I'll find that punk who sold me that phony desert land. I'll track them all down. Every last one of them. Your mother too. I'll track her down and shoot them in their bed. In their hotel bed. I'll splatter their brains all over the vibrating bed. I'll drag him into the hotel lobby and slit his throat. I was in the war. I know how to kill. I was over there. I know how to do it. I've done it before. It's no big deal. You just make an adjustment. You convince yourself it's all right. That's all. It's easy. You just slaughter them. Easy.
WESLEY: You don't have to kill him. It's illegal, what he's doing.
WESTON: HE'S WITH MY WIFE! THAT'S ILLEGAL!
WESLEY: She'll come back.

WESTON: He doesn't know what he's dealing with. He thinks I'm just like him. Cowardly. Sniveling. Sneaking around. He's not counting on what's in my blood. He doesn't realize the explosiveness. We don't belong to the same class. He doesn't realize that. He's not counting on that. He's counting on me to use my reason. To talk things out. To have a conversation. To go out and have a business lunch and talk things over. He's not counting on murder. Murder's the farthest thing from his mind.

WESLEY: Just take it easy, Pop. Try to get some sleep.

WESTON: I am sleeping! I'm sleeping right here. I'm falling away. I was a flyer you know.

WESLEY: I know.

WESTON: I flew giant machines in the air. Giants! Bombers. What a sight. Over Italy. The Pacific. Islands. Giants. Oceans. Blue oceans.

Slowly WESTON *goes unconscious again as* WESLEY *watches him lying on table.* WESLEY *moves toward him slightly.*

WESLEY: Pop? *He moves in a little closer.* You asleep?

He turns downstage and looks at the wood and tools. He looks toward the refrigerator. ELLA *enters from down right carrying a bag of groceries. She stops when she sees* WESLEY. WESLEY *turns toward her.* ELLA *looks at* WESTON *lying on the table.*

ELLA: How long's he been here?

WESLEY: Just got here. Where have you been?

ELLA *crossing to refrigerator:* Out.

WESLEY: Where's your boyfriend?

ELLA *opening refrigerator:* Don't get insulting. Who put all these artichokes in here? What's going on?

WESLEY: Dad. He brought them back from the desert.

ELLA: What desert?

WESLEY: Hot Springs.

ELLA: Oh. He went down to look at his pathetic piece of property, I guess.

ELLA *sets the bag of groceries on the stove, then starts throwing the artichokes out onto the floor from the refrigerator.*

WESLEY: What are you doing?

ELLA: Throwing these out. It's a joke bringing artichokes back here when we're out of food.

WESLEY: How do you know about his desert property?

ELLA: I just know, that's all.

WESLEY: He told you? He never told me about it.

ELLA: I just happen to know he was screwed out of five hundred bucks. Let's leave it at that. Another shrewd business deal.

WESLEY: Taylor.

ELLA *turning to* WESLEY: What?

WESLEY: Taylor sold it to him right?

ELLA: Don't be ridiculous. *Turns back to refrigerator.*

WESLEY: How else would you know?

ELLA: He's not the only person in the world involved in real estate, you know.

WESLEY: He's been sneaking around here for months.

ELLA: Sneaking? He doesn't sneak. He comes right to the front door every time. He's very polite.

WESLEY: He's venomous.

ELLA: You're just jealous of him, that's all.

WESLEY: Don't give me that shit! It was him, wasn't it? I remember seeing him with his briefcase, wandering around the property.

ELLA: He's a speculator. That's his job. It's very important in this day and age to have someone who can accurately assess the value of land. To see its potential for the future.

She starts putting all the groceries from her bag into the refrigerator.

WESLEY: What exactly is he anyway? You told me he was a lawyer.

ELLA: I don't delve into his private affairs.

WESLEY: You don't, huh?

ELLA: Why are you so bitter all of a sudden?

WESLEY: It's not all of a sudden.

ELLA: I should think you'd be very happy to leave this place. To travel. To see other parts of the world.

WESLEY: I'm not leaving!

ELLA: Oh, yes you are. We all are. I've sealed the deal. It just needs one last little signature from me and its finished. Everything. The beat-up cars, the rusted out tractor, the moldy avocados, the insane horse, the demented sheep, the chickens, the whole entire shooting match. The whole collection. Over.

WESLEY: Then you're free I suppose?

ELLA: Exactly.

WESLEY: Are you going off with him?

ELLA: I wish you'd get your mind out of the garbage. I'm on my own.

WESLEY: Where'd you get the groceries?

ELLA: I picked them up.

WESLEY *after pause:* You know, you're too late. All your wheeling and dealing and you've missed the boat.

ELLA *closing refrigerator, turning to* WESLEY: What do you mean?

WESLEY: Dad's already sold it.

ELLA: You must be crazy! He couldn't sell a shoestring! Look at him! Look at him lying there! Does that look like a man who could sell something as valuable as a piece of property? Does that look like competence to you? Take a look at him! He's pathetic!

WESLEY: I wouldn't wake him up if I were you.

ELLA: He can't hurt me now! I've got protection! If he lays a hand on me, I'll have him cut to ribbons! He's finished!

WESLEY: He's beat you to the punch and he doesn't even know it.

ELLA: Don't talk stupid! And get this junk out of here! I'm tired of looking at broken doors every time I come in here.

WESLEY: That's a new door.

ELLA: GET IT OUT OF HERE!

WESLEY *quietly:* I told you, you better not wake him up.

ELLA: I'm not tiptoeing around anymore. I'm finished with feeling like a foreigner in my own house. I'm not afraid of him anymore.

WESLEY: You should be. He's going to kill Taylor, you know.

ELLA: He's always going to kill somebody! Every day he's going to kill somebody!

WESLEY: He means it this time. He's got nothing to lose.

ELLA: That's for sure!

WESLEY: He's going to kill you, too.

ELLA *is silent for a while. They look at each other.*

ELLA: Do you know what this is? It's a curse. I can feel it. It's invisible but it's there. It's always there. It comes onto us like nighttime. Every day I can feel it. Every day I can see it coming. And it always comes. Repeats itself. It comes even when you do everything to stop it from coming. Even when you try to change it. And it goes back. Deep. It goes back and back to tiny little cells and genes. To atoms. To tiny little swimming things making up their minds without us. Plotting in the womb. Before that even. In the air. We're surrounded with it. It's bigger than government even. It goes forward too. We spread it. We pass it on. We inherit it and pass it down, and then pass it down again. It goes on and on like that without us.

ELLIS, *the owner of the "Alibi Club," enters from right and smiles at them. He is wearing a shiny yellow shirt, open at the collar, with a gold cross on a chain hanging from his neck. He's very burly, with tattooes all over his arms, tightfitting pants, shiny shoes, lots of rings. He looks around and notices* WESTON *still lying on the table.*

ELLIS: A few too many "boiler-makers," huh? I keep telling him to go light, but it's like fartin' in the wind. *Laughs at his own joke.* You must be the wife and kids. Name's Ellis, I run the "Alibi Club," down in town. You must know it, huh?

No reaction from ELLA *and* WESLEY.

ELLIS: Well, the old man knows it, that's for sure. Down there pretty near every night. Regular steady. Always wondered where he slept. What's that smell in here?

WESLEY: Artichokes.

ELLIS: Artichokes, huh? Smells like stale piss. *Bursts out laughing; no reaction from others.* Never was big on vegetables myself. I'm a steak man.

"Meat and blood," that's my motto. Keeps your bones hard as ivory.

ELLA: I know it may be asking a little bit too much to knock when there's no door to knock on, but do you always make a habit of just wandering into people's houses like you own them?

ELLIS: I do own it. *Pause.* That's right. Signed, sealed, and delivered. Got the cash right here.

He pulls out two big stacks of bills from his belt and waves them in the air.

ELLIS: Fifteen hundred in hard core mean green.

WESLEY: Fifteen hundred dollars? *Looks at* ELLA.

ELLIS: That's what he owes. That's the price we agreed on. Look, buddy, I didn't even have to show up here with it. Your old man's such a sap he signed the whole thing over to me without a dime even crossing the bar. I coulda' stung him easy. Just happens that I'm a man of honor.

ELLA *to* WESLEY: Get him out of here!

ELLIS *coldly to* WESLEY: I wouldn't try it, buddy boy.

ELLIS *and* WESLEY *stare at each other.* ELLIS *smiles.*

ELLIS: I've broken too many backs in my time, buddy. I'm not a hard man, but I'm strong as a bull calf, and I don't realize my own strength. It's terrible when that happens. You know? Before you know it, someone's hurt. Someone's lying there.

ELLA: This is a joke! You can't buy a piece of property from an alcoholic! He's not responsible for his actions!

ELLIS: He owns it, doesn't he?

ELLA: I OWN IT!

ELLIS: That's not what he told me.

ELLA: I own it and it's already been sold, so just get the hell out!

ELLIS: Well, I've got the deed right here. *He pulls deed out.* Right here. Signed, sealed, and delivered. How do you explain that?

ELLA: It's not legal!

WESLEY: Who does he owe money to?

ELLIS: Oh, well, now I don't stick my nose where it doesn't belong. I just happen to know that he owes to some pretty hard fellas.

WESLEY: Fifteen hundred bucks?

ELLIS: That's about the size of it.

ELLA: Wake him up! We'll get to the bottom of this.

WESLEY *to* ELLA: Are you crazy? If he sees you here he'll go off the deep end.

ELLA *going to* WESTON *and shaking him:* I'll wake him up, then!

WESLEY: Oh, Jesus!

WESTON *remains unconscious.* ELLA *keeps shaking him violently.*

ELLA: Weston! Weston get up! Weston!

ELLIS: I've seen some hard cases in my time, but he's dedicated. That's for sure. Drinks like a Canadian. Flat out.

WESLEY: You say these guys are tough? What does he owe them for?

ELLIS: Look, buddy, he borrows all the time. He's a borrowing fool. It could be anything. Payments on a car. Land in the desert. He's always got some fool scheme going. He's just let it slide too long this time, that's all.

WESLEY: What'll they do to him?

ELLIS: Nothing now. I've saved his hide. You should be kissing my feet.

ELLA: WESTON! GET UP!

She is tiring from shaking him. WESTON *remains unconscious.*

WESLEY: They'd kill him for fifteen hundred bucks?

ELLIS: Who said anything about killing? Did I say anything about killing?

WESLEY: No.

ELLIS: Then don't jump to conclusions. You can get in trouble that way.

WESLEY: Maybe you should deliver it to them.

ELLIS: Look, I've carried the ball this far, now he's gonna' have to do the rest. I'm not his bodyguard.

WESLEY: What if he takes off with it?

ELLIS: That's his problem.

WESLEY: Give it to me.

ELLIS: What?

WESLEY: The money. I'll deliver it.

ELLA *leaving* WESTON: Wesley, don't you touch that money! It's tainted! Don't you touch it!

ELLIS *and* WESLEY *look at each other.*

WESLEY: You've got the deed. I'm his oldest son.

ELLA: You're his only son!

WESLEY: Just give it to me. I'll take care of it.

ELLIS *handing money to* WESLEY: All right, buddy. Just don't go off half-cocked. That's a lot a' spendin' change for a young man.

WESLEY *takes it.*

ELLA: Wesley, it's illegal! You'll be an accomplice!

WESLEY *to* ELLIS: Where do I find them?

ELLIS: That's your business, buddy. I'm just the buyer.

ELLIS *walks around, looking over the place.* ELLA *crosses to* WESLEY *as* WESLEY *counts the money.*

ELLA: Wesley, you give me that money! It doesn't belong to you! Give it to me!

WESLEY *looking at her coldly:*   There's not enough here to go to Europe on, Mom.

ELLIS: I was thinkin' of turning this place into a steak house. What do you think? Make a nice little steak house, don't you think?

WESLEY *still counting money:* Sure.

ELLIS: People stop in off the highway, have a steak, a martini, afternoon cocktail, look out over the valley. Nice and peaceful. Might even put in a Japanese garden out front. Have a few goldfish swimming around. Maybe an eight-hole pitch-and-putt course right out there, too. Place is full of potential.

ELLA: Wesley!

TAYLOR *appears with attaché case stage right.* ELLA *turns and sees him.* WESLEY *keeps counting money.*

TAYLOR: Oh, I'm sorry. I didn't realize you had company. *To* ELLA. I've got the final draft drawn up.

TAYLOR *crosses toward table, sees* WESTON *lying on it, stops, looks for a place to set down his attaché case.*

ELLA *to* TAYLOR: It's too late.

TAYLOR: Excuse me? What's too late?

ELLA: The whole thing. Weston's sold it.

TAYLOR: That's silly. I've got the final draft right here in my case. All it needs is your signature.

ELLIS: Who's this character?

ELLA *to* TAYLOR: He sold it for fifteen hundred dollars.

TAYLOR *laughs:* That's impossible.

ELLA: There it is right there! Wesley's got it in his hands! Wesley's taking it!

TAYLOR: He can't sell this piece of property. He's incompetent. We've already been through that.

ELLIS *crossing to* TAYLOR: Hey, listen, buddy. I don't know what your story is, but I suggest you get the fuck outa' here because this is my deal here. Understand? This is my little package.

TAYLOR *to* ELLA: Who's this?

ELLA: He's the buyer.

WESLEY *to* TAYLOR: Too slow on the trigger, Taylor. Took it right out from under you, didn't he?

TAYLOR: Well, it's simply a matter of going to court then. He doesn't have a leg to stand on. Legally he's a ward of the state. He can't sell land.

ELLIS *waving deed:* Look, I checked this deed out at city hall, and everything's above board.

TAYLOR: The deed has nothing to do with it. I'm speaking of psychological responsibility.

WESLEY: Does that apply to buying the same as selling?

TAYLOR *to* ELLA: What's he talking about?

ELLA: Nothing. Wesley, you give that money back!

WESLEY: Does that apply to buying dried up land in the middle of the desert with no water and a hundred miles from the nearest gas pump?

TAYLOR *to* WESLEY: I think you're trying to divert the focus of the situation here. The point is that your father's psychologically and emotionally unfit to be responsible for his own actions, and, therefore, any legal negotiations issuing from him cannot be held binding. This can be easily proven in a court of law. We have first-hand evidence that he's prone to fits of violence. His license for driving has been revoked, and yet he still keeps driving. He's unable to get insurance. He's unable to hold a steady job. He's absent from his home ninety percent of the time. He has a jail record. It's an open and shut case.

ELLIS *to* TAYLOR: What are you anyway? A lawyer or something? Where do you get off talkin' like that in my house!

ELLA: IT'S NOT YOUR HOUSE! THAT'S WHAT HE'S SAYING! CAN'T YOU LISTEN? DON'T YOU HAVE A BRAIN IN YOUR HEAD?

ELLIS: Listen, lady, I sell booze. You know what I mean? A lot a' weird stuff goes on in my bar, but I never seen anything as weird as this character. I never seen anything I couldn't handle.

WESLEY: You best take off, Taylor, before it all catches up to you.

TAYLOR: I refuse to be intimidated any further! I put myself out on a limb for this project and all I'm met with is resistance!

ELLA: I'm not resisting.

TAYLOR *to* WESLEY: You may not realize it, but there's corporations behind me! Executive management! People of influence. People with ambition who realize the importance of investing in the future. Of building this country up, not tearing it down. You people carry on as though the whole world revolved around your petty little existence. As though everything was holding its breath, waiting for your next move. Well, it's not like that! Nobody's waiting! Everything's going forward! Everything's going ahead without you! The wheels are in motion. There's nothing you can do to turn it back. The only thing you can do is cooperate. To play ball. To become part of us. To invest in the future of this great land. Because if you don't, you'll all be left behind. Every last one of you. Left high and dry. And there'll be nothing to save you. Nothing and nobody.

A policeman appears stage right in highway patrol gear.

SERGEANT MALCOLM: Uh—excuse me. Mrs. Tate?

ELLA: Yes.

MALCOLM: Are you Mrs. Tate?

ELLA: Yes, I am.

MALCOLM: I'm sorry. I would have knocked but there's no door.

ELLA: That's all right.

TAYLOR *begins to move to stage left nervously.* WESLEY *watches him.*

MALCOLM: I'm Sergeant Malcolm, Highway Patrol.

ELLA: Well, what is it?

MALCOLM: You have a daughter, Emma Tate?

ELLA: Yes. What's wrong?

MALCOLM: She's been apprehended.

ELLA: What for?

MALCOLM: It seems she rode her horse through a bar downtown and shot the place full of holes with a rifle.

ELLA: What?

ELLIS: What bar?

MALCOLM: Place called the "Alibi Club." I wasn't there at the time, but they picked her up.

ELLIS: That's my club!

MALCOLM *to* ELLIS: Are you the owner?

ELLIS: THAT'S MY CLUB!

MALCOLM: Are you Mr. Ellis?

ELLIS: What kind of damages?

MALCOLM: Well, we'll have to get an estimate, but it's pretty severe. Shot the whole place up. Just lucky there was no one in it at the time.

ELLIS *to* WESLEY: Give me that money back!

ELLIS *grabs money out of* WESLEY's *hands.* TAYLOR *sneaks off stage left.*

WESLEY *to cop:* Hey! He's getting away! That guy's a crook!

MALCOLM: What guy?

WESLEY *moving toward stage left:* That guy! That guy who just ran out of here! He's an embezzler! A confidence man! Whatever you call it. He sold my old man phony land!

MALCOLM: That's not within my jurisdiction.

ELLIS *to* ELLA: I know he sent her down there. I wasn't born yesterday, ya' know! He's crazy if he thinks he can put that kind of muscle on me! What does he think he is anyway? I'm gonna' sue him blind for this! I'm gonna' take the shirt right off his back! I was trying to do him a favor! I was stickin' my neck out for him! You just tell him when he wakes up out of his stupor that he's in bigger trouble than he thinks! He ain't seen nothin' yet! You tell him. *Starts to leave.* And just remember that I own this place. It's mine! So don't try any more funny stuff. I got friends in high places, too. I deal directly with them all the time. Ain't that right, Sarge?

MALCOLM: I don't know about that. I'm here on other business.

ELLIS *to* ELLA: You just tell him! I'll teach him to mess around with me!

ELLIS *exits. Right.*

ELLA *to cop:* He's taking our money!

MALCOLM: Look, lady, your daughter's in jail. I don't know about any of this other stuff. I'm here about your daughter.

WESLEY *runs off right.* ELLA *yells after him.*

ELLA: WESLEY! WHERE ARE YOU GOING?

WESLEY'S VOICE *off:* I'M GONNA' GET THAT MONEY BACK!

ELLA: IT'S NOT YOUR MONEY! COME BACK HERE! WESLEY! *She stops and looks at* MALCOLM. Everybody's running off. Even Mr. Taylor. Did you hear the way he was talking to me? He was talking to me all different. All different than before. He wasn't nice at all.

MALCOLM: Mrs. Tate, what are we going to do about your daughter?

ELLA: I don't know. What should we do?

MALCOLM: Well, she has to stay in overnight, and if you don't want her back home she can be arraigned in juvenile court.

ELLA: We're all leaving here though. Everyone has to leave. She can't come home. There wouldn't be anyone here.

MALCOLM: You'll have to sign a statement then.

ELLA: What statement?

MALCOLM: Giving permission for the arraignment.

ELLA: All right.

MALCOLM: You'll have to come down with me unless you have a car.

ELLA: I have a car. *Pause.* Everyone's run away.

MALCOLM: Will you be all right by yourself?

ELLA: I am by myself.

MALCOLM: Yes, I know. Will you be all right or do you want to come with me in the patrol car?

ELLA: I'll be all right.

MALCOLM: I'll wait for you down at the station then.

MALCOLM *exits.* ELLA *just stands there.*

ELLA *to herself:* Everybody ran away.

WESTON *sits up with a jolt on the table.* ELLA *jumps. They look at each other for a moment, then* ELLA *runs off stage.* WESTON *just stays sitting up on the table. He looks around the stage. He gets to his feet and tries to steady himself. He walks toward the refrigerator and kicks the artichokes out of his way. He opens refrigerator and looks in. Lights slowly fade to black with* WESTON *standing there looking into refrigerator.*

ACT III

SCENE: *Same set. Stage is cleared of wood and tools and artichokes. Fence enclosure with the lamb inside is back, center stage. Pot of fresh coffee heating on the stove. All the laundry has been washed and* WESTON *is at the table to stage left folding it and stacking it in neat piles. He's minus his overcoat, baseball cap, and tennis shoes and wears a fresh clean shirt, new pants, shined shoes, and has had a shave. He seems sober now and in high spirits compared to before. The lamb is heard "baaing" in the dark as the lights slowly come up on* WESTON *at the table.*

WESTON *to lamb as he folds clothes:* There's worse things than maggots ya' know. Much worse. Maggots go away if they're properly attended to. If you got someone around who can take the time. Who can recognize the signs. Who brings ya' in out of the cold, wet pasture and sets ya' up in a cushy situation like this. No lamb ever had it better. It's warm. It's free of draft, now that I got the new door up. There's no varmints. No coyotes. No eagles. No—*Looks over at lamb.* Should I tell ya' something about eagles? This is a true story. This is a true account. One time I was out in the fields doing the castrating, which is a thing that has to be done. It's not my favorite job, but it's something that just has to be done. I'd set myself up right beside the lean-to out there. Just a little roof-shelter thing out there with my best knife, some boiling water, and a hot iron to cauterize with. It's a bloody job on all accounts. Well, I had maybe a dozen spring ram lambs to do out there. I had 'em all gathered up away from the ewes in much the same kinda' set up as you got right there. Similar fence structure like that. It was a crisp, bright type a' morning. Air was real thin and you could see all the way out across the pasture land. Frost was still well bit down on the stems, right close to the ground. Maybe a couple a' crows and the ewes carrying on about their babies, and that was the only sound. Well, I was working away out there when I feel this shadow cross over me. I could feel it even before I saw it take shape on the ground. Felt like the way it does when the clouds move across the sun. Huge and black and cold like. So I look up, half expecting a buzzard or maybe a red-tail, but what hits me across the eyes is this giant eagle. Now I'm a flyer and I'm used to aeronautics, but this sucker was doin' some downright suicidal antics. Real low down like he's coming in for a landing or something, then changing his mind and pulling straight up again and sailing out away from me. So I watch him going small for a while, then turn back to my work. I do a couple more lambs maybe, and the same thing happens. Except this time he's even lower yet. Like I could almost feel his feathers on my back. I could hear his sound real clear. A giant bird. His wings made a kind of cracking noise. Then up he went again. I watched him longer this time, trying to figure out his intentions. Then I put the whole thing together. He was after those testes. Those fresh little remnants of manlihood. So I decided to oblige him this time and threw a few a' them on top a' the shed roof. Then I just went back to work again, pretending to be preoccupied. I was waitin' for him this time though. I was listening hard for him, knowing he'd be coming in from behind me. I was watchin' the ground for any sign of blackness. Nothing happened for about three more lambs, when all of a sudden he comes. Just like a thunder clap. Blam! He's down on that shed roof with his talons taking half the tar paper with him, wings whippin' the air, screaming like a bred mare then climbing straight back up into the sky again. I had to stand up on that one. Somethin' brought me straight up off the ground and I started yellin' my head off. I don't know why it was comin' outa' me but I was standing there with this icy feeling up my backbone and just yelling my fool head off. Cheerin' for that eagle. I'd never felt like that since the first day I went up in a B-49. After a while I sat down again and went on workin'. And every time I cut a lamb I'd throw those balls up on top a' the shed roof. And every time he'd come down like the Cannonball Express on that roof. And every time I got that feeling.

WESLEY *appears stage right with his face and hands bloody.*

WESLEY: Then what?
WESTON: Were you listening to me?
WESLEY: What happens next?
WESTON: I was tellin' it to the lamb!
WESLEY: Tell it to me.
WESTON: You've already heard it. What happened to your face anyway?
WESLEY: Ran into a brick wall.
WESTON: Why don't ya' go clean up.
WESLEY: What happens next?
WESTON: I ain't tellin' it again!
WESLEY: Then I ain't cleaning up!
WESTON: What's the matter with you anyway? Are you drunk or something?
WESLEY: I was trying to get your money back.
WESTON: What money?
WESLEY: From Ellis.
WESTON: That punk. Don't waste your time. He's a punk crook.
WESLEY: He ran off with your money. And he's got the house too.
WESTON: I've got the house! I've decided to stay.
WESLEY: What?
WESTON: I'm stayin'. I finished the new door. Did you notice?
WESLEY: No.
WESTON: Well, you shoulda' noticed. You walked right through it. What's the matter with you? I'm fixin' the whole place up. I decided.
WESLEY: You're fixing it up?
WESTON: Yeah. That's what I said. What's so unusual about that? This could be a great place if somebody'd take some interest in it. Why don't you have some coffee and clean yourself up a little. You look like forty miles a' rough road. Go ahead. There's fresh coffee on the stove.

WESLEY *crosses slowly to the stove and looks at the coffee.*

WESTON: I got up and took a walk around the place. Bright and early. Don't think I've walked around the whole place for a couple a' years. I walked around and a funny thing started happening to me.
WESLEY *looking at coffee:*   What?
WESTON: I started wondering who this was walking around in the orchard at six-thirty in the morning. It didn't feel like me. It was some character in a dark overcoat and tennis shoes and a baseball cap and stickers comin' out of his face. It didn't feel like the owner of a piece a' property as nice as this. Then I started to wonder who the owner was. I mean if I didn't feel like the owner, then who was the owner? I started wondering if the real owner was gonna' pop up out of nowhere and

blast my brains out for trespassing. I started feeling like I should be running or hiding or something. Like I shouldn't be there in this kind of a neighborhood. Not that it's fancy or anything, but it's peaceful. It's real peaceful up here. Especially at that time a' the morning. Then it struck me that I actually was the owner. That somehow it was me and I was actually the one walking on my own piece of land. And that gave me a great feeling.

WESLEY *staring at coffee:*   It did?

WESTON: Yeah. So I came back in here, and the first thing I did was I took all my old clothes off and walked around here naked. Just walked through the whole damn house in my birthday suit. Tried to get the feeling of it really being me in my own house. It was like peeling off a whole person. A whole stranger. Then I walked straight in and made myself a hot bath. Hot as I could stand it. Just sank down into it and let it sink deep into the skin. Let it fog up all the windows and the glass on the medicine cabinet. Then I let all the water drain out, and then I filled the whole tub up again but this time with ice cold water. Just sat there and let it creep on me until I was in up to my neck. Then I got out and took a shave and found myself some clean clothes. Then I came in here and fixed myself a big old breakfast of ham and eggs.

WESLEY: Ham and eggs?

WESTON: Yeah. Somebody left a whole mess a' groceries in the ice box. Surprised the hell outa' me. Just like Christmas. Just like somebody knew I was gonna' be reborn this morning or something. Couldn't believe my eyes.

WESLEY *goes to refrigerator and looks in.*

WESTON: Then I started makin' coffee and found myself doing all this stuff I used to do. Like I was coming back to my life after a long time a' being away.

WESLEY *staring in refrigerator:*   Mom brought this stuff.

WESTON: Then I started doing the laundry. All the laundry. I went around the house and found all the piles of dirty clothes I could get my hands on. Emma's, Ella's, even some a' yours. Some a' your socks. Found everybody's clothes. And every time I bent down to pick up somebody's clothes I could feel that person like they were right there in the room. Like the clothes were still attached to the person they belonged to. And I felt like I knew every single one of you. Every one. Like I knew you through the flesh and blood. Like our bodies were connected and we could never escape that. But I didn't feel like escaping. I felt like it was a good thing. It was good to be connected by blood like that. That a family wasn't just a social thing. It was an animal thing. It was a reason of nature that we were all together under the same roof. Not that we had to be but that we were supposed to be. And I started feeling glad about it. I started feeling full of hope.

WESLEY *staring in refrigerator:*   I'm starving.

WESTON *crossing to* WESLEY: Look, go take a bath and get that crap off your face, and I'll make ya' some ham and eggs. What is that crap anyway?

WESLEY: Blood.

WESTON: He took a few swipes at ya', huh? Well go wash it off and come back in here. Go on!

WESLEY *turning to* WESTON: He wouldn't give me the money, you know.

WESTON: So what. The guy's a knuckle-head. Don't have the brains God gave a chicken. Now go in there and clean up before *I* start swingin' on you.

WESLEY *exits off left.* WESTON *starts taking ham and eggs out of refrigerator and fixing a breakfast at the stove. He yells off stage to* WESLEY *as he cooks.*

WESTON *yelling:*   So I was thinkin' about that avocado deal you were talkin' about before! You know, joining up with the "Growers Association" and everything! And I was thinkin' it might not be such a bad deal after all! I mean we don't have to hire Chicanos or nothin'! We could pick 'em ourselves and sell 'em direct to the company! How 'bout that idea! Cut down on the overhead! That tractor's still workin', isn't it? I mean the motor's not seized up or nothin', and we got plenty a' good pressure in the irrigation! I checked it this morning! Water's blastin' right through those pipes! Wouldn't take much to get the whole operation goin' full-tilt again! I'll resell that piece a' land out there! That'll give us somethin' to get us started! Somebody somewhere's gonna' want a good piece a' desert land! It's prime location even if it isn't being developed! Only a three-hour drive from Palm Springs, and you know what that's like! You know the kinda' people who frequent that place! One of 'em's bound to have some extra cash!

ELLA *enters from stage right. She looks haggard and tired. She stands there looking at* WESTON, *who keeps cooking the eggs. Then she looks at the lamb.* WESTON *knows she's there but doesn't look at her.*

ELLA *after pause:*   What's that lamb doing back in here?

WESTON: I got him back on his feet. It was nip and tuck there for a while. Didn't think he'd pull through. Maggots clear up into the small intestine.

ELLA *crossing to table:*   Spare me the details.

She pulls off her white gloves and sits exhausted into the chair at stage right. She looks at the piles of clean laundry.

WESTON *still cooking:*   Where you been anyway?

ELLA: Jail.

WESTON: Oh, they finally caught ya', huh? *Chuckles.*

ELLA: Very humorous.

WESTON: You want some breakfast? I was just fixin' something up for Wes, here.

ELLA: You're cooking?

WESTON: Yeah. What's it look like?

ELLA: Who did all this laundry?

WESTON: Yours truly.

ELLA: Are you having a nervous breakdown or what?

WESTON: Can't a man do his own laundry?

ELLA: As far as I know he can.

WESTON: Even did some a' yours too.

ELLA: Gee, thanks.

WESTON: Well, I coulda' just left it. I was doin' a load of my own, so I thought I'd throw everybody else's in to boot.

ELLA: I'm very grateful.

WESTON: So where you been? Off with that fancy lawyer?

ELLA: I've been to jail, like I said.

WESTON: Come on. What, on a visit? They throw you in the drunk tank? Out with it.

ELLA: I was visiting your daughter.

WESTON: Oh, yeah? What'd they nab her for?

ELLA: Possession of firearms. Malicious vandalism. Breaking and entering. Assault. Violation of equestrian regulations. You name it.

WESTON: Well, she always was a fireball.

ELLA: Part of the inheritance, right?

WESTON: Right. Direct descendant.

ELLA: Well, I'm glad you've found a way of turning shame into a source of pride.

WESTON: What's shameful about it? Takes courage to get charged with all that stuff. It's not everyone her age who can run up a list of credits like that.

ELLA: That's for sure.

WESTON: Could you?

ELLA: Don't be ridiculous! I'm not self-destructive. Doesn't run in my family line.

WESTON: That's right. I never thought about it like that. You're the only one who doesn't have it. Only us.

ELLA: Oh, so now I'm the outsider.

WESTON: Well, it's true. You come from a different class of people. Gentle. Artists. They were all artists, weren't they?

ELLA: My grandfather was a pharmacist.

WESTON: Well, scientists then. Members of the professions. Professionals. Nobody raised their voice.

ELLA: That's bad?

WESTON: No. Just different. That's all. Just different.

ELLA: Are we waxing philosophical over our eggs now? Is that the idea? Sobered up over night, have we? Awoken to a brand-new morning? What is this crap! I've been down there all night trying to pull Emma back together again and I come back to Mr. Hyde! Mr. "Goody Two-Shoes"! Mister Mia Copa himself! Well, you can kiss off with that crap because I'm not buying it!

WESTON: Would you like some coffee?

ELLA: NO, I DON'T WANT ANY GODDAMN COFFEE! AND GET
THAT SON-OF-A-BITCHING SHEEP OUT OF MY KITCHEN!!

WESTON *staying cool:*   You've picked up on the language okay, but your
inflection's off.

ELLA: There's nothing wrong with my inflection!

WESTON: Something doesn't ring true about it. Something deep in the
voice. At the heart of things.

ELLA: Oh, you are really something. How can you accuse me of not measuring up to your standards! You're a complete washout!

WESTON: It's got nothing to do with standards. It's more like fate.

ELLA: Oh, knock it off, would you? I'm exhausted.

WESTON: Try the table. Nice and hard. It'll do wonders for you.

ELLA *suddenly soft:*   The table?

WESTON: Yeah. Just stretch yourself out. You'll be amazed. Better than
any bed.

ELLA *looks at the table for a second, then starts pushing all the clean laundry
off it onto the floor. She pulls herself up onto it and stretches out on it.* WESTON
goes on cooking with his back to her. She watches him as she lies there.

WESTON: And when you wake up I'll have a great big breakfast of ham
and eggs, ready and waiting. You'll feel like a million bucks. You'll
wonder why you spent all those years in bed, once you feel that table.
That table will deliver you.

WESLEY *wanders on stage from stage left, completely naked, his hair wet. He
looks dazed.* WESTON *pays no attention but goes on preparing the breakfast and
talking as* WESLEY *wanders upstage and stares at* ELLA. *She looks at him but
doesn't react. He turns downstage and looks at* WESTON. *He looks at lamb and
crosses down to it. He bends over and picks it up, then carries it off stage right.*
WESTON *goes on cooking and talking.* ELLA *stays on table.*

WESTON: That's the trouble with too much comfort, you know? Makes
you forget where you come from. Makes you lose touch. You think
you're making headway but you're losing all the time. You're falling
behind more and more. You're going into a trance that you'll never
come back from. You're being hypnotized. Your body's being mesmer-
ized. You go into a coma. That's why you need a hard table once in a
while to bring you back. A good hard table to bring you back to life.

ELLA *still on table, sleepily:*   You should have been a preacher.

WESTON: You think so?

ELLA: Great voice you have. Deep. Resonates.

WESTON *putting eggs on plate:*   I'm not a public person.

ELLA: I'm so exhausted.

WESTON: You just sleep.

ELLA: You should have seen that jail, Weston.

WESTON: I have.

ELLA: Oh, that's right. How could you ever sleep in a place like that?

WESTON: If you're numb enough you don't feel a thing. *He yells off stage to* WESLEY. WES! YOUR BREAKFAST'S READY!
ELLA: He just went out.
WESTON: What?
ELLA: He just walked out stark naked with that sheep under his arm.

WESTON *looks at fence enclosure, sees lamb gone. He's still holding plate.*

WESTON: Were'd he go?
ELLA: Outside.
WESTON *crossing right, carrying plate:* WES! GODDAMN-IT, YOUR BREAKFAST'S READY!

WESTON *exits carrying plate off stage right.* ELLA *tries to keep her eyes open, still on table.*

ELLA *to herself:* Nothing surprises me any more.

She slowly falls asleep on table. Nothing happens for a while. Then WESTON *comes back on from right still carrying plate.* ELLA *stays asleep on table.*

WESTON *crossing to stove:* He's not out there. Wouldn't ya' know it? Just when it's ready, he walks out. *Turning to* ELLA. Why'd he take the lamb? That lamb needs to be kept warm. *Sees that* ELLA'S *sound asleep.* Great. *Turns and sets plate down on stove; looks at food.* Might as well eat it myself. A double breakfast. Why not? *He starts eating off the plate, talks to himself.* Can't expect the thing to get well if it's not kept warm. *He turns upstage again and looks at* ELLA *sleeping, then turns back to the plate of food.* Always was best at talkin' to myself. Always was the best thing. Nothing like it. Keeps ya' company at least.

WESLEY *enters from right dressed in* WESTON'S *baseball cap, overcoat, and tennis shoes. He stands there.* WESTON *looks at him.* ELLA *sleeps.*

WESTON: What in the hell's goin' on with you? I was yellin' for you just now. Didn't you hear me?
WESLEY *staring at* WESTON: No.
WESTON: Your breakfast was all ready. Now it's cold. I've eaten half of it already. Almost half gone.
WESLEY *blankly:* You can have it.
WESTON: What're you doin' in those clothes anyway?
WESLEY: I found them.
WESTON: I threw them out! What's got into you? You go take a bath and then put on some old bum's clothes that've been thrown-up in, pissed in, and God knows what all in?
WESLEY: They fit me.
WESTON: I can't fathom you, that's for sure. What'd you do with that lamb?

WESLEY: Butchered it.

WESTON *turning away from him, disgusted:*   I swear to God. *Pause, then turning to* WESLEY. WHAT'D YA' BUTCHER THE DUMB THING FOR!

WESLEY: We need some food.

WESTON: THE ICE BOX IS CRAMMED FULL A' FOOD!

WESLEY *crosses quickly to refrigerator, opens it, and starts pulling all kinds of food out and eating it ravenously.* WESTON *watches him, a little afraid of* WESLEY'S *state.*

WESTON: WHAT'D YA' GO AND BUTCHER IT FOR? HE WAS GETTING BETTER! *Watches* WESLEY *eating hungrily.* What's a' matter with you, boy? I made ya' a big breakfast. Why didn't ya' eat that? What's a' matter with you?

WESTON *moves cautiously, away from* WESLEY *to stage right.* WESLEY *keeps eating, throwing half-eaten food to one side and then digging into more. He groans slightly as he eats.*

WESTON *to* WESLEY: Look, I know I ignored some a' the chores around the place and you had to do it instead a' me. But I brought you some artichokes back, didn't I? Didn't I do that? I didn't have to do that. I went outa' my way. I saw the sign on the highway and drove two miles outa' my way just to bring you back some artichokes. *Pause, as he looks at* WESLEY *eating; he glances nervously up at* ELLA, *then back to* WESLEY. You couldn't be all that starving! We're not that bad off, goddamnit! I've seen starving people in my time, and we're not that bad off! *Pause, no reaction from* WESLEY, *who continues to eat ravenously.* You just been spoiled, that's all! This is a paradise for a young person! There's kids your age who'd give their eye-teeth to have an environment like this to grow up in! You've got everything! Everything! Opportunity is glaring you in the teeth here! *Turns toward* ELLA. ELLA! ELLA, WAKE UP! *No reaction from* ELLA; *turns back to* WESLEY, *still eating.* If this is supposed to make me feel guilty, it's not working! It's not working because I don't have to pay for my past now! Not now! Not after this morning! All that's behind me now! YOU UNDERSTAND ME? IT'S ALL OVER WITH BECAUSE I'VE BEEN REBORN! I'M A WHOLE NEW PERSON NOW! I'm a whole new person.

WESLEY *stops eating suddenly and turns to* WESTON.

WESLEY *coldly:*   They're going to kill you.

WESTON *pause:*   Who's going to kill me! What're you talking about! Nobody's going to kill me!

WESLEY: I couldn't get the money.

WESTON: What money?

WESLEY: Ellis.

WESTON: So what?

WESLEY: You owe it to them.

WESTON: Owe it to who? I don't remember anything. All that's over with now.

WESLEY: No, it's not. It's still there. Maybe you've changed, but you still owe them.

WESTON: I can't remember. Must've borrowed some for the car payment. Can't remember it.

WESLEY: They remember it.

WESTON: So, I'll get it to them. It's not that drastic.

WESLEY: How? Ellis has the house and everything now.

WESTON: How does he have the house? This is my house!

WESLEY: You signed it over.

WESTON: I never signed anything!

WESLEY: You were drunk.

WESTON: SHUT UP!

WESLEY: How're you going to pay them?

WESTON *pause:* I can sell that land.

WESLEY: It's phony land. The guy's run off to Mexico.

WESTON: What guy?

WESLEY: Taylor. The lawyer. The lawyer friend of Mom's.

WESTON *pause, looks at* ELLA *sleeping, then back to* WESLEY: Same guy?

WESLEY: Same guy. Ripped us all off.

WESTON: This isn't right. I was on a whole new track. I was getting right up on top of it all.

WESLEY: They've got it worked out so you can't.

WESTON: I was ready for a whole new attack. This isn't right!

WESLEY: They've moved in on us like a creeping disease. We didn't even notice.

WESTON: I just built a whole new door and everything. I washed all the laundry. I cleaned up all the artichokes. I started over.

WESLEY: You better run.

WESTON: Run? What do you mean, run? I can't run!

WESLEY: Take the Packard and get out of here.

WESTON: I can't run out on everything.

WESLEY: Why not?

WESTON: 'CAUSE THIS IS WHERE I SETTLED DOWN! THIS IS WHERE THE LINE ENDED! RIGHT HERE! I MIGRATED TO THIS SPOT! I GOT NOWHERE TO GO TO! THIS IS IT!

WESLEY: Take the Packard.

WESTON *stands there for a while. He looks around, trying to figure a way out.*

WESTON *after pause:* I remember now. I was in hock. I was in hock up to my elbows. See, I always figured on the future. I banked on it. I was banking on it getting better. It couldn't get worse, so I figured it'd just get better. I figured that's why everyone wants you to buy things. Buy refrigerators. Buy cars, houses, lots, invest. They wouldn't be so generous if they didn't figure you had it commin' in. At some point it had to be comin' in. So I went along with it. Why not borrow if you know it's coming in. Why not make a touch here and there. They all want you to borrow anyhow. Banks, car lots, investors. The whole thing's geared to invisible money. You never hear the sound of change any more. It's all plastic shuffling back and forth. It's all in everybody's heads. So I figured if that's the case, why not take advantage of it? Why not go in debt for a few grand if all it is is numbers? If it's all an idea and nothing's really there, why not take advantage? So I just went along with it, that's all. I just played ball.

WESLEY: You better go.

Pause, as WESTON *looks at* ELLA *sleeping.*

WESTON: Same guy, huh? She musta' known about it, too. She musta' thought I left her.

WESTON *turns and looks at* WESLEY. *Silence.*

WESLEY: You did.

WESTON: I just went off for a little while. Now and then. I couldn't stand it here. I couldn't stand the idea that everything would stay the same. That every morning it would be the same. I kept looking for it out there somewhere. I kept trying to piece it together. The jumps. I couldn't figure out the jumps. From being born, to growing up, to droppin' bombs, to having kids, to hittin' bars, to this. It all turned on me somehow. It all turned around on me. I kept looking for it out there somewhere. And all the time it was right inside this house.

WESLEY: They'll be coming for you here. They know where you live now.

WESTON: Where should I go?

WESLEY: How 'bout Mexico?

WESTON: Mexico? Yeah. That's where everyone escapes to, right? It's full of escape artists down there. I could go down there and get lost. I could disappear. I could start a whole new life down there.

WESLEY: Maybe.

WESTON: I could find that guy and get my money back. That real estate guy. What's his name?

WESLEY: Taylor.

WESTON: Yeah, Taylor. He's down there too, right? I could find him.

WESLEY: Maybe.

WESTON *looking over at* ELLA *again:*   I can't believe she knew and still went off with him. She musta' thought I was dead or something. She musta' thought I was never coming back.

WESTON *moves toward* ELLA, *then stops. He looks at* WESLEY, *then turns and exits off right.* WESLEY *just stands there.* WESLEY *bends down and picks some scraps of food up off the floor and eats them very slowly. He looks at the empty lamb pen.* EMMA *enters from left, dressed as she was in Act 2. She crosses into center, looking in the direction of where* WESTON *went.* WESLEY *seems dazed as he slowly chews the food.* ELLA *stays asleep on table.* EMMA *carries a riding crop. She taps her leg with it as she looks off right.*

EMMA: Mexico, huh? He won't last a day down there. They'll find him easy. Stupid going to Mexico. That's the first place they'll look. *To* WESLEY. What're you eating?

WESLEY: Food.

EMMA: Off the floor? You'll wind up just like him. Diseased!

WESLEY *dazed:*   I'm hungry.

EMMA: You're sick! What're you doing with his clothes on? Are you supposed to be the head of the family now or something? The Big Cheese? Daddy Bear?

WESLEY: I tried his remedy, but it didn't work.

EMMA: He's got a remedy?

WESLEY *half to himself:*   I tried taking a hot bath. Hot as I could stand it. Then freezing cold. Then walking around naked. But it didn't work. Nothing happened. I was waiting for something to happen. I went outside. I was freezing cold out there and I looked for something to put over me. I started digging around in the garbage and I found his clothes.

EMMA: Digging around in the garbage?

WESLEY: I had the lamb's blood dripping down my arms. I thought it was me for a second. I thought it was me bleeding.

EMMA: You're disgusting. You're even more disgusting than him. And that's pretty disgusting. *Looking at* ELLA, *still asleep.* What's she doing?

WESLEY: I started putting all his clothes on. His baseball cap, his tennis shoes, his overcoat. And every time I put one thing on it seemed like a part of him was growing on me. I could feel him taking over me.

EMMA *crossing up to table, tapping crop on her leg:*   What is she, asleep or something? *She whacks* ELLA *across the butt with the riding crop.* WAKE UP! ELLA *stays sleeping.*

WESLEY: I could feel myself retreating. I could feel him coming in and me going out. Just like the change of the guards.

EMMA: Well, don't eat your heart out about it. You did the best you could.

WESLEY: I didn't do a thing.

EMMA: That's what I mean.

WESLEY: I just grew up here.

EMMA *crossing down to* WESLEY: Have you got any money?

WESLEY *starts digging around in the pockets of the overcoat.*

EMMA: What're you fishing around in there for? That's *his* coat.

WESLEY: I thought you were supposed to be in jail?

EMMA *crossing back up to table:*   I was.

WESLEY: What happened?

EMMA *picking up* ELLA'S *handbag and going through it:* I used my ingenuity. I made use of my innate criminal intelligence.

EMMA *throws things onto the floor from* ELLA'S *pocket book as she searches through it.*

WESLEY: What'd you do?
EMMA: I got out.
WESLEY: I know, but how?
EMMA: I made sexual overtures to the sergeant. That's how. Easy.

She takes a big wad of money out of pocket book and a set of car keys, then throws the bag away. She holds up the money.

EMMA: I'm going into crime. It's the only thing that pays these days.
WESLEY *looking at roll of bills in* EMMA'S *hand:* Where'd she get that?
EMMA: Where do you think?
WESLEY: You're taking her car?
EMMA: It's the perfect self-employment. Crime. No credentials. No diplomas. No overhead. No upkeep. Just straight profit. Right off the top.
WESLEY: How come I'm going backwards?
EMMA *moving in toward* WESLEY: Because you don't look ahead. That's why. You don't see the writing on the wall. You gotta learn how to read these things, Wes. It's deadly otherwise. You can't believe people when they look you in the eyes. You gotta' look behind them. See what they're standing in front of. What they're hiding. Everybody's hiding, Wes. Everybody. Nobody looks like what they are.
WESLEY: What are you?
EMMA *moving away:* I'm gone. I'm gone! Never to return.

ELLA *suddenly wakes up on the table. She sits up straight.*

ELLA *as though waking from a bad dream:* EMMA!!

EMMA *looks at her, then runs off stage left.* ELLA *sits there on table staring in horror at* WESLEY. *She doesn't recognize him.*

ELLA *to* WESLEY: Weston! Was that Emma?
WESLEY: It's me, Mom.
ELLA *yelling off stage but still on table:* EMMA!! *She jumps off table and looks for a coat.* We've got to catch her! She can't run off like that! That horse will kill her! Where's my coat? *To* WESLEY. WHERE'S MY COAT?
WESLEY: You weren't wearing one.
ELLA *to* WESLEY: Go catch her, Weston! She's your daughter! She's trying to run away!
WESLEY: Let her go.
ELLA: I can't let her go! I'm responsible!

Huge explosion off stage. Flash of light, then silence. WESLEY *and* ELLA *just stand there staring.* EMERSON *enters from right, giggling. He's a small man in a suit.*

EMERSON: Jeeezus! Did you ever hear a thing like that? What a wallop! Jeezus Christ! *Giggles.*

WESLEY *and* ELLA *look at him.*

EMERSON: Old Slater musta' packed it brim full. I never heard such a godalmighty bang in my whole career.

SLATER, *his partner, enters from right, holding out the skinned lamb carcass. He's taller than* EMERSON, *also in a suit. They both giggle as though they'd pulled off a halloween stunt.*

SLATER: Emerson, get a load a'this! *Giggling.* Did you see this thing? *To* WESLEY. What is this, a skinned goat?
WESLEY *blank:*   Lamb.
SLATER: Oh, it's a lamb! *They laugh.* Looks like somebody's afterbirth to me! *They laugh hysterically.*
WESLEY: What was that bang?

They stop laughing and look at WESLEY. *They laugh again, then stop.*

EMERSON: Bang? What bang?
WESLEY: That explosion.
EMERSON: Oh that! That was just a little reminder. A kind of a post-hypnotic suggestion. *They laugh.*
ELLA: Who are these men, Weston?
EMERSON *to* WESLEY: Weston? You're Weston?
WESLEY: My father.
EMERSON *to* SLATER: Looks a little young, don't ya' think?
SLATER *dropping lamb carcass into fence enclosure:*   Well, if she says he's Weston, he must be Weston.
ELLA: What are these men doing here? *She moves away from them.*
EMERSON *to* WESLEY: So you're Weston? We had a different picture in mind. We had someone altogether different in mind.
WESLEY: What was it that blew up out there?
EMERSON: Something that wasn't paid for. Something past due.
SLATER: Long overdue.
WESLEY: The car. You blew up the car.
EMERSON: Bingo!

They crack up. WESLEY *moves upstage and looks out as though trying to see outside.*

ELLA: Get these men out of here, Weston! They're in my kitchen.

SLATER *looking around:*   Some mess in here, boy. I couldn't live like this if you paid me.

EMERSON: Well, that's what comes from not paying your bills. You let one thing slide; first thing you know you let everything slide. You let everything go downhill until you wind up in a dungheap like this.

WESLEY *looking out, upstage:*   There's a fire out there.

SLATER: It'll go out. It's just a gelignite-nitro mixture. Doesn't burn for long. May leave a few scars on the lawn but nothin' permanent.

WESLEY *without emotion, still looking out:*   Nothing left of the car.

SLATER: That's right. Very thorough. The Irish developed it. Beautiful stuff. Never know what hit ya'.

EMERSON *to* WESLEY: Well, we gotta' run, Weston. But you can get the general drift. *They start to leave;* EMERSON *stops.* Oh, and if you see your old man, you might pass on the info. We hate to keep repeating ourselves. The first time is great, but after that it gets pretty boring.

SLATER *to* WESLEY: Don't forget to give that lamb some milk. He looks pretty bad off.

They both laugh loudly, then exit. ELLA *is facing downstage now, staring at the lamb carcass in the pen.* WESLEY *has his back to her upstage. He looks out. Pause.*

ELLA *staring at dead lamb:*   I must've slept right through the day. How long did I sleep?

They stay in these positions facing away from each other.

WESLEY: Not so long.

ELLA: And Emma left. She really left on that horse. I didn't think she'd do it. I had a dream she was leaving. That's what woke me up.

WESLEY: She was right here in the kitchen.

ELLA: I must've slept right through it. *Pause, as she stares at lamb carcass.* Oh! You know what, Wes?

WESLEY: What?

ELLA: Something just went right through me. Just from looking at this lamb.

WESLEY: What?

ELLA: That story your father used to tell about that eagle. You remember that?

WESLEY: Yeah.

ELLA: You remember the whole thing?

WESLEY: Yeah.

ELLA: I don't. I remember something about it. But it just went right through me.

WESLEY: Oh.

ELLA *after pause:*   I remember he keeps coming back and swooping down on the shed roof and then flying off.

WESLEY: Yeah.

ELLA: What else?

WESLEY: I don't know.

ELLA: You remember. What happens next?

WESLEY: A cat comes.

ELLA: That's right. A big tom cat comes. Right out in the fields. And he jumps up on top of that roof to sniff around in all the entrails or whatever it was.

WESLEY *still with back to her:*   And that eagle comes down and picks up the cat in his talons and carries him screaming off into the sky.

ELLA *staring at lamb:*   That's right. And they fight. They fight like crazy in the middle of the sky. That cat's tearing his chest out, and the eagle's trying to drop him, but the cat won't let go because he knows if he falls he'll die.

WESLEY: And the eagle's being torn apart in midair. The eagle's trying to free himself from the cat, and the cat won't let go.

ELLA: And they come crashing down to the earth. Both of them come crashing down. Like one whole thing.

They stay like that with WESLEY *looking off upstage, his back to* ELLA, *and* ELLA *downstage, looking at the lamb. Lights fade very slowly to black.*

TENNESSEE WILLIAMS (1911–1983)

Cat on a Hot Tin Roof

Tennessee Williams was born in Columbus, Mississippi. His first play, *Battle of Angels*, was performed in 1940. His first major success came with *The Glass Menagerie* (1945). His plays are often studies of corruption in all its varied forms; two of them, *A Streetcar Named Desire* (1947) and *Cat on a Hot Tin Roof* (1955) won Pulitzer Prizes. Other major plays include *Summer and Smoke* (1948), *Suddenly Last Summer* (1958), and *The Night of the Iguana* (1961).

CHARACTERS

MARGARET

BRICK

MAE, sometimes called Sister Woman

BIG MAMA

DIXIE, a little girl

BIG DADDY

REVEREND TOOKER

GOOPER, sometimes called Brother Man

DOCTOR BAUGH, pronounced "Baw"

LACEY, a Negro servant
SOOKEY, another
Another little girl and two small boys
(The playing script of Act III also includes TRIXIE, another little girl, also
DAISY, BRIGHTIE and SMALL, servants.)

ACT I

*At the rise of the curtain someone is taking a shower in the bathroom, the door
of which is half open. A pretty young woman, with anxious lines in her face,
enters the bedroom and crosses to the bathroom door.*

MARGARET *shouting above roar of water:* One of those no-neck monsters
   hit me with a hot buttered biscuit so I have t' change!

MARGARET'S *voice is both rapid and drawling. In her long speeches she has the
vocal tricks of a priest delivering a liturgical chant, the lines are almost sung,
always continuing a little beyond her breath so she has to gasp for another. Sometimes she intersperses the lines with a little wordless singing, such as "Da-da-
daaaa!"*

Water turns off and BRICK *calls out to her, but is still unseen. A tone of politely
feigned interest, masking indifference, or worse, is characteristic of his speech
with* MARGARET.

BRICK: Wha'd you say, Maggie? Water was on s' loud I couldn't
   hearya. . . .
MARGARET: Well, I!—just remarked that!—one of th' no-neck monsters
   messed up m' lovely lace dress so I got t'—cha-a-ange. . . .

She opens and kicks shut drawers of the dresser.

BRICK: Why d'ya call Gooper's kiddies no-neck monsters?
MARGARET: Because they've got no necks! Isn't that a good enough rea-
   son?
BRICK: Don't they have any necks?
MARGARET: None visible. Their fat little heads are set on their fat little
   bodies without a bit of connection.
BRICK: That's too bad.
MARGARET: Yes, it's too bad because you can't wring their necks if
   they've got no necks to wring! Isn't that right, honey?

She steps out of her dress, stands in a slip of ivory satin and lace.

Yep, they're no-neck monsters, all no-neck people are monsters . . .

Children shriek downstairs.

Hear them? Hear them screaming? I don't know where their voice boxes are located since they don't have necks. I tell you I got so nervous at that table tonight I thought I would throw back my head and utter a scream you could hear across the Arkansas border an' parts of Louisiana an' Tennessee. I said to your charming sister-in-law, Mae, honey, couldn't you feed those precious little things at a separate table with an oilcloth cover? They make such a mess an' the lace cloth looks *so* pretty! She made enormous eyes at me and said, "Ohhh, noooooo! On Big Daddy's birthday? Why, he would never forgive me!" Well, I want you to know, Big Daddy hadn't been at the table two minutes with those five no-neck monsters slobbering and drooling over their food before he threw down his fork an' shouted, "Fo' God's sake, Gooper, why don't you put them pigs at a trough in th' kitchen?"—Well, I swear, I simply could have di-ieed!

Think of it, Brick, they've got five of them and number six is coming. They've brought the whole bunch down here like animals to display at a county fair. Why, they have those children doin' tricks all the time! "Junior, show Big Daddy how you do this, show Big Daddy how you do that, say your little piece fo' Big Daddy, Sister. Show your dimples, Sugar. Brother, show Big Daddy how you stand on your head!"—It goes on all the time, along with constant little remarks and innuendos about the fact that you and I have not produced any children, are totally childless and therefore totally useless!—Of course it's comical but it's also disgusting since it's so obvious what they're up to!

BRICK *without interest:*　What are they up to, Maggie?

MARGARET:　Why, you know what they're up to!

BRICK *appearing:*　No, I don't know what they're up to.

He stands there in the bathroom doorway drying his hair with a towel and hanging onto the towel rack because one ankle is broken, plastered and bound. He is still slim and firm as a boy. His liquor hasn't started tearing him down outside. He has the additional charm of that cool air of detachment that people have who have given up the struggle. But now and then, when disturbed, something flashes behind it, like lightning in a fair sky, which shows that at some deeper level he is far from peaceful. Perhaps in a stronger light he would show some signs of deliquescence, but the fading, still warm, light from the gallery treats him gently.

MARGARET:　I'll tell you what they're up to, boy of mine!—They're up to cutting you out of your father's estate, and—

She freezes momentarily before her next remark. Her voice drops as if it were somehow a personally embarrassing admission.

—Now we know that Big Daddy's dyin' of—*cancer.* . . .

There are voices on the lawn below: long-drawn calls across distance. MARGARET *raises her lovely bare arms and powders her armpits with a light sigh.*

She adjusts the angle of a magnifying mirror to straighten an eyelash, then rises fretfully saying:

There's so much light in the room it—
BRICK *softly but sharply:* Do we?
MARGARET: Do we what?
BRICK: Know Big Daddy's dyin' of cancer?
MARGARET: Got the report today.
BRICK: Oh . . .
MARGARET *letting down bamboo blinds which cast long, gold-fretted shadows over the room:* Yep, got th' report just now . . . it didn't surprise me, Baby. . . .

Her voice has range, and music; sometimes it drops low as a boy's and you have a sudden image of her playing boy's games as a child.

I recognized the symptoms soon's we got here last spring and I'm willin' to bet you that Brother Man and his wife were pretty sure of it, too. That more than likely explains why their usual summer migration to the coolness of the Great Smokies was passed up this summer in favor of—hustlin' down here ev'ry whipstitch with their whole screamin' tribe! And why so many allusions have been made to Rainbow Hill lately. You know what Rainbow Hill is? Place that's famous for treatin' alcoholics an dope fiends in the movies!
BRICK: I'm not in the movies.
MARGARET: No, and you don't take dope. Otherwise you're a perfect candidate for Rainbow Hill, Baby, and that's where they aim to ship you— over my dead body! Yep, over my dead body they'll ship you there, but nothing would please them better. Then Brother Man could get a-hold of the purse strings and dole out remittances to us, maybe get power of attorney and sign checks for us and cut off our credit wherever, whenever he wanted! Son-of-a-bitch!—How'd you like that, Baby?—Well, you've been doin' just about ev'rything in your power to bring it about, you've just been doin' ev'rything you can think of to aid and abet them in this scheme of theirs! Quittin' work, devoting yourself to the occupation of drinkin'!—Breakin' your ankle last night on the high school athletic field: doin' what? Jumpin' hurdles? At two or three in the morning? Just fantastic! Got in the paper. *Clarksdale Register* carried a nice little item about it, human interest story about a well-known former athlete stagin' a one-man track meet on the Glorious Hill High School athletic field last night, but was slightly out of condition and didn't clear the first hurdle! Brother Man Gooper claims he exercised his influence t' keep it from goin' out over AP or UP or every goddam "P."

But, Brick? You still have one big advantage!

During the above swift flood of words, BRICK *has reclined with contrapuntal leisure on the snowy surface of the bed and has rolled over carefully on his side or belly.*

BRICK *wryly:* Did you *say* something, Maggie?

MARGARET: Big Daddy dotes on you, honey. And he can't stand Brother Man and Brother Man's wife, that monster of fertility, Mae; she's downright odious to him! Know how I know? By little expressions that flicker over his face when that woman is holding fo'th on one of her choice topics such as—how she refused twilight sleep!—when the twins were delivered! Because she feels motherhood's an experience that a woman ought to experience fully!—in order to fully appreciate the wonder and beauty of it! HAH!

This loud "HAH!" is accompanied by a violent action such as slamming a drawer shut.

—and how she made Brother Man come in an' stand beside her in the delivery room so he would not miss out on the "wonder and beauty" of it either!—producin' those no-neck monsters. . . .

A speech of this kind would be antipathetic from almost anybody but MARGARET; *she makes it oddly funny, because her eyes constantly twinkle and her voice shakes with laughter which is basically indulgent.*

—Big Daddy shares my attitude toward those two! As for me, well—I give him a laugh now and then and he tolerates me. In fact!—I sometimes suspect that Big Daddy harbors a little unconscious "lech" fo' me. . . .

BRICK: What makes you think that Big Daddy has a lech for you, Maggie?

MARGARET: Way he always drops his eyes down my body when I'm talkin' to him, drops his eyes to my boobs an' licks his old chops! Ha Ha!

BRICK: That kind of talk is disgusting.

MARGARET: Did anyone ever tell you that you're an ass-aching Puritan, Brick?

I think it's mighty fine that that ole fellow, on the doorstep of death, still takes in my shape with what I think is deserved appreciation!

And you wanta know something else? Big Daddy didn't know how many little Maes and Goopers had been produced! "How many kids have you got?" he asked at the table, just like Brother Man and his wife were new acquaintances to him! Big Mama said he was jokin', but that ole boy wasn't jokin', Lord, no!

And when they infawmed him that they had five already and were turning out number six!—the news seemed to come as a sort of unpleasant surprise . . .

Children yell below.

Scream, monsters!

Turns to BRICK *with a sudden, gay, charming smile which fades as she notices that he is not looking at her but into fading gold space with a troubled expression.*

It is constant rejection that makes her humor "bitchy."

Yes, you should of been at that supper-table, Baby.

Whenever she calls him "baby" the word is a soft caress.

Y'know, Big Daddy, bless his ole sweet soul, he's the dearest ole thing in the world, but he does hunch over his food as if he preferred not to notice anything else. Well, Mae an' Gooper were side by side at the table, direckly across from Big Daddy, watchin' his face like hawks while they jawed an' jabbered about the cuteness an' brillance of th' no-neck monsters!

She giggles with a hand fluttering at her throat and her breast and her long throat arched.

She comes downstage and recreates the scene with voice and gesture.

And the no-neck monsters were ranged around the table, some in high chairs and some on th' *Books of Knowledge,* all in fancy little paper caps in honor of Big Daddy's birthday, and all through dinner, well, I want you to know that Brother Man an' his partner never once, for one moment, stopped exchanging pokes an' pinches an' kicks an' signs an' signals!—Why, they were like a couple of cardsharps fleecing a sucker.—Even Big Mama, bless her ole sweet soul, she isn't th' quickest an' brightest thing in the world, she finally noticed, at last, an' said to Gooper, "Gooper, what are you an' Mae makin' all these signs at each other about?"—I swear t' goodness, I nearly choked on my chicken!

MARGARET, *back at the dressing table, still doesn't see* BRICK. *He is watching her with a look that is not quite definable—Amused? shocked? contemptuous?— part of those and part of something else.*

Y'know—your brother Gooper still cherishes the illusion he took a giant step up on the social ladder when he married Miss Mae Flynn of the Memphis Flynns.

MARGARET *moves about the room as she talks, stops before the mirror, moves on.*

But I have a piece of Spanish news for Gooper. The Flynns never had a thing in this world but money and they lost that, they were nothing at all but fairly successful climbers. Of course, Mae Flynn came out in Memphis eight years before I made my debut in Nashville, but I had friends at Ward Belmont who came from Memphis and they used to come to see me and I used to go to see them for Christmas and spring vacations, and so I know who rates an' who doesn't rate in Memphis society. Why, y'know ole Papa Flynn, he barely escaped doing time in the Federal pen for shady manipulations on th' stock market when his chain stores crashed, and as for Mae having been a cotton carnival queen, as they remind us so often, lest we forget, well, that's one honor that I don't envy her for!—Sit on a brass throne on a tacky float an' ride down Main Street, smilin', bowin', and blowin' kisses to all the trash on the street—

She picks out a pair of jeweled sandals and rushes to the dressing table.

Why, year before last, when Susan McPheeters was singled out fo' that honor, y' know what happened to her? Y'know what happened to poor little Susie McPheeters?

BRICK *absently:*   No. What happened to little Susie McPheeters?

MARGARET: Somebody spit tobacco juice in her face.

BRICK *dreamily:*   Somebody spit tobacco juice in her face?

MARGARET: That's right, some old drunk leaned out of a window in the Hotel Gayoso and yelled, "Hey, Queen, hey, hey, there, Queenie!" Poor Susie looked up and flashed him a radiant smile and he shot out a squirt of tobacco juice right in poor Susie's face.

BRICK: Well, what d'you know about that.

MARGARET *gaily:*   What do I know about it? I was there, I saw it!

BRICK *absently:*   Must have been kind of funny.

MARGARET: Susie didn't think so. Had hysterics. Screamed like a banshee. They had to stop th' parade an' remove her from her throne an' go on with—

She catches sight of him in the mirror, gasps slightly, wheels about to face him. Count ten.

—Why are you looking at me like that?

BRICK *whistling softly, now:*   Like what, Maggie?

MARGARET *intensely, fearfully:*   The way y' were lookin' at me just now, befo' I caught your eye in the mirror and you started t' whistle! I don't know how t' describe it but it froze my blood!—I've caught you lookin' at me like that so often lately. What are you thinkin' of when you look at me like that?

BRICK: I wasn't conscious of lookin' at you, Maggie.

MARGARET: Well, I was conscious of it! What were you thinkin'?

BRICK: I don't remember thinking of anything, Maggie.

MARGARET: Don't you think I know that—? Don't you—?—Think I know that—?

BRICK *coolly:* Know *what*, Maggie?

MARGARET *struggling for expression:* That I've gone through this—*hideous!—transformation*, become—*hard! Frantic!*

Then she adds, almost tenderly:

—cruel!!

That's what you've been observing in me lately. How could y' help but observe it? That's all right. I'm not—thin-skinned any more, can't afford t' be thin-skinned any more.

She is now recovering her power.

—But Brick? Brick?

BRICK: Did you say something?

MARGARET: I was *goin' t'* say something: that I get—lonely. Very!

BRICK: Ev'rybody gets that . . .

MARGARET: Living with someone you love can be lonelier—than living entirely *alone!*—if the one that y' love doesn't love you. . . .

There is a pause. BRICK *hobbles downstage and asks, without looking at her:*

BRICK: Would you like to live alone, Maggie?

Another pause: then—after she has caught a quick, hurt breath:

MARGARET: *No!—God!—I wouldn't!*

Another gasping breath. She forcibly controls what must have been an impulse to cry out. We see her deliberately, very forcibly, going all the way back to the world in which you can talk about ordinary matters.

Did you have a nice shower?

BRICK: Uh-huh.

MARGARET: Was the water cool?

BRICK: No.

MARGARET: But it made y' feel fresh, huh?

BRICK: Fresher. . . .

MARGARET: I know something would make y' feel *much* fresher!

BRICK: What?

MARGARET: An alcohol rub. Or cologne, a rub with cologne!

BRICK: That's good after a workout but I haven't been workin' out, Maggie.

MARGARET: You've kept in good shape, though.

BRICK *indifferently:* You think so, Maggie?

MARGARET: I always thought drinkin' men lost their looks, but I was plainly mistaken.

BRICK *wryly:* Why, thanks, Maggie.

MARGARET: You're the only drinkin' man I know that it never seems t' put fat on.

BRICK: I'm gettin' softer, Maggie.

MARGARET: Well, sooner or later it's bound to soften you up. It was just beginning to soften up Skipper when—

She stops short.

I'm sorry. I never could keep my fingers off a sore—I wish you *would* lose your looks. If you did it would make the martyrdom of Saint Maggie a little more bearable. But no such goddam luck. I actually believe you've gotten better looking since you've gone on the bottle. Yeah, a person who didn't know you would think you'd never had a tense nerve in your body or a strained muscle.

There are sounds of croquet on the lawn below: the click of mallets, light voices, near and distant.

Of course, you always had that detached quality as if you were playing a game without much concern over whether you won or lost, and now that you've lost the game, not lost but just quit playing, you have that rare sort of charm that usually only happens in very old or hopelessly sick people, the charm of the defeated.—You look so cool, so cool, so enviably cool. *Music is heard.* They're playing croquet. The moon has appeared and it's white, just beginning to turn a little bit yellow. . . .

You were a wonderful lover. . . .

Such a wonderful person to go to bed with, and I think mostly because you were really indifferent to it. Isn't that right? Never had any anxiety about it, did it naturally, easily, slowly, with absolute confidence and perfect calm, more like opening a door for a lady or seating her at a table than giving expression to any longing for her. Your indifference made you wonderful at lovemaking—*strange?*—but true. . . .

You know, if I thought you would never, never, *never* make love to me again—I would go downstairs to the kitchen and pick out the longest and sharpest knife I could find and stick it straight into my heart, I swear that I would!

But one thing I don't have is the charm of the defeated, my hat is still in the ring, and I am determined to win!

There is the sound of croquet mallets hitting croquet balls.

—What is the victory of a cat on a hot tin roof?—I wish I knew. . . .

Just staying on it, I guess, as long as she can. . . .

More croquet sounds.

Later tonight I'm going to tell you I love you an' maybe by that time you'll be drunk enough to believe me. Yes, they're playing croquet. . . .

Big Daddy is dying of cancer. . . .

What were you thinking of when I caught you looking at me like that? Were you thinking of Skipper?

BRICK *takes up his crutch, rises.*

Oh, excuse me, forgive me, but laws of silence don't work! No, laws of silence don't work. . . .

BRICK *crosses to the bar, takes a quick drink, and rubs his head with a towel.*

Laws of silence don't work. . . .

When something is festering in your memory or your imagination, laws of silence don't work, it's just like shutting a door and locking it on a house on fire in hope of forgetting that the house is burning. But not facing a fire doesn't put it out. Silence about a thing just magnifies it. It grows and festers in silence, becomes malignant. . . .

Get dressed, Brick.

He drops his crutch.

BRICK: I've dropped my crutch.

He has stopped rubbing his hair dry but still stands hanging onto the towel rack in a white towel-cloth robe.

MARGARET: Lean on me.
BRICK: No, just give me my crutch.
MARGARET: Lean on my shoulder.
BRICK: *I don't want to lean on your shoulder, I want my crutch!*

This is spoken like sudden lightning.

Are you going to give me my crutch or do I have to get down on my knees on the floor and—
MARGARET: *Here, here, take it, take it!*

She has thrust the crutch at him.

BRICK *hobbling out:* Thanks . . .
MARGARET: We mustn't scream at each other, the walls in this house have
ears. . . .

He hobbles directly to liquor cabinet to get a new drink.

—but that's the first time I've heard you raise your voice in a long time,
Brick. A crack in the wall?—Of composure?

—I think that's a good sign. . . .

A sign of nerves in a player on the defensive!

BRICK *turns and smiles at her coolly over his fresh drink.*

BRICK: It just hasn't happened yet, Maggie.
MARGARET: What?
BRICK: The click I get in my head when I've had enough of this stuff to
make me peaceful. . . .

Will you do me a favor?
MARGARET: Maybe I will. What favor?
BRICK: Just, just keep your voice down!
MARGARET *in a hoarse whisper:* I'll do you that favor, I'll speak in a whis-
per, if not shut up completely, if *you* will do *me* a favor and make that
drink your last one till after the party.
BRICK: What party?
MARGARET: Big Daddy's birthday party.
BRICK: Is this Big Daddy's birthday?
MARGARET: You know this is Big Daddy's birthday!
BRICK: No, I don't, I forgot it.
MARGARET: Well, I remembered it for you. . . .

*They are both speaking as breathlessly as a pair of kids after a fight, drawing
deep exhausted breaths and looking at each other with faraway eyes, shaking
and panting together as if they had broken apart from a violent struggle.*

BRICK: Good for you, Maggie.
MARGARET: You just have to scribble a few lines on this card.
BRICK: You scribble something, Maggie.
MARGARET: It's got to be your handwriting; it's your present, I've given
him my present; it's got to be your handwriting!

The tension between them is building again, the voices becoming shrill once more.

BRICK: I didn't get him a present.
MARGARET: I got one for you.

BRICK: All right. You write the card, then.
MARGARET: And have him know you didn't remember his birthday?
BRICK: I didn't remember his birthday.
MARGARET: You don't have to prove you didn't!
BRICK: I don't want to fool him about it.
MARGARET: Just write "Love, Brick!" for God's—
BRICK: No.
MARGARET: You've *got* to!
BRICK: I don't have to do anything I don't want to do. You keep forgetting the conditions on which I agreed to stay on living with you.
MARGARET *out before she knows it:*   I'm not living with you. We occupy the same cage.
BRICK: You've got to remember the conditions agreed on.
MARGARET: They're impossible conditions!
BRICK: Then why don't you—?
MARGARET: HUSH! Who is out there? Is somebody at the door?

There are footsteps in hall.

MAE *outside:*   May I enter a moment?
MARGARET: Oh, *you!* Sure. Come in, Mae.

MAE *enters bearing aloft the bow of a young lady's archery set.*

MAE: Brick, is this thing yours?
MARGARET: Why, Sister Woman—that's my Diana Trophy. Won it at the intercollegiate archery contest on the Ole Miss campus.
MAE: It's a mighty dangerous thing to leave exposed round a house full of nawmal rid-blooded children attracted t'weapons.
MARGARET: "Nawmal rid-blooded children attracted t'weapons" ought t'be taught to keep their hands off things that don't belong to them.
MAE: Maggie, honey, if you had children of your own you'd know how funny that is. Will you please lock this up and put the key out of reach?
MARGARET: Sister Woman, nobody is plotting the destruction of your kiddies. —Brick and I still have our special archers' license. We're goin' deer-huntin' on Moon Lake as soon as the season starts. I love to run with dogs through chilly woods, run, run leap over obstructions—

She goes into the closet carrying the bow.

MAE: How's the injured ankle, Brick?
BRICK: Doesn't hurt. Just itches.
MAE: Oh, my! Brick—Brick, you should've been downstairs after supper! Kiddies put on a show. Polly played the piano, Buster an' Sonny drums, an' then they turned out the lights an' Dixie an' Trixie puhfawmed a toe dance in fairy costume with *spahkluhs!* Big Daddy just beamed! He just beamed!

MARGARET *from the closet with a sharp laugh:* Oh, I bet. It breaks my heart that we missed it!

She reenters.

But Mae? Why did y'give dawgs' names to all your kiddies?

MAE: *Dogs'* names?

MARGARET *has made this observation as she goes to raise the bamboo blinds, since the sunset glare has diminished. In crossing she winks at* BRICK.

MARGARET *sweetly:* Dixie, Trixie, Buster, Sonny, Polly!—Sounds like four dogs and a parrot . . . animal act in a circus!

MAE: Maggie? MARGARET *turns with a smile.* Why are you so catty?

MARGARET: Cause I'm a cat! But why can't *you* take a joke, Sister Woman?

MAE: Nothin' pleases me more than a joke that's funny. You know the real names of our kiddies. Buster's real name is Robert. Sonny's real name is Saunders. Trixie's real name is Marlene and Dixie's—

Someone downstairs calls for her. "Hey, Mae!"—She rushes to door, saying:

Intermission is over!

MARGARET *as* MAE *closes door:* I wonder what Dixie's real name is?

BRICK: Maggie, being catty doesn't help things any. . .

MARGARET: I know! WHY!—Am I so catty?—Cause I'm consumed with envy an' eaten up with longing?—Brick, I've laid out your beautiful Shantung silk suit from Rome and one of your monogrammed silk shirts. I'll put your cuff links in it, those lovely star sapphires I get you to wear so rarely. . . .

BRICK: I can't get trousers on over this plaster cast.

MARGARET: Yes, you can, I'll help you.

BRICK: I'm not going to get dressed, Maggie.

MARGARET: Will you just put on a pair of white silk pajamas?

BRICK: Yes, I'll do that, Maggie.

MARGARET: *Thank* you, thank you so *much!*

BRICK: Don't mention it.

MARGARET: *Oh, Brick!* How long does it have t' go on? This punishment? Haven't I done time enough, haven't I served my term, can't I apply for a—pardon?

BRICK: Maggie, you're spoiling my liquor. Lately your voice always sounds like you'd been running upstairs to warn somebody that the house was on fire!

MARGARET: Well, no wonder, no wonder. Y'know what I feel like, Brick?

Children's and grownups' voices are blended, below, in a loud but uncertain rendition of "My Wild Irish Rose."

I feel all the time like a cat on a hot tin roof!

BRICK: Then jump off the roof, jump off it, cats can jump off roofs and land on their four feet uninjured!

MARGARET: Oh, yes!

BRICK: Do it!—fo' God's sake, do it . . .

MARGARET: Do what?

BRICK: Take a lover!

MARGARET: I can't see a man but you! Even with my eyes closed, I just see you! Why don't you get ugly, Brick, why don't you please get fat or ugly or something so I could stand it?

She rushes to hall door, opens it, listens.

The concert is still going on! Bravo, no-necks, bravo!

She slams and locks door fiercely.

BRICK: What did you lock the door for?

MARGARET: To give us a little privacy for a while.

BRICK: You know better, Maggie.

MARGARET: No, I don't know better. . . .

She rushes to gallery doors, draws the rose-silk drapes across them.

BRICK: Don't make a fool of yourself.

MARGARET: I don't mind makin' a fool of myself over you!

BRICK: I mind, Maggie. I feel embarrassed for you.

MARGARET: Feel embarrassed! But don't continue my torture. I can't live on and on under these circumstances.

BRICK: You agreed to—

MARGARET: I know but—

BRICK: —Accept that condition!

MARGARET: I CAN'T! CAN'T! CAN'T!

She seizes his shoulder.

BRICK: Let go!

He breaks away from her and seizes the small boudoir chair and raises it like a lion-tamer facing a big circus cat.

Count five. She stares at him with her fist pressed to her mouth, then bursts into shrill, almost hysterical laughter. He remains grave for a moment, then grins and puts the chair down.

BIG MAMA *calls through the closed door.*

BIG MAMA: Son? Son? Son?

BRICK: What is it, Big Mama?

BIG MAMA *outside:*   Oh, son! We got the most wonderful news about Big Daddy. I just had t' run up an' tell you right this—

She rattles the knob.

—What's this door doin', locked, faw? You all think there's robbers in the house?

MARGARET: Big Mama, Brick is dressin', he's not dressed yet.

BIG MAMA: That's all right, it won't be the first time I've seen Brick not dressed. Come on, open this door!

MARGARET, *with a grimace, goes to unlock and open the hall door, as* BRICK *hobbles rapidly to the bathroom and kicks the door shut.* BIG MAMA *has disappeared from the hall.*

MARGARET: Big Mama?

BIG MAMA *appears through the opposite gallery doors behind* MARGARET, *huffing and puffing like an old bulldog. She is a short, stout woman; her sixty years and 170 pounds have left her somewhat breathless most of the time; she's always tensed like a boxer, or rather, a Japanese wrestler. Her "family" was maybe a little superior to* BIG DADDY'S, *but not much. She wears a black or silver lace dress and at least half a million in flashy gems. She is very sincere.*

BIG MAMA *loudly, startling* MARGARET: Here—I come through Gooper's and Mae's gall'ry door. Where's Brick? *Brick*—Hurry on out of there, son, I just have a second and want to give you the news about Big Daddy.—I hate locked doors in a house. . . .

MARGARET *with affected lightness:*   I've noticed you do, Big Mama, but people have got to have *some* moments of privacy, don't they?

BIG MAMA: No, ma'am, not in *my* house. *Without pause.* Whacha took off you' dress faw? I thought that little lace dress was so sweet on yuh, honey.

MARGARET: I thought it looked sweet on me, too, but one of m' cute little table-partners used it for a napkin so—!

BIG MAMA *picking up stockings on floor:*   What?

MARGARET: You know, Big Mama, Mae and Gooper's so touchy about those children—thanks, Big Mama . . .

BIG MAMA *has thrust the picked-up stockings in* MARGARET'S *hand with a grunt.*

—that you just don't dare to suggest there's any room for improvement in their—

BIG MAMA: Brick, hurry out!—Shoot, Maggie, you just don't like children.

MARGARET: I do SO like children! Adore them!—well brought up!

BIG MAMA *gentle—loving:*   Well, why don't you have some and bring them up well, then, instead of all the time pickin' on Gooper's an' Mae's?

GOOPER *shouting up the stairs:*   Hey, hey, Big Mama, Betsy an' Hugh got to go, waitin' t' tell yah g'by!

BIG MAMA: Tell 'em to hold their hawses, I'll be right down in a jiffy!

She turns to the bathroom door and calls out.

Son? Can you hear me in there?

There is a muffled answer.

We just got the full report from the laboratory at the Ochsner Clinic, completely negative, son, ev'rything negative, right on down the line! Nothin' a-tall's wrong with him but some little functional thing called a spastic colon. Can you hear me, son?

MARGARET: He can hear you, Big Mama.

BIG MAMA: Then why don't he say something? God Almighty, a piece of news like that should make him shout. It made *me* shout, I can tell you. I shouted and sobbed and fell right down on my knees!—Look!

She pulls up her skirt.

See the bruises where I hit my kneecaps? Took both doctors to haul me back on my feet!

She laughs—she always laughs like hell at herself.

Big Daddy was furious with me! But ain't that wonderful news?

Facing bathroom again, she continues:

After all the anxiety we been through to git a report like that on Big Daddy's birthday? Big Daddy tried to hide how much of a load that news took off his mind, but didn't fool *me.* He was mighty close to crying about it *himself!*

Goodbyes are shouted downstairs, and she rushes to door.

Hold those people down there, don't let them go!—Now, git dressed, we're all comin' up to this room fo' Big Daddy's birthday party because of your ankle.—How's his ankle, Maggie?

MARGARET: Well, he broke it, Big Mama.

BIG MAMA: I know he broke it.

A phone is ringing in hall. A Negro voice answers: "Mistuh Polly's res'dence."

I mean does it hurt him much still.

MARGARET: I'm afraid I can't give you that information, Big Mama.

You'll have to ask Brick if it hurts much still or not.
SOOKEY *in the hall:* It's Memphis, Mizz Polly, it's Miss Sally in Memphis.
BIG MAMA: Awright, Sookey.

BIG MAMA *rushes into the hall and is heard shouting on the phone:*

Hello, Miss Sally. How are you, Miss Sally?—Yes, well, I was just gonna call you about it. *Shoot!*—

She raises her voice to a bellow.

Miss Sally? Don't ever call me from the Gayoso Lobby, too much talk goes on in that hotel lobby, no wonder you can't hear me! Now listen, Miss Sally. They's nothin' serious wrong with Big Daddy. We got the report just now, they's nothin' wrong but a thing called a—spastic! *SPASTIC!*—colon . . .

She appears at the hall door and calls to Margaret.

—Maggie, come out here and talk to that fool on the phone. I'm shouted breathless!
MARGARET *goes out and is heard sweetly at phone:* Miss Sally? This is Brick's wife, Maggie. So nice to hear your voice. Can you hear *mine?* Well, *good!*—Big Mama just wanted you to know that they've got the report from the Ochsner Clinic and what Big Daddy has is a spastic colon. Yes. Spastic colon, Miss Sally. That's right, spastic colon. *G'bye, Miss Sally, hope I'll see you real soon!*

Hangs up a little before MISS SALLY *was probably ready to terminate the talk. She returns through the hall door.*

She heard me perfectly. I've discovered with deaf people the thing to do is not shout at them but just enunciate clearly. My rich old Aunt Cornelia was deaf as the dead but I could make her hear me just by sayin' each word slowly, distinctly, close to her ear. I read her the *Commercial Appeal* ev'ry night, read her the classified ads in it, even, she never missed a word of it. But was she a mean ole thing! Know what I got when she died? Her unexpired subscriptions to five magazines and the Book-of-the-Month Club and a LIBRARY full of ev'ry dull book ever written! All else went to her hellcat of a sister . . . meaner than she was, even!

BIG MAMA *has been straightening things up in the room during this speech.*

BIG MAMA *closing closet door on discarded clothes:* Miss Sally sure is a case! Big Daddy says she's always got her hand out fo' something. He's not mistaken. That poor ole thing always has her hand out fo' something. I don't think Big Daddy gives her as much as he should.

Somebody shouts for her downstairs and she shouts:

I'm comin'!

She starts out. At the hall door, turns and jerks a forefinger, first toward the bathroom door, then toward the liquor cabinet, meaning: "Has Brick been drinking?" MARGARET *pretends not to understand, cocks her head and raises her brows as if the pantomimic performance was completely mystifying to her.*

BIG MAMA *rushes back to* MARGARET

Shoot! Stop playin' so dumb!—I mean has he been drinkin' that stuff much yet?

MARGARET *with a little laugh:* Oh! I think he had a highball after supper.

BIG MAMA: Don't laugh about it!—Some single men stop drinkin' when they git married and others start! Brick never touched liquor before he—!

MARGARET *crying out:* *THAT'S NOT FAIR!*

BIG MAMA: Fair or not fair I want to ask you a question, one question: D'you make Brick happy in bed?

MARGARET: Why don't you ask if he makes *me* happy in bed?

BIG MAMA: Because I know that—

MARGARET: *It works both ways!*

BIG MAMA: Something's not right! You're childless and my son drinks!

Someone has called her downstairs and she has rushed to the door on the line above. She turns at the door and points at the bed.

—When a marriage goes on the rocks, the rocks are *there*, right *there!*

MARGARET: *That's—*

BIG MAMA *has swept out of the room and slammed the door.*

—not—*fair.* . .

MARGARET *is alone, completely alone, and she feels it. She draws in, hunches her shoulders, raises her arms with fists clenched, shuts her eyes tight as a child about to be stabbed with a vaccination needle. When she opens her eyes again, what she sees is the long oval mirror and she rushes straight to it, stares into it with a grimace and says: "Who are you?"—Then she crouches a little and answers herself in a different voice which is high, thin, mocking: "I am Maggie the Cat!"—Straightens quickly as bathroom door opens a little and* BRICK *calls out to her.*

BRICK: Has Big Mama gone?

MARGARET: She's gone.

He opens the bathroom door and hobbles out, with his liquor glass now empty, straight to the liquor cabinet. He is whistling softly. MARGARET'S *head pivots on her long, slender throat to watch him.*

She raises a hand uncertainly to the base of her throat, as if it was difficult for her to swallow, before she speaks:

You know, our sex life didn't just peter out in the usual way, it was cut off short, long before the natural time for it to, and it's going to revive again, just as sudden as that. I'm confident of it. That's what I'm keeping myself attractive for. For the time when you'll see me again like other men see me. Yes, like other men see me. They still see me, Brick, and they like what they see. Uh-huh. Some of them would give their—

Look, Brick!

She stands before the long oval mirror, touches her breast and then her hips with her two hands.

How high my body stays on me!—Nothing has fallen on me—not a fraction. . . .

Her voice is soft and trembling: a pleading child's. At this moment as he turns to glance at her—a look which is like a player passing a ball to another player, third down and goal to go—she has to capture the audience in a grip so tight that she can hold it till the first intermission without any lapse of attention.

Other men still want me. My face looks strained, sometimes, but I've kept my figure as well as you've kept yours, and men admire it. I still turn heads on the street. Why, last week in Memphis everywhere that I went men's eyes burned holes in my clothes, at the country club and in restaurants and department stores, there wasn't a man I met or walked by that didn't just eat me up with his eyes and turn around when I passed him and look back at me. Why, at Alice's party for her New York cousins, the best-lookin' man in the crowd—followed me upstairs and tried to force his way in the powder room with me, followed me to the door and tried to force his way in!
BRICK: Why didn't you let him, Maggie?
MARGARET: Because I'm not that common, for one thing. Not that I wasn't almost tempted to. You like to know who it was? It was Sonny Boy Maxwell, that's who!
BRICK: Oh, yeah, Sonny Boy Maxwell, he was a good end-runner but had a little injury to his back and had to quit.
MARGARET: He has no injury now and has no wife and still has a lech for me!
BRICK: I see no reason to lock him out of a powder room in that case.
MARGARET: And have someone catch me at it? I'm not that stupid. Oh,

I might sometime cheat on you with someone, since you're so insultingly eager to have me do it!—But if I do, you can be damned sure it will be in a place and a time where no one but me and the man could possibly know. Because I'm not going to give you any excuse to divorce me for being unfaithful or anything else. . . .

BRICK: Maggie, I wouldn't divorce you for being unfaithful or anything else. Don't you know that? Hell. I'd be relieved to know that you'd found yourself a lover.

MARGARET: Well, I'm taking no chances. No, I'd rather stay on this hot tin roof.

BRICK: A hot tin roof's 'n uncomfo'table place t' stay on. . . .

He starts to whistle softly.

MARGARET *through his whistle:*   Yeah, but I can stay on it just as long as I have to.

BRICK: You could leave me, Maggie.

He resumes whistle. She wheels about to glare at him.

MARGARET: *Don't want to and will not!* Besides if I did, you don't have a cent to pay for it but what you get from Big Daddy and he's dying of cancer!

For the first time a realization of BIG DADDY'S *doom seems to penetrate to* BRICK'S *consciousness, visibly, and he looks at* MARGARET.

BRICK: Big Mama just said he *wasn't*, that the report was okay.

MARGARET: That's what she thinks because she got the same story that they gave Big Daddy. And was just as taken in by it as he was, poor ole things. . . .

But tonight they're going to tell her the truth about it. When Big Daddy goes to bed, they're going to tell her that he is dying of cancer.

She slams the dresser drawer.

—It's malignant and it's terminal.

BRICK: Does Big Daddy know it?

MARGARET: Hell, do they *ever* know it? Nobody says, "You're dying." You have to fool them. They have to fool *themselves*.

BRICK: Why?

MARGARET: *Why?* Because human beings dream of life everlasting, that's the reason! But most of them want it on earth and not in heaven.

He gives a short, hard laugh at her touch of humor.

Well. . . . *She touches up her mascara.* That's how it is, anyhow. . . . *She looks about.* Where did I put down my cigarette? Don't want to burn up the home-place, at least not with Mae and Gooper and their five monsters in it!

She has found it and sucks at it greedily. Blows out smoke and continues:

So this is Big Daddy's last birthday. And Mae and Gooper, they know it, oh, *they* know it, all right. They got the first information from the Ochsner Clinic. That's why they rushed down here with their no-neck monsters. Because. Do you know something? Big Daddy's made no will? Big Daddy's never made out any will in his life, and so this campaign's afoot to impress him, forcibly as possible, with the fact that you drink and I've borne no children!

He continues to stare at her a moment, then mutters somethng sharp but not audible and hobbles rather rapidly out onto the long gallery in the fading, much faded, gold light.

MARGARET *continuing her liturgical chant:*   Y'know, I'm *fond* of Big Daddy, I am genuinely fond of that old man, I really *am*, you know. . . .
BRICK *faintly, vaguely:*   Yes, I know you are. . . .
MARGARET: I've always sort of admired him in spite of his coarseness, his four-letter words and so forth. Because Big Daddy *is* what he *is*, and he makes no bones about it. He hasn't turned gentleman farmer, he's still a Mississippi redneck, as much of a redneck as he must have been when he was just overseer here on the old Jack Straw and Peter Ochello place. But he got hold of it an' built it into th' biggest an' finest plantation in the Delta.—I've always *liked* Big Daddy. . . . *She crosses to the proscenium.* Well, this is Big Daddy's last birthday. I'm sorry about it. But I'm facing the facts. It takes money to take care of a drinker and that's the office that I've been elected to lately.
BRICK: You don't have to take care of me.
MARGARET: Yes, I do. Two people in the same boat have got to take care of each other. At least you want money to buy more Echo Spring when this supply is exhausted, or will you be satisfied with a ten-cent beer?

Mae an' Gooper are plannin' to freeze us out of Big Daddy's estate because you drink and I'm childless. But we can defeat that plan. We're *going* to defeat that plan!

Brick y'know, I've been so God damn disgustingly poor all my life!— That's the *truth*, Brick!
BRICK: I'm not sayin' it isn't.
MARGARET: Always had to suck up to people I couldn't stand because they had money and I was poor as Job's turkey. You don't know what that's like. Well, I'll tell you, it's like you would feel a thousand miles away from Echo Spring!—And had to get back to it on that broken ankle . . . without a crutch!

That's how it feels to be as poor as Job's turkey and have to suck up to relatives that you hated because they had money and all you had was a bunch of hand-me-down clothes and a few old moldly three-per-cent government bonds. My daddy loved his liquor, he fell in love with his liquor the way you've fallen in love with Echo Spring!—And my poor Mama, having to maintain some semblance of social position, to keep appearances up, on an income of one hundred and fifty dollars a month on those old government bonds!

When I came out, the year that I made my debut, I had just two evening dresses! One Mother made me from a pattern in *Vogue*, the other a hand-me-down from a snotty rich cousin I hated!

—The dress that I married you in was my grandmother's weddin' gown. . . .

So that's why I'm like a cat on a hot tin roof!

BRICK *is still on the gallery. Someone below calls up to him in a warm Negro voice, "Hiya, Mistuh Brick, how yuh feelin'?"* BRICK *raises his liquor glass as if that answered the question.*

MARGARET: You can be young without money, but you can't be old without it. You've got to be old *with* money because to be old without it is just too awful, you've got to be one or the other, either *young* or *with money*, you can't be old and *without* it.—That's the *truth*, Brick. . . .

BRICK *whistles softly, vaguely.*

Well, now I'm dressed, I'm all dressed, there's nothing else for me to do.

Forlornly, almost fearfully.

I'm dressed, all dressed, nothing else for me to do. . . .

She moves about restlessly, aimlessly, and speaks, as if to herself.

I know when I made my mistake.—What am I—? Oh!—my bracelets. . . .

She starts working a collection of bracelets over her hands onto her wrists, about six on each, as she talks.

I've thought a whole lot about it and now I know when I made my mistake. Yes, I made my mistake when I told you the truth about that thing with Skipper. Never should have confessed it, a fatal error, tellin' you about that thing with Skipper.

BRICK: Maggie, shut up about Skipper. I mean it, Maggie; you got to shut up about Skipper.

MARGARET: You ought to understand that Skipper and I—

BRICK: You don't think I'm serious, Maggie? You're fooled by the fact that I am saying this quiet? Look, Maggie. What you're doing is a dangerous thing to do. You're—you're—you're—foolin' with something that—nobody ought to fool with.

MARGARET: This time I'm going to finish what I have to say to you. Skipper and I made love, if love you could call it, because it made both of us feel a little bit closer to you. You see, you son of a bitch, you asked too much of people, of me, of him, of all the unlucky poor damned sons of bitches that happen to love you, and there was a whole pack of them, yes, there was a pack of them besides me and Skipper, you asked too goddam much of people that loved you, you—superior creature!— you godlike being—And so we made love to each other to dream it was you, both of us! Yes, yes, yes! Truth, truth! What's so awful about it? I like it, I think the truth is—yeah! I shouldn't have told you. . . .

BRICK *holding his head unnaturally still and uptilted a bit:* It was Skipper that told me about it. Not you, Maggie.

MARGARET: I told you!

BRICK: After he told me!

MARGARET: What does it matter who—?

Brick turns suddenly out upon the gallery and calls:

BRICK: Little girl! Hey, little girl!

LITTLE GIRL *at a distance:* What, Uncle Brick?

BRICK: Tell the folks to come up!—Bring everybody upstairs!

MARGARET: I can't stop myself! I'd go on telling you this in front of them all, if I had to!

BRICK: Little girl! Go on, go on, will you? Do what I told you, call them!

MARGARET: Because it's got to be told and you, you!—you never let me!

She sobs, then controls herself, and continues almost calmly.

It was one of those beautiful, ideal things they tell about in the Greek legends, it couldn't be anything else, you being you, and that's what made it so sad, that's what made it so awful, because it was love that never could be carried through to anything satisfying or even talked about plainly. Brick, I tell you, you got to believe me, Brick, I *do* understand all about it! I—I think it was—*noble!* Can't you tell I'm sincere when I say I respect it? My only point, the only point that I'm making, is life has got to be allowed to continue even after the *dream* of life is—all—over. . . .

BRICK *is without his crutch. Leaning on furniture, he crosses to pick it up as she continues as if possessed by a will outside herself:*

Why I remember when we double-dated at college, Gladys Fitzgerald and I and you and Skipper, it was more like a date between you and Skipper. Gladys and I were just sort of tagging along as if it was necessary to chaperone you!—to make a good public impression—

BRICK *turns to face her, half lifting his crutch:*   Maggie, you want me to hit you with this crutch? Don't you know I could kill you with this crutch?

MARGARET: Good Lord, man, d'you think I'd care if you did?

BRICK: One man has one great good true thing in his life. One great good thing which is true!—I had friendship with Skipper.—You are naming it dirty!

MARGARET: I'm not naming it dirty! I am naming it clean.

BRICK: Not love with you, Maggie, but friendship with Skipper was that one great true thing, and you are naming it dirty!

MARGARET: Then you haven't been listenin', not understood what I'm saying! I'm naming it so damn clean that it killed poor Skipper!—You two had something that had to be kept on ice, yes, incorruptible, yes!—and death was the only icebox where you could keep it. . . .

BRICK: I married you, Maggie. Why would I marry you, Maggie, if I was—?

MARGARET: Brick, don't brain me yet, let me finish!—I know, believe me I know, that it was only Skipper that harbored even any *unconscious* desire for anything not perfectly pure between you two!—Now let me skip a little. You married me early that summer we graduated out of Ole Miss, and we were happy, weren't we, we were blissful, yes, hit heaven together ev'ry time that we loved! But that fall you an' Skipper turned down wonderful offers of jobs in order to keep on bein' football heroes—pro-football heroes. You organized the Dixie Stars that fall, so you could keep on bein' teammates forever! But somethin' was not right with it!—*Me included!*—between you. Skipper began hittin' the bottle . . . you got a spinal injury—couldn't play the Thanksgivin' game in Chicago, watched it on TV from a traction bed in Toledo. I joined Skipper. The Dixie Stars lost because poor Skipper was drunk. We drank together that night all night in the bar of the Blackstone and when cold day was comin' up over the Lake an' we were comin' out drunk to take a dizzy look at it, I said, "SKIPPER! STOP LOVIN' MY HUSBAND OR TELL HIM HE'S GOT TO LET YOU ADMIT IT TO HIM!"—one way or another!

HE SLAPPED ME HARD ON THE MOUTH!—then turned and ran without stopping once, I am sure, all the way back into his room at the Blackstone. . . .

—When I came to his room that night, with a little scratch like a shy little mouse at his door, he made that pitiful, ineffectual little attempt to prove that what I had said wasn't true. . . .

BRICK *strikes at her with crutch, a blow that shatters the gemlike lamp on the table.*

—In this way, I destroyed him, by telling him truth that he and his world which he was born and raised in, yours and his world, had told him could not be told?

—From then on Skipper was nothing at all but a receptacle for liquor and drugs. . . .

—*Who shot cock robin? I with my*—

She throws back her head with tight shut eyes.

—*merciful arrow!*

BRICK *strikes at her; misses.*

Missed me!—Sorry,—I'm not tryin' to whitewash my behavior, Christ, no! Brick, I'm not good. I don't know why people have to pretend to be good, nobody's good. The rich or the well-to-do can afford to respect moral patterns, conventional moral patterns, but I could never afford to, yeah, but—I'm honest! Give me credit for just that, will you *please?*—Born poor, raised poor, expect to die poor unless I manage to get us something out of what Big Daddy leaves when he dies of cancer! But Brick?!—*Skipper is dead! I'm alive!* Maggie the cat is—

BRICK *hops awkwardly forward and strikes at her again with his crutch.*

—*alive! I am alive, alive! I am . . .*

He hurls the crutch at her, across the bed she took refuge behind, and pitches forward on the floor as she completes her speech.

—*alive!*

A little girl, DIXIE, *bursts into the room, wearing an Indian war bonnet and firing a cap pistol at* MARGARET *and shouting: "Bang, bang, bang!"*

Laughter downstairs floats through the open hall door. MARGARET *had crouched gasping to bed at child's entrance. She now rises and says with cool fury:*

Little girl, your mother or someone should teach you—*gasping*—to knock at a door before you come into a room. Otherwise people might think that you—lack—good breeding. . . .
DIXIE: Yanh, yanh, yanh, what is Uncle Brick doin' on th' floor?
BRICK: I tried to kill your Aunt Maggie, but I failed—and I fell. Little girl, give me my crutch so I can get up off th' floor.
MARGARET: Yes, give your uncle his crutch, he's a cripple, honey, he broke his ankle last night jumping hurdles on the high school athletic field!

DIXIE: What were you jumping hurdles for, Uncle Brick?

BRICK: Because I used to jump them, and people like to do what they used to do, even after they've stopped being able to do it. . . .

MARGARET: That's right, that's your answer, now go away, little girl.

DIXIE *fires cap pistol at* MARGARET *three times.*

Stop, you stop that, monster! You little no-neck monster!

She seizes the cap pistol and hurls it through gallery doors.

DIXIE *with a precocious instinct for the cruelest thing:* You're *jealous!*— You're just jealous because you can't have babies!

She sticks out her tongue at MARGARET *as she sashays past her with her stomach stuck out, to the gallery.* MARGARET *slams the gallery doors and leans panting against them. There is a pause.* BRICK *has replaced his spilt drink and sits, faraway, on the great four-poster bed.*

MARGARET: You see?—they gloat over us being childless, even in front of their five little no-neck monsters!

Pause. Voices approach on the stairs.

Brick?—I've been to a doctor in Memphis, a—a gynecologist. . . .

I've been completely examined, and there is no reason why we can't have a child whenever we want one. And this is my time by the calendar to conceive. Are you listening to me? Are you? Are you LISTEN-ING TO ME!

BRICK: Yes. I hear you, Maggie.

His attention returns to her inflamed face.

—But how in hell on earth do you imagine—that you're going to have a child by a man that can't stand you?

MARGARET: That's a problem that I will have to work out.

She wheels about to face the hall door.

Here they come!

The lights dim.

Curtain

ACT II

There is no lapse of time. MARGARET *and* BRICK *are in the same positions they held at the end of Act I.*

MARGARET *at door: Here they come!*

BIG DADDY *appears first, a tall man with a fierce, anxious look, moving carefully not to betray his weakness even, or especially, to himself.*

BIG DADDY: Well, Brick.
BRICK: Hello, Big Daddy.—Congratulations!
BIG DADDY: —Crap. . . .

Some of the people are approaching through the hall, others along the gallery: voices from both directions. GOOPER *and* REVEREND TOOKER *become visible outside gallery doors, and their voices come in clearly.*

They pause outside as GOOPER *lights a cigar.*

REVEREND TOOKER *vivaciously: Oh, but St. Paul's in Grenada has three memorial windows, and the latest one is a Tiffany stained-glass window that cost twenty-five hundred dollars, a picture of Christ the Good Shepherd with a Lamb in His arms.
GOOPER: Who give that window, Preach?
REVEREND TOOKER: Clyde Fletcher's widow. Also presented St. Paul's with a baptismal font.
GOOPER: Y'know what somebody ought t' give your church is a *coolin'* system, Preach.
REVEREND TOOKER: Yes, siree, Bob! And y'know what Gus Hamma's family gave in his memory to the church at Two Rivers? A complete new stone parish-house with a basketball court in the basement and a—

BIG DADDY *uttering a loud barking laugh which is far from truly mirthful:*   Hey, Preach! What's all this talk about memorials, Preach? Y' think somebody's about t' kick off around here? 'S that it?

Startled by this interjection, REVEREND TOOKER *decides to laugh at the question almost as loud as he can.*

How he would answer the question we'll never know, as he's spared that embarrassment by the voice of GOOPER'S *wife,* MAE, *rising high and clear as she appears with "*DOC*"* BAUGH, *the family doctor, through the hall door.*

MAE *almost religiously: —Let's see now, they've had their *tyyy*-phoid shots, and their tetanus shots, their diphtheria shots and their hepatitis shots and their polio shots, they got *those* shots every month from May through September, and—Gooper? Hey! Gooper!—What all have the kiddies been shot faw?

MARGARET *overlapping a bit:* Turn on the hi-fi, Brick! Let's have some music t' start off th' party with!

The talk becomes so general that the room sounds like a great aviary of chattering birds. Only BRICK *remains unengaged, leaning upon the liquor cabinet with his faraway smile, an ice cube in a paper napkin with which he now and then rubs his forehead. He doesn't respond to* MARGARET'S *command. She bounds forward and stoops over the instrument panel of the console.*

GOOPER: We gave 'em that thing for a third anniversary present, got three speakers in it.

The room is suddenly blasted by the climax of a Wagnerian opera or a Beethoven symphony.

BIG DADDY: *Turn that dam thing off!*

Almost instant silence, almost instantly broken by the shouting charge of BIG MAMA, *entering through hall door like a charging rhino.*

BIG MAMA: *Wha's my Brick, wha's mah precious baby!!*
BIG DADDY: *Sorry! Turn it back on!*

Everyone laughs very loud. BIG DADDY *is famous for his jokes at* BIG MAMA'S *expense, and nobody laughs louder at these jokes than* BIG MAMA *herself, though sometimes they're pretty cruel and* BIG MAMA *has to pick up or fuss with something to cover the hurt that the loud laugh doesn't quite cover.*

On this occasion, a happy occasion because the dread in her heart has also been lifted by the false report on BIG DADDY'S *condition, she giggles, grotesquely, coyly, in* BIG DADDY'S *direction and bears down upon* BRICK, *all very quick and alive.*

BIG MAMA: Here he is, here's my precious baby! What's that you've got in your hand? You put that liquor down, son, your hand was made fo' holdin' somethin' better than that!
GOOPER: Look at Brick put it down!

BRICK *has obeyed* BIG MAMA *by draining the glass and handing it to her. Again everyone laughs, some high, some low.*

BIG MAMA: Oh, you bad boy, you, you're my bad little boy. Give Big Mama a kiss, you bad boy, you!—Look at him shy away, will you? Brick never liked bein' kissed or made a fuss over, I guess because he's always had too much of it!

Son, you turn that thing off!

BRICK *has switched on the TV set.*

I can't stand TV, radio was bad enough but TV has gone it one better, I mean—*Plops wheezing in chair.*—one worse, ha ha! Now what'm I sittin' down here faw? I want t' sit next to my sweetheart on the sofa, hold hands with him and love him up a little!

BIG MAMA *has on a black and white figured chiffon. The large irregular patterns, like the markings of some massive animal, the luster of her great diamonds and many pearls, the brilliants set in the silver frames of her glasses, her riotous voice, booming laugh, have dominated the room since she entered.* BIG DADDY *has been regarding her with a steady grimace of chronic annoyance.*

BIG MAMA *still louder:* Preacher, Preacher, hey, Preach! Give me you' hand an' help me up from this chair!
REVEREND TOOKER: None of your tricks, Big Mama!
BIG MAMA: What tricks? You give me you' hand so I can get up an'—

REVEREND TOOKER *extends her his hand. She grabs it and pulls him into her lap with a shrill laugh that spans an octave in two notes.*

Ever seen a preacher in a fat lady's lap? Hey, hey, folks! Ever seen a preacher in a fat lady's lap?

BIG MAMA *is notorious throughout the Delta for this sort of inelegant horseplay.* MARGARET *looks on with indulgent humor, sipping Dubonnet "on the rocks" and watching* BRICK, *but* MAE *and* GOOPER *exchange signs of humorless anxiety over these antics, the sort of behavior which* MAE *thinks may account for their failure to quite get in with the smartest young married set in Memphis, despite all. One of the Negroes,* LACY *or* SOOKEY, *peeks in, cackling. They are waiting for a sign to bring in the cake and champagne. But* BIG DADDY'S *not amused. He doesn't understand why, in spite of the infinite mental relief he's received from the doctor's report, he still has these same old fox teeth in his guts. "This spastic thing sure is something," he says to himself, but aloud he roars at* BIG MAMA.

BIG DADDY: BIG MAMA, WILL YOU QUIT HORSIN'?—You're too old an' too fat fo' that sort of crazy kid stuff an' besides a woman with your blood pressure—she had two hundred last spring!—is riskin' a stroke when you mess around like that. . . .
BIG MAMA: *Here comes Big Daddy's birthday!*

Negroes in white jackets enter with an enormous birthday cake ablaze with candles and carrying buckets of champagne with satin ribbons about the bottle necks.

MAE *and* GOOPER *strike up song, and everybody, including the Negroes and Children, joins in. Only* BRICK *remains aloof.*

EVERYONE: Happy birthday to you.
  Happy birthday to you.
  Happy birthday, Big Daddy—

Some sing: "Dear, Big Daddy!"

  Happy birthday to you.

Some sing: "How old are you?"

MAE *has come down center and is organizing her children like a chorus. She gives them a barely audible: "One, two, three!" and they are off in the new tune.*

CHILDREN: Skinamarinka—dinka—dink
  Skinamarinka—do
  We love you.
  Skinamarinka—dinka—dink
  Skinamarinka—do.

All together, they turn to Big Daddy.

  Big Daddy, you!

They turn back front, like a musical comedy chorus.

  We love you in the morning;
  We love you in the night.
  We love you when we're with you,
  And we love you out of sight.
  Skinamarinka—dinka—dink
  Skinamarinka—do.

MAE *turns to* BIG MAMA.

  Big Mama, too!

BIG MAMA *bursts into tears. The Negroes leave.*

BIG DADDY: Now Ida, what the hell is the matter with you?
MAE: She's just so happy.
BIG MAMA: I'm just so happy, Big Daddy, I have to cry or something.

Sudden and loud in the hush:

Brick, do you know the wonderful news that Doc Baugh got from the clinic about Big Daddy? Big Daddy's one hundred per cent!

MARGARET: Isn't that wonderful?

BIG MAMA: He's just one hundred per cent. Passed the examination with flying colors. Now that we know there's nothing wrong with Big Daddy but a spastic colon, I can tell you something. I was worried sick, half out of my mind, for fear that Big Daddy might have a thing like—

MARGARET *cuts through this speech, jumping up and exclaiming shrilly:*

MARGARET: Brick, honey, aren't you going to give Big Daddy his birthday present?

Passing by him, she snatches his liquor glass from him.

She picks up a fancily wrapped package.

Here it is, Big Daddy, this is from Brick!

BIG MAMA: This is the biggest birthday Big Daddy's ever had, a hundred presents and bushels of telegrams from—

MAE *at same time:*   What is it, Brick?

GOOPER: I bet 500 to 50 that Brick don't *know* what it is.

BIG MAMA: The fun of presents is not knowing what they are till you open the package. Open your present, Big Daddy.

BIG DADDY: Open it you'self. I want to ask Brick somethin! Come here, Brick.

MARGARET: Big Daddy's callin' you, Brick.

She is opening the package.

BRICK: Tell Big Daddy I'm crippled.

BIG DADDY: I see you're crippled. I want to know how you got crippled.

MARGARET *making diversionary tactics:*   Oh, look, oh, look, why, it's a cashmere robe!

She holds the robe up for all to see.

MAE: You sound surprised, Maggie.

MARGARET: I never saw one before.

MAE: That's funny.—*Hah!*

MARGARET *turning on her fiercely, with a brilliant smile:*   Why is it funny? All my family ever had was family—and luxuries such as cashmere robes still surprise me!

BIG DADDY *ominously:*   Quiet!

MAE *heedless in her fury:*   I don't see how you could be so surprised when you bought it yourself at Loewenstein's in Memphis last Saturday. You know how I know?

BIG DADDY: I said, Quiet!

MAE: —I know because the salesgirl that sold it to you waited on me and said, Oh, Mrs. Pollitt, your sister-in-law just bought a cashmere robe for your husband's father!

MARGARET: Sister Woman! Your talents are wasted as a housewife and mother, you really ought to be with the FBI or—

BIG DADDY: QUIET!

REVEREND TOOKER'S *reflexes are slower than the others'. He finishes a sentence after the bellow.*

REVEREND TOOKER *to Doc Baugh:*   —the Stork and the Reaper are running neck and neck!

He starts to laugh gaily when he notices the silence and BIG DADDY'S *glare. His laugh dies falsely.*

BIG DADDY: Preacher, I hope I'm not butting in on more talk about memorial stained-glass windows, am I, Preacher?

REVEREND TOOKER *laughs feebly, then coughs dryly in the embarrassed silence.*

Preacher?

BIG MAMA: Now, Big Daddy, don't you pick on Preacher!

BIG DADDY *raising his voice:*   You ever hear that expression all hawk and no spit? You bring that expression to mind with that little dry cough of yours, all hawk an' no spit. . . .

The pause is broken only by a short startled laugh from Margaret, the only one there who is conscious of and amused by the grotesque.

MAE *raising her arms and jangling her bracelets:*   I wonder if the mosquitoes are active tonight?

BIG DADDY: What's that, Little Mama? Did you make some remark?

MAE: Yes, I said I wondered if the mosquitoes would eat us alive if we went out on the gallery for a while.

BIG DADDY: Well, if they do, I'll have your bones pulverized for fertilizer!

BIG MAMA *quickly:*   Last week we had an airplane spraying the place and I think it done some good, at least I haven't had a—

BIG DADDY *cutting her speech:*   Brick, they tell me, if what they tell me is true, that you done some jumping last night on the high school athletic field?

BIG MAMA: Brick, Big Daddy is talking to you, son.

BRICK *smiling vaguely over his drink:*   What was that, Big Daddy?

BIG DADDY: They said you done some jumping on the high school track field last night.

BRICK: That's what they told me, too.

BIG DADDY: Was it jumping or humping that you were doing out there? What were doing out there at three A.M., layin' a woman on that cinder track?

BIG MAMA: Big Daddy, you are off the sick-list now, and I'm not going to excuse you for talkin' so—
BIG DADDY: Quiet!
BIG MAMA: —*nasty in front of Preacher and*—
BIG DADDY: *QUIET!*—I ast you, Brick, if you was cuttin' you'self a piece o' poon-tang last night on that cinder track? I thought maybe you were chasin' poon-tang on that track an' tripped over something in the heat of the chase—'sthat it?

GOOPER *laughs, loud and false, others nervously following suit.* BIG MAMA *stamps her foot, and purses her lips, crossing to* MAE *and whispering something to her as* BRICK *meets his father's hard, intent, grinning stare with a slow, vague smile that he offers all situations from behind the screen of his liquor.*

BRICK: No, sir, I don't think so. . . .
MAE *at the same time, sweetly:*   Reverend Tooker, let's you and I take a stroll on the widow's walk.

She and the preacher go out on the gallery as BIG DADDY *says:*

BIG DADDY: Then what the hell were you doing out there at three o'clock in the morning?
BRICK: Jumping the hurdles, Big Daddy, runnin' and jumpin' the hurdles, but those high hurdles have gotten too high for me, now.
BIG DADDY: Cause you was drunk?
BRICK *his vague smile fading a little:*   Sober I wouldn't have tried to jump the *low* ones. . . .
BIG MAMA *quickly:*   Big Daddy, blow out the candles on your birthday cake!
MARGARET *at the same time:*   I want to propose a toast to Big Daddy Pollitt on his sixty-fifth birthday, the biggest cotton planter in—
BIG DADDY *bellowing with fury and disgust:*   *I told you to stop it, now stop it, quit this—!*
BIG MAMA *coming in front of Big Daddy with the cake:*   Big Daddy, I will not allow you to talk that way, not even on your birthday, I—
BIG DADDY: I'll talk like I want to on my birthday, Ida, or any other goddam day of the year and anybody here that don't like it knows what they can do!
BIG MAMA: You don't mean that!
BIG DADDY: What makes you think I don't mean it?

Meanwhile various discreet signals have been exchanged and GOOPER *has also gone out on the gallery.*

BIG MAMA: I just know you don't mean it.
BIG DADDY: You don't know a goddam thing and you never did!
BIG MAMA: Big Daddy, you don't mean that.
BIG DADDY: Oh, yes, I do, oh, yes, I do, I mean it! I put up with a whole lot of crap around here because I thought I was dying. And you

thought I was dying and you started taking over, well, you can stop taking over now, Ida, because I'm not gonna die, you can just stop now this business of taking over because you're not taking over because I'm not dying, I went through the laboratory and the goddam exploratory operation and there's nothing wrong with me but a spastic colon. And I'm not dying of cancer which you thought I was dying of. Ain't that so? Didn't you think that I was dying of cancer, Ida?

Almost everybody is out on the gallery but the two old people glaring at each other across the blazing cake.

BIG MAMA'S *chest heaves and she presses a fat fist to her mouth.*

BIG DADDY *continues, hoarsely:*

Ain't that so, Ida? Didn't you have an idea I was dying of cancer and now you could take control of this place and everything on it? I got that impression, I seemed to get that impression. Your loud voice everywhere, your fat old body butting in here and there!
BIG MAMA: Hush! The Preacher!
BIG DADDY: Rut the goddam preacher!

BIG MAMA *gasps loudly and sits down on the sofa which is almost too small for her.*

Did you hear what I said? I said rut the goddam preacher!

Somebody closes the gallery doors from outside just as there is a burst of fireworks and excited cries from the children.

BIG MAMA: I never seen you act like this before and I can't think what's got in you!
BIG DADDY: I went through all that laboratory and operation and all just so I would know if you or me was boss here! Well, now it turns out that I am and you ain't—and that's my birthday present—and my cake and champagne!—because for three years now you been gradually taking over. Bossing. Talking. Sashaying your fat old body around the place I made! I made this place! I was overseer on it! I was the overseer on the old Straw and Ochello plantation. I quit school at ten! I quit school at ten years old and went to work like a nigger in the fields. And I rose to be overseer of the Straw and Ochello plantation. And old Straw died and I was Ochello's partner and the place got bigger and bigger and bigger and bigger and bigger! I did all that myself with no goddam help from you, and now you think you're just about to take over. Well, I am just about to tell you that you are not just about to take over, you are not just about to take over a God damn thing. Is that clear to you, Ida? Is that very plain to you, now? Is that understood completely? I been through the laboratory from A to Z. I've had

the goddam exploratory operation, and nothing is wrong with me but a spastic colon—made spastic, I guess, by *disgust!* By all the goddam lies and liars that I have had to put up with, and all the goddam hypocrisy that I lived with all these forty years that we been livin' together!

Hey! Ida!! Blow out the candles on the birthday cake! Purse up your lips and draw a deep breath and blow out the goddam candles on the cake!

BIG MAMA: Oh, Big Daddy, oh, oh, oh, Big Daddy!

BIG DADDY: What's the matter with you?

BIG MAMA: *In all these years you never believed that I loved you??*

BIG DADDY: Huh?

BIG MAMA: *And I did, I did so much, I did love you!*—I even loved your hate and your hardness, Big Daddy!

She sobs and rushes awkwardly out onto the gallery.

BIG DADDY *to himself:* *Wouldn't it be funny if that was true. . . .*

A pause is followed by a burst of light in the sky from the fireworks.

BRICK! HEY, BRICK!

He stands over his blazing birthday cake.

After some moments, BRICK *hobbles in on his crutch, holding his glass.*

Margaret *follows him with a bright, anxious smile.*

I didn't call you, Maggie. I called Brick.

MARGARET: I'm just delivering him to you.

She kisses BRICK *on the mouth which he immediately wipes with the back of his hand. She flies girlishly back out.* BRICK *and his father are alone.*

BIG DADDY: Why did you do that?

BRICK: Do what, Big Daddy?

BIG DADDY: Wipe her kiss off your mouth like she'd spit on you.

BRICK: I don't know. I wasn't conscious of it.

BIG DADDY: That woman of yours has a better shape on her than Gooper's but somehow or other they got the same look about them.

BRICK: What sort of look is that, Big Daddy?

BIG DADDY: I don't know how to describe it but it's the same look.

BRICK: They don't look peaceful, do they?

BIG DADDY: No, they sure in hell don't.

BRICK: They look nervous as cats.

BIG DADDY: That's right, they look nervous as cats.

BRICK: Nervous as a couple of cats on a hot tin roof?

BIG DADDY: That's right, boy, they look like a couple of cats on a hot tin roof. It's funny that you and Gooper being so different would pick out the same type of woman.

BRICK: Both of us married into society, Big Daddy.

BIG DADDY: Crap . . . I wonder what gives them both that look?

BRICK: Well, they're sittin' in the middle of a big piece of land, Big Daddy, twenty-eight thousand acres is a pretty big piece of land and so they're squaring off on it, each determined to knock off a bigger piece of it than the other whenever you let it go.

BIG DADDY: I got a surprise for those women. I'm not gonna let it go for a long time yet if that's what they're waiting for.

BRICK: That's right, Big Daddy. You just sit tight and let them scratch each other's eyes out. . . .

BIG DADDY: You bet your life I'm going to sit tight on it and let those sons of bitches scratch their eyes out, ha ha ha. . . .

But Gooper's wife's a good breeder, you got to admit she's fertile. Hell, at supper tonight she had them all at the table and they had to put a couple of extra leafs in the table to make room for them, she's got five head of them, now, and another one's comin'.

BRICK: Yep, number six is comin'. . . .

BIG DADDY: Brick, you know, I swear to God, I don't know the way it happens?

BRICK: The way what happens, Big Daddy?

BIG DADDY: You git you a piece of land, by hook or crook, an' things start growin' on it, things accumulate on it, and the first thing you know it's completely out of hand, completely out of hand!

BRICK: Well, they say nature hates a vacuum, Big Daddy.

BIG DADDY: That's what they say, but sometimes I think that a vacuum is a hell of a lot better than some of the stuff that nature replaces it with.

Is someone out there by that door?

BRICK: Yep.

BIG DADDY: Who?

He has lowered his voice.

BRICK: Someone int'rested in what we say to each other.

BIG DADDY: Gooper?—*GOOPER!*

After a discreet pause, MAE *appears in the gallery door.*

MAE: Did you call Gooper, Big Daddy?

BIG DADDY: Aw, it was you.

MAE: Do you want Gooper, Big Daddy?

BIG DADDY: No, and I don't want you. I want some privacy here, while I'm having a confidential talk with my son Brick. Now it's too hot in here to close them doors, but if I have to close those rutten doors in order to have a private talk with my son Brick, just let me know and

I'll close 'em. Because I hate eavesdroppers, I don't like any kind of sneakin' an' spyin'.

MAE: Why, Big Daddy—

BIG DADDY: You stood on the wrong side of the moon, it threw your shadow!

MAE: I was just—

BIG DADDY: You was just nothing but *spyin'* an' you *know* it!

MAE *begins to sniff and sob:*   Oh, Big Daddy, you're so unkind for some reason to those that really love you!

BIG DADDY: Shut up, shut up, shut up! I'm going to move you and Gooper out of that room next to this! It's none of your goddam business what goes on in here at night between Brick an' Maggie. You listen at night like a couple of rutten peekhole spies and go and give a report on what you hear to Big Mama an' she comes to me and says they say such and such and so and so about what they heard goin' on between Brick an' Maggie, and Jesus, it makes me sick. I'm goin' to move you an' Gooper out of that room, I can't stand sneakin' an' spyin', it makes me sick. . . .

MAE *throws back her head and rolls her eyes heavenward and extends her arms as if invoking God's pity for this unjust martyrdom; then she presses a handkerchief to her nose and flies from the room with a loud swish of skirts.*

BRICK *now at the liquor cabinet:*   They listen, do they?

BIG DADDY: Yeah. They listen and give reports to Big Mama on what goes on in here between you and Maggie. They say that—

He stops as if embarrassed.

—You won't sleep with her, that you sleep on the sofa. Is that true or not true? If you don't like Maggie, get rid of Maggie!—What are you doin' there now?

BRICK: Fresh'nin' up my drink.

BIG DADDY: Son, you know you got a real liquor problem?

BRICK: Yes, sir, yes, I know.

BIG DADDY: Is that why you quit sports-announcing, because of this liquor problem?

BRICK: Yes, sir, yes, sir, I guess so.

He smiles vaguely and amiably at his father across his replenished drink.

BIG DADDY: Son, don't guess about it, it's too important.

BRICK *vaguely:*   Yes, sir.

BIG DADDY: And listen to me, don't look at the damn chandelier. . . .

Pause. BIG DADDY'S *voice is husky.*

—Somethin' else we picked up at th' big fire sale in Europe.

Another pause.

Life is important. There's nothing else to hold onto. A man that drinks is throwing his life away. Don't do it, hold onto your life. There's nothing else to hold onto. . . .

Sit down over here so we don't have to raise our voices, the walls have ears in this place.

BRICK *hobbling over to sit on the sofa beside him:* All right, Big Daddy.

BIG DADDY: Quit!—how'd that come about? Some disappointment?

BRICK: I don't know. Do you?

BIG DADDY: I'm askin' you, God damn it! How in hell would I know if you don't?

BRICK: I just got out there and found that I had a mouth full of cotton. I was always two or three beats behind what was goin' on on the field and so I—

BIG DADDY: Quit!

BRICK *amiably:* Yes, quit.

BIG DADDY: Son?

BRICK: Huh?

BIG DADDY *inhales loudly and deeply from his cigar; then bends suddenly a little forward, exhaling loudly and raising a hand to his forehead:* —Whew! —ha ha!—I took in too much smoke, it made me a little light-headed. . . .

The mantel clock chimes.

Why is it so damn hard for people to talk?

BRICK: Yeah. . . .

The clock goes on sweetly chiming till it has completed the stroke of ten.

—Nice peaceful-soundin' clock, I like to hear it all night. . . .

He slides low and comfortable on the sofa; BIG DADDY *sits up straight and rigid with some unspoken anxiety. All his gestures are tense and jerky as he talks. He wheezes and pants and sniffs through his nervous speech, glancing quickly, shyly, from time to time, at his son.*

BIG DADDY: We got that clock the summer we wint to Europe, me an' Big Mama on that damn Cook's Tour, never had such an awful time in my life, I'm tellin' you, son, those gooks over there, they gouge your eyeballs out in their grand hotels. And Big Mama bought more stuff than you could haul in a couple of boxcars, that's no crap. Everywhere she wint on this whirl-wind tour, she bought, bought, bought. Why, half that stuff she bought is still crated up in the cellar, under water last spring!

He laughs.

That Europe is nothin' on earth but a great big auction, that's all it is, that bunch of old worn-out places, it's just a big fire-sale, the whole rutten thing, an' Big Mama wint wild in it, why, you couldn't hold that woman with a mule's harness! Bought, bought, bought!—lucky I'm a rich man, yes siree, Bob, an' half that stuff is mildewin' in th' basement. It's lucky I'm a rich man, it sure is lucky, well, I'm a rich man, Brick, yep, I'm a mighty rich man.

His eyes light up for a moment.

Y'know how much I'm worth? Guess, Brick! Guess how much I'm worth!

BRICK *smiles vaguely over his drink.*

Close on ten million in cash an' blue-chip stocks, outside, mind you, of twenty-eight thousand acres of the richest land this side of the valley Nile!

A puff and crackle and the night sky blooms with an eerie greenish glow. Children shriek on the gallery.

But a man can't buy his life with it, he can't buy back his life with it when his life has been spent, that's one thing not offered in the Europe fire-sale or in the American markets or any markets on earth, a man can't buy his life with it, he can't buy back his life when his life is finished. . . .

That's a sobering thought, a very sobering thought, and that's a thought that I was turning over in my head, over and over and over—until today. . . .

I'm wiser and sadder, Brick, for this experience which I just gone through. They's one thing else that I remember in Europe.
BRICK: What is that, Big Daddy?
BIG DADDY: The hills around Barcelona in the country of Spain and the children running over those bare hills in their bare skins beggin' like starvin' dogs with howls and screeches, and how fat the priests are on the streets of Barcelona, so many of them and so fat and so pleasant, ha ha!—Y'know I could feed that country? I got money enough to feed that goddam country, but the human animal is a selfish beast and I don't reckon the money I passed out there to those howling children in the hills around Barcelona would more than upholster one of the chairs in this room, I mean pay to put a new cover on this chair!

Hell, I threw them money like you'd scatter feed corn for chickens, I threw money at them just to get rid of them long enough to climb back into th' car and—drive away. . . .

And then in Morocco, them Arabs, why, prostitution begins at four or five, that's no exaggeration, why, I remember one day in Marrakech, that old walled Arab city, I set on a broken-down wall to have a cigar, it was fearful hot there and this Arab woman stood in the road and looked at me till I was embarrassed, she stood stock still in the dusty hot road and looked at me till I was embarrassed. But listen to this. She had a naked child with her, a little naked girl with her, barely able to toddle, and after a while she set this child on the ground and give her a push and whispered something to her.

This child come toward me, barely able t' walk, come toddling up to me and—

Jesus, it makes you sick t' remember such a thing like this! It stuck out its hand and tried to unbutton my trousers!

That child was not yet five! Can you believe me? Or do you think that I am making this up? I wint back to the hotel and said to Big Mama, Git packed! We're clearing out of this country. . . .

BRICK: Big Daddy, you're on a talkin' jag tonight.

BIG DADDY *ignoring this remark:*   Yes, sir, that's how it is, the human animal is a beast that dies but the fact that he's dying don't give him pity for others, no, sir, it—

—Did you say something?

BRICK: Yes.

BIG DADDY: What?

BRICK: Hand me over that crutch so I can get up.

BIG DADDY: Where you goin'?

BRICK: I'm takin' a short little trip to Echo Spring.

BIG DADDY: To where?

BRICK: Liquor cabinet. . . .

BIG DADDY: Yes, sir, boy—

He hands BRICK *the crutch.*

—the human animal is a beast that dies and if he's got money he buys and buys and buys and I think the reason he buys everything he can buy is that in the back of his mind he has the crazy hope that one of his purchases will be life everlasting!—Which it never can be. . . .The human animal is a beast that—

BRICK *at the liquor cabinet:*   Big Daddy, you sure are shootin' th' breeze here tonight.

There is a pause and voices are heard outside.

BIG DADDY: I been quiet here lately, spoke not a word, just sat and stared into space. I had something heavy weighing on my mind but tonight that load was took off me. That's why I'm talking.—The sky looks diff'rent to me. . . .
BRICK: You know what I like to hear most?
BIG DADDY: What?
BRICK: Solid quiet. Perfect unbroken quiet.
BIG DADDY: Why?
BRICK: Because it's more peaceful.
BIG DADDY: Man, you'll hear a lot of that in the grave.

He chuckles agreeably.

BRICK: Are you through talkin' to me?
BIG DADDY: Why are you so anxious to shut me up?
BRICK: Well, sir, ever so often you say to me, Brick, I want to have a talk with you, but when we talk, it never materializes. Nothing is said. You sit in a chair and gas about this and that and I look like I listen. I try to look like I listen, but I don't listen, not much. Communication is— awful hard between people an'—somehow between you and me, it just don't—
BIG DADDY: Have you ever been scared? I mean have you ever felt down-right terror of something?

He gets up.

Just one moment. I'm going to close these doors. . . .

He closes doors on gallery as if he were going to tell an important secret.

BRICK: What?
BIG DADDY: Brick?
BRICK: Huh?
BIG DADDY: Son, I thought I had it!
BRICK: Had what? Had what, Big Daddy?
BIG DADDY: Cancer!
BRICK: Oh . . .
BIG DADDY: I thought the old man made out of bones had laid his cold and heavy hand on my shoulder!
BRICK: Well, Big Daddy, you kept a tight mouth about it.
BIG DADDY: A pig squeals. A man keeps a tight mouth about it, in spite of a man not having a pig's advantage.
BRICK: What advantage is that?
BIG DADDY: Ignorance—of mortality—is a comfort. A man don't have that comfort, he's the only living thing that conceives of death, that knows what it is. The others go without knowing which is the way that anything living should go, go without knowing, without any knowledge

of it, and yet a pig squeals, but a man sometimes, he can keep a tight mouth about it. Sometimes he—

There is a deep, smoldering ferocity in the old man.

—can keep a tight mouth about it. I wonder if—

BRICK: What, Big Daddy?

BIG DADDY: A whiskey highball would injure this spastic condition?

BRICK: No, sir, it might do it good.

BIG DADDY *grins suddenly, wolfishly: Jesus, I can't tell you! The sky is open! Christ, it's open again! It's open, boy, it's open!*

BRICK *looks down at his drink.*

BRICK: You feel better, Big Daddy?

BIG DADDY: Better? Hell! I can breathe!—All of my life I been like a doubled up fist. . . .

He pours a drink.

—Poundin', smashin', drivin'!—now I'm going to loosen these doubled-up hands and touch things *easy* with them. . . .

He spreads his hands as if caressing the air.

You know what I'm contemplating?

BRICK *vaguely: No, sir. What are you contemplating?*

BIG DADDY: Ha ha!—*Pleasure!*—pleasure with *women!*

BRICK'S *smile fades a little but lingers.*

Brick, this stuff burns me!—

—Yes, boy. I'll tell you something that you might not guess. I still have desire for women and this is my sixty-fifth birthday.

BRICK: I think that's mighty remarkable, Big Daddy.

BIG DADDY: Remarkable?

BRICK: *Admirable,* Big Daddy.

BIG DADDY: You're damn right it is, remarkable and admirable both. I realize now that I never had me enough. I let many chances slip by because of scruples about it, scruples, convention—crap . . . . All that stuff is bull, bull, bull!—It took the shadow of death to make me see it. Now that shadow's lifted, I'm going to cut loose and have, what is it they call it, have me a—ball!

BRICK: A ball, huh?

BIG DADDY: That's right, a ball, a ball! Hell!—I slept with Big Mama till, let's see, five years ago, till I was sixty and she was fifty-eight, and never even liked her, never did!

The phone has been ringing down the hall. BIG MAMA *enters, exclaiming:*

BIG MAMA: Don't you men hear that phone ring? I heard it way out on the gall'ry.
BIG DADDY: There's five rooms off this front gall'ry that you could go through. Why do you go through this one?

BIG MAMA *makes a playful face as she bustles out the hall door.*

Hunh!—Why, when Big Mama goes out of a room, I can't remember what that woman looks like, but when Big Mama comes back into the room, boy, then I see what she looks like, and I wish I didn't!

Bends over laughing at this joke till it hurts his guts and he straightens with a grimace. The laugh subsides to a chuckle as he puts the liquor glass a little distrustfully down on the table.

BRICK *has risen and hobbled to the gallery doors.*

Hey! Where you goin'?
BRICK: Out for a breather.
BIG DADDY: Not yet you ain't. Stay here till this talk is finished, young fellow.
BRICK: I thought it was finished, Big Daddy.
BIG DADDY: It ain't even begun.
BRICK: My mistake. Excuse me. I just wanted to feel that river breeze.
BIG DADDY: Turn on the ceiling fan and set back down in that chair.

BIG MAMA'S *voice rises, carrying down the hall.*

BIG MAMA: Miss Sally, you're a case! You're a caution, Miss Sally. Why didn't you give me a chance to explain it to you?
BIG DADDY: Jesus, she's talking to my old maid sister again.
BIG MAMA: Well, goodbye, now, Miss Sally. You come down real soon, Big Daddy's dying to see you! Yaisss, goodbye, Miss Sally. . . .

She hangs up and bellows with mirth. BIG DADDY *groans and covers his ears as she approaches.*

Bursting in:

Big Daddy, that was Miss Sally callin' from Memphis again! You know what she done, Big Daddy? She called her doctor in Memphis to git him to tell her what that spastic thing is! Ha-*HAAAA*!—And called back to tell me how relieved she was that—Hey! Let me in!

BIG DADDY *has been holding the door half closed against her.*

BIG DADDY: Naw I ain't. I told you not to come and go through this room. You just back out and go through those five other rooms.

BIG MAMA: Big Daddy? Big Daddy? Oh, big Daddy!—You didn't mean those things you said to me, did you?

He shuts door firmly against her but she still calls.

Sweetheart? Sweetheart? Big Daddy? You didn't mean those awful things you said to me?—I know you didn't. I know you didn't mean those things in your heart. . . .

The childlike voice fades with a sob and her heavy footsteps retreat down the hall. BRICK *has risen once more on his crutches and starts for the gallery again.*

BIG DADDY: All I ask of that woman is that she leave me alone. But she can't admit to herself that she makes me sick. That comes of having slept with her too many years. Should of quit much sooner but that old woman she never got enough of it—and I was good in bed . . . I never should of wasted so much of it on her. . . . They say you got just so many and each one is numbered. Well, I got a few left in me, a few, and I'm going to pick me a good one to spend 'em on! I'm going to pick me a choice one, I don't care how much she costs, I'll smother her in—minks! Ha ha! I'll strip her naked and smother her in minks and choke her with diamonds! Ha ha! I'll strip her naked and choke her with diamonds and smother her with minks and hump her from hell to breakfast. *Ha aha ha ha ha!*

MAE *gaily at door:*   Who's that laughin' in there?

GOOPER: Is Big Daddy laughin' in there?

BIG DADDY: Crap!—them two—*drips.* . . .

He goes over and touches BRICK'S *shoulder.*

Yes, son. Brick, boy.—I'm—*happy!* I'm happy, son, I'm happy!

He chokes a little and bites his under lip, pressing his head quickly, shyly against his son's head and then, coughing with embarrassment, goes uncertainly back to the table where he set down the glass. He drinks and makes a grimace as it burns his guts. BRICK *sighs and rises with effort.*

What makes you so restless? Have you got ants in your britches?

BRICK: Yes, sir . . .

BIG DADDY: Why?

BRICK: —Something—hasn't—happened. . . .

BIG DADDY: Yeah? What is that?

BRICK *sadly:*   —the click. . . .

BIG DADDY: Did you say click?

BRICK: Yes, click.

BIG DADDY: What click?

BRICK: A click that I get in my head that makes me peaceful.

BIG DADDY: I sure in hell don't know what you're talking about, but it disturbs me.

BRICK: It's just a mechanical thing.

BIG DADDY: What is a mechanical thing?

BRICK: This click that I get in my head that makes me peaceful. I got to drink till I get it. It's just a mechanical thing, something like a—like a—like a—

BIG DADDY: Like a—

BRICK: Switch clicking off in my head, turning the hot light off and the cool night on and—*He looks up, smiling sadly* —all of a sudden there's—peace!

BIG DADDY *whistles long and soft with astonishment; he goes back to Brick and clasps his son's two shoulders:*   Jesus! I didn't know it had gotten that bad with you. Why, boy, you're—*alcoholic!*

BRICK: That's the truth, Big Daddy. I'm alcoholic.

BIG DADDY: This shows how I—let things go!

BRICK: I have to hear that little click in my head that makes me peaceful. Usually I hear it sooner than this, sometimes as early as—noon, but—

—Today it's—dilatory. . . .

—I just haven't got the right level of alcohol in my bloodstream yet!

This last statement is made with energy as he freshens his drink.

BIG DADDY: Uh—huh. Expecting death made me blind. I didn't have no idea that a son of mine was turning into a drunkard under my nose.

BRICK *gently:*   Well, now you do, Big Daddy, the news has penetrated.

BIG DADDY: Uh-huh, yes, now I do, the news has—penetrated. . . .

BRICK: And so if you'll excuse me—

BIG DADDY: No, I won't excuse you.

BRICK: —I'd better sit by myself till I hear that click in my head, it's just a mechanical thing but it don't happen except when I'm alone or talking to no one. . . .

BIG DADDY: You got a long, long time to sit still, boy, and talk to no one, but now you're talkin' to me. At least I'm talking to you. And you set there and listen until I tell you the conversation is over!

BRICK: But this talk is like all the others we've ever had together in our lives! It's nowhere, nowhere!—it's—it's *painful*, Big Daddy. . . .

BIG DADDY: All right, then let it be painful, but don't you move from that chair!—I'm going to remove that crutch. . . .

He seizes the crutch and tosses it across room.

BRICK: I can hop on one foot, and if I fall, I can crawl!

BIG DADDY: If you ain't careful you're gonna crawl off this plantation and then, by Jesus, you'll have to hustle your drinks along Skid Row!

BRICK: That'll come, Big Daddy.

BIG DADDY: Naw, it won't. You're my son and I'm going to straighten you out; now that *I'm* straightened out, I'm going to straighten out you!

BRICK: Yeah?

BIG DADDY: Today the report come in from Ochsner Clinic. Y'know what they told me?

His face glows with triumph.

The only thing that they could detect with all the instruments of science in that great hospital is a little spastic condition of the colon! And nerves torn to pieces by all that worry about it.

A little girl bursts into room with a sparkler clutched in each fist, hops and shrieks like a monkey gone mad and rushes back out again as BIG DADDY *strikes at her.*

Silence. The two men stare at each other. A woman laughs gaily outside.

I want you to know I breathed a sigh of relief almost as powerful as the Vicksburg tornado!

BRICK: You weren't ready to go?

BIG DADDY: GO WHERE?—crap. . . .

—When you are gone from here, boy, you are long gone and no where! The human machine is not no different from the animal machine or the fish machine or the bird machine or the reptile machine or the insect machine! It's just a whole God damn lot more complicated and consequently more trouble to keep together. Yep. I thought I had it. The earth shook under my foot, the sky come down like the black lid of a kettle and I couldn't breathe!—Today!!—that lid was lifted, I drew my first free breath in—how many years?—*God!—three*. . . .

There is laughter outside, running footsteps, the soft, plushy sound and light of exploding rockets.

BRICK *stares at him soberly for a long moment; then makes a sort of startled sound in his nostrils and springs up on one foot and hops across the room to grab his crutch, swinging on the furniture for support. He gets the crutch and flees as if in horror for the gallery. His father seizes him by the sleeve of his white silk pajamas.*

Stay here, you son of a bitch!—till I say go!

BRICK: I can't.

BIG DADDY: You sure in hell will, God damn it.

BRICK: No, I can't. We talk, you talk, in—circles! We get no where, no where! It's always the same, you say you want to talk to me and don't have a ruttin' thing to say to me!

BIG DADDY: Nothin' to say when I'm tellin' you I'm going to live when I thought I was dying?!

BRICK: Oh—*that!*—Is that what you have to say to me?

BIG DADDY: Why, you son of a bitch! Ain't that, ain't that—*important?!*

BRICK: Well, you said that, that's said, and now I—

BIG DADDY: Now you set back down.

BRICK: You're all balled up, you—

BIG DADDY: I ain't balled up!

BRICK: You are, you're all balled up!

BIG DADDY: Don't tell me what I am, you drunken whelp! I'm going to tear this coat sleeve off if you don't set down!

BRICK: Big Daddy—

BIG DADDY: Do what I tell you! I'm the boss here, now! I want you to know I'm back in the driver's seat now!

BIG MAMA *rushes in, clutching her great heaving bosom.*

What in hell do you want in here, Big Mama?

BIG MAMA: Oh, Big Daddy! Why are you shouting like that? I just cain't stainnnnnnnd—it. . . .

BIG DADDY *raising the back of his hand above his head:*   GIT!—outa here.

She rushes back out, sobbing.

BRICK *softly, sadly:*   Christ. . . .

BIG DADDY *fiercely:*   Yeah! Christ!—is right . . .

BRICK *breaks loose and hobbles toward the gallery.*

BIG DADDY *jerks his crutch from under* BRICK *so he steps with the injured ankle. He utters a hissing cry of anguish, clutches a chair and pulls it over on top of him on the floor.*

Son of a—tub of—hog fat. . . .

BRICK: Big Daddy! Give me my crutch.

BIG DADDY *throws the crutch out of reach.*

Give me that crutch, Big Daddy.

BIG DADDY: Why do you drink?

BRICK: Don't know, give me my crutch!

BIG DADDY: You better think why you drink or give up drinking!

BRICK: Will you please give me my crutch so I can get up off this floor?

BIG DADDY: First you answer my question. Why do you drink? Why are you throwing your life away, boy, like somethin' disgusting you picked up on the street?

BRICK *getting onto his knees:*   Big Daddy, I'm in pain, I stepped on that foot.

BIG DADDY: Good! I'm glad you're not too numb with the liquor in you to feel some pain!

BRICK: You—spilled my—drink . . .

BIG DADDY: I'll make a bargain with you. You tell me why you drink and I'll hand you one. I'll pour you the liquor myself and hand it to you.

BRICK: Why do I drink?

BIG DADDY: Yea! Why?

BRICK: Give me a drink and I'll tell you.

BIG DADDY: Tell me first!

BRICK: I'll tell you in one word.

BIG DADDY: What word?

BRICK: DISGUST!

The clock chimes softly, sweetly. BIG DADDY *gives it a short, outraged glance.*

Now how about that drink?

BIG DADDY: What are you disgusted with? You got to tell me that, first. Otherwise being disgusted don't make no sense!

BRICK: Give me my crutch.

BIG DADDY: You heard me, you got to tell me what I asked you first.

BRICK: I told you, I said to kill my disgust!

BIG DADDY: DISGUST WITH WHAT!

BRICK: You strike a hard bargain.

BIG DADDY: What are you disgusted with?—an' I'll pass you the liquor.

BRICK: I can hop on one foot, and if I fall, I can crawl.

BIG DADDY: You want liquor that bad?

BRICK *dragging himself up, clinging to bedstead:*   Yeah, I want it that bad.

BIG DADDY: If I give you a drink, will you tell me what it is you're disgusted with, Brick?

BRICK: Yes, sir, I will try to.

The old man pours him a drink and solemnly passes it to him.

There is silence as BRICK *drinks.*

Have you ever heard the word "mendacity"?

BIG DADDY: Sure. Mendacity is one of them five dollar words that cheap politicians throw back and forth at each other.

BRICK: You know what it means?

BIG DADDY: Don't it mean lying and liars?

BRICK: Yes, sir, lying and liars.

BIG DADDY: Has someone been lying to you?

CHILDREN *chanting in chorus offstage:*   We want Big Dad-dee! We want Big Dad-dee!

GOOPER *appears in the gallery door.*

GOOPER: Big Daddy, the kiddies are shouting for you out there.

BIG DADDY *fiercely:*   Keep out, Gooper!
GOOPER: 'Scuse *me!*

BIG DADDY *slams the doors after* GOOPER.

BIG DADDY: Who's been lying to you, has Margaret been lying to you, has your wife been lying to you about something, Brick?
BRICK: Not her. That wouldn't matter.
BIG DADDY: Then who's been lying to you, and what about?
BRICK: No one single person and no one lie. . . .
BIG DADDY: Then what, what then, for Christ's sake?
BRICK: —The whole, the whole—thing. . . .
BIG DADDY: Why are you rubbing your head? You got a headache?
BRICK: No, I'm tryin' to—
BIG DADDY: —Concentrate, but you can't because your brain's all soaked with liquor, is that the trouble? Wet brain!

He snatches the glass from BRICK'S *hand.*

What do you know about this mendacity thing? Hell! I could write a book on it! Don't you know that? I could write a book on it and still not cover the subject? Well, I could, I could write a goddam book on it and still not cover the subject anywhere near enough!!—Think of all the lies I got to put up with!—Pretenses! Ain't that mendacity? Having to pretend stuff you don't think or feel or have any idea of? Having for instance to act like I care for Big Mama!—I haven't been able to stand the sight, sound, or smell of that woman for forty years now!—even when I *laid* her!—regular as a piston. . . .

Pretend to love that son of a bitch of a Gooper and his wife Mae and those five same screechers out there like parrots in a jungle? Jesus! Can't stand to look at 'em!

Church!—it bores the bejesus out of me but I go!—I go an' sit there and listen to the fool preacher!

Clubs!—Elks! Masons! Rotary!—*crap!*

A spasm of pain makes him clutch his belly. He sinks into a chair and his voice is softer and hoarser.

You I *do* like for some reason, did always have some kind of real feeling for—affection—respect—yes, always. . . .

You and being a success as a planter is all I ever had any devotion to in my whole life!—and that's the truth. . . .

I don't know why, but it is!

I've lived with mendacity!—Why can't *you* live with it? Hell, you *got* to live with it, there's nothing *else* to *live* with except mendacity, is there?

BRICK: Yes, sir. Yes, sir there is something else that you can live with!

BIG DADDY: What?

BRICK *lifting his glass:*   This!—Liquor. . . .

BIG DADDY: That's not living, that's dodging away from life.

BRICK: I want to dodge away from it.

BIG DADDY: Then why don't you kill yourself, man?

BRICK: I like to drink. . . .

BIG DADDY: Oh, God, I can't talk to you. . . .

BRICK: I'm sorry, Big Daddy.

BIG DADDY: Not as sorry as I am. I'll tell you something. A little while back when I thought my number was up—

This speech should have torrential pace and fury.

—before I found out it was just this—spastic—colon. I thought about you. Should I or should I not, if the jig was up, give you this place when I go—since I hate Gooper an' Mae an' know that they hate me, and since all five same monkeys are little Maes an' Goopers.—And I thought, No!—Then I thought, Yes!—I couldn't make up my mind. I hate Gooper and his five same monkeys and that bitch Mae! Why should I turn over twenty-eight thousand acres of the richest land this side of the valley Nile to not my kind?—But why in hell, on the other hand, Brick—should I subsidize a goddam fool on the bottle?—Liked or not liked, well, maybe even—*loved!*—Why should I do that?—Subsidize worthless behavior? Rot? Corruption?

BRICK *smiling:*   I understand.

BIG DADDY: Well, if you do, you're smarter than I am, God damn it, because I don't understand. And this I will tell you frankly. I didn't make up my mind at all on that question and still to this day I ain't made out no will!—Well, now I don't *have* to. The pressure is gone. I can just wait and see if you pull yourself together or if you don't.

BRICK: That's right, Big Daddy.

BIG DADDY: You sound like you thought I was kidding.

BRICK *rising:*   No, sir, I know you're not kidding.

BIG DADDY: But you don't care—?

BRICK *hobbling toward the gallery door:*   No, sir, I don't care. . . .

Now how about taking a look at your birthday fireworks and getting some of that cool breeze off the river?

He stands in the gallery doorway as the night sky turns pink and green and gold with successive flashes of light.

BIG DADDY: *WAIT!*—Brick. . . .

His voice drops. Suddenly there is something shy, almost tender, in his restraining gesture.

Don't let's—leave it like this, like them other talks we've had, we've always—talked around things, we've—just talked around things for some rutten reason, I don't know what, it's always like something was left not spoken, something avoided because neither of us was honest enough with the—other. . . .

BRICK: I never lied to you, Big Daddy.

BIG DADDY: Did I ever to *you*?

BRICK: No, sir. . . .

BIG DADDY: Then there is at least two people that never lied to each other.

BRICK: But we've never *talked* to each other.

BIG DADDY: We can *now*.

BRICK: Big Daddy, there don't seem to be anything much to say.

BIG DADDY: You say that you drink to kill your disgust with lying.

BRICK: You said to give you a reason.

BIG DADDY: Is liquor the only thing that'll kill this disgust?

BRICK: Now. Yes.

BIG DADDY: But not once, huh?

BRICK: Not when I was still young an' believing. A drinking man's someone who wants to forget he isn't still young an' believing.

BIG DADDY: Believing what?

BRICK: Believing. . . .

BIG DADDY: Believing *what?*

BRICK *stubbornly evasive:*   Believing. . . .

BIG DADDY: I don't know what the hell you mean by believing and I don't think you know what you mean by believing, but if you still got sports in your blood, go back to sports announcing and—

BRICK: Sit in a glass box watching games I can't play? Describing what I can't do while players do it? Sweating out their disgust and confusion in contests I'm not fit for? Drinkin' a coke, half bourbon, so I can stand it? That's no goddam good any more, no help—time just outran me, Big Daddy—got there first . . .

BIG DADDY: I think you're passing the buck.

BRICK: You know many drinkin' men?

BIG DADDY *with a slight, charming smile:*   I have known a fair number of that species.

BRICK: Could any of them tell you why he drank?

BIG DADDY: Yep, you're passin' the buck to things like time and disgust with "mendacity" and—crap!—if you got to use that kind of language about a thing, it's ninety-proof bull, and I'm not buying any.

BRICK: I had to give you a reason to get a drink!

BIG DADDY: You started drinkin' when your friend Skipper died.

Silence for five beats. Then BRICK *makes a startled movement, reaching for his crutch.*

BRICK: What are you suggesting?
BIG DADDY: I'm suggesting nothing.

The shuffle and clop of BRICK'S *rapid hobble away from his father's steady, grave attention.*

—But Gooper an' Mae suggested that there was something not right
exactly in your—
BRICK *stopping short downstage as if backed to a wall:*   "Not right"?
BIG DADDY: Not, well, exactly *normal* in your friendship with—
BRICK: They suggested that, too? I thought that was Maggie's suggestion.

BRICK'S *detachment is at last broken through. His heart is accelerated; his fore-head sweat-beaded; his breath becomes more rapid and his voice hoarse. The thing they're discussing, timidly and painfully on the side of* BIG DADDY, *fiercely, violently on* BRICK'S *side, is the inadmissible thing that Skipper died to disavow between them. The fact that if it existed it had to be disavowed to "keep face" in the world they lived in, may be at the heart of the "mendacity" that* BRICK *drinks to kill his disgust with. It may be the root of his collapse. Or maybe it is only a single manifestation of it, not even the most important. The bird that I hope to catch in the net of this play is not the solution of one man's psychological problem. I'm trying to catch the true quality of experience in a group of people, that cloudy, flickering, evanescent—fiercely charged!—inter-play of live human beings in the thundercloud of a common crisis. Some mystery should be left in the revelation of character in a play, just as a great deal of mystery is always left in the revelation of character in life, even in one's own character to himself. This does not absolve the playwright of his duty to observe and probe as clearly and deeply as he legitimately can: but it should steer him away from "pat" conclusions, facile definitions which make a play just a play, not a snare for the truth of human experience.*

The following scene should be played with great concentration, with most of the power leashed but palpable in what is left unspoken.

Who else's suggestion is it, is it *yours?* How many others thought that
Skipper and I were—
BIG DADDY *gently:*   Now, hold on, hold on a minute, son.—I knocked
around in my time.
BRICK: What's that got to do with—
BIG DADDY: I said "Hold on!"—I bummed, I bummed this country till I
was—
BRICK: Whose suggestion, who else's suggestion is it?
BIG DADDY: Slept in hobo jungles and railroad Y's and flophouses in all
cities before I—
BRICK: Oh, *you* think so, too, you call me your son and a queer. Oh!
Maybe that's why you put Maggie and me in this room that was Jack

Straw's and Peter Ochello's, in which that pair of old sisters slept in a double bed where both of 'em died!

BIG DADDY: *Now just don't go throwing rocks at—*

Suddenly REVEREND TOOKER *appears in the gallery doors, his head slightly, playfully, fatuously cocked, with a practised clergyman's smile, sincere as a bird call blown on a hunter's whistle, the living embodiment of the pious, conventional lie.*

BIG DADDY *gasps a little at this perfectly timed, but incongruous, apparition.*

—What're you lookin' for, Preacher?

REVEREND TOOKER: The gentleman's lavatory, ha ha!—heh, heh . . .

BIG DADDY *with strained courtesy:*   —Go back out and walk down to the other end of the gallery, Reverend Tooker, and use the bathroom connected with my bedroom, and if you can't find it, ask them where it is!

REVEREND TOOKER: Ah, thanks.

He goes out with a deprecatory chuckle.

BIG DADDY: It's hard to talk in this place . . .

BRICK: Son of a—!

BIG DADDY *leaving a lot unspoken:*   —I seen all things and understood a lot of them, till 1910. Christ, the year that—I had worn my shoes through, hocked my—I hopped off a yellow dog freight car half a mile down the road, slept in a wagon of cotton outside the gin—Jack Straw an' Peter Ochello took me in. Hired me to manage this place which grew into this one.—When Jack Straw died—why, old Peter Ochello quit eatin' like a dog does when its master's dead, and died, too!

BRICK: Christ!

BIG DADDY: I'm just saying I understand such—

BRICK *violently:*   Skipper is dead. I have not quit eating!

BIG DADDY: No, but you started drinking.

BRICK *wheels on his crutch and hurls his glass across the room shouting.*

BRICK: YOU THINK SO, TOO?

BIG DADDY: *Shhh!*

Footsteps run on the gallery. There are women's calls.

BIG DADDY *goes toward the door.*

Go way!—Just broke a glass. . . .

BRICK *is transformed, as if a quiet mountain blew suddenly up in volcanic flame.*

BRICK: You think so, too? You think so, too? You think me an' Skipper did, did, did!—*sodomy!*—together?

BIG DADDY: Hold—!
BRICK: That what you—
BIG DADDY: —ON—a minute!
BRICK: You think we did dirty things between us, Skipper an'—
BIG DADDY: Why are you shouting like that? Why are you—
BRICK: —Me, is that what you think of Skipper, is that—
BIG DADDY: —so excited? I don't think nothing. I don't know nothing.
   I'm simply telling you what—
BRICK: You think that Skipper and me were a pair of dirty old men?
BIG DADDY: Now that's—
BRICK: Straw? Ochello? A couple of—
BIG DADDY: Now just—
BRICK: —ducking sissies? Queers? Is that what you—
BIG DADDY: Shhh.
BRICK: —think?

He loses his balance and pitches to his knees without noticing the pain. He grabs the bed and drags himself up.

BIG DADDY: Jesus!—Whew. . . . Grab my hand!
BRICK: Naw, I don't want your hand. . . .
BIG DADDY: Well, I want yours. Git up!

He draws him up, keeps an arm about him with concern and affection.

You broken out in a sweat! You're panting like you'd run a race with—

BRICK *freeing himself from his father's hold:*   Big Daddy, you shock me, Big
   Daddy, you, you—*shock* me! Talkin' so—

He turns away from his father.

—casually!—about a—thing like that . . .

—Don't you know how people *feel* about things like that? How, how *disgusted* they are by things like that? Why, at Ole Miss when it was discovered a pledge to our fraternity, Skipper's and mine, did a, *attempted* to do a, unnatural thing with—

We not only dropped him like a hot rock!—We told him to git off the campus, and he did, he got!—All the way to—

He halts, breathless.

BIG DADDY: —Where?
BRICK: —North Africa, last I heard!
BIG DADDY: Well, I have come back from further away than that, I have just now returned from the other side of the moon, death's country, son, and I'm not easy to shock by anything here.

He comes downstage and faces out.

Always, anyhow, lived with too much space around me to be infected by ideas of other people. One thing you can grow on a big place more important than cotton!—is *tolerance!*—I grown it.

He returns toward BRICK.

BRICK: Why can't exceptional friendship, *real, real, deep, deep friendship!* between two men be respected as something clean and decent without being thought of as—
BIG DADDY: It can, it is, for God's sake.
BRICK: —*Fairies.* . . .

In his utterance of this word, we gauge the wide and profound reach of the conventional mores he got from the world that crowned him with early laurel.

BIG DADDY: I told Mae an' Gooper—
BRICK: Frig Mae and Gooper, frig all dirty lies and liars!—Skipper and me had a clean, true thing between us!—had a clean friendship, practically all our lives, till Maggie got the idea you're talking about. Normal? No!—It was too rare to be normal, any true thing between two people is too rare to be normal. Oh, once in a while he put his hand on my shoulder or I'd put mine on his, oh, maybe even, when we were touring the country in pro-football an' shared hotel-rooms we'd reach across the space between the two beds and shake hands to say goodnight, yeah, one or two times we—
BIG DADDY: Brick, nobody thinks that that's not normal!
BRICK: Well, they're mistaken, it was! It was a pure an' true thing an' that's not normal.

They both stare straight at each other for a long moment. The tension breaks and both turn away as if tired.

BIG DADDY: Yeah, it's—hard t'—talk. . . .
BRICK: All right, then, let's—let it go. . . .
BIG DADDY: Why did Skipper crack up? Why have you?

BRICK *looks back at his father again. He has already decided, without knowing that he has made this decision, that he is going to tell his father that he is dying of cancer. Only this could even the score between them: one inadmissible thing in return for another.*

BRICK *ominously:* All right. You're asking for it, Big Daddy. We're finally going to have that real true talk you wanted. It's too late to stop it, now, we got to carry it through and cover every subject.

He hobbles back to the liquor cabinet.

Uh-huh.

He opens the ice bucket and picks up the silver tongs with slow admiration of their frosty brightness.

Maggie declares that Skipper and I went into pro-football after we left "Ole Miss" because we were scared to grow up . . .

He moves downstage with the shuffle and clop of a cripple on a crutch. As MARGARET *did when her speech became "recitative," he looks out into the house, commanding its attention by his direct, concentrated gaze—a broken, "tragically elegant" figure telling simply as much as he knows of "the Truth":*

—Wanted to—keep on tossing—those long, long!—high, high!— passes that—couldn't be intercepted except by time, the aerial attack that made us famous! And so we did, we did, we kept it up for one season, that aerial attack, we held it high!—Yeah, but—

—that summer, Maggie, she laid the law down to me, said, Now or never, and so I married Maggie. . . .

BIG DADDY: How was Maggie in bed?

BRICK *wryly:*   Great! the greatest!

BIG DADDY *nods as if he thought so.*

She went on the road that fall with the Dixie Stars. Oh, she made a great show of being the world's best sport. She wore a—wore a—tall bearskin cap! A shako, they call it, a dyed moleskin coat, a moleskin coat dyed red!—Cut up crazy! Rented hotel ballrooms for victory celebrations, wouldn't cancel them when it—turned out—defeat. . . .

MAGGIE THE CAT! Ha ha!

BIG DADDY *nods.*

—But Skipper, he had some fever which came back on him which doctors couldn't explain and I got that injury—turned out to be just a shadow on the X-ray plate—and a touch of bursitis. . . .

I lay in a hospital bed, watched our games on TV, saw Maggie on the bench next to Skipper when he was hauled out of a game for stumbles, fumbles!—Burned me up the way she hung on his arm!—Y'know, I think that Maggie had always felt sort of left out because she and me never got any closer together than two people just get in bed, which is not much closer than two cats on a—fence humping. . . .

So! She took this time to work on poor dumb Skipper. He was a less than average student at Ole Miss, you know that, don't you?!—Poured in his mind the dirty, false idea that what we were, him and me, was a frustrated case of that ole pair of sisters that lived in this room, Jack Straw and Peter Ochello!—He, poor Skipper, went to bed with Maggie to prove it wasn't true, and when it didn't work out, he thought it *was* true!—Skipper broke in two like a rotten stick—nobody ever turned so fast to a lush—or died of it so quick. . . .

—Now are you satisfied?

BIG DADDY *has listened to this story, dividing the grain from the chaff. Now he looks at his son.*

BIG DADDY: Are *you* satisfied?
BRICK: With what?
BIG DADDY: That half-ass story!
BRICK: What's half-ass about it?
BIG DADDY: Something's left out of that story. What did you leave out?

The phone has started ringing in the hall. As if it reminded him of something, BRICK *glances suddenly toward the sound and says:*

BRICK: Yes!—I left out a long-distance call which I had from Skipper, in which he made a drunken confession to me and on which I hung up!—last time we spoke to each other in our lives. . . .

Muted ring stops as someone answers phone in a soft, indistinct voice in hall.

BIG DADDY: You hung up?
BRICK: Hung up. Jesus! Well—
BIG DADDY: Anyhow now!—we have tracked down the lie with which you're disgusted and which you are drinking to kill your disgust with, Brick. You been passing the buck. This disgust with mendacity is disgust with yourself.

You!—dug the grave of your friend and kicked him in it!—before you'd face truth with him!
BRICK: *His* truth, not *mine!*
BIG DADDY: His truth, okay! But you wouldn't face it with him!
BRICK: Who *can* face truth? Can *you?*
BIG DADDY: Now don't start passin' the rotten buck again, boy!
BRICK: *How about these birthday congratulations, these many, many happy returns of the day, when ev'rybody but you knows there won't be any!*

Whoever has answered the hall phone lets out a high, shrill laugh; the voice becomes audible saying: "No, no, you got it all wrong! Upside down! Are you crazy?"

BRICK *suddenly catches his breath as he realizes that he has made a shocking disclosure. He hobbles a few paces, then freezes, and without looking at his father's shocked face, says:*

Let's, let's—go out, now, and—

BIG DADDY *moves suddenly forward and grabs hold of the boy's crutch like it was a weapon for which they were fighting for possession.*

BIG DADDY: Oh, no, no! No one's going out! What did you start to say?
BRICK: I don't remember.
BIG DADDY: "Many happy returns when they know there won't be any"?
BRICK: Aw, hell, Big Daddy, forget it. Come on out on the gallery and look at the fireworks they're shooting off for your birthday. . . .
BIG DADDY: First you finish that remark you were makin' before you cut off. "Many happy returns when they know there won't be any"?— Ain't that what you just said?
BRICK: Look, now. I can get around without that crutch if I have to but it would be a lot easier on the furniture an' glassware if I didn' have to go swinging along like Tarzan of th'—
BIG DADDY: FINISH! WHAT YOU WAS SAYIN'!

An eerie green glow shows in sky behind him.

BRICK *sucking the ice in his glass, speech becoming thick:*   Leave th' place to Gooper and Mae an' their five little same little monkeys. All I want is—
BIG DADDY: "LEAVE TH' PLACE," did you say?
BRICK *vaguely:*   All twenty-eight thousand acres of the richest land this side of the valley Nile.
BIG DADDY: Who said I was "leaving the place" to Gooper or anybody? This is my sixty-fifth birthday! I got fifteen years or twenty years left in me! I'll outlive *you!* I'll bury you an' have to pay for your coffin!
BRICK: Sure. Many happy returns. Now let's go watch the fireworks, come on, let's—
BIG DADDY: Lying, have they been lying? About the report from th'— clinic? Did they, did they—find something?—*Cancer*. Maybe?
BRICK: Mendacity is a system that we live in. Liquor is one way out an' death's the other. . . .

He takes the crutch from BIG DADDY'S *loose grip and swings out on the gallery leaving the doors open.*

A song, "Pick a Bale of Cotton," is heard.

MAE *appearing in door:*   Oh, Big Daddy, the field hands are singin' fo' you!
BIG DADDY *shouting hoarsely:*   BRICK! BRICK!
MAE: He's outside drinkin', Big Daddy.
BIG DADDY: BRICK!

MAE *retreats, awed by the passion of his voice. Children call* BRICK *in tones mocking* BIG DADDY. *His face crumbles like broken yellow plaster about to fall into dust.*

There is a glow in the sky. BRICK *swings back through the doors, slowly, gravely, quite soberly.*

BRICK: I'm sorry, Big Daddy. My head don't work any more and it's hard for me to understand how anybody could care if he lived or died or was dying or cared about anything but whether or not there was liquor left in the bottle and so I said what I said without thinking. In some ways I'm no better than the others, in some ways worse because I'm less alive. Maybe it's being alive that makes them lie, and being almost *not* alive makes me sort of accidentally truthful—I don't know but—anyway—we've been friends . . .

—And being friends is telling each other the truth. . . .

There is a pause.

You told me! I told *you!*

A child rushes into the room and grabs a fistful of firecrackers and runs out again.

CHILD *screaming:*   Bang, bang, bang, bang, bang, bang, bang, bang, bang!
BIG DADDY *slowly and passionately:*   CHRIST—DAMN—ALL—LYING SONS OF—LYING BITCHES!

He straightens at last and crosses to the inside door. At the door he turns and looks back as if he had some desperate question he couldn't put into words. Then he nods reflectively and says in a hoarse voice:

Yes, all liars, all liars, all lying dying liars!

This is said slowly, slowly, with a fierce revulsion. He goes on out.

—Lying! Dying! Liars!

His voice dies out. There is the sound of a child being slapped. It rushes, hideously bawling, through room and out the hall door.

BRICK *remains motionless as the lights dim out and the curtain falls.*

Curtain

ACT III

There is no lapse of time. MAE *enters with* REVEREND TOOKER.

MAE: Where is Big Daddy! Big Daddy?

BIG MAMA *entering:*   Too much smell of burnt fireworks makes me feel a little bit sick at my stomach.—Where is Big Daddy?

MAE: That's what I want to know, where has Big Daddy gone?

BIG MAMA: He must have turned in, I reckon he went to baid. . . .

GOOPER *enters.*

GOOPER: Where is Big Daddy?

MAE: We don't know where he is!

BIG MAMA: I reckon he's gone to baid.

GOOPER: Well, then, now we can talk.

BIG MAMA: What *is* this talk, *what* talk?

MARGARET *appears on gallery, talking to* DR. BAUGH.

MARGARET *musically:*   My family freed their slaves ten years before abolition, my great-great-grandfather gave his slaves their freedom five years before the war between the States started!

MAE: Oh, for God's sake! Maggie's climbed back up in her family tree!

MARGARET *sweetly:*   What, Mae?—Oh, where's Big Daddy?!

The pace must be very quick. Great Southern animation.

BIG MAMA *addressing them all:*   I think Big Daddy was just worn out. He loves his family, he loves to have them around him, but it's a strain on his nerves. He wasn't himself tonight, Big Daddy wasn't himself, I could tell he was all worked up.

REVEREND TOOKER: I think he's remarkable.

BIG MAMA: Yaisss! Just remarkable. Did you all notice the food he ate at that table? Did you all notice the supper he put away? Why, he ate like a hawss!

GOOPER: I hope he doesn't regret it.

BIG MAMA: Why, that man—ate a huge piece of cawn-bread with molasses on it! Helped himself twice to hoppin' john.

MARGARET: Big Daddy loves hoppin' john.—We had a real country dinner.

BIG MAMA *overlapping Margaret:*   Yais, he simply adores it! An' candied yams? That man put away enough food at that table to stuff a nigger *field* hand!

GOOPER *with grim relish:*   I hope he don't have to pay for it later on. . . .

BIG MAMA *fiercely:*   What's *that,* Gooper?

MAE: Gooper says he hopes Big Daddy doesn't suffer tonight.

BIG MAMA: Oh, shoot, Gooper says, Gooper says! Why should Big Daddy suffer for satisfying a normal appetite? There's nothin' wrong with that man but nerves, he's sound as a dollar! And now he knows he is an' that's why he ate such a supper. He had a big load off his mind, knowin' he wasn't doomed t'—what he thought he was doomed to. . . .

MARGARET *sadly and sweetly:*   Bless his old sweet soul. . . .

BIG MAMA *vaguely:*   Yais, bless his heart, where's Brick?

MAE: Outside.

GOOPER: —Drinkin' . . .

BIG MAMA: I know he's drinkin'. You all don't have to keep tellin' me Brick is drinkin'. Cain't I see he's drinkin' without you continually tellin' me that boy's drinkin'?

MARGARET: Good for you, Big Mama!

She applauds.

BIG MAMA: Other people *drink* and *have* drunk an' will *drink*, as long as they make that stuff an' put it in bottles.

MARGARET: That's the truth. I never trusted a man that didn't drink.

MAE: Gooper never drinks. Don't you trust Gooper?

MARGARET: Why, Gooper don't you drink? If I'd known you didn't drink, I wouldn't of made that remark—

BIG MAMA: *Brick?*

MARGARET: —at least not in your presence.

She laughs sweetly.

BIG MAMA: *Brick!*

MARGARET: He's still on the gall'ry. I'll go bring him in so we can talk.

BIG MAMA *worriedly:*   I don't know what this mysterious family conference is about.

Awkward silence. BIG MAMA *looks from face to face, then belches slightly and mutters, "Excuse me. . . ." She opens an ornamental fan suspended about her throat, a black lace fan to go with her black lace gown and fans her wilting corsage, sniffing nervously and looking from face to face in the uncomfortable silence as* MARGARET *calls "Brick?" and* BRICK *sings to the moon on the gallery.*

I don't know what's wrong here, you all have such long faces! Open that door on the hall and let some air circulate through here, will you please, Gooper?

MAE: I think we'd better leave that door closed, Big Mama, till after the talk.

BIG MAMA: Reveren' Tooker, will *you* please open that door?!

REVEREND TOOKER: I sure will, Big Mama.

MAE: I just didn't think we ought t' take any chance of Big Daddy hearin' a word of this discussion.

BIG MAMA: I *swan!* Nothing's going to be said in Big Daddy's house that he cain't hear if he wants to!

GOOPER: Well, Big Mama, it's—

MAE *gives him a quick, hard poke to shut him up. He glares at her fiercely as she circles before him like a burlesque ballerina, raising her skinny bare arms over her head, jangling her bracelets, exclaiming:*

MAE: A breeze! A breeze!

REVEREND TOOKER: I think this house is the coolest house in the Delta.—Did you all know that Halsey Banks' widow put air-conditioning units in the church and rectory at Friar's Point in memory of Halsey?

General conversation has resumed; everybody is chatting so that the stage sounds like a big bird-cage.

GOOPER: Too bad nobody cools your church off for you. I bet you sweat in that pulpit these hot Sundays, Reverend Tooker.

REVEREND TOOKER: Yes, my vestments are drenched.

MAE *at the same time to* DR. BAUGH: You think those vitamin B_{12} injections are what they're cracked up t' be, Doc Baugh?

DOCTOR BAUGH: Well, if you want to be stuck with something I guess they're as good to be stuck with as anything else.

BIG MAMA *at gallery door:*   Maggie, Maggie, aren't you comin' with Brick?

MAE *suddenly and loudly, creating a silence:*   I have a strange feeling, I have a peculiar feeling!

BIG MAMA *turning from gallery:*   What feeling?

MAE: That Brick said somethin' he shouldn't of said t' Big Daddy.

BIG MAMA: Now what on earth could Brick of said t' Big Daddy that he shouldn't say?

GOOPER: Big Mama, there's somethin'—

MAE: NOW, WAIT!

She rushes up to BIG MAMA *and gives her a quick hug and kiss.* BIG MAMA *pushes her impatiently off as the* REVEREND TOOKER'S *voice rises serenely in a little pocket of silence:*

REVEREND TOOKER: Yes, last Sunday the gold in my chasuble faded into th' purple. . . .

GOOPER: Reveren' you must of been preachin' hell's fire last Sunday!

He guffaws at this witticism but the REVEREND *is not sincerely amused. At the same time* BIG MAMA *has crossed over to* DR. BAUGH *and is saying to him:*

BIG MAMA *her breathless voice rising high-pitched above the others:*   In my day they had what they call the Keeley cure for heavy drinkers. But now I understand they just take some kind of tablets, they call them "Annie

Bust" tablets. But *Brick* don't need to take *nothin'*.

BRICK *appears in gallery doors with* MARGARET *behind him.*

BIG MAMA *unaware of his presence behind her:* That boy is just broken up over Skipper's death. You know how poor Skipper died. They gave him a big, big dose of that sodium amytal stuff at his home and then they called the ambulance and give him another big, big dose of it at the hospital and that and all of the alcohol in his system fo' months an' months an' months just proved too much for his heart. . . . I'm scared of needles! I'm more scared of a needle than the knife. . . . I think more people have been needled out of this world than—

She stops short and wheels about.

OH!—here's Brick! My precious baby—

She turns upon BRICK *with short, fat arms extended, at the same time uttering a loud, short sob, which is both comic and touching.*

BRICK *smiles and bows slightly, making a burlesque gesture of gallantry for* MAGGIE *to pass before him into the room. Then he hobbles on his crutch directly to the liquor cabinet and there is absolute silence, with everybody looking at* BRICK *as everybody has always looked at* BRICK *when he spoke or moved or appeared. One by one he drops ice cubes in his glass, then suddenly, but not quickly, looks back over his shoulder with a wry, charming smile, and says:*

BRICK: I'm sorry! Anyone else?
BIG MAMA *sadly:* No, son. I *wish* you wouldn't!
BRICK: I wish I didn't have to, Big Mama, but I'm still waiting for that click in my head which makes it all smooth out!
BIG MAMA: Aw, Brick, you—BREAK MY HEART!
MARGARET *at the same time:* Brick, go sit with Big Mama!
BIG MAMA: I just cain't *staiiiiiiiii-nnnnnd*—it. . . .

She sobs.

MAE: Now that we're all assembled—
GOOPER: We kin talk. . . .
BIG MAMA: Breaks my heart. . . .
MARGARET: Sit with Big Mama, Brick, and hold her hand.

BIG MAMA *sniffs very loudly three times, almost like three drum beats in the pocket of silence.*

BRICK: You do that, Maggie. I'm a restless cripple. I got to stay on my crutch.

BRICK *hobbles to the gallery door; leans there as if waiting.*

MAE *sits beside* BIG MAMA, *while* GOOPER *moves in front and sits on the end of the couch, facing her.* REVEREND TOOKER *moves nervously into the space between them; on the other side,* DR. BAUGH *stands looking at nothing in particular and lights a cigar.* MARGARET *turns away.*

BIG MAMA: Why're you all *surroundin'* me—like this? Why're you all starin' at me like this an' makin' signs at each other?

REVEREND TOOKER *steps back startled.*

MAE: Calm yourself, Big Mama.
BIG MAMA: Calm you'self, *you'self,* Sister Woman. How could I calm myself with everyone starin' at me as if big drops of blood had broken out on m'face? What's this all about, annh! What?

GOOPER *coughs and takes a center position.*

GOOPER: Now, Doc Baugh.
MAE: Doc Baugh?
BRICK *suddenly:*   SHHH!—

Then he grins and chuckles and shakes his head regretfully.

   —Naw!—that wasn't th' click.
GOOPER: Brick, shut up or stay out there on the gallery with your liquor! We got to talk about a serious matter. Big Mama wants to know the complete truth about the report we got today from the Ochsner Clinic.
MAE *eagerly:*   —on Big Daddy's condition!
GOOPER: Yais, on Big Daddy's condition, we got to face it.
DOCTOR BAUGH: Well. . . .
BIG MAMA *terrified, rising:*   Is there? Something? Something that I? Don't—Know?

In these few words, this startled, very soft, question, BIG MAMA *reviews the history of her forty-five years with* BIG DADDY, *her great, almost embarrassingly true-hearted and simple-minded devotion to* BIG DADDY, *who must have had something* BRICK *has, who made himself loved so much by the "simple expedient" of not loving enough to disturb his charming detachment, also once coupled, like* BRICK'S, *with virile beauty.*

BIG MAMA *has a dignity at this moment: she almost stops being fat.*

DOCTOR BAUGH *after a pause, uncomfortably:*   Yes?—Well—
BIG MAMA: I!!!—want to—*knowwwwwww.* . . .

Immediately she thrusts her fist to her mouth as if to deny that statement.

Then, for some curious reason, she snatches the withered corsage from her breast and hurls it on the floor and steps on it with her short, fat feet.

   —Somebody must be lyin'!—I want to know!

MAE: Sit down, Big Mama, sit down on this sofa.
MARGARET *quickly:*   Brick, go sit with Big Mama.
BIG MAMA: *What is it, what is it?*
DOCTOR BAUGH: I never have seen a more thorough examination than Big Daddy Pollitt was given in all my experience with the Ochsner Clinic.
GOOPER: It's one of the best in the country.
MAE: It's *THE* best in the country—bar *none!*

For some reason she gives GOOPER *a violent poke as she goes past him. He slaps at her hand without removing his eyes from his mother's face.*

DOCTOR BAUGH: Of course they were ninety-nine and nine-tenths percent sure before they even started.
BIG MAMA: Sure of what, sure of what, sure of—*what?—what!*

She catches her breath in a startled sob. MAE *kisses her quickly. She thrusts* MAE *fiercely away from her, staring at the doctor.*

MAE: Mommy, be a brave girl!
BRICK *in the doorway, softly:*   "By the light, by the light,
   Of the sil-ve-ry mo-ooo-n . . ."
GOOPER: Shut up!—Brick.
BRICK: —Sorry. . . .

He wanders out on the gallery.

DOCTOR BAUGH: But now, you see, Big Mama, they cut a piece off this growth, a specimen of the tissue and—
BIG MAMA: Growth? You told Big Daddy—
DOCTOR BAUGH: Now wait.
BIG MAMA *fiercely:*   You told me and Big Daddy there wasn't a thing wrong with him but—
MAE: Big Mama, they always—
GOOPER: Let Doc Baugh talk, will yuh?
BIG MAMA: —little spastic condition of—

Her breath gives out in a sob.

DOCTOR BAUGH: Yes, that's what we told Big Daddy. But we had this bit of tissue run through the laboratory and I'm sorry to say the test was positive on it. It's—well—malignant. . . .

Pause.

BIG MAMA: —Cancer?! Cancer?!

DR. BAUGH *nods gravely.*

BIG MAMA *gives a long gasping cry.*

MAE AND GOOPER: Now, now, now, Big Mama, you had to know. . . .
BIG MAMA: WHY DIDN'T THEY CUT IT OUT OF HIM? HANH? HANH?
DOCTOR BAUGH: Involved too much, Big Mama, too many organs affected.
MAE: Big Mama, the liver's affected and so's the kidneys, both! It's gone way past what they call a—
GOOPER: A surgical risk.
MAE: —Uh-huh. . . .

Big Mama draws a breath like a dying gasp.

REVEREND TOOKER: Tch, tch, tch, tch, tch!
DOCTOR BAUGH: Yes, it's gone past the knife.
MAE: *That's why he's turned yellow, Mommy!*
BIG MAMA: *Git away from me, git away from me, Mae!*

She rises abruptly.

I want Brick! Where's Brick? Where is my only son?
MAE: Mama! Did she say "*only son*"?
GOOPER: What does that make *me?*
MAE: A sober responsible man with five precious children!—*Six!*
BIG MAMA: I want Brick to tell me! Brick! Brick!
MARGARET *rising from her reflections in a corner:*   Brick was so upset he went back out.
BIG MAMA: *Brick!*
MARGARET: Mama, let *me* tell you!
BIG MAMA: No, no, leave me alone, you're not my blood!
GOOPER: *Mama, I'm your son! Listen to me!*
MAE: Gooper's your son, Mama, he's your first-born!
BIG MAMA: Gooper never liked Daddy.
MAE *as if terribly shocked:*   *That's not TRUE!*

There is a pause. The minister coughs and rises.

REVEREND TOOKER *to Mae:*   I think I'd better slip away at this point.
MAE *sweetly and sadly:*   Yes, Reverend Tooker, you go.
REVEREND TOOKER *discreetly:*   Goodnight, goodnight, everybody, and God bless you all . . . on this place. . . .

He slips out.

DOCTOR BAUGH: That man is a good man but lacking in tact. Talking about people giving memorial windows—if he mentioned one memorial window, he must have spoke of a dozen, and saying how awful it was when somebody died intestate, the legal wrangles, and so forth.

MAE *coughs, and points at* BIG MAMA.

DOCTOR BAUGH: Well, Big Mama. . . .

He sighs.

BIG MAMA: It's all a mistake, I know it's just a bad dream.
DOCTOR BAUGH: We're gonna keep Big Daddy as comfortable as we can.
BIG MAMA: Yes, it's just a bad dream, that's all it is, it's just an awful dream.
GOOPER: In my opinion Big Daddy is having some pain but won't admit that he has it.
BIG MAMA: Just a dream, a bad dream.
DOCTOR BAUGH: That's what lots of them do, they think if they don't admit they're having the pain they can sort of escape the fact of it.
GOOPER *with relish:*   Yes, they get sly about it, they get real sly about it.
MAE: Gooper and I think—
GOOPER: Shut up, Mae!—Big Daddy ought to be started on morphine.
BIG MAMA: Nobody's going to give Big Daddy morphine.
DOCTOR BAUGH: Now, Big Mama, when that pain strikes it's going to strike mighty hard and Big Daddy's going to need the needle to bear it.
BIG MAMA: I tell you, nobody's going to give him morphine.
MAE: Big Mama, you don't want to see Big Daddy suffer, you know you—

GOOPER *standing beside her gives her a savage poke.*

DOCTOR BAUGH *placing a package on the table:*   I'm leaving this stuff here, so if there's a sudden attack you all won't have to send out for it.
MAE: I know how to give a hypo.
GOOPER: Mae took a course in nursing during the war.
MARGARET: Somehow I don't think Big Daddy would want Mae to give him a hypo.
MAE: You think he'd want *you* to do it?

DR. BAUGH *rises.*

GOOPER: Doctor Baugh is goin'.
DOCTOR BAUGH: Yes, I got to be goin'. Well, keep your chin up, Big Mama.

GOOPER *with jocularity:*   She's gonna keep *both* chins up, aren't you Big Mama?

BIG MAMA *sobs.*

Now stop that, Big Mama.

MAE: Sit down with me, Big Mama.

GOOPER *at door with* DR. BAUGH: Well, Doc, we sure do appreciate all you done. I'm telling you, we're surely obligated to you for—

DR. BAUGH *has gone out without a glance at him.*

GOOPER: —I guess that doctor has got a lot on his mind but it wouldn't hurt him to act a little more human. . . .

BIG MAMA *sobs.*

Now be a brave girl, Mommy.

BIG MAMA: It's not true, I know that it's just not true!

GOOPER: Mama, those tests are infallible!

BIG MAMA: Why are you so determined to see your father daid?

MAE: Big Mama!

MARGARET *gently:*   I know what Big Mama means.

MAE *fiercely:*   Oh, do you?

MARGARET *quietly and very sadly:*   Yes, I think I do.

MAE: For a newcomer in the family you sure do show a lot of understanding.

MARGARET: Understanding is needed on this place.

MAE: I guess you must have needed a lot of it in your family, Maggie, with your father's liquor problem and now you've got Brick with his!

MARGARET: Brick does not have a liquor problem at all. Brick is devoted to Big Daddy. This thing is a terrible strain on him.

BIG MAMA: Brick is Big Daddy's boy, but he drinks too much and it worries me and Big Daddy, and, Margaret, you've got to cooperate with us, you've got to cooperate with Big Daddy and me in getting Brick straightened out. Because it will break Big Daddy's heart if Brick don't pull himself together and take hold of things.

MAE: Take hold of *what* things, Big Mama?

BIG MAMA: The place.

There is a quick violent look between MAE *and* GOOPER.

GOOPER: Big, Mama, you've had a shock.

MAE: Yais, we've all had a shock, but . . .

GOOPER: Let's be realistic—

MAE: —Big Daddy would never, would *never*, be foolish enough to—

GOOPER: —put this place in irresponsible hands!

BIG MAMA: Big Daddy ain't going to leave the place in anybody's hands;

Big Daddy is *not* going to die. I want you to get that in your heads, all of you!

MAE: Mommy, Mommy, Big Mama, we're just as hopeful an' optimistic as you are about Big Daddy's prospects, we have faith in *prayer*—but nevertheless there are certain matters that have to be discussed an' dealt with, because otherwise—

GOOPER: Eventualities have to be considered and now's the time. . . . Mae, will you please get my briefcase out of our room?

MAE: Yes, honey.

She rises and goes out through the hall door.

GOOPER *standing over* BIG MAMA: Now Big Mom. What you said just now was not at all true and you know it. I've always loved Big Daddy in my own quiet way. I never made a show of it, and I know that Big Daddy has always been fond of me in a quiet way, too, and he never made a show of it neither.

MAE *returns with* GOOPER'S *briefcase.*

MAE: Here's your briefcase, Gooper, honey.

GOOPER *handing the briefcase back to her:*   Thank you. . . . Of ca'use, my relationship with Big Daddy is different from Brick's.

MAE: You're eight years older'n Brick an' always had t'carry a bigger load of th' responsibilities than Brick ever had t'carry. He never carried a thing in his life but a football or a highball.

GOOPER: Mae, will y' let me talk, please?

MAE: Yes, honey.

GOOPER: Now, a twenty-eight thousand acre plantation's a mighty big thing t'run.

MAE: Almost singlehanded.

MARGARET *has gone out onto the gallery, and can be heard calling softly to* BRICK.

BIG MAMA: You never had to run this place! What are you talking about? As if Big Daddy was dead and in his grave, you had to run it? Why, you just helped him out with a few business details and had your law practice at the same time in Memphis!

MAE: Oh, Mommy, Mommy, Big Mommy! Let's be fair! Why, Gooper has given himself body and soul to keeping this place up for the past five years since Big Daddy's health started failing. Gooper won't say it, Gooper never thought of it as a duty, he just did it. And what did Brick do? Brick kept living in his past glory at college! Still a football player at twenty-seven!

MARGARET *returning alone:*   Who are you talking about, now? Brick? A football player? He isn't a football player and you know it. Brick is a sport's announcer on TV and one of the best-known ones in the country!

MAE: I'm talking about what he was.

MARGARET: Well, I wish you would just stop talking about my husband.

GOOPER: I've got a right to discuss my brother with other members of MY OWN family which don't include *you*. Why don't you go out there and drink with Brick?

MARGARET: I've never seen such malice toward a brother.

GOOPER: How about his for me? Why, he can't stand to be in the same room with me!

MARGARET: This is a deliberate campaign of vilification for the most disgusting and sordid reason on earth, and I know what it is! It's *avarice, avarice, greed, greed!*

BIG MAMA: *Oh, I'll scream! I will scream in a moment unless this stops!*

GOOPER *has stalked up to* MARGARET *with clenched fists at his sides as if he would strike her.* MAE *distorts her face again into a hideous grimace behind* MARGARET'S *back.*

MARGARET: We only remain on the place because of Big Mom and Big Daddy. If it is true what they say about Big Daddy we are going to leave here just as soon as it's over. Not a moment later.

BIG MAMA *sobs:* Margaret. Child. Come here. Sit next to Big Mama.

MARGARET: Precious Mommy. I'm sorry, I'm so sorry, I—!

She bends her long graceful neck to press her forehead to BIG MAMA'S *bulging shoulder under its black chiffon.*

GOOPER: How beautiful, how touching, this display of devotion!

MAE: Do you know why she's childless? She's childless because that big beautiful athlete husband of hers won't go to bed with her!

GOOPER: You jest won't let me do this in a nice way, will yah? Aw right— Mae and I have five kids with another one coming! I don't give a goddam if Big Daddy likes me or don't like me or did or never did or will or will never! I'm just appealing to a sense of common decency and fair play. I'll tell you the truth. I've resented Big Daddy's partiality to Brick ever since Brick was born, and the way I've been treated like I was just barely good enough to spit on and sometimes not even good enough for that. Big Daddy is dying of cancer, and it's spread all through him and it's attacked all his vital organs incuding the kidneys and right now he is sinking into uremia, and you all know what uremia is, it's poisoning of the whole system due to the failure of the body to eliminate its poisons.

MARGARET *to herself, downstage, hissingly: Poisons, poisons! Venomous thoughts and words! In hearts and minds!—That's poisons!*

GOOPER *overlapping her:* I am asking for a square deal, and I expect to get one. But if I don't get one, if there's any peculiar shenanigans going on around here behind my back, or before me, well, I'm not a corporation lawyer for nothing, I know how to protect my own interests.—*OH! A late arrival!*

BRICK *enters from the gallery with a tranquil, blurred smile, carrying an empty glass with him.*

MAE: Behold the conquering hero comes!

GOOPER: The fabulous Brick Pollitt! Remember him?—Who could forget him!

MAE: He looks like he's been injured in a game!

GOOPER: Yep, I'm afraid you'll have to warm the bench at the Sugar Bowl this year, Brick!

MAE *laughs shrilly.*

Or was it the Rose Bowl that he made that famous run in?

MAE: The punch bowl, honey. It was in the punch bowl, the cut-glass punch bowl!

GOOPER: Oh, that's right, I'm getting the bowls mixed up!

MARGARET: Why don't you stop venting your malice and envy on a sick boy?

BIG MAMA: *Now you two hush, I mean it, hush, all of you, hush!*

GOOPER: All right, Big Mama. A family crisis brings out the best and the worst in every member of it.

MAE: *That's* the truth.

MARGARET: *Amen!*

BIG MAMA: *I said, hush!* I won't tolerate any more catty talk in my house.

MAE *gives* GOOPER *a sign indicating briefcase.*

BRICK'S *smile has grown both brighter and vaguer. As he prepares a drink, he sings softly:*

BRICK: *Show me the way to go home,*
  I'm tired and I wanta go to bed,
  I had a little drink about an hour ago—

GOOPER *at the same time:* Big Mama, you know it's necessary for me t'go back to Memphis in th' mornin' t'represent the Parker estate in a lawsuit.

MAE *sits on the bed and arranges papers she has taken from the briefcase.*

BRICK *continuing the song:* *Wherever I may roam,*
  On land or sea or foam.

BIG MAMA: Is it, Gooper?

MAE: Yaiss.

GOOPER: That's why I'm forced to—to bring up a problem that—

MAE: Somethin' that's too important t' be put off!

GOOPER: If Brick was sober, he ought to be in on this.

MARGARET: Brick is present; we're here.

GOOPER: Well, good. I will now give you this outline my partner, Tom Bullitt, an' me have drawn up—a sort of dummy—trusteeship.

MARGARET: Oh, that's it! You'll be in charge an' dole out remittances, will you?

GOOPER: This we did as soon as we got the report on Big Daddy from th' Ochsner Laboratories. We did this thing, I mean we drew up this dummy outline with the advice and assistance of the Chairman of the Boa'd of Directors of th' Southern Plantahs Bank and Trust Company in Memphis, C. C. Bellowes, a man who handles estates for all th' prominent fam'lies in West Tennessee and th' Delta.

BIG MAMA: Gooper?

GOOPER *crouching in front of* BIG MAMA: Now this is not—not final, or anything like it. This is just a preliminary outline. But it does provide a basis—a design—a—possible, feasible—*plan!*

MARGARET: Yes, I'll bet.

MAE: It's a plan to protect the biggest estate in the Delta from irresponsibility an'—

BIG MAMA: Now you listen to me, all of you, you listen here! They's not goin' to be any more catty talk in my house! And Gooper, you put that away before I grab it out of your hand and tear it right up! I don't know what the hell's in it, and I don't want to know what the hell's in it. I'm talkin' in Big Daddy's language now; I'm his *wife*, not his *widow*, I'm still his *wife!* And I'm talkin' to you in his language an'—

GOOPER: Big Mama, what I have here is—

MAE: Gooper explained that it's just a plan. . . .

BIG MAMA: I don't care what you got there. Just put it back where it came from, an' don't let me see it again, not even the outside of the envelope of it! Is that understood? Basis! Plan! Preliminary! Design! I say—what is it Big Daddy always says when he's disgusted?

BRICK *from the bar:*   Big Daddy says "crap" when he's disgusted.

BIG MAMA *rising:*   That's right—*CRAP!* I say *CRAP* too, like Big Daddy!

MAE: Coarse language doesn't seem called for in this—

GOOPER: Somethin' in me is *deeply outraged* by hearin' you talk like this.

BIG MAMA: *Nobody's goin' to take nothin'!*—till Big Daddy lets go of it, and maybe, just possibly, not—not even then! No, not even then!

BRICK: *You can always hear me singin' this song,*
Show me the way to go home.

BIG MAMA: Tonight Brick looks like he used to look when he was a little boy, just like he did when he played wild games and used to come home all sweaty and pink-cheeked and sleepy, with his—red curls shining. . . .

She comes over to him and runs her fat shaky hand through his hair. He draws aside as he does from all physical contact and continues the song in a whisper, opening the ice bucket and dropping in the ice cubes one by one as if he were mixing some important chemical formula.

BIG MAMA *continuing:*   Time goes by so fast. Nothin' can outrun it. Death commences too early—almost before you're half acquainted with life—you meet with the other. . . .

Oh, you know we just got to love each other an' stay together, all of us, just as close as we can, especially now that such a *black* thing has come and moved into this place without invitation.

Awkwardly embracing BRICK, *she presses her head to his shoulder.*

GOOPER *has been returning papers to* MAE *who has restored them to briefcase with an air of severely tried patience.*

GOOPER: Big Mama? Big Mama?

He stands behind her, tense with sibling envy.

BIG MAMA *oblivious of* GOOPER: Brick, you hear me, don't you?
MARGARET: Brick hears you, Big Mama, he understands what you're saying.
BIG MAMA: Oh, Brick, son of Big Daddy! Big Daddy does so love you! Y'know what would be his fondest dream come true? If before he passed on, if Big Daddy has to pass on, you gave him a child of yours, a grandson as much like his son as his son is like Big Daddy!
MAE *zipping briefcase shut; an incongruous sound:*   Such a pity that Maggie an' Brick can't oblige!
MARGARET *suddenly and quietly but forcefully:*   Everybody listen.

She crosses to the center of the room, holding her hands rigidly together.

MAE: Listen to what, Maggie?
MARGARET: I have an announcement to make.
GOOPER: A sports announcement, Maggie?
MARGARET: Brick and I are going to—*have a child!*

BIG MAMA *catches her breath in a loud gasp.*

Pause. BIG MAMA *rises.*

BIG MAMA: Maggie! Brick! This is too good to believe!
MAE: That's right, too good to believe.
BIG MAMA: Oh, my, my! This is Big Daddy's dream, his dream come true! I'm going to tell him right now before he—
MARGARET: We'll tell him in the morning. Don't disturb him now.
BIG MAMA: I want to tell him before he goes to sleep, I'm going to tell him his dream's come true this minute! And Brick! A child will make you pull yourself together and quit this drinking!

She seizes the glass from his hand.

The responsibilities of a father will—

Her face contorts and she makes an excited gesture; bursting into sobs, she rushes out, crying.

I'm going to tell Big Daddy right this minute!

Her voice fades out down the hall.

BRICK *shrugs slightly and drops an ice cube into another glass.* MARGARET *crosses quickly to his side, saying something under her breath, and she pours the liquor for him, staring up almost fiercely into his face.*

BRICK *cooly:*   Thank you, Maggie, that's a nice big shot.

MAE *has joined* GOOPER *and she gives him a fierce poke, making a low hissing sound and a grimace of fury.*

GOOPER *pushing her aside:*   Brick, could you possibly spare me one small shot of that liquor?
BRICK: Why, help yourself, Gooper boy.
GOOPER: I will.
MAE *shrilly:*   Of course we know that this is—
GOOPER: *Be still, Mae!*
MAE: I won't be still! I know she's made this up!
GOOPER: God damn it, I said to shut up!
MARGARET: Gracious! I didn't know that my little announcement was going to provoke such a storm!
MAE: *That* woman isn't *pregnant!*
GOOPER: Who said she was?
MAE: *She* did.
GOOPER: The doctor didn't. Doc Baugh didn't.
MARGARET: I haven't gone to Doc Baugh.
GOOPER: Then who'd you go to, Maggie?
MARGARET: One of the best gynecologists in the South.
GOOPER: Uh huh, uh huh!—I see. . . .

He takes out pencil and notebook.

—May we have his name, please?
MARGARET: No, you may not, Mister Prosecuting Attorney!
MAE: He doesn't have any name, he doesn't exist!
MARGARET: Oh, he exists all right, and so does my child, Brick's baby!
MAE: You can't conceive a child by a man that won't sleep with you unless you think you're—

BRICK *has turned on the phonograph. A scat song cuts* MAE'S *speech.*

GOOPER: *Turn that off!*
MAE: We know it's a lie because we hear you in here; he won't sleep with you, we hear you! So don't imagine you're going to put a trick over on us, to fool a dying man with a—

A long drawn cry of agony and rage fills the house. MARGARET *turns phonograph down to a whisper.*

The cry is repeated.

MAE *awed:*   Did you hear that, Gooper, did you hear that?
GOOPER: Sounds like the pain has struck.
MAE: Go see, Gooper!
GOOPER: Come along and leave these lovebirds together in their nest!

He goes out first. MAE *follows but turns at the door, contorting her face and hissing at* MARGARET.

MAE: *Liar!*

She slams the door.

MARGARET *exhales with relief and moves a little unsteadily to catch hold of* BRICK'S *arm.*

MARGARET: Thank you for—keeping still . . .
BRICK: OK, Maggie.
MARGARET: It was gallant of you to save my face!
BRICK: —It hasn't happened yet.
MARGARET: What?
BRICK: The click. . . .
MARGARET: —The click in your head that makes you peaceful, honey?
BRICK: Uh-huh. It hasn't happened. . . . I've got to make it happen before I can sleep. . . .
MARGARET: —I—know what you—mean. . . .
BRICK: Give me that pillow in the big chair, Maggie.
MARGARET: I'll put it on the bed for you.
BRICK: No, put it on the sofa, where I sleep.
MARGARET: Not tonight, Brick.
BRICK: I want it on the sofa. That's where I sleep.

He has hobbled to the liquor cabinet. He now pours down three shots in quick succession and stands waiting, silent. All at once he turns with a smile and says:

   There!
MARGARET: What?
BRICK: The *click.* . . .

His gratitude seems almost infinite as he hobbles out on the gallery with a drink. We hear his crutch as he swings out of sight. Then, at some distance, he begins singing to himself a peaceful song.

MARGARET *holds the big pillow forlornly as if it were her only companion, for a few moments, then throws it on the bed. She rushes to the liquor cabinet, gathers all the bottles in her arms, turns about undecidedly, then runs out of the room with them, leaving the door ajar on the dim yellow hall.* BRICK *is heard hobbling back along the gallery, singing his peaceful song. He comes back in, sees the pillow on the bed, laughs lightly, sadly, picks it up. He has it under his arm as* MARGARET *returns to the room.* MARGARET *softly shuts the door and leans against it, smiling softly at* BRICK.

MARGARET: Brick, I used to think that you were stronger than me and I didn't want to be overpowered by you. But now, since you've taken to liquor—you know what?—I guess it's bad, but now I'm stronger than you and I can love you more truly!

Don't move that pillow. I'll move it right back if you do!

—Brick?

She turns out all the lamps but a single rose-silk-shaded one by the bed.

I really have been to a doctor and I know what to do and—Brick?—this is my time by the calendar to conceive!
BRICK: Yes, I understand, Maggie. But how are you going to conceive a child by a man in love with his liquor?
MARGARET: By locking his liquor up and making him satisfy my desire before I unlock it!
BRICK: Is that what you've done, Maggie?
MARGARET: Look and see. That cabinet's mighty empty compared to before!
BRICK: Well, I'll be a son of a—

He reaches for his crutch but she beats him to it and rushes out on the gallery, hurls the crutch over the rail and comes back in, panting.

There are running footsteps. BIG MAMA *bursts into the room, her face all awry, gasping, stammering.*

BIG MAMA: Oh, my God, oh, my God, oh, my God, where is it?
MARGARET: Is this what you want, Big Mama?

MARGARET *hands her the package left by the doctor.*

BIG MAMA: I can't bear it, oh, God! Oh, Brick! Brick, baby!

She rushes at him. He averts his face from her sobbing kisses. MARGARET *watches with a tight smile.*

My son, Big Daddy's boy! Little Father!

The groaning cry is heard again. She runs out, sobbing.

MARGARET: And so tonight we're going to make the lie true, and when that's done, I'll bring the liquor back here and we'll get drunk together, here, tonight, in this place that death has come into. . . .

—What do you say?

BRICK: I don't say anything. I guess there's nothing to say.

MARGARET: Oh, you weak people, you weak, beautiful people!—who give up.—What you want is someone to—

She turns out the rose-silk lamp.

—take hold of you.—Gently, gently, with love! And—

The curtain begins to fall slowly.

I *do* love you, Brick, I *do!*

BRICK *smiling with charming sadness:* Wouldn't it be funny if that was true?

The Curtain Comes Down

The End

Critical Touchstones

ARISTOTLE (384–322 B.C.)

from The Poetics

Born at Stagira in northern Greece, Aristotle at the age of seventeen was sent to study with Plato in Athens. His *Poetics* (*c.* 336 B.C.), from which the following selections are taken, is in effect the earliest surviving work of sustained literary criticism in the western world. Aristotle's description of the nature and effects of tragic drama have proven to be astonishingly durable and suggestive. Here he argues the primary importance to tragedy of a unified plot that arouses pity and fear in the audience. The best plots will be those which involve *peripety* (or reversal of fortune) and *discovery* (anagnorisis, a change from ignorance to knowledge). A third important element of plot is suffering, or, harmful and destructive action. Aristotle ends by considering the kinds of plots most likely to arouse pity and fear.

8. The Unity of a Plot does not consist, as some suppose, in its having one man as its subject. An infinity of things befall that one man, some of which it is impossible to reduce to unity; and in like manner there are many actions of one man which cannot be made to form one action. One sees, therefore, the mistake of all the poets who have written a *Heracleid*, a *Theseid*, or similar poems; they suppose that, because Heracles was one man, the story also of Heracles must be one story. Homer, however, evidently understood this point quite well, whether by art or instinct, just in the same way as he excels the rest in every other respect. In writing an *Odyssey*, he did not make the poem cover all that ever befell his hero—it befell him, for instance, to get wounded on Parnassus and also to feign madness at the time of the call to arms, but the two incidents had no necessary or probable connexion with one another—instead of doing that, he took as the subject of the *Odyssey*, as also of the *Iliad*, an action with a Unity of the kind we are describing. The truth is that, just as in the other imitative arts one imitation is always of one thing, so in poetry the story, as an imitation of action, must represent one action, a complete whole, with its several incidents so closely connected that the transposal or withdrawal of any one of them will disjoin and dislocate the whole. For that which makes no perceptible difference by its presence or absence is no real part of the whole.

9. From what we have said it will be seen that the poet's function is to describe, not the thing that has happened, but a kind of thing that might happen, i.e. what is possible as being probable or necessary. The distinction between historian and poet is not in the one writing prose and the other verse—you might put the work of Herodotus into verse, and it would still be a species of history; it consists really in this, that the one describes the thing that has been, and the other a kind of thing that might be. Hence poetry is something more philosophic and of graver import than history,

since its statements are of the nature rather of universals, whereas those of history are singulars. By a universal statement I mean one as to what such or such a kind of man will probably or necessarily say or do—which is the aim of poetry, though it affixes proper names to the characters; by a singular statement, one as to what, say, Alcibiades did or had done to him. In Comedy this has become clear by this time; it is only when their plot is already made up of probable incidents that they give it a basis of proper names, choosing for the purpose any names that may occur to them, instead of writing like the old iambic poets about particular persons. In Tragedy, however, they still adhere to the historic names; and for this reason: what convinces is the possible; now whereas we are not yet sure as to the possibility of that which has not happened, that which has happened is manifestly possible, else it would not have come to pass. Nevertheless even in Tragedy there are some plays with but one or two known names in them, the rest being inventions; and there are some without a single known name, e.g., Agathon's *Antheus*, in which both incidents and names are of the poet's invention; and it is no less delightful on that account. So that one must not aim at a rigid adherence to the traditional stories on which tragedies are based. It would be absurd, in fact, to do so, as even the known stories are only known to a few, though they are a delight none the less to all.

It is evident from the above that the poet must be more the poet of his stories or Plots than of his verses, inasmuch as he is a poet by virtue of the imitative element in his work, and it is actions that he imitates. And if he should come to take a subject from actual history, he is none the less a poet for that; since some historic occurrences may very well be in the probable and possible order of things; and it is in that aspect of them that he is their poet.

Of simple Plots and actions the episodic are the worst. I call a Plot episodic when there is neither probability nor necessity in the sequence of its episodes. Actions of this sort bad poets construct through their own fault, and good ones on account of the players. His work being for public performance, a good poet often stretches out a Plot beyond its capabilities, and is thus obliged to twist the sequence of incident.

Tragedy, however, is an imitation not only of a complete action, but also of incidents arousing pity and fear. Such incidents have the very greatest effect on the mind when they occur unexpectedly and at the same time in consequence of one another; there is more of the marvellous in them then than if they happened of themselves or by mere chance. Even matters of chance seem most marvellous if there is an appearance of design as it were in them; as for instance the statue of Mitys at Argos killed the author of Mitys' death by falling down on him when a looker-on at a public spectacle; for incidents like that we think to be not without a meaning. A Plot therefore, of this sort is necessarily finer than others.

10. Plots are either simple or complex, since the actions they represent are naturally of this twofold description. The action, proceeding in the way defined, as one continuous whole, I call simple, when the change in the hero's fortunes takes place without Peripety or Discovery; and complex, when it involves one or the other, or both. These should each of them arise out of the structure of the Plot itself, so as to be the consequence, necessary or probable, of the antecedents. There is a great difference between a thing happening *propter hoc* and *post hoc*.

11. A Peripety is the change of the kind described from one state of things within the play to its opposite, and that too in the way we are saying, in the probable or necessary sequence of events; as it is for instance in *Oedipus*: here the opposite state of things is produced by the Messenger, who, coming to gladden Oedipus and to remove his fears as to his mother, reveals the secret of his birth. And in *Lynceus*: just as he is being led off for execution, with Danaus at his side to put him to death, the incidents preceding this bring it about that he is saved and Danaus put to death. A Discovery is, as the very word implies, a change from ignorance to knowledge, and thus to either love or hate, in the personages marked for good or evil fortune. The finest form of Discovery is one attended by Peripeties, like that which goes with the Discovery in *Oedipus*. There are no doubt other forms of it; what we have said may happen in a way in reference to inanimate things, even things of a very casual kind; and it is also possible to discover whether some one has done or not done something. But the form most directly connected with the Plot and the action of the piece is the first-mentioned. This, with a Peripety, will arouse either pity or fear—actions of that nature being what Tragedy is assumed to represent; and it will also serve to bring about the happy or unhappy ending. The Discovery, then, being of persons, it may be that of one party only to the other, the latter being already known; or both the parties may have to discover themselves. Iphigenia, for instance, was discovered to Orestes by sending the letter; and another Discovery was required to reveal him to Iphigenia.

Two parts of the Plot, then, Peripety and Discovery, are on matters of this sort. A third part is Suffering; which we may define as an action of a destructive or painful nature, such as murders on the stage, tortures, woundings, and the like. The other two have been already explained.

14. The tragic fear and pity may be aroused by the Spectacle; but they may also be aroused by the very structure and incidents of the play—which is the better way and shows the better poet. The Plot in fact should be so framed that, even without seeing the things take place, he who simply hears the account of them shall be filled with horror and pity at the incidents; which is just the effect that the mere recital of the story in *Oedipus* would have on one. To produce this same effect by means of the Spectacle is less

artistic, and requires extraneous aid. Those, however, who make use of the Spectacle to put before us that which is merely monstrous and not productive of fear, are wholly out of touch with Tragedy; not every kind of pleasure should be required of a tragedy, but only its own proper pleasure.

The tragic pleasure is that of pity and fear, and the poet has to produce it by a work of imitation; it is clear, therefore, that the causes should be included in the incidents of his story. Let us see, then, what kinds of incident strike one as horrible, or rather as piteous. In a deed of this description the parties must necessarily be either friends, or enemies, or indifferent to one another. Now when enemy does it on enemy, there is nothing to move us to pity either in his doing or in his meditating the deed, except so far as the actual pain of the sufferer is concerned; and the same is true when the parties are indifferent to one another. Whenever the tragic deed, however, is done within the family—when murder or the like is done or meditated by brother on brother, by son on father, by mother on son, or son on mother—these are the situations the poet should seek after. The traditional stories, accordingly, must be kept as they are, e.g., the murder of Clytaemnestra by Orestes and of Eriphyle by Alcmeon. At the same time even with these there is something left to the poet himself; it is for him to devise the right way of treating them. Let us explain more clearly what we mean by 'the right way'. The deed of horror may be done by the doer knowingly and consciously, as in the old poets, and in Medea's murder of her children in Euripides. Or he may do it, but in ignorance of his relationship, and discover that afterwards, as does the Oedipus in Sophocles. Here the deed is outside the play; but it may be within it, like the act of the Alcmeon in Astydamas, or that of the Telegonus in *Ulysses Wounded*. A third possibility is for one meditating some deadly injury to another, in ignorance of his relationship, to make the discovery in time to draw back. These exhaust the possibilities, since the deed must necessarily be either done or not done, and either knowingly or unknowingly.

The worst situation is when the personage is with full knowledge on the point of doing the deed, and leaves it undone. It is odious and also (through the absence of suffering) untragic; hence it is that no one is made to act thus except in some few instances, e.g., Haemon and Creon in *Antigone*. Next after this comes the actual perpetration of the deed meditated. A better situation than that, however, is for the deed to be done in ignorance, and the relationship discovered afterwards, since there is nothing odious in it, and the Discovery will serve to astound us. But the best of all is the last; what we have in *Cresphontes*, for example, where Merope, on the point of slaying her son, recognizes him in time; in *Iphigenia*, where sister and brother are in a like position; and in *Helle*, where the son recognizes his mother, when on the point of giving her up to her enemy.

This will explain why our tragedies are restricted (as we said just now) to such a small number of families. It was accident rather than art that led the poets in quest of subjects to embody this kind of incident in their Plots.

They are still obliged, accordingly, to have recourse to the families in which such horrors have occurred.

On the construction of the Plot, and the kind of Plot required for Tragedy, enough has now been said.

FRIEDRICH NIETZSCHE (1844–1900)

from The Birth of Tragedy

Friedrich Nietzsche was born in Rocken, Germany, and studied classical philology at the Universities of Bonn and Leipzig. He is known principally for his lyrical and unsystematic philosophical works such as *Beyond Good and Evil* (1886) and *Thus Spake Zarathustra* (1892). His work has had a profound influence on many modern writers and on the modern philosophy of existentialism. In the following excerpt from his first book, *The Birth of Tragedy* (1872), Nietzsche advances the theory that Greek tragedy arose from the worship of the suffering but joyous Dionysus, god of the grape and of the vine, who died and was reborn each year. Nietzsche implies that tragedy, by allowing us to witness and participate in the ennobling pain of others, offers us a glimpse of the possibility that all humans may achieve unity with one another.

The tradition is undisputed that Greek tragedy in its earliest form had for its sole theme the sufferings of Dionysus and that for a long time the only stage hero was Dionysus himself. But it may be claimed with equal confidence that until Euripides, Dionysus never ceased to be the tragic hero; that all the celebrated figures of the Greek stage—Prometheus, Oedipus, etc.—are mere masks of this original hero, Dionysus. That behind all these masks there is a deity, that is one essential reason for the typical "ideality" of these famous figures which has caused so much astonishment. Somebody, I do not know who, has claimed that all individuals, taken as individuals, are comic and hence untragic—from which it would follow that the Greeks simply *could* not suffer individuals on the tragic stage. In fact, this is what they seem to have felt; and the Platonic distinction and evaluation of the "idea" and the "idol," the mere image, is very deeply rooted in the Hellenic character.

Using Plato's terms we should have to speak of the tragic figures of the Hellenic stage somewhat as follows: the one truly real Dionysus appears in a variety of forms, in the mask of a fighting hero, and entangled, as it were, in the net of the individual will. The god who appears talks and acts so as to resemble an erring, striving, suffering individual. That he *appears* at all with such epic precision and clarity is the work of the dream-interpreter, Apollo, who through this symbolic appearance interprets to the chorus its Dionysian state. In truth, however, the hero is the suffering Dionysus of the Mysteries, the god experiencing in himself the agonies of individuation, of whom wonderful myths tell that as a boy he was torn to pieces by the Titans and now is worshiped in this state as Zagreus. Thus it is intimated that this dismemberment, the properly Dionysian *suffering*, is like a transformation into air, water, earth, and fire, that we are therefore to regard the state of individuation as the origin and primal cause of all suffering, as something objectionable in itself. From the smile of this Dionysus sprang the Olympian gods, from his tears sprang man. In this existence as a dismembered god, Dionysus possesses the dual nature of a cruel, barbarized demon and a mild, gentle ruler. But the hope of the epopts[1] looked toward a rebirth of Dionysus, which we must now dimly conceive as the end of individuation. It was for this coming third Dionysus that the epopts' roaring hymns of joy resounded. And it is this hope alone that casts a gleam of joy upon the features of a world torn asunder and shattered into individuals; this is symbolized in the myth of Demeter, sunk in eternal sorrow, who *rejoices* again for the first time when told that she may *once more* give birth to Dionysus. This view of things already provides us with all the elements of a profound and pessimistic view of the world, together with the *mystery doctrine of tragedy:* the fundamental knowledge of the oneness of everything existent, the conception of individuation as the primal cause of evil, and of art as the joyous hope that the spell of individuation may be broken in augury of a restored oneness.

We have already suggested that the Homeric epos is the poem of Olympian culture, in which this culture has sung its own song of victory over the terrors of the war of the Titans. Under the predominating influence of tragic poetry, these Homeric myths are now born anew; and this metempsychosis reveals that in the meantime the Olympian culture also has been conquered by a still more profound view of the world. The defiant Titan Prometheus has announced to his Olympian tormentor that some day the greatest danger will menace his rule, unless Zeus should enter into an alliance with him in time. In Aeschylus we recognize how the terrified Zeus, fearful of his end, allies himself with the Titan. Thus the former age of the Titans is once more recovered from Tartarus and brought to the light.

The philosophy of wild and naked nature beholds with the frank, undissembling gaze of truth the myths of the Homeric world as they dance past: they turn pale, they tremble under the piercing glance of this goddess—till the powerful fist of the Dionysian artist forces them into the service of the new deity. Dionysian truth takes over the entire domain of myth as the symbolism of *its* knowledge which it makes known partly in the public cult of tragedy and partly in the secret celebrations of dramatic mysteries, but always in the old mythical garb.

What power was it that freed Prometheus from his vultures and transformed the myth into a vehicle of Dionysian wisdom? It is the Heracleian power of music: having reached its highest manifestation in tragedy, it can

---

1. Those initiated into the mysteries.

invest myths with a new and most profound significance. This we have already characterized as the most powerful function of music. For it is the fate of every myth to creep by degrees into the narrow limits of some alleged historical reality, and to be treated by some later generation as a unique fact with historical claims: and the Greeks were already fairly on the way toward restamping the whole of their mythical juvenile dream sagaciously and arbitrarily into a historico-pragmatical *juvenile history*. For this is the way in which religions are wont to die out: under the stern, intelligent eyes of an orthodox dogmatism, the mythical premises of a religion are systematized as a sum total of historical events; one begins apprehensively to defend the credibility of the myths, while at the same time one opposes any continuation of their natural vitality and growth; the feeling for myth perishes, and its place is taken by the claim of religion to historical foundations. This dying myth was now seized by the new-born genius of Dionysian music; and in these hands it flourished once more with colors such as it had never yet displayed, with a fragrance that awakened a longing anticipation of a metaphysical world. After this final effulgence it collapses, its leaves wither, and soon the mocking Lucians of antiquity catch at the discolored and faded flowers carried away by the four winds. Through tragedy the myth attains its most profound content, its most expressive form; it rises once more like a wounded hero, and its whole excess of strength, together with the philosophic calm of the dying, burns in its eyes with a last powerful gleam.

What did you want, sacrilegious Euripides, when you sought to compel this dying myth to serve you once more? It died under your violent hands—and then you needed a copied, masked myth that, like the ape of Heracles, merely knew how to deck itself out in the ancient pomp. And just as the myth died on you, the genius of music died on you, too. Though with greedy hands you plundered all the gardens of music, you still managed only copied, masked music. And because you had abandoned Dionysus, Apollo abandoned you: rouse all the passions from their resting places and conjure them into your circle, sharpen and whet a sophistical dialectic for the speeches of your heroes—your heroes, too, have only copied, masked passions and speak only copied, masked speeches.

GEORGE BERNARD SHAW (1856–1950)

"The Lesson of [Ibsen's] Plays"

In addition to being an astonishingly prolific playwright, Dublin-born George Bernard Shaw was an important critic of art, music, and drama. His major plays—which led to his receiving the Nobel Prize in 1925— include *Arms and the Man* (1894), *Major Barbara* (1905), *Pgymalion* (1912), and *Saint Joan* (1923). His study of Ibsen, *The Quintessence of Ibsenism*, was first published in 1891. In this excerpt, taken from the Second Edition of 1913, Shaw argues against easy pronouncements about the morality of Ibsen's plays. He notes Ibsen's sympathetic portrayal of idealists, but he also notes Ibsen's belief in the dangers of slavery to ideals of goodness. When reading Ibsen—and certainly when reading plays like *The Wild Duck* (page 1167)—we must resist hasty judgments about his often attractive, but often failing, idealists. We must read Ibsen, that is, with a quality that Shaw ascribes to him: a "vigorous open-mindedness" which pays attention to the spirit of the law no less than to its letter.

In following this sketch of the plays written by Ibsen to illustrate his thesis that the real slavery of today is slavery to ideals of goodness, it may be that readers who have conned Ibsen through idealist spectacles have wondered that I could so pervert the utterances of a great poet. Indeed I know already that many of those who are most fascinated by the poetry of the plays will plead for any explanation of them rather than that given by Ibsen himself in the plainest terms through the mouths of Mrs. Alving, Relling, and the rest. No great writer uses his skill to conceal his meaning. There is a tale by a famous Scotch storyteller which would have suited Ibsen exactly if he had hit on it first. Jeanie Deans sacrificing her sister's life on the scaffold to ideal truthfulness is far more horrible than the sacrifice in *Rosmersholm*; and the *deus ex machina* expedient by which Scott makes the end of his story agreeable is no solution of the ethical problem raised, but only a puerile evasion of it. He dared not, when it came to the point, allow Effie to be hanged for the sake of Jeanie's ideals.[1] Nevertheless, if I were to pretend that Scott wrote *The Heart of Midlothian* to shew that people are led to do as mischievous, as unnatural, as murderous things by their religious and moral ideals as by their envy and ambition, it would be

---

1. The common-sense solution of the ethical problem has often been delivered by acclamation in the theatre. Many years ago I witnessed a performance of a melodrama founded on this story. After the painful trial scene, in which Jeanie Deans condemns her sister to death by refusing to swear to a perfectly innocent fiction, came a scene in the prison. "If it had been me," said the jailor, "I wad ha sworn a hole through an iron pot." The roar of applause which burst from the pit and gallery was thoroughly Ibsenist in sentiment. The speech, by the way, must have been a gag of the actor's: at all events I cannot find it in the acting edition of the play.

easy to confute me from the pages of the book itself. And Ibsen, like Scott, has made his opinion plain. If any one attempts to maintain that *Ghosts* is a polemic in favor of indissoluble monogamic marriage, or that *The Wild Duck* was written to inculcate that truth should be told for its own sake, they must burn the text of the plays if their contention is to stand. The reason that Scott's story is tolerated by those who shrink from *Ghosts* is not that it is less terrible, but that Scott's views are familiar to all well-brought-up ladies and gentlemen, whereas Ibsen's are for the moment so strange to them as to be unthinkable. He is so great a poet that the idealist finds himself in the dilemma of being unable to conceive that such a genius should have an ignoble meaning, and yet equally unable to conceive his real meaning otherwise than as ignoble. Consequently he misses the meaning altogether in spite of Ibsen's explicit and circumstantial insistence on it, and proceeds to substitute a meaning congenial to his own ideal of nobility.

Ibsen's deep sympathy with his idealist figures seems to countenance this confusion. Since it is on the weaknesses of the higher types of character that idealism seizes, his most tragic examples of vanity, selfishness, folly, and failure are not vulgar villains, but men who in an ordinary novel or melodrama would be heroes. Brand and Rosmer, who drive those they love to death, do so with all the fine airs of the Sophoclean or Shakespearean good man persecuted by Destiny. Hilda Wangel, who kills the Master Builder literally to amuse herself, is the most fascinating of sympathetic girl-heroines. The ordinary Philistine commits no such atrocities: he marries the woman he likes and lives with her more or less happily ever after; but that is not because he is greater than Brand or Rosmer: he is less. The idealist is a more dangerous animal than the Philistine just as a man is a more dangerous animal than a sheep. Though Brand virtually murdered his wife, I can understand many a woman, comfortably married to an amiable Philistine, reading the play and envying the victim her husband. For when Brand's wife, having made the sacrifice he has exacted, tells him that he was right; that she is happy now; that she sees God face to face; and then reminds him that "whoso sees Jehovah dies," he instinctively clasps his hands over her eyes; and that action raises him at once far above the criticism that sneers at idealism from beneath, instead of surveying it from the clear ether above, which can only be reached through its mists.

If, in my account of the plays, I have myself suggested false judgments by describing the errors of the idealists in the terms of the life they have risen above rather than in those of the life they fall short of, I can only plead, with but moderate disrespect for the general reader, that if I had done otherwise I should have failed wholly to make my exposition intelligible. Indeed accurate terms for realist morality, though they are to be found in the Bible, are so out of fashion and forgotten that in this very distinction between idealism and realism, I am forced to insist on a sense of the words which, had not Ibsen forced my hand, I should perhaps have conveyed otherwise, to avoid the conflict of many of its applications with the vernacular use of the words.

This, however, was a trifle compared to the difficulty which arose from our inveterate habit of labelling men with the abstract names of their qualities without the slightest reference to the underlying will which sets these qualities in action. At an anniversary celebration of the Paris Commune of 1871, I was struck by the fact that no speaker could find a eulogy for the Federals which would not have been equally appropriate to the peasants of La Vendée who fought for their tyrants against the French revolutionists, or to the Irishmen and Highlanders who fought for the Stuarts at the Boyne or Culloden. The statements that the slain members of the Commune were heroes who died for a noble ideal would have left a stranger quite as much in the dark about them as the counter statements, once common enough in our newspapers, that they were incendiaries and assassins. Our obituary notices are examples of the same ambiguity. Of all the public men lately deceased when Ibsenism was first discussed in England, none was made more interesting by strongly marked personal characteristics than the famous atheist orator Charles Bradlaugh. He was not in the least like any other notable member of the House of Commons. Yet when the obituary notices appeared, with the usual string of qualities: eloquence, determination, integrity, strong common-sense, and so on, it would have been possible, by merely expunging all names and other external details from these notices, to leave the reader entirely unable to say whether the subject of them was Gladstone, Lord Morley, William Stead, or any one else no more like Bradlaugh than Garibaldi or the late Cardinal Newman, whose obituary certificates of morality might nevertheless have been reprinted almost verbatim for the occasion without any gross incongruity. Bradlaugh had been the subject of many sorts of newspaper notices in his time. Thirty years ago, when the middle classes supposed him to be a revolutionist, the string of qualities which the press hung upon him were all evil ones, great stress being laid on the fact that as he was an atheist it would be an insult to God to admit him to Parliament. When it became apparent that he was an anti-socialist force in politics, he, without any recantation of his atheism, at once had the string of evil qualities exchanged for a rosary of good ones; but it is hardly necessary to add that neither the old badge nor the new could ever give any inquirer the least clue to the sort of man he actually was: he might have been Oliver Cromwell or Wat Tyler or Jack Cade, Penn or Wilberforce or Wellington, the late Mr. Hampden of flat-earth-theory notoriety or Proudhon or the Archbishop of Canterbury, for all the distinction such labels could give him one way or the other. The worthlessness of these abstract descriptions is recognized in practice every day. Tax a stranger before a crowd with being a thief, a coward, and a liar; and the crowd will suspend its judgment until you answer the question, "What's he done?" Attempt to take up a collection for him on the ground that he is an upright, fearless, high-principled hero; and the same question must be answered before a penny goes into the hat.

The reader must therefore discount those partialities which I have permitted myself to express in telling the stories of the plays. They are as much beside the mark as any other example of the sort of criticism which seeks to create an impression favorable or otherwise to Ibsen by simply pasting his characters all over with good or bad conduct marks. If any person cares to describe Hedda Gabler as a modern Lucretia who preferred death to dishonor, and Thea Elvsted as an abandoned perjured strumpet who deserted the man she had sworn before her God to love, honor, and obey until her death, the play contains conclusive evidence establishing both points. If the critic goes on to argue that as Ibsen manifestly means to recommend Thea's conduct above Hedda's by making the end happier for her, the moral of the play is a vicious one, that, again, cannot be gainsaid. If, on the other hand, *Ghosts* be defended, as the dramatic critic of *Piccadilly* did defend it, because it throws into divine relief the beautiful figure of the simple and pious Pastor Manders, the fatal compliment cannot be parried. When you have called Mrs. Alving an emancipated woman or an unprincipled one, Alving a debauchee or a victim of society, Nora a fearless and noble-hearted woman or a shocking little liar and an unnatural mother, Helmer a selfish hound or a model husband and father, according to your bias, you have said something which is at once true and false, and in both cases perfectly idle.

The statement that Ibsen's plays have an immoral tendency, is, in the sense in which it is used, quite true. Immorality does not necessarily imply mischievous conduct: it implies conduct, mischievous or not, which does not conform to current ideals. All religions begin with a revolt against morality, and perish when morality conquers them and stamps out such words as grace and sin, substituting for them morality and immorality. Bunyan places the town of Morality, with its respectable leading citizens Mr. Legality and Mr. Civility, close to the City of Destruction. In the United States today he would be imprisoned for this. Born as I was in the seventeenth century atmosphere of mid-nineteenth century Ireland, I can remember when men who talked about morality were suspected of reading Tom Paine, if not of being downright atheists. Ibsen's attack on morality is a symptom of the revival of religion, not of its extinction. He is on the side of the prophets in having devoted himself to shewing that the spirit or will of Man is constantly outgrowing the ideals, and that therefore thoughtless conformity to them is constantly producing results no less tragic than those which follow thoughtless violation of them. Thus the main effect of his plays is to keep before the public the importance of being always prepared to act immorally. He reminds men that they ought to be as careful how they yield to a temptation to tell the truth as to a temptation to hold their tongues, and he urges upon women who either cannot or will not marry that the inducements held out to them by society to preserve their virginity and refrain from motherhood, may be called temptations as logically as the inducements to the contrary held out by individuals and by their own temperaments, the practical decision depending on circumstances just as much as a decision between walking and taking a cab, however less trivial both the action and the circumstances may be. He protests against the ordinary assumption that there are certain moral institutions which justify all means used to maintain them, and insists that the supreme end shall be the inspired, eternal, ever growing one, not the external unchanging, artificial one; not the letter but the spirit; not the contract but the object of the contract; not the abstract law but the living will. And because the will to change our habits and thus defy morality arises before the intellect can reason out any racially beneficent purpose in the change, there is always an interval during which the individual can say no more than that he wants to behave immorally because he likes, and because he will feel constrained and unhappy if he acts otherwise. For this reason it is enormously important that we should "mind our own business" and let other people do as they like unless we can prove some damage beyond the shock to our feelings and prejudices. It is easy to put revolutionary cases in which it is so impossible to draw the line that they will always be decided in practice more or less by physical force; but for all ordinary purposes of government and social conduct the distinction is a common-sense one. The plain working truth is that it is not only good for people to be shocked occasionally, but absolutely necessary to the progress of society that they should be shocked pretty often. But it is not good for people to be garrotted occasionally, or at all. That is why it is a mistake to treat an atheist as you treat a garrotter, or to put "bad taste" on the footing of theft and murder. The need for freedom of evolution is the sole basis of toleration, the sole valid argument against Inquisitions and Censorships, the sole reason for not burning heretics and sending every eccentric person to the madhouse.

In short, our ideals, like the gods of old, are constantly demanding human sacrifices. Let none of them, says Ibsen, be placed above the obligation to prove itself worth the sacrifices it demands; and let everyone religiously refuse to sacrifice himself and others from the moment he loses his faith in the validity of the ideal. Of course it will be said here by incorrigibly slipshod readers that this, far from being immoral, is the highest morality; but I really will not waste further definition on those who will neither mean one thing or another by a word nor allow me to do so. Suffice it that among those who are not ridden by current ideals no question as to the ethical soundness of Ibsen's plays will ever arise; and among those who are so ridden his plays will be denounced as immoral, and cannot be defended against the accusation.

There can be no question as to the effect likely to be produced on an individual by his conversion from the ordinary acceptance of current ideals as safe standards of conduct, to the vigilant openmindedness of Ibsen. It must at once greatly deepen the sense of moral responsibility. Before conversion the individual anticipates nothing worse in the way of examination at the judgment bar of his conscience than such questions as, Have you kept the commandments? Have you obeyed the law? Have you attended church regularly? paid your rates and taxes to Caesar? and contributed, in reason, to charitable institutions? It may be hard to do all these things; but it is still harder not to do them, as our ninety-nine moral cowards in the hundred well know. And even a scoundrel can do them all and yet live a worse life than the smuggler or prostitute who must answer No all through the catechism. Substitute for such a technical examination one in which the whole point to be settled is, Guilty or Not Guilty? one in which there is no more and no less respect for virginity than for incontinence, for subordination than for rebellion, for legality than for illegality, for piety than for blasphemy: in short, for the standard qualities than for the standard faults, and immediately, instead of lowering the ethical standard by relaxing the tests of worth, you raise it by increasing their stringency to a point at which no mere Pharisaism or moral cowardice can pass them.

Naturally this does not please the Pharisee. The respectable lady of the strictest Church principles, who has brought up her children with such relentless regard to their ideal morality that if they have any spirit left in them by the time they arrive at years of independence they use their liberty to rush deliriously to the devil: this unimpeachable woman has always felt it unjust that the respect she wins should be accompanied by deep-seated detestation, whilst the latest spiritual heiress of Nell Gwynne, whom no respectable person dare bow to in the street, is a popular idol. The reason is—though the idealist lady does not know it—that Nell Gwynne is a better woman than she; and the abolition of the idealist test which brings her out a worse one, and its replacement by the realist test which would shew the true relation between them, would be a most desirable step forward in public morals, especially as it would act impartially, and set the good side of the Pharisee above the bad side of the Bohemian as ruthlessly as it would set the good side of the Bohemian above the bad side of the Pharisee.[2] For as long as convention goes counter to reality in these matters, people will be led into Hedda Gabler's error of making an ideal of vice. If we maintain the convention that the distinction between Catherine of Russia and Queen Victoria, between Nell Gwynne and Mrs. Proudie, is the distinction between a bad woman and a good woman, we need not be surprised when those who sympathize with Catherine and Nell conclude that it is better to be a loose woman than a strict one, and go on recklessly to conceive a

2. The warning implied in this sentence is less needed now than it was twenty years ago. The association of Bohemianism with the artistic professions and with revolutionary political views has been weakened by the revolt of the children of the Bohemians against its domestic squalor and social outlawry. Bohemianism is now rather one of the stigmata of the highly conservative "smart sets" of the idle rich than of the studio, the stage, and the Socialist organizations. (1912)

prejudice against teetotalism and monogamy, and a prepossession in favour of alcoholic excitement and promiscuous amours. Ibsen himself is kinder to the man who has gone his own way as a rake and a drunkard than to the man who is respectable because he dare not be otherwise. We find that the franker and healthier a boy is, the more certain is he to prefer pirates and highwaymen, or Dumas musketeers, to "pillars of society" as his favorite heroes of romance. We have already seen both Ibsenites and anti-Ibsenites who seem to think that the cases of Nora and Mrs. Elvsted are meant to establish a golden rule for women who wish to be "emancipated": the said golden rule being simply, Run away from your husband. But in Ibsen's view of life, that would come under the same condemnation as the ecclesiastical rule, Cleave to your husband until death do you part. Most people know of a case or two in which it would be wise for a wife to follow the example of Nora or even of Mrs. Elvsted. But they must also know cases in which the results of such a course would be as tragic-comic as those of Gregers Werle's attempt in *The Wild Duck* to do for the Ekdal household what Lona Hessel did for the Bernick household. What Ibsen insists on is that there is no golden rule; that conduct must justify itself by its effect upon life and not by its conformity to any rule or ideal. And since life consists in the fulfilment of the will, which is constantly growing, and cannot be fulfilled today under the conditions which secured its fulfilment yesterday, he claims afresh the old Protestant right of private judgment in questions of conduct as against all institutions, the so-called Protestant Churches themselves included.

Here I must leave the matter, merely reminding those who may think that I have forgotten to reduce Ibsenism to a formula for them, that its quintessence is that there is no formula.

ERNEST JONES (1879–1958)

[*The Theme of Matricide in* Hamlet]

The British psychoanalyst Ernest Jones is best known for his three-volume biography *The Life and Work of Sigmund Freud* (1953–1957). In the following excerpt from his provocative study *Hamlet and Oedipus* (1949), Jones emphasizes the importance, to Hamlet, of his mother's adulterous relationship with his uncle Claudius. Jones suggests that this adultery, even more than Claudius's murder of Hamlet's father, is what Hamlet seeks to avenge. Whether or not we agree with the notion that Hamlet must restrain himself from killing his own mother, Jones's speculations remind us of Gertrude's centrality to *Hamlet* and of the importance of the psychological relationships among this unusual triangle.

Even after the Ghost informs him of the adultery and murder, both of which he had evidently suspected, it is still his mother's incest that dominates his emotions. Waldock, indeed, would regard Hamlet's hesitancy as throughout secondary to his preoccupation with the horror at it. As Dover Wilson puts it: "It is the 'couch for luxury and damned incest' far more than the murder that transforms his imagination into 'as foul as Vulcan's stithy,' " and Furnivall before him took the same view. Both the King and Queen have sinned against his beloved father, but without doubt Hamlet was more horrified at his mother's sinning even than at his uncle's.

It is not surprising, therefore, that some critics, e.g. Mauerhof, Wulffen, and others, have wondered whether Hamlet did not feel the need to save his mother from her sin as more important than avenging his father's murder. Henderson gives the theme a romantic form by contending that Shakespeare used as his model for his hero the ideal courtier as portrayed by Castiglione, and that Hamlet's knightly sense of honour made him regard the salvation of his mother as more important than the killing of the King. The most obvious way of putting an end to the incest, and at the same time avenging his father, was of course to kill Claudius, but, as we saw in the previous chapter, there were paralysing reasons that made this impossible. Even if these could be overcome what would be the Queen's situation? Dover Wilson considers that she would inevitably be disgraced, a proposition which is in itself very questionable, and that Hamlet could not face such an eventuality. The same objection holds here as with so many explanations: why ever did not Hamlet debate this difficulty in his soliloquies, and why did he keep repeating that he had no idea of what it was that hindered him from proceeding with his task?

There would seem to be this much truth in all those suggestions: that Hamlet's conception of his task differed somewhat from his father's. The latter was clear about the avenging of the murder (i.e. by killing Claudius), but was emphatic about sparing his wife and not punishing or in any way injuring her. Hamlet, on the other hand, was more concerned about putting an end to the incestuous relationship than about avenging the murder, though he never doubted it was his duty to do so. His difficulty was what to do about his mother, and he was by no means so inclined as his father to let her off lightly; in fact, he keeps reminding himself to be careful not to injure her, as if that was a dangerous propensity he had to keep in check. Dover Wilson has even suggested that the Ghost's reappearance in the bedroom scene is for the purpose of urging him to confine his attentions to his uncle and to spare his mother.

There remained only the horrible idea of destroying his mother. Gelber seems to hint at this when he speaks of Hamlet's choice being between the ruin of his mother or the ruin of himself, but it was an American psychiatrist, Frederic Wertham, who first ventured to propound the idea in its naked form. He has made a study of matricide, and has published a book describing the investigation of an actual case where the sight of his mother's lechery and betrayal of his greatly loved father led a youth to this desperate expedient. Wertham gives the name of Orestes complex to indicate a son's impulse to kill his mother. Interestingly enough, it is by no means the only occasion in which the story of Orestes has been brought into connection with that of Hamlet. Sixty years ago a French writer compared the two and concluded that "the story of Hamlet is in reality only that of Orestes under another name and in another land." Gilbert Murray devoted a detailed study to the comparison between the two. In spite of the many similarities, however, notably what Murray delicately calls the "shyness about the mother-murder" and the "shadow of madness" that affects the two heroes, he cannot find any historical connection between the two legends, so presumably they owe their resemblance to a common appeal to something in human nature. He writes: "In plays like 'Hamlet' or the 'Agamemnon' or the 'Electra' we have certainly fine and flexible character study, a varied and well-wrought story, a full command of the technical instruments of the poet and the dramatist, but we have also, I suspect, an undercurrent of desires and fears and passions, long slumbering yet eternally familiar, which have for thousands of years lain near the root of our most intimate emotions and have been wrought into the fabric of our most magical dreams." This insight, however, deserts him when he concludes that both of the stories are ultimately based on "that prehistoric and world-wide ritual battle of Summer and Winter, of Life and Death." Florence Anderson also discusses the same comparison, and asserts, "I am sure that Shakespeare knew much about Orestes when he recast the rude Amleth as the subtle, melancholy Hamlet." She differs from Gilbert Murray in thinking that there must have been a very old relationship between the two traditions.

With Hamlet, Wertham advanced the idea in a one-sided fashion as the sole explanation of Hamlet's dilemma. Actually matricidal impulses, which are familiar to psycho-pathologists, always prove to emanate from the Oedipus complex of which they are one facet, or—to change the metaphor—for which they are an attempted solution. The topic is akin to the question with which this chapter opened; does an outraged man slay the woman or the rival?

Let us now return to the play in the light of these considerations. The crucial situation is evidently the bedroom scene. Before this, however, in the bitter talk with Ophelia, Hamlet says: "I could accuse me of such things that it were better my mother had not borne me." What does this dark saying portend? It sounds more sinister even than killing a king. And there is a slight difference between "had I never been borne" and "had my mother not borne me." Need the mother be mentioned, and for whom would it have been better? This faint hint could not claim attention in itself, but much more follows. Even in the same scene he tells Ophelia that "those that are married already, all but one shall live." It is generally assumed that the "one" is Claudius, but at the moment his thoughts are only about women, at whom he is railing. To the King and Queen the idea in question is not foreign. Claudius warns his wife, "His liberty is full of threats to all, To you yourself," and in the bedroom scene the Queen exclaims in alarm, "What wilt thou do? Thou wilt not murder me?" The curious slip of the tongue, deliberate or otherwise, in which he addresses Claudius as "dear mother" shows how similar are his feelings about the two. He even explains this:

Father and Mother is man and wife,
Man and Wife is one flesh, and so my mother.

In psychoanalysis this idea, common in infancy, is known by the somewhat portentous title of the "combined parent concept." It dates from the phantasy of the parents in coitus, i.e., as one flesh.

On his way to his mother's bedroom Hamlet (Act III, Sc. 2, line 361) speaks the savage words:

Now could I drink hot blood,
And do such bitter business as the day
Would quake to look on: soft, now to my mother—
O heart, lose not thy nature, let not ever
The soul of Nero enter this firm bosom,
Let me be cruel not unnatural.
I will speak daggers to her, but use none.

In this connection Dover Wilson, as with the matter of Hamlet's incestuous proclivities, approaches very close to the dreadful thought, though in neither case does he quite reach it. He writes: "For whom is this itching dagger intended?" He is going to his mother. But surely he does not intend to murder her? He is no Nero. "These murderous impulses must be kept in leash." He is no Nero in action, certainly, but has he Nero's heart? Why the allusion at this critical point to Nero of all people, the man who is reputed to have slept with his mother and then murdered her (presumably for a similar reason, inability to bear the guilt her continued presence evoked)?

T. S. Eliot writes: "The essential emotion of the play is the feeling of a son towards a guilty mother. . . . Hamlet is dominated by an emotion which is inexpressible, because it is in excess of the facts as they appear." As they appear, yes, but not as they actually exist in Hamlet's soul. His emotions are inexpressible not for that reason, but because there are thoughts and wishes that no one dares to express even to himself. We plumb here the darkest depths.

ARTHUR MILLER (b. 1915)
Tragedy and the Common Man

"Tragedy and the Common Man" first appeared in the New York
Times in 1949 and was later collected in *The Theater Essays Of Arthur
Miller* (1978). In this now classic essay, Miller argues against the idea
(largely derived from Greek practice and from Aristotle's *Poetics*) that
tragic heroes must be noble or high-born people. On the contrary, Miller
contends that in the modern world, the "common man" is most likely to
know "the fear of being displaced . . . . from our chosen image of what
and who we are in the world." Moreover, according to Miller, tragedy
should not be negative or pessimistic in its effect; rather, as it assumes the
perfectibility of humankind, it should be uplifting and ultimately
optimistic.

In this age few tragedies are written. It has often been held that the
lack is due to a paucity of heroes among us, or else that modern man has
had the blood drawn out of his organs of belief by the skepticism of science,
and the heroic attack on life cannot feed on an attitude of reserve and cir-
cumspection. For one reason or another, we are often held to be below
tragedy—or tragedy above us. The inevitable conclusion is, of course, that
the tragic mode is archaic, fit only for the very highly placed, the kings or
the kingly, and where this admission is not made in so many words it is
most often implied.

I believe that the common man is as apt a subject for tragedy in its
highest sense as kings were. On the face of it this ought to be obvious in
the light of modern psychiatry, which bases its analysis upon classic for-
mulations, such as the Oedipus and Orestes complexes, for instance, which
were enacted by royal beings, but which apply to everyone in similar emotional situations.

More simply, when the question of tragedy in art is not at issue, we
never hesitate to attribute to the well-placed and the exalted the very same
mental processes as the lowly. And finally, if the exaltation of tragic action
were truly a property of the high-bred character alone, it is inconceivable
that the mass of mankind should cherish tragedy above all other forms, let
alone be capable of understanding it.

As a general rule, to which there may be exceptions unknown to me, I
think the tragic feeling is evoked in us when we are in the presence of a
character who is ready to lay down his life, if need be, to secure one thing—
his sense of personal dignity. From Orestes to Hamlet, Medea to Macbeth,
the underlying struggle is that of the individual attempting to gain his
"rightful" position in his society.

Sometimes he is one who has been displaced from it, sometimes one
who seeks to attain it for the first time, but the fateful wound from which

the inevitable events spiral is the wound of indignity, and its dominant force is indignation. Tragedy, then, is the consequence of a man's total compulsion to evaluate himself justly.

In the sense of having been initiated by the hero himself, the tale always reveals what has been called his "tragic flaw," a failing that is not peculiar to grand or elevated characters. Nor is it necessarily a weakness. The flaw, or crack in the character, is really nothing—and need be nothing, but his inherent unwillingness to remain passive in the face of what he conceives to be a challenge to his dignity, his image of his rightful status. Only the passive, only those who accept their lot without active retaliation, are "flawless." Most of us are in that category.

But there are among us today, as there always have been, those who act against the scheme of things that degrades them, and in the process of action everything we have accepted out of fear or insensitivity or ignorance is shaken before us and examined, and from this total onslaught by an individual against the seemingly stable cosmos surrounding us—from this total examination of the "unchangeable" environment—comes the terror and the fear that is classically associated with tragedy.

More important, from this total questioning of what has previously been unquestioned, we learn. And such a process is not beyond the common man. In revolutions around the world, these past thirty years, he has demonstrated again and again this inner dynamic of all tragedy.

Insistence upon the rank of the tragic hero, or the so-called nobility of his character, is really but a clinging to the outward forms of tragedy. If rank or nobility of character was indispensable, then it would follow that the problems of those with rank were the particular problems of tragedy. But surely the right of one monarch to capture the domain from another no longer raises our passions, nor are our concepts of justice what they were to the mind of an Elizabethan king.

The quality in such plays that does shake us, however, derives from the underlying fear of being displaced, the disaster inherent in being torn away from our chosen image of what and who we are in this world. Among us today this fear is as strong, and perhaps stronger, than it ever was. In fact, it is the common man who knows this fear best.

Now, if it is true that tragedy is the consequence of a man's total compulsion to evaluate himself justly, his destruction in the attempt posits a wrong or an evil in his environment. And this is precisely the morality of tragedy and its lesson. The discovery of the moral law, which is what the enlightenment of tragedy consists of, is not the discovery of some abstract or metaphysical quantity.

The tragic right is a condition of life, a condition in which the human personality is able to flower and realize itself. The wrong is the condition which suppresses man, perverts the flowing out of his love and creative instinct. Tragedy enlightens—and it must, in that it points the heroic finger at the enemy of man's freedom. The thrust for freedom is the quality in tragedy which exalts. The revolutionary questioning of the stable environment is what terrifies. In no way is the common man debarred from such thoughts or such actions.

Seen in this light, our lack of tragedy may be partially accounted for by the turn which modern literature has taken toward the purely psychiatric view of life, or the purely sociological. If all our miseries, our indignities, are born and bred within our minds, then all action, let alone the heroic action, is obviously impossible.

And if society alone is responsible for the cramping of our lives, then the protagonist must needs be so pure and faultless as to force us to deny his validity as a character. From neither of these views can tragedy derive, simply because neither represents a balanced concept of life. Above all else, tragedy requires the finest appreciation by the writer of cause and effect.

No tragedy can therefore come about when its author fears to question absolutely everything, when he regards any institution, habit or custom as being either everlasting, immutable or inevitable. In the tragic view the need of man to wholly realize himself is the only fixed star, and whatever it is that hedges his nature and lowers it is ripe for attack and examination. Which is not to say that tragedy must preach revolution.

The Greeks could probe the very heavenly origin of their ways and return to confirm the rightness of laws. And Job could face God in anger, demanding his right and end in submission. But for a moment everything is in suspension, nothing is accepted, and in this stretching and tearing apart of the cosmos, in the very action of so doing, the character gains "size," the tragic stature which is spuriously attached to the royal or the highborn in our minds. The commonest of men may take on that stature to the extent of his willingness to throw all he has into the contest, the battle to secure his rightful place in his world.

There is a misconception of tragedy with which I have been struck in review after review, and in many conversations with writers and readers alike. It is the idea that tragedy is of necessity allied to pessimism. Even the dictionary says nothing more about the word than that it means a story with a sad or unhappy ending. This impression is so firmly fixed that I almost hesitate to claim that in truth tragedy implies more optimism in its author than does comedy, and that its final result ought to be the reinforcement of the onlooker's brightest opinions of the human animal.

For, if it is true to say that in essence the tragic hero is intent upon claiming his whole due as a personality, and if this struggle must be total and without reservation, then it automatically demonstrates the indestructible will of man to achieve his humanity.

The possibility of victory must be there in tragedy. Where pathos rules, where pathos is finally derived, a character has fought a battle he could not possibly have won. The pathetic is achieved when the protagonist is, by virtue of his witlessness, his insensitivity or the very air he gives off, incapable of grappling with a much superior force.

Pathos truly is the mode for the pessimist. But tragedy requires a nicer balance between what is possible and what is impossible. And it is curious, although edifying, that the plays we revere, century after century, are the tragedies. In them, and in them alone, lies the belief—optimistic, if you will, in the perfectibility of man.

It is time, I think, that we who are without kings, took up this bright thread of our history and followed it to the only place it can possible lead in our time—the heart and spirit of the average man.

NORTHROP FRYE (b. 1912)

[Genre in Drama]

Northrop Frye was born in Sherbrooke, Quebec, and taught for many years at the University of Toronto. Commonly considered one of the foremost literary critics of the twentieth century, his works include *Fearful Symmetry: A Study of William Blake* (1947) and *The Educated Imagination* (1963). In the following selection from *Anatomy of Criticism* (1957), Frye discusses the various sub-genres of drama and notes the importance of irony to both tragic and comic plays.

As tragedy moves over towards irony, the sense of inevitable event begins to fade out, and the sources of catastrophe come into view. In irony catastrophe is either arbitrary and meaningless, the impact of an unconscious (or, in the pathetic fallacy, malignant) world on conscious man, or the result of more or less definable social and psychological forces. Tragedy's "this must be" becomes irony's "this at least is," a concentration on foreground facts and a rejection of mythical superstructures. Thus the ironic drama is a vision of what in theology is called the fallen world, of simple humanity, man as natural man and in conflict with both human and non-human nature. In nineteenth century drama the tragic vision is often identical with the ironic one, hence nineteenth century tragedies tend to be either *Schicksal* dramas dealing with the arbitrary ironies of fate, or (clearly the more rewarding form) studies of the frustrating and smothering of human activity by the combined pressure of a reactionary society without and a disorganized soul within. Such irony is difficult to sustain in the theatre because it tends toward a stasis of action. In those parts of Chekhov, notably the last act of *The Three Sisters*, where the characters one by one withdraw from each other into their subjective prison-cells, we are coming about as close to pure irony as the stage can get.

The ironic play passes through a dead center of complete realism, a pure mime representing human life without comment and without imposing any sort of dramatic form beyond what is required for simple exhibition. This idolatrous form of mimesis is rare, but the thin line of its tradition can be traced from Classical mime-writers like Herodas to their *tranche-de-vie* descendants in recent times. The mime is somewhat commoner as an individual performance, and, outside the theatre, the Browning monodrama is a logical development of the isolating and soliloquizing tendencies of ironic conflict. In the theatre we usually find that the spectacle of "all too human" life is either oppressive or ridiculous, and that it tends to pass directly from one to the other. Irony, then, as it moves away from tragedy, begins to merge into comedy.

Ironic comedy presents us of course with "the way of the world," but as soon as we find sympathetic or even neutral characters in a comedy, we move into the more familiar comic area where we have a group of humors outwitted by the opposing group. Just as tragedy is a vision of the supremacy of *mythos* or thing done, and just as irony is a vision of *ethos*, or character individualized against environment, so comedy is a vision of *dianoia*, a significance which is ultimately social significance, the establishing of a desirable society. As an imitation of life, drama is, in terms of *mythos*, conflict; in terms of *ethos*, a representative image; in terms of *dianoia*, the final harmonic chord revealing the tonality under the narrative movement, it is community. The further comedy moves from irony, the more it becomes what we here call ideal comedy, the vision not of the way of the world, but of what you will, life as you like it. Shakespeare's main interest is in getting away from the son-father conflict of ironic comedy towards a vision of a serene community, a vision most prominent in *The Tempest*. Here the action is polarized around a younger and an older man working in harmony together, a lover and a benevolent teacher.

The next step brings us to the extreme limit of social comedy, the symposium, the structure of which is, as we should expect, clearest in Plato, whose Socrates is both teacher and lover, and whose vision moves toward an integration of society in a form like that of the symposium itself, the dialectic festivity which, as is explained in the opening of the *Laws*, is the controlling force that holds society together. It is easy to see that Plato's dialogue form is dramatic and has affinities with comedy and mime; and while there is much in Plato's thought that contradicts the spirit of comedy as we have outlined it, it is significant that he contradicts it directly, tries to kidnap it, so to speak. It seems almost a rule that the more he does this, the further he moves into pure exposition or dictatorial monologue and away from drama. The most dramatic of his dialogues, such as *Euthydemus*, are regularly the most indecisive in philosophical "position."

In our own day Bernard Shaw has tried hard to keep the symposium in the theatre. His early manifesto, *The Quintessence of Ibsenism*, states that a play should be an intelligent discussion of a serious problem, and in his preface to *Getting Married* he remarks approvingly on the fact that it observes the unities of time and place. For comedy of Shaw's type tends to a symposium form which occupies the same amount of time in its action that the audience consumes in watching it. However, Shaw discovered in practice that what emerges from the theatrical symposium is not a dialectic that compels to a course of action or thought, but one that emancipates from formulated principles of conduct. The shape of such a comedy is very clear in the bright little sketch *In Good King Charles's Golden Days*, where even the most highly developed human types, the saintly Fox and the philosophical Newton, are shown to be comic humors by the mere presence of other types of people. Yet the central symposium figure of the haranguing lover bulks formidably in *Man and Superman*, and even the renunciation of love for mathematics at the end of *Back to Methusaleh* is consistent with the symposium spirit.

The view of poetry which sees it as intermediate between history and philosophy, its images combining the temporal events of the one with the timeless ideas of the other, seems to be still involved in this exposition of dramatic forms. We can now see a mimetic or verbal drama stretching from the history-play to the philosophy-play (the act-play and the scene-play), with the mime, the pure image, halfway between. These three are specialized forms, cardinal points of drama rather than generic areas. But the whole mimetic area is only a part, a semicircle, let us say, of all drama. In the misty and unexplored region of the other semicircle of spectacular drama we have identified a quadrant that we have called the *auto*, and we have now to chart the fourth quadrant that lies between the *auto* and comedy, and establish the fourth cardinal point where it meets the *auto* again. When we think of the clutter of forms that belong here, we are strongly tempted to call our fourth area "miscellaneous" and let it go; but it is precisely here that new generic criticism is needed.

The further comedy moves from irony, and the more it rejoices in the free movement of its happy society, the more readily it takes to music and dancing. As music and scenery increase in importance, the ideal comedy crosses the boundary line of spectacular drama and becomes the masque. In Shakespeare's ideal comedies, especially *A Midsummer Night's Dream* and *The Tempest*, the close affinity with the masque is not hard to see. The masque—or at least the kind of masque that is nearest to comedy, and which we shall here call the ideal masque—is still in the area of *dianoia:* it is usually a compliment to the audience, or an important member of it, and leads up to an idealization of the society represented by that audience. Its plots and characters are fairly stock, as they exist only in relation to the significance of the occasion.

It thus differs from comedy in its more intimate attitude to the audience: there is more insistence on the connection between the audience and the community on the stage. The members of a masque are ordinarily disguised members of the audience, and there is a final gesture of surrender when the actors unmask and join the audience in a dance. The ideal masque is in fact a myth-play like the *auto*, to which it is related much as comedy is to tragedy. It is designed to emphasize, not the ideals to be achieved by discipline or faith, but ideals which are desired or considered to be already possessed. Its settings are seldom remote from magic and fairyland, from

Arcadias and visions of earthly Paradise. It uses gods freely, like the *auto*, but possessively, and without imaginative subjection. In Western drama, from the Renaissance to the end of the eighteenth century, masque and ideal comedy make great use of Classical mythology, which the audience is not obliged to accept as "true."

The rather limited masque throws some light on the structure and characteristics of its two far more important and versatile neighbors. For the masque is flanked on one side by the musically organized drama which we call opera, and on the other by a scenically organized drama, which has now settled in the movie. Puppet-plays and the vast Chinese romances where, as in the movie, the audience enters and leaves unpredictably, are examples of pre-camera scenic masques. Both opera and movie are, like the masque, proverbial for lavish display, and part of the reason for it in the movie is that many movies are actually bourgeois myth-plays, as half a dozen critics suddenly and almost simultaneously discovered a few years ago. The predominance of the private life of the actor in the imaginations of many moviegoers may perhaps have some analogy with the consciously assumed disguise of the masque.

MARTIN ESSLIN (b. 1918)

from The Theatre of the Absurd

Martin Esslin was born in Hungary and grew up in Vienna. He left Europe in 1938 to escape Nazism and eventually came to England, where he has worked as a script-writer and producer for the British Broadcasting Corporation. In the following selection from his seminal book *The Theatre of the Absurd* (1961, revised 1969), Esslin describes the essentially modern character of absurdist drama. In a world in which belief in God or in organized philosophical systems is in effect absent, the playwright presents his own view of humankind as it attempts to face the possible absurdity of reality. Esslin cites both the satirical and broadly religious orientation of the theater of the absurd. He also stresses the idea that, in the modern theater, language and discursive thought are devalued, while poetic images, "visual elements, movement, and light" take on increasing importance for the playwright.

When Nietzsche's Zarathustra descended from his mountains to preach to mankind, he met a saintly hermit in the forest. This old man invited him to stay in the wilderness rather than go into the cities of men. When Zarathustra asked the hermit how he passed his time in his solitude, he replied: 'I make up songs and sing them; and when I make up songs I laugh, I weep, and I growl; thus do I praise God.' Zarathustra declined the old man's offer and continued on his journey. But when he was alone, he spoke thus to his heart: 'Can it be possible! This old saint in the forest has not yet heard that God is dead!'

Zarathustra was first published in 1883. The number of people for whom God is dead has greatly increased since Nietzsche's day, and mankind has learned the bitter lesson of the falseness and evil nature of some of the cheap and vulgar substitutes that have been set up to take his place. And so, after two terrible wars, there are still many who are trying to come to terms with the implications of Zarathustra's message, searching for a way in which they can, with dignity, confront a universe deprived of what was once its centre and its living purpose, a world deprived of a generally accepted integrating principle, which has become disjointed, purposeless—absurd.

The Theatre of the Absurd is one of the expressions of this search. It bravely faces up to the fact that for those to whom the world has lost its central explanation and meaning, it is no longer possible to accept art forms still based on the continuation of standards and concepts that have lost their validity; that is, the possibility of knowing the laws of conduct and ultimate values, as deducible from a firm foundation of revealed certainty about the purpose of man in the universe.

In expressing the tragic sense of loss at the disappearance of ultimate certainties the Theatre of the Absurd, by a strange paradox, is also a symptom of what probably comes nearest to being a genuine religious quest in our age: an effort, however timid and tentative, to sing, to laugh, to weep—and to growl—if not in praise of God (whose name, in Adamov's phrase, has for so long been degraded by usage that it has lost its meaning), at least in search of a dimension of the Ineffable; an effort to make man aware of the ultimate realities of his condition, to instil in him again the lost sense of cosmic wonder and primeval anguish, to shock him out of an existence that has become trite, mechanical, complacent, and deprived of the dignity that comes of awareness. For God is dead, above all, to the masses who live from day to day and have lost all contact with the basic facts—and mysteries—of the human condition with which, in former times, they were kept in touch through the living ritual of their religion, which made them parts of a real community and not just atoms in an atomized society.

The Theatre of the Absurd forms part of the unceasing endeavour of the true artists of our time to breach this dead wall of complacency and automatism and to re-establish an awareness of man's situation when confronted with the ultimate reality of his condition. As such, the Theatre of the Absurd fulfils a dual purpose and presents its audience with a two-fold absurdity.

In one of its aspects it castigates, satirically, the absurdity of lives lived unaware and unconscious of ultimate reality. This is the feeling of the deadness and mechanical senselessness of half-unconscious lives, the feeling of 'human beings secreting inhumanity', which Camus describes in *The Myth of Sisyphus:*

> In certain hours of lucidity, the mechanical aspect of their gestures, their senseless pantomime, makes stupid everything around them. A man speaking

on the telephone behind a glass partition—one cannot hear him but observes his trivial gesturing. One asks oneself, why is he alive? This malaise in front of man's own inhumanity, this incalculable letdown when faced with the image of what we are, this 'nausea', as a contemporary writer calls it, also is the Absurd.

This is the experience that Ionesco expresses in plays like *The Bald Soprano* or *The Chairs*, Adamov in *La Parodie*, or N. F. Simpson in *A Resounding Tinkle*. It represents the satirical, parodistic aspect of the Theatre of the Absurd, its social criticism, its pillorying of an inauthentic, petty society. This may be the most easily accessible, and therefore most widely recognized, message of the Theatre of the Absurd, but it is far from being its most essential or most significant feature.

In its second, more positive aspect, behind the satirical exposure of the absurdity of inauthentic ways of life, the Theatre of the Absurd is facing up to a deeper layer of absurdity—the absurdity of the human condition itself in a world where the decline of religious belief has deprived man of certainties. When it is no longer possible to accept complete closed systems of values and revelations of divine purpose, life must be faced in its ultimate, stark reality. That is why, in the analysis of the dramatists of the Absurd in this book, we have always seen man stripped of the accidental circumstances of social position or historical context, confronted with the basic choices, the basic situations of his existence: man faced with time and therefore waiting, in Beckett's plays or Gelber's, waiting between birth and death; man running away from death, climbing higher and higher, in Vian's play, or passively sinking down toward death, in Buzzati's; man rebelling against death, confronting and accepting it, in Ionesco's *Tueur Sans Gages*; man inextricably entangled in a mirage of illusions, mirrors reflecting mirrors, and forever hiding ultimate reality, in the plays of Genet; man trying to establish his position, or to break out into freedom, only to find himself newly imprisoned, in the parables of Manuel de Pedrolo; man trying to stake out a modest place for himself in the cold and darkness that envelops him, in Pinter's plays; man vainly striving to grasp the moral law forever beyond his comprehension, in Arrabal's; man caught in the inescapable dilemma that strenuous effort leads to the same result as passive indolence—complete futility and ultimate death—in the earlier work of Adamov; man forever lonely, immured in the prison of his subjectivity, unable to reach his fellow-man, in the vast majority of these plays.

Concerned as it is with the ultimate realities of the human condition, the relatively few fundamental problems of life and death, isolation and communication, the Theatre of the Absurd, however grotesque, frivolous, and irreverent it may appear, represents a return to the original, religious function of the theatre—the confrontation of man with the spheres of myth and religious reality. Like ancient Greek tragedy and the medieval mystery plays and baroque allegories, the Theatre of the Absurd is intent on making its audience aware of man's precarious and mysterious position in the universe.

The difference is merely that in ancient Greek tragedy—and comedy—as well as in the medieval mystery play and the baroque *auto sacramental*, the ultimate realities concerned were generally known and universally accepted metaphysical systems, while the Theatre of the Absurd expresses the absence of any such generally accepted cosmic system of values. Hence, much more modestly, the Theatre of the Absurd makes no pretence at explaining the ways of God to man. It can merely present, in anxiety or with derision, an individual human being's intuition of the ultimate realities as he experiences them; the fruits of one man's descent into the depths of his personality, his dreams, fantasies, and nightmares.

While former attempts at confronting man with the ultimate realities of his condition projected a coherent and generally recognized version of the truth, the Theatre of the Absurd merely communicates one poet's most intimate and personal intuition of the human situation, his own *sense of being*, his individual vision of the world. This is the *subject-matter* of the Theatre of the Absurd, and it determines its *form*, which must, of necessity, represent a convention of the stage basically different from the 'realistic' theatre of our time.

As the Theatre of the Absurd is not concerned with conveying information or presenting the problems or destinies of characters that exist outside the author's inner world, as it does not expound a thesis or debate ideological propositions, it is not concerned with the representation of events, the narration of the fate or the adventures of characters, but instead with the presentation of one individual's basic situation. It is a theatre of situation as against a theatre of events in sequence, and therefore it uses a language based on patterns of concrete images rather than argument and discursive speech. And since it is trying to present a sense of being, it can neither investigate nor solve problems of conduct or morals.

Because the Theatre of the Absurd projects its author's personal world, it lacks objectively valid characters. It cannot show the clash of opposing temperaments or study human passions locked in conflict, and is therefore not dramatic in the accepted sense of the term. Nor is it concerned with telling a story in order to communicate some moral or social lesson, as is the aim of Brecht's narrative, 'epic' theatre. The action in a play of the Theatre of the Absurd is not intended to tell a story but to communicate a pattern of poetic images. To give but one example: things happen in *Waiting for Godot*, but these happenings do not constitute a plot or story; they are an image of Beckett's intuition that *nothing really ever happens* in man's existence. The whole play is a complex poetic image made up of a complicated pattern of subsidiary images and themes, which are interwoven like the themes of a musical composition, not, as in most well-made plays, to present a line of development, but to make in the spectator's mind a total, complex impression of a basic, and static, situation. In this, the Theatre of the Absurd is analogous to a Symbolist or Imagist poem, which also presents a pattern of images and associations in a mutually interdependent structure.

While the Brechtian epic theatre tries to widen the range of drama by introducing narrative, epic elements, the Theatre of the Absurd aims at concentration and depth in an essentially lyrical, poetic pattern. Of course, dramatic, narrative, and lyrical elements are present in all drama. Brecht's own theatre, like Shakespeare's, contains lyrical inserts in the form of songs; even at their most didactic, Ibsen and Shaw are rich in purely poetic moments. The Theatre of the Absurd, however, in abandoning psychology, subtlety of characterization, and plot in the conventional sense, gives the poetical element an incomparably greater emphasis. While the play with a linear plot describes a development in time, in a dramatic form that presents a concretized poetic image the play's extension in time is purely incidental. Expressing an *intuition in depth*, it should ideally be apprehended *in a single moment*, and only because it is physically impossible to present so complex an image in an instant does it have to be spread over a period of time. The formal structure of such a play is, therefore, merely a device to express a complex total image by unfolding it in a sequence of interacting elements.

The endeavour to communicate a total sense of being is an attempt to present a truer picture of reality itself, reality as apprehended by an individual. The Theatre of the Absurd is the last link in a line of development that started with naturalism. The idealistic, Platonic belief in immutable essences—ideal forms that it was the artist's task to present in a purer state than they could ever be found in nature—foundered in the philosophy of Locke and Kant, which based reality on perception and the inner structure of the human mind. Art then became mere imitation of external nature. Yet the imitation of surfaces was bound to prove unsatisfying and this inevitably led to the next step—the exploration of the reality of the mind. Ibsen and Strindberg exemplified that development during the span of their own lifetimes' exploration of reality. James Joyce began with minutely realistic stories and ended up with the vast multiple structure of *Finnegans Wake*. The work of the dramatists of the Absurd continues the same development. Each of these plays is an answer to the questions 'How does this individual feel when confronted with the human situation? What is the basic mood in which he faces the world? What does it feel like to be he?' And the answer is a single, total, but complex and contradictory poetic image—one play— or a succession of such images, complementing each other—the dramatist's *œuvre*.

In apprehending the world at any one moment, we receive simultaneously a whole complex of different perceptions and feelings. We can only communicate this instantaneous vision by breaking it down into different elements which can then be built up into a sequence in time, in a sentence or series of sentences. To convert our perception into conceptual terms, into logical thought and language, we perform an operation analogous to that of the scanner that analyses the pictures in a television camera into rows of single impulses. The poetic image, with its ambiguity and its simultaneous evocation of multiple elements of sense association, is one of the methods by which we can, however imperfectly, communicate the reality of our intuition of the world.

The highly eccentric German philosopher Ludwig Klages—who is almost totally unknown, and quite unjustly so, in the English-speaking world—formulated a psychology of perception based on the recognition that our senses present us with images (*Bilder*) built up of a multitude of simultaneous impressions that are subsequently analysed and disintegrated in the process of translation into conceptual thinking. For Klages, this is part of the insidious action of critical intellect upon the creative element of the mind—his philosophical *magnum opus* is called *Der Geist als Widersacher der Seele (The Intellect as Antagonist of the Soul)*—but however misguided his attempt to turn this opposition into a cosmic battle between the creative and the analytical may have been, the basic idea that conceptual and discursive thought impoverishes the ineffable fullness of the perceived image remains valid, at least as an illustration of the problem of what it is that is being communicated in poetic imagery.

And it is in this striving to communicate a basic and as yet undissolved totality of perception, an intuition of being, that we can find a key to the devaluation and disintegration of language in the Theatre of the Absurd. For if it is the translation of the total intuition of being into the logical and temporal sequence of conceptual thought that deprives it of its pristine complexity and poetic truth, it is understandable that the artist should try to find ways to circumvent this influence of discursive speech and logic. Here lies the chief difference between poetry and prose: poetry is ambiguous and associative, striving to approximate to the wholly unconceptual language of music. The Theatre of the Absurd, in carrying the same poetic endeavour into the concrete imagery of the stage, can go further than pure poetry in dispensing with logic, discursive thought, and language. The stage is a multidimensional medium; it allows the simultaneous use of visual elements, movement, light, and language. It is, therefore, particularly suited to the communication of complex images consisting of the contrapuntal interaction of all these elements.

In the 'literary' theatre, language remains the predominant component. In the anti-literary theatre of the circus or the music hall, language is reduced to a very subordinate role. The Theatre of the Absurd has regained the freedom of using language as merely one—sometimes dominant, sometimes submerged—component of its multidimensional poetic imagery. By putting the language of a scene in contrast to the action, by reducing it to meaningless patter, or by abandoning discursive logic for the poetic logic of association or assonance, the Theatre of the Absurd has opened up a new dimension of the stage.

Copyrights and Acknowledgments

The authors are grateful to the following publishers and copyright holders for permission to reprint material in this book.

FICTION

Fitzgerald. Copyright © 1931 by the Curtis Publishing Company. Copyright © renewed 1959 by Frances Scott Fitzgerald Lanahan. Both used by permission of the publisher.

SIMON & SCHUSTER For "Woman on a Roof" from *A Man and Two Women* by Doris Lessing. Copyright © 1958, 1962, 1963 by Doris Lessing. Reprinted by permission of Simon & Schuster.

ROSEMARY THURBER For "The Catbird Seat" from *The Thurber Carnival* by James Thurber. Copyright © 1945 by James Thurber. Copyright © 1973 by Helen W. Thurber and Rosemary A. Thurber. Used by permission.

UNIVERSITY OF CHICAGO PRESS For "Narrators and Their Qualities" from *The Rhetoric of Fiction* by Wayne C. Booth. Copyright © 1982 by the University of Chicago Press. Reprinted by permission.

UNIVERSITY PRESS OF VIRGINIA For "The Writer's Sources" from *Faulkner in the University: Class Conferences at the University of Virginia, 1957–1958*, edited by Frederick L. Gwynn and Joseph L. Blotner. Copyright © 1977. Used by permission.

VANGUARD PRESS For "Where Are You Going, Where Have You Been?" from *The Wheel of Love* by Joyce Carol Oates. Copyright © 1965, 1966, 1967, 1968, 1969, 1970 by Joyce Carol Oates. Reprinted by permission of Vanguard Press.

VIKING PENGUIN INC. For "Gimpel the Fool" by Isaac Bashevis Singer, translated by Saul Bellow, from *A Treasury of Yiddish Stories*, edited by Irving Howe and Eliezer Greenberg. Copyright © 1953 by The Viking Press, Inc. Copyright renewed © 1981 by Isaac Bashevis Singer. For "Counterparts" from *Dubliners* by James Joyce. Copyright © 1916 by B. W. Huebsch. Definitive text copyright © 1967 by the Estate of James Joyce. For "Odor of Chrysanthemums" from *The Complete Short Stories of D. H. Lawrence*, Vol. II. Copyright © 1934 by Frieda Lawrence, renewed copyright © 1962 by Angelo Ravagli and C. M. Weekley, Executors of the Estate of Frieda Lawrence Ravagli. All rights reserved. For excerpt from "The Virtues of Sloppy Writing," interview with John Updike by Charles Thomas Samuels, from *Writers at Work: The Paris Review Interviews*, Fourth Series, edited by George Plimpton. Copyright © 1974, 1976 by The Paris Review, Inc. All reprinted by permission of Viking Penguin Inc.

POETRY

ANGUS AND ROBERTSON (U.K.) LTD. For "Imperial Adam" from *Collected Poems of A. D. Hope*. Used by the kind permission of Angus and Robertson, Publishers.

ANTAEUS–ECCO PRESS For "Love Song: I and Thou" and "Fabrication of Ancestors" from *New and Collected Poems: 1961–1983* by Alan Dugan. Published by the Ecco Press. Copyright © 1983 by Alan Dugan. For "Horse" from *The Triumph of Achilles* by Louise Glück. Published by the Ecco Press. Copyright © 1985 by Louise Glück. All reprinted by permission of Antaeus–Ecco Press.

ATHENEUM PUBLISHERS, INC. For "The Grapes" from *The Venetian Vespers* by Anthony Hecht. Copyright © 1979 by Anthony E. Hecht. For "The Survivor" from *The Names of the Lost* by Philip Levine. Copyright © 1976 by Philip Levine. For "Bats" from *Shrapnel and a Poet's Year* by George MacBeth. Copyright © 1973 by George MacBeth. For "The Mad Scene" from *Nights and Days* by James Merrill. Copyright © 1966 by James Merrill. For "The Drunk in the Furnace" from *The First Four Books of Poems* by W. S. Merwin. Copyright © 1960 by

W. S. Merwin. For "Eating Poetry" from *Reasons for Moving* by Mark Strand. Copyright © 1968 by Mark Strand. All reprinted with the permission of Atheneum Publishers, Inc.

THE ATLANTIC MONTHLY PRESS   For "For the Eating of Swine" from *The Unborn* by Rodney Jones. Copyright © 1985 by Rodney Jones. Reprinted by permission of The Atlantic Monthly Press.

BLACK SPARROW PRESS   For "Yellow" from *The Days Run Away like Wild Horses over the Hills* by Charles Bukowski. Copyright © 1969 by Charles Bukowski. Used by permission of Black Sparrow Press.

BOA EDITIONS   For "To a Child" from *Remains* by W. D. Snodgrass. Copyright © 1985 by W. D. Snodgrass. Reprinted by permission of BOA Editions.

GEORGE BRAZILLER, INC.   For "Dismantling the Silence" from *Dismantling the Silence* and for "Breasts" from *Return to a Place Lit By a Glass of Milk,* both by Charles Simic. Used by permission of the publisher.

BROADSIDE PRESS   For "Nikki-Rosa" from *Black Judgment* by Nikki Giovanni. Copyright © 1969 by Broadside Press. For "Man Thinking About Woman" by Donald L. Lee. Both reprinted by permission of Broadside Press.

GWENDOLYN BROOKS   For "We Real Cool" and "First Fight. Then Fiddle." from *The World of Gwendolyn Brooks.* Copyright © 1949 by Harper & Row. Used by permission of the author.

CHATTO & WINDUS   For "Dulce et Decorum Est," "Strange Meeting," and "Anthem for Doomed Youth" from *Collected Poems of Wilfred Owen,* edited by C. Day Lewis. Used by permission of the author's estate and Chatto & Windus.

DEVIN–ADAIR PUBLISHERS   For "Inniskeen Road: July Evening" from *Collected Poems* by Patrick Kavanaugh. Copyright © 1964 by Patrick Kavanagh. Used by permission of the publisher.

DODD, MEAD & COMPANY, INC.   For "We Wear the Mask" from *The Complete Poems of Paul Laurence Dunbar.* Copyright © 1980. Reprinted by permission of Dodd, Mead & Co., Inc.

DOUBLEDAY & COMPANY, INC.   For "Mourning Pablo Neruda" from *The Man in the Black Coat Turns* by Robert Bly. Copyright © 1981 by Robert Bly. For "The Waking," "Elegy for Jane," and "I Knew a Woman" by Theodore Roethke, copyright © 1948, 1950, 1954 by Theodore Roethke. For "My Papa's Waltz" by Theodore Roethke, copyright © 1942 by Hearst Magazine, Inc. All four from *The Collected Poems of Theodore Roethke.* For "The Father of Our Country" from *Trilogy* by Diane Wakoski. Copyright © 1967 by Diane Wakoski. All reprinted by permission of Doubleday & Company, Inc.

FABER & FABER   For "Talking in Bed" from *The Whitsun Weddings* by Philip Larkin. Reprinted by permission of Faber & Faber Ltd.

FARRAR, STRAUS & GIROUX, INC.   For "Dream Song #4" from *The Dream Songs* by John Berryman. For "The Fish" and "The Map" from *The Complete Poems 1927–1979* by Elizabeth Bishop. Copyright © 1935, 1940, renewed copyright © 1963, 1968 by Elizabeth Bishop. For "The Byrnies" from *Selected Poems 1950–1975* by Thom Gunn. Copyright © 1957, 1958, 1961, 1967, 1971, 1973, 1974, 1975, 1976, 1979 by Thom Gunn. For "Digging," "Mid-Term Break," and "Punishment" from *Poems 1965–1975* by Seamus Heaney. Copyright © 1966, 1969, 1972, 1975, 1980 by Seamus Heaney. For "Feeling into Words" from *Preoccupations: Selected Prose 1968–1978* by Seamus Heaney. Copyright © 1980 by Seamus

LITTLE, BROWN AND COMPANY   For "The Animals in That Country" from *The Animals in That Country* by Margaret Atwood. Copyright © 1968 by Oxford University Press (Canadian Branch). For "Charming" from *A Happy Childhood: Poems by William Matthews*. Copyright © 1982 by William Matthews. First appeared in *The Atlantic Monthly*. Both used by permission of Little, Brown and Company in association with the Atlantic Monthly Press. For "Columbus" from *Verses from 1929 On* by Ogden Nash. Copyright © 1935 by the Curtis Publishing Company. First appeared in *The Saturday Evening Post*. Used by permission of Little, Brown and Company.

LIVERIGHT PUBLISHING CORPORATION   For "Proem: To Brooklyn Bridge" from *The Complete Poems and Selected Letters and Prose of Hart Crane*, edited by Brom Weber. Copyright © 1933, 1958, 1966 by Liveright Publishing Corporation. For "Buffalo Bill 's" from *Tulips & Chimneys* by E. E. Cummings. Copyright © 1923, 1925 and renewed 1951, 1953 by E. E. Cummings. Copyright © 1973, 1976 by The Trustees for the E. E. Cummings Trust. Copyright © 1973, 1976 by George James Firmage. For "Those Winter Sundays" from *Angle of Ascent: New and Selected Poems* by Robert Hayden. Copyright © 1966, 1970, 1972, 1975 by Robert Hayden. For "A Symposium: Apples" from *Aspects of Eve: Poems* by Linda Pastan. Copyright © 1970, 1971, 1972, 1973, 1974, 1975 by Linda Pastan. For "Reapers" from *Cane* by Jean Toomer. Copyright © 1923 by Boni & Liveright. Copyright renewed 1951 by Jean Toomer. All reprinted by permission of Liveright Publishing Corporation.

MACMILLAN PUBLISHING COMPANY   For "Poetry" from *Collected Poems* by Marianne Moore. Copyright © 1935 by Marianne Moore, renewed 1963 by Marianne Moore and T. S. Eliot. For "Eros Turannos" from *Collected Poems* by Edwin Arlington Robinson. Copyright © 1916 by Edwin Arlington Robinson, renewed 1944 by Ruth Nivison. For "Mr. Flood's Party" from *Collected Poems* by Edwin Arlington Robinson. Copyright © 1921 by Edwin Arlington Robinson, renewed 1949 by Ruth Nivison. For "Lapis Lazuli" and "The Circus Animals' Desertion" from *Collected Poems* by W. B. Yeats. Copyright © 1940 by Georgie Yeats, renewed 1968 by Bertha Georgie Yeats, Michael Butler Yeats, and Anne Yeats. For "Leda and the Swan" and "Sailing to Byzantium" from *Collected Poems* by W. B. Yeats. Copyright © 1928 by Macmillan Publishing Company, copyright © renewed 1956 by Georgie Yeats. For "The Second Coming" from *Collected Poems* by W. B. Yeats. Copyright © 1924 by Macmillan Publishing Company, renewed 1952 by Bertha Georgie Yeats. All reprinted with the permission of Macmillan Publishing Company.

RICHARD B. MILES   For "Reason" from *Poems 1930–1960* by Josephine Miles. Originally published by Indiana University Press. Copyright © by Richard B. Miles. Reprinted by permission of Richard B. Miles.

NEW DIRECTIONS   For "Dream of a Baseball Star" from *The Happy Birthday of Death* by Gregory Corso. Copyright © 1960 by New Directions Publishing Company. For "Stars Wheel in Purple" from *Selected Poems* by H. D. (Hilda Doolittle). Copyright © 1957 by Norman Holmes Pearson. For "Constantly risking absurdity" from *A Coney Island of the Mind* by Lawrence Ferlinghetti. Copyright © 1958 by Lawrence Ferlinghetti. For "An English Field in the Nuclear Age" from *Candles in Babylon* by Denise Levertov. Copyright © 1982 by Denise Levertov. For "The Ache of Marriage" and "Merrit Parkway" from *Poems 1960–1967* by Denise Levertov. Copyright © 1961, 1964 by Denise Levertov Goodman. For "Image of the Engine" from *Collected Poems* by George Oppen. Copyright © 1962

Glossary of Literary Terms

Absurdist drama (p. 1297): a form of twentieth century drama and part of the more general literature of the absurd that emerged after World War II. Among its features are antiheroic, isolated characters; abstract or surrealistic settings; and a grotesquely comic sense of the absurdity and irrationality of existence. Samuel Beckett's *Krapp's Last Tape* (p. 1359) is an exemplary absurdist drama.

Accentual meter (p. 680): a metrical system that uses the number of stressed or accented syllables to determine the length of a poetic line.

Accentual-syllabic meter (p. 682): a metrical system that uses both accent-count and syllable-count to determine the length of a poetic line.

Alexandrine (p. 737): a line of iambic hexameter.

Allegory (p. 171): a form of narrative that uses a direct and unambiguous system of equivalencies between characters or situations and the abstractions they represent. (See the chateracter Faith in Hawthorne's "Young Goodman Brown," p. 6.)

Alliteration (p. 714): a poetic term denoting the recurrence of identical (and usually initial) consonant sounds in nearby words.

Anagnorisis (p. 1246): Greek for "recognition"; commonly used to refer to a tragic protagonist's recognition of the tragic circumstances that will reverse his fortunes.

Anapest (p. 684): a metrical foot consisting of two unstressed syllables followed by a stressed syllable (for example, "in the hall").

Antagonist (pp. 30, 52, 1050): generic name for a character who opposes the protagonist or main character of a story or play.

Antistrophe (p. 1247): the part of a choral ode in a Greek tragedy that is chanted by the chorus as it retraces, toward the right of the stage, a pattern of movement made toward the left of the stage as it changed the preceding strophe. See *Strophe*.

Apostrophe (p. 600): a figure of speech in which an absent or non-living thing or person is addressed as though present or living.

Aside (p. 1051): a speech delivered by a dramatic character while others are present, but not intended to be "heard" by the others. That is, the words are intended for the audience only.

Assonance (p. 716): the repetition of stressed vowel sounds in nearby words.

Atmosphere (p. 82): the psychological environment or ambiance created by description in a work of fiction.

Ballad stanza (p. 738): a four-line stanza alternating iambic tetrameter and iambic trimeter lines, and rhyming a b x b (x standing for the uncompleted rhyme).

Black comedy (p. 1297): a "darker," more pessimistic version of Absurdist drama, often containing sardonic or bitter humor and a strong sense of alienation from the contemporary world.

Blank verse (p. 679): unrhymed iambic pentameter verse.

Burns stanza (p. 738): a six-line stanza rhyming a a a b a b, in which the "a" lines are written in iambic tetrameter, and the "b" lines in iambic dimeter or trimeter.

Caesura (p. 685): a heavy pause in the middle or at the end of a line of poetry, signalled by a mark of punctuation or resulting from the rhythm of the language.

Character (p. 51, 698): a personage whose experiences are recorded in a story, poem, or play.

Chaucerian stanza (p. 739): a seven-line stanza of iambic pentameter rhyming a b a b b c c. First used in the long poems of Geoffrey Chaucer.

Choragos (p. 1247): the leader of the chorus in a Greek tragedy.

Choral ode (p. 1246): a poem recited by the chorus between the scenes of a Greek play.

Chorus (p. 965): a group of actors (usually considered to be around fifteen in number) who, speaking in unison at regular intervals in a Greek tragedy, offer commentary and provide background about the dramatic action.

Climax (p. 31, 968, 1049): the crisis or culminating point of a narrative or dramatic plot; the point at which the main character's fortunes change, and where he or she becomes aware of what has happened.

Comedy (p. 971): a form of drama which is usually amusing and whose main characters usually end happily.

Comedy of manners (p. 1296): a form of comic drama which emphasizes (humorously) the main character's misdirected attempts to conform to the manners and conventions of an artificial society.

Common meter (p. 738): another name of the meter of a ballad stanza.

Complications (p. 31): incidents which serve to further the conflict in a story or play.

Conceit (p. 601): a figure of speech in which two radically dissimilar objects are compared to one another, often in an extended fashion.

Confidant(e) (p. 52): in a work of fiction, a minor character whose principal function is to serve as a listener for a more important character.

Conflict (p. 30): the opposition of forces or persons which animates the plot and action of a play or story.

Connotation (p. 581): the emotional overtones or associations of a word, as opposed to its dictionary definition.

Conventional rhyme (p. 717): rhyme in which identical stressed vowel sounds are followed by identical consonant sounds (or by no consonant sounds at all). For example, gin/pin or shoe/threw.

Conventional symbol (p. 604): a symbol whose meaning is agreed upon by all members of a culture or other sub-group. For example: the cross, the star of David, all national flags.

Couplet (p. 736): any pair of successive poetic lines, sometimes printed separately, and often rhymed.

Dactyl (p. 684): a poetic foot consisting of a stressed syllable followed by two unstressed syllables. For example: Tripoli.

Denotation (p. 581): the dictionary definition of a word, as compared with its connotation.

Denouement (p. 31, 968, 1050): French for "unknotting"; the portion of a plot which occurs after the conflict has been resolved. Sometimes used to explain or comment on the action.

Deus ex machina (p. 1248): Latin for "God out of a machine." A mechanical device used in some Greek tragedies to resolve the conflict by "rescuing" the main character. Any improbable device used to resolve a plot.

Dialogue (p. 964): talk between characters in a work of literature.

Diction (p. 576, 964): the words or style of language that an author uses.

Dimeter (p. 685): a poetic line consisting of two feet.

Domestic tragedy (p. 1349): a tragedy in which ordinary, commonplace people in families—not kings and queens—are the subjects.

Dramatic irony (p. 1248): a form of irony in which dramatic characters act or speak in ways that have a different significance from what the audience knows to be the case.

Dramatic monologue (p. 645): a poem spoken by one person to an audience whose "presence" is implied in the poem.

Dramatic point of view (p. 128): a form of fictional narration in which the only characters's speeches are given, with minimal commentary or description.

Dramatic unities (p. 1049): a set of often loosely followed precepts that demand that a play be about *one* action, take place in *one* day's time, and be confined to *one* place.

Dramatis personae (p. 963): Latin for "characters in the play." A list of roles usually given at the beginning of a dramatic script or text.

Eccyclema (p. 1248): a wheeled cart used to draw tableaux of characters out onto the stage in a Greek play.

Elegiac stanza (p. 738): also called the heroic quatrain, a four-line stanza of iambic pentameter rhyming a b a b.

Enjambment (p. 687): the "wrapping around" of one line of verse to the next without punctuation.

Exodos (p. 1246): the concluding ode spoken by the chorus in a Greek play, delivered as or just before they exit.

Exposition (p. 967, 1049): the part of a plot occurring before the conflict is introduced; it often provides background information and establishes the atmosphere.

Expressionistic drama (p. 972): a form of drama which flourished after World War I and which often attempted to dramatize fantasies, dreams, memories, or aberrant psychological states.

Fable (p. 171): a simple narrative that teaches a clear moral and whose characters are usually animals.

Falling action (p. 968, 1049): the part of a plot which occurs just after the climax and before the denouement. In this portion of the plot the conflict has been resolved, and affairs begin to stabilize.

Falling meter (p. 684): any meter (for example trochaic or dactylic) whose feet consist of a stressed syllable followed by one or more unstressed syllables.

Figure of speech (p. 590): a usage of language which differs from literal, customery usage, and which involves a comparison.

First person narrator (p. 126): a narrator who uses "I" or "We" in telling the action of a story.

Flat character (p. 52): in fiction or drama, a relatively undeveloped character who exhibits only one primary trait.

Foil (p. 52, 1050): a dramatic character who serves as a significant contrast to, and who thus enhances, a more important character.

Foreshadowing (p. 31): the use of a detail or incident that anticipates something that is about to happen.

Free verse (p. 690): a type of poetry that has no rhyme and no regular meter.

Genre (p. 3): a litery kind, such as poetry, drama, fiction, the novel, and so forth.

Ground (p. 596): in metaphor, the basis for a comparison between two things. In "my love is a rose," beauty (and perhaps fragility) is the ground of the mataphor.

Hamartia (p. 970): Greek for "tragic flaw." The trait or error that brings about the fall of a tragic hero.

Heroic couplet (p. 736): a pair of rhymed iambic pentameter lines.

Heroic quatrain (p. 738): also called an elegiac stanza; a four-line stanza in iambic pentameter rhyming a b a b.

Hexameter (p. 685): a line of poetry having six feet.

High comedy (p. 1296): comedy which appeals to the intellect and evokes thoughtful laughter through wit and sophisticated language, as opposed to slapstick or farce.

Horatian ode (p. 745): a kind of ode, named after the Roman poet Horace, which uses regular stanzic patterns.

Hyperbole (p. 601): a figure of speech in which more is said than intended; extravagant exaggeration.

Iamb (p. 684): a poetic foot consisting of an unstressed syllable followed by a stressed syllable; for example, "Elaine."

Imagery (p. 593): the sensory content of a work of literature (visual, auditory, gustatory, olfactory, tactile, thermal, kinetic, and so forth).

Immediate scene (p. 128): in narration, the presentation of events as they are happening, rather than through summary.

In Memoriam stanza (p. 738): a stanza employed by Tennyson in his elegy "In Memoriam." It consists of iambic tetrameter quatrains rhyming a b b a.

Interior monologue (p. 129): a form of narration in which the reader hears the thoughts of a character as though they were being spoken.

Irony (p. 1248): speeches or situations that mean or imply something different from (often the opposite of) what they are intended or from what they appear to mean, and so have a double significance.

Italian sonnet (p. 740): a fourteen line poem consisting of an octave and a sestet, and rhyming (most commonly) a b b a a b b a / c d e c d e.

Katharsis (also Catharsis, p. 971): Greek for purgation. The expression of the pity and fear felt by the audience as they watch a tragic performance.

Kothornoi (p. 1248): high shoes worn by actors in a Greek play.

Low comedy (p. 1296): a kind of comedy which creates humor by physical (as opposed to verbal) action; farce or slapstick.

Metaphor (p. 596): as a general term, figurative language. As a specific term, a figure of speech in which one object is equated to another though the use of a linking verb.

Meter (p. 678): the theoretically regular pattern of stressed and unstressed syllables in a line of poetry.

Metonymy (p. 598): Greek for "a change of name"; a figure of speech in which something associated with an object or person is used to stand for that object or person. For example: "oval office" is used to stand for the president.

Middle English (p. 577): a stage in the history of the English language covering the period from 100 A.D. (just after the Norman conquest) till roughly 1500.

Modern English (p. 578): a stage in the history of the English language from roughly 1500 to the present.

Monometer (p. 685): a poetic line consisting of one foot.

Mood (p. 82): the atmosphere of a story or play, arising from the language, the physical details of the setting, and the nature of the action.

Natural syumbols (p. 604): objects (like the sun) occurring in nature that are invested with similar meanings by virtually all cultures worldwide.

New Comedy (p. 1295): a later form of classical comedy, of the fourth and third centuries B.C., which employs stock characters and plots.

Nonce symbols (p. 604): symbols invented and used "for the nonce," or for the time being by individual authors.

Objective correlative (p. 84): a term used by the American poet T. S. Eliot to designate an external action or object that is equivalent to an internal condition or conflict.

Objective point of view (p. 128): in narration, a manner of exhibiting an action without any commentary by the narrator.

Octave (p. 740): technically, any eight-line stanza; more commonly, the first eight lines of an Italian sonnet.

Old Comedy (p. 1295): Greek comedy of the fifth century B.C., as written by the playwright Aristophanes; usually satiric.

Old English (p. 577): a stage in the history of the English language ranging from 440 A.D. (the time of the first Germanic settlements in England) until around 1100 A.D. (when the effects of the Norman conquest began to be felt).

Omniscient narrator (p. 125): in narration, the presentation of action by an all-knowing narrator who often comments freely on the action.

Onomatopoeia (p. 716): a device in which the sounds of words (for example "buzz" and "crackle") imitate their meaning.

Open forms (p. 747): loose poetic forms that do not follow the conventions of meter, rhyme, and stanza structure.

Orchestra (p. 1247): the open space upon which the action of a Greek play takes place.

Ottava rima (p. 739): an eight-line stanza of iambic pentameter rhyming a b a b a b c c.

Parable (p. 171): an unambiguous narrative, often loosely allegorical, that conveys a clear moral or spiritual message.

Parados (p. 1246): the first ode spoken by the chorus of a Greek play, delivered as (or just after) they enter.

Paradox (p. 600): a figure of speech in which a statement contradicts itself, but is still in some sense true.

Pentameter (p. 685): a poetic line having five feet.

Peripety (p. 1246): in Greek tragedy, the reversal that occurs in the fortunes of the main character.

Persona (p. 124, 640): the voice (or "mask") which tells a story or poem.

Personification (p. 597): a figure of speech in which animals or objects are given human characteristics or attributes; for example, "the whispering pines."

Petrarchan sonnet (p. 740): another name for the Italian sonnet, named after Francesco Petrarch, an early Italian master of the form.

Pindaric ode (p. 745): an ode, following the Greek poet Pindar, usually in units of three stanzas: a strophe and an antistrophe in the same stanza pattern, and an eopde in a different pattern.

Plot (p. 29, 967): the substance and structure of the actions in a narrative or drama.

Plot analysis (p. 48): a kind of essay which shows how a plot is constructed.

Plot summary (p. 47): a brief paraphrase of the main events of a story or play.

Point of view (p. 124): the way a story is narrated, including the narrator, the time at which the story is told, and the vantage point adopted.

Private symbol (p. 605): a symbol with special significance that is used recurrently by one author.

Prosody (p. 680): the study of meter, rhythm, and versification in poetry.

Protagonist (p. 30, 52, 1050) the main character in a story or play.

Pyrrhic (p. 684): a poetic foot, used only for metrical substitution, which consists of two unstressed syllables.

Quantitative meter (p. 680): a metrical system in which poetic feet are determined by the duration of their syllables in time.

Quatrain (p. 738): any four-line stanza.

Quintain (p. 738): any five-line stanza.

Realistic drama (p. 971): drama which, though its characters, actions, and stage settings, attempts to portray common, everyday life, often in domestic settings.

Resolution (p. 31): the events which follow the climax of the plot in a drama or narrative.

Rhyme (p. 710): similarity in vowel and consonant sounds in nearby words, usually at the ends of poetic lines.

Rhyme royal (p. 739): a seven-line stanza of iambic pentameter rhymed a b a b b c c.

Rhyme scheme (p. 720): the pattern in which rhyming words are repeated in a poem, usually represented by assigning a different letter to each new rhyme.

Rhythm (p. 680): the total quality of the motion of a line of poetry or prose, including meter, tempo, duration, pauses, and so forth.

Rich rhyme (p. 717): rhyme which is identical throughout all parts of two words with different meanings, for example, "their/there."

Rime couee (p. 738): see *Burns stanza.*

Rising action (p. 967, 1049): that portion of a plot where conflict is introduced and complications develop.

Rising meter (p. 684): a poetic foot consisting of one or more unstressed syllables followed by a stressed syllable (for example, iambic and anapestic).

Romantic comedy (p. 971, 1295): a kind of comedy whose plot centers around a thwarted love-match, and which usually concludes with the marriage of those who had been thwarted.

Round character (p. 52): a relatively complex, well-developed character presented from a number of perspectives.

Satiric comedy (p. 1295): a kind of comedy, usually humorous or witty, which portrays and criticizes human foibles or weaknesses.

Scansion (p. 683): the process of marking stressed and unstrssed syllables in a line of poetry to determine the meter.

Sestet (p. 740): technically, any six-line stanza; more commonly, the last six lines of an Italian sonnet.

Sestina (p. 743): a thirty-nine line poem consisting of six six-line stanzas followed by a three-line envoy. The sestina does not use rhyme, but employs an elaborate repetition of key words at the ends of lines.

Shakespearean sonnet (p. 741): the English sonnet; a fourteen line poem, often about love, written in iambic pentameter and rhyming a b a b / c d c d / e f e f / g g.

Simile (p. 596): an explicit comparison, usually limited, between two things, using "like" or "as." For example: her eyes are as bright as diamonds.

Situational humor (p. 1343): humor which arises more from coincidence than from language, and which usually plays upon the audience's expectations about a character's behavior..

Skene (p. 1247): the background, usually a facade, in front of which the action of a Greek play was presented.

Slant rhyme (p. 717): a form of partial rhyme in which there is not an exact congruence in the sounds of the rhyming words (for example, "blink/blank").

Social comedy (p. 971): plays which, while ending happily, make fun of or satarize various forms of human behavior in society.

Soliloquy (p. 1051): in drama, a speech delivered by a character alone on the stage, who thus makes his inner thoughts known to the audience without being heard by any other character.

Song (p. 970): a short lyric poem set to music.

Sonnet (p. 740): a fourteen line poem, usually about love, written in iambic pentameter and employing a conventional rhyme scheme. See *Italian sonnet* and *Shakespearean sonnet*.

Sophoclean irony (p. 1248): named for the Greek playwright Sophocles. A form of irony involving a discrepancy between what a character says or does and what the audience knows to be the true significance of the speech or action.

Spectacle (p. 970, 1161): the visual display of a drama, including costumery, stage settings, dancing, and so forth.

Spenserian stanza (p. 739): a stanza of nine lines—the first eight in iambic pentameter, the last in iambic hexameter—which rhyme a b a b b c b c c.

Spondee (p. 684): a poetic foot, usually used in metrical substitution, consisting of two stressed syllables (for example, "Babe Ruth").

Stage directions (p. 739): instructions in the printed text of a play which explain how the characters are to act, speak, or move.

Stanza (p. 735): a structural unit of a poem, often printed separately, and often employing a particular rhyme scheme.

Stereotypes (p. 53): flat characters who closely resemble types found in society.

Stichic verse (p. 768): poetry printed in a continuous series of lines, not divided into stanzas or other formal divisions.

Stock characters (p. 53, 969): flat characters who closely resemble stereotyped characters found commonly in literary works.

Stream of consciousness (p. 129): a form of narration which attempts to capture the exact "flow"—often seemingly chaotic—of the human mind or consciousness.

Strong rhyme (p. 717): rhyme which ends on a stressed syllable.

Strophe (p. 1247): the part of a choral ode in a Greek play that the chorus chanted as it executed a pattern of movement toward the left of the stage. See *Antistrophe*.

Strophic verse (p. 1247): poetry that is divided into stanzas or other formal divisions, as opposed to stichic verse.

Summary (p. 128): in narration, the presentation of events in abbreviated form after they have happened, as opposed to immediate scene.

Syllabic meter (p. 682): a metrical system in which lines are formed on the basis of the number of syllables they contain, without regard to stress.

Symbols (p. 170, 602): objects, people, or events which appear in literary works and which represent ideas significant to those works.

Synecdoche (p. 598): a figure of speech in which a part of something stands for the whole thing; for example a farm "hand."

Tenor (p. 596): in metaphor, the word which is being described by the comparison. In "he is an ox," "he" is the tenor.

Tercet (p. 737): any three-line stanza.

Terza rima (p. 737): a kind of poetry in three-line stanzas which employs inter-locking rhymes in the following pattern: a b a / b c b / c d c, and so forth.

Tetrameter (p. 685): a poetic line with four feet.

Theater of convention (p. 1048): a form of drama, often ritualistic, which does not insist upon surface realism in its presentation of character or setting.

Theatre of illusion (p. 1048): a form of drama which attempts to convey, through its characters, events, or settings, an air of realism or actuality.

Theme (p. 196, 771): the main idea, moral, or significance of a literary work.

Third person limited (p. 125): a kind of fictional point of view which, though told in the third person, is in some way restricted, usually by narrating the action through the eyes of one character.

Thought (p. 969): one of Aristotle's six elements of tragedy, referring to the ideas of the playwright or the characters.

Tone (p. 652): the attitude that an author adopts toward his or her subject matter or audience.

Tragedy (p. 970, 1240): a form of drama which usually ends unhappily with the downfall or misfortune of a significant character.

Trimeter (p. 685): a poetic line consisting of three feet.

Trochee (p. 684): a poetic foot consisting of a stressed syllable followed by an un-stressed syllable; for example, "after."

Trope (p. 594): a "turn" of language; that is, a figure of speech.

Understatement (p. 601): a figure of speech in which less is said than is intended. See *Hyperbole*.

Vehicle (p. 596): that part of a metaphor which "carries" the comparison and clarifies the term being described. In "he is an ox," "ox" is the vehicle. Compare with *Tenor*.

Venus and Adonis stanza (p. 738): a stanza employed by Shakespeare in *Venus and Adonis*. It consists of a quatrain followed by a couplet, and it rhymes a b a b c c.

Verbal humor (p. 1343): humor conveyed through witty language rather than through incident or action.

Verbal irony (p. 1248): a figure of speech in which the language means the opposite of (or something different from) what it apparently means. When a character says "You're looking wide awake this morning" to a sleepy-eyed person, he is employing verbal irony.

Vilanelle (p. 742): a nineteen-line poem employing only two rhymes and written in five tercets plus a quatrain. It also employs an elaborate repetition of two alternating refrains.

Weak rhyme (p. 717): rhyme which ends on an unstressed syllable.

Index of Authors, Titles, and First Lines of Poetry

Authors' names appear in capitals, titles of selections in italics, and first lines of poems in roman type.